Literature in Critical Perspectives:
AN ANTHOLOGY

Edited by
WALTER K. GORDON
Rutgers University, Camden

Literature in Critical Perspectives:
AN ANTHOLOGY

Prentice-Hall, Inc., Englewood Cliffs, New Jersey

©1968
by PRENTICE-HALL, Inc.,
Englewood Cliffs, New Jersey

All rights reserved. No part of this book
may be reproduced in any form or by any means,
without permission in writing from the publisher.

Printed in the United States of America

ISBN: 0-13-537613-0

Library of Congress Catalog Card Number: 68-15855

10 9 8 7

PRENTICE-HALL INTERNATIONAL, INC., *London*
PRENTICE-HALL OF AUSTRALIA, PTY. LTD., *Sydney*
PRENTICE-HALL OF CANADA, LTD., *Toronto*
PRENTICE-HALL OF INDIA PRIVATE LIMITED, *New Delhi*
PRENTICE-HALL OF JAPAN, INC., *Tokyo*

PREFACE

Literature in Critical Perspectives is an anthology of 4 plays, 17 short stories, 59 poems, and 23 essays. Its purpose is to teach principles and techniques of literary interpretation to freshman and sophomore college students in introduction-to-literature courses. The selections are not grouped primarily in the traditional manner according to genre—poetry, fiction, drama—but are organized by major critical perspectives: Social, Formalist, Psychological, and Archetypal.

Each of the first four sections is preceded by an introduction that outlines the strengths and weaknesses of the particular approach and discusses its historical development. The tenets of each critical mode are then discussed by one of its distinguished practitioners: David Daiches; Cleanth Brooks; Lionel Trilling; Leslie Fiedler. In each section a play follows, then an interpretative essay that scrutinizes the drama within the context of the section's critical bias.

With the critical theory and practice clearly in mind, the student then proceeds to stories and poems to which he can apply the critical principles already learned. Discussion questions in the temper of the appropriate critical perspective follow each selection to guide the student in his analysis.

To show that a work of literature can be examined profitably from several critical perspectives—singly and in combination—*Billy Budd* is reprinted in Section V and assessed by nine critics whose critical concerns and values vary markedly. This section is paginated for use as a casebook.

An appendix entitled "What to Say About Literature" instructs the less-experienced student in basic critical questions relative to the various approaches to literature and assists him in writing themes on literary topics.

In editing a volume of this type, one obviously stands on the shoulders of many who have gone before him. I should like to acknowledge debts both large and small to the scholarship of Cleanth Brooks, Murray Krieger, Lee Lemon, Austin Warren, William Handy, Jolande Jacobi, Lauriat Lane, Walter Sutton, Paul C. Obler, Stanley Edgar Hyman, and Mark Spilka. For allowing me to use them as sounding boards for ideas in this book, I wish to thank my friends and colleagues at Rutgers University in Camden, John Berkey, Irwin Gopnik, James Sanderson, and Everett Zimmerman. All have given willingly of their time, knowledge, and experience and have saved me from many an egregious error.

My wife Lydia has lived with *Literature in Critical Perspectives* for three years and has contributed to the book at every stage from its conception through proofreading to a degree amounting to collaboration. For sustaining my labors and for constant encouragement I acknowledge an unpayable debt.

W. K. G.

CONTENTS

Preface   v

I Critical Perspective: SOCIAL

Introduction		3
Criticism and Sociology	DAVID DAICHES	7
Suggestions for Additional Reading		18

Play and Criticism

Major Barbara	BERNARD SHAW	19
Major Barbara: Shaw's Challenge to Liberalism	LOUIS CROMPTON	67

Stories

Act of Faith	IRWIN SHAW	78
The Lottery	SHIRLEY JACKSON	87
A Bottle of Milk for Mother	NELSON ALGREN	92
Bartleby the Scrivener	HERMAN MELVILLE	101

Poems

I Will Arise and Go Now	OGDEN NASH	121
The Charge of the Light Brigade	ALFRED, LORD TENNYSON	122
To a Mouse	ROBERT BURNS	122
The World is Too Much with Us; Late and Soon	WILLIAM WORDSWORTH	124
next to of course god america i	E. E. CUMMINGS	124
Verses on the Death of Dr. Swift, D.S.P.D.	JONATHAN SWIFT	125
The Latest Decalogue	ARTHUR HUGH CLOUGH	137
Autobiography	LAWRENCE FERLINGHETTI	138
Dover Beach	MATTHEW ARNOLD	144
The Unknown Citizen	W. H. AUDEN	145
An Elementary School Classroom in a Slum	STEPHEN SPENDER	146
Elegy Written in a Country Churchyard	THOMAS GRAY	147
Again the Native Hour Lets Down the Locks	ALLEN TATE	150
Slave Quarters	JAMES DICKEY	151
A Song About Major Eatherly	JOHN WAIN	155

II Critical Perspective: FORMALIST

Introduction		163
The Formalist Critics	CLEANTH BROOKS	167
Suggestions for Additional Reading		172
Play and Criticism		
Oedipus Rex	SOPHOCLES	173
Oedipus Tyrannus	RICHMOND LATTIMORE	204
Stories		
Flight	JOHN STEINBECK	215
The Open Boat	STEPHEN CRANE	225
Araby	JAMES JOYCE	238
The Snows of Kilimanjaro	ERNEST HEMINGWAY	242
Poems		
"Ah, Are You Digging on My Grave?"	THOMAS HARDY	254
I Never Lost as Much but Twice	EMILY DICKINSON	255
Ars Poetica	ARCHIBALD MACLEISH	255
Tears, Idle Tears	ALFRED, LORD TENNYSON	256
The Death of the Ball Turret Gunner	RANDALL JARRELL	257
On First Looking into Chapman's Homer	JOHN KEATS	258
Song: Goe and Catche a Falling Starre	JOHN DONNE	258
Sonnet 73	WILLIAM SHAKESPEARE	259
Easter-Wings	GEORGE HERBERT	260
Sonnet 124	WILLIAM SHAKESPEARE	260
The Collar	GEORGE HERBERT	261
Ode to the West Wind	PERCY BYSSHE SHELLEY	262
To a Skylark	PERCY BYSSHE SHELLEY	264
After Apple-Picking	ROBERT FROST	267
When Lilacs Last in the Dooryard Bloom'd	WALT WHITMAN	268
The Windhover	GERARD MANLEY HOPKINS	274
The Force that Through the Green Fuse Drives the Flower	DYLAN THOMAS	275
Fern Hill	DYLAN THOMAS	276
A Valediction: Forbidding Mourning	JOHN DONNE	277
Ode on a Grecian Urn	JOHN KEATS	278

III Critical Perspective: PSYCHOLOGICAL

Introduction		283
The Dissection of the Psychical Personality	SIGMUND FREUD	288

Freud and Literature	LIONEL TRILLING	302
Suggestions for Additional Reading		314
Play and Criticism		
The Tragedy of Hamlet, Prince of Denmark	WILLIAM SHAKESPEARE	315
The Psycho-Analytic Solution to Hamlet's Character	ERNEST JONES	379
Stories		
The Secret Life of Walter Mitty	JAMES THURBER	388
William Wilson	EDGAR ALLAN POE	392
Mr. Arcularis	CONRAD AIKEN	403
The Turn of the Screw	HENRY JAMES	413
Poems		
The Buried Life	MATTHEW ARNOLD	468
I Saw a Chapel All of Gold	WILLIAM BLAKE	470
Kisses in the Train	D. H. LAWRENCE	470
My Last Duchess	ROBERT BROWNING	471
Soliloquy of the Spanish Cloister	ROBERT BROWNING	472
The Bishop Orders His Tomb at Saint Praxed's Church	ROBERT BROWNING	475
Daddy	SYLVIA PLATH	478
La Belle Dame Sans Merci	JOHN KEATS	480
Kubla Khan	SAMUEL TAYLOR COLERIDGE	481
Goblin Market	CHRISTINA ROSSETTI	483
Original Sin: A Short Story	ROBERT PENN WARREN	495

IV Critical Perspective: ARCHETYPAL

Introduction		499
The Concept of the Collective Unconscious	CARL JUNG	504
The Collective Unconscious, Myth, and the Archetype	CARL JUNG	510
Archetype and Signature	LESLIE FIEDLER	515
Suggestions for Additional Reading		525
Myth, Play, and Criticism		
The Myth of Orpheus	CATHERINE B. AVERY	527
Orpheus Descending	TENNESSEE WILLIAMS	529
Orpheus Descending	SIGNI L. FALK	574
Stories		
King Solomon	ISAAC ROSENFELD	579
Young Goodman Brown	NATHANIEL HAWTHORNE	587
Blackberry Winter	ROBERT PENN WARREN	594

My Kinsman, Major Molineux	NATHANIEL HAWTHORNE	606

Poems

Stopping by Woods on a Snowy Evening	ROBERT FROST	617
To Autumn	JOHN KEATS	617
Crossing the Bar	ALFRED, LORD TENNYSON	618
Ulysses	ALFRED, LORD TENNYSON	619
The Lotos-Eaters	ALFRED, LORD TENNYSON	620
Bacchus	RALPH WALDO EMERSON	625
Oedipus	EDWIN MUIR	626
Kilroy	PETER VIERECK	628
Corinna's Going A-Maying	ROBERT HERRICK	630
Sailing to Byzantium	WILLIAM BUTLER YEATS	631
The Rime of the Ancient Mariner	SAMUEL TAYLOR COLERIDGE	633
Lycidas	JOHN MILTON	649
The Waste Land	T. S. ELIOT	657

V Critical Perspectives on BILLY BUDD

Billy Budd	HERMAN MELVILLE	671

SOCIAL

Herman Melville and the Forms—Irony and Social Criticism in Billy Budd	KARL E. ZINK	713

FORMALIST

The Ceremony of Innocence	WILLIAM YORK TINDALL	719
Billy Budd: The Plot Against the Story	LEE T. LEMON	724

PSYCHOLOGICAL

The "Ineludible Gripe" of Billy Budd	ROBERT ROGERS	732

ARCHETYPAL

Innocence and Infamy	RICHARD CHASE	741
Billy Budd: Adam or Christ?	H. E. HUDSON, IV	753

MIXED

Billy Budd—Acceptance or Irony	RICHARD HARTER FOGLE	758
The Problem of Billy Budd	EDWARD H. ROSENBERRY	762

APPENDIX: What to Say About Literature

What to Say About a Play	DOUGALD B. MACEACHEN	777
What to Say About Fiction	ROBERT W. LEWIS, JR.	778
What to Say About a Poem	WILLIAM K. WIMSATT	781
Index		793

I Critical Perspective:
SOCIAL

Introduction

Social critics have long believed that authors do not write in an intellectual vacuum. Even those who work in physical isolation are influenced by the whole world of political, economic, philosophical, and religious ideas into which they are born, in which they develop, and to which they respond. For the social critic, the work of art is an imitation of life, an inseparable part of the social context which produces it. Particular times and places unfailingly make their distinct and idiosyncratic impressions upon the artist and therefore upon the products of his imagination. The social critic argues, for example, that Dickens's Hard Times cannot be understood without the Victorian context of the impact of the Industrial Revolution or his Bleak House fully appreciated without reference to the ineptitude of the Victorian judicial system. Nor must social influences be primary in the artist's mind, for the social critic asserts that the literary work will inevitably reflect its environment. For example, the fatal action of Thomas Hardy's Tess of the D'Urbervilles, not normally considered a "social" novel, is seen by critic Arnold Kettle as caused by the peasantry's disintegration, which results as the capitalistic system of farming is extended. Kettle interprets the characters, setting, and ultimate tragedy in the light of this hypothesis.

The classic statement of the social approach to literature was made by Hippolyte Taine (1828–1893), who set out to establish a scientific basis for literary criticism by applying the methods of the biological sciences to literary interpretation. He compared a literary work to a fossil shell. Just as the shell bears the imprint of the animal, the work bears the imprint of the author: "Under the shell there was an animal, and behind the document there was a man." Just as it would be a mistake to examine the shell without considering the animal, it would be a mistake to consider the work without considering the forces that shaped and fashioned it, for the work of art is not a "mere play of the imagination, the isolated caprice of an excited brain, but a transcript of contemporary manners and customs." Attempting to clarify his position and to isolate the major influences on the artist, Taine further argued that three major factors determine a work of art's particular character: biology ("race"), culture ("environment"), and history ("epoch"). It will be helpful to examine each factor briefly because it is to one or another of this triad that subsequent social approaches to literature owe their beginnings.

The first factor, race, is the vaguest and most controversial term in Taine's theory. He felt that there were certain racial—by which he frequently meant national—distinctions, certain native endowments of nationalities which like Lamarckian acquired characteristics were inherited from generation to generation and which gave a distinctive national character or tone to a work of art. Most people would probably admit that these national distinctions exist. For example, we frequently speak of the music of Richard Wagner as typically Germanic; of Debussy and Renoir as exhibiting the delicate sensibility that epitomizes French art; of the indigenous Americanism of George Gershwin. Certainly the action of Huckleberry Finn would be unimaginable if transported from its homeland on the Mississippi to the Nile, Ganges, or Yangtze. But beyond these impressionistic generalizations few modern critics care to venture. General acceptance of Taine's theory of race has led to such misguided applications as the concept of Aryan supremacy promulgated by Hitler's Third Reich. In justice to Taine, however, it must be pointed out that he never argued for the superiority of one race over another, but merely for recognition of temperamental differences among nations and their art.

Yet authors of the same race frequently have very different reactions to certain ideas or events. William Wordsworth, born and reared in the idyllic Lake Country of England, views Nature as teacher, nurse, and divinity; whereas Tennyson, resenting the loss of his dearest friend, describes Nature as "red in tooth and claw." Taine attempts to account for this range of differences among members of the same nationality by the second factor of his triad, environment. He writes in his introduction to History of English Literature:

> Having thus verified the internal structure of a race, we must consider the environment in which it lives. For man is not alone in the world; nature envelops him, and other men surround him; accidental and secondary folds come and overspread the primitive and permanent fold, while physical or social circumstances derange or complete the natural groundwork surrendered to them.

Environment, then, is viewed as the totality of the author's experiences. Whether the climate is hot or cold, the country at war or peace, the Church active or passive, the economy prosperous or depressed—all these are among the multiplicity of external forces that shape the creative imagination of the author and that Taine would include within the scope of his term "environment."

Environment gives way to epoch when the author is considered against his historical rather than his social background. Environment deals with immediate forces, usually of relatively short duration; epochal elements differ in that they are continuous, cumulative, progressive, and subject to a certain momentum. The author, writing against the background of a tradition, is seen as part of a literary continuum. He is bound to be influenced by his predecessors, and in his turn he will influence those who come after him. Whether he conforms or rebels against the traditional literary mode is unimportant—in either case he will respond to what Taine calls the "rule of intellect" or the master idea of his age. Taine's thesis that the author is a prisoner of his intellectual past and that a certain time-spirit exists at any given moment in history is a debatable one, but literary historians have generally accepted the concept of the epoch. They have attempted to define "periods," to identify the major intellectual movements in their field, and then to discuss various authors against the background of the unfolding panorama of literature and in terms of what they think the master idea of the period to be. Medievalism, the Renaissance, Neo-Classicism, Romanticism, Victorianism, Puritanism, Naturalism, the Cult of Unintelligibility, the Angry Young Men, and the Theater of the Absurd are all examples of the kind of useful classification resulting from Taine's concept of the epoch.

In the twentieth century, interest in Taine's race-environment-epoch theory has continued, but other theories have been advanced to describe an even stricter union between art and society than Taine had envisioned. The most influential of these has developed from the ideas of Karl Marx (1818–1883), a German economist who asserted that all forms of human society are in the last analysis based on the means of production of that society. From the economic base arises a superstructure of institutions, such as politics, government, law, religion, art, and literature. As Marx viewed them, technology, class structure, distribution of power, and political organization of the state, as well as literature and the other arts are completely determined by a society's economic structure.

All changes in economic structure stem from causes within the economic structure itself. But the relations between literature and society are especially complex because they are reciprocal. As critic Harry Levin notes, literature is not only affected by social causes, it causes social effects; it is both culture-ridden and culture-forming. Followers of Marx made applications of his thought that it is doubtful he fully intended; they proceeded to identify aesthetic and social values. For the Marxists literature became a tool in the hands of politicians, a propaganda device to insure social control.

Under this system, art developed into a weapon in the class struggle, to be used by the proletariat as an instrument of national policy. In 1933, Granville Hicks, perhaps the most articulate of the Marxist critics of the thirties, devised a list of characteristics for the ideal Marxist work of art: (1) it must lead the proletarian reader to recognize his role in the class struggle; (2) it must show the effects of the class struggle; (3) it must make the reader feel he is participating in the lives described; and (4) the author must take the point of view of the "vanguard of the proletariat; he should be or try to make himself a member of the proletariat."

Relegation of literature to the position of handmaiden to politics has resulted in modern Russia in strict governmental censorship of artistic expression. Consequently, all forms of art must be concerned, both in purpose and subject, with art's relevance to society: struggles and triumphs on collectivist farms, at socialist steel mills, at the people's hydroelectric plants. Rigid criteria for literary expression have, of course, been established by other societies, yet history shows that such criteria ultimately fail because their intent is to inhibit social change by controlling art, which is felt to be a major influence on society. But society itself is dynamic, not static. Such attempts at censorship, intended to freeze social institutions, are therefore doomed to failure from their very beginnings.

In the Theory of Literature, Austin Warren cites three major areas with which studies treating the relationship of literature and society have concerned themselves: (1) the heredity and environment of the writer; (2) the world about which he wrote; and (3) the world into which his work entered. The first approach treats the sociology of the writer, his family background, his social status, and his political allegiances. The importance of this material is based upon the assumption that such details will clarify and explain the social views expressed by the author in his writings. Taking this approach, one commentator claims that to understand the symbolic nature of the Houyhnhnms in the fourth book of Swift's Gulliver's Travels, the reader must know that Swift was a Tory and that the horse-people represent the political and social philosophy of John Locke as practiced by the Whigs. Viewed in this light, the Houyhnhnms become symbols of Whig rationalistic excesses and objects of Swift's satire. Others have examined Mark Twain's attitudes toward slavery in order to understand better Huckleberry Finn, Robert Burns's humble origins to interpret his "Cotter's Saturday Night," and James Boswell's political attitudes to account for his opinions and behavior in The Life of Samuel Johnson.

The second major subdivision of social criticism treats the social context of the work itself. Here, the work is assumed to mirror its world and is examined for its depiction of society. Medieval scholars, for example, have long considered Chaucer in this manner, extolling him for his ability to depict a microcosm of medieval society in the Prologue to the Canterbury Tales. Some critics, such as J. N. Manly, present persuasive evidence to show that Chaucer drew his portraits of the Host, Prioress, and others from live models. Again, Molière is justly praised for his ability to epitomize social types such as the religious hypocrite (Tartuffe), the self-deceiving social climber (Le Bourgeois Gentilhomme), and the hypochondriac (La Malade Imaginaire), examine them under the devastating scrutiny of his dramatic wit, and make them objects of ridicule. Gustave Flaubert's Madame Bovary, filled with memorable portraits of druggists, priests, merchants, and doctors, is a realistic portrayal—and some think indictment—of middle-class society in nineteenth-century France. The titles of social studies such as The Contemporary Negro Novel: A Study in Race Relations, Political Themes in Restoration Tragedy, and The Literary History of the American Revolution show the range and variety of this second critical perspective.

The third approach is concerned with the outer world to which the literary work is directed, the society for which it is written. There are few, if any, authors who do not have their audiences in mind as they write, and an author's concern for the group with whom he hopes to communicate inevitably affects the method of composition of his work. Social studies which consider a writer's public usually investigate the critical reception of a work of art, explore its influence on society, or attempt to define the artistic limitations imposed on the author by his audience. Some commentators think that the critical condemnation of Jude the Obscure so disappointed and embittered Thomas Hardy that he abandoned fiction and turned to poetry as a means of artistic expression. Much has also been made of the power of some fiction to initiate social reform; thus Oliver Twist and Uncle Tom's Cabin are said to have so shamed their societies with the inequities of the poorhouse system and with slavery that an outraged and enlightened public demanded legislative changes in the social system. Studies of the Elizabethan stage have shown that the physical characteristics of the stage such as the apron that extended into the audience and the lack of scenery were very much in Shakespeare's mind when he wrote his plays. He took advantage of the intimate actor-audience relationship afforded by the extended apron to make use of the soliloquy, and he compensated for the lack of scenery by using descriptive dialogue. A final example is Shakespeare's contemporary, John Lyly, who, seeking the preferment of Elizabeth and her court, addressed many of his works to her and would probably have been a very different author indeed but for his audience.

The halcyon days of social criticism were undoubtedly in the 1930's when major literary critics such as Stephen Spender, Archibald MacLeish, Granville Hicks, L. C. Knights, C. Day Lewis, V. F. Calverton, James T. Farrell, and Bernard Smith championed the cause of social criticism on both sides of the Atlantic; discussion groups flourished, and magazines like the New Masses and the Left Review were formed to provide outlets of expression for socially oriented criticism and art. Although still a major means of interpreting literature, social criticism has lost much of its appeal to contemporary readers, writers, and critics for several reasons. First, many persons are unwilling to accept the idea of society as a necessary cause for literary effects, and even those who do subscribe to such a view find it difficult to determine the degree of society's influence on literature. Secondly, doctrinaire social critics, overlooking other criteria, have attempted to judge the worth of literature solely in terms of its social relevance. Finally, some critics have been unable to resist the temptation of studying society rather than literature. They fail to satisfy the reader who seeks aesthetic enlightenment. Despite these limitations, excesses, and shortcomings, social interpretation can frequently throw the meaning of a work of literature into enlightening and rewarding perspectives.

Criticism and Sociology*

DAVID DAICHES

In modern criticism, investigation of a writer's social origins and of the effect which social factors had on his work, has been at least as common as psychological studies of a writer's state of mind, and the two have often gone together.

A GENETIC APPROACH

... Critics such as Edmund Wilson have inquired into the social factors affecting the attitude of Dickens, for example, or Kipling, thus seeking sociological causes of psychological phenomena, the psychological phenomena themselves being then used to explain or, genetically, to account for the characteristics of the writer's work. The problems which arise in any discussion of the relation between sociology and criticism are similar to, and in some respects identical with, those posed by the relation between criticism and psychology. In each case a genetic approach is involved, a consideration of the work in terms of its origins, whether individual or social or both. Three preliminary questions suggest themselves. First: Are the sciences (or pseudo-sciences), in terms of which these origins are explained, themselves normative or are they merely descriptive—do they enable us to pass relative judgments of worth and value, or do they merely tell us what goes on? Second: If they are normative—if we have criteria on which to form value judgments about states of mind and kinds of society—can judgments which are made about the conditions of origin of a literary work be transferred to the literary work itself? Third: If they are not normative, what kind of value can data concerning the psychological or sociological origin of a work possess for the literary critic as distinct from the literary historian? Let us consider these questions with references to sociology.

WHAT IS SOCIOLOGY?

Is sociology a normative science? To put the question in this way is to assume that it is at least a science, and though this can be debated, and the term "science" itself is not unambiguous in such a context, we can leave that point for the sociologists to wrangle over. We may at least agree that inquiry into the structure of society at any given period of history, and into the modes of behavior that result from that structure, does take place and does yield genuine knowledge. Does the knowledge thus made available provide automatic criteria of social sickness and health? Can the sociologist, in his capacity as sociologist, tell us what forms of social organization are better than others and what particular kinds of social behavior are more and less good? The sociologists themselves would probably be inclined to answer this question in the negative: they would prefer to think of their actions as purely descriptive and not in any degree normative. But though sociology may not in itself be a normative science, it can provide us with knowledge

---

* David Daiches, CRITICAL APPROACHES TO LITERATURE, © 1956. Reprinted by permission of Prentice-Hall, Inc., Englewood Cliffs, New Jersey.

towards which we, as rational and intelligent persons, may adopt a normative attitude. As far as the intelligent layman is concerned, sociology *is* normative, because the intelligent layman is concerned with more than just man as a social animal—he takes all aspects of man into his purview and brings political, ethical, and other notions to bear on the information with which the sociologist provides him. He is the non-specialist humanist, and as such is concerned with relating the specialized studies of the sociologist to man's status and needs as man. He may, for example, interpret sociological data ethically and approve of those social institutions which turn aggressive instincts into other channels or which help to increase the sense of responsibility shown by members of a community to each other while disapproving of institutions serving a contrary function. His criteria will not be drawn from sociology—he will be bringing to bear independently conceived standards of what is good and bad in human behavior—but sociology *will* have provided him with data immediately capable of such treatment. We might go further and say that the data provided by the sociologist cry out for such treatment. Sociology, then, though not in itself a normative science, demands immediate normative treatment as soon as it emerges from the hands of the specialist. We immediately want to ask, when hearing of different kinds of social structure and social convention, which is better, which is more conducive to the good life as we understand it.

SOCIOLOGICAL KNOWLEDGE AND THE LITERARY CRITIC

Suppose, then, that the experts tell us something about the structure of early eighteenth century society in England, and we—representing as far as sociology is concerned the intelligent layman—make up our minds about the value and significance of that structure: how are we going to apply this to, say, a criticism of the *Spectator* essays? We can, of course, easily relate this information to such questions as the social purpose of the periodical essay, and the reason why such a literary form should arise at this time rather than at any other; we could throw a good deal of light on the tone and choice of subjects of these essays by pointing out that they represent some of the first works of literature addressed specifically to that middle class whose rise in status and influence was symbolized by the revolution of 1689 and who were now faced with the problem of taking over an aristocratic function without an aristocratic tradition. We can use the data provided by the social historian in examining the reasons for reading which prevailed among the class which most eagerly bought the *Spectator* essays; this again will show an interesting correlation between what they read and why they read. These and similar points will be found most helpful by the literary historian in giving an account of the origins and nature of the eighteenth century periodical essay. But how will they help the critic? Can he say that because these essays performed a good social function effectively they are therefore good essays? Clearly, this would be an impossible oversimplification which would result in our treating all literature as rhetoric, the art of persuasion, and judging the rhetoric at least in some degree in accordance with the social worthiness of its objective. Such a view would certainly put *Uncle Tom's Cabin* above *Hamlet* (at least in the eyes of Northern critics).

Let us take another example. Suppose we are interested in the social origins of the "art for art's sake" theories that prevailed at the end of the last century. It would not be difficult (indeed, it has often been done) to relate these theories to the artist's feeling of maladjustment which in turn was produced by the development of industrial society in the nineteenth century and the resulting social attitude of the dominant middle class. These are illuminating facts, and no man of letters would wish to be without them. They advance understanding—but exactly how are they to be used by the critic? If we value art we are bound to take a poor view of a social organization which removes the artist further and further away from his fellow men and leaves him the position either of licensed clown or despised eccentric. Must the critic, then, assume that any new literary forms or devices introduced by writers at this time as a result of the operation of such factors are to be deplored?

As a final example, consider the breakdown of community belief, and the consequent development of private worlds, in modern society; this breakdown derives at least in part from social and economic causes, and it has certainly had an incalculable effect on literary techniques. It has meant, among other things, a remarkable enlargement of the scope of the novel through the writer's being forced to rely on a personal sense of insight rather than on a social sense of value. This has affected style, plot, vocabulary, subject matter—every aspect of the art of fiction. Or consider the modern poet's problem in trying to find a language of symbols to replace those communally held myths which for the first time in many centuries are now no longer tenable even without literal belief. Sociology can help us to see why Joyce wrote as he did, why so much of the most sensitive modern poetry is obscure—but what can it tell us about the value of Joyce's way of writing or of obscurity in poetry? Are we to disapprove of the enlargement of the scope of the novel because it has social origins which, on any reasonable standard of health in society, most of us would deplore? To take an analogy from medicine: if it could be shown (and the attempt has been made) that Keats' genius flowered as and when it did because he suffered from tuberculosis, are we to conclude that Keats' poetry is therefore bad—or that tuberculosis is therefore good?

SOCIOLOGICAL VALUE AND LITERARY VALUE

The answer to the second question posed above—can we transfer value judgments about kinds of society to the literary works produced by those kinds of society?—must thus be a tentative negative. We certainly cannot do so in any direct or simple way. Of course, if we believe that if the cause is undesirable the effect must automatically be so, then we shall return a clear affirmative answer to this question. If we believe that because a flood disaster is a bad thing any example of human courage which it provokes must also be bad; if we believe that value in the cause can be transferred unchanged to the effect and that any literary development that arises out of social conditions of which we disapprove must itself be worthy of disapproval—then we have a simple unicellular approach to life and all its problems and need not concern ourselves at all with literary value as distinct from other kinds of value. The Marxist critic who is often extremely illuminating when he points to causes (for example, explaining the attitude of Defoe in his novels as arising from his economic and class interests) has nothing to say as a *critic*, as someone appraising literary works on literary grounds, for he simply carries over his view of the social cause to his evaluation of the effect. Thus the Marxist, believing that the social conditions that helped produce the esthetic attitude of, say, James Joyce, were undesirable conditions, would have to assume that *Ulysses* is therefore an undesirable work. Similarly, a work which arises out of good social conditions, or good social attitudes, would be a good work. Many non-Marxists might agree that the social factors which helped to make Joyce look at life the way he did were factors we should like to eliminate, but they might at the same time recognize the literary interest and value of what these social factors led Joyce to do. The more serious and responsible Marxists have been satisfied to use their special view of social and economic history in order to explain why certain writers adopted the attitudes they did rather than to evaluate their work, and left it to their rasher followers to carry judgments of society into the literary realm.

If we believe in literary criticism at all—as distinct from literary history and from mere explanation and description—we must believe that there are criteria of literary excellence derived from the nature of literature itself. We know what a good table is, a good radio, a good loaf of bread. Now we may hold that an individual craftsman working with a pride in his own skill can turn out a better table than a man working in a mass production factory. We may make such a judgment because we know what we want in a table and we discover on inspection that a table made under the former conditions is a better table, according to our ideas of what a table should be, than that made under the latter. We may go on to show *why* mass production is a feature of modern civilization and why it is economically or socially impossible for us today to have our tables made by individual craftsmen: we may, that is to say, explain the conditions under which good and bad tables come to be made: but this explanation only adds to understanding because we started with an independent criterion of what a good table is. We cannot say that a table's badness consists in its being mass produced: we can say (if that is what we believe) that it is bad because of its design, because its shape, size, decoration or some other of its qualities as a table is of *this* kind rather than of *that*, and add the new knowledge that this kind of badness is liable to result when tables are made under modern conditions of manufacture. We have not gone outside our theory of tables in order to discover what a bad table is, but we *have* gone outside it in order to explain, at least partially, how this table came to be bad in this way.

The critic of tables who immediately sees a table as bad when told that it is made under conditions of which he disapproves either means that it is bad not as a table but as a social product—it is made possible by conditions that are socially undesirable—and that is not judging the table as a table at all; or, if he really thinks he is judging the table as a table, he is simply confused. And it is not only the Marxists who have fallen into one or other of these categories: the art criticism of John Ruskin continually falls into the confusion of a man who is sensitive to esthetic values as such yet keeps insisting that good art is only that which is produced by good social and ethical conditions. The point might be illustrated by another analogy. In the years after Hitler became the political leader of Germany, many people in America and elsewhere refused to buy, for example, Rhine wine because they did not want to give economic support to a régime they detested. They refused to buy wine from Germany because they thoroughly disapproved of the social and political conditions prevailing in Germany at the time. But they remained fond of Rhine wine, and few believed that the Liebfraumilch produced under Hitler was any worse than that produced under the Weimar Republic.

It is true that this is not a very accurate analogy, because a work of literary art often bears the stamp of its social origin in its very texture in a way that a table or a bottle of wine does not. We often, in fact, require the assistance of the social historian to explain to us what a work of art really is, as we have noted in discussing the relation to criticism of historical scholarship. Before we can evaluate anything we must know what it truly is, and that is one of the links between history (and sociology) and criticism and between the genetic and the evaluative approach. Sometimes (though by no means always) if we see how a thing has come to be what it is we are in a better position to appreciate what it really is and thus to evaluate it for what it is. Is a painting meant to hang in a gallery or to decorate the walls of a particular church? Is a lyric meant to be sung to the lute, read aloud, or meditated in the study? Is *Gulliver's Travels* a child's adventure story or a satire on mankind? If the first object of the critic is to see the work in itself as it really is, the sociologist, like the historian, can often help him. But once he has seen what it is, he must apply a criterion suitable to the nature of what he sees.

DESCRIPTIVE FUNCTION OF SOCIOLOGICAL CRITICISM

Sociological criticism can, then, help us to avoid making mistakes about the nature of the work of literature we have before us, by throwing light on its function or on the conventions with reference to which certain aspects of it are to be understood. It has therefore an important *descriptive* function, and as accurate description must precede evaluation it can be called a handmaid of criticism. And a very important handmaid it often is. If we read Chaucer's *Troilus and Criseyde* with a knowledge of the courtly love tradition in the light of which so much of its action is developed, we can see the work more clearly, we know better what we are dealing with, and we can proceed to evaluate it with all the more confidence.

SOCIOLOGICAL EXPLANATION OF THE CHARACTERISTICS OF AN AGE

But sociological criticism has perhaps a more important function than this. It can greatly advance knowledge by helping the reader to see why some faults are characteristic of works of a certain period—can even help to explain the nature of such faults, though the discovery that they are faults is made with reference to purely literary standards. One does not go to the social historian to discover that certain kinds of sentimentality—such as that which mars the ending of Barrie's *The Little Minister*—represent a literary fault; the social historian, however, by drawing our attention to the social causes of sentimentality, can assist us to a deeper understanding of what sentimentality really is. If we are puzzled by the difference in tone between the first part of the *Romance of the Rose*, written by Guillaume de Lorris, and its continuation by Jean de Meun, the social historian can help us by showing the tone of the first part as characteristic of a certain social class at a certain period and that of the second as deriving from an author whose mode of thought was to some extent conditioned by the mental habits of a new and rising class. This helps to explain what has been going on in the work, and in turn helps us to see it more clearly. The critic notes a quality (as fault or as virtue or as neutral); the social historian, like the psychologist, can help to explain why this particular quality can be found in that writer.

THE SOCIOLOGICAL CRITIC IN ACTION

Studies of the social background of an author's work, and of the influence of that background on that work, are of necessity of some length, for they involve first the description of that background and then the investigation of individual works with that description in mind. It is not easy, therefore, to do justice to this critical approach in a fairly brief quotation. *The Dickens World*, by Humphrey House,[1] an admirable example of sociological criticism, makes its points by alternating between sections giving accounts of the changing historical scene in Dickens' day and illustrations of the reflection of this changing scene in Dickens' novels. The author's statement of his purpose shows clearly what this kind of study hopes to achieve:

This book will attempt to show in a broad and simple way the connexion between what Dickens wrote and the times in which he wrote it, between his reformism and some of the things he wanted reformed, between the attitude to life shown in his books and the society in which he lived. It will be concerned a good deal with facts, and illustrated with quotations

[1] Oxford University Press, 1941. [Reprinted by permission of the publisher—Ed.]

from miscellaneous sources; for it is only in such details that a writer's environment can be seen and his purposes understood; the exact language of contemporaries alone can have the authentic tone and idiom necessary to conviction. With an author so variously and intricately wound into the history of his time the workings of his imagination can often best be seen from others' views of the events with which he started. . . .

Some notion of the sociological critic in action can be got from the following quotation from the sixth chapter ("The Changing Scene") of Mr. House's book:

Dickens lived through the years which saw the making of modern England, and of the middle-class oligarchy which is its government. His boyhood ended with the struggles for Catholic Emancipation and the Reform Bill: his writing life coincided almost exactly with the rule of the Ten-Pound Householders. Middle-class government then meant middle-class reform —the assault on obsolete privileges and procedure [Mr. House, in another chapter, discusses how such assaults enter into the very fabric of Dickens' novels], the abolition of restraints on trade, industry, and acquisitiveness, and the painful construction of a legal and administrative system adapted to the conditions which gave the middle classes their power.

The technical achievements of the years between 1812 and 1870 had a far greater effect on those who saw them than any such achievement since: railways altered the whole pattern of the country's life more deeply than cars or aeroplanes. For us, accustomed to ever-accelerating change, it is difficult to recover the mood of mixed utilitarian satisfaction and emotional excitement with which railway, telegraph, and submarine cable were greeted. Our grandfathers were enthralled by such books as Lardner's on the steam-engine and his *Museum of Science and Art* "illustrated by engravings on wood." The cuts of cranks and valves provoked them to something like aesthetic enthusiasm; the titbits of astronomy and geology made them think seriously, and often with disastrous result, about the Creation of the World; the chapters on cables and telegraphs urged them irresistibly to quote the boast of Puck. The more thoughtful perhaps shared something of Carlyle's apprehension, first voiced in 1829, that mechanization of external life might mean a baleful mechanization of the mind. But all alike, after a first hesitation or resistance, were compelled to accept the new world and the social changes that it brought: all were part if it, and there was no more escape for Dickens than for anybody else.

Some measure of the changes can be made if we compare *Pickwick* with *Our Mutual Friend*. The books are plainly by the same author; but when all allowances have been made for the obvious differences of form, theme, mood, and setting, for the influence of Dickens's private life upon his art, for developments in his art itself, it still remains clear that the two books are the product of different climates. It is sometimes said in discussions of Dickens's technique as a novelist that any of his great characters could step out of one book into another without materially disturbing the arrangement of either. But if we try to imagine Sam Weller in *Our Mutual Friend* the limitations of this formal criticism are at once plain. The physique, features, and complexion of the characters have changed between the two books almost as much as their clothes: the grimaces of villains have conformed to a new fashion; manners are so altered that one would as little expect that Boffin should get drunk as that John Harmon should fight a duel. We feel that people use knives and forks in a different style. Everybody is more restrained. The eccentrics and monsters in the earlier books walk through a crowd without exciting particular attention: in the latter they are likely to be pointed at in the streets, and are forced into bitter seclusion; social conformity has taken on a new meaning. Silas Wegg and Mr. Venus are at odds and ends with their world as Daniel Quilp was not. The middle classes are more self-important, the lower less self-assured. London, though vastly bigger in extent, is smaller in mystery: it has been opened up by the police. The whole scene seems narrower, more crowded, and, in a peculiar way, more stuffy. The very air seems to have changed in quality, and to tax the powers of Sanitary Reform to the uttermost. In *Pickwick* a bad smell was a bad smell; in *Our Mutual Friend* it is a problem.

These changes cannot be attributed to machinery only, nor to any one cause: but the cumulative effect of difference is so striking that it is impossible to understand Dickens without following in some detail the impact of external changes on his work. . . . [Mr. House then quotes from contemporary accounts of these external changes.]

The general chronology of *Dombey and Son* works out quite well if we assume that the book's plot ended with the writing of it in 1848. Florence was then the mother of a son old enough to talk intelligently about his "poor little uncle": supposing she was then twenty-one or two, Paul would have been born about 1833 and died 1840–1. This fits some of the main episodes that can be dated by historical events. The journey of Dombey and the Major to Leamington happened soon after Paul's death: the London and Birmingham Railway, by which they travelled, was fully opened in September 1838, and the Royal Hotel, Leamington, at which they stayed, was pulled down about 1841–2. In describing the Leamington scenes Dickens was obviously drawing on memories of a holiday he had there with Hablot Browne in the autumn of 1838; and Browne was their illustrator. Mr. Carker's death at Paddock Wood station was only possible after 1844, when the branch line was opened from there to Maidstone. The book and the period thus hang together without any serious problems of anachronism. In it there is still a lot from the 1820's. Sol Gills with his decaying, out-of-date business, and even the Dombey firm itself, living on the worn maxim, ill-observed, of a pushing eighteenth-century merchant, are intended to appear as survivals from another age. On the whole the book shows an emotional as well as a practical "consciousness of living in a world of change," an apprehension of what the changes meant in detail every day, the new quality of life they brought. *Dombey*, more than any other of his major works, shows how quickly and surely Dickens could sense the mood of his time, and incorporate new sensations in imaginative literature.

The new mood and atmosphere are very largely caused by the railways: the publication of the book coincided with the railway mania of the middle 'forties. It would be hard to exaggerate the effect of those years on English social life. Practically the whole country was money-mad; the public attitude to investment was quite altered, and it then first became clear that Joint Stock companies, however imperfectly managed, were certain to become a permanent and influential feature of finance. Railway works helped to absorb the unemployed and so to remove the fear of revolution. The growth of home consumption was enormously accelerated by improved transport: diet, furniture, fireplaces, and all the physical appurtenances of life changed character more rapidly; the very landscape was given a new aesthetic character—even perhaps a new standard—by embankments, cuttings, and viaducts. But, above all, the scope and tempo of individual living were revolutionized, even for a workman and his family, on a Parliamentary train.

Mr. House then goes on to note the impact of these changes on Dickens' novels, emphasizing particularly the effects he got by contrasting the new world of railways with the dying world of stagecoaches. He shows, too, how, by describing the changing countryside as viewed by a passenger sitting in a train and looking out of the window, he can give a panoramic picture of the new industrial England and point the contrast between living conditions in the congested factory areas and the spacious dwellings of the country landowners.

Against this detailed social background, Mr. House then discusses a number of the novels, which emerge with some of their features more clearly visible than they would be to the reader who has not had his attention drawn to the social and economic factors at work on their author's attitude. For example:

Great Expectations is the perfect expression of a phase of English society: it is a statement, to be taken as it stands, of what money can do, good and bad; of how it can change and make distinctions of class; how it can pervert virtue, sweeten manners, open up new fields of enjoyment and suspicion. The mood of the book belongs not to the imaginary date of its plot, but to the time in which it was written; for the unquestioned assumptions that Pip can be transformed by money and the minor graces it can buy, and that the loss of one fortune can be repaired on the strength of incidental gains in voice and friends, were only possible in a country secure in its internal economy, with expanding markets abroad: this could hardly be said of England in the 'twenties and 'thirties [when the action was supposed to have taken place].

Pip's acquired "culture" was an entirely bourgeois thing: it came to little more than accent, table manners, and clothes. In these respects a country gentleman with an estate in a remoter part of England would probably have been, even at Queen Victoria's accession, more like the neighbouring farmers than like Mr. Dombey. The process of diffusing standard "educated," London and Home Counties, speech as the norm expected of a gentleman was by no means complete: its rapid continuance through the Dickens period was an essential part of the increasing social uniformity between the middle and upper classes, helped on by the development of the "public" schools.

We are told that Pip "read" a great deal, and that he enjoyed it; but we do not know what he read, or how it affected his mind, or what kind of pleasures he got from it. He knew enough about Shakespeare and acting to realize that Mr. Wopsle turned Waldengarver was ridiculous; but what other delights he found in theatre-going in his prosperous days we are left to judge for ourselves; painting and music certainly had no large part in his life. People like Pip, Herbert Pocket, and Traddles have no culture but domestic comfort and moral decency. They are sensitive, lovable, and intelligent, but their normal activities are entirely limited to a profession and a fireside. When one of their kind extends his activities beyond this range it is in the direction of "social work," and even that is likely to be governed by his profession, as Allan Woodcourt is a good doctor, and Mr. Milvey a good parson. David Copperfield's other activity is to write novels like *Great Expectations* and *David Copperfield*: so we come full circle. . . .

Here the sociological critic has illuminated certain features of literary works by drawing our attention to the way in which social changes and other social factors are mirrored in them. He is not assessing value; he is throwing searchlights from new angles and, like the historical scholar and the psychological critic, spotlights aspects of the works he discusses by explaining how they came to be what they are. The pattern that emerges under this searchlight is not the "true" or the "complete" pattern of the work—no single pattern is. But it is a pattern which, if we bear it in mind when looking at the work from other points of view, can add its share to increased perception and enjoyment. For works of literary art are multiple things, with many meanings growing out of each other, and no one critic or school of critics can exhaust their significance.

WITH WHAT KINDS OF WORK IS SOCIOLOGICAL CRITICISM MOST HELPFUL?

It can be argued that sociological criticism is most usefully applied to certain kinds of prose works, and less usefully to lyric poetry. The prose novel in English has, until fairly recent times, been largely a public instrument, dependent for its pattern of meaning on agreement between the writer and his public about the significance of human action and the nature of morality (see Daiches, *The Novel and the Modern World*, 1939, chapter 1), while the lyric poet tends to communicate a more private vision of reality. Robinson Crusoe, on finding himself alone on his island, did not seek to exploit his loneliness by meditation on the relation between the individual and the universe: his task was to recreate in this distant isolation the skeleton at least of the civilization he had left behind him—complete with umbrella. For the English novel depended on society, and on public agreement about what, among the multifarious details of daily life, was worth picking out as significant. What was significant was what altered a social relationship —love and marriage, quarreling and reconciliation, gain or loss of money or of social status. You could, of course, criticize society, but you did it by showing how social convention did not in fact lead to that generally-approved practical morality which it professed to foster. You could explore the relation between spontaneity of feeling and social convention, as Jane Austen did, or the relation between gentility and morality, as Thackeray did, or the effect of industrial society on private character, as Dickens did, or investigate the possibilities of self-knowledge and vocation in a context of society at work, as George Eliot did, but in every case the plot would be carried forward by public symbols. And in every case society is *there*, to be taken account of and accepted as a basic fact about human life even when the author wishes to attack it or alter it. The eighteenth and nineteenth century novel is therefore a particularly happy hunting ground for the sociological critic, and the student might ask himself what sociological questions can profitably be asked about, for example, the novels of Richardson, Jane Austen, Dickens, Thackeray and George Eliot. But with such a novelist as Emily Brontë, who worked with a poet's kind of imagination, the sociological approach is perhaps less fruitful. Similarly, with the twentieth century novel, we can perhaps profitably ask sociological questions about Wells, Galsworthy, Dos Passos, even (though in his own way he operates as a poet) Faulkner, but what about Virginia Woolf, D. H. Lawrence, and Hemingway? (Hemingway, though he apparently deals with man in society, is, in his best novels, constructing heroic myths which derive from an essentially poetic sensibility. Lawrence's social origins can be usefully investigated by those interested in his psychology, but the relevance of such investigation to an understanding of the way in which his imagination works in his novels is surely dubious.) These are distinctions which the reader would do well to consider, whatever the conclusions he may reach.

On the other hand, a sociological approach has been brought to bear on poetry, not only by the Marxists (who endeavor to explain works of literature by relating them to their origins in the individual's response to the class situation in which he finds himself) but by such a critic as F. W. Bateson, in his *English Poetry: A Critical Introduction* (1950). Bateson's tenth chapter is a discussion of Gray's "Elegy" which contrasts sharply in method with Cleanth Brooks' analysis of the poem in *The Well Wrought Urn*. Bateson starts from the fact that the "Elegy" was composed in two installments, the second (which contains the last fifty-six lines) inferior to the first. The second part of the "Elegy," Bateson argues, is an unsuccessful attempt to depersonalize it after a brilliant first section in which the plangent contrast between "the natural, almost animal life of the village" and "the futile artificial life of the 'Proud'" presents the Gray of 1742 (friendless and dependent) arraigning the Gray of 1741 (before the death of his only intimate friend, Richard West). After an interesting analysis of the way in which symbolic images operate in the poem, Bateson concludes: "The *Elegy*, in addition to all the other things that it is, was a tract for the times. It was a plea for decentralization, recalling the over-urbanized ruling class to its roots in a rural society based upon the benevolent despotism of the manor-house."

Bateson divides the history of English poetry into six consecutive schools—Anglo-French, Chaucerian, Renaissance, Augustan, Romantic, and Modern, and distinguishes six consecutive social orders to which they correspond—the Period of Lawyers' Feudalism, the Local Democracy of the Yeomanry, the Centralized Absolutism of the Prince's Servants, the Oligarchy of the Landed Interests, the Plutocracy of Business, and the Managerial State. Then he proceeds to relate particular poems to the social organization of their period, showing how attitude, image, state of mind, are in each case related to the poet's response to the social world of which he was a part. The titles of his chapters are instructive: "The Yeoman Democracy and Chaucer's 'Miller's Tale,'" "The Money-Lender's Son: 'L'Allegro' and 'Il Penseroso,'" "The Quickest Way out of Manchester: Four Romantic Odes," and so on. Brief quotation does serious injustice to the cogency and closeness of Bateson's reasoning, but perhaps this conclusion to his essay on Waller will help to illustrate his method:

This central contradiction is the ultimate explanation of the pretentiousness and the emptiness of much Augustan poetry. With no mystical or traditional basis of authority on the one hand, and no rational basis on the other, except in the single field of agricultural improvement [Bateson has previously discussed in some detail the agricultural improvements of the period], the ruling class could only justify its privileges in the eyes of the nation by being an *aristocracy*, living in the best houses, eating the best food, reading the best books and patronizing the best poets. Hence their "ritual of conspicuous waste"—Palladian mansions that were too large to live in, Pindaric odes that were too dull to read. None of the Augustan poets entirely resolves the contradiction, and there is therefore no Augustan poem that can be quite be called great, but the better poets succeed in mitigating it. Waller's "Panegyric to my Lord Protector," Dryden's "Secular Masque," Rochester's "Satyr against Mankind," Pope's portrait of Lord Timon (in the fourth "Moral Essay"), and Gray's brilliant "On Lord Holland's Seat near Margate" go some way at any rate to salving the period's social conscience.[2]

Another important recent work which endeavors to explain the tone of works of literature with reference to the social context and to enable us to see their literary qualities more clearly by showing us how they reflect the writer looking at his world is *Poets on Fortune's Hill*, by John F. Danby (1952). The following quotation from Danby's introductory chapter will make clear his point of view.[3]

The picture of the Hill of Fortune, and of literature bound to the patronage of either Great House or Public Theatre, already makes the Elizabethan-Jacobean scene less monolithic than it is sometimes imagined. Taking the image further, increasing complications become evident. The Hill has different levels and different sides. Movements up and down, and around and about, or movements combining both these, are possible. Different views are to be expected from different positions on the Hill. Elizabethan society is as highly differentiated as any other. Literature is what happens "in" a man, certainly. What can happen "in" him, however, will be partly conditioned by what has happened "to" him in virtue of his place and behaviour on the Hill. Finally, literature is addressed by a man from his place to those of his contemporaries (on the same Hill) who are in a position to listen to him. . . . Literature has a three-dimensional setting. Very often it is reduced in the study to something as two-dimensional as the paper it is written on.

Some of the differences between specific works might best be accounted for in terms of social placing. The *Arcadia* is Great House literature, and Sidney the interpreter of the *ethos* of the Great House. Shakespeare's plays belong to the open town, the open Elizabethan country, and the unroofed commercial theatre. Beaumont and Fletcher are curious hybrids: second-generation scions of the Elizabethan *élite*, and second-generation exploiters of a theatre now no longer, possibly, open to the sky. . . .

A recognition of the social placing of the writers concerned helps, I think, towards a clearer view of how matters stand between them on these questions [of influence and impact and changes in style]. And not only that. The question of "influences" ceases to be academic, eccentrically driving away from the text. When "influences" are seen in relation to social placing, and when social place is seen to imply a whole *ethos*, intellectual, temperamental, and spiritual, the question of "influence" takes on a new significance. It is brought into relation with the essential quality of the work itself, as written by a man from his place. It is, in other words, made relevant to a just appreciation of what the work under consideration *is*, and not merely what it is "derived" from.

The pure formalist might say that Mr. Danby's investigations might show us "what the work under consideration *is*" but not what it is *qua* work of literary art. But there can be little doubt that this method, properly used, does help us to see why certain poets

---

[2] [Published by Longmans, Green & Co., Ltd.—Ed.]

[3] Reprinted by permission of Faber and Faber Limited.

and dramatists wrote as they did, and what the moral pattern of their work really is. It also illuminates differences between contemporary poets. Consider, for example, this statement:

> Sidney is on the top of Fortune's hill, whereas Spenser is not. Spenser's poetry must win him preferment, and then maintain him in place in the body of the world. For Sidney poetry is the private devotion to truth. For Spenser it must also be the public vindication of his claim to recognition as a poet, a proof that the poet as such is engaged on work of national importance. There is therefore in Spenser a professional earnestness, an earnestness not only about "truth" but also an earnestness to display his command over all the poetic crafts. His poetry requires the external occasion, the prescriptions of theory and form, the suggested topics; and in its most ambitious assay of skill it will load story with allegory, and allegory with morality, and morality with platonism, to form a massive assembly of all the by-products of renaissance learning and art. . . .

Such an approach, used in a discussion of Sidney's *Arcadia* as "the Great House Romance," of the relation between Sidney's work and the late-Shakespearean romance, and of other aspects of Shakespeare and of Beaumont and Fletcher, can not only explain the reasons for certain features of their work which we already know; it can also draw our attention to literary qualities in their work which we had not before clearly seen. Thus sociological criticism can help to increase literary perception as well as to explain origins.

Marxist criticism has been on the whole far less sensitive than this. It has been content either to explain literature in terms of its social origins, or to account for a writer's attitude in terms of his position in the class structure, or to pass judgment on a given work or writer in accordance with the tendency it or he displays to favor the political and economic cause favored by the critic. Nevertheless, some valuable genetic insights have been provided by Marxist or near-Marxist critics. Christopher Caudwell's *Illusion and Reality* (sub-titled "A Study of the Sources of Poetry") (1937), and *Studies in a Dying Culture* (1939) are among the best Marxist criticism, and Granville Hicks' *Great Tradition* (1933) and *Figures of Transition* (1939) are often illuminating in spite of their tendency to startling over-simplification and to the simple transference of political or economic judgment into the literary field. Marxism, being a theory of history, is more appropriate to literary criticism as a genetic explanation of social origins of works of literature (as it is in Caudwell) than as an evaluative tool.

EMPLOYING THE METHOD

The reader might profitably consider whether Danby's approach, described above, can be usefully applied to any other period of literature. Can, for example, Tennyson's *In Memoriam* be illuminated by a consideration of the poet's place on Fortune's Hill? And what of the Victorian novelist's relation to his public? How far are conditions of publication relevant to a critical discussion of a novel? (Kathleen Tillotson's *Novels of the Eighteen-Forties*, 1954, contains much interesting discussion of the position of the novelist with reference to both his public and his publisher, and then proceeds to discuss some specific novels. The reader might ask himself how far and in what way the earlier discussion illuminates the latter.)

FOR DISCUSSION:

1. What does Daiches mean when he says that although sociology is not a normative science, it demands normative treatment as soon as it comes into contact with the masses?

2. Is Daiches making a distinction between the literary critic and the literary historian? If so, what is it?

3. Daiches says the first object of the

critic is to see the work as it really is. What difficulties are inherent in this attempt?

4. What advantages does the social approach to literary interpretation have over other methods? What disadvantages does it have?

5. With what particular kinds of literature is the social approach most successful? Least successful?

6. What are the major pitfalls in the sociological criticism of literature?

SUGGESTIONS FOR ADDITIONAL READING:

An excellent bibliography of books and articles treating the relationship of literature and society can be found on pages 143–214 of Hugh D. Duncan, *Language and Literature in Society*, Chicago, 1953.

Arvin, Newton. "Fiction Mirrors America," *Current History*, XLII (September 1935), 610–616.

Daiches, David. *Literature and Society*. London, 1938.

Farrell, James. *A Note on Literary Criticism*. New York, 1936.

Henderson, Philip. *Literature and a Changing Civilization*. London, 1935.

Lerner, Max, and Edwin Mims. "Literature," *Encyclopaedia of Social Sciences*, IX (1933), 523–541.

Levin, Harry. "Literature as a Social Institution," *Accent*, VI (1946), 159–168.

Read, Herbert. *Art and Society*. London, 1937.

Witte, W. "The Sociological Approach to Literature," *Modern Language Review*, XXXVI (1941), 86–94.

Major Barbara*

BERNARD SHAW

STEPHEN UNDERSHAFT, son of Andrew Undershaft and Lady Britomart
LADY BRITOMART, daughter of the Earl of Stevenage and wife of Andrew Undershaft
BARBARA UNDERSHAFT, daughter of Andrew Undershaft and Lady Britomart; a Major in the Salvation Army
SARAH UNDERSHAFT, daughter of Andrew Undershaft and Lady Britomart
ADOLPHUS CUSINS, fiancé of Barbara Undershaft
CHARLES LOMAX, fiancé of Sarah Undershaft
MORRISON, Lady Britomart's butler
ANDREW UNDERSHAFT, husband of Lady Britomart; head of Undershaft and Lazarus, munitions makers
RUMMY (ROMOLA) MITCHENS, SNOBBY (BRONTERE O'BRIEN) PRICE, regulars at the West Ham Salvation Army Shelter
PETER SHIRLEY, a discharged workman, poor but honest
JENNY HILL, a Salvation Army lass
BILL WALKER, a young tough
MRS. BAINES, a Salvation Army Commissioner
BILTON, a foreman in Undershaft and Lazarus

ACT I

It is after dinner in January 1906, in the library in Lady Britomart Undershaft's house in Wilton Crescent. A large and comfortable settee is in the middle of the room, upholstered in dark leather. A person sitting on it (it is vacant at present) would have, on his right, Lady Britomart's writing table, with the lady herself busy at it; a smaller writing table behind him on his left; the door behind him on Lady Britomart's side; and a window with a window seat directly on his left. Near the window is an armchair.

LADY BRITOMART is a woman of fifty or thereabouts, well dressed and yet careless of her dress, well bred and quite reckless of her breeding, well mannered and yet appallingly outspoken and indifferent to the opinion of her interlocutors, amiable and yet peremptory, arbitrary, and high-tempered to the last bearable degree, and withal a very typical managing matron of the upper class, treated as a naughty child until she grew into a scolding mother, and finally settling down with plenty of practical ability and worldly experience, limited in the oddest way with domestic and class limitations, conceiving the universe exactly as if it were a large house in Wilton Crescent, though handling her corner of it very effectively on that assumption, and being quite enlightened and liberal as to the books in the library, the pictures on the walls, the music in the portfolios, and the articles in the papers.

Her son, STEPHEN, comes in. He is a gravely correct young man under 25, taking himself very seriously, but still in some awe of his mother, from childish habit and bachelor shyness rather than from any weakness of character.

STEPHEN. Whats the matter?

---

* Copyright 1913, 1941, George Bernard Shaw. Reprinted by permission of the Public Trustee as Executor of the Estate of George Bernard Shaw, and the Society of Authors.

LADY BRITOMART. Presently, Stephen.

Stephen submissively walks to the settee and sits down. He takes up a Liberal weekly called The Speaker.

LADY BRITOMART. Dont begin to read, Stephen. I shall require all your attention.
STEPHEN. It was only while I was waiting—
LADY BRITOMART. Dont make excuses, Stephen. [*He puts down* The Speaker.] Now! [*She finishes her writing; rises; and comes to the settee.*] I have not kept you waiting very long, I think.
STEPHEN. Not at all, mother.
LADY BRITOMART. Bring me my cushion. [*He takes the cushion from the chair at the desk and arranges it for her as she sits down on the settee.*] Sit down. [*He sits down and fingers his tie nervously.*] Dont fiddle with your tie, Stephen: there is nothing the matter with it.
STEPHEN. I beg your pardon. [*He fiddles with his watch chain instead.*]
LADY BRITOMART. Now are you attending to me, Stephen?
STEPHEN. Of course, mother.
LADY BRITOMART. No: it's not of course. I want something much more than your everyday matter-of-course attention. I am going to speak to you very seriously, Stephen. I wish you would let that chain alone.
STEPHEN. [*hastily relinquishing the chain*]. Have I done anything to annoy you, mother? If so, it was quite unintentional.
LADY BRITOMART [*astonished*]. Nonsense! [*With some remorse.*] My poor boy, did you think I was angry with you?
STEPHEN. What is it, then, mother? You are making me very uneasy.
LADY BRITOMART [*squaring herself at him rather aggressively*]. Stephen: may I ask how soon you intend to realize that you are a grown-up man, and that I am only a woman?
STEPHEN [*amazed*]. Only a—
LADY BRITOMART. Dont repeat my words, please: it is a most aggravating habit. You must learn to face life seriously, Stephen. I really cannot bear the whole burden of our family affairs any longer. You must advise me: you must assume the responsibility.
STEPHEN. I!

LADY BRITOMART. Yes, you, of course. You were 24 last June. Youve been at Harrow and Cambridge. Youve been to India and Japan. You must know a lot of things, now; unless you have wasted your time most scandalously. Well, advise me.
STEPHEN [*much perplexed*]. You know I have never interfered in the household —
LADY BRITOMART. No: I should think not. I dont want you to order the dinner.
STEPHEN. I mean in our family affairs.
LADY BRITOMART. Well, you must interfere now; for they are getting quite beyond me.
STEPHEN [*troubled*]. I have thought sometimes that perhaps I ought; but really, mother, I know so little about them; and what I do know is so painful! it is so impossible to mention some things to you— [*he stops, ashamed.*]
LADY BRITOMART. I suppose you mean your father.
STEPHEN [*almost inaudibly*]. Yes.
LADY BRITOMART. My dear: we cant go on all our lives not mentioning him. Of course you were quite right not to open the subject until I asked you to; but you are old enough now to be taken into my confidence, and to help me to deal with him about the girls.
STEPHEN. But the girls are all right. They are engaged.
LADY BRITOMART [*complacently*]. Yes: I have made a very good match for Sarah. Charles Lomax will be a millionaire at 35. But that is ten years ahead; and in the meantime his trustees cannot under the terms of his father's will allow him more than £800 a year.
STEPHEN. But the will says also that if he in-increases his income by his own exertions, they may double the increase.
LADY BRITOMART. Charles Lomax's exertions are much more likely to decrease his income than to increase it. Sarah will have to find at least another £800 a year for the next ten years; and even then they will be as poor as church mice. And what about Barbara? I thought Barbara was going to make the most brilliant career of all of you. And what does she do? Joins the Salvation Army; discharges her maid; lives on a pound a week; and walks in one evening with a professor of Greek whom she has picked up in the street, and who

pretends to be a Salvationist, and actually plays the big drum for her in public because he has fallen head over ears in love with her.

STEPHEN. I was certainly rather taken aback when I heard they were engaged. Cusins is a very nice fellow, certainly: nobody would ever guess that he was born in Australia; but—

LADY BRITOMART. Oh, Adolphus Cusins will make a very good husband. After all, nobody can say a word against Greek: it stamps a man at once as an educated gentleman. And my family, thank Heaven, is not a pig-headed Tory one. We are Whigs, and believe in liberty. Let snobbish people say what they please: Barbara shall marry, not the man they like, but the man *I* like.

STEPHEN. Of course I was thinking only of his income. However, he is not likely to be extravagant.

LADY BRITOMART. Dont be too sure of that, Stephen. I know your quiet, simple, refined, poetic people like Adolphus: quite content with the best of everything! They cost more than your extravagant people, who are always as mean as they are second rate. No: Barbara will need at least £2000 a year. You see it means two additional households. Besides, my dear, you must marry soon. I dont approve of the present fashion of philandering bachelors and late marriages; and I am trying to arrange something for you.

STEPHEN. It's very good of you, mother; but perhaps I had better arrange that for myself.

LADY BRITOMART. Nonsense! you are much too young to begin matchmaking: you would be taken in by some pretty little nobody. Of course I dont mean that you are not to be consulted: you know that as well as I do. [STEPHEN *closes his lips and is silent.*] Now dont sulk, Stephen.

STEPHEN. I am not sulking, mother. What has all this got to do with—with—with my father?

LADY BRITOMART. My dear Stephen: where is the money to come from? It is easy enough for you and the other children to live on my income as long as we are in the same house; but I cant keep four families in four separate houses. You know how poor my father is: he has barely seven thousand a year now; and really, if he were not the Earl of Stevenage, he would have to give up society. He can do nothing for us. He says, naturally enough, that it is absurd that he should be asked to provide for the children of a man who is rolling in money. You see, Stephen, your father must be fabulously wealthy, because there is always a war going on somewhere.

STEPHEN. You need not remind me of that, mother. I have hardly ever opened a newspaper in my life without seeing our name in it. The Undershaft torpedo! The Undershaft quick firers! The Undershaft ten inch! the Undershaft disappearing rampart gun! the Undershaft submarine! and now the Undershaft aerial battleship! At Harrow they called me the Woolwich Infant. At Cambridge it was the same. A little brute at King's who was always trying to get up revivals, spoilt my Bible—your first birthday present to me—by writing under my name, 'Son and heir to Undershaft and Lazarus, Death and Destruction Dealers: address Christendom and Judea.' But that was not so bad as the way I was kowtowed to everywhere because my father was making millions by selling cannons.

LADY BRITOMART. It is not only the cannons, but the war loans that Lazarus arranges under cover of giving credit for the cannons. You know, Stephen, it's perfectly scandalous. Those two men, Andrew Undershaft and Lazarus, positively have Europe under their thumbs. That is why your father is able to behave as he does. He is above the law. Do you think Bismarck or Gladstone or Disraeli could have openly defied every social and moral obligation all their lives as your father has? They simply wouldnt have dared. I asked Gladstone to take it up. I asked The Times to take it up. I asked the Lord Chamberlain to take it up. But it was just like asking them to declare war on the Sultan. They wouldnt. They said they couldnt touch him. I believe they were afraid.

STEPHEN. What could they do? He does not actually break the law.

LADY BRITOMART. Not break the law! He is always breaking the law. He broke the law when he was born: his parents were not married.

STEPHEN. Mother! Is that true?

LADY BRITOMART. Of course it's true: that was why we separated.

STEPHEN. He married without letting you know this!

LADY BRITOMART [*rather taken aback by this inference*]. Oh no. To do Andrew justice, that was not the sort of thing he did. Besides, you know the Undershaft motto: Unashamed. Everybody knew.

STEPHEN. But you said that was why you separated.

LADY BRITOMART. Yes, because he was not content with being a foundling himself: he wanted to disinherit you for another foundling. That was what I couldnt stand.

STEPHEN [*ashamed*]. Do you mean for—for—for—

LADY BRITOMART. Dont stammer, Stephen. Speak distinctly.

STEPHEN. But this is so frightful to me, mother. To have to speak to you about such things!

LADY BRITOMART. It's not pleasant for me, either, especially if you are still so childish that you must make it worse by a display of embarrassment. It is only in the middle classes, Stephen, that people get into a state of dumb helpless horror when they find that there are wicked people in the world. In our class, we have to decide what is to be done with wicked people; and nothing should disturb our self-possession. Now ask your question properly.

STEPHEN. Mother: have you no consideration for me? For Heaven's sake either treat me as a child, as you always do, and tell me nothing at all; or tell me everything and let me take it as best I can.

LADY BRITOMART. Treat you as a child! What do you mean? It is most unkind and ungrateful of you to say such a thing. You know I have never treated any of you as children. I have always made you my companions and friends, and allowed you perfect freedom to do and say whatever you liked, so long as you liked what I could approve of.

STEPHEN [*desperately*]. I daresay we have been the very imperfect children of a very perfect mother; but I do beg you to let me alone for once, and tell me about this horrible business of my father wanting to set me aside for another son.

LADY BRITOMART [*amazed*]. Another son! I never said anything of the kind. I never dreamt of such a thing. This is what comes of interrupting me.

STEPHEN. But you said—

LADY BRITOMART [*cutting him short*]. Now be a good boy, Stephen, and listen to me patiently. The Undershafts are descended from a foundling in the parish of St Andrew Undershaft in the city. That was long ago, in the reign of James the First. Well, this foundling was adopted by an armorer and gun-maker. In the course of time the foundling succeeded to the business; and from some notion of gratitude, or some vow or something, he adopted another foundling, and left the business to him. And that foundling did the same. Ever since that, the cannon business has always been left to an adopted foundling named Andrew Undershaft.

STEPHEN. But did they never marry? Were there no legitimate sons?

LADY BRITOMART. Oh yes: they married just as your father did; and they were rich enough to buy land for their own children and leave them well provided for. But they always adopted and trained some foundling to succeed them in the business; and of course they always quarrelled with their wives furiously over it. Your father was adopted in that way; and he pretends to consider himself bound to keep up the tradition and adopt somebody to leave the business to. Of course I was not going to stand that. There may have been some reason for it when the Undershafts could only marry women in their own class, whose sons were not fit to govern great estates. But there could be no excuse for passing over my son.

STEPHEN [*dubiously*]. I am afraid I should make a poor hand of managing a cannon foundry.

LADY BRITOMART. Nonsense! you could easily get a manager and pay him a salary.

STEPHEN. My father evidently had no great opinion of my capacity.

LADY BRITOMART. Stuff, child! you were only a baby: it had nothing to do with your capacity. Andrew did it on principle, just as he did every perverse and wicked thing on principle. When my father remonstrated, Andrew actually told him to his face that history tells us of only two successful institutions: one the Undershaft firm, and the other the Roman Empire under the Antonines. That was because the Antonine emperors all adopted their successors. Such rubbish! The Stevenages are as good as the Antonines, I hope; and you are a Stevenage. But that was Andrew all over. There you have the man! Always clever and unanswerable when he was defending nonsense and wickedness: always awkward and sullen when he had to behave sensibly and decently!

STEPHEN. Then it was on my account that your home life was broken up, mother. I am sorry.

LADY BRITOMART. Well, dear, there were other differences. I really cannot bear an immoral man. I am not a Pharisee, I hope; and I should not have minded his merely doing wrong things: we are none of us perfect. But your father didnt exactly do wrong things: he said them and thought them: that was what was so dreadful. He really had a sort of religion of wrongness. Just as one doesnt mind men practising immorality so long as they own that they are in the wrong by preaching morality; so I couldnt forgive Andrew for preaching immorality while he practised morality. You would all have grown up without principles, without any knowledge of right and wrong, if he had been in the house. You know, my dear, your father was a very attractive man in some ways. Children did not dislike him; and he took advantage of it to put the wickedest ideas into their heads, and make them quite unmanageable. I did not dislike him myself: very far from it; but nothing can bridge over moral disagreement.

STEPHEN. All this simply bewilders me, mother. People may differ about matters of opinion, or even about religion; but how can they differ about right and wrong? Right is right; and wrong is wrong; and if a man cannot distinguish them properly, he is either a fool or a rascal: thats all.

LADY BRITOMART [touched]. Thats my own boy [she pats his cheek]! Your father never could answer that: he used to laugh and get out of it under cover of some affectionate nonsense. And now that you understand the situation, what do you advise me to do?

STEPHEN. Well, what can you do?

LADY BRITOMART. I must get the money somehow.

STEPHEN. We cannot take money from him. I had rather go and live in some cheap place like Bedford Square or even Hampstead than take a farthing of his money.

LADY BRITOMART. But after all, Stephen, our present income comes from Andrew.

STEPHEN [shocked]. I never knew that.

LADY BRITOMART. Well, you surely didnt suppose your grandfather had anything to give me. The Stevenages could not do everything for you. We gave you social position. Andrew had to contribute something. He had a very good bargain, I think.

STEPHEN [bitterly]. We are utterly dependent on him and his cannons, then?

LADY BRITOMART. Certainly not: the money is settled. But he provided it. So you see it is not a question of taking money from him or not: it is simply a question of how much. I dont want any more for myself.

STEPHEN. Nor do I.

LADY BRITOMART. But Sarah does; and Barbara does. That is, Charles Lomax and Adolphus Cusins will cost them more. So I must put my pride in my pocket and ask for it, I suppose. That is your advice, Stephen, is it not?

STEPHEN. No.

LADY BRITOMART [sharply]. Stephen!

STEPHEN. Of course if you are determined—

LADY BRITOMART. I am not determined: I ask your advice; and I am waiting for it. I will not have all the responsibility thrown on my shoulders.

STEPHEN [obstinately]. I would die sooner than ask him for another penny.

LADY BRITOMART [resignedly]. You mean that I must ask him. Very well, Stephen: it shall be as you wish. You will be glad to know that your grandfather concurs. But he thinks I ought to ask Andrew to come here and see the girls. After all, he must have some natural affection for them.

STEPHEN. Ask him here!!!

LADY BRITOMART. Do not repeat my words, Stephen. Where else can I ask him?

STEPHEN. I never expected you to ask him at all.

LADY BRITOMART. Now dont tease, Stephen. Come! you see that it is necessary that he should pay us a visit, dont you?

STEPHEN [reluctantly]. I suppose so, if the girls cannot do without his money.

LADY BRITOMART. Thank you, Stephen: I knew you would give me the right advice when it was properly explained to you. I have asked your father to come this evening. [STEPHEN bounds from his seat.] Dont jump, Stephen: it fidgets me.

STEPHEN [in utter consternation]. Do you mean to say that my father is coming here tonight—that he may be here at any moment?

LADY BRITOMART [looking at her watch]. I said nine. [He gasps. She rises.] Ring the bell, please. [STEPHEN goes to the smaller writing table; presses a button on it; and sits at it with his elbows on the table and his head in his hands, outwitted and overwhelmed.] It is ten minutes to nine yet; and I have to prepare the girls. I asked Charles Lomax and Adolphus to dinner on purpose that they might be here. Andrew had better see them in case he should cherish any delusions as to their being capable of supporting their wives. [The butler enters: LADY BRITOMART goes behind the settee to speak to him.] Morrison: go up to the drawing room and tell everybody to come down here at once. [MORRISON withdraws. LADY BRITOMART turns to STEPHEN.] Now remember, Stephen: I shall need all your countenance and authority. [He rises and tries to recover some vestige of these attributes.] Give me a chair, dear. [He pushes a chair forward from the wall to where she stands, near the smaller writing table. She sits down; and he goes to the armchair, into which he throws himself.] I dont know how Barbara will take it. Ever since they made her a major in the Salvation Army she has developed a propensity to have her own way and order people about which quite cows me sometimes. It's not ladylike: I'm sure I dont know where she picked it up. Anyhow, Barbara shant bully me; but still it's just as well that your father should be here before she has time to refuse to meet him or make a fuss. Dont look nervous, Stephen: it will only encourage Barbara to make difficulties. I am nervous enough, goodness knows; but I dont shew it.

SARAH and BARBARA come in with their respective young men, CHARLES LOMAX and ADOLPHUS CUSINS. SARAH is slender, bored, and mundane. BARBARA is robuster, jollier, much more energetic. SARAH is fashionably dressed: BARBARA is in Salvation Army uniform. LOMAX, a young man about town, is like many other young men about town. He is afflicted with a frivolous sense of humor which plunges him at the most inopportune moments into paroxysms of imperfectly suppressed laughter. CUSINS is a spectacled student, slight, thin haired, and sweet voiced, with a more complex form of Lomax's complaint. His sense of humor is intellectual and subtle, and is complicated by an appalling temper. The lifelong struggle of a benevolent temperament and a high conscience against impulses of inhuman ridicule and fierce impatience has set up a chronic strain which has visibly wrecked his constitution. He is a most implacable, determined, tenacious, intolerant person who by mere force of character presents himself as—and indeed actually is—considerate, gentle, explanatory, even mild and apologetic, capable possibly of murder, but not of cruelty or coarseness. By the operation of some instinct which is not merciful enough to blind him with the illusions of love, he is obstinately bent on marrying BARBARA. LOMAX likes SARAH and thinks it will be rather a lark to marry her. Consequently he has not attempted to resist Lady Britomart's arrangements to that end.

All four look as if they had been having a good deal of fun in the drawing room. The girls enter first, leaving the swains outside. SARAH comes to the settee. BARBARA comes in after her and stops at the door.

BARBARA. Are Cholly and Dolly to come in?

LADY BRITOMART [forcibly]. Barbara: I will not have Charles called Cholly: the vulgarity of it positively makes me ill.

BARBARA. It's all right, mother: Cholly is quite correct nowadays. Are they to come in?

LADY BRITOMART. Yes, if they will behave themselves.

BARBARA [through the door]. Come in, Dolly; and behave yourself.

BARBARA comes to her mother's writing table. CUSINS enters smiling, and wanders towards LADY BRITOMART.

SARAH [*calling*]. Come in, Cholly. [LOMAX *enters, controlling his features very imperfectly, and places himself vaguely between* SARAH *and* BARBARA.]

LADY BRITOMART [*peremptorily*]. Sit down, all of you. [*They sit.* CUSINS *crosses to the window and seats himself there.* LOMAX *takes a chair.* BARBARA *sits at the writing table and* SARAH *on the settee.*] I dont in the least know what you are laughing at, Adolphus. I am surprised at you, though I expected nothing better from Charles Lomax.

CUSINS [*in a remarkably gentle voice*]. Barbara has been trying to teach me the West Ham Salvation March.

LADY BRITOMART. I see nothing to laugh at in that; nor should you if you are really converted.

CUSINS [*sweetly*]. You were not present. It was really funny, I believe.

LOMAX. Ripping.

LADY BRITOMART. Be quiet, Charles. Now listen to me, children. Your father is coming here this evening.

General stupefaction. LOMAX, SARAH, *and* BARBARA *rise:* SARAH *scared, and* BARBARA *amused and expectant.*

LOMAX [*remonstrating*]. Oh I say!

LADY BRITOMART. You are not called on to say anything, Charles.

SARAH. Are you serious, mother?

LADY BRITOMART. Of course I am serious. It is on your account, Sarah, and also on Charles's. [*Silence.* SARAH *sits, with a shrug.* CHARLES *looks painfully unworthy.*] I hope you are not going to object, Barbara.

BARBARA. I! why should I? My father has a soul to be saved like anybody else. He's quite welcome as far as I am concerned. [*She sits on the table, and softly whistles* 'Onward, Christian Soldiers.']

LOMAX [*still remonstrant*]. But really, dont you know! Oh I say!

LADY BRITOMART [*frigidly*]. What do you wish to convey, Charles?

LOMAX. Well, you must admit that this is a bit thick.

LADY BRITOMART [*turning with ominous suavity to* CUSINS]. Adolphus: you are a professor of Greek. Can you translate Charles Lomax's remarks into reputable English for us?

CUSINS [*cautiously*]. If I may say so, Lady Brit, I think Charles has rather happily expressed what we all feel. Homer, speaking of Autolycus, uses the same phrase. πυκινὸν δόμον ἐλθεῖν means a bit thick.

LOMAX [*handsomely*]. Not that I mind, you know, if Sarah dont. [*He sits.*]

LADY BRITOMART [*crushingly*]. Thank you. Have I your permission, Adolphus, to invite my own husband to my own house?

CUSINS [*gallantly*]. You have my unhesitating support in everything you do.

LADY BRITOMART. Tush! Sarah: have you nothing to say?

SARAH. Do you mean that he is coming regularly to live here?

LADY BRITOMART. *Certainly not.* The spare room is ready for him if he likes to stay for a day or two and see a little more of you; but there are limits.

SARAH. Well, he cant eat us, I suppose. I dont mind.

LOMAX [*chuckling*]. I wonder how the old man will take it.

LADY BRITOMART. Much as the old woman will, no doubt, Charles.

LOMAX [*abashed*]. I didnt mean—at least—

LADY BRITOMART. You didnt think, Charles. You never do; and the result is, you never mean anything. And now please attend to me, children. Your father will be quite a stranger to us.

LOMAX. I suppose he hasnt seen Sarah since she was a little kid.

LADY BRITOMART. Not since she was a little kid, Charles, as you express it with that elegance of diction and refinement of thought that seem never to desert you. Accordingly—er—[*impatiently*]. Now I have forgotten what I was going to say. That comes of your provoking me to be sarcastic, Charles. Adolphus: will you kindly tell me where I was.

CUSINS [*sweetly*]. You were saying that as Mr Undershaft has not seen his children since they were babies, he will form his opinion of the way you have brought them up from their behavior tonight, and that therefore you wish us all to be particularly careful to conduct ourselves well, especially Charles.

LADY BRITOMART [*with emphatic approval*]. Precisely.

LOMAX. Look here, Dolly: Lady Brit didnt say that.
LADY BRITOMART [*vehemently*]. I did, Charles. Adolphus's recollection is perfectly correct. It is most important that you should be good; and I do beg you for once not to pair off into opposite corners and giggle and whisper while I am speaking to your father.
BARBARA. All right, mother. We'll do you credit. [*She comes off the table, and sits in her chair with ladylike elegance.*]
LADY BRITOMART. Remember, Charles, that Sarah will want to feel proud of you instead of ashamed of you.
LOMAX. Oh I say! theres nothing to be exactly proud of, dont you know.
LADY BRITOMART. Well, try and look as if there was.

MORRISON, *pale and dismayed, breaks into the room in unconcealed disorder.*

MORRISON. Might I speak a word to you, my lady?
LADY BRITOMART. Nonsense! Shew him up.
MORRISON. Yes, my lady. [*He goes.*]
LOMAX. Does Morrison know who it is?
LADY BRITOMART. Of course. Morrison has always been with us.
LOMAX. It must be a regular corker for him, dont you know.
LADY BRITOMART. Is this a moment to get on my nerves, Charles, with your outrageous expressions?
LOMAX. But this is something out of the ordinary, really—
MORRISON [*at the door*]. The—er—Mr Undershaft. [*He retreats in confusion.*]

ANDREW UNDERSHAFT *comes in. All rise.* LADY BRITOMART *meets him in the middle of the room behind the settee.*

ANDREW *is, on the surface, a stoutish, easy-going elderly man, with kindly patient manners, and an engaging simplicity of character. But he has a watchful, deliberate, waiting, listening face, and formidable reserves of power, both bodily and mental, in his capacious chest and long head. His gentleness is partly that of a strong man who has learnt by experience that his natural grip hurts ordinary people unless he handles them very carefully, and partly the mellowness of age and success. He is also a little shy in his present very delicate situation.*

LADY BRITOMART. Good evening, Andrew.
UNDERSHAFT. How d'ye do, my dear.
LADY BRITOMART. You look a good deal older.
UNDERSHAFT [*apologetically*]. I am somewhat older. [*Taking her hand with a touch of courtship.*] Time has stood still with you.
LADY BRITOMART [*throwing away his hand*]. Rubbish! This is your family.
UNDERSHAFT [*surprised*]. Is it so large? I am sorry to say my memory is failing very badly in some things. [*He offers his hand with paternal kindness to* LOMAX.]
LOMAX [*jerkily shaking his hand*]. Ahdedoo.
UNDERSHAFT. I can see you are my eldest. I am very glad to meet you again, my boy.
LOMAX [*remonstrating*]. No, but look here dont you know—[*Overcome.*] Oh I say!
LADY BRITOMART [*recovering from momentary speechlessness*]. Andrew: do you mean to say that you dont remember how many children you have?
UNDERSHAFT. Well, I am afraid I—. They have grown so much—er. Am I making any ridiculous mistake? I may as well confess: I recollect only one son. But so many things have happened since, of course—er—
LADY BRITOMART [*decisively*]. Andrew: you are talking nonsense. Of course you have only one son.
UNDERSHAFT. Perhaps you will be good enough to introduce me, my dear.
LADY BRITOMART. That is Charles Lomax, who is engaged to Sarah.
UNDERSHAFT. My dear sir, I beg your pardon.
LOMAX. Notatall. Delighted, I assure you.
LADY BRITOMART. This is Stephen.
UNDERSHAFT [*bowing*]. Happy to make your acquaintance, Mr Stephen. Then [*going to Cusins*] you must be my son. [*Taking Cusins' hands in his.*] How are you, my young friend? [*To* LADY BRITOMART.] He is very like you, my love.
CUSINS. You flatter me, Mr Undershaft. My name is Cusins: engaged to Barbara. [*Very explicitly.*] That is Major Barbara Undershaft, of the Salvation Army. That is Sarah, your second daughter. This is Stephen Undershaft, your son.
UNDERSHAFT. My dear Stephen, I beg your pardon.
STEPHEN. Not at all.
UNDERSHAFT. Mr Cusins: I am much indebted to you for explaining so precisely. [*Turning to* SARAH.] Barbara, my dear—

SARAH [*prompting him*]. Sarah.
UNDERSHAFT. Sarah, of course. [*They shake hands. He goes over to* BARBARA.] Barbara—I am right this time, I hope?
BARBARA. Quite right. [*They shake hands.*]
LADY BRITOMART [*resuming command*]. Sit down, all of you. Sit down, Andrew. [*She comes forward and sits on the settee.* CUSINS *also brings his chair forward on her left.* BARBARA *and* STEPHEN *resume their seats.* LOMAX *gives his chair to* SARAH *and goes for another.*]
UNDERSHAFT. Thank you, my love.
LOMAX [*conversationally, as he brings a chair forward between the writing table and the settee, and offers it to* UNDERSHAFT]. Takes you some time to find out exactly where you are, dont it?
UNDERSHAFT [*accepting the chair, but remaining standing*]. That is not what embarrasses me, Mr Lomax. My difficulty is that if I play the part of a father, I shall produce the effect of an intrusive stranger; and if I play the part of a discreet stranger, I may appear a callous father.
LADY BRITOMART. There is no need for you to play any part at all, Andrew. You had much better be sincere and natural.
UNDERSHAFT [*submissively*]. Yes, my dear: I daresay that will be best. [*He sits down comfortably.*] Well, here I am. Now what can I do for you all?
LADY BRITOMART. You need not do anything, Andrew. You are one of the family. You can sit with us and enjoy yourself.

A painfully conscious pause. BARBARA *makes a face at* LOMAX, *whose too long suppressed mirth immediately explodes in agonized neighings.*

LADY BRITOMART [*outraged*]. Charles Lomax: if you can behave yourself; behave yourself. If not, leave the room.
LOMAX. I'm awfully sorry, Lady Brit; but really you know, upon my soul! [*He sits on the settee between* LADY BRITOMART *and* UNDERSHAFT, *quite overcome.*]
BARBARA. Why dont you laugh if you want to, Cholly? It's good for your inside.
LADY BRITOMART. Barbara: you have had the education of a lady. Please let your father see that; and dont talk like a street girl.
UNDERSHAFT. Never mind me, my dear. As you know, I am not a gentleman; and I was never educated.
LOMAX [*encouragingly*]. Nobody'd know it, I assure you. You look all right, you know.
CUSINS. Let me advise you to study Greek, Mr. Undershaft. Greek scholars are privileged men. Few of them know Greek; and none of them know anything else; but their position is unchallengeable. Other languages are the qualifications of waiters and commercial travellers: Greek is to a man of position what the hallmark is to silver.
BARBARA. Dolly: dont be insincere. Cholly: fetch your concertina and play something for us.
LOMAX [*jumps up eagerly, but checks himself to remark doubtfully to* UNDERSHAFT]. Perhaps that sort of thing isnt in your line, eh?
UNDERSHAFT. I am particularly fond of music.
LOMAX [*delighted*]. Are you? Then I'll get it. [*He goes upstairs for the instrument.*]
UNDERSHAFT. Do you play, Barbara?
BARBARA. Only the tambourine. But Cholly's teaching me the concertina.
UNDERSHAFT. Is Cholly also a member of the Salvation Army?
BARBARA. No: he says it's bad form to be a dissenter. But I dont despair of Cholly. I made him come yesterday to a meeting at the dock gates, and take the collection in his hat.
UNDERSHAFT [*looks whimsically at his wife*]!!
LADY BRITOMART. It is not my doing, Andrew. Barbara is old enough to take her own way. She has no father to advise her.
BARBARA. Oh yes she has. There are no orphans in the Salvation Army.
UNDERSHAFT. Your father there has a great many children and plenty of experience, eh?
BARBARA [*looking at him with quick interest and nodding*]. Just so. How did you come to understand that? [LOMAX *is heard at the door trying the concertina.*]
LADY BRITOMART. Come in, Charles. Play us something at once.
LOMAX. Righto! [*He sits down in his former place, and preludes.*]
UNDERSHAFT. One moment, Mr Lomax. I am rather interested in the Salvation Army. Its motto might be my own: Blood and Fire.

LOMAX [*shocked*]. But not your sort of blood and fire, you know.

UNDERSHAFT. My sort of blood cleanses: my sort of fire purifies.

BARBARA. So do ours. Come down tomorrow to my shelter—the West Ham shelter—and see what we're doing. We're going to march to a great meeting in the Assembly Hall at Mile End. Come and see the shelter and then march with us: it will do you a lot of good. Can you play anything?

UNDERSHAFT. In my youth I earned pennies, and even shillings occasionally, in the streets and in public house parlors by my natural talent for step-dancing. Later on, I became a member of the Undershaft orchestral society, and performed passably on the tenor trombone.

LOMAX [*scandalized—putting down the concertina*]. Oh I say!

BARBARA. Many a sinner has played himself into heaven on the trombone, thanks to the Army.

LOMAX [*to* BARBARA, *still rather shocked*]. Yes; but what about the cannon business, dont you know? [*To* UNDERSHAFT.] Getting into heaven is not exactly in your line, is it?

LADY BRITOMART. Charles!!!

LOMAX. Well; but it stands to reason, dont it? The cannon business may be necessary and all that: we cant get on without cannons; but it isnt right, you know. On the other hand, there may be a certain amount of tosh about the Salvation Army—I belong to the Established Church myself—but still you cant deny that it's religion; and you cant go against religion, can you? At least unless youre downright immoral, dont you know.

UNDERSHAFT. You hardly appreciate my position, Mr Lomax—

LOMAX [*hastily*]. I'm not saying anything against you personally—

UNDERSHAFT. Quite so, quite so. But consider for a moment. Here I am, a profiteer in mutilation and murder. I find myself in a specially amiable humor just now because, this morning, down at the foundry, we blew twenty-seven dummy soldiers into fragments with a gun which formerly destroyed only thirteen.

LOMAX [*leniently*]. Well, the more destructive war becomes, the sooner it will be abolished, eh?

UNDERSHAFT. Not at all. The more destructive war becomes the more fascinating we find it. No, Mr Lomax: I am obliged to you for making the usual excuse for my trade; but I am not ashamed of it. I am not one of those men who keep their morals and their business in watertight compartments. All the spare money my trade rivals spend on hospitals, cathedrals, and other receptacles for conscience money, I devote to experiments and researches in improved methods of destroying life and property. I have always done so; and I always shall. Therefore your Christmas card moralities of peace on earth and goodwill among men are of no use to me. Your Christianity, which enjoins you to resist not evil, and to turn the other cheek, would make me a bankrupt. My morality—my religion—must have a place for cannons and torpedoes in it.

STEPHEN [*coldly—almost sullenly*]. You speak as if there were half a dozen moralities and religions to choose from, instead of one true morality and one true religion.

UNDERSHAFT. For me there is only one true morality; but it might not fit you, as you do not manufacture aerial battleships. There is only one true morality for every man; but every man has not the same true morality.

LOMAX [*overtaxed*]. Would you mind saying that again? I didnt quite follow it.

CUSINS. It's quite simple. As Euripides says, one man's meat is another man's poison morally as well as physically.

UNDERSHAFT. Precisely.

LOMAX. Oh, that! Yes, yes, yes. True. True.

STEPHEN. In other words, some men are honest and some are scoundrels.

BARBARA. Bosh! There are no scoundrels.

UNDERSHAFT. Indeed? Are there any good men?

BARBARA. No. Not one. There are neither good men nor scoundrels: there are just children of one Father; and the sooner they stop calling one another names the better. You neednt talk to me: I know them. Ive had scores of them through my hands: scoundrels, criminals, infidels, philanthropists, missionaries, county councillors, all sorts. Theyre all just the same sort of sinner; and theres the same salvation ready for them all.

UNDERSHAFT. May I ask have you ever saved a maker of cannons?

BARBARA. No. Will you let me try?

UNDERSHAFT. Well, I will make a bargain with you. If I go to see you tomorrow in your Salvation Shelter, will you come the day after to see me in my cannon works?

BARBARA. Take care. It may end in your giving up the cannons for the sake of the Salvation Army.

UNDERSHAFT. Are you sure it will not end in your giving up the Salvation Army for the sake of the cannons?

BARBARA. I will take my chance of that.

UNDERSHAFT. And I will take my chance of the other. [*They shake hands on it.*] Where is your shelter?

BARBARA. In West Ham. At the sign of the cross. Ask anybody in Canning Town. Where are your works?

UNDERSHAFT. In Perivale St Andrews. At the sign of the sword. Ask anybody in Europe.

LOMAX. Hadnt I better play something?

BARBARA. Yes. Give us Onward, Christian Soldiers.

LOMAX. Well, thats rather a strong order to begin with, dont you know. Suppose I sing Thourt passing hence, my brother. It's much the same tune.

BARBARA. It's too melancholy. You get saved, Cholly; and youll pass hence, my brother, without making such a fuss about it.

LADY BRITOMART. Really, Barbara, you go on as if religion were a pleasant subject. Do have some sense of propriety.

UNDERSHAFT. I do not find it an unpleasant subject, my dear. It is the only one that capable people really care for.

LADY BRITOMART [*looking at her watch*]. Well, if you are determined to have it, I insist on having it in a proper and respectable way. Charles: ring for prayers.

General amazement. STEPHEN *rises in dismay.*

LOMAX [*rising*]. Oh I say!

UNDERSHAFT [*rising*]. I am afraid I must be going.

LADY BRITOMART. You cannot go now, Andrew: it would be most improper. Sit down. What will the servants think?

UNDERSHAFT. My dear: I have conscientious scruples. May I suggest a compromise? If Barbara will conduct a little service in the drawing room, with Mr Lomax as organist, I will attend it willingly. I will even take part, if a trombone can be procured.

LADY BRITOMART. Dont mock, Andrew.

UNDERSHAFT [*shocked—to* BARBARA]. You dont think I am mocking, my love, I hope.

BARBARA. No, of course not; and it wouldnt matter if you were: half the Army came to their first meeting for a lark. [*Rising.*] Come along. [*She throws her arm round her father and sweeps him out, calling to the others from the threshold.*] Come, Dolly. Come, Cholly.

CUSINS *rises.*

LADY BRITOMART. I will not be disobeyed by everybody. Adolphus: sit down. [*He does not.*] Charles: you may go. You are not fit for prayers: you cannot keep your countenance.

LOMAX. Oh I say! [*He goes out.*]

LADY BRITOMART [*continuing*]. But you, Adolphus, can behave yourself if you choose to. I insist on your staying.

CUSINS. My dear Lady Brit: there are things in the family prayer book that I couldnt bear to hear you say.

LADY BRITOMART. What things, pray?

CUSINS. Well, you would have to say before all the servants that we have done things we ought not to have done, and left undone things we ought to have done, and that there is no health in us. I cannot bear to hear you doing yourself such an injustice, and Barbara such an injustice. As for myself, I flatly deny it: I have done my best. I shouldnt dare to marry Barbara—I couldnt look you in the face—if it were true. So I must go to the drawing room.

LADY BRITOMART [*offended*]. Well, go. [*He starts for the door.*] And remember this, Adolphus [*he turns to listen*]: I have a very strong suspicion that you went to the Salvation Army to worship Barbara and nothing else. And I quite appreciate the very clever way in which you systematically humbug me. I have found you out. Take care Barbara doesnt. Thats all.

CUSINS [*with unruffled sweetness*]. Dont tell on me. [*He steals out.*]

LADY BRITOMART. Sarah: if you want to go, go. Anything's better than to sit there as if you wished you were a thousand miles away.

SARAH [*languidly*]. Very well, mamma. [*She goes.*]

LADY BRITOMART, *with a sudden flounce, gives way to a little gust of tears.*

STEPHEN [*going to her*]. Mother: whats the matter?

LADY BRITOMART [*swishing away her tears with her handkerchief*]. Nothing. Foolishness. You can go with him, too, if you like, and leave me with the servants.

STEPHEN. Oh, you mustnt think that, mother. I—I dont like him.

LADY BRITOMART. The others do. That is the injustice of a woman's lot. A woman has to bring up her children; and that means to restrain them, to deny them things they want, to set them tasks, to punish them when they do wrong, to do all the unpleasant things. And then the father, who has nothing to do but pet them and spoil them, comes in when all her work is done and steals their affection from her.

STEPHEN. He has not stolen our affection from you. It is only curiosity.

LADY BRITOMART [*violently*]. I wont be consoled, Stephen. There is nothing the matter with me. [*She rises and goes towards the door.*]

STEPHEN. Where are you going, mother?

LADY BRITOMART. To the drawing room, of course. [*She goes out. Onward, Christian Soldiers, on the concertina, with tambourine accompaniment, is heard when the door opens.*] Are you coming, Stephen?

STEPHEN. No. Certainly not. [*She goes. He sits down on the settee, with compressed lips and an expression of strong dislike.*]

ACT II

The yard of the West Ham shelter of the Salvation Army is a cold place on a January morning. The building itself, an old warehouse, is newly whitewashed. Its gabled end projects into the yard in the middle, with a door on the ground floor, and another in the loft above it without any balcony or ladder, but with a pulley rigged over it for hoisting sacks. Those who come from this central gable end into the yard have the gateway leading to the street on their left, with a stone horse-trough just beyond it, and, on the right, a penthouse shielding a table from the weather. There are forms at the table; and on them are seated a man and a woman, both much down on their luck, finishing a meal of bread (one thick slice each, with margarine and golden syrup) and diluted milk.

THE MAN, a workman out of employment, is young, agile, a talker, a poser, sharp enough to be capable of anything in reason except honesty or altruistic considerations of any kind. THE WOMAN is a commonplace old bundle of poverty and hard-worn humanity. She looks sixty and probably is forty-five. If they were rich people, gloved and muffed and well wrapped up in furs and overcoats, they would be numbed and miserable; for it is a grindingly cold raw January day; and a glance at the background of grimy warehouses and leaden sky visible over the whitewashed walls of the yard would drive any idle rich person straight to the Mediterranean. But these two, being no more troubled with visions of the Mediterranean than of the moon, and being compelled to keep more of their clothes in the pawnshop, and less on their persons, in winter than in summer, are not depressed by the cold: rather are they stung into vivacity, to which their meal has just now given an almost jolly turn. THE MAN takes a pull at his mug, and then gets up and moves about the yard with his hands deep in his pockets, occasionally breaking into a stepdance.

THE WOMAN. Feel better arter your meal, sir?

THE MAN. No. Call that a meal! Good enough for you, praps; but wot is it to me, an intelligent workin man.

THE WOMAN. Workin man! Wot are you?

THE MAN. Painter.

THE WOMAN [*sceptically*]. Yus, I dessay.

THE MAN. Yus, you dessay! I know. Every loafer that cant do nothink calls isself a painter. Well, I'm a real painter: grainer, finisher, thirty-eight bob a week when I can get it.

THE WOMAN. Then why dont you go and get it?

THE MAN. I'll tell you why. Fust: I'm intelligent—fffff! it's rotten cold here [*he dances a step or two*]—yes: intelligent beyond the station o life into which it has pleased the capitalists to call me; and they dont like a man that sees through em. Second, an intelligent bein needs a doo share of appiness; so I drink somethink cruel when I get the chawnce. Third, I stand by my class and do as little as I can so's to leave arf the job for me fellow workers. Fourth, I'm fly enough to know wots inside the law and wots outside it; and inside it I do as the capitalists do: pinch wot I can lay me ands on. In a proper state of society I am sober, industrious and honest: in Rome, so to speak, I do as the Romans do. Wots the consequence? When trade is bad—and it's rotten bad just now—and the employers az to sack arf their men, they generally start on me.

THE WOMAN. Whats your name?

THE MAN. Price. Bronterre O'Brien Price. Usually called Snobby Price, for short.

THE WOMAN. Snobby's a carpenter, aint it? You said you was a painter.

PRICE. Not that kind of snob, but the genteel sort. I'm too uppish, owing to my intelligence, and my father being a Chartist and a reading, thinking man: a stationer, too. I'm none of your common hewers of wood and drawers of water; and dont you forget it. [*He returns to his seat at the table, and takes up his mug.*] Wots your name?

THE WOMAN. Rummy Mitchens, sir.

PRICE [*quaffing the remains of his milk to her*]. Your elth, Miss Mitchens.

RUMMY [*correcting him*]. Missis Mitchens.

PRICE. Wot! Oh Rummy, Rummy! Respectable married woman, Rummy, gittin rescued by the Salvation Army by pretendin to be a bad un. Same old game!

RUMMY. What am I to do? I cant starve. Them Salvation lasses is dear good girls; but the better you are, the worse they likes to think you were before they rescued you. Why shouldnt they av a bit o credit, poor loves? theyre worn to rags by their work. And where would they get the money to rescue us if we was to let on we're no worse than other people? You know what ladies and gentlemen are.

PRICE. Thievin swine! Wish I ad their job, Rummy, all the same. Wot does Rummy stand for? Pet name praps?

RUMMY. Short for Romola.

PRICE. For wot!?

RUMMY. Romola. It was out of a new book. Somebody me mother wanted me to grow up like.

PRICE. We're companions in misfortune, Rummy. Both on us got names that nobody cawnt pronounce. Consequently I'm Snobby and youre Rummy because Bill and Sally wasnt good enough for our parents. Such is life!

RUMMY. Who saved you, Mr Price? Was it Major Barbara?

PRICE. No: I come here on my own. I'm going to be Bronterre O'Brien Price, the converted painter. I know wot they like. I'll tell em how I blasphemed and gambled and wopped my poor old mother—

RUMMY [*shocked*]. Used you to beat your mother?

PRICE. Not likely. She used to beat me. No matter: you come and listen to the converted painter, and youll hear how she was a pious woman that taught me me prayers at er knee, an how I used to come home drunk and drag her out o bed be er snow white airs, an lam into er with the poker.

RUMMY. Thats whats so unfair to us women. Your confessions is just as big lies as ours: you dont tell what you really done no more than us; but you men can tell your lies right out at the meetins and be made much of for it; while the sort o confessions we az to make az to be wispered to one lady at a time. It aint right, spite of all their piety.

PRICE. Right! Do you spose the Army'd be allowed if it went and did right? Not much. It combs our air and makes us good little blokes to be robbed and put upon. But I'll play the game as good as any of em. I'll see somebody struck by lightnin, or hear a voice sayin 'Snobby Price: where will you spend eternity?' I'll av a time of it, I tell you.

RUMMY. You wont be let drink, though.

PRICE. I'll take it out in gorspellin, then. I dont want to drink if I can get fun enough any other way.

JENNY HILL, *a pale, overwrought, pretty Salvation lass of 18, comes in through the yard gate, leading* PETER SHIRLEY, *a half hardened, half worn-out elderly man, weak with hunger.*

JENNY [*supporting him*]. Come! pluck up. I'll get you something to eat. Youll be all right then.
PRICE [*rising and hurrying officiously to take the old man off Jenny's hands*]. Poor old man! Cheer up, brother: youll find rest and peace and appiness ere. Hurry up with the food, miss: e's fair done. [JENNY *hurries into the shelter.*] Ere, buck up, daddy! she's fetchin y'a thick slice o breadn treacle, an a mug o skyblue. [*He seats him at the corner of the table.*]
RUMMY [*gaily*]. Keep up your old art! Never say die!
SHIRLEY. I'm not an old man. I'm ony 46. I'm as good as ever I was. The grey patch come in my hair before I was thirty. All it wants is three pennorth o hair dye: am I to be turned on the streets to starve for it? Holy God! Ive worked ten to twelve hours a day since I was thirteen, and paid my way all through; and now am I to be thrown into the gutter and my job given to a young man that can do it no better than me because Ive black hair that goes white at the first change?
PRICE [*cheerfully*]. No good jawrin about it. Youre ony a jumped-up, jerked-off, or-spittle-turned-out incurable of an ole workin man: who cares about you? Eh? Make the thievin swine give you a meal: theyve stole many a one from you. Get a bit o your own back. [JENNY *returns with the usual meal.*] There you are, brother. Awsk a blessin an tuck that into you.
SHIRLEY [*looking at it ravenously but not touching it, and crying like a child*]. I never took anything before.
JENNY [*petting him*]. Come, come! the Lord sends it to you: he wasnt above taking bread from his friends; and why should you be? Besides, when we find you a job you can pay us for it if you like.
SHIRLEY [*eagerly*]. Yes, yes: thats true. I can pay you back: it's only a loan. [*Shivering.*] Oh Lord! oh Lord! [*He turns to the table and attacks the meal ravenously.*]
JENNY. Well, Rummy, are you more comfortable now?
RUMMY. God bless you, lovey! youve fed my body and saved my soul, havnt you? [JENNY, *touched, kisses her.*] Sit down and rest a bit: you must be ready to drop.
JENNY. Ive been going hard since morning. But theres more work than we can do. I mustnt stop.
RUMMY. Try a prayer for just two minutes. Youll work all the better after.
JENNY [*her eyes lighting up*]. Oh isnt it wonderful how a few minutes prayer revives you! I was quite lightheaded at twelve o'clock, I was so tired; but Major Barbara just sent me to pray for five minutes; and I was able to go on as if I had only just begun. [*To* PRICE.] Did you have a piece of bread?
PRICE [*with unction*]. Yes, miss; but Ive got the piece that I value more; and thats the peace that passeth hall hannerstennin.
RUMMY [*fervently*]. Glory Hallelujah!

BILL WALKER, *a rough customer of about 25, appears at the yard gate and looks malevolently at* JENNY.

JENNY. That makes me so happy. When you say that, I feel wicked for loitering here. I must get to work again.

She is hurrying to the shelter, when the new-comer moves quickly up to the door and intercepts her. His manner is so threatening that she retreats as he comes at her truculently, driving her down the yard.

BILL. Aw knaow you. Youre the one that took awy maw girl. Youre the one that set er agen me. Well, I'm gowin to ev er aht. Not that Aw care a carse for er or you: see? Bat Aw'll let er knaow; and Aw'll let you knaow. Aw'm gowing to give her a doin thatll teach er to cat awy from me. Nah in wiv you and tell er to cam aht afore Aw cam in and kick er aht. Tell er Bill Walker wants er. She'll knaow wot thet means; and if she keeps me witin itll be worse. You stop to jawr beck at me; and Aw'll stawt on you: d'ye eah? Theres your wy. In you gow. [*He takes her by the arm and slings her towards the door of the shelter. She falls on her hand and knee. RUMMY helps her up again.]

PRICE [rising, and venturing irresolutely towards BILL]. Easy there, mate. She aint doin you no arm.

BILL. Oo are you callin mite? [Standing over him threateningly.] Youre gowin to stend ap for er, aw yer? Put ap your ends.

RUMMY [running indignantly to him to scold him]. Oh, you great brute—[He instantly swings his left hand back against her face. She screams and reels back to the trough, where she sits down, covering her bruised face with her hands and rocking herself and moaning with pain.]

JENNY [going to her]. Oh, God forgive you! How could you strike an old woman like that?

BILL [seizing her by the hair so violently that she also screams, and tearing her away from the old woman]. You Gawd forgimme again an Aw'll Gawk forgive you one on the jawr thetll stop you pryin for a week. [Holding her and turning fiercely on PRICE.] Ev you ennything to sy agen it?

PRICE [intimidated]. No, matey: she aint anything to do with me.

BILL. Good job for you! Aw'd pat two meals into you and fawt you with one finger arter, you stawved cur. [To JENNY.] Nah are you gowin to fetch aht Mog Ebbijem; or em Aw to knock your fice off you and fetch her meself?

JENNY [writhing in his grasp]. Oh please someone go in and tell Major Barbara—[she screams again as he wrenches her head down; and PRICE and RUMMY flee into the shelter.]

BILL. You want to gow in and tell your Mijor of me, do you?

JENNY. Oh please dont drag my hair. Let me go.

BILL. Do you or downt you? [She stifles a scream.] Yus or nao?

JENNY. God give me strength—

BILL [striking her with his fist in the face]. Gow an shaow her thet, and tell her if she wants one lawk it to cam and interfere with me. [JENNY, crying with pain, goes into the shed. He goes to the form and addresses the old man.] Eah: finish your mess; an git aht o maw wy.

SHIRLEY [springing up and facing him fiercely, with the mug in his hand]. You take a liberty with me, and I'll smash you over the face with the mug and cut your eye out. Aint you satisfied—young whelps like you—with takin the bread out o the mouths of your elders that have brought you up and slaved for you, but you must come shovin and cheekin and bullyin in here, where the bread o charity is sickenin in our stummicks?

BILL [contemptuously, but backing a little]. Wot good are you, you aold palsy mag? Wot good are you?

SHIRLEY. As good as you and better. I'll do a day's work agen you or any fat young soaker of your age. Go and take my job at Horrockses, where I worked for ten year. They want young men there: they cant afford to keep men over forty-five. Theyre very sorry—give you a character and happy to help you to get anything suited to your years—sure a steady man wont be long out of a job. Well, let em try you. Theyll find the differ. What do you know? Not as much as how to beeyave yourself—layin your dirty fist across the mouth of a respectable woman!

BILL. Downt provowk me to ly it acrost yours: d'ye eah?

SHIRLEY [with blighting contempt]. Yes: you like an old man to hit, dont you, when youve finished with the women. I aint seen you hit a young one yet.

BILL [stung]. You loy, you aold soup-kitchener, you. There was a yang menn eah. Did Aw offer to itt him or did Aw not?

SHIRLEY. Was he starvin or was he not? Was he a man or only a crosseyed thief an a loafer? Would you hit my son-in-law's brother?

BILL. Oo's ee?

SHIRLEY. Todger Fairmile o Balls Pond. Him that won £20 off the Japanese wrastler at the music hall by standin out 17 minutes 4 seconds agen him.

BILL [sullenly]. Aw'm nao music awl wrastler. Ken he box?

SHIRLEY. Yes: an you cant.

BILL. Wot! Aw cawnt, cawnt Aw? Wots thet you sy [threatening him]?

SHIRLEY [not budging an inch]. Will you box Todger Fairmile if I put him on to you? Say the word.

BILL [*subsiding with a slouch*]. Aw'll stend ap to enny menn alawv, if he was ten Todger Fairmawls. But Aw dont set ap to be a perfeshnal.

SHIRLEY [*looking down on him with unfathomable disdain*]. You box! Slap an old woman with the back o your hand! You hadnt even the sense to hit her where a magistrate couldnt see the mark of it, you silly young lump of conceit and ignorance. Hit a girl in the jaw and ony make her cry! If Todger Fairmile'd done it, she wouldnt a got up inside o ten minutes, no more than you would if he got on to you. Yah! I'd set about you myself if I had a week's feedin in me instead o two months' starvation. [*He turns his back on him and sits down moodily at the table.*]

BILL [*following him and stooping over him to drive the taunt in*]. You loy! youve the bread and treacle in you that you cam eah to beg.

SHIRLEY [*bursting into tears*]. Oh God! it's true: I'm only an old pauper on the scrap heap. [*Furiously.*] But youll come to it yourself; and then youll know. Youll come to it sooner than a teetotaller like me, fillin yourself with gin at this hour o the mornin!

BILL. Aw'm nao gin drinker, you oald lawr; bat wen Aw want to give my girl a bloomin good awdin Aw lawk to ev a bit o devil in me: see? An eah Aw emm, talkin to a rotten aold blawter like you sted o givin her wot for. [*Working himself into a rage.*] Aw'm gowin in there to fetch her aht. [*He makes vengefully for the shelter door.*]

SHIRLEY. Youre going to the station on a stretcher, more likely; and theyll take the gin and the devil out of you there when they get you inside. You mind what youre about: the major here is the Earl o Stevenage's granddaughter.

BILL [*checked*]. Garn!

SHIRLEY. Youll see.

BILL [*his resolution oozing*]. Well, Aw aint dan nathin to er.

SHIRLEY. Spose she said you did! who'd believe you?

BILL [*very uneasy, skulking back to the corner of the penthouse*]. Gawd! theres no jastice in this cantry. To think wot them people can do! Aw'm as good as er.

SHIRLEY. Tell her so. It's just what a fool like you would do.

BARBARA, *brisk and businesslike, comes from the shelter with a note book, and addresses herself to* SHIRLEY. BILL, *cowed, sits down in the corner on a form, and turns his back on them.*

BARBARA. Good morning.

SHIRLEY [*standing up and taking off his hat*]. Good morning, miss.

BARBARA. Sit down: make yourself at home. [*He hesitates; but she puts a friendly hand on his shoulder and makes him obey.*] Now then! since youve made friends with us, we want to know all about you. Names and addresses and trades.

SHIRLEY. Peter Shirley. Fitter. Chucked out two months ago because I was too old.

BARBARA [*not at all surprised*]. Youd pass still. Why didnt you dye your hair?

SHIRLEY. I did. Me age come out at a coroner's inquest on me daughter.

BARBARA. Steady?

SHIRLEY. Teetotaller. Never out of a job before. Good worker. And sent to the knackers like an old horse!

BARBARA. No matter: if you did your part God will do his.

SHIRLEY [*suddenly stubborn*]. My religion's no concern of anybody but myself.

BARBARA [*guessing*]. I know. Secularist?

SHIRLEY [*hotly*]. Did I offer to deny it?

BARBARA. Why should you? My own father's a Secularist, I think. Our Father—yours and mine—fulfills himself in many ways; and I daresay he knew what he was about when he made a Secularist of you. So buck up, Peter! we can always find a job for a steady man like you. [SHIRLEY, *disarmed and a little bewildered, touches his hat. She turns from him to* BILL.] Whats your name?

BILL [*insolently*]. Wots thet to you?

BARBARA [*calmly making a note*]. Afraid to give his name. Any trade?

BILL. Oo's afride to give is nime? [*Doggedly, with a sense of heroically defying the House of Lords in the person of Lord Stevenage.*] If you want to bring a chawge agen me, bring it. [*She waits, unruffled.*] Moy nime's Bill Walker.

BARBARA [*as if the name were familiar: trying to remember how*]. Bill Walker? [*Rec-

ollecting.] Oh, I know: youre the man that Jenny Hill was praying for inside just now. [*She enters his name in her note book.*]

BILL. Oo's Jenny Ill? And wot call as she to pry for me?

BARBARA. I dont know. Perhaps it was you that cut her lip.

BILL [*defiantly*]. Yus, it was me that cat her lip. Aw aint afride o you.

BARBARA. How could you be, since youre not afraid of God? Youre a brave man, Mr Walker. It takes some pluck to do our work here; but none of us dare lift our hand against a girl like that, for fear of her father in heaven.

BILL [*sullenly*]. I want nan o your kentin jawr. I spowse you think Aw cam eah to beg from you, like this demmiged lot eah. Not me. Aw downt want your bread and scripe and ketlep. Aw dont blieve in your Gawd, no more than you do yourself.

BARBARA [*sunnily apologetic and ladylike, as on a new footing with him*]. Oh, I beg your pardon for putting your name down, Mr Walker. I didnt understand. I'll strike it out.

BILL [*taking this as a slight, and deeply wounded by it*]. Eah! you let maw nime alown. Aint it good enaff to be in your book?

BARBARA [*considering*]. Well, you see, theres no use putting down your name unless I can do something for you, is there? Whats your trade?

BILL [*still smarting*]. Thets nao concern o yours.

BARBARA. Just so. [*Very businesslike*]. I'll put you down as [*writing*] the man who—struck—poor little Jenny Hill—in the mouth.

BILL [*rising threateningly*]. See eah. Awve ed enaff o this.

BARBARA [*quite sunny and fearless*]. What did you come to us for?

BILL. Aw cam for maw gel, see? Aw cam to tike her aht o this and to brike er jawr for er.

BARBARA [*complacently*]. You see I was right about your trade. [BILL, *on the point of retorting furiously, finds himself, to his great shame and terror, in danger of crying instead. He sits down again suddenly.*] Whats her name?

BILL [*dogged*]. Er nime's Mog Ebbijem: thets wot her nime is.

BARBARA. Mog Habbijam! Oh, she's gone to Canning Town, to our barracks there.

BILL [*fortified by his resentment of Mog's perfidy*]. Is she? [*Vindictively.*] Then Aw'm gowin to Kennintahn arter her. [*He crosses to the gate; hesitates; finally comes back at* BARBARA.] Are you loyin to me to git shat o me?

BARBARA. I dont want to get shut of you. I want to keep you here and save your soul. Youd better stay: youre going to have a bad time today, Bill.

BILL. Oo's gowin to give it to me? You, preps?

BARBARA. Someone you dont believe in. But youll be glad afterwards.

BILL [*slinking off*]. Aw'll gow to Kennintahn to be aht o reach o your tangue. [*Suddenly turning on her with intense malice.*] And if Aw downt fawnd Mog there, Aw'll cam beck and do two years for you, selp me Gawd if Aw downt!

BARBARA [*a shade kindlier, if possible*]. It's no use, Bill. She's got another bloke.

BILL. Wot!

BARBARA. One of her own converts. He fell in love with her when he saw her with her soul saved, and her face clean, and her hair washed.

BILL [*surprised*]. Wottud she wash it for, the carroty slat? It's red.

BARBARA. It's quite lovely now, because she wears a new look in her eyes with it. It's a pity youre too late. The new bloke has put your nose out of joint, Bill.

BILL. Aw'll put his nowse aht o joint for him. Not that Aw care a carse for er, mawnd thet. But Aw'll teach her to drop me as if Aw was dirt. And Aw'll teach him to meddle with maw judy. Wots iz bleedin nime?

BARBARA. Sergeant Todger Fairmile.

SHIRLEY [*rising with grim joy*]. I'll go with him, miss. I want to see them two meet. I'll take him to the infirmary when it's over.

BILL [*to* SHIRLEY, *with undissembled misgiving*]. Is thet im you was speakin on?

SHIRLEY. Thats him.

BILL. Im that wrastled in the music awl?

SHIRLEY. The competitions at the National Sportin Club was worth nigh a hundred a year to him. He's gev em up now for religion; so he's a bit fresh for want of the exercise he was accustomed to. He'll be glad to see you. Come along.

BILL. Wots is wight?

SHIRLEY. Thirteen four. [*Bill's last hope expires.*]

BARBARA. Go and talk to him, Bill. He'll convert you.

SHIRLEY. He'll convert your head into a mashed potato.

BILL [*sullenly*]. Aw aint afride of im. Aw aint afride of ennybody. Bat e can lick me. She's dan me. [*He sits down moodily on the edge of the horse trough.*]

SHIRLEY. You aint going. I thought not. [*He resumes his seat.*]

BARBARA [*calling*]. Jenny!

JENNY [*appearing at the shelter door with a plaster on the corner of her mouth*]. Yes, Major.

BARBARA. Send Rummy Mitchens out to clear away here.

JENNY. I think she's afraid.

BARBARA [*her resemblance to her mother flashing out for a moment*]. Nonsense! she must do as she's told.

JENNY [*calling into the shelter*]. Rummy: the Major says you must come.

JENNY *comes to* BARBARA, *purposely keeping on the side next* BILL, *lest he should suppose that she shrank from him or bore malice.*

BARBARA. Poor little Jenny! Are you tired? [*Looking at the wounded cheek.*] Does it hurt?

JENNY. No: it's all right now. It was nothing.

BARBARA [*critically*]. It was as hard as he could hit, I expect. Poor Bill! You dont feel angry with him, do you?

JENNY. Oh no, no, no: indeed I dont, Major, bless his poor heart! [BARBARA *kisses her; and she runs away merrily into the shelter.* BILL *writhes with an agonizing return of his new and alarming symptoms, but says nothing.* RUMMY MITCHENS *comes from the shelter.*]

BARBARA [*going to meet* RUMMY]. Now Rummy, bustle. Take in those mugs and plates to be washed; and throw the crumbs about for the birds.

RUMMY *takes the three plates and mugs; but* SHIRLEY *takes back his mug from her, as there is still some milk left in it.*

RUMMY. There aint any crumbs. This aint a time to waste good bread on birds.

PRICE [*appearing at the shelter door*]. Gentleman come to see the shelter, Major. Says he's your father.

BARBARA. All right. Coming. [SNOBBY *goes back into the shelter, followed by* BARBARA.]

RUMMY [*stealing across to* BILL *and addressing him in a subdued voice, but with intense conviction*]. I'd av the lor of you, you flat eared pignosed potwalloper, if she'd let me. Youre no gentleman, to hit a lady in the face. [BILL, *with greater things moving in him, takes no notice.*]

SHIRLEY [*following her*]. Here! in with you and dont get yourself into more trouble by talking.

RUMMY [*with hauteur*]. I aint ad the pleasure o being hintroduced to you, as I can remember. [*She goes into the shelter with the plates.*]

SHIRLEY. Thats the—

BILL [*savagely*]. Downt you talk to me, d'ye eah? You lea me alown, or Aw'll do you a mischief. Aw'm not dirt under your feet, ennywy.

SHIRLEY [*calmly*]. Dont you be afeerd. You aint such prime company that you need expect to be sought after. [*He is about to go into the shelter when* BARBARA *comes out, with* UNDERSHAFT *on her right.*]

BARBARA. Oh, there you are, Mr Shirley! [*Between them.*] This is my father: I told you he was a Secularist, didnt I? Perhaps youll be able to comfort one another.

UNDERSHAFT [*startled*]. A Secularist! Not the least in the world: on the contrary, a confirmed mystic.

BARBARA. Sorry, I'm sure. By the way, papa, what is your religion? in case I have to introduce you again.

UNDERSHAFT. My religion? Well, my dear, I am a Millionaire. That is my religion.

BARBARA. Then I'm afraid you and Mr Shirley wont be able to comfort one another after all. Youre not a Millionaire, are you, Peter?

SHIRLEY. No; and proud of it.

UNDERSHAFT [*gravely*]. Poverty, my friend, is not a thing to be proud of.

SHIRLEY [*angrily*]. Who made your millions

for you? Me and my like. Whats kep us poor? Keepin you rich. I wouldn't have your conscience, not for all your income.

UNDERSHAFT. I wouldnt have your income, not for all your conscience, Mr. Shirley. [*He goes to the penthouse and sits down on a form.*]

BARBARA [*stopping* SHIRLEY *adroitly as he is about to retort*]. You wouldnt think he was my father, would you, Peter? Will you go into the shelter and lend the lasses a hand for a while: we're worked off our feet.

SHIRLEY [*bitterly*]. Yes: I'm in their debt for a meal, aint I?

BARBARA. Oh, not because youre in their debt, but for love of them, Peter, for love of them. [*He cannot understand, and is rather scandalized.*] There! dont stare at me. In with you; and give that conscience of yours a holiday [*bustling him into the shelter*].

SHIRLEY [*as he goes in*]. Ah! it's a pity you never was trained to use your reason, miss. Youd have been a very taking lecturer on Secularism.

BARBARA *turns to her father.*

UNDERSHAFT. Never mind me, my dear. Go about your work; and let me watch it for a while.

BARBARA. All right.

UNDERSHAFT. For instance, whats the matter with that outpatient over there?

BARBARA [*looking at* BILL, *whose attitude has never changed, and whose expression of brooding wrath has deepened*]. Oh, we shall cure him in no time. Just watch. [*She goes over to* BILL *and waits. He glances up at her and casts his eyes down again, uneasy, but grimmer than ever.*] It would be nice to just stamp on Mog Habbijam's face, wouldnt it, Bill?

BILL [*starting up from the trough in consternation*]. It's a loy: Aw never said so. [*She shakes her head.*] Oo taold you wot was in moy mawnd?

BARBARA. Only your new friend.

BILL. Wot new friend?

BARBARA. The devil, Bill. When he gets round people they get miserable, just like you.

BILL [*with a heartbreaking attempt at devil-may-care cheerfulness*]. Aw aint miserable. [*He sits down again, and stretches his legs in an attempt to seem indifferent.*]

BARBARA. Well, if youre happy, why dont you look happy, as we do?

BILL [*his legs curling back in spite of him*]. Aw'm eppy enaff, Aw tell you. Woy cawnt you lea me alown? Wot ev I dan to you? Aw aint smashed your fice, ev Aw?

BARBARA [*softly: wooing his soul*]. It's not me thats getting at you, Bill.

BILL. Oo else is it?

BARBARA. Somebody that doesnt intend you to smash women's faces, I suppose. Somebody or something that wants to make a man of you.

BILL [*blustering*]. Mike a menn o me! Aint Aw a menn? eh? Oo sez Aw'm not a menn?

BARBARA. Theres a man in you somewhere, I suppose. But why did he let you hit poor little Jenny Hill? That wasnt very manly of him, was it?

BILL [*tormented*]. Ev dan wiv it, Aw tell you. Chack it. Aw'm sick o your Jenny Ill and er silly little fice.

BARBARA. Then why do you keep thinking about it? Why does it keep coming up against you in your mind? Youre not getting converted, are you?

BILL [*with conviction*]. Not ME. Not lawkly.

BARBARA. Thats right, Bill. Hold out against it. Put out your strength. Dont lets get you cheap. Todger Fairmile said he wrestled for three nights against his salvation harder than he ever wrestled with the Jap at the music hall. He gave in to the Jap when his arm was going to break. But he didnt give in to his salvation until his heart was going to break. Perhaps youll escape that. You havnt any heart, have you?

BILL. Wot d'ye mean? Woy aint Aw got a awt the sime as ennybody else?

BARBARA. A man with a heart wouldnt have bashed poor little Jenny's face, would he?

BILL [*almost crying*]. Ow, will you lea me alown? Ev Aw ever offered to meddle with you, that you cam neggin and provowkin me lawk this? [*He writhes convulsively from his eyes to his toes.*]

BARBARA [*with a steady soothing hand on his arm and a gentle voice that never lets him go*]. It's your soul thats hurting you,

BILL. Bill, and not me. Weve been through it all ourselves. Come with us, Bill. [*He looks wildly round.*] To brave manhood on earth and eternal glory in heaven. [*He is on the point of breaking down.*] Come. [*A drum is heard in the shelter; and* BILL, *with a gasp, escapes from the spell as* BARBARA *turns quickly.* ADOLPHUS *enters from the shelter with a big drum.*] Oh! there you are, Dolly. Let me introduce a new friend of mine, Mr Bill Walker. This is my bloke, Bill: Mr Cusins. [CUSINS *salutes with his drumstick.*]

BILL. Gowin to merry im?

BARBARA. Yes.

BILL [*fervently*]. Gawd elp im! Gaw-aw-aw-awd elp im!

BARBARA. Why? Do you think he wont be happy with me?

BILL. Awve aony ed to stend it for a mawnin: e'll ev to stend it for a lawftawm.

CUSINS. That is a frightful reflection, Mr. Walker. But I cant tear myself away from her.

BILL. Well, Aw ken. [*To* BARBARA.] Eah! do you knaow where Aw'm gowin to, and wot Aw'm gowin to do?

BARBARA. Yes: youre going to heaven; and youre coming back here before the week's out to tell me so.

BILL. You loy. Aw'm gowin to Kennintahn, to spit in Todger Fairmawl's eye. Aw beshed Jenny Ill's fice; an nar Aw'll git me aown fice beshed and cam beck and shaow it to er. Ee'll itt me ardern Aw itt her. Thatll mike us square. [*To* ADOLPHUS.] Is thet fair or is it not? Youre a genlmn: you oughter knaow.

BARBARA. Two black eyes wont make one white one, Bill.

BILL. Aw didnt awst you. Cawnt you never keep your mahth shat? Oy awst the genlmn.

CUSINS [*reflectively*]. Yes: I think youre right, Mr Walker. Yes: I should do it. It's curious: it's exactly what an ancient Greek would have done.

BARBARA. But what good will it do?

CUSINS. Well, it will give Mr Fairmile some exercise; and it will satisfy Mr Walker's soul.

BILL. Rot! there aint nao sach a thing as a saoul. Ah kin you tell wevver Awve a saoul or not? You never seen it.

BARBARA. Ive seen it hurting you when you went against it.

BILL [*with compressed aggravation*]. If you was maw gel and took the word aht o me mahth lawk thet, Aw'd give you sathink youd feel urtin, Aw would. [*To* ADOLPHUS.] You tike maw tip, mite. Stop er jawr; or youll doy afoah your tawm. [*With intense expression.*] Wore aht: thets wot youll be: wore aht. [*He goes away through the gate.*]

CUSINS [*looking after him*]. I wonder!

BARBARA. Dolly! [*indignant, in her mother's manner.*]

CUSINS. Yes, my dear, it's very wearing to be in love with you. If it lasts, I quite think I shall die young.

BARBARA. Should you mind?

CUSINS. Not at all. [*He is suddenly softened, and kisses her over the drum, evidently not for the first time, as people cannot kiss over a big drum without practice.* UNDERSHAFT *coughs.*]

BARBARA. It's all right, papa, weve not forgotten you. Dolly: explain the place to papa: I havnt time. [*She goes busily into the shelter.*]

UNDERSHAFT *and* ADOLPHUS *now have the yard to themselves.* UNDERSHAFT, *seated on a form, and still keenly attentive, looks hard at* ADOLPHUS. ADOLPHUS *looks hard at him.*

UNDERSHAFT. I fancy you guess something of what is in my mind, Mr. Cusins. [CUSINS *flourishes his drumsticks as if in the act of beating a lively rataplan, but makes no sound.*] Exactly so. But suppose Barbara finds you out!

CUSINS. You know, I do not admit that I am imposing on Barbara. I am quite genuinely interested in the views of the Salvation Army. The fact is, I am a sort of collector of religions; and the curious thing is that I find I can believe them all. By the way, have you any religion?

UNDERSHAFT. Yes.

CUSINS. Anything out of the common?

UNDERSHAFT. Only that there are two things necessary to Salvation.

CUSINS [*disappointed, but polite*]. Ah, the Church Catechism. Charles Lomax also belongs to the Established Church.

UNDERSHAFT. The two things are —

CUSINS. Baptism and —

UNDERSHAFT. No. Money and gunpowder.

CUSINS [*surprised, but interested*]. That is the general opinion of our governing classes. The novelty is in hearing any man confess it.

UNDERSHAFT. Just so.

CUSINS. Excuse me: is there any place in your religion for honor, justice, truth, love, mercy and so forth?

UNDERSHAFT. Yes: they are the graces and luxuries of a rich, strong, and safe life.

CUSINS. Suppose one is forced to choose between them and money or gunpowder?

UNDERSHAFT. Choose money and gunpowder; for without enough of both you cannot afford the others.

CUSINS. That is your religion?

UNDERSHAFT. Yes.

The cadence of this reply makes a full close in the conversation, CUSINS *twists his face dubiously and contemplates* UNDERSHAFT. UNDERSHAFT *contemplates him.*

CUSINS. Barbara wont stand that. You will have to choose between your religion and Barbara.

UNDERSHAFT. So will you, my friend. She will find out that that drum of yours is hollow.

CUSINS. Father Undershaft: you are mistaken: I am a sincere Salvationist. You do not understand the Salvation Army. It is the army of joy, of love, of courage: it has banished the fear and remorse and despair of the old hell-ridden evangelical sects: it marches to fight the devil with trumpet and drum, with music and dancing, with banner and palm, as becomes a sally from heaven by its happy garrison. It picks the waster out of the public house and makes a man of him: it finds a worm wriggling in a back kitchen, and lo! a woman! Men and women of rank too, sons and daughters of the Highest. It takes the poor professor of Greek, the most artificial and self-suppressed of human creatures, from his meal of roots, and lets loose the rhapsodist in him; reveals the true worship of Dionysos to him; sends him down the public street drumming dithyrambs [*he plays a thundering flourish on the drum*].

UNDERSHAFT. You will alarm the shelter.

CUSINS. Oh, they are accustomed to these sudden ecstasies. However, if the drum worries you—[*he pockets the drumsticks; unhooks the drum; and stands it on the ground opposite the gateway.*]

UNDERSHAFT. Thank you.

CUSINS. You remember what Euripides says about your money and gunpowder?

UNDERSHAFT. No.

CUSINS [*declaiming*].

> One and another
> In money and guns may outpass his brother;
> And men in their millions float and flow
> And seethe with a million hopes as leaven;
> And they win their will; or they miss their will;
> And their hopes are dead or are pined for still;
> But who'er can know
> As the long days go
> That to live is happy, has found his heaven.

My translation: what do you think of it?

UNDERSHAFT. I think, my friend, that if you wish to know, as the long days go, that to live is happy, you must first acquire money enough for a decent life, and power enough to be your own master.

CUSINS. You are damnably discouraging. [*He resumes his declamation.*]

> Is it so hard a thing to see
> That the spirit of God—whate'er it be—
> The law that abides and changes not, ages long,
> The Eternal and Nature-born: these things be strong?
> What else is Wisdom? What of Man's endeavor,
> Or God's high grace so lovely and so great?
> To stand from fear set free? to breathe and wait?
> To hold a hand uplifted over Fate?
> And shall not Barbara be loved for ever?

UNDERSHAFT. Euripides mentions Barbara, does he?

CUSINS. It is a fair translation. The word means Loveliness.

UNDERSHAFT. May I ask—as Barbara's father—how much a year she is to be loved for ever on?

CUSINS. As for Barbara's father, that is more your affair than mine. I can feed her by teaching Greek: that is about all.

UNDERSHAFT. Do you consider it a good match for her?

CUSINS [with polite obstinacy]. Mr Undershaft: I am in many ways a weak, timid, ineffectual person; and my health is far from satisfactory. But whenever I feel that I must have anything, I get it, sooner or later. I feel that way about Barbara. I dont like marriage: I feel intensely afraid of it; and I dont know what I shall do with Barbara or what she will do with me. But I feel that I and nobody else must marry her. Please regard that as settled.— Not that I wish to be arbitrary; but why should I waste your time in discussing what is inevitable?

UNDERSHAFT. You mean that you will stick at nothing: not even the conversion of the Salvation Army to the worship of Dionysos.

CUSINS. The business of the Salvation Army is to save, not to wrangle about the name of the pathfinder. Dionysos or another: what does it matter?

UNDERSHAFT [rising and approaching him]. Professor Cusins: you are a young man after my own heart.

CUSINS. Mr Undershaft: you are, as far as I am able to gather, a most infernal old rascal; but you appeal very strongly to my sense of ironic humor.

UNDERSHAFT mutely offers his hand. They shake.

UNDERSHAFT [suddenly concentrating himself]. And now to business.

CUSINS. Pardon me. We are discussing religion. Why go back to such an uninteresting and unimportant subject as business?

UNDERSHAFT. Religion is our business at present, because it is through religion alone that we can win Barbara.

CUSINS. Have you, too, fallen in love with Barbara?

UNDERSHAFT. Yes, with a father's love.

CUSINS. A father's love for a grown-up daughter is the most dangerous of all infatuations. I apologize for mentioning my own pale, coy, mistrustful fancy in the same breath with it.

UNDERSHAFT. Keep to the point. We have to win her; and we are neither of us Methodists.

CUSINS. That doesnt matter. The power Barbara wields here—the power that wields Barbara herself—is not Calvinism, not Presbyterianism, not Methodism —

UNDERSHAFT. Not Greek Paganism either, eh?

CUSINS. I admit that. Barbara is quite original in her religion.

UNDERSHAFT [triumphantly]. Aha! Barbara Undershaft would be. Her inspiration comes from within herself.

CUSINS. How do you suppose it got there?

UNDERSHAFT [in towering excitement]. It is the Undershaft inheritance. I shall hand on my torch to my daughter. She shall make my converts and preach my gospel—

CUSINS. What! Money and gunpowder!

UNDERSHAFT. Yes, money and gunpowder. Freedom and power. Command of life and command of death.

CUSINS [urbanely: trying to bring him down to earth]. This is extremely interesting, Mr Undershaft. Of course you know that you are mad.

UNDERSHAFT [with redoubled force]. And you?

CUSINS. Oh, mad as a hatter. You are welcome to my secret since I have discovered yours. But I am astonished. Can a madman make cannons?

UNDERSHAFT. Would anyone else than a madman make them? And now [with surging energy] question for question. Can a sane man translate Euripides?

CUSINS. No.

UNDERSHAFT [seizing him by the shoulder]. Can a sane woman make a man of a waster or a woman of a worm?

CUSINS [reeling before the storm]. Father Colossus—Mammoth Millionaire—

UNDERSHAFT [pressing him]. Are there two mad people or three in this Salvation shelter today?

CUSINS. You mean Barbara is as mad as we are?

UNDERSHAFT [pushing him lightly off and resuming his equanimity suddenly and completely]. Pooh, Professor! let us call things by their proper names. I am a millionaire; you are a poet: Barbara is a savior of souls. What have we three to do with the common mob of slaves and idolators?

[*He sits down again with a shrug of contempt for the mob.*]

CUSINS. Take care! Barbara is in love with the common people. So am I. Have you never felt the romance of that love?

UNDERSHAFT [*cold and sardonic*]. Have you ever been in love with Poverty, like St Francis? Have you ever been in love with Dirt, like St Simeon! Have you ever been in love with disease and suffering, like our nurses and philanthropists? Such passions are not virtues, but the most unnatural of all the vices. This love of the common people may please an earl's granddaughter and a university professor; but I have been a common man and a poor man; and it has no romance for me. Leave it to the poor to pretend that poverty is a blessing: leave it to the coward to make a religion of his cowardice by preaching humility: we know better than that. We three must stand together above the common people: how else can we help their children to climb up beside us? Barbara must belong to us, not to the Salvation Army.

CUSINS. Well, I can only say that if you think you will get her away from the Salvation Army by talking to her as you have been talking to me, you dont know Barbara.

UNDERSHAFT. My friend: I never ask for what I can buy.

CUSINS [*in a white fury*]. Do I understand you to imply that you can buy Barbara?

UNDERSHAFT. No; but I can buy the Salvation Army.

CUSINS. Quite impossible.

UNDERSHAFT. You shall see. All religious organizations exist by selling themselves to the rich.

CUSINS. Not the Army. That is the Church of the poor.

UNDERSHAFT. All the more reason for buying it.

CUSINS. I dont think you quite know what the Army does for the poor.

UNDERSHAFT. Oh yes I do. It draws their teeth: that is enough for me as a man of business.

CUSINS. Nonsense! It makes them sober—

UNDERSHAFT. I prefer sober workmen. The profits are larger.

CUSINS.—honest—

UNDERSHAFT. Honest workmen are the most economical.

CUSINS.—attached to their homes—

UNDERSHAFT. So much the better: they will put up with anything sooner than change their shop.

CUSINS.—happy—

UNDERSHAFT. An invaluable safeguard against revolution.

CUSINS.—unselfish—

UNDERSHAFT. Indifferent to their own interests, which suits me exactly.

CUSINS.—with their thoughts on heavenly things—

UNDERSHAFT [*rising*]. And not on Trade Unionism nor Socialism. Excellent.

CUSINS [*revolted*]. You really are an infernal old rascal.

UNDERSHAFT [*indicating* PETER SHIRLEY, *who has just come from the shelter and strolled dejectedly down the yard between them*]. And this is an honest man!

SHIRLEY. Yes; and what av I got by it? [*he passes on bitterly and sits on the form, in the corner of the penthouse*].

SNOBBY PRICE, *beaming sanctimoniously, and* JENNY HILL, *with a tambourine full of coppers, come from the shelter and go to the drum, on which* JENNY *begins to count the money.*

UNDERSHAFT [*replying to* SHIRLEY]. Oh, your employers must have got a good deal by it from first to last. [*He sits on the table, with one foot on the side form,* CUSINS, *overwhelmed, sits down on the same form nearer the shelter.* BARBARA *comes from the shelter to the middle of the yard. She is excited and a little overwrought.*]

BARBARA. Weve just had a splendid experience meeting at the other gate in Cripps's lane. Ive hardly ever seen them so much moved as they were by your confession, Mr Price.

PRICE. I could almost be glad of my past wickedness if I could believe that it would elp to keep hathers stright.

BARBARA. So it will, Snobby. How much, Jenny?

JENNY. Four and tenpence, Major.

BARBARA. Oh Snobby, if you had given your poor mother just one more kick, we should have got the whole five shillings!

PRICE. If she heard you say that, miss, she'd be sorry I didnt. But I'm glad. Oh what a joy it will be to her when she hears I'm saved!

UNDERSHAFT. Shall I contribute the odd twopence, Barbara? The millionaire's mite, eh? [*He takes a couple of pennies from his pocket.*]

BARBARA. How did you make that twopence?

UNDERSHAFT. As usual. By selling cannons, torpedoes, submarines, and my new patent Grand Duke hand grenade.

BARBARA. Put it back in your pocket. You cant buy your salvation here for twopence: you must work it out.

UNDERSHAFT. Is twopence not enough? I can afford a little more, if you press me.

BARBARA. Two million millions would not be enough. There is bad blood on your hands; and nothing but good blood can cleanse them. Money is no use. Take it away. [*She turns to* CUSINS.] Dolly: you must write another letter for me to the papers. [*He makes a wry face.*] Yes: I know you dont like it; but it must be done. The starvation this winter is beating us: everybody is unemployed. The General says we must close this shelter if we cant get more money. I force the collections at the meetings until I am ashamed: dont I, Snobby?

PRICE. It's a fair treat to see you work it, miss. The way you got them up from three-and-six to four-and-ten with that hymn, penny by penny and verse by verse, was a caution. Not a Cheap Jack on Mile End Waste could touch you at it.

BARBARA. Yes; but I wish we could do without it. I am getting at last to think more of the collection than of the people's souls. And what are those hatfuls of pence and halfpence? We want thousands! tens of thousands! hundreds of thousands! I want to convert people, not to be always begging for the Army in a way I'd die sooner than beg for myself.

UNDERSHAFT [*in profound irony*]. Genuine unselfishness is capable of anything, my dear.

BARBARA [*unsuspectingly, as she turns away to take the money from the drum and put it in a cash bag she carries*]. Yes, isnt it? [UNDERSHAFT *looks sardonically at* CUSINS.]

CUSINS [*aside to* UNDERSHAFT]. Mephistopheles! Machiavelli!

BARBARA [*tears coming into her eyes as she ties the bag and pockets it*]. How are we to feed them? I cant talk religion to a man with bodily hunger in his eyes. [*Almost breaking down.*] It's frightful.

JENNY [*running to her*]. Major, dear—

BARBARA [*rebounding*]. No: dont comfort me. It will be all right. We shall get the money.

UNDERSHAFT. How?

JENNY. By praying for it, of course. Mrs Baines says she prayed for it last night; and she has never prayed for it in vain: never once. [*She goes to the gate and looks out into the street.*]

BARBARA [*who has dried her eyes and regained her composure*]. By the way, dad, Mrs Baines has come to march with us to our big meeting this afternoon; and she is very anxious to meet you, for some reason or other. Perhaps she'll convert you.

UNDERSHAFT. I shall be delighted, my dear.

JENNY [*at the gate: excitedly*]. Major! Major! heres that man back again.

BARBARA. What man?

JENNY. The man that hit me. Oh, I hope he's coming back to join us.

BILL WALKER, *with frost on his jacket, comes through the gate, his hands deep in his pockets and his chin sunk between his shoulders, like a cleaned-out gambler. He halts between* BARBARA *and the drum.*

BARBARA. Hullo, Bill! Back already!

BILL [*nagging at her*]. Bin talkin ever sence, ev you?

BARBARA. Pretty nearly. Well, has Todger paid you out for poor Jenny's jaw?

BILL. Nao e aint.

BARBARA. I thought your jacket looked a bit snowy.

BILL. Sao it is snaowy. You want to knaow where the snaow cam from, downt you?

BARBARA. Yes.

BILL. Well, it cam from orf the grahnd in in Pawkinses Corner in Kennintahn. It got rabbed orf be maw shaoulders: see?

BARBARA. Pity you didnt rub some off with your knees, Bill! That would have done you a lot of good.

BILL [*with sour mirthless humor*]. Aw was sivin anather menn's knees at the tawm. E was kneelin on moy ed, e was.

JENNY. Who was kneeling on your head?

BILL. Todger was. E was pryin for me: pryin

camfortable wiv me as a cawpet. Sow was Mog. Sao was the aol bloomin meetin. Mog she sez 'Ow Lawd brike is stabborn sperrit; bat downt urt is dear art.' Thet was wot she said. 'Downt urt is dear art'! An er blowk—thirteen stun four!—kneelin wiv all is wight on me. Fanny, aint it?

JENNY. Oh no. We're so sorry, Mr Walker.

BARBARA [*enjoying it frankly*]. Nonsense! of course it's funny. Served you right, Bill! You must have done something to him first.

BILL [*doggedly*]. Aw did wot Aw said Aw'd do. Aw spit in is eye. E looks ap at the skoy and sez, 'Ow that Aw should be fahnd worthy to be spit upon for the gospel's sike!' e sez; an Mog sez 'Glaory Allelloolier!'; an then e called me Braddher, an dahned me as if Aw was a kid and e was me mather worshin me a Setterda nawt. Aw ednt jast nao shaow wiv im a tall. Arf the street pryed; an the tather arf larfed fit to split theirselves. [*To Barbara.*] There! are you settisfawd nah?

BARBARA [*her eyes dancing*]. Wish I'd been there, Bill.

BILL. Yus: youd a got in a hextra bit o talk on me, wouldnt you?

JENNY. I'm so sorry, Mr Walker.

BILL [*fiercely*]. Downt you gow being sorry for me: youve no call. Listen eah. Aw browk your jawr.

JENNY. No, it didnt hurt me: indeed it didnt, except for a moment. It was only that I was frightened.

BILL. Aw downt want to be forgive be you, or be ennybody. Wot Aw did Aw'll py for. Aw trawd to gat me aown jawr browk to settisfaw you —

JENNY [*distressed*]. Oh no —

BILL [*impatiently*]. Tell y' Aw did: cawnt you listen to wots bein taold you? All Aw got be it was bein mide a sawt of in the pablic street for me pines. Well, if Aw cawnt settisfaw you one wy, Aw ken anather. Listen eah! Aw ed two quid sived agen the frost; an Awve a pahnd of it left. A mite o mawn last week ed words with the judy e's gowing to merry. E give er wot-for; an e's bin fawnd fifteen bob. E ed a rawt to itt er cause they was gowin to be merrid; but Aw ednt nao rawt to itt you; sao put anather fawy bob on an call it a pahnd's worth. [*He produces a sovereign.*] Eahs the manney. Tike it; and lets ev no more o your forgivin an prying and your Mijor jawrin me. Let wot Aw dan be dan an pide for; and let there be a end of it.

JENNY. Oh, I couldnt take it, Mr Walker. But if you would give a shilling or two to poor Rummy Mitchens! you really did hurt her; and she's old.

BILL [*contemptuously*]. Not lawkly. Aw'd give her anather as soon as look at er. Let her ev the lawr o me as she threatened! She aint forgiven me: not mach. Wot Aw dan to er is not on me mawnd —wot she [*indicating* BARBARA] mawt call on me conscience—no more than stickin a pig. It's this Christian gime o yours that Aw wownt ev plyed agen me: this bloomin forgivin an neggin an jawrin that mikes a menn thet sore that iz lawf's a burdn to im. Aw wownt ev it, Aw tell you; sao tike your manney and stop thraowin your silly beshed fice hap agen me.

JENNY. Major: may I take a little of it for the Army?

BARBARA. No: the Army is not to be bought. We want your soul, Bill; and we'll take nothing less.

BILL [*bitterly*]. Aw knaow. Me an maw few shillins is not good enaff for you. Youre a earl's grendorter, you are. Nathink less than a andered pahnd for you.

UNDERSHAFT. Come, Barbara! you could do a great deal of good with a hundred pounds. If you will set this gentleman's mind at ease by taking his pound, I will give the other ninety-nine.

BILL, *dazed by such opulence, instinctively touches his cap.*

BARBARA. Oh, youre too extravagant, papa. Bill offers twenty pieces of silver. All you need offer is the other ten. That will make the standard price to buy anybody who's for sale. I'm not; and the Army's not. [*To* BILL.] Youll never have another quiet moment, Bill, until you come round to us. You cant stand out against your salvation.

BILL [*sullenly*]. Aw cawnt stend aht agen music awl wrastlers and awtful tangued women. Awve offered to py. Aw can do no more. Tike it or leave it. There it is. [*He throws the sovereign on the drum, and sits down on the horse-trough. The* coin fascinates Snobby Price, who takes an early opportunity of dropping his cap on it.]

MRS BAINES comes from the shelter. She is dressed as a Salvation Army Commissioner. She is an earnest looking woman of about 40, with a caressing, urgent voice, and an appealing manner.

BARBARA. This is my father, Mrs Baines. [UNDERSHAFT comes from the table, taking his hat off with marked civility.] Try what you can do with him. He wont listen to me, because he remembers what a fool I was when I was a baby. [She leaves them together and chats with JENNY.]

MRS BAINES. Have you been shewn over the shelter, Mr Undershaft? You know the work we're doing, of course.

UNDERSHAFT [very civilly]. The whole nation knows it, Mrs Baines.

MRS BAINES. No, sir: the whole nation does not know it, or we should not be crippled as we are for want of money to carry our work through the length and breadth of the land. Let me tell you that there would have been rioting this winter in London but for us.

UNDERSHAFT. You really think so?

MRS BAINES. I know it. I remember 1886, when you rich gentlemen hardened your hearts against the cry of the poor. They broke the windows of your clubs in Pall Mall.

UNDERSHAFT [gleaming with approval of their method]. And the Mansion House Fund went up next day from thirty thousand pounds to seventy-nine thousand! I remember quite well.

MRS BAINES. Well, wont you help me to get at the people? They wont break windows then. Come here, Price. Let me shew you to this gentleman [PRICE comes to be inspected]. Do you remember the window breaking?

PRICE. My ole father thought it was the revolution, maam.

MRS. BAINES. Would you break windows now?

PRICE. Oh no, maam. The windows of eaven av bin opened to me. I know now that the rich man is a sinner like myself.

RUMMY [appearing above at the loft door]. Snobby Price!

SNOBBY. Wot is it?

RUMMY. Your mother's askin for you at the other gate in Cripps's Lane. She's heard about your confession [PRICE turns pale].

MRS BAINES. Go, Mr Price; and pray with her.

JENNY. You can go through the shelter, Snobby.

PRICE [to MRS BAINES]. I couldnt face her now, maam, with all the weight of my sins fresh on me. Tell her she'll find her son at ome, waitin for her in prayer. [He sulks off through the gate, incidentally stealing the sovereign on his way out by picking up his cap from the drum.]

MRS BAINES [with swimming eyes]. You see how we take the anger and the bitterness against you out of their hearts, Mr Undershaft.

UNDERSHAFT. It is certainly most convenient and gratifying to all large employers of labor, Mrs Baines.

MRS BAINES. Barbara: Jenny: I have good news: most wonderful news. [JENNY runs to her.] My prayers have been answered. I told you they would, Jenny, didnt I?

JENNY. Yes, yes.

BARBARA [moving nearer to the drum]. Have we got money enough to keep the shelter open?

MRS BAINES. I hope we shall have enough to keep all the shelters open. Lord Saxmundham has promised us five thousand pounds —

BARBARA. Hooray!

JENNY. Glory!

MRS BAINES.—if—

BARBARA. 'If!' If what?

MRS BAINES.—if five other gentlemen will give a thousand each to make it up to ten thousand.

BARBARA. Who is Lord Saxmundham? I never heard of him.

UNDERSHAFT [who has pricked up his ears at the peer's name, and is now watching BARBARA curiously]. A new creation, my dear. You have heard of Sir Horace Bodger?

BARBARA. Bodger! Do you mean the distiller? Bodger's whisky!

UNDERSHAFT. That is the man. He is one of the greatest of our public benefactors. He restored the cathedral at Hakington. They made him a baronet for that. He gave half a million to the funds of his party: they made him a baron for that.

SHIRLEY. What will they give him for the five thousand?

UNDERSHAFT. There is nothing left to give him. So the five thousand, I should think, is to save his soul.

MRS BAINES. Heaven grant it may! Oh Mr Undershaft, you have some very rich friends. Cant you help us towards the other five thousand? We are going to hold a great meeting this afternoon at the Assembly Hall in the Mile End Road. If I could only announce that one gentleman had come forward to support Lord Saxmundham, others would follow. Dont you know somebody? couldnt you? wouldnt you? [her eyes fill with tears] oh, think of those poor people, Mr Undershaft: think of how much it means to them, and how little to a great man like you.

UNDERSHAFT [sardonically gallant]. Mrs Baines: you are irresistible. I cant disappoint you; and I cant deny myself the satisfaction of making Bodger pay up. You shall have your five thousand pounds.

MRS BAINES. Thank God!

UNDERSHAFT. You dont thank me?

MRS BAINES. Oh sir, dont try to be cynical: dont be ashamed of being a good man. The Lord will bless you abundantly; and our prayers will be like a strong fortification round you all the days of your life. [With a touch of caution.] You will let me have the cheque to shew at the meeting, wont you? Jenny: go in and fetch a pen and ink. [JENNY runs to the shelter door.]

UNDERSHAFT. Do not disturb Miss Hill: I have a fountain pen [JENNY halts. He sits at the table and writes the cheque. CUSINS rises to make room for him. They all watch him silently].

BILL [cynically, aside to BARBARA, his voice and accent horribly debased]. Wot prawce selvytion nah?

BARBARA. Stop. [UNDERSHAFT stops writing: they all turn to her in surprise.] Mrs Baines: are you really going to take this money?

MRS BAINES [astonished]. Why not, dear?

BARBARA. Why not! Do you know what my father is? Have you forgotten that Lord Saxmundham is Bodger the whisky man? Do you remember how we implored the County Council to stop him from writing Bodger's Whisky in letters of fire against the sky; so that the poor drink-ruined creatures on the Embankment could not wake up from their snatches of sleep without being reminded of their deadly thirst by that wicked sky sign? Do you know that the worst thing I have had to fight here is not the devil, but Bodger, Bodger, Bodger, with his whisky, his distilleries, and his tied houses? Are you going to make our shelter another tied house for him, and ask me to keep it?

BILL. Rotten dranken whisky it is too.

MRS BAINES. Dear Barbara: Lord Saxmundham has a soul to be saved like any of us. If heaven has found the way to make a good use of the money, are we to set ourselves up against the answer to our prayers?

BARBARA. I know he has a soul to be saved. Let him come down here; and I'll do my best to help him to his salvation. But he wants to send his cheque down to buy us, and go on being as wicked as ever.

UNDERSHAFT [with a reasonableness which CUSINS alone perceives to be ironical]. My dear Barbara: alcohol is a very necessary article. It heals the sick—

BARBARA. It does nothing of the sort.

UNDERSHAFT. Well, it assists the doctor: that is perhaps a less questionable way of putting it. It makes life bearable to millions of people who could not endure their existence if they were quite sober. It enables Parliament to do things at eleven at night that no sane person would do at eleven in the morning. Is it Bodger's fault that this inestimable gift is deplorably abused by less than one per cent of the poor? [He turns again to the table; signs the cheque; and crosses it.]

MRS BAINES. Barbara: will there be less drinking or more if all those poor souls we are saving come tomorrow and find the doors of our shelters shut in their faces? Lord Saxmundham gives us the money to stop drinking—to take his own business from him.

CUSINS [impishly]. Pure self-sacrifice on Bodger's part, clearly! Bless dear Bodger! [BARBARA almost breaks down as ADOLPHUS, too, fails her.]

UNDERSHAFT [tearing out the cheque and pocketing the book as he rises and goes past CUSINS to MRS BAINES]. I also, Mrs Baines, may claim a little disinterestedness. Think of my business! think of the widows and orphans! the men and lads torn to pieces with shrapnel and poisoned with lyddite! [MRS BAINES *shrinks; but he goes on remorselessly.*] the oceans of blood, not one drop of which is shed in a really just cause! the ravaged crops! the peaceful peasants forced, women and men, to till their fields under the fire of opposing armies on pain of starvation! the bad blood of the fierce little cowards at home who egg on others to fight for the gratification of their national vanity! All this makes money for me: I am never richer, never busier than when the papers are full of it. Well, it is your work to preach peace on earth and good will to men. [*Mrs Baines's face lights up again.*] Every convert you make is a vote against war. [*Her lips move in prayer.*] Yet I give you this money to help you to hasten my own commercial ruin. [*He gives her the cheque.*]

CUSINS [*mounting the form in an ecstasy of mischief*]. The millennium will be inaugurated by the unselfishness of Undershaft and Bodger. Oh be joyful! [*He takes the drum-sticks from his pocket and flourishes them.*]

MRS BAINES [*taking the cheque*]. The longer I live the more proof I see that there is an Infinite Goodness that turns everything to the work of salvation sooner or later. Who would have thought that any good could have come out of war and drink? And yet their profits are brought today to the feet of salvation to do its blessed work. [*She is affected to tears.*]

JENNY [*running to MRS BAINES and throwing her arms round her*]. Oh dear! how blessed, how glorious it all is!

CUSINS [*in a convulsion of irony*]. Let us seize this unspeakable moment. Let us march to the great meeting at once. Excuse me just an instant. [*He rushes into the shelter. JENNY takes her tambourine from the drum head.*]

MRS BAINES. Mr Undershaft: have you ever seen a thousand people fall on their knees with one impulse and pray? Come with us to the meeting. Barbara shall tell them that the Army is saved, and saved through you.

CUSINS [*returning impetuously from the shelter with a flag and a trombone, and coming between MRS BAINES and UNDERSHAFT*]. You shall carry the flag down the first street, Mrs. Baines [*he gives her the flag*]. Mr Undershaft is a gifted trombonist: he shall intone an Olympian diapason to the West Ham Salvation March. [*Aside to UNDERSHAFT, as he forces the trombone on him.*] Blow, Machiavelli, blow.

UNDERSHAFT [*aside to him, as he takes the trombone*]. The trumpet in Zion! [*CUSINS rushes to the drum, which he takes up and puts on. UNDERSHAFT continues, aloud.*] I will do my best. I could vamp a bass if I knew the tune.

CUSINS. It is a wedding chorus from one of Donizetti's operas; but we have converted it. We convert everything to good here, including Bodger. You remember the chorus. 'For thee immense rejoicing—immenso giubilo—immenso giubilo.' [*With drum obbligato.*] Rum tum ti tum tum, tum tum ti ta—

BARBARA. Dolly: you are breaking my heart.

CUSINS. What is a broken heart more or less here? Dionysos Undershaft has descended. I am possessed.

MRS BAINES. Come, Barbara: I must have my dear Major to carry the flag with me.

JENNY. Yes, yes, Major darling.

CUSINS [*snatches the tambourine out of Jenny's hand and mutely offers it to BARBARA*].

BARBARA [*coming forward a little as she puts the offer behind her with a shudder, whilst CUSINS recklessly tosses the tambourine back to JENNY and goes to the gate*]. I cant come.

JENNY. Not come!

MRS BAINES [*with tears in her eyes*]. Barbara: do you think I am wrong to take the money?

BARBARA [*impulsively going to her and kissing her*]. No, no: God help you, dear, you must: you are saving the Army. Go; and may you have a great meeting!

JENNY. But arnt you coming?

BARBARA. No. [*She begins taking off the silver S brooch from her collar.*]

MRS BAINES. Barbara: what are you doing?

JENNY. Why are you taking your badge off? You cant be going to leave us, Major.

BARBARA [*quietly*]. Father: come here.

UNDERSHAFT [*coming to her*]. My dear! [*Seeing that she is going to pin the badge on his collar, he retreats to the penthouse in some alarm.]

BARBARA [*following him*]. Dont be frightened. [*She pins the badge on and steps back towards the table, shewing him to the others.*] There! It's not much for £5000, is it?

MRS BAINES. Barbara: if you wont come and pray with us, promise me you will pray for us.

BARBARA. I cant pray now. Perhaps I shall never pray again.

MRS BAINES. Barbara!

JENNY. Major!

BARBARA [*almost delirious*]. I cant bear any more. Quick march!

CUSINS [*calling to the procession in the street outside*]. Off we go. Play up, there! Immenso giubilo. [*He gives the time with his drum; and the band strikes up the march, which rapidly becomes more distant as the procession moves briskly away.*]

MRS BAINES. I must go, dear. Youre overworked: you will be all right tomorrow. We'll never lose you. Now Jenny: step out with the old flag. Blood and Fire! [*She marches out through the gate with her flag.*]

JENNY. Glory Hallelujah! [*flourishing her tambourine and marching.*]

UNDERSHAFT [*to CUSINS, as he marches out past him easing the slide of his trombone*]. 'My ducats and my daughter'!

CUSINS [*following him out*]. Money and gunpowder!

BARBARA. Drunkenness and Murder! My God: why hast thou forsaken me?

She sinks on the form with her face buried in her hands. The march passes away into silence. BILL WALKER *steals across to her.*

BILL [*taunting*]. Wot prawce selvytion nah?
SHIRLEY. Dont you hit her when she's down.
BILL. She itt me wen aw wiz dahn. Waw shouldnt Aw git a bit o me aown beck?

BARBARA [*raising her head*]. I didnt take your money, Bill. [*She crosses the yard to the gate and turns her back on the two men to hide her face from them.*]

BILL [*sneering after her*]. Naow, it warnt enaff for you. [*Turning to the drum, he misses the money.*] Ellow! If you aint took it sammun else ez. Weres it gorn? Bly me if Jenny Ill didnt tike it arter all!

RUMMY [*screaming at him from the loft*]. You lie, you dirty blackguard! Snobby Price pinched it off the drum when he took up his cap. I was up here all the time an see im do it.

BILL. Wot! Stowl maw manney! Waw didnt you call thief on him, you silly aold macker you?

RUMMY. To serve you aht for ittin me acrost the fice. It's cost y'pahnd, that az. [*Raising a pæan of squalid triumph.*] I done you. I'm even with you. Uve ad it aht o y—[BILL *snatches up Shirley's mug and hurls it at her. She slams the loft door and vanishes. The mug smashes against the door and falls in fragments.*]

BILL [*beginning to chuckle*]. Tell us, aol menn, wot o'clock this mawnin was it wen im as they call Snobby Prawce was sived?

BARBARA [*turning to him more composedly, and with unspoiled sweetness*]. About half past twelve, Bill. And he pinched your pound at a quarter to two. *I* know. Well, you cant afford to lose it. I'll send it to you.

BILL [*his voice and accent suddenly improving*]. Not if Aw wiz to stawve for it. Aw aint to be bought.

SHIRLEY. Aint you? Youd sell yourself to the devil for a pint o beer; only there aint no devil to make the offer.

BILL [*unashamed*]. Sao Aw would, mite, and often ev, cheerful. But she cawnt baw me. [*Approaching* BARBARA.] You wanted maw saoul, did you? Well, you aint got it.

BARBARA. I nearly got it, Bill. But weve sold it back to you for ten thousand pounds.

SHIRLEY. And dear at the money!

BARBARA. No, Peter: it was worth more than money.

BILL [*salvationproof*]. It's nao good: you cawnt get rahnd me nah. Aw downt blieve in it; and Awve seen tody that Aw was rawt. [*Going*] Sao long, aol soupkitchener! Ta, ta, Mijor Earl's Grendorter! [*Turning at the gate.*] Wot prawce selvytion nah? Snobby Prawce! Ha! ha!

BARBARA [*offering her hand*]. Goodbye, Bill.
BILL [*taken aback, half plucks his cap off; then shoves it on again defiantly*]. Git aht. [BARBARA *drops her hand, discouraged. He has a twinge of remorse.*] But thets aw

rawt, you knaow. Nathink pasnl. Naow mellice. Sao long, Judy. [*He goes.*]

BARBARA. No malice. So long, Bill.

SHIRLEY [*shaking his head*]. You make too much of him, miss, in your innocence.

BARBARA [*going to him*]. Peter: I'm like you now. Cleaned out, and lost my job.

SHIRLEY. Youve youth an hope. Thats two better than me.

BARBARA. I'll get you a job, Peter. Thats hope for you: the youth will have to be enough for me. [*She counts her money.*] I have just enough left for two teas at Lockharts, a Rowton doss for you, and my tram and bus home. [*He frowns and rises with offended pride. She takes his arm.*] Dont be proud, Peter: it's sharing between friends. And promise me youll talk to me and not let me cry. [*She draws him towards the gate.*]

SHIRLEY. Well, I'm not accustomed to talk to the like of you—

BARBARA [*urgently*]. Yes, yes: you must talk to me. Tell me about Tom Paine's books and Bradlaugh's lectures. Come along.

SHIRLEY. Ah, if you would only read Tom Paine in the proper spirit, miss! [*They go out through the gate together.*]

ACT III

Next day after lunch LADY BRITOMART *is writing in the library in Wilton Crescent.* SARAH *is reading in the armchair near the window.* BARBARA, *in ordinary fashionable dress, pale and brooding, is on the settee.* CHARLES LOMAX *enters. He starts on seeing* BARBARA *fashionably attired and in low spirits.*

LOMAX. Youve left off your uniform!

BARBARA *says nothing; but an expression of pain passes over her face.*

LADY BRITOMART [*warning him in low tones to be careful*]. Charles!

LOMAX [*much concerned, coming behind the settee and bending sympathetically over* BARBARA]. I'm awfully sorry, Barbara. You know I helped you all I could with the concertina and so forth. [*Momentously.*] Still, I have never shut my eyes to the fact that there is a certain amount of tosh about the Salvation Army. Now the claims of the Church of England—

LADY BRITOMART. Thats enough, Charles. Speak of something suited to your mental capacity.

LOMAX. But surely the Church of England is suited to all our capacities.

BARBARA [*pressing his hand*]. Thank you for your sympathy, Cholly. Now go and spoon with Sarah.

LOMAX [*dragging a chair from the writing table and seating himself affectionately by Sarah's side*]. How is my ownest today?

SARAH. I wish you wouldnt tell Cholly to do things, Barbara. He always comes straight and does them. Cholly: we're going to the works this afternoon.

LOMAX. What works?

SARAH. The cannon works.

LOMAX. What? your governor's shop!

SARAH. Yes.

LOMAX. Oh I say!

CUSINS *enters in poor condition. He also starts visibly when he sees* BARBARA *without her uniform.*

BARBARA. I expected you this morning, Dolly. Didnt you guess that?

CUSINS [*sitting down beside her*]. I'm sorry. I have only just breakfasted.

SARAH. But weve just finished lunch.

BARBARA. Have you had one of your bad nights?

CUSINS. No: I had rather a good night: in fact, one of the most remarkable nights I have ever passed.

BARBARA. The meeting?

CUSINS. No: after the meeting.

LADY BRITOMART. You should have gone to bed after the meeting. What were you doing?

CUSINS. Drinking.

LADY BRITOMART. Adolphus!
SARAH. Dolly!
BARBARA. Dolly!
LOMAX. Oh I say!

LADY BRITOMART. What were you drinking, may I ask?

CUSINS. A most devilish kind of Spanish burgundy, warranted free from added alcohol: a Temperance burgundy in fact. Its richness in natural alcohol made any addition superfluous.

BARBARA. Are you joking, Dolly?

CUSINS [*patiently*]. No. I have been making a night of it with the nominal head of this household: that is all.

LADY BRITOMART. Andrew made you drunk!

CUSINS. No: he only provided the wine. I think it was Dionysos who made me drunk. [*To* BARBARA.] I told you I was possessed.

LADY BRITOMART. Youre not sober yet. Go home to bed at once.

CUSINS. I have never before ventured to reproach you, Lady Brit; but how could you marry the Prince of Darkness?

LADY BRITOMART. It was much more excusable to marry him than to get drunk with him. That is a new accomplishment of Andrew's, by the way. He usent to drink.

CUSINS. He doesnt now. He only sat there and completed the wreck of my moral basis, the rout of my convictions, the purchase of my soul. He cares for you, Barbara. That is what makes him so dangerous to me.

BARBARA. That has nothing to do with it, Dolly. There are larger loves and diviner dreams than the fireside ones. You know that, dont you?

CUSINS. Yes: that is our understanding. I know it. I hold to it. Unless he can win me on that holier ground he may amuse me for a while; but he can get no deeper hold, strong as he is.

BARBARA. Keep to that; and the end will be right. Now tell me what happened at the meeting?

CUSINS. It was an amazing meeting. Mrs Baines almost died of emotion. Jenny Hill simply gibbered with hysteria. The Prince of Darkness played his trombone like a madman: its brazen roarings were like the laughter of the damned. 117 conversions took place then and there. They prayed with the most touching sincerity and gratitude for Bodger, and for the anonymous donor of the £5000. Your father would not let his name be given.

LOMAX. That was rather fine of the old man, you know. Most chaps would have wanted the advertisement.

CUSINS. He said all the charitable institutions would be down on him like kites on a battle-field if he gave his name.

LADY BRITOMART. Thats Andrew all over. He never does a proper thing without giving an improper reason for it.

CUSINS. He convinced me that I have all my life been doing improper things for proper reasons.

LADY BRITOMART. Adolphus: now that Barbara has left the Salvation Army, you had better leave it too. I will not have you playing that drum in the streets.

CUSINS. Your orders are already obeyed, Lady Brit.

BARBARA. Dolly: were you ever really in earnest about it? Would you have joined if you had never seen me?

CUSINS [*disingenuously*]. Well—er—well, possibly, as a collector of religions—

LOMAX [*cunningly*]. Not as a drummer, though, you know. You are a very clear-headed brainy chap, Dolly; and it must have been apparent to you that there is a certain amount of tosh about—

LADY BRITOMART. Charles: if you must drivel, drivel like a grown-up man and not like a schoolboy.

LOMAX [*out of countenance*]. Well, drivel is drivel, dont you know, whatever a man's age.

LADY BRITOMART. In good society in England, Charles, men drivel at all ages by repeating silly formulas with an air of wisdom. Schoolboys make their own formulas out of slang, like you. When they reach your age, and get political private secretaryships and things of that sort, they drop slang and get their formulas out of the Spectator or The Times. You had better confine yourself to The Times. You will find that there is a certain amount of tosh about The Times; but at least its language is reputable.

LOMAX [*overwhelmed*]. You are so awfully strong-minded, Lady Brit—

LADY BRITOMART. Rubbish! [MORRISON *comes in.*] What is it?

MORRISON. If you please, my lady, Mr Undershaft has just drove up to the door.

LADY BRITOMART. Well, let him in. [MORRISON *hesitates.*] Whats the matter with you?

MORRISON. Shall I announce him, my lady;

or is he at home here, so to speak, my lady?

LADY BRITOMART. Announce him.

MORRISON. Thank you, my lady. You wont mind my asking, I hope. The occasion is in a manner of speaking new to me.

LADY BRITOMART. Quite right. Go and let him in.

MORRISON. Thank you, my lady. [*He withdraws.*]

LADY BRITOMART. Children: go and get ready. [SARAH *and* BARBARA *go upstairs for their out-of-door wraps.*] Charles: go and tell Stephen to come down here in five minutes: you will find him in the drawing room. [CHARLES *goes.*] Adolphus: tell them to send round the carriage in about fifteen minutes. [ADOLPHUS *goes.*]

MORRISON [*at the door*]. Mr Undershaft.

UNDERSHAFT *comes in.* MORRISON *goes out.*

UNDERSHAFT. Alone! How fortunate!

LADY BRITOMART [*rising*]. Dont be sentimental, Andrew. Sit down. [*She sits on the settee: he sits beside her, on her left. She comes to the point before he has time to breathe.*] Sarah must have £800 a year until Charles Lomax comes into his property. Barbara will need more, and need it permanently, because Adolphus hasnt any property.

UNDERSHAFT [*resignedly*]. Yes, my dear: I will see to it. Anything else? for yourself, for instance?

LADY BRITOMART. I want to talk to you about Stephen.

UNDERSHAFT [*rather wearily*]. Dont, my dear. Stephen doesnt interest me.

LADY BRITOMART. He does interest me. He is our son.

UNDERSHAFT. Do you really think so? He has induced us to bring him into the world; but he chose his parents very incongruously, I think. I see nothing of myself in him, and less of you.

LADY BRITOMART. Andrew: Stephen is an excellent son, and a most steady, capable, highminded young man. You are simply trying to find an excuse for disinheriting him.

UNDERSHAFT. My dear Biddy: the Undershaft tradition disinherits him. It would be dishonest of me to leave the cannon foundry to my son.

LADY BRITOMART. It would be most unnatural and improper of you to leave it to anyone else, Andrew. Do you suppose this wicked and immoral tradition can be kept up for ever? Do you pretend that Stephen could not carry on the foundry just as well as all the other sons of the big business houses?

UNDERSHAFT. Yes: he could learn the office routine without understanding the business, like all the other sons; and the firm would go on by its own momentum until the real Undershaft—probably an Italian or a German—would invent a new method and cut him out.

LADY BRITOMART. There is nothing that any Italian or German could do that Stephen could not do. And Stephen at least has breeding.

UNDERSHAFT. The son of a foundling! Nonsense!

LADY BRITOMART. My son, Andrew! And even you may have good blood in your veins for all you know.

UNDERSHAFT. True. Probably I have. That is another argument in favour of a foundling.

LADY BRITOMART. Andrew: dont be aggravating. And dont be wicked. At present you are both.

UNDERSHAFT. This consideration is part of the Undershaft tradition, Biddy. Every Undershaft's wife has treated him to it ever since the house was founded. It is mere waste of breath. If the tradition be ever broken it will be for an abler man than Stephen.

LADY BRITOMART [*pouting*]. Then go away.

UNDERSHAFT [*deprecatory*]. Go away!

LADY BRITOMART. Yes: go away. If you will do nothing for Stephen, you are not wanted here. Go to your foundling, whoever he is; and look after him.

UNDERSHAFT. The fact is, Biddy—

LADY BRITOMART. Dont call me Biddy. I dont call you Andy.

UNDERSHAFT. I will not call my wife Britomart: it is not good sense. Seriously, my love, the Undershaft tradition has landed me in a difficulty. I am getting on in years; and my partner Lazarus has at last made a stand and insisted that the succession must be settled one way or the other; and of course he is quite right. You see, I havent found a fit successor yet.

LADY BRITOMART [*obstinately*]. There is Stephen.

UNDERSHAFT. Thats just it: all the foundlings I can find are exactly like Stephen.

LADY BRITOMART. Andrew!!

UNDERSHAFT. I want a man with no relations and no schooling: that is, a man who would be out of the running altogether if he were not a strong man. And I cant find him. Every blessed foundling nowadays is snapped up in his infancy by Barnardo homes, or School Board officers, or Boards of Guardians; and if he shews the least ability he is fastened on by schoolmasters; trained to win scholarships like a racehorse; crammed with second-hand ideas; drilled and disciplined in docility and what they call good taste; and lamed for life so that he is fit for nothing but teaching. If you want to keep the foundry in the family, you had better find an eligible foundling and marry him to Barbara.

LADY BRITOMART. Ah! Barbara! Your pet! You would sacrifice Stephen to Barbara.

UNDERSHAFT. Cheerfully. And you, my dear, would boil Barbara to make soup for Stephen.

LADY BRITOMART. Andrew: this is not a question of our likings and dislikings: it is a question of duty. It is your duty to make Stephen your successor.

UNDERSHAFT. Just as much as it is your duty to submit to your husband. Come, Biddy! these tricks of the governing class are of no use with me. I am one of the governing class myself; and it is waste of time giving tracts to a missionary. I have the power in this matter; and I am not to be hum-bugged into using it for your purposes.

LADY BRITOMART. Andrew: you can talk my head off; but you cant change wrong into right. And your tie is all on one side. Put it straight.

UNDERSHAFT [*disconcerted*]. It wont stay unless it's pinned [*he fumbles at it with childish grimaces*]—

STEPHEN *comes in*.

STEPHEN [*at the door*]. I beg your pardon [*about to retire*].

LADY BRITOMART. No: come in, Stephen.

[STEPHEN *comes forward to his mother's writing table.*]

UNDERSHAFT [*not very cordially*]. Good afternoon.

STEPHEN [*coldly*]. Good afternoon.

UNDERSHAFT [*to* LADY BRITOMART]. He knows all about the tradition, I suppose?

LADY BRITOMART. Yes. [To STEPHEN.] It is what I told you last night, Stephen.

UNDERSHAFT [*sulkily*]. I understand you want to come into the cannon business.

STEPHEN. *I* go into trade! Certainly not.

UNDERSHAFT [*opening his eyes, greatly eased in mind and manner*]. Oh! in that case—

LADY BRITOMART. Cannons are not trade, Stephen. They are enterprise.

STEPHEN. I have no intention of becoming a man of business in any sense. I have no capacity for business and no taste for it. I intend to devote myself to politics.

UNDERSHAFT [*rising*]. My dear boy: this is an immense relief to me. And I trust it may prove an equally good thing for the country. I was afraid you would consider yourself disparaged and slighted. [*He moves towards* STEPHEN *as if to shake hands with him.*]

LADY BRITOMART [*rising and interposing*]. Stephen: I cannot allow you to throw away an enormous property like this.

STEPHEN [*stiffly*]. Mother: there must be an end of treating me as a child, if you please. [LADY BRITOMART *recoils, deeply wounded by his tone.*] Until last night I did not take your attitude seriously, because I did not think you meant it seriously. But I find now that you left me in the dark as to matters which you should have explained to me years ago. I am extremely hurt and offended. Any further discussion of my intentions had better take place with my father, as between one man and another.

LADY BRITOMART. Stephen! [*She sits down again, her eyes filling with tears.*]

UNDERSHAFT [*with grave compassion*]. You see, my dear, it is only the big men who can be treated as children.

STEPHEN. I am sorry, mother, that you have forced me—

UNDERSHAFT [*stopping him*]. Yes, yes, yes, yes: thats all right, Stephen. She wont interfere with you any more: your independence is achieved: you have won your latchkey. Dont rub it in; and above all, dont apologize. [*He resumes his seat.*] Now what about your future, as between one man and another—I beg your pardon, Biddy: as between two men and a woman.

LADY BRITOMART [*who has pulled herself together strongly*]. I quite understand, Stephen. By all means go your own way if you feel strong enough. [STEPHEN *sits down magisterially in the chair at the writing table with an air of affirming his majority.*]

UNDERSHAFT. It is settled that you do not ask for the succession to the cannon business.

STEPHEN. I hope it is settled that I repudiate the cannon business.

UNDERSHAFT. Come, come! dont be so devilishly sulky: it's boyish. Freedom should be generous. Besides, I owe you a fair start in life in exchange for disinheriting you. You cant become prime minister all at once. Havnt you a turn for something? What about literature, art, and so forth?

STEPHEN. I have nothing of the artist about me, either in faculty or character, thank Heaven!

UNDERSHAFT. A philosopher, perhaps? Eh?

STEPHEN. I make no such ridiculous pretension.

UNDERSHAFT. Just so. Well, there is the army, the navy, the Church, the Bar. The Bar requires some ability. What about the Bar?

STEPHEN. I have not studied law. And I am afraid I have not the necessary push—I believe that is the name barristers give to their vulgarity—for success in pleading.

UNDERSHAFT. Rather a difficult case, Stephen. Hardly anything left but the stage, is there? [STEPHEN *makes an impatient movement.*] Well, come! is there anything you know or care for?

STEPHEN [*rising and looking at him steadily*]. I know the difference between right and wrong.

UNDERSHAFT [*hugely tickled*]. You dont say so! What! no capacity for business, no knowledge of law, no sympathy with art, no pretension to philosophy; only a simple knowledge of the secret that has puzzled all the philosophers, baffled all the lawyers, muddled all the men of business, and ruined most of the artists: the secret of right and wrong. Why, man, youre a genius, a master of masters, a god! At twenty-four, too!

STEPHEN [*keeping his temper with difficulty*]. You are pleased to be facetious. I pretend to nothing more than any honorable English gentleman claims as his birthright [*he sits down angrily*].

UNDERSHAFT. Oh, thats everybody's birthright. Look at poor little Jenny Hill, the Salvation lassie! she would think you were laughing at her if you asked her to stand up in the street and teach grammar or geography or mathematics or even drawing room dancing; but it never occurs to her to doubt that she can teach morals and religion. You are all alike, you respectable people. You cant tell me the bursting strain of a ten-inch gun, which is a very simple matter; but you all think you can tell me the bursting strain of a man under temptation. You darent handle high explosives; but youre all ready to handle honesty and truth and justice and the whole duty of man, and kill one another at that game. What a country! What a world!

LADY BRITOMART [*uneasily*]. What do you think he had better do, Andrew?

UNDERSHAFT. Oh, just what he wants to do. He knows nothing and he thinks he knows everything. That points clearly to a political career. Get him a private secretaryship to someone who can get him an Under Secretaryship; and then leave him alone. He will find his natural and proper place in the end on the Treasury Bench.

STEPHEN [*springing up again*]. I am sorry, sir, that you force me to forget the respect due to you as my father. I am an Englishman and I will not hear the Government of my country insulted. [*He thrusts his hands in his pockets, and walks angrily across to the window.*]

UNDERSHAFT [*with a touch of brutality*]. The government of your country! *I* am the government of your country: I, and Lazarus. Do you suppose that you and half a dozen amateurs like you, sitting in a row in that foolish gabble shop, can govern Undershaft and Lazarus? No, my friend: you will do what pays us. You will make war when it suits us, and keep peace when it doesnt. You will find out that trade requires certain measures when we have decided on those measures. When I want anything to keep my dividends up, you will discover that my want is a national need. When other people want something to keep my dividends down, you will call out the police and military. And in return you shall have the support and applause of my newspapers, and the delight of imagining that you are a great statesman. Government of your country! Be off with you, my boy, and play with your caucuses and leading articles and historic parties and great leaders and burning questions and the rest of your toys. I am going back to my counting-house to pay the piper and call the tune.

STEPHEN [actually smiling, and putting his hand on his father's shoulder with indulgent patronage]. Really, my dear father, it is impossible to be angry with you. You dont know how absurd all this sounds to me. You are very properly proud of having been industrious enough to make money; and it is greatly to your credit that you have made so much of it. But it has kept you in circles where you are valued for your money and deferred to for it, instead of in the doubtless very old-fashioned and behind-the-times public school and university where I formed my habits of mind. It is natural for you to think that money governs England; but you must allow me to think I know better.

UNDERSHAFT. And what does govern England, pray?

STEPHEN. Character, father, character.

UNDERSHAFT. Whose character? Yours or mine?

STEPHEN. Neither yours nor mine, father, but the best elements in the English national character.

UNDERSHAFT. Stephen: Ive found your profession for you. Youre a born journalist. I'll start you with a high-toned weekly review. There!

Before STEPHEN can reply SARAH, BARBARA, LOMAX, and CUSINS come in ready for walking. BARBARA crosses the room to the window and looks out. CUSINS drifts amiably to the armchair. LOMAX remains near the door, whilst SARAH comes to her mother.

STEPHEN goes to the smaller writing table and busies himself with his letters.

SARAH. Go and get ready, mamma: the carriage is waiting. [LADY BRITOMART leaves the room.]

UNDERSHAFT [to SARAH]. Good day, my dear. Good afternoon, Mr Lomax.

LOMAX [vaguely]. Ahdedoo.

UNDERSHAFT [to CUSINS]. Quite well after last night, Euripides, eh?

CUSINS. As well as can be expected.

UNDERSHAFT. Thats right. [To BARBARA.] So you are coming to see my death and devastation factory, Barbara?

BARBARA [at the window]. You came yesterday to see my salvation factory. I promised you a return visit.

LOMAX [coming forward between SARAH and UNDERSHAFT]. Youll find it awfully interesting. Ive been through the Woolwich Arsenal; and it gives you a ripping feeling of security, you know, to think of the lot of beggars we could kill if it came to fighting. [To UNDERSHAFT, with sudden solemnity.] Still, it must be rather an awful reflection for you, from the religious point of view as it were. Youre getting on, you know, and all that.

SARAH. You dont mind Cholly's imbecility, papa, do you?

LOMAX [much taken aback]. Oh I say!

UNDERSHAFT. Mr Lomax looks at the matter in a very proper spirit, my dear.

LOMAX. Just so. Thats all I meant, I assure you.

SARAH. Are you coming, Stephen?

STEPHEN. Well, I am rather busy—er—[Magnanimously.] Oh well, yes: I'll come. That is, if there is room for me.

UNDERSHAFT. I can take two with me in a little motor I am experimenting with for field use. You wont mind its being rather unfashionable. It's not painted yet; but it's bullet proof.

LOMAX [appalled at the prospect of confronting Wilton Crescent in an unpainted motor]. Oh I say!

SARAH. The carriage for me, thank you. Barbara doesnt mind what she's seen in.

LOMAX. I say, Dolly, old chap: do you really mind the car being a guy? Because of course if you do I'll go in it. Still—

CUSINS. I prefer it.

LOMAX. Thanks awfully, old man. Come, my ownest. [He hurries out to secure his seat in the carriage. SARAH follows him.]

CUSINS [moodily walking across to Lady Britomart's writing table]. Why are we two coming to this Works Department of Hell? that is what I ask myself.

BARBARA. I have always thought of it as a sort of pit where lost creatures with blackened faces stirred up smoky fires and were driven and tormented by my father. Is it like that, dad?

UNDERSHAFT [scandalized]. My dear! It is a spotlessly clean and beautiful hillside town.

CUSINS. With a Methodist chapel? Oh do say theres a Methodist chapel.

UNDERSHAFT. There are two: a Primitive one and a sophisticated one. There is even an Ethical Society; but it is not much patronized, as my men are all strongly religious. In the High Explosives Sheds they object to the presence of Agnostics as unsafe.

CUSINS. And yet they dont object to you!

BARBARA. Do they obey all your orders?

UNDERSHAFT. I never give them any orders. When I speak to one of them it is 'Well, Jones, is the baby doing well? and has Mrs Jones made a good recovery?' 'Nicely, thank you, sir.' And thats all.

CUSINS. But Jones has to be kept in order. How do you maintain discipline among your men?

UNDERSHAFT. I dont. They do. You see, the one thing Jones wont stand is any rebellion from the man under him, or any assertion of social equality between the wife of the man with 4 shillings a week less than himself, and Mrs Jones! Of course they all rebel against me, theoretically. Practically, every man of them keeps the man just below him in his place. I never meddle with them. I never bully them. I dont even bully Lazarus. I say that certain things are to be done; but I dont order anybody to do them. I dont say, mind you, that there is no ordering about and snubbing and even bullying. The men snub the boys and order them about; the carmen snub the sweepers; the artisans snub the unskilled laborers; the foremen drive and bully both the laborers and artisans; the assistant engineers find fault with the foremen; the chief engineers drop on the assistants; the departmental managers worry the chiefs; and the clerks have tall hats and hymnbooks and keep up the social tone by refusing to associate on equal terms with anybody. The result is a colossal profit, which comes to me.

CUSINS [revolted]. You really are a—well, what I was saying yesterday.

BARBARA. What was he saying yesterday?

UNDERSHAFT. Never mind, my dear. He thinks I have made you unhappy. Have I?

BARBARA. Do you think I can be happy in this vulgar silly dress? I! who have worn the uniform. Do you understand what you have done to me? Yesterday I had a man's soul in my hand. I set him in the way of life with his face to salvation. But when we took your money he turned back to drunkenness and derision. [With intense conviction.] I will never forgive you that. If I had a child, and you destroyed its body with your explosives—if you murdered Dolly with your horrible guns—I could forgive you if my forgiveness would open the gates of heaven to you. But to take a human soul from me, and turn it into the soul of a wolf! that is worse than any murder.

UNDERSHAFT. Does my daughter despair so easily? Can you strike a man to the heart and leave no mark on him?

BARBARA [her face lighting up]. Oh, you are right: he can never be lost now: where was my faith?

CUSINS. Oh, clever clever devil!

BARBARA. You may be a devil; but God speaks through you sometimes. [She takes her father's hands and kisses them.] You have given me back my happiness: I feel it deep down now, though my spirit is troubled.

UNDERSHAFT. You have learnt something. That always feels at first as if you had lost something.

BARBARA. Well, take me to the factory of death; and let me learn something more. There must be some truth or other behind all this frightful irony. Come, Dolly. [She goes out.]

CUSINS. My guardian angel! [To UNDERSHAFT.] Avaunt! [He follows BARBARA.]

STEPHEN [quietly, at the writing table]. You must not mind Cusins, father. He is a very amiable good fellow; but he is a Greek scholar and naturally a little eccentric.

UNDERSHAFT. Ah, quite so, Thank you, Stephen. Thank you. [He goes out.]

STEPHEN *smiles patronizingly; buttons his coat responsibly; and crosses the room to the door.* LADY BRITOMART, *dressed for out-of-*

doors, opens it before he reaches it. She looks round for others; looks at STEPHEN; and turns to go without a word.

STEPHEN [embarrassed]. Mother —
LADY BRITOMART. Dont be apologetic, Stephen. And dont forget that you have outgrown your mother. [She goes out.]

Perivale St Andrews lies between two Middlesex hills, half climbing the northern one. It is an almost smokeless town of white walls, roofs of narrow green slates or red tiles, tall trees, domes, campaniles, and slender chimney shafts, beautifully situated and beautiful in itself. The best view of it is obtained from the crest of a slope about half a mile to the east, where the high explosives are dealt with. The foundry lies hidden in the depths between, the tops of its chimneys sprouting like huge skittles into the middle distance. Across the crest runs an emplacement of concrete, with a firestep, and a parapet which suggests a fortification, because there is a huge cannon of the obsolete Woolwich Infant pattern peering across it at the town. The cannon is mounted on an experimental gun carriage: possibly the original model of the Undershaft disappearing rampart gun alluded to by STEPHEN. *The firestep, being a convenient place to sit, is furnished here and there with straw disc cushions; and at one place there is the additional luxury of a fur rug.*

BARBARA *is standing on the firestep, looking over the parapet towards the town. On her right is the cannon; on her left the end of a shed raised on piles, with a ladder of three or four steps up to the door, which opens outwards and has a little wooden landing at the threshold, with a fire bucket in the corner of the landing. Several dummy soldiers more or less mutilated, with straw protruding from their gashes, have been shoved out of the way under the landing. A few others are nearly upright against the shed; and one has fallen forward and lies, like a grotesque corpse, on the emplacement. The parapet stops short of the shed, leaving a gap which is the beginning of the path down the hill through the foundry to the town. The rug is on the firestep near this gap. Down on the emplacement behind the cannon is a trolley carrying a huge conical bombshell with a red band painted on it. Further to the right is the door of an office, which, like the sheds, is of the lightest possible construction.*

CUSINS *arrives by the path from the town.*

BARBARA. Well?
CUSINS. Not a ray of hope. Everything perfect! wonderful! real! It only needs a cathedral to be a heavenly city instead of a hellish one.
BARBARA. Have you found out whether they have done anything for old Peter Shirley?
CUSINS. They have found him a job as gatekeeper and timekeeper. He's frightfully miserable. He calls the time-keeping brainwork, and says he isnt used to it; and his gate lodge is so splendid that he's ashamed to use the rooms, and skulks in the scullery.
BARBARA. Poor Peter!

STEPHEN *arrives from the town. He carries a fieldglass.*

STEPHEN [enthusiastically]. Have you two seen the place? Why did you leave us?
CUSINS. I wanted to see everything I was not intended to see; and Barbara wanted to make the men talk.
STEPHEN. Have you found anything discreditable?
CUSINS. No. They call him Dandy Andy and are proud of his being a cunning old rascal; but it's all horribly, frightfully, immorally, unanswerably perfect.

Sarah arrives.

SARAH. Heavens! what a place! [*She crosses to the trolley.*] Did you see the nursing home!? [*She sits down on the shell.*]
STEPHEN. Did you see the libraries and schools!?
SARAH. Did you see the ball room and the banqueting chamber in the Town Hall!?
STEPHEN. Have you gone into the insurance fund, the pension fund, the building society, the various applications of cooperation!?

UNDERSHAFT *comes from the office, with a sheaf of telegrams in his hand.*

UNDERSHAFT. Well, have you seen everything? I'm sorry I was called away. [Indicating the telegrams.] Good news from Manchuria.

STEPHEN. Another Japanese victory?

UNDERSHAFT. Oh, I dont know. Which side wins does not concern us here. No: the good news is that the aerial battleship is a tremendous success. At the first trial it has wiped out a fort with three hundred soldiers in it.

CUSINS [*from the platform*]. Dummy soldiers?

UNDERSHAFT [*striding across to* STEPHEN *and kicking the prostrate dummy brutally out of his way*]. No: the real thing.

CUSINS *and* BARBARA *exchange glances. Then* CUSINS *sits on the step and buries his face in his hands.* BARBARA *gravely lays her hand on his shoulder. He looks up at her in whimsical desperation.*

UNDERSHAFT. Well, Stephen, what do you think of the place?

STEPHEN. Oh, magnificent. A perfect triumph of modern industry. Frankly, my dear father, I have been a fool: I had no idea of what it all meant: of the wonderful forethought, the power of organization, the administrative capacity, the financial genius, the colossal capital it represents. I have been repeating to myself as I came through your streets 'Peace hath her victories no less renowned than War.' I have only one misgiving about it all.

UNDERSHAFT. Out with it.

STEPHEN. Well, I cannot help thinking that all this provision for every want of your workmen may sap their independence and weaken their sense of responsibility. And greatly as we enjoyed our tea at that splendid restaurant—how they gave us all that luxury and cake and jam and cream for threepence I really cannot imagine!—still you must remember that restaurants break up home life. Look at the continent, for instance! Are you sure so much pampering is really good for the men's characters?

UNDERSHAFT. Well you see, my dear boy, when you are organizing civilization you have to make up your mind whether trouble and anxiety are good things or not. If you decide that they are, then, I take it, you simply dont organize civilization; and there you are, with trouble and anxiety enough to make us all angels! But if you decide the other way, you may as well go through with it. However, Stephen, our characters are safe here. A sufficient dose of anxiety is always provided by the fact that we may be blown to smithereens at any moment.

SARAH. By the way, papa, where do you make the explosives?

UNDERSHAFT. In separate little sheds, like that one. When one of them blows up, it costs very little; and only the people quite close to it are killed.

STEPHEN, *who is quite close to it, looks at it rather scaredly, and moves away quickly to the cannon. At the same moment the door of the shed is thrown abruptly open; and a foreman in overalls and list slippers comes out on the little landing and holds the door for* LOMAX, *who appears in the doorway.*

LOMAX [*with studied coolness*]. My good fellow: you neednt get into a state of nerves. Nothing's going to happen to you; and I suppose it wouldnt be the end of the world if anything did. A little bit of British pluck is what you want, old chap. [*He descends and strolls across to* SARAH.]

UNDERSHAFT [*to the foreman*]. Anything wrong, Bilton?

BILTON [*with ironic calm*]. Gentleman walked into the high explosives shed and lit a cigaret, sir: thats all.

UNDERSHAFT. Ah, quite so. [*Going over to* LOMAX.] Do you happen to remember what you did with the match?

LOMAX. Oh come! I'm not a fool. I took jolly good care to blow it out before I chucked it away.

BILTON. The top of it was red hot inside, sir.

LOMAX. Well, suppose it was! I didn't chuck it into any of your messes.

UNDERSHAFT. Think no more of it, Mr Lomax. By the way, would you mind lending me your matches.

LOMAX [*offering his box*]. Certainly.

UNDERSHAFT. Thanks. [*He pockets the matches.*]

LOMAX [*lecturing to the company generally*]. You know, these high explosives dont go off like gunpowder, except when theyre in a gun. When theyre spread loose, you can put a match to them without the least risk: they just burn quietly like a bit of paper. [*Warming to the scientific interest of the subject.*] Did you know that, Undershaft? Have you ever tried?

UNDERSHAFT. Not on a large scale, Mr Lomax. Bilton will give you a sample of gun cotton when you are leaving if you ask him. You can experiment with it at home. [BILTON *looks puzzled.*]

SARAH. Bilton will do nothing of the sort, papa. I suppose it's your business to blow up the Russians and Japs; but you might really stop short of blowing up poor Cholly. [BILTON *gives it up and retires into the shed.*]

LOMAX. My ownest, there is no danger. [*He sits beside her on the shell.*]

LADY BRITOMART *arrives from the town with a bouquet.*

LADY BRITOMART [*impetuously*]. Andrew: you shouldnt have let me see this place.
UNDERSHAFT. Why, my dear?
LADY BRITOMART. Never mind why: you shouldnt have: thats all. To think of all that [*indicating the town*] being yours! and that you have kept it to yourself all these years!
UNDERSHAFT. It does not belong to me. I belong to it. It is the Undershaft inheritance.
LADY BRITOMART. It is not. Your ridiculous cannons and that noisy banging foundry may be the Undershaft inheritance; but all that plate and linen, all that furniture and those houses and orchards and gardens belong to us. They belong to me: they are not a man's business. I wont give them up. You must be out of your senses to throw them all away; and if you persist in such folly, I will call in a doctor.
UNDERSHAFT [*stooping to smell the bouquet*]. Where did you get the flowers, my dear?
LADY BRITOMART. Your men presented them to me in your William Morris Labor Church.
CUSINS. Oh! It needed only that. A Labor Church! [*he mounts the firestep distractedly, and leans with his elbows on the parapet, turning his back to them*].
LADY BRITOMART. Yes, with Morris's words in mosaic letters ten feet high round the dome. NO MAN IS GOOD ENOUGH TO BE ANOTHER MAN'S MASTER. The cynicism of it!

UNDERSHAFT. It shocked the men at first, I am afraid. But now they take no more notice of it than of the ten commandments in church.
LADY BRITOMART. Andrew: you are trying to put me off the subject of the inheritance by profane jokes. Well, you shant. I dont ask it any longer for Stephen: he has inherited far too much of your perversity to be fit for it. But Barbara has rights as well as Stephen. Why should not Adolphus succeed to the inheritance? I could manage the town for him; and he can look after the cannons, if they are really necessary.
UNDERSHAFT. I should ask nothing better if Adolphus were a foundling. He is exactly the sort of new blood that is wanted in English business. But he's not a foundling; and theres an end of it. [*He makes for the office door.*]
CUSINS [*turning to them*]. Not quite. [*They all turn and stare at him*]. I think—Mind! I am not committing myself in any way as to my future course—but I think the foundling difficulty can be got over. [*He jumps down to the emplacement*].
UNDERSHAFT [*coming back to him*]. What do you mean?
CUSINS. Well, I have something to say which is in the nature of a confession.
SARAH.
LADY BRITOMART.
BARBARA. } Confession!
STEPHEN.
LOMAX. Oh I say!
CUSINS. Yes, a confession. Listen, all. Until I met Barbara I thought myself in the main an honorable, truthful man, because I wanted the approval of my conscience more than I wanted anything else. But the moment I saw Barbara, I wanted her far more than the approval of my conscience.
LADY BRITOMART. Adolphus!
CUSINS. It is true. You accused me yourself, Lady Brit, of joining the Army to worship Barbara; and so I did. She bought my soul like a flower at a street corner; but she bought it for herself.
UNDERSHAFT. What! Not for Dionysos or another?
CUSINS. Dionysos and all the others are in herself. I adored what was divine in her, and was therefore a true worshipper. But

I was romantic about her too. I thought she was a woman of the people, and that a marriage with a professor of Greek would be far beyond the wildest social ambitions of her rank.
LADY BRITOMART. Adolphus!!
LOMAX. Oh I say!!!
CUSINS. When I learnt the horrible truth —
LADY BRITOMART. What do you mean by the horrible truth, pray?
CUSINS. That she was enormously rich; that her grandfather was an earl; that her father was the Prince of Darkness —
UNDERSHAFT. Chut!
CUSINS.—and that I was only an adventurer trying to catch a rich wife, then I stooped to deceive her about my birth.
BARBARA [rising]. Dolly!
LADY BRITOMART. Your birth! Now Adolphus, dont dare to make up a wicked story for the sake of these wretched cannons. Remember: I have seen photographs of your parents; and the Agent General for South Western Australia knows them personally and has assured me that they are most respectable married people.
CUSINS. So they are in Australia; but here they are outcasts. Their marriage is legal in Australia, but not in England. My mother is my father's deceased wife's sister; and in this island I am consequently a foundling. [Sensation.]
BARBARA. Silly! [She climbs to the cannon, and leans, listening, in the angle it makes with the parapet.]
CUSINS. Is the subterfuge good enough, Machiavelli?
UNDERSHAFT [thoughtfully]. Biddy: this may be a way out of the difficulty.
LADY BRITOMART. Stuff! A man cant make cannons any the better for being his own cousin instead of his proper self [she sits down on the rug with a bounce that expresses her downright contempt for their casuistry.]
UNDERSHAFT [to CUSINS]. You are an educated man. That is against the tradition.
CUSINS. Once in ten thousand times it happens that the schoolboy is a born master of what they try to teach him. Greek has not destroyed my mind: it has nourished it. Besides, I did not learn it at an English public school.
UNDERSHAFT. Hm! Well, I cannot afford to be too particular: you have cornered the foundling market. Let it pass. You are eligible, Euripides: you are eligible.
BARBARA. Dolly: yesterday morning, when Stephen told us all about the tradition, you became very silent; and you have been strange and excited ever since. Were you thinking of your birth then?
CUSINS. When the finger of Destiny suddenly points at a man in the middle of his breakfast, it makes him thoughtful.
UNDERSHAFT. Aha! You have had your eye on the business, my young friend, have you?
CUSINS. Take care! There is an abyss of moral horror between me and your accursed aerial battleships.
UNDERSHAFT. Never mind the abyss for the present. Let us settle the practical details and leave your final decision open. You know that you will have to change your name. Do you object to that?
CUSINS. Would any man named Adolphus—any man called Dolly!—object to be called something else?
UNDERSHAFT. Good. Now, as to money! I propose to treat you handsomely from the beginning. You shall start at a thousand a year.
CUSINS [with sudden heat, his spectacles twinkling with mischief]. A thousand! You dare offer a miserable thousand to the son-in-law of a millionaire! No, by Heavens, Machiavelli! you shall not cheat me. You cannot do without me; and I can do without you. I must have two thousand five hundred a year for two years. At the end of that time, if I am a failure, I go. But if I am a success, and stay on, you must give me the other five thousand.
UNDERSHAFT. What other five thousand?
CUSINS. To make the two years up to five thousand a year. The two thousand five hundred is only half pay in case I should turn out a failure. The third year I must have ten per cent on the profits.
UNDERSHAFT [taken aback]. Ten per cent! Why, man, do you know what my profits are?
CUSINS. Enormous, I hope: otherwise I shall require twenty-five per cent.
UNDERSHAFT. But, Mr Cusins, this is a serious matter of business. You are not bringing any capital into the concern.
CUSINS. What! no capital! Is my mastery of

Greek no capital? Is my access to the subtlest thought, the loftiest poetry yet attained by humanity, no capital? My character! my intellect! my life! my career! what Barbara calls my soul! are these no capital? Say another word; and I double my salary.

UNDERSHAFT. Be reasonable —

CUSINS [*peremptorily*]. Mr Undershaft: you have my terms. Take them or leave them.

UNDERSHAFT [*recovering himself*]. Very well. I note your terms; and I offer you half.

CUSINS [*disgusted*]. Half!

UNDERSHAFT [*firmly*]. Half.

CUSINS. You call yourself a gentleman; and you offer me half!!

UNDERSHAFT. I do not call myself a gentleman; but I offer you half.

CUSINS. This to your future partner! your successor! your son-in-law!

BARBARA. You are selling your own soul, Dolly, not mine. Leave me out of the bargain, please.

UNDERSHAFT. Come! I will go a step further for Barbara's sake. I will give you three fifths; but that is my last word.

CUSINS. Done!

LOMAX. Done in the eye! Why, *I* get only eight hundred, you know.

CUSINS. By the way, Mac, I am a classical scholar, not an arithmetical one. Is three fifths more than half or less?

UNDERSHAFT. More, of course.

CUSINS. I would have taken two hundred and fifty. How you can succeed in business when you are willing to pay all that money to a University don who is obviously not worth a junior clerk's wages!—well! What will Lazarus say?

UNDERSHAFT. Lazarus is a gentle romantic Jew who cares for nothing but string quartets and stalls at fashionable theatres. He will be blamed for your rapacity in money matters, poor fellow! as he has hitherto been blamed for mine. You are a shark of the first order, Euripides. So much the better for the firm!

BARBARA. Is the bargain closed, Dolly? Does your soul belong to him now?

CUSINS. No: the price is settled: that is all. The real tug of war is still to come. What about the moral question?

LADY BRITOMART. There is no moral question in the matter at all, Adolphus. You must simply sell cannons and weapons to people whose cause is right and just, and refuse them to foreigners and criminals.

UNDERSHAFT [*determinedly*]. No: none of that. You must keep the true faith of an Armorer, or you dont come in here.

CUSINS. What on earth is the true faith of an Armorer?

UNDERSHAFT. To give arms to all men who offer an honest price for them, without respect of persons or principles: to aristocrat and republican, to Nihilist and Tsar, to Capitalist and Socialist, to Protestant and Catholic, to burglar and policeman, to black man, white man and yellow man, to all sorts and conditions, all nationalities, all faiths, all follies, all causes and all crimes. The first Undershaft wrote up in his shop IF GOD GAVE THE HAND, LET NOT MAN WITHHOLD THE SWORD. The second wrote up ALL HAVE THE RIGHT TO FIGHT: NONE HAVE THE RIGHT TO JUDGE. The third wrote up TO MAN THE WEAPON: TO HEAVEN THE VICTORY. The fourth had no literary turn; so he did not write up anything; but he sold cannons to Napoleon under the nose of George the Third. The fifth wrote up PEACE SHALL NOT PREVAIL SAVE WITH A SWORD IN HER HAND. The sixth, my master, was the best of all. He wrote up NOTHING IS EVER DONE IN THIS WORLD UNTIL MEN ARE PREPARED TO KILL ONE ANOTHER IF IT IS NOT DONE. After that, there was nothing left for the seventh to say. So he wrote up, simply, UNASHAMED.

CUSINS. My good Machiavelli, I shall certainly write something up on the wall; only, as I shall write it in Greek, you wont be able to read it. But as to your Armorer's faith, if I take my neck out of the noose of my own morality I am not going to put it into the noose of yours. I shall sell cannons to whom I please and refuse them to whom I please. So there!

UNDERSHAFT. From the moment when you become Andrew Undershaft, you will never do as you please again. Dont come here lusting for power, young man.

CUSINS. If power were my aim I should not come here for it. You have no power.

UNDERSHAFT. None of my own, certainly.

CUSINS. I have more power than you, more will. You do not drive this place: it drives you. And what drives the place?

UNDERSHAFT [*enigmatically*]. A will of which I am a part.

BARBARA [*startled*]. Father! Do you know what you are saying; or are you laying a snare for my soul?

CUSINS. Dont listen to his metaphysics, Barbara. The place is driven by the most rascally part of society, the money hunters, the pleasure hunters, the military promotion hunters; and he is their slave.

UNDERSHAFT. Not necessarily. Remember the Armorer's Faith. I will take an order from a good man as cheerfully as from a bad one. If you good people prefer preaching and shirking to buying my weapons and fighting the rascals, dont blame me. I can make cannons: I cannot make courage and conviction. Bah! you tire me, Euripides, with your morality mongering. Ask Barbara: she understands. [*He suddenly reaches up and takes Barbara's hands, looking powerfully into her eyes.*] Tell him, my love, what power really means.

BARBARA [*hypnotized*]. Before I joined the Salvation Army, I was in my own power; and the consequence was that I never knew what to do with myself. When I joined it, I had not time enough for all the things I had to do.

UNDERSHAFT [*approvingly*]. Just so. And why was that, do you suppose?

BARBARA. Yesterday I should have said, because I was in the power of God. [*She resumes her self-possession, withdrawing her hands from his with a power equal to his own.*] But you came and shewed me that I was in the power of Bodger and Undershaft. Today I feel—oh! how can I put it into words? Sarah: do you remember the earthquake at Cannes, when we were little children?—how little the surprise of the first shock mattered compared to the dread and horror of waiting for the second? That is how I feel in this place today. I stood on the rock I thought eternal; and without a word of warning it reeled and crumbled under me. I was safe with an infinite wisdom watching me, an army marching to Salvation with me; and in a moment, at a stroke of your pen in a cheque book, I stood alone; and the heavens were empty. That was the first shock of the earthquake: I am waiting for the second.

UNDERSHAFT. Come, come, my daughter! dont make too much of your little tinpot tragedy. What do we do here when we spend years of work and thought and thousands of pounds of solid cash on a new gun or an aerial battleship that turns out just a hairsbreadth wrong after all? Scrap it. Scrap it without wasting another hour or another pound on it. Well, you have made for yourself something that you call a morality or a religion or what not. It doesnt fit the facts. Well, scrap it. Scrap it and get one that does fit. That is what is wrong with the world at present. It scraps its obsolete steam engines and dynamos; but it wont scrap its old prejudices and its old moralities and its old religions and its old political constitutions. Whats the result? In machinery it does very well; but in morals and religion and politics it is working at a loss that brings it nearer bankruptcy every year. Dont persist in that folly. If your old religion broke down yesterday, get a newer and a better one for tomorrow.

BARBARA. Oh how gladly I would take a better one to my soul! But you offer me a worse one. [*Turning on him with sudden vehemence.*] Justify yourself: shew me some light through the darkness of this dreadful place, with its beautifully clean workshops, and respectable workmen, and model homes.

UNDERSHAFT. Cleanliness and respectability do not need justification, Barbara: they justify themselves. I see no darkness here, no dreadfulness. In your Salvation shelter I saw poverty, misery, cold and hunger. You gave them bread and treacle and dreams of heaven. I give from thirty shillings a week to twelve thousand a year. They find their own dreams; but I look after the drainage.

BARBARA. And their souls?

UNDERSHAFT. I save their souls just as I saved yours.

BARBARA [*revolted*]. You saved my soul! What do you mean?

UNDERSHAFT. I fed you and clothed you and housed you. I took care that you should have money enough to live handsomely—more than enough; so that you could be wasteful, careless, generous. That saved your soul from the seven deadly sins.

BARBARA [*bewildered*]. The seven deadly sins!

UNDERSHAFT. Yes, the deadly seven. [*Counting on his fingers.*] Food, clothing, firing, rent, taxes, respectability and children. Nothing can lift those seven millstones from Man's neck but money; and the spirit cannot soar until the millstones are lifted. I lifted them from your spirit. I enabled Barbara to become Major Barbara; and I saved her from the crime of poverty.

CUSINS. Do you call poverty a crime?

UNDERSHAFT. The worst of crimes. All the other crimes are virtues beside it: all the other dishonors are chivalry itself by comparison. Poverty blights whole cities; spreads horrible pestilences; strikes dead the very souls of all who come within sight, sound, or smell of it. What you call crime is nothing: a murder here and a theft there, a blow now and a curse then: what do they matter? they are only the accidents and illnesses of life: there are not fifty genuine professional criminals in London. But there are millions of poor people, abject people, dirty people, ill fed, ill clothed people. They poison us morally and physically: they kill the happiness of society: they force us to do away with our own liberties and to organize unnatural cruelties for fear they should rise against us and drag us down into their abyss. Only fools fear crime: we all fear poverty. Pah! [*turning on* BARBARA] you talk of your half-saved ruffian in West Ham: you accuse me of dragging his soul back to perdition. Well, bring him to me here; and I will drag his soul back again to salvation for you. Not by words and dreams; but by thirtyeight shillings a week, a sound house in a handsome street, and a permanent job. In three weeks he will have a fancy waistcoat; in three months a tall hat and a chapel sitting; before the end of the year he will shake hands with a duchess at a Primrose League meeting, and join the Conservative Party.

BARBARA. And will he be the better for that?

UNDERSHAFT. You know he will. Dont be a hypocrite, Barbara. He will be better fed, better housed, better clothed, better behaved; and his children will be pounds heavier and bigger. That will be better than an American cloth mattress in a shelter, chopping firewood, eating bread and treacle, and being forced to kneel down from time to time to thank heaven for it: knee drill, I think you call it. It is cheap work converting starving men with a Bible in one hand and a slice of bread in the other. I will undertake to convert West Ham to Mahometanism on the same terms. Try your hand on my men: their souls are hungry because their bodies are full.

BARBARA. And leave the east end to starve?

UNDERSHAFT [*his energetic tone dropping into one of bitter and brooding remembrance*]. I was an east ender. I moralized and starved until one day I swore that I would be a full-fed free man at all costs; that nothing should stop me except a bullet, neither reason nor morals nor the lives of other men. I said 'Thou shalt starve ere I starve'; and with that word I became free and great. I was a dangerous man until I had my will: now I am a useful, beneficent, kindly person. That is the history of most self-made millionaires, I fancy. When it is the history of every Englishman we shall have an England worth living in.

LADY BRITOMART. Stop making speeches, Andrew. This is not the place for them.

UNDERSHAFT [*punctured*]. My dear: I have no other means of conveying my ideas.

LADY BRITOMART. Your ideas are nonsense. You got on because you were selfish and unscrupulous.

UNDERSHAFT. Not at all. I had the strongest scruples about poverty and starvation. Your moralists are quite unscrupulous about both: they make virtues of them. I had rather be a thief than a pauper. I had rather be a murderer than a slave. I dont want to be either; but if you force the alternative on me, then, by Heaven, I'll chose the braver and more moral one. I hate poverty and slavery worse than any other crimes whatsoever. And let me tell you this. Poverty and slavery have stood up for centuries to your sermons and leading articles: they will not stand up to my machine guns. Dont preach at them: dont reason with them. Kill them.

BARBARA. Killing. Is that your remedy for everything?

UNDERSHAFT. It is the final test of conviction, the only lever strong enough to overturn a social system, the only way of saying Must. Let six hundred and seventy fools loose in the streets; and three policemen can scatter them. But huddle them together in a certain house in Westminster; and let them go through certain ceremonies and call themselves certain names until at last they get the courage to kill; and your six hundred and seventy fools become a government. Your pious mob fills up ballot papers and imagines it is governing its masters; but the ballot paper that really governs is the paper that has a bullet wrapped up in it.

CUSINS. That is perhaps why, like most intelligent people, I never vote.

UNDERSHAFT. Vote! Bah! When you vote, you only change the names of the cabinet. When you shoot, you pull down governments, inaugurate new epochs, abolish old orders and set up new. Is that historically true, Mr Learned Man, or is it not?

CUSINS. It is historically true. I loathe having to admit it. I repudiate your sentiments. I abhor your nature. I defy you in every possible way. Still, it is true. But it ought not to be true.

UNDERSHAFT. Ought! ought! ought! ought! ought! Are you going to spend your life saying ought, like the rest of our moralists? Turn your oughts into shalls, man. Come and make explosives with me. Whatever can blow men up can blow society up. The history of the world is the history of those who had courage enough to embrace this truth. Have you the courage to embrace it, Barbara?

LADY BRITOMART. Barbara: I positively forbid you to listen to your father's abominable wickedness. And you, Adolphus, ought to know better than to go about saying that wrong things are true. What does it matter whether they are true if they are wrong?

UNDERSHAFT. What does it matter whether they are wrong if they are true?

LADY BRITOMART [rising]. Children: come home instantly. Andrew: I am exceedingly sorry I allowed you to call on us. You are wickeder than ever. Come at once.

BARBARA [shaking her head]. It's no use running away from wicked people, mamma.

LADY BRITOMART. It is every use. It shews your disapprobation of them.

BARBARA. It does not save them.

LADY BRITOMART. I can see that you are going to disobey me. Sarah: are you coming home or are you not?

SARAH. I daresay it's very wicked of papa to make cannons; but I dont think I shall cut him on that account.

LOMAX [pouring oil on the troubled waters]. The fact is, you know, there is a certain amount of tosh about this notion of wickedness. It doesnt work. You must look at facts. Not that I would say a word in favor of anything wrong; but then, you see, all sorts of chaps are always doing all sorts of things; and we have to fit them in somehow, dont you know. What I mean is that you cant go cutting everybody; and thats about what it comes to. [Their rapt attention to his eloquence makes him nervous.] Perhaps I dont make myself clear.

LADY BRITOMART. You are lucidity itself, Charles. Because Andrew is successful and has plenty of money to give to Sarah, you will flatter him and encourage him in his wickedness.

LOMAX [unruffled]. Well, where the carcase is, there will the eagles be gathered, dont you know. [To UNDERSHAFT.] Eh? What?

UNDERSHAFT. Precisely. By the way, may I call you Charles?

LOMAX. Delighted. Cholly is the usual ticket.

UNDERSHAFT [to LADY BRITOMART]. Biddy—

LADY BRITOMART [violently]. Dont dare call me Biddy. Charles Lomax: you are a fool. Adolphus Cusins: you are a Jesuit. Stephen: you are a prig. Barbara: you are a lunatic. Andrew: you are a vulgar tradesman. Now you all know my opinion; and my conscience is clear, at all events [she sits down with a vehemence that the rug fortunately softens].

UNDERSHAFT. My dear: you are the incarnation of morality. [She snorts.] Your conscience is clear and your duty done when you have called everybody names. Come, Euripides! it is getting late; and we all want to go home. Make up your mind.

CUSINS. Understand this, you old demon—

LADY BRITOMART. Adolphus!

UNDERSHAFT. Let him alone, Biddy. Proceed, Euripides.

CUSINS. You have me in a horrible dilemma. I want Barbara.

UNDERSHAFT. Like all young men, you greatly exaggerate the difference between one young woman and another.

BARBARA. Quite true, Dolly.

CUSINS. I also want to avoid being a rascal.

UNDERSHAFT [with biting contempt]. You lust for personal righteousness, for self-approval, for what you call a good conscience, for what Barbara calls salvation, for what I call patronizing people who are not so lucky as yourself.

CUSINS. I do not: all the poet in me recoils from being a good man. But there are things in me that I must reckon with. Pity—

UNDERSHAFT. Pity! The scavenger of misery.

CUSINS. Well, love.

UNDERSHAFT. I know. You love the needy and the outcast: you love the oppressed races, the negro, the Indian ryot, the underdog everywhere. Do you love the Japanese? Do you love the French? Do you love the English?

CUSINS. No. Every true Englishman detests the English. We are the wickedest nation on earth; and our success is a moral horror.

UNDERSHAFT. That is what comes of your gospel of love, is it?

CUSINS. May I not love even my father-in-law?

UNDERSHAFT. Who wants your love, man? By what right do you take the liberty of offering it to me? I will have your due heed and respect, or I will kill you. But your love! Damn your impertinence!

CUSINS [grinning]. I may not be able to control my affections, Mac.

UNDERSHAFT. You are fencing, Euripides. You are weakening: your grip is slipping. Come! try your last weapon. Pity and love have broken in your hand: forgiveness is still left.

CUSINS. No: forgiveness is a beggar's refuge. I am with you there: we must pay our debts.

UNDERSHAFT. Well said. Come! you will suit me. Remember the words of Plato.

CUSINS [starting]. Plato! You dare quote Plato to me!

UNDERSHAFT. Plato says, my friend, that society cannot be saved until either the Professors of Greek take to making gunpowder, or else the makers of gunpowder become Professors of Greek.

CUSINS. Oh, tempter, cunning tempter!

UNDERSHAFT. Come! choose, man, choose.

CUSINS. But perhaps Barbara will not marry me if I make the wrong choice.

BARBARA. Perhaps not.

CUSINS [desperately perplexed]. You hear!

BARBARA. Father: do you love nobody?

UNDERSHAFT. I love my best friend.

LADY BRITOMART. And who is that, pray?

UNDERSHAFT. My bravest enemy. That is the man who keeps me up to the mark.

CUSINS. You know, the creature is really a sort of poet in his way. Suppose he is a great man, after all!

UNDERSHAFT. Suppose you stop talking and make up your mind, my young friend.

CUSINS. But you are driving me against my nature. I hate war.

UNDERSHAFT. Hatred is the coward's revenge for being intimidated. Dare you make war on war? Here are the means: my friend Mr Lomax is sitting on them.

LOMAX [springing up]. Oh I say! You dont mean that this thing is loaded, do you?

My ownest: come off it.

SARAH [sitting placidly on the shell]. If I am to be blown up, the more thoroughly it is done the better. Dont fuss, Cholly.

LOMAX [to UNDERSHAFT, strongly remonstrant]. Your own daughter, you know!

UNDERSHAFT. So I see. [To CUSINS.] Well, my friend, may we expect you here at six tomorrow morning?

CUSINS [firmly]. Not on any account. I will see the whole establishment blown up with its own dynamite before I will get up at five. My hours are healthy, rational hours: eleven to five.

UNDERSHAFT. Come when you please: before a week you will come at six and stay until I turn you out for the sake of your health. [Calling.] Bilton! [He turns to LADY BRITOMART, who rises]. My dear: let us leave these two young people to themselves for a moment. [BILTON comes from the shed.] I am going to take you through the gun cotton shed.

BILTON [barring the way]. You cant take anything explosive in here, sir.

LADY BRITOMART. What do you mean? Are you alluding to me?

BILTON [unmoved]. No, maam. Mr Undershaft has the other gentleman's matches in his pocket.

LADY BRITOMART [*abruptly*]. Oh! I beg your pardon. [*She goes into the shed.*]
UNDERSHAFT. Quite right, Bilton, quite right: here you are. [*He gives* BILTON *the box of matches.*] Come, Stephen. Come, Charles. Bring Sarah. [*He passes into the shed.*]

BILTON *opens the box and deliberately drops the matches into the fire-bucket.*

LOMAX. Oh! I say [BILTON *stolidly hands him the empty box*]. Infernal nonsense! Pure scientific ignorance! [*He goes in.*]
SARAH. Am I all right, Bilton?
BILTON. Youll have to put on list slippers, miss: thats all. Weve got em inside. [*She goes in.*]
STEPHEN [*very seriously to* CUSINS]. Dolly, old fellow, think. Think before you decide. Do you feel that you are a sufficiently practical man? It is a huge undertaking, an enormous responsibility. All this mass of business will be Greek to you.
CUSINS. Oh, I think it will be much less difficult than Greek.
STEPHEN. Well, I just want to say this before I leave you to yourselves. Dont let anything I have said about right and wrong prejudice you against this great chance in life. I have satisfied myself that the business is one of the highest character and a credit to our country. [*Emotionally.*] I am very proud of my father. I—[*Unable to proceed, he presses Cusins' hand and goes hastily into the shed, followed by* BILTON.]

BARBARA *and* CUSINS, *left alone together, look at one another silently.*

CUSINS. Barbara: I am going to accept this offer.
BARBARA. I thought you would.
CUSINS. You understand, dont you, that I had to decide without consulting you. If I had thrown the burden of the choice on you, you would sooner or later have despised me for it.
BARBARA. Yes: I did not want you to sell your soul for me any more than for this inheritance.
CUSINS. It is not the sale of my soul that troubles me: I have sold it too often to care about that. I have sold it for a professorship. I have sold it for an income. I have sold it to escape being imprisoned for refusing to pay taxes for hangmen's ropes and unjust wars and things that I abhor. What is all human conduct but the daily and hourly sale of our souls for trifles? What I am now selling it for is neither money nor position nor comfort, but for reality and for power.
BARBARA. You know that you will have no power, and that he has none.
CUSINS. I know. It is not for myself alone. I want to make power for the world.
BARBARA. I want to make power for the world too; but it must be spiritual power.
CUSINS. I think all power is spiritual: these cannons will not go off by themselves. I have tried to make spiritual power by teaching Greek. But the world can never be really touched by a dead language and a dead civilization. The people must have power; and the people cannot have Greek. Now the power that is made here can be wielded by all men.
BARBARA. Power to burn women's houses down and kill their sons and tear their husbands to pieces.
CUSINS. You cannot have power for good without having power for evil too. Even mother's milk nourishes murderers as well as heroes. This power which only tears men's bodies to pieces has never been so horribly abused as the intellectual power, the imaginative power, the poetic, religious power that can enslave men's souls. As a teacher of Greek I gave the intellectual man weapons against the common man. I now want to give the common man weapons against the intellectual man. I love the common people. I want to arm them against the lawyers, the doctors, the priests, the literary men, the professors, the artists, and the politicians, who, once in authority, are more disastrous and tyrannical than all the fools, rascals, and impostors. I want a power simple enough for common men to use, yet strong enough to force the intellectual oligarchy to use its genius for the general good.
BARBARA. Is there no higher power than that [*pointing to the shell*]?
CUSINS. Yes; but that power can destroy the higher powers just as a tiger can destroy a man: therefore Man must master that power first. I admitted this when the

Turks and Greeks were last at war. My best pupil went out to fight for Hellas. My parting gift to him was not a copy of Plato's Republic, but a revolver and a hundred Undershaft cartridges. The blood of every Turk he shot—if he shot any—is on my head as well as on Undershaft's. That act committed me to this place for ever. Your father's challenge has beaten me. Dare I make war on war? I must. I will. And now, is it all over between us?

BARBARA [touched by his evident dread of her answer]. Silly baby Dolly! How could it be!

CUSINS [overjoyed]. Then you—you—you— Oh for my drum! [He flourishes imaginary drumsticks.]

BARBARA [angered by his levity]. Take care, Dolly, take care. Oh, if only I could get away from you and from father and from it all! if I could have the wings of a dove and fly away to heaven!

CUSINS. And leave me!

BARBARA. Yes, you, and all the other naughty mischievous children of men. But I cant. I was happy in the Salvation Army for a moment. I escaped from the world into a paradise of enthusiasm and prayer and soul saving; but the moment our money ran short, it all came back to Bodger: it was he who saved our people: he, and the Prince of Darkness, my papa. Undershaft and Bodger: their hands stretch everywhere: when we feed a starving fellow creature, it is with their bread, because there is no other bread; when we tend the sick, it is in the hospitals they endow; if we turn from the churches they build, we must kneel on the stones of the streets they pave. As long as that lasts, there is no getting away from them. Turning our backs on Bodger and Undershaft is turning our backs on life.

CUSINS. I thought you were determined to turn your back on the wicked side of life.

BARBARA. There is no wicked side: life is all one. And I never wanted to shirk my share in whatever evil must be endured, whether it be sin or suffering. I wish I could cure you of middle-class ideas, Dolly.

CUSINS [gasping]. Middle cl—! A snub! A social snub to me! from the daughter of a foundling!

BARBARA. That is why I have no class, Dolly: I come straight out of the heart of the whole people. If I were middle-class I should turn my back on my father's business; and we should both live in an artistic drawing room, with you reading the reviews in one corner, and I in the other at the piano, playing Schumann: both very superior persons, and neither of us a bit of use. Sooner than that, I would sweep out the guncotton shed, or be one of Bodger's barmaids. Do you know what would have happened if you had refused papa's offer?

CUSINS. I wonder!

BARBARA. I should have given you up and married the man who accepted it. After all, my dear old mother has more sense than any of you. I felt like her when I saw this place—felt that I must have it— that never, never, never could I let it go; only she thought it was the houses and the kitchen ranges and the linen and china, when it was really all the human souls to be saved: not weak souls in starved bodies, sobbing with gratitude for a scrap of bread and treacle, but fullfed, quarrelsome, snobbish, uppish creatures, all standing on their little rights and dignities, and thinking that my father ought to be greatly obliged to them for making so much money for him—and so he ought. That is where salvation is really wanted. My father shall never throw it in my teeth again that my converts were bribed with bread. [She is transfigured.] I have got rid of the bribe of bread. I have got rid of the bribe of heaven. Let God's work be done for its own sake: the work he had to create us to do because it cannot be done except by living men and women. When I die, let him be in my debt, not I in his; and let me forgive him as becomes a woman of my rank.

CUSINS. Then the way of life lies through the factory of death?

BARBARA. Yes, through the raising of hell to heaven and of man to God, through the unveiling of an eternal light in the Valley of The Shadow. [Seizing him with both hands.] Oh, did you think my courage would never come back? did you believe that I was a deserter? that I, who have stood in the streets, and taken my people to my heart, and talked of the holiest and greatest things with them, could ever turn back and chatter foolishly to fashionable people about nothing in a drawing room? Never, never, never, never: Major Barbara will die with the colors. Oh! and I have my dear little Dolly boy still; and he has found me my place and my work. Glory Hallelujah! [*She kisses him.*]

CUSINS. My dearest: consider my delicate health. I cannot stand as much happiness as you can.

BARBARA. Yes: it is not easy work being in love with me, is it? But it's good for you. [*She runs to the shed, and calls, childlike.*] Mamma! Mamma! [BILTON *comes out of the shed, followed by* UNDERSHAFT.] I want Mamma.

UNDERSHAFT. She is taking off her list slippers, dear. [*He passes on to* CUSINS.] Well? What does she say?

CUSINS. She has gone right up into the skies.

LADY BRITOMART [*coming from the shed and stopping on the steps, obstructing* SARAH, *who follows with* LOMAX. BARBARA *clutches like a baby at her mother's skirt*]. Barbara: when will you learn to be independent and to act and think for yourself? I know as well as possible what that cry of 'Mamma, Mamma,' means. Always running to me!

SARAH [*touching Lady Britomart's ribs with her finger tips and imitating a bicycle horn*]. Pip! pip!

LADY BRITOMART [*highly indignant*]. How dare you say Pip! pip! to me, Sarah? You are both very naughty children. What do you want, Barbara?

BARBARA. I want a house in the village to live in with Dolly. [*Dragging at the skirt.*] Come and tell me which one to take.

UNDERSHAFT [*to* CUSINS]. Six o'clock tomorrow morning, Euripides.

FOR DISCUSSION:

1. How does Shaw's description of Lady Britomart prepare the reader for her appearance in the beginning of Act I?

2. Is the exposition skillfully or clumsily handled? For example, is it likely that Lady Britomart would tell her son of the financial condition of Charles or of the activities of Barbara, or is this information he could reasonably be expected to already know?

3. How well does Lady Britomart know herself? How well does she know her children? Her husband?

4. Shaw is well known for urbane, witty dialogue that frequently carries a social barb. Cite examples of this from the speeches of Lady Britomart and Andrew Undershaft.

5. What is the thematic purpose of the lengthy scene in Act II at the Salvation Army shelter dealing with Price, Rummy, Shirley, and Bill Walker? Are these characters individuals or types? How does Shaw make them so?

6. Acts II and III are obviously meant to contrast with each other. In what specific ways does Shaw pair one against the other?

7. Comment on the statement, "The ballot paper that really governs is the paper that has a bullet wrapped up in it."

8. What does Cusins mean when he says, "The way of life lies through the factory of death"?

9. Comment on the statement, "The more destructive war becomes, the more fascinating we find it."

10. Shaw originally intended to entitle this play Andrew Undershaft's Profession. Would this have been a better title? Why?

11. How convincing are the "conversions" of Stephen, Cusins, and Barbara in Act III? Are they contrived and ill motivated, or does Shaw take pains to make their repudiation of early attitudes credible?

12. Critics have called Major Barbara "a triumph of immoral purpose," "a withering attack on the Salvation Army," "an exultation of capitalism," and "an assertion that the destruction of some good things must accompany the destruction of the bad." Which of these views seems best to suit the play? Why?

13. It is frequently said of Shaw, although he disclaims it in the preface to Major Barbara, that he looks to the despotism of a single Napoleonic Superman for the ultimate salvation of society. Assess Major Barbara in the light of this evaluation of Shaw's social views.

14. In Major Barbara Shaw packs opinions on an amazing number of social topics. By citing the relevant passages in the play, discuss his attitude toward each of the following: inheritance by birthright, religious conversion, genteel poverty, Christian morality, philanthropic altruism, absolute moral principles, the relation of religion to Big Business, the relation of government to Big Business, requirements for social reform.

Major Barbara: Shaw's Challenge To Liberalism*

LOUIS CROMPTON

Major Barbara, together with *Man and Superman* and *John Bull's Other Island*, forms part of a trilogy of philosophical comedies, all of which deal with the bankruptcy of nineteenth-century liberalism in the face of the brute facts of sex, nationalism, and poverty. This propagandistic purpose has been from the start a bone of contention. It is not by chance that critics holding a formalist position, from Shaw's friend A. B. Walkley down to Francis Fergusson[1] in our own day have denounced the play as a kind of literary monster, while philosopher-critics[2] have regarded it as one of the few dramas with anything serious to say on the subject of politics. Indeed, *Major Barbara* raises the central issue of modern aesthetics as squarely as any piece of writing can. This question—putting it in the simplest possible terms—I take to be whether art is to be regarded as autonomous and *sui generis* or whether it is to be judged in relation to some ulterior standard of reality, that is, as a form of science or knowledge. But even if you accept this second view of the nature of art—which is certainly Shaw's view—you will still have to ask yourself whether your conception of this ulterior reality corresponds to Shaw's. Thus the play presents a double challenge—first to the dominant literary theory of our day, and second to our political and social ideals.

Only the inordinate length of *Man and Superman* kept Shaw from publishing his three philosophical comedies together in a set as he did the *Plays Pleasant and Unpleasant* and the *Three Plays for Puritans*. For his German edition, Shaw suggested that they be grouped and given the title *Comedies of Science and Religion*. Like the grouped plays of the other cycles, these plays share, besides their common theme, a common mood and a common dramatic structure.

It is this latter feature—their unique dramatic form—which has first of all confused, puzzled, and exasperated critics. What Shaw does is to mix together in each play a Molièresque comedy and a Socratic dialogue. This is a heady mixture which has delighted many and infuriated not a few who have simply found these plays morally and aesthetically indigestible. But let us see first how this splicing of forms works in practice. Each play begins by presenting us with a high-minded idealist, who takes himself with earnest seriousness and looks upon himself as an enlightened reformer. He is then made the subject of a comedy in the style of Molière, not with the idea of unmasking his hypocrisy, but with the intention of exposing the comic contradictions within his ideals and temperament. Then the problems raised by this character, which appear originally in a farcical-

---

* Reprinted from *Literature and Society* edited by Bernice Slote by permission of University of Nebraska Press. Copyright © 1964 by the University of Nebraska Press.

[1] See Walkley, *Drama and Life* (New York: Brentano's, 1907); Fergusson, *The Idea of a Theater* (Princeton: Princeton University Press, 1949).

[2] Charles Frankel, "Efficient Power and Inefficient Virtue," in *Great Moral Dilemmas in Literature*, ed. R. M. MacIver (New York: Harper, 1956).

satirical light, are treated more and more seriously until they are shown to be bound up with what Shaw calls "the destiny of nations," and the audience which had settled down for a night of fun finds it must either transform itself from an audience of pleasure-seekers into a "pit of philosophers" or founder hopelessly in the dream sequence of *Man and Superman* or the last acts of *John Bull's Other Island* and *Major Barbara*. An impossible procedure, you will complain. But not, Shaw would answer, to someone who believed that "Every joke is an earnest in the womb of time," and who was firmly convinced that the prophet who did not make his audience laugh would suffer, at worst, the fate of Socrates and Christ, and, at best, that of Voltaire and Tom Paine.

The idealistic liberals who are the butts of the satire are Roebuck Ramsden in *Man and Superman*, Tom Broadbent in *John Bull's Other Island*, and Lady Britomart Undershaft in *Major Barbara*, but since our subject is the latter play let us look at Lady Britomart as a representative of her species. The character of Lady Britomart, like most of those in *Major Barbara*, was drawn from a real person. It is a well-known fact that Shaw based Adolphus Cusins, his professor of Greek, on Gilbert Murray, but it is less well known that he based Lady Britomart on Murray's real-life mother-in-law, Lady Rosalind Frances, Countess of Carlisle. (Indeed, Shaw jokingly told Murray in a letter that he was at work on a play to be called "Murray's Mother-in-Law.") The Countess of Carlisle was, like Lady Britomart, a Whig peeress; her father was the Liberal whip in Parliament, and she was herself a crusading temperance reformer and for eighteen years the leader of the national Woman's Liberal Federation. Her husband the earl being more interested in art than in estate management, she ran the extensive family estates like a private fiefdom, attending in minute detail to the farmers' personal welfare—and to their moral characters. Castle Howard and her house in Kensington were salons for the Liberal intelligentsia. Murray himself has paid tribute to her crusading enthusiasm and to the heartening quality of her formidable benevolence.

The clue to Shaw's treatment of the comic contradictions in Lady Britomart's character may be found in a remark by James Froude, Carlyle's biographer, on the subject of Lady Rosalind. Froude, who disapproved of her politics but admired her character, said that though she professed to be a Liberal, she was by temperament better fitted to be an "empress." Hence if Shaw had chosen to make her the central figure of the play he might have imitated Molière's "Bourgeois Gentleman" to the extent of calling it "The Imperious Liberal." By family tradition and personal conviction Lady Britomart is an avowed believer in free speech and a democratic franchise, but every speech that she utters shows her native aristocratic spirit and natural masterfulness at odds with these ideals. She thinks she is consulting her son Stephen about the family inheritance when she is in fact revealing her own firm convictions. She can no more be said to be consciously bullying Stephen than an avalanche can be accused of intending to obliterate a tree in its path, but the effect is just the same. She declares that her children are her friends and equals and in reality treats them like kindergarten toddlers unable to take care of themselves. If she were not as amiable as she is wilful and domineering, she would be an atrocious tyrant; but as her children are as strong-minded as herself, and as she is prevented by her affectionateness from acting as peremptorily as she talks, we even end by feeling something like pity for her as a well-intentioned mother balked in the pursuit of her heart's desire, and too heroic in temperament to take refuge in self-pity, sulking, or quarrels. *Major Barbara* has been glibly likened to *The Importance of Being Earnest* for its wit and farce, and there is indeed a superficial resemblance between Lady Britomart and Lady Bracknell in Wilde's play, but nothing could be more unlike Wilde than the stroke by which Shaw has the frustrated Lady Britomart burst into tears at the end of act one when her children desert her for their father.

But where, if we take Shaw's formula seriously, is the "earnest" of the particular joke which underlies this brilliant piece of high comedy? We do not have to look far for it. It lies in the fact that Lady Britomart represents the hereditary British governing class in its most enlightened and liberal aspect, but also under its limitations. For, with all her admirable civic energy her vision is circumscribed by two ironclad principles—her conventional "morality" and her belief in the divine right of the aristocracy to rule the country. Behind her reformism is an intense moral fervor, but she does not see that moral tyranny is in itself the most oppressive of all tyrannies and that moral indignation is no substitute for critical thought and action. When Stephen shows embarrassment when he thinks she is about to reveal some youthful indiscretion of his father's, she chides him: "It is only in the middle classes, Stephen, that people get into a state of dumb helpless horror when they find out that there are wicked people in the world. In our class, we have to decide what is to be done with wicked people; and nothing should disturb our self-possession." But, as we shall see later, "helpless horror" and moral indignation are almost all that Lady Britomart can oppose to the brutal facts of the Undershaft munitions works and the political power of a capitalist class out to realize its profits at whatever cost.

Where Lady Britomart's moralism is not an aristocratic Mrs. Grundyism, a Queen Victoria-ism so to speak, it is merely a rationalization of her class prejudices and privileges, "right" and "propriety" being whatever furthers the Stephenage family interests and "wrong" or "impropriety" being whatever conflicts with them. For the central issue of the first act, and indeed of the play as a whole, is who will inherit the armament factory owned by Lady Britomart's husband, Andrew Undershaft.

The question of the Undershaft inheritance has caused a rift between the husband and wife: according to the tradition of the firm, the inheritance must go not to a son of the owner but to some promising adopted heir. This condition, utterly at odds with aristocratic belief in birth and blood, so offends Lady Britomart that it is useless for Andrew to argue that the Roman Empire was run successfully on this scheme and that it brought to the throne Marcus Aurelius. She is so used to thinking of the Stephenages as governors by natural right that when Andrew had refused to break the firm's law of succession in favor of his son Stephen the resulting quarrel led to a legal separation. Lady Britomart's way of putting this is to declare that nothing can bridge fundamental "moral" disagreement.

We have only to spend two minutes in Stephen's presence to realize the soundness of his father's decision, for Stephen is a conscientious, thoroughly well-intentioned prig and moral pedant, tediously prating about "right" being "right" and "wrong" being "wrong"; in short, he is ten times the slave of conventional morality his mother is, with her spiritedness all soured into sulky petulance of the most high-toned sort. His sister Sarah lacks his pretentiousness, but also his starchy character, and is, in fact, no more than a fashionable nonentity. Only in their third child, Barbara, has the Undershaft-Stephenage marriage justified itself as an evolutionary experiment in the crossing of types and classes, for Barbara has Lady Britomart's genius for leadership and mothering, with none of her class limitations. So little is she concerned with mere propriety and good form and so intensely does she identify herself with the religious spirit of the race that she has thrown aristocratic prejudice to the winds and demonstrated the family independence of mind by joining the least snobbish of the reforming religious sects of the day, the Salvation Army.

As the play opens we learn that Sarah and Barbara have both become engaged, Sarah to Charles Lomax, an amiable aristocratic noodle as empty-headed as herself, and Barbara to a man as complex and subtle in his moral and intellectual perceptions as Lomax is silly. Shaw shows us in Cusins a representative of the humane conscience in its most tender and perceptive form. In writing to Gilbert Murray, his model for the part, Shaw pointed out that he had taken pains to make his professor "the reverse in every point of the theatrical strong man":

I want him to go on his quality wholly, and not to make the smallest show of physical robustness or brute determination. His selection by Undershaft should be a standing puzzle to the people who believe in the strong-silent still-waters-run-deep hero of melodrama. The very name Adolphus Cusins is selected to that end.[3]

In choosing Murray as his model, Shaw had in mind a type of Liberal in strong contrast to the active, bustling Lady Britomart. Cusins is the academic, cloistered, sympathetic, skeptical, ironic, supercivilized Liberal who shrinks instinctively from what E. M. Forster has called the world of "telegrams and anger."

Murray's liberalism sprang from several sources—from the radicalism of Castle Howard, from his Irish rebel background, and from a strain of Shelleyan humanitarianism that made him, like Shaw, a vegetarian and a hater of all forms of cruelty. The other side of the picture was his Hellenism. For Murray, Greek literature was a living force having direct bearing on modern politics, morals, and culture. Here is how he writes of Euripides, the Greek playwright to whom he felt especially drawn:

His contemporary public denounced him as dull, because he tortured them with personal problems; as malignant, because he made them see truths they wished not to see; as blasphemous and foul-minded, because he made demands on their spiritual and religious natures which they could neither satisfy nor overlook.[4]

In short, Murray regarded Euripides as standing in relation to the golden age of Athens as the "New Drama" of Shaw and Ibsen stood in relation to the age of Victoria and Edward VII. Shaw returned the compliment by hailing the production of Murray's translations of Euripides at the Court theatre as modern masterpieces that had earned their place on the contemporary stage through their own right.

During the Boer campaign of 1899–1901, Murray belonged, with his cousin by marriage Bertrand Russell, to the small but vocal Liberal minority who opposed the war. No doubt his anti-war sentiments endowed Euripides' *Andromache* and *The Trojan Women* with particular significance for him; at any rate these were two of his earliest choices for translation into English verse. In *Major Barbara* Shaw makes Undershaft give Cusins the nickname "Euripides," thus implying that he looks on human affairs with the same mixture of ironic pessimism and pity as did his Greek predecessor. When Cusins is brought face-to-face with the facts of armament-making, he tells Undershaft, "There is an abyss of moral horror between me and your accursed aerial battleships."

It is this group Lady Britomart has invited her estranged husband to meet in the drawing-room of her West End mansion. Her intention is the eminently practical one of extracting dowries from Andrew for the two brides-to-be, her estimate of the earning power of a feckless man-about-town and a classics professor being realistically small. But Lady Britomart's attempt to bring up once more the matter of the inheritance meets flinty resistance from Undershaft. Indeed, the family reunion appears headed for a fiasco, and only the unexpected interest Undershaft shows in Barbara's novel religious aspirations saves the meeting from shipwreck. It is an immense puzzle to both the naive and the

[3] October 7, 1905; printed in Murray, *An Unfinished Autobiography* (New York: Oxford, 1960), pp. 155–156. This whole letter is of great interest for the play.

[4] *A History of Ancient Greek Literature* (New York: D. Appleton, 1897), p. 250. See also Murray's *Euripides and His Age* (New York: Henry Holt, 1913).

sophisticated members of the family group that Undershaft should show such a concern with her new faith, particularly since he is resolutely unashamed of his destructive trade and even seems to glory in it, declaring, "Your Christianity, which enjoins you to resist not evil, and to turn the other cheek, would make me a bankrupt. My morality—my religion—must have a place for cannons and torpedoes in it." Barbara challenges him to maintain this faith after visiting her East End Salvation Army shelter. Her father accepts the invitation, and issues a counter-challenge: she shall, in return, pay a visit to his arms factory and face the temptation offered by a religion of "money and gun-powder." He warns her that she may end by giving up the Salvation Army for the sake of the cannons; strong in her conviction of the impossibility of any such enormity, she accepts his condition.

The scene at the Salvation Army shelter is a remarkable piece of low-life melodrama, equalled in English only by the works of O'Casey. The refugees at the barracks include a cynically smart young man and an old crone, both posing as redeemed sinners, and an unemployed older man who is brought in in a state of semistarvation. This man, Peter Shirley by name, has been turned out of his job as overage; he finds the necessity of accepting charity all the more bitter because he holds the faith of a secularist, in contrast to the others who believe in nothing but their right to bilk and exploit capitalist society as it has bilked and exploited them. Finally Bill Walker enters, a half-drunk, blustering bully in a very mean mood, who bawls angrily for his girl, and curses the Army for taking her from him.

It will be seen that this is not a particularly cheerful, amusing, or attractive group of slum dwellers. Unlike other writers who are sympathetic to the poor, Shaw does not sentimentalize or idealize them, his argument being that if poverty actually did improve people it would be the strongest argument for making poverty compulsory. Shaw insists rather that poverty is unequivocally demoralizing: its fruits are not simple piety, honest rectitude, and altruistic sentiment; they are more likely to be, at best, hypocrisy, cynicism, and shattered self-respect; and, at worst, conscienceless brutality.

Looking into this abyss, Lady Britomart would first of all be shocked at the total lack of respect of the poor for their governors—sincerely shocked, since she would be conscious of having their spiritual and physical welfare at heart. Barbara and Cusins as humanitarians are most appalled by the bitterness and violence of these lives. Moreover, Christianity itself must assume part of the blame for this moral debasement. For besides teaching humility and acquiescence, it also, through its Pauline theology, first preaches a retaliatory morality and then allows the blackguard to escape the consequences of his actions through a belief in a divine atonement.

Shaw's second act makes this last point through a moral parable in the vein of Tolstoy. Bill Walker, the bully, first strikes the old woman and then a young Salvation Army girl. When the old woman curses him he simply jeers at her, knowing that hard words break no bones and that she is, spiritually speaking, on the same level as himself in her vindictive desire for revenge. The young girl, by contrast, instead of reproaching him prays for him. This unexpected behavior has the effect of giving his anger time to cool, and then, as he reflects more soberly on his deed, causing a noticeable twinge of conscience. This sensitivity Barbara exploits skilfully, not scolding him, but keeping the naked fact of his deed inexorably before him. Finally he feels he must somehow make amends, and the way he tries to do this is highly significant. First, he tries to "atone" by getting himself pummeled by a Salvation Army officer who is a converted boxer: this is the Pauline–Christian method. When this fails, he then "fines" himself as he has seen other blackguards fined in lawcourts: this is, of course, only Pauline Christianity as we have institutionalized it with our legal system of penalties and prisons. But Barbara, whose Christianity is not that of Paul but of Christ—that is, a Christianity which scorns vengeance, retaliation, and punishment—is still inexorable; she will not play the role of Tetzel on any account. Bill Walker cannot "buy" salvation from the Salvation Army. The only way he can redeem himself is through a growth of conscience that will make it impossible for him to repeat his deed. Under no circumstances must he be encouraged to sin so that grace may abound.

Barbara's fight for Bill's soul comes very near to success and only fails through a stroke of diablerie on the part of her father. The latter frustrates her simply by demonstrating that although the Salvation Army can afford to refuse to sell the blackguard his salvation for twenty shillings, it cannot, no matter how scrupulous it affects to be, refuse to sell the millionaire his for, say, five thousand pounds. Barbara had refused to accept her father's tuppence in the collection plate because the money was earned through the creation of destructive forces far more brutal in their effect than anything the slum ruffian might aspire to. But when Mrs. Baines, the Army commissioner, comes to plead for money to carry on the Army's work in a hard winter, she is forced to accept Undershaft's proffer of the aforementioned thousands despite his sardonic emphasis on the terrifying nature of his enterprises. The ruffian, when he sees the rich man's gift accepted where his own conscience money was rejected, turns on Barbara with cynical scorn, and Barbara, facing at once the failure of her attempt at salvation and a realization that the Salvation Army, if it is to exist at all, can only exist as the pensioner of the distillery and cannon industries, utters her bitter and heart-rending cry of despair, "My God: why hast thou forsaken me?"

The melodrama of the scene at the Salvation Army barracks thus reaches its climax in this loss of faith. But it is at this point that the play takes the most surprising of its many surprising turns. For at the moment that Barbara's God, the God of Evangelical Christianity, appears to have failed her, the professor of Greek hails as a new deity the very man Barbara now fears as anti-Christ, her diabolical-seeming father. Cusins, in a transport of ecstasy, declares himself to be possessed by the spirit of Undershaft, whom he addresses as the new "Dionysos." Barbara, in the pain and confusion of her loss, can of course see nothing in this behavior but a piece of perverse irony.

Since the reader or spectator of the play may be left in the same puzzlement as Shaw's West End heiress, it may be well at this point to ask what Shaw means by his idea of a "new" Dionysos. What has the ancient Greek god to do with modern society? The answer is to be found in the meaning Dionysiac religion had in the Greek world. Historians and philosophers, of whom Nietzsche is the most famous, have repeatedly emphasized the strange disparity between the serene rationalism of Greek society as we usually conceive it and the wild barbarity of the Bacchic cult which entered Greece from Thrace and Macedonia in the tenth century before Christ. Nietzsche traces the birth of dramatic tragedy itself to this irruption of frenzied rites and ecstatic orgies into the calm order and moral rationalism of Greek life, which the new religion challenged with its worship of supernormal psychic energy and its identification of the worshipper both with the new God and with the life processes of the animal and vegetative world.

Cusins had earlier praised the services of the Salvation Army as the "true worship of Dionysos," finding in the Army's ecstasy and enthusiasm (literally, a standing outside oneself and possession by the divine will) an analogue of the uncouth religion that shocked the cultivated Greeks as the Army shocked the conventional Anglicanism of the West End. In its stirring religious music he had seen the primitive dithyramb reborn, its trombones, timbrels, and drums being the antithesis of both the tepid hymns sung in fashionable churches and the salon music of the fashionable drawing room. Even its symbols, Blood and Fire, Cusins points out, are Dionysiac symbols. Its joy and happiness are those of the God-possessed, as Barbara's later grief is that of the God-forsaken.

Thus Dionysianism is what Bergson calls a "dynamic religion,"[5] with its basis not in conventional morality or institutionalism but in a mystical union with the divine will. It breaks down social barriers, taking the intellectual into University Settlements in the slums, and pitting him actively against evil. It carries its devotees beyond the bounds of logic and reason. Aroused and lacking rational direction, it finds its expression in the frenzy of the revolutionary mob.

Cusins is a sophisticated intellectual who has joined the Army, as Lady Britomart puts it, to worship Barbara. (No bad object of worship, Shaw would insist.) As a student of comparative religion and a disciple of Sir James Frazer, his view of the Army is, to say the least, not that of a fundamentalist. But Barbara's obvious religious genius attracts him strongly, and her evangelicalism, on its practical side, is not at all incompatible with his own religion of love, pity, and forgiveness. Indeed, for all his sardonic irony, he faces a crisis of his own beliefs at the same moment Barbara faces hers. As we have already seen, Cusins, in his skepticism and humanitarianism is akin to the young Euripides who casts doubts on the traditional Greek attitudes to such questions as patriotism, religion, women, and slaves.

But the Greek playwright's later development has a strange and unforeseen twist to it. For Euripides, who first turned the Greek drama away from its roots in Dionysiac religion toward a critical and skeptical direction, does return to Dionysos at the end of his career. In what is generally regarded as the last work of his old age, *The Bacchae*, the humanistic and humanitarian playwright does come face to face with the religion in which the drama had its origin.

It is probably no exaggeration to say that *The Bacchae* is, by a good margin, the most terrifying, unedifying, and enigmatic of all Greek tragedies. You will recall that in this play Dionysos visits in disguise the city of Thebes where his rites have been forbidden by the moralistic King Pentheus and works a horrifying revenge. The problem Euripides' drama poses, put in the briefest terms, is this: what attitude are we to adopt to this new force in society, at once so terrible and so fascinating? Does Dionysos' ghastly triumph over Pentheus signify the rebirth of vital religion or does he symbolize some dark, demonic power from which we are to recoil in dread?

Now, like the Greeks of Euripides' day, Cusins has also been brought face to face with a brutal, primitive force of life and death which the cultivated, sensitive side of him recoils from, but which the clear-headed student of society is forced to take into account. This power is the destructive-creative energy of Cusins' prospective father-in-law, the arms maker. And Shaw, to emphasize the fact that he has had the parallel with Euripides' drama in mind all along, has Cusins quote some twenty or thirty lines from the play in the Salvation Army scene, in what Cusins identifies as his "own" (that is, Murray's) new translation.[6]

It is no exaggeration to say that Shaw's Undershaft has created the same bafflement in critics as Euripides' Dionysos, whether the critic be as naive as the *Time* reviewer who accused Shaw of making a "complete about-face" and firing on his own socialist ranks,[7] or as sophisticated as Mr. Francis Fergusson, who for all his learning and intelligence, denounces *Major Barbara* as a tissue of "unresolved paradoxes."

What then are we to make of this man who has so puzzled Shaw's commentators? It may perhaps be best to turn first to the living models from whom Shaw may have obtained hints for his millionaire munitions maker. One was a neighbor at Ayot Saint Lawrence,

---

[5] Henri Bergson, *The Two Sources of Morality and Religion* (New York: Henry Holt, 1935).

[6] The lines are quoted from page 126 of Murray's *The Bacchae of Euripides* (London: G. Allen and Sons, 1904).

[7] Nov. 12, 1956, p. 72.

Charles McEvoy, a quiet and gentle man, who had manufactured torpedoes for the North during the American Civil War. But I should like to suggest that Shaw, in drawing the sardonic side of Undershaft's character, seems to have had in mind the Swedish arms maker Alfred Nobel, the inventor of nitroglycerine. During the closing decades of the nineteenth century, Nobel's success in creating more and more powerful explosives had sent a wave of panic around the world. A leading figure in European business and international finance, Nobel was also a man of an intellectual and literary cast. Like Undershaft, he belonged to a munitions dynasty, his father having been an armaments maker before him. In thought and sentiment, Nobel was a Shelleyan radical and humanitarian, but this did not limit his hardheadedness in business, and he sold his patents indiscriminately to autocratic and liberal states alike. (In a manuscript draft of *Major Barbara* Shaw makes Undershaft boast that he has sold a new rifle to the Swedish, Italian, and German governments without any compunctions on the score of politics.[8]) Nobel's motto, "My home is where my work is, and my work is everywhere," might well have been Undershaft's. And, of course, one of the last deeds of this complex and enigmatic man was his endowment of the Nobel Peace Prize, which challenged the humanitarian liberals among his personal friends to solve the problem his discoveries had created. The Peace Prize was first awarded in 1901, four years before Shaw began his play.

This will perhaps explain in part one of the paradoxes of *Major Barbara*—that it is a dealer in lethal weapons who plays the role of Socrates in this socialist drama. But what of Undershaft's peculiar commercial ruthlessness, that specifically cold-blooded side of his personality that has so shocked and baffled critics and audiences? To unravel this puzzle we must begin by considering his background. Undershaft is an East End slum boy, reared in that wilderness of desolation that was East London in the middle of the nineteenth century. He has, like all the members of his dynasty, taken the name of the firm's founder, an abandoned orphan reared in the parish of St. Andrew Undershaft in the City.[9] His early career had resembled in its single-mindedness the career of the American industrial barons of the post-Civil War period. Determined to escape from the indignities of poverty, he had taken for his own the stern old Scots slogan: "Thou shalt starve ere I starve."

Here the second paradox appears, for as a Socialist we expect Shaw especially to condemn this spirit. But he condones it and even insists that for a poor person it is indeed the only possible "manly" attitude. (Undershaft's Christian name, "Andrew," means "manly.") For Shaw, the great cardinal virtues are courage and self-respect, and he believed that if the poor in a democracy let themselves be exploited, starved, and snubbed, it is only because of their own inveterate abjectness. Hence the cutting remarks which Undershaft, the ex-slum boy, addresses to Peter Shirley, the down-trodden, long-suffering worker, in the Salvation Army shelter:

SHIRLEY [*angrily*]. Who made your millions for you? Me and my like. Whats kep us poor? keepin you rich. I wouldn't have your conscience, not for all your income.
UNDERSHAFT. I wouldn't have your income, not for all your conscience, Mr Shirley.

Undershaft is driving home the point that the play makes over and over again, that a conviction of moral superiority is in itself the hollowest of consolations, the last resource of the weak and cowardly, and the treacherous quagmire in which true worth and manhood are lost.

[8] British Museum, MS 50616B, folio 53. The passage is cancelled. This draft of act one is dated "Sandgate 4/4/05."

[9] The odd epithet "Undershaft" was applied to the church because of the custom of setting up a maypole outside its doors.

Honor, justice, and truth are indeed part of Undershaft's religion, but he is firm in pointing out that these can be had only as the "graces and luxuries of a rich, strong, and safe life." Any liberal like Cusins who preaches these virtues to the poor without taking into account economic realities is a fool. Undershaft can even declare that his determinedly ruthless conduct satisfies the Kantian test, since the world would be an immeasurably better place if all the poor behaved exactly as he has. But first we must rid ourselves of the liberal belief that moral virtue by itself is ever capable of becoming a significant force in the world. Shaw made this point abundantly clear in a speech of Undershaft's in the unpublished Derry manuscript of the play:

Come, come, my young friends: let us live in the real world. Your moral world is a vacuum; nothing is done there, though a good deal is eaten and drunk by the moralists at the expense of the real world. It is nice to live in the vacuum and repeat the fine phrases and edifying sentiments a few literary people have manufactured for you: but you know as well as I do that your morality is tolerated only on the assumption that nothing is to come of it. Your Christmas carols about peace and goodwill to men are very pretty; but you order cannons from me just the same. You ring out the old, ring in the new: that is, you discard muzzle-loaders and introduce breachloaders. Barbara converts laborers whose conversion dont matter, because they have no responsibility and no power; but she does not convert the Secretary of State for war. Euripides abhors war, he says; but he will not stop it by Greek verses. It can be stopped only by a mighty power which is not in his class room.[10]

Undershaft soon makes it clear that this power is the power of bombs.

Liberal intellectuals frequently distrust power and decry the use of force. In so doing, they blind themselves to the fact that the authority of governments in liberal democracies rests on the police and army as surely as in any authoritarian state. Shaw, speaking through Undershaft, defines a government as a body of men with the courage to kill. Stephen, the conventionally-minded parliamentarian, must himself be as ready to kill his political opponents as Caesar, Cromwell, Washington, Lincoln, and Stalin were to kill theirs. Being a totally conventional young man with his head stuffed full of moral clichés and a conviction of the divinely righteous nature of upper-class British interests, he will kill stupidly and senselessly. How little his high-mindedness represents anything in the way of real scruples we see when the Undershaft party arrives at the factory. Stephen, who has earlier expressed priggish horror at his father's business, is now all admiration for this triumph of industry.

But for the intellectual humanitarian and the former Salvationist the reconciliation to the factory of death is not so easy. The last scene of the play is at once an intellectual argument and a religious wooing of the souls of Cusins and Barbara by Mephistopheles–Dionysos–Undershaft. Cusins may admit that force is the basis of present-day society and that a capitalist state exists for the sake of protecting the rich man's dividends, just as the Salvation Army inadvertently plays into the hands of the rich by diverting the attention of the poor from revolution. But perhaps the answer is not to use force against force but to abandon force completely and to appeal for social justice on the grounds of Christianity, love, and mercy? No: Undershaft inexorably insists, government and rule means killing: all political progress (not to mention political conservatism) rests ultimately on the willingness to kill.

Since this is the idea which readers and audiences of *Major Barbara* have found most puzzling and unintelligible, coming as it does in a work of a writer who can by no means be accused of lacking moral sensitivity and bowels of compassion, and who otherwise

---

[10] British Museum, MS 5061D, folios 35–36. This first "Irish" version is dated "Derry 8/9/1905."

hardly seems to be of the school of Hobbes and Machiavelli, let us see if we can determine exactly what Undershaft means before we raise the cry of "unresolved paradox." I think that Shaw's intention is clear enough if we give full weight to what Undershaft says in the final scene, but since these relatively straightforward statements have been for most people as music to the deaf and sunsets to the blind, we may profitably take another look at the unpublished manuscript version of the play in the possession of the British Museum. Here Undershaft does not, I think, depart from any of the positions he maintains in the final version of the play, but he is perhaps more explicit:

UNDERSHAFT [grimly]. Why do [the poor] starve? Because they have been taught that it is their duty to starve. "Blessed are the poor in spirit"—eh? But now mark my highest claim, my proudest boast. To those who are worth their salt as slaves I give the means of life. But to those who will not or cannot sell their manhood—to those who will not stand tamely and suffer their country to be ravaged by poverty and preyed upon by skulkers and idlers—I give the means of death. Poverty and slavery have stood up for centuries to sermons and Bibles and leading articles and pious platitudes: they will not stand up to my machine guns. Let every English citizen resolve to kill or be killed sooner than tolerate the existence of one poor person or one idler on English soil; and poverty and slavery will vanish tomorrow.
BARBARA. Killing! Is that your remedy?
UNDERSHAFT. It is the final test of conviction, the sole lever strong enough to lift a whole people. It is the right of every man who will stake his own life on his faith. It is the only way of saying Must.[11]

At this point it is perhaps natural to ask whether Shaw, in giving Undershaft these speeches, was expressing his own political philosophy or merely presenting an idea, so to speak, dramatically. Any doubts on this subject may be resolved by consideration of another British Museum manuscript, that which contains Shaw's notes for a lecture on Darwin delivered to the Fabian Society in 1906, the year after the production of *Major Barbara*:

Revolutions, remember, can only be made by men and women with courage enough to meet the ferocity and pugnacity of the common soldier and vanquish it. Do not let us delude ourselves with any dreams of a peaceful evolution of Capitalism into Socialism, of automatic Liberal Progress, of the conciliation of our American bosses, and South African Randlords and British county society and Pall Mall military caste by the Fabian Society. The man who is not a Socialist is quite prepared to fight for his private property, or at least to pay someone else to fight for him. He has no doubt whatever of the necessity and morality of such warfare. . . .
We must clear our minds from cant and cowardice on this subject. It is true that the old barricade revolutionists were childishly and romantically wrong in their methods; and the Fabians were right in making an end of them and formulating constitutional Socialism. But nothing is so constitutional as fighting. Rents cannot be collected now without force, nor are they socialized—to the small extent to which they are already socialized—without force.[12]

Shaw is here appealing to history to verify Undershaft's statement that "the ballot paper that really governs is the paper that has a bullet wrapped up in it." The bloody suppression of the Commune of 1871 had demonstrated the willingness of the proprietorial class to fight for their property rights. Later in this same Fabian lecture Shaw argues that the classic instance of non-violent change, the passage of the Reform Bill of 1832, is really an instance in favor of his view; for the Reform Bill passed only when the temper of the English nation reached the point where it was clearly a choice between passing the bill and facing a revolution.

[11] British Museum, MS 50616D, folio 18.   [12] British Museum, MS 50661, folios 81–82.

I have called the last act a religious wooing of souls. Undershaft, seeing in Cusins the brains and sensitivity he thinks necessary in anyone who is to run a factory of death (or let us say, a democratic, or any other kind of state) offers him the management of the munitions work. The intelligentsia is to undertake the responsibilities of political power, that is, the power of life and death over millions. Cusins finds himself in the position of a famous predecessor of academic fame; Mephistopheles has once again put in a bid for a professor's soul, and though Cusins, wiser than Faust, realizes that he has already sold his soul for his professorship, this does not make his dilemma less cruel.

For Barbara's engagement to Cusins is both a love match and something more again. That is to say, their marriage is to be a religious marriage in a sense of devoting them to something beyond themselves, to "larger loves and diviner dreams than the fireside ones." Their understanding is that unless their marriage can foster this religious side of themselves they are to part and seek other mates, or join the legion of the world's celibate saints and philosophers. If Cusins elects to sell his soul to Undershaft he thus jeopardizes his relation with Barbara, who is first of all a "salvationist" (in an unsectarian sense) and only secondly a fiancée.

At this point Shaw turns to an episode from real life to solve the dilemma. When an idealistic student[13] of Murray's set out for the Greco-Turkish War in 1897, Murray had given the young man, not a copy of Plato's *Republic*, but a revolver. Shaw ascribes this incident to Cusins, and makes Undershaft seize upon it to demonstrate to the professor that he is, for all his hatred of war, committed to the side of the industrialist. Cusins is forced to concur, and declares that he will choose the "reality and power" of the factory of death, even if it means losing Barbara.

But Barbara, for all her talk about turning her back on wickedness, can no more turn away from life than can Cusins. Now she will be able to preach to the well-fed, self-respecting men and women in Undershaft's model factory-town and know that, when they abandon their snobbishness and selfishness for higher ends, they are not simply being tempted by the bribe of bread. She has regained her faith and courage: the enthusiasm of the new Dionysianism possesses her and she goes "right up into the skies," saved forever from the fate she has most dreaded, the boredom and triviality of the genteel drawing room.

FOR DISCUSSION:

1. How does Crompton's essay make use of the social approach to literature as described by Daiches in "Criticism and Sociology"?

2. Explain what Crompton means when he says that the play "presents a double challenge."

3. What is the purpose of giving Cusins the nickname "Euripides" in the play?

4. How is Act III "a religious wooing of souls"?

5. How is Andrew Undershaft a spokesman for Shaw's own social ideas?

6. This essay points out several influences of real life on Shaw's play in terms of models for characters, historical events, etc. Enumerate these influences.

---

[18] The young man was H. N. Brailsford: see *An Unfinished Autobiography*, p. 97.

Act of Faith

IRWIN SHAW

"Present it to him in a pitiful light," Olson was saying as they picked their way through the almost frozen mud toward the orderly-room tent. "Three combat-scarred veterans, who fought their way from Omaha Beach to . . . What was the name of the town we fought our way to?"

"Königstein," Seeger said.

"Königstein." Olson lifted his right foot heavily out of a puddle and stared admiringly at the three pounds of mud clinging to his overshoe. "The backbone of the Army. The noncommissioned officer. We deserve better of our country. Mention our decorations, in passing."

"What decorations should I mention?" Seeger asked. "The Marksman's Medal?"

"Never quite made it," Olson said. "I had a cross-eyed scorer at the butts. Mention the Bronze Star, the Silver Star, the Croix de Guerre with palms, the Unit Citation, the Congressional Medal of Honor."

"I'll mention them all." Seeger grinned. "You don't think the C.O.'ll notice that we haven't won most of them, do you?"

"Gad, sir," Olson said with dignity, "do you think that one Southern military gentleman will dare doubt the word of another Southern military gentleman in the hour of victory?"

"I come from Ohio," Seeger said.

"Welch comes from Kansas," Olson said, coolly staring down a second lieutenant who was passing. The lieutenant made a nervous little jerk with his hand, as though he expected a salute, then kept it rigid, as a slight, superior smile of scorn twisted at the corner of Olson's mouth. The lieutenant dropped his eyes and splashed on through the mud. "You've heard of Kansas," Olson said. "Magnolia-scented Kansas."

"Of course," said Seeger. "I'm no fool."

"Do your duty by your men, Sergeant." Olson stopped to wipe the cold rain off his face and lectured him. "Highest-ranking noncom present took the initiative and saved his comrades, at great personal risk, above and beyond the call of you-know-what, in the best traditions of the American Army."

"I will throw myself in the breach," Seeger said.

"Welch and I can't ask more," said Olson.

They walked heavily through the mud on the streets between the rows of tents. The camp stretched drearily over the Reims plain, with the rain beating on the sagging tents. The division had been there over three weeks, waiting to be shipped home, and all the meagre diversions of the neighborhood had been sampled and exhausted, and there was an air of watchful suspicion and impatience with the military life hanging over the camp now, and there was even reputed to be a staff sergeant in C Company who was laying odds they would not get back to America before July 4th.

"I'm redeployable," Olson sang. "It's so enjoyable." It was a jingle he had composed, to no recognizable melody, in the early days after the victory in Europe, when he had added up his points and found they came to only sixty-three, but he persisted in singing it. He was a short, round boy who had been flunked out of air cadets' school and transferred to the infantry but whose spirits had not been damaged in the process. He had a high, childish voice and a pretty, baby face. He was very good-natured, and had a girl waiting for him at the University of California, where he intended to finish his course at government expense when he got out of the Army, and he was just the

---

* Copyright © 1946 by Irwin Shaw and reprinted by his permission. Originally published in the New Yorker, February 2, 1946.

type who is killed off early and predictably and sadly in moving pictures about the war, but he had gone through four campaigns and six major battles without a scratch.

Seeger was a large, lanky boy, with a big nose, who had been wounded at St.-Lô but had come back to his outfit in the Siegfried Line quite unchanged. He was cheerful and dependable and he knew his business. He had broken in five or six second lieutenants, who had later been killed or wounded, and the C.O. had tried to get him commissioned in the field, but the war had ended while the paperwork was being fumbled over at headquarters.

They reached the door of the orderly tent and stopped. "Be brave, Sergeant," Olson said. "Welch and I are depending on you."

"O.K.," Seeger said, and went in.

The tent had the dank, Army-canvas smell that had been so much a part of Seeger's life in the past three years. The company clerk was reading an October, 1945, issue of the Buffalo *Courier-Express*, which had just reached him, and Captain Taney, the company C.O., was seated at a sawbuck table which he used as a desk, writing a letter to his wife, his lips pursed with effort. He was a small, fussy man, with sandy hair that was falling out. While the fighting had been going on, he had been lean and tense and his small voice had been cold and full of authority. But now he had relaxed, and a little pot belly was creeping up under his belt and he kept the top button of his trousers open when he could do it without too public loss of dignity. During the war, Seeger had thought of him as a natural soldier—tireless, fanatic about detail, aggressive, severely anxious to kill Germans. But in the last few months, Seeger had seen him relapsing gradually and pleasantly into the small-town hardware merchant he had been before the war, sedentary and a little shy, and, as he had once told Seeger, worried, here in the bleak champagne fields of France, about his daughter, who had just turned twelve and had a tendency to go after the boys and had been caught by her mother kissing a fifteen-year-old neighbor in the hammock after school.

"Hello, Seeger," he said, returning the salute with a mild, offhand gesture. "What's on your mind?"

"Am I disturbing you, sir?"

"Oh, no. Just writing a letter to my wife. You married, Seeger?" He peered at the tall boy standing before him.

"No, sir."

"It's very difficult," Taney sighed, pushing dissatisfiedly at the letter before him. "My wife complains I don't tell her I love her often enough. Been married fifteen years. You'd think she'd know by now." He smiled at Seeger. "I thought you were going to Paris," he said. "I signed the passes yesterday."

"That's what I came to see you about, sir."

"I suppose something's wrong with the passes." Taney spoke resignedly, like a man who has never quite got the hang of Army regulations and has had requisitions, furloughs, and requests for courts-martial returned for correction in a baffling flood.

"No, sir," Seeger said. "The passes're fine. They start tomorrow. Well, it's just—" He looked around at the company clerk, who was on the sports page.

"This confidential?" Taney asked.

"If you don't mind, sir."

"Johnny," Taney said to the clerk, "go stand in the rain someplace."

"Yes, sir," the clerk said, and slowly got up and walked out.

Taney looked shrewdly at Seeger and spoke in a secret whisper. "You pick up anything?" he asked.

Seeger grinned. "No, sir, haven't had my hands on a girl since Strasbourg."

"Ah, that's good." Taney leaned back, relieved, happy that he didn't have to cope with the disapproval of the Medical Corps.

"It's—well," said Seeger, embarrassed, "It's hard to say—but it's money."

Taney shook his head sadly. "I know."

"We haven't been paid for three months, sir, and—"

"Damn it!" Taney stood up and shouted furiously. "I would like to take every bloody, chair-warming old lady in the Finance Department and wring their necks."

The clerk stuck his head into the tent. "Anything wrong? You call for me, sir?"

"No!" Taney shouted. "Get out of here!"

The clerk ducked out.

Taney sat down again. "I suppose," he said, in a more normal voice, "they have their problems. Outfits being broken up, being moved all over the place. But it's rugged."

"It wouldn't be so bad," Seeger said, "but we're going to Paris tomorrow. Olson, Welch, and myself. And you need money in Paris."

"Don't I know it?" Taney wagged his head. "Do you know what I paid for a bottle of champagne on the Place Pigalle in September?" He paused significantly. "I won't tell you. You wouldn't have any respect for me the rest of your life."

Seeger laughed. "Hanging is too good for the guy who thought up the rate of exchange," he said.

"I don't care if I never see another franc as long as I live." Taney waved his letter in the air, although it had been dry for a long time.

There was silence in the tent, and Seeger swallowed a little embarrassedly. "Sir," he said, "the truth is, I've come to borrow some money for Welch, Olson, and myself. We'll pay it back out of the first pay we get, and that can't be too long from now. If you don't want to give it to us, just tell me and I'll understand and get the hell out of here. We don't like to ask, but you might just as well be dead as be in Paris broke."

Taney stopped waving his letter and put it down thoughtfully. He peered at it, wrinkling his brow, looking like an aged bookkeeper in the single, gloomy light that hung in the middle of the tent.

"Just say the word, Captain," Seeger said, "and I'll blow."

"Stay where you are, son," said Taney. He dug in his shirt pocket and took out a worn, sweat-stained wallet. He looked at it for a moment. "Alligator," he said, with automatic, absent pride. "My wife sent it to me when we were in England. Pounds don't fit in it. However . . ." He opened it and took out all the contents. There was a small pile of francs on the table in front of him when he finished. He counted them. "Four hundred francs," he said. "Eight bucks."

"Excuse me," Seeger said humbly. "I shouldn't've asked."

"Delighted," Taney said vigorously. "Absolutely delighted." He started dividing the francs into two piles. "Truth is, Seeger, most of my money goes home in allotments. And the truth is, I lost eleven hundred francs in a poker game three nights ago, and I ought to be ashamed of myself. Here." He shoved one pile toward Seeger. "Two hundred francs."

Seeger looked down at the frayed, meretricious paper, which always seemed to him like stage money anyway. "No, sir," he said. "I can't take it."

"Take it," Taney said. "That's a direct order."

Seeger slowly picked up the money, not looking at Taney. "Sometime, sir," he said, "after we get out, you have to come over to my house, and you and my father and my brother and I'll go on a real drunk."

"I regard that," Taney said gravely, "as a solemn commitment."

They smiled at each other, and Seeger started out.

"Have a drink for me," said Taney, "at the Café de la Paix. A small drink." He was sitting down to tell his wife he loved her when Seeger went out of the tent.

Olson fell into step with Seeger and they walked silently through the mud between the tents.

"Well, mon vieux?" Olson said finally.

"Two hundred francs," said Seeger.

Olson groaned. "Two hundred francs! We won't be able to pinch a whore's behind on the Boulevard des Capucines for two hundred francs. That miserable, penny-loving Yankee!"

"He only had four hundred," Seeger said.

"I revise my opinion," said Olson.

They walked disconsolately and heavily back toward their tent.

Olson spoke only once before they got there. "These raincoats," he said, patting his. "Most ingenious invention of the war. Highest saturation point of any modern fabric. Collect more water per square inch, and hold it, than any material known to man. All hail the quartermaster!"

Welch was waiting at the entrance of their tent. He was standing there peering excitedly and shortsightedly out at the rain through his glasses, looking angry and tough, like a big-city hack driver, individual and incorruptible even in the ten-million colored uniform. Every time Seeger came upon Welch unexpectedly, he couldn't help smiling at the belligerent stance, the harsh stare through the steel-rimmed G.I. glasses, which had nothing at all to do with the way Welch really was. "It's a family inheritance," Welch had once explained. "My whole family stands as though we were getting ready to rap a drunk with a beer glass. Even my old lady." Welch had six brothers, all devout, according to Welch, and Seeger from time to time idly pictured them standing in a row, on Sunday mornings in church, seemingly on the verge of general violence, amid the hushed Latin and the Sabbath millinery.

"How much?" Welch asked loudly.

"Don't make us laugh," Olson said, pushing past him into the tent.

"What do you think I could get from the French for my combat jacket?" Seeger said. He went into the tent and lay down on his cot.

Welch followed them in and stood between the two of them. "Boys," he said, "on a man's errand."

"I can just see us now," Olson murmured, lying on his cot with his hands clasped behind his head, "painting Montmartre red. Please bring on the naked dancing girls. Four bucks' worth."

"I am not worried," Welch announced.

"Get out of here." Olson turned over on his stomach.

"I know where we can put our hands on sixty-five bucks." Welch looked triumphantly first at Olson, then at Seeger.

Olson turned over slowly and sat up. "I'll kill you," he said, "if you're kidding."

"While you guys are wasting your time fooling around with the infantry," Welch said, "I used my head. I went into Reems and used my head."

"Rance," Olson said automatically. He had had two years of French in college and he felt, now that the war was over, that he had to introduce his friends to some of his culture.

"I got to talking to a captain in the Air Force," Welch said eagerly. "A little, fat old paddle-footed captain that never got higher off the ground than the second floor of Com Z headquarters, and he told me that what he would admire to do more than anything else is take home a nice shiny German Luger pistol with him to show to the boys back in Pacific Grove, California."

Silence fell on the tent, and Welch and Olson looked at Seeger.

"Sixty-five bucks for a Luger, these days," Olson said, "is a very good figure."

"They've been sellin' for as low as thirty-five," said Welch hesitantly. "I'll bet," he said to Seeger, "you could sell yours now and buy another one back when you got some dough, and make a clear twenty-five on the deal."

Seeger didn't say anything. He had killed the owner of the Luger, an enormous S.S. major, in Coblenz, behind some bales of paper in a warehouse, and the major had fired at Seeger three times with it, once nicking his helmet, before Seeger hit him in the face at twenty feet. Seeger had kept the Luger, a heavy, well-balanced gun, lugging it with him, hiding it at the bottom of his bedroll, oiling it three times a week, avoiding all opportunities of selling it, although he had once been offered a hundred dollars for it and several times eighty and ninety, while the war was still on, before German weapons became a glut on the market.

"Well," said Welch, "there's no hurry. I told the captain I'd see him tonight around eight o'clock in front of the Lion d'Or Hotel. You got five hours to make up your mind. Plenty of time."

"Me," said Olson, after a pause, "I won't say anything."

Seeger looked reflectively at his feet, and the two other men avoided looking at him.

Welch dug in his pocket. "I forgot," he said. "I picked up a letter for you." He handed it to Seeger.

"Thanks," Seeger said. He opened it absently, thinking about the Luger.

"Me," said Olson, "I won't say a bloody word. I'm just going to lie here and think about that nice, fat Air Force captain."

Seeger grinned a little at him and went to the tent opening to read the letter in the light. The letter was from his father, and even from one glance at the handwriting, scrawly and hurried and spotted, so different from his father's usual steady, handsome, professorial script, he knew that something was wrong.

"Dear Norman," it read, "sometime in the future, you must forgive me for writing this letter. But I have been holding this in so long, and there is no one here I can talk to, and because of your brother's condition I must pretend to be cheerful and optimistic all the time at home, both with him and your mother, who has never been the same since Leonard was killed. You're the oldest now, and although I know we've never talked very seriously about anything before, you have been through a great deal by now, and I imagine you must have matured considerably, and you've seen so many different places and people. Norman, I need help. While the war was on and you were fighting, I kept this to myself. It wouldn't have been fair to burden you with this. But now the war is over, and I no longer feel I can stand up under this alone. And you will have to face it sometime when you get home, if you haven't faced it already, and perhaps we can help each other by facing it together."

"I'm redeployable. It's so enjoyable," Olson was singing softly, on his cot. He fell silent after his burst of song.

Seeger blinked his eyes in the gray, wintry, rainy light, and went on reading his father's letter, on the stiff white stationery with the university letterhead in polite engraving at the top of each page.

"I've been feeling this coming on for a long time," the letter continued, "but it wasn't until last Sunday morning that something happened to make me feel it in its full force. I don't know how much you've guessed about the reason for Jacob's discharge from the Army. It's true he was pretty badly wounded in the leg at Metz, but I've asked around, and I know that men with worse wounds were returned to duty after hospitalization. Jacob got a medical discharge, but I don't think it was for the shrapnel wound in his thigh. He is suffering now from what I suppose you call combat fatigue, and he is subject to fits of depression and hallucinations. Your mother and I thought that as time went by and the war and the Army receded, he would grow better. Instead, he is growing worse. Last Sunday morning when I came down into the living room from upstairs he was crouched in his old uniform, next to the window, peering out."

"What the hell," Olson was saying. "If we don't get the sixty-five bucks we can always go to the Louvre. I understand the Mona Lisa is back."

"I asked Jacob what he was doing," the letter went on. "He didn't turn around. 'I'm observing,' he said. 'V-1s and V-2s. Buzz bombs and rockets. They're coming in by the hundred.' I tried to reason with him and he told me to crouch and save myself from flying glass. To humor him I got down on the floor beside him and tried to tell him the war was over, that we were in Ohio, 4,000 miles away from the nearest spot where bombs had fallen, that America had never been touched. He wouldn't listen. 'These're the new rocket bombs,' he said, 'for the Jews.'"

"Did you ever hear of the Panthéon?" Olson asked loudly.

"No," said Welch.

"It's free."

"I'll go," said Welch.

Seeger shook his head a little and blinked his eyes before he went back to the letter.

"After that," his father went on, "Jacob seemed to forget about the bombs from time to time, but he kept saying that the mobs were coming up the street armed with bazookas and Browning automatic rifles. He mumbled incoherently a good deal of the time and kept walking back and forth saying, 'What's the situation? Do you know what the situation is?' And once he told me he wasn't worried about himself, he was a soldier and he expected to be killed, but he was worried about Mother and myself and Leonard and you. He seemed to forget that Leonard was dead. I tried to calm him and get him back to bed before your mother came down, but he refused and wanted to set out immediately to rejoin his division. It was all terribly disjointed, and at one time he took the ribbon he got for winning the Bronze Star and threw it in the fireplace, then he got down on his hands and knees and picked it out of the ashes and made me pin it on him again, and he kept repeating, 'This is when they are coming for the Jews.'"

"The next war I'm in," said Olson, "they don't get me under the rank of colonel."

It had stopped raining by now, and Seeger folded the unfinished letter and went outside. He walked slowly down to the end of the company street, and, facing out across the empty, soaked French fields, scarred and neglected by various armies, he stopped and opened the letter again.

"I don't know what Jacob went through in the Army," his father wrote, "that has done this to him. He never talks to me about the war and he refuses to go to a psychoanalyst, and from time to time he is his own bouncing, cheerful self, playing handball in the afternoons and going around with a large group of girls. But he has devoured all the concentration-camp reports, and I found him weeping when the newspapers reported that a hundred Jews were killed in Tripoli some time ago.

"The terrible thing is, Norman, that I find myself coming to believe that it is not neurotic for a Jew to behave like this today. Perhaps Jacob is the normal one, and I, going about my business, teaching economics in a quiet classroom, pretending to understand that the world is comprehensible and orderly, am really the mad one. I ask you once more to forgive me for writing you a letter like this, so different from any letter or any conversation I've ever had with you. But it is crowding me, too. I do not see rockets and bombs, but I see other things.

"Wherever you go these days—restaurants, hotels, clubs, trains—you seem to hear talk about the Jews, mean, hateful, murderous talk. Whatever page you turn to in the newspapers, you seem to find an article about Jews being killed somewhere on the face of the globe. And there are large, influential newspapers and well-known columnists who each day are growing more and more outspoken and more popular. The day that Roosevelt died I heard a drunken man yelling outside a bar, 'Finally they got the Jew out of the White House.' And some of the people who heard him merely laughed, and nobody stopped him. And on V-J Day, in celebration, hoodlums in Los Angeles savagely beat a Jewish writer. It's difficult to know what to do, whom to fight, where to look for allies.

"Three months ago, for example, I stopped my Thursday-night poker game, after playing with the same men for over ten years. John Reilly happened to say that the Jews got rich out of the war, and when I demanded an apology, he refused, and when I looked around at the faces of the men who had been my friends for so long, I could see they were not with me. And when I left the house, no one said good night to me. I know the poison was spreading from Germany before the war and during it, but I had not realized it had come so close.

"And in my economics class, I find myself idiotically hedging in my lectures. I discover that I am loath to praise any liberal writer or any liberal act, and find myself somehow annoyed and frightened to see an article of criticism of existing abuses signed by a Jewish name. And I hate to see Jewish names on important committees, and hate to read of Jews fighting for the poor, the oppressed, the cheated and hungry. Somehow, even in a country where my family has lived a hundred years, the enemy has won this subtle victory over me—he has made me disfranchise myself from honest causes by calling them foreign, Communist, using Jewish names connected with them as ammunition against them.

"Most hateful of all, I found myself looking for Jewish names in the casualty lists and secretly being glad when I saw them there, to prove that there, at least, among the dead and wounded, we belonged. Three times, thanks to you and your brothers, I found our name there, and, may God forgive me, at the expense of your blood and your brother's life, through my tears, I felt that same twitch of satisfaction.

"When I read the newspapers and see another story that Jews are still being killed in Poland, or Jews are requesting that they be given back their homes in France or that they be allowed to enter some country where they will not be murdered, I am annoyed with them. I feel that they are boring the rest of the world with their problems, that they are making demands upon the rest of the world by being killed, that they are disturbing everyone by being hungry and asking for the return of their property. If we could all fall in through the crust of the earth and vanish in one hour, with our heroes and poets and prophets and martyrs, perhaps we would be doing the memory of the Jewish race a service.

"This is how I feel today, son. I need some help. You've been to the war, you've fought and killed men, you've seen the people of other countries. Maybe you understand things that I don't understand. Maybe you see some hope somewhere. Help me. Your loving Father."

Seeger folded the letter slowly, not seeing what he was doing, because the tears were burning his eyes. He walked slowly and aimlessly across the dead, sodden grass of the empty field, away from the camp. He tried to wipe away his tears, because, with his eyes full and dark, he kept seeing his father and brother crouched in the old-fashioned living room in Ohio, and hearing his brother, dressed in the old, discarded uniform, saying, "These're the new rocket bombs. For the Jews."

He sighed, looking out over the bleak, wasted land. Now, he thought, now I have to think about it. He felt a slight, unreasonable twinge of anger at his father for presenting him with the necessity of thinking about it. The Army was good about serious problems. While you were fighting, you were too busy and frightened and weary to think about anything, and at other times you were relaxing, putting your brain on a shelf, postponing everything to that impossible time of clarity and beauty after the war. Well, now, here was the impossible, clear, beautiful time, and here was his father, demanding that he think. There are all sorts of Jews, he thought: there are the sort whose every waking moment is ridden by the knowledge of Jewishness; who see signs against the Jew in every smile on a streetcar, every whisper; who see pogroms in every newspaper article, threats in every change of the weather, scorn in every handshake, death behind each closed door. He had not been like that. He was young, he was big and healthy and easygoing, and people of all kinds had liked him all his life, in the Army and out. In America, especially, what was going on in Europe had been remote, unreal, unrelated to him. The chanting, bearded old men burning in the Nazi furnaces, and the dark-eyed women screaming prayers in Polish and Russian and German as they were pushed naked into the gas chambers, had seemed as shadowy and almost as unrelated to him, as he trotted out onto the stadium field for a football game, as they must have been to the men named O'Dwyer and Wickersham and Poole who played in the line beside him.

These tortured people had seemed more related to him in Europe. Again and again, in the towns that had been taken back from the Germans, gaunt, gray-faced men had stopped him humbly, looking searchingly at him, and had asked, peering at his long, lined, grimy face under the anonymous helmet, "Are you a Jew?" Sometimes they asked it in English, sometimes French, sometimes Yiddish. He didn't know French or Yiddish, but he learned to recognize that question. He had never understood exactly why they asked the question, since they never demanded anything of him, rarely even could speak to him. Then, one day in Strasbourg, a little, bent old man and a small, shapeless woman had stopped him and asked, in English, if he was Jewish. "Yes," he'd said, smiling at them. The two old people had smiled widely, like children. "Look," the old man had said to his wife. "A young American soldier. A Jew. And so large and strong." He had touched Seeger's arm reverently with the tips of his fingers, then had touched the Garand Seeger was carrying. "And such a beautiful rifle."

And there, for a moment, although he was not particularly sensitive, Seeger had got an inkling of why he had been stopped and questioned by so many before. Here, to these bent, exhausted old people, ravaged of their families, familiar with flight and death for so many years, was a symbol of continuing life. A large young man in the uniform of the liberator, blood, as they thought, of their blood, but not in hiding, not quivering in fear and helplessness, but striding secure and victorious down the street, armed and capable of inflicting terrible destruction on his enemies.

Seeger had kissed the old lady on the cheek and she had wept, and the old man had scolded her for it while shaking Seeger's hand fervently and thankfully before saying good-bye.

Thinking back on it, he knew that it

was silly to pretend that, even before his father's letter, he had been like any other American soldier going through the war. When he had stood over the huge, dead S.S. major with the face blown in by his bullets in the warehouse in Coblenz, and taken the pistol from the dead hand, he had tasted a strange little extra flavor of triumph. How many Jews, he'd thought, has this man killed? How fitting it is that I've killed him. Neither Olson nor Welch, who were like his brothers, would have felt that in picking up the Luger, its barrel still hot from the last shots its owner had fired before dying. And he had resolved that he was going to make sure to take this gun back with him to America, and plug it and keep it on his desk at home, as a kind of vague, half-understood sign to himself that justice had once been done and he had been its instrument.

Maybe, he thought, maybe I'd better take it back with me, but not as a memento. Not plugged, but loaded. America by now was a strange country for him. He had been away a long time and he wasn't sure what was waiting for him when he got home. If the mobs were coming down the street toward his house, he was not going to die singing and praying.

When he had been taking basic training, he'd heard a scrawny, clerkish soldier from Boston talking at the other end of the PX bar, over the watered beer. "The boys at the office," the scratchy voice was saying, "gave me a party before I left. And they told me one thing. 'Charlie,' they said, 'hold onto your bayonet. We're going to be able to use it when you get back. On the Yids.'"

He hadn't said anything then, because he'd felt it was neither possible nor desirable to fight against every random overheard voice raised against the Jews from one end of the world to the other. But again and again, at odd moments, lying on a barracks cot, or stretched out trying to sleep on the floor of a ruined French farmhouse, he had heard that voice, harsh, satisfied, heavy with hate and ignorance, saying above the beery grumble of apprentice soldiers at the bar, "Hold onto your bayonet."

And the other stories. Jews collected stories of hatred and injustice and inklings of doom like a special, lunatic kind of miser.

The story of the Navy officer, commander of a small vessel off the Aleutians, who in the officers' wardroom had complained that he hated the Jews because it was the Jews who had demanded that the Germans be beaten first, and the forces in the Pacific had been starved in consequence. And when one of his junior officers, who had just come aboard, had objected and told the commander that he was a Jew, the commander had risen from the table and said, "Mister, the Constitution of the United States says I have to serve in the same Navy with Jews, but it doesn't say I have to eat at the same table with them." In the fogs and the cold, swelling Arctic seas off the Aleutians, in a small boat, subject to sudden, mortal attack at any moment. . . . And the million other stories. Jews, even the most normal and best adjusted, became living treasuries of them, scraps of malice and bloodthirstiness, clever and confusing and cunningly twisted so that every act by every Jew became suspect and blameworthy and hateful. Seeger had heard the stories and had made an almost conscious effort to forget them. Now, holding his father's letter in his hand, he remembered them all.

He stared unseeingly out in front of him. Maybe, he thought, maybe it would've been better to have been killed in the war, like Leonard. Simpler. Leonard would never have to face a crowd coming for his mother and father. Leonard would not have to listen and collect these hideous, fascinating little stories that made of every Jew a stranger in any town, on any field, on the face of the earth. He had come so close to being killed so many times; it would have been so easy, so neat and final. Seeger shook his head. It was ridiculous to feel like that, and he was ashamed of himself for the weak moment. At the age of twenty-one, death was not an answer.

"Seeger!" It was Olson's voice. He and Welch had sloshed silently up behind Seeger, standing in the open field. "Seeger, mon vieux, what're you doing—grazing?"

Seeger turned slowly to them. "I wanted to read my letter," he said.

Olson looked closely at him. They had been together so long, through so many things, that flickers and hints of expression on each other's faces were recognized and acted upon. "Anything wrong?" Olson asked.

"No," said Seeger. "Nothing much."

"Norman," Welch said, his voice young and solemn. "Norman, we've been talking, Olson and me. We decided—you're pretty attached to that Luger, and maybe, if you—well—"

"What he's trying to say," said Olson, "is we withdraw the request. If you want to sell it, O.K. If you don't, don't do it for our sake. Honest."

Seeger looked at them standing there, disreputable and tough and familiar. "I haven't made up my mind yet," he said.

"Anything you decide," Welch said oratorically, "is perfectly all right with us. Perfectly."

The three of them walked aimlessly and silently across the field, away from camp. As they walked, their shoes making a wet, sliding sound in the damp, dead grass, Seeger thought of the time Olson had covered him in the little town outside Cherbourg, when Seeger had been caught, going down the side of a street, by four Germans with a machine gun in the second story of a house on the corner and Olson had had to stand out in the middle of the street with no cover at all for more than a minute, firing continuously, so that Seeger could get away alive. And he thought of the time outside St.-Lô when he had been wounded and had lain in a minefield for three hours and Welch and Captain Taney had come looking for him in the darkness and had found him and picked him up and run for it, all of them expecting to get blown up any second. And he thought of all the drinks they'd had together, and the long marches and the cold winter together, and all the girls they'd gone out with together, and he thought of his father and brother crouching behind the window in Ohio waiting for the rockets and the crowds armed with Browning automatic rifles.

"Say." He stopped and stood facing them. "Say, what do you guys think of the Jews?"

Welch and Olson looked at each other, and Olson glanced down at the letter in Seeger's hand.

"Jews?" Olson said finally. "What're they? Welch, you ever hear of the Jews?"

Welch looked thoughtfully at the gray sky. "No," he said. "But remember, I'm an uneducated fellow."

"Sorry, bud," Olson said, turning to Seeger. "We can't help you. Ask us another question. Maybe we'll do better."

Seeger peered at the faces of his friends. He would have to rely upon them, later on, out of uniform, on their native streets, more than he had ever relied on them on the bullet-swept street and in the dark minefield in France. Welch and Olson stared back at him, troubled, their faces candid and tough and dependable.

"What time," Seeger asked, "did you tell that captain you'd meet him?"

"Eight o'clock," Welch said. "But we don't have to go. If you have any feeling about that gun—"

"We'll meet him," Seeger said. "We can use that sixty-five bucks."

"Listen," Olson said, "I know how much you like that gun, and I'll feel like a heel if you sell it."

"Forget it," Seeger said, starting to walk again. "What could I use it for in America?"

FOR DISCUSSION:

1. "Act of Faith" attempts to seize a moment in time and space, to depict realistically a world within a world—the social climate of the G.I. in the days following the close of World War II. Show how the attitudes, interests, and values of the enlisted man are presented by Shaw.

2. One of the major shortcomings of social fiction is that once the social scene depicted in the story no longer exists, the story can seem limited and dated. Is "Act of Faith" limited by its specific locale and time, or does it manage to describe a fundamental, unchanging aspect of the human condition?

3. What is the effect of juxtaposing segments of Professor Seeger's letter with the speech of Olson and Welch?

4. What is the significance of the title?

The Lottery*

SHIRLEY JACKSON

The morning of June 27th was clear and sunny, with the fresh warmth of a full-summer day; the flowers were blossoming profusely and the grass was richly green. The people of the village began to gather in the square, between the post office and the bank, around ten o'clock; in some towns there were so many people that the lottery took two days and had to be started on June 26th, but in this village, where there were only about three hundred people, the whole lottery took less than two hours, so it could begin at ten o'clock in the morning and still be through in time to allow the villagers to get home for noon dinner.

The children assembled first, of course. School was recently over for the summer, and the feeling of liberty sat uneasily on most of them; they tended to gather together quietly for a while before they broke into boisterous play, and their talk was still of the classroom and the teacher, of books and reprimands. Bobby Martin had already stuffed his pockets full of stones, and the other boys soon followed his example, selecting the smoothest and roundest stones; Bobby and Harry Jones and Dickie Delacroix—the villagers pronounced this name "Dellacroy"—eventually made a great pile of stones in one corner of the square and guarded it against the raids of the other boys. The girls stood aside, talking among themselves, looking over their shoulders at the boys, and the very small children rolled in the dust or clung to the hands of their older brothers or sisters.

Soon the men began to gather, surveying their own children, speaking of planting and rain, tractors and taxes. They stood together, away from the pile of stones in the corner, and their jokes were quiet and they smiled rather than laughed. The women, wearing faded house dresses and sweaters, came shortly after their menfolk. They greeted one another and exchanged bits of gossip as they went to join their husbands. Soon the women, standing by their husbands, began to call to their children, and the children came reluctantly, having to be called four or five times. Bobby Martin ducked under his mother's grasping hand and ran, laughing, back to the pile of stones. His father spoke up sharply, and Bobby came quickly and took his place between his father and his oldest brother.

The lottery was conducted—as were the square dances, the teen-age club, the Halloween program—by Mr. Summers, who had time and energy to devote to civic activities. He was a round-faced jovial man and he ran the coal business, and people were sorry for him, because he had no children and his wife was a scold. When he arrived in the square, carrying the black wooden box, there was a murmur of conversation among the villagers, and he waved and called, "Little late today, folks." The postmaster, Mr. Graves, followed him, carrying a three-legged stool, and the stool was put in the center of the square and Mr. Summers set the black box down on it. The villagers kept their distance, leaving a space between themselves and the stool, and when Mr. Summers said, "Some of you fellows want to give me a hand?" there was a hesitation before two men, Mr. Martin and his oldest son, Baxter, came forward to hold the box steady on the stool while Mr. Summers stirred up the papers inside it.

The original paraphernalia for the lottery had been lost long ago, and the black box now resting on the stool had been put

---

* Reprinted from THE LOTTERY by Shirley Jackson, by permission of FARRAR, STRAUS & GIROUX, INC. Copyright 1948 by the New Yorker Magazine, Copyright 1949 by Shirley Jackson. Also by permission of Brandt & Brandt.

into use even before Old Man Warner, the oldest man in town, was born. Mr. Summers spoke frequently to the villagers about making a new box, but no one liked to upset even as much tradition as was represented by the black box. There was a story that the present box had been made with some pieces of the box that had preceded it, the one that had been constructed when the first people settled down to make a village here. Every year, after the lottery, Mr. Summers began talking again about a new box, but every year the subject was allowed to fade off without anything's being done. The black box grew shabbier each year; by now it was no longer completely black but splintered badly along one side to show the original wood color, and in some places faded or stained.

Mr. Martin and his oldest son, Baxter, held the black box securely on the stool until Mr. Summers had stirred the papers thoroughly with his hand. Because so much of the ritual had been forgotten or discarded, Mr. Summers had been successful in having slips of paper substituted for the chips of wood that had been used for generations. Chips of wood, Mr. Summers had argued, had been all very well when the village was tiny, but now that the population was more than three hundred and likely to keep on growing, it was necessary to use something that would fit more easily into the black box. The night before the lottery, Mr. Summers and Mr. Graves made up the slips of paper and put them in the box, and it was then taken to the safe of Mr. Summers' coal company and locked up until Mr. Summers was ready to take it to the square next morning. The rest of the year, the box was put away, sometimes one place, sometimes another; it had spent one year in Mr. Graves's barn and another year underfoot in the post office, and sometimes it was set on a shelf in the Martin grocery and left there.

There was a great deal of fussing to be done before Mr. Summers declared the lottery open. There were the lists to make up —of heads of families, heads of households in each family, members of each household in each family. There was the proper swearing-in of Mr. Summers by the postmaster, as the official of the lottery; at one time, some people remembered, there had been a recital of some sort, performed by the official of the lottery, a perfunctory, tuneless chant that had been rattled off duly each year; some people believed that the official of the lottery used to stand just so when he said or sang it, others believed that he was supposed to walk among the people, but years and years ago this part of the ritual had been allowed to lapse. There had been, also, a ritual salute, which the official of the lottery had had to use in addressing each person who came up to draw from the box, but this also had changed with time, until now it was felt necessary only for the official to speak to each person approaching. Mr. Summers was very good at all this; in his clean white shirt and blue jeans, with one hand resting carelessly on the black box, he seemed very proper and important as he talked interminably to Mr. Graves and the Martins.

Just as Mr. Summers finally left off talking and turned to the assembled villagers, Mrs. Hutchinson came hurriedly along the path to the square, her sweater thrown over her shoulders, and slid into place in the back of the crowd. "Clean forgot what day it was," she said to Mrs. Delacroix, who stood next to her, and they both laughed softly. "Thought my old man was out back stacking wood," Mrs. Hutchinson went on, "and then I looked out the window and the kids was gone, and then I remembered it was the twenty-seventh and came a-running." She dried her hands on her apron, and Mrs. Delacroix said, "You're in time, though. They're still talking away up there."

Mrs. Hutchinson craned her neck to see through the crowd and found her husband and children standing near the front. She tapped Mrs. Delacroix on the arm as a farewell and began to make her way through the crowd. The people separated good-humoredly to let her through; two or three people said, in voices just loud enough to be heard across the crowd, "Here comes your Missus, Hutchinson," and "Bill, she made it after all." Mrs. Hutchinson reached her husband, and Mr. Summers, who had been waiting, said cheerfully, "Thought we were going to have to get on without you, Tessie." Mrs. Hutchinson said, grinning, "Wouldn't have me leave m'dishes in the sink, now, would you, Joe?," and soft laughter ran through the crowd as the people stirred back into position after Mrs. Hutchinson's arrival.

"Well, now," Mr. Summers said soberly, "guess we better get started, get this over with, so's we can go back to work. Anybody ain't here?"

"Dunbar," several people said. "Dunbar, Dunbar."

Mr. Summers consulted his list. "Clyde Dunbar," he said. "That's right. He's broke his leg, hasn't he? Who's drawing for him?"

"Me, I guess," a woman said, and Mr. Summers turned to look at her. "Wife draws for her husband," Mr. Summers said. "Don't you have a grown boy to do it for you, Janey?" Although Mr. Summers and everyone else in the village knew the answer perfectly well, it was the business of the official of the lottery to ask such questions formally. Mr. Summers waited with an expression of polite interest while Mrs. Dunbar answered.

"Horace's not but sixteen yet," Mrs. Dunbar said regretfully. "Guess I gotta fill in for the old man this year."

"Right," Mr. Summers said. He made a note on the list he was holding. Then he asked, "Watson boy drawing this year?"

A tall boy in the crowd raised his hand. "Here," he said. "I'm drawing for m'mother and me." He blinked his eyes nervously and ducked his head as several voices in the crowd said things like "Good fellow, Jack," and "Glad to see your mother's got a man to do it."

"Well," Mr. Summers said, "guess that's everyone. Old Man Warner make it?"

"Here," a voice said, and Mr. Summers nodded.

A sudden hush fell on the crowd as Mr. Summers cleared his throat and looked at the list. "All ready?" he called. "Now, I'll read the names—heads of families first—and the men come up and take a paper out of the box. Keep the paper folded in your hand without looking at it until everyone has had a turn. Everything clear?"

The people had done it so many times that they only half listened to the directions; most of them were quiet, wetting their lips, not looking around. Then Mr. Summers raised one hand high and said, "Adams." A man disengaged himself from the crowd and came forward. "Hi, Steve," Mr. Summers said, and Mr. Adams said, "Hi, Joe." They grinned at one another humorously and nervously. Then Mr. Adams reached into the black box and took out a folded paper. He held it firmly by one corner as he turned and went hastily back to his place in the crowd, where he stood a little apart from his family, not looking down at his hand.

"Allen," Mr. Summers said. "Anderson. . . . Bentham."

"Seems like there's no time at all between lotteries any more," Mrs. Delacroix said to Mrs. Graves in the back row. "Seems like we got through with the last one only last week."

"Time sure goes fast," Mrs. Graves said.

"Clark. . . . Delacroix."

"There goes my old man," Mrs. Delacroix said. She held her breath while her husband went forward.

"Dunbar," Mr. Summers said, and Mrs. Dunbar went steadily to the box while one of the women said, "Go on, Janey," and another said, "There she goes."

"We're next," Mrs. Graves said. She watched while Mr. Graves came around from the side of the box, greeted Mr. Summers gravely, and selected a slip of paper from the box. By now, all through the crowd there were men holding the small folded papers in their large hands, turning them over and over nervously. Mrs. Dunbar and her two sons stood together, Mrs. Dunbar holding the slip of paper.

"Harburt. . . . Hutchinson."

"Get up there, Bill," Mrs. Hutchinson said, and the people near her laughed.

"Jones."

"They do say," Mr. Adams said to Old Man Warner, who stood next to him, "that over in the north village they're talking of giving up the lottery."

Old Man Warner snorted. "Pack of crazy fools," he said. "Listening to the young folks, nothing's good enough for *them*. Next thing you know, they'll be wanting to go back to living in caves, nobody work any more, live *that* way for a while. Used to be a saying about 'Lottery in June, corn be heavy soon.' First thing you know, we'd all be eating stewed chickweed and acorns. There's *always* been a lottery," he added petulantly. "Bad enough to see young Joe Summers up there joking with everybody."

"Some places have already quit lotteries," Mrs. Adams said.

"Nothing but trouble in *that*," Old Man Warner said stoutly. "Pack of young fools."

"Martin." And Bobby Martin watched his father go forward. "Overdyke.... Percy."

"I wish they'd hurry," Mrs. Dunbar said to her older son. "I wish they'd hurry."

"They're almost through," her son said.

"You get ready to run tell Dad," Mrs. Dunbar said.

Mr. Summers called his own name and then stepped forward precisely and selected a slip from the box. Then he called, "Warner."

"Seventy-seventh year I been in the lottery," Old Man Warner said as he went through the crowd. "Seventy-seventh time."

"Watson." The tall boy came awkwardly through the crowd. Someone said, "Don't be nervous, Jack," and Mr. Summers said, "Take your time, son."

"Zanini."

After that, there was a long pause, a breathless pause, until Mr. Summers, holding his slip of paper in the air, said, "All right, fellows." For a minute, no one moved, and then all the slips of paper were opened. Suddenly, all the women began to speak at once, saying, "Who is it?," "Who's got it?," "Is it the Dunbars?," "Is it the Watsons?" Then the voices began to say, "It's Hutchinson. It's Bill," "Bill Hutchinson's got it."

"Go tell your father," Mrs. Dunbar said to her older son.

People began to look around to see the Hutchinsons. Bill Hutchinson was standing quiet, staring down at the paper in his hand. Suddenly, Tessie Hutchinson shouted to Mr. Summers, "You didn't give him time enough to take any paper he wanted. I saw you. It wasn't fair!"

"Be a good sport, Tessie," Mrs. Delacroix called, and Mrs. Graves said, "All of us took the same chance."

"Shut up, Tessie," Bill Hutchinson said.

"Well, everyone," Mr. Summers said, "that was done pretty fast, and now we've got to be hurrying a little more to get done in time." He consulted his next list. "Bill," he said, "you draw for the Hutchinson family. You got any other households in the Hutchinsons?"

"There's Don and Eva," Mrs. Hutchinson yelled. "Make *them* take their chance!"

"Daughters draw with their husbands' families, Tessie," Mr. Summers said gently. "You know that as well as anyone else."

"It wasn't *fair*," Tessie said.

"I guess not, Joe," Bill Hutchinson said regretfully. "My daughter draws with her husband's family, that's only fair. And I've got no other family except the kids."

"Then, as far as drawing for families is concerned, it's you," Mr. Summers said in explanation, "and as far as drawing for households is concerned, that's you, too. Right?"

"Right," Bill Hutchinson said.

"How many kids, Bill?" Mr. Summers asked formally.

"Three," Bill Hutchinson said. "There's Bill, Jr., and Nancy, and little Dave. And Tessie and me."

"All right, then," Mr. Summers said. "Harry, you got their tickets back?"

Mr. Graves nodded and held up the slips of paper. "Put them in the box, then," Mr. Summers directed. "Take Bill's and put it in."

"I think we ought to start over," Mrs. Hutchinson said, as quietly as she could. "I tell you it wasn't *fair*. You didn't give him time enough to choose. *Everybody* saw that."

Mr. Graves had selected the five slips and put them in the box, and he dropped all the papers but those onto the ground, where the breeze caught them and lifted them off.

"Listen, everybody," Mrs. Hutchinson was saying to the people around her.

"Ready, Bill?" Mr. Summers asked, and Bill Hutchinson, with one quick glance around at his wife and children, nodded.

"Remember," Mr. Summers said, "take the slips and keep them folded until each person has taken one. Harry, you help little Dave." Mr. Graves took the hand of the little boy, who came willingly with him up to the box. "Take a paper out of the box, Davy," Mr. Summers said. Davy put his hand into the box and laughed. "Take just *one* paper," Mr. Summers said. "Harry, you hold it for him." Mr. Graves took the child's hand and removed the folded paper from the tight fist and held it while little Dave stood next to him and looked up at him wonderingly.

"Nancy next," Mr. Summers said. Nancy was twelve, and her school friends breathed heavily as she went forward, switching her skirt, and took a slip daintily from the box. "Bill, Jr.," Mr. Summers said, and

Billy, his face red and his feet over-large, nearly knocked the box over as he got a paper out. "Tessie," Mr. Summers said. She hesitated for a minute, looking around defiantly, and then set her lips and went up to the box. She snatched a paper out and held it behind her.

"Bill," Mr. Summers said, and Bill Hutchinson reached into the box and felt around, bringing his hand out at last with the slip of paper in it.

The crowd was quiet. A girl whispered, "I hope it's not Nancy," and the sound of the whisper reached the edges of the crowd.

"It's not the way it used to be," Old Man Warner said clearly. "People ain't the way they used to be."

"All right," Mr. Summers said. "Open the papers. Harry, you open little Dave's."

Mr. Graves opened the slip of paper and there was a general sigh through the crowd as he held it up and everyone could see that it was blank. Nancy and Bill, Jr., opened theirs at the same time, and both beamed and laughed, turning around to the crowd and holding their slips of paper above their heads.

"Tessie," Mr. Summers said. There was a pause, and then Mr. Summers looked at Bill Hutchinson, and Bill unfolded his paper and showed it. It was blank.

"It's Tessie," Mr. Summers said, and his voice was hushed. "Show us her paper, Bill."

Bill Hutchinson went over to his wife and forced the slip of paper out of her hand. It had a black spot on it, the black spot Mr. Summers had made the night before with the heavy pencil in the coal-company office. Bill Hutchinson held it up, and there was a stir in the crowd.

"All right, folks," Mr. Summers said. "Let's finish quickly."

Although the villagers had forgotten the ritual and lost the original black box, they still remembered to use stones. The pile of stones the boys had made earlier was ready; there were stones on the ground with the blowing scraps of paper that had come out of the box. Mrs. Delacroix selected a stone so large she had to pick it up with both hands and turned to Mrs. Dunbar. "Come on," she said. "Hurry up."

Mrs. Dunbar had small stones in both hands, and she said, gasping for breath, "I can't run at all. You'll have to go ahead and I'll catch up with you."

The children had stones already, and someone gave little Davey Hutchinson a few pebbles.

Tessie Hutchinson was in the center of a cleared space by now, and she held her hands out desperately as the villagers moved in on her. "It isn't fair," she said. A stone hit her on the side of the head.

Old Man Warner was saying, "Come on, come on, everyone." Steve Adams was in the front of the crowd of villagers, with Mrs. Graves beside him.

"It isn't fair, it isn't right," Mrs. Hutchinson screamed, and then they were upon her.

FOR DISCUSSION:

1. Miss Jackson sets out in the first four paragraphs to make the lottery appear a trivial, routine, commonplace activity. What are the devices she uses toward this end?

2. What is the first hint that the lottery is a horrible thing, the object of which is to lose, not win?

3. The lottery is described as a "civic activity," in the same sense as square dances, teenage clubs, and Halloween programs. What is meant by this description?

4. What comment is Miss Jackson making on the nature of man and the society in which he lives?

5. Account for the horror of the tale and its shocking effect on the reader.

6. In contrast to Shaw's "Act of Faith" the setting of "The Lottery" is vague in place and indeterminate in time. How does this work to the advantage of "The Lottery"?

A Bottle of Milk for Mother*

NELSON ALGREN

I feel I am of them—
I belong to those convicts and prostitutes myself,
And henceforth I will not deny them—
For how can I deny myself?

WHITMAN

Two months after the Polish Warriors S.A.C. had had their heads shaved, Bruno Lefty Bicek got into his final difficulty with the Racine Street police. The arresting officers and a reporter from the *Dziennik Chicagoski* were grouped about the captain's desk when the boy was urged forward into the room by Sergeant Adamovitch, with two fingers wrapped about the boy's broad belt: a full-bodied boy wearing a worn and sleeveless blue work shirt grown too tight across the shoulders; and the shoulders themselves with a loose swing to them. His skull and face were shining from a recent scrubbing, so that the little bridgeless nose glistened between the protective points of the cheekbones. Behind the desk sat Kozak, eleven years on the force and brother to an alderman. The reporter stuck a cigarette behind one ear like a pencil.

"We spotted him followin' the drunk down Chicago—" Sergeant Comiskey began.

Captain Kozak interrupted. "Let the jackroller tell us how he done it hisself."

"I ain't no jackroller."

"What you doin' here, then?"

Bicek folded his naked arms.

"Answer me. If you ain't here for jackrollin' it must be for strong-arm robb'ry—'r you one of them Chicago Av'noo moll-buzzers?"

"I ain't neither."

"C'mon, c'mon, I seen you in here before—what were you up to, followin' that poor old man?"

"I ain't been in here before."

Neither Sergeant Milano, Comiskey, nor old Adamovitch moved an inch; yet the boy felt the semicircle about him drawing closer. Out of the corner of his eye he watched the reporter undoing the top button of his mangy raccoon coat, as though the barren little query room were already growing too warm for him.

"What were you doin' on Chicago Av'noo in the first place when you live up around Division? Ain't your own ward big enough you have to come down here to get in trouble? What do you *think* you're here for?"

"Well, I was just walkin' down Chicago like I said, to get a bottle of milk for Mother, when the officers jumped me. I didn't even see 'em drive up, they wouldn't let me say a word, I got no idea what I'm here for. I was just doin' a errand for Mother 'n—"

"All right, son, you want us to book you as a pickup 'n hold you overnight, is that it?"

"Yes sir."

"What about this, then?"

Kozak flipped a spring-blade knife with a five-inch blade onto the police blotter; the boy resisted an impulse to lean forward and take it. His own double-edged double-

---

* "A Bottle of Milk for Mother," copyright 1941 by Nelson Algren from NEON WILDERNESS. Reprinted by permission of Doubleday & Company, Inc.

jointed spring-blade cuts-all genuine Filipino twisty-handled all-American gut-ripper.

"Is it yours or ain't it?"

"Never seen it before, Captain."

Kozak pulled a billy out of his belt, spread the blade across the bend of the blotter before him, and with one blow clubbed the blade off two inches from the handle. The boy winced as though he himself had received the blow. Kozak threw the broken blade into a basket and the knife into a drawer.

"Know why I did that, son?"

"Yes sir."

"Tell me."

"'Cause it's three inches to the heart."

"No. 'Cause it's against the law to carry more than three inches of knife. C'mon, Lefty, tell us about it. 'N it better be good."

The boy began slowly, secretly gratified that Kozak appeared to know he was the Warriors' first-string left-hander: maybe he'd been out at that game against the Knothole Wonders the Sunday he'd finished his own game and then had relieved Dropkick Kodadek in the sixth in the second. Why hadn't anyone called him "Iron-Man Bicek" or "Fire-ball Bruno" for that one?

"Everythin' you say can be used against you," Kozak warned him earnestly. "Don't talk unless you want to." His lips formed each syllable precisely.

Then he added absently, as though talking to someone unseen, "We'll just hold you on an open charge till you do."

And his lips hadn't moved at all.

The boy licked his own lips, feeling a dryness coming into his throat and a tightening in his stomach. "We seen this boobatch with his collar turned inside out cash'n his check by Konstanty Stachula's Tonsorial Palace of Art on Division. So I followed him a way, that was all. Just break'n the old monotony was all. Just a notion, you might say, that come over me. I'm just a neighborhood kid, Captain."

He stopped as though he had finished the story. Kozak glanced over the boy's shoulder at the arresting officers and Lefty began again hurriedly.

"Ever' once in a while he'd pull a little single-shot of Scotch out of his pocket, stop a second t' toss it down, 'n toss the bottle at the car tracks. I picked up a bottle that didn't bust but there wasn't a spider left in 'er, the boobatch'd drunk her dry. 'N do you know, he had his pockets *full* of them little bottles? 'Stead of buyin' hisself a fifth in the first place. Can't understand a man who'll buy liquor that way. Right before the corner of Walton 'n Noble he popped into a hallway. That was Chiney-Eye-the-Princinct-Captain's hallway, so I popped right in after him. Me'n Chiney-Eye 'r just like that." The boy crossed two fingers of his left hand and asked innocently, "Has the alderman been in to straighten this out, Captain?"

"What time was all this, Lefty?"

"Well, some of the street lamps was lit awready 'n I didn't see nobody either way down Noble. It'd just started spitt'n a little snow 'n I couldn't see clear down Walton account of Wojciechowski's Tavern bein' in the way. He was a old guy, a dino you. He couldn't speak a word of English. But he started in cryin' about how every time he gets a little drunk the same old thing happens to him 'n he's gettin' fed up, he lost his last three checks in the very same hallway 'n it's gettin' so his family don't believe him no more . . ."

Lefty paused, realizing that his tongue was going faster than his brain. He unfolded his arms and shoved them down his pants pockets; the pants were turned up at the cuffs and the cuffs were frayed. He drew a colorless cap off his hip pocket and stood clutching it in his left hand.

"I didn't take him them other times, Captain," he anticipated Kozak.

"Who did?"

Silence.

"What's Benkowski doin' for a livin' these days, Lefty?"

"Just nutsin' around."

"What's Nowogrodski up to?"

"Goes wolfin' on roller skates by Riverview. The rink's open all year round."

"Does he have much luck?"

"Never turns up a hair. They go by too fast."

"What's that evil-eye up to?"

Silence.

"You know who I mean. Idzikowski."

"The Finger?"

"You know who I mean. Don't stall."

"He's hexin' fights, I heard."

"Seen Kodadek lately?"

"I guess. A week 'r two 'r a month ago."

"What was *he* up to?"

"Sir?"

"What was Kodadek doin' the last time you seen him?"

"You mean Dropkick? He was nutsin' around."

"Does he nuts around drunks in hallways?"

Somewhere in the room a small clock or wrist watch began ticking distinctly.

"Nutsin' around ain't jackrollin'."

"You mean Dropkick ain't a jackroller but you are."

The boy's blond lashes shuttered his eyes.

"All right, get ahead with your lyin' a little faster."

Kozak's head came down almost neckless onto his shoulders, and his face was molded like a flatiron, the temples narrow and the jaws rounded. Between the jaws and the open collar, against the graying hair of the chest, hung a tiny crucifix, slender and golden, a shade lighter than his tunic's golden buttons.

"I told him I wasn't gonna take his check, I just needed a little change, I'd pay it back someday. But maybe he didn't understand. He kept hollerin' how he lost his last check, please to let him keep this one. 'Why you drink'n it all up, then,' I put it to him, 'if you're that anxious to hold onto it?' He gimme a foxy grin then 'n pulls out four of them little bottles from four different pockets, 'n each one was a different kind of liquor. I could have one, he tells me in Polish, which do I want, 'n I slapped all four out of his hands. All four. I don't like to see no full-grown man drinkin' that way. A Polak hillbilly he was, 'n certain'y no citizen.

"'Now let me have that change,' I asked him, 'n that wasn't so much t' ask. I don't go around just lookin' fer trouble, Captain. 'N my feet was slop-full of water 'n snow. I'm just a neighborhood fella. But he acted like I was gonna kill him 'r somethin'. I got one hand over his mouth 'n a half nelson behind him 'n talked polite-like in Polish in his ear, 'n he begun sweatin' 'n tryin' t' wrench away on me. 'Take it easy,' I asked him. 'Be reas'nable, we're both in this up to our necks now.' 'N he wasn't drunk no more then, 'n he was plenty t' hold onto. You wouldn't think a old boobatch like that'd have so much stren'th left in him, boozin' down Division night after night, year after year, like he didn't have no home to go to. He pulled my hand off his mouth 'n started hollerin', '*Mlody bandyta! Mlody bandyta!*' 'n I could feel him slippin'. He was just too strong fer a kid like me to hold—"

"Because you were reach'n for his wallet with the other hand?"

"Oh no. The reason I couldn't hold him was my right hand had the nelson 'n I'm not so strong there like in my left 'n even my left ain't what it was before I thrun it out pitchin' that double-header."

"So you kept the rod in your left hand?"

The boy hesitated. Then: "Yes sir." And felt a single drop of sweat slide down his side from under his armpit. Stop and slide again down to the belt.

"What did you get off him?"

"I tell you, I had my hands too full to get *anythin'*—that's just what I been tryin' to tell you. I didn't get so much as one of them little single-shots for all my trouble."

"How many slugs did you fire?"

"Just one, Captain. That was all there was in 'er. I didn't really fire, though. Just at his feet. T' scare him so's he wouldn't jump me. I fired in self-defense. I just wanted to get out of there." He glanced helplessly around at Comiskey and Adamovitch. "You do crazy things sometimes, fellas—well, that's all I was doin'."

The boy caught his tongue and stood mute. In the silence of the query room there was only the scraping of the reporter's pencil and the unseen wrist watch. "I'll ask Chiney-Eye if it's legal, a reporter takin' down a confession, that's my out," the boy thought desperately, and added aloud, before he could stop himself: "'N beside I had to show him—"

"Show him what, son?"

Silence.

"Show him what, Left-hander?"

"That I wasn't just another greenhorn sprout like he thought."

"Did he say you were just a sprout?"

"No. But I c'd tell. Lot of people think I'm just a green kid. I show 'em. I guess I showed 'em now all right." He felt he should be apologizing for something and couldn't tell whether it was for strong-arming a man or for failing to strong-arm him.

"I'm just a neighborhood kid. I belonged to the Keep-Our-City-Clean Club at St. John Cant'us. I told him polite-like, like a Polish-American citizen, this was Chiney-Eye-a-Friend-of-Mine's hallway. 'No more after this one,' I told him. 'This is your last time gettin' rolled, old man. After this I'm pertectin' you, I'm seein' to it nobody touches you—but the people who live here don't like this sort of thing goin' on any more'n you 'r I do. There's gotta be a stop to it, old man—'n we all gotta live, don't we?' That's what I told him in Polish."

Kozak exchanged glances with the prim-faced reporter from the *Chicagoski*, who began cleaning his black tortoise-shell spectacles hurriedly yet delicately, with the fringed tip of his cravat. They depended from a black ribbon; he snapped them back onto his beak.

"You shot him in the groin, Lefty. He's dead."

The reporter leaned slightly forward, but perceived no special reaction and so relaxed. A pretty comfy old chair for a dirty old police station, he thought lifelessly. Kozak shaded his eyes with his gloved hand and looked down at his charge sheet. The night lamp on the desk was still lit, as though he had been working all night; as the morning grew lighter behind him lines came out below his eyes, black as though packed with soot, and a curious droop came to the St. Bernard mouth.

"You shot him through the groin—zip." Kozak's voice came, flat and unemphatic, reading from the charge sheet as though without understanding. "Five children. Stella, Mary, Grosha, Wanda, Vincent. Thirteen, ten, six, six, and one two months. Mother invalided since last birth, name of Rose. WPA fifty-five dollars. You told the truth about *that*, at least."

Lefty's voice came in a shout: "You know *what*? That bullet must of bounced, that's what!"

"Who was along?"

"I was singlin'. Lone-wolf stuff." His voice possessed the first faint touch of fear.

"You said, 'We seen the man.' Was he a big man? How big a man was he?"

"I'd judge two hunerd twenty pounds," Comiskey offered, "at least. Fifty pounds heavier 'n this boy, just about. 'N half a head taller."

"Who's 'we,' Left-hander?"

"Captain, I said, 'We seen.' Lots of people, fellas, seen him is all I meant, cashin' his check by Stachula's when the place was crowded. Konstanty cashes checks if he knows you. Say, I even know the project that old man was on, far as that goes, because my old lady wanted we should give up the store so's I c'd get on it. But it was just me done it, Captain."

The raccoon coat readjusted his glasses. He would say something under a by-line like "This correspondent has never seen a colder gray than that in the eye of the wanton killer who arrogantly styles himself the *lone wolf of Potomac Street*." He shifted uncomfortably, wanting to get farther from the wall radiator but disliking to rise and push the heavy chair.

"Where was that bald-headed pal of yours all this time?"

"Don't know the fella, Captain. Nobody got hair any more around the neighborhood, it seems. The whole damn Triangle went 'n got army haircuts by Stachula's."

"Just you 'n Benkowski, I mean. Don't be afraid, son—we're not tryin' to ring in anythin' you done afore this. Just this one you were out cowboyin' with Benkowski on; were you help'n him 'r was he help'n you? Did you 'r him have the rod?"

Lefty heard a Ford V-8 pull into the rear of the station, and a moment later the splash of the gas as the officers refueled. Behind him he could hear Milano's heavy breathing. He looked down at his shoes, carefully buttoned all the way up and tied with a double bowknot. He'd have to have new laces mighty soon or else start tying them with a single bow.

"That Benkowski's sort of a toothless monkey used to go on at the City Garden at around a hundred an' eighteen pounds, ain't he?"

"Don't know the fella well enough t' say."

"Just from seein' him fight once 'r twice is all. 'N he wore a mouthpiece, I couldn't tell about his teeth. Seems to me he came in about one thirty-three, if he's the same fella you're thinkin' of, Captain."

"I guess you fought at the City Garden once 'r twice yourself, ain't you?"

"Oh, once 'r twice."

"How'd you make out, Left'?"

"Won 'em both on K.O.s. Stopped both fights in the first. One was against that boogie from the Savoy. If he woulda got up I woulda killed him fer life. Fer Christ I would. I didn't know I could hit like I can."

"With Benkowski in your corner both times?"

"Oh no, sir."

"That's a bloodsuck'n lie. I seen him in your corner with my own eyes the time you won off Cooney from the C.Y.O. He's your manager, jackroller."

"I didn't say he wasn't."

"You said he wasn't secondin' you."

"He don't."

"Who does?"

"The Finger."

"You told me the Finger was your hex-man. Make up your mind."

"He does both, Captain. He handles the bucket 'n sponge 'n in between he fingers the guy I'm fightin', 'n if it's close he fingers the ref 'n judges. Finger, he never losed a fight. He waited for the boogie outside the dressing room 'n pointed him clear to the ring. He win that one for me awright." The boy spun the frayed greenish cap in his hand in a concentric circle about his index finger, remembering a time when the cap was new and had earlaps. The bright checks were all faded now, to the color of worn pavement, and the earlaps were tatters.

"What possessed your mob to get their heads shaved, Lefty?"

"I strong-armed him myself, I'm rugged as a bull." The boy began to swell his chest imperceptibly; when his lungs were quite full he shut his eyes, like swimming under water at the Oak Street beach, and let his breath out slowly, ounce by ounce.

"I didn't ask you that. I asked you what happened to your hair."

Lefty's capricious mind returned abruptly to the word "possessed" that Kozak had employed. That had a randy ring, sort of: "What possessed you boys?"

"I forgot what you just asked me."

"I asked you why you didn't realize it'd be easier for us to catch up with your mob when all of you had your heads shaved."

"I guess we figured there'd be so many guys with heads shaved it'd be harder to catch a finger than if we all had hair. But that was some accident all the same. A fella was gonna lend Ma a barber chair 'n go fifty-fifty with her shavin' all the Polaks on P'tom'c Street right back of the store, for relief tickets. So she started on me, just to show the fellas, but the hair made her sicker 'n ever 'n back of the store's the only place she got to lie down 'n I hadda finish the job myself.

"The fellas begun giv'n me a Christ-awful razzin' then, ever' day. God oh God, wherever I went around the Triangle, all the neighborhood fellas 'n little niducks 'n old-time hoods by the Broken Knuckle, whenever they seen me they was pointin' 'n laughin' 'n sayin', 'Hi, Baldy Bicek!' So I went home 'n got the clippers 'n the first guy I seen was Bibleback Watrobinski, you wouldn't know him. I jumps him 'n pushes the clip right through the middle of his hair—he ain't had a haircut since the alderman got indicted you—'n then he took one look at what I done in the drugstore window 'n we both bust out laughin' 'n laughin', 'n fin'lly Bible says I better finish what I started. So he set down on the curb 'n I finished him. When I got all I could off that way I took him back to the store 'n heated water 'n shaved him close 'n Ma couldn't see the point at all.

"Me 'n Bible prowled around a couple days 'n here come Catfoot Nowogrodski from Fry Street you, out of Stachula's with a spanty-new sideburner haircut 'n a green tie. I grabbed his arms 'n let Bible run it through the middle just like I done him. Then it was Catfoot's turn, 'n we caught Chester Chekhovka fer *him*, 'n fer Chester we got Cowboy Okulanis from by the Nort'western Viaduct you, 'n fer him we got Mustang, 'n fer Mustang we got John from the Joint, 'n fer John we got Snake Baranowski, 'n we kep' right on goin' that way till we was doin' guys we never seen before even, Wallios 'n Greeks 'n a Flip from Clark Street he musta been, walkin' with a white girl we done it to. 'N fin'lly all the sprouts in the Triangle start comin' around with their heads shaved, they want to join up with the Baldheads A.C., they called it. They thought it was a club you.

"It got so a kid with his head shaved could beat up on a bigger kid because the big one'd be a-scared to fight back hard, he thought the Baldheads'd get him. So that's why we changed our name then, that's why we're not the Warriors any more, we're the Baldhead True American Social 'n Athletic Club.

"I played first for the Warriors when I wasn't on the mound," he added cautiously, "'n I'm enterin' the Gold'n Gloves next year 'less I go to collitch instead. I went to St. John Cant'us all the way through. Eight' grade, that is. If I keep on gainin' weight I'll be a hunerd ninety-eight this time next year 'n be five-foot-ten—I'm a fair-size light-heavy right this minute. That's what in England they call a cruiser weight you."

He shuffled a step and made as though to unbutton his shirt to show his proportions. But Adamovitch put one hand on his shoulders and slapped the boy's hand down. He didn't like this kid. This was a low-class Polak. He himself was a high-class Polak because his name was Adamovitch and not Adamowski. This sort of kid kept spoiling things for the high-class Polaks by always showing off instead of just being good citizens like the Irish. That was why the Irish ran the City Hall and Police Department and the Board of Education and the Post Office while the Polaks stayed on relief and got drunk and never got anywhere and had everybody down on them. All they could do like the Irish, old Adamovitch reflected bitterly, was to fight under Irish names to get their ears knocked off at the City Garden.

"That's why I want to get out of this jam," this one was saying beside him. "So's it don't ruin my career in the rope' arena. I'm goin' straight. This has sure been one good lesson fer me. Now I'll go to a big-ten collitch 'n make good you."

Now, if the college-coat asked him, "What big-ten college?" he'd answer something screwy like "The Boozological Stoodent-Collitch." That ought to set Kozak back awhile, they might even send him to a bug doc. He'd have to be careful—not *too* screwy. Just screwy enough to get by without involving Benkowski.

He scuffed his shoes and there was no sound in the close little room save his uneasy scuffling; square-toed boy's shoes, laced with a button-hook. He wanted to look more closely at the reporter but every time he caught the glint of the fellow's glasses he felt awed and would have to drop his eyes; he'd never seen glasses on a string like that before and would have given a great deal to wear them a moment. He took to looking steadily out of the barred window behind Kozak's head, where the January sun was glowing sullenly, like a flame held steadily in a fog. Heard an empty truck clattering east on Chicago, sounding like either a '38 Chevvie or a '37 Ford dragging its safety chain against the car tracks; closed his eyes and imagined sparks flashing from the tracks as the iron struck, bounced, and struck again. The bullet had bounced too. Wow.

"What do you think we ought to do with a man like you, Bicek?"

The boy heard the change from the familiar "Lefty" to "Bicek" with a pang; and the dryness began in his throat again.

"One to fourteen is all I can catch fer manslaughter." He appraised Kozak as coolly as he could.

"You like farm work the next fourteen years? Is that okay with you?"

"I said that's all I could get, at the most. This is a first offense 'n self-defense too. I'll plead the unwritten law."

"Who give you *that* idea?"

"Thought of it myself. Just now. You ain't got a chance to send me over the road 'n you know it."

"We can send you to St. Charles, Bicek. 'N transfer you when you come of age. Unless we can make it first-degree murder."

The boy ignored the latter possibility.

"Why, a few years on a farm'd true me up fine. I planned t' cut out cigarettes 'n whisky anyhow before I turn pro—a farm'd be just the place to do that."

"By the time you're released you'll be thirty-two, Bicek—too late to turn pro then, ain't it?"

"I wouldn't wait that long. Hungry Piontek-from-by-the-Warehouse you, he lammed twice from that St. Charles farm. 'N Hungry don't have all his marbles even. He ain't even a citizen."

"Then let's talk about somethin' you couldn't lam out of so fast 'n easy. Like the chair. Did you know that Bogatski from Noble Street, Bicek? The boy that burned last summer, I mean."

A plain-clothes man stuck his head in

the door and called confidently: "That's the man, Captain. That's the man."

Bicek forced himself to grin good-naturedly. He was getting pretty good, these last couple days, at grinning under pressure. When a fellow got sore he couldn't think straight, he reflected anxiously. And so he yawned in Kozak's face with deliberateness, stretching himself as effortlessly as a cat.

"Captain, I ain't been in serious trouble like this before . . ." he acknowledged, and paused dramatically. He'd let them have it straight from the shoulder now: "So I'm mighty glad to be so close to the alderman. Even if he is indicted."

There. Now they know. He'd told them.

"You talkin' about my brother, Bicek?"

The boy nodded solemnly. Now they knew who they had hold of at last.

The reporter took the cigarette off his ear and hung it on his lower lip. And Adamovitch guffawed.

The boy jerked toward the officer: Adamovitch was laughing openly at him. Then they were all laughing openly at him. He heard their derision, and a red rain danced one moment before his eyes; when the red rain was past, Kozak was sitting back easily, regarding him with the expression of a man who has just been swung at and missed and plans to use the provocation without undue haste. The captain didn't look like the sort who'd swing back wildly or hurriedly. He didn't look like the sort who missed. His complacency for a moment was as unbearable to the boy as Adamovitch's guffaw had been. He heard his tongue going, trying to regain his lost composure by provoking them all.

"Hey, Stingywhiskers!" He turned on the reporter. "Get your Eversharp goin' there, write down I plugged the old rumpot, write down Bicek carries a rod night 'n day 'n don't care where he points it. You, I go around slappin' the crap out of whoever I feel like—"

But they all remained mild, calm, and unmoved: for a moment he feared Adamovitch was going to pat him on the head and say something fatherly in Polish.

"Take it easy, lad," Adamovitch suggested. "You're in the query room. We're here to help you, boy. We want to see you through this thing so's you can get back to pugging. You just ain't letting us help you, son."

Kozak blew his nose as though that were an achievement in itself, and spoke with the false friendliness of the insurance man urging a fleeced customer toward the door.

"Want to tell us where you got that rod now, Lefty?"

"I don't want to tell you anything." His mind was setting hard now, against them all. Against them all in here and all like them outside. And the harder it set, the more things seemed to be all right with Kozak: he dropped his eyes to his charge sheet now and everything was all right with everybody. The reporter shoved his notebook into his pocket and buttoned the top button of his coat as though the questioning were over.

It was all too easy. They weren't going to ask him anything more, and he stood wanting them to. He stood wishing them to threaten, to shake their heads ominously, wheedle and cajole and promise him mercy if he'd just talk about the rod.

"I ain't mad, Captain. I don't blame you men either. It's your job, it's your bread 'n butter to talk tough to us neighborhood fellas—ever'body got to have a racket, 'n yours is talkin' tough." He directed this last at the captain, for Comiskey and Milano had left quietly. But Kozak was studying the charge sheet as though Bruno Lefty Bicek were no longer in the room. Nor anywhere at all.

"I'm still here," the boy said wryly, his lip twisting into a dry and bitter grin.

Kozak looked up, his big, wind-beaten, impassive face looking suddenly to the boy like an autographed pitcher's mitt he had once owned. His glance went past the boy and no light of recognition came into his eyes. Lefty Bicek felt a panic rising in him: a desperate fear that they weren't going to press him about the rod, about the old man, about his feelings. "Don't look at me like I ain't nowheres," he asked. And his voice was struck flat by fear.

Something else! The time he and Dropkick had broken into a slot machine! The time he and Casey had played the attention racket and made four dollars! Something! Anything else!

The reporter lit his cigarette.

"Your case is well disposed of," Kozak said, and his eyes dropped to the charge sheet forever.

"I'm born in this country. I'm educated here—"

But no one was listening to Bruno Lefty Bicek any more.

He watched the reporter leaving with regret—at least the guy could have offered him a drag—and stood waiting for someone to tell him to go somewhere now, shifting uneasily from one foot to the other. Then he started slowly, backward, toward the door: he'd make Kozak tell Adamovitch to grab him. Halfway to the door he turned his back on Kozak.

There was no voice behind him. Was this what "well disposed of" meant? He turned the knob and stepped confidently into the corridor; at the end of the corridor he saw the door that opened into the courtroom, and his heart began shaking his whole body with the impulse to make a run for it. He glanced back and Adamovitch was five yards behind, coming up catfooted like only an old man who has been a citizen-dress man can come up catfooted, just far enough behind and just casual enough to make it appear unimportant whether the boy made a run for it or not.

The Lone Wolf of Potomac Street waited miserably, in the long unlovely corridor, for the sergeant to thrust two fingers through the back of his belt. Didn't they realize that he might have Dropkick and Catfoot and Benkowski with a sub-machine gun in a streamlined cream-colored roadster right down front, that he'd zigzag through the courtroom onto the courtroom fire escape and—swish—down off the courtroom roof three stories with the chopper still under his arm and through the car's roof and into the driver's seat? Like that George Raft did that time he was innocent at the Chopin, and cops like Adamovitch had better start ducking when Lefty Bicek began making a run for it. He felt the fingers thrust overfamiliarly between his shirt and his belt.

A cold draft came down the corridor when the door at the far end opened; with the opening of the door came the smell of disinfectant from the basement cells. Outside, far overhead, the bells of St. John Cantius were beginning. The boy felt the winding steel of the staircase to the basement beneath his feet and heard the whining screech of a Chicago Avenue streetcar as it paused on Ogden for the traffic lights and then screeched on again, as though a cat were caught beneath its back wheels. Would it be snowing out there still? he wondered, seeing the whitewashed basement walls.

"Feel all right son?" Adamovitch asked in his most fatherly voice, closing the cell door while thinking to himself: "The kid don't *feel* guilty is the whole trouble. You got to make them *feel* guilty or they'll never go to church at all. A man who goes to church without feeling guilty for *something* is wasting his time, I say." Inside the cell he saw the boy pause and go down on his knees in the cell's gray light. The boy's head turned slowly toward him, a pious oval in the dimness. Old Adamovitch took off his hat.

"This place'll rot down 'n mold over before Lefty Bicek starts prayin', boobatch. Prays, squeals, 'r bawls. So run along 'n I'll see you in hell with yer back broke. I'm lookin' for my cap I dropped is all."

Adamovitch watched him crawling forward on all fours, groping for the pavement-colored cap; when he saw Bicek find it he put his own hat back on and left feeling vaguely dissatisfied.

He did not stay to see the boy, still on his knees, put his hands across his mouth and stare at the shadowed wall.

Shadows were there within shadows.

"I knew I'd never get to be twenty-one anyhow," Lefty told himself softly at last.

FOR DISCUSSION:

1. What is the significance of the quotation from Whitman which precedes the story? How does this quotation define Algren's attitude toward the social problem described in "A Bottle of Milk for Mother"?

2. Briefly describe Lefty's education, home life, ambitions, and companions. Why does Algren spend so much time on these aspects of Lefty's past?

3. What is the significance of the refer-

ences to the shaved heads of the members of the club to which Lefty belongs?

4. Lefty gives as his motive for the crime, "I had to show him—. . . That I wasn't just another greenhorn sprout like he thought." In what ways are his fight for identity and recognition revealed in his answers to the policemen's questions? How does it account for such romantic improbabilities as his illusion of an escape from the courtroom and his desire to be questioned about previous crimes?

5. Of Polish origin himself, Adamovitch despises Lefty as much for being a "low-class Polak" as for any other reason. Comment on the detective's attitude as a subordinate social theme in the story.

6. Lefty makes several rather pathetic attempts to defend himself against the charges of the police (he considers pleading the unwritten law, hints at political influence with the alderman, expresses a desire to attend college). What is the effect of these inept defenses on the reader?

7. Comment on the meaning of the next to last sentence of the story, "Shadows were there within shadows."

Bartleby the Scrivener

HERMAN MELVILLE

I am a rather elderly man. The nature of my avocations, for the last thirty years, has brought me into more than ordinary contact with what would seem an interesting and somewhat singular set of men, of whom, as yet, nothing, that I know of, has ever been written—I mean, the law-copyists, or scriveners. I have known very many of them, professionally and privately, and, if I pleased, could relate divers histories, at which good-natured gentlemen might smile, and sentimental souls might weep. But I waive the biographies of all other scriveners, for a few passages in the life of Bartleby who was a scrivener, the strangest I ever saw, or heard of. While, of other law-copyists, I might write the complete life, of Bartleby nothing of that sort can be done. I believe that no materials exist, for a full and satisfactory biography of this man. It is an irreparable loss to literature. Bartleby was one of those beings of whom nothing is ascertainable, except from the original sources, and, in his case, those are very small. What my own astonished eyes saw of Bartleby, *that* is all I know of him, except, indeed, one vague report, which will appear in the sequel.

Ere introducing the scrivener, as he first appeared to me, it is fit I make some mention of myself, my *employés*, my business, my chambers, and general surroundings; because some such description is indispensable to an adequate understanding of the chief character about to be presented. Imprimis: I am a man who, from his youth upwards, has been filled with a profound conviction that the easiest way of life is the best. Hence, though I belong to a profession proverbially energetic and nervous, even to turbulence, at times, yet nothing of that sort have I ever suffered to invade my peace. I am one of those unambitious lawyers who never address a jury, or in any way draw down public applause; but, in the cool tranquillity of a snug retreat, do a snug business among rich men's bonds, and mortgages, and title-deeds. All who know me, consider me an eminently *safe* man. The late John Jacob Astor, a personage little given to poetic enthusiasm, had no hesitation in pronouncing my first grand point to be prudence; my next, method. I do not speak it in vanity, but simply record the fact, that I was not unemployed in my profession by the late John Jacob Astor; a name which, I admit, I love to repeat; for it hath a rounded and orbicular sound to it, and rings like unto bullion. I will freely add, that I was not insensible to the late John Jacob Astor's good opinion.

Some time prior to the period at which this little history begins, my avocations had been largely increased. The good old office, now extinct in the State of New York, of a Master in Chancery, had been conferred upon me. It was not a very arduous office, but very pleasantly remunerative. I seldom lose my temper; much more seldom indulge in dangerous indignation at wrongs and outrages; but I must be permitted to be rash here and declare, that I consider the sudden and violent abrogation of the office of Master in Chancery, by the new Constitution, as a —— premature act; inasmuch as I had counted upon a life-lease of the profits, whereas I only received those of a few short years. But this is by the way.

My chambers were up stairs, at No. — Wall Street. At one end, they looked upon the white wall of the interior of a spacious skylight shaft, penetrating the building from top to bottom.

This view might have been considered rather tame than otherwise, deficient in what landscape painters call "life." But, if so, the view from the other end of my chambers offered, at least, a contrast, if nothing more. In that direction, my windows commanded an unobstructed view of a lofty brick wall, black by age and everlasting shade; which wall required no spy-glass to bring out its lurking beauties, but, for the benefit of all near-sighted spectators, was pushed up to within ten feet of my window-panes. Owing to the great height of the surrounding buildings, and my chambers being on the second floor, the interval between this wall and mine not a little resembled a huge square cistern.

At the period just preceding the advent of Bartleby, I had two persons as copyists in my employment, and a promising lad as an office-boy. First, Turkey; second, Nippers; third, Ginger Nut. These may seem names, the like of which are not usually found in the Directory. In truth, they were nicknames, mutually conferred upon each other by my three clerks, and were deemed expressive of their respective persons or characters. Turkey was a short, pursy Englishman, of about my own age—that is, somewhere not far from sixty. In the morning, one might say, his face was of a fine florid hue, but after twelve o'clock, meridian—his dinner hour—it blazed like a grate full of Christmas coals; and continued blazing—but, as it were, with a gradual wane—till six o'clock, P.M., or thereabouts; after which, I saw no more of the proprietor of the face, which, gaining its meridian with the sun, seemed to set with it, to rise, culminate, and decline the following day, with the like regularity and undiminished glory. There are many singular coincidences I have known in the course of my life, not the least among which was the fact, that, exactly when Turkey displayed his fullest beams from his red and radiant countenance, just then, too, at that critical moment, began the daily period when I considered his business capacities as seriously disturbed for the remainder of the twenty-four hours. Not that he was absolutely idle, or averse to business then; far from it. The difficulty was, he was apt to be altogether too energetic. There was a strange, inflamed, flurried, flighty recklessness of activity about him. He would be incautious in dipping his pen into his inkstand. All his blots upon my documents were dropped there after twelve o'clock, meridian. Indeed, not only would he be reckless, and sadly given to making blots in the afternoon, but, some days, he went further, and was rather noisy. At such times, too, his face flamed with augmented blazonry, as if cannel coal had been heaped on anthracite. He made an unpleasant racket with his chair; spilled his sand-box; in mending his pens, impatiently split them all to pieces, and threw them on the floor in a sudden passion; stood up, and leaned over his table, boxing his papers about in a most indecorous manner, very sad to behold in an elderly man like him. Nevertheless, as he was in many ways a most valuable person to me, and all the time before twelve o'clock, meridian, was the quickest, steadiest creature, too, accomplishing a great deal of work in a style not easily to be matched—for these reasons, I was willing to overlook his eccentricities, though, indeed, occasionally, I remonstrated with him. I did this very gently, however, because, though the civilest, nay, the blandest and most reverential of men in the morning, yet, in the afternoon, he was disposed, upon provocation, to be slightly rash with his tongue—in fact, insolent. Now, valuing his morning services as I did, and resolved not to lose them—yet, at the same time, made uncomfortable by his inflamed ways after twelve o'clock—and being a man of peace, unwilling by my admonitions to call forth unseemly retorts from him, I took upon me, one Saturday noon (he was always worse on Saturdays) to hint to him, very kindly, that, perhaps, now that he was growing old, it might be well to abridge his labors; in short, he need not come to my chambers after twelve o'clock, but, dinner over, had best go home to his lodgings, and rest himself till tea-time. But no; he insisted upon his afternoon devotions. His countenance became intolerably fervid, as he oratorically assured me—gesticulating with a long ruler at the other end of the room—that if his services in the morning were useful, how indispensable, then, in the afternoon?

"With submission, sir," said Turkey, on this occasion, "I consider myself your right-hand man. In the morning I but marshal and deploy my columns; but in the afternoon I put myself at their head, and gallantly charge the foe, thus"—and he made a violent thrust with the ruler.

"But the blots, Turkey," intimated I.

"True; but, with submission, sir, behold

these hairs! I am getting old. Surely, sir, a blot or two of a warm afternoon is not to be severely urged against gray hairs. Old age —even if it blot the page—is honorable. With submission, sir, we *both* are getting old."

This appeal to my fellow-feeling was hardly to be resisted. At all events, I saw that go he would not. So, I made up my mind to let him stay, resolving, nevertheless, to see to it that, during the afternoon, he had to do with my less important papers.

Nippers, the second on my list, was a whiskered, sallow, and, upon the whole, rather piratical-looking young man, of about five-and-twenty. I always deemed him the victim of two evil powers—ambition and indigestion. The ambition was evinced by a certain impatience of the duties of a mere copyist, an unwarrantable usurpation of strictly professional affairs, such as the original drawing up of legal documents. The indigestion seemed betokened in an occasional nervous testiness and grinning irritability, causing the teeth to audibly grind together over mistakes committed in copying; unnecessary maledictions, hissed, rather than spoken, in the heat of business; and especially by a continual discontent with the height of the table where he worked. Though of a very ingenious mechanical turn, Nippers could never get this table to suit him. He put chips under it, blocks of various sorts, bits of pasteboard, and at last went so far as to attempt an exquisite adjustment, by final pieces of folded blotting-paper. But no invention would answer. If, for the sake of easing his back, he brought the table-lid at a sharp angle well up towards his chin, and wrote there like a man using the steep roof of a Dutch house for his desk, then he declared that it stopped the circulation in his arms. If now he lowered the table to his waistbands, and stooped over it in writing, then there was a sore aching in his back. In short, the truth of the matter was, Nippers knew not what he wanted. Or, if he wanted anything, it was to be rid of a scrivener's table altogether. Among the manifestations of his diseased ambition was a fondness he had for receiving visits from certain ambiguous-looking fellows in seedy coats, whom he called his clients. Indeed, I was aware that not only was he, at times, considerable of a ward-politician, but he occasionally did a little business at the justices' courts, and was not unknown on the steps of the Tombs. I have good reason to believe, however, that one individual who called upon him at my chambers, and who, with a grand air, he insisted was his client, was no other than a dun, and the alleged title-deed, a bill. But, with all his failings, and the annoyances he caused me, Nippers, like his compatriot Turkey, was a very useful man to me; wrote a neat, swift hand; and, when he chose, was not deficient in a gentlemanly sort of deportment. Added to this, he always dressed in a gentlemanly sort of way; and so, incidentally, reflected credit upon my chambers. Whereas, with respect to Turkey, I had much ado to keep him from being a reproach to me. His clothes were apt to look oily, and smell of eating-houses. He wore his pantaloons very loose and baggy in summer. His coats were execrable; his hat not to be handled. But while the hat was a thing of indifference to me, inasmuch as his natural civility and deference, as a dependent Englishman, always led him to doff it the moment he entered the room, yet his coat was another matter. Concerning his coats, I reasoned with him; but with no effect. The truth was, I suppose, that a man with so small an income could not afford to sport such a lustrous face and a lustrous coat at one and the same time. As Nippers once observed, Turkey's money went chiefly for red ink. One winter day, I presented Turkey with a highly respectable-looking coat of my own—a padded gray coat, of a most comfortable warmth, and which buttoned straight up from the knee to the neck. I thought Turkey would appreciate the favor, and abate his rashness and obstreperousness of afternoons. But no; I verily believe that buttoning himself up in so downy and blanket-like a coat had a pernicious effect upon him—upon the same principle that too much oats are bad for horses. In fact, precisely as a rash, restive horse is said to feel his oats, so Turkey felt his coat. It made him insolent. He was a man whom prosperity harmed.

Though, concerning the self-indulgent habits of Turkey, I had my own private surmises, yet, touching Nippers, I was well persuaded that, whatever might be his faults in other respects, he was, at least, a temperate young man. But, indeed, nature herself seemed to have been his vintner, and, at his birth, charged him so thoroughly with an irritable, brandy-like disposition, that all subsequent potations were needless. When I consider how, amid the stillness of my chambers, Nippers would sometimes impatiently rise from his seat, and stooping over his table, spread his arms wide apart, seize the whole desk, and move it, and jerk it, with a grim, grinding motion on the floor, as if the table were a perverse voluntary agent, intent on thwarting and vexing him, I plainly perceive that, for Nippers, brandy-and-water were altogether superfluous.

It was fortunate for me that, owing to its peculiar cause—indigestion—the irritability and consequent nervousness of Nippers were mainly observable in the morning, while in the afternoon he was comparatively mild. So that, Turkey's paroxysms only coming on about twelve o'clock, I never had to do with their eccentricities at one time. Their fits relieved each other, like guards. When Nipper's was on, Turkey's was off; and vice versa. This was a good natural arrangement, under the circumstances.

Ginger Nut, the third on my list, was a lad, some twelve years old. His father was a carman, ambitious of seeing his son on the bench instead of a cart, before he died. So he sent him to my office, as student at law, errand-boy, cleaner and sweeper, at the rate of one dollar a week. He had a little desk to himself, but he did not use it much. Upon inspection, the drawer exhibited a great array of the shells of various sorts of nuts. Indeed, to this quick-witted youth, the whole noble science of the law was contained in a nut-shell. Not the least among the employments of Ginger Nut, as well as one which he discharged with the most alacrity, was his duty as cake and apple purveyor for Turkey and Nippers. Copying law-papers being proverbially a dry, husky sort of business, my two scriveners were fain to moisten their mouths very often with Spitzenbergs, to be had at the numerous stalls nigh the Custom House and Post Office. Also, they sent Ginger Nut very frequently for that peculiar cake—small, flat, round, and very spicy—after which he had been named by them. Of a cold morning, when business was but dull, Turkey would gobble up scores of these cakes, as if they were mere wafers—indeed, they sell them at the rate of six or eight for a penny—the scrape of his pen blending with the crunching of the crisp particles in his mouth. Of all the fiery afternoon blunders and flurried rashness of Turkey, was his once moistening a ginger-cake between his lips, and clapping it on to a mortgage, for a seal. I came within an ace of dismissing him then. But he mollified me by making an oriental bow, and saying—

"With submission, sir, it was generous of me to find you in stationery on my own account."

Now my original business—that of a conveyancer and title hunter, and drawer-up of recondite documents of all sorts—was considerably increased by receiving the Master's office. There was now great work for scriveners. Not only must I push the clerks already with me, but I must have additional help.

In answer to my advertisement, a motionless young man one morning stood upon my office threshold, the door being open, for it was summer. I can see that figure now —pallidly neat, pitiably respectable, incurably forlorn! It was Bartleby.

After a few words touching his qualifications, I engaged him, glad to have among my corps of copyists a man of so singularly sedate an aspect, which I thought might operate beneficially upon the flighty temper of Turkey, and the fiery one of Nippers.

I should have stated before that ground-glass folding-doors divided my premises into two parts, one of which was occupied by my scriveners, the other by myself. According to my humor, I threw open these doors, or closed them. I resolved to assign Bartleby a corner by the folding-doors, but on my side of them, so as to have this quiet man within easy call, in case any trifling thing was to be done. I placed his desk close up to a small side-window in that part of the room, a window which originally had afforded a lateral view of certain grimy brick-yards and bricks, but which, owing to subsequent erections, commanded at present no view at all, though it gave some light. Within three feet of the panes was a wall, and the light came down from far above, between two lofty buildings, as from a very small opening in a dome. Still further to a satisfactory arrangement, I procured a high green folding screen, which might entirely isolate Bartleby from my sight, though not remove him from my voice. And thus, in a manner, privacy and society were conjoined.

At first, Bartleby did an extraordinary quantity of writing. As if long famishing for something to copy, he seemed to gorge himself on my documents. There was no pause for digestion. He ran a day and night line, copying by sunlight and by candle-light. I should have been quite delighted with his application, had he been cheerfully industrious. But he wrote on silently, palely, mechanically.

It is, of course, an indispensable part of a scrivener's business to verify the accuracy of his copy, word by word. Where there are two or more scriveners in an office, they assist each other in this examination, one reading from the copy, the other holding the original. It is a very dull, wearisome, and lethargic affair. I can readily imagine that, to some sanguine temperaments, it would be altogether intolerable. For example, I cannot credit that the mettlesome poet, Byron, would have contentedly sat down with Bartleby to examine a law document of, say five hundred pages, closely written in a crimpy hand.

Now and then, in the haste of business, it had been my habit to assist in comparing some brief document myself, calling Turkey or Nippers for this purpose. One object I had, in placing Bartleby so handy to me behind the screen, was, to avail myself of his services on such trivial occasions. It was on the third day, I think, of his being with me, and before any necessity had arisen for having his own writing examined, that, being much hurried to complete a small affair I had in hand, I abruptly called to Bartleby. In my haste and natural expectancy of instant compliance, I sat with my head bent over the original on my desk, and my right hand sideways, and somewhat nervously extended with the copy, so that, immediately upon emerging from his retreat, Bartleby might snatch it and proceed to business without the least delay.

In this very attitude did I sit when I called to him, rapidly stating what it was I wanted him to do—namely, to examine a small paper with me. Imagine my surprise, nay, my consternation, when, without moving from his privacy, Bartleby, in a singularly mild, firm voice, replied, "I would prefer not to."

I sat awhile in perfect silence, rallying my stunned faculties. Immediately it occurred to me that my ears had deceived me, or Bartleby had entirely misunderstood my meaning. I repeated my request in the clearest tone I could assume; but in quite as clear a one came the previous reply, "I would prefer not to."

"Prefer not to," echoed I, rising in high excitement, and crossing the room with a stride. "What do you mean? Are you moonstruck? I want you to help me compare this sheet here—take it," and I thrust it towards him.

"I would prefer not to," said he.

I looked at him steadfastly. His face was leanly composed; his gray eye dimly calm. Not a wrinkle of agitation rippled him. Had there been the least uneasiness, anger, impatience or impertinence in his manner; in other words, had there been anything ordinarily human about him, doubtless I should have violently dismissed him from the premises. But as it was, I should have as soon thought of turning my pale plaster-of-paris bust of Cicero out of doors. I stood gazing at him awhile, as he went on with his own writing, and then reseated myself at my desk. This is very strange, thought I. What had one best do? But my business hurried me. I concluded to forget the matter for the present, reserving it for my future leisure. So, calling Nippers from the other room, the paper was speedily examined.

A few days after this, Bartleby concluded four lengthy documents, being quadruplicates of a week's testimony taken before me in my High Court of Chancery. It became necessary to examine them. It was an important suit, and great accuracy was imperative. Having all things arranged, I called Turkey, Nippers and Ginger Nut, from the next room, meaning to place the four copies in the hands of my four clerks, while I should read from the original. Accordingly, Turkey, Nippers, and Ginger Nut had taken their seats in a row, each with his document in his hand, when I called to Bartleby to join this interesting group.

"Bartleby! quick, I am waiting."

I heard a slow scrape of his chair legs on the uncarpeted floor, and soon he appeared standing at the entrance of his hermitage.

"What is wanted?" said he, mildly.

"The copies, the copies," said I, hurriedly. "We are going to examine them. There"—and I held towards him the fourth quadruplicate.

"I would prefer not to," he said, and gently disappeared behind the screen.

For a few moments I was turned into a pillar of salt, standing at the head of my seated column of clerks. Recovering myself, I advanced towards the screen, and demanded the reason for such extraordinary conduct.

"Why do you refuse?"

"I would prefer not to."

With any other man I should have flown outright into a dreadful passion, scorned all further words, and thrust him ignominiously from my presence. But there was something about Bartleby that not only strangely disarmed me, but, in a wonderful manner, touched and disconcerted me. I began to reason with him.

"These are your own copies we are about to examine. It is labor saving to you, because one examination will answer for your four papers. It is common usage. Every copyist is bound to help examine his copy. Is it not so? Will you not speak? Answer!"

"I prefer not to," he replied in a flutelike tone. It seemed to me that, while I had been addressing him, he carefully revolved every statement that I made; fully comprehended the meaning; could not gainsay the irresistible conclusion; but, at the same time, some paramount consideration prevailed with him to reply as he did.

"You are decided, then, not to comply with my request—a request made according to common usage and common sense?"

He briefly gave me to understand, that on that point my judgment was sound. Yes: his decision was irreversible.

It is not seldom the case that, when a man is browbeaten in some unprecedented and violently unreasonable way, he begins to stagger in his own plainest faith. He begins, as it were, vaguely to surmise that, wonderful as it may be, all the justice and all the reason is on the other side. Accordingly, if any disinterested persons are present, he turns to them for some reinforcement for his own faltering mind.

"Turkey," said I, "what do you think of this? Am I not right?"

"With submission, sir," said Turkey, in his blandest tone, "I think that you are."

"Nippers," said I, "what do you think of it?"

"I think I should kick him out of the office."

(The reader of nice perceptions will here perceive that, it being morning, Turkey's answer is couched in polite and tranquil terms, but Nippers replies in ill-tempered ones. Or, to repeat a previous sentence, Nipper's ugly mood was on duty, and Turkey's off.)

"Ginger Nut," said I, willing to enlist the smallest suffrage in my behalf, "what do you think of it?"

"I think, sir, he's a little *luny*," replied Ginger Nut, with a grin.

"You hear what they say," said I, turning towards the screen, "come forth and do your duty."

But he vouchsafed no reply. I pondered a moment in sore perplexity. But once more business hurried me. I determined again to postpone the consideration of this dilemma to my future leisure. With a little trouble we made out to examine the papers without Bartleby, though at every page or two Turkey deferentially dropped his opinion, that this proceeding was quite out of the common; while Nippers, twitching in his chair with a dyspeptic nervousness, ground out, between his set teeth, occasional hissing maledictions against the stubborn oaf behind the screen. And for his (Nipper's) part, this was the first and the last time he would do another man's business without pay.

Meanwhile Bartleby sat in his hermitage, oblivious to everything but his own peculiar business there.

Some days passed, the scrivener being employed upon another lengthy work. His late remarkable conduct led me to regard his ways narrowly. I observed that he never went to dinner; indeed, that he never went anywhere. As yet I had never, of my personal knowledge, known him to be outside of my office. He was a perpetual sentry in the corner. At about eleven o'clock though, in the morning, I noticed that Ginger Nut would advance toward the opening in Bartleby's screen, as if silently beckoned thither by a gesture invisible to me where I sat. The boy would then leave the office, jingling a few pence, and reappear with a handful of ginger-nuts, which he delivered in the hermitage, receiving two of the cakes for his trouble.

He lives, then, on ginger-nuts, thought I; never eats a dinner, properly speaking; he must be a vegetarian, then, but no; he never eats even vegetables, he eats nothing but ginger-nuts. My mind then ran on in reveries concerning the probable effects upon the human constitution of living entirely on ginger-nuts. Ginger-nuts are so called, because they contain ginger as one of their peculiar constituents, and the final flavoring one. Now, what was ginger? A hot, spicy thing. Was Bartleby hot and spicy? Not at all. Ginger, then, had no effect upon Bartleby. Probably he preferred it should have none.

Nothing so aggravates an earnest person as a passive resistance. If the individual so resisted be of a not inhumane temper, and the resisting one perfectly harmless in his passivity, then, in the better moods of the former, he will endeavor charitably to construe to his imagination what proves impossible to be solved by his judgment. Even so, for the most part, I regarded Bartleby and his ways. Poor fellow! thought I, he means no mischief; it is plain he intends no insolence; his aspect sufficiently evinces that his eccentricities are involuntary. He is useful to me. I can get along with him. If I turn him away, the chances are he will fall in with some less indulgent employer, and then he will be rudely treated, and perhaps driven forth miserably to starve. Yes. Here I can cheaply purchase a delicious self-approval. To befriend Bartleby; to humor him in his strange wilfulness, will cost me little or nothing, while I lay up in my soul what will eventually prove a sweet morsel for my conscience. But this mood was not invariable with me. The passiveness of Bartleby sometimes irritated me. I felt strangely goaded on to encounter him in new opposition—to elicit some angry spark from him answerable to my own. But, indeed, I might as well have essayed to strike fire with my knuckles against a bit of Windsor soap. But one afternoon the evil impulse in me mastered me, and the following little scene ensued:

"Bartleby," said I, "when those papers are all copied, I will compare them with you."

"I would prefer not to."

"How? Surely you do not mean to persist in that mulish vagary?"

No answer.

I threw open the folding-doors near by, and, turning upon Turkey and Nippers, exclaimed:

"Bartleby a second time says, he won't examine his papers. What do you think of it, Turkey?"

It was afternoon, be it remembered. Turkey sat glowing like a brass boiler; his bald head steaming; his hands reeling among his blotted papers.

"Think of it?" roared Turkey. "I think I'll just step behind his screen, and black his eyes for him!"

So saying, Turkey rose to his feet and threw his arms into a pugilistic position. He was hurrying away to make good his promise, when I detained him, alarmed at the effect of incautiously rousing Turkey's combativeness after dinner.

"Sit down, Turkey," said I, "and hear what Nippers has to say. What do you think of it, Nippers? Would I not be justified in immediately dismissing Bartleby?"

"Excuse me, that is for you to decide, sir. I think his conduct quite unusual, and, indeed, unjust, as regards Turkey and myself. But it may only be a passing whim."

"Ah," exclaimed I, "you have strangely changed your mind, then—you speak very gently of him now."

"All beer," cried Turkey; "gentleness is effects of beer—Nippers and I dined together to-day. You see how gentle *I* am, sir. Shall I go and black his eyes?"

"You refer to Bartleby, I suppose. No, not to-day, Turkey," I replied; "pray, put up your fists."

I closed the doors, and again advanced towards Bartleby. I felt additional incentives tempting me to my fate. I burned to be rebelled against again. I remembered that Bartleby never left the office.

"Bartleby," said I, "Ginger Nut is away; just step around to the Post Office, won't you?" (it was but a three minutes' walk) "and see if there is anything for me."

"I would prefer not to."

"You *will* not?"

"I *prefer* not."

I staggered to my desk, and sat there in a deep study. My blind inveteracy returned. Was there any other thing in which I could procure myself to be ignominiously repulsed by this lean, penniless wight?—my hired clerk? What added thing is there, perfectly reasonable, that he will be sure to refuse to do?

"Bartleby!"

No answer.

"Bartleby," in a louder tone.

No answer.

"Bartleby," I roared.

Like a very ghost, agreeably to the laws of magical invocation, at the third summons, he appeared at the entrance of his hermitage.

"Go to the next room, and tell Nippers to come to me."

"I prefer not to," he respectfully and slowly said, and mildly disappeared.

"Very good, Bartleby," said I, in a quiet sort of serenely-severe self-possessed tone, intimating the unalterable purpose of some terrible retribution very close at hand. At the moment I half intended something of the kind. But upon the whole, as it was drawing towards my dinner-hour, I thought it best to put on my hat and walk home for the day, suffering much from perplexity and distress of mind.

Shall I acknowledge it? The conclusion of this whole business was, that it soon became a fixed fact of my chambers, that a pale young scrivener, by the name of Bartleby, had a desk there; that he copied for me at the usual rate of four cents a folio (one hundred words); but he was permanently exempt from examining the work done by him, that duty being transferred to Turkey and Nippers, out of compliment, doubtless, to their superior acuteness; moreover, said Bartleby was never, on any account, to be dispatched on the most trivial errand of any sort; and that even if entreated to take upon him such a matter, it was generally understood that he would "prefer not to"—in other words, that he would refuse point-blank.

As days passed on, I became considerably reconciled to Bartleby. His steadiness, his freedom from all dissipation, his incessant industry (except when he chose to throw himself into a standing revery behind his screen), his great stillness, his unalterableness of demeanor under all circumstances, made him a valuable acquisition. One prime thing was this—*he was always there*—first in the morning, continually through the day, and the last at night. I had a singular confidence in his honesty. I felt my most precious papers perfectly safe in his hands. Sometimes, to be sure, I could not, for the very soul of me, avoid falling into sudden spasmodic passions with him. For it was exceeding difficult to bear in mind all the time those strange peculiarities, privileges, and unheard-of exemptions, forming the tacit stipulations on Bartleby's part under which he remained in my office. Now and then, in the eagerness of dispatching pressing business, I would inadvertently summon Bartleby, in a short, rapid tone, to put his finger, say, on the incipient tie of a bit of red tape with which I was about compressing some papers. Of course, from behind the screen the usual answer, "I prefer not to," was sure to come; and then, how could a human creature, with the common infirmities of our nature, refrain from bitterly exclaiming upon such perverseness—such unreasonableness? However, every added repulse of this sort which I received only tended to lessen the probability of my repeating the inadvertence.

Here it must be said, that, according to the custom of most legal gentlemen occupying chambers in densely-populated law buildings, there were several keys to my door. One was kept by a woman residing in the attic, which person weekly scrubbed and daily swept and dusted my apartments. Another was kept by Turkey for convenience sake. The third I sometimes carried in my own pocket. The fourth I knew not who had.

Now, one Sunday morning I happened to go to Trinity Church, to hear a celebrated preacher, and finding myself rather early on the ground I thought I would walk round to my chambers for a while. Luckily I had my key with me; but upon applying it to the lock, I found it resisted by something inserted from the inside. Quite surprised, I called out; when to my consternation a key was turned from within; and thrusting his lean visage at me, and holding the door ajar, the apparition of Bartleby appeared, in his shirt-sleeves, and otherwise in a strangely tattered deshabille, saying quietly that he was sorry, but he was deeply engaged just then, and—preferred not admitting me at present. In a brief word or two, he moreover added, that perhaps I had better walk round the block two or three times, and by that time he would probably have concluded his affairs.

Now, the utterly unsurmised appearance of Bartleby, tenanting my law-chambers of a Sunday morning, with his cadaverously gentlemanly *nonchalance*, yet withal firm and self-possessed, had such a strange effect upon me, that incontinently I slunk away from my own door, and did as desired. But not without sundry twinges of impotent rebellion against the mild effrontery of this unaccountable scrivener. Indeed, it was his wonderful mildness chiefly, which not only disarmed me, but unmanned me, as it were. For I consider that one, for the time, is somehow unmanned when he tranquilly permits his hired clerk to dictate to him, and order him away from his own premises. Furthermore, I was full of uneasiness as to what Bartleby could possibly be doing in my office in his shirt-sleeves, and in an otherwise dismantled condition of a Sunday morning. Was anything amiss going on? Nay, that was out of the question. It was not to be thought of for a moment that Bartleby was an immoral person. But what could he be doing there?—copying? Nay again, whatever might be his eccentricities, Bartleby was an eminently decorous person. He would be the last man to sit down to his desk in any state approaching to nudity. Besides, it was Sunday; and there was something about Bartleby that forbade the supposition that he would by any secular occupation violate the proprieties of the day.

Nevertheless, my mind was not pacified; and full of a restless curiosity, at last I returned to the door. Without hindrance I inserted my key, opened it, and entered. Bartleby was not to be seen. I looked round anxiously, peeped behind his screen; but it was very plain that he was gone. Upon more closely examining the place, I surmised that for an indefinite period Bartleby must have ate, dressed, and slept in my office, and that too without plate, mirror, or bed. The cushioned seat of a rickety old sofa in one corner bore the faint impress of a lean, reclining form. Rolled away under his desk, I found a blanket; under the empty grate, a blacking box and brush; on a chair, a tin basin, with soap and a ragged towel; in a newspaper a few crumbs of ginger-nuts and a morsel of cheese. Yes, thought I, it is evident enough that Bartleby has been making his home here, keeping bachelor's hall all by himself. Immediately then the thought came sweeping across me, what miserable friendlessness and loneliness are here revealed! His poverty is great; but his solitude, how horrible! Think of it. Of a Sunday, Wall Street is deserted as Petra; and every night of every day it is an emptiness. This building, too, which of week-days hums with industry and life, at nightfall echoes with sheer vacancy, and all through Sunday is forlorn. And here Bartleby makes his home; sole spectator of a solitude which he has seen all populous—a sort of innocent and transformed Marius brooding among the ruins of Carthage!

For the first time in my life a feeling of overpowering stinging melancholy seized me. Before, I had never experienced aught but a not unpleasing sadness. The bond of a common humanity now drew me irresistibly to bloom. A fraternal melancholy! For both I and Bartleby were sons of Adam. I remembered the bright silks and sparkling faces I had seen that day, in gala trim, swan-like sailing down the Mississippi of Broadway; and I contrasted them with the pallid copyist, and thought to myself, Ah, happiness courts the light, so we deem the world is gay; but misery hides aloof, so we deem that misery there is none. These sad fancyings—chimeras, doubtless, of a sick and silly brain—led on to other and more special thoughts, concerning the eccentricities of Bartleby. Presentiments of strange discoveries hovered round me. The scrivener's pale form appeared to me laid out, among uncaring strangers, in its shivering winding-sheet.

Suddenly I was attracted by Bartleby's closed desk, the key in open sight left in the lock.

I mean no mischief, seek the gratification of no heartless curiosity, thought I; besides, the desk is mine, and its contents, too, so I will make bold to look within. Everything was methodically arranged, the papers smoothly placed. The pigeon-holes were deep, and removing the files of documents, I groped into their recesses. Presently I felt something there, and dragged it out. It was an old bandanna handkerchief, heavy and knotted. I opened it, and saw it was a saving's bank.

I now recalled all the quiet mysteries which I had noted in the man. I remembered that he never spoke but to answer; that, though at intervals he had considerable time to himself, yet I had never seen him reading—no, not even a newspaper; that for long periods he would stand looking out, at his pale window behind the screen, upon the dead brick wall; I was quite sure he never visited any refectory or eating-house; while his pale face clearly indicated that he never drank beer like Turkey, or tea and coffee even, like other men; that he never went anywhere in particular that I could learn; never went out for a walk, unless, indeed, that was the case at present; that he had declined telling who he was, or whence he came, or whether he had any relatives in the world; that though so thin and pale, he never complained of ill-health. And more than all, I remembered a certain unconscious air of pallid—how shall I call it?—of pallid haughtiness, say, or rather an austere reserve about him, which had positively awed me into my tame compliance with his eccentricities, when I had feared to ask him to do the slightest incidental thing for me, even though I might know, from his long-continued motionlessness, that behind his screen he must be standing in one of those dead-wall reveries of his.

Revolving all these things, and coupling them with the recently discovered fact, that he made my office his constant abiding place and home, and not forgetful of his morbid moodiness; revolving all these things, a prudential feeling began to steal over me. My first emotions had been those of pure melancholy and sincerest pity; but just in proportion as the forlornness of Bartleby grew and grew to my imagination, did that same melancholy merge into fear, that pity into repulsion. So true it is, and so terrible, too, that up to a certain point the thought or sight of misery enlists our best affections; but, in certain special cases, beyond that point it does not. They err who would assert that invariably this is owing to the inherent selfishness of the human heart. It rather proceeds from a certain hopelessness of remedying excessive and organic ill. To a sensitive being, pity is not seldom pain. And when at last it is perceived that such pity cannot lead to effectual succor, common sense bids the soul be rid of it. What I saw that morning persuaded me that the scrivener was the victim of innate and incurable disorder. I might give alms to his body; but his body did not pain him; it was his soul that suffered, and his soul I could not reach.

I did not accomplish the purpose of going to Trinity Church that morning. Somehow, the things I had seen disqualified me for the time from church-going. I walked homeward, thinking what I would do with Bartleby. Finally, I resolved upon this—I would put certain calm questions to him the next morning, touching his history, etc., and if he declined to answer them openly and unreservedly (and I supposed he would prefer not), then to give him a twenty dollar bill over and above whatever I might owe him, and tell him his services were no longer required; but that if in any other way I could assist him, I would be happy to do so, especially if he desired to return to his native place, wherever that might be, I would willingly help to defray the expenses. Moreover, if, after reaching home, he found himself at any time in want of aid, a letter from him would be sure of a reply.

The next morning came.

"Bartleby," said I, gently calling to him behind his screen.

No reply.

"Bartleby," said I, in a still gentler tone, "come here; I am not going to ask you to do anything you would prefer not to do—I simply wish to speak to you."

Upon this he noiselessly slid into view.

"Will you tell me, Bartleby, where you were born?"

"I would prefer not to."

"Will you tell me *anything* about yourself?"

"I would prefer not to."

"But what reasonable objection can you have to speak to me? I feel friendly towards you."

He did not look at me while I spoke, but kept his glance fixed upon my bust of Cicero, which, as I then sat, was directly behind me, some six inches above my head.

"What is your answer, Bartleby?" said I, after waiting a considerable time for a reply, during which his countenance remained immovable, only there was the faintest conceivable tremor of the white attenuated mouth.

"At present I prefer to give no answer," he said, and retired into his hermitage.

It was rather weak in me I confess, but his manner, on this occasion, nettled me. Not only did there seem to lurk in it a certain calm disdain, but his perverseness seemed ungrateful, considering the undeniable good usage and indulgence he had received from me.

Again I sat ruminating what I should do. Mortified as I was at his behavior, and resolved as I had been to dismiss him when I entered my office, nevertheless I strangely felt something superstitious knocking at my heart, and forbidding me to carry out my purpose, and denouncing me for a villain if I dared to breathe one bitter word against this forlornest of mankind. At last, familiarly drawing my chair behind his screen, I sat down and said: "Bartleby, never mind, then, about revealing your history; but let me entreat you, as a friend, to comply as far as may be with the usages of this office. Say now, you will help to examine papers to-morrow or next day: in short, say now, that in a day or two you will begin to be a little reasonable:—say so, Bartleby."

"At present I would prefer not to be a little reasonable," was his mildly cadaverous reply.

Just then the folding-doors opened, and Nippers approached. He seemed suffering from an unusually bad night's rest, induced by severer indigestion than common. He overheard those final words of Bartleby.

"Prefer not, eh?" gritted Nippers—"I'd prefer him, if I were you, sir," addressing me—"I'd prefer him; I'd give him preferences, the stubborn mule! What is it, sir, pray, that he prefers not to do now?"

Bartleby moved not a limb.

"Mr. Nippers," said I, "I'd prefer that you would withdraw for the present."

Somehow, of late, I had got into the way of involuntarily using this word "prefer" upon all sorts of not exactly suitable occasions. And I trembled to think that my contact with the scrivener had already and seriously affected me in a mental way. And what further and deeper aberration might it not yet produce? This apprehension had not been without efficacy in determining me to summary measures.

As Nippers, looking very sour and sulky, was departing, Turkey blandly and deferentially approached.

"With submission, sir," said he, "yesterday I was thinking about Bartleby here, and I think that if he would but prefer to take a quart of good ale every day, it would do much towards mending him, and enabling him to assist in examining his papers."

"So you have got the word, too," said I, slightly excited.

"With submission, what word, sir?" asked Turkey, respectfully crowding himself into the contracted space behind the screen, and by so doing, making me jostle the scrivener. "What word, sir?"

"I would prefer to be left alone here," said Bartleby, as if offended at being mobbed in his privacy.

"That's the word, Turkey," said I—"that's it."

"Oh, prefer? oh yes—queer word. I never use it myself. But, sir, as I was saying, if he would but prefer—"

"Turkey," interrupted I, "you will please withdraw."

"Oh certainly, sir, if you prefer that I should."

As he opened the folding-door to retire, Nippers at his desk caught a glimpse of me, and asked whether I would prefer to have a certain paper copied on blue paper or white. He did not in the least roguishly accent the word "prefer." It was plain that it involuntarily rolled from his tongue. I thought to myself, surely I must get rid of a demented man, who already has in some degree turned the tongues, if not the heads of myself and clerks. But I thought it prudent not to break the dismission at once.

The next day I noticed that Bartleby did nothing but stand at his window in his dead-wall revery. Upon asking him why he did not write, he said that he had decided upon doing no more writing.

"Why, how now? what next?" exclaimed I, "do no more writing?"

"No more."

"And what is the reason?"

"Do you not see the reason for yourself?" he indifferently replied.

I looked steadfastly at him, and perceived that his eyes looked dull and glazed. Instantly it occurred to me, that his unexampled diligence in copying by his dim window for the first few weeks of his stay with me might have temporarily impaired his vision.

I was touched. I said something in condolence with him. I hinted that of course he did wisely in abstaining from writing for a while; and urged him to embrace that opportunity of taking wholesome exercise in the open air. This, however, he did not do. A few days after this, my other clerks being absent, and being in a great hurry to dispatch certain letters by the mail, I thought that, having nothing else earthly to do, Bartleby would surely be less inflexible than usual, and carry these letters to the post-office. But he blankly declined. So, much to my inconvenience, I went myself.

Still added days went by. Whether Bartleby's eyes improved or not, I could not say. To all appearance, I thought they did. But when I asked him if they did, he vouchsafed no answer. At all events, he would do no copying. At last, in reply to my urgings, he informed me that he had permanently given up copying.

"What!" exclaimed I; "suppose your eyes should get entirely well—better than ever before—would you not copy then?"

"I have given up copying," he answered, and slid aside.

He remained as ever, a fixture in my chamber. Nay—if that were possible—he became still more of a fixture than before. What was to be done? He would do nothing in the office; why should he stay there? In plain fact, he had now become a millstone to me, not only useless as a necklace, but afflictive to bear. Yet I was sorry for him. I speak less than truth when I say that, on his own account, he occasioned me uneasiness. If he would but have named a single relative or friend, I would instantly have written, and urged their taking the poor fellow away to some convenient retreat. But he seemed alone, absolutely alone in the universe. A bit of wreck in the mid-Atlantic. At length, necessities connected with my business tyrannized over all other considerations. Decently as I could, I told Bartleby that in six days' time he must unconditionally leave the office. I warned him to take measures, in the interval, for procuring some other abode. I offered to assist him in this endeavor, if he himself would but take the first step towards a removal. "And when you finally quit me, Bartleby," added I, "I shall see that you go not away entirely unprovided. Six days from this hour, remember."

At the expiration of that period, I peeped behind the screen, and lo! Bartleby was there.

I buttoned up my coat, balanced myself; advanced slowly towards him, touched his shoulder, and said, "The time has come; you must quit this place; I am sorry for you; here is money; but you must go."

"I would prefer not," he replied, with his back still towards me.

"You *must*."

He remained silent.

Now I had an unbounded confidence in this man's common honesty. He had frequently restored to me sixpences and shillings carelessly dropped upon the floor, for I am apt to be very reckless in such shirt-button affairs. The proceeding, then, which followed will not be deemed extraordinary.

"Bartleby," said I, "I owe you twelve dollars on account; here are thirty-two; the odd twenty are yours—Will you take it?" and I handed the bills towards him.

But he made no motion.

"I will leave them here, then," putting them under a weight on the table. Then taking my hat and cane and going to the door, I tranquilly turned and added—"After you have removed your things from these offices, Bartleby, you will of course lock the door—since every one is now gone for the day but you—and if you please, slip your key underneath the mat, so that I may have it in the morning. I shall not see you again; so good-bye to you. If, hereafter, in your new place of abode, I can be of any service to you, do not fail to advise me by letter. Good-bye, Bartleby, and fare you well."

But he answered not a word; like the last column of some ruined temple, he remained standing mute and solitary in the middle of the otherwise deserted room.

As I walked home in a pensive mood, my vanity got the better of my pity. I could not but highly plume myself on my masterly management in getting rid of Bartleby. Masterly I call it, and such it must appear to any dispassionate thinker. The beauty of my procedure seemed to consist in its perfect quietness. There was no vulgar bullying, no bravado of any sort, no choleric hectoring, and striding to and fro across the apartment, jerking out vehement commands for Bartleby to bundle himself off with his beggarly traps. Nothing of the kind. Without loudly bidding Bartleby depart—as an inferior genius might have done—I *assumed* the ground that depart he must; and upon that assumption built all I had to say. The more I thought over my procedure, the more I was charmed with it. Nevertheless, next morning, upon awakening, I had my doubts—I had somehow slept off the fumes of vanity. One of the coolest and wisest hours a man has, is just after he awakes in the morning. My procedure seemed as sagacious as ever—but only in theory. How it would prove in practice—there was the rub. It was truly a beautiful thought to have assumed Bartleby's departure; but, after all, that assumption was simply my own, and none of Bartleby's. The great point was, not whether I had assumed that he would quit me, but whether he would prefer so to do. He was more a man of preferences than assumptions.

After breakfast, I walked down town, arguing the probabilities *pro and con*. One moment I thought it would prove a miserable failure, and Bartleby would be found all alive at my office as usual; the next moment it seemed certain that I should find his chair empty. And so I kept veering about. At the corner of Broadway and Canal Street, I saw quite an excited group of people standing in earnest conversation.

"I'll take odds he doesn't," said a voice as I passed.

"Doesn't go?—done!" said I, "put up your money."

I was instinctively putting my hand in my pocket to produce my own, when I remembered that this was an election day. The words I had overheard bore no reference to Bartleby, but to the success or nonsuccess of some candidate for the mayoralty. In my intent frame of mind, I had, as it were, imagined that all Broadway shared in my excitement, and were debating the same question with me. I passed on, very thankful that the uproar of the street screened my momentary absent-mindedness.

As I had intended, I was earlier than usual at my office door. I stood listening for a moment. All was still. He must be gone. I tried the knob. The door was locked. Yes, my procedure had worked to a charm; he indeed must be vanished. Yet a certain melancholy mixed with this: I was almost sorry for my brilliant success. I was fumbling under the door mat for the key, which Bartleby was to have left there for me, when accidentally my knee knocked against a panel, producing a summoning sound, and in response a voice came to me from within —"Not yet; I am occupied."

It was Bartleby.

I was thunderstruck. For an instant I stood like the man who, pipe in mouth, was killed one cloudness afternoon long ago in Virginia, by summer lightning; at his own warm open window he was killed, and remained leaning out there upon the dreamy afternoon, till some one touched him, when he fell.

"Not gone!" I murmured at last. But again obeying that wondrous ascendancy which the inscrutable scrivener had over me, and from which ascendancy, for all my chafing, I could not completely escape, I slowly went down stairs and out into the street, and while walking round the block, considered what I should next do in this unheard-of perplexity. Turn the man out by an actual thrusting I could not; to drive him away by calling him hard names would not do; calling in the police was an unpleasant idea; and yet, permit him to enjoy his cadaverous triumph over me—this, too, I could not think of. What was to be done? or, if nothing could be done, was there anything further that I could *assume* in the matter? Yes, as before I had prospectively assumed that Bartleby would depart, so now I might retrospectively assume that departed he was. In the legitimate carrying out of this assumption, I might enter my office in a great hurry, and pretending not to see Bartleby at all, walk straight against him as if he were air. Such a proceeding would in a singular degree have the appearance of a homethrust. It was hardly possible that Bartleby could withstand such an application of the doctrine of assumptions. But upon second thoughts the success of the plan seemed rather dubious. I resolved to argue the matter over with him again.

"Bartleby," said I, entering the office, with a quietly severe expression, "I am seriously displeased. I am pained, Bartleby. I had thought better of you. I had imagined you of such a gentlemanly organization, that in any delicate dilemma a slight hint would suffice—in short, an assumption. But it appears I am deceived. Why," I added, unaffectedly starting, "you have not even touched that money yet," pointing to it, just where I had left it the evening previous.

He answered nothing.

"Will you, or will you not, quit me?" I now demanded in a sudden passion, advancing close to him.

"I would prefer *not* to quit you," he replied, gently emphasizing the *not*.

"What earthly right have you to stay here? Do you pay any rent? Do you pay my taxes? Or is this property yours?"

He answered nothing.

"Are you ready to go on and write now? Are your eyes recovered? Could you copy a small paper for me this morning? or help examine a few lines? or step round to the post-office? In a word, will you do anything at all, to give a coloring to your refusal to depart the premises?"

He silently retired into his hermitage.

I was now in such a state of nervous resentment that I thought it but prudent to check myself at present from further demonstrations. Bartleby and I were alone. I remembered the tragedy of the unfortunate Adams and the still more unfortunate Colt in the solitary office of the latter; and how poor Colt, being dreadfully incensed by Adams, and imprudently permitting himself to get wildly excited, was at unawares hurried into his fatal act—an act which certainly no man could possibly deplore more than the actor himself. Often it had occurred to me in my ponderings upon the subject that had that altercation taken place in the public street, or at a private residence, it would not have terminated as it did. It was the circumstance of being alone in a solitary office, up stairs, of a building entirely unhallowed by humanizing domestic associations—an uncarpeted office, doubtless, of a dusty, haggard sort of appearance—this it must have been, which greatly helped to enhance the irritable desperation of the hapless Colt.

But when this old Adam of resentment rose in me and tempted me concerning Bartleby, I grappled him and threw him. How? Why, simply by recalling the divine injunction: "A new commandment give I unto you, that ye love one another." Yes, this it was that saved me. Aside from higher considerations, charity often operates as a vastly wise and prudent principle—a great safeguard to its possessor. Men have committed murder for jealousy's sake, and anger's sake, and hatred's sake, and selfishness' sake, and spiritual pride's sake; but no man, that ever I heard of, ever committed a diabolical murder for sweet charity's sake. Mere self-interest, then, if no better motive can be enlisted, should, especially with high-tempered men, prompt all beings to charity and philanthropy. At any rate, upon the occasion in question, I strove to drown my exasperated feelings towards the scrivener by benevolently construing his conduct. Poor fellow, poor fellow! thought I, he don't mean anything; and besides, he has seen hard times, and ought to be indulged.

I endeavored, also, immediately to occupy myself, and at the same time to comfort my despondency. I tried to fancy, that in the course of the morning, at such time as might prove agreeable to him, Bartleby, of his own free accord, would emerge from his hermitage and take up some decided line of march in the direction of the door. But no. Half-past twelve o'clock came; Turkey began to glow in the face, overturn his inkstand, and become generally obstreperous; Nippers abated down into quietude and courtesy; Ginger Nut munched his noon apple; and Bartleby remained standing at his window in one of his profoundest dead-wall reveries. Will it be credited? Ought I to acknowledge it? That afternoon I left the office without saying one further word to him.

Some days now passed, during which, at leisure intervals I looked a little into "Edwards on the Will," and "Priestley on Necessity." Under the circumstances, those books induced a salutary feeling. Gradually I slid into the persuasion that these troubles of mine, touching the scrivener, had been all predestinated from eternity, and Bartleby was billeted upon me for some mysterious purpose of an all-wise Providence, which it was not for a mere mortal like me to fathom. Yes, Bartleby, stay there behind your screen, thought I; I shall persecute you no more; you are harmless and noiseless as any of these old chairs; in short, I never feel so private as when I know you are here. At last I see it, I feel it; I penetrate to the predestinated purpose of my life. I am content. Others may have loftier parts to enact; but my mission in this world, Bartleby, is to furnish you with office-room for such period as you may see fit to remain.

I believe that this wise and blessed frame of mind would have continued with me, had it not been for the unsolicited and uncharitable remarks obtruded upon me by my professional friends who visited the rooms. But thus it often is, that the constant friction of illiberal minds wears out at last the best resolves of the more generous. Though to be sure, when I reflected upon it, it was not strange that people entering my office should be struck by the peculiar aspect of the unaccountable Bartleby, and so be tempted to throw out some sinister observations concerning him. Sometimes an attorney, having business with me, and calling at my office, and finding no one but the scrivener there, would undertake to obtain some sort of precise information from him touching my whereabouts; but without heeding his idle talk, Bartleby would remain standing immovable in the middle of the room. So after contemplating him in that position for a time, the attorney would depart, no wiser than he came.

Also, when a reference was going on, and the room full of lawyers and witnesses, and business driving fast, some deeply-occupied legal gentleman present, seeing Bartleby wholly unemployed, would request him to run round to his (the legal gentleman's) office and fetch some papers for him. Thereupon, Bartleby would tranquilly decline, and yet remain idle as before. Then the lawyer would give a great stare, and turn to me. And what could I say? At last I was made aware that all through the circle of my professional acquaintance, a whisper of wonder was running round, having reference to the strange creature I kept at my office. This worried me very much. And as the idea came upon me of his possibly turning out a long-lived man, and keep occupying my chambers, and denying my authority; and perplexing my visitors; and scandalizing my professional reputation; and casting a general gloom over the premises; keeping soul and body together to the last upon his savings (for doubtless he spent but half a dime a day), and in the end perhaps outlive me, and claim possession of my office by right of his perpetual occupancy: as all these dark anticipations crowded upon me more and more, and my friends continually intruded their relentless remarks upon the apparition in my room; a great change was wrought in me. I resolved to gather all my faculties together, and forever rid me of this intolerable incubus.

Ere revolving any complicated project, however, adapted to this end, I first simply suggested to Bartleby the propriety of his permanent departure. In a calm and serious tone, I commended the idea to his careful and mature consideration. But, having taken three days to meditate upon it, he apprised me, that his original determination remained the same; in short, that he still preferred to abide with me.

What shall I do? I now said to myself, buttoning up my coat to the last button. What shall I do? what ought I to do? what does conscience say I *should* do with this man, or, rather, ghost? Rid myself of him, I must; go, he shall. But how? You will not thrust him, the poor, pale, passive mortal—you will not thrust such a helpless creature out of your door? you will not dishonor yourself by such cruelty? No, I will not, I cannot do that. Rather would I let him live and die here, and then mason up his remains in the wall. What, then, will you do? For all your coaxing, he will not budge. Bribes he leaves under your own paperweight on your table; in short, it is quite plain that he prefers to cling to you.

Then something severe, something unusual must be done. What! surely you will not have him collared by a constable, and commit his innocent pallor to the common jail? And upon what ground could you procure such a thing to be done?—a vagrant, is he? What! he a vagrant, a wanderer, who refuses to budge? It is because he will *not* be a vagrant, then, that you seek to count him as a vagrant. That is too absurd. No visible means of support: there I have him. Wrong again: for indubitably he *does* support himself, and that is the only unanswerable proof that any man can show of his possessing the means so to do. No more, then. Since he will not quit me, I must quit him. I will change my offices; I will move elsewhere, and give him fair notice, that if I find him on my new premises I will then proceed against him as a common trespasser.

Acting accordingly, next day I thus addressed him: "I find these chambers too far from the City Hall; the air is unwholesome. In a word, I propose to remove my offices next week, and shall no longer require your services. I tell you this now, in order that you may seek another place."

He made no reply, and nothing more was said.

On the appointed day I engaged carts and men, proceeded to my chambers, and, having but little furniture, everything was removed in a few hours. Throughout, the scrivener remained standing behind the screen, which I directed to be removed the last thing. It was withdrawn; and, being folded up like a huge folio, left him the motionless occupant of a naked room. I stood in the entry watching him a moment, while something from within me upbraided me.

I re-entered, with my hand in my pocket—and—and my heart in my mouth.

"Good-bye, Bartleby; I am going—good-bye, and God some way bless you; and take that," slipping something in his hand. But it dropped upon the floor, and then—strange to say—I tore myself from him whom I had so longed to be rid of.

Established in my new quarters, for a day or two I kept the door locked, and started at every footfall in the passages. When I returned to my rooms, after any little absence, I would pause at the threshold for an instant, and attentively listen, ere applying my key. But these fears were needless. Bartleby never came nigh me.

I thought all was going well, when a perturbed-looking stranger visited me, inquiring whether I was the person who had recently occupied rooms at No. — Wall Street.

Full of forebodings, I replied that I was.

"Then, sir," said the stranger, who proved a lawyer, "you are responsible for the man you left there. He refuses to do any copying; he refuses to do anything; he says he prefers not to; and he refuses to quit the premises."

"I am very sorry, sir," said I, with assumed tranquility, but an inward tremor, "but, really, the man you allude to is nothing to me—he is no relation or apprentice of mine, that you should hold me responsible for him."

"In mercy's name, who is he?"

"I certainly cannot inform you. I know nothing about him. Formerly I employed him as a copyist; but he has done nothing for me now for some time past."

"I shall settle him, then—good morning, sir."

Several days passed, and I heard nothing more; and, though I often felt a charitable prompting to call at the place and see poor Bartleby, yet a certain squeamishness, of I know not what, withheld me.

All is over with him, by this time, thought I, at last, when, through another week, no further intelligence reached me. But, coming to my room the day after, I found several persons waiting at my door in a high state of nervous excitement.

"That's the man—here he comes," cried the foremost one, whom I recognized as the lawyer who had previously called upon me alone.

"You must take him away, sir, at once," cried a portly person among them, advancing upon me, and whom I knew to be the landlord of No. — Wall Street. "These gentlemen, my tenants, cannot stand it any longer; Mr. B——," pointing to the lawyer, "has turned him out of his room, and he now persists in haunting the building generally, sitting upon the banisters of the stairs by day, and sleeping in the entry by night. Everybody is concerned; clients are leaving the offices; some fears are entertained of a mob; something you must do, and that without delay."

Aghast at this torrent, I fell back before it, and would fain have locked myself in my new quarters. In vain I persisted that Bartleby was nothing to me—no more than to any one else. In vain—I was the last person known to have anything to do with him, and they held me to the terrible account. Fearful, then, of being exposed in the papers (as one person present obscurely threatened), I considered the matter, and, at length, said, that if the lawyer would give me a confidential interview with the scrivener, in his (the lawyer's) own room, I would, that afternoon, strive my best to rid them of the nuisance they complained of.

Going up stairs to my old haunt, there was Bartleby silently sitting upon the banister at the landing.

"What are you doing here, Bartleby?" said I.

"Sitting upon the banister," he mildly replied.

I motioned him into the lawyer's room, who then left us.

"Bartleby," said I, "are you aware that you are the cause of great tribulation to me, by persisting in occupying the entry after being dismissed from the office?"

No answer.

"Now one of two things must take place. Either you must do something, or something must be done to you. Now what sort of business would you like to engage in? Would you like to re-engage in copying for some one?"

"No; I would prefer not to make any change."

"Would you like a clerkship in a dry-goods store?"

"There is too much confinement about that. No, I would not like a clerkship; but I am not particular."

"Too much confinement," I cried, "why, you keep yourself confined all the time!"

"I would prefer not to take a clerkship," he rejoined, as if to settle that little item at once.

"How would a bar-tender's business suit you? There is no trying of the eye-sight in that."

"I would not like it at all; though, as I said before, I am not particular."

His unwonted wordiness inspired me. I returned to the charge.

"Well, then, would you like to travel through the country collecting bills for the merchants? That would improve your health."

"No, I would prefer to be doing something else."

"How, then, would going as a companion to Europe, to entertain some young gentleman with your conversation—how would that suit you?"

"Not at all. It does not strike me that there is anything definite about that. I like to be stationary. But I am not particular."

"Stationary you shall be, then," I cried, now losing all patience, and, for the first time in all my exasperating connection with him, fairly flying into a passion. "If you do not go away from these premises before night, I shall feel bound—indeed, I am bound—to—to—to quit the premises myself!" I rather absurdly concluded, knowing not with what possible threat to try to frighten his immobility into compliance. Despairing of all further efforts, I was precipitately leaving him, when a final thought occurred to me—one which had not been wholly unindulged before.

"Bartleby," said I, in the kindest tone I could assume under such exciting circumstances, "will you go home with me now—not to my office, but my dwelling—and remain there till we can conclude upon some convenient arrangement for you at our leisure? Come, let us start now, right away."

"No: at present I would prefer not to make any change at all."

I answered nothing; but, effectually dodging every one by the suddenness and rapidity of my flight, rushed from the building, ran up Wall Street towards Broadway, and, jumping into the first omnibus, was soon removed from pursuit. As soon as tranquility returned, I distinctly perceived that I had now done all that I possibly could, both in respect to the demands of the landlord and his tenants, and with regard to my own desire and sense of duty, to benefit Bartleby, and shield him from rude persecution. I now strove to be entirely care-free and quiescent; and my conscience justified me in the attempt; though, indeed, it was not so successful as I could have wished. So fearful was I of being again hunted out by the incensed landlord and his exasperated tenants, that, surrendering my business to Nippers, for a few days, I drove about the upper part of the town and through the suburbs, in my rockaway; crossed over to Jersey City and Hoboken, and paid fugitive visits to Manhattanville and Astoria. In fact, I almost lived in my rockaway for the time.

When again I entered my office, lo, a note from the landlord lay upon the desk. I opened it with trembling hands. It informed me that the writer had sent to the police, and had Bartleby removed to the Tombs as a vagrant. Moreover, since I knew more about him than any one else, he wished me to appear at that place, and make a suitable statement of the facts. These tidings had a conflicting effect upon me. At first I was indignant; but, at last, almost approved. The landlord's energetic, summary disposition, had led him to adopt a procedure which I do not think I would have decided upon myself; and yet, as a last resort, under such peculiar circumstances, it seemed the only plan.

As I afterwards learned, the poor scrivener, when told that he must be conducted to the Tombs, offered not the slightest obstacle, but, in his pale, unmoving way, silently acquiesced.

Some of the compassionate and curious by-standers joined the party; and headed by one of the constables arm-in-arm with Bartleby, the silent procession filed its way through all the noise, and heat, and joy of the roaring thoroughfares at noon.

The same day I received the note, I went to the Tombs, or, to speak more properly, the Halls of Justice. Seeking the right officer, I stated the purpose of my call, and was informed that the individual I described was, indeed, within. I then assured the functionary that Bartleby was a perfectly honest man, and greatly to be compassionated, however unaccountably eccentric. I narrated all I knew, and closed by suggesting the idea of letting him remain in as indulgent confinement as possible, till something less harsh might be done—though, indeed, I hardly knew what. At all events, if nothing else could be decided upon, the alms-house must receive him. I then begged to have an interview.

Being under no disgraceful charge, and quite serene and harmless in all his ways, they had permitted him freely to wander about the prison, and, especially, in the inclosed grass-platted yards thereof. And so I found him there, standing all alone in the quietest of the yards, his face towards a high wall, while all around, from the narrow slits of the jail windows, I thought I saw peering out upon him the eyes of murderers and thieves.

"Bartleby!"

"I know you," he said, without looking round—"and I want nothing to say to you."

"It was not I that brought you here, Bartleby," said I, keenly pained at his implied suspicion. "And to you, this should not be so vile a place. Nothing reproachful attaches to you by being here. And see, it is not so sad a place as one might think. Look, there is the sky, and here is the grass."

"I know where I am," he replied, but would say nothing more, and so I left him.

As I entered the corridor again, a broad meat-like man, in an apron, accosted me, and, jerking his thumb over his shoulder, said—"Is that your friend?"

"Yes."

"Does he want to starve? If he does, let him live on the prison fare, that's all."

"Who are you?" asked I, not knowing what to make of such an unofficially speaking person in such a place.

"I am the grub-man. Such gentlemen as have friends here, hire me to provide them with something good to eat."

"Is this so?" said I, turning to the turnkey.

He said it was.

"Well, then," said I, slipping some silver into the grub-man's hands (for so they called him), "I want you to give particular attention to my friend there; let him have the best dinner you can get. And you must be as polite to him as possible."

"Introduce me, will you?" said the grub-man, looking at me with an expression which seemed to say he was all impatience for an opportunity to give a specimen of his breeding.

Thinking it would prove of benefit to the scrivener, I acquiesced; and, asking the grub-man his name, went up with him to Bartleby.

"Bartleby, this is a friend; you will find him very useful to you."

"Your sarvant, sir, your sarvant," said the grub-man, making a low salutation behind his apron. "Hope you find it pleasant here, sir; nice grounds—cool apartments—hope you'll stay with us some time—try to make it agreeable. What will you have for dinner today?"

"I prefer not to dine to-day," said Bartleby, turning away. "It would disagree with me; I am unused to dinners." So saying, he slowly moved to the other side of the inclosure, and took up a position fronting the dead-wall.

"How's this?" said the grub-man, addressing me with a stare of astonishment. "He's odd, ain't he?"

"I think he is a little deranged," said I, sadly.

"Deranged? deranged is it? Well, now, upon my word, I thought that friend of yourn was a gentleman forger; they are always pale and genteel-like, them forgers. I can't help pity 'em—can't help it, sir. Did you know Monroe Edwards?" he added, touchingly, and paused. Then, laying his hand piteously on my shoulder, sighed, "he died of consumption at Sing-Sing. So you weren't acquainted with Monroe?"

"No, I was never socially acquainted with any forgers. But I cannot stop longer. Look to my friend yonder. You will not lose by it. I will see you again."

Some few days after this, I again obtained admission to the Tombs, and went through the corridors in quest of Bartleby; but without finding him.

"I saw him coming from his cell not long ago," said a turnkey, "may be he's gone to loiter in the yards."

So I went in that direction.

"Are you looking for the silent man?" said another turnkey, passing me. "Yonder he lies—sleeping in the yard there. 'Tis not twenty minutes since I saw him lie down."

The yard was entirely quiet. It was not accessible to the common prisoners. The surrounding walls, of amazing thickness, kept off all sounds behind them. The Egyptian character of the masonry weighed upon me with its gloom. But a soft imprisoned turf grew under foot. The heart of the eternal pyramids, it seemed, wherein, by some strange magic, through the clefts, grass-seed, dropped by birds, had sprung.

Strangely huddled at the base of the wall, his knees drawn up, and lying on his side, his head touching the cold stones, I saw the wasted Bartleby. But nothing stirred. I paused; then went close up to him; stooped over, and saw that his dim eyes were open; otherwise he seemed profoundly sleeping. Something prompted me to touch him. I felt his hand, when a tingling shiver ran up my arm and down my spine to my feet.

The round face of the grub-man peered upon me now. "His dinner is ready. Won't he dine to-day, either? Or does he live without dining?"

"Lives without dining," said I, and closed the eyes.

"Eh!—He's asleep, ain't he?"

"With kings and counselors," murmured I.

There would seem little need for proceeding further in this history. Imagination will readily supply the meagre recital of poor Bartleby's interment. But, ere parting with the reader, let me say, that if this little narrative has sufficiently interested him, to awaken curiosity as to who Bartleby was, and what manner of life he led prior to the present narrator's making his acquaintance, I can only reply, that in such curiosity I fully share, but am wholly unable to gratify it. Yet here I hardly know whether I should divulge one little item of rumor, which came to my ear a few months after the scrivener's decease. Upon what basis it rested, I could never ascertain; and hence, how true it is I cannot now tell. But, inasmuch as this vague report has not been without a certain suggestive interest to me, however sad, it may prove the same with some others; and so I will briefly mention it. The report was this: that Bartleby had been a subordinate clerk in the Dead Letter Office at Washington, from which he had been suddenly removed by a change in the administration. When I think over this rumor, hardly can I express the emotions which seize me. Dead letters! does it not sound like dead men? Conceive a man by nature and misfortune prone to a pallid hopelessness, can any business seem more fitted to heighten it than that of continually handling these dead letters, and assorting them for the flames? For by the cart-load they are annually burned. Sometimes from out the folded paper the pale clerk takes a ring—the finger it was meant for, perhaps, moulders in the grave; a bank-note sent in swiftest charity—he whom it would relieve, now eats nor hungers any more; pardon for those who died despairing; hope for those who died unhoping; good tidings for those who died stifled by unrelieved calamities. On errands of life, these letters speed to death.

Ah, Bartleby! Ah, humanity!

FOR DISCUSSION:

1. What is the significance of the story's setting—on Wall Street, the financial district of New York City?

2. Several critics view Bartleby as the prototype of the artist in society. In what ways is Bartleby like an artist? What role does the lawyer-narrator play in a social interpretation of the story?

3. How is society responsible for Bartleby's tragedy?

4. The final line of the story links Bartleby with humanity. What does Melville suggest by this association?

5. This story has been interpreted as (a) Melville's affirmation of passive resistance, (b) his criticism of the sterility of the business world, (c) a dramatization of the conflict between free will and absolutism, and (d) an insight into the destructive power of irrationality. Which of these readings is best supported by the text?

I Will Arise and Go Now

OGDEN NASH

In far Tibet
There live a lama,
He got no pappa,
Got no momma,

He got no wife,
He got no chillun,
Got no use
For penicillun,

He got no soap,
He got no opera,
He don't know Irium
From copra,

He got no songs,
He got no banter,
Don't know Jolson
Don't know Cantor,

He got no teeth,
He got no gums,
Don't eat no Spam,
Don't need no Tums.

He love to nick him
When he shave;
He also got
No hair to save.

Got no distinction
No clear head,
Don't call for Calvert,
Drink milk instead.

He use no lotions
For allurance,
He got no car
And no insurance.

No Winchell facts,
No Pearson rumor
For this self-centered
Non-consumer.

Indeed, the
Ignorant Have-Not
Don't even know
What he don't got.

If you will mind
The Philco, comma,
I think I'll go
And join that lama.

FOR DISCUSSION:

1. Why is the lama a particularly good symbol for Nash in this poem?
2. Nash's title, "I Will Arise and Go Now," is taken from the first line of Yeats's "Lake Isle of Innisfree," a borrowing intended to suggest comparison between the two poems. What is Nash's point in inviting this comparison?
3. Nash is the foremost comic versifier in the United States today. In this poem, however, as in many of his others, a serious theme underlies his veneer of humor. What is the theme of the poem, and what are the comic devices Nash uses to give "I Will Arise and Go Now" its flavor?
4. What particular aspects of contemporary life does Nash find objectionable?
5. How is Nash's use of grammar, syntax, and spelling integrally related to his message?
6. This poem appeared originally in the New Yorker in 1948. Is it in any way dated?

*Reprinted by permission of the Author. Copyright 1948 by Ogden Nash. Originally published in the New Yorker, February 7, 1948.

The Charge of the Light Brigade

ALFRED, LORD TENNYSON

Half a league, half a league,
  Half a league onward,
All in the valley of Death
  Rode the six hundred.
"Forward, the Light Brigade!
Charge for the guns!" he said.
Into the valley of Death
  Rode the six hundred.

"Forward, the Light Brigade!"
Was there a man dismayed?   10
Not though the soldier knew
  Someone had blundered.
Theirs not to make reply,
Theirs not to reason why,
Theirs but to do and die.
Into the valley of Death
  Rode the six hundred.

Cannon to right of them,
Cannon to left of them,
Cannon in front of them   20
  Volleyed and thundered;
Stormed at with shot and shell,
Boldly they rode and well,
Into the jaws of Death,
Into the mouth of Hell
  Rode the six hundred.

Flashed all their sabers bare,
Flashed as they turned in air
Sabring the gunners there,
Charging an army, while   30
  All the world wondered.
Plunged in the battery-smoke
Right through the line they broke;
Cossack and Russian
Reeled from the saber-stroke
  Shattered and sundered.
Then they rode back, but not,
  Not the six hundred.

Cannon to right of them,
Cannon to left of them,   40
Cannon behind them
  Volleyed and thundered;
Stormed at with shot and shell,
While horse and hero fell,
They that had fought so well
Came through the jaws of Death,
Back from the mouth of Hell,
All that was left of them,
  Left of six hundred.

When can their glory fade?   50
O the wild charge they made!
  All the world wondered.
Honor the charge they made!
Honor the Light Brigade,
  Noble six hundred!

FOR DISCUSSION:

1. Do you find this an inspirational poem or one in which the desired effect simply is not achieved?
2. What devices does Tennyson employ to heighten the reader's emotional intensity for the men who gallantly gave their lives in a useless sacrifice?

To a Mouse

ON TURNING HER UP IN HER NEST
WITH THE PLOUGH, NOVEMBER, 1785

ROBERT BURNS

Wee, sleekit, cowrin, tim'rous beastie,
  O, what a panic's in thy breastie!
Thou need na start awa sae hasty,

                    Wi' bickering brattle!
I wad be laith to rin an' chase thee,
                    Wi' murd'ring pattle!

I'm truly sorry Man's dominion
Has broken Nature's social union,
An' justifies that ill opinion
                    Which makes thee startle
At me, thy poor, earth-born companion,
                    An' fellow-mortal!

I doubt na, whyles, but thou may thieve
What then? poor beastie, thou maun live!
A daimen icker in a thrave
                    'S a sma' request.
I'll get a blessin wi' the lave,
                    And never miss't!

Thy wee bit housie, too, in ruin!
Its silly wa's the win's are strewin!
An' naething, now, to big a new ane,
                    O' foggage green!
An' bleak December's winds ensuin,
                    Baith snell and keen!

Thou saw the fields laid bare an' waste,
An' weary Winter comin fast,
An' cozie here, beneath the blast,
                    Thou thought to dwell,
Till crash! the cruel coulter past
                    Out thro' thy cell.

That wee bit heap o' leaves an' stibble,
Has cost thee mony a weary nibble!
Now thou's turned out, for a' thy trouble,
                    But house or hald,
To thole the Winter's sleety dribble,
                    An' cranreuch cauld!

But, Mousie, thou art no thy lane,
In proving foresight may be vain:
The best-laid schemes o' Mice an' Men,
                    Gang aft a-gley,
An' lea'e us nought but grief and pain,
                    For promised joy.

Still thou art blest, compared wi' me!
The present only toucheth thee;
But, Och! I backward cast my e'e,
                    On prospects drear!
An' forward, tho' I canna see,
                    I guess an' fear!

---

4. *bickering* hurrying; *brattle* bustle 6. *pattle* plough staff 13. *whyles* sometimes 15. *daimen* odd; *icker* ear of corn; *thrave* twenty-four sheaves 17. *lave* remainder 21. *big* build 22. *foggage* coarse grass 23. *snell* sharp 29. *coulter* blade of a plow 34. *But* without 35. *thole* endure 36. *cranreuch* frost 37. *no thy lane* not alone 40. *Gang aft a-gley* oftentimes go astray

CRITICAL PERSPECTIVE: SOCIAL

FOR DISCUSSION:

1. Burns's poetry frequently deals with everyday, commonplace events which give insight into the nature of man and his position in life. What similarity does Burns see between mankind and the dispossessed mouse?

2. In what way does Burns believe the mouse to be more fortunate than himself?

The World is Too Much with Us; Late and Soon

WILLIAM WORDSWORTH

The world is too much with us; late and soon,
Getting and spending, we lay waste our powers:
Little we see in Nature that is ours;
We have given our hearts away, a sordid boon!
This sea that bares her bosom to the moon;
The winds that will be howling at all hours,
And are up-gathered now like sleeping flowers;
For this, for everything, we are out of tune;
It moves us not.—Great God! I'd rather be
A Pagan suckled in a creed outworn;   10
So might I, standing on this pleasant lea,
Have glimpses that would make me less forlorn;
Have sight of Proteus rising from the sea;
Or hear old Triton blow his wreathèd horn.

FOR DISCUSSION:

1. What is the "creed outworn" to which Wordsworth refers in line 10?
2. What statement is Wordsworth making on the spiritual condition of modern man?

3. The imagery in the sestet is predominantly concerned with perception (sight, hearing). How is this imagery suited to the theme of the poem?

next to of course god america i*

E. E. CUMMINGS

"next to of course god america i
love you land of the pilgrims' and so forth oh
say can you see by the dawn's early my
country 'tis of centuries come and go

* Copyright, 1926, by Horace Liveright; copyright, 1954, by E. E. Cummings. Reprinted from POEMS 1923–1954 by E. E. Cummings by permission of Harcourt, Brace & World, Inc. and Faber & Faber Ltd.

and are no more what of it we should worry
in every language even deafanddumb
thy sons acclaim your glorious name by gorry
by jingo by gee by gosh by gum
why talk of beauty what could be more beautiful than these heroic happy dead   10
who rushed like lions to the roaring slaughter
they did not stop to think they died instead
then shall the voice of liberty be mute?"

He spoke. And drank rapidly a glass of water

FOR DISCUSSION:

1. What is the dramatic situation depicted in this poem?
2. Cummings is well-known for typographic idiosyncrasy in his poetry. Is the almost total lack of punctuation in this poem merely an ostentatious technical device, or does it relate to the poem's theme?
3. What is the effect of the break between lines 13 and 14?

Verses on the Death of Dr. Swift, D.S.P.D.*

JONATHAN SWIFT

As *Rochefoucault* his Maxims drew
From Nature, I believe 'em true:
They argue no corrupted Mind
In him; the Fault is in Mankind.

This Maxim more than all the rest
Is thought too base for human Breast;
"In all Distresses of our Friends
We first consult our private Ends,
While Nature kindly bent to ease us,
Points out some Circumstance to please us."   10

If this perhaps your Patience move
Let Reason and Experience prove.

We all behold with envious Eyes,
Our *Equal* rais'd above our *Size*;
Who wou'd not at a crowded Show,
Stand high himself, keep others low?
I love my Friend as well as you,
But would not have him stop my View;
Then let him have the higher Post;
I ask but for an Inch at most.   20

* [These verses were occasioned by reading a maxim of Rochefoucauld, "In the adversity of our best Friends, we find something that doth not displease us." Both the text and Swift's notes follow the version of Sir Harold Williams—Ed.]

If in a Battle you should find,
One, whom you love of all Mankind,
Had some heroick Action done,
A Champion kill'd, or Trophy won;
Rather than thus be over-topt,
Would you not wish his Lawrels cropt?

Dear honest Ned is in the Gout,
Lies rackt with Pain, and you without:
How patiently you hear him groan!
How glad the Case is not your own!   30

What Poet would not grieve to see,
His Brethren write as well as he?
But rather than they should excel,
He'd wish his Rivals all in Hell.

Her End when Emulation misses,
She turns to Envy, Stings and Hisses:
The strongest Friendship yields to Pride,
Unless the Odds be on our Side.

Vain human Kind! Fantastick Race!
Thy various Follies, who can trace?   40
Self-love, Ambition, Envy, Pride,
Their Empire in our Hearts divide:
Give others Riches, Power, and Station,
'Tis all on me an Usurpation.
I have no Title to aspire;
Yet, when you sink, I seem the higher.
In POPE, I cannot read a Line,
But with a Sigh, I wish it mine:
When he can in one Couplet fix
More Sense than I can do in Six: 50
It gives me such a jealous Fit,
I cry, Pox take him, and his Wit.

Why must I be outdone by GAY,
In my own hum'rous biting Way?

ARBUTHNOT is no more my Friend,
Who dares to Irony pretend;
Which I was born to introduce,
Refin'd it first, and shew'd its Use.

ST. JOHN, as well as PULTNEY knows,
That I had some repute for Prose;   60
And till they drove me out of Date,
Could maul a Minister of State:
If they have mortify'd my Pride,
And made me throw my Pen aside;
If with such Talents Heav'n hath blest 'em
Have I not Reason to detest 'em?

To all my Foes, dear Fortune, send
Thy Gifts, but never to my Friend:
I tamely can endure the first,
But, this with Envy makes me burst. 70

Thus much may serve by way of Proem,
Proceed we therefore to our Poem.

The Time is not remote, when I
Must by the Course of Nature dye:
When I foresee my special Friends,
Will try to find their private Ends:
Tho' it is hardly understood,
Which way my Death can do them good;
Yet, thus methinks, I hear 'em speak;
"See, how the Dean begins to break:
Poor Gentleman, he droops apace,
You plainly find it in his Face:
That old Vertigo in his Head,
Will never leave him, till he's dead:
Besides, his Memory decays,
He recollects not what he says;
He cannot call his Friends to Mind;
Forgets the Place where last he din'd:
Plyes you with Stories o'er and o'er,
He told them fifty Times before. 90
How does he fancy we can sit,
To hear his out-of-fashion'd Wit?
But he takes up with younger Fokes,
Who for his Wine will bear his Jokes:
Faith, he must make his Stories shorter,
Or change his Comrades once a Quarter:
In half the Time, he talks them round;
There must another Sett be found.

"For Poetry, he's past his Prime,
He takes an Hour to find a Rhime: 100
His Fire is out, his Wit decay'd,
His Fancy sunk, his Muse a Jade.
I'd have him throw away his Pen;
But there's no talking to some Men."

And, then their Tenderness appears,
By adding largely to my Years:
"He's older than he would be reckon'd,
And well remembers *Charles* the Second.

"He hardly drinks a Pint of Wine;
And that, I doubt, is no good Sign. 110
His Stomach too begins to fail:
Last Year we thought him strong and hale;
But now, he's quite another Thing;
I wish he may hold out till Spring."

Then hug themselves, and reason thus;
"It is not yet so bad with us."

In such a Case they talk in Tropes,
And, by their Fears express their Hopes:
Some great Misfortune to portend,
No Enemy can match a Friend;
With all the Kindness they profess,
The Merit of a lucky Guess,
(When daily Howd'y's come of Course,
And Servants answer; *Worse and Worse*)
Wou'd please 'em better than to tell,
That, GOD be prais'd, the Dean is well.
Then he who prophecy'd the best,
Approves his Foresight to the rest:
"You know, I always fear'd the worst,
And often told you so at first:"
He'd rather chuse that I should dye,
Than his Prediction prove a Lye.
Not one foretels I shall recover;
But, all agree, to give me over.

Yet shou'd some Neighbour feel a Pain,
Just in the Parts, where I complain;
How many a Message would he send?
What hearty Prayers that I should mend?
Enquire what Regimen I kept;
What gave me Ease, and how I slept?
And more lament, when I was dead,
Than all the Sniv'llers round my Bed.

My good Companions, never fear,
For though you may mistake a Year;
Though your Prognosticks run too fast,
They must be verify'd at last.

Behold the fatal Day arrive!
"How is the Dean?" "He's just alive."
Now the departing Prayer is read:
"He hardly breathes. The Dean is dead."
Before the Passing-Bell begun,
The News thro' half the Town has run.
"O, may we all for Death prepare!
What has he left? And who's his Heir?"
"I know no more than what the News is,
'Tis all bequeath'd to publick Uses."
"To publick Use! A perfect Whim!
What had the Publick done for him!
Meer Envy, Avarice, and Pride!
He gave it all:—But first he dy'd.
And had the Dean, in all the Nation,
No worthy Friend, no poor Relation?
So ready to do Strangers good,
Forgetting his own Flesh and Blood?"

Now Grub-Street Wits are all employ'd;
With Elegies, the Town is cloy'd:
Some Paragraph in ev'ry Paper,
To curse the *Dean*, or *bless* the *Drapier*.

The Doctors tender of their Fame,
Wisely on me lay all the Blame: 170
"We must confess his Case was nice;
But he would never take Advice:
Had he been rul'd, for ought appears,
He might have liv'd these Twenty Years:
For when we open'd him we found,
That all his vital Parts were sound."

From *Dublin* soon to *London* spread,
'Tis told at Court, the Dean is dead.

Kind Lady *Suffolk* in the Spleen,
Runs laughing up to tell the Queen. 180
The Queen, so Gracious, Mild, and Good,
Cries, "Is he gone? 'Tis time he shou'd.
He's dead you say; why let him rot;
I'm glad the Medals were forgot.
I promis'd them, I own; but when?
I only was the Princess then;
But now as Consort of the King,
You know 'tis quite a different Thing."

Now, *Chartres* at Sir *Robert's* Levee,
Tells, with a Sneer, the Tidings heavy: 190
"Why, is he dead without his Shoes?"
(Cries *Bob*) "I'm Sorry for the News;

168. The author imagines, that the Scriblers of the prevailing Party, which he always opposed, will libel him after his Death; but that others will remember him with Gratitude, who consider the Service he had done to *Ireland*, under the Name of M. B. Drapier, by utterly defeating the destructive Project of *Wood's* Half-pence, in five Letters to the People of Ireland, at that Time read universally, and convincing every Reader.

178. The Dean supposeth himself to dye in *Ireland*.

179. Mrs. *Howard*, afterwards Countess of *Suffolk*, then of the Bed-chamber to the Queen, professed much Friendship for the Dean. The Queen then Princess, sent a dozen times to the Dean (then in *London*) with her Command to attend her; which at last he did, by Advice of all his Friends. She often sent for him afterwards, and always treated him very Graciously. He taxed her with a Present worth Ten Pounds, which she promised before he should return to Ireland, but on his taking Leave, the Medals were not ready.

183. The Medals were to be sent to the Dean in four Months, but she forgot them, or thought them too dear. The Dean, being in Ireland, sent Mrs. *Howard* a Piece of *Indian* Plad made in that Kingdom: which the Queen seeing took from her, and wore it herself, and sent to the Dean for as much as would cloath herself and Children, desiring he would send the Charge of it. He did the former. It cost thirty-five Pounds, but he said he would have nothing except the Medals. He was the Summer following in England, was treated as usual, and she being then Queen, the Dean was promised a Settlement in England, but returned as he went, and, instead of Favour or Medals, hath been ever since under her Majesty's Displeasure.

189. *Chartres*, is a most infamous, vile Scoundrel, grown from a Foot-Boy, or worse, to a prodigious Fortune both in *England* and *Scotland:* He had a Way of insinuating himself into all Ministers under every Change, either as Pimp, Flatterer, or Informer. He was Tryed at Seventy for a Rape, and came off by sacrificing a great Part of his Fortune (he is since dead, but this Poem still preserves the Scene and Time it was writ in.)

192. Sir Robert Walpole, Chief Minister of State, treated the *Dean* in 1726, with great Distinction, invited him to Dinner at Chelsea, with the *Dean's* Friends chosen on Purpose; appointed an Hour to talk with him of *Ireland*, to which *Kingdom* and *People* the *Dean* found him no great Friend; for he defended Wood's Project of Halfpence, &c. The *Dean* would see him no more; and upon his next Year's return to England, Sir Robert on an accidental Meeting, only made a civil Compliment, and never invited him again.

Oh, were the Wretch but living still,
And in his Place my good Friend *Will*;
Or, had a Mitre on his Head
Provided *Bolingbroke* were dead."

Now *Curl* his Shop from Rubbish drains;
Three genuine Tomes of *Swift*'s Remains.
And then to make them pass the glibber,
Revis'd by *Tibbalds, Moore, and Cibber*.   200
He'll treat me as he does my Betters.
Publish my Will, my Life, my Letters.
Revive the Libels born to dye;
Which POPE must bear, as well as I.

Here shift the Scene, to represent
How those I love, my Death lament.
Poor POPE will grieve a Month; and GAY
A Week; and ARBUTHNOTT a Day.

ST. JOHN himself will scarce forbear,
To bite his Pen, and drop a Tear.   210
The rest will give a Shrug and cry,
I'm sorry; but we all must dye.
Indifference clad in Wisdom's Guise,
All Fortitude of Mind supplies:
For how can stony Bowels melt,
In those who never Pity felt;
When We are lash'd, *They* kiss the Rod;
Resigning to the Will of God.

The Fools, my Juniors by a Year,
Are tortur'd with Suspence and Fear.   220
Who wisely thought my Age a Screen,
When Death approach'd to stand between:
The Screen remov'd, their Hearts are trembling,
They mourn for me without dissembling.

---

194. Mr. *William Pultney*, from being Mr. *Walpole*'s intimate Friend, detesting his Administration, opposed his Measures, and joined with my Lord Bolingbroke, to represent his Conduct in an excellent Paper, called the *Craftsman*, which is still continued.

196. Henry St. John, Lord Viscount *Bolingbroke*, Secretary of State to Queen Anne of blessed Memory. He is reckoned the most Universal Genius in Europe; Walpole dreading his Abilities, treated him most injuriously, working with King *George*, who forgot his Promise of restoring the said Lord, upon the restless Importunity of *Walpole*.

197. Curl hath been the most infamous Bookseller of any Age or Country: His Character in Part may be found in Mr. *Pope*'s Dunciad. He published three Volumes all charged on the Dean, who never writ three Pages of them: He hath used many of the Dean's Friends in almost as vile a Manner.

200. Three stupid Verse Writers in *London*, the last to the Shame of the Court, and the highest Disgrace to Wit and Learning, was made Laureat. Moore, commonly called *Jemmy Moore*, Son of Arthur Moore, whose Father was Jaylor of *Monaghan* in *Ireland*. See the Character of *Jemmy Moore*, and *Tibbalds, Theobald* in the Dunciad.

202. Curl is notoriously infamous for publishing the Lives, Letters, and last Wills and Testaments of the Nobility and Ministers of State, as well as of all the Rogues, who are hanged at *Tyburn*. He hath been in Custody of the House of Lords for publishing or forging the Letters of many Peers; which made the Lords enter a Resolution in their Journal Book, that no Life or Writings of any Lord should be published without the Consent of the next Heir at Law, or Licence from their House.

My female Friends, whose tender Hearts
Have better learn'd to act their Parts.
Receive the News in *doleful Dumps,*
"The Dean is dead, (*and what is Trumps?*)
Then Lord have Mercy on his Soul.
(Ladies I'll venture for the *V*ole.)   230
Six Deans they say must bear the Pall.
(I wish I knew what *King* to call.)
Madam, your Husband will attend
The Funeral of so good a Friend.
No Madam, 'tis a shocking Sight,
And he's engag'd To-morrow Night!
My Lady *Club* wou'd take it ill,
If he shou'd fail her at *Q*uadrill.
He lov'd the Dean. (*I lead a Heart.*)
But dearest Friends, they say, must part.   240
His Time was come, he ran his Race;
We hope he's in a better Place."

   Why do we grieve that Friends should dye?
No Loss more easy to supply.
One Year is past; a different Scene;
No further mention of the Dean;
Who now, alas, no more is mist,
Than if he never did exist.
Where's now this Fav'rite of *Apollo?*
Departed; *and his Works must follow:*   250
Must undergo the common Fate;
His Kind of Wit is out of Date.
Some Country Squire to *Lintot* goes,
Enquires for Swift in Verse and Prose:
Says *Lintot,* "I have heard the Name:
"He dy'd a Year ago." The same.
He searcheth all his Shop in vain;
"Sir you may find them in *Duck-lane:*
I sent them with a Load of Books,
Last *M*onday to the Pastry-cooks.   260
To fancy they cou'd live a Year!
I find you're but a Stranger here.
The Dean was famous in his Time;
And had a Kind of Knack at Rhyme:
His way of Writing now is past;
The Town hath got a better Taste:
I keep no antiquated Stuff;
But, spick and span I have enough.
Pray, do but give me leave to shew 'em;
Here's *Colley Cibber's* Birth-day Poem.   270
This Ode you never yet have seen,
By *Stephen Duck,* upon the Queen.
Then, here's a Letter finely penn'd
Against the *Craftsman* and his Friend;
It clearly shews that all Reflection

---

253. Bernard Lintot, a Bookseller in *London.*   258. A Place in *London* where old Books are
Vide Mr. *Pope's* Dunciad.   sold.

On Ministers, is disaffection.
Next, here's Sir *Robert's* Vindication,
And Mr. *Henly's* last Oration:
The Hawkers have not got 'em yet,
Your Honour please to buy a Set?   280

"Here's *Wolston's* Tracts, the twelfth Edition;
'Tis read by ev'ry Politician:
The Country Members, when in Town,
To all their Boroughs send them down:
You never met a Thing so smart;
The Courtiers have them all by Heart:
Those Maids of Honour (who can read)
Are taught to use them for their Creed.
The Rev'rend Author's good Intention,
Hath been rewarded with a Pension: 290
He doth an Honour to his Gown,
By bravely running *Priest-craft* down:
He shews, as sure as GOD's in *Gloc'ster*,
That *Jesus* was a Grand Impostor:
That all his Miracles were Cheats,
Perform'd as Juglers do their Feats:
The Church had never such a Writer:
A Shame, he hath not got a Mitre!"

Suppose me dead; and then suppose
A Club assembled at the *Rose*;   300
Where from Discourse of this and that,
I grow the Subject of their Chat:
And, while they toss my Name about,
With Favour some, and some without;
One quite indiff'rent in the Cause,
My Character impartial draws:

"The Dean, if we believe Report,
Was never ill receiv'd at Court:
As for his Works in Verse and Prose,
I own my self no Judge of those: 310
Nor, can I tell what Criticks thought 'em;
But, this I know, all People bought 'em;
As with a moral View design'd
To cure the Vices of Mankind:
His Vein, ironically grave,
Expos'd the Fool, and lash'd the Knave:
To steal a Hint was never known,
But what he writ was all his own.

277. Walpole hires a Set of Party Scriblers, who do nothing else but write in his Defence.
278. Henly is a Clergyman who wanting both Merit and Luck to get Preferment, or even to keep his Curacy in the Established Church, formed a new Conventicle, which he calls an Oratory. There, at set Times, he delivereth strange Speeches compiled by himself and his Associates, who share the Profit with him: Every Hearer pays a Shilling each Day for Admittance. He is an absolute Dunce, but generally reputed crazy.
281. Wolston was a Clergyman, but for want of Bread, hath in several Treatises, in the most blasphemous Manner, attempted to turn Our Saviour and his Miracles into Ridicule. He is much caressed by many great Courtiers, and by all the Infidels, and his Books read generally by the Court Ladies.

"He never thought an Honour done him,
Because a Duke was proud to own him: 320
Would rather slip aside, and chuse
To talk with Wits in dirty Shoes:
Despis'd the Fools with Stars and Garters,
So often seen caressing *Chartres:*
He never courted Men in Station,
Nor Persons had in Admiration;
Of no Man's Greatness was afraid,
Because he sought for no Man's Aid.
Though trusted long in great Affairs,
He gave himself no haughty Airs: 330
Without regarding private Ends,
Spent all his Credit for his Friends:
And only chose the Wise and Good;
No Flatt'rers; no Allies in Blood;
But succour'd Virtue in Distress,
And seldom fail'd of good Success;
As Numbers in their Hearts must own,
Who, but for him, had been unknown.

"With Princes kept a due Decorum,
But never stood in Awe before 'em: 340
He follow'd *David's* Lesson just,
In Princes never put thy Trust.
And, would you make him truly sower;
Provoke him with *a slave in Power:*
The *Irish* Senate, if you nam'd,
With what Impatience he declaim'd!
Fair LIBERTY was all his Cry;
For her he stood prepar'd to die;
For her he boldly stood alone;
For her he oft expos'd his own. 350
Two Kingdoms, just as Faction led,
Had set a Price upon his Head;
But, not a Traytor cou'd be found,
To sell him for Six Hundred Pound.

"Had he but spar'd his Tongue and Pen,
He might have rose like other Men:
But, Power was never in his Thought;
And, Wealth he valu'd not a Groat:
Ingratitude he often found,
And pity'd those who meant the Wound: 360
But, kept the Tenor of his Mind,
To merit well of human Kind:
Nor made a Sacrifice of those

324. See the notes before on Chartres. [Line 189—Ed.]

351. In the Year 1713, the late Queen was prevailed with by an Address of the House of Lords in *England,* to publish a Proclamation, promising Three Hundred Pounds to whatever Person would discover the Author of a Pamphlet called, *The Publick Spirit of the Whiggs;* and in Ireland, in the Year 1724, my Lord Carteret at his first coming into the Government, was prevailed on to issue a Proclamation for promising the like Reward of Three Hundred Pounds, to any Person who could discover the Author of a Pamphlet called, *The Drapier's Fourth Letter,* &c. writ against that destructive Project of coining Half-pence for *Ireland;* but in neither Kingdoms was the Dean discovered.

Who still were true, to please his Foes.
He labour'd many a fruitless Hour
To reconcile his Friends in Power;
Saw Mischief by a Faction brewing,
While they pursu'd each others Ruin.
But, finding vain was all his Care,
He left the Court in meer Despair. 370

"And, oh! how short are human Schemes!
Here ended all our golden Dreams.
What St. John's Skill in State Affairs,
What Ormond's *Valour*, Oxford's Cares,
To save their sinking Country lent,
Was all destroy'd by one Event.
Too soon that precious Life was ended,
On which alone, our Weal depended.
When up a dangerous Faction starts,
With Wrath and Vengeance in their Hearts: 380
By solemn League and Cov'nant bound,
To ruin, slaughter, and confound;
To turn Religion to a Fable,
And make the Government a *Babel*:
Pervert the Law, disgrace the Gown,
Corrupt the Senate, rob the Crown;
To sacrifice old *England's* Glory,
And make her infamous in Story.
When such a Tempest shook the Land,
How could unguarded Virtue stand? 390

"With Horror, Grief, Despair the Dean
Beheld the dire destructive Scene:
His Friends in Exile, or the Tower,
Himself within the Frown of Power;
Pursu'd by base envenom'd Pens,
Far to the Land of Slaves and Fens;
A servile Race in Folly nurs'd,
Who truckle most, when treated worst.

365. Queen ANNE's Ministry fell to Variance from the first Year after their Ministry began: *Harcourt* the Chancellor, and Lord *Bolingbroke* the Secretary, were discontented with the Treasurer *Oxford*, for his too much Mildness to the Whig Party; this Quarrel grew higher every Day till the Queen's Death: The Dean, who was the only Person that endeavoured to reconcile them, found it impossible; and thereupon retired to the Country about ten Weeks before that fatal Event: Upon which he returned to his Deanry in *Dublin*, where for many Years he was worried by the new People in Power, and had Hundreds of Libels writ against him in England.

377. In the Height of the Quarrel between the Ministers, the Queen died.

379. Upon Queen ANNE's Death the Whig Faction was restored to Power, which they exercised with the utmost Rage and Revenge; impeached and banished the Chief Leaders of the Church Party, and stripped all their Adherents of what Employments they had, after which *England* was never known to make so mean a Figure in *Europe*. The greatest Preferments in the Church in both Kingdoms were given to the most ignorant Men, Fanaticks were publickly caressed, *Ireland* utterly ruined and enslaved, only great Ministers heaping up Millions, and so Affairs continue until this present third Day of May, 1732, and are likely to go on in the same Manner.

394. Upon the Queen's Death, the Dean returned to live in *Dublin*, at his Deanry-House: Numberless Libels were writ against him in *England*, as a Jacobite; he was insulted in the Street, and at Nights was forced to be attended by his Servants armed.

396. The Land of Slaves and Fens, is *Ireland*.

"By Innocence and Resolution,
He bore continual Persecution;
While Numbers to Preferment rose;
Whose Merits were, to be his Foes.
When, ev'n his own familiar Friends
Intent upon their private Ends;
Like Renegadoes now he feels,
Against him lifting up their Heels.

"The Dean did by his Pen defeat
An infamous destructive Cheat.
Taught Fools their Int'rest how to know;
And gave them Arms to ward the Blow.
Envy hath own'd it was his doing,
To save that helpless Land from Ruin,
While they who at the Steerage stood,
And reapt the Profit, sought his Blood.

"To save them from their evil Fate,
In him was held a Crime of State.
A wicked Monster on the Bench,
Whose Fury Blood could never quench;
As vile and profligate a Villain,
As modern *Scroggs*, or old *Tressilian*;
Who long all Justice had discarded,
Nor fear'd he GOD, nor Man regarded;
Vow'd on the Dean his Rage to vent,
And make him of his Zeal repent;
But Heav'n his Innocence defends,
The grateful People stand his Friends:
Not Strains of Law, nor Judges Frown,
Nor Topicks brought to please the Crown,
Nor Witness hir'd, nor Jury pick'd,
Prevail to bring him in convict.

"In Exile with a steady Heart,
He spent his Life's declining Part;
Where, Folly, Pride, and Faction sway,
Remote from ST. JOHN, POPE, and GAY.

---

408. One *Wood*, a Hardware-man from England, had a Patent for coining Copper Half-pence in Ireland, to the Sum of 108,000 l. which in the Consequence, must leave that Kingdom without Gold or Silver (See *Drapier's Letters*.)

417. One *Whitshed* was then Chief Justice: He had some Years before prosecuted a Printer for a Pamphlet writ by the Dean, to perswade the people of Ireland to wear their own Manufactures. Whitshed sent the Jury down eleven Times, and kept them nine Hours, until they were forced to bring in a special Verdict. He sat as Judge afterwards on the Tryal of the Printer of the *Drapier's* Fourth Letter; but the Jury, against all he could say or swear, threw out the Bill: All the Kingdom took the *Drapier's* Part, except the Courtiers, or those who expected Places. The *Drapier* was celebrated in many Poems and Pamphlets: His Sign was set up in most Streets of *Dublin* (where many of them still continue) and in several Country Towns.

420. *Scroggs* was Chief Justice under King *Charles* the Second: His Judgment always varied in State Tryals, according to Directions from Court. *Tressilian* was a wicked Judge, hanged above three hundred Years ago.

431. In *Ireland*, which he had Reason to call a Place of Exile; to which Country nothing could have driven him, but the Queen's Death, who had determined to fix him in England, in Spight of the Dutchess of Somerset, &c.

434. Henry St. John, Lord Viscount Bolingbroke, mentioned before. [Line 196—Ed.]

"His Friendship there to few confin'd,
Were always of the midling Kind:
No Fools of Rank, a mungril Breed,
Who fain would pass for Lords indeed:
Where Titles give no Right or Power,
And Peerage is a wither'd Flower,   440
He would have held it a Disgrace,
If such a Wretch had known his Face.
On Rural Squires, that Kingdom's Bane,
He vented oft his Wrath in vain:
Biennial Squires, to Market brought;
Who sell their Souls and Votes for Naught;
The Nation stript go joyful back,
To rob the Church, their Tenants rack,
Go Snacks with Thieves and Rapparees,
And, keep the Peace, to pick up Fees: 450
In every Jobb to have a Share,
A Jayl or Barrack to repair;
And turn the Tax for publick Roads
Commodious to their own Abodes.

"Perhaps I may allow, the Dean
Had too much Satyr in his Vein;
And seem'd determin'd not to starve it,
Because no Age could more deserve it.
Yet, Malice never was his Aim;
He lash'd the Vice but spar'd the Name.   460
No Individual could resent,
Where Thousands equally were meant.
His Satyr points at no Defect,
But what all Mortals may correct;
For he abhorr'd that senseless Tribe,
Who call it Humour when they jibe:
He spar'd a Hump or crooked Nose,
Whose Owners set not up for Beaux.
True genuine Dulness mov'd his Pity,
Unless it offer'd to be witty.   470
Those, who their Ignorance confess'd,
He ne'er offended with a Jest;
But laugh'd to hear an Idiot quote,
A Verse from *Horace*, learn'd by Rote.

"He knew an hundred pleasant Stories,
With all the Turns of *Whigs* and *Tories*:

435. In *Ireland* the Dean was not acquainted with one single Lord Spiritual or Temporal. He only conversed with private Gentlemen of the Clergy or Laity, and but a small Number of either.

439. The Peers of Ireland lost a great Part of their Jurisdiction by one single Act, and tamely submitted to this infamous Mark of Slavery without the least Resentment, or Remonstrance.

445. The Parliament (as they call it) in *Ireland* meet but once in two Years; and, after giving five Times more than they can afford, return Home to reimburse themselves by all Country Jobs and Oppressions, of which some few only are here mentioned.

449. The Highway-Men in *Ireland* are, since the late Wars there, usually called Rapparees, which was a Name given to those *Irish* Soldiers who in small Parties used, at that Time, to plunder the Protestants.

452. The Army in *Ireland* is lodged in Barracks, the building and repairing whereof, and other Charges, have cost a prodigious Sum to that unhappy Kingdom.

Was chearful to his dying Day,
And Friends would let him have his Way.
   "He gave the little Wealth he had,
To build a House for Fools and Mad: 480
And shew'd by one satyric Touch,
No Nation wanted it so much:
That Kingdom he hath left his Debtor,
I wish it soon may have a Better."

FOR DISCUSSION:

1. How does Swift view himself in lines 299–484? How does his view of himself compare with his view of mankind in general?

2. There are several contemporary references in this poem. Do they limit the effectiveness of the poem's commentary, or does Swift hit at a universal characteristic of the human animal?

483. Meaning *Ireland*, where he now lives, and probably may dye.

The Latest Decalogue

ARTHUR HUGH CLOUGH

Thou shalt have one God only; who
Would be at the expense of two?
No graven images may be
Worshiped, except the currency.
Swear not at all; for, for thy curse
Thine enemy is none the worse.
At church on Sunday to attend
Will serve to keep the world thy friend.
Honor thy parents; that is, all
From whom advancement may befall.   10
Thou shalt not kill; but need'st not strive
Officiously to keep alive.
Do not adultery commit;
Advantage rarely comes of it.
Thou shalt not steal; an empty feat,
When it's so lucrative to cheat.
Bear not false witness; let the lie
Have time on its own wings to fly.
Thou shalt not covet, but tradition
Approves all forms of competition.   20

FOR DISCUSSION:

1. The tone of this poem is bitter and sarcastic. Specifically how does Clough achieve this effect?

2. "The Latest Decalogue" was thought by many Victorians to be shocking and in poor taste. What accounts for this critical response?

Autobiography

LAWRENCE FERLINGHETTI

I am leading a quiet life
in Mike's Place every day
watching the champs
of the Dante Billiard Parlor
and the French pinball addicts.
I am leading a quiet life
on lower East Broadway.
I am an American.
I was an American boy.
I read the American Boy Magazine
and became a boy scout
in the suburbs.
I thought I was Tom Sawyer
catching crayfish in the Bronx River
and imagining the Mississippi.
I had a baseball mit
and an American Flyer bike.
I delivered the Woman's Home Companion
at five in the afternoon
or the Herald Trib
at five in the morning.
I still can hear the paper thump
on lost porches.
I had an unhappy childhood.
I saw Lindberg land.
I looked homeward
and saw no angel.
I got caught stealing pencils
from the Five and Ten Cent Store
the same month I made Eagle Scout.
I chopped trees for the CCC
and sat on them.
I landed in Normandy
in a rowboat that turned over.
I have seen the educated armies
on the beach at Dover.
I have seen Egyptian pilots in purple clouds
shopkeepers rolling up their blinds
at midday
potato salad and dandelions
at anarchist picnics.
I am reading 'Lorna Doone'
and a life of John Most
terror of the industrialist

* From A CONEY ISLAND OF THE MIND by Lawrence Ferlinghetti. Copyright 1955, ©1958 by Lawrence Ferlinghetti. Reprinted by permission of the publisher, New Directions Publishing Corporation.

a bomb on his desk at all times.
I have seen the garbagemen parade
in the Columbus Day Parade
behind the glib
farting trumpeters.
I have not been out to the Cloisters
in a long time
nor to the Tuileries
but I still keep thinking
of going.
I have seen the garbagemen parade
when it was snowing.
I have eaten hotdogs in ballparks.
I have heard the Gettyburg Address
and the Ginsberg Address.
I like it here
and I won't go back
where I came from.
I too have ridden boxcars boxcars boxcars.
I have travelled among unknown men.
I have been in Asia
with Noah in the Ark.
I was in India
when Rome was built.
I have been in the Manger
with an Ass.
I have seen the Eternal Distributor
from a White Hill
in South San Francisco
and the Laughing Woman at Loona Park
outside the Fun House
in a great rainstorm
still laughing.
I have heard the sound of revelry
by night.
I have wandered lonely
as a crowd.
I am leading a quiet life
outside of Mike's Place every day
watching the world walk by
in its curious shoes.
I once started out
to walk around the world
but ended up in Brooklyn.
That Bridge was too much for me.
I have engaged in silence
exile and cunning.
I flew too near the sun
and my wax wings fell off.
I am looking for my Old Man
whom I never knew.
I am looking for the Lost Leader
with whom I flew.
Young men should be explorers.
Home is where one starts from.

But Mother never told me
there'd be scenes like this.
Womb-weary
I rest
I have travelled.
I have seen goof city.
I have seen the mass mess.
I have heard Kid Ory cry.
I have heard a trombone preach.
I have heard Debussy
strained thru a sheet.
I have slept in a hundred islands
where books were trees.
I have heard the birds
that sound like bells.
I have worn grey flannel trousers
and walked upon the beach of hell.
I have dwelt in a hundred cities
where trees were books.
What subways what taxis what cafes!
What women with blind breasts
limbs lost among skyscrapers!
I have seen the statues of heroes
at carrefours.
Danton weeping at a metro entrance
Columbus in Barcelona
pointing Westward up the Ramblas
toward the American Express
Lincoln in his stony chair
And a great Stone Face
in North Dakota.
I know that Columbus
did not invent America.
I have heard a hundred housebroken Ezra Pounds.
They should all be freed.
It is long since I was a herdsman.
I am leading a quiet life
in Mike's Place every day
reading the Classified columns.
I have read the Reader's Digest
from cover to cover
and noted the close identification
of the United States and the Promised Land
where every coin is marked
In God We Trust
but the dollar bills do not have it
being gods unto themselves.
I read the Want Ads daily
looking for a stone a leaf
an unfound door.
I hear America singing
in the Yellow Pages.
One could never tell
the soul has its rages.
I read the papers every day

and hear humanity amiss
in the sad plethora of print.
I see where Walden Pond has been drained
to make an amusement park.
I see they're making Melville
eat his whale.
I see another war is coming
but I won't be there to fight it.
I have read the writing
on the outhouse wall.
I helped Kilroy write it.
I marched up Fifth Avenue
blowing on a bugle in a tight platoon
but hurried back to the Casbah
looking for my dog.
I see a similarity
between dogs and me.
Dogs are the true observers
walking up and down the world
thru the Molloy country.
I have walked down alleys
too narrow for Chryslers.
I have seen a hundred horseless milkwagons
in a vacant lot in Astoria.
Ben Shahn never painted them
but they're there
askew in Astoria.
I have heard the junkman's obbligato.
I have ridden superhighways
and believed the billboard's promises
Crossed the Jersey Flats
and seen the Cities of the Plain
And wallowed in the wilds of Westchester
with its roving bands of natives
in stationwagons.
I have seen them.
I am the man.
I was there.
I suffered
somewhat.
I am an American.
I have a passport.
I did not suffer in public.
And I'm too young to die.
I am a selfmade man.
And I have plans for the future.
I am in line
for a top job.
I may be moving on
to Detroit.
I am only temporarily
a tie salesman.
I am a good Joe.
I am an open book
to my boss.

I am a complete mystery
to my closest friends.
I am leading a quiet life
in Mike's Place every day
contemplating my navel.
I am a part
of the body's long madness.
I have wandered in various nightwoods.
I have leaned in drunken doorways.
I have written wild stories
without punctuation.
I am the man.
I was there.
I suffered
somewhat.
I have sat in an uneasy chair.
I am a tear of the sun.
I am a hill
where poets run.
I invented the alphabet
after watching the flight of cranes
who made letters with their legs.
I am a lake upon a plain.
I am a word
in a tree.
I am a hill of poetry.
I am a raid
on the inarticulate.
I have dreamt
that all my teeth fell out
but my tongue lived
to tell the tale.
For I am a still
of poetry.
I am a bank of song.
I am a playerpiano
in an abandoned casino
on a seaside esplanade
in a dense fog
still playing.
I see a similarity
between the Laughing Woman
and myself.
I have heard the sound of summer
in the rain.
I have seen girls on boardwalks
have complicated sensations.
I understand their hesitations.
I am a gatherer of fruit.
I have seen how kisses
cause euphoria.
I have risked enchantment.
I have seen the Virgin
in an appletree at Chartres
And Saint Joan burn

at the Bella Union.
I have seen giraffes in junglejims
their necks like love
wound around the iron circumstances
of the world.
I have seen the Venus Aphrodite
armless in her drafty corridor.
I have heard a siren sing
at One Fifth Avenue.
I have seen the White Goddess dancing
in the Rue des Beaux Arts
on the Fourteenth of July
and the Beautiful Dame Without Mercy
picking her nose in Chumley's.
She did not speak English.
She had yellow hair
and a hoarse voice
and no bird sang.
I am leading a quiet life
in Mike's Place every day
watching the pocket pool players
making the minestrone scene
wolfing the macaronis
and I have read somewhere
the Meaning of Existence
yet have forgotten
just exactly where.
But I am the man
And I'll be there.
And I may cause the lips
of those who are asleep
to speak.
And I may make my notebooks
into sheaves of grass.
And I may write my own
eponymous epitaph
instructing the horsemen
to pass.

FOR DISCUSSION:

1. Whitmanesque in technique, "Autobiography" attempts to show a great many facets of American life in a short space. Is it successful? How great is the range of American life depicted in the poem?

2. There are echoes and allusions to Wolfe, Arnold, Wordsworth, Browning, T. S. Eliot, and Thoreau in the poem. What is the effect and purpose of these references?

3. What is meant by lines 150-151, "I hear America singing/in the Yellow Pages"?

4. Despite the repetition of the pronoun "I," this is not a self-centered poem. How does Ferlinghetti avoid egotism in "Autobiography"?

5. Why is this poem not a conventional autobiography?

Dover Beach

MATTHEW ARNOLD

The sea is calm to-night.
The tide is full, the moon lies fair
Upon the straits;—on the French coast, the light
Gleams, and is gone; the cliffs of England stand,
Glimmering and vast, out in the tranquil bay.
Come to the window, sweet is the night air!
Only, from the lone line of spray
Where the sea meets the moon-blanch'd land,
Listen! you hear the grating roar
Of pebbles which the waves draw back, and fling,   10
At their return, up the high strand,
Begin, and cease, and then again begin,
With tremulous cadence slow, and bring
The eternal note of sadness in.

Sophocles long ago
Heard it on the Ægæan, and it brought
Into his mind the turbid ebb and flow
Of human misery; we
Find also in the sound a thought,
Hearing it by this distant northern sea.   20

The Sea of Faith
Was once, too, at the full, and round earth's shore
Lay like the folds of a bright girdle furl'd.
But now I only hear
Its melancholy, long, withdrawing roar,
Retreating, to the breath
Of the night-wind down the vast edges drear
And naked shingles of the world.
Ah, love, let us be true
To one another! for the world, which seems   30
To lie before us like a land of dreams,
So various, so beautiful, so new,
Hath really neither joy, nor love, nor light,
Nor certitude, nor peace, nor help for pain;
And we are here as on a darkling plain
Swept with confused alarms of struggle and flight,
Where ignorant armies clash by night.

FOR DISCUSSION:

1. What are the meanings of "shingles" in line 28 and "darkling" in line 35?

2. The sea of faith is compared in line 23 to "the folds of a bright girdle furl'd." What does Arnold mean by this simile?

3. Critics complain that the dominant image of the poem, the sea, is completely forgotten after line 28 in favor of the darkling plain image of the final stanza. Is this really an inconsistency, or does one image lead thematically to the other?

4. Trace the light and sound imagery throughout the poem. How does it relate to the theme? Notice how the depiction of light and sound moves from the literal in the early part of the poem to the metaphorical in the final sections.

The Unknown Citizen

W. H. AUDEN

(TO JS/07/M/378
THIS MARBLE MONUMENT
IS ERECTED BY THE STATE)

He was found by the Bureau of Statistics to be
One against whom there was no official complaint,
And all the reports on his conduct agree
That, in the modern sense of an old-fashioned word, he was a saint,
For in everything he did he served the Greater Community.
Except for the War till the day he retired
He worked in a factory and never got fired,
But satisfied his employers, Fudge Motors Inc.
Yet he wasn't a scab or odd in his views,
For his Union reports that he paid his dues,
(Our report on his Union shows it was sound)
And our Social Psychology workers found
That he was popular with his mates and liked a drink.
The Press are convinced that he bought a paper every day
And that his reactions to advertisements were normal in every way.
Policies taken out in his name prove that he was fully insured,
And his Health-card shows he was once in hospital but left it cured.
Both Producers Research and High-Grade Living declare
He was fully sensible to the advantages of the Installment Plan
And had everything necessary to the Modern Man,
A phonograph, a radio, a car and a frigidaire.
Our researchers into Public Opinion are content
That he held the proper opinions for the time of year;
When there was peace, he was for peace; when there was war, he went.
He was married and added five children to the population,
Which our Eugenist says was the right number for a parent of his generation,
And our teachers report that he never interfered with their education.
Was he free? Was he happy? The question is absurd:
Had anything been wrong, we should certainly have heard.

FOR DISCUSSION:

1. This is a poem in which the tone conveys the poet's meaning more than his words. Specifically, how do we know that line 29, "Had anything been wrong, we should certainly have heard" is meant to be taken as sarcastic?

2. Like Nash in "I Will Arise and Go Now," Auden is attacking specific aspects of modern life. What exactly does Auden dislike about the life lived by the unknown citizen?

* Copyright 1940 by W. H. Auden. Reprinted from THE COLLECTED POETRY OF W. H. AUDEN, by permission of Random House, Inc. and Faber & Faber Ltd.

An Elementary School Classroom in a Slum*

STEPHEN SPENDER

Far far from gusty waves, these children's faces
Like rootless weeds the torn hair round their paleness.
The tall girl with her weighed-down head. The paper-
seeming boy with rat's eyes. The stunted unlucky heir
Of twisted bones, reciting a father's gnarled disease,
His lesson from his desk. At back of the dim class
One unnoted, mild and young: his eyes live in a dream
Of squirrels' game, in tree room, other than this.

On sour cream walls, donations. Shakespeare's head
Cloudless at dawn, civilized dome riding all cities.   10
Belled, flowery, Tyrolese valley. Open-handed map
Awarding the world its world. And yet, for these

Children, these windows, not this world, are world,
Where all their future's painted with a fog,
A narrow street sealed in with a lead sky,
Far far from rivers, capes, and stars of words.

Surely Shakespeare is wicked, the map a bad example
With ships and sun and love tempting them to steal—
For lives that slyly turn in their cramped holes
From fog to endless night? On their slag heap, these children   20
Wear skins peeped through by bones, and spectacles of steel
With mended glass, like bottle bits in slag.
Tyrol is wicked; map's promising a fable:
All of their time and space are foggy slum,
So blot their maps with slums as big as doom.

Unless, governor, teacher, inspector, visitor,
This map becomes their window and these windows
That open on their lives like crouching tombs
Break, O break open, till they break the town
And show the children to the fields and all their world   30
Azure on their sands, to let their tongues
Run naked into books, the white and green leaves open
The history theirs whose language is the sun.

FOR DISCUSSION:

1. To whom is the poem addressed? When do we know?
2. What is the double meaning of "reciting" in line 5?
3. In what sense does Spender mean that Shakespeare and Tyrol are wicked and that the map promises a fable?
4. What is meant by lines 11–12, "Open-handed map/Awarding the world its world"?
5. The final stanza is a plea for social reform. Specifically what does Spender want done to alleviate the plight of the slum schoolchildren?
6. How are the windows of the classroom used both literally and metaphorically?

* Copyright 1942 by Stephen Spender. Reprinted from COLLECTED POEMS 1928–1953, by Stephen Spender, by permission of Random House, Inc. and Faber & Faber Ltd.

Elegy Written in a Country Churchyard

THOMAS GRAY

The curfew tolls the knell of parting day,
The lowing herd wind slowly o'er the lea,
The plowman homeward plods his weary way,
And leaves the world to darkness and to me.

Now fades the glimmering landscape on the sight,
And all the air a solemn stillness holds,
Save where the beetle wheels his droning flight,
And drowsy tinklings lull the distant folds;

Save that from yonder ivy-mantled tow'r
The moping owl does to the moon complain
Of such, as wand'ring near her secret bow'r,
Molest her ancient solitary reign.

Beneath those rugged elms, that yew-tree's shade,
Where heaves the turf in many a mould'ring heap,
Each in his narrow cell for ever laid,
The rude forefathers of the hamlet sleep.

The breezy call of incense-breathing morn,
The swallow twitt'ring from the straw-built shed,
The cock's shrill clarion, or the echoing horn,
No more shall rouse them from their lowly bed.

For them no more the blazing hearth shall burn,
Or busy housewife ply her evening care:
No children run to lisp their sire's return,
Or climb his knees the envied kiss to share.

Oft did the harvest to their sickle yield,
Their furrow oft the stubborn glebe has broke;
How jocund did they drive their team afield!
How bowed the woods beneath their sturdy stroke!

Let not Ambition mock their useful toil,
Their homely joys, and destiny obscure;
Nor Grandeur hear with a disdainful smile,
The short and simple annals of the poor.

The boast of heraldry, the pomp of pow'r,
And all that beauty, all that wealth e'er gave,
Awaits alike th' inevitable hour.
The paths of glory lead but to the grave.

Nor you, ye Proud, impute to these the fault,
If Mem'ry o'er their tomb no trophies raise,
Where thro' the long-drawn aisle and fretted vault
The pealing anthem swells the note of praise.

Can storied urn or animated bust
Back to its mansion call the fleeting breath?
Can Honour's voice provoke the silent dust,
Or Flatt'ry soothe the dull cold ear of Death?

Perhaps in this neglected spot is laid
Some heart once pregnant with celestial fire;
Hands that the rod of empire might have swayed,
Or waked to ecstasy the living lyre.

But Knowledge to their eyes her ample page
Rich with the spoils of time did ne'er unroll: 50
Chill Penury repressed their noble rage,
And froze the genial current of the soul.

Full many a gem of purest ray serene,
The dark unfathomed caves of ocean bear:
Full many a flower is born to blush unseen,
And waste its sweetness on the desert air.

Some village-Hampden, that with dauntless breast
The little tyrant of his fields withstood;
Some mute inglorious Milton here may rest,
Some Cromwell guiltless of his country's blood.   60

Th' applause of list'ning senates to command,
The threats of pain and ruin to despise,
To scatter plenty o'er a smiling land,
And read their hist'ry in a nation's eyes,

Their lot forbad: nor circumscribed alone
Their growing virtues, but their crimes confined;
Forbad to wade through slaughter to a throne,
And shut the gates of mercy on mankind,

The struggling pangs of conscious truth to hide,
To quench the blushes of ingenuous shame,   70
Or heap the shrine of Luxury and Pride
With incense kindled at the Muse's flame.

Far from the madding crowd's ignoble strife,
Their sober wishes never learned to stray;
Along the cool sequestered vale of life
They kept the noiseless tenor of their way.

Yet ev'n these bones from insult to protect
Some frail memorial still erected nigh,
With uncouth rhymes and shapeless sculpture decked,
Implores the passing tribute of a sigh.   80

Their name, their years, spelt by th' unlettered muse,
The place of fame and elegy supply:
And many a holy text around she strews,
That teach the rustic moralist to die.

For who to dumb forgetfulness a prey,
This pleasing anxious being e'er resigned,
Left the warm precincts of the cheerful day,
Nor cast one longing ling'ring look behind?

On some fond breast the parting soul relies,
Some pious drops the closing eye requires;
Ev'n from the tomb the voice of Nature cries,
Ev'n in our ashes live their wonted fires.

For thee, who mindful of th' unhonoured dead
Dost in these lines their artless tale relate;
If chance, by lonely contemplation led,
Some kindred spirit shall inquire thy fate,

Haply some hoary-headed swain may say,
"Oft have we seen him at the peep of dawn
Brushing with hasty steps the dews away
To meet the sun upon the upland lawn.

"There at the foot of yonder nodding beech
That wreathes its old fantastic roots so high,
His listless length at noontide would he stretch,
And pore upon the brook that babbles by.

"Hard by yon wood, now smiling as in scorn,
Mutt'ring his wayward fancies he would rove,
Now drooping, woeful wan, like one forlorn,
Or crazed with care, or crossed in hopeless love.

"One morn I missed him on the customed hill,
Along the heath and near his fav'rite tree;
Another came; nor yet beside the rill,
Nor up the lawn, nor at the wood was he;

"The next with dirges due in sad array
Slow thro' the church-way path we saw him borne.
Approach and read (for thou canst read) the lay,
Graved on the stone beneath yon agèd thorn."

THE EPITAPH

Here rests his head upon the lap of Earth
A Youth to Fortune and to Fame unknown.
Fair Science frowned not on his humble birth,
And Melancholy marked him for her own.

Large was his bounty, and his soul sincere,
Heav'n did a recompence as largely send:
He gave to Mis'ry all he had, a tear,
He gained from Heav'n ('twas all he wished) a friend.

No farther seek his merits to disclose,
Or draw his frailties from their dread abode,
(There they alike in trembling hope repose,)
The bosom of his Father and his God.

FOR DISCUSSION:

1. Traditionally, the English elegiac poet is more concerned with himself than with the individual whose death occasions his poem. In other elegies Milton, Shelley, and Tennyson, for example, are only superficially concerned with the deaths of Edward King, John Keats, and Arthur Henry Hallam. To what extent is Gray's lamentation a sincere mourning for the deaths of the peasants? To what extent is the poem about Gray himself?

2. In what specific ways are the first three stanzas preparation for the melancholic tone that permeates the poem?

3. Examine and explicate the personifications in stanza 11 (lines 41–44).

4. As originally written, stanza 15 (lines 57–60) made reference to Cato and Caesar rather than Hampden and Cromwell. What is the effect of these changes?

5. Examine carefully the poem's attitude toward the peasants and the aristocracy.

6. Most critics agree that the last half of the poem is weaker than the first half. Do you agree? Why?

7. Is Gray able to avoid being overly sentimental? If so, how?

Again the Native Hour Lets Down the Locks*

ALLEN TATE

Again the native hour lets down the locks
Uncombed and black, but gray the bobbing beard;
Ten years ago His eyes, fierce shuttlecocks,
Pierced the close net of what I failed: I feared
The belly-cold, the grave-clout, that betrayed
Me dithering in the drift of cordial seas;
Ten years are time enough to be dismayed
By mummy Christ, head crammed between his knees.

Suppose I taken an arrogant bomber, stroke
By stroke, up to the frazzled sun to hear   10
Sun-ghostlings whisper: Yes, the capital yoke—
Remove it and there's not a ghost to fear
This crucial day, whose decapitate joke
Languidly winds into the inner ear.

FOR DISCUSSION:

1. This sonnet comments on the celebration of Christmas in 1942, when the world was embroiled in war. What social attitudes does it express?

2. Is it necessary to assume that the "I" of line 4 is the poet?

3. What puns are inherent in "native" (line 1), "cordial" (line 6), "capital" (line 11), and "crucial" (line 13)?

4. Is the poet saying that war belies our belief in Christianity, or that our economic system is responsible for our misery, or both?

---

* "Again the Native Hour Lets Down the Locks" (Copyright 1945 Allen Tate) is reprinted with the permission of Charles Scribner's Sons from POEMS by Allen Tate. Also by permission of Associated Book Publishers Ltd.

3. Ten years ago a reference to Tate's Sonnets at Christmas, written ten years before this poem

Slave Quarters

JAMES DICKEY

In the great place the great house is gone from   in the sun
Room, near the kitchen of air   I look across at low walls
Of slave quarters, and feel my imagining loins

Rise with the madness of Owners
To take off the Master's white clothes
And slide all the way into moonlight
Two hundred years old with this moon.
Let me go,

Ablaze with my old me-
scent, in moonlight made by the mind
From the dusk sun, in the yard where my dogs would smell
For once what I totally am,
Flaming up in their brains as the Master
They but dimly had sensed through my clothes:
Let me stand as though moving

At midnight, now at the instant of sundown
When the wind turns

From sea wind to land, and the marsh grass
Hovers, changing direction:
                      there was this house
That fell before I got out. I can pull
It over me where I stand, up from the earth,
Back out of the shells
Of the sea:
          become with the change of this air
A coastal islander, proud of his grounds,
His dogs, his spinet
From Savannah, his pale daughters,
His war with the sawgrass, pushed back into
The sea it crawled from. Nearer dark, unseen,
I can begin to dance
Inside my gabardine suit
As though I had left my silk nightshirt

In the hall of mahogany, and crept
To slave quarters to live out
The secret legend of Owners. Ah, stand up,
Blond loins, another
Love is possible! My thin wife would be sleeping
Or would not mention my absence:
                          the moonlight

---

* Copyright © 1965 by James Dickey. Reprinted from BUCKDANCER'S CHOICE, by James Dickey, by permission of Wesleyan University Press.

On these rocks can be picked like cotton
By a crazed Owner dancing-mad
With the secret repossession of his body

Phosphorescent and mindless, shedding
Blond-headed shadow on the sand,
Hounds pressing in their sleep
Around him, smelling his footblood
On the strange ground that lies between skins
With the roof blowing off slave quarters
To let the moon in burning   50
The years away
In just that corner where crabgrass proves it lives
Outside of time
Who seeks the other color of his body,
His loins giving off a frail light
On the dark lively shipwreck of grass   sees
Water live where
The half-moon touches,
The moon made whole in one wave
Very far from the silent piano   the copy of Walter Scott   60
Closed on its thin-papered battles
Where his daughter practiced, decorum preventing the one
Bead of sweat in all that lace   collected at her throat
From breaking and humanly running
Over Mozart's unmortal keys—

                          I come past
A sand crab pacing sideways   his eyes out
On stalks   the bug-eyed vision of fiddler
Crabs sneaking a light on the run
From the split moon   holding in it a white man stepping   70
Down the road of clamshells and cotton   his eyes out
On stems   the tops of the sugar
Cane soaring   the sawgrass walking:
                                  I come past
The stale pools left
Over from high tide   where the crab in the night sand
Is basting himself with his claws   moving ripples outward
Feasting on brightness
                   and above
A gull also crabs slowly,   80
Tacks, jibes   then turning the corner
Of wind, receives himself like a brother
As he glides down upon his reflection:

My body has a color not yet freed:
In that ruined house let me throw
Obsessive gentility off;
Let Africa rise upon me like a man
Whose instincts are delivered from their chains
Where they lay close-packed and wide-eyed
In muslin sheets   90
As though in the miserly holding
Of too many breaths by one ship.   Now

Worked in silver   their work lies all
Around me   the fields dissolving
Into the sea   and   not on a horse
I stoop to the soil   working
Gathering   moving to the rhythm of a music
That has crossed the ocean in chains

In the grass the great singing void of slave

Labor about me   the moonlight bringing
Sweat out of my back as though   the sun
Changed skins upon me   some other
Man moving near me on horseback   whom I look in the eyes
Once a day:
        there in that corner

Her bed turned to grass. Unsheltered by these walls
The outside fields form slowly
Anew, in a kind of barrelling blowing,
Bend in all the right places   as faintly Michael rows
The boat ashore   his spiritual lungs
Entirely filling the sail.   How take on the guilt

Of slavers? How shudder like one who made
Money from buying a people
To work as ghosts
In this blowing solitude?
I only stand here upon shells   dressed poorly
For nakedness   poorly
For the dark wrecked hovel of rebirth

Picking my way in thought
To the black room
Where starlight blows off the roof
And the great beasts that died with the minds
Of the first slaves, stand at the door, asking
For death, asking to be
Forgotten: the sadness of elephants
The visionary pain in the heads
Of incredibly poisonous snakes
Lion   wildebeest   giraffe   all purchased also
When one wished only
Labor
      those beasts becoming
For the white man the animals of Eden
Emblems of sexual treasure   all beasts attending
Me now   my dreamed dogs snarling at the shades
Of eland and cheetah
On the dispossessed ground where I dance
In my clothes beyond movement:

In nine months she would lie
With a knife between her teeth to cut the pain
Of bearing
A child who belongs in no world   my hair in that boy

Turned black   my skin
Darkened by half   his, lightened
By that half exactly   the beasts of Africa reduced
To cave shadows flickering on his brow
As I think of him: a child would rise from that place
With half my skin. He could for an instant
Of every day   when the wind turns   look
Me in the eyes.   What do you feel when passing

Your blood beyond death   150
To another in secret: into
Another who takes your features   and adds
A misplaced Africa to them,
Changing them forever
As they must live? What happens
To you, when such a one bears
You after your death into rings
Of battling light   a heavyweight champion
Through the swirling glass of four doors,
In epauletted coats   into places   160
Where you learn to wait
On tables   into sitting in all-night cages
Of parking lots   into raising
A sun-sided spade in a gang
Of men on a tar road working
Until the crickets give up?
What happens when the sun goes down

And the white man's loins still stir
In a house of air   still draw him toward
Slave quarters? When Michael's voice is heard   170
Bending the sail like grass,
The real moon begins to come
Apart on the water
And two hundred years are turned back
On with the headlights of a car?
When you learn that there is no hatred
Like love in the eyes
Of a wholly owned face? When you think of what
It would be like   what it has been
What it is to look once a day   180
Into an only
Son's brown, waiting, wholly possessed
Amazing eyes, and not
Acknowledge, but own?

FOR DISCUSSION:

1. Comment on the effectiveness of the device of first-person narration in a poem of this type.

2. What does Dickey especially deplore in the white man's relations with the Negro? Hypocrisy? Injustice? Condescension?

A Song About Major Eatherly*

JOHN WAIN

The book (Fernard Gigon's *Formula for Death—The Atom Bombs and After*) also describes how Major Claude R. Eatherly, pilot of the aircraft which carried the second bomb to Nagasaki, later started having nightmares. His wife is quoted as saying: 'He often jumps up in the middle of the night and screams out in an inhuman voice which makes me feel ill: "Release it, release it".'

Major Eatherly began to suffer brief periods of madness, says Gigon. The doctors diagnosed extreme nervous depression, and Eatherly was awarded a pension of 237 dollars a month.

This he appears to have regarded 'as a premium for murder, as a payment for what had been done to the two Japanese cities'. He never touched the money, and took to petty thievery, for which he was committed to Fort Worth prison.

Report in The Observer, August 1958.

I

Good news. It seems he loved them after all.
His orders were to fry their bones to ash.
He carried up the bomb and let it fall.
And then his orders were to take the cash,

A hero's pension. But he let it lie.
It was in vain to ask him for the cause.
Simply that if he touched it he would die.
He fought his own, and not his country's wars.

His orders told him he was not a man:
An instrument, fine-tempered, clear of stain,　　　　10
All fears and passions closed up like a fan:
No more volition than his aeroplane.

But now he fought to win his manhood back.
Steep from the sunset of his pain he flew
Against the darkness in that last attack.
It was for love he fought, to make that true.

II

To take life is always to die a little: to stop
any feeling and moving contrivance, however ugly,
unnecessary, or hateful, is to reduce by so much the total
of life there is. And that is to die a little.　　　　20

To take the life of an enemy is to help him,
a little, towards destroying your own. Indeed, that is why
we hate our enemies: because they force us to kill them.

---

* From WEEP BEFORE GOD, Copyright ©1961 by John Wain. Reprinted by permission of St. Martin's Press, Inc., Macmillan & Company Ltd., The Macmillan Company of Canada Ltd., and the author.

A murderer hides the dead man in the ground:
but his crime rears up and topples on to the living,
for it is they who now must hunt the murderer,
murder him, and hide him in the ground: it is they
who now feel the touch of death cold in their bones.

Animals hate death. A trapped fox will gnaw
through his own leg: it is so important to live
that he forgives himself the agony,
consenting, for life's sake, to the desperate teeth
grating through bone and pulp, the gasping yelps.

That is the reason the trapper hates the fox.
You think the trapper doesn't hate the fox?
But he does, and the fox can tell how much.
It is not the fox's teeth that grind his bones,
It is the trapper's. It is the trapper, there,
Who keeps his head down, gnawing, hour after hour.

And the people the trapper works for, they are there too,
heads down beside the trap, gnawing away.
Why shouldn't they hate the fox? Their cheeks are smeared
with his rank blood, and on their tongues his bone
being splintered, feels uncomfortably sharp.

So once Major Eatherly hated the Japanese.

III

Hell is a furnace, so the wise men taught.
The punishment for sin is to be broiled.
A glowing coal for every sinful thought.

The heat of God's great furnace ate up sin,
Which whispered up in smoke or fell in ash:
So that each hour a new hour could begin.

So fire was holy, though it tortured souls,
The sinners' anguish never ceased, but still
Their sin was burnt from them by shining coals.

Hell fried the criminal but burnt the crime,
Purged where it punished, healed where it destroyed:
It was a stove that warmed the rooms of time.

No man begrudged the flames their appetite.
All were afraid of fire, yet none rebelled.
The wise men taught that hell was just and right.

'The soul desires its necessary dread:
Only among the thorns can patience weave
A bower where the mind can make its bed.'

Even the holy saints whose patient jaws
Chewed bitter rind and hands raised up the dead
Were chestnuts roasted at God's furnace doors.

The wise men passed. The clever men appeared.
They ruled that hell be called a pumpkin face.
They robbed the soul of what it justly feared.

Coal after coal the fires of hell went out.
Their heat no longer warmed the rooms of time,
Which glistened now with fluorescent doubt.

The chilly saints went striding up and down
To warm their blood with useful exercise.
They rolled like conkers through the draughty town.

Those emblematic flames sank down to rest,
But metaphysical fire can not go out:
Men ran from devils they had dispossessed,

And felt within their skulls the dancing heat
No longer stored in God's deep boiler-room.
Fire scorched their temples, frostbite chewed their feet.

That parasitic fire could race and climb
More swiftly than the stately flames of hell.
Its fuel gone, it licked the beams of time.

So time dried out and youngest hearts grew old.
The smoky minutes cracked and broke apart.
The world was roasting but the men were cold.

Now from this pain worse pain was brought to birth,
More hate, more anguish, till at last they cried,
'Release this fire to gnaw the crusty earth:

Make it a flame that's obvious to sight
And let us say we kindled it ourselves,
To split the skulls of men and let in light.

Since death is camped among us, wish him joy,
Invite him to our table and our games.
We cannot judge, but we can still destroy'.

And so the curtains of the mind were drawn.
Men conjured hell a first, a second time:
And Major Eatherly took off at dawn.

IV

Suppose a sea-bird,
its wings stuck down with oil, riding the waves
in no direction, under the storm-clouds, helpless,
lifted for an instant by each moving billow
to scan the meaningless horizon, helpless,
helpless, and the storms coming, and its wings dead,
its bird-nature dead:
                Imagine this castaway,
loved, perhaps, by the Creator, and yet abandoned,

mocked by the flashing scales of the fish beneath it,
who leap, twist, dive, as free of the wide sea
as formerly the bird of the wide sky,
now helpless, starving, a prisoner of the surface,
unable to dive or rise:
                      this is your emblem.
Take away the bird, let it be drowned
in the steep black waves of the storm, let it be broken
against rocks in the morning light, too faint to swim:
take away the bird, but keep the emblem.

It is the emblem of Major Eatherly,
who looked round quickly from the height of each wave,
but saw no land, only the rim of the sky
into which he was not free to rise, or the silver
gleam of the mocking scales of the fish diving
where he was not free to dive.

Men have clung always to emblems,
to tokens of absolution from their sins.
Once it was the scapegoat driven out, bearing
its load of guilt under the empty sky
until its shape was lost, merged in the scrub.

Now we are civilized, there is no wild heath.
Instead of the nimble scapegoat running out
to be lost under the wild and empty sky,
the load of guilt is packed into prison walls,
and men file inward through the heavy doors.

But now that image, too, is obsolete.
The Major entering prison is no scapegoat.
His penitence will not take away our guilt,
nor sort with any consoling ritual:
this is penitence for its own sake, beautiful,
uncomprehending, inconsolable, unforeseen.
He is not in prison for his penitence:
it is no outrage to our law that he wakes
with cries of pity on his parching lips.
We do not punish him for cries or nightmares.
We punish him for stealing things from stores.

O, give his pension to the storekeeper.
Tell him it is the price of all our souls.
But do not trouble to unlock the door
and bring the Major out into the sun.
Leave him: it is all one: perhaps his nightmares
grow cooler in the twilight of the prison.
Leave him; if he is sleeping, come away.
But lay a folded paper by his head,
nothing official or embossed, a page
torn from your notebook, and the words in pencil.
Say nothing of love, or thanks, or penitence:
say only 'Eatherly, we have your message.'

FOR DISCUSSION:
1. Why did Eatherly reject the pension?
2. Is the quotation from The Observer what one usually thinks of as subject matter for poetry?
3. Why does Wain think that the helpless seabird is an appropriate symbol for Major Eatherly?
4. What is Eatherly's message?

II Critical Perspective:
FORMALIST

Introduction

Formalism is the most influential of the twentieth-century critical movements. Not only has it caused a revolution in the teaching of literature in secondary schools and colleges but it has redefined standards of quality in literature for professional critics and casual readers alike. Its theories have fashioned the literary taste of two generations and measurably contributed to the reputation of authors like Donne, Keats, Conrad, Joyce, and Dylan Thomas, whose works adapt particularly well to the formalist critical approach.

Like all intellectual movements that span half a century, formalism is difficult to define and characterize. Even the name of the movement has undergone change during its growth. But whether formalism has called itself New Criticism, structuralism, analytic criticism, or contextualism, certain aesthetic principles have guided its development and distinguished it from its predecessors. These principles derive ultimately from the aesthetic theories of Aristotle, Kant, and Coleridge, but the particular qualities that characterize formalism were imparted primarily by two groups. The first was a group of scholar-critics at Kenyon College and Vanderbilt University who published their views in a magazine called The Fugitive in the early 1920's: John Crowe Ransom, Allen Tate, Donald Davidson, and Robert Penn Warren. The second was an English group of academicians and critics who expanded and elaborated upon the ideas of The Fugitive group and who put many formalist theories into critical practice: I. A. Richards, T. S. Eliot, and William Empson.

Formalism began as a reaction against the excesses of social and biographical criticism, which assumes literature to be the outgrowth of an historical period or the life of the author, and which stipulates that literary criticism must focus on these forces. Dissatisfied with these attitudes toward criticism, the formalists sought a theory of literature which would not only preserve the integrity of the work of art but which would also provide the critic with a methodology for understanding meaning in literature.

The formalists began by insisting that there is an essential dichotomy between the language of science and the language of art. By this they meant that scientific meaning and discourse were very different from poetic meaning and discourse. Science, according to Richards, is concerned with a statement that "may be used for the sake of the reference, true or false, which it causes." Poetry, on the other hand, uses language "for the sake of the effects in emotion and attitude produced by the reference it occasions."

Conceived in this manner, the work of art is a verbal fact, unique in its ability to communicate man's experiences by means of a set of symbols whose referents do not exist in a one-to-one relationship; a word can have several meanings in a literary work. The scientist's purpose is to consciously avoid multiple meanings, emotional attitudes, and a plurality of implications. He tries to describe his world with verbal symbols that are as totally denotative as possible, whose meanings are agreed upon in advance, and which change very little in different contexts. On the other hand, the vocabulary of the artist, which seeks to describe human values and subjective experiences rather than things, is necessarily connotative, suggestive, and evocative. In fact, formalists believe art derives its being, purpose, and value from the very limitations imposed by scientific attitudes and scientific uses of language.

Formalists are in complete agreement in their assertion that the words of a poem do not operate referentially in the same manner as the words of a treatise on the physical description of matter. Thus, for example, when T. S. Eliot sets the scene for his "Love Song of J. Alfred Prufrock" on a night when the "evening is spread out against the sky/Like a patient etherised upon a table," he does not mean that the temperature is 75°, the humidity 72%, the barometer 30.02 and falling, the cloud coverage 10%, and the winds from the Northeast at 2 m.p.h. His diction, totally connotative, suggests an unnatural calm, a pervasive stillness, a clinically detached dreamlike state of expectancy that is totally absent from and irrelevant to the meteorologist's report, but which is completely appropriate—and one might add necessary—to Eliot's purpose in the poem. Because of the special nature of the language of art, the formalist insists on the primacy of the text. More than any of the other critical perspectives, formalism asserts the essential autonomy of the work of art and assiduously defends this autonomy against subordination to external considerations. In short, the bases of formalism are an emphasis on the verbal rather than the biographical, historical, or social context and an insistence on an ontological criticism, that is, a criticism that recognizes the work of art as a separate entity with its own laws of being and design.

Growing out of this concept of the work of art as a distinct, self-contained entity with rules of being unto itself is the formalist assertion that a literary work "means" not only by its content but by its form as well. Indeed, the two are not separate, but identical: form is content. To the social critic the meaning of literature lies in its relation to social causes; the formalist critic, however, demands that literature be judged in literary terms and sees artistic meaning as inherent in the specific ordering, relation, structuring, and development of the work's component parts. Meaning and value are therefore intrinsic rather than extrinsic qualities, and the author is to be judged on the basis of how well he has unified his work. The form of literature is not a mere container into which ideas are put, but an integral part of a work's total meaning.

Thus the structure of a work of art is as important as the structure of a building. Just as the architect solves problems of relating one room to another, of integrating the hall, kitchen, and living room into a meaningful, functional, and pleasing whole, so the author solves problems of "internal consistency" by planning a particular verbal framework within which he patterns his episodes, unifies his themes, and orders his images.

All kinds of unifying devices are the concern of the formalist, especially the devices that concern thematic unity and that tie together seemingly unrelated episodes in a poem, play, or novel. Critical inquiries into themes of maturation and retrogression are common. Joyce's A Portrait of the Artist as a Young Man is thus viewed as the orderly evolution of a youth struggling toward manhood with each successive scene showing the novel's protagonist coming closer to his goal of adulthood. Huckleberry Finn, episodic though it may seem on first reading, reveals under formalist scrutiny the force of the Mississippi River in shaping the subtle spiritual and psychological development of its young protagonist. Formalism has also shown Gulliver's Travels to be comprised not of four separate and distinct books unrelated to each other, but of four books which form a unified whole portraying the irretraceable steps in the deterioration and retrogression of Lemuel Gulliver. Similar unity can be found in Golding's Lord of the Flies where a recurring motif of the hunt and chase is employed to show the gradual movement of a group of young boys from a civilized state to one bordering on savagery and cannibalism.

Not only patterns of grand design have interested the formalist critic but smaller structural elements as well. Cyclical or recurring patterns in novels, interrelationships between characters in plays, development of certain poetic images and possibilities for multiple interpretation of individual words have all received much attention from this school of criticism. Thus, the scaffold in The Scarlet Letter is not only an appropriate symbol of crime and punishment but also a unifying device linking together the beginning, middle, and end of Hawthorne's novel. In like manner, formalists note that Hamlet's predicament—the obligation to avenge a father's death—is shared by two other characters in the play, Laertes and Fortinbras, and that their impulsive actions stand in vivid contrast to Hamlet's indecision. Shakespeare's Sonnet 73 (p. 259) contains three major images —a bare tree in autumn, the twilight of a day, and a pile of dying embers—each a poetic statement of oncoming death and a preparation for the poem's final couplet. Critics of the formalist school have also observed that the word "buckle" in line 10 of Hopkins's "The Windhover" (p. 274) makes sense in any of its traditional meanings: fasten, crumple, or struggle.

Few critics have been as concerned with formal aspects of literary criticism as Cleanth Brooks, who has been largely responsible for establishing formalism as a methodology and as a practical approach to literary interpretation. His technique is that of close textual analysis: how does the particular word, image, phrase, or stanza convey a meaning that no replacement could? In poetry he has insisted that imagery be fresh, consistent, and functional; that the meter be consistent with the sense of the poem; and that all parts of the poem (tone, imagery, structure, meter) co-relate and contribute to the total effect or point. Equally demanding in his criticism of fiction, Brooks has analyzed matters of plot unity, atmosphere, internal conflict, suspense, climax, and narrative point of view. As a critic of drama he has focused on patterns of exposition, act division, techniques of characterization, and functional uses of setting and dialogue. Recognizing the individuality and special character of each work of art, he has always emphasized materials and methods inherent in the work itself.

Indeed, Brooks believes the individual work is so special that to reword a passage, to use words other than the author's, or to place words in a different arrangement or order from the author's is to commit the heresy of paraphrase. Any alteration in the unique structural and semantic pattern of a work of art changes its meaning unavoidably. The diction and order of presentation selected by an author set up a unity based upon a multiplicity of rhetorical and linguistic devices, such as ambiguity, paradox, and irony, which is damaged if the inner core of the work is paraphrased. For Brooks, the coherence of a work of art is unique and inimitable.

If paraphrase is unacceptable to the formalists as a critical device because it fails to recognize the integrity of the work of art, considering the intention of the author in writing the work is even more damaging. To analyze art in terms of the author's attitude toward his work, the way he felt when he was writing it, what made him write it, and what he thought he was attempting to do is to commit what William K. Wimsatt and Monroe C. Beardsley have called the intentional fallacy. They begin by asserting that what the author intended is, for the most part, unknowable or at best questionable. Authors themselves are hardly infallible judges of their own actions, motives, and intentions. Even if their statements can be accepted as true, they are open to question because motive and intent are frequently subconscious, unknown even to the author himself. Again, intentions are not always carried out, or carried out in the exact fashion the author intends. No, the formalist asserts, achieved intention is the only measurable critical guide, and if the author has succeeded, his intent will be shown in the work itself; if he has not, then whatever he originally intended is irrelevant and therefore of no consequence to the critic.

Related to the intentional fallacy is the use of biographical information about the author to interpret his work. Formalists believe that biography can be an attractive, interesting, and rewarding study in itself, but to confuse the study of the man with the study of his work is to misunderstand totally the nature of literary creation and to bring to bear on the poem, play, or novel, external considerations which can not solve problems that yield only to internal approaches. It is therefore not very helpful as a tool to interpretation to know whether Bacon, Marlowe, or Shakespeare wrote Hamlet when one analyzes the "To Be Or Not To Be" soliloquy, or to investigate Coleridge's attraction to Dorothy Wordsworth as a clue to the meaning of his "Kubla Khan," or to know that Donne was preparing for a trip to Europe when he wrote "A Valediction Forbidding Mourning." Interesting though these approaches may be, they are fallacious because they establish a critical standard that leads away from the work itself.

Just as the intentional fallacy and biographical criticism confuse the literary work and its causes, another erroneous critical attitude, which Wimsatt and Beardsley call the affective fallacy, confuses the literary work and its results. Here, they point out, the critic is concerned with the emotional result (or affect) the work of art has on its audience. On the one hand, this critical perspective produces the relativity of Aristotle's theory of catharsis and the impressionism of Emily Dickinson's definition of poetry ("If I feel physically as if the top of my head were blown off, I know that is poetry"). On the other hand, it has been responsible for historical investigation into the critical reception of novels, studies of the Victorian reading public and the attitudes of the Elizabethan theatergoer.

Because formalism has been outspoken in its assessment of shortcomings in earlier modes of criticism, it has been common—despite the statements of many formalists—to view it as totally antithetical to traditional social, historical, and biographical attitudes. Cleanth Brooks has been especially vocal in attempts to clarify the relationship between the traditional critical schools (which he calls scholarship) and formalist criticism:

> It is easy therefore for even well informed people to conceive that the "new" criticism is somehow hostile to historical scholarship. Some of the limitations of the orthodox scholarship have been pointed out and the claims of that critical discipline have been properly urged. I have urged them myself. But to ask that more attention be given to criticism is not to demand that we abandon training in linguistics or in textual criticism or in literary history or in the history of ideas. Such a conclusion is entirely unwarranted. Yet for good reason or bad many people have leaped to this conclusion and perhaps the best service therefore that could be rendered the "new" criticism . . . is to attempt to clear up this confusion.

As might be expected, objections to formalism from articulate representatives of other views of criticism have not been lacking. David Daiches attacks the fundamental premise of formalism—the self-sufficiency and integrity of art—and argues that a literary work is many things at the same time: a reflection of its social climate; a record of the mental history of its author; a consciously structured arrangement of words, ideas, and techniques; and a document that can provide unique insights into human experiences and values. To become obsessed with one of these aspects to the exclusion of others, he believes, is to distort the process of criticism.

Others have suggested that by their insistence upon the omission of the author and audience from the process of literary criticism, the formalists have adopted an art-for-art's-sake attitude. When literature is divorced from people and from life, when criticism concerns itself only with the how, not the why or what, the work of art becomes barren and sterile. By emphasizing structural elements in a poem, play or novel, opponents say, the formalists have made an end of technique rather than a means. Literature in this guise, they lament, is perhaps suitable for the laboratory but not for the world.

The Formalist Critics*

CLEANTH BROOKS

Here are some articles of faith I could subscribe to:
That literary criticism is a description and an evaluation of its object.
That the primary concern of criticism is with the problem of unity—the kind of whole which the literary work forms or fails to form, and the relation of the various parts to each other in building up this whole.
That the formal relations in a work of literature may include, but certainly exceed, those of logic.
That in a successful work, form and content cannot be separated.
That form is meaning.
That literature is ultimately metaphorical and symbolic.
That the general and the universal are not seized upon by abstraction, but got at through the concrete and the particular.
That literature is not a surrogate for religion.
That, as Allen Tate says, "specific moral problems" are the subject matter of literature, but that the purpose of literature is not to point a moral.
That the principles of criticism define the area relevant to literary criticism; they do not constitute a method for carrying out the criticism.

Such statements as these would not, however, even though greatly elaborated, serve any useful purpose here. The interested reader already knows the general nature of the critical position adumbrated—or, if he does not, he can find it set forth in writings of mine or of other critics of like sympathy. Moreover, a condensed restatement of the position here would probably beget as many misunderstandings as have past attempts to set it forth. It seems much more profitable to use the present occasion for dealing with some persistent misunderstandings and objections.

In the first place, to make the poem or the novel the central concern of criticism has appeared to mean cutting it loose from its author and from his life as a man, with his own particular hopes, fears, interests, conflicts, etc. A criticism so limited may seem bloodless and hollow. It will seem so to the typical professor of literature in the graduate school, where the study of literature is still primarily a study of the ideas and personality of the author as revealed in his letters, his diaries, and the recorded conversations of his friends. It will certainly seem so to literary gossip columnists who purvey literary chitchat. It may also seem so to the young poet or novelist, beset with his own problems of composition and with his struggles to find a subject and a style and to get a hearing for himself.

In the second place, to emphasize the work seems to involve severing it from those who actually read it, and this severance may seem drastic and therefore disastrous. After all, literature is written to be read. Wordsworth's poet was a man speaking to men. In

---

* Reprinted from *The Kenyon Review*, XIII (Winter 1951), 72–81, by permission of the editors and the author.

each Sunday *Times*, Mr. J. Donald Adams points out that the hungry sheep look up and are not fed; and less strenuous moralists than Mr. Adams are bound to feel a proper revulsion against "mere aestheticism." Moreover, if we neglect the audience which reads the work, including that for which it was presumably written, the literary historian is prompt to point out that the kind of audience that Pope had did condition the kind of poetry that he wrote. The poem has its roots in history, past or present. Its place in the historical context simply cannot be ignored.

I have stated these objections as sharply as I can because I am sympathetic with the state of mind which is prone to voice them. Man's experience is indeed a seamless garment, no part of which can be separated from the rest. Yet if we urge this fact of inseparability against the drawing of distinctions, then there is no point in talking about criticism at all. I am assuming that distinctions are necessary and useful and indeed inevitable.

The formalist critic knows as well as anyone that poems and plays and novels are written by men—that they do not somehow happen—and that they are written as expressions of particular personalities and are written from all sorts of motives—for money, from a desire to express oneself, for the sake of a cause, etc. Moreover, the formalist critic knows as well as anyone that literary works are merely potential until they are read—that is, that they are recreated in the minds of actual readers, who vary enormously in their capabilities, their interests, their prejudices, their ideas. But the formalist critic is concerned primarily with the work itself. Speculation on the mental processes of the author takes the critic away from the work into biography and psychology. There is no reason, of course, why he should not turn away into biography and psychology. Such explorations are very much worth making. But they should not be confused with an account of the work. Such studies describe the process of composition, not the structure of the thing composed, and they may be performed quite as validly for the poor work as for the good one. They may be validly performed for any kind of expression—nonliterary as well as literary.

On the other hand, exploration of the various readings which the work has received also takes the critic away from the work into psychology and the history of taste. The various imports of a given work may well be worth studying. I. A. Richards has put us all in his debt by demonstrating what different experiences may be derived from the same poem by an apparently homogeneous group of readers; and the scholars have pointed out, all along, how different Shakespeare appeared to an 18th Century as compared with a 19th Century audience; or how sharply divergent are the estimates of John Donne's lyrics from historical period to historical period. But such work, valuable and necessary as it may be, is to be distinguished from a criticism of the work itself. The formalist critic, because he wants to criticize the work itself, makes two assumptions: (1) he assumes that the revelant part of the author's intention is what he got actually into his work; that is, he assumes that the author's intention as *realized* is the "intention" that counts, not necessarily what he was conscious of trying to do, or what he now remembers he was then trying to do. And (2) the formalist critic assumes an ideal reader: that is, instead of focusing on the varying spectrum of possible readings, he attempts to find a central point of reference from which he can focus upon the structure of the poem or novel.

But there *is* no ideal reader, someone is prompt to point out, and he will probably add that it is sheer arrogance that allows the critic, with his own blindsides and prejudices, to put himself in the position of that ideal reader. There is no ideal reader, of course, and I suppose that the practising critic can never be too often reminded of the gap between his reading and the "true" reading of the poem. But for the purpose of focusing upon the poem rather than upon his own reactions, it is a defensible strategy. Finally, of course, it is the strategy that all critics of whatever persuasion are forced to adopt. (The alternatives are desperate: either we say that one person's reading is as good as another's and equate those readings on a basis of absolute equality and thus deny the possibility of any standard reading. Or else we take a lowest common denominator of the various readings that have been made; that is, we frankly move from literary criticism into socio-psychology. To propose taking a consensus of the opinions of "qualified" readers is simply to split the ideal reader into a group of ideal readers.) As consequences of the distinction just referred to, the formalist critic rejects two popular tests for literary value. The first proves the value of the work from the author's "sincerity" (or the intensity of the author's feelings as he composed it). If we heard that Mr. Guest testified that he put his heart and soul into his poems, we would not be very much impressed, though I should see no reason to doubt such a statement from Mr. Guest. It would simply be critically irrelevant. Ernest Hemingway's statement in a recent issue of *Time* magazine that he counts his last novel his best is of interest for Hemingway's biography, but most readers of *Across the River and Into the Trees* would agree that it proves nothing at all about the value of the novel—that in this case the judgment is simply pathetically inept. We discount also such tests for poetry as that proposed by A. E. Housman—the bristling of his beard at the reading of a good poem. The intensity of his reaction has critical significance only in proportion as we have already learned to trust him as a reader. Even so, what it tells us is something about Housman—nothing decisive about the poem.

It is unfortunate if this playing down of such responses seems to deny humanity to either writer or reader. The critic may enjoy certain works very much and may be indeed intensely moved by them. I am, and I have no embarrassment in admitting the fact; but a detailed description of my emotional state on reading certain works has little to do with indicating to an interested reader what the work is and how the parts of it are related.

Should all criticism, then, be self-effacing and analytic? I hope that the answer is implicit in what I have already written, but I shall go on to spell it out. Of course not. That will depend upon the occasion and the audience. In practice, the critic's job is rarely a purely critical one. He is much more likely to be involved in dozens of more or less related tasks, some of them trivial, some of them important. He may be trying to get a hearing for a new author, or to get the attention of the freshman sitting in the back row. He may be comparing two authors, or editing a text; writing a brief newspaper review or reading a paper before the Modern Language Association. He may even be simply talking with a friend, talking about literature for the hell of it. Parable, anecdote, epigram, metaphor—these and a hundred other devices may be thoroughly legitimate for his varying purposes. He is certainly not to be asked to suppress his personal enthusiasms or his interest in social history or in politics. Least of all is he being asked to *present* his criticisms as the close reading of a text. Tact, common sense, and uncommon sense if he has it, are all requisite if the practising critic is to do his various jobs well.

But it will do the critic no harm to have a clear idea of what his specific job as a critic is. I can sympathize with writers who are tired of reading rather drab "critical analyses," and who recommend brighter, more amateur, and more "human" criticism. As ideals, these are excellent; as recipes for improving criticism, I have my doubts. Appropriate vulgarizations of these ideals are already flourishing, and have long flourished —in the class room presided over by the college lecturer of infectious enthusiasm, in the gossipy Book-of-the-Month Club bulletins, and in the columns of the *Saturday Review of Literature*.

I have assigned the critic a modest, though I think an important, role. With reference to the help which the critic can give to the practising artist, the role is even more modest. As critic, he can give only negative help. Literature is not written by formula: he can have no formula to offer. Perhaps he can do little more than indicate whether in his opinion the work has succeeded or failed. Healthy criticism and healthy creation do tend to go hand in hand. Everything else being equal, the creative artist is better off for being in touch with a vigorous criticism. But the other considerations are never equal, the case is always special, and in a given case the proper advice *could* be: quit reading criticism altogether, or read political science or history or philosophy —or join the army, or join the church.

There is certainly no doubt that the kind of specific and positive help that someone like Ezra Pound was able to give to several writers of our time is in one sense the most important kind of criticism that there can be. I think that it is not unrelated to the kind of criticism that I have described: there is the same intense concern with the text which is being built up, the same concern with "technical problems." But many other things are involved—matters which lie outside the specific ambit of criticism altogether; among them a knowledge of the personality of the particular writer, the ability to stimulate, to make positive suggestions.

A literary work is a document and as a document can be analysed in terms of the forces that have produced it, or it may be manipulated as a force in its own right. It mirrors the past, it may influence the future. These facts it would be futile to deny, and I know of no critic who does deny them. But the reduction of a work of literature to its causes does not constitute literary criticism; nor does an estimate of its effects. Good literature is more than effective rhetoric applied to true ideas—even if we could agree upon a philosophical yardstick for measuring the truth of ideas and even if we could find some way that transcended nose-counting for determining the effectiveness of the rhetoric.

A recent essay by Lionel Trilling bears very emphatically upon this point. (I refer to him the more readily because Trilling has registered some of his objections to the critical position that I maintain.) In the essay entitled "The Meaning of a Literary Idea," Trilling discusses the debt to Freud and Spengler of four American writers, O'Neill, Dos Passos, Wolfe, and Faulkner. Very justly, as it seems to me, he chooses Faulkner as the contemporary writer who, along with Ernest Hemingway, best illustrates the power and importance of ideas in literature. Trilling is thoroughly aware that his choice will seem shocking and perhaps perverse, "because," as he writes, "Hemingway and Faulkner have insisted on their indifference to the conscious intellectual tradition of our time and have acquired the reputation of achieving their effects by means that have the least possible connection with any sort of intellectuality or even with intelligence."

Here Trilling shows not only acute discernment but an admirable honesty in electing to deal with the hard cases—with the writers who do not clearly and easily make the case for the importance of ideas. I applaud the discernment and the honesty, but I wonder whether the whole discussion in his essay does not indicate that Trilling is really much closer to the so-called "new critics" than perhaps he is aware. For Trilling, one notices, rejects any simple one-to-one relation between the truth of the idea and the value of the literary work in which it is embodied. Moreover, he does not claim that "recognizable ideas of a force or weight are 'used' in the work," or "new ideas of a certain force and weight are 'produced' by the work." He praises rather the fact that we feel that Hemingway and Faulkner are "intensely at work upon the recalcitrant stuff of life." The last point is made the matter of real importance. Whereas Dos Passos, O'Neill, and Wolfe make us "feel that *they* feel that they have said the last word," "we seldom have the sense that [Hemingway and Faulkner] . . . have misrepresented to themselves the nature and the difficulty of the matter they work on."

Trilling has chosen to state the situation in terms of the writer's activity (Faulkner is intensely at work, etc.). But this judgment is plainly an inference from the quality of Faulkner's novels—Trilling has not simply heard Faulkner say that he has had to struggle with his work. (I take it Mr. Hemingway's declaration about the effort he put into the last novel impresses Trilling as little as it impresses the rest of us.)

Suppose, then, that we tried to state Mr. Trilling's point, not in terms of the effort of the artist, but in terms of the structure of the work itself. Should we not get something very like the terms used by the formalist critics? A description in terms of "tensions," of symbolic development, of ironies and their resolution? In short, is not the formalist critic trying to describe in terms of the dynamic form of the work itself how the recalcitrancy of the material is acknowledged and dealt with?

Trilling's definition of "ideas" makes it still easier to accommodate my position to his. I have already quoted a passage in which he repudiates the notion that one has to show how recognizable ideas are "used" in the work, or new ideas are "produced" by the work. He goes on to write: "All that we need to do is account for a certain aesthetic effect as being in some important part achieved by a mental process which is not different from the process by which discursive ideas are conceived, and which is to be judged by some of the criteria by which an idea is judged." One would have to look far to find a critic "formal" enough to object to this. What some of us have been at pains to insist upon is that literature does not simply "exemplify" ideas or "produce" ideas—as Trilling acknowledges. But no one claims that the writer is an inspired idiot. He uses his mind and his reader ought to use his, in processes "not different from the process by which discursive ideas are conceived." Literature is not inimical to ideas. It thrives upon ideas, but it does not present ideas patly and neatly. It involves them with the "recalcitrant stuff of life." The literary critic's job is to deal with that involvement.

The mention of Faulkner invites a closing comment upon the critic's specific job. As I have described it, it may seem so modest that one could take its performance for granted. But consider the misreadings of Faulkner now current, some of them the work of the most brilliant critics that we have, some of them quite wrong-headed, and demonstrably so. What is true of Faulkner is only less true of many another author, including many writers of the past. Literature has many "uses"—and critics propose new uses, some of them exciting and spectacular. But all the multiform uses to which literature can be put rest finally upon our knowing what a given work "means." That knowledge is basic.

FOR DISCUSSION:

1. Do you agree with Brooks's statement that the primary concern of criticism should be with unity?

2. Specifically, what does Brooks mean by "form is meaning"? Cite examples of works of literature where the two coalesce.

3. What qualifications and reservations are inherent in Brooks's rejection of the social criticism of literature?

4. Do you agree that the author's intention—what he thought he was trying to do—is irrelevant in the criticism of literature?

5. Is Brooks's approach an attempt to bring objective criteria to bear on the analysis of literature?

SUGGESTIONS FOR ADDITIONAL READING:

Brooks, Cleanth. "The New Criticism: A Brief for the Defense," *American Scholar,* XIII (Summer 1944), 435–449.

———. *The Well Wrought Urn: Studies in the Structure of Poetry.* New York, 1947.

Burke, Kenneth. *Philosophy of Literary Form.* Baton Rouge, 1941.

Daiches, David. "The New Criticism: Some Qualifications," *College English,* XXXIX (February 1950), 64–72.

Elton, William. *A Glossary of New Criticism.* New York, 1949.

Empson, William. *Seven Types of Ambiguity.* New York, 1930.

Foster, Richard. *The New Romantics.* Bloomington, 1962.

Handy, William J. *Kant and the Southern New Critics.* Austin, 1963.

Krieger, Murray. *The New Apologists for Poetry.* Minneapolis, 1956.

Ransom, John Crowe. *The New Criticism.* New York, 1941.

Richards, I. A. *Practical Criticism.* New York, 1929.

Stallman, Robert. "The New Critics," in *Critiques and Essays in Criticism,* pp. 488–506, New York, 1949.

Wimsatt, William K. and Monroe C. Beardsley. "The Intentional Fallacy," in *The Verbal Icon,* pp. 3–21, Lexington, 1954.

Oedipus Rex

SOPHOCLES

OEDIPUS, King of Thebes
A PRIEST
CREON, brother of Iocastê
TEIRESIAS, a blind prophet
IOCASTE, wife of Oedipus

MESSENGER
SHEPHERD OF LAÏOS
SECOND MESSENGER
CHORUS OF THEBAN ELDERS

Scene. Before the palace of Oedipus, King of Thebes. A central door and two lateral doors open onto a platform which runs the length of the façade. On the platform, right and left, are altars; and three steps lead down into the "orchestra," or chorus-ground. At the beginning of the action these steps are crowded by suppliants who who have brought branches and chaplets of olive leaves and who lie in various attitudes of despair. OEDIPUS enters.

Prologue

OEDIPUS. My children, generations of the living
In the line of Kadmos, nursed at his ancient hearth:
Why have you strewn yourselves before these altars
In supplication, with your boughs and garlands?
The breath of incense rises from the city
With a sound of prayer and lamentation.
                      Children,
I would not have you speak through messengers,
And therefore I have come myself to hear you—
I, Oedipus, who bear the famous name.
  [To a PRIEST.]
You, there, since you are eldest in the company,
Speak for them all, tell me what preys upon you,
Whether you come in dread, or crave some blessing:
Tell me, and never doubt that I will help you
In every way I can; I should be heartless
Were I not moved to find you suppliant here.

PRIEST. Great Oedipus, O powerful King of Thebes!
You see how all the ages of our people
Cling to your altar steps: here are boys
Who can barely stand alone, and here are priests
By weight of age, as I am a priest of God,
And young men chosen from those yet unmarried;
As for the others, all that multitude,
They wait with olive chaplets in the squares,

---

* OEDIPUS REX: An English Version by Dudley Fitts and Robert Fitzgerald, copyright, 1949, by Harcourt, Brace & World, Inc. and reprinted with their permission. Also by permission of Faber & Faber Ltd.
    CAUTION: All rights, including professional, amateur, motion picture, recitation, lecturing, public reading, radio broadcasting, and television are strictly reserved. Inquiries on all rights should be addressed to Harcourt, Brace & World, Inc., 750 Third Avenue, New York 17, New York.

At the two shrines of Pallas, and where
  Apollo
Speaks in the glowing embers.
                    Your own eyes
Must tell you: Thebes is tossed on a
  murdering sea
And can not lift her head from the death
  surge.
A rust consumes the buds and fruits of
  the earth;
The herds are sick; children die unborn,
And labor is vain. The god of plague and
  pyre
Raids like detestable lightning through
  the city,
And all the house of Kadmos is laid
  waste,
All emptied, and all darkened: Death
  alone
Battens upon the misery of Thebes.

You are not one of the immortal gods,
  we know;
Yet we have come to you to make our
  prayer
As to the man surest in mortal ways
And wisest in the ways of God. You
  saved us
From the Sphinx, that flinty singer, and
  the tribute
We paid to her so long; yet you were
  never
Better informed than we, nor could we
  teach you:
It was some god breathed in you to set
  us free.

Therefore, O mighty King, we turn to you:
Find us our safety, find us a remedy,
Whether by counsel of the gods or men.
A king of wisdom tested in the past
Can act in a time of troubles, and act
  well.
Noblest of men, restore
Life to your city! Think how all men
  call you
Liberator for your triumph long ago;
Ah, when your years of kingship are re-
  membered,
Let them not say *We rose, but later fell*—
Keep the State from going down in the
  storm!
Once, years ago, with happy augury,
You brought us fortune; be the same
  again!

No man questions your power to rule the
  land:
But rule over men, not over a dead city!
Ships are only hulls, citadels are nothing,
When no life moves in the empty pas-
  sageways.

OEDIPUS. Poor children! You may be sure I
  know
All that you longed for in your coming
  here.
I know that you are deathly sick; and yet,
Sick as you are, not one is as sick as I.
Each of you suffers in himself alone
His anguish, not another's; but my spirit
Groans for the city, for myself, for you.

I was not sleeping, you are not waking
  me.
No, I have been in tears for a long while
And in my restless thought walked many
  ways.
In all my search, I found one helpful
  course,
And that I have taken: I have sent Creon,
Son of Menoikeus, brother of the Queen,
To Delphi, Apollo's place of revelation,
To learn there, if he can,
What act or pledge of mine may save the
  city.
I have counted the days, and now, this
  very day,
I am troubled, for he has overstayed his
  time.
What is he doing? He has been gone too
  long.
Yet whenever he comes back, I should
  do ill
To scant whatever duty God reveals.

PRIEST. It is a timely promise. At this instant
They tell me Creon is here.

OEDIPUS.   O Lord Apollo!
May his news be fair as his face is radiant!

PRIEST. It could not be otherwise: he is
  crowned with bay,
The chaplet is thick with berries.

OEDIPUS.   We shall soon know;
He is near enough to hear us now.
  [*Enter* CREON.]
                    O Prince:
Brother: son of Menoikeus:

What answer do you bring us from the god?

CREON. A strong one. I can tell you, great afflictions
Will turn out well, if they are taken well.

OEDIPUS. What was the oracle? These vague words
Leave me still hanging between hope and fear.

CREON. Is it your pleasure to hear me with all these
Gathered around us? I am prepared to speak,
But should we not go in?

OEDIPUS.   Let them all hear it.
It is for them I suffer, more than for myself.

CREON. Then I will tell you what I heard at Delphi.

In plain words
The god commands us to expel from the land of Thebes
An old defilement we are sheltering.
It is a deathly thing, beyond cure;
We must not let it feed upon us longer.

OEDIPUS. What defilement? How shall we rid ourselves of it?

CREON. By exile or death, blood for blood. It was
Murder that brought the plague-wind on the city.

OEDIPUS. Murder of whom? Surely the god has named him?

CREON. My lord: long ago Laïos was our king,
Before you came to govern us.

OEDIPUS.   I know;
I learned of him from others; I never saw him.

CREON. He was murdered; and Apollo commands us now
To take revenge upon whoever killed him.

OEDIPUS. Upon whom? Where are they? Where shall we find a clue
To solve that crime, after so many years?

CREON. Here in this land, he said.
                    If we make enquiry,
We may touch things that otherwise escape us.

OEDIPUS. Tell me: Was Laïos murdered in his house,
Or in the fields, or in some foreign country?

CREON. He said he planned to make a pilgrimage.
He did not come home again.

OEDIPUS.   And was there no one,
No witness, no companion, to tell what happened?

CREON. They were all killed but one, and he got away
So frightened that he could remember one thing only.

OEDIPUS. What was that one thing? One may be the key
To everything, if we resolve to use it.

CREON. He said that a band of highwaymen attacked them,
Outnumbered them, and overwhelmed the King.

OEDIPUS. Strange, that a highwayman should be so daring—
Unless some faction here bribed him to do it.

CREON. We thought of that. But after Laïos' death
New troubles arose and we had no avenger.

OEDIPUS. What troubles could prevent your hunting down the killers?

CREON. The riddling Sphinx's song
Made us deaf to all mysteries but her own.

OEDIPUS. Then once more I must bring what is dark to light.

It is most fitting that Apollo shows,
As you do, this compunction for the dead.
You shall see how I stand by you, as I
    should,
To avenge the city and the city's god,
And not as though it were for some dis-
    tant friend,
But for my own sake, to be rid of evil.
Whoever killed King Laïos might—who
    knows?—
Decide at any moment to kill me as well.
By avenging the murdered king I protect
    myself.

Come, then, my children: leave the altar
    steps,
Lift up your olive boughs!
                          One of you go
And summon the people of Kadmos to
    gather here.

I will do all that I can; you may tell them
    that.
        [*Exit a* PAGE.]
So, with the help of God,
We shall be saved—or else indeed we are
    lost.

PRIEST. Let us rise, children. It was for this
    we came,
And now the King has promised it him-
    self.
Phoibos has sent us an oracle; may he
    descend
Himself to save us and drive out the
    plague.

[*Exeunt* OEDIPUS *and* CREON *into the palace
by the central door. The* PRIEST *and the*
SUPPLIANTS *disperse R. and L. After a short
pause the* CHORUS *enters the orchestra.*]

Párodos

                         [STROPHE 1]
CHORUS. What is God singing in his pro-
    found
Delphi of gold and shadow?
What oracle for Thebes, the sunwhipped
    city?

Fear unjoints me, the roots of my heart
    tremble.

Now I remember, O Healer, your power,
    and wonder:
Will you send doom like a sudden cloud,
    or weave it
Like nightfall of the past?

Speak, speak to us, issue of holy sound:
Dearest to our expectancy: be tender!
                         [ANTISTROPHE 1]
Let me pray to Athenê, the immortal
    daughter of Zeus,
And to Artemis her sister
Who keeps her famous throne in the
    market ring,
And to Apollo, bowman at the far butts
    of heaven—

O gods, descend! Like three streams leap
    against

The fires of our grief, the fires of darkness;
Be swift to bring us rest!

As in the old time from the brilliant
    house
Of air you stepped to save us, come again!
                           [STROPHE 2]
Now our afflictions have no end,
Now all our stricken host lies down
And no man fights off death with his
    mind;

The noble plowland bears no grain,
And groaning mothers can not bear—

See, how our lives like birds take wing,
Like sparks that fly when a fire soars,
To the shore of the god of evening.
                        [ANTISTROPHE 2]
The plague burns on, it is pitiless,
Though pallid children laden with death
Lie unwept in the stony ways,

And old gray women by every path
Flock to the strand about the altars

There to strike their breasts and cry
Worship of Phoibos in wailing prayers:
Be kind, God's golden child!

[STROPHE 3]

There are no swords in this attack by fire,
No shields, but we are ringed with cries.
Send the besieger plunging from our homes
Into the vast sea-room of the Atlantic
Or into the waves that foam eastward of Thrace—

For the day ravages what the night spares—

Destroy our enemy, lord of the thunder!
Let him be riven by lightning from heaven!

[ANTISTROPHE 3]

Phoibos Apollo, stretch the sun's bowstring,
That golden cord, until it sing for us,
Flashing arrows in heaven!
                    Artemis, Huntress,
Race with flaring lights upon our mountains!

O scarlet god, O golden-banded brow,
O Theban Bacchos in a storm of Maenads,
[Enter OEDIPUS, C.]
Whirl upon Death, that all the Undying hate!
Come with blinding torches, come in joy!

Scene I

OEDIPUS. Is this your prayer? It may be answered. Come,
Listen to me, act as the crisis demands,
And you shall have relief from all these evils.

Until now I was a stranger to this tale,
As I had been a stranger to the crime.
Could I track down the murderer without a clue?
But now, friends,
As one who became a citizen after the murder,
I make this proclamation to all Thebans:
If any man knows by whose hand Laïos, son of Labdakos,
Met his death, I direct that man to tell me everything,
No matter what he fears for having so long withheld it.
Let it stand as promised that no further trouble
Will come to him, but he may leave the land in safety.

Moreover: If anyone knows the murderer to be foreign,
Let him not keep silent: he shall have his reward from me.
However, if he does conceal it; if any man
Fearing for his friend or for himself disobeys this edict,
Hear what I propose to do:

I solemnly forbid the people of this country,
Where power and throne are mine, ever to receive that man
Or speak to him, no matter who he is, or let him
Join in sacrifice, lustration, or in prayer.
I decree that he be driven from every house,
Being, as he is, corruption itself to us: the Delphic
Voice of Zeus has pronounced this revelation.
Thus I associate myself with the oracle
And take the side of the murdered king.

As for the criminal, I pray to God—
Whether it be a lurking thief, or one of a number—
I pray that that man's life be consumed in evil and wretchedness.
And as for me, this curse applies no less
If it should turn out that the culprit is my guest here,
Sharing my hearth.
            You have heard the penalty.
I lay it on you now to attend to this
For my sake, for Apollo's, for the sick
Sterile city that heaven has abandoned.
Suppose the oracle had given you no command:

Should this defilement go uncleansed for ever?
You should have found the murderer: your king,
A noble king, had been destroyed!
                              Now I,
Having the power that he held before me,
Having his bed, begetting children there
Upon his wife, as he would have, had he lived—
Their son would have been my children's brother,
If Laïos had had luck in fatherhood!
(But surely ill luck rushed upon his reign)—
I say I take the son's part, just as though
I were his son, to press the fight for him
And see it won! I'll find the hand that brought
Death to Labdakos' and Polydoros' child,
Heir of Kadmos' and Agenor's line.
And as for those who fail me,
May the gods deny them the fruit of the earth,
Fruit of the womb, and may they rot utterly!
Let them be wretched as we are wretched, and worse!

For you, for loyal Thebans, and for all
Who find my actions right, I pray the favor
Of justice, and of all the immortal gods.

CHORAGOS. Since I am under oath, my lord, I swear
I did not do the murder, I can not name
The murderer. Might not the oracle
That has ordained the search tell where to find him?

OEDIPUS. An honest question. But no man in the world
Can make the gods do more than the gods will.

CHORAGOS. There is one last expedient—

OEDIPUS.   Tell me what it is.
Though it seem slight, you must not hold it back.

CHORAGOS. A lord clairvoyant to the lord Apollo,
As we all know, is the skilled Teiresias.
One might learn much about this from him, Oedipus.

OEDIPUS. I am not wasting time:
Creon spoke of this, and I have sent for him—
Twice, in fact; it is strange that he is not here.

CHORAGOS. The other matter—that old report—seems useless.

OEDIPUS. Tell me. I am interested in all reports.

CHORAGOS. The King was said to have been killed by highwaymen.

OEDIPUS. I know. But we have no witnesses to that.

CHORAGOS. If the killer can feel a particle of dread,
Your curse will bring him out of hiding!

OEDIPUS.   No.
The man who dared that act will fear no curse.
   [*Enter the blind seer* TEIRESIAS, *led by a* PAGE.]

CHORAGOS. But there is one man who may detect the criminal.
This is Teiresias, this is the holy prophet
In whom, alone of all men, truth was born.

OEDIPUS. Teiresias: seer: student of mysteries,
Of all that's taught and all that no man tells,
Secrets of Heaven and secrets of the earth:
Blind though you are, you know the city lies
Sick with plague; and from this plague, my lord,
We find that you alone can guard or save us.

Possibly you did not hear the messengers?
Apollo, when we sent to him,
Sent us back word that this great pestilence

310 Would lift, but only if we established clearly
The identity of those who murdered Laïos.
They must be killed or exiled.
             Can you use
Birdflight or any art of divination
To purify yourself, and Thebes, and me
From this contagion? We are in your hands.
There is no fairer duty
Than that of helping others in distress.

TEIRESIAS. How dreadful knowledge of the truth can be
320 When there's no help in truth! I knew this well,
But made myself forget. I should not have come.

OEDIPUS. What is troubling you? Why are your eyes so cold?

TEIRESIAS. Let me go home. Bear your own fate, and I'll
Bear mine. It is better so: trust what I say.

OEDIPUS. What you say is ungracious and unhelpful
To your native country. Do not refuse to speak.

TEIRESIAS. When it comes to speech, your own is neither temperate
Nor opportune. I wish to be more prudent.

OEDIPUS. In God's name, we all beg you—

330 TEIRESIAS.   You are all ignorant.
No; I will never tell you what I know.
Now it is my misery; then, it would be yours.

OEDIPUS. What! You do know something, and will not tell us?
You would betray us all and wreck the State?

TEIRESIAS. I do not intend to torture myself, or you.
Why persist in asking? You will not persuade me.

OEDIPUS. What a wicked old man you are! You'd try a stone's
Patience! Out with it! Have you no feeling at all?

TEIRESIAS. You call me unfeeling. If you could only see
The nature of your own feelings . . .   340

OEDIPUS.   Why,
Who would not feel as I do? Who could endure
Your arrogance toward the city?

TEIRESIAS.   What does it matter!
Whether I speak or not, it is bound to come.

OEDIPUS. Then, if "it" is bound to come, you are bound to tell me.

TEIRESIAS. No, I will not go on. Rage as you please.

OEDIPUS. Rage? Why not!
      And I'll tell you what I think:
You planned it, you had it done, you all but   350
Killed him with your own hands: if you had eyes,
I'd say the crime was yours, and yours alone.

TEIRESIAS. So? I charge you, then,
Abide by the proclamation you have made:
From this day forth
Never speak again to these men or to me;
You yourself are the pollution of this country.

OEDIPUS. You dare say that! Can you possibly think you have
Some way of going free, after such insolence?

TEIRESIAS. I have gone free. It is the truth sustains me.   360

OEDIPUS. Who taught you shamelessness? It was not your craft.

TEIRESIAS. You did. You made me speak. I did not want to.

OEDIPUS. Speak what? Let me hear it again more clearly.

TEIRESIAS. Was it not clear before? Are you tempting me?

OEDIPUS. I did not understand it. Say it again.

TEIRESIAS. I say that you are the murderer whom you seek.

OEDIPUS. Now twice you have spat out infamy. You'll pay for it!

TEIRESIAS. Would you care for more? Do you wish to be really angry?

OEDIPUS. Say what you will. Whatever you say is worthless.

TEIRESIAS. I say you live in hideous shame with those
Most dear to you. You can not see the evil.

OEDIPUS. It seems you can go on mouthing like this for ever.

TEIRESIAS. I can, if there is power in truth.

OEDIPUS.   There is:
But not for you, not for you,
You sightless, witless, senseless, mad old man!

TEIRESIAS. You are the madman. There is no one here
Who will not curse you soon, as you curse me.

OEDIPUS. You child of endless night! You can not hurt me
Or any other man who sees the sun.

TEIRESIAS. True: it is not from me your fate will come.
That lies within Apollo's competence,
As it is his concern.

OEDIPUS.   Tell me:
Are you speaking for Creon, or for yourself?

TEIRESIAS. Creon is no threat. You weave your own doom.

OEDIPUS. Wealth, power, craft of statesmanship!
Kingly position, everywhere admired!
What savage envy is stored up against these,
If Creon, whom I trusted, Creon my friend,
For this great office which the city once
Put in my hands unsought—if for this power
Creon desires in secret to destroy me!

He has bought this decrepit fortune-teller, this
Collector of dirty pennies, this prophet fraud—
Why, he is no more clairvoyant than I am!
      Tell us:
Has your mystic mummery ever approached the truth?
When that hellcat the Sphinx was performing here,
What help were you to these people?
Her magic was not for the first man who came along:
It demanded a real exorcist. Your birds—
What good were they? or the gods, for the matter of that?
But I came by,
Oedipus, the simple man, who knows nothing—
I thought it out for myself, no birds helped me!
And this is the man you think you can destroy,
That you may be close to Creon when he's king!
Well, you and your friend Creon, it seems to me,
Will suffer most. If you were not an old man,
You would have paid already for your plot.

CHORAGOS. We can not see that his words or yours
Have been spoken except in anger, Oedipus,
And of anger we have no need. How can God's will

Be accomplished best? That is what most
  concerns us.

TEIRESIAS. You are a king. But where argument's concerned
I am your man, as much a king as you.
I am not your servant, but Apollo's.
I have no need of Creon to speak for me.

Listen to me. You mock my blindness, do you?
But I say that you, with both your eyes, are blind:
You can not see the wretchedness of your life,
Nor in whose house you live, no, nor with whom.
Who are your father and mother? Can you tell me?
You do not even know the blind wrongs
That you have done them, on earth and in the world below.
But the double lash of your parents' curse will whip you
Out of this land some day, with only night
Upon your precious eyes.
Your cries then—where will they not be heard?
What fastness of Kithairon will not echo them?
And that bridal-descent of yours—you'll know it then,
The song they sang when you came here to Thebes
And found your misguided berthing.
All this, and more, that you can not guess at now,
Will bring you to yourself among your children.

Be angry, then. Curse Creon. Curse my words.
I tell you, no man that walks upon the earth
Shall be rooted out more horribly than you.

OEDIPUS. Am I to bear this from him?—Damnation
Take you! Out of this place! Out of my sight!

TEIRESIAS. I would not have come at all if you had not asked me.

OEDIPUS. Could I have told that you'd talk nonsense, that
You'd come here to make a fool of yourself, and of me?

TEIRESIAS. A fool? Your parents thought me sane enough.

OEDIPUS. My parents again!—Wait: who were my parents?

TEIRESIAS. This day will give you a father, and break your heart.

OEDIPUS. Your infantile riddles! Your damned abracadabra!

TEIRESIAS. You were a great man once at solving riddles.

OEDIPUS. Mock me with that if you like; you will find it true.

TEIRESIAS. It was true enough. It brought about your ruin.

OEDIPUS. But if it saved this town?

TEIRESIAS [To the PAGE].
        Boy, give me your hand.

OEDIPUS. Yes, boy; lead him away.
        —While you are here
We can do nothing. Go; leave us in peace.

TEIRESIAS. I will go when I have said what I have to say.
How can you hurt me? And I tell you again:
The man you have been looking for all this time,
The damned man, the murderer of Laïos,
That man is in Thebes. To your mind he is foreign-born,
But it will soon be shown that he is a Theban,
A revelation that will fail to please.
            A blind man
Who has his eyes now; a penniless man, who is rich now;
And he will go tapping the strange earth with his staff
To the children with whom he lives now he will be
Brother and father—the very same; to her

Who bore him, son and husband—the very same
Who came to his father's bed, wet with his father's blood.

Enough. Go think that over.

If later you find error in what I have said,
You may say that I have no skill in prophecy.

[*Exit* TEIRESIAS, *led by his* PAGE. OEDIPUS *goes into the palace.*]

Ode I

[STROPHE 1]

CHORUS. The Delphic stone of prophecies
  Remembers ancient regicide
  And a still bloody hand.
  That killer's hour of flight has come.
  He must be stronger than riderless
  Coursers of untiring wind,
  For the son of Zeus armed with his father's thunder
  Leaps in lightning after him;
  And the Furies follow him, the sad Furies.

[ANTISTROPHE 1]

Holy Parnassos' peak of snow
Flashes and blinds that secret man,
That all shall hunt him down:
Though he may roam the forest shade
Like a bull gone wild from pasture
To rage through glooms of stone.
Doom comes down on him; flight will not avail him;
For the world's heart calls him desolate,
And the immortal Furies follow, for ever follow.

[STROPHE 2]

But now a wilder thing is heard
From the old man skilled at hearing Fate in the wing-beat of a bird.
Bewildered as a blown bird, my soul hovers and can not find
Foothold in this debate, or any reason or rest of mind.
But no man ever brought—none can bring
Proof of strife between Thebes' royal house,
Labdakos' line, and the son of Polybos;
And never until now has any man brought word
Of Laïos' dark death staining Oedipus the King.

[ANTISTROPHE 2]

Divine Zeus and Apollo hold
Perfect intelligence alone of all tales ever told;
And well though this diviner works, he works in his own night;
No man can judge that rough unknown or trust in second sight,
For wisdom changes hands among the wise.
Shall I believe my great lord criminal
At a raging word that a blind old man let fall?
I saw him, when the carrion woman faced him of old,
Prove his heroic mind! These evil words are lies.

Scene 2

CREON. Men of Thebes:
  I am told that heavy accusations
  Have been brought against me by King Oedipus.

  I am not the kind of man to bear this tamely.

  If in these present difficulties
He holds me accountable for any harm to him
Through anything I have said or done—why, then,
I do not value life in this dishonor.
It is not as though this rumor touched upon
Some private indiscretion. The matter is grave.

520 The fact is that I am being called disloyal
To the State, to my fellow citizens, to my friends.

CHORAGOS. He may have spoken in anger, not from his mind.

CREON. But did you not hear him say I was the one
Who seduced the old prophet into lying?

CHORAGOS. The thing was said; I do not know how seriously.

CREON. But you were watching him! Were his eyes steady?
Did he look like a man in his right mind?

CHORAGOS. I do not know.
I can not judge the behavior of great men.
530 But here is the King himself.
[*Enter* OEDIPUS.]

OEDIPUS. So you dared come back
Why? How brazen of you to come to my house,
You murderer!
Do you think I do not know
That you plotted to kill me, plotted to steal my throne?
Tell me, in God's name: am I coward, a fool,
That you should dream you could accomplish this?
A fool who could not see your slippery game?
A coward, not to fight back when I saw it?
540 You are the fool, Creon, are you not? hoping
Without support or friends to get a throne?
Thrones may be won or bought: you could do neither.

CREON. Now listen to me. You have talked; let me talk, too.
You can not judge unless you know the facts.

OEDIPUS. You speak well: there is one fact; but I find it hard
To learn from the deadliest enemy I have.

CREON. That above all I must dispute with you.

OEDIPUS. That above all I will not hear you deny.

CREON. If you think there is anything good in being stubborn
Against all reason, then I say you are wrong. 550

OEDIPUS. If you think a man can sin against his own kind
And not be punished for it, I say you are mad.

CREON. I agree. But tell me: what have I done to you?

OEDIPUS. You advised me to send for that wizard, did you not?

CREON. I did. I should do it again.

OEDIPUS. Very well. Now tell me:
How long has it been since Laïos—

CREON. What of Laïos?

OEDIPUS. Since he vanished in that onset by the road?

CREON. It was long ago, a long time. 560

OEDIPUS. And this prophet,
Was he practicing here then?

CREON. He was; and with honor, as now.

OEDIPUS. Did he speak of me at that time?

CREON. He never did;
At least, not when I was present.

OEDIPUS. But . . . the enquiry?
I suppose you held one?

CREON. We did, but we learned nothing.

OEDIPUS. Why did the prophet not speak against me then? 570

CREON. I do not know; and I am the kind of man
Who holds his tongue when he has no facts to go on.

OEDIPUS. There's one fact that you know,
and you could tell it.

CREON. What fact is that? If I know it, you
shall have it.

OEDIPUS. If he were not involved with you,
he could not say
That it was I who murdered Laïos.

CREON. If he says that, you are the one that
knows it!—
But now it is my turn to question you.

OEDIPUS. Put your questions. I am no murderer.

CREON. First, then: You married my sister?

OEDIPUS.   I married your sister.

CREON. And you rule the kingdom equally
with her?

OEDIPUS. Everything that she wants she has
from me.

CREON. And I am the third, equal to both
of you?

OEDIPUS. That is why I call you a bad friend.

CREON. No. Reason it out, as I have done.
Think of this first: Would any sane man
prefer
Power, with all a king's anxieties,
To that same power and the grace of
sleep?
Certainly not I.
I have never longed for the king's power—
only his rights.
Would any wise man differ from me in
this?
As matters stand, I have my way in everything
With your consent, and no responsibilities.
If I were king, I should be a slave to
policy.

How could I desire a scepter more
Than what is now mine—untroubled influence?
No, I have not gone mad; I need no
honors,
Except those with the perquisites I have
now.
I am welcome everywhere; every man
salutes me,
And those who want your favor seek my
ear,
Since I know how to manage what they
ask.
Should I exchange this ease for that anxiety?
Besides, no sober mind is treasonable.
I hate anarchy
And never would deal with any man who
likes it.

Test what I have said. Go to the priestess
At Delphi, ask if I quoted her correctly.
And as for this other thing: if I am found
Guilty of treason with Teiresias,
Then sentence me to death! You have
my word
It is a sentence I should cast my vote
for—
But not without evidence!
                    You do wrong
When you take good men for bad, bad
men for good.
A true friend thrown aside—why, life itself
Is not more precious!
          In time you will know this well:
For time, and time alone, will show the
just man,
Though scoundrels are discovered in a
day.

CHORAGOS. This is well said, and a prudent
man would ponder it.
Judgments too quickly formed are dangerous.

OEDIPUS. But is he not quick in his duplicity?
And shall I not be quick to parry him?
Would you have me stand still, hold my
peace, and let
This man win everything, through my
inaction?

CREON. And you want—what is it, then? To
banish me?

OEDIPUS. No, not exile. It is your death I
want,
So that all the world may see what treason
means.

CREON. You will persist, then? You will not believe me?

OEDIPUS. How can I believe you?

CREON. Then you are a fool.

OEDIPUS. To save myself?

CREON. In justice, think of me.

OEDIPUS. You are evil incarnate.

CREON. But suppose that you are wrong?

OEDIPUS. Still I must rule.

CREON. But not if you rule badly.

OEDIPUS. O city, city!

CREON. It is my city, too!

CHORAGOS. Now, my lords, be still. I see the Queen,
Iocastê, coming from her palace chambers;
And it is time she came, for the sake of you both.
This dreadful quarrel can be resolved through her.
[Enter IOCASTE.]

IOCASTE. Poor foolish men, what wicked din is this?
With Thebes sick to death, is it not shameful
That you should rake some private quarrel up?
[To OEDIPUS.]
Come into the house.
—And you, Creon, go now:
Let us have no more of this tumult over nothing.

CREON. Nothing? No, sister: what your husband plans for me
Is one of two great evils: exile or death.

OEDIPUS. He is right.
Why, woman I have caught him squarely
Plotting against my life.

CREON. No! Let me die
Accurst if ever I have wished you harm!

IOCASTE. Ah, believe it, Oedipus!
In the name of the gods, respect this oath of his
For my sake, for the sake of these people here!

[STROPHE 1]
CHORAGOS. Open your mind to her, my lord.
Be ruled by her, I beg you!

OEDIPUS. What would you have me do?

CHORAGOS. Respect Creon's word. He has never spoken like a fool,
And now he has sworn an oath.

OEDIPUS. You know what you ask?

CHORAGOS. I do.

OEDIPUS. Speak on, then.

CHORAGOS. A friend so sworn should not be baited so,
In blind malice, and without final proof.

OEDIPUS. You are aware, I hope, that what you say
Means death for me, or exile at the least.

[STROPHE 2]
CHORAGOS. No, I swear by Helios, first in Heaven!
May I die friendless and accurst,
The worst of deaths, if ever I meant that!
It is the withering fields
That hurt my sick heart:
Must we bear all these ills,
And now your bad blood as well?

OEDIPUS. Then let him go. And let me die, if I must,
Or be driven by him in shame from the land of Thebes.
It is your unhappiness, and not his talk,
That touches me.
As for him—
Wherever he goes, hatred will follow him.

CREON. Ugly in yielding, as you were ugly in rage!
Natures like yours chiefly torment themselves.

OEDIPUS. Can you not go? Can you not leave me?

CREON. I can.
  You do not know me; but the city knows me,
  And in its eyes I am just, if not in yours.
  [Exit CREON.]

  [ANTISTROPHE 1]
CHORAGOS. Lady Iocastê, did you not ask the King to go to his chambers?

IOCASTE. First tell me what has happened.

CHORAGOS. There was suspicion without evidence; yet it rankled
  As even false charges will.

IOCASTE.   On both sides?

CHORAGOS.   On both.

IOCASTE.   But what was said?

CHORAGOS. Oh let it rest, let it be done with! Have we not suffered enough?

OEDIPUS. You see to what your decency has brought you:
  You have made difficulties where my heart saw none.

  [ANTISTROPHE 2]
CHORAGOS. Oedipus, it is not once only I have told you—
  You must know I should count myself unwise
  To the point of madness, should I now forsake you—
    You, under whose hand,
    In the storm of another time,
    Our dear land sailed out free.
    But now stand fast at the helm!

IOCASTE. In God's name, Oedipus, inform your wife as well:
  Why are you so set in this hard anger?

OEDIPUS. I will tell you, for none of these men deserves
  My confidence as you do. It is Creon's work,
  His treachery, his plotting against me.

IOCASTE. Go on, if you can make this clear to me.

OEDIPUS. He charges me with the murder of Laïos.

IOCASTE. Has he some knowledge? Or does he speak from hearsay?

OEDIPUS. He would not commit himself to such a charge,
  But he has brought in that damnable soothsayer
  To tell his story.

IOCASTE.   Set your mind at rest.
  If it is a question of soothsayers, I tell you
  That you will find no man whose craft gives knowledge
  Of the unknowable.

    Here is my proof:

  An oracle was reported to Laïos once
  (I will not say from Phoibos himself, but from
  His appointed ministers, at any rate)
  That his doom would be death at the hands of his own son—
  His son, born of his flesh and of mine!

  Now, you remember the story: Laïos was killed
  By marauding strangers where three highways meet;
  But his child had not been three days in this world
  Before the King had pierced the baby's ankles
  And left him to die on a lonely mountainside.

  Thus, Apollo never caused that child
  To kill his father, and it was not Laïos' fate
  To die at the hands of his son, as he had feared.
  This is what prophets and prophecies are worth!
  Have no dread of them.
        It is God himself
  Who can show us what he wills, in his own way.

OEDIPUS. How strange a shadowy memory crossed my mind,
  Just now while you were speaking; it chilled my heart.

IOCASTE. What do you mean? What memory do you speak of?

OEDIPUS. If I understand you, Laïos was killed
At a place where three roads meet.

IOCASTE. So it was said;
We have no later story.

OEDIPUS. Where did it happen?

IOCASTE. Phokis, it is called: at a place where the Theban Way
Divides into the roads toward Delphi and Daulia.

OEDIPUS. When?

IOCASTE. We had the news not long before you came
And proved the right to your succession here.

OEDIPUS. Ah, what net has God been weaving for me?

IOCASTE. Oedipus! Why does this trouble you?

OEDIPUS. Do not ask me yet.
First, tell me how Laïos looked, and tell me
How old he was.

IOCASTE. He was tall, his hair just touched
With white; his form was not unlike your own.

OEDIPUS. I think that I myself may be accurst
By my own ignorant edict.

IOCASTE. You speak strangely.
It makes me tremble to look at you, my King.

OEDIPUS. I am not sure that the blind man can not see.
But I should know better if you were to tell me—

IOCASTE. Anything—though I dread to hear you ask it.

OEDIPUS. Was the King lightly escorted, or did he ride
With a large company, as a ruler should?

IOCASTE. There were five men with him in all: one was a herald,
And a single chariot, which he was driving.

OEDIPUS. Alas, that makes it plain enough!
But who—
Who told you how it happened?

IOCASTE. A household servant,
The only one to escape.

OEDIPUS. And is he still
A servant of ours?

IOCASTE. No; for when he came back at last
And found you enthroned in the place of the dead king,
He came to me, touched my hand with his, and begged
That I would send him away to the frontier district
Where only the shepherds go—
As far away from the city as I could send him.
I granted his prayer; for although the man was a slave,
He had earned more than this favor at my hands.

OEDIPUS. Can he be called back quickly?

IOCASTE. Easily.
But why?

OEDIPUS. I have taken too much upon myself
Without enquiry; therefore I wish to consult him.

IOCASTE. Then he shall come.
But am I not one also
To whom you might confide these fears of yours?

OEDIPUS. That is your right; it will not be denied you,
Now least of all; for I have reached a pitch
Of wild foreboding. Is there anyone
To whom I should sooner speak?

Polybos of Corinth is my father.
My mother is a Dorian: Meropê.
I grew up chief among the men of Corinth
Until a strange thing happened—
Not worth my passion, it may be, but strange.

At a feast, a drunken man maundering in his cups
Cries out that I am not my father's son!

I contained myself that night, though I felt anger
And a sinking heart. The next day I visited
My father and mother, and questioned them. They stormed,
Calling it all the slanderous rant of a fool;
And this relieved me. Yet the suspicion
Remained always aching in my mind;
I knew there was talk; I could not rest;
And finally, saying nothing to my parents,
I went to the shrine at Delphi.
The god dismissed my question without reply;
He spoke of other things.
                Some were clear,
Full of wretchedness, dreadful, unbearable:
As, that I should lie with my own mother, breed
Children from whom all men would turn their eyes;
And that I should be my father's murderer.

I heard all this, and fled. And from that day
Corinth to me was only in the stars
Descending in that quarter of the sky,
As I wandered farther and farther on my way
To a land where I should never see the evil
Sung by the oracle. And I came to this country
Where, so you say, King Laïos was killed.

I will tell you all that happened there, my lady.

There were three highways
Coming together at a place I passed;
And there a herald came towards me, and a chariot
Drawn by horses, with a man such as you describe
Seated in it. The groom leading the horses
Forced me off the road at his lord's command;
But as this charioteer lurched over towards me
I struck him in my rage. The old man saw me
And brought his double goad down upon my head
As I came abreast.
                He was paid back, and more!
Swinging my club in this right hand I knocked him
Out of his car, and he rolled on the ground.
            I killed him.

I killed them all.
Now if that stranger and Laïos were—kin,
Where is a man more miserable than I?
More hated by the gods? Citizen and alien alike
Must never shelter me or speak to me—
I must be shunned by all.
                And I myself
Pronounced this malediction upon myself!

Think of it: I have touched you with these hands,
These hands that killed your husband. What defilement!

Am I all evil, then? It must be so,
Since I must flee from Thebes, yet never again
See my own countrymen, my own country,
For fear of joining my mother in marriage
And killing Polybos, my father.
                    Ah,
If I was created so, born to this fate,
Who could deny the savagery of God?

O holy majesty of heavenly powers!
May I never see that day! Never!
Rather let me vanish from the race of men
Than know the abomination destined me!

CHORAGOS. We too, my lord, have felt dismay at this.
But there is hope: you have yet to hear the shepherd.

OEDIPUS. Indeed, I fear no other hope is left me.

IOCASTE. What do you hope from him when he comes?

OEDIPUS.   This much:
If his account of the murder tallies with yours,
Then I am cleared.

IOCASTE.   What was it that I said
Of such importance?

OEDIPUS.   Why, "marauders," you said,
Killed the King, according to this man's story.
If he maintains that still, if there were several,
Clearly the guilt is not mine: I was alone.
But if he says one man, singlehanded, did it,
Then the evidence all points to me.

IOCASTE. You may be sure that he said there were several;
And can he call back that story now? He cán not.
The whole city heard it as plainly as I.
But suppose he alters some detail of it:
He can not ever show that Laïos' death
Fulfilled the oracle: for Apollo said
My child was doomed to kill him; and my child—
Poor baby!—it was my child that died first.

No. From now on, where oracles are concerned,
I would not waste a second thought on any.

OEDIPUS. You may be right.
          But come: let someone go
For the shepherd at once. This matter must be settled.

IOCASTE. I will send for him.
I would not wish to cross you in anything,
And surely not in this.—Let us go in.
[*Exeunt into the palace.*]

Ode II

[STROPHE 1]
CHORUS. Let me be reverent in the ways of right,
Lowly the paths I journey on;
Let all my words and actions keep
The laws of the pure universe
From highest Heaven handed down.
For Heaven is their bright nurse,
Those generations of the realms of light;
Ah, never of mortal kind were they begot,
Nor are they slaves of memory, lost in sleep:
Their Father is greater than Time, and ages not.

[ANTISTROPHE 1]
The tyrant is a child of Pride
Who drinks from his great sickening cup
Recklessness and vanity,
Until from his high crest headlong
He plummets to the dust of hope.
That strong man is not strong.
But let no fair ambition be denied;
May God protect the wrestler for the State
In government, in comely policy,
Who will fear God, and on His ordinance wait.

[STROPHE 2]
Haughtiness and the high hand of disdain
Tempt and outrage God's holy law;
And any mortal who dares hold
No immortal Power in awe
Will be caught up in a net of pain:
The price for which his levity is sold.
Let each man take due earnings, then,
And keep his hands from holy things,
And from blasphemy stand apart—
Else the crackling blast of heaven
Blows on his head, and on his desperate heart;
Though fools will honor impious men,
In their cities no tragic poet sings.

[ANTISTROPHE 2]
Shall we lose faith in Delphi's obscurities,
We who have heard the world's core
Discredited, and the sacred wood
Of Zeus at Elis praised no more?
The deeds and the strange prophecies
Must make a pattern yet to be understood.

Zeus, if indeed you are lord of all,
Throned in light over night and day,
Mirror this in your endless mind:
Our masters call the oracle
Words on the wind, and the Delphic vision blind!
Their hearts no longer know Apollo,
And reverence for the gods has died away.

Scene 3

[*Enter* IOCASTE.]

IOCASTE. Princes of Thebes, it has occurred to me
To visit the altars of the gods, bearing
These branches as a suppliant, and this incense.
Our King is not himself: his noble soul
Is overwrought with fantasies of dread,
Else he would consider
The new prophecies in the light of the old.
He will listen to any voice that speaks disaster,
And my advice goes for nothing.
[*She approaches the altar, R.*]
To you, then, Apollo,
Lycean lord, since you are nearest, I turn in prayer.
Receive these offerings, and grant us deliverance
From defilement. Our hearts are heavy with fear
When we see our leader distracted, as helpless sailors
Are terrified by the confusion of their helmsman.
[*Enter* MESSENGER.]

MESSENGER. Friends, no doubt you can direct me:
Where shall I find the house of Oedipus,
Or, better still, where is the King himself?

CHORAGOS. It is this very place, stranger; he is inside.
This is his wife and mother of his children.

MESSENGER. I wish her happiness in a happy house,
Blest in all the fulfillment of her marriage.

IOCASTE. I wish as much for you: your courtesy
Deserves a like good fortune. But now, tell me:
Why have you come? What have you to say to us?

MESSENGER. Good news, my lady, for your house and your husband.

IOCASTE. What news? Who sent you here?

MESSENGER. I am from Corinth.
The news I bring ought to mean joy for you,
Though it may be you will find some grief in it.

IOCASTE. What is it? How can it touch us in both ways?

MESSENGER. The word is that the people of the Isthmus
Intend to call Oedipus to be their king.

IOCASTE. But old King Polybos—is he not reigning still?

MESSENGER. No. Death holds him in his sepulchre.

IOCASTE. What are you saying? Polybos is dead?

MESSENGER. If I am not telling the truth, may I die myself.

IOCASTE [*To a* MAIDSERVANT].
Go in, go quickly; tell this to your master.

O riddlers of God's will, where are you now!
This was the man whom Oedipus, long ago,
Feared so, fled so, in dread of destroying him—
But it was another fate by which he died.
[Enter OEDIPUS, C.]

OEDIPUS. Dearest Iocastê, why have you sent for me?

IOCASTE. Listen to what this man says, and then tell me
What has become of the solemn prophecies.

OEDIPUS. Who is this man? What is his news for me?

IOCASTE. He has come from Corinth to announce your father's death!

OEDIPUS. Is it true, stranger? Tell me in your own words.

MESSENGER. I can not say it more clearly: the King is dead.

OEDIPUS. Was it by treason? Or by an attack of illness?

MESSENGER. A little thing brings old men to their rest.

OEDIPUS. It was sickness, then?

MESSENGER. Yes, and his many years.

OEDIPUS. Ah!
Why should a man respect the Pythian hearth, or
Give heed to the birds that jangle above his head?
They prophesied that I should kill Polybos,
Kill my own father; but he is dead and buried,
And I am here—I never touched him, never,
Unless he died of grief for my departure,
And thus, in a sense, through me. No. Polybos
Has packed the oracles off with him underground.
They are empty words.

IOCASTE. Had I not told you so?

OEDIPUS. You had; it was my faint heart that betrayed me.

IOCASTE. From now on never think of those things again.

OEDIPUS. And yet—must I not fear my mother's bed?

IOCASTE. Why should anyone in this world be afraid,
Since Fate rules us and nothing can be foreseen?
A man should live only for the present day.

Have no more fear of sleeping with your mother:
How many men, in dreams, have lain with their mothers!
No reasonable man is troubled by such things.

OEDIPUS. That is true; only—
If only my mother were not still alive!
But she is alive. I can not help my dread.

IOCASTE. Yet this news of your father's death is wonderful.

OEDIPUS. Wonderful. But I fear the living woman.

MESSENGER. Tell me, who is this woman that you fear?

OEDIPUS. It is Meropê, man; the wife of King Polybos.

MESSENGER. Meropê? Why should you be afraid of her?

OEDIPUS. An oracle of the gods, a dreadful saying.

MESSENGER. Can you tell me about it or are you sworn to silence?

OEDIPUS. I can tell you, and I will.
Apollo said through his prophet that I was the man

Who should marry his own mother, shed his father's blood
With his own hands. And so, for all these years
I have kept clear of Corinth, and no harm has come—
Though it would have been sweet to see my parents again.

MESSENGER. And is this the fear that drove you out of Corinth?

OEDIPUS. Would you have me kill my father?

MESSENGER. As for that
You must be reassured by the news I gave you.

OEDIPUS. If you could reassure me, I would reward you.

MESSENGER. I had that in mind, I will confess: I thought
I could count on you when you returned to Corinth.

OEDIPUS. No: I will never go near my parents again.

MESSENGER. Ah, son, you still do not know what you are doing—

OEDIPUS. What do you mean? In the name of God tell me!

MESSENGER. —If these are your reasons for not going home.

OEDIPUS. I tell you, I fear the oracle may come true.

MESSENGER. And guilt may come upon you through your parents?

OEDIPUS. That is the dread that is always in my heart.

MESSENGER. Can you not see that all your fears are groundless?

OEDIPUS. How can you say that? They are my parents, surely?

MESSENGER. Polybos was not your father.

OEDIPUS. Not my father?

MESSENGER. No more your father than the man speaking to you.

OEDIPUS. But you are nothing to me!

MESSENGER. Neither was he.

OEDIPUS. Then why did he call me son?

MESSENGER. I will tell you:
Long ago he had you from my hands, as a gift.

OEDIPUS. Then how could he love me so, if I was not his?

MESSENGER. He had no children, and his heart turned to you.

OEDIPUS. What of you? Did you buy me? Did you find me by chance?

MESSENGER. I came upon you in the crooked pass of Kithairon.

OEDIPUS. And what were you doing there?

MESSENGER. Tending my flocks.

OEDIPUS. A wandering shepherd?

MESSENGER. But your savior, son, that day.

OEDIPUS. From what did you save me?

MESSENGER. Your ankles should tell you that.

OEDIPUS. Ah, stranger, why do you speak of that childhood pain?

MESSENGER. I cut the bonds that tied your ankles together.

OEDIPUS. I have had the mark as long as I can remember.

MESSENGER. That was why you were given the name you bear.

OEDIPUS. God! Was it my father or my mother who did it?
Tell me!

MESSENGER. I do not know. The man who gave you to me
Can tell you better than I.

OEDIPUS. It was not you that found me, but another?

MESSENGER. It was another shepherd gave you to me.

OEDIPUS. Who was he? Can you tell me who he was?

MESSENGER. I think he was said to be one of Laïos' people.

OEDIPUS. You mean the Laïos who was king here years ago?

MESSENGER. Yes; King Laïos; and the man was one of his herdsmen.

OEDIPUS. Is he still alive? Can I see him?

MESSENGER.   These men here 1080
Know best about such things.

OEDIPUS.   Does anyone here
Know this shepherd that he is talking about?
Have you seen him in the fields, or in the town?
If you have, tell me. It is time things were made plain.

CHORAGOS. I think the man he means is that same shepherd
You have already asked to see. Iocastê perhaps
Could tell you something.

OEDIPUS.   Do you know anything
About him, Lady? Is he the man we have summoned? 1090
Is that the man this shepherd means?

IOCASTE.   Why think of him?
Forget this herdsman. Forget it all.
This talk is a waste of time.

OEDIPUS.   How can you say that,
When the clues to my true birth are in my hands?

IOCASTE. For God's love, let us have no more questioning!
Is your life nothing to you?
My own is pain enough for me to bear.

OEDIPUS. You need not worry. Suppose my mother a slave, 1100
And born of slaves: no baseness can touch you.

IOCASTE. Listen to me, I beg you: do not do this thing!

OEDIPUS. I will not listen; the truth must be made known.

IOCASTE. Everything that I say is for your own good!

OEDIPUS.   My own good
Snaps my patience, then; I want none of it.

IOCASTE. You are fatally wrong! May you never learn who you are!

OEDIPUS. Go, one of you, and bring the shepherd here.
Let us leave this woman to brag of her royal name.

IOCASTE. Ah, miserable!
That is the only word I have for you now. 1110
That is the only word I can ever have.
[*Exit into the palace.*]

CHORAGOS. Why has she left us, Oedipus? Why has she gone
In such a passion of sorrow? I fear this silence:
Something dreadful may come of it.

OEDIPUS.   Let it come!
However base my birth, I must know about it.
The Queen, like a woman, is perhaps ashamed
To think of my low origin. But I
Am a child of Luck; I can not be dishonored.
Luck is my mother; the passing months, my brothers, 1120
Have seen me rich and poor.

If this is so,
How could I wish that I were someone else?
How could I not be glad to know my birth?

Ode III

[STROPHE]

CHORUS. If ever the coming time were known
To my heart's pondering,
Kithairon, now by Heaven I see the torches
At the festival of the next full moon,
And see the dance, and hear the choir sing
A grace to your gentle shade:
Mountain where Oedipus was found,
O mountain guard of a noble race!
May the god who heals us lend his aid,
And let that glory come to pass
For our king's cradling-ground.

[ANTISTROPHE]

Of the nymphs that flower beyond the years,
Who bore you, royal child,
To Pan of the hills or the timberline Apollo,
Cold in delight where the upland clears,
Or Hermês for whom Kyllenê's heights are piled?
Or flushed as evening cloud,
Great Dionysos, roamer of mountains,
He—was it he who found you there,
And caught you up in his own proud
Arms from the sweet god-ravisher
Who laughed by the Muses' fountains?

Scene 4

OEDIPUS. Sirs: though I do not know the man,
I think I see him coming, this shepherd we want:
He is old, like our friend here, and the men
Bringing him seem to be servants of my house.
But you can tell, if you have ever seen him.

[Enter SHEPHERD escorted by servants.]

CHORAGOS. I know him, he was Laïos' man. You can trust him.

OEDIPUS. Tell me first, you from Corinth: is this the shepherd
We were discussing?

MESSENGER.   This is the very man.

OEDIPUS [To SHEPHERD]. Come here. No, look at me. You must answer
Everything I ask.—You belonged to Laïos?

SHEPHERD. Yes: born his slave, brought up in his house.

OEDIPUS. Tell me: what kind of work did you do for him?

SHEPHERD. I was a shepherd of his, most of my life.

OEDIPUS. Where mainly did you go for pasturage?

SHEPHERD. Sometimes Kithairon, sometimes the hills near-by.

OEDIPUS. Do you remember ever seeing this man out there?

SHEPHERD. What would he be doing there? This man?

OEDIPUS. This man standing here. Have you ever seen him before?

SHEPHERD. No. At least, not to my recollection.

MESSENGER. And that is not strange, my lord. But I'll refresh
His memory: he must remember when we two

Spent three whole seasons together, March to September,
On Kithairon or thereabouts. He had two flocks;
I had one. Each autumn I'd drive mine home
And he would go back with his to Laïos' sheepfold.—
Is this not true, just as I have described it?

SHEPHERD. True, yes; but it was all so long ago.

MESSENGER. Well, then: do you remember, back in those days,
That you gave me a baby boy to bring up as my own?

SHEPHERD. What if I did? What are you trying to say?

MESSENGER. King Oedipus was once that little child.

SHEPHERD. Damn you, hold your tongue!

OEDIPUS. No more of that!
It is your tongue needs watching, not this man's.

SHEPHERD. My King, my Master, what is it I have done wrong?

OEDIPUS. You have not answered his question about the boy.

SHEPHERD. He does not know . . . He is only making trouble . . .

OEDIPUS. Come, speak plainly, or it will go hard with you.

SHEPHERD. In God's name, do not torture an old man!

OEDIPUS. Come here, one of you; bind his arms behind him.

SHEPHERD. Unhappy king! What more do you wish to learn?

OEDIPUS. Did you give this man the child he speaks of?

SHEPHERD. I did.
And I would to God I had died that very day.

OEDIPUS. You will die now unless you speak the truth.

SHEPHERD. Yet if I speak the truth, I am worse than dead.

OEDIPUS. Very well; since you insist upon delaying—

SHEPHERD. No! I have told you already that I gave him the boy.

OEDIPUS. Where did you get him? From your house? From somewhere else?

SHEPHERD. Not from mine, no. A man gave him to me.

OEDIPUS. Is that man here? Do you know whose slave he was?

SHEPHERD. For God's love, my King, do not ask me any more!

OEDIPUS. You are a dead man if I have to ask you again.

SHEPHERD. Then . . . Then the child was from the palace of Laïos.

OEDIPUS. A slave child? or a child of his own line?

SHEPHERD. Ah, I am on the brink of dreadful speech!

OEDIPUS. And I of dreadful hearing. Yet I must hear.

SHEPHERD. If you must be told, then . . .
They said it was Laïos' child;
But it is your wife who can tell you about that.

OEDIPUS. My wife!—Did she give it to you?

SHEPHERD. My lord, she did.

OEDIPUS. Do you know why?

SHEPHERD. I was told to get rid of it.

OEDIPUS. An unspeakable mother!

SHEPHERD.　　There had been prophecies...

OEDIPUS. Tell me.

SHEPHERD. It was said that the boy would kill his own father.

OEDIPUS. Then why did you give him over to this old man?

SHEPHERD. I pitied the baby, my King,
And I thought that this man would take him far away
To his own country.
　　　　He saved him—but for what a fate!

For if you are what this man says you are,
No man living is more wretched than Oedipus.

OEDIPUS. Ah God!
It was true!
　　　　All the prophecies!
　　　　　　　　　　　—Now,
O Light, may I look on you for the last time!
I, Oedipus,
Oedipus, damned in his birth, in his marriage damned,
Damned in the blood he shed with his own hand!
[He rushes into the palace.]

Ode IV

[STROPHE 1]
CHORUS. Alas for the seed of men.

What measure shall I give these generations
That breathe on the void and are void
And exist and do not exist?

Who bears more weight of joy
Than mass of sunlight shifting in images,
Or who shall make his thought stay on
That down time drifts away?

Your splendor is all fallen.

O naked brow of wrath and tears,
O change of Oedipus!
I who saw your days call no man blest—
Your great days like ghósts góne.
　　　　　　　　　[ANTISTROPHE 1]
That mind was a strong bow.

Deep, how deep you drew it then, hard archer,
At a dim fearful range,
And brought dear glory down!

You overcame the stranger—
The virgin with her hooking lion claws—
And though death sang, stood like a tower
To make pale Thebes take heart.

Fortress against our sorrow!

True king, giver of laws,
Majestic Oedipus!
No prince in Thebes had ever such renown,
No prince won such grace of power.
　　　　　　　　　[STROPHE 2]
And now of all men ever known
Most pitiful is this man's story:
His fortunes are most changed, his state
Fallen to a low slave's
Ground under bitter fate.

O Oedipus, most royal one!
The great door that expelled you to the light
Gave at night—ah, gave night to your glory:
As to the father, to the fathering son.

All understood too late.

How could that queen whom Laïos won,
The garden that he harrowed at his height,
Be silent when that act was done?
　　　　　　　　　[ANTISTROPHE 2]
But all eyes fail before time's eye,
All actions come to justice there.
Though never willed, though far down the deep past,
Your bed, your dread sirings,

Are brought to book at last.
Child by Laïos doomed to die,
Then doomed to lose that fortunate little death,
Would God you never took breath in this air
That with my wailing lips I take to cry:

For I weep the world's outcast.

I was blind, and now I can tell why: 1280
Asleep, for you had given ease of breath
To Thebes, while the false years went by.

Éxodos

[*Enter, from the palace,* SECOND MESSENGER.]

SECOND MESSENGER. Elders of Thebes, most honored in this land,
What horrors are yours to see and hear, what weight
Of sorrow to be endured, if, true to your birth,
You venerate the line of Labdakos!
I think neither Istros nor Phasis, those great rivers,
Could purify this place of the corruption
It shelters now, or soon must bring to light—
1290 Evil not done unconsciously, but willed.

The greatest griefs are those we cause ourselves.

CHORAGOS. Surely, friend, we have grief enough already;
What new sorrow do you mean?

SECOND MESSENGER. The Queen is dead.

CHORAGOS. Iocastê? Dead? But at whose hand?

SECOND MESSENGER. Her own.
The full horror of what happened you can not know,
For you did not see it; but I, who did, will tell you
As clearly as I can how she met her death.

1300 When she had left us,
In passionate silence, passing through the court,
She ran to her apartment in the house,
Her hair clutched by the fingers of both hands.
She closed the doors behind her; then, by that bed
Where long ago the fatal son was conceived—
That son who should bring about his father's death—
We heard her call upon Laïos, dead so many years,
And heard her wail for the double fruit of her marriage,
A husband by her husband, children by her child.

Exactly how she died I do not know: 1310
For Oedipus burst in moaning and would not let us
Keep vigil to the end: it was by him
As he stormed about the room that our eyes were caught.
From one to another of us he went, begging a sword,
Cursing the wife who was not his wife, the mother
Whose womb had carried his own children and himself.
I do not know: it was none of us aided him,
But surely one of the gods was in control!
For with a dreadful cry
He hurled his weight, as though wrenched 1320
out of himself,
At the twin doors: the bolts gave, and he rushed in.
And there we saw her hanging, her body swaying
From the cruel cord she had noosed about her neck.
A great sob broke from him, heartbreaking to hear,
As he loosed the rope and lowered her to the ground.

I would blot out from my mind what happened next!
For the King ripped from her gown the

golden brooches
That were her ornament, and raised them, and plunged them down
Straight into his own eyeballs, crying, "No more,
No more shall you look on the misery about me,
The horrors of my own doing! Too long you have known
The faces of those whom I should never have seen,
Too long been blind to those for whom I was searching!
From this hour, go in darkness!" And as he spoke,
He struck at his eyes—not once, but many times;
And the blood spattered his beard,
Bursting from his ruined sockets like red hail.

So from the unhappiness of two this evil has sprung,
A curse on the man and woman alike. The old
Happiness of the house of Labdakos
Was happiness enough: where is it today?
It is all wailing and ruin, disgrace, death —all
The misery of mankind that has a name—
And it is wholly and for ever theirs.

CHORAGOS. Is he in agony still? Is there no rest for him?

SECOND MESSENGER. He is calling for someone to lead him to the gates
So that all the children of Kadmos may look upon
His father's murderer, his mother's—no, I can not say it!
And then he will leave Thebes,
Self-exiled, in order that the curse
Which he himself pronounced may depart from the house.
He is weak, and there is none to lead him,
So terrible is his suffering.
But you will see:
Look, the doors are opening; in a moment
You will see a thing that would crush a heart of stone.
[*The central door is opened;* OEDIPUS, *blinded, is led in.*]

CHORAGOS. Dreadful indeed for men to see.
Never have my own eyes
Looked on a sight so full of fear.

Oedipus!
What madness came upon you, what daemon
Leaped on your life with heavier
Punishment than a mortal man can bear?
No: I can not even
Look at you, poor ruined one.
And I would speak, question, ponder,
If I were able. No.
You make me shudder.

OEDIPUS. God.   God.
Is there a sorrow greater?
Where shall I find harbor in this world?
My voice is hurled far on a dark wind.
What has God done to me?

CHORAGOS. Too terrible to think of, or to see.

[STROPHE 1]
OEDIPUS. O cloud of night,
Never to be turned away: night coming on,
I can not tell how: night like a shroud!

My fair winds brought me here.
                    O God. Again
The pain of the spikes where I had sight,
The flooding pain
Of memory, never to be gouged out.

CHORAGOS. This is not strange.
You suffer it all twice over, remorse in pain,
Pain in remorse.

[ANTISTROPHE 1]
OEDIPUS. Ah dear friend
Are you faithful even yet, you alone?
Are you still standing near me, will you stay here,
Patient, to care for the blind?
                    The blind man!
Yet even blind I know who it is attends me,
By the voice's tone—
Though my new darkness hide the comforter.

CHORAGOS. Oh fearful act!

What god was it drove you to rake black
Night across your eyes?

[STROPHE 2]

OEDIPUS. Apollo. Apollo. Dear
Children, the god was Apollo.
He brought my sick, sick fate upon me.
But the blinding hand was my own!
How could I bear to see
When all my sight was horror everywhere?

CHORAGOS. Everywhere; that is true.

OEDIPUS. And now what is left?
Images? Love? A greeting even,
Sweet to the senses? Is there anything?
Ah, no, friends: lead me away.
Lead me away from Thebes.
             Lead the great wreck
And hell of Oedipus, whom the gods hate.

CHORAGOS. Your fate is clear, you are not blind to that.
Would God you had never found it out!

[ANTISTROPHE 2]

OEDIPUS. Death take the man who unbound
My feet on that hillside
And delivered me from death to life! What life?
If only I had died,
This weight of monstrous doom
Could not have dragged me and my darlings down.

CHORAGOS. I would have wished the same.

OEDIPUS. Oh never to have come here
With my father's blood upon me! Never
To have been the man they call his mother's husband!
Oh accurst! Oh child of evil,
To have entered that wretched bed—
             the selfsame one!
More primal than sin itself, this fell to me.

CHORAGOS. I do not know how I can answer you.
You were better dead than alive and blind.

OEDIPUS. Do not counsel me any more. This punishment
That I have laid upon myself is just.
If I had eyes,
I do not know how I could bear the sight
Of my father, when I came to the house of Death,
Or my mother: for I have sinned against them both
So vilely that I could not make my peace
By strangling my own life.
             Or do you think my children,
Born as they were born, would be sweet to my eyes?
Ah never, never! Nor this town with its high walls,
Nor the holy images of the gods.
             For I,
Thrice miserable!—Oedipus, noblest of all the line
Of Kadmos, have condemned myself to enjoy
These things no more, by my own malediction
Expelling that man whom the gods declared
To be a defilement in the house of Laïos.
After exposing the rankness of my own guilt,
How could I look men frankly in the eyes?
No, I swear it,
If I could have stifled my hearing at its source,
I would have done it and made all this body
A tight cell of misery, blank to light and sound:
So I should have been safe in a dark agony
Beyond all recollection.
             Ah Kithairon!
Why did you shelter me? When I was cast upon you,
Why did I not die? Then I should never
Have shown the world my execrable birth.

Ah Polybos! Corinth, city that I believed
The ancient seat of my ancestors: how fair
I seemed, your child! And all the while this evil
Was cancerous within me!
             For I am sick
In my daily life, sick in my origin.

O three roads, dark ravine, woodland and way

Where three roads met: you, drinking my father's blood,
My own blood, spilled by my own hand: can you remember
The unspeakable things I did there, and the things
I went on from there to do?
     O marriage, marriage!
The act that engendered me, and again the act
Performed by the son in the same bed—
     Ah, the net
Of incest, mingling fathers, brothers, sons,
With brides, wives, mothers: the last evil
That can be known by men: no tongue can say
How evil!
  No. For the love of God, conceal me
Somewhere far from Thebes; or kill me; or hurl me
Into the sea, away from men's eyes for ever.

Come, lead me. You need not fear to touch me.
Of all men, I alone can bear this guilt.
 [*Enter* CREON.]

CHORAGOS. We are not the ones to decide; but Creon here
May fitly judge of what you ask. He only
Is left to protect the city in your place.

OEDIPUS. Alas, how can I speak to him? What right have I
To beg his courtesy whom I have deeply wronged?

CREON. I have not come to mock you, Oedipus,
Or to reproach you, either.
 [*To* ATTENDANTS.]
     —You, standing there:
If you have lost all respect for man's dignity,
At least respect the flame of Lord Helios:
Do not allow this pollution to show itself
Openly here, an affront to the earth
And Heaven's rain and the light of day.
No, take him
Into the house as quickly as you can.
For it is proper
That only the close kindred see his grief.

OEDIPUS. I pray you in God's name, since your courtesy
Ignores my dark expectation, visiting
With mercy this man of all men most execrable:
Give me what I ask—for your good, not for mine.

CREON. And what is it that you would have me do?

OEDIPUS. Drive me out of this country as quickly as may be
To a place where no human voice can ever greet me.

CREON. I should have done that before now—only,
God's will had not been wholly revealed to me.

OEDIPUS. But his command is plain: the parricide
Must be destroyed. I am that evil man.

CREON. That is the sense of it, yes; but as things are,
We had best discover clearly what is to be done.

OEDIPUS. You would learn more about a man like me?

CREON. You are ready now to listen to the god.

OEDIPUS. I will listen. But it is to you
That I must turn for help. I beg you, hear me.

The woman in there—
Give her whatever funeral you think proper:
She is your sister.
     —But let me go, Creon!
Let me purge my father's Thebes of the pollution
Of my living here, and go out to the wild hills,
To Kithairon, that has won such fame with me,
The tomb my mother and father appointed for me,

And let me die there, as they willed I should.
And yet I know
Death will not ever come to me through sickness
Or in any natural way: I have been preserved
For some unthinkable fate. But let that be.

As for my sons, you need not care for them.
They are men, they will find some way to live.
But my poor daughters, who have shared my table,
Who never before have been parted from their father—
Take care of them, Creon; do this for me.
And will you let me touch them with my hands
A last time, and let us weep together?
Be kind, my lord,
Great prince, be kind!
          Could I but touch them,
They would be mine again, as when I had my eyes.
[*Enter* ANTIGONE *and* ISMENE, *attended.*]
Ah, God!
Is it my dearest children I hear weeping?
Has Creon pitied me and sent my daughters?

CREON. Yes, Oedipus: I knew that they were dear to you
In the old days, and know you must love them still.

OEDIPUS. May God bless you for this—and be a friendlier
Guardian to you than he has been to me!

Children, where are you?
Come quickly to my hands: they are your brother's—
Hands that have brought your father's once clear eyes
To this way of seeing—
          Ah, dearest ones,
I had neither sight nor knowledge then, your father
By the woman who was the source of his own life!
And I weep for you—having no strength to see you—,
I weep for you when I think of the bitterness
That men will visit upon you all your lives.
What homes, what festivals can you attend
Without being forced to depart again in tears?
And when you come to marriageable age,
Where is the man, my daughters, who would dare
Risk the bane that lies on all my children?
Is there any evil wanting? Your father killed
His father; sowed the womb of her who bore him;
Engendered you at the fount of his own existence!
That is what they will say of you.

          Then, whom
Can you ever marry? There are no bridegrooms for you,
And your lives must wither away in sterile dreaming.

O Creon, son of Menoikeus!
You are the only father my daughters have,
Since we, their parents, are both of us gone for ever.
They are your own blood: you will not let them
Fall into beggary and loneliness;
You will keep them from the miseries that are mine!
Take pity on them; see, they are only children,
Friendless except for you. Promise me this,
Great Prince, and give me your hand in token of it.
[CREON *clasps his right hand.*]

Children:
I could say much, if you could understand me,
But as it is, I have only this prayer for you:
Live where you can, be as happy as you can—

Happier, please God, than God has made your father!

CREON. Enough. You have wept enough. Now go within.

OEDIPUS. I must; but it is hard.

CREON. Time eases all things.

OEDIPUS. But you must promise—

CREON. Say what you desire.

OEDIPUS. Send me from Thebes!

CREON. God grant that I may!

OEDIPUS. But since God hates me . . .

CREON. No, he will grant your wish.

OEDIPUS. You promise?

CREON. I can not speak beyond my knowledge.

OEDIPUS. Then lead me in.

CREON. Come now, and leave your children.

OEDIPUS. No! Do not take them from me!

CREON. Think no longer
That you are in command here, but rather think
How, when you were, you served your own destruction.

[*Exeunt into the house all but the* CHORUS; *the* CHORAGOS *chants directly to the audience.*]

CHORAGOS. Men of Thebes: look upon Oedipus.

This is the king who solved the famous riddle
And towered up, most powerful of men.
No mortal eyes but looked on him with envy,
Yet in the end ruin swept over him.

Let every man in mankind's frailty
Consider his last day; and let none
Presume on his good fortune until he find
Life, at his death, a memory without pain.

FOR DISCUSSION:

1. Clever direction can do much to provide the audience with information not known to characters in the play. For instance, when this play is performed, Oedipus usually walks with a telltale limp. Why is this effective? What other techniques not explicit in the text could a good director employ to clarify Sophocles' play?

2. The chorus in a Greek play functions in a variety of possible ways: it can be an expository device; or a mouthpiece for the author; or it can operate as a character in the play, responding to other characters' words and actions. In which of these ways does Sophocles use his chorus?

3. What is the dramatic function of the plague which afflicts Thebes in the opening of the play?

4. When does Jocasta recognize that Oedipus is in fact her son and her first husband's killer? What does she do about it?

5. Irony and paradox are major literary devices in Oedipus Rex, e.g., Tiresias, though blind, is a seer; Oedipus is really seeking himself. Cite four other uses of these devices.

6. One of the central problems in the play is the philosophical issue of individual free will versus determinism. From the audience's point of view is Oedipus' tragic reversal of fortune attributable to his own conduct, or is he merely a pawn in the hands of divine powers whose inexorable will is carried out? From Oedipus' point of view?

7. A secondary theme is concerned with the nature of guilt. Is Oedipus guilty? If so, of what?

8. What are the weak points in Oedipus' character? The strong points? Specifically how do his scenes with Tiresias, Jocasta, Creon, and the Messenger reveal these strengths and weaknesses?

9. Is there a discernible structure, unity, or pattern of development to the play? If so, what is it?

10. Critic James Schroeter observes that Oedipus like many other protagonists of national literatures (e.g., Christ, King Arthur, Moses, Mohammed) is a foster child, reared in a home other than that of his biological parents. How does this double background account for many of Oedipus' actions?

11. Voltaire attacked the play on the

grounds of its credibility. He believed that no king would be ignorant of the manner in which his predecessor died, that Oedipus should certainly have been aware of the place of Laius' death and that based on the evidence produced, Oedipus' recognition of the truth should have taken place long before it did. How damaging is this criticism of the play?

12. Bernard Knox sees the imagery in the play paralleling its actions. Thus, as Oedipus unravels the mystery only to find himself the object of his search, the imagery shifts from that of hunter to prey, from doctor to patient, from investigator to criminal, from the finder to the thing found. Trace these changes in imagery in the play.

13. Several image-chains run throughout Oedipus Rex. Cite several examples of each of the following and show how each series of images is integrated with the theme of the play: (a) ship metaphors and harbor-haven symbolism, (b) metaphors of vision and blindness, (c) hunting or tracking metaphors.

14. What is the reaction of the reader to the ending? Tragic waste? Indignation at innocence punished? An increased awareness of the necessity of submission to divine authority? Account for this response.

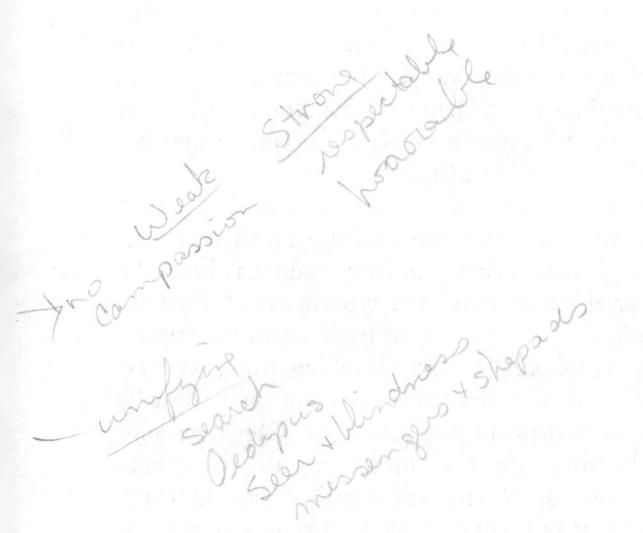

Oedipus Tyrannus*

RICHMOND LATTIMORE

> But let it never be thought right that I should stay
> in the city of my father, and be part of it,
> but let me go to the mountains and live there, where stands
> Cithaeron, called my mountain, which, when they still lived,
> my mother and my father gave me, for my final tomb.
> So let them kill me at last, for they destroyed my life.

Such lines, spoken near the end of Oedipus Tyrannus (hereafter simply Oedipus) after the catastrophe has taken place and all is out, are a kind of Sophoclean anōmalia. They are scarcely led to by the action; they lead nowhere, for the drama does not even tell us whether or not Oedipus got his wish, and there is no story we know of Oedipus dying on the mountain wilderness. Thus the lines do not tie the action to the establishment of a cult, or annual ceremony, in the manner of Euripides. They frame no moral precept. They seem, so taken, to escape from the structure of a play which is fastened together with a special coherence that leaves few loose ends, and none that are important. The most popular modern acting version practically wipes the passage out. But it will be seen to be, after all, a part of the larger action of the tragedy.

The plot of Oedipus, beginning with the prologue and continuing through the next to the last episode, or act, concerns itself with the investigation of events which have already happened. It consists essentially in the joining together of pieces of information (symbola or "clues") until the last piece has been put in, the pattern completed, the puzzle solved. There are two principal problems: the detection of the murderer of Laius and the discovery of the identity of Oedipus himself; a manhunt combined with what might be called a rescue party. But both searches turn out to be after the same game, and the solution—discovery—is complete when the two are identified.

Thus, the drama belongs to the general story pattern of the lost one found. The lost one may be a lost husband, wife, brother, sister, or any close philos, thought dead far away but discovered to be present, unknown. A particularly popular variant has been the one that makes the lost one the lost baby or the foundling: the type to which Oedipus belongs. Whichever variant happens to be followed, the pattern of itself seems to generate certain features that are required, or almost required. For the foundling story, we may note the following: the child is noble; the child is unwanted and is put away (usually for destruction) and thought dead; but the method is always indirect (in Greek versions, a servant is usually delegated to do the dirty work) and the child is rescued, sometimes miraculously nursed by animals. The child grows up in the wilds, and is thought to be plebeian, but is at last recognized by infallible tests or unmistakable tokens and restored to its proper station. Thus the story is in part a story of the triumph of truth over rumor or opinion, and the triumph is pretty likely to come after the darkest moment, when error is on the point of prevailing.

---

* From THE POETRY OF GREEK TRAGEDY by Richmond Lattimore. Copyright 1958 by The Johns Hopkins Press and reprinted by its permission. [Footnotes omitted—Ed.]

A brief consideration of *Oedipus* will show that it follows the pattern almost perfectly. The tokens are not used by Sophocles toward the solution—he has another use for them—but they are there in the form of those otherwise so superfluously cruel pins stuck through the baby's ankles. It is also true that Oedipus is believed to be noble, though of the wrong noble stock: instead of being raised as the peasant's son, he is adopted by the great. In this, Oedipus resembles Ernest Moncrieff, alias Jack Worthing, in his black handbag deposited in the cloak room of Charing Cross Station. The resemblance is important. From the stories of Iamus, the young Cyrus, and Romulus, to the stories of Ernest and Ralph Rackstraw, the foundling story is a success story, a theme for what we call comedy or romantic comedy. But *Oedipus* is a true tragedy.

The tragically fulfilled story, mounted on so articulate a scheme for comedy, accounts for much of the essential nature of *Oedipus*. No extant tragedy so bristles with tragic irony. It opposes Oedipus—possessed of rumor, opinion, or, that is, error—against those who know—Tiresias, the Theban Shepherd—the latter two pulling back against revelation, because they know it is bad, as insistently as Oedipus, armed with his native wit (*gnōmē*) goes plunging forward. Where characters themselves are not omniscient, the audience is. They know the gist of the story and can be surprised only in the means by which the necessary ends are achieved. They know, for instance, that when Oedipus says [217–218]:

> I shall speak, as a stranger to the whole question
> and stranger to the action

he is, in all sincerity, speaking falsehood, though the falsehood is qualified in the term stranger (*xenos*, outlander): the stranger who met and killed the king, the stranger who met and married the queen, who was no true stranger at all. Or when, at the outset, he says [63–64]:

> For I know well
> that all of you are sick, but though you are sick, there's none
> of you who is so sick as I

he is, indeed, speaking the truth, but more truth than he knows, since he is using sickness metaphorically to describe the mental distress of a leader, himself sound, in a stricken kingdom. Oedipus keeps circling back on the truth and brushing against it, as if he subconsciously knew where it was; the omniscient audience can only wonder when the shock of contact will come.

In addition to this irony of detail, there is a larger irony in the inversion of the whole action. Tragic themes may mock the comic by matching them in reverse. Bassanio's three caskets are Lear's three daughters. Bassanio, marked for fortune, chooses the precious lead; Lear rejects it because he must suffer. The triumph of truth and virtue in the foundling play is the joyful recognition: "Our Perdita is found!" But to Oedipus, Tiresias says [458–466]:

> I tell you: that man whom you have long been searching for
> with threats and proclamations for the murderer
> of Laius: that man is here.
> Supposed a stranger come to live with us, he shall
> be shown to be a genuine Theban, and will not
> be pleased with this solution.
>   Blind, who once saw clear,
> beggared, who once was rich, he shall feel out his way
> into a foreign country, with a stick.

The homeless wanderer by delivering the land from the monster and marrying the princess became prince in fact and then was shown to be prince by right, but this revelation turned him once more into a homeless wanderer. But the wanderer, who had once gone bright-eyed with his strong traveler's staff, now uses the staff to tap out the way before him, because he is now old, and eyeless.

The reversed pattern shows again in the fact that the malignant oracles have their darkest moment just before they come clear, with Jocasta's [982]

> O prophesyings of the gods,
> where are you now?

echoed and amplified in Oedipus' typical tyrant-speech of scepticism. Or consider the design of the helpers. The pattern story of the foundling requires a helper or rescuer: the merciful forester or herdsman who refuses to kill the baby outright, or who finds it and saves it from exposure (sometimes this is a wild animal). Sophocles provides at least one helper, or rescuer, for every act. The appeal in the prologue is to Oedipus, himself a rescuer (*sōtēr*) in the past; and Oedipus appeals to Creon, who comes from and represents Apollo and Delphi. It is as rescuer that Tiresias is called, Jocasta intervenes to help, so does the Corinthian Herdsman, and the last helper, the Theban Herdsman, is the true and original rescuer. Those who do not know are eager to help, those who know are reluctant, but all helpers alike push Oedipus over the edge into disaster. Again, it is the story as design which seems to dictate the actual ceremony of the blinding. The Greek word *arthron*, which means a socket, means also a piece which moves within a socket. The infant Oedipus was pinned through the ankles, the joints (*arthra*) of his feet, and while we would not speak of the joints of the eyes, *arthra* serves again for the eyeballs through which Oedipus sticks his wife's pins. Thus the foundling-property of the pinned feet is ignored for its original purpose as means of recognition and transposed into a means of dramatic justice in Oedipus' self-vengeance, by which the strong man renders himself helpless as the baby was rendered helpless.

The fundamental story pattern demands precision in all detail where repeated words are positive, not suggestive, and nowhere else in tragedy is language so precise as here. Consider this piece in Jocasta's résumé [730–734]:

> But Laius, so the report goes, was murdered
> by foreign brigands at a place where three roads meet.
> And for his son, only three days had passed since birth
> when Laius, pinning his feet together at the joints,
> gave him to other hands, and these abandoned him
> upon the mountain wilderness.

The lines are stiff with clues, which though they involve material facts (the three roads, the pinned feet, the mountain side), yet have holes in them (the reported brigands, the second-hand casting away), and they are arranged so that the clue of the three roads forces Oedipus to fix on the fight with the king, and ignore the still more glaring clue that should lead to his own identification with the cast-away baby.

The plausibility of this, if it stands, is a case of the probable-impossible, or drama more perfect than actual life. The pattern story demands tailoring; and if this were a true report of real action, we could ask some awkward questions. For example: Why did the servant of Laius (Theban Shepherd) give the false report of *a body of brigands*? Why did he say nothing when he saw Oedipus in Thebes, but ask to go to the country? Why was he treated so well, when he had run away and left his master and fellow-servants dead on the road? One may answer these: he suspected the truth all the time, beginning with the encounter on the road, for he knew that the son of Laius had not died, and recognized him in this young man who looked like Laius; he was loyal to his protégé, and perhaps disliked Laius, of whom no good has ever been told, here or elsewhere; the story of a body of brigands protected both him and Oedipus. These answers are plausible, but are we intended to work them out, or is there even time to consider them in the rapid progress of the action? This is not the tragedy of the Theban Shepherd. He is an agent, not a principal. There are other points of verisimilitude it would be possible but tedious to raise.

But Sophocles himself raised a couple of questions which he did not answer. Why, if Tiresias was wise and inspired, positively omniscient, did *he* not answer the Sphinx? Why, after the death of Laius and arrival of Oedipus, did he say nothing about the connection? Creon's answer to this last is sage and temperate [571–572]:

> I do not know. And where I have no idea I prefer
> to keep quiet.

But it does not take us far. Is it not, rather, that Oedipus is the man who must find, and condemn, and punish himself? As for the question, why did Tiresias not answer the Sphinx? Grant that it was awkward of Sophocles to raise this, or the other question, when he would not, or could not, answer. In this second case, the Sphinx is one of those barbarous primeval figures who haunt the edges of tragedy. An amorous she-fiend who asks childish riddles and destroys those who cannot answer serves with effect as a vaguely indicated background bogey, or as a blazon on a shield by Aeschylus, but scrutinized close-up she must turn ludicrous; so, in the tetralogy of Aeschylus, she draws the satyr-play. But if the question *were* answered: again, it was not for Tiresias to solve this. As Perdita is lost, so she can be found; so the Sphinx is there for Oedipus to answer. To say he was "fated" to is to overstate it with prejudice toward the grand designs of heaven; but it is a part of his pattern or story- *tychē*, which in Greek does not mean "fate," "chance," or "fortune" so strictly as it means "contact," or, say, "coincidence," the way things are put together.

The pieces fit. The missing one who has been hunted is found. This is the special sense sometimes implicated in the cry *iou iou*, the cry which Oedipus and Jocasta, and Heracles in *The Women of Trachis*, give when the truth is out, the hunter's cry of Socrates in the *Republic* when the quarry for which he and his friends have beaten far bushes is seen to be grovelling right at their feet.

But after discovery, Oedipus does one more thing to complete the pattern. He blinds himself, as reported in the one true messenger-scene of the drama, from the anonymous Messenger who gives us, not the fact of the ruin of Oedipus, for we knew that already, but only the cruel ceremonies through which that ruin is displayed [1310–1337]:

> And how she perished after that I do not know,
> for Oedipus burst in, shouting aloud, and made
> it impossible to watch the rest of her agony
> because our eyes were on him as he stalked the court
> and ranged among us, crying to be given a sword,
> crying to find that wife who was no wife, that field
> that bore a double crop, himself and his children.
> As the man raved, it was some spirit showed him.
> It was not any man of us who stood close by.
> With a fierce cry, as if something were guiding him,

> he drove against the double doors, and from their bases
> buckled the panels inward and burst into the room.
> There we looked in, and saw the woman hanging, caught
> in a noose of rope. But he
> when he looked at her, moaning horribly, he loosed
> the knot from her throat. Then, when the poor woman was laid
> upon the ground, the rest was terrible to see.
> Tearing the golden pins by which her dress was clasped
> out of the robes she wore
> he raised them, stabbed them into the balls of both his eyes,
> crying that they should never more look on himself,
> nor on the evils done to him, or what he had done,
> but that their sight of those they should not look upon
> must darken, lest they recognize whom they should not.
> To such an incantation, many times, not once,
> he dashed the pins into his eyes, and from the eyeballs
> the blood ran down his chin, nor was the storm an ooze
> and drip, but there came both
> a dark clear rain and clotted hail, and all was blood.

What was the sword for? The question is left flying in the air as Oedipus sees Jocasta, already dead. But why does Oedipus blind himself? Students of motivation will find their answer. So that the eyes should no longer look upon the people, the things, that they should not. Sophocles says so. He repeats it: how could Oedipus share sensibilities with his fellow citizens, with whom he can now share nothing? If he could have shut off the sources of hearing, he would have: thus making himself, we might add, the outcast who was to be banned from the community, because the murderer was to be that outcast, and Oedipus is the murderer. We add this; but Sophocles adds that it would be sweet for Oedipus to cut himself loose from all evils, from all his life he knows now as evil; and then seems to contradict himself when Oedipus cries for his daughters and calls them into his arms. But by then, the mood of frenzy has ebbed along with the strength of fury, and Oedipus is himself again, reasoning, and justifying.

Then, for the wildness of Oedipus when he stabbed his eyes, could we say that reasoning of any kind is too reasonable? At least we can say that Oedipus' self-blinding can be seen from various angles. It seems to be a punishment of what is evil (*kakon*), for Oedipus does not deign to call himself *kakodaimōn*, unlucky, ill-starred, but just evil (or vile), *kakos*. The evil Jocasta has escaped; the fury turns on himself with, as we have seen, the formal mode of transfixing those socketed balls of his eyes.

But blinding still serves one more purpose. The riddle of the Sphinx spoke of man feeble as a baby, man strong as grown man (walking on two feet), man feeble in old age. And we have had Oedipus as baby, and Oedipus as grown man, a strong traveler walking on his two feet. We need Oedipus old and enfeebled, and he is still a man in his prime, and appallingly strong. Only such a catastrophic self-punishment can break him so that, within moments, he has turned into an old man, who [1356]

> needs strength now, and needs someone to lead him.

So he has lived the three stages. The riddle of the Sphinx was the mystery of man. But it was the specially private mystery of Oedipus. This—the Sphinx might have meant to him —is the mystery of you. Solve it. *Gnōthi sauton*.

In this sense, but I think in this sense only, Oedipus is Everyman. Stories such as these have shapes of their own which force action rather than shapes which are forced by reason or character; and hence, romantic comedy tends to refine plot at the expense of personality, with stock or pattern situations generating stock characters. But this does not have to happen. Eteocles in *The Seven* is also bent by the shape of the story but generates a momentum which makes his necessary act his own. So is Oedipus. He is the tragedy tyrant driven by his plot, but he is more, a unique individual and, somehow, a great man, who drives himself.

Oedipus Tyrannus is a tragical tragedy despite its frame of romantic comedy, and we should be slow to type Oedipus himself. He is an intellectual man, but not *the* intellectual of the time (Pericles or another). He prides himself on his insight and wit, but for a man of great intelligence he makes disastrous mistakes. Partly, it is a combination of hasty temper and a passionate reliance on quick judgments, which makes him rush to Delphi, then rush away from Delphi indignant with Apollo for not answering his question, or jump to the conclusion that Jocasta's distress is caused by snobbery and anguish for having married a man who was not, after all, a king's son. When he leaves Delphi, he is so sure of his assumptions that he does the two things he should never do: he kills a man who could well be his father, and marries a woman old enough to be his mother. Partly, he makes mistakes through the obsessions of a tyrant—that others are jealous and work through bribery and treachery to unseat him. This makes him assume, wrongly, that the outside brigands who killed Laius must have been suborned from inside Thebes, and suspect that Polybus died through conspiracy. It makes him break into the whole action against Creon and Tiresias. So far, he is the tragedy tyrant, like Creon in *Antigone* or Theseus in *Hippolytus*. But no farther. Oedipus condemns Creon without trial, but lets him off at the pleading of the Chorus, though he is sure they are wrong. And Oedipus can answer to the vague threats of Tiresias against him [452]:

> I do not care <what happens to me> if I save this city.

No tragedy tyrant could say that; and such a man is rewarded by the love and respect of his people (the Chorus) such as no tragedy tyrant ever earns or gets. Oedipus is a tyrant, not *the* tyrant, and unique as he is, he is unique again because he adds one more aspect: the lost child, the strange, hunted creature who came from the mountain and will go back to the mountain.

All combine in the most puzzling stasimon in *Oedipus*—the second—after all has been called into question: the honesty of Creon, the good sense of Oedipus, the official report of the murder of Laius, the identity of the murderer, the truth of oracles, the value of religion [898–943]:

> May it be always given me to know
> guarded purity in all speech,
> in all action. For this, ordinances stand high
> in the bright mountain
> air where they were born. Olympus
> is their sole father. It was no
> mortal growth of men brought
> them forth: nor shall indifference
> store them away in sleep.
> Here the god stands great, ageless forever.
>
> Lust breeds the tyrant man. Lust,
> when fed and puffed with vanity
> on what disaccords with the time's advantage,

> clambering the sheer height
> goes over the drop, where nothing breaks his fall,
> where no firm foothold serves
> longer. But I pray god
> not to break that hand hold which serves
> well the community.
> I shall not loose my hold upon the god, my guide.
>
> But if one, gazing too high
> for thought and action, advances
> without fear of justice, without
> caution, where spirits live,
> may a bad fate seize him,
> his wages for ill starred lusting,
> if he gains unfairly his advantage,
> nor refrains from the forbidden,
> if he lays lewd hands on secret things.
> What man shall hold off the bolts of god
> from his life, in such action,
> or if such works go unpunished, why
> should I go through the ceremonies of worship?
>
> No longer shall I go to the earth's
> secret centerstone, religiously,
> nor to the temple which is at Abae,
> nor yet to Olympia,
> no, unless this code is put together
> to be manifest before mortals.
> Then, oh Power, if Power is what you should be called,
> Zeus, lord of all, oh give heed,
> let your domain, ever immortal, not ignore.
> For the old oracles for Laius are dying
> out; men throw them aside
> now, and nowhere is Apollo regarded.
> God's worship is going.

To begin with the last: we are almost irresistibly forced to think that this belongs to the time, about 426, after the death of Pericles and after the plague came out of nowhere to waste Athens. Apollo had promised the Peloponnesians he would help them against Athens; the city was full of oracles; the enlightened, one supposes, ignored them. Apollo must show them. He showed them. He struck, absurdly, unpredictably. The plague came. The failure of the intellectual, as of the tyrant, is to insist on his own *gnōmē*. Pericles was both intellectual and essentially tyrannical. But I go no further, for Oedipus was not Pericles. But his tragedy is the intellectual's tragedy: his tragic flaw, if you must, that his wit can not cover, foresee, account for all, and nonsensical forces can make nonsense of it; or, as Aeschylus put it, "Science is weaker than Nature is."

Now to go back. The intellectual's tragedy is the tyrant's tragedy. "Lust breeds the tyrant man." Or is it "lust"? The word is *hybris*. Should we say "violence"? We have just emerged from the scene where Oedipus is most tyrannical. In the famous debate on forms of government in the third book of Herodotus, *hybris*, "lawless violence," marks the tyrant, both the insane, bloody acts of Cambyses and the unscrupulous intrigues of Magian nobodies. *Hybris* combines with "jealousy" (*phthonos*) to make the tyrant suspicious of good men, vindictive, one who kills without due process of law, as Oedipus has just been saved from killing Creon. Oedipus is too great to refuse his Chorus, but this is a personal favor; the almost crazy, uneasy suspicion remains. But *hybris* not only characterizes the tyrant in action, it produces him; for escaping the violent tyrant, we may fall into the hands of the violent rabble or the violent nobles who by their violent disorder set up the situation for a redeemer and liberator—the tyrant again. Violence breeds the tyrant.

In a general sense. But we can get a still stricter meaning on another interpretation: the reference is to Jocasta and (it is only fair to add) Laius. The tragedy of incontinence: lust breeds (plants, begets) the tyrant. Against this, it can be argued that the citizens (the Chorus) do not know that the child of Jocasta and Laius, who lusted and must breed, is now their tyrannical tyrant; they do not even think he is alive; and they and Jocasta have been working together in complete sympathy so that it would be strange for them to turn suddenly on her.

Yet I think it does apply to Jocasta, since Sophocles fits the words to her, and the audience can pick up and follow. Like Oedipus again and again through the ironies of the play, the Chorus say more than they know. All meanings are combined: the civic violence which breeds the tyrant, the tyrant's violence which makes him tyrannical in action, with the violence of lust breeding the tyrant, the child who should never have been born and who, born in defiance, lays hands on secret places and defiles his mother, the wife who is no wife.

Along with this, we have the persistent imagery of the climber on the mountain, in high places where spirits live and the overdrop is sheer, danger natural and supernatural, where the climber must use not only feet but hands, and needs a guide—ideally a divine guide. No recorded Greek ever climbed a mountain for the sport of mountain-climbing, and the notion of finding the hardest way up a peak is peculiarly gothic or baroque for an Athenian, or, as Spengler would say, Faustian; but there were occasions, religious and military occasions at least, when mountains had to be climbed. The mountain-climb figured early, from Hesiod on, as a symbol of the slippery, punishing, dangerous quest for achievement or excellence (*aretē*) which stood at the top; just as, in this stasimon, the laws of righteousness stand in the thin, pure Olympian air.

The Greek wilderness is the mountains. All cultures have their wildernesses. The northern foundling might be a child of the great forest, but Greece is not a land of flat forests; its wilderness, whether of woods or scrubby barrens or cliff and boulder, is of the big mountains which are scarcely ever out of sight anywhere in mainland Greece. These were the domain of emptiness, spirits, wild beasts, and tough shepherds; the Athenian city man knew little of them, not that he did not lead a hardy life of military service that would seem impossibly strenuous today, but the citizen-spearman was a fighter of the plains and more at home on a warship than on a mountain top.

The mountains were the wilderness. To Athenians thinking of Thebes, *the* mountain was Cithaeron, visible from Athens; invisible in fact from Thebes, but seen from the near hills as a bold black trapezoid dominating the Asopus Valley. Parnassus is higher, steeper, and snowier, but a sacred mountain with civilized Delphi perched in its underslopes. Cithaeron is all wild.

On such mountain sides the Chorus imagine the outcast murderer [474–491]:

> Who is he, whom the magic-singing
> Delphian rock proclaimed
> the bloody-handed murderer
> whose crimes were too deep to tell?
> Run, he must run now
> harder than stormy horses,
> feet flying in flight,
> for the armed god is after him, leaping

> with fire and flash, Apollo, Zeus' own,
> and the forbidding Death-
> Spirits horribly haunt him.
>
> The message shone, it showed
> even now from the snows
> of Parnassus. Manhunt the hidden
> man. After him all.
> He lurks, a wild bull
> in the wild wood, in the holes
> of the rock side
> lonely-footed, forlorn wandering,
> dodging aside from the mid-centered
> prophecies, which, things alive,
> hover to haunt him.

In the first long angry response of Tiresias, where the chief image is of a ship come home to harbor (obvious enough), the mountain, and the stalker on the mountain, project, even obtrude [420–434]:

> I tell you, since you have baited me with my blindness:
> you have your eyes, and do not see where you are standing
> in evil, nor where you are living, nor whom you are living with.
> Do you know whose son you are? Unconscious enemy
> of your own people, here on earth, and under the ground,
> the double-goading curse, father's and mother's in one,
> shall stalk you on its feet of horror from this land,
> you who see straight now, but shall then see only dark.
> What harbor shall not be full of your cries,
> what Mount Cithaeron shall not echo to them soon
> when you learn what that marriage is, that awful haven
> where, after your fair voyage, you brought in your ship?

The foundling, in Greece, was the child of the mountain side. The foundling was often protected by divine wild spirits of the place, or he might have been a spirit himself, or even a great god, Dionysus, Hermes, even Zeus. The Chorus fancy Oedipus, the mountain-child, fosterling of Cithaeron, as by-blow of some mountain-walking god, Pan, Apollo, Hermes, or Dionysus, by one of the nymphs of the mountains. Oedipus, in answer to the doubts, as he thinks, of Jocasta, identifies himself with nature [1115–1124]:

> Let her break forth her tempers as she will, but I
> will still find out what seed made me, although it be
> humble. She being proud, perhaps, as women are,
> thinks the obscurity of my birth is some disgrace.
> I count myself the child of Fortune. While her gifts
> are good, I shall not call myself degraded. I
> am born of her. She is my mother. And the months
> my brothers marked me small, and they have marked me great.
> So born, I would not ever wish I had been born
> anything else, to keep me from learning who I am.

Tychē, Fortune or Coincidence, is here the way in which things come out or work, that is, another Greek way of saying Nature. The natural son is the child of Nature. After the catastrophe, it is to nature and the pathos of places that Oedipus chiefly appeals [1456–1470]:

> Cithaeron oh Cithaeron, why did you take me? Why
> did you not kill me when you took me? Thus had I
> never made clear to men the place where I was born.
> O Polybus and Corinth and my father's house
> of old, as men then called it, what a festering sore
> you fed beneath my outward splendor, I who now
> have been found evil in myself, and evil born.
> O three roads, hidden valley,
> oak wood and narrow meeting at the threeway cross,
> who drank the blood of my own father which was spilled
> by my own hands, do you remember still
> what things I did to you, and then, when I came here,
> what things I did again?

It is as if Oedipus had been set free from ordinary city life when he was put away into the hands of the mountain Shepherd. It is natural that the child of the wilderness who lived in the city should go home to his wilderness to die—to ask to go, even though the story has not told that he did so; and thus we have come back to our beginning 1521–1525]:

> But let it never be thought right that I should stay
> in the city of my father, and be part of it,
> but let me go to the mountains and live there, where stands
> Cithaeron, called *my* mountain, which, when they still lived
> my mother and my father gave me, for my final tomb.
> So let them kill me at last, for they destroyed my life.

We have completed the circle but we have not resolved all the play. Never think that. We can read *Oedipus* as many times as we like, and every time find new truths and throw away old falsehoods that once seemed to be true. There is always a dimension that escapes.

While it is true that *Oedipus* is a particularly compact combination of themes, where themes of foundling, mountain-spirit, murder, manhunt, tyrant cohere because we are constantly led from one into the other, yet in this play one can, perhaps more clearly than elsewhere in Sophocles, separate the poetic from the dramatic. Or at least we can separate the "daemonic" or "barbaric," because it is not absolutely needed. There are splendid characterizing lines and rhetorical effects, without this kind of poetic material. And the daemonic is not "so." The finished play is not about any nature-child or mountain-spirit. He exists only in the imagination of the players. The Oedipus of the action is a perfectly plausible, too human man, and the closest he has ever come to being a child of Fortune or Nature, or Year Spirit with the months for brothers, is to be handed from one kindhearted Shepherd to another, in a summer of babyhood on the high pastures. The play King, with his greatnesses and his faults, does not need to be a splendid barbarian at heart, like Ajax. He is a homicide: but on the level of discourse we may see him as thinking himself so set upon, so right in his defense, that the deadly brawl at the crossroads has scarcely troubled his conscience since. He never was a hunted monster, something like a great, wild beast, fierce but scary, driven among the high rocks. That is all the imagination of old men. We can so play trenchant characters that all seems motivated, and we can forget that what first drove the action was the shape of a universal pattern story from the childhood of men.

Oedipus is acted today, often professionally, and more frequently, I believe, than any other Greek play. It is commonly given in what almost passes as an authorized version—that of Yeats—which has cut down or cut out those daemonic passages we have been considering. It is good theatre, and it is truly dramatic, but it is no longer haunted.

In a stasimon of *Antigone*, also, among the moralities we see an image of the high snows of Olympus where Zeus is forever, deathless and sleepless, with his laws; and by contrast, an image of the pit below, this time the darkness of the sea stirred to waves that batter the promontories. The gods of Sophocles are there, but remote, unattainable as the snows of Olympus; we can only see the effects, and are closer to the dark underpit. The tragedies of Sophocles concern resolute, intelligent, civilized people, determined to understand everything; they never do, because there is a dark nonsensical element in things, which eludes their comprehension and, often, destroys them; but which has its own wild beauty.

FOR DISCUSSION:

1. Lattimore finds that Oedipus Rex is a play which "is fastened together with a special kind of coherence that leaves few loose ends." What are the unifying elements in Sophocles' play?

2. Specifically, how does Sophocles employ a story pattern usually portrayed as a comedy—the identification of the foundling—and recast it as a tragedy?

3. Lattimore notes some of the inconsistencies of the play. How important does he think they are? Why?

4. How does Lattimore integrate the play's theme and imagery?

5. Is Lattimore's analysis of Oedipus Rex entirely internal? If not, what use of material outside the play itself does he make?

Flight*

JOHN STEINBECK

About fifteen miles below Monterey, on the wild coast, the Torres family had their farm, a few sloping acres above a cliff that dropped to the brown reefs and to the hissing white waters of the ocean. Behind the farm the stone mountains stood up against the sky. The farm buildings huddled like little clinging aphids on the mountain skirts, crouched low to the ground as though the wind might blow them into the sea. The little shack, the rattling, rotting barn were gray-bitten with sea salt, beaten by the damp wind until they had taken on the color of the granite hills. Two horses, a red cow and a red calf, half a dozen pigs and a flock of lean, multi-colored chickens stocked the place. A little corn was raised on the sterile slope, and it grew short and thick under the wind, and all the cobs formed on the landward sides of the stalks.

Mama Torres, a lean, dry woman with ancient eyes, had ruled the farm for ten years ever since her husband tripped over a stone in the field one day and fell full length on a rattlesnake. When one is bitten on the chest there is not much that can be done.

Mama Torres had three children, two undersized black ones of twelve and fourteen, Emilio and Rosy, whom Mama kept fishing on the rocks below the farm when the sea was kind and when the truant officer was in some distant part of Monterey County. And there was Pepé, the tall smiling son of nineteen, a gentle, affectionate boy, but very lazy. Pepé had a tall head, pointed at the top, and from its peak, coarse black hair grew down like a thatch all around. Over his smiling little eyes Mama cut a straight bang so he could see. Pepé had sharp Indian cheekbones and an eagle nose, but his mouth was as sweet and shapely as a girl's mouth, and his chin was fragile and chiseled.

He was loose and gangling, all legs and feet and wrists, and he was very lazy. Mama thought him fine and brave, but she never told him so. She said, "Some lazy cow must have got into thy father's family, else how could I have a son like thee." And she said, "When I carried thee, a sneaking lazy coyote came out of the brush and looked at me one day. That must have made thee so."

Pepé smiled sheepishly and stabbed at the ground with his knife to keep the blade sharp and free from rust. It was his inheritance, that knife, his father's knife. The long heavy blade folded back into the black handle. There was a button on the handle. When Pepé pressed the button, the blade leaped out ready for use. The knife was with Pepé always, for it had been his father's knife.

One sunny morning when the sea below the cliff was glinting and blue and the white surf creamed on the reef, when even the stone mountains looked kindly, Mama Torres called out the door of the shack, "Pepé, I have a labor for thee."

There was no answer. Mama listened. From behind the barn she heard a burst of laughter. She lifted her full long skirt and walked in the direction of the noise.

Pepé was sitting on the ground with his back against a box. His white teeth glistened. On either side of him stood the two black ones, tense and expectant. Fifteen feet away a redwood post was set in the ground. Pepé's right hand lay limply in his lap, and in the palm the big black knife rested. The blade was closed back into the handle. Pepé looked smiling at the sky.

Suddenly Emilio cried, "Ya!"

Pepé's wrist flicked like the head of a snake. The blade seemed to fly open in mid-air, and with a thump the point dug

---

* From THE LONG VALLEY by John Steinbeck. Copyright 1938, copyright © renewed 1966 by John Steinbeck. Reprinted by permission of The Viking Press, Inc. and McIntosh and Otis, Inc.

into the redwood post, and the black handle quivered. The three burst into excited laughter. Rosy ran to the post and pulled out the knife and brought it back to Pepé. He closed the blade and settled the knife carefully in his listless palm again. He grinned self-consciously at the sky.

"Ya!"

The heavy knife lanced out and sunk into the post again. Mama moved forward like a ship and scattered the play.

"All day you do foolish things with the knife, like a toy-baby," she stormed. "Get up on thy huge feet that eat up shoes. Get up!" She took him by one loose shoulder and hoisted at him. Pepé grinned sheepishly and came half-heartedly to his feet. "Look!" Mama cried. "Big lazy, you must catch the horse and put on him thy father's saddle. You must ride to Monterey. The medicine bottle is empty. There is no salt. Go thou now, Peanut! Catch the horse."

A revolution took place in the relaxed figure of Pepé. "To Monterey, me? Alone? Sí, Mama."

She scowled at him. "Do not think, big sheep, that you will buy candy. No, I will give you only enough for the medicine and the salt."

Pepé smiled. "Mama, you will put the hatband on the hat?"

She relented then. "Yes, Pepé. You may wear the hatband."

His voice grew insinuating, "And the green handkerchief, Mama?"

"Yes, if you go quickly and return with no trouble, the silk green handkerchief will go. If you make sure to take off the handkerchief when you eat so no spot may fall on it. . . ."

"Sí, Mama. I will be careful. I am a man."

"Thou? A man? Thou art a peanut."

He went into the rickety barn and brought out a rope, and he walked agilely enough up the hill to catch the horse.

When he was ready and mounted before the door, mounted on his father's saddle that was so old that the oaken frame showed through torn leather in many places, then Mama brought out the round black hat with the tooled leather band, and she reached up and knotted the green silk handkerchief about his neck. Pepé's blue denim coat was much darker than his jeans, for it had been washed much less often.

Mama handed up the big medicine bottle and the silver coins. "That for the medicine," she said, "and that for the salt. That for a candle to burn for the papa. That for *dulces* for the little ones. Our friend Mrs. Rodriguez will give you dinner and maybe a bed for the night. When you go to the church say only ten Paternosters and only twenty-five Ave Marias. Oh! I know, big coyote. You would sit there flapping your mouth over Aves all day while you looked at the candles and the holy pictures. That is not good devotion to stare at the pretty things."

The black hat, covering the high pointed head and black thatched hair of Pepé, gave him dignity and age. He sat the rangy horse well. Mama thought how handsome he was, dark and lean and tall. "I would not send thee now alone, thou little one, except for the medicine," she said softly. "It is not good to have no medicine, for who knows when the toothache will come, or the sadness of the stomach. These things are."

"*Adios*, Mama," Pepé cried. "I will come back soon. You may send me often alone. I am a man."

"Thou art a foolish chicken."

He straightened his shoulders, flipped the reins against the horse's shoulder and rode away. He turned once and saw that they still watched him, Emilio and Rosy and Mama. Pepé grinned with pride and gladness and lifted the tough buckskin horse to a trot.

When he had dropped out of sight over a little dip in the road, Mama turned to the black ones, but she spoke to herself. "He is nearly a man now," she said. "It will be a nice thing to have a man in the house again." Her eyes sharpened on the children. "Go to the rocks now. The tide is going out. There will be abalones to be found." She put the iron hooks into their hands and saw them down the steep trail to the reefs. She brought the smooth stone *metate* to the doorway and sat grinding her corn to flour and looking occasionally at the road over which Pepé had gone. The noonday came and then the afternoon, when the little ones beat the abalones on a rock to make them tender and Mama patted the tortillas to make them thin. They ate their dinner as the red sun was plunging down toward the ocean. They sat on the doorsteps and watched the big white moon come over the mountain tops.

Mama said, "He is now at the house of our friend Mrs. Rodriguez. She will give him nice things to eat and maybe a present."

Emilio said, "Some day I too will ride to Monterey for medicine. Did Pepé come to be a man today?"

Mama said wisely, "A boy gets to be a man when a man is needed. Remember this thing. I have known boys forty years old because there was no need for a man."

Soon afterwards they retired, Mama in her big oak bed on one side of the room. Emilio and Rosy in their boxes full of straw and sheepskins on the other side of the room.

The moon went over the sky and the surf roared on the rocks. The roosters crowed the first call. The surf subsided to a whispering surge against the reef. The moon dropped toward the sea. The roosters crowed again.

The moon was near down to the water when Pepé rode on a winded horse to his home flat. His dog bounced out and circled the horse yelping with pleasure. Pepé slid off the saddle to the ground. The weathered little shack was silver in the moonlight and the square shadow of it was black to the north and east. Against the east the piling mountains were misty with light; their tops melted into the sky.

Pepé walked wearily up the three steps and into the house. It was dark inside. There was a rustle in the corner.

Mama cried out from her bed. "Who comes? Pepé, is it thou?"

"Sí, Mama."

"Did you get the medicine?"

"Sí, Mama."

"Well, go to sleep, then. I thought you would be sleeping at the house of Mrs. Rodriguez." Pepé stood silently in the dark room. "Why do you stand there, Pepé? Did you drink wine?"

"Sí, Mama."

"Well, go to bed then and sleep out the wine."

His voice was tired and patient, but very firm. "Light the candle, Mama. I must go away into the mountains."

"What is this, Pepé? You are crazy." Mama struck a sulphur match and held the little blue burr until the flame spread up the stick. She set light to the candle on the floor beside her bed. "Now, Pepé, what is this you say?" She looked anxiously into his face.

He was changed. The fragile quality seemed to have gone from his chin. His mouth was less full than it had been, the lines of the lips were straighter, but in his eyes the greatest change had taken place. There was no laughter in them any more nor any bashfulness. They were sharp and bright and purposeful.

He told her in a tired monotone, told her everything just as it had happened. A few people came into the kitchen of Mrs. Rodriguez. There was wine to drink. Pepé drank wine. The little quarrel—the man started toward Pepé and then the knife—it went almost by itself. It flew, it darted before Pepé knew it. As he talked, Mama's face grew stern, and it seemed to grow more lean. Pepé finished. "I am a man now, Mama. The man said names to me I could not allow."

Mama nodded. "Yes, thou art a man, my poor little Pepé. Thou art a man. I have seen it coming on thee. I have watched you throwing the knife into the post, and I have been afraid." For a moment her face had softened, but now it grew stern again. "Come! We must get you ready. Go. Awaken Emilio and Rosy. Go quickly."

Pepé stepped over to the corner where his brother and sister slept among the sheepskins. He leaned down and shook them gently. "Come, Rosy! Come, Emilio! The mama says you must arise."

The little black ones sat up and rubbed their eyes in the candlelight. Mama was out of bed now, her long black skirt over her nightgown. "Emilio," she cried. "Go up and catch the other horse for Pepé. Quickly now! Quickly." Emilio put his legs in his overalls and stumbled sleepily out the door.

"You heard no one behind you on the road?" Mama demanded.

"No, Mama. I listened carefully. No one was on the road."

Mama darted like a bird about the room. From a nail on the wall she took a canvas water bag and threw it on the floor. She stripped a blanket from her bed and rolled it into a tight tube and tied the ends with string. From a box beside the stove she lifted a flour sack half full of black stringy jerky. "Your father's black coat, Pepé. Here, put it on."

Pepé stood in the middle of the floor watching her activity. She reached behind the door and brought out the rifle, a long 38-56, worn shiny the whole length of the barrel. Pepé took it from her and held it in the crook of his elbow. Mama brought a little leather bag and counted the cartridges into his hand. "Only ten left," she warned. "You must not waste them."

Emilio put his head in the door. "*'Qui 'st 'l caballo, Mama.*"

"Put on the saddle from the other horse. Tie on the blanket. Here, tie the jerky to the saddle horn."

Still Pepé stood silently watching his mother's frantic activity. His chin looked hard, and his sweet mouth was drawn and thin. His little eyes followed Mama about the room almost suspiciously.

Rosy asked softly, "Where goes Pepé?"

Mama's eyes were fierce. "Pepé goes on a journey. Pepé is a man now. He has a man's thing to do."

Pepé straightened his shoulders. His mouth changed until he looked very much like Mama.

At last the preparation was finished. The loaded horse stood outside the door. The water bag dripped a line of moisture down the bay shoulder.

The moonlight was being thinned by the dawn and the big white moon was near down to the sea. The family stood by the shack. Mama confronted Pepé. "Look, my son! Do not stop until it is dark again. Do not sleep even though you are tired. Take care of the horse in order that he may not stop of weariness. Remember to be careful with the bullets—there are only ten. Do not fill thy stomach with jerky or it will make thee sick. Eat a little jerky and fill thy stomach with grass. When thou comest to the high mountains, if thou seest any of the dark watching men, go not near to them nor try to speak to them. And forget not thy prayers." She put her lean hands on Pepé's shoulders, stood on her toes and kissed him formally on both cheeks, and Pepé kissed her on both cheeks. Then he went to Emilio and Rosy and kissed both of their cheeks.

Pepé turned back to Mama. He seemed to look for a little softness, a little weakness in her. His eyes were searching, but Mama's face remained fierce. "Go now," she said. "Do not wait to be caught like a chicken."

Pepé pulled himself into the saddle. "I am a man," he said.

It was the first dawn when he rode up the hill toward the little canyon which let a trail into the mountains. Moonlight and daylight fought with each other, and the two warring qualities made it difficult to see. Before Pepé had gone a hundred yards, the outlines of his figure were misty; and long before he entered the canyon, he had become a gray, indefinite shadow.

Mama stood stiffly in front of her doorstep, and on either side of her stood Emilio and Rosy. They cast furtive glances at Mama now and then.

When the gray shape of Pepé melted into the hillside and disappeared, Mama relaxed. She began the high, whining keen of the death wail. "Our beautiful—our brave," she cried. "Our protector, our son is gone." Emilio and Rosy moaned beside her. "Our beautiful—our brave, he is gone." It was the formal wail. It rose to a high piercing whine and subsided to a moan. Mama raised it three times and then she turned and went into the house and shut the door.

Emilio and Rosy stood wondering in the dawn. They heard Mama whimpering in the house. They went out to sit on the cliff above the ocean. They touched shoulders. "When did Pepé come to be a man?" Emilio asked.

"Last night," said Rosy. "Last night in Monterey." The ocean clouds turned red with the sun that was behind the mountains.

"We will have no breakfast," said Emilio. "Mama will not want to cook." Rosy did not answer him. "Where is Pepé gone?" he asked.

Rosy looked around at him. She drew her knowledge from the quiet air. "He has gone on a journey. He will never come back."

"Is he dead? Do you think he is dead?"

Rosy looked back at the ocean again. A little steamer, drawing a line of smoke sat on the edge of the horizon. "He is not dead," Rosy explained. "Not yet."

Pepé rested the big rifle across the saddle in front of him. He let the horse walk up the hill and he didn't look back. The stony slope took on a coat of short brush so that Pepé found the entrance to a trail and entered it.

When he came to the canyon opening, he swung once in his saddle and looked back, but the houses were swallowed in the misty light. Pepé jerked forward again. The high shoulder of the canyon closed in on him. His horse stretched out its neck and sighed and settled to the trail.

It was a well-worn path, dark soft leaf-mold earth strewn with broken pieces of sandstone. The trail rounded the shoulder of the canyon and dropped steeply into the bed of the stream. In the shallows the water ran smoothly, glinting in the first morning sun. Small round stones on the bottom were as brown as rust with sun moss. In the sand along the edges of the stream the tall, rich wild mint grew, while in the water itself the cress, old and tough, had gone to heavy seed.

The path went into the stream and emerged on the other side. The horse sloshed into the water and stopped. Pepé dropped his bridle and let the beast drink of the running water.

Soon the canyon sides became steep and the first giant sentinel redwoods guarded the trail, great round red trunks bearing foliage as green and lacy as ferns. Once Pepé was among the trees, the sun was lost. A perfumed and purple light lay in the pale green of the underbrush. Gooseberry bushes and blackberries and tall ferns lined the stream, and overhead the branches of the redwoods met and cut off the sky.

Pepé drank from the water bag, and he reached into the flour sack and brought out a black string of jerky. His white teeth gnawed at the string until the tough meat parted. He chewed slowly and drank occasionally from the water bag. His little eyes were slumberous and tired, but the muscles of his face were hard set. The earth of the trail was black now. It gave up a hollow sound under the walking hoofbeats.

The stream fell more sharply. Little waterfalls splashed on the stones. Five-fingered ferns hung over the water and dripped spray from their fingertips. Pepé rode half over in his saddle, dangling one leg loosely. He picked a bay leaf from a tree beside the way and put it into his mouth for a moment to flavor the dry jerky. He held the gun loosely across the pommel.

Suddenly he squared in his saddle, swung the horse from the trail and kicked it hurriedly up behind a big redwood tree. He pulled up the reins tight against the bit to keep the horse from whinnying. His face was intent and his nostrils quivered a little.

A hollow pounding came down the trail, and a horseman rode by, a fat man with red cheeks and a white stubble beard. His horse put down its head and blubbered at the trail when it came to the place where Pepé had turned off. "Hold up!" said the man and he pulled up his horse's head.

When the last sound of the hoofs died away, Pepé came back into the trail again. He did not relax in the saddle any more. He lifted the big rifle and swung the lever to throw a shell into the chamber, and then he let down the hammer to half cock.

The trail grew very steep. Now the redwood trees were smaller and their tops were dead, bitten dead where the wind reached them. The horse plodded on; the sun went slowly overhead and started down toward the afternoon.

Where the stream came out of a side canyon, the trail left it. Pepé dismounted and watered his horse and filled up his water bag. As soon as the trail had parted from the stream, the trees were gone and only the thick brittle sage and manzanita and chaparral edged the trail. And the soft black earth was gone, too, leaving only the light tan broken rock for the trail bed. Lizards scampered away into the brush as the horse rattled over the little stones.

Pepé turned in his saddle and looked back. He was in the open now: he could be seen from a distance. As he ascended the trail the country grew more rough and terrible and dry. The way wound about the bases of great square rocks. Little gray rabbits skittered in the brush. A bird made a monotonous high creaking. Eastward the bare rock mountaintops were pale and powder-dry under the dropping sun. The horse plodded up and up the trail toward a little V in the ridge which was the pass.

Pepé looked suspiciously back every minute or so, and his eyes sought the tops of the ridges ahead. Once, on a white barren spur, he saw a black figure for a moment, but he looked quickly away, for it was one of the dark watchers. No one knew who the watchers were, nor where they lived, but it was better to ignore them and never to show interest in them. They did not bother one who stayed on the trail and minded his own business.

The air was parched and full of light dust blown by the breeze from the eroding mountains. Pepé drank sparingly from his bag and corked it tightly and hung it on the horn again. The trail moved up the dry shale hillside, avoiding rocks, dropping under clefts, climbing in and out of old water scars. When he arrived at the little pass he stopped and looked back for a long time. No dark watchers were to be seen now. The trail behind was empty. Only the high tops of the redwoods indicated where the stream flowed.

Pepé rode on through the pass. His little eyes were nearly closed with weariness, but his face was stern, relentless and manly. The high mountain wind coasted sighing through the pass and whistled on the edges of the big blocks of broken granite. In the air, a red-tailed hawk sailed over close to the ridge and screamed angrily. Pepé went slowly through the broken jagged pass and looked down on the other side.

The trail dropped quickly, staggering among broken rock. At the bottom of the slope there was a dark crease, thick with brush, and on the other side of the crease a little flat, in which a grove of oak trees grew. A scar of green grass cut across the flat. And behind the flat another mountain rose, desolate with dead rocks and starving little black bushes. Pepé drank from the bag again for the air was so dry that it encrusted his nostrils and burned his lips. He put the horse down the trail. The hooves slipped and struggled on the steep way, starting little stones that rolled off into the brush. The sun was gone behind the westward mountain now, but still it glowed brilliantly on the oaks and on the grassy flat. The rocks and the hillsides still sent up waves of the heat they had gathered from the day's sun.

Pepé looked up to the top of the next dry withered ridge. He saw a dark form against the sky, a man's figure standing on top of a rock, and he glanced away quickly not to appear curious. When a moment later he looked up again, the figure was gone.

Downward the trail was quickly covered. Sometimes the horse floundered for footing, sometimes set his feet and slid a little way. They came at last to the bottom where the dark chaparral was higher than Pepé's head. He held up his rifle on one side and his arm on the other to shield his face from the sharp brittle fingers of the brush.

Up and out of the crease he rode, and up a little cliff. The grassy flat was before him, and the round comfortable oaks. For a moment he studied the trail down which he had come, but there was no movement and no sound from it. Finally he rode out over the flat, to the green streak, and at the upper end of the damp he found a little spring welling out of the earth and dropping into a dug basin before it seeped out over the flat.

Pepé filled his bag first, and then he let the thirsty horse drink out of the pool. He led the horse to the clump of oaks, and in the middle of the grove, fairly protected from sight on all sides, he took off the saddle and the bridle and laid them on the ground. The horse stretched his jaws sideways and yawned. Pepé knotted the lead rope about the horse's neck and tied him to a sapling among the oaks, where he could graze in a fairly large circle.

When the horse was gnawing hungrily at the dry grass, Pepé went to the saddle and took a black string of jerky from the sack and strolled to an oak tree on the edge of the grove, from under which he could watch the trail. He sat down in the crisp dry oak leaves and automatically felt for his big black knife to cut the jerky, but he had no knife. He leaned back on his elbow and gnawed at the tough strong meat. His face was blank, but it was a man's face.

The bright evening light washed the eastern ridge, but the valley was darkening. Doves flew down from the hills to the spring, and the quail came running out of the brush and joined them, calling clearly to one another.

Out of the corner of his eye Pepé saw a shadow grow out of the bushy crease. He turned his head slowly. A big spotted wildcat was creeping toward the spring, belly to the ground, moving like thought.

Pepé cocked his rifle and edged the muzzle slowly around. Then he looked apprehensively up the trail and dropped the hammer again. From the ground beside him he picked an oak twig and threw it toward the spring. The quail flew up with a roar and the doves whistled away. The big cat stood up: for a long moment he looked at Pepé with cold yellow eyes, and then fearlessly walked back into the gulch.

The dusk gathered quickly in the deep valley. Pepé muttered his prayers, put his head down on his arm and went instantly to sleep.

The moon came up and filled the valley with cold blue light, and the wind swept rustling down from the peaks. The owls worked up and down the slopes looking for rabbits. Down in the brush of the gulch a coyote gabbled. The oak trees whispered softly in the night breeze.

Pepé started up, listening. His horse had whinnied. The moon was just slipping behind the western ridge, leaving the valley in darkness behind it. Pepé sat tensely gripping his rifle. From far up the trail he heard an answering whinny and the crash of shod hooves on the broken rock. He jumped to his feet, ran to his horse and led it under the trees. He threw on the saddle and cinched it tight for the steep trail, caught the unwilling head and forced the bit into the mouth. He felt the saddle to make sure the water bag and the sack of jerky were there. Then he mounted and turned up the hill.

It was velvet dark. The horse found the entrance to the trail where it left the flat, and started up, stumbling and slipping on the rocks. Pepé's hand rose up to his head. His hat was gone. He had left it under the oak tree.

The horse had struggled far up the trail when the first change of dawn came into the air, a steel grayness as light mixed thoroughly with dark. Gradually the sharp snaggled edge of the ridge stood out above them, rotten granite tortured and eaten by the winds of time. Pepé had dropped his reins on the horn, leaving direction to the horse. The brush grabbed at his legs in the dark until one knee of his jeans was ripped.

Gradually the light flowed down over the ridge. The starved brush and rocks stood out in the half light, strange and lonely in high perspective. Then there came warmth into the light. Pepé drew up and looked back, but he could see nothing in the darker valley below. The sky turned blue over the coming sun. In the waste of the mountainside, the poor dry brush grew only three feet high. Here and there, big outcroppings of unrotted granite stood up like moldering houses. Pepé relaxed a little. He drank from his water bag and bit off a piece of jerky. A single eagle flew over, high in the light.

Without warning Pepé's horse screamed and fell on its side. He was almost down before the rifle crash echoed up from the valley. From a hole behind the struggling shoulder, a stream of bright crimson blood pumped and stopped and pumped and stopped. The hooves threshed on the ground. Pepé lay half stunned beside the horse. He looked slowly down the hill. A piece of sage clipped off beside his head and another crash echoed up from side to side of the canyon. Pepé flung himself frantically behind a bush.

He crawled up the hill on his knees and on one hand. His right hand held the rifle up off the ground and pushed it ahead of him. He moved with the instinctive care of an animal. Rapidly he wormed his way toward one of the big outcroppings of granite on the hill above him. Where the brush was high he doubled up and ran, but where the cover was slight he wriggled forward on his stomach, pushing the rifle ahead of him. In the last little distance there was no cover at all. Pepé poised and then he darted across the space and flashed around the corner of the rock.

He leaned panting against the stone. When his breath came easier he moved along behind the big rock until he came to a narrow split that offered a thin section of vision down the hill. Pepé lay on his stomach and pushed the rifle barrel through the slit and waited.

The sun reddened the western ridges now. Already the buzzards were settling down toward the place where the horse lay. A small brown bird scratched in the dead sage leaves directly in front of the rifle muzzle. The coasting eagle flew back toward the rising sun.

Pepé saw a little movement in the brush far below. His grip tightened on the gun. A little brown doe stepped daintily out on the trail and crossed it and disappeared into the brush again. For a long time Pepé waited. Far below he could see the little flat and the oak trees and the slash of green. Suddenly his eyes flashed back at the trail again. A quarter of a mile down there had been a quick movement in the chaparral. The rifle swung over. The front sight nestled in the V of the rear sight. Pepé studied for a moment and then raised the rear sight a notch. The little movement in the brush came again. The sight settled on it. Pepé squeezed the trigger. The explosion crashed down the mountain and up the other side, and came rattling back. The whole side of the slope grew still. No more movement. And then a white streak cut into the granite of the slit and a bullet whined away and a crash sounded up from below. Pepé felt a sharp pain in his right hand. A sliver of granite was sticking out from between his first and second knuckles and the point protruded from his palm. Carefully he pulled out the sliver of stone. The wound bled evenly and gently. No vein nor artery was cut.

Pepé looked into a little dusty cave in the rock and gathered a handful of spider web, and he pressed the mass into the cut, plastering the soft web into the blood. The flow stopped almost at once.

The rifle was on the ground. Pepé picked it up, levered a new shell into the chamber. And then he slid into the brush on his stomach. Far to the right he crawled, and then up the hill, moving slowly and carefully, crawling to cover and resting and then crawling again.

In the mountains the sun is high in its arc before it penetrates the gorges. The hot face looked over the hill and brought instant heat with it. The white light beat on the rocks and reflected from them and rose up quivering from the earth again, and the rocks and bushes seemed to quiver behind the air.

Pepé crawled in the general direction of the ridge peak, zig-zagging for cover. The deep cut between his knuckles began to throb. He crawled close to a rattlesnake before he saw it, and when it raised its dry head and made a soft beginning whirr, he backed up and took another way. The quick gray lizards flashed in front of him, raising a tiny line of dust. He found another mass of spider web and pressed it against his throbbing hand.

Pepé was pushing the rifle with his left hand now. Little drops of sweat ran to the ends of his coarse black hair and rolled down his cheeks. His lips and tongue were growing thick and heavy. His lips writhed to draw saliva into his mouth. His little dark eyes were uneasy and suspicious. Once when a gray lizard paused in front of him on the parched ground and turned its head sideways he crushed it flat with a stone.

When the sun slid past noon he had not gone a mile. He crawled exhaustedly a last hundred yards to a patch of high sharp manzanita, crawled desperately, and when the patch was reached he wriggled in among the tough gnarly trunks and dropped his head on his left arm. There was little shade in the meager brush, but there was cover and safety. Pepé went to sleep as he lay and the sun beat on his back. A few little birds hopped close to him and peered and hopped away. Pepé squirmed in his sleep and he raised and dropped his wounded hand again and again.

The sun went down behind the peaks and the cool evening came, and then the dark. A coyote yelled from the hillside, Pepé started awake and looked about with misty eyes. His hand was swollen and heavy; a little thread of pain ran up the inside of his arm and settled in a pocket in his armpit. He peered about and then stood up, for the mountains were black and the moon had not yet risen. Pepé stood up in the dark. The coat of his father pressed on his arm. His tongue was swollen until it nearly filled his mouth. He wriggled out of the coat and dropped it in the brush, and then he struggled up the hill, falling over rocks and tearing his way through the brush. The rifle knocked against stones as he went. Little dry avalanches of gravel and shattered stone went whispering down the hill behind him.

After a while the old moon came up and showed the jagged ridge top ahead of him. By moonlight Pepé traveled more easily. He bent forward so that his throbbing arm hung away from his body. The journey uphill was made in dashes and rests, a frantic rush up a few yards and then a rest. The wind coasted down the slope rattling the dry stems of the bushes.

The moon was at meridian when Pepé came at last to the sharp backbone of the ridge top. On the last hundred yards of the rise no soil had clung under the wearing winds. The way was on solid rock. He clambered to the top and looked down on the other side. There was a draw like the last below him, misty with moonlight, brushed with dry struggling sage and chaparral. On the other side the hill rose up sharply and at the top the jagged rotten teeth of the mountain showed against the sky. At the bottom of the cut the brush was thick and dark.

Pepé stumbled down the hill. His throat was almost closed with thirst. At first he tried to run, but immediately he fell and rolled. After that he went more carefully. The moon was just disappearing behind the mountains when he came to the bottom. He crawled into the heavy brush feeling with his fingers for water. There was no water in the bed of the stream, only damp earth. Pepé laid his gun down and scooped up a handful of mud and put it in his mouth, and then he spluttered and scraped the earth from his tongue with his finger, for the mud drew at his mouth like a poultice. He dug a hole in the stream bed with his fingers, dug a little basin to catch water; but before it was very deep his head fell forward on the damp ground and he slept.

The dawn came and the heat of the day fell on the earth, and still Pepé slept. Late in the afternoon his head jerked up. He looked slowly around. His eyes were slits of wariness. Twenty feet away in the heavy brush a big tawny mountain lion stood looking at him. Its long thick tail waved gracefully, its ears erect with interest, not laid back dangerously. The lion squatted down on its stomach and watched him.

Pepé looked at the hole he had dug in the earth. A half inch of muddy water had collected in the bottom. He tore the sleeve from his hurt arm, with his teeth ripped out a little square, soaked it in the water and put it in his mouth. Over and over he filled the cloth and sucked it.

Still the lion sat and watched him. The evening came down but there was no movement on the hills. No birds visited the dry bottom of the cut. Pepé looked occasionally at the lion. The eyes of the yellow beast drooped as though he were about to sleep. He yawned and his long thin red tongue curled out. Suddenly his head jerked around and his nostrils quivered. His big tail lashed. He stood up and slunk like a tawny shadow into the thick brush.

A moment later Pepé heard the sound, the faint far crash of horses' hooves on gravel. And he heard something else, a high whining yelp of a dog.

Pepé took his rifle in his left hand and he glided into the brush almost as quietly as the lion had. In the darkening evening he crouched up the hill toward the next ridge. Only when the dark came did he stand up. His energy was short. Once it was dark he fell over the rocks and slipped to his knees on the steep slope, but he moved on and on up the hill, climbing and scrabbling over the broken hillside.

When he was far up toward the top, he lay down and slept for a little while. The withered moon, shining on his face, awakened him. He stood up and moved up the hill. Fifty yards away he stopped and turned back, for he had forgotten his rifle. He walked heavily down and poked about in the brush, but he could not find his gun. At last he lay down to rest. The pocket of pain in his armpit had grown more sharp. His arm seemed to swell out and fall with every heartbeat. There was no position lying down where the heavy arm did not press against his armpit.

With the effort of a hurt beast, Pepé got up and moved again toward the top of the ridge. He held his swollen arm away from his body with his left hand. Up the steep hill he dragged himself, a few steps and a rest, and a few more steps. At last he was nearing the top. The moon showed the uneven sharp back of it against the sky.

Pepé's brain spun in a big spiral up and away from him. He slumped to the ground and lay still. The rock ridge top was only a hundred feet above him.

The moon moved over the sky. Pepé half turned on his back. His tongue tried to make words, but only a thick hissing came from between his lips.

When the dawn came, Pepé pulled himself up. His eyes were sane again. He drew his great puffed arm in front of him and looked at the angry wound. The black line ran up from his wrist to his armpit. Automatically he reached in his pocket for the big black knife, but it was not there. His eyes searched the ground. He picked up a sharp blade of stone and scraped at the wound, sawed at the proud flesh and then squeezed the green juice out in big drops. Instantly he threw back his head and whined like a dog. His whole right side shuddered at the pain, but the pain cleared his head.

In the gray light he struggled up the last slope to the ridge and crawled over and lay down behind a line of rocks. Below him lay a deep canyon exactly like the last, waterless and desolate. There was no flat, no oak trees, not even heavy brush in the bottom of it. And on the other side a sharp ridge stood up, thinly brushed with starving sage, littered with broken granite. Strewn over the hill there were giant outcroppings, and on the top the granite teeth stood out against the sky.

The new day was light now. The flame of sun came over the ridge and fell on Pepé where he lay on the ground. His coarse black hair was littered with twigs and bits of spider web. His eyes had retreated back in to his head. Between his lips the tip of his black tongue showed.

He sat up and dragged his great arm into his lap and nursed it, rocking his body and moaning in his throat. He threw back his head and looked up into the pale sky.

A big black bird circled nearly out of sight, and far to the left another was sailing near.

He lifted his head to listen, for a familiar sound had come to him from the valley he had climbed out of; it was the crying yelp of hounds, excited and feverish, on a trail.

Pepé bowed his head quickly. He tried to speak rapid words but only a thick hiss came from his lips. He drew a shaky cross on his breast with his left hand. It was a long struggle to get to his feet. He crawled slowly and mechanically to the top of a big rock on the ridge peak. Once there, he arose slowly, swaying to his feet, and stood erect. Far below he could see the dark brush where he had slept. He braced his feet and stood there, black against the morning sky.

There came a ripping sound at his feet. A piece of stone flew up and a bullet droned off into the next gorge. The hollow crash echoed up from below. Pepé looked down for a moment and then pulled himself straight again.

His body jarred back. His left hand fluttered helplessly toward his breast. The second crash sounded from below. Pepé swung forward and toppled from the rock. His body struck and rolled over and over, starting a little avalanche. And when at last he stopped against a bush, the avalanche slid slowly down and covered up his head.

FOR DISCUSSION:

1. Is the theme of "Flight" maturation or regression; that is, does the action of the story trace Pepé's evolution from boyhood to manhood, or his retrogression from a member of the human race through brute animality to an inanimate part of the natural landscape?

2. What is the significance of the loss of the hat, knife, and coat on Pepé's flight to elude his pursuers?

3. We are not specifically told whether Pepé has committed murder or not. Why is Steinbeck purposefully vague about Pepé's crime?

4. Is this a story of crime and punishment? If so, of what is Pepé guilty?

5. How do you interpret Pepé's religious gesture of making the sign of the cross immediately before exposing himself to the posse?

6. Some critics think Pepé is mentally retarded. Is there anything in the story to substantiate this?

7. What is the function of Mama Torres, Rosy, and Emilio? Are they spokesmen for the author?

The Open Boat

A TALE INTENDED TO BE AFTER THE FACT:
BEING THE EXPERIENCE OF FOUR MEN
FROM THE SUNK STEAMER *Commodore*

STEPHEN CRANE

I

None of them knew the colour of the sky. Their eyes glanced level, and were fastened upon the waves that swept toward them. These waves were of the hue of slate, save for the tops, which were of foaming white, and all of the men knew the colours of the sea. The horizon narrowed and widened, and dipped and rose, and at all times its edge was jagged with waves that seemed thrust up in points like rocks.

Many a man ought to have a bathtub larger than the boat which here rode upon the sea. These waves were most wrongfully and barbarously abrupt and tall, and each froth-top was a problem in small-boat navigation.

The cook squatted in the bottom, and looked with both eyes at the six inches of gunwale which separated him from the ocean. His sleeves were rolled over his fat forearms, and the two flaps of his unbuttoned vest dangled as he bent to bail out the boat. Often he said, "Gawd! that was a narrow clip." As he remarked it he invariably gazed eastward over the broken sea.

The oiler, steering with one of the two oars in the boat, sometimes raised himself suddenly to keep clear of water that swirled in over the stern. It was a thin little oar, and it seemed often ready to snap.

The correspondent, pulling at the other oar, watched the waves and wondered why he was there.

The injured captain, lying in the bow, was at this time buried in that profound dejection and indifference which comes, temporarily at least, to even the bravest and most enduring when, willy-nilly, the firm fails, the army loses, the ship goes down. The mind of the master of a vessel is rooted deep in the timbers of her, though he command for a day or a decade; and this captain had on him the stern impression of a scene in the greys of dawn of seven turned faces, and later a stump of a topmast with a white ball on it, that slashed to and fro at the waves, went low and lower, and down. Thereafter there was something strange in his voice. Although steady, it was deep with mourning, and of a quality beyond oration or tears.

"Keep 'er a little more south, Billie," said he.

"A little more south, sir," said the oiler in the stern.

A seat in his boat was not unlike a seat upon a bucking broncho, and by the same token a broncho is not much smaller. The craft pranced and reared and plunged like an animal. As each wave came, and she rose for it, she seemed like a horse making at a fence outrageously high. The manner of her scramble over these walls of water is a mystic thing, and, moreover, at the top of them were ordinarily these problems in white water, the foam racing down from the summit of each wave requiring a new leap, and a leap from the air. Then, after scornfully bumping a crest, she would slide and race and splash down a long incline, and arrive bobbing and nodding in front of the next menace.

A singular disadvantage of the sea lies in the fact that after successfully surmounting one wave you discover that there is another behind it just as important and just as nervously anxious to do something effective in the way of swamping boats. In a ten-foot dinghy one can get an idea of the resources of the sea in the line of waves that is not probable to the average experience which is never at sea in a dinghy. As each slaty wall of water approached, it shut all else from the view of the men in the boat, and it was not difficult to imagine that this particular wave was the final outburst of the ocean, the last effort of the grim water. There was a terrible grace in the move of the waves, and they came in silence, save for the snarling of the crests.

In the wan light the faces of the men must have been grey. Their eyes must have glinted in strange ways as they gazed steadily astern. Viewed from a balcony, the whole thing would doubtless have been weirdly picturesque. But the men in the boat had no time to see it, and if they had had leisure, there were other things to occupy their minds. The sun swung steadily up the sky, and they knew it was broad day because the colour of the sea changed from slate to emerald green streaked with amber lights, and the foam was like tumbling snow. The process of the breaking day was unknown to them. They were aware only of this effect upon the colour of the waves that rolled toward them.

In disjointed sentences the cook and the correspondent argued as to the difference between a life-saving station and a house of refuge. The cook had said: "There's a house of refuge just north of the Mosquito Inlet Light, and as soon as they see us they'll come off in their boat and pick us up."

"As soon as who see us?" said the correspondent.

"The crew," said the cook.

"Houses of refuge don't have crews," said the correspondent. "As I understand them, they are only places where clothes and grub are stored for the benefit of shipwrecked people. They don't carry crews."

"Oh, yes, they do," said the cook.

"No, they don't," said the correspondent.

"Well, we're not there yet, anyhow," said the oiler, in the stern.

"Well," said the cook, "perhaps it's not a house of refuge that I'm thinking of as being near Mosquito Inlet Light; perhaps it's a life-saving station."

"We're not there yet," said the oiler in the stern.

II

As the boat bounced from the top of each wave the wind tore through the hair of the hatless men, and as the craft plopped her stern down again the spray slashed past them. The crest of each of these waves was a hill, from the top of which the men surveyed for a moment a broad tumultuous expanse, shining and wind-riven. It was probably splendid, it was probably glorious, this play of the free sea, wild with lights of emerald and white and amber.

"Bully good thing it's an on-shore wind," said the cook. "If not, where would we be? Wouldn't have a show."

"That's right," said the correspondent.

The busy oiler nodded his assent.

Then the captain, in the bow, chuckled in a way that expressed humour, contempt, tragedy, all in one. "Do you think we've got much of a show now, boys?" said he.

Whereupon the three were silent, save for a trifle of hemming and hawing. To express any particular optimism at this time they felt to be childish and stupid, but they all doubtless possessed this sense of the situation in their minds. A young man thinks doggedly at such times. On the other hand, the ethics of their condition was decidedly against any open suggestion of hopelessness. So they were silent.

"Oh, well," said the captain, soothing his children, "we'll get ashore all right."

But there was that in his tone which made them think; so the oiler quoth, "Yes! if this wind holds."

The cook was bailing. "Yes! if we don't catch hell in the surf."

Canton-flannel gulls flew near and far. Sometimes they sat down on the sea, near patches of brown seaweed that rolled over the waves with a movement like carpets on a line in a gale. The birds sat comfortably in groups, and they were envied by some in the dinghy, for the wrath of the sea was no more to them than it was to a covey of prairie chickens a thousand miles inland. Often they came very close and stared at the men with black bead-like eyes. At these times they were uncanny and sinister in their unblinking scrutiny, and the men hooted angrily at them, telling them to be gone. One came, and evidently decided to alight on the top of the captain's head. The bird flew parallel to the boat and did not circle, but made short sidelong jumps in the air in chicken-fashion. His black eyes were wistfully fixed upon the captain's head. "Ugly brute," said the oiler to the bird. "You look as if you were made with a jack-knife." The cook and the correspondent swore darkly at the creature. The captain naturally wished to knock it away with the end of the heavy painter, but he did not dare do it, because anything resembling an emphatic gesture would have capsized this freighted boat; and so, with his open hand, the captain gently and carefully waved the gull away. After it had been discouraged from the pursuit the captain breathed easier on account of his hair, and others breathed easier because the bird struck their minds at this time as being somehow gruesome and ominous.

In the meantime the oiler and the correspondent rowed. And also they rowed. They sat together in the same seat, and each rowed an oar. Then the oiler took both oars; then the correspondent took both oars; then the oiler; then the correspondent. They rowed and they rowed. The very ticklish part of the business was when the time came for the reclining one in the stern to take his turn at the oars. By the very last star of truth, it is easier to steal eggs from under a hen than it was to change seats in the dinghy. First the man in the stern slid his hand along the thwart and moved with care, as if he were of Sèvres. Then the man in the rowing-seat slid his hand along the other thwart. It was all done with the most extraordinary care. As the two sidled past each other, the whole party kept watchful eyes on the coming wave, and the captain cried: "Look out, now! Steady, there!"

The brown mats of seaweed that appeared from time to time were like islands, bits of earth. They were travelling, apparently, neither one way nor the other. They were, to all intents, stationary. They informed the men in the boat that it was making progress slowly toward the land.

The captain, rearing cautiously in the bow after the dinghy soared on a great swell, said that he had seen the lighthouse at Mosquito Inlet. Presently the cook remarked that he had seen it. The correspondent was at the oars then, and for some reason he too wished to look at the lighthouse; but his back was toward the far shore, and the waves were important, and for some time he could not seize an opportunity to turn his head. But at last there came a wave more gentle than the others, and when at the crest of it he swiftly scoured the western horizon.

"See it?" said the captain.

"No," said the correspondent, slowly; "I didn't see anything."

"Look again," said the captain. He pointed. "It's exactly in that direction."

At the top of another wave the correspondent did as he was bid, and this time his eyes chanced on a small, still thing on the edge of the swaying horizon. It was precisely like the point of a pin. It took an anxious eye to find a lighthouse so tiny.

"Think we'll make it, Captain?"

"If this wind holds and the boat don't swamp, we can't do much else," said the captain.

The little boat, lifted by each towering sea and splashed viciously by the crests, made progress that in the absence of seaweed was not apparent to those in her. She seemed just a wee thing wallowing, miraculously top up, at the mercy of five oceans. Occasionally a great spread of water, like white flames, swarmed into her.

"Bail her, cook," said the captain, serenely.

"All right, Captain," said the cheerful cook.

III

It would be difficult to describe the subtle brotherhood of men that was here established on the seas. No one said that it was so. No one mentioned it. But it dwelt in the boat, and each man felt it warm him. They were a captain, an oiler, a cook, and a correspondent, and they were friends—friends in a more curiously iron-bound degree than may be common. The hurt captain, lying against the water-jar in the bow, spoke always in a low voice and calmly; but he could never command a more ready and swiftly obedient crew than the motley three of the dinghy. It was more than a mere recognition of what was best for the common safety. There was surely in it a quality that was personal and heart-felt. And after this devotion to the commander of the boat, there was this comradeship, that the correspondent, for instance, who had been taught to be cynical of men, knew even at the time was the best experience of his life. But no one said that it was so. No one mentioned it.

"I wish we had a sail," remarked the captain. "We might try my overcoat on the end of an oar, and give you two boys a chance to rest." So the cook and the correspondent held the mast and spread wide the overcoat; the oiler steered; and the little boat made good way with her new rig. Sometimes the oiler had to scull sharply to keep a sea from breaking into the boat, but otherwise sailing was a success.

Meanwhile the lighthouse had been growing slowly larger. It had now almost assumed colour, and appeared like a little grey shadow on the sky. The man at the oars could not be prevented from turning his head rather often to try for a glimpse of this little grey shadow.

At last, from the top of each wave, the men in the tossing boat could see land. Even as the lighthouse was an upright shadow on the sky, this land seemed but a long black shadow on the sea. It certainly was thinner than paper. "We must be about opposite New Smyrna," said the cook, who had coasted this shore often in schooners. "Captain, by the way, I believe they abandoned that life-saving station there about a year ago."

"Did they?" said the captain.

The wind slowly died away. The cook and the correspondent were not now obliged to slave in order to hold high the oar. But the waves continued their old impetuous swooping at the dinghy, and the little craft, no longer under way, struggled woundily over them. The oiler or the correspondent took the oars again.

Shipwrecks are apropos of nothing. If men could only train for them and have them occur when the men had reached pink condition, there would be less drowning at sea. Of the four in the dinghy none had slept any time worth mentioning for two days and two nights previous to embarking in the dinghy, and in the excitement of clambering about the deck of a foundering ship they had also forgotten to eat heartily.

For these reasons, and for others, neither the oiler nor the correspondent was fond of rowing at this time. The correspondent wondered ingenuously how in the name of all that was sane could there be people who thought it amusing to row a boat. It was not an amusement; it was a diabolical punishment, and even a genius of mental aberrations could never conclude that it was anything but a horror to the muscles and a crime against the back. He mentioned to the boat in general how the amusement of rowing struck him, and the weary-faced oiler smiled in full sympathy. Previously to the foundering, by the way, the oiler had worked a double watch in the engine-room of the ship.

"Take her easy now, boys," said the captain. "Don't spend yourselves. If we have to run a surf you'll need all your strength, because we'll sure have to swim for it. Take your time."

Slowly the land arose from the sea. From a black line it became a line of black and a line of white—trees and sand. Finally the captain said that he could make out a house on the shore. "That's the house of refuge, sure," said the cook. "They'll see us before long, and come out after us."

The distant lighthouse reared high. "The keeper ought to be able to make us out now, if he's looking through a glass," said the captain. "He'll notify the life-saving people."

"None of those other boats could have got ashore to give word of this wreck," said the oiler, in a low voice, "else the life-boat would be out hunting us."

Slowly and beautifully the land loomed out of the sea. The wind came again. It had veered from the north-east to the south-east. Finally a new sound struck the ears of the men in the boat. It was the low thunder of the surf on the shore. "We'll never be able to make the lighthouse now," said the captain. "Swing her head a little more north, Billie."

"A little more north, sir," said the oiler.

Whereupon the little boat turned her nose once more down the wind, and all but the oarsman watched the shore grow. Under the influence of this expansion doubt and direful apprehension were leaving the minds of the men. The management of the boat was still most absorbing, but it could not prevent a quiet cheerfulness. In an hour, perhaps, they would be ashore.

Their backbones had become thoroughly used to balancing in the boat, and they now rode this wild colt of a dinghy like circus men. The correspondent thought that he had been drenched to the skin, but happening to feel in the top pocket of his coat, he found therein eight cigars. Four of them were soaked with sea-water; four were perfectly scatheless. After a search, somebody produced three dry matches; and thereupon the four waifs rode impudently in their little boat and, with an assurance of an impending rescue shining in their eyes, puffed at the big cigars, and judged well and ill of all men. Everybody took a drink of water.

IV

"Cook," remarked the captain, "there don't seem to be any signs of life about your house of refuge."

"No," replied the cook. "Funny they don't see us!"

A broad stretch of lowly coast lay before the eyes of the men. It was of low dunes topped with dark vegetation. The roar of the surf was plain, and sometimes they could see the white lip of a wave as it spun up the beach. A tiny house was blocked out black upon the sky. Southward, the slim lighthouse lifted its little grey length.

Tide, wind, and waves were swinging the dinghy northward. "Funny they don't see us," said the men.

The surf's roar was here dulled, but its tone was nevertheless thunderous and mighty. As the boat swam over the great rollers the men sat listening to this roar. "We'll swamp sure," said everybody.

It is fair to say here that there was not a life-saving station within twenty miles in either direction; but the men did not know this fact, and in consequence they made dark and opprobrious remarks concerning the eyesight of the nation's life-savers. Four scowling men sat in the dinghy and surpassed records in the invention of epithets.

"Funny they don't see us."

The light-heartedness of a former time had completely faded. To their sharpened minds it was easy to conjure pictures of all kinds of incompetency and blindness and, indeed, cowardice. There was the shore of the populous land, and it was bitter and bitter to them that from it came no sign.

"Well," said the captain, ultimately, "I suppose we'll have to make a try for ourselves. If we stay out here too long, we'll none of us have strength left to swim after the boat swamps."

And so the oiler, who was at the oars, turned the boat straight for the shore. There was a sudden tightening of muscles. There was some thinking.

"If we don't all get ashore," said the captain—"if we don't all get ashore, I suppose you fellows know where to send news of my finish?"

They then briefly exchanged some addresses and admonitions. As for the reflections of the men, there was a great deal of rage in them. Perchance they might be formulated thus: "If I am going to be drowned—if I am going to be drowned—if I am going to be drowned, why, in the name of the seven mad gods who rule the sea, was I allowed to come thus far and contemplate sand and trees? Was I brought here merely to have my nose dragged away as I was about to nibble the sacred cheese of life? It is preposterous. If this old ninny-woman, Fate, cannot do better than this, she should be deprived of the management of men's fortunes. She is an old hen who knows not her intention. If she has decided to drown me, why did she not do it in the beginning and save me all this trouble? The whole affair is absurd.—But no; she cannot mean to drown me. She dare not drown me. She cannot drown me. Not after all this work." Afterward the man might have had an impulse to shake his fist at the clouds. "Just you drown me, now, and then hear what I call you!"

The billows that came at this time were more formidable. They seemed always just about to break and roll over the little boat in a turmoil of foam. There was a preparatory and long growl in the speech of them. No mind unused to the sea would have concluded that the dinghy could ascend these sheer heights in time. The shore was still afar. The oiler was a wily surfman. "Boys," he said swiftly, "she won't live three minutes more, and we're too far out to swim. Shall I take her to sea again, Captain?"

"Yes; go ahead!" said the captain.

This oiler, by a series of quick miracles and fast and steady oarsmanship, turned the boat in the middle of the surf and took her safely to sea again.

There was a considerable silence as the boat bumped over the furrowed sea to deeper water. Then somebody in gloom spoke: "Well, anyhow, they must have seen us from the shore by now."

The gulls went in slanting flight up the wind toward the grey, desolate east. A squall, marked by dingy clouds and clouds brick-red like smoke from a burning building, appeared from the south-east.

"What do you think of those life-saving people? Ain't they peaches?"

"Funny they haven't seen us."

"Maybe they think we're out here for sport! Maybe they think we're fishin'. Maybe they think we're damned fools."

It was a long afternoon. A changed tide tried to force them southward, but wind and wave said northward. Far ahead, where coast-line, sea, and sky formed their mighty angle, there were little dots which seemed to indicate a city on the shore.

"St. Augustine?"

The captain shook his head. "Too near Mosquito Inlet."

And the oiler rowed, and then the correspondent rowed; then the oiler rowed. It was a weary business. The human back can become the seat of more aches and pains than are registered in books for the composite anatomy of a regiment. It is a limited area, but it can become the theatre of innumerable muscular conflicts, tangles, wrenches, knots, and other comforts.

"Did you ever like to row, Billie?" asked the correspondent.

"No," said the oiler; "hang it!"

When one exchanged the rowing-seat for a place in the bottom of the boat, he suffered a bodily depression that caused him to be careless of everything save an obligation to wiggle one finger. There was cold sea-water swashing to and fro in the boat, and he lay in it. His head, pillowed on a thwart, was within an inch of the swirl of a wave-crest, and sometimes a particularly obstreperous sea came inboard and drenched him once more. But these matters did not annoy him. It is almost certain that if the boat had capsized he would have tumbled comfortably out upon the ocean as if he felt sure that it was a great soft mattress.

"Look! There's a man on the shore!"

"Where?"

"There! See 'im? See 'im?"

"Yes, sure! He's walking along."

"Now he's stopped. Look! He's facing us!"

"He's waving at us!"

"So he is! By thunder!"

"Ah, now we're all right! Now we're all right! There'll be a boat out here for us in half an hour."

"He's going on. He's running. He's going up to that house there."

The remote beach seemed lower than the sea, and it required a searching glance to discern the little black figure. The captain saw a floating stick, and they rowed to it. A bath towel was by some weird chance in the boat, and, tying this on the stick, the captain waved it. The oarsman did not dare turn his head, so he was obliged to ask questions.

"What's he doing now?"

"He's standing still again. He's looking, I think.—There he goes again—toward the house.—Now he's stopped again."

"Is he waving at us?"

"No, not now; he was, though."

"Look! There comes another man!"

"He's running."

"Look at him go, would you!"

"Why, he's on a bicycle. Now he's met the other man. They're both waving at us. Look!"

"There comes something up the beach."

"What the devil is that thing?"

"Why, it looks like a boat."

"Why, certainly, it's a boat."

"No; it's on wheels."

"Yes, so it is. Well, that must be the life-boat. They drag them along shore on a wagon."

"That's the life-boat, sure."

"No, by God, it's—it's an omnibus."

"I tell you it's a life-boat."

"It is not! It's an omnibus. I can see it plain. See? One of these big hotel omnibuses."

"By thunder, you're right. It's an omnibus, sure as fate. What do you suppose they are doing with an omnibus? Maybe they are going around collecting the life-crew, hey?"

"That's it, likely. Look! There's a fellow waving a little black flag. He's standing on the steps of the omnibus. There come those other two fellows. Now they're all talking together. Look at the fellow with the flag. Maybe he ain't waving it!"

"That ain't a flag, is it? That's his coat. Why, certainly, that's his coat."

"So it is; it's his coat. He's taken it off and is waving it around his head. But would you look at him swing it!"

"Oh, say, there isn't any life-saving station there. That's just a winter-resort hotel omnibus that has brought over some of the boarders to see us drown."

"What's that idiot with the coat mean? What's he signalling, anyhow?"

"It looks as if he were trying to tell us to go north. There must be a life-saving station up there."

"No; he thinks we're fishing. Just giving us a merry hand. See? Ah, there, Willie!"

"Well, I wish I could make something out of those signals. What do you suppose he means?"

"He don't mean anything; he's just playing."

"Well, if he'd just signal us to try the surf again, or to go to sea and wait, or go north, or go south, or go to hell, there would be some reason in it. But look at him! He just stands there and keeps his coat revolving like a wheel. The ass!"

"There come more people."

"Now there's quite a mob. Look! Isn't that a boat?"

"Where? Oh, I see where you mean. No, that's no boat."

"That fellow is still waving his coat."

"He must think we like to see him do that. Why don't he quit it? It don't mean anything."

"I don't know. I think he is trying to make us go north. It must be that there's a life-saving station there somewhere."

"Say, he ain't tired yet. Look at 'im wave!"

"Wonder how long he can keep that up. He's been revolving his coat ever since he caught sight of us. He's an idiot. Why aren't they getting men to bring a boat out? A fishing-boat—one of those big yawls—could come out here all right. Why don't he do something?"

"Oh, it's all right now."

"They'll have a boat out here for us in less than no time, now that they've seen us."

A faint yellow tone came into the sky over the low land. The shadows on the sea slowly deepened. The wind bore coldness with it, and the men began to shiver.

"Holy smoke!" said one, allowing his voice to express his impious mood, "if we keep on monkeying out here! If we've got to flounder out here all night!"

"Oh, we'll never have to stay here all night! Don't you worry. They've seen us now, and it won't be long before they'll come chasing out after us."

The shore grew dusky. The man waving a coat blended gradually into this gloom, and it swallowed in the same manner the omnibus and the group of people. The spray, when it dashed uproariously over the side, made the voyagers shrink and swear like men who were being branded.

"I'd like to catch the chump who waved the coat. I feel like socking him one, just for luck."

"Why? What did he do?"

"Oh, nothing, but then he seemed so damned cheerful."

In the meantime the oiler rowed, and then the correspondent rowed, and then the oiler rowed. Grey-faced and bowed forward, they mechanically, turn by turn, plied the leaden oars. The form of the lighthouse had vanished from the southern horizon, but finally a pale star appeared, just lifting from the sea. The streaked saffron in the west passed before the all-merging darkness, and the sea to the east was black. The land had vanished, and was expressed only by the low and drear thunder of the surf.

"If I am going to be drowned—if I am going to be drowned—if I am going to be drowned, why, in the name of the seven mad gods who rule the sea, was I allowed to come thus far and contemplate sand and trees? Was I brought here merely to have my nose dragged away as I was about to nibble the sacred cheese of life?"

The patient captain, drooped over the water-jar, was sometimes obliged to speak to the oarsman.

"Keep her head up! Keep her head up!"

"Keep her head up, sir." The voices were weary and low.

This was surely a quiet evening. All save the oarsman lay heavily and listlessly in the boat's bottom. As for him, his eyes were just capable of noting the tall black waves that swept forward in a most sinister silence, save for an occasional subdued growl of a crest.

The cook's head was on a thwart, and he looked without interest at the water under his nose. He was deep in other scenes. Finally he spoke. "Billie," he murmured, dreamfully, "what kind of pie do you like best?"

V

"Pie!" said the oiler and the correspondent, agitatedly. "Don't talk about those things, blast you!"

"Well," said the cook, "I was just thinking about ham sandwiches and—"

A night on the sea in an open boat is a long night. As darkness settled finally, the shine of the light, lifting from the sea in the south, changed to full gold. On the northern horizon a new light appeared, a small bluish gleam on the edge of the waters. These two lights were the furniture of the world. Otherwise there was nothing but waves.

Two men huddled in the stern, and distances were so magnificent in the dinghy that the rower was enabled to keep his feet partly warm by thrusting them under his companions. Their legs indeed extended far under the rowing-seat until they touched the feet of the captain forward. Sometimes, despite the efforts of the tired oarsman, a wave came piling into the boat, an icy wave of the night, and the chilling water soaked them anew. They would twist their bodies for a moment and groan, and sleep the dead sleep once more, while the water in the boat gurgled about them as the craft rocked.

The plan of the oiler and the correspondent was for one to row until he lost the ability, and then arouse the other from his sea-water couch in the bottom of the boat.

The oiler plied the oars until his head drooped forward and the overpowering sleep blinded him; and he rowed yet afterward. Then he touched a man in the bottom of the boat, and called his name. "Will you spell me for a little while?" he said, meekly.

"Sure, Billie," said the correspondent, awaking and dragging himself to a sitting position. They exchanged places carefully, and the oiler, cuddling down in the sea-water at the cook's side, seemed to go to sleep instantly.

The particular violence of the sea had ceased. The waves came without snarling. The obligation of the man at the oars was to keep the boat headed so that the tilt of the rollers would not capsize her, and to preserve her from filling when the crests rushed past. The black waves were silent and hard to be seen in the darkness. Often one was almost upon the boat before the oarsman was aware.

In a low voice the correspondent addressed the captain. He was not sure that the captain was awake, although this iron man seemed to be always awake. "Captain, shall I keep her making for that light north, sir?"

The same steady voice answered him. "Yes. Keep it about two points off the port bow."

The cook had tied a life-belt around himself in order to get even the warmth which this clumsy cork contrivance could donate, and he seemed almost stove-like when a rower, whose teeth invariably chattered wildly as soon as he ceased his labour, dropped down to sleep.

The correspondent, as he rowed, looked down at the two men sleeping underfoot. The cook's arm was around the oiler's shoulders, and, with their fragmentary clothing and haggard faces, they were the babes of the sea—a grotesque rendering of the old babes in the wood.

Later he must have grown stupid at his work, for suddenly there was a growling of water, and a crest came with a roar and a swash into the boat, and it was a wonder that it did not set the cook afloat in his life-belt. The cook continued to sleep, but the oiler sat up, blinking his eyes and shaking with the new cold.

"Oh, I'm awful sorry, Billie," said the correspondent, contritely.

"That's all right, old boy," said the oiler, and lay down again and was asleep.

Presently it seemed that even the captain dozed, and the correspondent thought that he was the one man afloat on all the oceans. The wind had a voice as it came over the waves, and it was sadder than the end.

There was a long, loud swishing astern of the boat, and a gleaming trail of phosphorescence, like blue flame, was furrowed on the black waters. It might have been made by a monstrous knife.

Then there came a stillness, while the correspondent breathed with open mouth and looked at the sea.

Suddenly there was another swish and another long flash of bluish light, and this time it was alongside the boat, and might almost been reached with an oar. The correspondent saw an enormous fin speed like a shadow through the water, hurling the crystalline spray and leaving the long glowing trail.

The correspondent looked over his shoulder at the captain. His face was hidden, and he seemed to be asleep. He looked at the babes of the sea. They certainly were asleep. So, being bereft of sympathy, he leaned a little way to one side and swore softly into the sea.

But the thing did not then leave the vicinity of the boat. Ahead or astern, on one side or the other, at intervals long or short, fled the long sparkling streak, and there was to be heard the whirroo of the dark fin. The speed and power of the thing was greatly to be admired. It cut the water like a gigantic and keen projectile.

The presence of this biding thing did not affect the man with the same horror that it would if he had been a picnicker. He simply looked at the sea dully and swore in an undertone.

Nevertheless, it is true that he did not wish to be alone with the thing. He wished one of his companions to awake by chance and keep him company with it. But the captain hung motionless over the water-jar, and the oiler and the cook in the bottom of the boat were plunged in slumber.

VI

"If I am going to be drowned—if I am going to be drowned—if I am going to be drowned, why, in the name of the seven mad gods who rule the sea, was I allowed to come thus far and contemplate sand and trees?"

During this dismal night, it may be remarked that a man would conclude that it was really the intention of the seven mad gods to drown him, despite the abominable injustice of it. For it was certainly an abominable injustice to drown a man who had worked so hard, so hard. The man felt it would be a crime most unnatural. Other people had drowned at sea since galleys swarmed with painted sails, but still—

When it occurs to a man that nature does not regard him as important, and that she feels she would not maim the universe by disposing of him, he at first wishes to throw bricks at the temple, and he hates deeply the fact that there are no bricks and no temples. Any visible expression of nature would surely be pelleted with his jeers.

Then, if there be no tangible thing to hoot, he feels, perhaps, the desire to confront a personification and indulge in pleas, bowed to one knee, and with hands supplicant, saying, "Yes, but I love myself."

A high cold star on a winter's night is the word he feels that she says to him. Thereafter he knows the pathos of his situation.

The men in the dinghy had not discussed these matters, but each had, no doubt, reflected upon them in silence and according to his mind. There was seldom any expression upon their faces save the general one of complete weariness. Speech was devoted to the business of the boat.

To chime the notes of his emotion, a verse mysteriously entered the correspondent's head. He had even forgotten that he had forgotten this verse, but it suddenly was in his mind.

A soldier of the Legion lay dying in Algiers;
There was lack of woman's nursing, there was
    dearth of woman's tears;
But a comrade stood beside him, and he took
    that comrade's hand,
And he said, "I never more shall see my own,
    my native land."

In his childhood the correspondent had been made acquainted with the fact that a soldier of the Legion lay dying in Algiers, but he had never regarded the fact as important. Myriads of his school-fellows had informed him of the soldier's plight, but the dinning had naturally ended by making him perfectly indifferent. He had never considered it his affair that a soldier of the Legion lay dying in Algiers, nor had it appeared to him as a matter for sorrow. It was less to him than the breaking of a pencil's point.

Now, however, it quaintly came to him as a human, living thing. It was no longer merely a picture of a few throes in the breast of a poet, meanwhile drinking tea and warming his feet at the grate; it was an actuality—stern, mournful, and fine.

The correspondent plainly saw the soldier. He lay on the sand with his feet out straight and still. While his pale left hand was upon his chest in an attempt to thwart the going of his life, the blood came between his fingers. In the far Algerian distance, a city of low square forms was set against a sky that was faint with the last sunset hues. The correspondent, plying the oars and dreaming of the slow and slower movements of the lips of the soldier, was moved by a profound and perfectly impersonal comprehension. He was sorry for the soldier of the Legion who lay dying in Algiers.

The thing which had followed the boat and waited had evidently grown bored at the delay. There was no longer to be heard the slash of the cutwater, and there was no longer the flame of the long trail. The light in the north still glimmered, but it was apparently no nearer to the boat. Sometimes the boom of the surf rang in the correspondent's ears, and he turned the craft seaward then and rowed harder. Southward, some one had evidently built a watch-fire on the beach. It was too low and too far to be seen, but it made a shimmering, roseate reflection upon the bluff in back of it, and this could be discerned from the boat. The wind came stronger, and sometimes a wave suddenly raged out like a mountain cat, and there was to be seen the sheen and sparkle of a broken crest.

The captain, in the bow, moved on his water-jar and sat erect. "Pretty long night," he observed to the correspondent. He looked at the shore. "Those life-saving people take their time."

"Did you see that shark playing around?"

"Yes, I saw him. He was a big fellow, all right."

"Wish I had known you were awake."

Later the correspondent spoke into the bottom of the boat. "Billie!" There was a slow and gradual disentanglement. "Billie, will you spell me?"

"Sure," said the oiler.

As soon as the correspondent touched the cold, comfortable sea-water in the bottom of the boat and had huddled close to the cook's life-belt he was deep in sleep, despite the fact that his teeth played all the popular airs. This sleep was so good to him that it was but a moment before he heard a voice call his name in a tone that demonstrated the last stages of exhaustion. "Will you spell me?"

"Sure, Billie."

The light in the north had mysteriously vanished, but the correspondent took his course from the wide-awake captain.

Later in the night they took the boat farther out to sea, and the captain directed the cook to take one oar at the stern and keep the boat facing the seas. He was to call out if he should hear the thunder of the surf. This plan enabled the oiler and the correspondent to get respite together. "We'll give those boys a chance to get into shape again," said the captain. They curled down and, after a few preliminary chatterings and trembles, slept once more the dead sleep. Neither knew they had bequeathed to the cook the company of another shark, or perhaps the same shark.

As the boat caroused on the waves, spray occasionally bumped over the side and gave them a fresh soaking, but this had no power to break their repose. The ominous slash of the wind and the water affected them as it would have affected mummies.

"Boys," said the cook, with the notes of every reluctance in his voice, "she's drifted in pretty close. I guess one of you had better take her to sea again." The correspondent, aroused, heard the crash of the toppled crests.

As he was rowing, the captain gave him some whisky-and-water, and this steadied the chills out of him. "If I ever get ashore and anybody shows me even a photograph of an oar—"

At last there was a short conversation.

"Billie!—Billie, will you spell me?"

"Sure," said the oiler.

VII

When the correspondent again opened his eyes, the sea and the sky were each of the grey hue of the dawning. Later, carmine and gold was painted upon the waters. The morning appeared finally, in its splendour, with a sky of pure blue, and the sunlight flamed on the tips of the waves.

On the distant dunes were set many little black cottages, and a tall white windmill reared above them. No man, nor dog, nor bicycle appeared on the beach. The cottages might have formed a deserted village.

The voyagers scanned the shore. A conference was held in the boat. "Well," said the captain, "if no help is coming, we might better try a run through the surf right away. If we stay out here much longer we will be too weak to do anything for ourselves at all." The others silently acquiesced in this reasoning. The boat was headed for the beach. The correspondent wondered if none ever ascended the tall wind-tower, and if then they never looked seaward. This tower was a giant, standing with its back to the plight of the ants. It represented in a degree, to the correspondent, the serenity of nature amid the struggles of the individual —nature in the wind, and nature in the vision of men. She did not seem cruel to him then, nor beneficent, nor treacherous, nor wise. But she was indifferent, flatly indifferent. It is, perhaps, plausible that a man in this situation, impressed with the unconcern of the universe, should see the innumerable flaws of his life, and have them taste wickedly in his mind, and wish for another chance. A distinction between right and wrong seems absurdly clear to him, then, in this new ignorance of the grave-edge, and he understands that if he were given another opportunity he would mend his conduct and his words, and be better and brighter during an introduction or at a tea.

"Now, boys," said the captain, "she is going to swamp sure. All we can do is to work her in as far as possible, and then when she swamps, pile out and scramble for the beach. Keep cool now, and don't jump until she swamps sure."

The oiler took the oars. Over his shoulders he scanned the surf. "Captain," he said, "I think I'd better bring her about and keep her head-on to the seas and back her in."

"All right, Billie," said the captain. "Back her in." The oiler swung the boat then, and, seated in the stern, the cook and the correspondent were obliged to look over their shoulders to contemplate the lonely and indifferent shore.

The monstrous inshore rollers heaved the boat high until the men were again enabled to see the white sheets of water scudding up the slanted beach. "We won't get in very close," said the captain. Each time a man could wrest his attention from the rollers, he turned his glance toward the shore, and in the expression of the eyes during this contemplation there was a singular quality. The correspondent, observing the others, knew that they were not afraid, but the full meaning of their glances was shrouded.

As for himself, he was too tired to grapple fundamentally with the fact. He tried to coerce his mind into thinking of it, but the mind was dominated at this time by the muscles, and the muscles said they did not care. It merely occurred to him that if he should drown it would be a shame.

There were no hurried words, no pallor, no plain agitation. The men simply looked at the shore. "Now, remember to get well clear of the boat when you jump," said the captain.

Seaward the crest of a roller suddenly fell with a thunderous crash, and the long white comber came roaring down upon the boat.

"Steady now," said the captain. The men were silent. They turned their eyes from the shore to the comber and waited. The boat slid up the incline, leaped at the furious top, bounced over it, and swung down the long back of the wave. Some water had been shipped, and the cook bailed it out.

But the next crest crashed also. The tumbling, boiling flood of white water caught the boat and whirled it almost perpendicular. Water swarmed in from all sides. The correspondent had his hands on the gunwale at this time, and when the water entered at that place he swiftly withdrew his fingers, as if he objected to wetting them.

The little boat, drunken with this weight of water, reeled and snuggled deeper into the sea.

"Bail her out, cook! Bail her out!" said the captain.

"All right, Captain," said the cook.

"Now, boys, the next one will do for us sure," said the oiler. "Mind to jump clear of the boat."

The third wave moved forward, huge, furious, implacable. It fairly swallowed the dinghy, and almost simultaneously the men tumbled into the sea. A piece of life-belt had lain in the bottom of the boat, and as the correspondent went overboard he held this to his chest with his left hand.

The January water was icy, and he reflected immediately that it was colder than he had expected to find it off the coast of Florida. This appeared to his dazed mind as a fact important enough to be noted at the time. The coldness of the water was sad; it was tragic. This fact was somehow mixed and confused with his opinion of his own situation, so that it seemed almost a proper reason for tears. The water was cold.

When he came to the surface he was conscious of little but the noisy water. Afterward he saw his companions in the sea. The oiler was ahead in the race. He was swimming strongly and rapidly. Off to the correspondent's left, the cook's great white and corked back bulged out of the water; and in the rear the captain was hanging with his one good hand to the keel of the overturned dinghy.

There is a certain immovable quality to a shore, and the correspondent wondered at it amid the confusion of the sea.

It seemed also very attractive; but the correspondent knew that it was a long journey, and he paddled leisurely. The piece of life-preserver lay under him, and sometimes he whirled down the incline of a wave as if he were on a hand-sled.

But finally he arrived at a place in the sea where travel was beset with difficulty. He did not pause swimming to inquire what manner of current had caught him, but there his progress ceased. The shore was set before him like a bit of scenery on a stage, and he looked at it and understood with his eyes each detail of it.

As the cook passed, much farther to the left, the captain was calling to him, "Turn over on your back, cook! Turn over on your back and use the oar."

"All right, sir." The cook turned on his back, and, paddling with an oar, went ahead as if he were a canoe.

Presently the boat also passed to the left of the correspondent, with the captain clinging with one hand to the keel. He would have appeared like a man raising himself to look over a board fence if it were not for the extraordinary gymnastics of the boat. The correspondent marvelled that the captain could still hold to it.

They passed on nearer to shore—the oiler, the cook, the captain—and following them went the water-jar, bouncing gaily over the seas.

The correspondent remained in the grip of this strange new enemy—a current. The shore, with its white slope of sand and its green bluff topped with little silent cottages, was spread like a picture before him. It was very near to him then, but he was impressed as one who, in a gallery, looks at a scene from Brittany or Algiers.

He thought: "I am going to drown? Can it be possible? Can it be possible? Can it be possible?" Perhaps an individual must consider his own death to be the final phenomenon of nature.

But later a wave perhaps whirled him out of this small deadly current, for he found suddenly that he could again make progress toward the shore. Later still he was aware that the captain, clinging with one hand to the keel of the dinghy, had his face turned away from the shore and toward him, and was calling his name. "Come to the boat! Come to the boat!"

In his struggle to reach the captain and the boat, he reflected that when one gets properly wearied drowning must really be a comfortable arrangement—a cessation of hostilities accompanied by a large degree of relief; and he was glad of it, for the main thing in his mind for some moments had been horror of the temporary agony. He did not wish to be hurt.

Presently he saw a man running along the shore. He was undressing with most remarkable speed. Coat, trousers, shirt, everything flew magically off him.

"Come to the boat!" called the captain.

"All right, Captain." As the correspondent paddled, he saw the captain let himself down to bottom and leave the boat. Then the correspondent performed his one little marvel of the voyage. A large wave caught him and flung him with ease and supreme speed completely over the boat and far beyond it. It struck him even then as an event in gymnastics and a true miracle of the sea. An overturned boat in the surf is not a plaything to a swimming man.

The correspondent arrived in water that reached only to his waist, but his condition did not enable him to stand for more than a moment. Each wave knocked him into a heap, and the undertow pulled at him.

Then he saw the man who had been running and undressing, and undressing and running, come bounding into the water. He dragged ashore the cook, and then waded toward the captain; but the captain waved him away and sent him to the correspondent. He was naked—naked as a tree in winter; but a halo was about his head, and he shone like a saint. He gave a strong pull, and a long drag, and a bully heave at the correspondent's hand. The correspondent, schooled in the minor formulæ, said, "Thanks, old man." But suddenly the man cried, "What's that?" He pointed a swift finger. The correspondent said, "Go."

In the shallows, face downward, lay the oiler. His forehead touched sand that was periodically, between each wave, clear of the sea.

The correspondent did not know all that transpired afterward. When he achieved safe ground he fell, striking the sand with each particular part of his body. It was as if he had dropped from a roof, but the thud was grateful to him.

It seemed that instantly the beach was populated with men with blankets, clothes, and flasks, and women with coffee-pots and all the remedies sacred to their minds. The welcome of the land to the men from the sea was warm and generous; but a still and dripping shape was carried slowly up the beach, and the land's welcome for it could only be the different and sinister hospitality of the grave.

When it came night, the white waves paced to and fro in the moonlight, and the wind brought the sound of the great sea's voice to the men on the shore, and they felt that they could then be interpreters.

FOR DISCUSSION:

1. How is the first paragraph an introduction to Crane's views on nature, life, and the extent of man's understanding of his place in the universe?

2. "The Open Boat" employs three different points of view as means of narration: the group, the omniscient narrator, and the correspondent. Trace Crane's use of each and show its appropriateness to the situation in which he uses it.

3. What is the purpose of the seven-part structure of this story? Discuss the significance of each part.

4. Irony is the employment of a circumstance that is the opposite of what is expected or considered appropriate. In "The Open Boat" Crane uses irony as a recurring motif to unify his story. Show how he uses it as a structural device, linking one episode to another.

5. Joseph Conrad said of "The Open Boat," "By the deep and simple humanity of presentation [it] seems somehow to illustrate the essentials of life itself, like a symbolic tale." What did he mean?

Araby

JAMES JOYCE

North Richmond Street, being blind, was a quiet street except at the hour when the Christian Brothers' School set the boys free. An uninhabited house of two storeys stood at the blind end, detached from its neighbours in a square ground. The other houses of the street, conscious of decent lives within them, gazed at one another with brown imperturbable faces.

The former tenant of our house, a priest, had died in the back drawing-room. Air, musty from having been long enclosed, hung in all the rooms, and the waste room behind the kitchen was littered with old useless papers. Among these I found a few paper-covered books, the pages of which were curled and damp: *The Abbot*, by Walter Scott, *The Devout Communicant* and *The Memoirs of Vidocq*. I liked the last best because its leaves were yellow. The wild garden behind the house contained a central apple-tree and a few straggling bushes under one of which I found the late tenant's rusty bicycle-pump. He had been a very charitable priest; in his will he had left all his money to institutions and the furniture of his house to his sister.

When the short days of winter came dusk fell before we had well eaten our dinners. When we met in the street the houses had grown sombre. The space of sky above us was the colour of ever-changing violet and towards it the lamps of the street lifted their feeble lanterns. The cold air stung us and we played till our bodies glowed. Our shouts echoed in the silent street. The career of our play brought us through the dark muddy lanes behind the houses where we ran the gauntlet of the rough tribes from the cottages, to the back doors of the dark dripping gardens where odours arose from the ashpits, to the dark odorous stables where a coachman smoothed and combed the horse or shook music from the buckled harness. When we returned to the street light from the kitchen windows had filled the areas. If my uncle was seen turning the corner we hid in the shadow until we had seen him safely housed. Or if Mangan's sister came out on the doorstep to call her brother in to his tea we watched her from our shadow peer up and down the street. We waited to see whether she would remain or go in and, if she remained, we left our shadow and walked up to Mangan's steps resignedly. She was waiting for us, her figure defined by the light from the half-opened door. Her brother always teased her before he obeyed and I stood by the railings looking at her. Her dress swung as she moved her body and the soft rope of her hair tossed from side to side.

Every morning I lay on the floor in the front parlour watching her door. The blind was pulled down to within an inch of the sash so that I could not be seen. When she came out on the doorstep my heart leaped. I ran to the hall, seized my books and followed her. I kept her brown figure always in my eye and, when we came near the point at which our ways diverged, I quickened my pace and passed her. This happened morning after morning. I had never spoken to her, except for a few casual words, and yet her name was like a summons to all my foolish blood.

Her image accompanied me even in places the most hostile to romance. On Saturday evenings when my aunt went marketing I had to go to carry some of the parcels. We walked through the flaring streets, jostled by drunken men and bargaining

---

* From DUBLINERS by James Joyce. Originally published by B. W. Huebsch, Inc. in 1916. All rights reserved. Reprinted by permission of The Viking Press, Inc., Jonathan Cape Ltd. and the executors of the James Joyce Estate.

women, amid the curses of labourers, the shrill litanies of shop-boys who stood on guard by the barrels of pigs' cheeks, the nasal chanting of street-singers, who sang a *come-all-you* about O'Donovan Rossa, or a ballad about the troubles in our native land. These noises converged in a single sensation of life for me: I imagined that I bore my chalice safely through a throng of foes. Her name sprang to my lips at moments in strange prayers and praises which I myself did not understand. My eyes were often full of tears (I could not tell why) and at times a flood from my heart seemed to pour itself out into my bosom. I thought little of the future. I did not know whether I would ever speak to her or not or, if I spoke to her, how I could tell her of my confused adoration. But my body was like a harp and her words and gestures were like fingers running upon the wires.

One evening I went into the back drawing-room in which the priest had died. It was a dark rainy evening and there was no sound in the house. Through one of the broken panes I heard the rain impinge upon the earth, the fine incessant needles of water playing in the sodden beds. Some distant lamp or lighted window gleamed below me. I was thankful that I could see so little. All my senses seemed to desire to veil themselves and, feeling that I was about to slip from them, I pressed the palms of my hands together until they trembled, murmuring: "O love! O love!" many times.

At last she spoke to me. When she addressed the first words to me I was so confused that I did not know what to answer. She asked me was I going to *Araby*. I forgot whether I answered yes or no. It would be a splendid bazaar, she said she would love to go.

"And why can't you?" I asked.

While she spoke she turned a silver bracelet round and round her wrist. She could not go, she said, because there would be a retreat that week in her convent. Her brother and two other boys were fighting for their caps and I was alone at the railings. She held one of the spikes, bowing her head towards me. The light from the lamp opposite our door caught the white curve of her neck, lit up her hair that rested there and, falling, lit up the hand upon the railing. It fell over one side of her dress and caught the white border of a petticoat, just visible as she stood at ease.

"It's well for you," she said.

"If I go," I said, "I will bring you something."

What innumerable follies laid waste my waking and sleeping thoughts after that evening! I wished to annihilate the tedious intervening days. I chafed against the work of school. At night in my bedroom and by day in the classroom her image came between me and the page I strove to read. The syllables of the word *Araby* were called to me through the silence in which my soul luxuriated and cast an Eastern enchantment over me. I asked for leave to go to the bazaar on Saturday night. My aunt was surprised and hoped it was not some Freemason affair. I answered few questions in class. I watched my master's face pass from amiability to sternness; he hoped I was not beginning to idle. I could not call my wandering thoughts together. I had hardly any patience with the serious work of like which, now that it stood between me and my desire, seemed to me child's play, ugly monotonous child's play.

On Saturday morning I reminded my uncle that I wished to go to the bazaar in the evening. He was fussing at the hallstand, looking for the hat-brush, and answered me curtly:

"Yes, boy, I know."

As he was in the hall I could not go into the front parlour and lie at the window. I left the house in bad humour and walked slowly towards the school. The air was pitilessly raw and already my heart misgave me.

When I came home to dinner my uncle had not yet been home. Still it was early. I sat staring at the clock for some time and, when its ticking began to irritate me, I left the room. I mounted the staircase and gained the upper part of the house. The high cold empty gloomy rooms liberated me and I went from room to room singing. From the front window I saw my companions playing below in the street. Their cries reached me weakened and indistinct and, leaning my forehead against the cool glass, I looked over at the dark house where she lived. I may have stood there for an hour, seeing nothing but the brown-clad figure cast by my imagination, touched discreetly by the lamplight at the curved neck, at the hand upon the railings and at the border below the dress.

When I came downstairs again I found Mrs. Mercer sitting at the fire. She was an old garrulous woman, a pawnbroker's widow, who collected used stamps for some pious purpose. I had to endure the gossip of the tea-table. The meal was prolonged beyond an hour and still my uncle did not come. Mrs. Mercer stood up to go: she was sorry she couldn't wait any longer, but it was after eight o'clock and she did not like to be out late, as the night air was bad for her. When she had gone I began to walk up and down the room, clenching my fists. My aunt said:

"I'm afraid you may put off your bazaar for this night of Our Lord."

At nine o'clock I heard my uncle's latchkey in the halldoor. I heard him talking to himself and heard the hallstand rocking when it had received the weight of his overcoat. I could interpret these signs. When he was midway through his dinner I asked him to give me the money to go to the bazaar. He had forgotten.

"The people are in bed and after their first sleep now," he said.

I did not smile. My aunt said to him energetically:

"Can't you give him the money and let him go? You've kept him late enough as it is."

My uncle said he was very sorry he had forgotten. He said he believed in the old saying: "All work and no play makes Jack a dull boy." He asked me where I was going and, when I had told him a second time he asked me did I know *The Arab's Farewell to his Steed.* When I left the kitchen he was about to recite the opening lines of the piece to my aunt.

I held a florin tightly in my hand as I strode down Buckingham Street towards the station. The sight of the streets thronged with buyers and glaring with gas recalled to me the purpose of my journey. I took my seat in a third-class carriage of a deserted train. After an intolerable delay the train moved out of the station slowly. It crept onward among ruinous houses and over the twinkling river. At Westland Row Station a crowd of people pressed to the carriage doors; but the porters moved them back, saying that it was a special train for the bazaar. I remained alone in the bare carriage. In a few minutes the train drew up beside an improvised wooden platform. I passed out on to the road and saw by the lighted dial of a clock that it was ten minutes to ten. In front of me was a large building which displayed the magical name.

I could not find any sixpenny entrance and, fearing that the bazaar would be closed, I passed in quickly through a turnstile, handing a shilling to a weary-looking man. I found myself in a big hall girdled at half its height by a gallery. Nearly all the stalls were closed and the greater part of the hall was in darkness. I recognised a silence like that which pervades a church after a service. I walked into the centre of the bazaar timidly. A few people were gathered about the stalls which were still open. Before a curtain, over which the words *Café Chantant* were written in coloured lamps, two men were counting money on a salver. I listened to the fall of the coins.

Remembering with difficulty why I had come I went over to one of the stalls and examined porcelain vases and flowered tea-sets. At the door of the stall a young lady was talking and laughing with two young gentlemen. I remarked their English accents and listened vaguely to their conversation.

"O, I never said such a thing!"

"O, but you did!"

"O, but I didn't!"

"Didn't she say that?"

"Yes. I heard her."

"O, there's a . . . fib!"

Observing me the young lady came over and asked me did I wish to buy anything. The tone of her voice was not encouraging; she seemed to have spoken to me out of a sense of duty. I looked humbly at the great jars that stood like eastern guards at either side of the dark entrance to the stall and murmured:

"No, thank you."

The young lady changed the position of one of the vases and went back to the two young men. They began to talk of the same subject. Once or twice the young lady glanced at me over her shoulder.

I lingered before her stall, though I knew my stay was useless, to make my interest in her wares seem the more real. Then I turned away slowly and walked down the middle of the bazaar. I allowed the two pennies to fall against the sixpence in my pocket. I heard a voice call from one end of the gallery that the light was out. The upper part of the hall was now completely dark.

Gazing up into the darkness I saw myself as a creature driven and derided by vanity; and my eyes burned with anguish and anger.

FOR DISCUSSION:

1. How does the setting as described in the first two paragraphs prepare the reader for the theme of the story?

2. Of what significance is the fact that the journey to the fair is a solitary one and no passengers other than the boy are allowed on the train?

3. What are the connotations of the word "Araby"? What is Araby's symbolic function in the story?

4. Why does the boy see himself at the end of the story as "a creature driven and derided by vanity." What is the meaning of "vanity" in this context?

5. The story is told partly in the first person. What are the advantages of this device in "Araby"?

The Snows of Kilimanjaro*

ERNEST HEMINGWAY

Kilimanjaro is a snow covered mountain 19,710 feet high, and is said to be the highest mountain in Africa. Its western summit is called the Masai "Ngàje Ngài," the House of God. Close to the western summit there is the dried and frozen carcass of a leopard. No one has explained what the leopard was seeking at that altitude.

"The marvellous thing is that it's painless," he said. "That's how you know when it starts."

"Is it really?"

"Absolutely. I'm awfully sorry about the odor though. That must bother you."

"Don't! Please don't."

"Look at them," he said. "Now is it sight or is it scent that brings them like that?"

The cot the man lay on was in the wide shade of a mimosa tree and as he looked out past the shade onto the glare of the plain there were three of the big birds squatted obscenely, while in the sky a dozen more sailed, making quick-moving shadows as they passed.

"They've been there since the day the truck broke down," he said. "Today's the first time any have lit on the ground. I watched the way they sailed very carefully at first in case I ever wanted to use them in a story. That's funny now."

"I wish you wouldn't," she said.

"I'm only talking," he said. "It's much easier if I talk. But I don't want to bother you."

"You know it doesn't bother me," she said. "It's that I've gotten so very nervous not being able to do anything. I think we might make it as easy as we can until the plane comes."

"Or until the plane doesn't come."

"Please tell me what I can do. There must be something I can do."

"You can take the leg off and that might stop it, though I doubt it. Or you can shoot me. You're a good shot now. I taught you to shoot didn't I?"

"Please don't talk that way. Couldn't I read to you?"

"Read what?"

"Anything in the book bag that we haven't read."

"I can't listen to it," he said. "Talking is the easiest. We quarrel and that makes the time pass."

"I don't quarrel. I never want to quarrel. Let's not quarrel any more. No matter how nervous we get. Maybe they will be back with another truck today. Maybe the plane will come."

"I don't want to move," the man said. "There is no sense in moving now except to make it easier for you."

"That's cowardly."

"Can't you let a man die as comfortably as he can without calling him names? What's the use of slanging me?"

"You're not going to die."

"Don't be silly. I'm dying now. Ask those bastards." He looked over to where the huge, filthy birds sat, their naked heads sunk in the hunched feathers. A fourth planed down, to run quick-legged and then waddle slowly toward the others.

"They are around every camp. You never notice them. You can't die if you don't give up."

"Where did you read that? You're such a bloody fool."

"You might think about some one else."

---

* "The Snows of Kilimanjaro" (Copyright 1936 Ernest Hemingway; renewal copyright ©1964 Mary Hemingway) is reprinted with the permission of Charles Scribner's Sons from THE SHORT STORIES OF ERNEST HEMINGWAY. Also by permission of the executors of the Ernest Hemingway Estate and Jonathan Cape Ltd.

"For Christ's sake," he said, "That's been my trade."

He lay then and was quiet for a while and looked across the heat shimmer of the plain to the edge of the bush. There were a few Tommies that showed minute and white against the yellow and, far off, he saw a herd of zebra, white against the green of the bush. This was a pleasant camp under big trees against a hill, with good water, and close by, a nearly dry water hole where sand grouse flighted in the mornings.

"Wouldn't you like me to read?" she asked. She was sitting on a canvas chair beside his cot. "There's a breeze coming up."

"No thanks."

"Maybe the truck will come."

"I don't give a damn about the truck."

"I do."

"You give a damn about so many things that I don't."

"Not so many, Harry."

"What about a drink?"

"It's supposed to be bad for you. It said in Black's to avoid all alcohol. You shouldn't drink."

"Molo!" he shouted.

"Yes Bwana."

"Bring whiskey-soda."

"Yes Bwana."

"You shouldn't," she said. "That's what I mean by giving up. It says it's bad for you. I know it's bad for you."

"No," he said. "It's good for me."

So now it was all over, he thought. So now he would never have a chance to finish it. So this was the way it ended in a bickering over a drink. Since the gangrene started in his right leg he had no pain and with the pain the horror had gone and all he felt now was a great tiredness and anger that this was the end of it. For this, that now was coming, he had very little curiosity. For years it had obsessed him; but now it meant nothing in itself. It was strange how easy being tired enough made it.

Now he would never write the things that he had saved to write until he knew enough to write them well. Well, he would not have to fail at trying to write them either. Maybe you could never write them, and that was why you put them off and delayed the starting. Well he would never know, now.

"I wish we'd never come," the woman said. She was looking at him holding the glass and biting her lip. "You never would have gotten anything like this in Paris. You always said you loved Paris. We could have stayed in Paris or gone anywhere. I'd have gone anywhere. I said I'd go anywhere you wanted. If you wanted to shoot we could have gone shooting in Hungary and been comfortable."

"Your bloody money," he said.

"That's not fair," she said. "It was always yours as much as mine. I left everything and I went wherever you wanted to go and I've done what you wanted to do. But I wish we'd never come here."

"You said you loved it."

"I did when you were all right. But now I hate it. I don't see why that had to happen to your leg. What have we done to have that happen to us?"

"I suppose what I did was to forget to put iodine on it when I first scratched it. Then I didn't pay any attention to it because I never infect. Then, later, when it got bad, it was probably using that weak carbolic solution when the other antiseptics ran out that paralyzed the minute blood vessels and started the gangrene." He looked at her, "What else?"

"I don't mean that."

"If we would have hired a good mechanic instead of a half baked kikuyu driver, he would have checked the oil and never burned out that bearing in the truck."

"I don't mean that."

"If you hadn't left your own people, your goddamned Old Westbury, Saratoga, Palm Beach people to take me on——"

"Why, I loved you. That's not fair. I love you now. I'll always love you. Don't you love me?"

"No," said the man. "I don't think so. I never have."

"Harry, what are you saying? You're out of your head."

"No. I haven't any head to go out of."

"Don't drink that," she said. "Darling, please don't drink that. We have to do everything we can."

"You do it," he said. "I'm tired."

Now in his mind he saw a railway station at Karagatch and he was standing with his pack and that was the headlight of the Simplon-Orient cutting the dark now and he was leaving Thrace then after the retreat. That was one of the things he had saved to write, with, in the morning at breakfast, looking out the window and seeing snow on the mountains in Bulgaria and Nansen's Secretary asking the old man if it were snow and the old man looking at it and saying, No, that's not snow. It's too early for snow. And the Secretary repeating to the other girls, No, you see. It's not snow and them all saying, It's not snow we were mistaken. But it was the snow all right and he sent them on into it when he evolved exchange of populations. And it was snow they tramped along in until they died that winter.

It was snow too that fell all Christmas week that year up in the Gauertal, that year they lived in the woodcutter's house with the big square porcelain stove that filled half the room, and they slept on mattresses filled with beech leaves, the time the deserter came with his feet bloody in the snow. He said the police were right behind him and they gave him woolen socks and held the gendarmes talking until the tracks had drifted over.

In Schrunz, on Christmas day, the snow was so bright it hurt your eyes when you looked out from the weinstube and saw every one coming home from church. That was where they walked up the sleigh-smoothed urine-yellowed road along the river with the steep pine hills, skis heavy on the shoulder, and where they ran that great run down the glacier above the Madlener-haus, the snow as smooth to see as cake frosting and as light as powder and he remembered the noiseless rush the speed made as you dropped down like a bird.

They were snow-bound a week in the Madlener-haus that time in the blizzard playing cards in the smoke by the lantern light and the stakes were higher all the time as Herr Lent lost more. Finally he lost it all. Everything, the skischule money and all the season's profit and then his capital. He could see him with his long nose, picking up the cards and then opening, "Sans Voir." There was always gambling then. When there was no snow you gambled and when there was too much you gambled. He thought of all the time in his life he had spent gambling.

But he had never written a line of that, nor of that cold, bright Christmas day with the mountains showing across the plain that Barker had flown across the lines to bomb the Austrian officers' leave train, machine-gunning them as they scattered and ran. He remembered Barker afterwards coming into the mess and starting to tell about it. And how quiet it got and then somebody saying, "You bloody murderous bastard."

Those were the same Austrians they killed then that he skied with later. No not the same. Hans, that he skied with all that year, had been in the Kaiser-Jägers and when they went hunting hares together up the little valley above the saw-mill they had talked of the fighting on Pasubio and of the attack on Pertica and Asalone and he had never written a word of that. Nor of Monte Corno, nor the Siete Commum, nor of Arsiedo.

How many winters had he lived in the Voralberg and the Arlberg? It was four and then he remembered the man who had the fox to sell when they had walked into Bludenz, that time to buy presents, and the cherry-pit taste of good kirsch, the fast-slipping rush of running powder-snow on crust, singing "Hi! Ho! said Rolly!" as you ran down the last stretch to the steep drop, taking it straight, then running the orchard in three turns and out across the ditch and onto the icy road behind the inn. Knocking your bindings loose, kicking the skis free and leaning them up against the wooden wall of the inn, the lamplight coming from the window, where inside, in the smoky, new-wine smelling warmth, they were playing the accordion.

"Where did we stay in Paris?" he asked the woman who was sitting by him in a canvas chair, now, in Africa.

"At the Crillon. You know that."

"Why do I know that?"

"That's where we always stayed."

"No. Not always."

"There and at the Pavillion Henri-Quatre in St. Germain. You said you loved it there."

"Love is a dunghill," said Harry. "And I'm the cock that gets on it to crow."

"If you have to go away," she said, "is it absolutely necessary to kill off everything you leave behind? I mean do you have to take away everything? Do you have to kill your horse, and your wife and burn your saddle and your armour?"

"Yes," he said. "Your damned money was my armour. My Swift and my Armour."

"Don't."

"All right. I'll stop that. I don't want to hurt you."

"It's a little bit late now."

"All right then. I'll go on hurting you. It's more amusing. The only thing I ever really liked to do with you I can't do now."

"No, that's not true. You liked to do many things and everything you wanted to do I did."

"Oh, for Christ sake stop bragging, will you?"

He looked at her and saw her crying.

"Listen," he said. "Do you think that it is fun to do this? I don't know why I'm doing it. It's trying to kill to keep yourself alive, I imagine. I was all right when we started talking. I didn't mean to start this, and now I'm crazy as a coot and being as cruel to you as I can be. Don't pay any attention, darling, to what I say. I love you, really. You know I love you. I've never loved any one else the way I love you."

He slipped into the familiar lie he made his bread and butter by.

"You're sweet to me."

"You bitch," he said. "You rich bitch. That's poetry. I'm full of poetry now. Rot and poetry. Rotten poetry."

"Stop it. Harry, why do you have to turn into a devil now?"

"I don't like to leave anything," the man said. "I don't like to leave things behind."

It was evening now and he had been asleep. The sun was gone behind the hill and there was a shadow all across the plain and the small animals were feeding close to camp; quick dropping heads and switching tails, he watched them keeping well out away from the bush now. The birds no longer waited on the ground. They were all perched heavily in a tree. There were many more of them. His personal boy was sitting by the bed.

"Memsahib's gone to shoot," the boy said. "Does Bwana want?"

"Nothing."

She had gone to kill a piece of meat and, knowing how he liked to watch the game, she had gone well away so she would not disturb this little pocket of the plain that he could see. She was always thoughtful, he thought. On anything she knew about, or had read, or that she had ever heard.

It was not her fault that when he went to her he was already over. How could a woman know that you meant nothing that you said; that you spoke only from habit and to be comfortable? After he no longer meant what he said, his lies were more successful with women than when he had told them the truth.

It was not so much that he lied as that there was no truth to tell. He had had his life and it was over and then he went on living it again with different people and more money, with the best of the same places, and some new ones.

You kept from thinking and it was all marvellous. You were equipped with good insides so that you did not go to pieces that way, the way most of them had, and you made an attitude that you cared nothing for the work you used to do, now that you could no longer do it. But, in yourself, you said that you would write about these people; about the very rich; that you were really not of them but a spy in their country; that you would leave it and write of it and for once it would be written by some one who knew what he was writing of. But he would never do it, because each day of not writing, of comfort, of being that which he despised, dulled his ability and softened his will to work so that, finally, he did no work at all. The people he knew now were all much more comfortable when he did not work. Africa was where he had been happiest in the good time of his life, so he had come out here to start again. They had made this safari with the minimum of comfort. There was no hardship; but there was no luxury and he had thought he could get back into training that way. That in some way he could work the fat off his soul the way a fighter went into the mountains to work and train in order to burn it out of his body.

She had liked it. She said she loved it. She loved anything that was exciting, that involved a change of scene, where there were new people and where things were pleasant. And he had felt the illusion of returning strength of will to work. Now if this was how it ended, and he knew it was, he must not turn like some snake biting itself because its back was broken. It wasn't this woman's fault. If it had not been she it would have been another. If he lived by a lie he should try to die by it. He heard a shot beyond the hill.

She shot very well this good, this rich bitch, this kindly caretaker and destroyer of his talent. Nonsense. He had destroyed his talent himself. Why should he blame this woman because she kept him well? He had destroyed his talent by not using it, by betrayals of himself and what he believed in, by drinking so much that he blunted the edge of his perceptions, by laziness, by sloth, and by snobbery, by pride and by prejudice, by hook and by crook. What was this? A catalogue of old books? What was his talent anyway? It was a talent all right but instead of using it, he had traded on it. It was never what he had done, but always what he could do. And he had chosen to make his living with something else instead of a pen or a pencil. It was strange, too, wasn't it, that when he fell in love with another woman, that woman should always have more money than the last one? But when he no longer was in love, when he was only lying, as to this woman, now, who had the most money of all, who had all the money there was, who had had a husband and children, who had taken lovers and been dissatisfied with them, and who loved him dearly as a writer, as a man, as a companion and as a proud possession; it was strange that when he did not love her at all and was lying, that he should be able to give her more for her money than when he had really loved.

We must all be cut out for what we do, he thought. However you make your living is where your talent lies. He had sold vitality, in one form or another, all his life and when your affections are not too involved you give much better value for the money. He had found that out but he would never write that, now, either. No, he would not write that, although it was well worth writing.

Now she came in sight, walking across the open toward the camp. She was wearing jodphurs and carrying her rifle. The two boys had a Tommie slung and they were coming along behind her. She was still a good-looking woman, he thought, and she had a pleasant body. She had a great talent and appreciation for the bed, she was not pretty, but he liked her face, she read enormously, liked to ride and shoot and, certainly, she drank too much. Her husband had died when she was still a comparatively young woman and for a while she had devoted herself to her two just-grown children, who did not need her and were embarrassed at having her about, to her stable of horses, to books, and to bottles. She liked to read in the evening before dinner and she drank Scotch and soda while she read. By dinner she was fairly drunk and after a bottle of wine at dinner she was usually drunk enough to sleep.

That was before the lovers. After she had the lovers she did not drink so much because she did not have to be drunk to sleep. But the lovers bored her. She had been married to a man who had never bored her and these people bored her very much.

Then one of her two children was killed in a plane crash and after that was over she did not want the lovers, and drink being no anæsthetic she had to make another life. Suddenly, she had been acutely frightened of being alone. But she wanted some one that she respected with her.

It had begun very simply. She liked what he wrote and she had always envied the life he led. She thought he did exactly what he wanted to. The steps by which she had acquired him and the way in which she had finally fallen in love with him were all part of a regular progression in which she had built herself a new life and he had traded away what remained of his old life.

He had traded it for security, for comfort too, there was no denying that, and for what else? He did not know. She would have bought him anything he wanted. He knew that. She was a damned nice woman too. He would as soon be in bed with her as any one; rather with her, because she was richer, because she was very pleasant and appreciative and because she never made scenes. And now this life that she had built again was coming to a term because he had not used iodine two weeks ago when a thorn had scratched his knee as they moved forward trying to photograph a herd of waterbuck standing, their heads up, peering while their nostrils searched the air, their ears spread wide to hear the first noise that would send them rushing into the bush. They had bolted, too, before he got the picture.

Here she came now.

He turned his head on the cot to look toward her. "Hello," he said.

"I shot a Tommy ram," she told him. "He'll make you good broth and I'll have them mash some potatoes with the Klim. How do you feel?"

"Much better."

"Isn't that lovely? You know I thought perhaps you would. You were sleeping when I left."

"I had a good sleep. Did you walk far?"

"No. Just around behind the hill. I made quite a good shot on the Tommy."

"You shoot marvellously, you know."

"I love it. I've loved Africa. Really. If you're all right it's the most fun that I've ever had. You don't know the fun it's been to shoot with you. I've loved the country."

"I love it too."

"Darling, you don't know how marvellous it is to see you feeling better. I couldn't stand it when you felt that way. You won't talk to me like that again, will you? Promise me?"

"No," he said. "I don't remember what I said."

"You don't have to destroy me. Do you? I'm only a middle-aged woman who loves you and wants to do what you want to do. I've been destroyed two or three times already. You wouldn't want to destroy me again, would you?"

"I'd like to destroy you a few times in bed," he said.

"Yes. That's the good destruction. That's the way we're made to be destroyed. The plane will be here tomorrow."

"How do you know?"

"I'm sure. It's bound to come. The boys have the wood all ready and the grass to make the smudge. I went down and looked at it again today. There's plenty of room to land and we have the smudges ready at both ends."

"What makes you think it will come tomorrow?"

"I'm sure it will. It's overdue now. Then, in town, they will fix up your leg and then we will have some good destruction. Not that dreadful talking kind."

"Should we have a drink? The sun is down."

"Do you think you should?"

"I'm having one."

"We'll have one together. *Molo, letti dui whiskey-soda!*" she called.

"You'd better put on your mosquito boots," he told her.

"I'll wait till I bathe . . ."

While it grew dark they drank and just before it was dark and there was no longer enough light to shoot, a hyena crossed the open on his way around the hill.

"That bastard crosses there every night," the man said. "Every night for two weeks."

"He's the one makes the noise at night. I don't mind it. They're a filthy animal though."

Drinking together, with no pain now except the discomfort of lying in the one position, the boys lighting a fire, its shadow jumping on the tents, he could feel the return of acquiescence in this life of pleasant surrender. She was very good to him. He had been cruel and unjust in the afternoon. She was a fine woman, marvellous really. And just then it occurred to him that he was going to die.

It came with a rush; not as a rush of water nor of wind; but of a sudden evil-smelling emptiness and the odd thing was that the hyena slipped lightly along the edge of it.

"What is it, Harry?" she asked him.

"Nothing," he said. "You had better move over to the other side. To windward."

"Did Molo change the dressing?"

"Yes. I'm just using the boric now."

"How do you feel?"

"A little wobbly."

"I'm going in to bathe," she said. "I'll be right out. I'll eat with you and then we'll put the cot in."

So, he said to himself, we did well to stop the quarrelling. He had never quarrelled much with this woman, while with the women that he loved he had quarrelled so much they had finally, always, with the corrosion of the quarrelling, killed what they had together. He had loved too much, demanded too much, and he wore it all out.

He thought about alone in Constantinople that time, having quarrelled in Paris before he had gone out. He had whored the whole time and then, when that was over, and he had failed to kill his loneliness, but only made it worse, he had written her, the first one, the one who left him, a letter telling her how he had never been able to kill it. . . . How when he thought he saw her outside the Regence one time it made him go all faint and sick inside, and that he would follow a woman who looked like her in some way, along the Boulevard, afraid to see it was not she, afraid to lose the feeling it gave him. How every one he had slept with had only made him miss her more. How what she had done could never matter since he knew he could not cure himself of loving her. He wrote this letter at the Club, cold sober, and mailed it to New York asking her to write him at the office in Paris. That seemed safe. And that night missing her so much it made him feel hollow sick inside, he wandered up past Taxim's, picked a girl up and took her out to supper. He had gone to a place to dance with her afterward, she danced badly, and left her for a hot Armenian slut, that swung her belly against him so it almost scalded. He took her away from a British gunner subaltern after a row. The gunner asked him outside and they fought in the street on the cobbles in the dark. He'd hit him twice, hard, on the side of the jaw and when he didn't go down he knew he was in for a fight. The gunner hit him in the body, then beside his eye. He swung with his left again and landed and the gunner fell on him and grabbed his coat and tore the sleeve off and he clubbed him twice behind the ear and then smashed him with his right as he pushed him away. When the gunner went down his head hit first and he ran with the girl because they heard the M. P.'s coming They got into a taxi and drove out to Rimmily Hissa along the Bosphorus, and around, and back in the cool night and went to bed and she felt as over-ripe as she looked but smooth, rose-petal, syrupy, smooth-bellied, big-breasted and needed no pillow under her buttocks, and he left her before she was awake looking blousy enough in the first daylight and turned up at the Pera Palace with a black eye, carrying his coat because one sleeve was missing.

That same night he left for Anatolia and he remembered, later on that trip, riding all day through fields of the poppies that they raised for opium and how strange it made you feel, finally, and all the distances seemed wrong, to where they had made the attack with the newly arrived Constantine officers, that did not know a god-damned thing, and the artillery had fired into the troops and the British observer had cried like a child.

That was the day he'd first seen dead men wearing white ballet skirts and upturned shoes with pompons on them. The Turks had come steadily and lumpily and he had seen the skirted men running and the officers shooting into them and running then themselves and he and the British observer had run too until his lungs ached and his mouth was full of the taste of pennies and they stopped behind some rocks and there were the Turks coming as lumpily as ever. Later he had seen the things that he could never think of and later still he had seen much worse. So when he got back to Paris that time he could not talk about it or stand to have it mentioned. And there in the café as he passed was that American poet with a pile of saucers in front of him and a stupid look on his potato face talking about the Dada movement with a Roumanian who said his name was Tristan Tzara, who always wore a monocle and had a headache, and, back at the apartment with his wife that now he loved again, the quarrel all over, the madness all over, glad to be home, the office sent his mail up to the flat. So then the letter in answer to the one he'd written came in on a platter one morning and when he saw the handwriting he went cold all over and tried to slip the letter underneath another. But his wife said, "Who is that letter from, dear?" and that was the end of the beginning of that.

He remembered the good times with them all, and the quarrels. They always picked the finest places to have the quarrels. And why had they always quarrelled when he was feeling best? He had never written any of that because, at first, he never wanted to hurt any one and then it seemed as though there was enough to write without it. But he had always thought that he would write it finally. There was so much to write. He had seen the world change; not just the events; although he had seen many of them and had watched the people, but he had seen the subtler change and he could remember how the people were at different times. He had been in it and he had watched it and it was his duty to write of it; but now he never would.

"How do you feel?" she said. She had come out from the tent now after her bath.

"All right."

"Could you eat now?" He saw Molo behind her with the folding table and the other boy with the dishes.

"I want to write," he said.

"You ought to take some broth to keep your strength up."

"I'm going to die tonight," he said. "I don't need my strength up."

"Don't be melodramatic, Harry, please," she said.

"Why don't you use your nose? I'm rotted half way up my thigh now. What the hell should I fool with broth for? Molo bring whiskey-soda."

"Please take the broth," she said gently.

"All right."

The broth was too hot. He had to hold it in the cup until it cooled enough to take it and then he just got it down without gagging.

"You're a fine woman," he said. "Don't pay any attention to me."

She looked at him with her well-known, well-loved face from *Spur* and *Town and Country*, only a little the worse for drink, only a little the worse for bed, but *Town and Country* never showed those good breasts and those useful thighs and those lightly small-of-back-caressing hands, and as he looked and saw her well known pleasant smile, he felt death come again. This time there was no rush. It was a puff, as of a wind that makes a candle flicker and the flame go tall.

"They can bring my net out later and hang it from the tree and build the fire up. I'm not going in the tent tonight. It's not worth moving. It's a clear night. There won't be any rain."

So this was how you died, in whispers that you did not hear. Well, there would be no more quarrelling. He could promise that. The one experience that he had never had he was not going to spoil now. He probably would. You spoiled everything. But perhaps he wouldn't.

"You can't take dictation, can you?"

"I never learned," she told him.

"That's all right."

There wasn't time, of course, although it seemed as though it telescoped so that you might put it all into one paragraph if you could get it right.

There was a log house, chinked white with mortar, on a hill above the lake. There was a bell on a pole by the door to call the people in to meals. Behind the house were fields and behind the fields was the timber. A line of lombardy poplars ran from the house to the dock. Other poplars ran along the point. A road went up to the hills along the edge of the timber and along that road he picked blackberries. Then that log house was burned down and all the guns that had been on deer foot racks above the open fire place were burned and afterwards their barrels, with the lead melted in the magazines, and the stocks burned away, lay out on the heap of ashes that were used to make lye for the big iron soap kettles, and you asked Grandfather if you could have them to play with, and he said, no. You see they were his guns still and he never bought any others. Nor did he hunt any more. The house was rebuilt in the same place out of lumber now and painted white and from its porch you saw the poplars and the lake beyond; but there were never any more guns. The barrels of the guns that had hung on the deer feet on the wall of the log house lay out there on the heap of ashes and no one ever touched them.

In the Black Forest, after the war, we rented a trout stream and there were two ways to walk it. One was down the valley from Triberg and around the valley road in the shade of the trees that bordered the white road, and then up a side road that went up through the hills past many small farms, with the big Schwarzwald houses, until that road crossed the stream. That was where our fishing began.

The other way was to climb steeply up to the edge of the woods and then go across the top of the hills through the pine woods, and then out to the edge of a meadow and down across this meadow to the bridge. There were birches along the stream and it was not big, but narrow, clear and fast, with pools where it had cut under the roots of the birches. At the Hotel in Triberg the proprietor had a fine season. It was very pleasant and we were all great friends. The next year came the inflation and the money he had made the year before was not enough to buy supplies to open the hotel and he hanged himself.

You could dictate that, but you could not dictate the Place Contrescarpe where the flower sellers dyed their flowers in the street and the dye ran over the paving where the autobus started and the old men and the women, always drunk on wine and bad marc; and the children with their noses running in the cold; the smell of dirty sweat and poverty and drunkenness at the Café des Amateurs and the whores at the Bal Musette they lived above. The Concierge who entertained the trooper of the Garde Republicaine in her loge, his horse-hair plumed helmet on a chair. The locataire across the hall whose husband was a bicycle racer and her joy that morning at the Cremerie when she had opened L'Auto and seen where he placed third in Paris-Tours, his first big race. She had blushed and laughed and then gone upstairs crying with the yellow sporting paper in her hand. The husband of the woman who ran the Bal Musette drove a taxi and when he, Harry, had to take an early plane the husband knocked upon the door to wake him and they each drank a glass of white wine at the zinc of the bar before they started. He knew his neighbors in that quarter then because they all were poor.

Around that Place there were two kinds; the drunkards and the sportifs. The drunkards killed their poverty that way; the sportifs took it out in exercise. They were the descendants of the Communards and it was no struggle for them to know their politics. They knew who had shot their fathers, their relatives, their brothers, and their friends when the Versailles troops came in and took the town after the Commune and executed any one they could catch with calloused hands, or who wore a cap, or carried any other sign he was a working man. And in that poverty, and in that quarter across the street from a Boucherie Chevaline and a wine co-operative he had written the start of all he was to do. There never was another part of Paris that he loved like that, the sprawling trees, the old white plastered houses painted brown below, the long green of the autobus in that round square, the purple flower dye upon the paving, the sudden drop down the hill of the rue Cardinal Lemoine to the River, and the other way the narrow crowded world of the rue Mouffetard. The street that ran up toward the Pantheon and the other that he always took with the bicycle, the only asphalted street in all that quarter, smooth under the tires, with the high narrow houses and the cheap tall hotel where Paul Verlaine had died. There were only two rooms in the apartments where they lived and he had a room on the top floor of that hotel that cost him sixty francs a month where he did his writing, and from it he could see the roofs and chimney pots and all the hills of Paris.

From the apartment you could only see the wood and coal man's place. He sold wine too, bad wine. The golden horse's head outside the Boucherie Chevaline where the carcasses hung yellow gold and red in the open window, and the green painted co-operative where they bought their wine; good wine and cheap. The rest was plaster walls and the windows of the neighbors. The neighbors who, at night, when some one lay drunk in the street, moaning and groaning in that typical French ivresse that you were propaganded to believe did not exist, would open their windows and then the murmur of talk.

"Where is the policeman? When you don't want him the bugger is always there. He's sleeping with come concierge. Get the Agent." Till some one threw a bucket of water from a window and the moaning stopped. "What's that? Water. Ah, that's intelligent." And the windows shutting. Marie, his femme de menage, protesting against the eight-hour day saying, "If a husband works until six he gets only a little drunk on the way home and does not waste too much. If he works only until five he is drunk every night and one has no money. It is the wife of the working man who suffers from this shortening of hours."

"Wouldn't you like some more broth?" the woman asked him now.

"No, thank you very much. It is awfully good."

"Try just a little."

"I would like a whiskey-soda."

"It's not good for you."

"No. It's bad for me. Cole Porter wrote

the words and the music. This knowledge that you're going mad for me."

"You know I like you to drink."

"Oh yes. Only it's bad for me."

When she goes, he thought. I'll have all I want. Not all I want but all there is. Ayee he was tired. Too tired. He was going to sleep a little while. He lay still and death was not there. It must have gone around another street. It went in pairs, on bicycles, and moved absolutely silently on the pavements.

No, he had never written about Paris. Not the Paris that he cared about. But what about the rest that he had never written?

What about the ranch and the silvered gray of the sage brush, the quick, clear water in the irrigation ditches, and the heavy green of the alfalfa. The trail went up into the hills and the cattle in the summer were shy as deer. The bawling and the steady noise and slow moving mass raising a dust as you brought them down in the fall. And behind the mountains, the clear sharpness of the peak in the evening light and, riding down along the trail in the moonlight, bright across the valley. Now he remembered coming down through the timber in the dark holding the horse's tail when you could not see and all the stories that he meant to write.

About the half-wit chore boy who was left at the ranch that time and told not to let any one get any hay, and that old bastard from the Forks who had beaten the boy when he had worked for him stopping to get some feed. The boy refusing and the old man saying he would beat him again. The boy got the rifle from the kitchen and shot him when he tried to come into the barn and when they came back to the ranch he'd been dead a week, frozen in the corral, and the dogs had eaten part of him. But what was left you packed on a sled wrapped in a blanket and roped on and you got the boy to help you haul it, and the two of you took it out over the road on skis, and sixty miles down to town to turn the boy over. He having no idea that he would be arrested. Thinking he had done his duty and that you were his friend and he would be rewarded. He'd helped to haul the old man in so everybody could know how bad the old man had been and how he'd tried to steal some feed that didn't belong to him, and when the sheriff put the handcuffs on the boy he couldn't believe it. Then he'd started to cry. That was one story he had saved to write. He knew at least twenty good stories from out there and he had never written one. Why?

"You tell them why," he said.

"Why what, dear?"

"Why nothing."

She didn't drink so much, now, since she had him. But if he lived he would never write about her, he knew that now. Nor about any of them. The rich were dull and they drank too much, or they played too much backgammon. They were dull and they were repetitious. He remembered poor Julian and his romantic awe of them and how he had started a story once that began, "The very rich are different from you and me." And how some one had said to Julian, Yes, they have more money. But that was not humorous to Julian. He thought they were a special glamourous race and when he found they weren't it wrecked him just as much as any other thing that wrecked him.

He had been contemptuous of those who wrecked. You did not have to like it because you understood it. He could beat anything, he thought, because no thing could hurt him if he did not care.

All right. Now he would not care for death. One thing he had always dreaded was the pain. He could stand pain as well as any man, until it went on too long, and wore him out, but here he had something that had hurt frightfully and just when he had felt it breaking him, the pain had stopped.

He remembered long ago when Williamson, the bombing officer, had been hit by a stick bomb some one in a German patrol had thrown as he was coming in through the wire that night and, screaming, had begged every one to kill him. He was a fat man, very brave, and a good officer, although addicted to fantastic shows. But that night he was caught in the wire, with a flare lighting him up and his bowels spilled out into the wire, so when they brought him in, alive, they had to cut him loose. Shoot me, Harry. For Christ sake shoot me. They had had an argument one time about our Lord never sending you anything you could not bear and some one's theory had been that meant that at a certain time the pain passed you out automatically. But he had always remembered Williamson, that night. Nothing passed out Williamson until he gave him all his morphine tablets that he had always saved to use himself and then they did not work right away.

Still this now, that he had, was very easy; and if it was no worse as it went on there was nothing to worry about. Except that he would rather be in better company.

He thought a little about the company that he would like to have.

No, he thought, when everything you do, you do too long, and do too late, you can't expect to find the people still there. The people all are gone. The party's over and you are with your hostess now.

I'm getting as bored with dying as with everything else, he thought.

"It's a bore," he said out loud.

"What is, my dear?"

"Anything you do too bloody long."

He looked at her face between him and the fire. She was leaning back in the chair and the firelight shone on her pleasantly lined face and he could see that she was sleepy. He heard the hyena make a noise just outside the range of the fire.

"I've been writing," he said. "But I got tired."

"Do you think you will be able to sleep?"

"Pretty sure. Why don't you turn in?"

"I like to sit here with you."

"Do you feel anything strange?" he asked her.

"No. Just a little sleepy."

"I do," he said.

He had just felt death come by again.

"You know the only thing I've never lost is curiosity," he said to her.

"You've never lost anything. You're the most complete man I've ever known."

"Christ," he said. "How little a woman knows. What is that? Your intuition?"

Because, just then, death had come and rested its head on the foot of the cot and he could smell its breath.

"Never believe any of that about a scythe and a skull," he told her. "It can be two bicycle policemen as easily, or be a bird. Or it can have a wide snout like a hyena."

It had moved up on him now, but it had no shape any more. It simply occupied space.

"Tell it to go away."

It did not go away but moved a little closer.

"You've got a hell of a breath," he told it. "You stinking bastard."

It moved up closer to him still and now he could not speak to it, and when it saw he could not speak it came a little closer, and now he tried to send it away without speaking, but it moved in on him so its weight was all upon his chest, and while it crouched there and he could not move, or speak, he heard the woman say, "Bwana is asleep now. Take the cot up very gently and carry it into the tent."

He could not speak to tell her to make it go away and it crouched now, heavier, so he could not breathe. And then, while they lifted the cot, suddenly it was all right and the weight went from his chest.

It was morning and had been morning for some time and he heard the plane. It showed very tiny and then made a wide circle and the boys ran out and lit the fires, using kerosene, and piled on grass so there were two big smudges at each end of the level place and the morning breeze blew them toward the camp and the plane circled twice more, low this time, and then glided down and levelled off and landed smoothly and, coming walking toward him, was old Compton in slacks, a tweed jacket and a brown felt hat.

"What's the matter, old cock?" Compton said.

"Bad leg," he told him. "Will you have some breakfast?"

"Thanks. I'll just have some tea. It's the Puss Moth you know. I won't be able to take the Memsahib. There's only room for one. Your lorry is on the way."

Helen had taken Compton aside and was speaking to him. Compton came back more cheery than ever.

"We'll get you right in," he said. "I'll be back for the Mem. Now I'm afraid I'll have to stop at Arusha to refuel. We'd better get going."

"What about the tea?"

"I don't really care about it you know."

The boys had picked up the cot and carried it around the green tents and down along the rock and out onto the plain and along past the smudges that were burning brightly now, the grass all consumed, and the wind fanning the fire, to the little plane. It was difficult getting him in, but once in he lay back in the leather seat, and the leg was stuck straight out to one side of the seat where Compton sat. Compton started the motor and got in. He waved to Helen and to the boys and, as the clatter moved into the old familiar roar, they swung around with Compie watching for wart-hog holes and roared, bumping, along the stretch between the fires and with the last bump rose and he saw them all standing below, waving, and the camp beside the hill, flattening now, and the plain spreading, clumps of trees, and the bush flattening, while the game trails ran now smoothly to the dry waterholes, and there was a new water that he had never known of. The zebra, small rounded backs now, and the wildebeeste, big-headed dots seeming to climb as they moved in long fingers across the plain, now scattering as the shadow came toward them, they were tiny now, and the movement had no gallop, and the plain as far as you could see, gray-yellow now and ahead old Compie's tweed back and the brown felt hat. Then they were over the first hills and the wildebeeste were trailing up them, and then they were over mountains with sudden depths of green-rising forest and the solid bamboo slopes, and then the heavy forest again, sculptured into peaks and hollows until they crossed, and hills sloped down and then another plain, hot now, and purple brown, bumpy with heat and Compie looking back to see how he was riding. Then there were other mountains dark ahead.

And then instead of going on to Arusha they turned left, he evidently figured that they had the gas, and looking down he saw a pink sifting cloud, moving over the ground, and in the air, like the first snow in a blizzard, that comes from nowhere, and he knew the locusts were coming up from the South. Then they began to climb and they were going to the East it seemed, and then it darkened and they were in a storm, the rain so thick it seemed like flying through a waterfall, and then they were out and Compie turned his head and grinned and pointed and there, ahead, all he could see, as wide as all the world, great, high, and unbelievably white in the sun, was the square top of Kilimanjaro. And then he knew that there was where he was going.

Just then the hyena stopped whimpering in the night and started to make a strange, human, almost crying sound. The woman heard it and stirred uneasily. She did not wake. In her dream she was at the house on Long Island and it was the night before her daughter's début. Somehow her father was there and he had been very rude. Then the noise the hyena made was so loud she woke and for a moment she did not know where she was and she was very afraid. Then she took the flashlight and shone it on the other cot that they had carried in after Harry had gone to sleep. She could see his bulk under the mosquito bar but somehow he had gotten his leg out and it hung down alongside the cot. The dressings had all come down and she could not look at it.

"Molo," she called, "Molo! Molo!"

Then she said, "Harry, Harry!" Then her voice rising, "Harry! Please, Oh Harry!"

There was no answer and she could not hear him breathing.

Outside the tent the hyena made the same strange noise that had awakened her. But she did not hear him for the beating of her heart.

FOR DISCUSSION:

1. How important is the epigraph to an understanding of the story?
2. What is the literary effect of juxtaposing the present and the past?
3. What does each of the following symbolize: the leopard? the hyena? the snow? Kilimanjaro? Helen?
4. Philip Young, a frequent commentator on Hemingway's life and works, calls this story "an exercise in personal and aesthetic hygiene." What does he mean?
5. The leopard is found close to the western summit of Kilimanjaro, a summit whose name means in English "House of God." Is there any religious significance to this? Why the western summit?
6. What significance do you attach to the fact that Harry dreams he sees the summit of Kilimanjaro just at the moment of his death?

"Ah, Are You Digging on My Grave?"*

THOMAS HARDY

"Ah, are you digging on my grave
My beloved one?—planting rue?"
—"No: yesterday he went to wed
One of the brightest wealth has bred,
'It cannot hurt her now,' he said,
'That I should not be true.'"

"Then who is digging on my grave?
My nearest, dearest kin?"
—"Ah, no: they sit and think, 'What use!
What good will planting flowers produce?   10
No tendance of her mound can loose
Her spirit from Death's gin.'"

"But someone digs upon my grave?
My enemy?—prodding sly?"
—"Nay: when she heard you had passed the Gate
That shuts on all flesh soon or late,
She thought you no more worth her hate,
And cares not where you lie."

"Then, who is digging on my grave?
Say—since I have not guessed!"   20
—"O it is I, my mistress dear,
Your little dog, who still lives near,
And much I hope my movements here
Have not disturbed your rest?"

"Ah, yes! You dig upon my grave . . . .
Why flashed it not on me
That one true heart was left behind!
What feeling do we ever find
To equal among human kind
A dog's fidelity!"   30

"Mistress, I dug upon your grave
To bury a bone, in case
I should be hungry near this spot
When passing on my daily trot.
I am sorry, but I quite forgot
It was your resting-place."

---

* Reprinted by permission of The Macmillan Company from COLLECTED POEMS by Thomas Hardy. Also by permission of Macmillan & Company Ltd., The Macmillan Company of Canada Ltd., and the trustees of the Hardy Estate.

FOR DISCUSSION:

1. Is the question-and-answer technique used in this poem more effective than a straight narrative device? Why?
2. Comment on Hardy's use of tone and irony.

3. Each of the first four stanzas considers a different possible digger on the grave. What is the significance of the order of these stanzas?

I Never Lost as Much but Twice*

EMILY DICKINSON

I never lost as much but twice,
And that was in the sod.
Twice have I stood a beggar
Before the door of God!

Angels, twice descending,
Reimbursed my store.
Burglar, banker, father!
I am poor once more!

FOR DISCUSSION:

1. What is the meaning of "in the sod"?
2. To whom is line 7 addressed?
3. What is the significance of the order of the three words in line 7?
4. Is the poem optimistic, resentful and accepting, pessimistic, personal, universal?

Ars Poetica†

ARCHIBALD MacLEISH

I

A poem should be palpable and mute
As a globed fruit,

Dumb
As old medallions to the thumb,

Silent as the sleeve-worn stone
Of casement ledges where the moss has grown —

---

* Reprinted by permission of the publishers and the Trustees of Amherst College from Thomas H. Johnson, Editor, THE POEMS OF EMILY DICKINSON, Cambridge, Mass.: Belknap Press of Harvard University Press, Copyright, 1951, 1955, by the President and Fellows of Harvard College.

† From COLLECTED POEMS OF ARCHIBALD MACLEISH, 1917–1952, copyright 1952 by Houghton Mifflin Company. Reprinted by permission of Houghton Mifflin Company and The Bodley Head Ltd.

A poem should be wordless
As the flight of birds.

II

A poem should be motionless in time
As the moon climbs,   10

Leaving, as the moon releases
Twig by twig the night-entangled trees,

Leaving, as the moon behind the winter leaves,
Memory by memory the mind —

A poem should be motionless in time
As the moon climbs.

III

A poem should be equal to:
Not true.

For all the history of grief
An empty doorway and a maple leaf.   20

For love
The leaning grasses and two lights above the sea —

A poem should not mean
But be.

FOR DISCUSSION:

1. Show how the conclusions reached in section III proceed from the premises set forth in sections I and II.

2. MacLeish is saying that meaning is not a quality of a poem, but is the poem. To what extent does "Ars Poetica" itself follow this dictum?

3. Why does the author use similes in sections I and II, but metaphors in section III?

Tears, Idle Tears

ALFRED, LORD TENNYSON

Tears, idle tears, I know not what they mean,
Tears from the depth of some divine despair
Rise in the heart, and gather to the eyes,
In looking on the happy Autumn-fields,
And thinking of the days that are no more.

Fresh as the first beam glittering on a sail,
That brings our friends up from the underworld,
Sad as the last which reddens over one
That sinks with all we love below the verge;
So sad, so fresh, the days that are no more.   10

Ah, sad and strange as in dark summer dawns
The earliest pipe of half-awakened birds
To dying ears, when unto dying eyes
The casement slowly grows a glimmering square;
So sad, so strange, the days that are no more.

Dear as remembered kisses after death,
And sweet as those by hopeless fancy feigned
On lips that are for others; deep as love,
Deep as first love, and wild with all regret;
O Death in Life, the days that are no more!   20

FOR DISCUSSION:

1. Why are the tears described as "idle," "fresh," "sad," "strange," and "dear"?
2. What is meant by "underworld" in line 7?
3. Each of the first three stanzas contains at least one major image. What do these images have in common?
4. What is the theme of the poem and how do the successive images contribute to it?

The Death of the Ball Turret Gunner*

RANDALL JARRELL

From my mother's sleep I fell into the State,
And I hunched in its belly till my wet fur froze.
Six miles from earth, loosed from its dream of life,
I woke to black flak and the nightmare fighters.
When I died they washed me out of the turret with a hose.

FOR DISCUSSION:

1. What is the meaning and effect of the verb "fell" in line 1?
2. What is the antecedent of "its" in line 2?
3. Why is the fur described as wet and frozen in line 2?
4. What is the "dream of life" referred to in line 3?
5. Comment on the effectiveness of the alliteration and internal rhyme in the poem.
6. Poets frequently draw a series of images from a particular field of human activity, such as the agricultural, military, or economic world. Are Jarrell's images so chosen? If so, what do they have in common? Are they appropriate to his theme?

* From LITTLE FRIEND, LITTLE FRIEND, Copyright 1945 by Harcourt, Brace & World, Inc. Reprinted by permission of Mrs. Randall Jarrell.

On First Looking into Chapman's Homer

JOHN KEATS

    Much have I travelled in the realms of gold,
And many goodly states and kingdoms seen;
Round many western islands have I been
Which bards in fealty to Apollo hold.
Oft of one wide expanse had I been told
That deep-browed Homer ruled as his demesne;
Yet did I never breathe its pure serene
Till I heard Chapman speak out loud and bold:
Then felt I like some watcher of the skies
When a new planet swims into his ken;   10
Or like stout Cortez when with eagle eyes
He stared at the Pacific—and all his men
Looked at each other with a wild surmise—
Silent, upon a peak in Darien.

FOR DISCUSSION:

1. This poem is written in the form of a modified Petrarchan sonnet. What is the relation of the idea expressed in the octave to that expressed in the sestet?
2. What is the effect of the use of such archaisms as "bards," "fealty," and "demesne"?
3. What are the "realms of gold" referred to in line 1?
4. In what sense is Keats like "the watcher of the skies" (line 9) and "stout Cortez" (line 11)?
5. Is Keats suggesting that Cortez discovered the Pacific? If not, what is his point?
6. How does Keats integrate theme and imagery in this sonnet?

Song: Goe and Catche a Falling Starre

JOHN DONNE

    Goe, and catche a falling starre,
      Get with child a mandrake roote,
    Tell me, where all past yeares are,
      Or who cleft the Divels foot,
Teach me to heare Mermaides singing,
Or to keep off envies stinging,
        And finde
      What winde
Serves to advance an honest minde.

    If thou beest borne to strange sights,   10
      Things invisible to see,

Ride ten thousand daies and nights,
    Till age snow white haires on thee,
Thou, when thou retorn'st, wilt tell mee
All strange wonders that befell thee,
        And sweare
        No where
Lives a woman true, and faire.

If thou findst one, let mee know,
    Such a Pilgrimage were sweet;   20
Yet doe not, I would not goe,
    Though at next doore wee might meet,
Though shee were true, when you met her,
And last, till you write your letter,
        Yet shee
        Will bee
False, ere I come, to two, or three.

FOR DISCUSSION:

1. What do the images in stanza 1 (lines 1–9) have in common?
2. What part of speech is "snow" in line 13?
3. Does "faire" in line 18 mean "beautiful" or "just"? Does its meaning make any difference?
4. What is the relation between the first and the last stanza?
5. Comment on the speaker's tone. Is it cynical, worldly wise, amused?

Sonnet 73

WILLIAM SHAKESPEARE

That time of year thou mayst in me behold
When yellow leaves, or none, or few, do hang
Upon those boughs which shake against the cold,
Bare ruined choirs, where late the sweet birds sang.
In me thou see'st the twilight of such day
As after sunset fadeth in the west,
Which by and by black night doth take away,
Death's second self that seals up all in rest.
In me thou see'st the glowing of such fire,
That on the ashes of his youth doth lie,   10
As the death-bed, whereon it must expire
Consumed with that which it was nourished by.
    This thou perceiv'st, which makes thy love more strong
    To love that well, which thou must leave ere long.

FOR DISCUSSION:

1. Each of the three quatrains of this sonnet has a major image. What do these images have in common?
2. How does the couplet relate to the three quatrains that precede it?
3. To what does "that" in line 14 refer?

Easter-Wings

GEORGE HERBERT

    Lord, who createdst man in wealth and store,
       Though foolishly he lost the same,
          Decaying more and more,
            Till he became
              Most poore:
              With   thee
           O let me rise
         As larks, harmoniously,
      And sing this day thy victories:
   Then shall the fall further the flight in me.   10

    My tender age in sorrow did beginne:
      And still with sicknesses and shame
        Thou didst so punish sinne,
           That I became
             Most thinne.
            With   thee
          Let me combine
       And feel this day thy victorie:
     For, if I imp my wing on thine,
   Affliction shall advance the flight in me.   20

FOR DISCUSSION:

1. Is the unusual typography of "Easter-Wings" merely an attention-getting device, or is it integrally related to the content of the poem? Trace the poem's content and external form, line by line. Is this poem an example of what Cleanth Brooks means when he writes, "Form is meaning"?

2. What is the structural and thematic relationship between stanza 1 (lines 1–10) and stanza 2 (lines 11–20)?

3. Does the word "flight" in lines 10 and 20 have a special significance?

Sonnet 124

WILLIAM SHAKESPEARE

If my dear love were but the child of state,
It might for Fortune's bastard be unfather'd,
As subject to Time's love or to Time's hate,
Weeds among weeds, or flowers with flowers gather'd.
No, it was builded far from accident;
It suffers not in smiling pomp, nor falls
Under the blow of thralled discontent,
Whereto the inviting time our fashion calls:
It fears not policy, that heretic,

Which works on leases of short-number'd hours, 10
But all alone stands hugely politic,
That it nor grows with heat nor drowns with showers.
   To this I witness call the fools of time,
Which die for goodness, who have lived for crime.

FOR DISCUSSION:

1. The imagery in the first quatrain is genealogical, that of the second and third quatrains, mainly political. Is there a logical connection between the two sets of images, or is there a discontinuity?

2. Specifically, what does the image of the weeds and flowers in line 4 mean?

3. To what does "this" in line 13 refer?

4. How does Shakespeare employ the device of rhetorical balance and contrast in this sonnet? Is the main idea developed in any way, or is it merely stated and restated in different ways throughout the sonnet?

The Collar

GEORGE HERBERT

I struck the board, and cry'd, No more.
     I will abroad.
What? shall I ever sigh and pine?
My lines and life are free; free as the rode,
   Loose as the winde, as large as store.
     Shall I be still in suit?
Have I no harvest but a thorn
To let me bloud, and not restore
What I have lost with cordiall fruit?
     Sure there was wine 10
Before my sighs did drie it: there was corn
    Before my tears did drown it.
   Is the yeare onely lost to me?
    Have I no bayes to crown it?
No flowers, no garlands gay? all blasted?
     All wasted?
Not so, my heart: but there is fruit,
    And thou hast hands.
Recover all thy sigh-blown age
On double pleasures: leave thy cold dispute 20
Of what is fit, and not. Forsake thy cage,
    Thy rope of sands,
Which pettie thoughts have made, and made to thee
   Good cable, to enforce and draw,
    And be thy law,
While thou didst wink and wouldst not see.
    Away; take heed:
    I will abroad.
Call in thy deaths head there: tie up thy fears.
    He that forbears 30

To suit and serve his need,
Deserves his load.
But as I rav'd and grew more fierce and wilde
At every word,
Me thoughts I heard one calling, *Child!*
And I reply'd, *My Lord.*

FOR DISCUSSION:

1. What is the significance of the title? Is there a possible pun on "collar" and "choler" in the poem? One critic suggests that "Herbert is in a choler because he wears the collar of religious discipline." Another suggests a further pun: "Herbert is in a choler because he wears a collar only until he hears the voice of the caller, God." How likely are these possibilities?

2. What is the meaning of "still" in line 6?

3. Does "At every word" in line 34 modify line 33 or line 35? Does it make any difference?

4. Define the conflict in the mind of the speaker.

5. Comment on the changing tone of the poem.

Ode to the West Wind

PERCY BYSSHE SHELLEY

I

O wild West Wind, thou breath of Autumn's being,
Thou, from whose unseen presence the leaves dead
Are driven, like ghosts from an enchanter fleeing,

Yellow, and black, and pale, and hectic red,
Pestilence-stricken multitudes: O thou,
Who chariotest to their dark wintry bed

The wingèd seeds, where they lie cold and low,
Each like a corpse within its grave, until
Thine azure sister of the Spring shall blow

Her clarion o'er the dreaming earth, and fill   10
(Driving sweet buds like flocks to feed in air)
With living hues and odours plain and hill:

Wild Spirit, which art moving everywhere;
Destroyer and preserver; hear, oh, hear!

II

Thou on whose stream, mid the steep sky's commotion,
Loose clouds like earth's decaying leaves are shed,
Shook from the tangled boughs of Heaven and Ocean,

Angels of rain and lightning: there are spread
On the blue surface of thine aëry surge,
Like the bright hair uplifted from the head   20

Of some fierce Maenad, even from the dim verge
Of the horizon to the zenith's height,
The locks of the approaching storm. Thou dirge

Of the dying year, to which this closing night
Will be the dome of a vast sepulchre,
Vaulted with all thy congregated might

Of vapours, from whose solid atmosphere
Black rain, and fire, and hail will burst: oh, hear!

III

Thou who didst waken from his summer dreams
The blue Mediterranean, where he lay,
Lulled by the coil of his crystàlline streams,

Beside a pumice isle in Baiae's bay,
And saw in sleep old palaces and towers
Quivering within the wave's intenser day,

All overgrown with azure moss and flowers
So sweet, the sense faints picturing them! Thou
For whose path the Atlantic's level powers

Cleave themselves into chasms, while far below
The sea-blooms and the oozy woods which wear
The sapless foliage of the ocean, know

Thy voice, and suddenly grow gray with fear
And tremble and despoil themselves: oh, hear!

IV

If I were a dead leaf thou mightest bear;
If I were a swift cloud to fly with thee;
A wave to pant beneath thy power, and share

The impulse of thy strength, only less free
Than thou, O uncontrollable! If even
I were as in my boyhood, and could be

The comrade of thy wanderings over Heaven,
As then, when to outstrip thy skiey speed
Scarce seemed a vision; I would ne'er have striven

As thus with thee in prayer in my sore need.
Oh, lift me as a wave, a leaf, a cloud!
I fall upon the thorns of life! I bleed!

A heavy weight of hours has chained and bowed
One too like thee: tameless, and swift, and proud.

V

Make me thy lyre, even as the forest is:
What if my leaves are falling like its own!
The tumult of thy mighty harmonies

Will take from both a deep, autumnal tone,   60
Sweet though in sadness. Be thou, Spirit fierce,
My spirit! Be thou me, impetuous one!

Drive my dead thoughts over the universe
Like withered leaves to quicken a new birth!
And, by the incantation of this verse,

Scatter, as from an unextinguished hearth
Ashes and sparks, my words among mankind!
Be through my lips to unawakened earth

The trumpet of a prophecy! O, Wind,
If Winter comes, can Spring be far behind?   70

FOR DISCUSSION:

1. In what verse form is this poem written?

2. In what sense are the leaves in line 5 "pestilence-stricken multitudes"? How is the West Wind both a destroyer and preserver?

3. How do sections I, II, and III relate to each other? How do the first three sections relate to the fourth? How do the first four relate to the fifth? Comment upon internal and external structural patterns in this poem.

4. What is the function of the first tercet of section IV?

5. Modern critics generally think line 54, "I fall upon the thorns of life! I bleed!" is excessively emotional. Is there any justification for it within the context of the poem?

6. Comment on the thematic appropriateness of the embers image in lines 66–67.

7. All four seasons are explicitly mentioned in this poem. What is each season's symbolic function?

To a Skylark

PERCY BYSSHE SHELLEY

 Hail to thee, blithe spirit!
  Bird thou never wert,
 That from heaven, or near it,
  Pourest thy full heart
In profuse strains of unpremeditated art.

 Higher still and higher
  From the earth thou springest
 Like a cloud of fire;
  The blue deep thou wingest,
And singing still dost soar, and soaring ever singest.   10

In the golden lightning
  Of the sunken sun,
O'er which clouds are bright'ning,
  Thou dost float and run;
Like an unbodied joy whose race is just begun.

The pale purple even
  Melts around thy flight;
Like a star of heaven
  In the broad daylight
Thou art unseen, but yet I hear thy shrill delight,   20

Keen as are the arrows
  Of that silver sphere,
Whose intense lamp narrows
  In the white dawn clear,
Until we hardly see, we feel that it is there.

All the earth and air
  With thy voice is loud,
As, when night is bare,
  From one lonely cloud
The moon rains out her beams, and Heaven is overflowed.   30

What thou art we know not;
  What is most like thee?
From rainbow clouds there flow not
  Drops so bright to see
As from thy presence showers a rain of melody.

Like a poet hidden
  In the light of thought,
Singing hymns unbidden,
  Till the world is wrought
To sympathy with hopes and fears it heeded not;   40

Like a high-born maiden
  In a palace-tower,
Soothing her love-laden
  Soul in secret hour
With music sweet as love, which overflows her bower;

Like a glowworm golden
  In a dell of dew,
Scattering unbeholden
  Its aëreal hue
Among the flowers and grass which screen it from the view;   50

Like a rose embowered
  In its own green leaves,
By warm winds deflowered,
  Till the scent it gives
Makes faint with too much sweet those heavy-wingèd thieves.

Sound of vernal showers
   On the twinkling grass,
Rain-awakened flowers,
   All that ever was
Joyous, and clear, and fresh, thy music doth surpass.   60

Teach us, sprite or bird,
   What sweet thoughts are thine;
I have never heard
   Praise of love or wine
That panted forth a flood of rapture so divine.

Chorus Hymeneal,
   Or triumphal chaunt,
Matched with thine, would be all
   But an empty vaunt,
A thing wherein we feel there is some hidden want.   70

What objects are the fountains
   Of thy happy strain?
What fields, or waves, or mountains?
   What shapes of sky or plain?
What love of thine own kind? what ignorance of pain?

With thy clear keen joyance
   Languor cannot be—
Shadow of annoyance
   Never came near thee—
Thou lovest—but ne'er knew love's sad satiety.   80

Waking or asleep,
   Thou of death must deem
Things more true and deep
   Than we mortals dream,
Or how could thy notes flow in such a crystal stream?

We look before and after,
   And pine for what is not;
Our sincerest laughter
   With some pain is fraught;
Our sweetest songs are those that tell of saddest thought.   90

Yet if we could scorn
   Hate, and pride, and fear;
If we were things born
   Not to shed a tear,
I know not how thy joy we ever should come near.

Better than all measures
   Of delightful sound—
Better than all treasures
   That in books are found—
Thy skill to poet were, thou scorner of the ground!   100

Teach me half the gladness
    That thy brain must know,
Such harmonious madness
    From my lips would flow
The world should listen then—as I am listening now.

FOR DISCUSSION:

1. Show how the imagery in stanza 4 (lines 16–20) and stanza 6 (lines 26–30) attempts to describe sound in terms of light. Is this successful?

2. Like most Romantic poets, Shelley makes extensive use of sense imagery. To what senses does he appeal in stanza 10 (lines 46–50)? Stanza 12 (lines 56–60)?

3. What is it that the poet would like to learn from the bird?

4. Comment on the organization and unity of this poem. What are its major divisions?

After Apple-Picking*

ROBERT FROST

My long two-pointed ladder's sticking through a tree
Toward heaven still,
And there's a barrel that I didn't fill
Beside it, and there may be two or three
Apples I didn't pick upon some bough.
But I am done with apple-picking now.
Essence of winter sleep is on the night,
The scent of apples: I am drowsing off.
I cannot rub the strangeness from my sight
I got from looking through a pane of glass   10
I skimmed this morning from the drinking trough
And held against the world of hoary grass.
It melted, and I let it fall and break.
But I was well
Upon my way to sleep before it fell,
And I could tell
What form my dreaming was about to take.
Magnified apples appear and disappear,
Stem end and blossom end,
And every fleck of russet showing clear.   20
My instep arch not only keeps the ache,
It keeps the pressure of a ladder-round.
I feel the ladder sway as the boughs bend.
And I keep hearing from the cellar bin
The rumbling sound
Of load on load of apples coming in.
For I have had too much
Of apple-picking: I am overtired

---

* From COMPLETE POEMS OF ROBERT FROST. Copyright 1923, 1930, 1939 by Holt, Rinehart and Winston, Inc. Copyright 1951, ©1958 by Robert Frost. Reprinted by permission of Holt, Rinehart and Winston, Inc. and Jonathan Cape Ltd.

Of the great harvest I myself desired.
There were ten thousand thousand fruit to touch,
Cherish in hand, lift down, and not let fall.
For all
That struck the earth,
No matter if not bruised or spiked with stubble,
Went surely to the cider-apple heap
As of no worth
One can see what will trouble
This sleep of mine, whatever sleep it is.
Were he not gone,
The woodchuck could say whether it's like his
Long sleep, as I describe its coming on,
Or just some human sleep.

FOR DISCUSSION:

1. What is the tone of this poem? How does Frost achieve it?
2. How is "After Apple-Picking" unified?
3. The temptation to read this poem symbolically is strong. Robert Penn Warren, for instance, believes the harvest refers to the task of writing poetry. Is this position tenable? What other symbolic readings are possible?
4. Is sleep in the poem a metaphor for death? If so, what is Frost's attitude toward death? How does the hibernation of the woodchuck relate to the human sleep of the final line?

When Lilacs Last in the Dooryard Bloom'd

WALT WHITMAN

I

When lilacs last in the dooryard bloom'd,
And the great star early droop'd in the western sky in the night,
I mourn'd, and yet shall mourn with ever-returning spring.

Ever-returning spring, trinity sure to me you bring,
Lilac blooming perennial and drooping star in the west,
And thought of him I love.

II

O powerful western fallen star!
O shades of night—O moody, tearful night!
O great star disappear'd—O the black murk that hides the star!
O cruel hands that hold me powerless—O helpless soul of me!
O harsh surrounding cloud that will not free my soul.

III

In the dooryard fronting an old farm-house near the white-wash'd palings,
Stands the lilac-bush tall-growing with heart-shaped leaves of rich green,
With many a pointed blossom rising delicate, with the perfume strong I love,

With every leaf a miracle—and from this bush in the dooryard,
With delicate-color'd blossoms and heart-shaped leaves of rich green,
A sprig with its flower I break.

IV

In the swamp in secluded recesses,
A shy and hidden bird is warbling a song.

Solitary the thrush,
The hermit withdrawn to himself, avoiding the settlements,
Sings by himself a song.

Song of the bleeding throat,
Death's outlet song of life, (for well dear brother I know,
If thou wast not granted to sing thou would'st surely die.)

V

Over the breast of the spring, the land, amid cities,
Amid lanes and through old woods, where lately the violets peep'd from the ground, spotting the gray debris,
Amid the grass in the fields each side of the lanes, passing the endless grass,
Passing the yellow-spear'd wheat, every grain from its shroud in the dark-brown fields uprisen,
Passing the apple-tree blows of white and pink in the orchards,
Carrying a corpse to where it shall rest in the grave,
Night and day journeys a coffin.

VI

Coffin that passes through lanes and streets,
Through day and night with the great cloud darkening the land,
With the pomp of the inloop'd flags with the cities draped in black,
With the show of the States themselves as of crape-veil'd women standing,
With processions long and winding and the flambeaus of the night,
With the countless torches lit, with the silent sea of faces and the unbared heads,
With the waiting depot, the arriving coffin, and the sombre faces,
With dirges through the night, with the thousand voices rising strong and solemn,
With all the mournful voices of the dirges pour'd around the coffin,
The dim-lit churches and the shuddering organs—where amid these you journey,
With the tolling tolling bells' perpetual clang,
Here, coffin that slowly passes,
I give you my sprig of lilac.

VII

(Nor for you, for one alone,
Blossoms and branches green to coffins all I bring,
For fresh as the morning, thus would I chant a song for you O sane and sacred death.
All over bouquets of roses,
O death, I cover you over with roses and early lilies,
But mostly and now the lilac that blooms the first,

Copious I break, I break the sprigs from the bushes,
With loaded arms I come, pouring for you,
For you and the coffins all of you O death.)

VIII

O western orb sailing the heaven,
Now I know what you must have meant as a month since I walk'd,
As I walk'd in silence the transparent shadowy night,
As I saw you had something to tell as you bent to me night after night,
As you droop'd from the sky low down as if to my side, (while the other stars all look'd on,)
As we wander'd together the solemn night, (for something I know not what kept me from sleep,)
As the night advanced, and I saw on the rim of the west how full you were of woe,
As I stood on the rising ground in the breeze in the cool transparent night,
As I watch'd where you pass'd and was lost in the netherward black of the night,
As my soul in its trouble dissatisfied sank, as where you sad orb,
Concluded, dropt in the night, and was gone.

IX

Sing on there in the swamp,
O singer bashful and tender, I hear your notes, I hear your call,
I hear, I come presently, I understand you,
But a moment I linger, for the lustrous star has detain'd me,
The star my departing comrade holds and detains me.

X

O how shall I warble myself for the dead one there I loved?
And how shall I deck my song for the large sweet soul that has gone?
And what shall my perfume be for the grave of him I love?

Sea-winds blown from east and west,
Blown from the Eastern sea and blown from the Western sea, till there on the prairies meeting,
These and with these and the breath of my chant,
I'll perfume the grave of him I love.

XI

O what shall I hang on the chamber walls?
And what shall the pictures be that I hang on the walls,
To adorn the burial-house of him I love?

Pictures of growing spring and farms and homes,
With the Fourth-month eve at sundown, and the gray smoke lucid and bright,
With floods of the yellow gold of the gorgeous, indolent, sinking sun, burning, expanding the air,
With the fresh sweet herbage under foot, and the pale green leaves of the trees prolific,
In the distance the flowing glaze, the breast of the river, with a wind-dapple here and there,
With ranging hills on the banks, with many a line against the sky, and shadows,
And the city at hand with dwellings so dense, and stacks of chimneys,
And all the scenes of life and the workshops, and the workmen homeward returning.

XII

Lo, body and soul—this land,
My own Manhattan with spires, and the sparkling and hurrying tides, and the ships,
The varied and ample land, the South and the North in the light, Ohio's shores and
        flashing Missouri,
And ever the far-spreading prairies cover'd with grass and corn.

Lo, the most excellent sun so calm and haughty,
The violet and purple morn with just-felt breezes,
The gentle soft-born measureless light,
The miracle spreading bathing all, the fulfill'd noon,
The coming eve delicious, the welcome night and the stars,
Over my cities shining all, enveloping man and land.

XIII

Sing on, sing on you gray-brown bird,
Sing from the swamps, the recesses, pour your chant from the bushes,
Limitless out of the dusk, out of the cedars and pines.

Sing on dearest brother, warble your reedy song,
Loud human song, with voice of uttermost woe.

O liquid and free and tender!
O wild and loose to my soul—O wondrous singer!
You only I hear—yet the star holds me, (but will soon depart,)
Yet the lilac with mastering odor holds me.

XIV

Now while I sat in the day and look'd forth,
In the close of the day with its light and the fields of spring, and the farmers preparing
        their crops,
In the large unconscious scenery of my land with its lakes and forests,
In the heavenly aerial beauty, (after the perturb'd winds and the storms,)
Under the arching heavens of the afternoon swift passing, and the voices of children and
        women,
The many-moving sea-tides, and I saw the ships how they sail'd,
And the summer approaching with richness, and the fields all busy with labor,
And the infinite separate houses, how they all went on, each with its meals and minutia of
        daily usages,
And the streets how their throbbings throbb'd, and the cities pent—lo, then and there,
Falling upon them all and among them all, enveloping me with the rest,
Appear'd the cloud, appear'd the long black trail,
And I knew death, its thought, and the sacred knowledge of death.

Then with the knowledge of death as walking one side of me,
And the thought of death close-walking the other side of me,
And I in the middle as with companions, and as holding the hands of companions,
I fled forth to the hiding receiving night that talks not,
Down to the shores of the water, the path by the swamp in the dimness,
To the solemn shadowy cedars and ghostly pines so still.

And the singer so shy to the rest receiv'd me,
The gray-brown bird I know receiv'd us comrades three,
And he sang the carol of death, and a verse for him I love.

From deep secluded recesses,
From the fragrant cedars and the ghostly pines so still,
Came the carol of the bird.

And the charm of the carol rapt me,
As I held as if by their hands my comrades in the night,
And the voice of my spirit tallied the song of the bird.

Come lovely and soothing death,
Undulate round the world, serenely arriving, arriving,
In the day, in the night, to all, to each,
Sooner or later delicate death.

Prais'd be the fathomless universe,
For life and joy, and for objects and knowledge curious,
And for love, sweet love—but praise! praise! praise!
For the sure-enwinding arms of cool-enfolding death.

Dark mother always gliding near with soft feet,
Have none chanted for thee a chant of fullest welcome?
Then I chant it for thee, I glorify thee above all,
I bring thee a song that when thou must indeed come, come unfalteringly.

Approach strong deliveress,
When it is so, when thou hast taken them I joyously sing the dead,
Lost in the loving floating ocean of thee,
Laved in the flood of thy bliss O death.

From me to thee glad serenades,
Dances for thee I propose saluting thee, adornments and feastings for thee,
And the sights of the open landscape and the high-spread sky are fitting,
And life and the fields, and the huge and thoughtful night.

The night in silence under many a star,
The ocean store and the husky whispering wave whose voice I know,
And the soul turning to thee O vast and well-veil'd death,
And the body gratefully nestling close to thee.

Over the tree-tops I float thee a song,
Over the rising and sinking waves, over the myriad fields and the prairies wide,
Over the dense-pack'd cities all and the teeming wharves and ways,
I float this carol with joy, with joy to thee O death.

XV

To the tally of my soul,
Loud and strong kept up the gray-brown bird,
With pure deliberate notes spreading filling the night.

Loud in the pines and cedars dim,
Clear in the freshness moist and the swamp-perfume,
And I with my comrades there in the night.

While my sight that was bound in my eyes unclosed,
As to long panoramas of visions.

And I saw askant the armies,
I saw as in noiseless dreams hundreds of battle-flags,
Borne through the smoke of the battles and pierc'd with missiles I saw them,
And carried hither and yon through the smoke, and torn and bloody,
And at last but a few shreds left on the staffs, (and all in silence,)
And the staffs all splinter'd and broken.
I saw battle-corpses, myriads of them,
And the white skeletons of young men, I saw them,
I saw the debris and debris of all the slain soldiers of the war,
But I saw they were not as was thought,
They themselves were fully at rest, they suffer'd not,
The living remain'd and suffer'd, the mother suffer'd,
And the wife and the child and the musing comrade suffer'd,
And the armies that remain'd suffer'd.

XVI

Passing the visions, passing the night,
Passing, unloosing the hold of my comrades' hands,
Passing the song of the hermit bird and the tallying song of my soul,
Victorious song, death's outlet song, yet varying ever-altering song,
As low and wailing, yet clear the notes, rising and falling, flooding the night,
Sadly sinking and fainting, as warning and warning, and yet again bursting with joy,
Covering the earth and filling the spread of the heaven,
As that powerful psalm in the night I heard from recesses,
Passing, I leave thee lilac with heart-shaped leaves,
I leave thee there in the dooryard, blooming, returning with spring.

I cease from my song for thee,
From my gaze on thee in the west, fronting the west, communing with thee,
O comrade lustrous with silver face in the night.

Yet each to keep and all, retrievements out of the night,
The song, the wondrous chant of the gray-brown bird,
And the tallying chant, the echo arous'd in my soul,
With the lustrous and drooping star with the countenance full of woe,
With the holders holding my hand nearing the call of the bird,
Comrades mine and I in the midst, and their memory ever to keep, for the dead I loved so well,
For the sweetest, wisest soul of all my days and lands—and this for his dear sake,
Lilac and star and bird twined with the chant of my soul,
There in the fragrant pines and the cedars dusk and dim.

FOR DISCUSSION:

1. The major symbols in this poem are the lilac, star, thrush, and night. What particular attributes of each does Whitman emphasize in his elegy for Lincoln?

2. What are the advantages of waiting until the last word of section V to make explicit that this is a poem about death?

3. What echoes of the major symbols are to be found in section VI? Section X?

4. Section VIII is devoted to intensive development of the star image. Show how Whitman associates the star with grief, Lincoln, night, and death in this section.

5. Section XVI recapitulates and fuses the major symbols. Comment on the final two lines of the poem in this connection.

6. Is Whitman able at any point in the poem to emotionally accept Lincoln's death? In what, if anything, does he take consolation?

7. To what extent is this poem a lamentation of death in general rather than of the death of Lincoln?

The Windhover:*

TO CHRIST OUR LORD

GERARD MANLEY HOPKINS

I caught this morning morning's minion, king-
    dom of daylight's dauphin, dapple-dawn-drawn Falcon, in his riding
  Of the rolling level underneath him steady air, and striding
High there, how he rung upon the rein of a wimpling wing
In his ecstasy! then off, off forth on swing,   5
    As a skate's heel sweeps smooth on a bow-bend: the hurl and gliding
  Rebuffed the big wind. My heart in hiding
Stirred for a bird,—the achieve of, the mastery of the thing!

Brute beauty and valor and act, oh, air, pride, plume, here
    Buckle! AND the fire that breaks from thee then, a billion   10
Times told lovelier, more dangerous, O my chevalier!

    No wonder of it: shéer plód makes plough down sillion
Shine, and blue-bleak embers, ah my dear,
    Fall, gall themselves, and gash gold-vermilion.

FOR DISCUSSION:

1. What is the form of this poem?

2. Note that the use of one-syllable and two-syllable end rhymes mirrors the abba abba pattern of the Petrarchan octave. How does this use of stress contribute to the effect of the poem?

3. Much of the diction is drawn from the medieval period and is intentionally feudal in tone, i.e., "dauphin," "chevalier," "sillion." What is the effect of this device?

4. To whom is "O my chevalier!" in line 11 directed? What is the meaning of "here" in line 9? Identify "thee" in line 10.

5. Many critics, F. R. Leavis, I. A. Richards, and William Empson among them, interpret "The Windhover" as a stoic, ascetic, defeatist poem. What is there to substantiate their view?

6. The word "buckle" can mean "to collapse," "to connect," and "to engage." Which meaning is most likely within the context of the poem?

7. Do the plough and embers images of the sestet provide a parallel or a contrast to the falcon image of the octave?

8. Does the poem's dedication "To Christ Our Lord" assist in interpreting Hopkins's meaning in "The Windhover"? How?

---

* From *Poems of Gerard Manley Hopkins*, Third Edition, edited by W. H. Gardner. Copyright 1948 by Oxford University Press, Inc. Reprinted by permission.

The Force that Through the Green Fuse Drives the Flower*

DYLAN THOMAS

The force that through the green fuse drives the flower
Drives my green age; that blasts the roots of trees
Is my destroyer.
And I am dumb to tell the crooked rose
My youth is bent by the same wintry fever.

The force that drives the water through the rocks
Drives my red blood; that dries the mouthing streams
Turns mine to wax.
And I am dumb to mouth unto my veins
How at the mountain spring the same mouth sucks.

The hand that whirls the water in the pool
Stirs the quicksand; that ropes the blowing wind
Hauls my shroud sail.
And I am dumb to tell the hanging man
How of my clay is made the hangman's lime.

The lips of time leech to the fountain head;
Love drips and gathers, but the fallen blood
Shall calm her sores.
And I am dumb to tell a weather's wind
How time has ticked a heaven round the stars.

And I am dumb to tell the lover's tomb
How at my sheet goes the same crooked worm.

FOR DISCUSSION:

1. Gunpowder is a major image in stanza 1 (lines 1–5). In what sense is the stem of the flower a "fuse"? And does an explosion "blast" the roots of trees in the same sense that the human body ages?

2. What is the meaning of "wintry fever," the oxymoron in line 5.

3. Stanza 2 (lines 6–10) compares mountain streams with the human bloodstream. How forceful and consistent is this comparison?

4. Many readers see Christian imagery in the third and fourth stanzas (the hanging man, fountain head, fallen blood, sores, heaven). Is this poem "religious" in nature, or does Thomas employ such images solely for their connotative value?

5. Is the "crooked worm" in the final stanza an echo of the "crooked rose" in the first? What are the possibilities of multiple interpretations of "dumb," "sheet," "worm"?

6. Does the poem have any discernible structure or pattern of development?

* From THE COLLECTED POEMS OF DYLAN THOMAS. Copyright 1939 by New Directions; 1946 by Dylan Thomas. Reprinted by permission of the publisher, New Directions Publishing Corporation, J. M. Dent & Sons, Ltd., and the literary executors of the Dylan Thomas Estate.

Fern Hill*

DYLAN THOMAS

Now as I was young and easy under the apple boughs
About the lilting house and happy as the grass was green,
   The night above the dingle starry,
     Time let me hail and climb
   Golden in the heydays of his eyes,
And honoured among wagons I was prince of the apple towns
And once below a time I lordly had the trees and leaves
     Trail with daisies and barley
   Down the rivers of the windfall light.

And as I was green and carefree, famous among the barns
About the happy yard and singing as the farm was home,
   In the sun that is young once only,
     Time let me play and be
   Golden in the mercy of his means,
And green and golden I was huntsman and herdsman, the calves
Sang to my horn, the foxes on the hills barked clear and cold,
     And the sabbath rang slowly
   In the pebbles of the holy streams.

All the sun long it was running, it was lovely, the hay
Fields high as the house, the tunes from the chimneys, it was air
   And playing, lovely and watery
     And fire green as grass.
   And nightly under the simple stars
As I rode to sleep the owls were bearing the farm away,
All the moon long I heard, blessed among stables, the nightjars
     Flying with the ricks, and the horses
   Flashing into the dark.

And then to awake, and the farm, like a wanderer white
With the dew, come back, the cock on his shoulder: it was all
   Shining, it was Adam and maiden,
     The sky gathered again
   And the sun grew round that very day.
So it must have been after the birth of the simple light
In the first, spinning place, the spellbound horses walking warm
     Out of the whinnying green stable
   On to the fields of praise.

And honoured among foxes and pheasants by the gay house
Under the new made clouds and happy as the heart was long,
   In the sun born over and over,
     I ran my heedless ways,

---

* From THE COLLECTED POEMS OF DYLAN THOMAS. Copyright 1939 by New Directions; 1946 by Dylan Thomas. Reprinted by permission of the publisher, New Directions Publishing Corporation, J. M. Dent & Sons Ltd., and the literary executors of the Dylan Thomas Estate.

My wishes raced through the house high hay
And nothing I cared, at my sky blue trades, that time allows
In all his tuneful turning so few and such morning songs
   Before the children green and golden
     Follow him out of grace,

Nothing I cared, in the lamb white days, that time would take me
Up to the swallow thronged loft by the shadow of my hand,
   In the moon that is always rising,
     Nor that riding to sleep
   I should hear him fly with the high fields
And wake to the farm forever fled fom the childless land.
Oh as I was young and easy in the mercy of his means,
   Time held me green and dying
     Though I sang in my chains like the sea.

FOR DISCUSSION:

1. What are the similarities in tone, theme, and technique between "Fern Hill" and "The Force that through the Green Fuse Drives the Flower"?

2. William Moynihan in The Craft and Art of Dylan Thomas calls "Fern Hill" the culmination of Thomas's intonational development. In this connection he notes Thomas's employment of prepositionals (over, under, about), syllabic compounds (soundfall, light), and variations on folk sayings (once below a time, all the sun long). What other literary techniques does Thomas use in this poem? What is their effect?

3. Some commentators see four patterns of images in this poem: (a) lordliness, (b) day and dark, (c) greenness, and (d) religious reality. Trace these throughout the poem showing how Thomas integrates each with the major symbol of the farm and the major theme of the transience of youth and joy.

4. "Fern Hill" is a poem about time. What is Thomas's attitude toward the process of maturation?

5. Do the final two lines mean that as the sea is chained to natural forces (the moon), so Thomas is subject to the chains of time? Or do they mean that perfect experiences can take place only in time but time is eventually responsible for the destruction of both the experience and the one who experiences, and that this struggle between happiness and transience is as eternal as the sea?

A Valediction: Forbidding Mourning

JOHN DONNE

As virtuous men passe mildly away,
   And whisper to their soules, to goe,
Whilst some of their sad friends doe say,
   The breath goes now, and some say, no:

So let us melt, and make no noise,
   No teare-floods, nor sigh-tempests move,
T'were prophanation of our joyes
   To tell the layetie our love.

Moving of th'earth brings harmes and feares,
   Men reckon what it did and meant,   10
But trepidation of the spheares,
   Though greater farre, is innocent.

Dull sublunary lovers love
   (Whose soule is sense) cannot admit
Absence because it doth remove
   Those things which elemented it.

But we by a love, so much refin'd,
   That our selves know not what it is,
Inter-assured of the mind,
   Care less, eyes, lips, and hands to misse.   20

Our two soules therefore, which are one,
   Though I must goe, endure not yet
A breach, but an expansion,
   Like gold to ayery thinnesse beate.

If they be two, they are two so
   As stiffe twin compasses are two,
Thy soule the fixt foot, makes no show
   To move, but doth, if the'other doe.

And though it in the center sit,
   Yet when the other far doth rome,   30
It leanes, and hearkens after it,
   And growes erect, as that comes home.

Such wilt thou be to mee, who must
   Like th'other foot, obliquely runne;
Thy firmnes makes my circle just,
   And makes me end, where I begunne.

FOR DISCUSSION:

1. What is a valediction?
2. The titular word "mourning" and the opening image seem to suggest the subject of this poem is death. Is this necessarily true, or is Donne speaking of absence of any kind?
3. Comment on Donne's use of chemical and religious imagery.
4. A conceit is a farfetched comparison or metaphor. Perhaps the most famous of all metaphysical conceits, the image in lines 25–36 compares the poet's love to a draftsman's compass. Is this a good comparison? What does Donne mean by lines 31–32, "It leanes and hearkens after it,/And growes erect as that comes home"? Does the comparison break down in the final stanza?

Ode on a Grecian Urn

JOHN KEATS

I

Thou still unravish'd bride of quietness,
   Thou foster-child of silence and slow time,
Sylvan historian, who canst thus express
   A flowery tale more sweetly than our rhyme:

What leaf-fring'd legend haunts about thy shape
  Of deities or mortals, or both,
    In Tempe or the dales of Arcady?
  What men or gods are these? What maidens loth?
What mad pursuit? What struggle to escape?
    What pipes and timbrels? What wild ecstasy?

II

Heard melodies are sweet, but those unheard
  Are sweeter; therefore, ye soft pipes, play on;
Not to the sensual ear, but, more endear'd,
  Pipe to the spirit ditties of no tone:
Fair youth, beneath the trees, thou canst not leave
  Thy song, nor ever can those trees be bare;
    Bold Lover, never, never canst thou kiss,
Though winning near the goal—yet, do not grieve;
  She cannot fade, though thou hast not thy bliss,
    For ever wilt thou love, and she be fair!

III

Ah, happy, happy boughs! that cannot shed
  Your leaves, nor ever bid the Spring adieu;
And, happy melodist, unwearied,
  For ever piping songs for ever new;
More happy love! more happy, happy love!
  For ever warm and still to be enjoy'd,
    For ever panting, and for ever young;
All breathing human passion far above,
  That leaves a heart high-sorrowful and cloy'd,
    A burning forehead, and a parching tongue.

IV

Who are these coming to the sacrifice?
  To what green altar, O mysterious priest,
Lead'st thou that heifer lowing at the skies,
  And all her silken flanks with garlands drest?
What little town by river or sea shore,
  Or mountain-built which peaceful citadel,
    Is emptied of this folk, this pious morn?
And, little town, thy streets for evermore
  Will silent be; and not a soul to tell
    Why thou art desolate, can e'er return.

V

O Attic shape! Fair attitude! with brede
  Of marble men and maidens overwrought,
With forest branches and the trodden weed;
  Thou, silent form, dost tease us out of thought
As doth eternity: Cold Pastoral!

When old age shall this generation waste,
　Thou shalt remain, in midst of other woe
　Than ours, a friend to man, to whom thou say'st,
"Beauty is truth, truth beauty,"—that is all
　Ye know on earth, and all ye need to know.　　50

FOR DISCUSSION:

1. The first two stanzas are structured around a series of paradoxes and contrasts. Identify them and show how Keats unifies his poem by the use of these devices.

2. What is the meaning of "still" in line 1; of "brede" in line 41?

3. How is the last stanza related to the first four?

4. In what way is the urn a "sylvan historian"?

5. Does the identification of truth and beauty in line 49 mean (a) art is always ready to ennoble man by lifting him above his transient life if even for a brief period, (b) ultimate reality is apprehended not by reason but by the imagination, (c) all ideals harmonize in a world of Platonic reality, (d) something else?

6. Who is the "ye" of the final line?

III Critical Perspective: PSYCHOLOGICAL

Introduction

Psychology, because it explores man's mental life in order to explain the growth, development, and structure of the human mind, has become a convenient tool for investigators in a number of different fields—philosophy, medicine, and sociology to name only a few. Interest in the nature of man's mental makeup, the relation of his body to his mind, and the causes for his behavior are as old as Aristotle. Not until comparatively recently, however, has literary criticism adapted the theories and findings of psychologists to the analysis of literature in a systematic and formal manner.

Psychology began to evolve as a science in its own right only at the close of the nineteenth century. Since then, it has done much to add to our understanding of the human animal. Always alert to nonliterary sources for ideas relevant to their field, literary critics have paid increasing attention to developments in modern psychology. In searching to understand as best they can artistic expression and its makers, critics have used Carl Jung's theories of the collective unconscious and introversion-extraversion; Alfred Adler's views on man's will to power and the inferiority complex; and Otto Rank's investigations into the role played by the will as the main integrative power of man's personality.

Of prime interest, however, to critics of literature are the theories of modern psychoanalysis which deal mainly with the treatment of psychologically maladjusted persons and focus on the reasons for their disturbances. This aspect of psychology explores the forces affecting personality development and emphasizes the conflicts, anxieties, frustrations, and inadequacies that make the individual what he is. Psychoanalysis has emphasized abnormalities and disturbances in the psychic world rather than mental health because it is primarily a therapeutic discipline and seeks causes for irrational behavior as a means toward treatment and cure. The foremost figure in psychoanalysis, and the strongest influence on the psychological criticism of literature, is Sigmund Freud (1856–1939).

The psychological implications of literature have long been recognized by creative writers, who seem to have intuitively perceived that in their observations of human behavior they deal with the basic drives, anxieties, and motivating forces of human nature. In their literary works the world's great writers—Sophocles, Shakespeare, Cervantes, and Dostoyevsky among others—provide modern scientists with case histories of various mental processes that are of great value in improving our understanding of ourselves. Freud himself often acknowledged his debt to the great literary artists of the world. He looked upon his own contribution as the collecting of clinical evidence to support what they had already revealed. And when he wrote, "Not I, but the poets discovered the unconscious," he fully understood that in their descriptions of the actions of men, literary artists have increased our perception of man.

Not all of Freud's work, of course, is adaptable to literary criticism. At least five of his basic ideas, however, have been influential in altering the critical thinking of the twentieth century. They are (1) the primacy of the unconscious, (2) the threefold organization of the psyche into the id, ego, and superego, (3) the assertion that dreams are an expression of the unconscious mind, (4) the conception of infantile behavior as essentially sexual, and (5) the relation between neurosis and creativity. These concepts are not really separate but interdependent, one leading to another. Let us examine these fundamental tenets of Freudian psychology and note briefly how each has been applied in literary criticism.

Freud's interest in man's mental makeup started in Vienna in the 1880's as he began to realize that dynamic forces were causing the distress of his patients. Unable to find physical causes to account for their complaints, he assumed the possibility that psychological factors unknown to the patients caused their disorders. He was to devote his entire life to exploring and developing his hypothesis and its implications. Referring to the central concern of his life many years later Freud wrote, "My life has been aimed at one goal only: to infer or guess how the mental apparatus is constructed and what forces interplay and counteract in it."

His investigation led him to what has become the most influential single idea of modern psychiatry: the primacy of the unconscious. Freud believed that the mind of man was like an iceberg. Consciousness was represented by the small upper section, and the larger part, the unconscious mind, was hidden in the murky blackness below the surface of awareness. Not only did he divide the mind into conscious and unconscious portions, but he argued for the supremacy of the latter as the determining force in human behavior.

The role played by the unconscious is especially difficult to assess accurately because on the surface the individual may seem to be aware of his desires, goals, and objectives. Freud found, however, that often great differences exist between real and apparent motives for behavior and that even the individual—or indeed especially the individual—is unable to tell the difference. The accident-prone individual, for instance, attributes his misfortunes to carelessness, but his accidents may be the result of an unconscious desire to bring harm upon himself and thereby inflict self-punishment for some guilt deeply seated in his unconscious mind. Or to take another example, the overweight girl who is unable to diet despite her obvious need to restrict her food intake defends her inability to control her appetite by saying that she simply likes food. Her compulsion to eat, however, may mask an unconscious fear of men and a consequent need to appear physically unattractive to them so that the occasion for intimacy will never arise.

Feeling the need to define the relationship of the conscious to the unconscious mind more clearly, Freud developed the concept of the tripartite division of the human psyche: the id, ego, and superego (pp. 288–301). He defined the id as the seat of man's pleasure principle and libidinous drives. Unconscious, instinctual, amoral, illogical, and totally without precaution or anxiety, it is the source of all repressed desires and is relentless in its demands for total satisfaction and fulfillment of its biological demands. But if a force such as the id were let loose in the world unbridled and unrestrained, it would ultimately destroy the total personality of the individual, who can survive only in an orderly social structure of other individuals. Because we live in communion with other men, total satisfaction of basic drives is rarely if ever possible. It is here that the ego serves a necessary function in the Freudian psychic superstructure.

Just as the id is governed by the pleasure principle, the ego is dominated by the reality principle, that is, since pleasure is not always immediately attainable in a manner that is advantageous to the total personality, the id's demands must be postponed or altered into drives that are attainable. The ego's function is to recognize the opportune moment for gratification of the id's drives or to channel them into socially acceptable channels. In a well-balanced individual, the ego and id are in harmony; repression and neurosis result, however, when the two are in severe conflict.

Because of its very nature, the unconscious is not susceptible to direct examination or investigation. At times, however, as in hypnosis, sleep, or during "unintentional" slips of the tongue the unconscious reveals itself and information about it can be obtained. Upon these occasions, whether in literature or life, critics and psychoanalysts attempt to understand an individual's behavior. The conscious mind is then not completely in control of the body and the censorial functions of the ego are relaxed, allowing the id to express itself with a directness not normally permitted.

To think that the unconscious can express itself directly in sleep, however, is a mistake. So powerful is the censorial capacity of the ego that even in dreams it must usually express itself indirectly—in symbols. Freud believed that dreams are the language of the unconscious and that they speak of repressions and unfulfilled desires. For this reason critics view dream analysis as a major avenue into the unconscious mind of an author or literary character. When the dream veers too close to reality, when the symbolism becomes too transparent, the dreamer usually awakens. Once awake, with the ego again in complete control of the psyche, the dreamer finds that he is sure that he has dreamt but is unable to remember what he has dreamt.

Since the ego is most likely to repress sexual drives, disciples of Freud believe physical objects in dreams are sexual symbols. These objects, as they bear formal resemblances to male and female sexual parts, serve sexual roles in an individual's psychic landscape. Thus, wells, tunnels, rings, domes, cups, and mountains are female symbols; trees, arrows, lances, and keys are male symbols. This aspect of Freudian psychology has suffered the wildest exploitation and abuse. Freud himself always argued that the dream symbols were highly personal and individualistic and therefore not reducible to interpretation on a universal scale. Despite his disavowal of the "dream book" approach to psychology, sexual symbols remain common tools in modern psychoanalytic criticism, and one need only read the dream visions of medieval literature, the somnolent visions of Shelley and Keats, the adventures of Alice in Wonderland, or the dreams of Lockwood in Wuthering Heights and Raskolnikov in Crime and Punishment to appreciate the variety of literature which lends itself to this sort of critical treatment.

The third major subdivision of the psyche is the superego. The major source of guilt feelings in the Freudian system, the superego is an outgrowth of the ego. Formed by the parental standards of behavior instilled in the individual in his youth, the superego functions as conscience, or moral observer of the ego's activities and decisions. Freud believed that the developing child tends to identify with his parents, and that during this period of time the parental image, commands, and moral values are internalized and assimilated by the child. The superego is receptive in later life to other outside moral influences (e.g., church and school), but fundamentally it preserves the ethical character given by early parental domination.

Indeed, Freud believed that the sexual nature of the infantile stage in personality development was largely overlooked by his predecessors. This period, when the id is being formed along lines that will influence behavior for the entire life of the individual, was for Freud the most important stage in the development of personality. Repressions and neuroses formed at this time act as tyrannical forces that demand expression in later life against the wishes of a mature ego and superego. The infant's mind, in Freud's view, is also animated by sexual and hostile motives toward one parent or the other. Small boys, for instance, go through an Oedipal phase, that is, a period when they desire sexual possession of their mother and view their father with the hostility due a rival for her affections. This is a central point in Ernest Jones's interpretation of Hamlet, and Freud, seeing the Oedipal stage as fairly common in literature, noted its appearance not only in Shakespeare's play but in Oedipus Rex and The Brothers Karamazov as well.

From his dual interest in the unconscious mind and in literature, Freud turned his attention to the psychological nature of creative expression itself. He frequently insisted that science has no real explanation for the gift of creativity, that the sources of inspiration are too many, too varied, and too deeply imbedded in the psyche to yield to the probing of the investigator. Despite this attitude, much of his writing is directly or indirectly concerned with artistic expression. Not only did he write monographs on Michelangelo, Goethe, Shakespeare, Dostoyevsky, and Da Vinci but his essays are filled with literary allusions, images, and techniques.

Freud's attitude toward art is curiously ambivalent. On the one hand, he conceives of artistic expression as a harmless escape into a world of daydreams, fantasies, and illusions. The author, an introverted personality to begin with, transfers his psychosexual drives from the real world into a world of wish fulfillment. Thus conceived, art becomes almost pure pleasure principle. The artist is seen as an unstable personality whose artistic expression is a kind of therapy which allows him to express his neurosis in a socially acceptable manner. In Lectures on Psycho-Analysis, Freud wrote:

I should like to direct your attention for a moment to a side of fantasy-life of very general interest. There is in fact a path from fantasy back again to reality, and that is—art. The artist has also an introverted disposition and has not far to go to become a neurotic. He is one who is urged on by instinctual needs which are too clamorous. He longs to attain to honor, power, riches, fame, and the love of women; but he lacks the means of achieving these gratifications. So, like any other with an unsatisfied longing, he turns away from reality and transfers all his interest, and all his libido too, to the creation of his wishes in the life of fantasy, from which the way might readily lead to neurosis.

At the same time, however, Freud believed that in solving his own psychic problems, the author frequently not only relieves his neurotic tensions but provides insights and revelations into the nature of reality not allowed less gifted men. "Creative writers," he declared in Delusions and Dreams, "are valuable allies and their evidence is to be prized highly, for they are apt to know a whole host of things between heaven and earth of which our philosophy has not yet let us dream."

Freud's theories have proven especially popular with a group of literary critics who make use of his findings in two ways; one group focuses on the writer and the other focuses on his creations. The first approach is based upon the conception of literature as an expression of the author's unconscious mind and uses the work of art as a tool in psychoanalyzing its author. This approach is most effective with writers whose biographies are well known and who have had histories of severe mental distress or who were unable to relate to their parents, wives, friends, or lovers in what society considers normal fashion. Using this application of Freudian psychology, critics have scrutinized the works of such writers and have written studies of the sadomasochism of Algernon Swinburne, the latent homosexuality of Walt Whitman, the schizophrenia of August Strindberg, the Oedipal attachment of Marcel Proust, and the manic depression of Jonathan Swift.

The second approach accepts for critical purposes fictional characters as real, as having had an infancy and early childhood which may not be described in the work of art but which the critic thinks are implied by the characters' actions. This type of psychoanalytic criticism emphasizes the unconscious motivations of fictional characters. It is particularly effective in analyzing characters who are in mental turmoil, who vacillate between several courses of action, or who are unable to account for their own behavior. The classic example of this application of psychology to literature is Ernest Jones's essay on Hamlet (pp. 379–387), where Hamlet's treatment of Ophelia, his killing of Polonius in Gertrude's boudoir, and his reluctance to take revenge against his mother despite her probable complicity in the murder are all explained by an unconscious childhood desire to possess his mother sexually, a drive which still demands fulfillment.

The union between psychology and literature has not always been a happy one. Disturbed by what they consider critical excesses, some commentators have advanced serious objections to this critical mode. They resent some literary critics' tendencies toward misapplication and oversimplification of Freud's ideas. At its worst psychological criticism has resulted in a frenetic search for phallic symbols with little or no attempt to integrate the symbols into any coherent plan or overview of the work. Even the practice of psychoanalyzing fictional characters has been attacked as a perversion of clinical techniques by those professional analysts who think that analysis of a literary hero is not at all like analysis of a real patient. In real life the analyst develops a rapport with the patient, notes his facial reactions to questions, is able to direct the topic into whatever channels he desires, and usually has available the patient's childhood memories and documents that corroborate or controvert those memories. None of these techniques is available to the literary critic. To reach conclusions, therefore, about the psychic disturbances of Oedipus, Hamlet, or Raskolnikov based upon limited acquaintance at a distance of centuries with a character who does not exist is, many believe, an improper use of psychoanalysis.

When psychology focuses its attention on the dead author rather than his creations, the analytic process has all the above shortcomings and another besides. Even when the subject is an avowed follower of Freudian doctrine such as Sherwood Anderson, Eugene O'Neill, or D. H. Lawrence, the analysis of the author rather than of *Winesburg, Ohio*, *Mourning Becomes Electra*, or *Sons and Lovers* is simply not literary criticism. Literature is more than a vehicle for psychological insight into creative writers. As the formalists believe, such analytical activity may be enjoyable, profitable, educational, and valuable, but it is not literary because it moves a step away from the work of art into the realm of biography.

Despite these shortcomings, the influence of Sigmund Freud on literary criticism has generally been a beneficial one. By emphasizing matters of human personality and behavior, he illuminated the dark corners of our innermost worlds. Critics would surely be remiss in their search for truth if they did not apply the findings of modern science to literary interpretation, the better to reveal us to ourselves.

The Dissection of the Psychical Personality*[1]

SIGMUND FREUD

Ladies and Gentlemen,—I know you are aware in regard to your own relations, whether with people or things, of the importance of your starting-point. This was also the case with psycho-analysis. It has not been a matter of indifference for the course of its development or for the reception it met with that it began its work on what is, of all the contents of the mind, most foreign to the ego—on symptoms. Symptoms are derived from the repressed, they are, as it were, its representatives before the ego; but the repressed is foreign territory to the ego—internal foreign territory—just as reality (if you will forgive the unusual expression) is external foreign territory. The path led from symptoms to the unconscious, to the life of the instincts, to sexuality; and it was then that psycho-analysis was met by the brilliant objection that human beings are not merely sexual creatures but have nobler and higher impulses as well. It might have been added that, exalted by their consciousness of these higher impulses, they often assume the right to think nonsense and to neglect facts.

You know better. From the very first we have said that human beings fall ill of a conflict between the claims of instinctual life and the resistance which arises within them against it; and not for a moment have we forgotten this resisting, repelling, repressing agency, which we thought of as equipped with its special forces, the ego-instincts, and which coincides with the ego of popular psychology. The truth was merely that, in view of the laborious nature of the progress made by scientific work, even psycho-analysis was not able to study every field simultaneously and to express its views on every problem in a single breath. But at last the point was reached when it was possible for us to divert our attention from the repressed to the repressing forces, and we faced this ego, which had seemed so self-evident, with the secure expectation that here once again we should find things for which we could not have been prepared. It was not easy, however, to find a first approach; and that is what I intend to talk to you about to-day.

I must, however, let you know of my suspicion that this account of mine of ego-psychology will affect you differently from the introduction into the psychical underworld which preceded it. I cannot say with certainty why this should be so. I thought first that you would discover that whereas what I reported to you previously were, in the main, facts, however strange and peculiar, now you will be listening principally to opinions—that is, to speculations. But that does not meet the position. After further consideration

---

* Reprinted from *New Introductory Lectures on Psycho-Analysis* . . . , THE STANDARD EDITION OF THE COMPLETE PSYCHOLOGICAL WORKS OF SIGMUND FREUD, Translated from the German under the General Editorship of James Strachey, XXII, 57–80. Reprinted by permission of The Hogarth Press Ltd., Sigmund Freud Copyrights Ltd., and W. W. Norton & Company, Inc. Copyright © 1965, 1964 by James Strachey. [Notes are from the *Standard Ed.*, unless otherwise indicated—Ed.]

[1] [The greater part of the material in this lecture is derived (with some amplifications) from Chapters I, II, III and V of *The Ego and the Id* (1923b).]

I must maintain that the amount of intellectual working-over of the factual material in our ego-psychology is not much greater than it was in the psychology of the neuroses. I have been obliged to reject other explanations as well of the result I anticipate: I now believe that it is somehow a question of the nature of the material itself and of our being unaccustomed to dealing with it. In any case, I shall not be surprised if you show yourselves even more reserved and cautious in your judgement than hitherto.

The situation in which we find ourselves at the beginning of our enquiry may be expected itself to point the way for us. We wish to make the ego the matter of our enquiry, our very own ego. But is that possible? After all, the ego is in its very essence a subject; how can it be made into an object? Well, there is no doubt that it can be. The ego can take itself as an object, can treat itself like other objects, can observe itself, criticize itself, and do Heaven knows what with itself. In this, one part of the ego is setting itself over against the rest. So the ego can be split; it splits itself during a number of its functions—temporarily at least. Its parts can come together again afterwards. That is not exactly a novelty, though it may perhaps be putting an unusual emphasis on what is generally known. On the other hand, we are familiar with the notion that pathology, by making things larger and coarser, can draw our attention to normal conditions which would otherwise have escaped us. Where it points to a breach or a rent, there may normally be an articulation present. If we throw a crystal to the floor, it breaks; but not into haphazard pieces. It comes apart along its lines of cleavage into fragments whose boundaries, though they were invisible, were predetermined by the crystal's structure. Mental patients are split and broken structures of this same kind. Even we cannot withhold from them something of the reverential awe which peoples of the past felt for the insane. They have turned away from external reality, but for that very reason they know more about internal, psychical reality and can reveal a number of things to us that would otherwise be inaccessible to us.

We describe one group of these patients as suffering from delusions of being observed. They complain to us that perpetually, and down to their most intimate actions, they are being molested by the observation of unknown powers—presumably persons—and that in hallucinations they hear these persons reporting the outcome of their observation: 'now he's going to say this, now he's dressing to go out' and so on. Observation of this sort is not yet the same thing as persecution, but it is not far from it; it presupposes that people distrust them, and expect to catch them carrying out forbidden actions for which they would be punished. How would it be if these insane people were right, if in each of us there is present in his ego an agency like this which observes and threatens to punish, and which in them has merely become sharply divided from their ego and mistakenly displaced into external reality?

I cannot tell whether the same thing will happen to you as to me. Ever since, under the powerful impression of this clinical picture, I formed the idea that the separation of the observing agency from the rest of the ego might be a regular feature of the ego's structure, that idea has never left me, and I was driven to investigate the further characteristics and connections of the agency which was thus separated off. The next step is quickly taken. The content of the delusions of being observed already suggests that the observing is only a preparation for judging and punishing, and we accordingly guess that another function of this agency must be what we call our conscience. There is scarcely anything else in us that we so regularly separate from our ego and so easily set over against it as precisely our conscience. I feel an inclination to do something that I think will give me pleasure, but I abandon it on the ground that my conscience does not allow it. Or I have let myself be persuaded by too great an expectation of pleasure into doing something to which the voice of conscience has objected and after the deed my conscience punishes me with distressing reproaches and causes me to feel remorse for the deed. I might simply say that the special agency which I am beginning to distinguish in the ego is conscience. But it is more prudent to keep the agency as something independent and to suppose that conscience is one of its functions and that self-observation, which is an essential preliminary to the judging activity of conscience, is another of them. And since when we recognize that something has a separate existence we give it a name of its own, from this time forward I will describe this agency in the ego as the 'super-ego'.

I am now prepared to hear you ask me scornfully whether our ego-psychology comes down to nothing more than taking commonly used abstractions literally and in a crude sense, and transforming them from concepts into things—by which not much would be gained. To this I would reply that in ego-psychology it will be difficult to escape what is universally known; it will rather be a question of new ways of looking at things and new ways of arranging them than of new discoveries. So hold to your contemptuous criticism for the time being and await further explanations. The facts of pathology give our efforts a background that you would look for in vain in popular psychology. So I will proceed.

Hardly have we familiarized ourselves with the idea of a super-ego like this which enjoys a certain degree of autonomy, follows its own intentions and is independent of the ego for its supply of energy, than a clinical picture forces itself on our notice which throws a striking light on the severity of this agency and indeed its cruelty, and on its changing relations to the ego. I am thinking of the condition of melancholia,[2] or, more precisely, of melancholic attacks, which you too will have heard plenty about, even if you are not psychiatrists. The most striking feature of this illness, of whose causation and mechanism we know much too little, is the way in which the super-ego—'conscience', you may call it, quietly—treats the ego. While a melancholic can, like other people, show a greater or lesser degree of severity to himself in his healthy periods, during a melancholic attack his super-ego becomes over-severe, abuses the poor ego, humiliates it and ill-treats it, threatens it with the direst punishments, reproaches it for actions in the remotest past which had been taken lightly at the time—as though it had spent the whole interval in collecting accusations and had only been waiting for its present access of strength in order to bring them up and make a condemnatory judgement on their basis. The super-ego applies the strictest moral standard to the helpless ego which is at its mercy; in general it represents the claims of morality, and we realize all at once that our moral sense of guilt is the expression of the tension between the ego and the super-ego. It is a most remarkable experience to see morality, which is supposed to have been given us by God and thus deeply implanted in us, functioning [in these patients] as a periodic phenomenon. For after a certain number of months the whole moral fuss is over, the criticism of the super-ego is silent, the ego is rehabilitated and again enjoys all the rights of man till the next attack. In some forms of the disease, indeed, something of a contrary sort occurs in the intervals; the ego finds itself in a blissful state of intoxication, it celebrates a triumph, as though the super-ego had lost all its strength or had melted into the ego; and this liberated, manic ego permits itself a truly uninhibited satisfaction of all its appetites. Here are happenings rich in unsolved riddles!

No doubt you will expect me to give you more than a mere illustration when I inform you that we have found out all kinds of things about the formation of the super-ego —that is to say, about the origin of conscience. Following a well-known pronouncement of Kant's which couples the conscience within us with the starry Heavens, a pious man

---

[2] [Modern terminology would probably speak of 'depression'.]

might well be tempted to honour these two things as the masterpieces of creation. The stars are indeed magnificent, but as regards conscience God has done an uneven and careless piece of work, for a large majority of men have brought along with them only a modest amount of it or scarcely enough to be worth mentioning. We are far from overlooking the portion of psychological truth that is contained in the assertion that conscience is of divine origin; but the thesis needs interpretation. Even if conscience is something 'within us', yet it is not so from the first. In this it is a real contrast to sexual life, which is in fact there from the beginning of life and not only a later addition. But, as is well known, young children are amoral and possess no internal inhibitions against their impulses striving for pleasure. The part which is later taken on by the super-ego is played to begin with by an external power, by parental authority. Parental influence governs the child by offering proofs of love and by threatening punishments which are signs to the child of loss of love and are bound to be feared on their own account. This realistic anxiety is the precursor of the later moral anxiety.[3] So long as it is dominant there is no need to talk of a super-ego and of a conscience. It is only subsequently that the secondary situation develops (which we are all too ready to regard as the normal one), where the external restraint is internalized and the super-ego takes the place of the parental agency and observes, directs and threatens the ego in exactly the same way as earlier the parents did with the child.

The super-ego, which thus takes over the power, function and even the methods of the parental agency, is however not merely its successor but actually the legitimate heir of its body. It proceeds directly out of it, we shall learn presently by what process. First, however, we must dwell upon a discrepancy between the two. The super-ego seems to have made a one-sided choice and to have picked out only the parents' strictness and severity, their prohibiting and punitive function, whereas their loving care seems not to have been taken over and maintained. If the parents have really enforced their authority with severity we can easily understand the child's in turn developing a severe super-ego. But, contrary to our expectation, experience shows that the super-ego can acquire the same characteristic of relentless severity even if the upbringing had been mild and kindly and had so far as possible avoided threats and punishments. We shall come back later to this contradiction when we deal with the transformations of instinct during the formation of the super-ego.

I cannot tell you as much as I should like about the metamorphosis of the parental relationship into the super-ego, partly because that process is so complicated that an account of it will not fit into the framework of an introductory course of lectures such as I am trying to give you, but partly also because we ourselves do not feel sure that we understand it completely. So you must be content with the sketch that follows.

The basis of the process is what is called an 'identification'—that is to say, the assimilation of one ego to another one,[4] as a result of which the first ego behaves like the second in certain respects, imitates it and in a sense takes it up into itself. Identification has been not unsuitably compared with the oral, cannibalistic incorporation of the other person. It is a very important form of attachment to someone else, probably the very first; and not the same thing as the choice of an object. The difference between the two can be expressed in some such way as this. If a boy identifies himself with his father, he wants to *be like* his father; if he makes him the object of his choice, he wants to *have*

---

[3] ['*Gewissensangst*', literally 'conscience anxiety'. Some discussion of the word will be found in an Editor's footnote to *Inhibitions, Symptoms and Anxiety, Standard Ed.*, 20, 128.]

[4] [I.e. one ego coming to resemble another one.]

him, to possess him. In the first case his ego is altered on the model of his father; in the second case that is not necessary. Identification and object-choice are to a large extent independent of each other; it is however possible to identify oneself with someone whom, for instance, one has taken as a sexual object, and to alter one's ego on his model. It is said that the influencing of the ego by the sexual object occurs particularly often with women and is characteristic of femininity. I must already have spoken to you in my earlier lectures of what is by far the most instructive relation between identification and object-choice. It can be observed equally easily in children and adults, in normal as in sick people. If one has lost an object or has been obliged to give it up, one often compensates oneself by identifying oneself with it and by setting it up once more in one's ego, so that here object-choice regresses, as it were, to identification.[5]

I myself am far from satisfied with these remarks on identification; but it will be enough if you can grant me that the installation of the super-ego can be described as a successful instance of identification with the parental agency. The fact that speaks decisively for this view is that this new creation of a superior agency within the ego is most intimately linked with the destiny of the Oedipus complex, so that the super-ego appears as the heir of that emotional attachment which is of such importance for childhood. With his abandonment of the Oedipus complex a child must, as we can see, renounce the intense object-cathexes which he has deposited with his parents, and it is as a compensation for this loss of objects that there is such a strong intensification of the identifications with his parents which have probably long been present in his ego. Identifications of this kind as precipitates of object-cathexes that have been given up will be repeated often enough later in the child's life; but it is entirely in accordance with the emotional importance of this first instance of such a transformation that a special place in the ego should be found for its outcome. Close investigation has shown us, too, that the super-ego is stunted in its strength and growth if the surmounting of the Oedipus complex is only incompletely successful. In the course of development the super-ego also takes on the influences of those who have stepped into the place of parents—educators, teachers, people chosen as ideal models. Normally it departs more and more from the original parental figures; it becomes, so to say, more impersonal. Nor must it be forgotten that a child has a different estimate of its parents at different periods of its life. At the time at which the Oedipus complex gives place to the super-ego they are something quite magnificent; but later they lose much of this. Identifications then come about with these later parents as well, and indeed they regularly make important contributions to the formation of character; but in that case they only affect the ego, they no longer influence the super-ego, which has been determined by the earliest parental imagos.[6]

I hope you have already formed an impression that the hypothesis of the super-ego really describes a structural relation and is not merely a personification of some such abstraction as that of conscience. One more important function remains to be mentioned which we attribute to this super-ego. It is also the vehicle of the ego ideal by which the ego measures itself, which it emulates, and whose demand for ever greater perfection it strives to fulfil. There is no doubt that this ego ideal is the precipitate of the old picture

---

[5] [The matter is in fact only very briefly alluded to in the Introductory Lectures (see the later part of Lecture XXVI, Standard Ed., 16, 427–428). Identification was the subject of Chapter VII of Group Psychology (1921c), ibid., 18, 150 ff. The formation of the super-ego was discussed at length in Chapter III of The Ego and the Id (1823b), ibid., 19, 28 ff.] [The Ego and the Id is also available in an edition published by Norton in 1961—Ed.]

[6] [This point was discussed by Freud in a paper on 'The Economic Problem of Masochism' (1924c), Standard Ed., 19, 168, where, incidentally, an Editorial footnote deals with Freud's use of the term 'imago'.]

of the parents, the expression of admiration for the perfection which the child then attributed to them.[7]

I am sure you have heard a great deal of the sense of inferiority which is supposed particularly to characterize neurotics. It especially haunts the pages of what are known as *belles lettres*. An author who uses the term 'inferiority complex' thinks that by so doing he has fulfilled all the demands of psycho-analysis and has raised his composition to a higher psychological plane. In fact 'inferiority complex' is a technical term that is scarcely used in psycho-analysis. For us it does not bear the meaning of anything simple, let alone elementary. To trace it back to the self-perception of possible organic defects, as the school of what are known as 'Individual Psychologists'[8] likes to do, seems to us a short-sighted error. The sense of inferiority has strong erotic roots. A child feels inferior if he notices that he is not loved, and so does an adult. The only bodily organ which is really regarded as inferior is the atrophied penis, a girl's clitoris.[9] But the major part of the sense of inferiority derives from the ego's relation to its super-ego; like the sense of guilt it is an expression of the tension between them. Altogether, it is hard to separate the sense of inferiority and the sense of guilt. It would perhaps be right to regard the former as the erotic complement to the moral sense of inferiority. Little attention has been given in psycho-analysis to the question of the delimitation of the two concepts.

If only because the inferiority complex has become so popular, I will venture to entertain you here with a short digression. A historical personality of our own days, who is still alive though at the moment he has retired into the background, suffers from a defect in one of his limbs owing to an injury at the time of his birth. A very well-known contemporary writer who is particularly fond of compiling the biographies of celebrities has dealt, among others, with the life of the man I am speaking of.[10] Now in writing a biography it may well be difficult to suppress a need to plumb the psychological depths. For this reason our author has ventured on an attempt to erect the whole of the development of his hero's character on the sense of inferiority which must have been called up by his physical defect. In doing so, he has overlooked one small but not insignificant fact. It is usual for mothers whom Fate has presented with a child who is sickly or otherwise at a disadvantage to try to compensate him for his unfair handicap by a superabundance of love. In the instance before us, the proud mother behaved otherwise; she withdrew her love from the child on account of his infirmity. When he had grown up into a man of great power, he proved unambiguously by his actions that he had never forgiven his mother. When you consider the importance of a mother's love for the mental life of a child, you will no doubt make a tacit correction of the biographer's inferiority theory.

---

[7] [There is some obscurity in this passage, and in particular over the phrase 'der Träger des Ichideals', here translated 'the vehicle of the ego ideal'. When Freud first introduced the concept in his paper on narcissism (1914c), he distinguished between the ego ideal itself and 'a special psychical agency which performs the task of seeing that narcissistic satisfaction from the ego ideal is ensured and which, with this end in view, constantly watches the actual ego and measures it by that ideal' (Standard Ed., 14, 95). Similarly in Lecture XXVI of the Introductory Lectures (1916–17), Standard Ed., 16, 429, he speaks of a person sensing 'an agency holding sway in his ego which measures his actual ego and each of its activities by an ideal ego that he has created for himself in the course of his development.' In some of Freud's later writings this distinction between the ideal and the agency enforcing it became blurred. It seems possible that it is revived here and that the super-ego is being identified with the enforcing agency. The use of the term '*Idealfunktion*' three paragraphs lower down (p. 294) raises the same question. The whole subject was discussed in the Editor's Introduction to *The Ego and the Id* (1923b) (ibid., 19, 9–10).]

[8] [Their views are discussed in Lecture XXXIV.]

[9] [Cf. a footnote of Freud's to his paper on the anatomical distinction between the sexes (1925j), Standard Ed., 19, 253–254.]

[10] [*Wilhelm II*, by Emil Ludwig (1926).]

But let us return to the super-ego. We have allotted it the functions of self-observation, of conscience and of [maintaining] the ideal.[11] It follows from what we have said about its origin that it presupposes an immensely important biological fact and a fateful psychological one: namely, the human child's long dependence on its parents and the Oedipus complex, both of which, again, are intimately interconnected. The super-ego is the representative for us of every moral restriction, the advocate of a striving towards perfection— it is, in short, as much as we have been able to grasp psychologically of what is described as the higher side of human life. Since it itself goes back to the influence of parents, educators and so on, we learn still more of its significance if we turn to those who are its sources. As a rule parents and authorities analogous to them follow the precepts of their own super-egos in educating children. Whatever understanding their ego may have come to with their super-ego, they are severe and exacting in educating children. They have forgotten the difficulties of their own childhood and they are glad to be able now to identify themselves fully with their own parents who in the past laid such severe restrictions upon them. Thus a child's super-ego is in fact constructed on the model not of its parents but of its parents' super-ego; the contents which fill it are the same and it becomes the vehicle of tradition and of all the time-resisting judgements of value which have propagated themselves in this manner from generation to generation. You may easily guess what important assistance taking the super-ego into account will give us in our understanding of the social behaviour of mankind—in the problem of delinquency, for instance—and perhaps even what practical hints on education. It seems likely that what are known as materialistic views of history sin in under-estimating this factor. They brush it aside with the remark that human 'ideologies' are nothing other than the product and superstructure of their contemporary economic conditions. That is true, but very probably not the whole truth. Mankind never lives entirely in the present. The past, the tradition of the race and of the people, lives on in the ideologies of the super-ego, and yields only slowly to the influences of the present and to new changes; and so long as it operates through the super-ego it plays a powerful part in human life, independently of economic conditions.

In 1921 I endeavoured to make use of the differentiation between the ego and the super-ego in a study of group psychology. I arrived at a formula such as this: a psychological group is a collection of individuals who have introduced the same person into their super-ego and, on the basis of this common element, have identified themselves with one another in their ego.[12] This applies, of course, only to groups that have a leader. If we possessed more applications of this kind, the hypothesis of the super-ego would lose its last touch of strangeness for us, and we should become completely free of the embarrassment that still comes over us when, accustomed as we are to the atmosphere of the underworld, we move in the more superficial, higher strata of the mental apparatus. We do not suppose, of course, that with the separation off of the super-ego we have said the last word on the psychology of the ego. It is rather a first step; but in this case it is not only the first step that is hard.

Now, however, another problem awaits us—at the opposite end of the ego, as we might put it. It is presented to us by an observation during the work of analysis, an observation which is actually a very old one. As not infrequently happens, it has taken a long time to come to the point of appreciating its importance. The whole theory of psycho-analysis is, as you know, in fact built up on the perception of the resistance offered to us by the patient when we attempt to make his unconscious conscious to him. The objective sign of this resistance is that his associations fail or depart widely from the topic

[11] ['Idealfunktion.' Cf. footnote 7 above.] [12] [Group Psychology (1921c), Standard Ed., 18, 116.]

that is being dealt with. He may also recognize the resistance *subjectively* by the fact that he has distressing feelings when he approaches the topic. But this last sign may also be absent. We then say to the patient that we infer from his behaviour that he is now in a state of resistance; and he replies that he knows nothing of that, and is only aware that his associations have become more difficult. It turns out that we were right; but in that case his resistance was unconscious too, just as unconscious as the repressed, at the lifting of which we were working. We should long ago have asked the question: from what part of his mind does an unconscious resistance like this arise? The beginner in psycho-analysis will be ready at once with the answer: it is, of course, the resistance of the unconscious. An ambiguous and unserviceable answer! If it means that the resistance arises from the repressed, we must rejoin: certainly not! We must rather attribute to the repressed a strong upward drive, an impulsion to break through into consciousness. The resistance can only be a manifestation of the ego, which originally put the repression into force and now wishes to maintain it. That, moreover, is the view we always took. Since we have come to assume a special agency in the ego, the super-ego, which represents demands of a restrictive and rejecting character, we may say that repression is the work of this super-ego and that it is carried out either by itself or by the ego in obedience to its orders. If then we are met by the case of the resistance in analysis not being conscious to the patient, this means either that in quite important situations the super-ego and the ego can operate unconsciously, or—and this would be still more important—that portions of both of them, the ego and the super-ego themselves, are unconscious. In both cases we have to reckon with the disagreeable discovery that on the one hand (super-) ego and conscious and on the other hand repressed and unconscious are far from coinciding.

And here, Ladies and Gentlemen, I feel that I must make a pause to take breath—which you too will welcome as a relief—and, before I go on, to apologize to you. My intention is to give you some addenda to the introductory lectures on psycho-analysis which I began fifteen years ago, and I am obliged to behave as though you as well as I had in the interval done nothing but practise psycho-analysis. I know that that assumption is out of place; but I am helpless, I cannot do otherwise. This is no doubt related to the fact that it is in general so hard to give anyone who is not himself a psycho-analyst an insight into psycho-analysis. You can believe me when I tell you that we do not enjoy giving an impression of being members of a secret society and of practising a mystical science. Yet we have been obliged to recognize and express as our conviction that no one has a right to join in a discussion of psycho-analysis who has not had particular experiences which can only be obtained by being analysed oneself. When I gave you my lectures fifteen years ago I tried to spare you certain speculative portions of our theory; but it is precisely from them that are derived the new acquisitions of which I must speak to you to-day.

I return now to our topic. In face of the doubt whether the ego and super-ego are themselves unconscious or merely produce unconscious effects, we have, for good reasons, decided in favour of the former possibility. And it is indeed the case that large portions of the ego and super-ego can remain unconscious and are normally unconscious. That is to say, the individual knows nothing of their contents and it requires an expenditure of effort to make them conscious. It is a fact that ego and conscious, repressed and unconscious do not coincide. We feel a need to make a fundamental revision of our attitude to the problem of conscious-unconscious. At first we are inclined greatly to reduce the value of the criterion of being conscious since it has shown itself so untrustworthy. But we should be doing it an injustice. As may be said of our life, it is not worth much, but it is all we have. Without the illumination thrown by the quality of consciousness, we should be lost in the obscurity of depth-psychology; but we must attempt to find our bearings afresh.

There is no need to discuss what is to be called conscious: it is removed from all doubt. The oldest and best meaning of the word 'unconscious' is the descriptive one; we call a psychical process unconscious whose existence we are obliged to assume—for some such reason as that we infer it from its effects—, but of which we know nothing. In that case we have the same relation to it as we have to a psychical process in another person, except that it is in fact one of our own. If we want to be still more correct, we shall modify our assertion by saying that we call a process unconscious if we are obliged to assume that it is being activated *at the moment*, though *at the moment* we know nothing about it. This qualification makes us reflect that the majority of conscious processes are conscious only for a short time; very soon they become *latent*, but can easily become conscious again. We might also say that they had become unconscious, if it were at all certain that in the condition of latency they are still something psychical. So far we should have learnt nothing new; nor should we have acquired the right to introduce the concept of an unconscious into psychology. But then comes the new observation that we were already able to make in parapraxes. In order to explain a slip of the tongue, for instance, we find ourselves obliged to assume that the intention to make a particular remark was present in the subject. We infer it with certainty from the interference with his remark which has occurred; but the intention did not put itself through and was thus unconscious. If, when we subsequently put it before the speaker, he recognizes it as one familiar to him, then it was only temporarily unconscious to him; but if he repudiates it as something foreign to him, then it was permanently unconscious.[13] From this experience we retrospectively obtain the right also to pronounce as something unconscious what had been described as latent. A consideration of these dynamic relations permits us now to distinguish two kinds of unconscious —one which is easily, under frequently occurring circumstances, transformed into something conscious, and another with which this transformation is difficult and takes place only subject to a considerable expenditure of effort or possibly never at all. In order to escape the ambiguity as to whether we mean the one or the other unconscious, whether we are using the word in the descriptive or in the dynamic sense, we make use of a permissible and simple way out. We call the unconscious which is only latent, and thus easily becomes conscious, the 'preconscious' and retain the term 'unconscious' for the other. We now have three terms, 'conscious', 'preconscious' and 'unconscious', with which we can get along in our description of mental phenomena. Once again: the preconscious is also unconscious in the purely descriptive sense, but we do not give it that name, except in talking loosely or when we have to make a defence of the existence in mental life of unconscious processes in general.

You will admit, I hope, that so far that is not too bad and allows of convenient handling. Yes, but unluckily the work of psycho-analysis has found itself compelled to use the word 'unconscious' in yet another, third, sense, and this may, to be sure, have led to confusion. Under the new and powerful impression of there being an extensive and important field of mental life which is normally withdrawn from the ego's knowledge so that the processes occurring in it have to be regarded as unconscious in the truly dynamic sense, we have come to understand the term 'unconscious' in a topographical or systematic sense as well; we have come to speak of a 'system' of the preconscious and a 'system' of the unconscious, of a conflict between the ego and the system Ucs., and have used the word more and more to denote a mental province rather than a quality of what is mental. The discovery, actually an inconvenient one, that portions of the ego and super-ego as well are unconscious in the dynamic sense, operates at this point as a relief—it makes possible the

---

[13] [Cf. *Introductory Lectures*, IV, Standard Ed., 15, 64.]

removal of a complication. We perceive that we have no right to name the mental region that is foreign to the ego 'the system *Ucs.*', since the characteristic of being unconscious is not restricted to it. Very well; we will no longer use the term 'unconscious' in the systematic sense and we will give what we have hitherto so described a better name and one no longer open to misunderstanding. Following a verbal usage of Nietzsche's and taking up a suggestion by Georg Groddeck [1923],[14] we will in future call it the 'id'.[15] This impersonal pronoun seems particularly well suited for expressing the main characteristic of this province of the mind—the fact of its being alien to the ego. The super-ego, the ego and the id—these, then, are the three realms, regions, provinces, into which we divide an individual's mental apparatus, and with the mutual relations of which we shall be concerned in what follows.[16]

But first a short interpolation. I suspect that you feel dissatisfied because the three qualities of the characteristic of consciousness and the three provinces of the mental apparatus do not fall together into three peaceable couples, and you may regard this as in some sense obscuring our findings. I do not think, however, that we should regret it, and we should tell ourselves that we had no right to expect any such smooth arrangement. Let me give you an analogy; analogies, it is true, decide nothing, but they can make one feel more at home. I am imagining a country with a landscape of varying configuration—hill-country, plains, and chains of lakes—, and with a mixed population: it is inhabited by Germans, Magyars and Slovaks, who carry on different activities. Now things might be partitioned in such a way that the Germans, who breed cattle, live in the hill-country, the Magyars, who grow cereals and wine, live in the plains, and the Slovaks, who catch fish and plait reeds, live by the lakes. If the partitioning could be neat and clear-cut like this, a Woodrow Wilson would be delighted by it;[17] it would also be convenient for a lecture in a geography lesson. The probability is, however, that you will find less orderliness and more mixing, if you travel through the region. Germans, Magyars and Slovaks live interspersed all over it; in the hill-country there is agricultural land as well, cattle are bred in the plains too. A few things are naturally as you expected, for fish cannot be caught in the mountains and wine does not grow in the water. Indeed, the picture of the region that you brought with you may on the whole fit the facts; but you will have to put up with deviations in the details.

You will not expect me to have much to tell you that is new about the id apart from its new name. It is the dark, inaccessible part of our personality; what little we know of it we have learnt from our study of the dream-work and of the construction of neurotic symptoms, and most of that is of a negative character and can be described only as a contrast to the ego. We approach the id with analogies: we call it a chaos, a cauldron full of seething excitations. We picture it as being open at its end to somatic influences, and as there taking up into itself instinctual needs which find their physical expression in it,[18]

---

[14] [A German physician by whose unconventional ideas Freud was much attracted.]

[15] [In German '*Es*', the ordinary word for 'it'.]

[16] [A discussion of the development of Freud's views on this subject is given in the Editor's Introduction to *The Ego and the Id* (1923b), *Standard Ed.*, 19, 4–11. It may be remarked that the abbreviation '*Ucs.*', apart from this passage, was not used by Freud after *The Ego and the Id* until a single appearance in *Moses and Monotheism* (1939a), Essay III, Part I, Section E.]

[17] [It may be remarked that only a year or so before writing this Freud had finished his collaboration with W. C. Bullitt (then American Ambassador in Berlin) on a study of President Wilson, of whose political judgement he was highly critical.] [*Thomas Woodrow Wilson* is available in an edition published by Houghton Mifflin in 1967—Ed.]

[18] [Freud is here regarding instincts as something physical, of which mental processes are the representatives. A long discussion of this will be found in the Editor's Note to 'Instincts and their Vicissitudes' (1915c), *Standard Ed.*, 14, 111 ff.]

but we cannot say in what substratum. It is filled with energy reaching it from the instincts, but it has no organization, produces no collective will, but only a striving to bring about the satisfaction of the instinctual needs subject to the observance of the pleasure principle. The logical laws of thought do not apply in the id, and this is true above all of the law of contradiction. Contrary impulses exist side by side, without cancelling each other out or diminishing each other: at the most they may converge to form compromises under the dominating economic pressure towards the discharge of energy. There is nothing in the id that could be compared with negation; and we perceive with surprise an exception to the philosophical theorem that space and time are necessary forms of our mental acts.[19] There is nothing in the id that corresponds to the idea of time; there is no recognition of the passage of time, and—a thing that is most remarkable and awaits consideration in philosophical thought—no alteration in its mental processes is produced by the passage of time.[20] Wishful impulses which have never passed beyond the id, but impressions, too, which have been sunk into the id by repression, are virtually immortal; after the passage of decades they behave as though they had just occurred. They can only be recognized as belonging to the past, can only lose their importance and be deprived of their cathexis of energy, when they have been made conscious by the work of analysis, and it is on this that the therapeutic effect of analytic treatment rests to no small extent.

Again and again I have had the impression that we have made too little theoretical use of this fact, established beyond any doubt, of the unalterability by time of the repressed. This seems to offer an approach to the most profound discoveries. Nor, unfortunately, have I myself made any progress here.

The id of course knows no judgements of value: no good and evil, no morality. The economic or, if you prefer, the quantitative factor, which is intimately linked to the pleasure principle, dominates all its processes. Instinctual cathexes seeking discharge—that, in our view, is all there is in the id. It even seems that the energy of these instinctual impulses is in a state different from that in the other regions of the mind, far more mobile and capable of discharge;[21] otherwise the displacements and condensations would not occur which are characteristic of the id and which so completely disregard the *quality* of what is cathected—what in the ego we should call an idea. We would give much to understand more about these things! You can see, incidentally, that we are in a position to attribute to the id characteristics other than that of its being unconscious, and you can recognize the possibility of portions of the ego and super-ego being unconscious without possessing the same primitive and irrational characteristics.[22]

We can best arrive at the characteristics of the actual ego, in so far as it can be distinguished from the id and from the super-ego, by examining its relation to the outermost superficial portion of the mental apparatus, which we describe as the system *Pcpt.-Cs.*[23] This system is turned towards the external world, it is the medium for the perceptions arising thence, and during its functioning the phenomenon of consciousness arises in it. It is the sense-organ of the entire apparatus; moreover it is receptive not only to excitations from outside but also to those arising from the interior of the mind. We need scarcely look for a justification of the view that the ego is that portion of the id which was modified

---

[19] [The reference is to Kant. Cf. *Beyond the Pleasure Principle* (1920g), Standard Ed., 18, 28.]

[20] [A full list of Freud's very frequent references to this matter, going back to his earliest writings, is given in Section V of 'The Unconscious' (1915e), Standard Ed., 14, 187.]

[21] [This difference was referred to by Freud in many passages. See, in particular, Section V of the metapsychological paper on 'The Unconscious' (1915e), Standard Ed., 14, 188 and *Beyond the Pleasure Principle* (1920g), ibid., 18, 26-7. In both these passages Freud attributes the distinction to Breuer, apparently having in mind a footnote to Breuer's theoretical contribution to *Studies on Hysteria* (1895d), ibid., 2, 194 n. In 'The Unconscious' he remarks that in his opinion this distinction represents the deepest insight we have gained up to the present into the nature of nervous energy.]

[22] [This account of the id is in the main based on Section V of the paper on 'The Unconscious'.]

[23] [Perceptual conscious.]

by the proximity and influence of the external world, which is adapted for the reception of stimuli and as a protective shield against stimuli, comparable to the cortical layer by which a small piece of living substance is surrounded. The relation to the external world has become the decisive factor for the ego; it has taken on the task of representing the external world to the id—fortunately for the id, which could not escape destruction if, in its blind efforts for the satisfaction of its instincts, it disregarded that supreme external power. In accomplishing this function, the ego must observe the external world, must lay down an accurate picture of it in the memory-traces of its perceptions, and by its exercise of the function of 'reality-testing' must put aside whatever in this picture of the external world is an addition derived from internal sources of excitation. The ego controls the approaches to motility under the id's orders; but between a need and an action it has interposed a postponement in the form of the activity of thought, during which it makes use of the mnemic residues of experience. In that way it has dethroned the pleasure principle which dominates the course of events in the id without any restriction and has replaced it by the reality principle, which promises more certainty and greater success.

The relation to time, which is so hard to describe, is also introduced into the ego by the perceptual system; it can scarcely be doubted that the mode of operation of that system is what provides the origin of the idea of time.[24] But what distinguishes the ego from the id quite especially is a tendency to synthesis in its contents, to a combination and unification in its mental processes which are totally lacking in the id. When presently we come to deal with the instincts in mental life we shall, I hope, succeed in tracing this essential characteristic of the ego back to its source.[25] It alone produces the high degree of organization which the ego needs for its best achievements. The ego develops from perceiving the instincts to controlling them; but this last is only achieved by the [psychical] representative of the instinct[26] being allotted its proper place in a considerable assemblage, by its being taken up into a coherent context. To adopt a popular mode of speaking, we might say that the ego stands for reason and good sense while the id stands for the untamed passions.

So far we have allowed ourselves to be impressed by the merits and capabilities of the ego; it is now time to consider the other side as well. The ego is after all only a portion of the id, a portion that has been expediently modified by the proximity of the external world with its threat of danger. From a dynamic point of view it is weak, it has borrowed its energies from the id, and we are not entirely without insight into the methods—we might call them dodges—by which it extracts further amounts of energy from the id. One such method, for instance, is by identifying itself with actual or abandoned objects. The object-cathexes spring from the instinctual demands of the id. The ego has in the first instance to take note of them. But by identifying itself with the object it recommends itself to the id in place of the object and seeks to divert the id's libido on to itself. We have already seen [p. 292] that in the course of its life the ego takes into itself a large number of precipitates like this of former object-cathexes. The ego must on the whole carry out the id's intentions, it fulfils its task by finding out the circumstances in which those intentions can best be achieved. The ego's relation to the id might be compared with that of a rider

---

[24] [Freud gave some indication of what he had in mind by this in his paper on the 'Mystic Writing-Pad' (1925a), Standard Ed., 19, 231.]

[25] [Freud does not seem, in fact, to have returned to the subject in these lectures.—He had discussed this characteristic of the ego at length in Chapter III of *Inhibitions, Symptoms and Anxiety* (1926d), Standard Ed., 20, 97–100. Though he had stressed the synthetic tendency of the ego particularly in his later writings (e.g. among many others in *The Question of Lay Analysis* (1926e), ibid., 196), the concept was implicit in his picture of the ego from the earliest times. See, for instance, the term he almost invariably used during the Breuer period for ideas that had to be repressed: 'incompatible'—i.e. that could not be synthesized by the ego. So in the first paper on the neuro-psychoses of defence (1894a), Standard Ed., 3, 51 n.]

[26] [See footnote 18.]

to his horse. The horse supplies the locomotive energy, while the rider has the privilege of deciding on the goal and of guiding the powerful animal's movement. But only too often there arises between the ego and the id the not precisely ideal situation of the rider being obliged to guide the horse along the path by which it itself wants to go.

There is one portion of the id from which the ego has separated itself by resistances due to repression. But the repression is not carried over into the id: the repressed merges into the remainder of the id.

We are warned by a proverb against serving two masters at the same time. The poor ego has things even worse: it serves three severe masters and does what it can to bring their claims and demands into harmony with one another. These claims are always divergent and often seem incompatible. No wonder that the ego so often fails in its task. Its three tyrannical masters are the external world, the super-ego and the id. When we follow the ego's efforts to satisfy them simultaneously—or rather, to obey them simultaneously—we cannot feel any regret at having personified this ego and having set it up as a separate organism. It feels hemmed in on three sides, threatened by three kinds of danger, to which, if it is hard pressed, it reacts by generating anxiety. Owing to its origin from the experiences of the perceptual system, it is earmarked for representing the demands of the external world, but it strives too to be a loyal servant of the id, to remain on good terms with it, to recommend itself to it as an object and to attract its libido to itself. In its attempts to mediate between the id and reality, it is often obliged to cloak the *Ucs.* commands of the id with its own *Pcs.* rationalizations, to conceal the id's conflicts with reality, to profess, with diplomatic disingenuousness, to be taking notice of reality even when the id has remained rigid and unyielding. On the other hand it is observed at every step it takes by the strict super-ego, which lays down definite standards for its conduct, without taking any account of its difficulties from the direction of the id and the external world, and which, if those standards are not obeyed, punishes it with tense feelings of inferiority and of guilt. Thus the ego, driven by the id, confined by the super-ego, repulsed by reality, struggles to master its economic task of bringing about harmony among the forces and influences working in and upon it; and we can understand how it is that so often we cannot suppress a cry: 'Life is not easy!' If the ego is obliged to admit its weakness, it breaks out in anxiety—realistic anxiety regarding the external world, moral anxiety regarding the super-ego and neurotic anxiety regarding the strength of the passions in the id.

I should like to portray the structural relations of the mental personality, as I have described them to you, in the unassuming sketch which I now present you with:

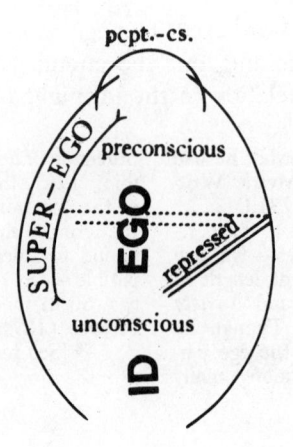

As you see here, the super-ego merges into the id; indeed, as heir to the Oedipus complex it has intimate relations with the id; it is more remote than the ego from the perceptual system.[27] The id has intercourse with the external world only through the ego—at least, according to this diagram. It is certainly hard to say to-day how far the drawing is correct. In one respect it is undoubtedly not. The space occupied by the unconscious id ought to have been incomparably greater than that of the ego or the preconscious. I must ask you to correct it in your thoughts.

And here is another warning, to conclude these remarks, which have certainly been exacting and not, perhaps, very illuminating. In thinking of this division of the personality into an ego, a super-ego and an id, you will not, of course, have pictured sharp frontiers like the artificial ones drawn in political geography. We cannot do justice to the characteristics of the mind by linear outlines like those in a drawing or in primitive painting, but rather by areas of colour melting into one another as they are presented by modern artists. After making the separation we must allow what we have separated to merge together once more. You must not judge too harshly a first attempt at giving a pictorial representation of something so intangible as psychical processes. It is highly probable that the development of these divisions is subject to great variations in different individuals; it is possible that in the course of actual functioning they may change and go through a temporary phase of involution. Particularly in the case of what is phylogenetically the last and most delicate of these divisions—the differentiation between the ego and the super-ego—something of the sort seems to be true. There is no question but that the same thing results from psychical illness. It is easy to imagine, too, that certain mystical practices may succeed in upsetting the normal relations between the different regions of the mind, so that, for instance, perception may be able to grasp happenings in the depths of the ego and in the id which were otherwise inaccessible to it. It may safely be doubted, however, whether this road will lead us to the ultimate truths from which salvation is to be expected. Nevertheless it may be admitted that the therapeutic efforts of psycho-analysis have chosen a similar line of approach. Its intention is, indeed, to strengthen the ego, to make it more independent of the super-ego, to widen its field of perception and enlarge its organization, so that it can appropriate fresh portions of the id.[28] Where id was, there ego shall be. It is a work of culture—not unlike the draining of the Zuider Zee.

FOR DISCUSSION:

1. What relationship does Freud see between parental authority and the development of the superego?

2. What is meant by "identification"? What role does it play in the formation of the superego?

3. What significance does Freud place on "slips" of the tongue?

4. In what three senses does Freud speak of the unconscious?

5. What is the distinction between the conscious, preconscious, and unconscious parts of the psyche?

6. Who are the ego's "three tyrannical masters"?

7. What is meant by "Where id was, there ego shall be"?

8. It has often been noted that for a scientist Freud employs a decidedly literary style. Comment on his style, noting the figurative devices which clarify, emphasize, and develop his ideas.

---

[27] [If this diagram is compared with the similar one in *The Ego and the Id* (1923b), Standard Ed., 19, 24, it will be seen that the earlier diagram differs principally from the present one in the fact that the super-ego is not indicated in it. Its absence is justified in a later passage in the same work (ibid., 36). In the original edition of these lectures this picture was printed upright, like its predecessor in *The Ego and the Id*. For some reason, perhaps to economize space, it was turned over on to its side, though otherwise unchanged, in both G.S. and G.W.]

[28] [Freud had said something similar in the last chapter of *The Ego and the Id*, Standard Ed., 19, 56.]

Freud and Literature*

LIONEL TRILLING

I

The Freudian psychology is the only systematic account of the human mind which in point of subtlety and complexity, of interest and tragic power, deserves to stand beside the chaotic mass of psychological insights which literature has accumulated through the centuries. To pass from the reading of a great literary work to a treatise of academic psychology is to pass from one order of perception to another, but the human nature of the Freudian psychology is exactly the stuff upon which the poet has always exercised his art. It is therefore not surprising that the psychoanalytical theory has had a great effect upon literature. Yet the relationship is reciprocal, and the effect of Freud upon literature has been no greater than the effect of literature upon Freud. When, on the occasion of the celebration of his seventieth birthday, Freud was greeted as the "discoverer of the unconscious," he corrected the speaker and disclaimed the title. "The poets and philosophers before me discovered the unconscious," he said. "What I discovered was the scientific method by which the unconscious can be studied."

A lack of specific evidence prevents us from considering the particular literary "influences" upon the founder of psychoanalysis; and, besides, when we think of the men who so clearly anticipated many of Freud's own ideas—Schopenhauer and Nietzsche, for example—and then learn that he did not read their works until after he had formulated his own theories, we must see that particular influences cannot be in question here but that what we must deal with is nothing less than a whole *Zeitgeist*, a direction of thought. For psychoanalysis is one of the culminations of the Romanticist literature of the nineteenth century. If there is perhaps a contradiction in the idea of a science standing upon the shoulders of a literature which avows itself inimical to science in so many ways, the contradiction will be resolved if we remember that this literature, despite its avowals, was itself scientific in at least the sense of being passionately devoted to a research into the self.

In showing the connection between Freud and this Romanticist tradition, it is difficult to know where to begin, but there might be a certain aptness in starting even back of the tradition, as far back as 1762 with Diderot's *Rameau's Nephew*. At any rate, certain men at the heart of nineteenth-century thought were agreed in finding a peculiar importance in this brilliant little work: Goethe translated it, Marx admired it, Hegel—as Marx reminded Engels in the letter which announced that he was sending the book as a gift—praised and expounded it at length, Shaw was impressed by it, and Freud himself, as we know from a quotation in his *Introductory Lectures*, read it with the pleasure of agreement.

The dialogue takes place between Diderot himself and a nephew of the famous composer. The protagonist, the younger Rameau, is a despised, outcast, shameless fellow; Hegel calls him the "disintegrated consciousness" and credits him with great wit, for it is

---

* From THE LIBERAL IMAGINATION by Lionel Trilling. Copyright 1940, 1947, copyright © renewed 1968 by Lionel Trilling. Reprinted by permission of The Viking Press, Inc. and Martin Secker & Warburg Ltd.

he who breaks down all the normal social values and makes new combinations with the pieces. As for Diderot, the deuteragonist, he is what Hegel calls the "honest consciousness," and Hegel considers him reasonable, decent, and dull. It is quite clear that the author does not despise his Rameau and does not mean us to. Rameau is lustful and greedy, arrogant yet self-abasing, perceptive yet "wrong," like a child. Still, Diderot seems actually to be giving the fellow a kind of superiority over himself, as though Rameau represents the elements which, dangerous but wholly necessary, lie beneath the reasonable decorum of social life. It would perhaps be pressing too far to find in Rameau Freud's id and in Diderot Freud's ego; yet the connection does suggest itself; and at least we have here the perception which is to be the common characteristic of both Freud and Romanticism, the perception of the hidden element of human nature and of the opposition between the hidden and the visible. We have too the bold perception of just what lies hidden: "If the little savage [i.e., the child] were left to himself, if he preserved all his foolishness and combined the violent passions of a man of thirty with the lack of reason of a child in the cradle, he'd wring his father's neck and go to bed with his mother."

From the self-exposure of Rameau to Rousseau's account of his own childhood is no great step; society might ignore or reject the idea of the "immorality" which lies concealed in the beginning of the career of the "good" man, just as it might turn away from Blake struggling to expound a psychology which would include the forces beneath the propriety of social man in general, but the idea of the hidden thing went forward to become one of the dominant notions of the age. The hidden element takes many forms and it is not necessarily "dark" and "bad"; for Blake the "bad" was the good, while for Wordsworth and Burke what was hidden and unconscious was wisdom and power, which work in despite of the conscious intellect.

The mind has become far less simple; the devotion to the various forms of autobiography—itself an important fact in the tradition—provides abundant examples of the change that has taken place. Poets, making poetry by what seems to them almost a freshly discovered faculty, find that this new power may be conspired against by other agencies of the mind and even deprived of its freedom; the names of Wordsworth, Coleridge, and Arnold at once occur to us again, and Freud quotes Schiller on the danger to the poet that lies in the merely analytical reason. And it is not only the poets who are threatened; educated and sensitive people throughout Europe become aware of the depredations that reason might make upon the affective life, as in the classic instance of John Stuart Mill.

We must also take into account the preoccupation—it began in the eighteenth century, or even in the seventeenth—with children, women, peasants, and savages, whose mental life, it is felt, is less overlaid than that of the educated adult male by the proprieties of social habit. With this preoccupation goes a concern with education and personal development, so consonant with the historical and evolutionary bias of the time. And we must certainly note the revolution in morals which took place at the instance (we might almost say) of the *Bildungsroman*, for in the novels fathered by *Wilhelm Meister* we get the almost complete identification of author and hero and of the reader with both, and this identification almost inevitably suggests a leniency of moral judgment. The autobiographical novel has a further influence upon the moral sensibility by its exploitation of all the modulations of motive and by its hinting that we may not judge a man by any single moment in his life without taking into account the determining past and the expiating and fulfilling future.

It is difficult to know how to go on, for the further we look the more literary affinities to Freud we find, and even if we limit ourselves to bibliography we can at best be incomplete. Yet we must mention the sexual revolution that was being demanded—by Shelley, for example, by the Schlegel of *Lucinde*, by George Sand, and later and more critically by

Ibsen; the belief in the sexual origin of art, baldly stated by Tieck, more subtly by Schopenhauer; the investigation of sexual maladjustment by Stendhal, whose observations on erotic feeling seem to us distinctly Freudian. Again and again we see the effective, utilitarian ego being relegated to an inferior position and a plea being made on behalf of the anarchic and self-indulgent id. We find the energetic exploitation of the idea of the mind as a divisible thing, one part of which can contemplate and mock the other. It is not a far remove from this to Dostoevski's brilliant instances of ambivalent feeling. Novalis brings in the preoccupation with the death wish, and this is linked on the one hand with sleep and on the other hand with the perception of the perverse, self-destroying impulses, which in turn leads us to that fascination by the horrible which we find in Shelley, Poe, and Baudelaire. And always there is the profound interest in the dream—"Our dreams," said Gerard de Nerval, "are a second life"—and in the nature of metaphor, which reaches its climax in Rimbaud and the later Symbolists, metaphor becoming less and less communicative as it approaches the relative autonomy of the dream life.

But perhaps we must stop to ask, since these are the components of the *Zeitgeist* from which Freud himself developed, whether it can be said that Freud did indeed produce a wide literary effect. What is it that Freud added that the tendency of literature itself would not have developed without him? If we were looking for a writer who showed the Freudian influence, Proust would perhaps come to mind as readily as anyone else; the very title of his novel, in French more than in English, suggests an enterprise of psychoanalysis and scarcely less so does his method—the investigation of sleep, of sexual deviation, of the way of association, the almost obsessive interest in metaphor; at these and at many other points the "influence" might be shown. Yet I believe it is true that Proust did not read Freud. Or again, exegesis of *The Waste Land* often reads remarkably like the psychoanalytic interpretation of a dream, yet we know that Eliot's methods were prepared for him not by Freud but by other poets.

Nevertheless, it is of course true that Freud's influence on literature has been very great. Much of it is so pervasive that its extent is scarcely to be determined; in one form or another, frequently in perversions or absurd simplifications, it had been infused into our life and become a component of our culture of which it is now hard to be specifically aware. In biography its first effect was sensational but not fortunate. The early Freudian biographers were for the most part Guildensterns who seemed to know the pipes but could not pluck out the heart of the mystery, and the same condemnation applies to the early Freudian critics. But in recent years, with the acclimatization of psychoanalysis and the increased sense of its refinements and complexity, criticism has derived from the Freudian system much that is of great value, most notably the license and the injunction to read the work of literature with a lively sense of its latent and ambiguous meanings, as if it were, as indeed it is, a being no less alive and contradictory than the man who created it. And this new response to the literary work has had a corrective effect upon our conception of literary biography. The literary critic or biographer who makes use of the Freudian theory is no less threatened by the dangers of theoretical systematization than he was in the early days, but he is likely to be more aware of these dangers; and I think it is true to say that now the motive of his interpretation is not that of exposing the secret shame of the writer and limiting the meaning of his work, but, on the contrary, that of finding grounds for sympathy with the writer and for increasing the possible significances of the work.

The names of the creative writers who have been more or less Freudian in tone or assumption would of course be legion. Only a relatively small number, however, have made serious use of the Freudian ideas. Freud himself seems to have thought this was as it should be: he is said to have expected very little of the works that were sent to him by writers with inscriptions of gratitude for all they had learned from him. The Surrealists have, with a certain inconsistency, depended upon Freud for the "scientific" sanction of their program. Kafka, with an apparent awareness of what he was doing, has explored the Freudian conceptions of guilt and punishment, of the dream, and of the fear of the father. Thomas Mann, whose tendency, as he himself says, was always in the direction of Freud's interests, has been most susceptible to the Freudian anthropology, finding a special charm in the theories of myths and magical practices. James Joyce, with his interest in the numerous states of receding consciousness, with his use of words as things and of words which point to more than one thing, with his pervading sense of the interrelation and interpenetration of all things, and, not least important, his treatment of familial themes, has perhaps most thoroughly and consciously exploited Freud's ideas.

II

It will be clear enough how much of Freud's thought has significant affinity with the anti-rationalist element of the Romanticist tradition. But we must see with no less distinctness how much of his system is militantly rationalistic. Thomas Mann is at fault when, in his first essay on Freud, he makes it seem that the "Apollonian," the rationalistic, side of psychoanalysis is, while certainly important and wholly admirable, somehow secondary and even accidental. He gives us a Freud who is committed to the "night side" of life. Not at all: the rationalistic element of Freud is foremost; before everything else he is positivistic. If the interpreter of dreams came to medical science through Goethe, as he tells us he did, he entered not by way of the *Walpurgisnacht* but by the essay which played so important a part in the lives of so many scientists of the nineteenth century, the famous disquisition on Nature.

This correction is needed not only for accuracy but also for any understanding of Freud's attitude to art. And for that understanding we must see how intense is the passion with which Freud believes that positivistic rationalism, in its golden-age pre-Revolutionary purity, is the very form and pattern of intellectual virtue. The aim of psychoanalysis, he says, is the control of the night side of life. It is "to strengthen the ego, to make it more independent of the super-ego, to widen its field of vision, and so to extend the organization of the id." "Where id was,"—that is, where all the irrational, non-logical, pleasure-seeking dark forces were—"there shall ego be,"—that is, intelligence and control. "It is," he concludes, with a reminiscence of Faust, "reclamation work, like the draining of the Zuyder Zee." This passage is quoted by Mann when, in taking up the subject of Freud a second time, he does indeed speak of Freud's positivistic program; but even here the bias induced by Mann's artistic interest in the "night side" prevents him from giving the other aspect of Freud its due emphasis. Freud would never have accepted the role which Mann seems to give him as the legitimizer of the myth and the dark irrational ways of the mind. If Freud discovered the darkness for science he never endorsed it. On the contrary, his rationalism supports all the ideas of the Enlightenment that deny validity to myth or religion; he holds to a simple materialism, to a simple determinism, to a rather limited sort of epistemology. No great scientist of our day has thundered so articulately and so fiercely against all those who would sophisticate with metaphysics the scientific principles that were good enough for the nineteenth century. Conceptualism or pragmatism is anathema to him through the greater part of his intellectual career, and this, when we consider the nature of his own brilliant scientific methods, has surely an element of paradox in it.

From his rationalistic positivism comes much of Freud's strength and what weakness he has. The strength is the fine, clear tenacity of his positive aims, the goal of therapy, the desire to bring to men a decent measure of earthly happiness. But upon the rationalism must also be placed the blame for the often naïve scientific principles which characterize his early thought—they are later much modified—and which consist largely of claiming for his theories a perfect correspondence with an external reality, a position which, for those who admire Freud and especially for those who take seriously his views on art, is troublesome in the extreme.

Now Freud has, I believe, much to tell us about art, but whatever is suggestive in him is not likely to be found in those of his works in which he deals expressly with art itself. Freud is not insensitive to art—on the contrary—nor does he ever intend to speak of it with contempt. Indeed, he speaks of it with a real tenderness and counts it one of the true charms of the good life. Of artists, especially of writers, he speaks with admiration and even a kind of awe, though perhaps what he most appreciates in literature are specific emotional insights and observations; as we have noted, he speaks of literary men, because they have understood the part played in life by the hidden motives, as the precursors and coadjutors of his own science.

And yet eventually Freud speaks of art with what we must indeed call contempt. Art, he tells us, is a "substitute gratification," and as such is "an illusion in contrast to reality." Unlike most illusions, however, art is "almost always harmless and beneficent" for the reason that "it does not seek to be anything but an illusion. Save in the case of a few people who are, one might say, obsessed by Art, it never dares make any attack on the realm of reality." One of its chief functions is to serve as a "narcotic." It shares the characteristics of the dream, whose element of distortion Freud calls a "sort of inner dishonesty." As for the artist, he is virtually in the same category with the neurotic. "By such separation of imagination and intellectual capacity," Freud says of the hero of a novel, "he is destined to be a poet or a neurotic, and he belongs to that race of beings whose realm is not of this world."

Now there is nothing in the logic of psychoanalytical thought which requires Freud to have these opinions. But there is a great deal in the practice of the psychoanalytical therapy which makes it understandable that Freud, unprotected by an adequate philosophy, should be tempted to take the line he does. The analytical therapy deals with illusion. The patient comes to the physician to be cured, let us say, of a fear of walking in the street. The fear is real enough, there is no illusion on that score, and it produces all the physical symptoms of a more rational fear, the sweating palms, pounding heart, and shortened breath. But the patient knows that there is no cause for the fear, or rather that there is, as he says, no "real cause": there are no machine guns, man traps, or tigers in the street. The physician knows, however, that there is indeed a "real" cause for the fear, though it has nothing at all to do with what is or is not in the street; the cause is within the patient, and the process of the therapy will be to discover, by gradual steps, what this real cause is and so free the patient from its effects.

Now the patient in coming to the physician, and the physician in accepting the patient, make a tacit compact about reality; for their purpose they agree to the limited reality by which we get our living, win our loves, catch our trains and our colds. The therapy will undertake to train the patient in proper ways of coping with this reality. The patient, of course, has been dealing with this reality all along, but in the wrong way. For Freud there are two ways of dealing with external reality. One is practical, effective, positive; this is the way of the conscious self, of the ego which must be made independent of the super-ego and extend its organization over the id, and it is the right way. The antithetical way may be called, for our purpose now, the "fictional" way. Instead of doing something about, or to, external reality, the individual who uses this way does something to, or about, his affective states. The most common and "normal" example of this is daydreaming, in which we give ourselves a certain pleasure by imagining our difficulties solved or our desires gratified. Then, too, as Freud discovered, sleeping dreams are, in much more complicated ways, and even though quite unpleasant, at the service of this same "fictional" activity. And in ways yet more complicated and yet more unpleasant, the actual neurosis from which our patient suffers deals with an external reality which the mind considers still more unpleasant than the painful neurosis itself.

For Freud as psychoanalytic practitioner there are, we may say, the polar extremes of reality and illusion. Reality is an honorific word, and it means what is *there*; illusion is a pejorative word, and it means a response to what is *not there*. The didactic nature of a course of psychoanalysis no doubt requires a certain firm crudeness in making the distinction; it is after all aimed not at theoretical refinement but at practical effectiveness. The polar extremes are practical reality and neurotic illusion, the latter judged by the former. This, no doubt, is as it should be; the patient is not being trained in metaphysics and epistemology.

This practical assumption is not Freud's only view of the mind in its relation to reality. Indeed what may be called the essentially Freudian view assumes that the mind, for good as well as bad, helps create its reality by selection and evaluation. In this view, reality is malleable and subject to creation; it is not static but is rather a series of situations which are dealt with in their own terms. But beside this conception of the mind stands the conception which arises from Freud's therapeutic-practical assumptions; in this view, the mind deals with a reality which is quite fixed and static, a reality that is wholly "given" and not (to use a phrase of Dewey's) "taken." In his epistemological utterances, Freud insists on this second view, although it is not easy to see why he should do so. For the reality to which he wishes to reconcile the neurotic patient is, after all, a "taken" and not a "given" reality. It is the reality of social life and of value, conceived and maintained by the human mind and will. Love, morality, honor, esteem—these are the components of a created reality. If we are to call art an illusion then we must call most of the activities and satisfactions of the ego illusions; Freud, of course, has no desire to call them that.

What, then, is the difference between, on the one hand, the dream and the neurosis, and, on the other hand, art? That they have certain common elements is of course clear; that unconscious processes are at work in both would be denied by no poet or critic; they share too, though in different degrees, the element of fantasy. But there is a vital difference between them which Charles Lamb saw so clearly in his defense of the sanity of true genius: "The . . . poet dreams being awake. He is not possessed by his subject but he has dominion over it."

That is the whole difference: the poet is in command of his fantasy, while it is exactly the mark of the neurotic that he is possessed by his fantasy. And there is a further difference which Lamb states; speaking of the poet's relation to reality (he calls it Nature), he says, "He is beautifully loyal to that sovereign directress, even when he appears most to betray her"; the illusions of art are made to serve the purpose of a closer and truer relation with reality. Jacques Barzun, in an acute and sympathetic discussion of Freud, puts the matter well: "A good analogy between art and *dreaming* has led him to a false one between art and *sleeping*. But the difference between a work of art and a dream is precisely this, that the work of art *leads us back to the outer reality by taking account of it*." Freud's assumption of the almost exclusively hedonistic nature and purpose of art bar him from the perception of this.

Of the distinction that must be made between the artist and the neurotic Freud is of course aware; he tells us that the artist is not like the neurotic in that he knows how to find a way back from the world of imagination and "once more get a firm foothold in reality." This however seems to mean no more than that reality is to be dealt with when the artist suspends the practice of his art; and at least once when Freud speaks of art dealing with reality he actually means the rewards that a successful artist can win. He does not deny to art its function and its usefulness; it has a therapeutic effect in releasing mental tension; it serves the cultural purpose of acting as a "substitute gratification" to reconcile men to the sacrifices they have made for culture's sake; it promotes the social sharing of highly valued emotional experiences; and it recalls men to their cultural ideals. This is not everything that some of us would find that art does, yet even this is a good deal for a "narcotic" to do.

III

I started by saying that Freud's ideas could tell us something about art, but so far I have done little more than try to show that Freud's very conception of art is inadequate. Perhaps, then, the suggestiveness lies in the application of the analytic method to specific works of art or to the artist himself? I do not think so, and it is only fair to say that Freud himself was aware both of the limits and the limitations of psychoanalysis in art, even though he does not always in practice submit to the former or admit the latter.

Freud has, for example, no desire to encroach upon the artist's autonomy; he does not wish us to read his monograph on Leonardo and then say of the "Madonna of the Rocks" that it is a fine example of homosexual, autoerotic painting. If he asserts that in investigation the "psychiatrist cannot yield to the author," he immediately insists that the "author cannot yield to the psychiatrist," and he warns the latter not to "coarsen everything" by using for all human manifestations the "substantially useless and awkward terms" of clinical procedure. He admits, even while asserting that the sense of beauty probably derives from sexual feeling, that psychoanalysis "has less to say about beauty than about most other things." He confesses to a theoretical indifference to the form of art and restricts himself to its content. Tone, feeling, style, and the modification that part makes upon part he does not consider. "The layman," he says, "may expect perhaps too much from analysis . . . for it must be admitted that it throws no light upon the two problems which probably interest him the most. It can do nothing toward elucidating the nature of the artistic gift, nor can it explain the means by which the artist works—artistic technique."

What, then, does Freud believe that the analytical method can do? Two things: explain the "inner meanings" of the work of art and explain the temperament of the artist as man.

A famous example of the method is the attempt to solve the "problem" of *Hamlet* as suggested by Freud and as carried out by Dr. Ernest Jones, his early and distinguished follower. Dr. Jones's monograph is a work of painstaking scholarship and of really masterly ingenuity. The research undertakes not only the clearing up of the mystery of Hamlet's character, but also the discovery of "the clue to much of the deeper workings of Shakespeare's mind." Part of the mystery in question is of course why Hamlet, after he had so definitely resolved to do so, did not avenge upon his hated uncle his father's death. But there is another mystery to the play—what Freud calls "the mystery of its effect," its magical appeal that draws so much interest toward it. Recalling the many failures to solve the riddle of the play's charm, he wonders if we are to be driven to the conclusion "that its magical appeal rests solely upon the impressive thoughts in it and the splendor of its language." Freud believes that we can find a source of power beyond this.

We remember that Freud has told us that the meaning of a dream is its intention, and we may assume that the meaning of a drama is its intention, too. The Jones research undertakes to discover what it was that Shakespeare intended to say about Hamlet. It finds that the intention was wrapped by the author in a dreamlike obscurity because it touched so deeply both his personal life and the moral life of the world; what Shakespeare intended to say is that Hamlet cannot act because he is incapacitated by the guilt he feels at his unconscious attachment to his mother. There is, I think, nothing to be quarreled with in the statement that there is an Oedipus situation in *Hamlet*; and if psychoanalysis has indeed added a new point of interest to the play, that is to its credit.[1] And, just so, there is no reason to quarrel with Freud's conclusion when he undertakes to give us the meaning of *King Lear* by a tortuous tracing of the mythological implications of the theme of the three caskets, of the relation of the caskets to the Norns, the Fates, and the Graces, of the connection of these triadic females with Lear's daughters, of the transmogrification of the death goddess into the love goddess and the identification of Cordelia with both, all to the conclusion that the meaning of *King Lear* is to be found in the tragic refusal of an old man to "renounce love, choose death, and make friends with the necessity of dying." There is something both beautiful and suggestive in this, but it is not *the* meaning of *King Lear* any more than the Oedipus motive is *the* meaning of *Hamlet*.

It is not here a question of the validity of the evidence, though that is of course important. We must rather object to the conclusions of Freud and Dr. Jones on the ground that their proponents do not have an adequate conception of what an artistic meaning is. There is no single meaning to any work of art; this is true not merely because it is better that it should be true, that is, because it makes art a richer thing, but because historical and personal experience show it to be true. Changes in historical context and in personal mood change the meaning of a work and indicate to us that artistic understanding is not a question of fact but of value. Even if the author's intention were, as it cannot be, precisely determinable, the meaning of a work cannot lie in the author's intention alone. It must also lie in its effect. We can say of a volcanic eruption on an inhabited island that it "means terrible suffering," but if the island is uninhabited or easily evacuated it means something else. In short, the audience partly determines the meaning of the work. But although Freud sees something of this when he says that in addition to the author's intention we must take into account the mystery of *Hamlet's* effect, he nevertheless goes on to speak as if, historically, *Hamlet's* effect had been single and brought about solely by the "magical" power of the Oedipus motive to which, unconsciously, we so violently respond. Yet there was, we know, a period when *Hamlet* was relatively in eclipse, and it has always been scandalously true of the French, a people not without filial feeling, that they have been somewhat indifferent to the "magical appeal" of *Hamlet*.

I do not think that anything I have said about the inadequacies of the Freudian method of interpretation limits the number of ways we can deal with a work of art. Bacon remarked that experiment may twist nature on the rack to wring out its secrets, and criticism may use any instruments upon a work of art to find its meanings. The elements of art are not limited to the world of art. They reach into life, and whatever extraneous knowledge of them we gain—for example, by research into the historical context of the work—may quicken our feelings for the work itself and even enter legitimately into those feelings. Then, too, anything we may learn about the artist himself may be enriching and legitimate. But one research into the mind of the artist is simply not practicable, however legitimate it may theoretically be. That is, the investigation of his unconscious intention

---

[1] However, A. C. Bradley, in his discussion of Hamlet (*Shakespearean Tragedy*), states clearly the intense sexual disgust which Hamlet feels and which, for Bradley, helps account for his uncertain purpose; and Bradley was anticipated in this view by Löning. It is well known, and Dover Wilson has lately emphasized the point, that to an Elizabethan audience Hamlet's mother was not merely tasteless, as to a modern audience she seems, in hurrying to marry Claudius, but actually adulterous in marrying him at all because he was, as her brother-in-law, within the forbidden degrees.

as it exists apart from the work itself. Criticism understands that the artist's statement of his conscious intention, though it is sometimes useful, cannot finally determine meaning. How much less can we know from his unconscious intention considered as something apart from the whole work? Surely very little that can be called conclusive or scientific. For, as Freud himself points out, we are not in a position to question the artist; we must apply the technique of dream analysis to his symbols, but, as Freud says with some heat, those people do not understand his theory who think that a dream may be interpreted without the dreamer's free association with the multitudinous details of his dream.

We have so far ignored the aspect of the method which finds the solution to the "mystery" of such a play as *Hamlet* in the temperament of Shakespeare himself and then illuminates the mystery of Shakespeare's temperament by means of the solved mystery of the play. Here it will be amusing to remember that by 1935 Freud had become converted to the theory that it was not Shakespeare of Stratford but the Earl of Oxford who wrote the plays, thus invalidating the important bit of evidence that Shakespeare's father died shortly before the composition of *Hamlet*. This is destructive enough to Dr. Jones's argument, but the evidence from which Dr. Jones draws conclusions about literature fails on grounds more relevant to literature itself. For when Dr. Jones, by means of his analysis of *Hamlet*, takes us into "the deeper workings of Shakespeare's mind," he does so with a perfect confidence that he knows what *Hamlet* is and what its relation to Shakespeare is. It is, he tells us, Shakespeare's "chief masterpiece," so far superior to all his other works that it may be placed on "an entirely separate level." And then, having established his ground on an entirely subjective literary judgment, Dr. Jones goes on to tell us that *Hamlet* "probably expresses the core of Shakespeare's philosophy and outlook as no other work of his does." That is, all the contradictory or complicating or modifying testimony of the other plays is dismissed on the basis of Dr. Jones's acceptance of the peculiar position which, he believes, *Hamlet* occupies in the Shakespeare canon. And it is upon this quite inadmissible judgment that Dr. Jones bases his argument: "It may be expected *therefore* that anything which will give us the key to the inner meaning of the play will *necessarily* give us the clue to much of the deeper workings of Shakespeare's mind." (The italics are mine.)

I should be sorry if it appeared that I am trying to say that psychoanalysis can have nothing to do with literature. I am sure that the opposite is so. For example, the whole notion of rich ambiguity in literature, of the interplay between the apparent meaning and the latent—not "hidden"—meaning, has been reinforced by the Freudian concepts, perhaps even received its first impetus from them. Of late years, the more perceptive psychoanalysts have surrendered the early pretensions of their teachers to deal "scientifically" with literature. That is all to the good, and when a study as modest and precise as Dr. Franz Alexander's essay on *Henry IV* comes along, an essay which pretends not to "solve" but only to illuminate the subject, we have something worth having. Dr. Alexander undertakes nothing more than to say that in the development of Prince Hal we see the classic struggle of the ego to come to normal adjustment, beginning with the rebellion against the father, going on to the conquest of the super-ego (Hotspur, with his rigid notions of honor and glory), then to the conquests of the *id* (Falstaff, with his anarchic self-indulgence) then to the identification with the father (the crown scene) and the assumption of mature responsibility. An analysis of this sort is not momentous and not exclusive of other meanings; perhaps it does no more than point up and formulate what we all have already seen. It has the tact to accept the play and does not, like Dr. Jones's study of *Hamlet*, search for a "hidden motive" and a "deeper working," which implies that there is a reality to which the play stands in the relation that a dream stands to the wish that generates it and from which it is separable; it is this reality, this "deeper working," which, according to Dr. Jones, produced the play. But *Hamlet* is not merely the product of Shakespeare's thought, it is the very instrument of his thought, and if meaning is intention, Shakespeare did not intend the Oedipus motive or anything less than *Hamlet*; if meaning is effect then it is *Hamlet* which affects us, not the Oedipus motive. *Coriolanus* also deals, and very terribly, with the Oedipus motive, but the effect of the one drama is very different from the effect of the other.

IV

If, then, we can accept neither Freud's conception of the place of art in life nor his application of the analytical method, what is it that he contributes to our understanding of art or to its practice? In my opinion, what he contributes outweighs his errors; it is of the greatest importance, and it lies in no specific statement that he makes about art but is, rather, implicit in his whole conception of the mind.

For, of all mental systems, the Freudian psychology is the one which makes poetry indigenous to the very constitution of the mind. Indeed, the mind, as Freud sees it, is in the greater part of its tendency exactly a poetry-making organ. This puts the case too strongly, no doubt, for it seems to make the working of the unconscious mind equivalent to poetry itself, forgetting that between the unconscious mind and the finished poem there supervene the social intention and the formal control of the conscious mind. Yet the statement has at least the virtue of counterbalancing the belief, so commonly expressed or implied, that the very opposite is true, and that poetry is a kind of beneficent aberration of the mind's right course.

Freud has not merely naturalized poetry; he has discovered its status as a pioneer settler, and he sees it as a method of thought. Often enough he tries to show how, as a method of thought, it is unreliable and ineffective for conquering reality; yet he himself is forced to use it in the very shaping of his own science, as when he speaks of the topography of the mind and tells us what a kind of defiant apology that the metaphors of space relationship which he is using are really most inexact since the mind is not a thing of space at all, but that there is no other way of conceiving the difficult idea except by metaphor. In the eighteenth century Vico spoke of the metaphorical, imagistic language of the early stages of culture; it was left to Freud to discover how, in a scientific age, we still feel and think in figurative formations, and to create, what psychoanalysis is, a science of tropes, of metaphor and its variants, synecdoche and metonymy.

Freud showed, too, how the mind, in one of its parts, could work without logic, yet not without that directing purpose, that control of intent from which, perhaps it might be said, logic springs. For the unconscious mind works without the syntactical conjunctions which are logic's essence. It recognizes no *because*, no *therefore*, no *but*; such ideas as similarity, agreement, and community are expressed in dreams imagistically by compressing the elements into a unity. The unconscious mind in its struggle with the conscious always turns from the general to the concrete and finds the tangible trifle more congenial than the large abstraction. Freud discovered in the very organization of the mind those mechanisms by which art makes its effects, such devices as the condensations of meanings and the displacement of accent.

All this is perhaps obvious enough and, though I should like to develop it in proportion both to its importance and to the space I have given to disagreement with Freud, I will not press it further. For there are two other elements in Freud's thought which, in conclusion, I should like to introduce as of great weight in their bearing on art.

Of these, one is a specific idea which, in the middle of his career (1920), Freud put forward in his essay *Beyond the Pleasure Principle*. The essay itself is a speculative attempt to solve a perplexing problem in clinical analysis, but its relevance to literature is inescapable, as Freud sees well enough, even though his perception of its critical importance is not sufficiently strong to make him revise his earlier views of the nature and function of art. The idea is one which stands besides Aristotle's notion of the catharsis, in part to supplement, in part to modify it.

Freud has come upon certain facts which are not to be reconciled with his earlier theory of the dream. According to this theory, all dreams, even the unpleasant ones, could be understood upon analysis to have the intention of fulfilling the dreamer's wishes. They are in the service of what Freud calls the pleasure principle, which is opposed to the reality principle. It is, of course, this explanation of the dream which had so largely conditioned Freud's theory of art. But now there is thrust upon him the necessity for reconsidering the theory of the dream, for it was found that in cases of war neurosis—what we once called shellshock—the patient, with the utmost anguish, recurred in his dreams to the very situation, distressing as it was, which had precipitated his neurosis. It seemed impossible to interpret these dreams by any assumption of a hedonistic intent. Nor did there seem to be the usual amount of distortion in them: the patient recurred to the terrible initiatory situation with great literalness. And the same pattern of psychic behavior could be observed in the play of children; there were some games which, far from fulfilling wishes, seemed to concentrate upon the representation of those aspects of the child's life which were most unpleasant and threatening to his happiness.

To explain such mental activities Freud evolved a theory for which he at first refused to claim much but to which, with the years, he attached an increasing importance. He first makes the assumption that there is indeed in the psychic life a repetition-compulsion which goes beyond the pleasure principle. Such a compulsion cannot be meaningless, it must have an intent. And that intent, Freud comes to believe, is exactly and literally the developing of fear. "These dreams," he says, "are attempts at restoring control of the stimuli by developing apprehension, the pretermission of which caused the traumatic neurosis." The dream, that is, is the effort to reconstruct the bad situation in order that the failure to meet it may be recouped; in these dreams there is no obscured intent to evade but only an attempt to meet the situation, to make a new effort of control. And in the play of children it seems to be that "the child repeats even the unpleasant experiences because through his own activity he gains a far more thorough mastery of the strong impression than was possible by mere passive experience."

Freud, at this point, can scarcely help being put in mind of tragic drama; nevertheless, he does not wish to believe that this effort to come to mental grips with a situation is involved in the attraction of tragedy. He is, we might say, under the influence of the Aristotelian tragic theory which emphasizes a qualified hedonism through suffering. But the pleasure involved in tragedy is perhaps an ambiguous one; and sometimes we must feel that the famous sense of cathartic resolution is perhaps the result of glossing over terror with beautiful language rather than an evacuation of it. And sometimes the terror even bursts through the language to stand stark and isolated from the play, as does Oedipus's sightless and bleeding face. At any rate, the Aristotelian theory does not deny another function for tragedy (and for comedy, too) which is suggested by Freud's theory of the traumatic neurosis—what might be called the mithridatic function, by which tragedy is used as the homeopathic administration of pain to inure ourselves to the greater pain which life will force upon us. There is in the cathartic theory of tragedy, as it is usually understood, a conception of tragedy's function which is too negative and which inadequately suggests the sense of active mastery which tragedy can give.

In the same essay in which he sets forth the conception of the mind embracing its own pain for some vital purpose, Freud also expresses a provisional assent to the idea (earlier stated, as he reminds us, by Schopenhauer) that there is perhaps a human drive which makes of death the final and desired goal. The death instinct is a conception that is rejected by many of even the most thoroughgoing Freudian theorists (as, in his last book, Freud mildly noted); the late Otto Fenichel in his authoritative work on the neurosis argues cogently against it. Yet even if we reject the theory as not fitting the facts in any operatively useful way, we still cannot miss its grandeur, its ultimate tragic courage in acquiescence to fate. The idea of the reality principle and the idea of the death instinct form the crown of Freud's broader speculation on the life of man. Their quality of grim poetry is characteristic of Freud's system and the ideas it generates for him.

And as much as anything else that Freud gives to literature, this quality of his thought is important. Although the artist is never finally determined in his work by the intellectual systems about him, he cannot avoid their influence; and it can be said of various competing systems that some hold more promise for the artist than others. When for example, we think of the simple humanitarian optimism which, for two decades, has been so pervasive, we must see that not only has it been politically and philosophically inadequate, but also that it implies, by the smallness of its view of the varieties of human possibility, a kind of check on the creative faculties. In Freud's view of life no such limitation is implied. To be sure, certain elements of his system seem hostile to the usual notions of man's dignity. Like every great critic of human nature—and Freud is that—he finds in human pride the ultimate cause of human wretchedness, and he takes pleasure in knowing that his ideas stand with those of Copernicus and Darwin in making pride more difficult to maintain. Yet the Freudian man is, I venture to think, a creature of far more dignity and far more interest than the man which any other modern system has been able to conceive. Despite popular belief to the contrary, man, as Freud conceives him, is not to be understood by any simple formula (such as sex) but is rather an inextricable tangle of culture and biology. And not being simple, he is not simply good; he has, as Freud says somewhere, a kind of hell within him from which rise everlastingly the impulses which threaten his civilization. He has the faculty of imagining for himself more in the way of pleasure and satisfaction than he can possibly achieve. Everything that he gains he pays for in more than equal coin; compromise and the compounding with defeat constitute his best way of getting through the world. His best qualities are the result of a struggle whose outcome is tragic. Yet he is a creature of love; it is Freud's sharpest criticism of the Adlerian psychology that to aggression it gives everything and to love nothing at all.

One is always aware in reading Freud how little cynicism there is in his thought. His desire for man is only that he should be human, and to this end his science is devoted. No view of life to which the artist responds can insure the quality of his work, but the poetic qualities of Freud's own principles, which are so clearly in the line of the classic tragic realism, suggest that this is a view which does not narrow and simplify the human world for the artist but on the contrary opens and complicates it.

FOR DISCUSSION:

1. Why does Trilling place Freud in the Romantic tradition? What does Freud owe to his predecessors in the seventeenth, eighteenth, and nineteenth centuries?

2. Comment briefly on Freud's influence on twentieth-century literature.

3. According to Freud what are the two ways of dealing with external reality?

4. Discuss the statement, "Reality is malleable and subject to creation."

5. Trilling objects to Freud's thesis that artistic expression is essentially neurotically inspired. Why?

6. How can art and literary criticism make use of Freud's analytic method? What inadequacies and limitations are there in his technique?

7. Comment on the statement that man is "an inextricable tangle of culture and biology."

SUGGESTIONS FOR ADDITIONAL READING:

Basler, Roy P. *Sex, Symbolism, and Psychology in Literature.* New Brunswick, 1948.

Bergler, Edmund. *The Writer and Psychoanalysis.* New York, 1954.

Fraiberg, Louis. *Psychoanalysis and Literary Criticism.* Detroit, 1960.

Griffin, William J. "The Use and Abuse of Psychoanalysis in the Study of Literature," *Literature and Psychology,* I (Winter 1951), 3–20.

Hoffman, Frederick J. *Freudianism and the Literary Mind.* New York, 1945.

Lesser, Simon O. *Fiction and the Unconscious.* Boston, 1957.

Manheim, Leonard and Eleanor. *Hidden Patterns: Studies in Psychoanalytic Literary Criticism.* New York, 1966.

Mordell, Albert. *The Erotic Motive in Literature.* New York, 1919.

Phillips, William, ed. *Art and Psychoanalysis.* New York, 1963.

Ruitenbeck, Hendrik, ed. *The Creative Imagination.* Chicago, 1965.

Trilling, Lionel. *Freud and the Crisis of Our Culture.* Boston, 1955.

The Tragedy of Hamlet, Prince of Denmark*

WILLIAM SHAKESPEARE

CLAUDIUS, King of Denmark
HAMLET, son to the former, and nephew to the present King
POLONIUS, lord chamberlain
HORATIO, friend to Hamlet
LAERTES, son to Polonius
VOLTIMAND,
CORNELIUS,
ROSENCRANTZ, } courtiers
GUILDENSTERN,
OSRIC,
A GENTLEMAN
A PRIEST
MARCELLUS, } officers
BERNARDO,

FRANCISCO, a soldier
REYNALDO, servant to Polonius
PLAYERS
TWO CLOWNS, gravediggers
FORTINBRAS, Prince of Norway
A CAPTAIN
ENGLISH AMBASSADORS
GERTRUDE, Queen of Denmark, and mother to Hamlet
OPHELIA, daughter to Polonius
LORDS, LADIES, OFFICERS, SOLDIERS, SAILORS, MESSENGERS, and other ATTENDANTS
GHOST OF HAMLET'S FATHER

Scene. Denmark

ACT I

Scene I

Enter BERNARDO and FRANCISCO, two Sentinels.

BERNARDO. Who's there?
FRANCISCO. Nay, answer me. Stand and unfold yourself.
BERNARDO. Long live the king!
FRANCISCO. Bernardo?
BERNARDO. He.
FRANCISCO. You come most carefully upon your hour.
BERNARDO. 'Tis now struck twelve; get thee to bed, Francisco.
FRANCISCO. For this relief much thanks: 'tis bitter cold,
 And I am sick at heart.
BERNARDO. Have you had quiet guard?
FRANCISCO.   Not a mouse stirring.
BERNARDO. Well, good night:
 If you do meet Horatio and Marcellus,
 The rivals of my watch, bid them make haste.
FRANCISCO. I think I hear them. Stand, ho! Who is there?

Enter HORATIO and MARCELLUS.

HORATIO. Friends to this ground.
MARCELLUS.   And liegemen to the Dane.
FRANCISCO. Give you good night.
MARCELLUS.   O, farewell, honest soldier: Who hath relieved you?

---

* From HAMLET by William Shakespeare, edited by R. C. Bald. Copyright 1946 by F. S. Crofts & Co., Inc. Reprinted by permission of Appleton-Century-Crofts, Division of Meredith Corporation.

13. *rivals* partners

FRANCISCO. Bernardo hath my place;
  Give you good night.
  Exit.
MARCELLUS. Holla, Bernardo!
BERNARDO. Say—
  What, is Horatio there?
HORATIO. A piece of him.
BERNARDO. Welcome, Horatio: welcome, good Marcellus.
MARCELLUS. What, has this thing appeared again tonight?
BERNARDO. I have seen nothing.
MARCELLUS. Horatio says 'tis but our fantasy,
  And will not let belief take hold of him
  Touching this dreaded sight twice seen of us;
  Therefore I have entreated him along
  With us to watch the minutes of this night,
  That, if again this apparition come,
  He may approve our eyes and speak to it.
HORATIO. Tush, tush, 'twill not appear.
BERNARDO. Sit down awhile,
  And let us once again assail your ears,
  That are so fortified against our story,
  What we have two nights seen.
HORATIO. Well, sit we down,
  And let us hear Bernardo speak of this.
BERNARDO. Last night of all,
  When yond same star that's westward from the pole
  Had made his course to illume that part of heaven
  Where now it burns, Marcellus and myself,
  The bell then beating one—

Enter GHOST.

MARCELLUS. Peace, break thee off, look where it comes again!
BERNARDO. In the same figure like the king that's dead.
MARCELLUS. Thou art a scholar, speak to it, Horatio.
BERNARDO. Looks a' not like the king? mark it, Horatio.
HORATIO. Most like; it harrows me with fear and wonder.
BERNARDO. It would be spoke to.
MARCELLUS. Question it, Horatio.
HORATIO. What art thou that usurp't this time of night,
  Together with that fair and warlike form
  In which the majesty of buried Denmark
  Did sometimes march? by heaven I charge thee, speak!
MARCELLUS. It is offended.
BERNARDO. See, it stalks away.
HORATIO. Stay! speak, speak, I charge thee, speak!
  Exit GHOST.
MARCELLUS. 'Tis gone, and will not answer.
BERNARDO. How now, Horatio? you tremble and look pale.
  Is not this something more than fantasy?
  What think you on't?
HORATIO. Before my God, I might not this believe
  Without the sensible and true avouch
  Of mine own eyes.
MARCELLUS. It is not like the king?
HORATIO. As thou art to thyself.
  Such was the very armor he had on
  When he the ambitious Norway combated;
  So frowned he once, when in an angry parle
  He smote the sledded Polacks on the ice.
  'Tis strange.
MARCELLUS. Thus twice before, and jump at this dead hour,
  With martial stalk hath he gone by our watch.
HORATIO. In what particular thought to work I know not,
  But, in the gross and scope of my opinion,
  This bodes some strange eruption to our state. *Something must be wrong*
MARCELLUS. Good now, sit down, and tell me, he that knows,
  Why this same strict and most observant watch
  So nightly toils the subject of the land,
  And why such daily cast of brazen cannon
  And foreign mart for implements of war,
  Why such impress of shipwrights, whose sore task
  Does not divide the Sunday from the week,
  What might be toward that this sweaty haste

29. *approve* corroborate 48. *Denmark* King of Denmark 49. *sometimes* formerly 61. *Norway* King of Norway 65. *jump* just 68. *gross and scope* general range 72. *toils* makes toil 74. *mart* trading 75. *impress* conscription 77. *toward* imminent

Doth make the night joint laborer with the day;
Who is't that can inform me?
HORATIO. That can I;
At least the whisper goes so. Our last king,
Whose image even but now appeared to us,
Was as you know by Fortinbras of Norway,
Thereto pricked on by a most emulate pride,
Dared to the combat; in which our valiant Hamlet—
For so this side of our known world esteemed him—
Did slay this Fortinbras, who, by a sealed compact
Well ratified by law and heraldry,
Did forfeit, with his life, all those his lands
Which he stood seized of to the conqueror;
Against the which a moiety competent
Was gagéd by our king, which had returned
To the inheritance of Fortinbras,
Had he been vanquisher; as, by the same co-mart
And carriage of the article designed,
His fell to Hamlet. Now sir, young Fortinbras,
Of unimprovéd mettle hot and full,
Hath in the skirts of Norway here and there
Sharked up a list of lawless resolutes,
For food and diet, to some enterprise
That hath a stomach in't; which is no other—
As it doth well appear unto our state—
But to recover of us, by strong hand
And terms compulsatory, those foresaid lands
So by his father lost; and this, I take it,
Is the main motive of our preparations,
The source of this our watch, and the chief head
Of this posthaste and romage in the land.
BERNARDO. I think it be no other but e'en so;
Well may it sort that this portentous figure
Comes arméd through our watch so like the king
That was and is the question of these wars.
HORATIO. A mote it is to trouble the mind's eye.
In the most high and palmy state of Rome,
A little ere the mightiest Julius fell,
The graves stood tenantless and the sheeted dead
Did squeak and gibber in the Roman streets,
And even the like precurse of feared events,
As harbingers preceding still the fates
And prologue to the omen coming on,
Have heaven and earth together demonstrated
Unto our climatures and countrymen,
As stars with trains of fire, and dews of blood,
Disasters in the sun; and the moist star,
Upon whose influence Neptune's empire stands,
Was sick almost to doomsday with eclipse.
But soft, behold, lo where it comes again!

Enter GHOST.

I'll cross it though it blast me. Stay, illusion;
He spreads his arms.
If thou hast any sound or use of voice,
Speak to me.
If there be any good thing to be done
That may to thee do ease and grace to me,
Speak to me.
If thou art privy to thy country's fate,
Which, happily, foreknowing may avoid,
O speak!
Or if thou hast uphoarded in thy life
Extorted treasure in the womb of earth,
For which they say you spirits oft walk in death,
The cock crows.

---

83. emulate ambitious 87. heraldry law of arms 89. seized possessed 90. moiety competent sufficient quantity 91. gagéd pledged 93. co-mart joint bargain 94. carriage effect 96. unimprovéd unused 97. skirts outlying parts 98. list company 100. stomach show of daring 106. head cause 107. romage activity 109. sort happen 117. precurse foretokening 118. harbingers forerunners 119. omen dire event 121. climatures regions of the earth 123. the moist star the moon

Speak of it. Stay and speak! Stop it, Marcellus.
MARCELLUS. Shall I strike at it with my partisan?
HORATIO. Do if it will not stand.
BERNARDO. 'Tis here!
HORATIO. 'Tis here!
[*Exit* GHOST.]
MARCELLUS. 'Tis gone!
We do it wrong, being so majestical,
To offer it the show of violence,
For it is as the air invulnerable,
And our vain blows malicious mockery.
BERNARDO. It was about to speak when the cock crew.
HORATIO. And then it started like a guilty thing
Upon a fearful summons. I have heard,
The cock, that is the trumpet to the morn,
Doth with his lofty and shrill-sounding throat
Awake the god of day and at his warning,
Whether in sea or fire, in earth or air,
The extravagant and erring spirit hies
To his confine; and of the truth herein
This present object made probation.
MARCELLUS. It faded on the crowing of the cock.
Some say that ever 'gainst that season comes
Wherein our Savior's birth is celebrated
This bird of dawning singeth all night long,
And then they say no spirit dare stir abroad;
The nights are wholesome; then no planets strike,
No fairy takes, nor witch hath power to charm,
So hallowed and so gracious is the time.
HORATIO. So have I heard, and do in part believe it.
But look, the morn, in russet mantle clad,
Walks o'er the dew of yon high eastern hill.
Break we our watch up, and by my advice
Let us impart what we have seen tonight
Unto young Hamlet, for upon my life
This spirit, dumb to us, will speak to him:
Do you consent we shall acquaint him with it,
As needful in our loves, fitting our duty?
MARCELLUS. Let's do't, I pray; and I this morning know
Where we shall find him most conveniently.
Exeunt.

Scene 2

Flourish. Enter CLAUDIUS, *King of Denmark,* GERTRUDE *the Queen, Councillors,* POLONIUS *and his son* LAERTES, HAMLET, *and others* [*including* VOLTIMAND *and* CORNELIUS].

KING. Though yet of Hamlet our dear brother's death
The memory be green, and that it us befitted
To bear our hearts in grief, and our whole kingdom
To be contracted in one brow of woe;
Yet so far hath discretion fought with nature,
That we with wisest sorrow think on him
Together with remembrance of ourselves:
Therefore our sometime sister, now our queen,
The imperial jointress to this warlike state,
Have we, as 'twere with a defeated joy,
With an auspicious and a dropping eye,
With mirth in funeral and with dirge in marriage,
In equal scale weighing delight and dole,
Taken to wife: nor have we herein barred
Your better wisdoms, which have freely gone
With this affair along. For all, our thanks.
Now follows that you know, young Fortinbras,
Holding a weak supposal of our worth,
Or thinking by our late dear brother's death

---

140. *partisan* spear   154. *extravagant* wandering out of bounds   155. *confine* place of confinement   156. *probation* proof   162. *strike* exercise evil influence   163. *takes* enchants   9. *jointress* a widow who holds a jointure, or life-interest, in an estate   14. *barred* ignored

Our state to be disjoint and out of frame,
Colleaguéd with this dream of his advantage,
He hath not failed to pester us with message
Importing the surrender of those lands
Lost by his father, with all bonds of law,
To our most valiant brother. So much for him.
Now for ourself, and for this time of meeting.
Thus much the business is: we have here writ
To Norway, uncle of young Fortinbras—
Who, impotent and bedrid, scarcely hears
Of this his nephew's purpose—to suppress
His further gait herein, in that the levies,
The lists, and full proportions are all made
Out of his subject, and we here dispatch
You, good Cornelius, and you, Voltimand,
For bearers of this greeting to old Norway,
Giving to you no further personal power
To business with the king, more than the scope
Of these delated articles allow.
Farewell, and let your haste commend your duty.
CORNELIUS. ⎱ In that, and all things, will
VOLTIMAND. ⎰ we show our duty.
KING. We doubt it nothing; heartily farewell.
          Exeunt VOLTIMAND *and* CORNELIUS.
And now, Laertes, what's the news with you?
You told us of some suit, what is't, Laertes?
You cannot speak of reason to the Dane
And lose your voice; what wouldst thou beg, Laertes,
That shall not be my offer, not thy asking?
The head is not more native to the heart,
The hand more instrumental to the mouth,
Than is the throne of Denmark to thy father.
What wouldst thou have, Laertes?
LAERTES.   My dread lord,
Your leave and favor to return to France,
From whence though willingly I came to Denmark,
To show my duty in your coronation;
Yet now, I must confess, that duty done,
My thoughts and wishes bend again toward France
And bow them to your gracious leave and pardon.
KING. Have you your father's leave? What says Polonius?
POLONIUS. He hath, my lord, wrung from me my slow leave
By laborsome petition, and at last
Upon his will I sealed my hard consent;
I do beseech you give him leave to go.
KING. Take thy fair hour, Laertes; time be thine,
And thy best graces spend it at thy will!
But now, my cousin Hamlet, and my son—
HAMLET [*aside*]. A little more than kin, and less than kind.
KING. How is it that the clouds still hang on you?
HAMLET. Not so, my lord; I am too much in the sun.
QUEEN. Good Hamlet, cast thy nightéd color off
And let thine eye look like a friend on Denmark,
Do not for ever with thy vailéd lids
Seek for thy noble father in the dust;
Thou know'st 'tis common; all that live must die,
Passing through nature to eternity.
HAMLET. Ay, madam, it is common.
QUEEN.   If it be,
Why seems it so particular with thee?
HAMLET. Seems, madam, nay it is; I know not "seems."
'Tis not alone, my inky cloak, good mother,
Nor customary suits of solemn black,
Nor windy suspiration of forced breath,
No, nor the fruitful river in the eye,
Nor the dejected havior of the visage,
Together with all forms, moods, shapes of grief,
That can denote me truly; these indeed seem,

---

20. *disjoint* disorganized 21. *colleaguéd* combined 31. *gait* progress 32. *proportions* estimates of forces and supplies 38. *delated* extended 44. *Dane* King of Denmark 45. *lose your voice* speak in vain 47. *native* linked by nature to 48. *instrumental* serviceable 67. *sun* notice the pun with son 69. *Denmark* King of Denmark 70. *vailéd* lowered 79. *suspiration* breathing

For they are actions that a man might play,
But I have that within which passes show;
These but the trappings and the suits of woe.
KING. 'Tis sweet and commendable in your nature, Hamlet,
To give these mourning duties to your father,
But you must know your father lost a father,
That father lost, lost his, and the survivor bound
In filial obligation for some term
To do obsequious sorrow; but to persever
In obstinate condolement is a course
Of impious stubbornness, 'tis unmanly grief;
It shows a will most incorrect to heaven,
A heart unfortified, a mind impatient,
An understanding simple and unschooled
For what we know must be, and is as common
As any the most vulgar thing to sense;
Why should we in our peevish opposition
Take it to heart? Fie, 'tis a fault to heaven,
A fault against the dead, a fault to nature,
To reason most absurd, whose common theme
Is death of fathers, and who still hath cried,
From the first corse till he that died today,
"This must be so." We pray you throw to earth
This unprevailing woe, and think of us
As of a father, for let the world take note
You are the most immediate to our throne,
And with no less nobility of love
Than that which dearest father bears his son,
Do I impart toward you. For your intent
In going back to school in Wittenberg,
It is most retrograde to our desire,
And we beseech you bend you to remain
Here in the cheer and comfort of our eye,
Our chiefest courtier, cousin, and our son.
QUEEN. Let not thy mother lose her prayers, Hamlet;
I pray thee stay with us, go not to Wittenberg.
HAMLET. I shall in all my best obey you, madam.
KING. Why, 'tis a loving and a fair reply;
Be as ourself in Denmark. Madam, come;
This gentle and unforced accord of Hamlet
Sits smiling to my heart, in grace whereof,
No jocund health that Denmark drinks today
But the great cannon to the clouds shall tell,
And the king's rouse the heavens shall bruit again,
Re-speaking earthly thunder. Come away.
Flourish. Exeunt all except HAMLET.
HAMLET. O that this too too sullied flesh would melt,
Thaw and resolve itself into a dew,
Or that the Everlasting had not fixed
His canon 'gainst self slaughter! O God, O God,
How weary, stale, flat, and unprofitable
Seem to me all the uses of this world!
Fie on't, ah fie, 'tis an unweeded garden
That grows to seed, things rank and gross in nature
Possess it merely. That it should come to this—
But two months dead, nay not so much, not two—
So excellent a king, that was to this
Hyperion to a satyr, so loving to my mother,
That he might not beteem the winds of heaven
Visit her face too roughly. Heaven and earth,
Must I remember? why, she would hang on him
As if increase of appetite had grown
By what it fed on, and yet within a month—
Let me not think on't, frailty, thy name is woman—
A little month, or ere those shoes were old
With which she followed my poor father's body,
Like Niobe all tears, why she, even she—

92. *obsequious* dutiful   114. *retrograde* opposed   127. *rouse* carousal; *bruit again* echo   132. *canon* ordinance   140. *Hyperion* the sun-god   141. *beteem* permit   149. *Niobe* After the gods had killed all her children Niobe was turned into stone from which tears gushed continually

150 O God, a beast, that wants discourse of reason,
Would have mourned longer—married with my uncle,
My father's brother, but no more like my father
Than I to Hercules, within a month,
Ere yet the salt of most unrighteous tears
Had left the flushing in her gallèd eyes,
She married. O most wicked speed, to post
With such dexterity to incestuous sheets!
It is not, nor it cannot come to good;
But break, my heart, for I must hold my tongue.

Enter HORATIO, MARCELLUS, *and* BERNARDO.

HORATIO. Hail to your lordship!
160 HAMLET. I am glad to see you well; Horatio—or I do forget myself.
HORATIO. The same, my lord, and your poor servant ever.
HAMLET. Sir, my good friend; I'll change that name with you;
And what make you from Wittenberg, Horatio?
Marcellus!
MARCELLUS. My good lord!
HAMLET. I am very glad to see you; good even, sir.
But what, in faith, make you from Wittenberg?
HORATIO. A truant disposition, good my lord.
HAMLET. I would not hear your enemy say so,
170 Nor shall you do my ear that violence
To make it truster of your own report
Against yourself; I know you are no truant.
But what is your affair in Elsinore?
We'll teach you to drink deep ere you depart.
HORATIO. My lord, I came to see your father's funeral.
HAMLET. I prithee do not mock me, fellow student;
I think it was to see my mother's wedding.
HORATIO. Indeed, my lord, it followed hard upon.
HAMLET. Thrift, thrift, Horatio, the funeral baked meats
Did coldly furnish forth the marriage tables. 180
Would I had met my dearest foe in heaven
Or ever I had seen that day, Horatio!
My father—methinks I see my father.
HORATIO. Where, my lord?
HAMLET. In my mind's eye, Horatio.
HORATIO. I saw him once, a' was a goodly king.
HAMLET. A' was a man, take him for all in all,
I shall not look upon his like again.
HORATIO. My lord, I think I saw him yesternight.
HAMLET. Saw who?
HORATIO. My lord, the king your father.
HAMLET. The king my father! 190
HORATIO. Season your admiration for a while
With an attent ear till I may deliver,
Upon the witness of these gentlemen,
This marvel to you.
HAMLET. For God's love let me hear.
HORATIO. Two nights together had these gentlemen,
Marcellus and Bernardo, on their watch
In the dead waste and middle of the night
Been thus encountered: a figure like your father,
Armèd at point exactly, cap-a-pe,
Appears before them, and with solemn march 200
Goes slow and stately by them; thrice he walked
By their oppressed and fear-surprisèd eyes,
Within his truncheon's length, whilst they, distilled
Almost to jelly with the act of fear,
Stand dumb and speak not to him; this to me
In dreadful secrecy impart they did,
And I with them the third night kept the watch,
Where as they had delivered both in time,
Form of the thing, each word made true and good,
The apparition comes: I knew your father; 210
These hands are not more like.
HAMLET. But where was this?

---

150. *discourse* process 155. *gallèd* rubbed, inflamed 181. *dearest* bitterest 191. *season* moderate; *admiration* astonishment 192. *attent* attentive 199. *at point* completely; *cap-a-pe* from head to foot

MARCELLUS. My lord, upon the platform where we watched.
HAMLET. Did you not speak to it?
HORATIO. My lord, I did,
But answer made it none; yet once methought
It lifted up it head, and did address
Itself to motion like as it would speak:
But even then the morning cock crew loud,
And at the sound it shrunk in haste away
And vanished from our sight.
HAMLET. 'Tis very strange.
HORATIO. As I do live, my honored lord, 'tis true,
And we did think it writ down in our duty
To let you know of it.
HAMLET. Indeed, indeed, sirs, but this troubles me.
Hold you the watch tonight?
ALL. We do, my lord.
HAMLET. Armed, say you?
ALL. Armed, my lord.
HAMLET. From top to toe?
ALL. My lord, from head to foot.
HAMLET. Then saw you not his face?
HORATIO. O yes, my lord, he wore his beaver up.
HAMLET. What, looked he frowningly?
HORATIO. A countenance more in sorrow than in anger.
HAMLET. Pale or red?
HORATIO. Nay, very pale.
HAMLET. And fixed his eyes upon you?
HORATIO. Most constantly.
HAMLET. I would I had been there.
HORATIO. It would have much amazed you.
HAMLET. Very like, very like. Stayed it long?
HORATIO. While one with moderate haste might tell a hundred.
BOTH. Longer, longer.
HORATIO. Not when I saw't.
HAMLET. His beard was grizzled, no?
HORATIO. It was as I have seen it in his life, A sable silvered.
HAMLET. I will watch tonight, Perchance 'twill walk again.
HORATIO. I warrant it will.
HAMLET. If it assume my noble father's person,
I'll speak to it though hell itself should gape
And bid me hold my peace; I pray you all,
If you have hitherto concealed this sight,
Let it be tenable in your silence still,
And whatsomever else shall hap tonight,
Give it an understanding but no tongue.
I will requite your loves; so fare you well:
Upon the platform 'twixt eleven and twelve
I'll visit you.
ALL. Our duty to your honor.
HAMLET. Your loves, as mine to you; farewell.
Exeunt.
My father's spirit in arms! all is not well;
I doubt some foul play; would the night were come!
Till then sit still, my soul; foul deeds will rise,
Though all the earth o'erwhelm them, to men's eyes.
Exit.

Scene 3

Enter LAERTES *and* OPHELIA *his sister.*

LAERTES. My necessaries are embarked; farewell.
And sister, as the winds give benefit,
And convoy is assistant, do not sleep,
But let me hear from you.
OPHELIA. Do you doubt that?
LAERTES. For Hamlet and the trifling of his favor,
Hold it a fashion and a toy in blood,
A violet in the youth of primy nature,
Forward, not permanent, sweet, not lasting,
The perfume and suppliance of a minute,
No more.

215. *it* its   229. *beaver* visor   237. *tell* count   241. *sable* black   247. *tenable* held back   255. *doubt* suspect   3. *convoy* means of conveyance   7. *primy* early

OPHELIA. No more but so?
LAERTES. Think it no more.
For nature crescent does not grow alone
In thews and bulk, but as this temple waxes
The inward service of the mind and soul
Grows wide withal. Perhaps he loves you now,
And now no soil nor cautel doth besmirch
The virtue of his will; but you must fear,
His greatness weighed, his will is not his own,
For he himself is subject to his birth.
He may not, as unvalued persons do,
Carve for himself, for on his choice depends
The safety and health of this whole state,
And therefore must his choice be circumscribed
Unto the voice and yielding of that body
Whereof he is the head. Then if he says he loves you,
It fits your wisdom so far to believe it
As he in his particular act and place
May give his saying deed, which is no further
Than the main voice of Denmark goes withal.
Then weigh what loss your honor may sustain
If with too credent ear you list his songs,
Or lose your heart, or your chaste treasure open
To his unmastered importunity.
Fear it, Ophelia, fear it, my dear sister,
And keep you in the rear of your affection,
Out of the shot and danger of desire.
The chariest maid is prodigal enough
If she unmask her beauty to the moon;
Virtue itself scapes not calumnious strokes;
The canker galls the infants of the spring
Too oft before their buttons be disclosed;
And in the morn and liquid dew of youth
Contagious blastments are most imminent.
Be wary, then best safety lies in fear;
Youth to itself rebels, though none else near.

OPHELIA. I shall the effect of this good lesson keep
As watchman to my heart. But, good my brother,
Do not, as some ungracious pastors do,
Show me the steep and thorny way to heaven,
Whiles like a puffed and reckless libertine
Himself the primrose path of dalliance treads,
And recks not his own rede.
LAERTES. O fear me not.
I stay too long; but here my father comes.

Enter POLONIUS.

A double blessing is a double grace;
Occasion smiles upon a second leave.
POLONIUS. Yet here, Laertes! aboard, aboard, for shame!
The wind sits in the shoulder of your sail,
And you are stayed for. There, my blessing with thee!
And these few precepts in thy memory
Look thou character. Give thy thoughts no tongue,
Nor any unproportioned thought his act.
Be thou familiar, but by no means vulgar.
The friends thou hast, and their adoption tried,
Grapple them unto thy soul with hoops of steel,
But do not dull thy palm with entertainment
Of each new-hatched, unfledged comrade. Beware
Of entrance to a quarrel, but being in,
Bear't that th' opposéd may beware of thee.
Give every man thy ear, but few thy voice;
Take each man's censure, but reserve thy judgment.
Costly thy habit as thy purse can buy,
But not expressed in fancy; rich, not gaudy;
For the apparel oft proclaims the man,
And they in France of the best rank and station

---

11. *crescent* growing 12. *this temple* the body 15. *soil* blemish; *cautel* deceit 23. *yielding* consent 30. *credent* trustful 34-35. *keep . . . desire* do not go as far forward as affection will lead you, but avoid danger by staying out of range. 36. *chariest* most sparing 39. *canker* grub, caterpillar; *galls* injures; *infants of the spring* young flowers 40. *buttons* buds 42. *blastments* blights 51. *recks* heeds; *rede* advice 59. *character* engrave 60. *unproportioned* unbalanced 69. *censure* opinion

Are often most select and generous, chief in that.
Neither a borrower nor a lender be,
For loan oft loses both itself and friend,
And borrowing dulls the edge of husbandry.
This above all, to thine ownself be true
And it must follow, as the night the day,
Thou canst not then be false to any man.
Farewell; my blessing season this in thee!
LAERTES. Most humbly do I take my leave, my lord.
POLONIUS. The time invites you; go, your servants tend.
LAERTES. Farewell, Ophelia, and remember well
What I have said to you.
OPHELIA.   'Tis in my memory locked
And you yourself shall keep the key of it.
LAERTES. Farewell.
    Exit LAERTES.
POLONIUS. What is't, Ophelia, he hath said to you?
OPHELIA. So please you, something touching the Lord Hamlet.
POLONIUS. Marry, well bethought.
'Tis told me he hath very oft of late
Given private time to you, and you yourself
Have of your audience been most free and bounteous;
If it be so—as so 'tis put on me,
And that in way of caution—I must tell you
You do not understand yourself so clearly
As it behoves my daughter and your honor.
What is between you? give me up the truth.
OPHELIA. He hath, my lord, of late made many tenders
Of his affection to me.
POLONIUS. Affection, pooh! you speak like a green girl
Unsifted in such perilous circumstance.
Do you believe his tenders, as you call them?
OPHELIA. I do not know, my lord, what I should think.
POLONIUS. Marry, I will teach you: think yourself a baby
That you have ta'en these tenders for true pay,
Which are not sterling. Tender yourself more dearly,
Or (not to crack the wind of the poor phrase,
Running it thus) you'll tender me a fool.
OPHELIA. My lord, he hath importuned me with love
In honorable fashion.
POLONIUS. Ay, fashion, you may call it; go to, go to.
OPHELIA. And hath given countenance to his speech, my lord,
With almost all the holy vows of heaven.
POLONIUS. Ay, springes to catch woodcocks. I do know,
When the blood burns, how prodigal the soul
Lends the tongue vows; these blazes, daughter,
Giving more light than heat, extinct in both,
Even in their promise, as it is a-making,
You must not take for fire. From this time
Be something scanter of your maiden presence;
Set your entreatments at a higher rate
Than a command to parley. For Lord Hamlet,
Believe so much in him that he is young,
And with a larger tether may he walk
Than may be given you: in few, Ophelia,
Do not believe his vows, for they are brokers,
Not of that dye which their investments show,
But mere implorators of unholy suits,
Breathing like sanctified and pious bawds,
The better to beguile. This is for all:
I would not, in plain terms, from this time forth
Have you so slander any moment leisure
As to give words or talk with the Lord Hamlet.
Look to't, I charge you; come your ways.
OPHELIA. I shall obey, my lord.
    Exeunt.

77. *husbandry* economy   83. *tend* attend   99. *tenders* offers   102. *unsifted* untried   113. *countenance* confirmation   115. *springes* snares   122. *entreatments* interviews   123. *parley* conference under a truce   127. *brokers* go-betweens   128. *investments* vestments, clothes   129. *implorators* solicitors   133. *slander* misuse; *moment* momentary

Scene 4

Enter HAMLET, HORATIO, *and* MARCELLUS.

HAMLET. The air bites shrewdly, it is very cold.
HORATIO. It is a nipping and an eager air.
HAMLET. What hour now?
HORATIO.   I think it lacks of twelve.
MARCELLUS. No, it is struck.
HORATIO. Indeed? I heard it not; it then draws near the season
  Wherein the spirit held his wont to walk.
  A flourish of trumpets, and two pieces go off.
  What does this mean, my lord?
HAMLET. The king doth wake tonight and takes his rouse,
  Keeps wassail, and the swaggering upspring reels;
  And as he drains his draughts of Rhenish down
  The kettledrum and trumpet thus bray out
  The triumph of his pledge.
HORATIO.   Is it a custom?
HAMLET. Ay, marry, is't;
  But to my mind, though I am native here
  And to the manner born, it is a custom
  More honored in the breach than the observance.
  This heavy-headed revel east and west
  Makes us traduced and taxed of other nations;
  They clepe us drunkards, and with swinish phrase
  Soil our addition, and indeed it takes
  From our achievements, though performed at height,
  The pith and marrow of our attribute.
  So, oft it chances in particular men
  That for some vicious mole of nature in them,
  As in their birth, wherein they are not guilty,
  (Since nature cannot choose his origin)
  By the o'ergrowth of some complexion,
  Oft breaking down the pales and forts of reason,
  Or by some habit that too much o'erleavens
  The form of plausive manners—that these men,
  Carrying, I say, the stamp of one defect,
  Being nature's livery, or fortune's star,
  His virtues else—be they as pure as grace,
  As infinite as man may undergo—
  Shall in the general censure take corruption
  From that particular fault: the dram of evil
  Doth all the noble substance often dout
  To his own scandal.
HORATIO.   Look, my lord, it comes!

Enter GHOST.

HAMLET. Angels and ministers of grace defend us!
  Be thou a spirit of health or goblin damned,
  Bring with thee airs from heaven or blasts from hell,
  Be thy intents wicked or charitable,
  Thou com'st in such a questionable shape,
  That I will speak to thee; I'll call thee Hamlet,
  King, father, royal Dane; O, answer me!
  Let me not burst in ignorance, but tell
  Why thy canonized bones hearsèd in death
  Have burst their cerements; why the sepulchre,
  Wherein we saw thee quietly inurned,
  Hath oped his ponderous and marble jaws
  To cast thee up again! What may this mean
  That thou, dead corse, again in complete steel

---

2. *eager* sharp 9. *up-spring* a dance 10. *Rhenish* Rhine wine 18. *taxed of* upbraided by 19. *clepe* call 20. *addition* title, honor 21. *at height* at the highest pitch of excellence 24. *mole of nature* natural defect 26. *his* its 27. *complexion* disposition 28. *pales* fences 29. *o'erleavens* modifies 30. *plausive* plausible 32. *livery* badge; *fortune's star* accidental mark 35. *censure* opinion 36. *dram* particle 37. *dout* extinguish 38. *his* its; *scandal* harm 48. *cerements* grave-cloths

Revisits thus the glimpses of the moon,
Making night hideous, and we fools of
   nature
So horridly to shake our disposition
With thoughts beyond the reaches of our
   souls?
Say, why is this? wherefore? what should
   we do?
   GHOST beckons HAMLET.
HORATIO. It beckons you to go away with it
As if it some impartment did desire
To you alone.
MARCELLUS. Look with what courteous
   action
It waves you to a more removéd ground;
But do not go with it.
HORATIO.   No, by no means.
HAMLET. It will not speak; then I will follow
   it.
HORATIO. Do not, my lord.
HAMLET.   Why, what should be the fear?
I do not set my life at a pin's fee,
And for my soul, what can it do to that,
Being a thing immortal as itself?
It waves me forth again, I'll follow it.
HORATIO. What if it tempt you toward the
   flood, my lord,
Or to the dreadful summit of the cliff
That beetles o'er his base into the sea,
And there assume some other horrible
   form,
Which might deprive your sovereignty of
   reason,
And draw you into madness? think of it:
The very place puts toys of desperation,
Without more motive, into every brain
That looks so many fathoms to the sea
And hears it roar beneath.
HAMLET.   It waves me still;
Go on, I'll follow thee.
MARCELLUS. You shall not go, my lord.
HAMLET.   Hold off your hands.
HORATIO. Be ruled, you shall not go.
HAMLET.   My fate cries out,
And makes each petty artere in this body
As hardy as the Nemean lion's nerve;
Still am I call'd; unhand me, gentlemen;
By heaven, I'll make a ghost of him that
   lets me;
I say, away! go on, I'll follow thee.
   Exeunt GHOST and HAMLET.
HORATIO. He waxes desperate with imagination.
MARCELLUS. Let's follow; 'tis not fit thus to
   obey him.
HORATIO. Have after. To what issue will this
   come?
MARCELLUS. Something is rotten in the state
   of Denmark.
HORATIO. Heaven will direct it.
MARCELLUS.   Nay, let's follow him.
   Exeunt.

Scene 5

Enter GHOST and HAMLET.

HAMLET. Whither wilt thou lead me? speak,
   I'll go no further.
GHOST. Mark me.
HAMLET.   I will.
GHOST.   My hour is almost come,
When I to sulphurous and tormenting
   flames
Must render up myself.
HAMLET.   Alas, poor ghost!
GHOST. Pity me not, but lend thy serious
   hearing
To what I shall unfold.
HAMLET.   Speak, I am bound to hear.
GHOST. So art thou to revenge, when thou
   shalt hear.
HAMLET. What?
GHOST. I am thy father's spirit,
Doomed for a certain term to walk the
   night,
And for the day confined to fast in fires,
Till the foul crimes done in my days of
   nature
Are burnt and purged away: but that I
   am forbid
To tell the secrets of my prison house,
I could a tale unfold whose lightest word
Would harrow up thy soul, freeze thy
   young blood,
Make thy two eyes like stars start from
   their spheres,

---

55. *disposition* normal habit of thought 65. *fee* value 71. *beetles* projects 73. *sovereignty of reason* supreme control exercised by reason 75. *toys* trifles, fancies 82. *artere* artery 83. *Nemean lion* the lion slain by Hercules; *nerve* sinew 85. *lets* hinders

Thy knotted and combinéd locks to part,
And each particular hair to stand an end,
Like quills upon the fretful porpentine.
But this eternal blazon must not be
To ears of flesh and blood. List, list, O list!
If thou didst ever thy dear father love—
HAMLET. O God!
GHOST. Revenge his foul and most unnatural murder.
HAMLET. Murder!
GHOST. Murder most foul, as in the best it is,
But this most foul, strange and unnatural.
HAMLET. Haste me to know't, that I with wings as swift
As meditation or the thoughts of love
May sweep to my revenge.
GHOST.   I find thee apt,
And duller shouldst thou be than the fat weed
That roots itself in ease on Lethe wharf,
Wouldst thou not stir in this. Now, Hamlet, hear:
'Tis given out that, sleeping in my orchard,
A serpent stung me; so the whole ear of Denmark
Is by a forgéd process of my death
Rankly abused: but know, thou noble youth,
The serpent that did sting thy father's life
Now wears his crown.
HAMLET.   O my prophetic soul!
My uncle?
GHOST. Ah, that incestuous, that adulterate beast,
With witchcraft of his wit, with traitorous gifts—
O wicked wit and gifts, that have the power
So to seduce!—won to his shameful lust
The will of my most seeming-virtuous queen;
O Hamlet, what a falling-off was there!
From me, whose love was of that dignity
That it went hand in hand even with the vow
I made to her in marriage, and to decline
Upon a wretch whose natural gifts were poor
To those of mine;
But virtue, as it never will be moved,
Though lewdness court it in a shape of heaven,
So lust, though to a radiant angel linked,
Will sate itself in a celestial bed
And prey on garbage.
But soft, methinks I scent the morning air;
Brief let me be. Sleeping within my orchard,
My custom always of the afternoon,
Upon my secure hour thy uncle stole
With juice of curséd hebenon in a vial,
And in the porches of mine ears did pour
The leperous distilment, whose effect
Holds such an enmity with blood of man,
That swift as quicksilver it courses through
The natural gates and alleys of the body,
And with a sudden vigor it doth posset
And curd, like eager droppings into milk,
The thin and wholesome blood; so did it mine,
And a most instant tetter barked about,
Most lazar-like, with vile and loathsome crust
All my smooth body.
Thus was I sleeping by a brother's hand
Of life, of crown, of queen at once dispatched,
Cut off even in the blossoms of my sin,
Unhouseled, disappointed, unaneled,
No reckoning made, but sent to my account
With all my imperfections on my head;
O horrible, O horrible, most horrible!
If thou hast nature in thee, bear it not;
Let not the royal bed of Denmark be
A couch for luxury and damnéd incest.
But howsomever thou pursues this act,
Taint not thy mind, nor let thy soul contrive
Against thy mother aught; leave her to heaven,
And to those thorns that in her bosom lodge
To prick and sting her. Fare thee well at once;

19. *an end* on end   20. *porpetine* porcupine   21. *eternal blazon* proclamation of the secrets of eternity   33. *Lethe* the river of oblivion   68. *posset* curdle   69. *eager* bitter   71. *tetter* eruption of the skin; *barked* crusted   72. *lazar-like* like a leper   77. *unhouseled* without sacrament; *unaneled* without extreme unction

The glowworm shows the matin to be near,
And gins to pale his uneffectual fire.
Adieu, adieu, adieu: remember me.
Exit.
HAMLET. O all you host of heaven! O earth! what else?
And shall I couple hell? O fie! Hold, hold my heart,
And you, my sinews, grow not instant old,
But bear me stiffly up. Remember thee?
Ay, thou poor ghost, whiles memory holds a seat
In this distracted globe. Remember thee?
Yea, from the table of my memory
I'll wipe away all trivial fond records,
All saws of books, all forms, all pressures past,
That youth and observation copied there;
And thy commandment all alone shall live
Within the book and volume of my brain
Unmixed with baser matter; yes by heaven!
O most pernicious woman!
O villain, villain, smiling, damnéd villain!
My tables—meet it is I set it down
That one may smile, and smile, and be a villain;
At least I'm sure it may be so in Denmark. [*Writing.*]
So uncle, there you are. Now to my word;
It is "Adieu, adieu, remember me:"
I have sworn't.
MARCELLUS. ⎱ [*within*]
HORATIO. ⎰ My lord, my lord!

Enter HORATIO *and* MARCELLUS.

MARCELLUS. Lord Hamlet!
HORATIO. Heavens secure him!
HAMLET. So be it!
HORATIO. Illo, ho, ho, my lord!
HAMLET. Hillo, ho, ho, boy! come, bird, come.
MARCELLUS. How is't, my noble lord?
HORATIO. What news, my lord?
HAMLET. O, wonderful.
HORATIO. Good my lord, tell it.
HAMLET. No, you will reveal it.
HORATIO. Not I, my lord, by heaven.
MARCELLUS. Nor I, my lord.
HAMLET. How say you then, would heart of man once think it?
But you'll be secret?
BOTH. Ay, by heaven, my lord.
HAMLET. There's never a villain dwelling in all Denmark
But he's an arrant knave.
HORATIO. There needs no ghost, my lord, come from the grave
To tell us this.
HAMLET. Why right, you are in the right;
And so, without more circumstance at all,
I hold it fit that we shake hands and part;
You, as your business and desire shall point you,
For every man hath business and desire,
Such as it is, and for my own poor part,
Look you, I will go pray.
HORATIO. These are but wild and whirling words, my lord.
HAMLET. I'm sorry they offend you, heartily;
Yes, faith, heartily.
HORATIO. There's no offence, my lord.
HAMLET. Yes, by Saint Patrick, but there is, Horatio,
And much offence too. Touching this vision here,
It is an honest ghost, that let me tell you;
For your desire to know what is between us
O'ermaster't as you may; and now, good friends,
As you are friends, scholars and soldiers,
Give me one poor request.
HORATIO. What is't, my lord? we will.
HAMLET. Never make known what you have seen tonight.
BOTH. My lord, we will not.
HAMLET. Nay, but swear't.
HORATIO. In faith, My lord, not I.
MARCELLUS. Nor I, my lord, in faith.
HAMLET. Upon my sword.
MARCELLUS. We have sworn, my lord, already.
HAMLET. Indeed, upon my sword, indeed.

GHOST *cries under the stage.*

GHOST. Swear.
HAMLET. Ha, ha, boy, say'st thou so? art thou there, truepenny?

98. *table* writing tablet 100. *saws* maxims; *forms* sketches; *pressures* impressions 115. *Illo, ho, ho* the falconer's call to his hawk 127. *circumstance* formality

Come on, you hear this fellow in the cellarage,
Consent to swear.
HORATIO. Propose the oath, my lord.
HAMLET. Never to speak of this that you have seen,
Swear by my sword.
GHOST. Swear.
HAMLET. *Hic et ubique?* then we'll shift our ground.
Come hither, gentlemen,
And lay your hands again upon my sword.
Swear by my sword
Never to speak of this that you have heard.
GHOST. Swear by his sword.
HAMLET. Well said, old mole, canst work i' the earth so fast?
A worthy pioner! Once more remove, good friends.
HORATIO. O day and night, but this is wondrous strange!
HAMLET. And therefore as a stranger give it welcome.
There are more things in heaven and earth, Horatio,
Than are dreamt of in your philosophy.
But come:
Here as before, never, so help you mercy,
How strange or odd some'er I bear myself—
As I perchance hereafter shall think meet
To put an antic disposition on—
That you, at such times seeing me, never shall
With arms encumbered thus, or this headshake,
Or by pronouncing of some doubtful phrase,
As "Well, well, we know," or "We could, an if we would,"
Or "If we list to speak," or "There be, an if they might,"
Or such ambiguous giving out, to note
That you know aught of me: this do swear,
So grace and mercy at your most need help you.
GHOST. Swear.
HAMLET. Rest, rest, perturbéd spirit: [*They swear.*] so, gentlemen,
With all my love I do commend me to you,
And what so poor a man as Hamlet is
May do to express his love and friending to you,
God willing, shall not lack. Let us go in together,
And still your fingers on your lips, I pray.
The time is out of joint; O cursed spite
That ever I was born to set it right!
Nay come, let's go together.
Exeunt.

ACT II

Scene I

Enter old POLONIUS, *with his man* REYNALDO.

POLONIUS. Give him this money and these notes, Reynaldo.
REYNALDO. I will, my lord.
POLONIUS. You shall do marvellous wisely, good Reynaldo,
Before you visit him, to make inquire
Of his behavior.
REYNALDO. My lord, I did intend it.
POLONIUS. Marry, well said, very well said.
Look you, sir,
Inquire me first what Danskers are in Paris,
And how, and who, what means, and where they keep,
What company, at what expense, and finding,
By this encompassment and drift of question,
That they do know my son, come you more nearer

---

156. *hic et ubique* here and everywhere 163. *pioner* miner 172. *antic* odd, strange 174. *encumbered* folded 7. *Danskers* Danes 8. *keep* resort 10. *encompassment* circuitous route

Than your particular demands will touch it;
Take you as 'twere some distant knowledge of him,
As thus, "I know his father and his friends,
And in part him;" do you mark this, Reynaldo?
REYNALDO. Ay, very well, my lord.
POLONIUS. "And in part him, but," you may say, "not well;
But if't be he I mean he's very wild,
Addicted so and so," and there put on him
What forgeries you please; marry, none so rank
As may dishonor him, take heed of that,
But, sir, such wanton, wild and usual slips
As are companions noted and most known
To youth and liberty.
REYNALDO. As gaming, my lord.
POLONIUS. Ay, or drinking, fencing, swearing, quarreling,
Drabbing—you may go so far.
REYNALDO. My lord, that would dishonor him.
POLONIUS. Faith, no, as you may season it in the charge.
You must not put another scandal on him,
That he is open to incontinency—
That's not my meaning; but breathe his faults so quaintly
That they may seem the taints of liberty,
The flash and outbreak of a fiery mind,
A savageness in unreclaimèd blood,
Of general assault.
REYNALDO. But, my good lord—
POLONIUS. Wherefore should you do this?
REYNALDO. Ay, my lord,
I would know that.
POLONIUS. Marry, sir, here's my drift,
And I believe it is a fetch of warrant:
You laying these slight sullies on my son,
As 'twere a thing a little soiled i' the working,
Mark you,
Your party in converse, him you would sound,
Having ever seen in the prenominate crimes
The youth you breathe of guilty, be assured
He closes with you in this consequence,
"Good sir," or so, or "friend," or "gentleman,"
According to the phrase or the addition
Of man and country.
REYNALDO. Very good, my lord.
POLONIUS. And then, sir, does a' this—a' does—
What was I about to say? By the mass, I was
About to say something; where did I leave?
REYNALDO. At "closes in the consequence,"
At "friend or so, and gentleman."
POLONIUS. At "closes in the consequence,"
ay, marry;
He closes with you thus: "I know the gentleman,
I saw him yesterday, or th'other day,
Or then, or then, with such, or such, and, as you say,
There was a' gaming, there o'ertook in's rouse,
There falling out at tennis," or perchance
"I saw him enter such a house of sale,"
Videlicet, a brothel, or so forth. See you now,
Your bait of falsehood takes this carp of truth,
And thus do we of wisdom and of reach,
With windlasses and with assays of bias,
By indirections find directions out;
So by my former lecture and advice
Shall you my son. You have me, have you not?
REYNALDO. My lord, I have.
POLONIUS. God be wi' ye, fare ye well.
REYNALDO. Good my lord!
POLONIUS. Observe his inclination in yourself.
REYNALDO. I shall, my lord.
POLONIUS. And let him ply his music.
REYNALDO. Well, my lord.
POLONIUS. Farewell!
Exit REYNALDO.

28. *season* modify; *charge* accusation 31. *quaintly* skilfully 32. *taints* faults 34. *unreclaimèd* unrestrained 35. *of general assault* which attack everyone 38. *fetch* device; *of warrant* justifiable 43. *prenominate* aforementioned 45. *in this consequence* to this effect 47. *addition* title 58. *o'ertook* overcome; *rouse* carousal, cups 63. *reach* capacity 64. *windlasses* crafty devices; *assays of bias* roundabout attempts 65. *indirections* indirect means

Enter OPHELIA.

How now, Ophelia, what's the matter?
OPHELIA. O my lord, my lord, I have been so affrighted!
POLONIUS. With what, i' the name of God?
OPHELIA. My lord, as I was sewing in my closet,
Lord Hamlet with his doublet all unbraced,
No hat upon his head, his stockings fouled,
Ungartered and down-gyvéd to his ankle,
Pale as his shirt, his knees knocking each other,
And with a look so piteous in purport
As if he had been loosèd out of hell
To speak of horrors—he comes before me.
POLONIUS. Mad for thy love?
OPHELIA.   My lord, I do not know,
But truly I do fear it.
POLONIUS.   What said he?
OPHELIA. He took me by the wrist and held me hard,
Then goes he to the length of all his arm,
And with his other hand thus o'er his brow
He falls to such perusal of my face
As a' would draw it. Long stayed he so;
At last, a little shaking of mine arm
And thrice his head thus waving up and down,
He raised a sigh so piteous and profound
As it did seem to shatter all his bulk
And end his being; that done, he lets me go:
And with his head over his shoulder turned
He seemed to find his way without his eyes,
For out o' doors he went without their helps,
And to the last bended their light on me.
POLONIUS. Come, go with me; I will go seek the king.
This is the very ecstasy of love,
Whose violent property fordoes itself,
And leads the will to desperate undertakings,
As oft as any passion under heaven
That does afflict our natures. I am sorry.
What, have you given him any hard words of late?
OPHELIA. No, my good lord, but as you did command
I did repel his letters, and denied
His access to me.
POLONIUS.   That hath made him mad.
I am sorry that with better heed and judgment
I had not quoted him; I feared he did but trifle
And meant to wreck thee; but, beshrew my jealousy,
By heaven it is as proper to our age
To cast beyond ourselves in our opinions,
As it is common for the younger sort
To lack discretion. Come, go we to the king,
This must be known; which, being kept close, might move
More grief to hide than hate to utter love.
Come.
Exeunt.

Scene 2

Flourish. Enter KING *and* QUEEN, ROSENCRANTZ *and* GUILDENSTERN, *with others*.

KING. Welcome, dear Rosencrantz and Guildenstern.
Moreover that we much did long to see you,
The need we have to use you did provoke
Our hasty sending. Something have you heard
Of Hamlet's transformation—so I call it,
Sith nor the exterior nor the inward man
Resembles that it was. What it should be,
More than his father's death, that thus hath put him

---

77. *doublet* jacket 79. *down-gyvéd* hanging down like gyves or fetters 101. *ecstasy* madness 102. *property* propensity; *fordoes* ruins 111. *quoted* observed 114. *cast beyond ourselves* go too far 117. *move* cause 118. *to hide* if hidden; *to utter love* if love is told

So much from the understanding of himself
I cannot dream of: I entreat you both
That, being of so young days brought up with him
And sith so neighbored to his youth and havior,
That you vouchsafe your rest here in our court
Some little time; so by your companies
To draw him on to pleasures, and to gather
So much as from occasion you may glean,
Whether aught to us unknown afflicts him thus,
That opened lies within our remedy.

QUEEN. Good gentlemen, he hath much talked of you,
And sure I am two men there are not living
To whom he more adheres. If it will please you
To show us so much gentry and good will
As to expend your time with us awhile,
For the supply and profit of our hope,
Your visitation shall receive such thanks
As fits a king's remembrance.

ROSENCRANTZ.   Both your majesties
Might, by the sovereign power you have of us,
Put your dread pleasures more into command
Than to entreaty.

GUILDENSTERN.   But we both obey,
And here give up ourselves in the full bent
To lay our service freely at your feet,
To be commanded.

KING. Thanks, Rosencrantz and gentle Guildenstern.
QUEEN. Thanks, Guildenstern and gentle Rosencrantz,
And I beseech you instantly to visit
My too much changéd son. Go, some of you,
And bring these gentlemen where Hamlet is.

GUILDENSTERN. Heavens make our presence and our practices
Pleasant and helpful to him!
QUEEN.   Ay, amen!

Exeunt ROSENCRANTZ, GUILDENSTERN
[*and some Attendants.*]

Enter POLONIUS.

POLONIUS. The ambassadors from Norway, my good lord,
Are joyfully returned.
KING. Thou still hast been the father of good news.
POLONIUS. Have I, my lord? Assure you, my good liege,
I hold my duty, as I hold my soul,
Both to my God and to my gracious king;
And I do think, or else this brain of mine
Hunts not the trail of policy so sure
As it hath used to do, that I have found
The very cause of Hamlet's lunacy.
KING. O speak of that, that do I long to hear.
POLONIUS. Give first admittance to the ambassadors;
My news shall be the fruit to that great feast.
KING. Thyself do grace to them, and bring them in.
[*Exit* POLONIUS.]
He tells me, my dear Gertrude, he hath found
The head and source of all your son's distemper.
QUEEN. I doubt it is no other but the main,
His father's death and our o'erhasty marriage.
KING. Well, we shall sift him.

Enter POLONIUS, VOLTIMAND *and* CORNELIUS.

           Welcome, my good friends.
Say, Voltimand, what from our brother Norway?
VOLTIMAND. Most fair return of greetings and desires.
Upon our first, he sent out to suppress
His nephew's levies, which to him appeared
To be a preparation 'gainst the Polack,
But better looked into, he truly found
It was against your highness; whereat grieved
That so his sickness, age, and impotence

---

12. *havior* way of life 18. *opened* made known
21. *adheres* is attached 22. *gentry* courtesy 30. *in the full bent* to the full 47. *policy* conduct of public affairs 53. *grace* honor 61. *upon our first* on our first raising the issue

Was falsely borne in hand, sends out arrests
On Fortinbras; which he in brief obeys,
Receives rebuke from Norway, and in fine
Makes vow before his uncle never more
To give the assay of arms against your majesty:
Whereon old Norway, overcome with joy,
Gives him threescore thousand crowns in annual fee,
And his commission to employ those soldiers,
So levied as before, against the Polack,
With an entreaty, herein further shown, [*Gives a paper.*]
That it might please you to give quiet pass
Through your dominions for this enterprise
On such regards of safety and allowance
As therein are set down.

KING. It likes us well;
And at our more considered time we'll read,
Answer, and think upon this business.
Meantime we thank you for your well-took labor.
Go to your rest; at night we'll feast together;
Most welcome home!
                Exeunt AMBASSADORS.

POLONIUS. This business is well ended.
My liege and madam, to expostulate
What majesty should be, what duty is,
Why day is day, night night, and time is time,
Were nothing but to waste night, day and time.
Therefore, since brevity is the soul of wit,
And tediousness the limbs and outward flourishes,
I will be brief. Your noble son is mad;
Mad call I it, for, to define true madness,
What is't but to be nothing else but mad?
But let that go.

QUEEN. More matter with less art.

POLONIUS. Madam, I swear I use no art at all.
That he is mad 'tis true; 'tis true 'tis pity,
And pity 'tis 'tis true; a foolish figure,
But farewell it, for I will use no art.
Mad let us grant him then, and now remains
That we find out the cause of this effect,
Or rather say, the cause of this defect,
For this effect defective comes by cause:
Thus it remains, and the remainder thus.
Perpend:
I have a daughter—have while she is mine—
Who in her duty and obedience, mark,
Hath given me this; now gather, and surmise.
    [*Reads*] *the letter.*
"To the celestial and my soul's idol, the most beautified Ophelia,"—
That's an ill phrase, a vile phrase, "beautified" is a vile phrase; but you shall hear. Thus: [*Reads.*]
"In her excellent white bosom, these," &c.—

QUEEN. Came this from Hamlet to her?

POLONIUS. Good madam, stay awhile; I will be faithful. [*Reads.*]
"Doubt thou the stars are fire,
    Doubt that the sun doth move,
Doubt truth to be a liar,
    But never doubt I love.
"O dear Ophelia, I am ill at these numbers, I have not art to reckon my groans; but that I love thee best, O most best, believe it. Adieu.
"Thine evermore, most dear lady, whilst this machine is to him, HAMLET."
This in obedience hath my daughter shown me,
And more above, hath his solicitings,
As they fell out by time, by means and place,
All given to mine ear.

KING. But how hath she Received his love?

POLONIUS. What do you think of me?

KING. As of a man faithful and honorable.

POLONIUS. I would fain prove so. But what might you think,
When I had seen this hot love on the wing—
As I perceived it, I must tell you that,
Before my daughter told me—what might you,
Or my dear majesty your queen here, think,
If I had played the desk or table-book,
Or given my heart a winking, mute and dumb,

---

67. *falsely borne in hand* deceived; *arrests* staying orders   69. *in fine* in conclusion   79. *regards* conditions   86. *expostulate* explain   98. *figure* trope, figure of speech   120. *numbers* verses   137. *given my heart a winking* shut the eyes of my heart

Or looked upon this love with idle sight—
What might you think? No, I went round to work,
And my young mistress thus I did bespeak:
"Lord Hamlet is a prince, out of thy star;
This must not be:" and then I prescripts gave her
That she should lock herself from his resort,
Admit no messengers, receive no tokens.
Which done, she took the fruits of my advice;
And he repelled (a short tale to make)—
Fell into a sadness, then into a fast,
Thence to a watch, thence into a weakness,
Thence to a lightness, and by this declension
Into the madness wherein now he raves,
And all we mourn for.
KING.   Do you think 'tis this?
QUEEN. It may be, very like.
POLONIUS. Hath there been such a time, I would fain know that,
That I have positively said " 'Tis so,"
When it proved otherwise?
KING.   Not that I know.
POLONIUS [pointing to his head and shoulder]. Take this from this, if this be otherwise;
If circumstances lead me, I will find
Where truth is hid, though it were hid indeed
Within the centre.
KING.   How may we try it further?
POLONIUS. You know sometimes he walks four hours together
Here in the lobby.
QUEEN.   So he does, indeed.
POLONIUS. At such a time I'll loose my daughter to him;
Be you and I behind an arras then;
Mark the encounter; if he love her not,
And be not from his reason fallen thereon,
Let me be no assistant for a state
But keep a farm and carters.
KING.   We will try it.

Enter HAMLET *reading on a book.*

QUEEN. But look where sadly the poor wretch comes reading.
POLONIUS. Away, I do beseech you both, away;
I'll board him presently.
Exeunt KING *and* QUEEN.
          O give me leave,
How does my good Lord Hamlet?
HAMLET. Well, God-a-mercy.
POLONIUS. Do you know me, my lord?
HAMLET. Excellent well, you are a fishmonger.
POLONIUS. Not I, my lord.
HAMLET. Then I would you were so honest a man.
POLONIUS. Honest, my lord!
HAMLET. Ay sir, to be honest, as this world goes, is to be one man picked out of ten thousand.
POLONIUS. That's very true, my lord.
HAMLET. For if the sun breed maggots in a dead dog, being a good kissing carrion —Have you a daughter?
POLONIUS. I have, my lord.
HAMLET. Let her not walk i' the sun; conception is a blessing, but as your daughter may conceive—friend, look to't.
POLONIUS [*aside*]. How say you by that? Still harping on my daughter. Yet he knew me not at first; a' said I was a fishmonger: A' is far gone, far gone, and truly in my youth I suffered much extremity for love, very near this. I'll speak to him again.—What do you read, my lord?
HAMLET. Words, words, words.
POLONIUS. What is the matter, my lord?
HAMLET. Between who?
POLONIUS. I mean the matter that you read, my lord.
HAMLET. Slanders, sir; for the satirical rogue says here, that old men have gray beards, that their faces are wrinkled, their eyes purging thick amber and plum-tree gum, and that they have a plentiful lack of wit, together with most weak hams; all of which, sir, though I most powerfully and potently believe, yet I hold it not honesty to have it

---

139. round directly 141. star sphere 142. prescripts orders 148. watch sleeplessness 149. lightness lightheadedness; declension decline 159. centre centre of the earth 165. thereon for this reason 170. board accost; presently at once 172. God-a-mercy thank-you 182. good kissing carrion flesh good for kissing 191. matter (1) subject matter (2) subject of a quarrel 196. purging oozing

thus set down; for yourself, sir, shall grow old as I am, if, like a crab, you could go backward.

POLONIUS [aside]. Though this be madness, yet there is method in't.—Will you walk out of the air, my lord?

HAMLET. Into my grave?

POLONIUS. Indeed, that's out of the air.— [Aside.] How pregnant sometimes his replies are! a happiness that often madness hits on, which reason and sanity could not so prosperously be delivered of. I will leave him, and suddenly contrive the means of meeting between him and my daughter.—My honorable lord, I will most humbly take my leave of you.

HAMLET. You cannot, sir, take from me any thing that I will more willingly part withal: except my life, except my life, except my life.

POLONIUS. Fare you well, my lord.

HAMLET. These tedious old fools!

Enter ROSENCRANTZ *and* GUILDENSTERN.

POLONIUS. You go to seek the Lord Hamlet; there he is.

ROSENCRANTZ [to POLONIUS]. God save you, sir!

[*Exit* POLONIUS.]

GUILDENSTERN. My most honored lord!

ROSENCRANTZ. My dear lord!

HAMLET. My excellent good friends! How dost thou, Guildenstern? Ah, Rosencrantz! Good lads, how do you both?

ROSENCRANTZ. As the indifferent children of the earth.

GUILDENSTERN. Happy, in that we are not overhappy; On Fortune's cap we are not the very button.

HAMLET. Nor the soles of her shoe?

ROSENCRANTZ. Neither, my lord.

HAMLET. Then you live about her waist, or in the middle of her favors.

GUILDENSTERN. Faith, her privates we.

HAMLET. In the secret parts of Fortune? O most true, she is a strumpet. What news?

ROSENCRANTZ. None, my lord, but that the world's grown honest.

HAMLET. Then is doomsday near; but your news is not true. Let me question more in particular: what have you, my good friends, deserved at the hands of Fortune, that she sends you to prison hither?

GUILDENSTERN. Prison, my lord?

HAMLET. Denmark's a prison.

ROSENCRANTZ. Then is the world one.

HAMLET. A goodly one, in which there are many confines, wards and dungeons, Denmark being one o' the worst.

ROSENCRANTZ. We think not so, my lord.

HAMLET. Why then 'tis none to you; for there is nothing either good or bad, but thinking makes it so: to me it is a prison.

ROSENCRANTZ. Why then your ambition makes it one; 'tis too narrow for your mind.

HAMLET. O God, I could be bounded in a nutshell, and count myself a king of infinite space, were it not that I have bad dreams.

GUILDENSTERN. Which dreams indeed are ambition; for the very substance of the ambitious is merely the shadow of a dream.

HAMLET. A dream itself is but a shadow.

ROSENCRANTZ. Truly, and I hold ambition of so airy and light a quality, that it is but a shadow's shadow.

HAMLET. Then are our beggars bodies, and our monarchs and outstretched heroes the beggars' shadows. Shall we to the court? for, by my fay, I cannot reason.

BOTH. We'll wait upon you.

HAMLET. No such matter; I will not sort you with the rest of my servants, for, to speak to you like an honest man, I am most dreadfully attended. But in the beaten way of friendship, what make you at Elsinore?

ROSENCRANTZ. To visit you, my lord, no other occasion.

HAMLET. Beggar that I am, I am even poor in thanks, but I thank you; and sure, dear friends, my thanks are too dear a halfpenny. Were you not sent for? Is

---

206. *pregnant* apt   213. *withal* with   224. *indifferent* ordinary   226. *button* top   243. *confines* cells; *wards* sections of a prison   258. *beggars* i.e., the men without ambition; *monarchs and . . . heroes,* i.e., ambitious men   259. *outstretched* enlarged, i.e., larger than ordinary men   269. *too dear a halfpenny* of little worth

it your own inclining? Is it a free visitation? Come, come, deal justly with me, come, come; nay, speak.
GUILDENSTERN. What should we say, my lord?
HAMLET. Why, any thing but to the purpose. You were sent for, and there is a kind of confession in your looks, which your modesties have not craft enough to color; I know the good king and queen have sent for you.
ROSENCRANTZ. To what end, my lord?
HAMLET. That you must teach me. But let me conjure you, by the rights of our fellowship, by the consonancy of our youth, by the obligation of our ever-preserved love, and by what more dear a better proposer can charge you withal, be even and direct with me whether you were sent for or no.
ROSENCRANTZ [aside to GUILDENSTERN]. What say you?
HAMLET [aside]. Nay then, I have an eye of you.—If you love me, hold not off.
GUILDENSTERN. My lord, we were sent for.
HAMLET. I will tell you why; so shall my anticipation prevent your discovery, and your secrecy to the king and queen molt no feather. I have of late—but wherefore I know not—lost all my mirth, foregone all custom of exercises; and indeed it goes so heavily with my disposition, that this goodly frame the earth seems to me a sterile promontory; this most excellent canopy the air, look you, this brave o'erhanging firmament, this majestical roof fretted with golden fire, why, it appeareth no thing to me but a foul and pestilent congregation of vapors. What a piece of work is man, how noble in reason, how infinite in faculties, in form and moving, how express and admirable in action, how like an angel in apprehension, how like a god! the beauty of the world, the paragon of animals! And yet to me what is this quintessence of dust? man delights not me, no, nor woman neither, though by your smiling you seem to say so.
ROSENCRANTZ. My lord, there was no such stuff in my thoughts.
HAMLET. Why did you laugh then, when I said "man delights not me"?
ROSENCRANTZ. To think, my lord, if you delight not in man, what lenten entertainment the players shall receive from you; we coted them on the way, and hither are they coming, to offer you service.
HAMLET. He that plays the king shall be welcome, his majesty shall have tribute of me; the adventurous knight shall use his foil and target, the lover shall not sigh gratis, the humorous man shall end his part in peace, the clown shall make those laugh whose lungs are tickle o' the sere, and the lady shall say her mind freely, or the blank verse shall halt for't. What players are they?
ROSENCRANTZ. Even those you were wont to take such delight in, the tragedians of the city.
HAMLET. How chances it they travel? their residence, both in reputation and profit, was better both ways.
ROSENCRANTZ. I think their inhibition comes by the means of the late innovation.
HAMLET. Do they hold the same estimation they did when I was in the city? are they so followed?
ROSENCRANTZ. No indeed, are they not.
HAMLET. How comes it? do they grow rusty?
ROSENCRANTZ. Nay, their endeavor keeps in the wonted pace; but there is, sir, an eyrie of children, little eyases, that cry out on the top of question, and are most tyrannically clapped for't: these are now the fashion, and so berattle the common stages (so they call them) that many wearing rapiers are afraid of goosequills, and dare scarce come thither.
HAMLET. What, are they children? who maintains 'em? how are they escoted? Will they pursue the quality no longer than they can sing? will they not say afterwards, if they should grow themselves to common players (as it is most

270. *free* unforced 279. *consonancy* accord 281. *proposer* questioner 282. *even* fair 289. *prevent come* before; *discovery* disclosure 290. *molt no feather* suffer no loss 291. *forgone* given up 296. *fretted* adorned 299. *express* well-devised 301. *paragon* model of excellence 309. *lenten* meagre 310. *coted* overtook 314. *target* shield 315. *humorous* eccentric 316. *tickle o' the sere* ready to go off at any moment 323. *inhibition* prohibition 330. *eyrie* nest, brood; *eyases* young hawks 333. *berattle* berate 334. *goosequills* pens 337. *escoted* supported; *quality* profession

like, if their means are no better) their writers do them wrong, to make them exclaim against their own succession?

ROSENCRANTZ. Faith, there has been much to do on both sides, and the nation holds it no sin to tarre them to controversy; there was for a while no money bid for argument, unless the poet and the player went to cuffs in the question.

HAMLET. Is't possible?

GUILDENSTERN. O, there has been much throwing about of brains.

HAMLET. Do the boys carry it away?

ROSENCRANTZ. Ay, that they do, my lord— Hercules and his load too.

HAMLET. It is not very strange, for my uncle is king of Denmark, and those that would make mows at him while my father lived, give twenty, forty, fifty, and hundred ducats apiece for his picture in little. 'Sblood, there is something in this more than natural, if philosophy could find it out.

Flourish for the players.

GUILDENSTERN. There are the players.

HAMLET. Gentlemen, you are welcome to Elsinore. Your hands, come then. The appurtenance of welcome is fashion and ceremony; let me comply with you in this garb, lest my extent to the players which, I tell you, must show fairly outwards, should more appear like entertainment than yours. You are welcome: but my uncle-father and aunt-mother are deceived.

GUILDENSTERN. In what, my dear lord?

HAMLET. I am but mad north-north-west; when the wind is southerly I know a hawk from a handsaw.

Enter POLONIUS.

POLONIUS. Well be with you, gentlemen.

HAMLET. Hark you, Guildenstern, and you too, at each ear a hearer; that great baby you see there is not yet out of his swaddling-clouts.

ROSENCRANTZ. Happily he is the second time come to them, for they say an old man is twice a child.

HAMLET. I will prophesy he comes to tell me of the players; mark it. You say right, sir; o' Monday morning, 'twas then indeed.

POLONIUS. My lord, I have news to tell you.

HAMLET. My lord, I have news to tell you. When Roscius was an actor in Rome—

POLONIUS. The actors are come hither, my lord.

HAMLET. Buz, buz!

POLONIUS. Upon my honor—

HAMLET. Then came each actor on his ass—

POLONIUS. The best actors in the world, either for tragedy, comedy, history, pastoral, pastoral-comical, historical-pastoral, tragical-historical, tragical-comical-historical-pastoral, scene individable, or poem unlimited; Seneca cannot be too heavy, nor Plautus too light for the law of writ and the liberty. These are the only men.

HAMLET. O Jephthah, judge of Israel, what a treasure hadst thou!

POLONIUS. What a treasure had he, my lord?

HAMLET. Why,
"One fair daughter and no more,
The which he lovéd passing well."

POLONIUS [*aside*]. Still on my daughter.

HAMLET. Am I not i' the right, old Jephthah?

POLONIUS. If you call me Jephthah, my lord, I have a daughter that I love passing well.

HAMLET. Nay, that follows not.

POLONIUS. What follows then, my lord?

HAMLET. Why,
"As by lot, God wot,"
and then, you know,
"It came to pass, as most like it was";
the first row of the pious chanson will show you more, for look where my abridgment comes.

Enter four or five PLAYERS.

You are welcome, masters, welcome all; I am glad to see thee well. Welcome,

---

342. *succession* future 344. *tarre* incite 345. *argument* plot of a play 350. *Hercules and his load* the sign outside the Globe Theater 352. *mows* faces, grimaces 358. *appurtenance* accompaniment 359. *comply* observe the formalities 361. *outwards* on the outside; *entertainment* welcome 366. *hawk* (1) falcon (2) plasterer's mortarboard; *handsaw* (1) heron (2) carpenter's tool 370. *clouts* clothes 386. *individable* unchanged; *unlimited* i.e., ignoring the unities 388. *writ* writing; *liberty* the area outside city jurisdiction, i.e., those who do not heed the rules 405. *chanson* song 406. *my abridgement* that which cuts me short

good friends. O my old friend, thy face is valanced since I saw thee last; comest thou to beard me in Denmark? What, my young lady and mistress! by'r lady, your ladyship is nearer to heaven than when I saw you last by the altitude of a chopine. Pray God your voice, like a piece of uncurrent gold, be not cracked within the ring. Masters, you are all welcome. We'll e'en to't like French falconers, fly at any thing we see; we'll have a speech straight; come, give us a taste of your quality, come, a passionate speech.

FIRST PLAYER. What speech, my good lord?

HAMLET. I heard thee speak me a speech once, but it was never acted, or if it was, not above once, for the play, I remember, pleased not the million; 'twas caviary to the general, but it was—as I received it, and others whose judgments in such matters cried in the top of mine—an excellent play, well digested in the scenes, set down with as much modesty as cunning. I remember one said there were no sallets in the lines to make the matter savory, nor no matter in the phrase that might indict the author of affection, but called it an honest method, as wholesome as sweet, and by very much more handsome than fine. One speech in't I chiefly loved; 'twas Æneas' tale to Dido, and thereabout of it especially where he speaks of Priam's slaughter. If it live in your memory, begin at this line—let me see, let me see:

"The rugged Pyrrhus, like the Hyrcanian beast,"

—'tis not so; it begins with Pyrrhus:

"The rugged Pyrrhus, he whose sable arms,
Black as his purpose, did the night resemble
When he lay couchéd in the ominous horse,
Hath now this dread and black complexion smearéd
With heraldry more dismal; head to foot
Now is he total gules, horridly tricked
With blood of fathers, mothers, daughters, sons,
Baked and impasted with the parching streets
That lend a tyrannous and damnéd light
To their lord's murder· roasted in wrath and fire
And thus o'er-sizéd with coagulate gore,
With eyes like carbuncles, the hellish Pyrrhus
Old grandsire Priam seeks."—
So proceed you.

POLONIUS. 'Fore God, my lord, well spoken, with good accent and good discretion.

FIRST PLAYER. "Anon he finds him
Striking too short at Greeks; his antique sword,
Rebellious to his arm, lies where it falls,
Repugnant to command; unequal matched,
Pyrrhus at Priam drives, in rage strikes wide,
But with the whiff and wind of his fell sword
The unnervéd father falls. Then senseless Ilium,
Seeming to feel this blow, with flaming top
Stoops to his base, and with a hideous crash
Takes prisoner Pyrrhus' ear, for lo! his sword,
Which was declining on the milky head
Of reverend Priam, seemed i' the air to stick;
So, as a painted tyrant, Pyrrhus stood
And, like a neutral to his will and matter,
Did nothing.
But as we often see against some storm
A silence in the heavens, the rack stand still,

---

409. *valanced* fringed   410. *young lady and mistress* the boy who played the leading female parts   412. *chopine* high-heeled shoe   413. *uncurrent* not legal tender   414. *ring* (1) tone (2) outer ring round the design of a coin   422. *general* public   423. *cried in the top of* spoke with more authority than   424. *digested* arranged   425. *modesty* moderation   426. *sallets* salads   428. *affection* affectation   429. *handsome* stately   431. *Aeneas' tale to Dido* In the *Aeneid* Aeneas relates to Dido the story of the fall of Troy   434. *Hyrcanian beast* tiger   436. *sable* black   440. *heraldry* heraldic device   441. *gules* the heraldic word for 'red'; *tricked* colored (another heraldic term)   446. *o'er-sizéd* glued over; *coagulate* clotted   447. *carbuncles* red semi-precious stones   457. *fell* fierce   458. *unnervéd* feeble in sinew; *Illium* the citadel of Troy   460. *stoops to his base* collapses to the ground   467. *against* in expectation of   468. *rack* clouds

The bold winds speechless, and the orb below
As hush as death, anon the dreadful thunder
Doth rend the region; so, after Pyrrhus' pause,
A rouséd vengeance sets him new a-work,
And never did the Cyclops' hammers fall
On Mars's armour, forged for proof eterne,
With less remorse than Pyrrhus' bleeding sword
Now falls on Priam.
Out, out, thou strumpet Fortune! All you gods
In general synod take away her power,
Break all the spokes and fellies from her wheel,
And bowl the round nave down the hill of heaven,
As low as to the fiends!"

POLONIUS. This is too long.

HAMLET. It shall to the barber's with your beard; prithee, say on, he's for a jig or a tale of bawdry, or he sleeps; say on, come to Hecuba.

FIRST PLAYER. "But who, ah woe! had seen the mobled queen—"

HAMLET. "The mobled queen"?

POLONIUS. That's good, "mobled queen" is good.

FIRST PLAYER. "Run barefoot up and down, threatening the flames
With bisson rheum, a clout upon that head
Where late the diadem stood, and for a robe
About her lank and all o'er-teeméd loins
A blanket in the alarm of fear caught up;
Who this had seen, with tongue in venom steeped,
'Gainst Fortune's state would treason have pronounced;
But if the gods themselves did see her then,
When she saw Pyrrhus make malicious sport
In mincing with his sword her husband's limbs,
The instant burst of clamor that she made—
Unless things mortal move them not at all—
Would have made milch the burning eyes of heaven,
And passion in the gods."

POLONIUS. Look whether he has not turned his color, and has tears in's eyes. Prithee no more.

HAMLET. 'Tis well; I'll have thee speak out the rest soon. Good my lord, will you see the players well bestowed? Do you hear, let them be well used, for they are the abstract and brief chronicles of the time; after your death you were better have a bad epitaph than their ill report while you live.

POLONIUS. My lord, I will use them according to their desert.

HAMLET. God's bodkin, man, much better; use every man after his desert, and who shall scape whipping? Use them after your own honor and dignity; the less they deserve, the more merit is in your bounty. Take them in.

POLONIUS. Come, sirs.

HAMLET. Follow him, friends; we'll hear a play tomorrow.
Exit POLONIUS [*with all the* PLAYERS *except the First*].
Dost thou hear me, old friend; can you play the Murder of Gonzago?

FIRST PLAYER. Ay, my lord.

HAMLET. We'll ha't tomorrow night. You could for a need study a speech of some dozen or sixteen lines, which I would set down and insert in't, could you not?

FIRST PLAYER. Ay, my lord.

HAMLET. Very well. Follow that lord, and look you mock him not. [*Exit* FIRST PLAYER.] My good friends, I'll leave you till night; you are welcome to Elsinore. *Exeunt.*

ROSENCRANTZ. Good my lord!

HAMLET. Ay, so, God bye to you.
　　Now I am alone.
O what a rogue and peasant slave am I!
Is it not monstrous that this player here
But in a fiction, in a dream of passion,

---

473. *Cyclops* the workmen of Vulcan 474. *proof* invulnerability 479. *fellies* rim 480. *nave* hub 484. *jig* comic dialogue in song 486. *mobled* muffled 490. *bisson* blinding; *rheum* moisture, tears; *clout* cloth 492. *o'erteeméd* (because, it was said, Hecuba had had fifty children) 501. *milch* tearful; *burning eyes of heaven* the stars 506. *bestowed* lodged

Could force his soul so to his own conceit
That from her working all his visage wanned,
Tears in his eyes, distraction in his aspect,
A broken voice, and his whole function suiting
With forms to his conceit? and all for nothing,
For Hecuba.
What's Hecuba to him, or he to Hecuba,
That he should weep for her? What would he do
Had he the motive and the cue for passion
That I have? He would drown the stage with tears,
And cleave the general ear with horrid speech,
Make mad the guilty and appal the free,
Confound the ignorant, and amaze indeed
The very faculties of eyes and ears;
Yet I,
A dull and muddy-mettled rascal, peak
Like John-a-dreams, unpregnant of my cause,
And can say nothing; no, not for a king,
Upon whose property and most dear life
A damned defeat was made. Am I a coward?
Who calls me villain, breaks my pate across,
Plucks off my beard and blows it in my face,
Tweaks me by the nose, gives me the lie i' the throat
As deep as to the lungs? who does me this, ha?
'Swounds, I should take it: for it cannot be
But I am pigeon-livered, and lack gall
To make oppression bitter, or ere this
I should ha' fatted all the region kites
With this slave's offal. Bloody, bawdy villain!
Remorseless, treacherous, lecherous, kindless villain!
O, vengeance!
Why, what an ass am I! This is most brave,
That I, the son of a dear father murdered,
Prompted to my revenge by heaven and hell,
Must like a whore, unpack my heart with words,
And fall a-cursing, like a very drab,
A stallion!
Fie upon't, foh! About, my brains; hum, I have heard
That guilty creatures sitting at a play
Have by the very cunning of the scene
Been struck so to the soul, that presently
They have proclaimed their malefactions;
For murder, though it have no tongue, will speak
With most miraculous organ. I'll have these players
Play something like the murder of my father
Before mine uncle; I'll observe his looks,
I'll tent him to the quick; if a' do blench
I know my course. The spirit that I have seen
May be a devil, and the devil hath power
To assume a pleasing shape; yea, and perhaps
Out of my weakness and melancholy,
As he is very potent with such spirits,
Abuses me to damn me; I'll have grounds
More relative than this; the play's the thing
Wherein I'll catch the conscience of the king.
Exit.

ACT III

Scene I

Enter KING, QUEEN, POLONIUS, OPHELIA, ROSENCRANTZ, GUILDENSTERN, LORDS.

KING. And can you by no drift of circumstance

536. *conceit* feeling, imagination 539. *function* behavior 551. *muddy-mettled* poor-spirited; *peak* mope 552. *John-a-dreams* a dreamy fellow; *un-* *pregnant* unproductive 555. *defeat* destruction 565. *kindless* unnatural 576. *presently* at once 582. *tent* probe 589. *relative* relevant

Get from him why he puts on this confusion,
Grating so harshly all his days of quiet
With turbulent and dangerous lunacy?
ROSENCRANTZ. He does confess he feels himself distracted,
But from what cause a' will by no means speak.
GUILDENSTERN. Nor do we find him forward to be sounded,
But with a crafty madness keeps aloof
When we would bring him on to some confession
Of his true state.
QUEEN.   Did he receive you well?
ROSENCRANTZ. Most like a gentleman.
GUILDENSTERN. But with much forcing of his disposition.
ROSENCRANTZ. Niggard of question, but of our demands
Most free in his reply.
QUEEN.   Did you assay him.
To any pastime?
ROSENCRANTZ. Madam, it so fell out, that certain players
We o'er-raught on the way; of these we told him,
And there did seem in him a kind of joy
To hear of it: they are here about the court
And, as I think, they have already order
This night to play before him.
POLONIUS. 'Tis most true,
And he beseeched me to entreat your majesties
To hear and see the matter.
KING. With all my heart; and it doth much content me
To hear him so inclined.
Good gentlemen, give him a further edge,
And drive his purpose into these delights.
ROSENCRANTZ. We shall, my lord.
Exeunt ROSENCRANTZ *and* GUILDENSTERN.
KING. Sweet Gertrude, leave us too,
For we have closely sent for Hamlet hither,
That he, as 'twere by accident, may here
Affront Ophelia;
Her father and myself, lawful espials,
Will so bestow ourselves that, seeing unseen,
We may of their encounter frankly judge,
And gather by him, as he is behaved,
If't be the affliction of his love or no
That thus he suffers for.
QUEEN. I shall obey you;
And for your part, Ophelia, I do wish
That your good beauties be the happy cause
Of Hamlet's wildness; so shall I hope your virtues
Will bring him to his wonted way again,
To both your honors.
OPHELIA.   Madam, I wish it may.
[*Exit* QUEEN.]
POLONIUS. Ophelia, walk you here. Gracious, so please you.
We will bestow ourselves. [*To* OPHELIA] Read on this book,
That show of such an exercise may color
Your loneliness. We are oft to blame in this—
'Tis too much proved—that with devotion's visage
And pious action we do sugar o'er
The devil himself.
KING. [*aside*]. O 'tis too true;
How smart a lash that speech doth give my conscience!
The harlot's cheek, beautied with plastering art,
Is not more ugly to the thing that helps it
Than is my deed to my most painted word:
O heavy burden!
POLONIUS. I hear him coming; let's withdraw, my lord.
Exeunt.

Enter HAMLET.

HAMLET. To be or not to be, that is the question,
Whether 'tis nobler in the mind to suffer
The slings and arrows of outrageous fortune,
Or to take arms against a sea of troubles,
And by opposing end them? To die, to sleep—
No more; and by a sleep to say we end
The heartache and the thousand natural shocks
That flesh is heir to, 'tis a consummation
Devoutly to be wished. To die, to sleep;
To sleep, perchance to dream; ay, there's the rub,
For in that sleep of death what dreams may come

17. o'er-raught overtook   31. affront confront   32. espials spies   45. color excuse   65. rub obstruction

Could be worse after death

When we have shuffled off this mortal coil
Must give us pause; there's the respect
That makes calamity of so long life;
For who would bear the whips and scorns of time,
The oppressor's wrong, the proud man's contumely,
The pangs of despised love, the law's delay,
The insolence of office and the spurns
That patient merit of the unworthy takes,
When he himself might his quietus make
With a bare bodkin? who would fardels bear,
To grunt and sweat under a weary life,
But that the dread of something after death,
The undiscovered country, from whose bourn
No traveler returns, puzzles the will,
And makes us rather bear those ills we have
Than fly to others that we know not of?
Thus conscience does make cowards of us all,
And thus the native hue of resolution
Is sicklied o'er with the pale cast of thought,
And enterprises of great pitch and moment
With this regard their currents turn awry,
And lose the name of action. Soft you now,
The fair Ophelia! Nymph, in thy orisons
Be all my sins remembered.

OPHELIA. Good my lord,
How does your honor for this many a day?

HAMLET. I humbly thank you, well, well, well.

OPHELIA. My lord, I have remembrances of yours
That I have longéd long to re-deliver;
I pray you now receive them.

HAMLET. No, not I,
I never gave you aught.

OPHELIA. My honored lord, you know right well you did,
And with them words of so sweet breath composed
As made these things more rich; their perfume lost,
Take these again, for to the noble mind
Rich gifts wax poor when givers prove unkind.
There, my lord.

HAMLET. Ha, ha, are you honest?

OPHELIA. My lord?

HAMLET. Are you fair?

OPHELIA. What means your lordship?

HAMLET. That if you be honest and fair, your honesty should admit no discourse to your beauty.

OPHELIA. Could beauty, my lord, have better commerce than with honesty?

HAMLET. Ay, truly, for the power of beauty will sooner transform honesty from what it is to a bawd than the force of honesty can translate beauty into his likeness; this was sometime a paradox, but now the time gives it proof. I did love you once.

OPHELIA. Indeed, my lord, you made me believe so.

HAMLET. You should not have believed me, for virtue cannot so inoculate our old stock, but we shall relish of it; I loved you not.

OPHELIA. I was the more deceived.

HAMLET. Get thee to a nunnery; why wouldst thou be a breeder of sinners? I am myself indifferent honest, but yet I could accuse me of such things, that it were better my mother had not borne me: I am very proud, revengeful, ambitious, with more offences at my beck than I have thoughts to put them in, imagination to give them shape, or time to act them in. What should such fellows as I do crawling between earth and heaven? We are arrant knaves, all; believe none of us; go thy ways to a nunnery. Where's your father?

OPHELIA. At home, my lord.

HAMLET. Let the doors be shut upon him, that he may play the fool no where but in's own house. Farewell.

OPHELIA. O help him, you sweet heavens!

HAMLET. If thou dost marry, I'll give thee this plague for thy dowry: be thou as chaste as ice, as pure as snow, thou shalt not escape calumny. Get thee to a nun-

---

71. *contumely* scorn 75. *quietus* settlement 76. *bodkin* dagger; *fardels* burdens 79. *bourn* boundary 86. *pitch* height 87. *awry* aside 89. *orisons* prayers

109. *commerce* association 118. *inoculate* engraft; *relish of* smack of, have a trace of

nery, go: farewell. Or if thou wilt needs marry, marry a fool, for wise men know well enough what monsters you make of them. To a nunnery go, and quickly too. Farewell.

OPHELIA. O heavenly powers restore him!

HAMLET. I have heard of your paintings too, well enough; God hath given you one face, and you make yourselves another; you jig, you amble, and you lisp; you nickname God's creatures, and make your wantonness your ignorance. Go to, I'll no more on't; it hath made me mad. I say we will have no more marriage; those that are married already, all but one, shall live; the rest shall keep as they are. To a nunnery, go.
Exit.

OPHELIA. O what a noble mind is here o'erthrown!
The courtier's, soldier's, scholar's eye, tongue, sword,
The expectancy and rose of the fair state,
The glass of fashion and the mould of form,
The observed of all observers, quite, quite down,
And I of ladies most deject and wretched,
That sucked the honey of his music vows,
Now see that noble and most sovereign reason
Like sweet bells jangled, out of tune and harsh,
That unmatched form and feature of blown youth
Blasted with ecstasy; O woe is me
To have seen what I have seen, see what I see!

Re-enter KING *and* POLONIUS.

KING. Love! his affections do not that way tend,
Nor what he spake, though it lacked form a little,
Was not like madness. There's something in his soul
O'er which his melancholy sits on brood,
And I do doubt the hatch and the disclose
Will be some danger; which for to prevent
I have in quick determination
Thus set it down: he shall with speed to England,
For the demand of our neglected tribute.
Haply the seas, and countries different,
With variable objects, shall expel
This something-settled matter in his heart,
Whereon his brains still beating puts him thus
From fashion of himself. What think you on't?

POLONIUS. It shall do well; but yet do I believe
The origin and commencement of his grief
Sprung from neglected love. How now, Ophelia?
You need not tell us what Lord Hamlet said;
We heard it all. My lord, do as you please,
But, if you hold it fit, after the play
Let his queen mother all alone entreat him
To show his grief; let her be round with him,
And I'll be placed, so please you, in the ear
Of all their conference. If she find him not,
To England send him, or confine him where
Your wisdom best shall think.

KING. It shall be so;
Madness in great ones must not unwatch'd go.
Exeunt.

Scene 2

Enter HAMLET *and three of the* PLAYERS.

HAMLET. Speak the speech, I pray you, as I pronounced it to you, trippingly on the tongue; but if you mouth it, as many of our players do, I had as lief the town crier spoke my lines. Nor do not saw the air too much with your hand, thus,

153. *glass* mirror; *mould* model; *form* behavior   160. *ecstasy* madness   173. *something-settled* somewhat settled   183. *round* direct   3. *had as lief* would as soon

but use all gently, for in the very torrent, tempest, and as I may say whirlwind of your passion, you must acquire and beget a temperance that may give it smoothness. O, it offends me to the soul to hear a robustious periwig-pated fellow tear a passion to tatters, to very rags, to split the ears of the groundlings, who for the most part are capable of nothing but inexplicable dumb shows and noise: I would have such a fellow whipped for o'erdoing Termagant; it out-herods Herod: pray you avoid it.
FIRST PLAYER. I warrant your honor.
HAMLET. Be not too tame neither, but let your own discretion be your tutor; suit the action to the word, the word to the action, with this special observance, that you o'erstep not the modesty of nature: for any thing so o'erdone is from the purpose of playing, whose end, both at the first and now, was and is, to hold as 'twere the mirror up to nature, to show virtue her own feature, scorn her own image, and the very age and body of the time his form and pressure. Now this overdone or come tardy off, though it make the unskilful laugh, cannot but make the judicious grieve; the censure of the which one must in your allowance o'erweigh a whole theatre of others. O there be players that I have seen play—and heard others praise, and that highly—not to speak it profanely, that neither having the accent of Christians nor the gait of Christian, pagan, nor man, have so strutted and bellowed, that I have thought some of nature's journeymen had made men, and not made them well, they imitated humanity so abominably.
FIRST PLAYER. I hope we have reformed that indifferently with us, sir.
HAMLET. O reform it altogether, and let those that play your clowns speak no more than is set down for them, for there be of them that will themselves laugh, to set on some quantity of barren spectators to laugh too, though in the mean time some necessary question of the play be then to be considered; that's villanous, and shows a most pitiful ambition in the fool that uses it. Go, make you ready.
Exeunt PLAYERS.

Enter POLONIUS, ROSENCRANTZ, *and* GUILDENSTERN.

How now, my lord? will the king hear this piece of work?
POLONIUS. And the queen too, and that presently.
HAMLET. Bid the players make haste.
Exit POLONIUS.
Will you two help to hasten them?
ROSENCRANTZ. } We will, my lord.
GUILDENSTERN. }
lord.
Exeunt they two.
HAMLET. What, ho, Horatio!

Enter HORATIO.

HORATIO. Here, sweet lord, at your service.
HAMLET. Horatio, thou art e'en as just a man
As e'er my conversation coped withal.
HORATIO. O my dear lord—
HAMLET.   Nay, do not think I flatter,
For what advancement may I hope from thee
That no revenue hast but thy good spirits
To feed and clothe thee? Why should the poor be flattered?
No, let the candied tongue lick absurd pomp,
And crook the pregnant hinges of the knee
Where thrift may follow fawning. Dost thou hear?
Since my dear soul was mistress of her choice,
And could of men distinguish her election,
She hath sealed thee for herself, for thou hast been
As one in suffering all that suffers nothing,
A man that fortune's buffets and rewards

---

9. *robustious* burly; *periwig-pated* bewigged 10. *groundlings* those who paid the cheapest rate of admission 13. *Termagant . . . Herod* characters in old scriptural plays, noted for their violence 19. *modesty* moderation 24. *pressure* shape; *tardy* imperfectly 32. *journeymen* laborers 35. *indifferently* fairly well 38. *clowns* comic rustics 46. *presently* immediately 53. *withal* with 59. *pregnant* supple 60. *thrift* profit 62. *election* choice

Hast ta'en with equal thanks; and blessed are those
Whose blood and judgment are so well co-medled,
That they are not a pipe for fortune's finger
To sound what stop she please. Give me that man
That is not passion's slave, and I will wear him
In my heart's core, ay, in my heart of heart,
As I do thee. Something too much of this.
There is a play tonight before the king;
One scene of it comes near the circumstance
Which I have told thee of my father's death;
I prithee, when thou seest that act a-foot,
Even with the very comment of thy soul
Observe my uncle. If his occulted guilt
Do not itself unkennel in one speech,
It is a damnéd ghost that we have seen,
And my imaginations are as foul
As Vulcan's stithy. Give him heedful note,
For I mine eyes will rivet to his face,
And after we will both our judgments join
In censure of his seeming.
HORATIO.   Well, my lord;
If he steal aught the whilst this play is playing,
And scape detecting, I will pay the theft.
HAMLET. They are coming to the play, I must be idle;
Get you a place.

Enter Trumpets and Kettledrums, KING, QUEEN, POLONIUS, OPHELIA, ROSENCRANTZ, GUILDENSTERN, *and other Lords attendant with his Guard carrying torches. Danish march. Sound a flourish.*

KING. How fares our cousin Hamlet?
HAMLET. Excellent, i' faith, of the chameleon's dish; I eat the air, promise-crammed: you cannot feed capons so.
KING. I have nothing with this answer, Hamlet; these words are not mine.
HAMLET. No, nor mine now. [*To* POLONIUS] My lord, you played once i' the university, you say?
POLONIUS. That did I, my lord, and was accounted a good actor.
HAMLET. What did you enact?
POLONIUS. I did enact Julius Cæsar; I was killed i' the Capitol; Brutus killed me.
HAMLET. It was a brute part of him to kill so capital a calf there. Be the players ready?
ROSENCRANTZ. Ay, my lord, they stay upon your patience.
QUEEN. Come hither, my dear Hamlet, sit by me.
HAMLET. No, good mother, here's metal more attractive.
[*Lying down at* OPHELIA's *feet.*]
POLONIUS [*to the* KING]. O ho, do you mark that?
HAMLET. Lady, shall I lie in your lap?
OPHELIA. No, my lord.
HAMLET. I mean, my head upon your lap?
OPHELIA. Ay, my lord.
HAMLET. Do you think I meant country matters?
OPHELIA. I think nothing, my lord.
HAMLET. That's a fair thought to lie between maids' legs.
OPHELIA. What is, my lord?
HAMLET. Nothing.
OPHELIA. You are merry, my lord.
HAMLET. Who, I?
OPHELIA. Ay, my lord.
HAMLET. O God, your only jig-maker. What should a man do but be merry? for, look you, how cheerfully my mother looks, and my father died within's two hours.
OPHELIA. Nay, 'tis twice two months, my lord.
HAMLET. So long? Nay then, let the devil wear black, for I'll have a suit of sables. O heavens, die two months ago, and not forgotten yet? Then there's hope a great man's memory may outlive his life half a year, but by'r lady a' must build churches then, or else shall a' suffer not thinking on, with the hobbyhorse, whose epitaph is, "For O, for O, the hobbyhorse is forgot."

---

67. *blood* passion; *co-medled* blended   78. *occulted* hidden   82. *stithy* smithy   85. *censure* judging; *seeming* behavior   88. *idle* insane   91. *the chameleon's dish* air, on which the chameleon was supposed to live   94. *are not mine* are not an answer to my question   104. *stay upon your patience* await your leisure   127. *sables* furs

Hautboys play. The dumb-show enters. Enter a King and a Queen very lovingly; the Queen embracing him, and he her. She kneels, and makes show of protestation unto him. He takes her up, and declines his head upon her neck: he lays him down upon a bank of flowers: she, seeing him asleep, leaves him. Anon comes in another man, takes off his crown, kisses it, pours poison in the sleeper's ears, and leaves him. The Queen returns; finds the King dead, and makes passionate action. The Poisoner with some three or four comes in again, seems to condole with her. The dead body is carried away. The Poisoner woos the Queen with gifts: she seems harsh awhile, but in the end accepts his love.
Exeunt.

OPHELIA. What means this, my lord?
HAMLET. Marry, this is miching mallecho, it means mischief.
OPHELIA. Belike this show imports the argument of the play.

Enter PROLOGUE.

HAMLET. We shall know by this fellow; the players cannot keep counsel, they'll tell all.
140 OPHELIA. Will a' tell us what this show meant?
HAMLET. Ay, or any show that you'll show him; be not you ashamed to show, he'll not shame to tell you what it means.
OPHELIA. You are naught, you are naught; I'll mark the play.
PROLOGUE. For us and for our tragedy,
  Here stooping to your clemency,
  We beg your hearing patiently.
    [*Exit.*]
HAMLET. Is this a prologue, or the posy of a ring?
150 OPHELIA. 'Tis brief, my lord.
HAMLET. As woman's love.

Enter [two PLAYERS *as]* King *and* Queen.

PLAYER KING. Full thirty times hath Phœbus' cart gone round
  Neptune's salt wash and Tellus' orbèd ground,
And thirty dozen moons with borrowed sheen
About the world have times twelve thirties been
Since love our hearts, and Hymen did our hands
Unite commutual in most sacred bands.
PLAYER QUEEN. So many journeys may the sun and moon
Make us again count o'er ere love be done!
But woe is me, you are so sick of late, 160
So far from cheer and from your former state,
That I distrust you. Yet, though I distrust,
Discomfort you my lord, it nothing must,
For women fear too much, even as they love,
And women's fear and love hold quantity:
In neither aught, or in extremity.
Now what my love is proof hath made you know,
And as my love is sized, my fear is so;
Where love is great, the littlest doubts are fear;
Where little fears grow great, great love 170
grows there.
PLAYER KING. Faith, I must leave thee, love, and shortly too;
My operant powers their functions leave to do;
And thou shalt live in this fair world behind,
Honored, beloved, and haply one as kind
For husband shalt thou—
PLAYER QUEEN.   O confound the rest!
Such love must needs be treason in my breast.
In second husband let me be accurst,
None wed the second but who killed the first.
HAMLET [*aside*]. Wormwood, wormwood.
PLAYER QUEEN. The instances that second 180
marriage move
Are base respects of thrift, but none of love;
A second time I kill my husband dead
When second husband kisses me in bed.
PLAYER KING. I do believe you think what now you speak,
But what we do determine oft we break.
Purpose is but the slave to memory,
Of violent birth but poor validity,

---

134. *miching mallecho* skulking mischief   144. *naught* indecent   149. *posy* inscription   152. *Phœbus' cart* the sun   157. *commutual* mutually   162. *distrust* fear for   172. *operant* active

Which now like fruit unripe sticks on the tree,
But fall unshaken when they mellow be.
Most necessary 'tis that we forget
To pay ourselves what to ourselves is debt;
What to ourselves in passion we propose,
The passion ending, doth the purpose lose.
The violence of either grief or joy
Their own enactures with themselves destroy;
Where joy most revels, grief doth most lament;
Grief joys, joy grieves, on slender accident.
This world is not for aye, nor 'tis not strange
That even our loves should with our fortunes change;
For 'tis a question left us yet to prove,
Whether love lead fortune, or else fortune love.
The great man down, you mark his favorite flies;
The poor advanced makes friends of enemies.
And hitherto doth love on fortune tend,
For who not needs shall never lack a friend,
And who in want a hollow friend doth try,
Directly seasons him his enemy.
But, orderly to end where I begun,
Our wills and fates do so contrary run,
That our devices still are overthrown;
Our thoughts are ours, their ends none of our own;
So think thou wilt no second husband wed,
But die thy thoughts when thy first lord is dead.

PLAYER QUEEN. Nor earth to me give food, nor heaven light,
Sport and repose lock from me day and night,
To desperation turn my trust and hope,
An anchor's cheer in prison be my scope,
Each opposite that blanks the face of joy,
Meet what I would have well, and it destroy,
Both here and hence pursue me lasting strife,
If once a widow ever I be wife!

HAMLET. If she should break it now!

PLAYER KING. 'Tis deeply sworn. Sweet, leave me here a while;
My spirits grow dull, and fain I would beguile
The tedious day with sleep.   *Sleeps.*

PLAYER QUEEN.   Sleep rock thy brain,
And never come mischance between us twain!
    Exit.

HAMLET. Madam, how like you this play?

QUEEN. The lady doth protest too much, methinks.

HAMLET. O, but she'll keep her word.

KING. Have you heard the argument? Is there no offence in't?

HAMLET. No, no, they do but jest, poison in jest; no offence i' the world.

KING. What do you call the play?

HAMLET. The Mousetrap. Marry, how? Tropically. This play is the image of a murder done in Vienna; Gonzago is the duke's name, his wife Baptista; you shall see anon 'tis a knavish piece of work, but what o' that? your majesty and we that have free souls, it touches us not; let the galled jade wince, our withers are unwrung.

Enter LUCIANUS.

This is one Lucianus, nephew to the king.

OPHELIA. You are as good as a chorus, my lord.

HAMLET. I could interpret between you and your love, if I could see the puppets dallying.

OPHELIA. You are keen, my lord, you are keen.

HAMLET. It would cost you a groaning to take off mine edge.

OPHELIA. Still better and worse.

HAMLET. So you must take your husbands. Begin murderer, leave the damnable faces, and begin. Come: "the croaking raven doth bellow for revenge."

LUCIANUS. Thoughts black, hands apt, drugs fit, and time agreeing,

---

195. enactures fulfilment, performances   207. seasons ripens   217. anchor's hermit's   218. blanks turns pale   230. argument outline of the plot   235. tropically figuratively   240. galled chafed; jade horse; withers shoulders of horse; unwrung not irritated

  Confederate season, else no creature seeing,
  Thou mixture rank, of midnight weeds
   collected,
  With Hecate's ban thrice blasted, thrice
   infected,
  Thy natural magic and dire property
  On wholesome life usurps immediately.
   Pours the poison in his ears.
HAMLET. A' poisons him i' the garden for
  his estate. His name's Gonzago; the
  story is extant, and written in very
  choice Italian; you shall see anon how
  the murderer gets the love of Gon-
  zago's wife.
OPHELIA. The king rises.
HAMLET. What, frighted with false fire?
QUEEN. How fares my lord?
POLONIUS. Give o'er the play.
KING. Give me some light; away!
POLONIUS. Lights, lights, lights!
   Exeunt all but HAMLET *and* HORATIO.
HAMLET. Why, let the stricken deer go weep,
   The hart ungallèd play,
  For some must watch while some must
   sleep;
   Thus runs the world away.
  Would not this, sir, and a forest of
  feathers—if the rest of my fortunes turn
  Turk with me—with two Provincial
  roses on my razed shoes, get me a
  fellowship in a cry of players, sir?
HORATIO. Half a share.
HAMLET. A whole one, I.
  For thou dost know, O Damon dear,
   This realm dismantled was
  Of Jove himself, and now reigns here
   A very, very—pajock.
HORATIO. You might have rhymed.
HAMLET. O good Horatio, I'll take the
  ghost's word for a thousand pound.
  Didst perceive?
HORATIO. Very well, my lord.
HAMLET. Upon the talk of the poisoning?
HORATIO. I did very well note him.
HAMLET. Ah, ha! Come, some music! come,
  the recorders!
  For if the king like not the comedy,
  Why then belike—he likes it not, perdy.
  Come, some music!

Enter ROSENCRANTZ *and* GUILDENSTERN.

GUILDENSTERN. Good my lord, vouchsafe me
  a word with you.
HAMLET. Sir, a whole history.
GUILDENSTERN. The king, sir—
HAMLET. Ay, sir, what of him?
GUILDENSTERN. Is in his retirement marvel-
  lous distempered.
HAMLET. With drink, sir?
GUILDENSTERN. No, my lord, with choler.
HAMLET. Your wisdom should show itself
  more richer to signify this to the doctor,
  for for me to put him to his purgation
  would perhaps plunge him into more
  choler.
GUILDENSTERN. Good my lord, put your discourse into some frame, and start not
  so wildly from my affair.
HAMLET. I am tame, sir; pronounce.
GUILDENSTERN. The queen your mother, in
  most great affliction of spirit, hath sent
  me to you.
HAMLET. You are welcome.
GUILDENSTERN. Nay, good my lord, this courtesy is not of the right breed. If it shall
  please you to make me a wholesome answer, I will do your mother's commandment; if not, your pardon and my
  return shall be the end of my business.
HAMLET. Sir, I cannot.
GUILDENSTERN. What, my lord?
HAMLET. Make you a wholesome answer—
  my wit's diseased; but, sir, such answer
  as I can make, you shall command, or
  rather, as you say, my mother; therefore no more, but to the matter: my
  mother, you say,—
ROSENCRANTZ. Then thus she says: your behavior hath struck her into amazement
  and admiration.
HAMLET. O wonderful son, that can so
  stonish a mother! But is there no sequel at the heels of this mother's admiration? impart.
ROSENCRANTZ. She desires to speak with you
  in her closet ere you go to bed.
HAMLET. We shall obey, were she ten times
  our mother. Have you any further trade
  with us?

---

255. *Hecate* goddess of witchcraft 272. *forest of feathers* bunch of feathers sometimes part of an actor's costume 273. *Provincial roses* large rosettes worn by actors 274. *razed* slashed; *cry* pack 281. *pajok* peacock 289. *recorders* flageolets 297. *distempered* out of sorts 304. *frame* coherent form 311. *wholesome* reasonable 325. *closet* private room

ROSENCRANTZ. My lord, you once did love me.
HAMLET. And do still, by these pickers and stealers.
ROSENCRANTZ. Good my lord, what is your cause of distemper? you do surely bar the door upon your own liberty, if you deny your griefs to your friend.
HAMLET. Sir, I lack advancement.
ROSENCRANTZ. How can that be, when you have the voice of the king himself for your succession in Denmark?
HAMLET. Ay, sir, but "while the grass grows" the proverb is something musty.

Enter the PLAYERS *with recorders.*

O, the recorders: let me see one. To withdraw with you—why do you go about to recover the wind of me, as if you would drive me into a toil?
GUILDENSTERN. O, my lord, if my duty be too bold, my love is too unmannerly.
HAMLET. I do not well understand that. Will you play upon this pipe?
GUILDENSTERN. My lord, I cannot.
HAMLET. I pray you.
GUILDENSTERN. Believe me, I cannot.
HAMLET. I do beseech you.
GUILDENSTERN. I know no touch of it, my lord.
HAMLET. 'Tis as easy as lying; govern these ventages with your fingers and thumb, give it breath with your mouth, and it will discourse most eloquent music. Look you, these are the stops.
GUILDENSTERN. But these cannot I command to any utterance of harmony; I have not the skill.
HAMLET. Why, look you now, how unworthy a thing you make of me! You would play upon me, you would seem to know my stops, you would pluck out the heart of my mystery, you would sound me from my lowest note to the top of my compass; and there is much music, excellent voice, in this little organ, yet cannot you make it speak. 'Sblood, do you think I am easier to be played on than a pipe? Call me what instrument you will, though you can fret me, yet you cannot play upon me.

Enter POLONIUS.

God bless you, sir!
POLONIUS. My lord, the queen would speak with you, and presently.
HAMLET. Do you see yonder cloud that's almost in shape of a camel?
POLONIUS. By the mass and 'tis, like a camel indeed.
HAMLET. Methinks it is like a weasel.
POLONIUS. It is backed like a weasel.
HAMLET. Or like a whale?
POLONIUS. Very like a whale.
HAMLET. Then I will come to my mother by and by. They fool me to the top of my bent. I will come by and by.
POLONIUS. I will say so.
  Exit.
HAMLET. By and by is easily said.
  Leave me, friends.
  [*Exeunt all but* HAMLET.]
'Tis now the very witching time of night,
When churchyards yawn, and hell itself breathes out
Contagion to this world: now could I drink hot blood,
And do such bitter business as the day
Would quake to look on. Soft, now to my mother.
O heart, lose not thy nature, let not ever
The soul of Nero enter this firm bosom;
Let me be cruel, not unnatural.
I will speak daggers to her, but use none;
My tongue and soul in this be hypocrites;
How in my words somever she be shent,
To give them seals never, my soul, consent!
  Exit.

Scene 3

Enter KING, ROSENCRANTZ, *and* GUILDENSTERN.

KING. I like him not, nor stands it safe with us

---

330. *pickers and stealers* hands 337. *'while the grass grows'*—the proverb continues 'oft starves the silly steed' 340. *recover the wind* get to windward 341. *toil* trap 343. *unmannerly* extreme 351. *ventages* wind-holes, stops 362. *organ* instrument 388. *Nero* (who had his mother Agrippina put to death) 392. *shent* reproved 393. *give them seals* ratify by means of actions

To let his madness range. Therefore prepare you;
I your commission will forthwith dispatch,
And he to England shall along with you:
The terms of our estate may not endure
Hazard so near us as doth hourly grow
Out of his brawls.
GUILDENSTERN. We will ourselves provide.
Most holy and religious fear it is
To keep those many many bodies safe
That live and feed upon your majesty.
ROSENCRANTZ. The single and peculiar life is bound,
With all the strength and armor of the mind,
To keep itself from noyance, but much more
That spirit upon whose weal depends and rests
The lives of many. The cess of majesty
Dies not alone, but like a gulf doth draw
What's near it with it; or it is a massy wheel
Fixed on the summit of the highest mount,
To whose huge spokes ten thousand lesser things
Are mortised and adjoined; which, when it falls,
Each small annexment, petty consequence,
Attends the boisterous ruin. Never alone
Did the king sigh, but with a general groan.
KING. Arm you, I pray you, to this speedy voyage,
For we will fetters put upon this fear
Which now goes too free-footed.
ROSENCRANTZ.   We will haste us.
Exeunt ROSENCRANTZ *and* GUILDENSTERN.

Enter POLONIUS.

POLONIUS. My lord, he's going to his mother's closet.
Behind the arras I'll convey myself
To hear the process; I'll warrant she'll tax him home,
And as you said, and wisely was it said,
'Tis meet that some more audience than a mother,
Since nature makes them partial, should o'erhear
The speech, of vantage. Fare you well, my liege;
I'll call upon you ere you go to bed
And tell you what I know.
KING.   Thanks, dear my lord.
Exit [POLONIUS].
O, my offence is rank, it smells to heaven;
It hath the primal eldest curse upon't,
A brother's murder! Pray can I not,
Though inclination be as sharp as will;
My stronger guilt defeats my strong intent,
And, like a man to double business bound,
I stand in pause where I shall first begin,
And both neglect. What if this curséd hand
Were thicker than itself with brother's blood,
Is there not rain enough in the sweet heavens
To wash it white as snow? Whereto serves mercy
But to confront the visage of offence?
And what's in prayer but this twofold force,
To be forestalléd ere we come to fall,
Or pardoned being down? Then I'll look up;
My fault is past. But O, what form of prayer
Can serve my turn? "Forgive me my foul murder"?
That cannot be, since I am still possess'd
Of those effects for which I did the murder,
My crown, mine own ambition, and my queen.
May one be pardoned, and retain the offence?
In the corrupted currents, of this world
Offence's gilded hand may shove by justice,
And oft 'tis seen the wicked prize itself
Buys out the law, but 'tis not so above;
There is no shuffling, there the action lies

5. *terms* conditions; *estate* rank   7. *provide* prepare   11. *peculiar* individual   13. *noyance* harm   15. *cess* cessation   16. *gulf* whirlpool   20. *mortised* fitted   21. *annexment* attachment   22. *ruin* crash   29. *process* proceedings; *tax* take to task   33. *of vantage* from a vantage point   37. *primal eldest curse* the curse of Cain   47. *offence* guilt   56. *offence* results of guilt   58. *gilded* furnished with bribes   61. *shuffling* trickery

In his true nature, and we ourselves compelled,
Even to the teeth and forehead of our faults,
To give in evidence. What then? what rests?
Try what repentance can; what can it not?
Yet what can it when one can not repent?
O wretched state! O bosom black as death!
O liméd soul, that, struggling to be free,
Art more engaged! Help, angels! make assay;
Bow, stubborn knees, and, heart with strings of steel,
Be soft as sinews of the new-born babe!
All may be well.   [*Retires and kneels.*]

Enter HAMLET.

HAMLET. Now might I do it pat, now a' is a-praying,
And now I'll do't, and so a' goes to heaven,
And so am I revenged. That would be scann'd:
A villain kills my father, and for that I, his sole son, do this same villain send
To heaven.
Why, this is hire and salary, not revenge.
A' took my father grossly, full of bread,
With all his crimes broad blown, as flush as May,
And how his audit stands who knows save heaven?
But in our circumstance and course of thought
'Tis heavy with him: and am I then revenged
To take him in the purging of his soul,
When he is fit and seasoned for his passage?
No.
Up, sword, and know thou a more horrid hent:
When he is drunk, asleep, or in his rage,
Or in the incestuous pleasure of his bed,
At game a-swearing, or about some act
That has no relish of salvation in't;
Then trip him, that his heels may kick at heaven,
And that his soul may be as damned and black
As hell, whereto it goes. My mother stays;
This physic but prolongs thy sickly days.
Exit.
KING. My words fly up, my thoughts remain below;
Words without thoughts never to heaven go.
Exit.

Scene 4

Enter QUEEN *and* POLONIUS.

POLONIUS. A' will come straight. Look you lay home to him;
Tell him his pranks have been too broad to bear with,
And that your grace hath screened and stood between
Much heat and him. I'll silence me even here.
Pray you, be round with him.
HAMLET [*within*]. Mother, mother, mother!
QUEEN.   I'll warrant you;
Fear me not: withdraw, I hear him coming.

[POLONIUS *goes behind the arras.*]

Enter HAMLET.

HAMLET. Now, mother, what's the matter?
QUEEN. Hamlet, thou hast thy father much offended.
HAMLET. Mother, you have my father much offended.
QUEEN. Come, come, you answer with an idle tongue.
HAMLET. Go, go, you question with a wicked tongue.
QUEEN. Why, how now, Hamlet?
HAMLET.   What's the matter now?

---

68. *liméd* entrapped 69. *engaged* entangled 73. *pat* readily 80. *full of bread* in full enjoyment of pleasure 81. *broad blown* in full bloom; *flush* vigorous 82. *audit* account 86. *seasoned* prepared 88. *hent* opportunity 1. *lay home* speak severely 2. *broad* unrestrained 5. *round* downright

QUEEN. Have you forgot me?
HAMLET.   No, by the rood, not so!
You are the queen, your husband's brother's wife,
And—would it were not so!—you are my mother.
QUEEN. Nay, then I'll set those to you that can speak.
HAMLET. Come, come, and sit you down; you shall not budge;
You go not till I set you up a glass
Where you may see the inmost part of you.
QUEEN. What wilt thou do? thou wilt not murder me?
Help, help, ho!
POLONIUS [behind]. What, ho! help, help, help!
HAMLET [drawing]. How now? a rat? Dead for a ducat, dead!
[Makes a pass through the arras and kills POLONIUS.]
POLONIUS [behind]. O, I am slain!
QUEEN. O me, what hast thou done?
HAMLET.   Nay, I know not;
Is it the king?
QUEEN. O, what a rash and bloody deed is this!
HAMLET. A bloody deed! almost as bad, good mother,
As kill a king, and marry with his brother.
QUEEN. As kill a king!
HAMLET.   Ay, lady, it was my word.
[Lifts up the arras, and sees POLONIUS.]
Thou wretched, rash, intruding fool, farewell!
I took thee for thy better; take thy fortune;
Thou find'st to be too busy is some danger.
Leave wringing of your hands; peace sit you down
And let me wring your heart, for so I shall,
If it be made a penetrable stuff,
If damnèd custom have not brassed it so
That it be proof and bulwark against sense.
QUEEN. What have I done, that thou darest wag thy tongue
In noise so rude against me?
HAMLET.   Such an act
That blurs the grace and blush of modesty,
Calls virtue hypocrite, takes off the rose
From the fair forehead of an innocent love,
And sets a blister there, makes marriage-vows
As false as dicers' oaths; O, such a deed
As from the body of contraction plucks
The very soul, and sweet religion makes
A rhapsody of words. Heaven's face does glow,
And this solidity and compound mass,
With heated visage as against the doom,
Is thought-sick at the act.
QUEEN.   Ay me, what act,
That roars so loud and thunders in the index?
HAMLET. Look here upon this picture, and on this,
The counterfeit presentment of two brothers.
See what a grace was seated on this brow:
Hyperion's curls, the front of Jove himself,
An eye like Mars, to threaten and command,
A station like the herald Mercury
New-lighted on a heaven-kissing hill,
A combination and a form indeed,
Where every god did seem to set his seal,
To give the world assurance of a man;
This was your husband. Look you now what follows;
Here is your husband, like a mildewed ear
Blasting his wholesome brother. Have you eyes?
Could you on this fair mountain leave to feed,
And batten on this moor? Ha! have you eyes?
You cannot call it love, for at your age
The heyday in the blood is tame, it's humble,
And waits upon the judgment; and what judgment

14. *rood* cross 33. *busy* prying, meddlesome 37. *custom* habit 38. *proof* armor; *sense* feeling 46. *contraction* contract, obligation 48. *glow* redden, *blush* for shame 50. *against* at the approach of 52. *index* preliminaries, table of contents 54. *presentment* representation 56. *Hyperion* the sun god; *front* forehead 58. *station* attitude 64. *ear* (of wheat) 67. *batten* gorge, pasture 69. *heyday* youth 70. *waits upon* defers to

Would step from this to this? Sense sure you have,
Else could you not have motion, but sure that sense
Is apoplexed, for madness would not err,
Nor sense to ecstasy was ne'er so thralled
But it reserved some quantity of choice
To serve in such a difference. What devil was't
That thus hath cozened you at hoodman-blind?
Eyes without feeling, feeling without sight,
Ears without hands or eyes, smelling sans all,
Or but a sickly part of one true sense
Could not so mope.
O shame, where is thy blush? Rebellious hell,
If thou canst mutine in a matron's bones,
To flaming youth let virtue be as wax
And melt in her own fire; proclaim no shame
When the compulsive ardor gives the charge,
Since frost itself as actively doth burn,
And reason panders will.
QUEEN.   O Hamlet, speak no more;
Thou turn'st my eyes into my very soul,
And there I see such black and grainéd spots
As will not leave their tinct.
HAMLET.   Nay, but to live
In the rank sweat of an enseaméd bed,
Stewed in corruption, honeying and making love
Over the nasty sty—
QUEEN.   O speak to me no more;
These words like daggers enter in mine ears;
No more, sweet Hamlet.
HAMLET.   A murderer and a villain,
A slave that is not twentieth part the tithe
Of your precedent lord, a vice of kings,
A cutpurse of the empire and the rule,
That from a shelf the precious diadem stole
And put it in his pocket—
QUEEN.   No more.
HAMLET. A king of shreds and patches—

Enter GHOST.

Save me, and hover o'er me with your wings,
You heavenly guards! What would your gracious figure?
QUEEN. Alas, he's mad.
HAMLET. Do you not come your tardy son to chide,
That, lapsed in time and passion, lets go by
The important acting of your dread command?
O, say!
GHOST. Do not forget; this visitation
Is but to whet thy almost blunted purpose.
But look, amazement on thy mother sits.
O step between her and her fighting soul;
Conceit in weakest bodies strongest works.
Speak to her, Hamlet.
HAMLET.   How is it with you, lady?
QUEEN. Alas, how is't with you,
That you do bend your eye on vacancy,
And with the incorporal air do hold discourse?
Forth at your eyes your spirits wildly peep,
And, as the sleeping soldiers in the alarm,
Your bedded hairs like life in excrements,
Start up and stand an end. O gentle son,
Upon the heat and flame of thy distemper
Sprinkle cool patience. Whereon do you look?
HAMLET. On him, on him! Look you, how pale he glares!
His form and cause conjoined, preaching to stones,
Would make them capable. Do not look upon me,
Lest with this piteous action you convert
My stern effects; then what I have to do
Will want true color—tears perchance for blood.

---

73. *apoplexed* subject to aberrations or fits 74. *ecstasy* madness; *thralled* in bondage 76. *serve* employ; *difference* power of distinguishing 77. *cozened* deceived; *hoodman-blind* blind-man's-bluff 81. *so mope* be so uncertain 83. *mutine* mutiny, rebel 86. *compulsive* compelling; *gives the charge* orders the attack 88. *panders* is subservient to 90. *grainéd* ingrained 91. *tinct* color, dye 92. *enseaméd* greasy 97. *tithe* tenth part 98. *precedent* previous; *vice* clown 99. *cutpurse* pickpocket 113. *fighting* struggling 114. *conceit* imagination 121. *excrements* outgrowths 122. *an* on 127. *capable* able to feel 129. *effects* deeds 130. *color* appearance; *for* instead of

QUEEN. To whom do you speak this?
HAMLET. Do you see nothing there?
QUEEN. Nothing at all; yet all that is I see.
HAMLET. Nor did you nothing hear?
QUEEN. No, nothing but ourselves.
HAMLET. Why, look you there! look, how it steals away!
My father, in his habit as he lived!
Look, where he goes, even now, out at the portal!
Exit GHOST.
QUEEN. This is the very coinage of your brain;
This bodiless creation ecstasy
Is very cunning in.
HAMLET. Ecstasy!
My pulse as yours doth temperately keep time
And makes as healthful music; it is not madness
That I have uttered. Bring me to the test,
And I the matter will reword, which madness
Would gambol from. Mother, for love of grace
Lay not that flattering unction to your soul,
That not your trespass but my madness speaks;
It will but skin and film the ulcerous place
Whiles rank corruption, mining all within,
Infects unseen. Confess yourself to heaven,
Repent what's past, avoid what is to come,
And do not spread the compost on the weeds
To make them ranker. Forgive me this my virtue,
For in the fatness of these pursy times
Virtue itself of vice must pardon beg,
Yea, curb and woo for leave to do him good.
QUEEN. O Hamlet, thou hast cleft my heart in twain.
HAMLET. O, throw away the worser part of it,
And live the purer with the other half.
Good night, but go not to my uncle's bed;
Assume a virtue, if you have it not.
That monster custom, who all sense doth eat
Of habits evil, is angel yet in this,
That to the use of actions fair and good
He likewise gives a frock or livery
That aptly is put on. Refrain tonight,
And that shall lend a kind of easiness
To the next abstinence; the next more easy,
For use almost can change the stamp of nature,
And either curb the devil, or throw him out
With wondrous potency. Once more, good night,
And when you are desirous to be blessed,
I'll blessing beg of you.—For this same lord,
[*Pointing to* POLONIUS.]
I do repent; but heaven hath pleased it so,
To punish me with this, and this with me,
That I must be their scourge and minister.
I will bestow him and will answer well
The death I gave him. So again, good night.
I must be cruel only to be kind;
Thus bad begins, and worse remains behind.
One word more, good lady.
QUEEN. What shall I do?
HAMLET. Not this, by no means, that I bid you do;
Let the bloat king tempt you again to bed,
Pinch wanton on your cheek, call you his mouse,
And let him for a pair of reechy kisses,
Or paddling in your neck with his damned fingers,
Make you to ravel all this matter out
That I essentially am not in madness,
But mad in craft. 'Twere good you let him know,

145. unction ointment 148. mining undermining 152. virtue apparent self-righteousness 153. fatness grossness; pursy corpulent 155. curb bow 161. sense feeling, sensitiveness 162. of from 164. livery uniform 165. aptly easily 168. use habit; stamp form, impression 175. scourge instrument of punishment; minister agent 176. bestow hide 182. bloat bloated 183. wanton wantonly 184. reechy reeking, dirty 186. ravel . . . out unravel 188. in craft, i.e., pretendedly

For who, that's but a queen, fair, sober, wise,
Would from a paddock, from a bat, a gib,
Such dear concernings hide? who would do so?
No, in despite of sense and secrecy,
Unpeg the basket on the house's top,
Let the birds fly, and like the famous ape,
To try conclusions, in the basket creep
And break your own neck down.
QUEEN. Be thou assured, if words be made of breath
And breath of life, I have no life to breathe
What thou hast said to me.
HAMLET. I must to England; you know that?
QUEEN.   Alack,
I had forgot; 'tis so concluded on.
HAMLET. There's letters sealed, and my two schoolfellows,
Whom I will trust as I will adders fanged,
They bear the mandate; they must sweep my way
And marshal me to knavery. Let it work,
For 'tis the sport to have the enginer
Hoist with his own petar, and't shall go hard
But I will delve one yard below their mines,
And blow them at the moon: O 'tis most sweet
When in one line two crafts directly meet.
This man shall set me packing;
I'll lug the guts into the neighbor room.
Mother, good night indeed. This counsellor
Is now most still, most secret, and most grave,
Who was in life a foolish prating knave.
Come, sir, to draw toward an end with you.
Good night, mother.
    Exit HAMLET *tugging in* POLONIUS.

ACT IV

Scene I

Enter KING, *and* QUEEN, *with* ROSENCRANTZ *and* GUILDENSTERN.

KING. There's matter in these sighs, these profound heaves,
You must translate; 'tis fit we understand them.
Where is your son?
QUEEN. Bestow this place on us a little while.
    [*Exeunt* ROSENCRANTZ *and* GUILDENSTERN.]
Ah, mine own lord, what have I seen tonight!
KING. What, Gertrude, how does Hamlet?
QUEEN. Mad as the sea and wind when both contend
Which is the mightier; in his lawless fit,
Behind the arras hearing something stir,
Whips out his rapier, cries "a rat, a rat!"
And in this brainish apprehension kills
The unseen good old man.
KING.   O heavy deed!
It had been so with us had we been there.
His liberty is full of threats to all—
To you yourself, to us, to every one.
Alas, how shall this bloody deed be answered?
It will be laid to us, whose providence
Should have kept short, restrained, and out of haunt
This mad young man; but so much was our love,
We would not understand what was most fit;
But like the owner of a foul disease,
To keep it from divulging, let it feed
Even on the pith of life. Where is he gone?

190. paddock toad; gib cat   191. dear concernings matters of personal importance   204. mandate orders; sweep prepare   205. marshal lead   206. enginer engineer   207. hoist blown up; petar mine, bomb   208. delve dig, tunnel   11. brainish apprehension imaginary fear   18. out of haunt out of the way

QUEEN. To draw apart the body he hath killed,
　O'er whom his very madness, like some ore
　Among a mineral of metals base,
　Shows itself pure; a' weeps for what is done.
KING. O Gertrude, come away!
　The sun no sooner shall the mountains touch,
　But we will ship him hence, and this vile deed
　We must, with all our majesty and skill,
　Both countenance and excuse. Ho, Guildenstern!

Enter ROSENCRANTZ *and* GUILDENSTERN.

Friends both, go join you with some further aid;
Hamlet in madness hath Polonius slain,
And from his mother's closet hath he dragged him.
Go seek him out; speak fair, and bring the body
Into the chapel. I pray you haste in this.
Exeunt ROSENCRANTZ *and* GUILDENSTERN.
Come, Gertrude, we'll call up our wisest friends,
And let them know both what we mean to do
And what's untimely done; [so haply slander—]
Whose whisper o'er the world's diameter,
As level as the cannon to his blank,
Transports his poisoned shot—may miss our name,
And hit the woundless air. O, come away!
My soul is full of discord and dismay.
Exeunt.

Scene 2

Enter HAMLET.

HAMLET. Safely stowed.
GENTLEMEN [*within*]. Hamlet, Lord Hamlet!
HAMLET. What noise? who calls on Hamlet? O, here they come.

Enter ROSENCRANTZ *and* GUILDENSTERN.

ROSENCRANTZ. What have you done, my lord, with the dead body?
HAMLET. Compounded it with dust, whereto 'tis kin.
ROSENCRANTZ. Tell us where 'tis that we may take it thence,
　And bear it to the chapel.
HAMLET. Do not believe it.
ROSENCRANTZ. Believe what?
HAMLET. That I can keep your counsel and not mine own. Besides, to be demanded of a sponge! what replication should be made by the son of a king?
ROSENCRANTZ. Take you me for a sponge, my lord?
HAMLET. Ay, sir, that soaks up the king's countenance, his rewards, his authorities. But such officers do the king best service in the end: he keeps them, like an ape, in the corner of his jaw—first mouthed, to be last swallowed; when he needs what you have gleaned, it is but squeezing you, and sponge, you shall be dry again.
ROSENCRANTZ. I understand you not, my lord.
HAMLET. I am glad of it; a knavish speech sleeps in a foolish ear.
ROSENCRANTZ. My lord, you must tell us where the body is, and go with us to the king.
HAMLET. The body is with the king, but the king is not with the body. The king is a thing—
GUILDENSTERN. A thing, my lord!
HAMLET. Of nothing; bring me to him. Hide fox, and all after.
Exeunt.

---

25. ore precious metal　26. mineral vein　32. countenance acknowledge　42. blank target　6. compounded mixed　15. countenance favor　22. sleeps is not understood

Scene 3

Enter KING, *and two or three.*

KING. I have sent to seek him, and to find the body.
    How dangerous is it that this man goes loose;
    Yet must not we put the strong law on him;
    He's loved of the distracted multitude,
    Who like not in their judgment, but their eyes,
    And where 'tis so, the offender's scourge is weighed,
    But never the offence. To bear all smooth and even,
    This sudden sending him away must seem
    Deliberate pause; diseases desperate grown
10   By desperate appliance are relieved,
    Or not at all.

Enter ROSENCRANTZ.

              How now, what hath befallen?
ROSENCRANTZ. Where the dead body is bestowed, my lord,
    We cannot get from him.
KING.   But where is he?
ROSENCRANTZ. Without, my lord; guarded, to know your pleasure.
KING. Bring him before us.
ROSENCRANTZ. Ho, Guildenstern! bring in my lord.

Enter HAMLET *and* GUILDENSTERN.

KING. Now, Hamlet, where's Polonius?
HAMLET. At supper.
KING. At supper! where?
HAMLET. Not where he eats, but where a'
20   is eaten; a certain convocation of politic worms are e'en at him. Your worm is your only emperor for diet; we fat all creatures else to fat us, and we fat ourselves for maggots; your fat king and your lean beggar is but variable service—two dishes, but to one table; that's the end.
KING. Alas, alas!
HAMLET. A man may fish with the worm that hath eat of a king, and eat of the fish that hath fed of that worm.
KING. What dost thou mean by this?
HAMLET. Nothing but to show you how a 30 king may go a progress through the guts of a beggar.
KING. Where is Polonius?
HAMLET. In heaven. Send thither to see; if your messenger find him not there, seek him i' the other place yourself. But if indeed you find him not within this month, you shall nose him as you go up the stairs into the lobby.
KING. Go seek him there.
    [*To some Attendants.*]
HAMLET. A' will stay till you come.
    [*Exeunt Attendants.*]
KING. Hamlet, this deed, for thine especial safety—
    Which we do tender, as we dearly grieve 40
    For that which thou hast done—must send thee hence
    With fiery quickness; therefore prepare thyself;
    The bark is ready, and the wind at help,
    The associates tend, and every thing is bent
    For England.
HAMLET.   For England!
KING.   Ay, Hamlet.
HAMLET.   Good.
KING. So is it, if thou knew'st our purposes.
HAMLET. I see a cherub that sees them. But come; for England! Farewell, dear mother.
KING. Thy loving father, Hamlet.
HAMLET. My mother; father and mother is 50 man and wife, man and wife is one flesh, and so my mother. Come, for England!
    [*Exit.*]

---

4. *distracted* unstable   6. *scourge* punishment   10. *appliance* medical treatment   21. *convocation of politic worms . . . emperor for diet* (a punning allusion to the Diets of the Holy Roman Empire held at Worms)   24. *variable service* different courses   31. *progress* state journey made by a king   40. *tender* care for; *dearly* deeply   44. *tend* wait

KING. Follow him at foot; tempt him with
  speed aboard.
Delay it not; I'll have him hence tonight.
Away! for every thing is sealed and done
That else leans on the affair; pray you,
  make haste.
  [Exeunt ROSENCRANTZ and GUILDEN-
  STERN.]
And, England, if my love thou hold'st at
  aught—
As my great power thereof may give thee
  sense,
Since yet thy cicatrice looks raw and red
After the Danish sword, and thy free awe
Pays homage to us—thou mayst not coldly
  set
Our sovereign process, which imports at
  full
By letters congruing to that effect
The present death of Hamlet. Do it,
  England;
For like the hectic in my blood he rages,
And thou must cure me; till I know 'tis
  done,
Howe'er my haps, my joys were ne'er be-
  gun.
Exit.

Scene 4

Enter FORTINBRAS, with his Army over the stage.

FORTINBRAS. Go, captain, from me greet the
  Danish king;
Tell him that by his license Fortinbras
Claims the conveyance of a promised
  march
Over his kingdom. You know the rendez-
  vous.
If that his majesty would aught with us,
We shall express our duty in his eye;
And let him know so.
CAPTAIN.   I will do't, my lord.
FORTINBRAS. Go softly on.
  [Exeunt FORTINBRAS and his Forces.]

Enter HAMLET, ROSENCRANTZ, [GUILDEN-
STERN and others.]

HAMLET. Good sir, whose powers are these?
CAPTAIN. They are of Norway, sir.
HAMLET. How purposed, sir, I pray you?
CAPTAIN. Against some part of Poland.
HAMLET. Who commands them, sir?
CAPTAIN. The nephew to old Norway, For-
  tinbras.
HAMLET. Goes it against the main of Poland,
  sir,
Or for some frontier?
CAPTAIN. Truly to speak, and with no addi-
  tion,
We go to gain a little patch of ground
That hath in it no profit but the name.
To pay five ducats, five, I would not farm
  it,
Nor will it yield to Norway or the Pole
A ranker rate, should it be sold in fee.
HAMLET. Why then, the Polack never will
  defend it.
CAPTAIN. Yes, it is already garrisoned.
HAMLET. Two thousand souls and twenty
  thousand ducats
Will not debate the question of this
  straw;
This is the imposthume of much wealth
  and peace,
That inward breaks, and shows no cause
  without
Why the man dies. I humbly thank you,
  sir.
CAPTAIN. God be wi' you, sir.
  [Exit.]
ROSENCRANTZ. Will't please you go, my lord?
HAMLET. I'll be with you straight. Go a little
  before.
  [Exeunt all except HAMLET.]
How all occasions do inform against me,
And spur my dull revenge! What is a
  man
If his chief good and market of his time
Be but to sleep and feed? a beast, no
  more.

56. leans on concerns   57. England King of England; hold'st at aught valuest at all   58. give thee
sense make thee perceive   59. cicatrice scar   61.
coldly set disregard   62. process command   63.
congruing amounting   64. present immediate   65.
hectic fever   67. haps fortunes   3. conveyance convoy   9. powers forces   15. main principal part   17.
addition exaggeration   22. ranker higher; in fee outright   27. imposthume ulcer   32. inform against
denounce   34. market profit

Sure, he that made us with such large discourse
Looking before and after, gave us not
That capability and godlike reason
To fust in us unused. Now, whether it be
Bestial oblivion, or some craven scruple
Of thinking too precisely on the event—
A thought which, quartered, hath but one part wisdom,
And ever three parts coward—I do not know
Why yet I live to say "This thing's to do,"
Sith I have cause, and will, and strength, and means
To do't. Examples gross as earth exhort me:
Witness this army of such mass and charge,
Led by a delicate and tender prince,
Whose spirit, with divine ambition puffed,
Makes mouths at the invisible event,
Exposing what is mortal and unsure
To all that fortune, death and danger dare,
Even for an eggshell. Rightly to be great
Is not to stir without great argument,
But greatly to find quarrel in a straw
When honor's at the stake. How stand I then
That have a father killed, a mother stained,
Excitements of my reason and my blood,
And let all sleep? while to my shame I see
The imminent death of twenty thousand men,
That for a fantasy and trick of fame
Go to their graves like beds, fight for a plot
Whereon the numbers cannot try the cause,
Which is not tomb enough and continent
To hide the slain? O, from this time forth
My thoughts be bloody, or be nothing worth!
Exit.

Scene 5

Enter QUEEN, HORATIO, *and a* GENTLEMAN.

QUEEN. I will not speak with her.
GENTLEMAN. She is importunate, indeed distract;
Her mood will needs be pitied.
QUEEN.   What would she have?
GENTLEMAN. She speaks much of her father, says she hears
There's tricks i' the world, and hems, and beats her heart,
Spurns enviously at straws, speaks things in doubt
That carry but half sense; her speech is nothing,
Yet the unshapéd use of it doth move
The hearers to collection; they aim at it,
And botch the words up fit to their own thoughts,
Which, as her winks and nods and gestures yield them,
Indeed would make one think there might be thought,
Though nothing sure, yet much unhappily.
HORATIO. 'Twere good she were spoken with, for she may strew
Dangerous conjectures in ill-breeding minds;
Let her come in.
[*Exit* GENTLEMAN.]
QUEEN. To my sick soul, as sin's true nature is,
Each toy seems prologue to some great amiss;

---

36. *discourse* power of reasoning 39. *fust* grow mouldy 40. *oblivion* forgetfulness 41. *event* outcome 47. *charge* expense 50. *makes mouths at* makes faces at, defies 58. *blood* passion, anger 61. *trick* whim 64. *continent* receptacle 2. *distract* distracted, unbalanced 5. *tricks* deceits 6. *spurns enviously at straws* takes offence at trifles 7. *nothing* nonsense 8. *unshapéd* incoherent 9. *collection* attempt to collect some meaning from it 10. *botch* patch 15. *ill-breeding* liable to misinterpret 18. *toy* trifle; *amiss* misfortune

So full of artless jealousy is guilt,
It spills itself in fearing to be spilt.

Enter OPHELIA *distracted.*

OPHELIA. Where is the beauteous majesty of Denmark?
QUEEN. How now, Ophelia?
OPHELIA [*sings*].
   How should I your true love know
      From another one?
   By his cockle hat and staff,
      And his sandal shoon.
QUEEN. Alas, sweet lady, what imports this song?
OPHELIA. Say you? Nay, pray you, mark.
[*Sings.*] He is dead and gone, lady,
      He is dead and gone;
   At his read a grass-green turf,
      At his heels a stone
         O, ho!
QUEEN. Nay, but Ophelia—
OPHELIA. Pray you, mark.
[*Sings.*] White his shroud as the mountain snow—

Enter KING.

QUEEN. Alas, look here, my lord.
OPHELIA [*sings*].
      Larded all with sweet flowers,
   Which beswept to the grave did not go
      With true-love showers.
KING. How do you, pretty lady?
OPHELIA. Well, God 'ild you! They say the owl was a baker's daughter. Lord, we know what we are, but know not what we may be. God be at your table!
KING. Conceit upon her father.
OPHELIA. Pray you, let's have no words of this; but when they ask you what it means, say you this:
[*Sings.*] To-morrow is Saint Valentine's day,
      All in the morning betime,
   And I a maid at your window,
      To be your Valentine.
   Then up he rose, and donned his clo'es,
      And dupped the chamber door.
   Let in the maid, that out a maid
      Never departed more.
KING. Pretty Ophelia!
OPHELIA. Indeed, la, without an oath I'll make an end on't:
[*Sings.*] By Gis and by Saint Charity,
      Alack and fie for shame!
   Young men will do't if they come to't,
      By Cock, they are to blame.

   Quoth she, "Before you tumbled me,
      You promised me to wed."
He answers
   So would I ha' done by yonder sun,
      And thou hadst not come to my bed.
KING. How long hath she been thus?
OPHELIA. I hope all will be well. We must be patient, but I cannot choose but weep to think they would lay him i' the cold ground. My brother shall know of it; and so I thank you for your good counsel. Come, my coach! Good night, ladies; good night, sweet ladies; good night, good night.
Exit.
KING. Follow her close; give her good watch, I pray you.
[*Exit* HORATIO.]
O, this is the poison of deep grief; it springs
All from her father's death—and now behold!
O Gertrude, Gertrude,
When sorrows come, they come not single spies,
But in battalions: first, her father slain;
Next, your son gone, and he most violent author
Of his own just remove; the people muddied,
Thick and unwholesome in their thoughts and whispers
For good Polonius' death; and we have done but greenly
In hugger-mugger to inter him; poor Ophelia

19. *artless* uncontrolled; *jealousy* suspicion 25. *cockle hat and staff* the insignia of a pilgrim 26. *shoon* shoes 27. *imports* means 37. *larded* decked 41. *'ild* yield, i.e., reward 44. *conceit* thought 48. *betime* early 52. *dupped* opened 58. *Gis* Jesus 80. *muddied* confused 82. *greenly* unskilfully 83. *hugger-mugger* surreptitious haste

Divided from herself and her fair judgment,
Without the which we are pictures, or mere beasts;
Last, and as much containing as all these,
Her brother is in secret come from France,
Feeds on his wonder, keeps himself in clouds,
And wants not buzzers to infect his ear
With pestilent speeches of his father's death, 90
Wherein necessity, of matter beggared,
Will nothing stick our person to arraign
In ear and ear. O my dear Gertrude, this,
Like to a murdering-piece, in many places
Gives me superfluous death.
   A noise within.
QUEEN.   Alack, what noise is this?
KING. Where are my Switzers? Let them guard the door.

Enter a MESSENGER.

What is the matter?
GENTLEMAN.   Save yourself, my lord;
The ocean, overpeering of his list,
Eats not the flats with more impiteous haste
Than young Laertes, in a riotous head, 100
O'erbears your officers. The rabble call him lord,
And, as the world were now but to begin,
Antiquity forgot, custom not known,
The ratifiers and props of every word,
They cry, "Choose we; Laertes shall be king!"
Caps, hands, and tongues applaud it to the clouds,
"Laertes shall be king, Laertes king!"
   A noise within.
QUEEN. How cheerfully on the false trail they cry!
O, this is counter, you false Danish dogs!
KING. The doors are broke. 110

Enter LAERTES *with others.*

LAERTES. Where is this king? Sirs, stand you all without.
DANES. No, let's come in.
LAERTES.   I pray you, give me leave.
DANES. We will, we will.
   [*They retire without the door.*]
LAERTES. I thank you; keep the door. O thou vile king,
Give me my father.
QUEEN.   Calmly, good Laertes.
LAERTES. That drop of blood that's calm proclaims me bastard,
Cries cuckold to my father, brands the harlot
Even here between the chaste unsmirchéd brow
Of my true mother.
KING.   What is the cause, Laertes,
That thy rebellion looks so giant-like? 120
Let him go, Gertrude, do not fear our person;
There's such divinity doth hedge a king,
That treason can but peep to what it would,
Acts little of his will. Tell me, Laertes,
Why thou art thus incensed. Let him go, Gertrude.
Speak, man.
LAERTES. Where is my father?
KING.   Dead.
QUEEN.   But not by him.
KING. Let him demand his fill.
LAERTES. How came he dead? I'll not be juggled with.
To hell allegiance, vows to the blackest devil, 130
Conscience and grace to the profoundest pit!
I dare damnation. To this point I stand,
That both the worlds I give to negligence,
Let come what comes, only I'll be revenged
Most throughly for my father.
KING.   Who shall stay you?
LAERTES. My will, not all the world's:
And for my means, I'll husband them so well,
They shall go far with little.
KING.   Good Laertes,
If you desire to know the certainty

---

88. *wonder* uncertainty; *in clouds* secluded 89. *buzzers* those who repeat rumors 92. *nothing stick* hesitate not at all; *arraign* accuse 94. *murdering-piece* piece of artillery loaded so as to scatter its shot 96. *Switzers* Swiss guards 98. *overpeering* pressing across; *list* boundary 99. *impiteous* pitiless 100. *head* armed band 104. *word* pledge 109. *counter* following the scent backwards 121. *fear* fear for 123. *peep* have a glimpse of; *would* desires 132. *to this point I stand* I stand firm on this one thing 133. *both the worlds*, i.e., this and the next; *give to negligence* am indifferent to 135. *throughly* thoroughly

140 Of your dear father's death, is't writ in
your revenge
That swoopstake you will draw both
friend and foe,
Winner and loser?
LAERTES. None but his enemies.
KING. Will you know them then?
LAERTES. To his good friends thus wide I'll
ope my arms,
And, like the kind life-rendering pelican,
Repast them with my blood.
KING. Why, now you speak
Like a good child and a true gentleman.
That I am guiltless of your father's death,
And am most sensibly in grief for it,
150 It shall as level to your judgment 'pear
As day does to your eye.
[A noise within.] Let her come in.
LAERTES. How now, what noise is that?

Enter OPHELIA.

O heat, dry up my brains; tears seven-
times salt,
Burn out the sense and virtue of mine
eye!
By heaven, thy madness shall be paid
with weight,
Till our scale turn the beam. O rose of
May,
Dear maid, kind sister, sweet Ophelia!
O heavens, is't possible a young maid's
wits
Should be as mortal as an old man's life?
160 Nature is fine in love, and where 'tis
fine,
It sends some precious instance of itself
After the thing it loves.
OPHELIA [sings]. They bore him barefaced
on the bier,
(Hey non nonny, nonny, hey
nonny)
And in his grave rained many
a tear—
Fare you well, my dove!
LAERTES. Hadst thou thy wits, and didst
persuade revenge,
It could not move thus.
OPHELIA. You must sing "A-down a-down,
an you call him a-down-a."

O, how the wheel becomes it! It is the
false steward, that stole his master's
daughter.
LAERTES. This nothing's more than matter.
OPHELIA. There's rosemary, that's for remembrance—pray you, love, remember; and
there is pansies, that's for thoughts.
LAERTES. A document in madness, thoughts
and remembrance fitted.
OPHELIA. There's fennel for you, and columb-
ines; there's rue for you, and here's
some for me—we may call it herb of
grace o' Sundays. O, you must wear
your rue with a difference. There's a
daisy; I would give you some violets,
but they withered all when my father
died. They say a' made a good end—
[Sings.] For bonny sweet Robin is all my
joy.
LAERTES. Thought and afflictions, passion,
hell itself,
She turns to favor and to prettiness.
OPHELIA [sings].
And will a' not come again?
And will a' not come again?
No, no, he is dead;
Go to thy death-bed;
He never will come again.
His beard was as white as snow,
All flaxen was his poll;
He is gone, he is gone,
And we cast away moan;
God ha' mercy on his soul!
And of all Christian souls, I pray God.
God be wi' you.
Exit.
LAERTES. Do you see this, O God?
KING. Laertes, I must commune with your
grief,
Or you deny me right. Go but apart,
Make choice of whom your wisest friends
you will,
And they shall hear and judge 'twixt you
and me.
If by direct or by collateral hand
They find us touched, we will our king-
dom give,
Our crown, our life, and all that we call
ours,
To you in satisfaction; but if not,

141. *swoopstake* at random 145. *life-rendering*, i.e., because it was supposed to feed its young on its own blood 146. *repast* feed 149. *sensibly* feelingly 156. *beam* balance 160. *fine* sensitive 161. *instance* token 172. *nothing* nonsense; *matter* sense 176. *document* piece of instruction 186. *favor* beauty 193. *poll* head 199. *commune with* share 203. *collateral hand* indirect means 204. *touched* involved

Be you content to lend your patience to us,
And we shall jointly labor with your soul
To give it due content.
LAERTES. Let this be so.
His means of death, his obscure funeral,
No trophy, sword, nor hatchment o'er his bones,
No noble rite nor formal ostentation,
Cry to be heard, as 'twere from heaven to earth,
That I must call't in question.
KING. So you shall,
And where the offence is let the great axe fall.
I pray you, go with me.
Exeunt.

Scene 6

Enter HORATIO *with an* ATTENDANT.

HORATIO. What are they that would speak with me?
SERVANT. Seafaring men, sir; they say they have letters for you.
HORATIO. Let them come in.
 [*Exit* ATTENDANT.]
 I do not know from what part of the world
 I should be greeted, if not from Lord Hamlet.

Enter SAILORS.

SAILOR. God bless you, sir.
HORATIO. Let him bless thee too.
SAILOR. A' shall, sir, an't please him. There's a letter for you, sir; it came from the ambassador that was bound for England; if your name be Horatio, as I am let to know it is.
HORATIO [*reads*]. "Horatio, when thou shalt have overlooked this, give these fellows some means to the king; they have letters for him. Ere we were two days old at sea, a pirate of very warlike appointment gave us chase. Finding ourselves too slow of sail, we put on a compelled valor, and in the grapple I boarded them; on the instant they got clear of our ship, so I alone became their prisoner. They have dealt with me like thieves of mercy, but they knew what they did; I am to do a good turn for them. Let the king have the letters I have sent, and repair thou to me with as much speed as thou wouldest fly death. I have words to speak in thine ear will make thee dumb, yet are they much too light for the bore of the matter. These good fellows will bring thee where I am. Rosencrantz and Guildenstern hold their course for England; of them I have much to tell thee. Farewell.
He that thou knowest thine, HAMLET."
Come, I will make you way for these your letters,
And do't the speedier, that you may direct me
To him from whom you brought them.
Exeunt.

Scene 7

Enter KING *and* LAERTES.

KING. Now must your conscience my acquittance seal,
And you must put me in your heart for friend,
Sith you have heard, and with a knowing ear,

---

211. *hatchment* coat of arms 212. *ostentation* ceremony 213. *cry to be heard* demand explanation 215. *axe*, i.e., of vengeance 20. *thieves of mercy* merciful robbers 25. *bore* caliber, i.e., importance 1. *acquittance* acquittal; *seal* confirm

       That he which hath your noble father slain
       Pursued my life.
LAERTES.   It well appears: but tell me
       Why you proceeded not against these feats,
       So crimeful and so capital in nature,
       As by your safety, greatness, wisdom, all things else,
       You mainly were stirred up.
KING.   O, for two special reasons,
10   Which may to you perhaps seem much unsinewed,
       But yet to me they are strong. The queen his mother
       Lives almost by his looks; and for myself—
       My virtue or my plague, be't either which—
       She is so conjunctive to my life and soul
       That, as the star moves not but in his sphere,
       I could not but by her. The other motive,
       Why to a public count I might not go,
       Is the great love the general gender bear him,
       Who, dipping all his faults in their affection,
20   Would, like the spring that turneth wood to stone,
       Convert his gyves to graces, so that my arrows,
       Too slightly timbered for so loud a wind,
       Would have reverted to my bow again,
       And not where I had aimed them.
LAERTES. And so have I a noble father lost,
       A sister driven into desperate terms,
       Whose worth, if praises may go back again,
       Stood challenger on mount of all the age
       For her perfections; but my revenge will come.
30 KING. Break not your sleeps for that; you must not think
       That we are made of stuff so flat and dull
       That we can let our beard be shook with danger
       And think it pastime. You shortly shall hear more;
       I loved your father, and we love ourself,
       And that, I hope, will teach you to imagine—

Enter a MESSENGER *with letters.*

       How now! what news?
MESSENGER. Letters, my lord, from Hamlet;
       This to your majesty, this to the queen.
KING. From Hamlet? who brought them?
MESSENGER. Sailors, my lord, they say; I saw them not.
       They were given me by Claudio; he received them
       Of him that brought them.
KING.   Laertes, you shall hear them.
       Leave us.
       Exit MESSENGER.
[*Reads.*] "High and mighty, You shall know I am set naked on your kingdom. Tomorrow shall I beg leave to see your kingly eyes, when I shall, first asking your pardon thereunto, recount the occasion of my sudden and more strange return.
       HAMLET."
       What should this mean? Are all the rest come back?
       Or is it some abuse, and no such thing?
LAERTES. Know you the hand?
KING.   'Tis Hamlet's character. "Naked"—
       And in a postscript here, he says "alone."
       Can you devise me?
LAERTES. I am lost in it, my lord; but let him come.
       It warms the very sickness in my heart
       That I shall live and tell him to his teeth,
       "Thus diddest thou."
KING.   If it be so, Laertes—
       As how should it be so? how otherwise?—
       Will you be ruled by me?
LAERTES.   Ay, my lord;
       So you will not o'errule me to a peace.
KING. To thine own peace. If he be now returned,
       As checking at his voyage, and that he means
       No more to undertake it, I will work him
       To an exploit, now ripe in my device,
       Under the which he shall not choose but fall:

---

6. *feats* deeds 9. *mainly* powerfully 10. *much unsinewed* very weak 14. *conjunctive* united 17. *count* trial 18. *general gender* common people 21. *gyves* fetters 26. *terms* straits 27. *go back again*, i.e., to what she once was 28. *on mount* on high 29. *for* to defend 50. *abuse* deceit 51. *character* handwriting 62. *checking at* fighting shy of

And for his death no wind of blame shall breathe,
But even his mother shall uncharge the practice,
And call it accident.
LAERTES. My lord, I will be ruled;
The rather if you could devise it so
That I might be the organ.
KING. It falls right.
You have been talked of since your travel much,
And that in Hamlet's hearing, for a quality
Wherein they say you shine; your sum of parts
Did not together pluck such envy from him
As did that one, and that, in my regard,
Of the unworthiest siege.
LAERTES. What part is that, my lord?
KING. A very riband in the cap of youth,
Yet needful too, for youth no less becomes
The light and careless livery that it wears
Than settled age his sables and his weeds,
Importing health and graveness. Two months since,
Here was a gentleman of Normandy.
I have seen myself, and served against, the French,
And they can well on horseback, but this gallant
Had witchcraft in't; he grew unto his seat,
And to such wondrous doing brought his horse
As he had been incorpsed and demi-natured
With the brave beast, so far he topped my thought
That I, in forgery of shapes and tricks,
Come short of what he did.
LAERTES. A Norman was't?
KING. A Norman.
LAERTES. Upon my life, Lamord.
KING. The very same.
LAERTES. I know him well; he is the brooch indeed
And gem of all the nation.
KING. He made confession of you,
And gave you such a masterly report
For art and exercise in your defence,
And for your rapier most especial,
That he cried out 'twould be a sight indeed
If one could match you; the scrimers of their nation
He swore had neither motion, guard, nor eye,
If you opposed them. Sir, this report of his
Did Hamlet so envenom with his envy,
That he could nothing do but wish and beg
Your sudden coming o'er to play with him.
Now, out of this—
LAERTES. What out of this, my lord?
KING. Laertes, was your father dear to you?
Or are you like the painting of a sorrow,
A face without a heart?
LAERTES. Why ask you this?
KING. Not that I think you did not love your father,
But that I know love is begun by time,
And that I see, in passages of proof,
Time qualifies the spark and fire of it.
There lives within the very flame of love
A kind of wick or snuff that will abate it
And nothing is at a like goodness still,
For goodness, growing to a plurisy,
Dies in his own too-much; that we would do
We should do when we would, for this "would" changes
And hath abatements and delays as many
As there are tongues, are hands, are accidents,
And then this "should" is like a spendthrift sigh,
That hurts by easing. But, to the quick of the ulcer—
Hamlet comes back; what would you undertake
To show yourself in deed your father's son

---

67. *uncharge* fail to suspect; *practice* plot 70. *organ* instrument 73. *parts* talents 76. *siege* rank 77. *riband* ornament 78. *becomes* is appropriately clad in 79. *livery* costume 80. *sables* blacks (or furs); *weeds* garments 87. *incorpsed and deminatured* united and made half 88. *topped* exceeded 89. *forgery* invention, imagination 93. *brooch* ornament 96. *masterly report* report of mastery or skill 97. *art* skill; *exercise* agility 100. *scrimers* fencers 112. *passages of proof* incidents which test 113. *qualifies* weakens 115. *snuff* burnt part of the wick 116. *still* always 117. *plurisy* excess 118. *that* what 123. *hurts by easing* damages while it gives relief (because sighs were supposed to draw blood from the heart); *quick* sensitive part

    More than in words?
LAERTES.   To cut his throat i' the church.
KING. No place, indeed, should murder sanctuarize;
    Revenge should have no bounds. But, good Laertes,
    Will you do this, keep close within your chamber.
130   Hamlet returned shall know you are come home;
    We'll put on those shall praise your excellence,
    And set a double varnish on the fame
    The Frenchman gave you, bring you in fine together
    And wager on your heads. He, being remiss,
    Most generous, and free from all contriving,
    Will not peruse the foils, so that with ease,
    Or with a little shuffling, you may choose
    A sword unbated, and in a pass of practice
    Requite him for your father.
LAERTES.   I will do't,
140   And for that purpose I'll anoint my sword.
    I bought an unction of a mountebank,
    So mortal, that but dip a knife in it,
    Where it draws blood no cataplasm so rare,
    Collected from all simples that have virtue
    Under the moon, can save the thing from death
    That is but scratched withal. I'll touch my point
    With this contagion, that, if I gall him slightly,
    It may be death.
KING.   Let's further think of this,
    Weigh what convenience both of time and means
150   May fit us to our shape. If this should fail,
    And that our drift look through our bad performance,
'Twere better not assayed; therefore this project
Should have a back or second that might hold
If this should blast in proof. Soft, let me see;
We'll make a solemn wager on your cunnings.
I ha't;
When in your motion you are hot and dry—
As make your bouts more violent to that end—
And that he calls for drink, I'll have preferred him
A chalice for the nonce, whereon but sipping,   160
If he by chance escape your venomed stuck,
Our purpose may hold there.

Enter QUEEN.

                  But stay, what noise?
QUEEN. One woe doth tread upon another's heel,
So fast they follow; your sister's drowned, Laertes.
LAERTES. Drowned! O where?
QUEEN. There is a willow grows askant the brook
That shows his hoary leaves in the glassy stream;
Therewith fantastic garlands did she make
Of crowflowers, nettles, daisies, and long purples
That liberal shepherds give a grosser name,   170
But our cold maids do dead men's fingers call them.
There, on the pendent boughs her crownet weeds
Clambering to hang, an envious sliver broke,
When down her weedy trophies and herself

---

133. *in fine* eventually   135. *contriving* plotting
136. *peruse* scan carefully   138. *unbated* not blunted
141. *unction* ointment; *mountebank* pedlar of patent medicines   142. *mortal* deadly   143. *cataplasm* poultice   144. *simples* herbs   146. *withal* with
147. *gall* scratch   150. *shape* plan   151. *drift* purpose; *look* become visible   153. *back* supporter
154. *blast* come to ruin; *in proof* when put to the test   155. *cunnings* skills   157. *motion* activity
159. *preferred* offered   160. *chalice* cup; *nonce* occasion   161. *stuck* thrust   166. *askant* alongside
172. *pendent* hanging   173. *crownet* coronet; *sliver* bough

Fell in the weeping brook. Her clothes spread wide,
And mermaid-like awhile they bore her up,
Which time she chanted snatches of old lauds,
As one incapable of her own distress,
Or like a creature native and indued
Unto that element; but long it could not be
Till that her garments, heavy with their drink,
Pulled the poor wretch from her melodious lay
To muddy death.
LAERTES.   Alas then, she is drowned?
QUEEN. Drowned, drowned.
LAERTES. Too much of water hast thou, poor Ophelia,
And therefore I forbid my tears; but yet
It is our trick; nature her custom holds,
Let shame say what it will; when these are gone,
The woman will be out. Adieu, my lord;
I have a speech of fire, that fain would blaze,
But that this folly douts it.
    Exit.
KING.   Let's follow, Gertrude.
How much I had to do to calm his rage!
Now fear I this will give it start again;
Therefore let's follow.
    Exeunt.

ACT V

Scene I

Enter two CLOWNS, [*with spades, etc.*]

FIRST CLOWN. Is she to be buried in Christian burial when she wilfully seeks her own salvation?
SECOND CLOWN. I tell thee she is; therefore make her grave straight. The crowner hath sat on her, and finds it Christian burial.
FIRST CLOWN. How can that be, unless she drowned herself in her own defence?
SECOND CLOWN. Why, 'tis found so.
FIRST CLOWN. It must be *se offendendo*; it cannot be else. For here lies the point: if I drown myself wittingly, it argues an act, and an act hath three branches; it is, to act, to do, to perform: argal, she drowned herself wittingly.
SECOND CLOWN. Nay, but hear you, goodman delver—
FIRST CLOWN. Give me leave. Here lies the water—good; here stands the man—good; if the man go to this water and drown himself, it is, will he nill he, he goes—mark you that; but if the water come to him and drown him, he drowns not himself; argal, he that is not guilty of his own death shortens not his own life.
SECOND CLOWN. But is this law?
FIRST CLOWN. Ay marry, is't—crowner's quest law.
SECOND CLOWN. Will you ha' the truth on't? If this had not been a gentlewoman, she should have been buried out o' Christian burial.
FIRST CLOWN. Why, there thou say'st; and the more pity that great folk should have countenance in this world to drown or hang themselves, more than their even Christian. Come, my spade; there is no ancient gentlemen but gardeners, ditchers, and gravemakers—they hold up Adam's profession.

---

177. lauds hymns 178. incapable unconscious 179. indued accustomed 180. that element, i.e., water 191. douts puts out 4. straight immediately; crowner coroner 9. se offendendo a blunder for 'se defendendo,' in self-defence 12. argal ergo, therefore 13. delver digger 16. will he nill he willy-nilly 21. quest inquest 25. there thou say'st there you're saying something 26. countenance permission 27. even fellow

SECOND CLOWN. Was he a gentleman?
FIRST CLOWN. A' was the first that ever bore arms.
SECOND CLOWN. Why, he had none.
FIRST CLOWN. What, art a heathen? How dost thou understand the Scripture? The Scripture says Adam digged; could he dig without arms? I'll put another question to thee; if thou answerest me not to the purpose, confess thyself—
SECOND CLOWN. Go to.
FIRST CLOWN. What is he that builds stronger than either the mason, the shipwright, or the carpenter?
SECOND CLOWN. The gallowsmaker, for that frame outlives a thousand tenants.
FIRST CLOWN. I like thy wit well, in good faith; the gallows does well, but how does it well? it does well to those that do ill; now, thou dost ill to say the gallows is built stronger than the church; argal, the gallows may do well to thee. To't again, come.
SECOND CLOWN. "Who builds stronger than a mason, a shipwright, or a carpenter?"
FIRST CLOWN. Ay, tell me that and unyoke.
SECOND CLOWN. Marry, now I can tell.
FIRST CLOWN. To't.
SECOND CLOWN. Mass, I cannot tell.

Enter HAMLET and HORATIO afar off.

FIRST CLOWN. Cudgel thy brains no more about it, for your dull ass will not mend his pace with beating, and when you are asked this question next, say "a gravemaker;" the houses he makes lasts till doomsday. Go, get thee to Yaughan, and fetch me a stoup of liquor.
[*Exit* SECOND CLOWN. *He digs, and sings.*]
    In youth when I did love, did love,
      Methought it was very sweet
    To contract—O—the time for—a—my behove,
      O—methought there—a—was nothing—a—meet.
HAMLET. Has this fellow no feeling of his business, that a' sings in gravemaking?
HORATIO. Custom hath made it in him a property of easiness.
HAMLET. 'Tis e'en so; the hand of little employment hath the daintier sense.
FIRST CLOWN.   *Sings.*
    But age with his stealing steps
      Hath clawed me in his clutch,
    And hath shipped me intil the land,
      As if I had never been such.
[*Throws up a skull.*]
HAMLET. That skull had a tongue in it, and could sing once; how the knave jowls it to the ground, as if it were Cain's jawbone, that did the first murder! This might be the pate of a politician, which this ass now o'er-reaches; one that would circumvent God, might it not?
HORATIO. It might, my lord.
HAMLET. Or of a courtier, which could say "Good morrow, sweet lord! How dost thou, good lord?" This might be my lord such-a-one, that praised my lord such-a-one's horse, when a' meant to beg it—might it not?
HORATIO. Ay, my lord.
HAMLET. Why, e'en so—and now my Lady Worm's, chapless, and knocked about the mazzard with a sexton's spade; here's fine revolution, and we had the trick to see't. Did these bones cost no more the breeding, but to play at loggats with 'em? mine ache to think on't.
FIRST CLOWN.   *Sings.*
    A pickaxe and a spade, a spade,
      For and a shrouding-sheet;
    O, a pit of clay for to be made
      For such a guest is meet.
[*Throws up another skull.*]
HAMLET. There's another; why may not that be the skull of a lawyer? Where be his quiddities now, his quillets, his cases, his tenures, and his tricks? why does he suffer this mad knave now to knock him about the sconce with a dirty shovel, and will not tell him of his action of battery? Hum! This fellow might be in's time a great buyer of land, with his statutes, his recog-

---

32. *bore arms* (a pun) had a coat of arms, the sign of gentle birth 51. *unyoke* make an end to it 59. *stoup* mug 62. *behove* benefit 63. *meet* fitting 66. *custom* habit; *property* characteristic 68. *easiness* indifference 69. *daintier sense* finer feeling 72. *intil* into 75. *jowls* flings 77. *o'erreaches* gets the better of 86. *chapless* without a jawbone; *mazzard* pate 89. *loggats* a game like bowls 95. *quiddities* definitions; *quillets* quibbles 96. *tenures* terms of holding land 97. *sconce* skull 99. *battery* assault 100. *statutes* and *recognisances* two different kinds of bonds

nizances, his fines, his double vouchers, his recoveries; is this the fine of his fines, and the recovery of his recoveries, to have his fine pate full of fine dirt? will his vouchers vouch him no more of his purchases, and double ones too, than the length and breadth of a pair of indentures? The very conveyances of his lands will scarcely lie in this box, and must the inheritor himself have no more, ha?

HORATIO. Not a jot more, my lord.

HAMLET. Is not parchment made of sheepskins?

HORATIO. Ay, my lord, and of calfskins too.

HAMLET. They are sheep and calves which seek out assurance in that. I will speak to this fellow. Whose grave's this, sirrah?

FIRST CLOWN. Mine, sir. [Sings.]
    O, a pit of clay for to be made
      For such a guest is meet.

HAMLET. I think it be thine indeed, for thou liest in't.

FIRST CLOWN. You lie out on't, sir, and therefore 'tis not yours; for my part, I do not lie in't, yet it is mine.

HAMLET. Thou dost lie in't, to be in't and say it is thine; 'tis for the dead, not for the quick; therefore thou liest.

FIRST CLOWN. 'Tis a quick lie, sir; 'twill away again from me to you.

HAMLET. What man dost thou dig it for?

FIRST CLOWN. For no man, sir.

HAMLET. What woman, then?

FIRST CLOWN. For none, neither.

HAMLET. Who is to be buried in't?

FIRST CLOWN. One that was a woman, sir; but, rest her soul, she's dead.

HAMLET. How absolute the knave is! we must speak by the card, or equivocation will undo us. By the Lord, Horatio, this three years I have took note of it, the age is grown so picked that the toe of the peasant comes so near the heel of the courtier he galls his kibe. How long hast thou been gravemaker?

FIRST CLOWN. Of all the days i' the year, I came to't that day that our last king Hamlet overcame Fortinbras.

HAMLET. How long is that since?

FIRST CLOWN. Cannot you tell that? every fool can tell that; it was the very day that young Hamlet was born—he that is mad and sent into England.

HAMLET. Ay, marry, why was he sent into England?

FIRST CLOWN. Why, because a' was mad: a' shall recover his wits there or, if a' do not, 'tis no great matter there.

HAMLET. Why?

FIRST CLOWN. 'Twill not be seen in him there; there the men are as mad as he.

HAMLET. How came he mad?

FIRST CLOWN. Very strangely, they say.

HAMLET. How strangely?

FIRST CLOWN. Faith, e'en with losing his wits.

HAMLET. Upon what ground?

FIRST CLOWN. Why, here in Denmark: I have been sexton here, man and boy, thirty years.

HAMLET. How long will a man lie i' the earth ere he rot?

FIRST CLOWN. Faith, if a' be not rotten before a' die—as we have many pocky corses nowadays that will scarce hold the laying in—he will last you some eight year or nine year. A tanner will last you nine year.

HAMLET. Why he more than another?

FIRST CLOWN. Why sir, his hide is so tanned with his trade that a' will keep out water a great while; and your water is a sore decayer of your whoreson dead body. Here's a skull now; this skull hath lien yon i' the earth three-and-twenty years.

HAMLET. Whose was it?

FIRST CLOWN. A whoreson mad fellow's it was; whose do you think it was?

HAMLET. Nay, I know not.

FIRST CLOWN. A pestilence on him for a mad rogue! a' poured a flagon of Rhenish on my head once. This same skull, sir, was Yorick's skull, the king's jester.

HAMLET. This?

FIRST CLOWN. E'en that.

HAMLET. Let me see. [Takes the skull.] Alas,

---

101. fines . . . double vouchers various types of procedure for transferring land; *fine* end   *105. indentures* legal documents on parchment   *106. conveyances* deeds   *111. seek out assurance* put their trust   *118. out on't* outside it   *121. quick* living   *131. absolute* positive   *132. by the card* by the compass, precisely; *equivocation* double meanings   *134. picked* fastidious   *135. galls his kibe* scrapes the chilblains on his heels   *154. upon what ground* for what cause   *160. pocky* diseased.   *161. hold the laying in* last till burial   *174. Rhenish* Rhine wine

poor Yorick! I knew him, Horatio: a fellow of infinite jest, of most excellent fancy; he hath borne me on his back a thousand times, and now how abhorred in my imagination it is! my gorge rises at it. Here hung those lips that I have kissed I know not how oft. Where be your gibes now? your gambols, your songs, your flashes of merriment that were wont to set the table on a roar? Not one now to mock your own grinning? quite chapfallen? Now get you to my lady's chamber, and tell her, let her paint an inch thick, to this favor she must come; make her laugh at that. Prithee, Horatio, tell me one thing.
HORATIO. What's that, my lord?
HAMLET. Dost thou think Alexander looked o' this fashion i' the earth?
HORATIO. E'en so.
HAMLET. And smelt so? pah.
[Puts down the skull.]
HORATIO. E'en so, my lord.
HAMLET. To what base uses we may return, Horatio! Why may not imagination trace the noble dust of Alexander till a' find it stopping a bunghole?
HORATIO. 'Twere to consider too curiously to consider so.
HAMLET. No, faith, not a jot; but to follow him thither with modesty enough, and likelihood to lead it, as thus: Alexander died, Alexander was buried, Alexander returneth to dust; the dust is earth, of earth we make loam, and why of that loam whereto he was converted might they not stop a beer barrel?
Imperious Cæsar, dead and turned to clay,
Might stop a hole to keep the wind away.
O, that that earth which kept the world in awe
Should patch a wall to expel the winter's flaw!
But soft, but soft awhile; here comes the king,

Enter KING, QUEEN, LAERTES, *and a Coffin, with Lords Attendant,* [*a* DOCTOR OF DIVINITY *following*].

The queen, the courtiers. Who is this they follow?

And with such maiméd rites? This doth betoken
The corse they follow did with desperate hand
Fordo it own life; 'twas of some estate.
Couch we awhile, and mark.
[*Retiring with* HORATIO.]
LAERTES. What ceremony else?
HAMLET. That is Laertes,
A very noble youth; mark.
LAERTES. What ceremony else?
DOCTOR. Her obsequies have been as far enlarged
As we have warranty. Her death was doubtful
And, but that great command o'ersways the order,
She should in ground unsanctified have lodged
Till the last trumpet; for charitable prayers,
Shards, flints and pebbles should be thrown on her:
Yet here she is allowed her virgin crants,
Her maiden strewments, and the bringing home
Of bell and burial.
LAERTES. Must there no more be done?
DOCTOR. No more be done.
We should profane the service of the dead
To sing a requiem and such rest to her
As to peace-parted souls.
LAERTES. Lay her i' the earth,
And from her fair and unpolluted flesh
May violets spring! I tell thee, churlish priest,
A ministering angel shall my sister be,
When thou liest howling.
HAMLET. What, the fair Ophelia!
QUEEN. Sweets to the sweet; farewell!
[*Scattering flowers*]
I hoped thou shouldst have been my Hamlet's wife;
I thought thy bride-bed to have decked, sweet maid,
And not have strewed thy grave.
LAERTES. O, treble woe
Fall ten times treble on that curséd head
Whose wicked deed thy most ingenious sense

186. *chapfallen* (1) jawless (2) dejected   188. *favor* appearance   201. *modesty* moderation   212. *maiméd rites* incomplete ceremonial   214. *fordo* destroy; *estate* rank   215. *couch* hide   220. *have warranty* are permitted; *doubtful* uncertain   221. *great command,* i.e., that of the King; *o'ersways* overrules   223. *for* instead of   224. *shards* broken pottery   225. *crants* garland   226. *strewments* strewments of flowers on the grave; *bringing home* laying to rest   241. *sense* senses

Deprived thee of! Hold off the earth awhile,
Till I have caught her once more in mine arms;
Leaps in the grave.
Now pile your dust upon the quick and dead,
Till of this flat a mountain you have made
To o'ertop old Pelion or the skyish head
Of blue Olympus.
HAMLET [*advancing*]. What is he whose grief
Bears such an emphasis, whose phrase of sorrow
Conjures the wandering stars and makes them stand
Like wonder-wounded hearers? This is I,
Hamlet the Dane.
Leaps in after LAERTES.
LAERTES.   The devil take thy soul!
[*Grappling with him.*]
HAMLET. Thou pray'st not well.
I prithee take thy fingers from my throat,
For, though I am not splenitive and rash,
Yet have I in me something dangerous,
Which let thy wisdom fear. Hold off thy hand!
KING. Pluck them asunder.
QUEEN.   Hamlet, Hamlet!
ALL. Gentlemen—
HORATIO.   Good my lord, be quiet.
[*The Attendants part them, and they come out of the grave.*]
HAMLET. Why, I will fight with him upon this theme
Until my eyelids will no longer wag.
QUEEN. O my son, what theme?
HAMLET. I loved Ophelia; forty thousand brothers
Could not with all their quantity of love
Make up my sum. What wilt thou do for her?
KING. O, he is mad, Laertes.
QUEEN. For love of God, forbear him.
HAMLET. 'Swounds, show me what thou'lt do:
Woo't weep? woo't fight? woo't fast? woo't tear thyself?
Woo't drink up eisel? eat a crocodile?
I'll do't. Dost thou come here to whine,
To outface me with leaping in her grave?
Be buried quick with her, and so will I:
And if thou prate of mountains, let them throw
Millions of acres on us, till our ground,
Singeing his pate against the burning zone,
Make Ossa like a wart! Nay, an thou'lt mouth,
I'll rant as well as thou.
QUEEN.   This is mere madness:
And thus awhile the fit will work on him;
Anon, as patient as the female dove
When that her golden couplets are disclosed,
His silence will sit drooping.
HAMLET.   Hear you, sir;
What is the reason that you use me thus?
I loved you ever: but it is no matter;
Let Hercules himself do what he may,
The cat will mew, and dog will have his day.
Exit.
KING. I pray you, good Horatio, wait upon him.
Exit HORATIO.
[*To* LAERTES] Strengthen your patience in our last night's speech;
We'll put the matter to the present push.
Good Gertrude, set some watch over your son.
This grave shall have a living monument:
An hour of quiet shortly shall we see;
Till then, in patience our proceeding be.
Exeunt.

Scene 2

Enter HAMLET *and* HORATIO.

HAMLET. So much for this, sir; now shall you see the other.

You do remember all the circumstance?
HORATIO. Remember it, my lord!
HAMLET. Sir, in my heart there was a kind of fighting

---

244. *quick* living 246. *Pelion . . . Olympus* (according to the Greek legend, the Titans piled Mt. Pelion on Mt. Ossa in their attempt to storm Mt. Olympus) 254. *splenitive* excitable 266. *forbear him* leave him alone 269. *eisel* vinegar 271. *outface* outdo 280. *couplets* twins; *disclosed* hatched 288. *present push* immediate test

That would not let me sleep; methought
   I lay
Worse than the mutines in the bilboes.
   Rashly,
And praised be rashness for it—let us
   know
Our indiscretion sometimes serves us well
When our deep plots do pall, and that
   should learn us
There's a divinity that shapes our ends,
Rough-hew them how we will—
HORATIO.   That is most certain.
HAMLET. Up from my cabin,
My sea-gown scarfed about me, in the
   dark
Groped I to find out them, had my de-
   sire,
Fingered their packet, and in fine with-
   drew
To mine own room again, making so
   bold,
My fears forgetting manners, to unseal
Their grand commission; where I found,
   Horatio—
O royal knavery!—an exact command,
Larded with many several sorts of rea-
   sons,
Importing Denmark's health and Eng-
   land's too,
With, ho! such bugs and goblins in my
   life,
That on the supervise, no leisure bated,
No, not to stay the grinding of the axe,
My head should be struck off.
HORATIO.   Is't possible?
HAMLET. Here's the commission; read it at
   more leisure.
But wilt thou hear now how I did pro-
   ceed?
HORATIO. I beseech you.
HAMLET. Being thus benetted round with
   vallanies—
Or I could make a prologue to my brains,
They had begun the play—I sat me down,
Devised a new commission, wrote it fair;
I once did hold it, as our statists do,
A baseness to write fair, and labored
   much
How to forget that learning, but, sir, now

It did me yeoman's service; wilt thou
   know
The effect of what I wrote?
HORATIO.   Ay, good my lord.
HAMLET. An earnest conjuration from the
   king,
As England was his faithful tributary,
As love between them like the palm
   might flourish,
As peace should still her wheaten garland
   wear
And stand a comma 'tween their amities,
And many such-like "as'es" of great
   charge,
That, on the view and knowing of these
   contents,
Without debatement further, more or
   less,
He should the bearers put to sudden
   death,
Not shriving-time allowed.
HORATIO.   How was this sealed?
HAMLET. Why, even in that was heaven
   ordinant.
I had my father's signet in my purse,
Which was the model of that Danish seal;
Folded the writ up in the form of the
   other,
Subscribed it, gave't the impression,
   placed it safely,
The changeling never known. Now, the
   next day
Was our seafight, and what to this was
   sequent
Thou know'st already.
HORATIO. So Guildenstern and Rosencrantz
   go to't.
HAMLET. Why, man, they did make love
   to this employment;
They are not near my conscience; their
   defeat
Does by their own insinuation grow;
'Tis dangerous when the baser nature
   comes
Between the pass and fell incensèd points
Of mighty opposites.
HORATIO.   Why, what a king is this!
HAMLET. Does it not, think thee, stand me
   now upon—

---

6. *mutines* mutineers; *bilboes* irons   9. *pall* fail
15. *fine* conclusion   20. *larded* adorned   21. *importing* concerning   22. *bugs* bugbears   23. *supervise* perusal; *bated* subtracted   30. *or* ere, before
33. *statists* statesmen   36. *yeoman's service* sturdy service   38. *conjuration* exhortation   39. *tributary* vassal   42. *comma* connecting link   43. *charge* force

47. *shriving-time* time for confession   48. *ordinant* propitious   52. *subscribed* signed; *impression* (of the seal)   54. *sequent* subsequent   58. *defeat* destruction   59. *insinuation* intrusion   60. *baser* of lower rank   61. *pass* thrust; *fell* fierce   63. *does it not . . . stand me now upon* am I not now obliged

He that hath killed my king, and whored my mother,
Popped in between the election and my hopes,
Thrown out his angle for my proper life,
And with such cozenage—is't not perfect conscience
To quit him with this arm? and is't not to be damned
To let this canker of our nature come In further evil?
HORATIO. It must be shortly known to him from England
What is the issue of the business there.
HAMLET. It will be short; the interim is mine,
And a man's life no more than to say "one."
But I am very sorry, good Horatio,
That to Laertes I forgot myself;
For, by the image of my cause, I see
The portraiture of his; I'll court his favors;
But sure the bravery of his grief did put me
Into a towering passion.
HORATIO. Peace, who comes here?

Enter young OSRIC, *a courtier.*

OSRIC. Your lordship is right welcome back to Denmark.
HAMLET. I humbly thank you, sir. [*Aside to* HORATIO.]
Dost know this water-fly?
HORATIO [*aside to* HAMLET]. No, my good lord.
HAMLET [*aside to* HORATIO]. Thy state is the more gracious, for 'tis a vice to know him. He hath much land, and fertile: let a beast be lord of beasts, and his crib shall stand at the king's mess; 'tis a chough, but, as I say, spacious in the possession of dirt.
OSRIC. Sweet lord, if your lordship were at leisure, I should impart a thing to you from his majesty.
HAMLET. I will receive it, sir, with all diligence of spirit. Put your bonnet to his right use; 'tis for the head.
OSRIC. I thank your lordship, it is very hot.
HAMLET. No, believe me, 'tis very cold; the wind is northerly.
OSRIC. It is indifferent cold, my lord, indeed.
HAMLET. But yet methinks it is very sultry and hot, or my complexion—
OSRIC. Exceedingly, my lord; it is very sultry—as 'twere—I cannot tell how. But, my lord, his majesty bade me signify to you, that a' has laid a great wager on your head; sir, this is the matter—
HAMLET. I beseech you, remember—
[HAMLET *motions him to put on his hat.*]
OSRIC. Nay, good my lord; for my ease, in good faith. Sir, here is newly come to court Laertes; believe me, an absolute gentleman, full of most excellent differences, of very soft society and great showing: indeed, to speak feelingly of him, he is the card or calendar of gentry, for you shall find in him the continent of what parts a gentleman would see.
HAMLET. Sir, his definement suffers no perdition in you, though I know to divide him inventorially would dizzy the arithmetic of memory, and yet but yaw neither, in respect of his quick sail. But, in the verity of extolment, I take him to be a soul of great article, and his infusion of such dearth and rareness as, to make true diction of him, his semblable is his mirror, and who else would trace him, his umbrage, nothing more.
OSRIC. Your lordship speaks most infallibly of him.
HAMLET. The concernancy, sir? why do we wrap the gentleman in our more rawer breath?
OSRIC. Sir?

---

66. *angle* fishing-line; *proper* own 67. *cozenage* deceit; *conscience* justice 68. *quit* repay 69. *canker* cancer 73. *interim* time between 78. *portraiture* picture, portrayal 79. *bravery* display, ostentation 88. *mess* table; *chough* jackdaw 96. *indifferent* moderately 106. *differences* accomplishments 107. *of very soft society* pleasant company; *great showing* fine appearance 108. *card or calendar* pattern; *gentry* gentlemanliness 109. *continent* sum total; *parts* good qualities 111. *definement* description; *perdition* loss 112. *divide him inventorially* make a list of his qualities 113. *arithmetic* reckoning power; *but only*; *yaw* fail to hold its course, i.e., come short of the mark 114. *in the verity of extolment* to praise him accurately 115. *article* scope; *infusion* character 116. *dearth* scarcity; *make true diction* speak truly 117. *semblable* resemblance, equal 118. *trace* copy; *umbrage* shadow 120. *concernancy* purport 121. *rawer* cruder

HORATIO. Is't not possible to understand in another tongue? You will to't, sir, really.
HAMLET. What imports the nomination of this gentleman?
OSRIC. Of Laertes?
HORATIO. His purse is empty already; all's golden words are spent.
HAMLET. Of him, sir.
OSRIC. I know you are not ignorant—
HAMLET. I would you did, sir; yet, in faith, if you did, it would not much approve me; well, sir.
OSRIC. You are not ignorant of what excellence Laertes is—
HAMLET. I dare not confess that, lest I should compare with him in excellence; but to know a man well were to know himself.
OSRIC. I mean, sir, for his weapon; but in the imputation laid on him by them, in his meed he's unfellowed.
HAMLET. What's his weapon?
OSRIC. Rapier and dagger.
HAMLET. That's two of his weapons: but, well.
OSRIC. The king, sir, hath wagered with him six Barbary horses, against the which he has impawned, as I take it, six French rapiers and poniards, with their assigns, as girdle, hangers, and so. Three of the carriages, in faith, are very dear to fancy, very responsive to the hilts, most delicate carriages, and of very liberal conceit.
HAMLET. What call you the carriages?
HORATIO. I knew you must be edified by the margent ere you had done.
OSRIC. The carriages, sir, are the hangers.
HAMLET. The phrase would be more germane to the matter, if we could carry a cannon by our sides; I would it might be hangers till then. But, on: six Barbary horses against six French swords, their assigns, and three liberal-conceited carriages; that's the French bet against the Danish. Why is this "impawned," as you call it?
OSRIC. The king, sir, hath laid, sir, that in a dozen passes between yourself and him, he shall not exceed you three hits; he hath laid on twelve for nine, and it would come to immediate trial, if your lordship would vouchsafe the answer.
HAMLET. How if I answer no?
OSRIC. I mean, my lord, the opposition of your person in trial.
HAMLET. Sir, I will walk here in the hall. If it please his majesty, it is the breathing time of day with me. Let the foils be brought, the gentleman willing, and the king hold his purpose, I will win for him an I can; if not, I will gain nothing but my shame and the odd hits.
OSRIC. Shall I redeliver you e'en so?
HAMLET. To this effect, sir; after what flourish your nature will.
OSRIC. I commend my duty to your lordship.
HAMLET. Yours, yours. [*Exit* OSRIC.] He does well to commend it himself; there are no tongues else for's turn.
HORATIO. This lapwing runs away with the shell on his head.
HAMLET. A' did comply with his dug before a' sucked it. Thus has he—and many more of the same bevy that I know the drossy age dotes on—only got the tune of the time and, out of an habit of encounter, a kind of yesty collection, which carries them through and through the most fanned and winnowed opinions, and do but blow them to their trial, the bubbles are out.

Enter a LORD.

LORD. My lord, his majesty commended him to you by young Osric, who brings back to him that you attend him in the hall; he sends to know if your pleasure hold to play with Laertes, or that you will take longer time.
HAMLET. I am constant to my purposes; they follow the king's pleasure; if his fitness speaks, mine is ready, now or whensoever, provided I be so able as now.

125. *nomination* mention 132. *approve me* be to my advantage 134. *compare with* rival 137. *imputation* reputation 138. *meed* desert; *unfellowed* unequalled 143. *impawned* staked 144. *assigns* appurtenances 145. *carriages* hangers 146. *dear* pleasing; *fancy* taste; *responsive* well-matched 147. *liberal conceit* elegant design 149. *edified* instructed; *margent* marginal note 152. *germane* suitable 153. *cannon* (Hamlet is referring to 'guncarriages') 160. *laid* stipulated; *for* instead of 167. *breathing* exercise 171. *redeliver you* take back your reply 177. *lapwing* a bird said to be able to run as soon as it was hatched 179. *comply* compliment 181. *drossy* degenerate 182. *encounter* formal greeting; *yesty* frothy 183. *carries them through* makes them impress 184. *fanned and winnowed* experienced

LORD. The king and queen and all are coming down.
HAMLET. In happy time.
LORD. The queen desires you to use some gentle entertainment to Laertes before you fall to play.
HAMLET. She well instructs me.
[*Exit* LORD.]
HORATIO. You will lose this wager, my lord.
HAMLET. I do not think so; since he went into France, I have been in continual practice; I shall win at the odds. But thou wouldst not think how ill all's here about my heart—but it is no matter.
HORATIO. Nay, good my lord—
HAMLET. It is but foolery, but it is such a kind of gain-giving as would perhaps trouble a woman.
HORATIO. If your mind dislike anything, obey it; I will forestall their repair hither, and say you are not fit.
HAMLET. Not a whit, we defy augury. There is special providence in the fall of a sparrow. If it be now, 'tis not to come; if it be not to come, it will be now; if it be not now, yet it will come—the readiness is all. Since no man has aught of what he leaves, what is't to leave betimes? Let be.

A table prepared with flagons of wine on it. Trumpets and drums. [Enter] officers with cushions. Then enter KING, QUEEN, [OSRIC] *and all the state. Foils and daggers [brought in]. [Then enter]* LAERTES.

KING. Come, Hamlet, come and take this hand from me.
[*The* KING *puts* LAERTES' *hand into* HAMLET'S.]
HAMLET. Give me your pardon, sir. I have done you wrong,
But pardon't, as you are a gentleman.
This presence knows,
And you must needs have heard, how I am punished
With sore distraction. What I have done
That might your nature, honor and exception
Roughly awake, I here proclaim was madness.
Was't Hamlet wronged Laertes? never Hamlet.
If Hamlet from himself be ta'en away,
And when he's not himself does wrong Laertes,
Then Hamlet does it not, Hamlet denies it.
Who does it then? his madness. If't be so,
Hamlet is of the faction that is wronged;
His madness is poor Hamlet's enemy.
Sir, in this audience,
Let my disclaiming from a purposed evil
Free me so far in your most generous thoughts,
That I have shot my arrow o'er the house,
And hurt my brother.
LAERTES.   I am satisfied in nature,
Whose motive, in this case, should stir me most
To my revenge; but in my terms of honor
I stand aloof, and will no reconcilement
Till by some elder masters of known honor
I have a voice and precedent of peace
To keep my name ungored. But till that time
I do receive your offered love like love,
And will not wrong it.
HAMLET.   I embrace it freely,
And will this brother's wager frankly play.
Give us the foils. Come on.
LAERTES.   Come, one for me.
HAMLET. I'll be your foil, Laertes; in mine ignorance
Your skill shall, like a star i' the darkest night,
Stick fiery off indeed.
LAERTES.   You mock me, sir.
HAMLET. No, by this hand.
KING. Give them the foils, young Osric. Cousin Hamlet,
You know the wager?
HAMLET.   Very well, my lord;
Your grace has laid the odds o' the weaker side.
KING. I do not fear it; I have seen you both;
But since he's bettered, we have therefore odds.

195. *entertainment* greeting, welcome   204. *gain-giving* misgiving   207. *repair* coming   213. *betimes* early   217. *this presence* those present   220. *exception* objection   227. *of the faction* on the side   233. *in nature,* i.e., as a son   239. *ungored* uninjured   244. *foil* something that sets off another by contrast   246. *stick fiery off* stand out brilliantly

LAERTES. This is too heavy; let me see another.
HAMLET. This likes me well. These foils have all a length?
Prepare to play.
OSRIC. Ay, my good lord.
KING. Set me the stoups of wine upon that table.
If Hamlet give the first or second hit,
Or quit in answer of the third exchange,
Let all the battlements their ordnance fire;
The king shall drink to Hamlet's better breath,
And in the cup an union shall he throw,
Richer than that which four successive kings
In Denmark's crown have worn. Give me the cups,
And let the kettle to the trumpet speak,
The trumpet to the cannoneer without,
The cannons to the heavens, the heaven to earth,
"Now the king drinks to Hamlet." Come begin;
And you, the judges, bear a wary eye.
Trumpets the while.
HAMLET. Come on, sir.
They play.
LAERTES. Come, my lord.
HAMLET. One.
LAERTES. No.
HAMLET. Judgment.
OSRIC. A hit, a very palpable hit.
Drums; flourish of trumpets; a piece goes off.
LAERTES. Well; again.
KING. Stay, give me drink. Hamlet, this pearl is thine;
Here's to thy health. Give him the cup.
HAMLET. I'll play this bout first; set it by awhile.
Come. [*They play.*] Another hit; what say you?
LAERTES. A touch, a touch, I do confess't.
KING. Our son shall win.
QUEEN. He's fat, and scant of breath.
Here, Hamlet take my napkin, rub thy brows;
The queen carouses to thy fortune, Hamlet.
HAMLET. Good madam!
KING. Gertrude, do not drink.
QUEEN. I will, my lord; I pray you, pardon me.
[*Drinks.*]
KING [*aside*]. It is the poisoned cup; it is too late.
HAMLET. I dare not drink yet, madam; by and by.
QUEEN. Come, let me wipe thy face.
LAERTES. My lord, I'll hit him now.
KING. I do not think't.
LAERTES [*aside*]. And yet it is almost against my conscience.
HAMLET. Come, for the third, Laertes, you but dally;
I pray you, pass with your best violence;
I am afeared you make a wanton of me.
Play.
LAERTES. Say you so? come on.
OSRIC. Nothing, neither way.
LAERTES. Have at you now!

[LAERTES *wounds* HAMLET; *then*] *in scuffling, they change rapiers,* [*and* HAMLET *wounds* LAERTES.]

KING. Part them; they are incensed.
The QUEEN *falls.*
HAMLET. Nay, come, again.
OSRIC. Look to the queen there, ho!
HORATIO. They bleed on both sides. How is it, my lord?
OSRIC. How is't, Laertes?
LAERTES. Why, as a woodcock to mine own springe, Osric; I am justly killed with mine own treachery.
HAMLET. How does the queen?
KING. She swoons to see them bleed.
QUEEN. No, no, the drink, the drink—O my dear Hamlet—
The drink, the drink!—I am poisoned.
[*Dies.*]
HAMLET. O villany! Ho! let the door be locked;
Treachery! seek it out.
LAERTES. It is here, Hamlet; Hamlet, thou art slain;
No medicine in the world can do thee good,
In thee there is not half an hour of life;
The treacherous instrument is in thy hand,
Unbated and envenomed. The foul practice

256. *stoups* goblets 258. *quit in answer of score a hit in* 261. *union* pearl 264. *kettle* kettledrum 276. *fat* sweaty; *scant* short 288. *wanton* spoilt child 295. *woodcock* the silliest of all birds; *springe* snare 306. *unbated* unblunted; *practice* plot

Hath turned itself on me; lo, here I lie,
Never to rise again. Thy mother's poisoned.
I can no more; the king, the king's to blame.
HAMLET. The point envenomed too!
Then, venom, to thy work.
Hurts the KING.
ALL. Treason! treason!
KING. O yet defend me, friends; I am but hurt.
HAMLET. Here, thou incestuous, murderous, damnéd Dane,
Drink off this potion; is thy union here?
Follow my mother.
KING *dies.*
LAERTES. He is justly served;
It is a poison tempered by himself.
Exchange forgiveness with me, noble Hamlet;
Mine and my father's death come not upon thee,
Nor thine on me!
Dies.
HAMLET. Heaven make thee free of it! I follow thee.
I am dead, Horatio. Wretched queen, adieu!
You that look pale and tremble at this chance,
That are but mutes or audience to this act,
Had I but time—as this fell sergeant, death,
Is strict in his arrest—O, I could tell you—
But let it be.—Horatio, I am dead,
Thou livest; report me and my cause aright
To the unsatisfied.
HORATIO. Never believe it;
I am more an antique Roman than a Dane.
Here's yet some liquor left.
HAMLET. As thou'rt a man,
Give me the cup. Let go; by heaven, I'll have't.
O good Horatio, what a wounded name,
Things standing thus unknown, shall live behind me!
If thou didst ever hold me in thy heart,
Absent thee from felicity awhile,
And in this harsh world draw thy breath in pain
To tell my story.
March afar off, and shout within.
What warlike noise is this?
OSRIC. Young Fortinbras, with conquest come from Poland,
To the ambassadors of England gives
This warlike volley.
HAMLET. O, I die, Horatio;
The potent poison quite o'er-crows my spirit;
I cannot live to hear the news from England,
But I do prophesy the election lights
On Fortinbras; he has my dying voice;
So tell him, with the occurrents, more and less,
Which have solicited—the rest is silence.
Dies.
HORATIO. Now cracks a noble heart; good night, sweet prince,
And flights of angels sing thee to thy rest!
Why does the drum come hither?

Enter FORTINBRAS, *the* ENGLISH AMBASSADORS *with drum, colors, and Attendants.*

FORTINBRAS. Where is this sight?
HORATIO. What is it you would see?
If aught of woe or wonder, cease your search.
FORTINBRAS. This quarry cries on havoc. O proud Death,
What feast is toward in thin eternal cell,
That thou so many princes at a shot
So bloodily hast struck?
FIRST AMBASSADOR. The sight is dismal,
And our affairs from England come too late;
The ears are senseless that should give us hearing,
To tell him his commandment is fulfilled,
That Rosencrantz and Guildenstern are dead;
Where should we have our thanks?
HORATIO. Not from his mouth,
Had it the ability of life to thank you;
He never gave commandment for their death.

---

325. sergeant a sheriff's officer 342. o'ercrows overcomes 345. voice vote 346. occurrents occurrences 347. solicited prompted (this) 353. quarry heap of dead; cries proclaims; havoc slaughter

But since, so jump upon this bloody question,
You from the Polack wars, and you from England,
Are here arrived, give order that these bodies
High on a stage be placéd to the view,
And let me speak to the yet unknowing world
How these things came about; so shall you hear
Of carnal, bloody and unnatural acts, 370
Of accidental judgments, casual slaughters,
Of deaths put on by cunning and forced cause,
And, in this upshot, purposes mistook
Fall'n on the inventors' heads: all this can I
Truly deliver.
FORTINBRAS. Let us haste to hear it,
And call the noblest to the audience.
For me, with sorrow I embrace my fortune;
I have some rights of memory in this kingdom,
Which now to claim my vantage doth invite me.
HORATIO. Of that I shall have also cause to speak, 380
And from his mouth whose voice will draw on more;
But let this same be presently performed,
Even while men's minds are wild; lest more mischance
On plots and errors happen.
FORTINBRAS.   Let four captains
Bear Hamlet like a soldier to the stage,
For he was likely, had he been put on,
To have proved most royally; and for his passage
The soldiers' music and the rites of war
Speak loudly for him.
Take up the bodies; such a sight as this 390
Becomes the field, but here shows much amiss.
Go bid the soldiers shoot.
Exeunt marching; after the which, a peal of ordnance are shot off.

FOR DISCUSSION:

1. Does Hamlet believe the ghost's story in Act I? How do we know?
2. Note each appearance of the ghost and consider the possibility that the apparition is merely a figment of Hamlet's deranged mind. Is there objective evidence in each case to corroborate Hamlet's seeing the ghost?
3. Which disturbs Hamlet more—the murder of his father or his mother's incestuous relationship with Claudius?
4. One of the central problems in the play concerns Hamlet's mental state. Cite evidence to support the view that his madness is (a) real, (b) feigned.
5. Various motives have been suggested for Hamlet's delay in killing Claudius and avenging the murder of his father. Some are (a) he was uncertain of Claudius' guilt; (b) he had no opportunity; (c) he feared retribution in the hereafter; (d) he feared the populace would punish him for regicide; (e) his philosophic cast of mind inhibited action; (f) he was a sensitive scholar who inherently detested violence. Examine each of these in the light of the play and determine the degree to which it explains Hamlet's procrastination.
6. What reasons for his delay does Hamlet himself advance? Does he believe them? How do we know?
7. Comment on evidence of severe mental disturbance in the "To be or not to be" soliloquy [III, i, 56–90].
8. Carefully trace Hamlet's attitudes toward his mother throughout the play.
9. How do you account for (a) Hamlet's harsh treatment of Ophelia, (b) his impulsive killing of Polonius, (c) his uncharacteristic recklessness in accepting Laertes' challenge, (d) his final murder of Claudius after so long a delay?
10. What does Hamlet mean when he says, "The readiness is all" [V, ii, 212].
11. There are several father-son relationships depicted in Hamlet. In what way do these fathers and sons interact?
12. The idea of mental and physical sickness, ulceration, decay, and corruption permeates both the language and action of Hamlet. Trace this idea through the imagery of the speeches and the incidents of the play.
13. To what extent does Hamlet's inability to distinguish between what appears to be true and what really is true contribute to his ultimate tragedy?

364. jump exactly; question affair 367. stage platform 371. casual chance 372. put on brought about 378. of memory not forgotten 379. vantage opportunity 382. presently immediately 383. wild disturbed 384. on over and above

The Psycho-Analytic Solution to Hamlet's Character*

ERNEST JONES

... That Hamlet is suffering from an internal conflict the essential nature of which is inaccessible to his introspection is evidenced by the following considerations. Throughout the play we have the clearest picture of a man who sees his duty plain before him, but who shirks it at every opportunity and suffers in consequence the most intense remorse. To paraphrase Sir James Paget's well-known description of hysterical paralysis: Hamlet's advocates say he cannot do his duty, his detractors say he will not, whereas the truth is that he cannot will. Further than this, the deficient will-power is localized to the one question of killing his uncle; it is what may be termed a *specific aboulia*. Now instances of such specific aboulias in real life invariably prove, when analysed, to be due to an unconscious repulsion against the act that cannot be performed (or else against something closely associated with the act, so that the idea of the act becomes also involved in the repulsion). In other words, whenever a person cannot bring himself to do something that every conscious consideration tells him he should do—and which he may have the strongest conscious desire to do—it is always because there is some hidden reason why a part of him doesn't want to do it; this reason he will not own to himself and is only dimly if at all aware of. That is exactly the case with Hamlet. Time and again he works himself up, points out to himself his obvious duty, with the cruellest self-reproaches lashes himself to agonies of remorse—and once more falls away into inaction. He eagerly seizes at every excuse for occupying himself with any other matter than the performance of his duty—even in the last scene of the last act entering on the distraction of a quite irrelevant fencing-match with a man who he must know wants to kill him, an eventuality that would put an end to all hope of fulfilling his task: just as on a lesser plane a person faced with a distasteful task, e.g. writing a difficult letter, will whittle away his time in arranging, tidying, and fidgeting with any little occupation that may serve as a pretext for procrastination. Bradley even goes as far as to make out a case for the view that Hamlet's self-accusation of "bestial oblivion" is to be taken in a literal sense, his unconscious detestation of his task being so intense as to enable him actually to forget it for periods.

Highly significant is the fact that the grounds Hamlet gives for his hesitancy are grounds none of which will stand any serious consideration, and which continually change from one time to another. One moment he pretends he is too cowardly to perform the deed, at another he questions the truthfulness of the ghost, at another—when the opportunity presents itself in its naked form—he thinks the time is unsuited, it would be better to wait till the King was at some evil act and then to kill him, and so on. They have each of them, it is true, a certain plausibility—so much so that some writers have accepted them at face value; but surely no pretext would be of any use if it were not plausible. As

---

* Reprinted from *Hamlet and Oedipus* by Ernest Jones, M.D. By permission of W. W. Norton & Company, Inc. Copyright 1949 by Ernest Jones. Also by permission of Victor Gollancz Ltd. [Footnote references to foreign sources omitted. Other footnotes renumbered—Ed.]

Madariaga truly says: "The argument that the reasons given by Hamlet not to kill the king at prayers are cogent is irrelevant. For the man who wants to procrastinate cogent arguments are more valuable than mere pretexts." Take, for instance, the matter of the credibility of the ghost. There exists an extensive and very interesting literature concerning Elizabethan beliefs in supernatural visitation. It was doubtless a burning topic, a focal point of the controversies about the conflicting theologies of the age, and moreover, affecting the practical question of how to treat witches. But there is no evidence of Hamlet (or Shakespeare!) being specially interested in theology, and from the moment when the ghost confirms the slumbering suspicion in his mind ("O, my prophetic soul! My uncle!") his intuition must indubitably have convinced him of the ghost's veridical nature. He never really doubted the villainy of his uncle.

When a man gives at different times a different reason for his conduct it is safe to infer that, whether consciously or not, he is concealing the true reason. Wetz, discussing a similar problem in reference to Iago, truly observes: "Nothing proves so well how false are the motives with which Iago tries to persuade himself as *the constant change in these motives.*" We can therefore safely dismiss all the alleged motives that Hamlet propounds, as being more or less successful attempts on his part to blind himself with self-deception. Loening's summing-up of them is not too emphatic when he says: "They are all mutually contradictory; *they are one and all false pretexts.*" The alleged motives excellently illustrate the psychological mechanisms of evasion and rationalization I have elsewhere described. It is not necessary, however, to discuss them here individually, for Loening has with the greatest perspicacity done this in full detail and has effectually demonstrated how utterly untenable they all are.

Still, in his moments of self-reproach Hamlet sees clearly enough the recalcitrancy of his conduct and renews his efforts to achieve action. It is noticeable how his outbursts of remorse are evoked by external happenings which bring back to his mind that which he would so gladly forget, and which, according to Bradley, he does at times forget: particularly effective in this respect are incidents that contrast with his own conduct, as when the player is so moved over the fate of Hecuba (Act II, Sc. 2), or when Fortinbras takes the field and "finds quarrel in a straw when honour's at the stake" (Act IV, Sc. 4). On the former occasion, stung by the monstrous way in which the player pours out his feeling at the thought of Hecuba, he arraigns himself in words which surely should effectually dispose of the view that he has any doubt where his duty lies.

> What's Hecuba to him, or he to Hecuba,
> That he should weep for her? What would he do,
> Had he the motive and the cue for passion
> That I have? He would drown the stage with tears
> And cleave the general ear with horrid speech,
> Make mad the guilty and appal the free,
> Confound the ignorant, and amaze indeed
> The very faculties of eyes and ears; yet I,
> A dull and muddy-mettled rascal, peak
> Like John-a-dreams, unpregnant of my cause,[1]
> And can say nothing; no, not for a king
> Upon whose property and most dear life
> A damn'd defeat was made: Am I a coward?
> Who calls me villain, breaks my pate across,
> Plucks off my beard and blows it in my face,

---

[1] How the essence of the situation is conveyed in these four words.

> Tweaks me by the nose, gives me the lie i' the throat
> As deep as to the lungs? Who does me this?
> Ha, 'swounds, I should take it: for it cannot be
> But I am pigeon-liver'd, and lack gall
> To make oppression bitter, or ere this
> I should ha' fatted all the region kites
> With this slave's offal. Bloody, bawdy villain!
> Remorseless, treacherous, lecherous, kindless villain!
> O, vengeance!
> Why, what an ass am I! This is most brave,
> That I, the son of a dear father murder'd,
> *Prompted to my revenge by heaven and hell,*
> Must like a whore unpack my heart with words,
> And fall a-cursing like a very drab;
> A scullion![2]

The readiness with which his guilty conscience is stirred into activity is again evidenced on the second appearance of the Ghost, when Hamlet cries,

> Do you not come your tardy son to chide,
> That lapsed in time and passion lets go by
> Th'important acting of your dread command?
> O, say!

The Ghost at once confirms this misgiving by answering,

> Do not forget! this visitation
> Is but to whet thy almost blunted purpose.

In short, the whole picture presented by Hamlet, his deep depression, the hopeless note in his attitude towards the world and towards the value of life, his dread of death,[3] his repeated reference to bad dreams, his self-accusations, his desperate efforts to get away from the thoughts of his duty, and his vain attempts to find an excuse for his procrastination: all this unequivocally points to a *tortured* conscience, to some hidden ground for shirking his task, a ground which he dare not or cannot avow to himself. We have, therefore, to take up the argument again at this point, and to seek for some evidence that may serve to bring to light the hidden counter-motive.

The extensive experience of the psycho-analytic researches carried out by Freud and his school during the past half-century has amply demonstrated that certain kinds of mental process show a greater tendency to be inaccessible to consciousness (put technically, to be "repressed") than others. In other words, it is harder for a person to realize the existence in his mind of some mental trends than it is of others. In order therefore to gain a proper perspective it is necessary briefly to inquire into the relative frequency with which various sets of mental processes are "repressed." Experience shows that this can be correlated with the degree of compatibility of these various sets with the ideals and standards accepted by the conscious ego; the less compatible they are with these the more likely

---

[2] Dover Wilson considers this a misprint for "stallion."

[3] Tieck saw in Hamlet's cowardly fear of death a chief reason for his hesitancy in executing his vengeance. How well Shakespeare understood what this fear was like may be inferred from Claudio's words in *Measure for Measure*:

> The weariest and most loathed wordly life
> That age, ache, penury and imprisonment
> Can lay on nature is a paradise
> To what we fear of death.

are they to be "repressed." As the standards acceptable to consciousness are in considerable measure derived from the immediate environment, one may formulate the following generalization: those processes are most likely to be "repressed" by the individual which are most disapproved of by the particular circle of society to whose influence he has chiefly been subjected during the period when his character was being formed. Biologically stated, this law would run: "That which is unacceptable to the herd becomes unacceptable to the individual member," it being understood that the term herd is intended here in the sense of the particular circle defined above, which is by no means necessarily the community at large. It is for this reason that moral, social, ethical, or religious tendencies are seldom "repressed," for, since the individual originally received them from his herd, they can hardly ever come into conflict with the dicta of the latter. This merely says that a man cannot be ashamed of that which he respects; the apparent exceptions to this rule need not be here explained.

The language used in the previous paragraph will have indicated that by the term "repression" we denote an active dynamic process. Thoughts that are "repressed" are actively kept from consciousness by a definite force and with the expenditure of more or less mental effort, though the person concerned is rarely aware of this. Further, what is thus kept from consciousness typically possesses an energy of its own; hence our frequent use of such expressions as "trend," "tendency," etc. A little consideration of the genetic aspects of the matter will make it comprehensible that the trends most likely to be "repressed" are those belonging to what are called the innate impulses, as contrasted with secondarily acquired ones. Loening seems very discerningly to have grasped this, for, in commenting on a remark of Kohler's to the effect that "where a feeling impels us to action or to omission, it is replete with a hundred reasons—with reasons that are as light as soap-bubbles, but which through self-deception appear to us as highly respectable and compelling motives, because they are hugely magnified in the (concave) mirror of our own feeling," he writes: "But this does not hold good, as Kohler and others believe, when we are impelled by *moral* feelings of which reason *approves* (for these we admit to ourselves, they need no excuse), for feelings that arise from our *natural man,* those the gratification of which is *opposed by our reason.*" It only remains to add the obvious corollary that, as the herd unquestionably selects from the "natural" instincts the sexual one on which to lay its heaviest ban, so it is the various psycho-sexual trends that are most often "repressed" by the individual. We have here the explanation of the clinical experience that the more intense and the more obscure is a given case of deep mental conflict the more certainly will it be found on adequate analysis to centre about a sexual problem. On the surface, of course, this does not appear so, for, by means of various psychological defensive mechanisms, the depression, doubt, despair, and other manifestations of the conflict are transferred on to more tolerable and permissible topics, such as anxiety about worldly success or failure, about immortality and the salvation of the soul, philosophical considerations about the value of life, the future of the world, and so on.

Bearing these considerations in mind, let us return to Hamlet. It should now be evident that the conflict hypotheses discussed above, which see Hamlet's conscious impulse towards revenge inhibited by an unconscious misgiving of a highly ethical kind, are based on ignorance of what actually happens in real life, since misgivings of this order belong in fact to the more conscious layers of the mind rather than to the deeper, unconscious ones. Hamlet's intense self-study would speedily have made him aware of any such misgivings and, although he might subsequently have ignored them, it would almost certainly have been by the aid of some process of rationalization which would have enabled him to deceive himself into believing that they were ill-founded; he would in any case have remained conscious of the nature of them. We have therefore to invert these hypotheses and realize—as his words so often indicate—that the positive striving for vengeance, the pious task laid on him by his father, was to him the moral and social one, the one approved of by his consciousness, and that the "repressed" inhibiting striving against the act of vengeance arose in some hidden source connected with his more personal, natural instincts. The former striving has already been considered, and indeed is manifest in every speech in which Hamlet debates the matter: the second is, from its nature, more obscure and has next to be investigated.

This is perhaps most easily done by inquiring more intently into Hamlet's precise attitude towards the object of his vengeance, Claudius, and towards the crimes that have to be avenged. These are two: Claudius' incest with the Queen,[4] and his murder of his brother. Now it is of great importance to note the profound difference in Hamlet's attitude towards these two crimes. Intellectually of course he abhors both, but there can be no question as to which arouses in him the deeper loathing. Whereas the murder of his father evokes in him indignation and a plain recognition of his obvious duty to avenge it, his mother's guilty conduct awakes in him the intensest horror. Furnivall[5] remarks, in speaking of the Queen, "Her disgraceful adultery and incest, and treason to his noble father's memory, Hamlet has felt in his inmost soul. Compared to their ingrain die, Claudius' murder of his father—notwithstanding all his protestations—is only a skin-deep stain."

Now, in trying to define Hamlet's attitude towards his uncle we have to guard against assuming off-hand that this is a simple one of mere execration, for there is a possibility of complexity arising in the following way: The uncle has not merely committed *each* crime, he has committed *both* crimes, a distinction of considerable importance, since the *combination* of crimes allows the admittance of a new factor, produced by the possible inter-relation of the two, which may prevent the result from being simply one of summation. In addition, it has to be borne in mind that the perpetrator of the crimes is a relative, and an exceedingly near relative. The possible inter-relationship of the crimes, and the fact that the author of them is an actual member of the family, give scope for a confusion in their influence on Hamlet's mind which may be the cause of the very obscurity we are seeking to clarify.

Let us first pursue further the effect on Hamlet of his mother's misconduct. Before he even knows with any certitude, however much he may suspect it, that his father has been murdered he is in the deepest depression, and evidently on account of this misconduct. The connection between the two is unmistakable in the monologue in Act I, Sc. 2, in reference to which Furnivall[6] writes: "One must insist on this, that before any revelation of his father's murder is made to Hamlet, before any burden of revenging that murder is laid upon him, he thinks of suicide as a welcome means of escape from this fair world of God's, made abominable to his diseased and weak imagination by his mother's lust, and the dishonour done by her to his father's memory."

> O that this too too solid[7] flesh would melt,
> Thaw and resolve itself into a dew,
> Or that the Everlasting had not fix'd
> His canon 'gainst self-slaughter, O God, God,
> How weary, stale, flat, and unprofitable

[4] Had this relationship not counted as incestuous, then Queen Elizabeth would have had no right to the throne; she would have been a bastard, Katherine of Aragon being still alive at her birth.

[5] Furnivall: Introduction to the "Leopold" Shakespeare, p. 72.

[6] Furnivall: op. cit., p. 70.

[7] Dover Wilson (*Times Literary Supplement*, May 16, 1918) brings forward excellent reasons for thinking that this word is a misprint for "sullied." I use the Shakespearean punctuation he has restored.

Seem to me all the uses of this world!
Fie on 't, O fie, 'tis an unweeded garden
That grows to seed, things rank and gross in nature
Possess it merely, that it should come to this,
But two months dead, nay, not so much, not two,
So excellent a king; that was to this
Hyperion to a satyr, so loving to my mother,
That he might not beteem the winds of heaven
Visit her face too roughly—heaven and earth
Must I remember? why, she would hang on him
As if increase of appetite had grown
By what it fed on, and yet within a month,
Let me not think on 't; frailty thy name is woman!
A little month or ere those shoes were old
With which she follow'd my poor father's body
Like Niobe all tears, why she, even she—
O God, a beast that wants discourse of reason
Would have mourn'd longer—married with my uncle,
My father's brother, but no more like my father
Than I to Hercules, within a month,
Ere yet the salt of most unrighteous tears
Had left the flushing in her galled eyes,
She married. O most wicked speed . . . to post
With such dexterity to incestuous sheets!
It is not, nor it cannot come to good,
But break my heart, for I must hold my tongue.

According to Bradley, Hamlet's melancholic disgust at life was the cause of his aversion from "any kind of decided action." His explanation of the whole problem of Hamlet is "the moral shock of the sudden ghastly disclosure of his mother's true nature," and he regards the effect of this shock, as depicted in the play, as fully comprehensible. He says: "Is it possible to conceive an experience more desolating to a man such as we have seen Hamlet to be; and is its result anything but perfectly natural? It brings bewildered horror, then loathing, then despair of human nature. His whole mind is poisoned . . . A nature morally blunter would have felt even so dreadful a revelation less keenly. A slower and more limited and positive mind might not have extended so widely through the world the disgust and disbelief that have entered it."

But we can rest satisfied with this seemingly adequate explanation of Hamlet's weariness of life only if we accept unquestioningly the conventional standards of the causes of deep emotion. Many years ago Connolly, a well-known psychiatrist, pointed out the disproportion here existing between cause and effect, and gave as his opinion that Hamlet's reaction to his mother's marriage indicated in itself a mental instability, "a predisposition to actual unsoundness"; he writes: "The circumstances are not such as would at once turn a healthy mind to the contemplation of suicide, the last resource of those whose reason has been overwhelmed by calamity and despair." In T. S. Eliot's opinion, also, Hamlet's emotion is in excess of the facts as they appear, and he specially contrasts it with Gertrude's negative and insignificant personality. Wihan attributes the exaggerated effect of his misfortunes to Hamlet's "Masslosigkeit" (lack of moderation), which is displayed in every direction. We have unveiled only the exciting cause, not the predisposing cause. The very fact that Hamlet is apparently content with the explanation arouses our misgiving, for, as will presently be expounded, from the very nature of the emotion he cannot be aware of the true cause of it. If we ask, not what ought to produce such soul-paralysing grief and distaste for life, but what in actual fact does produce it, we are compelled to go beyond this explanation and seek for some deeper cause. In real life speedy second marriages occur commonly enough without leading to any such result as is here depicted, and when we see them followed by this result we invariably find, if the opportunity for an analysis of the subject's mind presents itself, that there is some other and more hidden reason why the event is followed by this inordinately great effect. The reason always is that the event has awakened to increased activity mental processes that have been "repressed" from the subject's consciousness. His mind has been specially prepared for the catastrophe by previous mental processes with which those directly resulting from the event have entered into association. This is perhaps what Furnivall means when he speaks of the world being made abominable to Hamlet's "diseased imagination." In short, the special nature of the reaction presupposes some special feature in the mental predisposition. Bradley himself has to qualify his hypothesis by inserting the words "to a man such as we have seen Hamlet to be."

We come at this point to the vexed question of Hamlet's sanity, about which so many controversies have raged. Dover Wilson authoritatively writes: "I agree with Loening, Bradley and others that Shakespeare meant us to imagine Hamlet as suffering from some kind of mental disorder throughout the play." The question is what kind of mental disorder and what is its significance dramatically and psychologically. The matter is complicated by Hamlet's frequently displaying simulation (the Antic Disposition), and it has been asked whether this is to conceal his real mental disturbance or cunningly to conceal his purposes in coping with the practical problems of this task? This is a topic that presently will be considered at some length, but there can be few who regard it as a comprehensive statement of Hamlet's mental state. As T. S. Eliot has neatly expressed it, "Hamlet's 'madness' is less than madness and more than feigned."

But what of the mental disorder itself? In the past this little problem in clinical diagnosis seems to have greatly exercised psychiatrists. Some of them, e.g. Thierisch, Sigismund, Stenger, and many others, have simply held that Hamlet was insane, without particularizing the form of insanity. Rosner labelled Hamlet as a hystero-neurasthenic, an opinion contradicted by Rubinstein and Landmann. Most, however, including Kellog, de Boismon, Heuse, Nicholson, and others, have committed themselves to the view that Hamlet was suffering from melancholia, though there are not failing psychiatrists, e.g. Ominus, who reject this. Schücking attributes the delay in his action to Hamlet's being paralysed by melancholia. Laehr has a particularly ingenious hypothesis which maintains that Shakespeare, having taken over the Ghost episode from the earlier play, was obliged to depict Hamlet as a melancholiac because this was theatrically the most presentable form of insanity in which hallucinations occur. Long ago Dowden made it seem probable that Shakespeare had made use of an important study of melancholia by Timothe Bright, but, although he may have adapted a few phrases to his own use, the clinical picture of Hamlet differs notably from that delineated by Bright.

More to the point is the actual account given in the play by the King, the Queen, Ophelia, and above all Polonius. In his description, for example, we note—if the Elizabethan language is translated into modern English—the symptoms of dejection, refusal of food, insomnia, crazy behaviour, fits of delirium, and finally of raving madness; Hamlet's poignant parting words to Polonius ("except my life," etc.) cannot mean other than a craving for death. These are undoubtedly suggestive of certain forms of melancholia, and the likeness to manic-depressive insanity, of which melancholia is now known to be but a part, is completed by the occurrence of attacks of great excitement that would nowadays be called "hypomanic," of which Dover Wilson counts no fewer than eight. This modern diagnosis has indeed been suggested, e.g. by Brock, Somerville, and others. Nevertheless, the rapid and startling oscillations between intense excitement and profound depression do not accord with the accepted picture of this disorder, and if I had to describe such a condition as Hamlet's in clinical terms—which I am not particularly inclined to —it would have to be as a severe case of hysteria on a cyclothymic basis.

All this, however, is of academic interest only. What we are essentially concerned with is the psychological understanding of the dramatic effect produced by Hamlet's personality and behaviour. That effect would be quite other were the central figure in the play to represent merely a "case of insanity." When that happens, as with Ophelia, such a person passes beyond our ken, is in a sense no more human, whereas Hamlet successfully claims our interest and sympathy to the very end. Shakespeare certainly never intended us to regard Hamlet as insane, so that the "mind o'erthrown" must have some other meaning than its literal one. Robert Bridges[8] has described the matter with exquisite delicacy:

> Hamlet himself would never have been aught to us, or we
> To Hamlet, wer't not for the artful balance whereby
> Shakespeare so gingerly put his sanity in doubt
> Without the while confounding his Reason.

I would suggest that in this Shakespeare's extraordinary powers of observation and penetration granted him a degree of insight that it has taken the world three subsequent centuries to reach. Until our generation (and even now in the juristic sphere) a dividing line separated the sane and responsible from the irresponsible insane. It is now becoming more and more widely recognized that much of mankind lives in an intermediate and unhappy state charged with what Dover Wilson well calls "that sense of frustration, futility and human inadequacy which is the burden of the whole symphony" and of which Hamlet is the supreme example in literature. This intermediate plight, in the toils of which perhaps the greater part of mankind struggles and suffers, is given the name of psychoneurosis, and long ago the genius of Shakespeare depicted it for us with faultless insight.

Extensive studies of the past half century, inspired by Freud, have taught us that a psychoneurosis means a state of mind where the person is unduly, and often painfully, driven or thwarted by the "unconscious" part of his mind, that buried part that was once the infant's mind and still lives on side by side with the adult mentality that has developed out of it and should have taken its place. It signifies *internal* mental conflict. We have here the reason why it is impossible to discuss intelligently the state of mind of anyone suffering from a psychoneurosis, whether the description is of a living person or an imagined one, without correlating the manifestations with what must have operated in his infancy and is *still operating*. That is what I propose to attempt here.

For some deep-seated reason, which is to him unacceptable, Hamlet is plunged into anguish at the thought of his father being replaced in his mother's affections by someone else. It is as if his devotion to his mother had made him so jealous for her affection that he had found it hard enough to share this even with his father and could not endure to share it with still another man. Against this thought, however, suggestive as it is, may be urged three objections. First, if it were in itself a full statement of the matter, Hamlet would have been aware of the jealousy, whereas we have concluded that the mental process we are seeking is hidden from him. Secondly, we see in it no evidence of the arousing of an old and forgotten memory. And, thirdly, Hamlet is being deprived by Claudius of no greater share in the Queen's affection than he had been by his own father, for the two brothers made exactly similar claims in this respect—namely, those of a loved hus-

[8] Robert Bridges: *The Testament of Beauty*, I, 577.

band. The last-named objection, however, leads us to the heart of the situation. How if, in fact, Hamlet had in years gone by, as a child, bitterly resented having had to share his mother's affection even with his own father, had regarded him as a rival, and had secretly wished him out of the way so that he might enjoy undisputed and undisturbed the monopoly of that affection? If such thoughts had been present in his mind in childhood days they evidently would have been "repressed," and all traces of them obliterated, by filial piety and other educative influences. The actual realization of his early wish in the death of his father at the hands of a jealous rival would then have stimulated into activity these "repressed" memories, which would have produced, in the form of depression and other suffering, an obscure aftermath of his childhood's conflict. This is at all events the mechanism that is actually found in the real Hamlets who are investigated psychologically.[9]

The explanation, therefore, of the delay and self-frustration exhibited in the endeavour to fulfill his father's demand for vengeance is that to Hamlet the thought of incest and parricide combined is too intolerable to be borne. One part of him tries to carry out the task, the other flinches inexorably from the thought of it. How fain would he blot it out in that "bestial oblivion" which unfortunately for him his conscience contemns. He is torn and tortured in an insoluble inner conflict.

FOR DISCUSSION:

1. Jones claims that Hamlet has an unconscious repulsion to killing Claudius. Why?

2. What evidence does Jones cite to support his view that Hamlet's conscience is tortured by some secret motivation for the procrastination in avenging his father?

3. Which psychological drives are most likely to be repressed? Why?

4. According to Freud, infancy and adolescence are the periods when Oedipal attachments are formed. Is Jones's theory invalidated because Shakespeare tells almost nothing of Hamlet's life in these early periods?

5. What objection does Jones advance to the idea that Hamlet is consciously jealous of Claudius for supplanting him in his mother's affections?

[9] See, for instance, Wulf Sachs, *Black Hamlet,* 1937.

The Secret Life of Walter Mitty*

JAMES THURBER

"We're going through!" The Commander's voice was like thin ice breaking. He wore his full-dress uniform, with the heavily braided white cap pulled down rakishly over one cold gray eye. "We can't make it, sir. It's spoiling for a hurricane, if you ask me." "I'm not asking you, Lieutenant Berg," said the Commander. "Throw on the power lights! Rev her up to 8,500! We're going through!" The pounding of the cylinders increased: ta-pocketa-pocketa-pocketa-pocketa-pocketa. The Commander stared at the ice forming on the pilot window. He walked over and twisted a row of complicated dials "Switch on No. 8 auxiliary!" he shouted. "Switch on No. 8 auxiliary!" repeated Lieutenant Berg. "Full strength in No. 3 turret!" shouted the Commander. "Full strength in No. 3 turret!" The crew, bending to their various tasks in the huge, hurtling eight-engined Navy hydroplane, looked at each other and grinned. "The Old Man'll get us through," they said to one another. "The Old Man ain't afraid of Hell!" . . .

"Not so fast! You're driving too fast!" said Mrs. Mitty. "What are you driving so fast for?"

"Hmm?" said Walter Mitty. He looked at his wife, in the seat beside him, with shocked astonishment. She seemed grossly unfamiliar, like a strange woman who had yelled at him in a crowd. "You were up to fifty-five," she said. "You know I don't like to go more than forty. You were up to fifty-five." Walter Mitty drove on toward Waterbury in silence, the roaring of the SN202 through the worst storm in twenty years of Navy flying fading in the remote, intimate airways of his mind. "You're tensed up again," said Mrs. Mitty. "It's one of your days. I wish you'd let Dr. Renshaw look you over."

Walter Mitty stopped the car in front of the building where his wife went to have her hair done. "Remember to get those overshoes while I'm having my hair done," she said. "I don't need overshoes," said Mitty. She put her mirror back into her bag. "We've been all through that," she said, getting out of the car. "You're not a young man any longer." He raced the engine a little. "Why don't you wear your gloves? Have you lost your gloves?" Walter Mitty reached in a pocket and brought out the gloves. He put them on, but after she had turned and gone into the building and he had driven on to a red light, he took them off again. "Pick it up, brother!" snapped a cop as the light changed, and Mitty hastily pulled on his gloves and lurched ahead. He drove around the streets aimlessly for a time, and then he drove past the hospital on his way to the parking lot.

. . . "It's the millionaire banker, Wellington McMillan," said the pretty nurse. "Yes?" said Walter Mitty, removing his gloves slowly. "Who has the case?" "Dr. Renshaw and Dr. Benbow, but there are two specialists here, Dr. Remington from New York and Mr. Pritchard-Mitford from London. He flew over." A door opened down a long, cool corridor and Dr. Renshaw came out. He looked distraught and haggard. "Hello, Mitty," he said. "We're having the devil's own time with McMillan,

---

* Copyright ©1942 James Thurber. From *My World—and Welcome to It*, published by Harcourt, Brace & World, New York, and from VINTAGE THURBER copyright ©1963 Hamish Hamilton, London. By permission of Mrs. Helen Thurber and Hamish Hamilton. Originally published in the *New Yorker*, March 18, 1939.

the millionaire banker and close personal friend of Roosevelt. Obstreosis of the ductal tract. Tertiary. Wish you'd take a look at him." "Glad to," said Mitty.

In the operating room there were whispered introductions: Dr. Remington, Dr. Mitty. Mr. Pritchard-Mitford, Dr. Mitty." "I've read your book on streptothricosis," said Pritchard-Mitford, shaking hands. "A brilliant performance, sir." "Thank you," said Walter Mitty. "Didn't know you were in the States, Mitty," grumbled Remington. "Coals to Newcastle, bringing Mitford and me here for a tertiary." "You are very kind," said Mitty. A huge, complicated machine, connected to the operating table, with many tubes and wires, began at this moment to go pocketa-pocketa-pocketa. "The new anesthetizer is giving way!" shouted an interne. "There is no one in the East who knows how to fix it!" "Quiet man!" said Mitty, in a low, cool voice. He sprang to the machine, which was now going pocketa-pocketa-queep-pocketa-queep. He began fingering delicately a row of glistening dials. "Give me a fountain pen!" he snapped. Someone handed him a fountain pen. He pulled a faulty piston out of the machine and inserted the pen in its place. "That will hold for ten minutes," he said. "Get on with the operation." A nurse hurried over and whispered to Renshaw, and Mitty saw the man turn pale. "Coreopsis has set in," said Renshaw nervously. "If you would take over, Mitty?" Mitty looked at him and at the craven figure of Benbow, who drank, and at the grave, uncertain faces of the two great specialists. "If you wish," he said. They slipped a white gown on him; he adjusted a mask and drew on thin gloves; nurses handed him shining . . .

"Back it up, Mac! Look out for that Buick!" Walter Mitty jammed on the brakes, "Wrong lane, Mac," said the parking-lot attendant, looking at Mitty closely. "Gee. Yeh," muttered Mitty. He began cautiously to back out of the lane marked "Exit Only." "Leave her sit there," said the attendant. "I'll put her away." Mitty got out of the car. "Hey, better leave the key." "Oh," said Mitty, handing the man the ignition key. The attendant vaulted into the car, backed it up with insolent skill, and put it where it belonged.

They're so damn cocky, thought Walter Mitty, walking along Main Street; they think they know everything. Once he had tried to take his chains off, outside New Milford, and he had got them wound around the axles. A man had had to come out in a wrecking car and unwind them, a young, grinning garageman. Since then Mrs. Mitty always made him drive to a garage to have the chains taken off. The next time, he thought, I'll wear my right arm in a sling; they won't grin at me then. I'll have my right arm in a sling and they'll see I couldn't possibly take the chains off myself. He kicked at the slush on the sidewalk. "Overshoes," he said to himself, and he began looking for a shoe store.

When he came out into the street again, with the overshoes in a box under his arm, Walter Mitty began to wonder what the other thing was his wife had told him to get. She told him twice, before they set out from their house for Waterbury. In a way he hated these weekly trips to town—he was always getting something wrong. Kleenex, he thought, Squibb's, razor blades? No. Toothpaste, toothbrush, bicarbonate, carborundum, initiative and referendum? He gave it up. But she would remember it. "Where's the what's-its-name?" she would ask. "Don't tell me you forgot the what's-its-name." A newsboy went by shouting something about the Waterbury trial.

. . . "Perhaps this will refresh your memory." The District Attorney suddenly thrust a heavy automatic at the quiet figure on the witness stand. "Have you ever seen this before?" Walter Mitty took the gun and examined it expertly. "This is my Webley-Vickers 50.80," he said calmly. An excited buzz ran around the courtroom. The judge rapped for order. "You are a crack shot with any sort of firearms, I believe?" said the District Attorney, insinuatingly. "Objection!" shouted Mitty's attorney. "We have shown that the defendant could not have fired the shot. We have shown that he wore his right arm in a sling on the night of the fourteenth of July." Walter Mitty raised his hand briefly and the bickering attorneys were stilled. "With any known make of gun," he said evenly, "I could have killed Gregory Fitzhurst at three hundred feet *with my left hand*." Pandemonium broke loose in the courtroom. A woman's scream rose above the bedlam and suddenly a lovely, dark-haired girl was in Walter Mitty's arms. The District Attorney struck at her savagely. Without rising from his chair, Mitty let the man have it on the point of the chin. "You miserable cur!" . . .

"Puppy biscuit," said Walter Mitty. He stopped walking and the buildings of Waterbury rose up out of the misty courtroom and surrounded him again. A woman who was passing laughed. "He said 'Puppy biscuit,'" she said to her companion. "That man said 'Puppy biscuit' to himself." Walter Mitty hurried on. He went into an A. & P., not the first one he came to but a smaller one farther up the street. "I want some biscuit for small, young dogs," he said to the clerk. "Any special brand, sir?" The greatest pistol shot in the world thought a moment. "It says 'Puppies Bark for It' on the box," said Walter Mitty.

His wife would be through at the hairdresser's in fifteen minutes, Mitty saw in looking at his watch, unless they had trouble drying it; sometimes they had trouble drying it. She didn't like to get to the hotel first; she would want him to be there waiting for her as usual. He found a big leather chair in the lobby, facing a window, and he put the overshoes and the puppy biscuit on the floor beside it. He picked up an old copy of *Liberty* and sank down into the chair. "Can Germany Conquer the World Through the Air?" Walter Mitty looked at the pictures of bombing planes and of ruined streets.

. . . "The cannonading has got the wind up in young Raleigh, sir," said the sergeant. Captain Mitty looked up at him through tousled hair. "Get him to bed," he said wearily. "With the others. I'll fly alone." "But you can't, sir," said the sergeant anxiously. "It takes two men to handle that bomber and the Archies are pounding hell out of the air. Von Richtman's circus is between here and Saulier." "Somebody's got to get that ammunition dump," said Mitty. "I'm going over. Spot of brandy?" He poured a drink for the sergeant and one for himself. War thundered and whined around the dugout and battered at the door. There was a rending of wood and splinters flew through the room. "A bit of a near thing," said Captain Mitty carelessly. "The box barrage is closing in," said the sergeant. "We only live once, Sergeant," said Mitty, with his faint, fleeting smile. "Or do we?" He poured another brandy and tossed it off. "I never see a man could hold his brandy like you, sir," said the sergeant. "Begging your pardon, sir." Captain Mitty stood up and strapped on his huge Webley-Vickers automatic. "It's forty kilometers through hell, sir," said the sergeant. Mitty finished one last brandy. "After all," he said softly, "what isn't?" The pounding of the cannon increased; there was the rat-tat-tatting of machine guns, and from somewhere came the menacing pocketa-pocketa-pocketa of the new flame-throwers. Walter Mitty walked to the door of the dugout humming "Auprés de Ma Blonde." He turned and waved to the sergeant. "Cheerio!" he said. . . .

Something struck his shoulder. "I've been looking all over this hotel for you," said Mrs. Mitty. "Why do you have to hide in this old chair? How did you expect me to find you?" "Things close in," said Walter Mitty vaguely. "What?" Mrs. Mitty said. "Did you get the what's-its-name? The puppy biscuit? What's in that box?" "Overshoes," said Mitty. "Couldn't you have put them on in the store?" "I was thinking," said Walter Mitty. "Does it ever occur to you that I am sometimes thinking?" She looked at him. "I'm going to take your temperature when I get you home," she said.

They went out through the revolving doors that made a faintly derisive whistling sound when you pushed them. It was two blocks to the parking lot. At the drugstore on the corner she said, "Wait here for me. I forgot something. I won't be a minute." She was more than a minute. Walter Mitty lighted a cigarette. It began to rain, rain with sleet in it. He stood up against the wall of the drugstore, smoking. . . . He put his shoulders back and his heels together. "To hell with the handkerchief," said Walter Mitty scornfully. He took one last drag on his cigarette and snapped it away. Then, with that faint, fleeting smile playing about his lips, he faced the firing squad; erect and motionless, proud and disdainful, Walter Mitty the Undefeated, inscrutable to the last.

FOR DISCUSSION:

1. Discuss the relationship between reality and Mitty's illusions. How does Thurber lead from one to the other?

2. The final two paragraphs seem to suggest the possibility that Mitty may rebel against his wife's domination. Is this likely? Or is this idea itself merely another illusion?

3. How does Thurber unify the daydreams and integrate them into the framework of the story as a whole?

4. Account for the continuing appeal of this story.

William Wilson

EDGAR ALLAN POE

> What say of it? what say [of] CONSCIENCE grim,
> That spectre in my path?
>
> Chamberlayne's *Pharronida*.

Let me call myself, for the present, William Wilson. The fair page now lying before me need not be sullied with my real appellation. This has been already too much an object for the scorn—for the horror—for the detestation of my race. To the uttermost regions of the globe have not the indignant winds bruited its unparalleled infamy? Oh, outcast of all outcasts most abandoned!—to the earth art thou not forever dead? to its honors, to its flowers, to its golden aspirations?—and a cloud, dense, dismal, and limitless, does it not hang eternally between thy hopes and heaven?

I would not, if I could, here or to-day, embody a record of my later years of unspeakable misery, and unpardonable crime. This epoch—these later years—took unto themselves a sudden elevation in turpitude, whose origin alone it is my present purpose to assign. Men usually grow base by degrees. From me, in an instant, all virtue dropped bodily as a mantle. From comparatively trivial wickedness I passed, with the stride of a giant, into more than the enormities of an Elah-Gabalus. What chance—what one event brought this evil thing to pass, bear with me while I relate. Death approaches; and the shadow which foreruns him has thrown a softening influence over my spirit. I long, in passing through the dim valley, for the sympathy—I had nearly said for the pity—of my fellow men. I would fain have them believe that I have been, in some measure, the slave of circumstances beyond human control. I would wish them to seek out for me, in the details I am about to give, some little oasis of *fatality* amid a wilderness of error. I would have them allow—what they cannot refrain from allowing—that, although temptation may have erewhile existed as great, man was never *thus*, at least, tempted before—certainly, never *thus* fell. And is it therefore that he has never thus suffered? Have I not indeed been living in a dream? And am I not now dying a victim to the horror and the mystery of the wildest of all sublunary visions?

I am the descendant of a race whose imaginative and easily excitable temperament has at all times rendered them remarkable; and, in my earliest infancy, I gave evidence of having fully inherited the family character. As I advanced in years it was more strongly developed; becoming, for many reasons, a cause of serious disquietude to my friends, and of positive injury to myself. I grew self-willed, addicted to the wildest caprices, and a prey to the most ungovernable passions. Weak-minded, and beset with constitutional infirmities akin to my own, my parents could do but little to check the evil propensities which distinguished me. Some feeble and ill-directed efforts resulted in complete failure on their part, and, of course, in total triumph on mine. Thenceforward my voice was a household law; and at an age when few children have abandoned their leading-strings, I was left to the guidance of my own will, and became, in all but name, the master of my own actions.

My earliest recollections of a school-life, are connected with a large, rambling Elizabethan house, in a misty-looking village of England, where were a vast number of gigantic and gnarled trees, and where all the houses were excessively ancient. In truth, it was a dream-like and spirit-soothing place, that venerable old town. At this moment, in fancy, I feel the refreshing chilliness of its deeply-shadowed avenues, inhale the fragrance of its thousand shrubberies, and thrill anew with undefinable delight, at the deep hollow note of the church-bell, breaking, each hour, with sullen and sudden roar, upon the stillness of the dusky atmosphere in which the fretted Gothic steeple lay imbedded and asleep.

It gives me, perhaps, as much of pleasure as I can now in any manner experience, to dwell upon minute recollections of the school and its concerns. Steeped in misery as I am—misery, alas! only too real—I shall be pardoned for seeking relief, however slight and temporary, in the weakness of a few rambling details. These, moreover, utterly trivial, and even ridiculous in themselves, assume, to my fancy, adventitious importance, as connected with a period and a locality when and where I recognise the first ambiguous monitions of the destiny which afterwards so fully overshadowed me. Let me then remember.

The house, I have said, was old and irregular. The grounds were extensive, and a high and solid brick wall, topped with a bed of mortar and broken glass, encompassed the whole. This prison-like rampart formed the limit of our domain; beyond it we saw but thrice a week—once every Saturday afternoon, when, attended by two ushers, we were permitted to take brief walks in a body through some of the neighbouring fields—and twice during Sunday, when we were paraded in the same formal manner to the morning and evening service in the one church of the village. Of this church the principal of our school was pastor. With how deep a spirit of wonder and perplexity was I wont to regard him from our remote pew in the gallery, as, with step solemn and slow, he ascended the pulpit! This reverend man, with countenance so demurely benign, with robes so glossy and so clerically flowing, with wig so minutely powdered, so rigid and so vast,—could this be he who, of late, with sour visage, and in snuffy habiliments, administered, ferule in hand, the Draconian laws of the academy? Oh, gigantic paradox, too utterly monstrous for solution!

At an angle of the ponderous wall frowned a more ponderous gate. It was riveted and studded with iron bolts, and surmounted with jagged iron spikes. What impressions of deep awe did it inspire! It was never opened save for the three periodical egressions and ingressions already mentioned; then, in every creak of its mighty hinges, we found a plenitude of mystery— a world of matter for solemn remark, or for more solemn meditation.

The extensive enclosure was irregular in form, having many capacious recesses. Of these, three or four of the largest constituted the play-ground. It was level, and covered with fine hard gravel. I well remember it had no trees, nor benches, nor anything similar within it. Of course it was in the rear of the house. In front lay a small parterre, planted with box and other shrubs; but through this sacred division we passed only upon rare occasions indeed—such as a first advent to school or final departure thence, or perhaps, when a parent or friend having called for us, we joyfully took our way home for the Christmas or Midsummer holy-days.

But the house!—how quaint an old building was this!—to me how veritably a palace of enchantment! There was really no end to its windings—to its incomprehensible subdivisions. It was difficult, at any given time, to say with certainty upon which of its two stories one happened to be. From each room to every other there were sure to be found three or four steps either in ascent or descent. Then the lateral branches were innumerable—inconceivable —and so returning in upon themselves, that our most exact ideas in regard to the whole mansion were not very far different from those with which we pondered upon infinity. During the five years of my residence here, I was never able to ascertain with precision, in what remote locality lay the little sleeping apartment assigned to myself and some eighteen or twenty other scholars.

The school-room was the largest in the house—I could not help thinking, in the world. It was very long, narrow, and dismally low, with pointed Gothic windows and a ceiling of oak. In a remote and terror-inspiring angle was a square enclosure of eight or ten feet, comprising the *sanctum*, "during hours," of our principal, the Reverend Dr. Bransby. It was a solid structure, with massy door, sooner than open which in the absence of the "Dominie," we would all have willingly perished by the *peine forte et dure*. In other angles were two other similar boxes, far less reverenced, indeed, but still greatly matters of awe. One of these was the pulpit of the "classical" usher, one of the "English and mathematical." Interspersed about the room, crossing and recrossing in endless irregularity, were innumerable benches and desks, black, ancient, and time-worn, piled desperately with much-bethumbed books, and so beseamed with initial letters, names at full length, grotesque figures, and other multiplied efforts of the knife, as to have entirely lost what little of original form might have been their portion in days long departed. A huge bucket with water stood at one extremity of the room, and a clock of stupendous dimensions at the other.

Encompassed by the massy walls of this venerable academy, I passed, yet not in tedium or disgust, the years of the third lustrum of my life. The teeming brain of childhood requires no external world of incident to occupy or amuse it; and the apparently dismal monotony of a school was replete with more intense excitement than my riper youth has derived from luxury, or my full manhood from crime. Yet I must believe that my first mental development had in it much of the uncommon—even much of the *outré*. Upon mankind at large the events of very early existence rarely leave in mature age any definite impression. All is gray shadow—a weak and irregular remembrance —an indistinct regathering of feeble pleasures and phantasmagoric pains. With me this is not so. In childhood I must have felt with the energy of a man what I now find stamped upon memory in lines as vivid, as deep, and as durable as the exergues of the Carthaginian medals.

Yet in fact—in the fact of the world's view—how little was there to remember! The morning's awakening, the nightly summons to bed; the connings, the recitations; the periodical half-holidays, and perambulations; the play-ground, with its broils, its pastimes, its intrigues;—these, by a mental sorcery long forgotten, were made to involve a wilderness of sensation, a world of rich incident, an universe of varied emotion, of excitement the most passionate and spirit-stirring. *"Oh, le bon temps, que ce siècle de fer!"*

In truth, the ardor, the enthusiasm, and the imperiousness of my disposition, soon rendered me a marked character among my schoolmates, and by slow, but natural gradations, gave me an ascendancy over all not greatly older than myself;—over all with a single exception. This exception was found in the person of a scholar, who, although no relation, bore the same Christian and surname as myself;—a circumstance, in fact, little remarkable; for, notwithstanding a noble descent, mine was one of those everyday appellations which seem, by prescriptive right, to have been, time out of mind, the common property of the mob. In this narrative I have therefore designated myself as William Wilson,—a fictitious title not very dissimilar to the real. My namesake alone, of those who in school phraseology constituted "our set," presumed to compete with me in the studies of the class—in the sports and broils of the play-ground—to refuse implicit belief in my assertions, and submission to my will—indeed, to interfere with my arbitrary dictation in any respect whatsoever. If there is on earth a supreme and unqualified despotism, it is the despotism of a master mind in boyhood over the less energetic spirits of its companions.

Wilson's rebellion was to me a source of the greatest embarrassment;—the more so as, in spite of the bravado with which in public I made a point of treating him and his pretensions, I secretly felt that I feared him, and could not help thinking the equality which he maintained so easily with myself, a proof of his true superiority; since not to be overcome cost me a perpetual struggle. Yet this superiority—even this equality—was in truth acknowledged by no one but myself; our associates, by some unaccountable blindness, seemed not even to suspect it. Indeed, his competition, his resistance, and especially his impertinent and dogged interference with my purposes, were not more pointed than private. He appeared to be destitute alike of the ambition which urged, and of the passionate energy of mind which enabled me to excel. In his rivalry he might have been supposed actuated solely by a whimsical desire to thwart, astonish, or mortify myself; although there were times when I could not help observing, with a feeling made up of wonder, abasement, and pique, that he mingled with his injuries, his insults, or his contradictions, a certain most inappropriate, and assuredly most unwelcome *affectionateness* of manner. I could only conceive this singular behavior to arise from a consummate self-conceit assuming the vulgar airs of patronage and protection.

Perhaps it was this latter trait in Wilson's conduct, conjoined with our identity of name, and the mere accident of our having entered the school upon the same day, which set afloat the notion that we were brothers, among the senior classes in the academy. These do not usually inquire with much strictness into the affairs of their juniors. I have before said, or should have said, that Wilson was not, in the most remote degree, connected with my family. But assuredly if we *had* been brothers we must have been twins; for, after leaving Dr. Bransby's, I casually learned that my namesake was born on the nineteenth of January, 1813—and this is a somewhat remarkable coincidence; for the day is precisely that of my own nativity.

It may seem strange that in spite of the continual anxiety occasioned me by the rivalry of Wilson, and his intolerable spirit of contradiction, I could not bring myself to hate him altogether. We had, to be sure, nearly every day a quarrel in which, yielding me publicly the palm of victory, he, in some manner, contrived to make me feel that it was he who had deserved it; yet a sense of pride on my part, and a veritable dignity on his own, kept us always upon what are called "speaking terms," while there were many points of strong congeniality in our tempers, operating to awake in me a sentiment which our position alone, perhaps, prevented from ripening into friendship. It is difficult, indeed, to define, or even to describe, my real feelings towards him. They formed a motley and heterogeneous admixture;—some petulant animosity, which was not yet hatred, some esteem, more respect, much fear, with a world of uneasy curiosity. To the moralist it will be unnecessary to say, in addition, that Wilson and myself were the most inseparable of companions.

It was no doubt the anomalous state of affairs existing between us, which turned all my attacks upon him, (and they were many, either open or covert) into the channel of banter or practical joke (giving pain while assuming the aspect of mere fun) rather than into a more serious and determined hostility. But my endeavours on this head were by no means uniformly successful, even when my plans were the most wittily concocted; for my namesake had much about him, in character, of that unassuming and quiet austerity which, while enjoying the poignancy of its own jokes, has no heel of Achilles in itself, and absolutely refuses to be laughed at. I could find, indeed, but one vulnerable point, and that, lying in a personal peculiarity, arising, perhaps, from constitutional disease, would have been spared by any antagonist less at his wit's end than myself;—my rival had a weakness in the faucial or guttural organs, which precluded him from raising his voice at any time *above a very low whisper.* Of this defect I did not fail to take what poor advantage lay in my power.

Wilson's retaliations in kind were many; and there was one form of his practical wit that disturbed me beyond measure. How his sagacity first discovered at all that so petty a thing would vex me, is a question I never could solve; but, having discovered, he habitually practised the annoyance. I had always felt aversion to my uncourtly patronymic, and its very common, if not plebeian prænomen. The words were venom in my ears; and when, upon the day of my arrival, a second William Wilson came also to the academy, I felt angry with him for bearing the name, and doubly disgusted with the name because a stranger bore it, who would be the cause of its twofold repetition, who would be constantly in my presence, and whose concerns, in the ordinary routine of the school business, must inevitably, on account of the detestable coincidence, be often confounded with my own.

The feeling of vexation thus engendered grew stronger with every circumstance tending to show resemblance, moral or physical, between my rival and myself. I had not then discovered the remarkable fact that we were of the same age; but I saw that we were of the same height, and I perceived that we were even singularly alike in general contour of person and outline of feature. I was galled, too, by the rumor touching a relationship, which had grown current in the upper forms. In a word, nothing could more seriously disturb me, (although I scrupulously concealed such disturbance,) than any allusion to a similarity of mind, person, or condition existing between us. But, in truth, I had no reason to believe that (with the exception of the matter of relationship, and in the case of Wilson himself,) this similarity had ever been made a subject of comment, or even observed at all by our schoolfellows. That *he* observed it in all its bearings, and as fixedly as I, was apparent; but that he could discover in such circumstances so fruitful a field of annoyance, can only be attributed, as I said before, to his more than ordinary penetration.

His cue, which was to perfect an imitation of myself, lay both in words and in actions; and most admirably did he play his part. My dress it was an easy matter to copy; my gait and general manner were, without difficulty, appropriated; in spite of his constitutional defect, even my voice did not escape him. My louder tones were, of course, unattempted, but then the key, it was identical; and *his singular whisper*, *it grew the very echo of my own.*

How greatly this most exquisite portraiture harassed me, (for it could not justly be termed a caricature,) I will not now venture to describe. I had but one consolation—in the fact that the imitation, apparently, was noticed by myself alone, and that I had to endure only the knowing and strangely sarcastic smiles of my namesake himself. Satisfied with having produced in my bosom the intended effect, he seemed to chuckle in secret over the sting he had inflicted, and was characteristically disregardful of the public applause which the success of his witty endeavours might have so easily elicited. That the school, indeed, did not feel his design, perceive its accomplishment, and participate in his sneer, was, for many anxious months, a riddle I could not resolve. Perhaps the *gradation* of his copy rendered it not so readily perceptible; or, more possibly, I owed my security to the masterly air of the copyist, who, disdaining the letter, (which in a painting is all the obtuse can see,) gave but the full spirit of his original for my individual contemplation and chagrin.

I have already more than once spoken of the disgusting air of patronage which he assumed toward me, and of his frequent officious interference with my will. This interference often took the ungracious character of advice; advice not openly given, but hinted or insinuated. I received it with a repugnance which gained strength as I grew in years. Yet, at this distant day, let me do him the simple justice to acknowledge that I can recall no occasion when the suggestions of my rival were on the side of those errors or follies so usual to his immature age and seeming inexperience; that his moral sense, at least, if not his general talents and worldly wisdom, was far keener than my own; and that I might, to-day, have been a better, and thus a happier man, had I less frequently rejected the counsels embodied in those meaning whispers which I then but too cordially hated and too bitterly despised.

As it was, I at length grew restive in the extreme under his distasteful supervision, and daily resented more and more openly what I considered his intolerable arrogance. I have said that, in the first years of our connexion as schoolmates, my feelings in regard to him might have been easily ripened into friendship: but, in the latter months of my residence at the academy, although the intrusion of his ordinary manner had, beyond doubt, in some measure, abated, my sentiments, in nearly similar proportion, partook very much of positive hatred. Upon one occasion he saw this, I think, and afterwards avoided, or made a show of avoiding me.

It was about the same period, if I remember aright, that, in an altercation of violence with him, in which he was more than usually thrown off his guard, and spoke and acted with an openness of demeanor rather foreign to his nature, I discovered, or fancied I discovered, in his accent, his air, and general appearance, a something which first startled, and then deeply interested me, by bringing to mind dim visions of my earliest infancy—wild, confused and thronging memories of a time when memory herself was yet unborn. I cannot better describe the sensation which oppressed me than by saying that I could with difficulty shake off the belief of my having been acquainted with the being who stood before me, at some epoch very long ago—some point of the past even infinitely remote. The delusion, however, faded rapidly as it came; and I mention it at all but to define the day of the last conversation I there held with my singular namesake.

The huge old house, with its countless subdivisions, had several large chambers communicating with each other, where slept the greater number of the students. There were, however, (as must necessarily happen in a building so awkwardly planned,) many little nooks or recesses, the odds and ends of the structure; and these the economic ingenuity of Dr. Bransby had also fitted up as dormitories; although, being the merest closets, they were capable of accommodating but a single individual. One of these small apartments was occupied by Wilson.

One night, about the close of my fifth year at the school, and immediately after the altercation just mentioned, finding every one wrapped in sleep, I arose from bed, and, lamp in hand, stole through a wilderness of narrow passages from my own bedroom to that of my rival. I had long been plotting one of those ill-natured pieces of practical wit at his expense in which I had hitherto been so uniformly unsuccessful. It was my intention, now, to put my scheme in operation, and I resolved to make him feel the whole extent of the malice with which I was imbued. Having reached his closet, I noiselessly entered, leaving the lamp, with a shade over it, on the outside. I advanced a step, and listened to the sound of his tranquil breathing. Assured of his being asleep, I returned, took the light, and with it again approached the bed. Close curtains were around it, which, in the prosecution of my plan, I slowly and quietly withdrew, when the bright rays fell vividly upon the sleeper, and my eyes, at the same moment, upon his countenance. I looked;—and a numbness, an iciness of feeling instantly pervaded my frame. My breast heaved, my knees tottered, my whole spirit became possessed with an objectless yet intolerable horror. Gasping for breath, I lowered the lamp in still nearer proximity to the face. Were these—*these* the lineaments of William Wilson? I saw, indeed, that they were his, but I shook as if with a fit of the ague in fancying they were not. What *was* there about them to confound me in this manner? I gazed;—while my brain reeled with a multitude of incoherent thoughts. Not thus he appeared—assuredly not *thus*—in the vivacity of his waking hours. The same name! the same contour of person! the same day of arrival at the academy! And then his dogged and meaningless imitation of my gait, my voice, my habits, and my manner! Was it, in truth, within the bounds of human possibility, that *what I now saw* was the result, merely, of the habitual practice of this sarcastic imitation? Awe-stricken, and with a creeping shudder, I extinguished the lamp, passed silently from the chamber, and left, at once, the halls of that old academy, never to enter them again.

After a lapse of some months, spent at home in mere idleness, I found myself a student at Eton. The brief interval had been sufficient to enfeeble my remembrance of the events at Dr. Bransby's, or at least to effect a material change in the nature of the feelings with which I remembered them. The truth—the tragedy—of the drama was no more. I could now find room to doubt the evidence of my senses; and seldom called up the subject at all but with wonder at the extent of human credulity, and a smile at the vivid force of the imagination which I hereditarily possessed. Neither was this species of scepticism likely to be diminished by the character of the life I led at Eton. The vortex of thoughtless folly into which I there so immediately and so recklessly plunged, washed away all but the froth of my past hours, engulfed at once every solid or serious impression, and left to memory only the veriest levities of a former existence.

I do not wish, however, to trace the course of my miserable profligacy here—a profligacy which set at defiance the laws, while it eluded the vigilance of the institution. Three years of folly, passed without profit, had but given me rooted habits of vice, and added, in a somewhat unusual degree, to my bodily stature, when, after a week of soulless dissipation, I invited a small party of the most dissolute students to a secret carousal in my chambers. We met at a late hour of the night; for our debaucheries were to be faithfully protracted until morning. The wine flowed freely, and there were not wanting other and perhaps more dangerous seductions; so that the grey dawn had already faintly appeared in the east, while our delirious extravagance was at its height. Madly flushed with cards and intoxication, I was in the act of insisting upon a toast of more than wonted profanity, when my attention was suddenly diverted by the violent, although partial unclosing of the door of the apartment, and by the eager voice of a servant from without. He said that some person, apparently in great haste, demanded to speak with me in the hall.

Wildly excited with wine, the unexpected interruption rather delighted than surprised me. I staggered forward at once, and a few steps brought me to the vestibule of the building. In this low and small room there hung no lamp; and now no light at all was admitted, save that of the exceedingly feeble dawn which made its way through the semi-circular window. As I put my foot over the threshold, I became aware of the figure of a youth about my own height, and habited in a white kerseymere morning frock, cut in the novel fashion of the one I myself wore at the moment. This the faint light enabled me to perceive; but the features of his face I could not distinguish. Upon my entering he strode hurriedly up to me, and, seizing me by the arm with a gesture of petulant impatience, whispered the words "William Wilson!" in my ear.

I grew perfectly sober in an instant.

There was that in the manner of the stranger, and in the tremulous shake of his uplifted finger, as he held it between my eyes and the light, which filled me with unqualified amazement; but it was not this which had so violently moved me. It was the pregnancy of solemn admonition in the singular, low, hissing utterance; and, above all, it was the character, the tone, *the key*, of those few, simple, and familiar, yet *whispered* syllables, which came with a thousand thronging memories of bygone days, and struck upon my soul with the shock of a galvanic battery. Ere I could recover the use of my senses he was gone.

Although this event failed not of a vivid effect upon my disordered imagination, yet was it evanescent as vivid. For some weeks, indeed, I busied myself in earnest inquiry, or was wrapped in a cloud of morbid speculation. I did not pretend to disguise from my perception the identity of the singular individual who thus perseveringly interfered with my affairs, and harassed me with his insinuated counsel. But who and what was this Wilson?—and whence came he?—and what were his purposes? Upon neither of these points could I be satisfied; merely ascertaining, in regard to him, that a sudden accident in his family had caused his removal from Dr. Bransby's academy on the afternoon of the day in which I myself had eloped. But in a brief period I ceased to think upon the subject; my attention being all absorbed in a contemplated departure for Oxford. Thither I soon went; the uncalculating vanity of my parents furnishing me with an outfit and annual establishment, which would enable me to indulge at will in the luxury already so dear to my heart,—to vie in profuseness of expenditure with the haughtiest heirs of the wealthiest earldoms in Great Britain.

Excited by such appliances to vice, my constitutional temperament broke forth with redoubled ardor, and I spurned even the common restraints of decency in the mad infatuation of my revels. But it were absurd to pause in the detail of my extravagance. Let it suffice, that among spendthrifts I out-Heroded Herod, and that, giving name to a multitude of novel follies, I added no brief appendix to the long catalogue of vices then usual in the most dissolute university of Europe.

It could hardly be credited, however, that I had, even here, so utterly fallen from the gentlemanly estate, as to seek acquaintance with the vilest arts of the gambler by profession, and, having become an adept in his despicable science, to practise it habitually as a means of increasing my already enormous income at the expense of the weak-minded among my fellow-collegians. Such, nevertheless, was the fact. And the very enormity of this offence against all manly and honourable sentiment proved, beyond doubt, the main if not the sole reason of the impunity with which it was committed. Who, indeed, among my most abandoned associates, would not rather have disputed the clearest evidence of his senses, than have suspected of such courses, the gay, the frank, the generous William Wilson—the noblest and most liberal commoner at Oxford—him whose follies (said his parasites) were but the follies of youth and unbridled fancy—whose errors but inimitable whim—whose darkest vice but a careless and dashing extravagance?

I had been now two years successfully busied in this way, when there came to the university a young *parvenu* nobleman, Glendinning—rich, said report, as Herodes Atticus—his riches, too, as easily acquired. I soon found him of weak intellect, and, of course, marked him as a fitting subject for my skill. I frequently engaged him in play, and contrived, with the gambler's usual art, to let him win considerable sums, the more effectually to entangle him in my snares. At length, my schemes being ripe, I met him (with the full intention that this meeting should be final and decisive) at the chambers of a fellow-commoner, (Mr. Preston,) equally intimate with both, but who, to do him justice, entertained not even a remote suspicion of my design. To give to this a better coloring, I had contrived to have assembled a party of some eight or ten, and was solicitously careful that the introduction of cards should appear accidental, and originate in the proposal of my contemplated dupe himself. To be brief upon a vile topic, none of the low finesse was omitted, so customary upon similar occasions that it is a just matter for wonder how any are still found so besotted as to fall its victim.

We had protracted our sitting far into the night, and I had at length effected the manœuvre of getting Glendinning as my sole antagonist. The game, too, was my favorite écarté. The rest of the company, interested in the extent of our play, had abandoned their own cards, and were standing around us as spectators. The parvenu, who had been induced by my artifices in the early part of the evening, to drink deeply, now shuffled, dealt, or played, with a wild nervousness of manner for which his intoxication, I thought, might partially, but could not altogether account. In a very short period he had become my debtor to a large amount, when, having taken a long draught of port, he did precisely what I had been coolly anticipating—he proposed to double our already extravagant stakes. With a well-feigned show of reluctance, and not until after my repeated refusal had seduced him into some angry words which gave a color of *pique* to my compliance, did I finally comply. The result, of course, did but prove how entirely the prey was in my toils; in less than an hour he had quadrupled his debt. For some time his countenance had been losing the florid tinge lent it by the wine; but now, to my astonishment, I perceived that it had grown to a pallor truly fearful. I say to my astonishment. Glendinning had been represented to my eager inquiries as immeasurably wealthy; and the sums which he had as yet lost, although in themselves vast, could not, I supposed, very seriously annoy, much less so violently affect him. That he was overcome by the wine just swallowed, was the idea which most readily presented itself; and, rather with a view to the preservation of my own character in the eyes of my associates, than from any less interested motive, I was about to insist, peremptorily, upon a discontinuance of the play, when some expressions at my elbow from among the company, and an ejaculation evincing utter despair on the part of Glendinning, gave me to understand that I had effected his total ruin under circumstances which, rendering him an object for the pity of all, should have protected him from the ill offices even of a fiend.

What now might have been my conduct it is difficult to say. The pitiable condition of my dupe had thrown an air of embarrassed gloom over all; and, for some moments a profound silence was maintained, during which I could not help feeling my cheeks tingle with the many burning glances of scorn or reproach cast upon me by the less abandoned of the party. I will even own that an intolerable weight of anxiety was for a brief instant lifted from my bosom by the sudden and extraordinary interruption which ensued. The wide, heavy folding doors of the apartment were all at once thrown open, to their full extent, with a vigorous and rushing impetuosity that extinguished, as if by magic, every candle in the room. Their light, in dying, enabled us just to perceive that a stranger had entered, about my own height, and closely muffled in a cloak. The darkness, however, was now total; and we could only *feel* that he was standing in our midst. Before any one of us could recover from the extreme astonishment into which this rudeness had thrown all, we heard the voice of the intruder.

"Gentlemen," he said, in a low, distinct, and never-to-be-forgotten *whisper* which thrilled to the very marrow of my bones, "Gentlemen, I make no apology for this behaviour, because in thus behaving, I am but fulfilling a duty. You are, beyond doubt, uninformed of the true character of the person who has to-night won at écarté a large sum of money from Lord Glendinning. I will therefore put you upon an expeditious and decisive plan of obtaining this very necessary information. Please to examine, at your leisure, the inner linings of the cuff of his left sleeve, and the several little packages which may be found in the somewhat capacious pockets of his embroidered morning wrapper."

While he spoke, so profound was the stillness that one might have heard a pin drop upon the floor. In ceasing, he departed at once, and as abruptly as he had entered. Can I—shall I describe my sensations?—must I say that I felt all the horrors of the damned? Most assuredly I had little time given for reflection. Many hands roughly seized me upon the spot, and lights were immediately reprocured. A search ensued. In the lining of my sleeve were found all the court cards essential in *écarté*, and, in the pockets of my wrapper, a number of packs, fac-similes of those used at our sittings, with the single exception that mine were of the species called, technically, *arrondées*; the honours being slightly convex at the ends, the lower cards slightly convex at the sides. In this disposition, the dupe who cuts, as customary, at the length of the pack, will invariably find that he cuts his antagonist an honor; while the gambler, cutting at the breath, will, as certainly, cut nothing for his victim which may count in the records of the game.

Any burst of indignation upon this discovery would have affected me less than the silent contempt, or the sarcastic composure, with which it was received.

"Mr. Wilson," said our host, stooping to remove from beneath his feet an exceedingly luxurious cloak of rare furs, "Mr. Wilson, this is your property." (The weather was cold; and, upon quitting my own room, I had thrown a cloak over my dressing wrapper, putting it off upon reaching the scene of play.) "I presume it is supererogatory to seek here (eyeing the folds of the garment with a bitter smile) for any farther evidence of your skill. Indeed, we have had enough. You will see the necessity, I hope, of quitting Oxford—at all events, of quitting instantly my chambers."

Abased, humbled to the dust as I then was, it is probable that I should have resented this galling language by immediate personal violence, had not my whole attention been at the moment arrested by a fact of the most startling character. The cloak which I had worn was of a rare description of fur; how rare, how extravagantly costly, I shall not venture to say. Its fashion, too, was of my own fantastic invention; for I was fastidious to an absurd degree of coxcombry, in matters of this frivolous nature. When, therefore, Mr. Preston reached me that which he had picked up upon the floor, and near the folding doors of the apartment, it was with an astonishment nearly bordering upon terror, that I perceived my own already hanging on my arm, (where I had no doubt unwittingly placed it,) and that the one presented me was but its exact counterpart in every, in even the minutest possible particular. The singular being who had so disastrously exposed me, had been muffled, I remembered, in a cloak; and none had been worn at all by any of the members of our party with the exception of myself. Retaining some presence of mind, I took the one offered me by Preston; placed it, unnoticed, over my own; left the apartment with a resolute scowl of defiance; and, next morning ere dawn of day, commenced a hurried journey from Oxford to the continent, in a perfect agony of horror and of shame.

I fled in vain. My evil destiny pursued me as if in exultation, and proved, indeed, that the exercise of its mysterious dominion had as yet only begun. Scarcely had I set foot in Paris ere I had fresh evidence of the detestable interest taken by this Wilson in my concerns. Years flew, while I experienced no relief. Villain!—at Rome, with how untimely, yet with how spectral an officiousness, stepped he in between me and my ambition! At Vienna, too—at Berlin—and at Moscow! Where, in truth, had I *not* bitter cause to curse him within my heart? From his inscrutable tyranny did I at length flee, panic-stricken, as from a pestilence; and to the very ends of the earth *I fled in vain.*

And again, and again, in secret communion with my own spirit, would I demand the questions "Who is he?—whence came he?—and what are his objects?" But no answer was there found. And then I scrutinized, with a minute scrutiny, the forms, and the methods, and the leading traits of his impertinent supervision. But even here there was very little upon which to base a conjecture. It was noticeable, indeed, that, in no one of the multiplied instances in which he had of late crossed my path, had he so crossed it except to frustrate those schemes, or to disturb those actions, which, if fully carried out, might have resulted in bitter mischief. Poor justification this, in truth, for an authority so imperiously assumed! Poor indemnity for natural rights of self-agency so pertinaciously, so insultingly denied!

I had also been forced to notice that my tormentor, for a very long period of time, (while scrupulously and with miraculous dexterity maintaining his whim of an identity of apparel with myself,) had so continued it in the execution of his varied interference with my will, that I saw not, at any moment, in the execution of his varied interference with my will, that I saw not, at any moment, the features of his face. Be Wilson what he might, *this*, at least, was but the veriest of affectation, or of folly. Could he, for an instant, have supposed that, in my admonisher at Eton—in the destroyer of my honor at Oxford,—in him who thwarted my ambition at Rome, my revenge at Paris, my passionate love at Naples, or what he falsely termed my avarice in Egypt,—that in this, my arch-enemy and evil genius, I could fail to recognise the William Wilson of my school-boy days,—the namesake, the companion, the rival,—the hated and dreaded rival at Dr. Bransby's? Impossible!—But let me hasten to the last eventful scene of the drama.

Thus far I had succumbed supinely to this imperious domination. The sentiment of deep awe with which I habitually regarded the elevated character, the majestic wisdom, the apparent omnipresence and omnipotence of Wilson, added to a feeling of even terror, with which certain other traits in his nature and assumptions inspired me, had operated, hitherto, to impress me with an idea of my own utter weakness and helplessness, and to suggest an implicit, although bitterly reluctant submission to his arbitrary will. But, of late days, I had given myself up entirely to wine; and its maddening influence upon my hereditary temper rendered me more and more impatient of control. I began to murmur,—to hesitate,—to resist. And was it only fancy which induced me to believe that, with the increase of my own firmness, that of my tormentor underwent a proportional diminution? Be this as it may, I now began to feel the inspiration of a burning hope, and at length nurtured in my secret thoughts a stern and desperate resolution that I would submit no longer to be enslaved.

It was at Rome, during the Carnival of 18—, that I attended a masquerade in the palazzo of the Neapolitan Duke Di Broglio. I had indulged more freely than usual in the excesses of the wine-table; and now the suffocating atmosphere of the crowded rooms irritated me beyond endurance. The difficulty, too, of forcing my way through the mazes of the company contributed not a little to the ruffling of my temper; for I was anxiously seeking, (let me not say with what unworthy motive) the young, the gay, the beautiful wife of the aged and doting Di Broglio. With a too unscrupulous confidence she had previously communicated to me the secret of the costume in which she would be habited, and now, having caught a glimpse of her person, I was hurrying to make my way into her presence.—At this moment I felt a light hand placed upon my shoulder, and that ever-remembered, low, damnable *whisper* within my ear.

In an absolute phrenzy of wrath, I turned at once upon him who had thus interrupted me, and seized him violently by the collar. He was attired, as I had expected, in a costume altogether similar to my own; wearing a Spanish cloak of blue velvet, begirt about the waist with a crimson belt sustaining a rapier. A mask of black silk entirely covered his face.

"Scoundrel!" I said, in a voice husky with rage, while every syllable I uttered seemed as new fuel to my fury, "scoundrel! impostor! accursed villain! you shall not— you *shall not* dog me unto death! Follow me, or I stab you where you stand!"—and I broke my way from the ball-room into a small ante-chamber adjoining—dragging him unresistingly with me as I went.

Upon entering, I thrust him furiously from me. He staggered against the wall, while I closed the door with an oath, and commanded him to draw. He hesitated but for an instant; then, with a slight sigh, drew in silence, and put himself upon his defence.

The contest was brief indeed. I was frantic with every species of wild excitement, and felt within my single arm the energy and power of a multitude. In a few seconds I forced him by sheer strength against the wainscoting, and thus, getting him at mercy, plunged my sword, with brute ferocity, repeatedly through and through his bosom.

At that instant some person tried the latch of the door. I hastened to prevent an intrusion, and then immediately returned to my dying antagonist. But what human language can adequately portray *that* astonishment, *that* horror which possessed me at the spectacle then presented to view? The brief moment in which I averted my eyes had been sufficient to produce, apparently, a material change in the arrangements at the upper or farther end of the room. A large mirror,—so at first it seemed to me in my confusion—now stood where none had been perceptible before; and, as I stepped up to it in extremity of terror, mine own image, but with features all pale and dabbled in blood, advanced to meet me with a feeble and tottering gait.

Thus it appeared, I say, but was not. It was my antagonist—it was Wilson, who then stood before me in the agonies of his dissolution. His mask and cloak lay, where he had thrown them, upon the floor. Not a thread in all his raiment—not a line in all the marked and singular lineaments of his face which was not, even in the most absolute identity, *mine own!*

It was Wilson; but he spoke no longer in a whisper, and I could have fancied that I myself was speaking while he said:

"You have conquered, and I yield. Yet, henceforward art thou also dead—dead to the World, to Heaven and to Hope! In me didst thou exist—and, in my death, see by this image, which is thine own, how utterly thou hast murdered thyself."

FOR DISCUSSION:

1. How do the first three paragraphs prepare the reader for the psychological nature of this tale?
2. In what particular way is the description of the school grounds and house appropriate for a journey into the unconscious?
3. Summarize the various hints given by Poe that William Wilson and his twin are one and the same.
4. Of what significance is the fact that the second Wilson could not speak "above a very low whisper"?
5. In his tendency toward immorality and debauchery William Wilson may be viewed as a personification of the id. Conversely, in his concern for ethics and in his attitude of restraint, Wilson's twin can be interpreted as a representation of man's ego and superego. Trace this relationship between Wilson and his double throughout the story.

Mr. Arcularis*

CONRAD AIKEN

Mr. Arcularis stood at the window of his room in the hospital and looked down at the street. There had been a light shower, which had patterned the sidewalks with large drops, but now again the sun was out, blue sky was showing here and there between the swift white clouds, a cold wind was blowing the poplar trees. An itinerant band had stopped before the building and was playing, with violin, harp, and flute, the finale of "Cavalleria Rusticana." Leaning against the window-sill—for he felt extraordinarily weak after his operation—Mr. Arcularis suddenly, listening to the wretched music, felt like crying. He rested the palm of one hand against a cold window-pane and stared down at the old man who was blowing the flute, and blinked his eyes. It seemed absurd that he should be so weak, so emotional, so like a child—and especially now that everything was over at last. In spite of all their predictions, in spite, too, of his own dreadful certainty that he was going to die, here he was, as fit as a fiddle—but what a fiddle it was, so out of tune!—with a long life before him. And to begin with, a voyage to England ordered by the doctor. What could be more delightful? Why should he feel sad about it and want to cry like a baby? In a few minutes Harry would arrive with his car to take him to the wharf; in an hour he would be on the sea, in two hours he would see the sunset behind him, where Boston had been, and his new life would be opening before him. It was many years since he had been abroad. June, the best of the year to come—England, France, the Rhine—how ridiculous that he should already be homesick!

There was a light footstep outside the door, a knock, the door opened, and Harry came in.

"Well, old man, I've come to get you. The old bus actually got here. Are you ready? Here, let me take your arm. You're tottering like an octogenarian!"

Mr. Arcularis submitted gratefully, laughing, and they made the journey slowly along the bleak corridor and down the stairs to the entrance hall. Miss Hoyle, his nurse, was there, and the Matron, and the charming little assistant with freckles who had helped to prepare him for the operation. Miss Hoyle put out her hand.

"Goodbye, Mr. Arcularis," she said, "and bon voyage."

"Goodbye, Miss Hoyle, and thank you for everything. You were very kind to me. And I fear I was a nuisance."

The girl with the freckles, too, gave him her hand, smiling. She was very pretty, and it would have been easy to fall in love with her. She reminded him of someone. Who was it? He tried in vain to remember while he said goodbye to her and turned to the Matron.

"And not too many latitudes with the young ladies, Mr. Arcularis!" she was saying.

Mr. Arcularis was pleased, flattered, by all this attention to a middle-aged invalid, and felt a joke taking shape in his mind, and no sooner in his mind than on his tongue.

"Oh, no latitudes," he said, laughing. "I'll leave the latitudes to the ship!"

"Oh, come now," said the Matron, "we don't seem to have hurt him much, do we?"

"I think we'll have to operate on him again and *really* cure him," said Miss Hoyle.

He was going down the front steps, between the potted palmettos, and they all laughed and waved. The wind was cold,

---

* From THE COLLECTED SHORT STORIES OF CONRAD AIKEN. Copyright 1931, 1960 by Conrad Aiken. Published by arrangement with The World Publishing Company, Cleveland and New York.

very cold for June, and he was glad he had put on his coat. He shivered.

"Damned cold for June!" he said. "Why should it be so cold?"

"East wind," Harry said, arranging the rug over his knees. "Sorry it's an open car, but I believe in fresh air and all that sort of thing. I'll drive slowly. We've got plenty of time."

They coasted gently down the long hill toward Beacon Street, but the road was badly surfaced, and despite Harry's care Mr. Arcularis felt his pain again. He found that he could alleviate it a little by leaning to the right, against the arm-rest, and not breathing too deeply. But how glorious to be out again! How strange and vivid the world looked! The trees had innumerable green fresh leaves—they were all blowing and shifting and turning and flashing in the wind; drops of rainwater fell downward sparkling; the robins were singing their absurd, delicious little four-noted songs; even the street cars looked unusually bright and beautiful, just as they used to look when he was a child and had wanted above all things to be a motorman. He found himself smiling foolishly at everything, foolishly and weakly, and wanted to say something about it to Harry. It was no use, though—he had no strength, and the mere finding of words would be almost more than he could manage. And even if he should succeed in saying it, he would then most likely burst into tears. He shook his head slowly from side to side.

"Ain't it grand?" he said.

"I'll bet it looks good," said Harry.

"Words fail me."

"You wait till you get out to sea. You'll have a swell time."

"Oh, swell! . . . I hope not. I hope it'll be calm."

"Tut tut."

When they passed the Harvard Club Mr. Arcularis made a slow and somewhat painful effort to turn in his seat and look at it. It might be the last chance to see it for a long time. Why this sentimental longing to stare at it, though? There it was, with the great flag blowing in the wind, the Harvard seal now concealed by the swift folds and now revealed, and there were the windows in the library, where he had spent so many delightful hours reading—Plato, and Kipling, and the Lord knows what—and the balconies from which for so many years he had watched the Marathon. Old Talbot might be in there now, sleeping with a book on his knee, hoping forlornly to be interrupted by anyone, for anything.

"Goodbye to the old club," he said.

"The bar will miss you," said Harry, smiling with friendly irony and looking straight ahead.

"But let there be no moaning," said Mr. Arcularis.

"What's *that* a quotation from?"

"'The Odyssey.'"

In spite of the cold, he was glad of the wind on his face, for it helped to dissipate the feeling of vagueness and dizziness that came over him in a sickening wave from time to time. All of a sudden everything would begin to swim and dissolve, the houses would lean their heads together, he had to close his eyes, and there would be a curious and dreadful humming noise, which at regular intervals rose to a crescendo and then drawlingly subsided again. It was disconcerting. Perhaps he still had a trace of fever. When he got on the ship he would have a glass of whisky. . . . From one of these spells he opened his eyes and found that they were on the ferry, crossing to East Boston. It must have been the ferry's engines that he had heard. From another spell he woke to find himself on the wharf, the car at a standstill beside a pile of yellow packing cases.

"We're here because we're here because we're here," said Harry.

"Because we're here," added Mr. Arcularis.

He dozed in the car while Harry—and what a good friend Harry was!—attended to all the details. He went and came with tickets and passports and baggage checks and porters. And at last he unwrapped Mr. Arcularis from the rugs and led him up the steep gangplank to the deck, and thence by devious windings to a small cold stateroom with a solitary porthole like the eye of a cyclops.

"Here you are," he said, "and now I've got to go. Did you hear the whistle?"

"No."

"Well, you're half asleep. It's sounded the all-ashore. Goodbye, old fellow, and take care of yourself. Bring me back a spray of edelweiss. And send me a picture postcard from the Absolute."

"Will you have it finite or infinite?"

"Oh, infinite. But with your signature on it. Now you'd better turn in for a while and have a nap. Cheerio!"

Mr. Arcularis took his hand and pressed it hard, and once more felt like crying. Absurd! Had he become a child again?

"Goodbye," he said.

He sat down in the little wicker chair, with his overcoat still on, closed his eyes, and listened to the humming of the air in the ventilator. Hurried footsteps ran up and down the corridor. The chair was not too comfortable, and his pain began to bother him again, so he moved, with his coat still on, to the narrow berth and fell asleep. When he woke up, it was dark, and the porthole had been partly opened. He groped for the switch and turned on the light. Then he rang for the steward.

"It's cold in here," he said. "Would you mind closing the port?"

The girl who sat opposite him at dinner was charming. Who was it she reminded him of? Why, of course, the girl at the hospital, the girl with the freckles. Her hair was beautiful, not quite red, not quite gold, nor had it been bobbed; arranged with a sort of graceful untidiness, it made him think of a Melozzo da Forli angel. Her face was freckled, she had a mouth which was both humorous and voluptuous. And she seemed to be alone.

He frowned at the bill of fare and ordered the thick soup.

"No hors d'oeuvres?" asked the steward.

"I think not," said Mr. Arcularis. "They might kill me."

The steward permitted himself to be amused and deposited the menu card on the table against the water bottle. His eyebrows were lifted. As he moved away, the girl followed him with her eyes and smiled.

"I'm afraid you shocked him," she said.

"Impossible," said Mr. Arcularis. "These stewards, they're dead souls. How could they be stewards otherwise? And they think they've seen and known everything. They suffer terribly from the *déjà vu*. Personally, I don't blame them."

"It must be a dreadful sort of life."

"It's because they're dead that they accept it."

"Do you think so?"

"I'm sure of it. I'm enough of a dead soul myself to know the signs!"

"Well, I don't know what you mean by that!"

"But nothing mysterious! I'm just out of hospital, after an operation. I was given up for dead. For six months I had given myself up for dead. If you've ever been seriously ill you know the feeling. You have a posthumous feeling—a mild, cynical tolerance for everything and everyone. What is there you haven't seen or done or understood? Nothing."

Mr. Arcularis waved his hands and smiled.

"I wish I could understand you," said the girl, "but I've never been ill in my life."

"Never?"

"Never."

"Good God!"

The torrent of the unexpressed and inexpressible paralyzed him and rendered him speechless. He stared at the girl, wondering who she was and then, realizing that he had perhaps stared too fixedly, averted his gaze, gave a little laugh, rolled a pill of bread between his fingers. After a second or two he allowed himself to look at her again and found her smiling.

"Never pay any attention to invalids," he said, "or they'll drag you to the hospital."

She examined him critically, with her head tilted a little to one side, but with friendliness.

"You don't *look* like an invalid," she said.

Mr. Arcularis thought her charming. His pain ceased to bother him, the disagreeable humming disappeared, or rather, it was dissociated from himself and became merely, as it should be, the sound of the ship's engines, and he began to think the voyage was going to be really delightful. The parson on his right passed him the salt.

"I fear you will need this in your soup," he said.

"Thank you. Is it as bad as that?"

The steward, overhearing, was immediately apologetic and solicitous. He explained that on the first day everything was at sixes and sevens. The girl looked up at him and asked him a question.

"Do you think we'll have a good voyage?" she said.

He was passing the hot rolls to the parson, removing the napkins from them with a deprecatory finger.

"Well, madam, I don't like to be a Jeremiah, but——"

"Oh, come," said the parson, "I hope we have no Jeremiahs."

"What do you mean?" said the girl.

Mr. Arcularis ate his soup with gusto —it was nice and hot.

"Well, maybe I shouldn't say it, but there's a corpse on board, going to Ireland; and I never yet knew a voyage with a corpse on board that we didn't have bad weather."

"Why, steward, you're just superstitious! What nonsense!"

"That's a very ancient superstition," said Mr. Arcularis. "I've heard it many times. Maybe it's true. Maybe we'll be wrecked. And what does it matter, after all?" He was very bland.

"Then let's be wrecked," said the parson coldly.

Nevertheless, Mr. Arcularis felt a shudder go through him on hearing the steward's remark. A corpse in the hold—a coffin? Perhaps it was true. Perhaps some disaster would befall them. There might be fogs. There might be icebergs. He thought of all the wrecks of which he had read. There was the *Titanic*, which he had read about in the warm newspaper room at the Harvard Club—it had seemed dreadfully real, even there. That band, playing "Nearer My God to Thee" on the after-deck while the ship sank! It was one of the darkest of his memories. And the *Empress of Ireland*—all those poor people trapped in the smoking room, with only one door between them and life, and that door locked for the night by the deck steward, and the deck steward nowhere to be found! He shivered, feeling a draft, and turned to the parson.

"How do these strange delusions arise?" he said.

The parson looked at him searchingly, appraisingly—from chin to forehead, from forehead to chin—and Mr. Arcularis, feeling uncomfortable, straightened his tie.

"From nothing but fear," said the parson. "Nothing on earth but fear."

"How strange!" said the girl.

Mr. Arcularis again looked at her—she had lowered her face—and again tried to think of whom she reminded him. It wasn't only the little freckle-faced girl at the hospital—both of them had reminded him of someone else. Someone far back in his life: remote, beautiful, lovely. But he couldn't think. The meal came to an end, they all rose, the ship's orchestra played a feeble foxtrot, and Mr. Arcularis, once more alone, went to the bar to have his whisky. The room was stuffy, and the ship's engines were both audible and palpable. The humming and throbbing oppressed him, the rhythm seemed to be the rhythm of his own pain, and after a short time he found his way, with slow steps, holding on to the walls in his moments of weakness and dizziness, to his forlorn and white little room. The port had been—thank God!—closed for the night; it was cold enough anyway. The white and blue ribbons fluttered from the ventilator, the bottle and glasses clicked and clucked as the ship swayed gently to the long, slow motion of the sea. It was all very peculiar—it was all like something he had experienced somewhere before. What was it? Where was it? . . . He untied his tie, looking at his face in the glass, and wondered, and from time to time put his hand to his side to hold in the pain. It wasn't at Portsmouth, in his childhood, nor at Salem, nor in the rose garden at his Aunt Julia's, nor in the schoolroom at Cambridge. It was something very queer, very intimate, very precious. The jackstones, the Sunday-school cards which he had loved when he was a child. . . . He fell asleep.

The sense of time was already hopelessly confused. One hour was like another, the sea looked always the same, morning was indistinguishable from afternoon—and was it Tuesday or Wednesday? Mr. Arcularis was sitting in the smoking room, in his favorite corner, watching the parson teach Miss Dean to play chess. On the deck outside he could see the people passing and repassing in their restless round of the ship. The red jacket went by, then the black hat with the white feather, then the purple scarf, the brown tweed coat, the Bulgarian mustache, the monocle, the Scotch cap with fluttering ribbons, and in no time at all the red jacket again, dipping past the windows with its own peculiar rhythm, followed once more by the black hat and the purple scarf. How odd to reflect on the fixed little orbits of these things—as definite and profound, perhaps, as the orbits of the stars, and as important to God or the Absolute. There was a kind of tyranny in this fixedness, too—to think of it too much made one uncomfortable. He closed his eyes for a moment, to avoid seeing for the fortieth time the Bulgarian mustache and the pursuing monocle. The parson was explaining the movements of knights. Two forward and one to the side. Eight possible moves, always to the opposite color from that on which the piece stands. Two forward and one to the side: Miss Dean repeated the words several times with reflective emphasis. Here, too, was the terrifying fixed curve of the infinite, the creeping curve of logic which at last must become the final signpost at the edge of nothing. After that—the deluge. The great white light of annihilation. The bright flash of death. . . . Was it merely the sea which made these abstractions so insistent, so intrusive? The mere notion of *orbit* had somehow become extraordinarily naked; and to rid himself of the discomfort and also to forget a little the pain which bothered his side whenever he sat down, he walked slowly and carefully into the writing room, and examined a pile of superannuated magazines and catalogues of travel. The bright colors amused him, the photographs of remote islands and mountains, savages in sampans or sarongs or both—it was all very far off and delightful, like something in a dream or a fever. But he found that he was too tired to read and was incapable of concentration. Dreams! Yes, that reminded him. That rather alarming business—sleep-walking!

Later in the evening—at what hour he didn't know—he was telling Miss Dean about it, as he had intended to do. They were sitting in deck chairs on the sheltered side. The sea was black, and there was a cold wind. He wished they had chosen to sit in the lounge.

Miss Dean was extremely pretty—no, beautiful. She looked at him, too, in a very strange and lovely way, with something of inquiry, something of sympathy, something of affection. It seemed as if, between the question and the answer, they had sat thus for a very long time, exchanging an unspoken secret, simply looking at each other quietly and kindly. Had an hour or two passed? And was it at all necessary to speak?

"No," she said, "I never have."

She breathed into the low words a note of interrogation and gave him a slow smile.

"That's the funny part of it. I never had either until last night. Never in my life. I hardly ever even dream. And it really rather frightens me."

"Tell me about it, Mr. Arcularis."

"I dreamed at first that I was walking, alone, in a wide plain covered with snow. It was growing dark, I was very cold, my feet were frozen and numb, and I was lost. I came then to a signpost—at first it seemed to me there was nothing on it. Nothing but ice. Just before it grew finally dark, however, I made out on it the one word 'Polaris.'"

"The Pole Star."

"Yes—and you see, I didn't myself know that. I looked it up only this morning. I suppose I must have seen it somewhere? And of course it rhymes with my name."

"Why, so it does!"

"Anyway, it gave me—in the dream—an awful feeling of despair, and the dream changed. This time, I dreamed I was standing *outside* my stateroom in the little dark corridor, or *cul-de-sac*, and trying to find the door-handle to let myself in. I was in my pajamas, and again I was very cold. And at this point I woke up. . . . The extraordinary thing is that's exactly where I was!"

"Good heavens. How strange!"

"Yes. And now the question is, Where had I been? I was frightened, when I came to—not unnaturally. For among other things I *did* have, quite definitely, the feeling that I *had been* somewhere. Somewhere where it was very cold. It doesn't sound very proper. Suppose I had been seen!"

"That might have been awkward," said Miss Dean.

"Awkward! It might indeed. It's very singular. I've never done such a thing before. It's this sort of thing that reminds one—rather wholesomely, perhaps, don't you think?"—and Mr. Arcularis gave a nervous little laugh—"how extraordinarily little we know about the workings of our own minds or souls. After all, what *do* we know?"

"Nothing—nothing—nothing—nothing," said Miss Dean slowly.

"*Absolutely* nothing."

Their voices had dropped, and again they were silent; and again they looked at each other gently and sympathetically, as if for the exchange of something unspoken and perhaps unspeakable. Time ceased. The orbit—so it seemed to Mr. Arcularis—once more became pure, became absolute. And once more he found himself wondering who it was that Miss Dean—Clarice Dean—reminded him of. Long ago and far away. Like those pictures of the islands and mountains. The little freckle-faced girl at the hospital was merely, as it were, the stepping stone, the signpost, or, as in algebra, the "equals" sign. But what was it they both "equaled"? The jackstones came again into his mind and his Aunt Julia's rose garden —at sunset; but this was ridiculous. It couldn't be simply that they reminded him of his childhood! And yet why not?

They went into the lounge. The ship's orchestra, in the oval-shaped balcony among faded palms, was playing the finale of "Cavalleria Rusticana," playing it badly.

"Good God!" said Mr. Arcularis, "can't I ever escape from that damned sentimental tune? It's the last thing I heard in America, and the last thing I *want* to hear."

"But don't you like it?"

"As music? No! It moves me too much, but in the wrong way."

"What, exactly, do you mean?"

"Exactly? Nothing. When I heard it at the hospital—when was it?—it made me feel like crying. Three old Italians tootling it in the rain. I suppose, like most people, I'm afraid of my feelings."

"Are they so dangerous?"

"Now then, young woman! Are you pulling my leg?"

The stewards had rolled away the carpets, and the passengers were beginning to dance. Miss Dean accepted the invitation of a young officer, and Mr. Arcularis watched them with envy. Odd, that last exchange of remarks—very odd; in fact, everything was odd. Was it possible that they were falling in love? Was that what it was all about—all these concealed references and recollections? He had read of such things. But at his age! And with a girl of twenty-two! It was ridiculous.

After an amused look at his old friend Polaris from the open door on the sheltered side, he went to bed.

The rhythm of the ship's engines was positively a persecution. It gave one no rest, it followed one like the Hound of Heaven, it drove on, out into space and across the Milky Way and then back home by way of Betelgeuse. It was cold there, too. Mr. Arcularis, making the round trip by way of Betelgeuse and Polaris, sparkled with frost. He felt like a Christmas tree. Icicles on his fingers and icicles on his toes. He tinkled and spangled in the void, hallooed to the waste echoes, rounded the buoy on the verge of the Unknown, and tacked glitteringly homeward. The wind whistled. He was barefooted. Snowflakes and tinsel blew past him. Next time, by George, he would go farther still—for altogether it was rather a lark. Forward into the untrodden! as somebody said. Some intrepid explorer of his own backyard, probably, some middle-aged professor with an umbrella: those were the fellows for courage! But give us time, thought Mr. Arcularis, give us time, and we will bring back with us the night-rime of the Obsolute. Or was it Absolete? If only there weren't this perpetual throbbing, this iteration of sound, like a pain, these circles and repetitions of light—the feeling as of everything coiling inward to a center of misery. . . .

Suddenly it was dark, and he was lost. He was groping, he touched the cold, white, slippery woodwork with his fingernails, looking for an electric switch. The throbbing, of course, was the throbbing of the ship. But he was almost home—almost home. Another corner to round, a door to be opened, and there he would be. Safe and sound. Safe in his father's home.

It was at this point that he woke up: in the corridor that led to the dining saloon. Such pure terror, such horror, seized him as he had never known. His heart felt as if it would stop beating. His back was toward the dining saloon; apparently he had just come from it. He was in his pajamas. The corridor was dim, all but two lights having been turned out for the night, and—thank God!—deserted. Not a soul, not a sound. He was perhaps fifty yards from his room.

With luck he could get to it unseen. Holding tremulously to the rail that ran along the wall, a brown, greasy rail, he began to creep his way forward. He felt very weak, very dizzy, and his thoughts refused to concentrate. Vaguely he remembered Miss Dean—Clarice—and the freckled girl, as if they were one and the same person. But he wasn't in the hospital, he was on the ship. Of course. How absurd. The Great Circle. Here we are, old fellow . . . steady round the corner . . . hold hard to your umbrella. . . .

In his room, with the door safely shut behind him, Mr. Arcularis broke into a cold sweat. He had no sooner got into his bunk, shivering, than he heard the night watchman pass.

"But where"—he thought, closing his eyes in agony—"have I been? . . ."

A dreadful idea had occurred to him.

"It's nothing serious—how could it be anything serious? Of course, it's nothing serious," said Mr. Arcularis.

"No, it's nothing serious," said the ship's doctor urbanely.

"I knew you'd think so. But just the same——"

"Such a condition is the result of worry," said the doctor. "Are you worried—do you mind telling me—about something? Just try to think."

"Worried?"

Mr. Arcularis knitted his brows. Was there something? Some little mosquito of a cloud disappearing into the southwest, the northeast? Some little gnat-song of despair? But no, that was all over. All over.

"Nothing," he said, "nothing whatever."

"It's very strange," said the doctor.

"Strange! I should say so. I've come to sea for a rest, not for a nightmare! What about a bromide?"

"Well, I can give you a bromide, Mr. Arcularis——"

"Then, please, if you don't mind, give me a bromide."

He carried the little phial hopefully to his stateroom, and took a dose at once. He could see the sun through his porthole. It looked northern and pale and small, like a little peppermint, which was only natural enough, for the latitude was changing with every hour. But why was it that doctors were all alike? And all, for that matter, like his father, or that other fellow at the hospital? Smythe, his name was. Doctor Smythe. A nice, dry little fellow, and they said he was a writer. Wrote poetry, or something like that. Poor fellow—disappointed. Like everybody else. Crouched in there, in his cabin, night after night, writing blank verse or something—all about the stars and flowers and love and death; ice and the sea and the infinite; time and tide—well, every man to his own taste.

"But it's nothing serious," said Mr. Arcularis, later, to the parson. "How could it be?"

"Why, of course not, my dear fellow," said the parson, patting his back. "How could it be?"

"I know it isn't and yet I worry about it."

"It would be ridiculous to think it serious," said the parson. Mr. Arcularis shivered; it was colder than ever. It was said that they were near icebergs. For a few hours in the morning there had been a fog, and the siren had blown—devastatingly—at three-minute intervals. Icebergs caused fog —he knew that.

These things always come," said the parson, "from a sense of guilt. You feel guilty about something. I won't be so rude as to inquire what it is. But if you could rid yourself of the sense of guilt——"

And later still, when the sky was pink:

"But is it anything to worry about?" said Miss Dean. "Really?"

"No, I suppose not."

"Then don't worry. We aren't children any longer!"

"Aren't we? I wonder!"

They leaned, shoulders touching, on the deck-rail, and looked at the sea, which was multitudinously incarnadined. Mr. Arcularis scanned the horizon in vain for an iceberg.

"Anyway," he said, "the colder we are the less we feel!"

"I hope that's no reflection on you," said Miss Dean.

"Here . . . feel my hand," said Mr. Arcularis.

"Heaven knows, it's cold!"

"It's been to Polaris and back! No wonder."

"Poor thing, poor thing!"
"Warm it."
"May I?"
"You can."
"I'll try."

Laughing, she took his hand between both of hers, one palm under and one palm over, and began rubbing it briskly. The decks were deserted, no one was near them, everyone was dressing for dinner. The sea grew darker, the wind blew colder.

"I wish I could remember who you are," he said.

"And you—who are you?"

"Myself."

"Then perhaps I am yourself."

"Don't be metaphysical!"

"But I am metaphysical!"

She laughed, withdrew, pulled the light coat about her shoulders.

The bugle blew the summons for dinner—"The Roast Beef of Old England"— and they walked together along the darkening deck toward the door, from which a shaft of soft light fell across the deck-rail. As they stepped over the brass door-sill Mr. Arcularis felt the throb of the engines again; he put his hand quickly to his side.

"Auf wiedersehen," he said. "Tomorrow and tomorrow and tomorrow."

Mr. Arcularis was finding it impossible, absolutely impossible, to keep warm. A cold fog surrounded the ship, had done so, it seemed, for days. The sun had all but disappeared, the transition from day to night was almost unnoticeable. The ship, too, seemed scarcely to be moving—it was as if anchored among walls of ice and rime. Monstrous that, merely because it was June, and supposed, therefore, to be warm, the ship's authorities should consider it unnecessary to turn on the heat! By day, he wore his heavy coat and sat shivering in the corner of the smoking room. His teeth chattered, his hands were blue. By night, he heaped blankets on his bed, closed the porthole's black eye against the sea, and drew the yellow curtains across it, but in vain. Somehow, despite everything, the fog crept in, and the icy fingers touched his throat. The steward, questioned about it, merely said, "Icebergs." Of course—any fool knew that. But how long, in God's name, was it going to last? They surely ought to be past the Grand Banks by this time! And surely it wasn't necessary to sail to England by way of Greenland and Iceland!

Miss Dean—Clarice—was sympathetic.

"It's simply because," she said, "your vitality has been lowered by your illness. You can't expect to be your normal self so soon after an operation! When *was* your operation, by the way?"

Mr. Arcularis considered. Strange—he couldn't be quite sure. It was all a little vague—his sense of time had disappeared.

"Heavens knows!" he said. "Centuries ago. When I was a tadpole and you were a fish. I should think it must have been at about the time of the Battle of Teutoburg Forest. Or perhaps when I was a Neanderthal man with a club!"

"Are you sure it wasn't farther back still?"

What did she mean by that?

"Not at all. Obviously, we've been on this damned ship for ages—for eras—for æons. And even on this ship, you must remember, I've had plenty of time, in my nocturnal wanderings, to go several times to Orion and back. I'm thinking, by the way, of going farther still. There's a nice little star off to the left, as you round Betelgeuse, which looks as if it might be right at the edge. The last outpost of the finite. I think I'll have a look at it and bring you back a frozen rime-feather."

"It would melt when you got it back."

"Oh, no, it wouldn't—not on *this* ship!"

Clarice laughed.

"I wish I could go with you," she said. "If only you would! If only——"

He broke off his sentence and looked hard at her—how lovely she was, and how desirable! No such woman had ever before come into his life; there had been no one with whom he had at once felt so profound a sympathy and understanding. It was a miracle, simply—a miracle. No need to put his arm around her or to kiss her—delightful as such small vulgarities would be. He had only to look at her, and to feel, gazing into those extraordinary eyes, that she knew him, had always known him. It was as if, indeed, she might be his own soul.

But as he looked thus at her, reflecting, he noticed that she was frowning.

"What is it?" he said.

She shook her head, slowly.

"I don't know."

"Tell me."

"Nothing. It just occurred to me that perhaps you weren't looking quite so well."

Mr. Arcularis was startled. He straightened himself up.

"What nonsense! Of course, this pain bothers me—and I feel astonishingly weak——"

"It's more than that—much more than that. Something is worrying you horribly." She paused, and then with an air of challenging him, added, "Tell me, did you—"

Her eyes were suddenly asking him blazingly the question he had been afraid of. He flinched, caught his breath, looked away. But it was no use, as he knew; he would have to tell her. He had known all along that he would have to tell her.

"Clarice," he said—and his voice broke in spite of his effort to control it—"it's killing me, it's ghastly! Yes, I did."

His eyes filled with tears, he saw that her own had done so also. She put her hand on his arm.

"I knew," she said. "I knew. But tell me."

"It's happened twice again—twice—and each time I was farther away. The same dream of going round a star, the same terrible coldness and helplessness. That awful whistling curve. . . ." He shuddered.

"And when you woke up"—she spoke quietly—"where were you when you woke up? Don't be afraid!"

"The first time I was at the farther end of the dining saloon. I had my hand on the door that leads into the pantry."

"I see. Yes. And the next time?"

Mr. Arcularis wanted to close his eyes in terror—he felt as if he were going mad. His lips moved before he could speak, and when at last he did speak it was in a voice so low as to be almost a whisper.

"I was at the bottom of the stairway that leads down from the pantry to the hold, past the refrigerating plant. It was dark, and I was crawling on my hands and knees . . . crawling on my hands and knees! . . ."

"Oh!" she said, and again, "Oh!"

He began to tremble violently; he felt the hand on his arm trembling also. And then he watched a look of unmistakable horror come slowly into Clarice's eyes, and a look of understanding, as if she saw. . . . She tightened her hold on his arm.

"Do you think. . . ." she whispered.

They stared at each other.

"I know," he said. "And so do you. . . . Twice more—three times—and I'll be looking down into an empty. . . ."

It was then that they first embraced—then, at the edge of the infinite, at the last signpost of the finite. They clung together desperately, forlornly, weeping as they kissed each other, staring hard one moment and closing their eyes the next. Passionately, passionately, she kissed him, as if she were indeed trying to give him her warmth, her life.

"But what nonsense!" she cried, leaning back, and holding his face between her hands, her hands which were wet with his tears. "What nonsense! It can't be!"

"It is," said Mr. Arcularis slowly.

"But how do you know? . . . How do you know where the——"

For the first time Mr. Arcularis smiled.

"Don't be afraid, darling—you mean the coffin?"

"How could you know where it is?"

"I don't need to," said Mr. Arcularis. . . . "I'm already almost there."

Before they separated for the night, in the smoking room, they had several whisky cocktails.

"We must make it gay!" Mr. Arcularis said. "Above all, we must make it gay. Perhaps even now it will turn out to be nothing but a nightmare from which both of us will wake! And even at the worst, at my present rate of travel, I ought to need two more nights! It's a long way, still, to that little star."

The parson passed them at the door.

"What! turning in so soon?" he said. "I was hoping for a game of chess."

"Yes, both turning in. But tomorrow?"

"Tomorrow, then, Miss Dean! And good night!"

"Good night."

They walked once round the deck, then leaned on the railing and stared into the fog. It was thicker and whiter than ever. The ship was moving barely perceptibly, the rhythm of the engines was slower, more subdued and remote, and at regular intervals, mournfully, came the long reverberating cry of the foghorn. The sea was calm, and lapped only very tenderly against the side of the ship, the sound coming up to them clearly, however, because of the profound stillness.

"'On such a night as this—'" quoted Mr. Arcularis grimly.

"'On such a night as this——'"

Their voices hung suspended in the night, time ceased for them, for an eternal instant they were happy. When at last they parted it was by tacit agreement on a note of the ridiculous.

"Be a good boy and take your bromide!" she said.

"Yes, mother, I'll take my medicine!"

In his stateroom, he mixed himself a strong potion of bromide, a very strong one, and got into bed. He would have no trouble in falling asleep; he felt more tired, more supremely exhausted, than he had ever been in his life; nor had bed ever seemed so delicious. And that long, magnificent, delirious swoop of dizziness . . . the Great Circle . . . the swift pathway to Arcturus. . . .

It was all as before, but infinitely more rapid. Never had Mr. Arcularis achieved such phenomenal, such supernatural, speed. In no time at all he was beyond the moon, shot past the North Star as if it were standing still (which perhaps it was?), swooped in a long, bright curve round the Pleiades, shouted his frosty greetings to Betelgeuse, and was off to the little blue star which pointed the way to the Unknown. Forward into the untrodden! Courage, old man, and hold on to your umbrella! Have you got your garters on? Mind your hat! In no time at all we'll be back to Clarice with the frozen rime-feather, the time-feather, the snowflake of the Absolute, the Obsolete. If only we don't wake . . . if only we needn't wake . . . if only we don't wake in that—in that—time and space . . . somewhere or nowhere . . . cold and dark . . . "Cavalleria Rusticana" sobbing among the palms; if a lonely . . . if only . . . the coffers of the poor —not coffers, not coffers, not coffers, Oh, God, not coffers, but light, delight, supreme white and brightness, whirling lightness above all—and freezing—freezing—freezing. . . .

At this point in the void the surgeon's last effort to save Mr. Arcularis's life had failed. He stood back from the operating table and made a tired gesture with a rubber-gloved hand.

"It's all over," he said. "As I expected."

He looked at Miss Hoyle, whose gaze was downward, at the basin she held. There was a moment's stillness, a pause, a brief flight of unexchanged comment, and then the ordered life of the hospital was resumed.

FOR DISCUSSION:

1. At what point does the reader become aware that Mr. Arcularis is not on a sea voyage to England but on an operating table in a hospital?

2. Are there any early hints that Mr. Arcularis is dying? Enumerate them.

3. What are the effects of the dreams-within-a-dream?

4. Most critics see this story as a study in consciousness. Is it successful? Why?

The Turn of the Screw

HENRY JAMES

The story had held us, round the fire, sufficiently breathless, but except the obvious remark that it was gruesome, as, on Christmas Eve in an old house, a strange tale should essentially be, I remember no comment uttered till somebody happened to say that it was the only case he had met in which such a visitation had fallen on a child. The case, I may mention, was that of an apparition in just such an old house as had gathered us for the occasion—an appearance, of a dreadful kind, to a little boy sleeping in the room with his mother and waking her up in the terror of it; waking her not to dissipate his dread and soothe him to sleep again, but to encounter also, herself, before she had succeeded in doing so, the same sight that had shaken him. It was this observation that drew from Douglas—not immediately, but later in the evening—a reply that had the interesting consequence to which I call attention. Someone else told a story not particularly effective, which I saw he was not following. This I took for a sign that he had himself something to produce and that we should only have to wait. We waited in fact till two nights later; but that same evening, before we scattered, he brought out what was in his mind.

"I quite agree—in regard to Griffin's ghost, or whatever it was—that its appearing first to the little boy, at so tender an age, adds a particular touch. But it's not the first occurrence of its charming kind that I know to have involved a child. If the child gives the effect another turn of the screw, what do you say to two children——?"

"We say, of course," somebody exclaimed, "that they give two turns! Also that we want to hear about them."

I can see Douglas there before the fire, to which he had got up to present his back, looking down at his interlocutor with his hands in his pockets. "Nobody but me, till now, has ever heard. It's quite too horrible."

This, naturally, was declared by several voices to give the thing the utmost price, and our friend, with quiet art, prepared his triumph by turning his eyes over the rest of us and going on: "It's beyond everything. Nothing at all that I know touches it."

"For sheer terror?" I remember asking.

He seemed to say it was not so simple as that; to be really at a loss how to qualify it. He passed his hand over his eyes, made a little wincing grimace. "For dreadful—dreadfulness!"

"Oh, how delicious!" cried one of the women.

He took no notice of her; he looked at me, but as if, instead of me, he saw what he spoke of. "For general uncanny ugliness and horror and pain."

"Well then," I said, "just sit right down and begin."

He turned round to the fire, gave a kick to a log, watched it an instant. Then as he faced us again: "I can't begin, I shall have to send to town." There was a unanimous groan at this, and much reproach; after which, in his preoccupied way, he explained. "The story's written. It's in a locked drawer—it has not been out for years. I could write to my man and enclose the key; he could send down the packet as he finds it." It was to me in particular that he appeared to propound this—appeared almost to appeal for aid not to hesitate. He had broken a thickness of ice, the formation of many a winter: had had his reasons for a long silence. The others resented postponement, but it was just his scruples that charmed me. I adjured him to write by the first post and to agree with us for an early hearing; then I asked him if the experience in question had been his own. To this his answer was prompt. "Oh, thank God, no!"

"And is the record yours? You took the thing down?"

"Nothing but the impression. I took that *here*"—he tapped his heart. "I've never lost it."

"Then your manuscript——?"

"Is in old, faded ink, and in the most beautiful hand." He hung fire again. "A woman's. She has been dead these twenty years. She sent me the pages in question before she died." They were all listening now, and of course there was somebody to be arch, or at any rate to draw the inference. But if he put the inference by without a smile it was also without irritation. "She was a most charming person, but she was ten years older than I. She was my sister's **governess**," he quietly said. "**She was the most agreeable woman I've ever known in her position; she would have been worthy of any whatever. It was long ago, and this episode was long before. I was at Trinity, and I found her at home on my coming down the second summer.** I was much there that year—it was a beautiful one; and we had, in her off-hours, some strolls and talks in the garden—talks in which she struck me as awfully clever and nice. Oh yes; don't grin: I liked her extremely and am glad to this day to think she liked me, too. If she hadn't she wouldn't have told me. She had never told anyone. It wasn't simply that she said so, but that I knew she hadn't. I was sure; I could see. You'll easily judge why when you hear."

"Because the thing had been such a scare?"

He continued to fix me. "You'll easily judge," he repeated: "you will."

I fixed him, too. "I see. She was in love."

He laughed for the first time. "You are acute. Yes, she was in love. That is, she had been. That came out—she couldn't tell her story without its coming out. I saw it, and she saw I saw it; but neither of us spoke of it. I remember the time and the place—the corner of the lawn, the shade of the great beeches and the long, hot summer afternoon. It wasn't a scene for a shudder; but oh——!" He quitted the fire and dropped back into his chair.

"You'll receive the packet Thursday morning?" I inquired.

"Probably not till the second post."

"Well then; after dinner——"

"You'll all meet me here?" He looked us round again. "Isn't anybody going?" It was almost the tone of hope.

"Everybody will stay!"

"*I* will—and *I* will!" cried the ladies whose departure had been fixed. Mrs. Griffin, however, expressed the need for a little more light. "Who was it she was in love with?"

"The story will tell," I took upon myself to reply.

"Oh, I can't wait for the story!"

"The story *won't* tell," said Douglas; "not in any literal, vulgar way."

"More's the pity, then. That's the only way I ever understand."

"Won't you tell, Douglas?" somebody else inquired.

He sprang to his feet again. "Yes—tomorrow. Now I must go to bed. Good night." And quickly catching up a candlestick, he left us slightly bewildered. From our end of the great brown hall we heard his step on the stair; whereupon Mrs. Griffin spoke. "Well, if I don't know who she was in love with, I know who *he* was."

"She was ten years older," said her husband.

"*Raison de plus*—at that age! But it's rather nice, his long reticence."

"Forty years!" Griffin put in.

"With this outbreak at last."

"The outbreak," I returned, "will make a tremendous occasion of Thursday night;" and everyone so agreed with me that, in the light of it, we lost all attention for everything else. The last story, however incomplete and like the mere opening of a serial, had been told; we handshook and "candlestuck," as somebody said, and went to bed.

I knew the next day that a letter containing the key had, by the first post, gone off to his London apartments; but in spite of—or perhaps just on account of—the eventual diffusion of this knowledge we quite let him alone till after dinner, till such an hour of the evening, in fact, as might best accord with the kind of emotion on which our hopes were fixed. Then he became as communicative as we could desire and indeed gave us his best reason for being so. We had it from him again before the fire in the hall, as we had had our mild wonders of the previous night. It appeared that the narrative he had promised to read us really required for a proper intelligence a few words of prologue. Let me say here distinctly, to have done with it, that this narrative, from an exact transcript of my own made much later, is what I shall presently give. Poor Douglas, before his death —when it was in sight—committed to me the manuscript that reached him on the third of these days and that, on the same spot, with immense effect, he began to read to our hushed little circle on the night of the fourth. The departing ladies who had said they would stay didn't, of course, thank heaven, stay: they departed, in consequence of arrangements made, in a rage of curiosity, as they professed, produced by the touches with which he had already worked us up. But that only made his little final auditory more compact and select, kept it, round the hearth, subject to a common thrill.

The first of these touches conveyed that the written statement took up the tale at a point after it had, in a manner, begun. The fact to be in possession of was therefore that his old friend, the youngest of several daughters of a poor country parson, had, at the age of twenty, on taking service for the first time in the schoolroom, come up to London, in trepidation, to answer in person an advertisement that had already placed her in brief correspondence with the advertiser. This person proved, on her presenting herself, for judgment, at a house in Harley Street, that impressed her as vast and imposing—this prospective patron proved a gentleman, a bachelor in the prime of life, such a figure as had never risen, save in a dream of an old novel, before a fluttered, anxious girl out of a Hampshire vicarage. One could easily fix his type; it never, happily, dies out. He was handsome and bold and pleasant, offhand and gay and kind. He struck her, inevitably, as gallant and splendid, but what took her most of all and gave her the courage she afterward showed was that he put the whole thing to her as a kind of favor, an obligation he should gratefully incur. She conceived him as rich, but as fearfully extravagant—saw him all in a glow of high fashion, of good looks, of expensive habits, of charming ways with women. He had for his own town residence a big house filled with the spoils of travel and the trophies of the chase; but it was to his country home, an old family place in Essex, that he wished her immediately to proceed.

He had been left, by the death of their parents in India, guardian to a small nephew and a small niece, children of a younger, a military brother, whom he had lost two years before. These children were, by the strangest of chances for a man in his position—a lone man without the right sort of experience or a grain of patience—very heavily on his hands. It had all been a great worry and, on his own part doubtless, a series of blunders, but he immensely pitied the poor chicks and had done all he could; had in particular sent them down to his other house, the proper place for them being of course the country, and kept them there, from the first, with the best people he could find to look after them, parting even with his own servants to wait on them and going down himself, whenever he might, to see how they were doing. The awkward thing was that they had practically no other relations and that his own affairs took up all his time. He had put them in possession of Bly, which was healthy and secure, and had placed at the head of their little establishment—but below stairs only— an excellent woman, Mrs. Grose, whom he was sure his visitor would like and who had formerly been maid to his mother. She was now housekeeper and was also acting for the time as superintendent to the little girl, of whom, without children of her own, she was, by good luck, extremely fond. There were plenty of people to help, but of course the young lady who should go down as governess would be in supreme authority. She would also have, in holidays, to look after the small boy, who had been for a term at school—young as he was to be sent, but what else could be done?—and who, as the holidays were about to begin, would be back from one day to the other. There had been for the two children at first a young lady whom they had had the misfortune to lose. She had done for them quite beautifully— she was a most respectable person—till her death, the great awkwardness of which had, precisely, left no alternative but the school for little Miles. Mrs. Grose, since then, in the way of manners and things, had done as she could for Flora; and there were, further, a cook, a housemaid, a dairywoman, an old pony, an old groom, and an old gardener, all likewise thoroughly respectable.

So far had Douglas presented his picture when someone put a question. "And what did the former governess die of?—of so much respectability?"

Our friend's answer was prompt. "That will come out. I don't anticipate."

"Excuse me—I thought that was just what you are doing."

"In her successor's place," I suggested, "I should have wished to learn if the office brought with it——"

"Necessary danger to life?" Douglas completed my thought. "She did wish to learn, and she did learn. You shall hear tomorrow what she learned. Meanwhile, of course, the prospect struck her as slightly grim. She was young, untried, nervous: it was a vision of serious duties and little company, of really great loneliness. She hesitated —took a couple of days to consult and consider. But the salary offered much exceeded her modest measure, and on a second interview she faced the music, she engaged." And Douglas, with this, made a pause that, for the benefit of the company, moved me to throw in—

"The moral of which was of course the seduction exercised by the splendid young man. She succumbed to it."

He got up and, as he had done the night before, went to the fire, gave a stir to a log with his foot, then stood a moment with his back to us. "She saw him only twice."

"Yes, but that's just the beauty of her passion."

A little to my surprise, on this, Douglas turned round to me. "It was the beauty of it. There were others," he went on, "who hadn't succumbed. He told her frankly all his difficulty—that for several applicants the conditions had been prohibitive. They were, somehow, simply afraid. It sounded dull— it sounded strange; and all the more so because of his main condition."

"Which was——?"

"That she should never trouble him— but never, never: neither appeal nor complain nor write about anything; only meet all questions herself, receive all moneys from his solicitor, take the whole thing over and let him alone. She promised to do this, and she mentioned to me that when, for a moment, disburdened, delighted, he held her hand, thanking her for the sacrifice, she already felt rewarded."

"But was that all her reward?" one of the ladies asked.

"She never saw him again."

"Oh!" said the lady; which, as our friend immediately left us again, was the only other word of importance contributed to the subject till, the next night, by the corner of the hearth, in the best chair, he opened the faded red cover of a thin oldfashioned gilt-edged album. The whole thing took indeed more nights than one, but on the first occasion the same lady put another question. "What is your title?"

"I haven't one."

"Oh, *I* have!" I said. But Douglas, without heeding me, had begun to read with a fine clearness that was like a rendering to the ear of the beauty of his author's hand.

I

I remember the whole beginning as a succession of flights and drops, a little seesaw of the right throbs and the wrong. After rising, in town, to meet his appeal, I had at all events a couple of very bad days— found myself doubtful again, felt indeed sure I had made a mistake. In this state of mind I spent the long hours of bumping, swinging coach that carried me to the stopping place at which I was to be met by a vehicle from the house. This convenience, I was told, had been ordered, and I found, toward the close of the June afternoon, a commodious fly in waiting for me. Driving at that hour, on a lovely day, through a country to which the summer sweetness seemed to offer me a friendly welcome, my fortitude mounted afresh and, as we turned into the avenue, encountered a reprieve that was probably but a proof of the point to which it had sunk. I suppose I had expected, or had dreaded, something so melancholy that what greeted me was a good surprise. I remember as a most pleasant impression the broad, clear front, its open windows and fresh curtains and the pair of maids looking out; I remember the lawn and the bright flowers and the crunch of my wheels on the gravel and the clustered treetops over which the rooks circled and cawed in the golden sky. The scene had a greatness that made it a different affair from my own scant home, and there immediately appeared at the door, with a little girl in her hand, a civil person who dropped me as decent a curtsy as if I had been the mistress or a distinguished visitor. I had received in Harley Street a narrower notion of the place, and that, as I recalled it, made me think the proprietor still more of a gentleman, suggested that what I was to enjoy might be something beyond his promise.

I had no drop again till the next day, for I was carried triumphantly through the following hours by my introduction to the younger of my pupils. The little girl who accompanied Mrs. Grose appeared to me on the spot a creature so charming as to make it a great fortune to have to do with her. She was the most beautiful child I had ever seen, and I afterward wondered that my employer had not told me more of her. I slept little that night—I was too much excited; and this astonished me, too, I recollect, remained with me, adding to my sense of the liberality with which I was treated. The large, impressive room, one of the best in the house, the great state bed, as I almost felt it, the full, figured draperies, the long glasses in which, for the first time, I could see myself from head to foot, all struck me—like the extraordinary charm of my small charge—as so many things thrown in. It was thrown in as well, from the first moment, that I should get on with Mrs. Grose in a relation over which, on my way, in the coach, I fear I had rather brooded. The only thing indeed that in this early outlook might have made me shrink again was the clear circumstance of her being so glad to see me. I perceived within half an hour that she was so glad—stout, simple, plain, clean, wholesome woman—as to be positively on her guard against showing it too much. I wondered even then a little why she should wish not to show it, and that, with reflection, with suspicion, might of course have made me uneasy.

But it was a comfort that there could be no uneasiness in a connection with anything so beatific as the radiant image of my little girl, the vision of whose angelic beauty had probably more than anything else to do with the restlessness that, before morning, made me several times rise and wander about my room to take in the whole picture and prospect; to watch, from my open window, the faint summer dawn, to look at such portions of the rest of the house as I could catch, and to listen, while, in the fading dusk, the first birds began to twitter, for the possible recurrence of a sound or two, less natural and not without, but within, that I had fancied I heard. There had been a moment when I believed I recognized, faint and far, the cry of a child; there had been another when I found myself just consciously starting as at the passage, before my door, of a light footstep. But these fancies were not marked enough not to be thrown off, and it is only in the light, or the gloom, I should rather say, of other and subsequent matters that they now come back to me. To watch, teach, "form" little Flora would too evidently be the making of a happy and useful life. It had been agreed between us downstairs that after this first occasion I should have her as a matter of course at night, her small white bed being already arranged, to that end, in my room. What I had undertaken was the whole care of her, and she had remained, just this last time, with Mrs. Grose only as an effect of our consideration for my inevitable strangeness and her natural timidity. In spite of this timidity—which the child herself, in the oddest way in the world, had been perfectly frank and brave about, allowing it, without a sign of uncomfortable consciousness, with the deep, sweet serenity indeed of one of Raphael's holy infants, to be discussed, to be imputed to her, and to determine us—I felt quite sure she would presently like me. It was part of what I already liked Mrs. Grose herself for, the pleasure I could see her feel in my admiration and wonder as I sat at supper with four tall candles and with my pupil, in a high chair and a bib, brightly facing me, between them, over bread and milk. There were naturally things that in Flora's presence could pass between us only as prodigious and gratified looks, obscure and roundabout allusions.

"And the little boy—does he look like her? Is he too so very remarkable?"

One wouldn't flatter a child. "Oh, miss, *most* remarkable. If you think well of this one!"—and she stood there with a plate in her hand, beaming at our companion, who looked from one of us to the other with placid heavenly eyes that contained nothing to check us.

"Yes; if I do——?"

"You *will* be carried away by the little gentleman!"

"Well, that, I think, is what I came for—to be carried away. I'm afraid, however," I remember feeling the impulse to add, "I'm rather easily carried away. I was carried away in London!"

I can still see Mrs. Grose's broad face as she took this in. "In Harley Street?"

"In Harley Street."

"Well, miss, you're not the first—and you won't be the last."

"Oh, I've no pretension," I could laugh, "to being the only one. My other pupil, at any rate, as I understand, comes back tomorrow?"

"Not tomorrow—Friday, miss. He arrives, as you did, by the coach, under care of the guard, and is to be met by the same carriage."

I forthwith expressed that the proper as well as the pleasant and friendly thing would be therefore that on the arrival of the public conveyance I should be in waiting for him with his little sister; an idea in which Mrs. Grose concurred so heartily that I somehow took her manner as a kind of comforting pledge—never falsified, thank heaven!—that we should on every question be quite at one. Oh, she was glad I was there!

What I felt the next day was, I suppose, nothing that could be fairly called a reaction from the cheer of my arrival; it was probably at the most only a slight oppression produced by a fuller measure of the scale, as I walked round them, gazed up at them, took them in, of my new circumstances. They had, as it were, an extent and mass for which I had not been prepared and in the presence of which I found myself, freshly, a little scared as well as a little proud. Lessons, in this agitation, certainly suffered some delay; I reflected that my first duty was, by the gentlest arts I could contrive, to win the child into the sense of knowing me. I spent the day with her out-of-doors; I arranged with her, to her great satisfaction, that it should be she, she only, who might show me the place. She showed it step by step and room by room and secret by secret, with droll, delightful, childish talk about it and with the result, in half an hour, of our becoming immense friends. Young as she was, I was struck, throughout our little tour, with her confidence and courage with the way, in empty chambers and dull corridors, on crooked staircases that made me pause and even on the summit of an old machicolated square tower that made me dizzy, her morning music, her disposition to tell me so many more things than she asked, rang out and led me on. I have not seen Bly since the day I left it, and I daresay that to my older and more informed eyes it would now appear sufficiently contracted. But as my little conductress, with her hair of gold and her frock of blue, danced before me round corners and pattered down passages, I had the view of a castle of romance inhabited by a rosy sprite, such a place as would somehow, for diversion of the young idea, take all color out of storybooks and fairytales. Wasn't it just a storybook over which I had fallen adoze and adream? No; it was a big, ugly, antique, but convenient house, embodying a few features of a building still older, half-replaced and half-utilized, in which I had the fancy of our being almost as lost as a handful of passengers in a great drifting ship. Well, I was, strangely, at the helm!

II

This came home to me when, two days later, I drove over with Flora to meet, as Mrs. Grose said, the little gentleman; and all the more for an incident that, presenting itself the second evening, had deeply disconcerted me. The first day had been, on the whole, as I have expressed, reassuring; but I was to see it wind up in keen apprehension. The postbag, that evening—it came late—contained a letter for me, which, however, in the hand of my employer, I found to be composed but of a few words enclosing another, addressed to himself, with a seal still unbroken. "This, I recognize, is from the headmaster, and the headmaster's an awful bore. Read him, please; deal with him; but mind you don't report. Not a word. I'm off!" I broke the seal with a great effort—so great a one that I was a long time coming to it; took the unopened missive at last up to my room and only attacked it just before going to bed. I had better have let it wait till morning, for it gave me a second sleepless night. With no counsel to take, the next day, I was full of distress; and it finally got so the better of me that I determined to open myself at least to Mrs. Grose.

"What does it mean? The child's dismissed his school."

She gave me a look that I remarked at the moment; then, visibly, with a quick blankness, seemed to try to take it back. "But aren't they all——?"

"Sent home—yes. But only for the holidays. Miles may never go back at all."

Consciously, under my attention, she reddened. "They won't take him?"

"They absolutely decline."

At this she raised her eyes, which she had turned from me; I saw them fill with good tears. "What has he done?"

I hesitated; then I judged best simply to hand her my letter—which, however, had the effect of making her, without taking it, simply put her hands behind her. She shook her head sadly. "Such things are not for me, miss."

My counselor couldn't read! I winced at my mistake, which I attenuated as I could and opened my letter again to repeat it to her; then, faltering in the act and folding it up once more, I put it back in my pocket. "Is he really *bad?*"

The tears were still in her eyes. "Do the gentlemen say so?"

"They go into no particulars. They simply express their regret that it should be impossible to keep him. That can have only one meaning." Mrs. Grose listened with dumb emotion; she forbore to ask me what this meaning might be; so that, presently, to put the thing with some coherence and with the mere aid of her presence to my own mind, I went on: "That he's an injury to the others."

At this, with one of the quick turns of simple folk, she suddenly flamed up. "Master Miles! *him* an injury?"

There was such a flood of good faith in it that, though I had not yet seen the child, my very fears made me jump to the absurdity of the idea. I found myself, to meet my friend the better, offering it, on the spot, sarcastically. "To his poor little innocent mates!"

"It's too dreadful," cried Mrs. Grose, "to say such cruel things! Why, he's scarce ten years old."

"Yes, yes; it would be incredible."

She was evidently grateful for such a profession. "See him, miss, first. *Then* believe it!" I felt forthwith a new impatience to see him; it was the beginning of a curiosity that, for all the next hours, was to deepen almost to pain. Mrs. Grose was aware, I could judge, of what she had produced in me, and she followed it up with assurance. "You might as well believe it of the little lady. Bless her," she added the next moment—"*look* at her!"

I turned and saw that Flora, whom, ten minutes before, I had established in the schoolroom with a sheet of white paper, a pencil, and a copy of nice "round o's," now presented herself to view at the open door. She expressed in her little way an extraordinary detachment from disagreeable duties, looking to me, however, with a great childish light that seemed to offer it as a mere result of the affection she had conceived for my person, which had rendered necessary that she should follow me. I needed nothing more than this to feel the full force of Mrs. Grose's comparison, and, catching my pupil in my arms, covered her with kisses in which there was a sob of atonement.

Nonetheless, the rest of the day I watched for further occasion to approach my colleague, especially as, toward evening, I began to fancy she rather sought to avoid me. I overtook her, I remember, on the staircase; we went down together, and at the bottom I detained her, holding her there with a hand on her arm. "I take what you said to me at noon as a declaration that you've never known him to be bad."

She threw back her head; she had clearly, by this time, and very honestly, adopted an attitude. "Oh, never known him—I don't pretend *that!*"

I was upset again. "Then you *have* known him——?"

"Yes indeed, miss, thank God!"

On reflection I accepted this. "You mean that a boy who never is——?"

"Is no boy for *me!*"

I held her tighter. "You like them with the spirit to be naughty?" Then, keeping pace with her answer, "So do I!" I eagerly brought out. "But not to the degree to contaminate—"

"To contaminate?"—my big word left her at a loss. I explained it. "To corrupt."

She stared, taking my meaning in; but it produced in her an odd laugh. "Are you afraid he'll corrupt you?" She put the question with such a fine bold humor that, with a laugh, a little silly doubtless, to match her own, I gave way for the time to the apprehension of ridicule.

But the next day, as the hour for my drive approached, I cropped up in another place. "What was the lady who was here before?"

"The last governess? She was also young and pretty—almost as young and almost as pretty, miss, even as you."

"Ah, then, I hope her youth and her beauty helped her!" I recollect throwing off. "He seems to like us young and pretty!"

"Oh, he *did*," Mrs. Grose assented: "it was the way he liked everyone!" She had no sooner spoken indeed than she caught herself up. "I mean that's *his* way—the master's."

I was struck. "But of whom did you speak first?"

She looked blank, but she colored. "Why, of *him*."

"Of the master?"

"Of who else?"

There was so obviously no one else that the next moment I had lost my impression of her having accidentally said more than she meant; and I merely asked what I wanted to know. "Did *she* see anything in the boy——?"

"That wasn't right? She never told me."

I had a scruple, but I overcame it. "Was she careful—particular?"

Mrs. Grose appeared to try to be conscientious. "About some things—yes."

"But not about all?"

Again she considered. "Well, miss—she's gone. I won't tell tales."

"I quite understand your feeling," I hastened to reply; but I thought it, after an instant, not opposed to this concession to pursue: "Did she die here?"

"No—she went off."

I don't know what there was in this brevity of Mrs. Grose's that struck me as ambiguous. "Went off to die?" Mrs. Grose's looked straight out of the window, but I felt that, hypothetically, I had a right to know what young persons engaged for Bly were expected to do. "She was taken ill, you mean, and went home?"

"She was not taken ill, so far as appeared, in this house. She left it, at the end of the year, to go home, as she said, for a short holiday, to which the time she had put in had certainly given her a right. We had then a young woman—a nursemaid who had stayed on and who was a good girl and clever; and she took the children altogether for the interval. But our young lady never came back, and at the very moment I was expecting her I heard from the master that she was dead."

I turned this over. "But of what?"

"He never told me! But please, miss," said Mrs. Grose, "I must get to my work."

III

Her thus turning her back on me was fortunately not, for my just preoccupations, a snub that could check the growth of our mutual esteem. We met, after I had brought home little Miles, more intimately than ever on the ground of my stupefaction, my general emotion: so monstrous was I then ready to pronounce it that such a child as had now been revealed to me should be under an interdict. I was a little late on the scene, and I felt, as he stood wistfully looking out for me before the door of the inn at which the coach had put him down, that I had seen him, on the instant, without and within, in the great glow of freshness, the same positive fragrance of purity, in which I had, from the first moment, seen his little sister. He was incredibly beautiful, and Mrs. Grose had put her finger on it: everything but a sort of passion of tenderness for him was swept away by his presence. What I then and there took him to my heart for was something divine that I have never found to the same degree in any child —his indescribable little air of knowing nothing in the world but love. It would have been impossible to carry a bad name with a greater sweetness of innocence, and by the time I had got back to Bly with him I remained merely bewildered—so far, that is, as I was not outraged—by the sense of the horrible letter locked up in my room, in a drawer. As soon as I could compass a private word with Mrs. Grose I declared to her that it was grotesque.

She promptly understood me. "You mean the cruel charge——?"

"It doesn't live an instant. My dear woman, *look* at him!"

She smiled at my pretention to have discovered his charm. "I assure you, miss, I do nothing else! What will you say, then?" she immediately added.

"In answer to the letter?" I had made up my mind. "Nothing."

"And to his uncle?"

I was incisive. "Nothing."

"And to the boy himself?"

I was wonderful. "Nothing."

She gave with her apron a great wipe to her mouth. "Then I'll stand by you. We'll see it out."

"We'll see it out!" I ardently echoed, giving her my hand to make it a vow.

She held me there a moment, then whisked up her apron again with her detached hand. "Would you mind, miss, if I used the freedom——"

"To kiss me? No!" I took the good creature in my arms and, after we had embraced like sisters, felt still more fortified and indignant.

This, at all events, was for the time: a time so full that, as I recall the way it went, it reminds me of all the art I now need to make it a little distinct. What I look back at with amazement is the situation I accepted. I had undertaken, with my companion, to see it out, and I was under a charm, apparently, that could smooth away the extent and the far and difficult connections of such an effort. I was lifted aloft on a great wave of infatuation and pity. I found it simple, in my ignorance, my confusion, and perhaps my conceit, to assume that I could deal with a boy whose education for the world was all on the point of beginning. I am unable even to remember at this day what proposal I framed for the end of his holidays and the resumption of his studies. Lessons with me, indeed, that charming summer, we all had a theory that he was to have; but I now feel that, for weeks, the lessons must have been rather my own. I learned something—at first, certainly—that had not been one of the teachings of my small, smothered life; learned to be amused, and even amusing, and not to think for the morrow. It was the first time, in a manner, that I had known space and air and freedom, all the music of summer and all the mystery of nature. And then there was consideration—and consideration was sweet. Oh, it was a trap—not designed, but deep—to my imagination, to my delicacy, perhaps to my vanity; to whatever, in me, was most excitable. The best way to picture it all is to say that I was off my guard. They gave me so little trouble—they were of a gentleness so extraordinary. I used to speculate—but even this with a dim disconnectedness—as to how the rough future (for all futures are rough!) would handle them and might bruise them. They had the bloom of health and happiness; and yet, as if I had been in charge of a pair of little grandees, of princes of the blood, for whom everything, to be right, would have to be enclosed and protected, the only form that, in my fancy, the afteryears could take for them was that of a romantic, a really royal extension of the garden and the park. It may be, of course, above all, that what suddenly broke into this gives the previous time a charm of stillness—that hush in which something gathers or crouches. The change was actually like the spring of a beast.

In the first weeks the days were long; they often, at their finest, gave me what I used to call my own hour, the hour when, for my pupils, teatime and bedtime having come and gone, I had, before my final retirement, a small interval alone. Much as I liked my companions, this hour was the thing in the day I liked most; and I liked it best of all when, as the light faded—or rather, I should say, the day lingered and the last calls of the last birds sounded, in a flushed sky, from the old trees—I could take a turn into the grounds and enjoy, almost with a sense of property that amused and flattered me, the beauty and dignity of the place. It was a pleasure at these moments to feel myself tranquil and justified; doubtless, perhaps, also to reflect that by my discretion, my quiet good sense and general high propriety, I was giving pleasure—if he ever thought of it!—to the person to whose pressure I had responded. What I was doing was what he had earnestly hoped and directly asked of me, and that I *could*, after all, do it proved even a greater joy than I had expected. I daresay I fancied myself, in short, a remarkable young woman and took comfort in the faith that this would more publicly appear. Well, I needed to be remarkable to offer a front to the remarkable things that presently gave their first sign.

It was plump, one afternoon, in the middle of my very hour: the children were tucked away, and I had come out for my stroll. One of the thoughts that, as I don't in the least shrink now from noting, used to be with me in these wanderings was that it would be as charming as a charming story suddenly to meet someone. Someone would appear there at the turn of a path and would stand before me and smile and approve. I didn't ask more than that—I only asked that he should *know*; and the only way to be sure he knew would be to see it, and the kind light of it, in his handsome face. That was exactly present to me—by which I mean the face was—when, on the first of these occasions, at the end of a long June day, I stopped short on emerging from one of the plantations and coming into view of the house. What arrested me on the spot —and with a shock much greater than any vision had allowed for—was the sense that my imagination had, in a flash, turned real. He did stand there!—but high up, beyond the lawn and at the very top of the tower to which, on that first morning, little Flora had conducted me. This tower was one of a pair—square, incongruous, crenelated structures—that were distinguished, for some reason, though I could see little difference, as the new and the old. They flanked opposite ends of the house and were probably architectural absurdities, redeemed in a measure indeed by not being wholly disengaged nor of a height too pretentious, dating, in their gingerbread antiquity, from a romantic revival that was already a respectable past. I admired them, had fancies about them, for we could all profit in a degree, especially when they loomed through the dusk, by the grandeur of their actual battlements; yet it was not at such an elevation that the figure I had so often invoked seemed most in place.

It produced in me, this figure, in the clear twilight, I remember, two distinct gasps of emotion, which were, sharply, the shock of my first and that of my second surprise. My second was a violent perception of the mistake of my first: the man who met my eyes was not the person I had precipitately supposed. There came to me thus a bewilderment of vision of which, after these years, there is no living view that I can hope to give. An unknown man in a lonely place is a permitted object of fear to a young woman privately bred; and the figure that faced me was—a few more seconds assured me—as little anyone else I knew as it was the image that had been in my mind. I had not seen it in Harley Street —I had not seen it anywhere. The place, moreover, in the strangest way in the world, had, on the instant, and by the very fact of its appearance, become a solitude. To me at least, making my statement here with a deliberation with which I have never made it, the whole feeling of the moment returns. It was as if, while I took in—what I did take in—all the rest of the scene had been stricken with death. I can hear again, as I write, the intense hush in which the sounds of evening dropped. The rooks stopped cawing in the golden sky, and the friendly hour lost, for the minute, all its voice. But there was no other change in nature, unless indeed it were a change that I saw with a stranger sharpness. The gold was still in the sky, the clearness in the air, and the man who looked at me over the battlements was as definite as a picture in a frame. That's how I thought, with extraordinary quickness, of each person that he might have been and that he was not. We were confronted across our distance quite long enough for me to ask myself with intensity who then he was and to feel, as an effect of my inability to say, a wonder that in a few instants more became intense.

The great question, or one of these, is, afterward, I know, with regard to certain matters, the question of how long they have lasted. Well, this matter of mine, think what you will of it, lasted while I caught at a dozen possibilities, none of which made a difference for the better, that I could see, in there having been in the house—and for how long, above all?— a person of whom I was in ignorance. It lasted while I just bridled a little with the sense that my office demanded that there should be no such ignorance and no such person. It lasted while this visitant, at all events—and there was a touch of the strange freedom, as I remember, in the sign of familiarity of his wearing no hat—seemed to fix me, from his position, with just the question, just the scrutiny through the fading light, that his own presence provoked. We were too far apart to call to each other, but there was a moment at which, at shorter range, some challenge between us, breaking the hush, would have been the right result of our straight mutual stare. He was in one of the angles, the one away from the house, very erect, as it struck me, and with both hands on the ledge. So I saw him as I see the letters I form on this page; then, exactly, after a minute, as if to add to the spectacle, he slowly changed his place —passed, looking at me hard all the while, to the opposite corner of the platform. Yes, I had the sharpest sense that during this transit he never took his eyes from me, and I can see at this moment the way his hand, as he went, passed from one of the crenelations to the next. He stopped at the other corner, but less long, and even as he turned away still markedly fixed me. He turned away; that was all I knew.

IV

It was not that I didn't wait, on this occasion, for more, for I was rooted as deeply as I was shaken. Was there a "secret" at Bly—a mystery of Udolpho or an insane, an unmentionable relative kept in unsuspected confinement? I can't say how long I turned it over, or how long, in a confusion of curiosity and dread, I remained where I had had my collision; I only recall that when I re-entered the house darkness had quite closed in. Agitation, in the interval, certainly had held me and driven me, for I must, in circling about the place, have walked three miles; but I was to be, later on, so much more overwhelmed that this mere dawn of alarm was a comparatively human chill. The most singular part of it, in fact —singular as the rest had been—was the part I became, in the hall, aware of in meeting Mrs. Grose. This picture comes back to me in the general train—the impression, as I received it on my return, of the wide white panelled space, bright in the lamplight and with its portraits and red carpet, and of the good surprised look of my friend, which immediately told me she had missed me. It came to me straightway, under her contact, that, with plain heartiness, mere relieved anxiety at my appearance, she knew nothing whatever that could bear upon the incident I had there ready for her. I had not suspected in advance that her comfortable face would pull me up, and I somehow measured the importance of what I had seen by my thus finding myself hesitate to mention it. Scarce anything in the whole history seems to me so odd as this fact that my real beginning of fear was one, as I may say, with the instinct of sparing my companion. On the spot, accordingly, in the pleasant hall and with her eyes on me, I, for a reason that I couldn't then have phrased, achieved an inward resolution—offered a vague pretext for my lateness and, with the plea of the beauty of the night and of the heavy dew and wet feet, went as soon as possible to my room.

Here it was another affair; here, for many days after, it was a queer affair enough. There were hours, from day to day—or at least there were moments, snatched even from clear duties—when I had to shut myself up to think. It was not so much yet that I was more nervous than I could bear to be as that I was remarkably afraid of becoming so; for the truth I had now to turn over was, simply and clearly, the truth that I could arrive at no account whatever of the visitor with whom I had been so inexplicably and yet, as it seemed to me, so intimately concerned. It took little time to see that I could sound without forms of inquiry and without exciting remark any domestic complication. The shock I had suffered must have sharpened all my senses; I felt sure, at the end of three days and as the result of mere closer attention, that I had not been practiced upon by the servants nor made the object of any "game." Of whatever it was that I knew, nothing was known around me. There was but one sane inference: someone had taken a liberty rather gross. That was what, repeatedly, I dipped into my room and locked the door to say to myself. We had been, collectively, subject to an intrusion; some unscrupulous traveler, curious in old houses, had made his way in unobserved, enjoyed the prospect from the best point of view, and then stolen out as he came. If he had given me such a bold hard stare, that was but a part of his indiscretion. The good thing, after all, was that we should surely see no more of him.

This was not so good a thing, I admit,

as not to leave me to judge that what, essentially, made nothing else much signify was simply my charming work. My charming work was just my life with Miles and Flora, and through nothing could I so like it as through feeling that I could throw myself into it in trouble. The attraction of my small charges was a constant joy, leading me to wonder afresh at the vanity of my original fears, the distaste I had begun by entertaining for the probable gray prose of my office. There was to be no gray prose, it appeared, and no long grind; so how could work not be charming that presented itself as daily beauty? It was all the romance of the nursery and the poetry of the schoolroom. I don't mean by this, of course, that we studied only fiction and verse; I mean I can express no otherwise the sort of interest my companions inspired. How can I describe that except by saying that instead of growing used to them—and it's a marvel for a governess: I call the sisterhood to witness!—I made constant fresh discoveries. There was one direction, assuredly, in which these discoveries stopped: deep obscurity continued to cover the region of the boy's conduct at school. It had been promptly given me, I have noted, to face that mystery without a pang. Perhaps even it would be nearer the truth to say that—without a word—he himself had cleared it up. He had made the whole charge absurd. My conclusion bloomed there with the real rose flush of his innocence: he was only too fine and fair for the little horrid, unclean school world, and he had paid a price for it. I reflected acutely that the sense of such differences, such superiorities of quality, always, on the part of the majority—which could include even stupid, sordid headmasters—turns infallibly to the vindictive.

Both the children had a gentleness (it was their only fault, and it never made Miles a muff) that kept them—how shall I express it?—almost impersonal and certainly quite unpunishable. They were like the cherubs of the anecdote, who had—morally, at any rate—nothing to whack! I remember feeling with Miles in especial as if he had had, as it were, no history. We expect of a small child a scant one, but there was in this beautiful little boy something extraordinarily sensitive, yet extraordinarily happy, that, more than in any creature of his age I have seen, struck me as beginning anew each day. He had never for a second suffered. I took this as a direct disproof of his having really been chastised. If he had been wicked he would have "caught" it, and I should have caught it by the rebound—I should have found the trace. I found nothing at all, and he was therefore an angel. He never spoke of his school, never mentioned a comrade or a master; and I, for my part, was quite too much disgusted to allude to them. Of course I was under the spell, and the wonderful part is that, even at the time, I perfectly knew I was. But I gave myself up to it; it was an antidote to any pain, and I had more pains than one. I was in receipt in these days of disturbing letters from home, where things were not going well. But with my children, what things in the world mattered? That was the question I used to put to my scrappy retirements. I was dazzled by their loveliness.

There was a Sunday—to get on—when it rained with such force and for so many hours that there could be no procession to church; in consequence of which, as the day declined, I had arranged with Mrs. Grose that, should the evening show improvement, we would attend together the late service. The rain happily stopped, and I prepared for our walk, which, through the park and by the good road to the village, would be a matter of twenty minutes. Coming downstairs to meet my colleague in the hall, I remembered a pair of gloves that had required three stitches and that had received them—with a publicity perhaps not edifying—while I sat with the children at their tea, served on Sundays, by exception, in that cold, clean temple of mahogany and brass, the "grown-up" dining room. The gloves had been dropped there, and I turned in to recover them. The day was gray enough, but the afternoon light still lingered, and it enabled me, on crossing the threshold, not only to recognize, on a chair near the wide window, then closed, the articles I wanted, but to become aware of a person on the other side of the window and looking straight in. One step into the room had sufficed; my vision was instantaneous; it was all there. The person looking straight in was the person who had already appeared to me. He appeared thus again with I won't say greater distinctness, for that was impossible, but with a nearness that represented a forward stride in our intercourse and made me, as I met him, catch my breath and turn cold. He was the same—, he was the same, and seen, this time, as he had been seen before, from the waist up, the window, though the dining room was on the ground floor, not going down to the terrace on which he stood. His face was close to the glass, yet the effect of this better view was, strangely, only to show me how intense the former had been. He remained but a few seconds—long enough to convince me he also saw and recognized; but it was as if I had been looking at him for years and had known him always. Something, however, happened this time that had not happened before; his stare into my face, through the glass and across the room, was as deep and hard as then, but it quitted me for a moment during which I could still watch it, see it fix successively several other things. On the spot there came to me the added shock of a certitude that it was not for me he had come there. He had come for someone else.

The flash of this knowledge—for it was knowledge in the midst of dread—produced in me the most extraordinary effect, started, as I stood there, a sudden vibration of duty and courage. I say courage because I was beyond all doubt already far gone. I bounded straight out of the door again, reached that of the house, got, in an instant, upon the drive, and, passing along the terrace as fast as I could rush, turned a corner and came full in sight. But it was in sight of nothing now—my visitor had vanished. I stopped, I almost dropped, with the real relief of this; but I took in the whole scene —I gave him time to reappear. I call it time, but how long was it? I can't speak to the purpose today of the duration of these things. That kind of measure must have left me: they couldn't have lasted as they actually appeared to me to last. The terrace and the whole place, the lawn and the garden beyond it, all I could see of the park, were empty with a great emptiness. There were shrubberies and big trees, but I remember the clear assurance I felt that none of them concealed him. He was there or was not there: not there if I didn't see him. I got hold of this; then, instinctively, instead of returning as I had come, went to the window. It was confusedly present to me that I ought to place myself where he had stood. I did so; I applied my face to the pane and looked, as he had looked, into the room. As if, at this moment, to show me exactly what his range had been, Mrs. Grose, as I had done for himself just before, came in from the hall. With this I had the full image of a repetition of what had already occurred. She saw me as I had seen my own visitant; she pulled up short as I had done; I gave her something of the shock that I had received. She turned white, and this made me ask myself if I had blanched as much. She stared, in short, and retreated on just my lines, and I knew she had then passed out and come round to me and that I should presently meet her. I remained where I was, and while I waited I thought of more things than one. But there's only one I take space to mention. I wondered why *she* should be scared.

V

Oh, she let me know as soon as, round the corner of the house, she loomed again into view. "What in the name of goodness is the matter——?" She was now flushed and out of breath.

I said nothing till she came quite near. "With me?" I must have made a wonderful face. "Do I show it?"

"You're as white as a sheet. You look awful."

I considered; I could meet on this, without scruple, any innocence. My need to respect the bloom of Mrs. Grose's had dropped, without a rustle, from my shoulders, and if I wavered for the instant it was not with what I kept back. I put out my hand to her and she took it; I held her hard a little, liking to feel her close to me. There was a kind of support in the shy heave of her surprise. "You came for me for church, of course, but I can't go."

"Has anything happened?"

"Yes. You must know now. Did I look very queer?"

"Through this window? Dreadful!"

"Well," I said, "I've been frightened." Mrs. Grose's eyes expressed plainly that *she* had no wish to be, yet also that she knew too well her place not to be ready to share with me any marked inconvenience. Oh, it was quite settled that she *must* share! "Just what you saw from the dining room a minute ago was the effect of that. What *I* saw —just before—was much worse."

Her hand tightened. "What was it?"

"An extraordinary man. Looking in."

"What extraordinary man?"

"I haven't the least idea."

Mrs. Grose gazed round us in vain. "Then where is he gone?"

"I know still less."

"Have you seen him before?"

"Yes—once. On the old tower."

She could only look at me harder. "Do you mean he's a stranger?"

"Oh, very much!"

"Yet you didn't tell me?"

"No—for reasons. But now that you've guessed——"

Mrs. Grose's round eyes encountered this charge. "Ah, I haven't guessed!" she said very simply. "How can I if you don't imagine?"

"I don't in the very least."

"You've seen him nowhere but on the tower?"

"And on this spot just now."

Mrs. Grose looked round again. "What was he doing on the tower?"

"Only standing there and looking down at me."

She thought a minute. "Was he a gentleman?"

I found I had no need to think. "No." She gazed in deeper wonder. "No."

"Then nobody about the place? Nobody from the village?"

"Nobody—nobody. I didn't tell you, but I made sure."

She breathed a vague relief: this was, oddly, so much to the good. It only went indeed a little way. "But if he isn't a gentleman——"

"What *is* he? He's a horror."

"A horror?"

"He's—God help me if I know *what* he is!"

Mrs. Grose looked round once more; she fixed her eyes on the duskier distance, then, pulling herself together, turned to me with abrupt inconsequence. "It's time we should be at church."

"Oh, I'm not fit for church!"

"Won't it do you good?"

"It won't do *them*——!" I nodded at the house.

"The children?"

"I can't leave them now."

"You're afraid——?"

I spoke boldly. "I'm afraid of *him*."

Mrs. Grose's large face showed me, at this, for the first time, the faraway faint glimmer of a consciousness more acute: I somehow made out in it the delayed dawn of an idea I myself had not given her and that was as yet quite obscure to me. It comes back to me that I thought instantly of this as something I could get from her; and I felt it to be connected with the desire she presently showed to know more. "When was it—on the tower?"

"About the middle of the month. At this same hour."

"Almost at dark," said Mrs. Grose.

"Oh, no, not nearly. I saw him as I see you."

"Then how did he get in?"

"And how did he get out?" I laughed. "I had no opportunity to ask him! This evening, you see," I pursued, "he has not been able to get in."

"He only peeps?"

"I hope it will be confined to that!" She had now let go my hand; she turned away a little. I waited an instant; then I brought out: "Go to church. Goodbye. I must watch."

Slowly she faced me again. "Do you fear for them?"

We met in another long look. "Don't you?" Instead of answering she came nearer to the window and, for a minute, applied her face to the glass. "You see how he could see," I meanwhile went on.

She didn't move. "How long was he here?"

"Till I came out. I came to meet him."

Mrs. Grose at last turned round, and there was still more in her face. "*I* couldn't have come out."

"Neither could I!" I laughed again. "But I did come. I have my duty."

"So have I mine," she replied; after which she added: "What is he like?"

"I've been dying to tell you. But he's like nobody."

"Nobody?" she echoed.

"He has no hat." Then seeing in her face that she already, in this, with a deeper dismay, found a touch of picture, I quickly added stroke to stroke. "He has red hair, very red, close-curling, and a pale face, long in shape, with straight, good features and little, rather queer whiskers that are as red as his hair. His eyebrows are, somehow, darker; they look particularly arched and as if they might move a good deal. His eyes are sharp, strange—awfully; but I only know clearly that they're rather small and very fixed. His mouth's wide, and his lips are thin, and except for his little whiskers he's quite clean-shaven. He gives me a sort of sense of looking like an actor."

"An actor!" It was impossible to resemble one less, at least, than Mrs. Grose at that moment.

"I've never seen one, but so I suppose them. He's tall, active, erect," I continued, "but never—no, never!—a gentleman."

My companion's face had blanched as I went on; her round eyes started and her mild mouth gaped. "A gentleman?" she gasped, confounded, stupefied: "a gentleman *he*?"

"You know him then?"

She visibly tried to hold herself. "But he *is* handsome?"

I saw the way to help her. "Remarkably!"

"And dressed——?"

"In somebody's clothes. They're smart, but they're not his own."

She broke into a breathless affirmative groan: "They're the master's!"

I caught it up. "You *do* know him?"

She faltered but a second. "Quint!" she cried.

"Quint?"

"Peter Quint—his own man, his valet, when he was here!"

"When the master was?"

Gaping still, but meeting me, she pieced it all together. "He never wore his hat, but he did wear—well, there were waistcoats missed. They were both here—last year. Then the master went, and Quint was alone."

I followed, but halting a little. "Alone?"

"Alone with us." Then, as from a deeper depth, "In charge," she added.

"And what became of him?"

She hung fire so long that I was still more mystified. "He went, too," she brought out at last.

"Went where?"

Her expression, at this, became extraordinary. "God knows where! He died."

"Died?" I almost shrieked.

She seemed fairly to square herself, plant herself more firmly to utter the wonder of it. "Yes. Mr. Quint is dead."

VI

It took of course more than that particular passage to place us together in presence of what we had now to live with as we could—my dreadful liability to impressions of the order so vividly exemplified, and my companion's knowledge, henceforth—a knowledge half consternation and half compassion—of that liability. There had been, this evening, after the revelation that left me, for an hour, so prostrate—there had been, for either of us, no attendance on any service but a little service of tears and vows, of prayers and promises, a climax to the series of mutual challenges and pledges that had straightway ensued on our retreating together to the schoolroom and shutting ourselves up there to have everything out. The result of our having everything out was simply to reduce our situation to the last rigor of its elements. She herself had seen nothing, not the shadow of a shadow, and nobody in the house but the governess was in the governess's plight; yet she accepted without directly impugning my sanity the truth as I gave it to her, and ended by showing me, on this ground, an awestricken tenderness, an expression of the sense of my more than questionable privilege, of which the very breath has remained with me as that of the sweetest of human charities.

What was settled between us, accordingly, that night, was that we thought we might bear things together; and I was not even sure that, in spite of her exemption, it was she who had the best of the burden. I knew at this hour, I think, as well as I knew later, what I was capable of meeting to shelter my pupils; but it took me some time to be wholly sure of what my honest ally was prepared for to keep terms with so compromising a contract. I was queer company enough—quite as queer as the company

I received; but as I trace over what we went through I see how much common ground we must have found in the one idea that, by good fortune, *could* steady us. It was the idea, the second movement, that led me straight out, as I may say, of the inner chamber of my dread. I could take the air in the court, at least, and there Mrs. Grose could join me. Perfectly can I recall now the particular way strength came to me before we separated for the night. We had gone over and over every feature of what I had seen.

"He was looking for someone else, you say—someone who was not you?"

"He was looking for little Miles." A portentous clearness now possessed me. "*That's* whom he was looking for."

"But how do you know?"

"I know, I know, I know!" My exaltation grew. "And you know, my dear!"

She didn't deny this, but I required, I felt, not even so much telling as that. She resumed in a moment, at any rate: "What if *he* should see him?"

"Little Miles? That's what he wants!"

She looked immensely scared again. "The child?"

"Heaven forbid! The man. He wants to appear to *them*." That he might was an awful conception, and yet, somehow, I could keep it at bay; which, moreover, as we lingered there, was what I succeeded in practically proving. I had an absolute certainty that I should see again what I had already seen, but something within me said that by offering myself bravely as the sole subject of such experience, by accepting, by inviting, by surmounting it all, I should serve as an expiatory victim and guard the tranquility of my companions. The children, in especial, I should thus fence about and absolutely save. I recall one of the last things I said that night to Mrs. Grose.

"It does strike me that my pupils have never mentioned——"

She looked at me hard as I musingly pulled up. "His having been here and the time they were with him?"

"The time they were with him, and his name, his presence, his history, in any way."

"Oh, the little lady doesn't remember. She never heard or knew."

"The circumstances of his death?" I thought with some intensity. "Perhaps not. But Miles would remember—Miles would know."

"Ah, don't try him!" broke from Mrs. Grose.

I returned her the look she had given me. "Don't be afraid." I continued to think. "It *is* rather odd."

"That he has never spoken of him?"

"Never by the least allusion. And you tell me they were 'great friends'?"

"Oh, it wasn't *him!*" Mrs. Grose with emphasis declared. "It was Quint's own fancy. To play with him, I mean—to spoil him." She paused a moment; then she added: "Quint was much too free."

This gave me, straight from my vision of his face—*such* a face!—a sudden sickness of disgust. "Too free with *my* boy?"

"Too free with everyone!"

I forbore, for the moment, to analyze this description further than by the reflection that a part of it applied to several of the members of the household, of the half-dozen maids and men who were still of our small colony. But there was everything, for our apprehension, in the lucky fact that no discomfortable legend, no perturbation of scullions, had ever, within anyone's memory attached to the kind old place. It had neither bad name nor ill fame, and Mrs. Grose, most apparently, only desired to cling to me and to quake in silence. I even put her, the very last thing of all, to the test. It was when, at midnight, she had her hand on the schoolroom door to take leave. "I have it from you then—for it's of great importance—that he was definitely and admittedly bad?"

"Oh, not admittedly. *I* knew it—but the master didn't."

"And you never told him?"

"Well, he didn't like tale-bearing—he hated complaints. He was terribly short with anything of that kind, and if people were all right to *him*——"

"He wouldn't be bothered with more?" This squared well enough with my impression of him: he was not a trouble-loving gentleman, nor so very particular perhaps about some of the company *he* kept. All the same, I pressed my interlocutress. "I promise you *I* would have told!"

She felt my discrimination. "I daresay I was wrong. But, really, I was afraid."

"Afraid of what?"

"Of things that man could do. Quint was so clever—he was so deep."

I took this in still more than, probably, I showed. "You weren't afraid of anything else? Not of his effect——?"

"His effect?" she repeated with a face of anguish and waiting while I faltered.

"On innocent little precious lives. They were in your charge."

"No, they were not in mine!" she roundly and distressfully returned. "The master believed in him and placed him here because he was supposed not to be well and the country air so good for him. So he had everything to say. Yes"—she let me have it—"even about *them*."

"Them—that creature?" I had to smother a kind of howl. "And you could bear it!"

"No. I couldn't—and I can't now!" And the poor woman burst into tears.

A rigid control, from the next day, was, as I have said, to follow them; yet how often and how passionately, for a week, we came back together to the subject! Much as we had discussed it that Sunday night, I was, in the immediate later hours in especial—for it may be imagined whether I slept —still haunted with the shadow of something she had not told me. I myself had kept back nothing, but there was a word Mrs. Grose had kept back. I was sure, moreover, by morning, that this was not from a failure of frankness, but because on every side there were fears. It seems to me indeed, in retrospect, that by the time the morrow's sun was high I had restlessly read into the fact before us almost all the meaning they were to receive from subsequent and more cruel occurrences. What they gave me above all was just the sinister figure of the living man—the dead one would keep awhile!—and of the months he had continuously passed at Bly, which, added up, made a formidable stretch. The limit of this evil time had arrived only when, on the dawn of a winter's morning, Peter Quint was found, by a laborer going to early work, stone dead on the road from the village: a catastrophe explained—superficially at least—by a visible wound to his head; such a wound as might have been produced—and as, on the final evidence, *had* been—by a fatal slip, in the dark and after leaving the public house, on the steepish icy slope, a wrong path altogether, at the bottom of which he lay. The icy slope, the turn mistaken at night and in liquor, accounted for much—practically, in the end and after the inquest and boundless chatter, for everything; but there had been matters in his life—strange passages and perils, secret disorders, vices more than suspected—that would have accounted for a good deal more.

I scarce know how to put my story into words that shall be a credible picture of my state of mind; but I was in these days literally able to find a joy in the extraordinary flight of heroism the occasion demanded of me. I now saw that I had been asked for a service admirable and difficult; and there would be a greatness in letting it be seen— oh, in the right quarter!—that I could succeed where many another girl might have failed. It was an immense help to me—I confess I rather applaud myself as I look back!—that I saw my service so strongly and so simply. I was there to protect and defend the little creatures in the world the most bereaved and the most lovable, the appeal of whose helplessness had suddenly become only too explicit, a deep, constant ache of one's own committed heart. We were cut off, really, together; we were united in our danger. They had nothing but me, and I—well, I had *them*. It was in short a magnificent chance. This chance presented itself to me in an image richly material. I was a screen—I was to stand before them. The more I saw, the less they would. I began to watch them in a stifled suspense, a disguised excitement that might well, had it continued too long, have turned to something like madness. What saved me, as I now see, was that it turned to something else altogether. It didn't last as suspense— it was superseded by horrible proofs. Proofs, I say, yes—from the moment I really took hold.

This moment dated from an afternoon hour that I happened to spend in the grounds with the younger of my pupils alone. We had left Miles indoors, on the red cushion of a deep window seat; he had wished to finish a book, and I had been glad to encourage a purpose so laudable in a young man whose only defect was an occasional excess of the restless. His sister, on the contrary, had been alert to come out, and I strolled with her half an hour, seeking the shade, for the sun was still high and the day exceptionally warm. I was aware afresh, with her, as we went, of how, like her brother, she contrived—it was the charming thing in both children—to let me alone without appearing to drop me and to accompany me without appearing to surround. They were never importunate and yet never listless. My attention to them all really went to seeing them amuse themselves immensely without me: this was a spectacle they seemed actively to prepare and that engaged me as an active admirer. I walked in a world of their invention—they had no occasion whatever to draw upon mine; so that my time was taken only with being, for them, some remarkable person or thing that the game of the moment required and that was merely, thanks to my superior, my exalted stamp, a happy and highly distinguished sinecure. I forget what I was on the present occasion; I only remember that I was something very important and very quiet and that Flora was playing very hard. We were on the edge of the lake, and, as we had lately begun geography, the lake was the Sea of Azof.

Suddenly, in these circumstances, I became aware that, on the other side of the Sea of Azof, we had an interested spectator. The way this knowledge gathered in me was the strangest thing in the world—the strangest, that is, except the very much stranger in which it quickly merged itself. I had sat down with a piece of work—for I was something or other that could sit—on the old stone bench which overlooked the pond; and in this position I began to take in with certitude, and yet without direct vision, the presence, at a distance, of a third person. The old trees, the thick shrubbery, made a great and pleasant shade, but it was all suffused with the brightness of the hot, still hour. There was no ambiguity in anything; none whatever, at least, in the conviction I from one moment to another found myself forming as to what I should see straight before me and across the lake as a consequence of raising my eyes. They were attached at this juncture to the stitching in which I was engaged, and I can feel once more the spasm of my effort not to move them till I should so have steadied myself as to be able to make up my mind what to do. There was an alien object in view—a figure whose right of presence I instantly, passionately questioned. I recollect counting over perfectly the possibilities, reminding myself that nothing was more natural, for instance, than the appearance of one of the men about the place, or even of a messenger, a postman, or a tradesman's boy, from the village. That reminder had as little effect on my practical certitude as I was conscious—still even without looking—of its having upon the character and attitude of our visitor. Nothing was more natural than that these things should be the other things that they absolutely were not.

Of the positive identity of the apparition I would assure myself as soon as the small clock of my courage should have ticked out the right second; meanwhile, with an effort that was already sharp enough, I transferred my eyes straight to little Flora, who, at the moment, was about ten yards away. My heart had stood still for an instant with the wonder and terror of the question whether she too would see; and I held my breath while I waited for what a cry from her, what some sudden innocent sign either of interest or of alarm, would tell me. I waited, but nothing came; then, in the first place—and there is something more dire in this, I feel, than in anything I have to relate—I was determined by a sense that, within a minute, all sounds from her had previously dropped; and, in the second, by the circumstance that, also within the minute, she had, in her play, turned her back to the water. This was her attitude when I at last looked at her—looked with the confirmed conviction that we were still, together, under direct personal notice. She had picked up a small flat piece of wood, which happened to have in it a little hole that had evidently suggested to her the idea of sticking in another fragment that might figure as a mast and make the thing a boat. This second morsel, as I watched her, she was very markedly and intently attempting to tighten in its place. My apprehension of what she was doing sustained me so that after some seconds I felt I was ready for more. Then I again shifted my eyes—I faced what I had to face.

VII

I got hold of Mrs. Grose as soon after this as I could; and I can give no intelligible account of how I fought out the interval. Yet I still hear myself cry as I fairly threw myself into her arms: "They know—it's too monstrous: they know, they know!"

"And what on earth——?" I felt her incredulity as she held me.

"Why, all that we know—and heaven knows what else besides!" Then, as she released me, I made it out to her, made it out perhaps only now with full coherency even to myself. "Two hours ago, in the garden"—I could scarce articulate—"Flora *saw!*"

Mrs. Grose took it as she might have taken a blow in the stomach. "She has told you?" she panted.

"Not a word—that's the horror. She kept it to herself! The child of eight, *that* child!" Unutterable still, for me, was the stupefaction of it.

Mrs. Grose, of course, could only gape the wider. "Then how do you know?"

"I was there—I saw with my eyes: saw that she was perfectly aware."

"Do you mean aware of *him*?"

"No—of *her*." I was conscious as I spoke that I looked prodigious things, for I got the slow reflection of them in my companion's face. "Another person—this time; but a figure of quite as unmistakable horror and evil: a woman in black, pale and dreadful—with such an air also, and such a face! —on the other side of the lake. I was there with the child—quiet for the hour; and in the midst of it she came."

"Came how—from where?"

"From where they come from! She just appeared and stood there—but not so near."

"And without coming nearer?"

"Oh, for the effect and the feeling, she might have been as close as you!"

My friend, with an odd impulse, fell back a step. "Was she someone you've never seen?"

"Yes. But someone the child has. Someone *you* have." Then, to show how I had thought it all out: "My predecessor—the one who died."

"Miss Jessel?"

"Miss Jessel. You don't believe me?" I pressed.

She turned right and left in her distress. "How can you be sure?"

This drew from me, in the state of my nerves, a flash of impatience. "Then ask Flora—*she's* sure!" But I had no sooner spoken than I caught myself up. "No, for God's sake, *don't!* She'll say she isn't—she'll lie!"

Mrs. Grose was not too bewildered instinctively to protest. "Ah, how *can* you?"

"Because I'm clear. Flora doesn't want me to know."

"It's only then to spare you."

"No, no—there are depths, depths! The more I go over it, the more I see in it, and the more I see in it, the more I fear. I don't know what I *don't* see—what I *don't* fear!"

Mrs. Grose tried to keep up with me. "You mean you're afraid of seeing her again?"

"Oh, no; that's nothing—now!" Then I explained. "It's of *not* seeing her."

But my companion only looked wan. "I don't understand you."

"Why, it's that the child may keep it up—and that the child assuredly *will*—without my knowing it."

At the image of this possibility Mrs. Grose for a moment collapsed, yet presently to pull herself together again, as if from the positive force of the sense of what, should we yield an inch, there would really be to give way to. "Dear, dear—we must keep our heads! And after all, if she doesn't mind it—!" She even tried a grim joke. "Perhaps she likes it!"

"Likes *such* things—a scrap of an infant!"

"Isn't it just a proof of her blessed innocence?" my friend bravely inquired.

She brought me, for the instant, almost round. "Oh, we must clutch at *that*—we must cling to it! If it isn't a proof of what you say, it's a proof of—God knows what! For the woman's a horror of horrors."

Mrs. Grose, at this, fixed her eyes a minute on the ground; then at last raising them, "Tell me how you know," she said.

"Then you admit it's what she was?" I cried.

"Tell me how you know," my friend simply repeated.

"Know? By seeing her! By the way she looked."

"At you, do you mean—so wickedly?"

"Dear me, no—I could have borne that. She gave me never a glance. She only fixed the child."

Mrs. Grose tried to see it. "Fixed her?"

"Ah, with such awful eyes!"

She stared at mine as if they might really have resembled them. "Do you mean of dislike?"

"God help us, no. Of something much worse."

"Worse than dislike?"—this left her indeed at a loss.

"With a determination—indescribable. With a kind of fury of intention."

I made her turn pale. "Intention?"

"To get hold of her." Mrs. Grose—her eyes just lingering on mine—gave a shudder and walked to the window; and while she stood there looking out I completed my statement. "*That's* what Flora knows."

After a little she turned round. "The person was in black, you say?"

"In mourning—rather poor, almost shabby. But — yes — with extraordinary beauty." I now recognized to what I had at last, stroke by stroke, brought the victim of my confidence, for she quite visibly weighed this. "Oh, handsome—very, very," I insisted; "wonderfully handsome. But infamous."

She slowly came back to me. "Miss Jessel—*was* infamous." She once more took my hand in both her own, holding it as tight as if to fortify me against the increase of alarm I might draw from this disclosure. "They were both infamous," she finally said.

So, for a little, we faced it once more together; and I found absolutely a degree of help in seeing it now so straight. "I appreciate," I said, "the great decency of your not having hitherto spoken; but the time has certainly come to give me the whole thing." She appeared to assent to this, but still only in silence; seeing which I went on: "I must have it now. Of what did she die? Come, there was something between them."

"There was everything."

"In spite of the difference——?"

"Oh, of their rank, their condition"—she brought it woefully out. "*She* was a lady."

I turned it over; I again saw. "Yes—she was a lady."

"And he so dreadfully below," said Mrs. Grose.

I felt that I doubtless needn't press too hard, in such company, on the place of a servant in the scale; but there was nothing to prevent an acceptance of my companion's own measure of my predecessor's abasement. There was a way to deal with that, and I dealt; the more readily for my full vision—on the evidence—of our employer's late clever, good-looking "own" man; impudent, assured, spoiled, depraved. "The fellow was a hound."

Mrs. Grose considered as if it were perhaps a little a case for a sense of shades. "I've never seen one like him. He did what he wished."

"With *her?*"

"With them all."

It was as if now in my friend's own eyes Miss Jessel had again appeared. I seemed at any rate, for an instant, to see their evocation of her as distinctly as I had seen her by the pond; and I brought out with decision: "It must have been also what *she* wished!"

Mrs. Grose's face signified that it had been indeed, but she said at the same time: "Poor woman—she paid for it!"

"Then you do know what she died of?" I asked.

"No—I know nothing. I wanted not to know; I was glad enough I didn't; and I thanked heaven she was well out of this!"

"Yet you had, then, your idea——"

"Of her real reason for leaving? Oh, yes—as to that. She couldn't have stayed. Fancy it here—for a governess! And afterward I imagined—and I still imagine. And what I imagine is dreadful."

"Not so dreadful as what *I* do," I replied; on which I must have shown her—as I was indeed but too conscious—a front of miserable defeat. It brought out again all her compassion for me, and at the renewed touch of her kindness my power to resist broke down. I burst, as I had, the other time, made her burst, into tears; she took me to her motherly breast, and my lamentation overflowed. "I don't do it!" I sobbed in despair; "I don't save or shield them! It's far worse than I dreamed—they're lost!"

VIII

What I had said to Mrs. Grose was true enough: there were in the matter I had put before her depths and possibilities that I lacked resolution to sound; so that when we met once more in the wonder of it we were of a common mind about the duty of resistance to extravagant fancies. We were to keep our heads if we should keep nothing else—difficult indeed as that might be in the face of what, in our prodigious experience, was least to be questioned. Late that night, while the house slept, we had another talk in my room, when she went all the way with me as to its being beyond doubt that I had seen exactly what I had seen. To hold her perfectly in the pinch of that, I found I had only to ask her how, if I had "made it up," I came to be able to give, of each of the persons appearing to me, a picture disclosing, to the last detail, their special marks —a portrait on the exhibition of which she had instantly recognized and named them. She wished of course—small blame to her! —to sink the whole subject; and I was quick to assure her that my own interest in it had now violently taken the form of a search for the way to escape from it. I encountered her on the ground of a probability that with recurrence—for recurrence we took for granted—I should get used to my danger, distinctly professing that my personal exposure had suddenly become the least of my discomforts. It was my new suspicion that was intolerable; and yet even to this complication the later hours of the day had brought a little ease.

On leaving her, after my first outbreak, I had of course returned to my pupils, associating the right remedy for my dismay with that sense of their charm which I had already found to be a thing I could positively cultivate and which had never failed me yet. I had simply, in other words, plunged afresh into Flora's special society and there become aware—it was almost a luxury!—that she could put her little conscious hand straight upon the spot that ached. She had looked at me in sweet speculation and then had accused me to my face of having "cried." I had supposed I had brushed away the ugly signs: but I could literally—for the time, at all events—rejoice, under this fathomless charity, that they had not entirely disappeared. To gaze into the depths of blue of the child's eyes and pronounce their loveliness a trick of premature cunning was to be guilty of a cynicism in preference to which I naturally preferred to abjure my judgment and, so far as might be, my agitation. I couldn't abjure for merely wanting to, but I could repeat to Mrs. Grose—as I did there, over and over, in the small hours—that with their voices in the air, their pressure on one's heart, and their fragrant faces against one's cheek, everything fell to the ground but their incapacity and their beauty. It was a pity that, somehow, to settle this once for all, I had equally to re-enumerate the signs of subtlety that, in the afternoon, by the lake, had made a miracle of my show of self-possession. It was a pity to be obliged to reinvestigate the certitude of the moment itself and repeat how it had come to me as a revelation that the inconceivable communion I then surprised was a matter, for either party, of habit. It was a pity that I should have had to quaver out again the reasons for my not having, in my delusion, so much as questioned that the little girl saw our visitant even as I actually saw Mrs. Grose herself, and that she wanted, by just so much as she did thus see, to make me suppose she didn't, and at the same time, without showing anything, arrive at a guess as to whether I myself did! It was a pity that I needed once more to describe the portentous little activity by which she sought to divert my attention—the perceptible increase of movement, the greater intensity of play, the singing, the gabbling of nonsense, and the invitation to romp.

Yet if I had not indulged, to prove there was nothing in it, in this review, I should have missed the two or three dim elements of comfort that still remained to me. I should not for instance have been able to asseverate to my friend that I was certain—which was so much to the good— that *I* at least had not betrayed myself. I should not have been prompted, by stress of need, by desperation of mind—I scarce know what to call it—to invoke such further aid to intelligence as might spring from pushing my colleague fairly to the wall. She had told me, bit by bit, under pressure, a great deal; but a small shifty spot on the wrong side of it all still sometimes brushed my brow like the wing of a bat; and I remember how on this occasion—for the sleeping house and the concentration alike of our danger and our watch seemed to help—I felt the importance of giving the last jerk to the curtain. "I don't believe anything so horrible," I recollect saying; "no, let us put it definitely, my dear, that I don't. But if I did, you know, there's a thing I should require now, just without sparing you the least bit more—oh, not a scrap, come! —to get out of you. What was it you had in mind when, in our distress, before Miles came back, over the letter from his school, you said, under my insistence, that you didn't pretend for him that he had not literally ever been 'bad'? He has *not* literally 'ever,' in these weeks that I myself have lived with him and so closely watched him; he has been an imperturbable little prodigy of delightful, lovable goodness. Therefore you might perfectly have made the claim for him if you had not, as it happened, seen an exception to take. What was your exception, and to what passage in your personal observation of him did you refer?"

It was a dreadfully austere inquiry, but levity was not our note, and, at any rate, before the gray dawn admonished us to separate I had got my answer. What my friend had had in mind proved to be immensely to the purpose. It was neither more nor less than the circumstance that for a period of several months Quint and the boy had been perpetually together. It was in fact the very appropriate truth that she had ventured to criticize the propriety, to hint at the incongruity, of so close an alliance, and even to go so far on the subject as a frank overture to Miss Jessel. Miss Jessel had, with a most strange manner, requested her to mind her business, and the good woman had, on this, directly approached little Miles. What she had said to him, since I pressed, was that *she* liked to see young gentlemen not forget their station.

I pressed again, of course, at this. "You reminded him that Quint was only a base menial?"

"As you might say! And it was his answer, for one thing, that was bad."

"And for another thing?" I waited. "He repeated your words to Quint?"

"No, not that. It's just what he *wouldn't!*" she could still impress upon me. "I was sure, at any rate," she added, "that he didn't. But he denied certain occasions."

"What occasions?"

"When they had been about together quite as if Quint were his tutor—and a very grand one—and Miss Jessel only for the little lady. When he had gone off with the fellow, I mean, and spent hours with him."

"He then prevaricated about it—he said he hadn't?" Her assent was clear enough to cause me to add in a moment: "I see. He lied."

"Oh!" Mrs. Grose mumbled. This was a suggestion that it didn't matter; which indeed she backed up by a further remark. "You see, after all, Miss Jessel didn't mind. She didn't forbid him."

I considered. "Did he put that to you as a justification?"

At this she dropped again. "No, he never spoke of it."

"Never mentioned her in connection with Quint?"

She saw, visibly flushing, where I was coming out. "Well, he didn't show anything. He denied," she repeated; "he denied."

Lord, how I pressed her now! "So that you could see he knew what was between the two wretches?"

"I don't know—I don't know!" the poor woman groaned.

"You do know, you dear thing," I replied; "only you haven't my dreadful boldness of mind, and you keep back, out of timidity and modesty and delicacy, even the impression that, in the past, when you had, without my aid, to flounder about in silence, most of all made you miserable. But I shall get it out of you yet! There was something in the boy that suggested to you," I continued, "that he covered and concealed their relation."

"Oh, he couldn't prevent——"

"Your learning the truth? I daresay! But, heavens," I fell, with vehemence, athinking, "what it shows that they must, to that extent, have succeeded in making of him!"

"Ah, nothing that's not nice *now!*" Mrs. Grose lugubriously pleaded.

"I don't wonder you looked queer," I persisted, "when I mentioned to you the letter from his school!"

"I doubt if I looked as queer as you!" she retorted with homely force. "And if he was so bad then as that comes to, how is he such an angel now?"

"Yes, indeed—and if he was a fiend at school! How, how, how? Well," I said in my torment, "you must put it to me again, but I shall not be able to tell you for some days. Only, put it to me again!" I cried in a way that made my friend stare. "There are directions in which I must not for the present let myself go." Meanwhile I returned to her first example—the one to which she had just previously referred—of the boy's happy capacity for an occasional slip. "If Quint—on your remonstrance at the time you speak of—was a base menial, one of the things Miles said to you, I find myself guessing, was that you were another." Again her admission was so adequate that I continued: "And you forgave him that?"

"Wouldn't you?"

"Oh, yes!" And we exchanged there, in the stillness, a sound of the oddest amusement. Then I went on: "At all events, while he was with the man——"

"Miss Flora was with the woman. It suited them all."

It suited me, too, I felt, only too well; by which I mean that it suited exactly the particularly deadly view I was in the very act of forbidding myself to entertain. But I so far succeeded in checking the expression of this view that I will throw, just here, no further light on it than may be offered by the mention of my final observation to Mrs. Grose. "His having lied and been impudent are, I confess, less engaging specimens than I had hoped to have from you of the outbreak in him of the little natural man. Still," I mused, "they must do, for they make me feel more than ever that I must watch."

It made me blush, the next minute, to see in my friend's face how much more unreservedly she had forgiven him than her anecdote struck me as presenting to my own tenderness an occasion for doing. This came out when, at the schoolroom door, she quitted me. "Surely you don't accuse him——"

"Of carrying on an intercourse that he conceals from me? Ah, remember that, until further evidence, I now accuse nobody." Then, before shutting her out to go, by another passage, to her own place, "I must just wait," I wound up.

IX

I waited and waited, and the days, as they elapsed, took something from my consternation. A very few of them, in fact, passing, in constant sight of my pupils, without a fresh incident, sufficed to give to grievous fancies and even to odious memories a kind of brush of the sponge. I have spoken of the surrender to their extraordinary childish grace as a thing I could actively cultivate, and it may be imagined if I neglected now to address myself to this source for whatever it would yield. Stranger than I can express, certainly, was the effort to struggle against my new lights; it would doubtless have been, however, a greater tension still had it not been so frequently successful. I used to wonder how my little charges could help guessing that I thought strange things about them; and the circumstance that these things only made them more interesting was not by itself a direct aid to keeping them in the dark. I trembled lest they should see that they were so immensely more interesting. Putting things at the worst, at all events, as in meditation I so often did, any clouding of their innocence could only be —blameless and foredoomed as they were —a reason the more for taking risks. There were moments when, by an irresistible impulse, I found myself catching them up and pressing them to my heart. As soon as I had done so I used to say to myself: "What will they think of that? Doesn't it betray too much?" It would have been easy to get into a sad, wild tangle about how much I might betray; but the real account, I feel, of the hours of peace that I could still enjoy was that the immediate charm of my companions was a beguilement still effective even under the shadow of the possibility that it was studied. For if it occurred to me that I might occasionally excite suspicion by the little outbreaks of my sharper passion for them, so too I remember wondering if I mightn't see a queerness in the traceable increase of their own demonstrations.

They were at this period extravagantly

and preternaturally fond of me; which, after all, I could reflect, was no more than a graceful response in children perpetually bowed over and hugged. The homage of which they were so lavish succeeded, in truth, for my nerves, quite as well as if I never appeared to myself, as I may say, literally to catch them at a purpose in it. They had never, I think, wanted to do so many things for their poor protectress; I mean—though they got their lessons better and better, which was naturally what would please her most—in the way of diverting, entertaining, surprising her; reading her passages, telling her stories, acting her charades, pouncing out at her, in disguises, as animals and historical characters, and above all astonishing her by the "pieces" they had secretly got by heart and could interminably recite. I should never get to the bottom—were I to let myself go even now—of the prodigious private commentary, all under still more private correction, with which, in these days, I overscored their full hours. They had shown me from the first a facility for everything, a general faculty which, taking a fresh start, achieved remarkable flights. They got their little tasks as if they loved them, and indulged, from the mere exuberance of the gift, in the most unimposed little miracles of memory. They not only popped out at me as tigers and as Romans, but as Shakespeareans, astronomers, and navigators. This was so singularly the case that it had presumably much to do with the fact as to which, at the present day, I am at a loss for a different explanation: I allude to my unnatural composure on the subject of another school for Miles. What I remember is that I was content not, for the time, to open the question, and that contentment must have sprung from the sense of his perpetually striking show of cleverness. He was too clever for a bad governess, for a parson's daughter, to spoil; and the strangest if not the brightest thread in the pensive embroidery I just spoke of was the impression I might have got, if I had dared to work it out, that he was under some influence operating in his small intellectual life as a tremendous incitement.

If it was easy to reflect, however, that such a boy could postpone school, it was at least as marked that for such a boy to have been "kicked out" by a schoolmaster was a mystification without end. Let me add that in their company now—and I was careful almost never to be out of it—I could follow no scent very far. We lived in a cloud of music and love and success and private theatricals. The musical sense in each of the children was of the quickest, but the elder in especial had a marvelous knack of catching and repeating. The schoolroom piano broke into all gruesome fancies; and when that failed there were confabulations in corners, with a sequel of one of them going out in the highest spirits in order to "come in" as something new. I had had brothers myself, and it was no revelation to me that little girls could be slavish idolaters of little boys. What surpassed everything was that there was a little boy in the world who could have for the inferior age, sex, and intelligence so fine a consideration. They were extraordinarily at one, and to say that they never either quarreled or complained is to make the note of praise coarse for their quality of sweetness. Sometimes, indeed, when I dropped into coarseness, I perhaps came across traces of little understandings between them by which one of them should keep me occupied while the other slipped away. There is a naïve side, I suppose, in all diplomacy; but if my pupils practiced upon me, it was surely with the minimum of grossness. It was all in the other quarter that, after a lull, the grossness broke out.

I find that I really hang back; but I must take my plunge. In going on with the record of what was hideous at Bly, I not only challenge the most liberal faith—for which I little care; but—and this is another matter—I renew what I myself suffered, I again push my way through it to the end. There came suddenly an hour after which, as I look back, the affair seems to me to have been all pure suffering; but I have at least reached the heart of it, and the straightest road out is doubtless to advance. One evening—with nothing to lead up or to prepare it—I felt the cold touch of the impression that had breathed on me the night of my arrival and which, much lighter then, as I have mentioned, I should probably have made little of in memory had my subsequent sojourn been less agitated. I had not gone to bed; I sat reading by a couple of candles. There was a roomful of old books at Bly—last-century fiction, some of it, which, to the extent of a distinctly deprecated renown, but never to so much as that of a stray specimen, had reached the sequestered home and appealed to the unavowed curiosity of my youth. I remember that the book I had in my hand was Fielding's *Amelia*; also that I was wholly awake. I recall further both a general conviction that it was horribly late and a particular objection to looking at my watch. I figure, finally, that the white curtain draping, in the fashion of those days, the head of Flora's little bed, shrouded, as I had assured myself long before, the perfection of childish rest. I recollect in short that, though I was deeply interested in my author, I found myself, at the turn of a page and with his spell all scattered, looking straight up from him and hard at the door of my room. There was a moment during which I listened, reminded of the faint sense I had had, the first night, of there being something undefinably astir in the house, and noted the soft breath of the open casement just move the half-drawn blind. Then, with all the marks of a deliberation that must have seemed magnificent had there been anyone to admire it, I laid down my book, rose to my feet, and taking a candle, went straight out of the room and, from the passage, on which my light made little impression, noiselessly closed and locked the door.

I can say now neither what determined nor what guided me, but I went straight along the lobby, holding my candle high, till I came within sight of the tall window that presided over the great turn of the staircase. At this point I precipitately found myself aware of three things. They were practically simultaneous, yet they had flashes of succession. My candle, under a bold flourish, went out, and I perceived, by the uncovered window, that the yielding dusk of earliest morning rendered it unnecessary. Without it, the next instant, I saw that there was someone on the stair. I speak of sequences, but I required no lapse of seconds to stiffen myself for a third encounter with Quint. The apparition had reached the landing halfway up and was therefore on the spot nearest the window, where at sight of me, it stopped short and fixed me exactly as it had fixed me from the tower and from the garden. He knew me as well as I knew him; and so, in the cold, faint twilight, with a glimmer in the high glass and another on the polish of the oak stair below, we faced each other in our common intensity. He was absolutely, on the occasion, a living, detestable, dangerous presence. But that was not the wonder of wonders; I reserve this distinction for quite another circumstance: the circumstance that dread had unmistakably quitted me and that there was nothing in me there that didn't meet and measure him.

I had plenty of anguish after that extraordinary moment, but I had, thank God, no terror. And he knew I had not—I found myself at the end of an instant magnificently aware of this. I felt, in a fierce rigor of confidence, that if I stood my ground a minute I should cease—for the time, at least—to have him to reckon with; and during the minute, accordingly, the thing was as human and hideous as a real interview: hideous just because it was human, as human as to have met alone, in the small hours, in a sleeping house, some enemy, some adventurer, some criminal. It was the dead silence of our long gaze at such close quarters that gave the whole horror, huge as it was, its only note of the unnatural. If I had met a murderer in such a place and at such an hour, we still at least would have spoken. Something would have passed, in life, between us; if nothing had passed, one of us would have moved. The moment was so prolonged that it would have taken but little more to make me doubt if even I were in life. I can't express what followed it save by saying that the silence itself—which was indeed in a manner an attestation of my strength—became the element into which I saw the figure disappear; in which I definitely saw it turn as I might have seen the low wretch to which it had once belonged on receipt of an order, and pass, with my eyes on the villainous back that no hunch could have more disfigured, straight down the staircase and into the darkness in which the next bend was lost.

X

I remained awhile at the top of the stair, but with the effect presently of understanding that when my visitor had gone, he had gone: then I returned to my room. The foremost thing I saw there by the light of the candle I had left burning was that Flora's little bed was empty; and on this I caught my breath with all the terror that, five minutes before, I had been able to resist. I dashed at the place in which I had left her lying and over which (for the small silk counterpane and the sheets were disarranged) the white curtains had been deceivingly pulled forward; then my step, to my unutterable relief, produced an answering sound: I perceived an agitation of the window blind, and the child, ducking down, emerged rosily from the other side of it. She stood there in so much of her candor and so little of her nightgown, with her pink bare feet and the golden glow of her curls. She looked intensely grave, and I had never had such a sense of losing an advantage acquired (the thrill of which had just been so prodigious) as on my consciousness that she addressed me with a reproach. "You naughty: where *have* you been?"—instead of challenging her own irregularity I found myself arraigned and explaining. She herself explained, for that matter, with the loveliest, eagerest simplicity. She had known suddenly, as she lay there, that I was out of the room, and had jumped up to see what had become of me. I had dropped, with the joy of her reappearance, back into my chair—feeling then, and then only, a little faint; and she had pattered straight over to me, thrown herself upon my knee, given herself to be held with the flame of the candle full in the wonderful little face that was still flushed with sleep. I remember closing my eyes an instant, yieldingly, consciously, as before the excess of something beautiful that shone out of the blue of her own. "You were looking for me out of the window?" I said. "You thought I might be walking in the grounds?"

"Well, you know, I thought someone was"—she never blanched as she smiled out that at me.

Oh, how I looked at her now! "And did you see anyone?"

"Ah, *no!*" she returned, almost with the full privilege of childish inconsequence, resentfully, though with a long sweetness in her little drawl of the negative.

At that moment, in the state of my nerves, I absolutely believed she lied; and if I once more closed my eyes it was before the dazzle of the three or four possible ways in which I might take this up. One of these, for a moment, tempted me with such singular intensity that, to withstand it, I must have gripped my little girl with a spasm that, wonderfully, she submitted to without a cry or a sign of fright. Why not break out at her on the spot and have it all over?—give it to her straight in her lovely little lighted face? "You see, you see, you *know* that you do and that you already quite suspect I believe it; therefore, why not frankly confess it to me, so that we may at least live with it together and learn perhaps, in the strangeness of our fate, where we are and what it means?" This solicitation dropped, alas, as it came: if I could immediately have succumbed to it I might have spared myself—well, you'll see what. Instead of succumbing I sprang again to my feet, looked at her bed, and took a helpless middle way. "Why did you pull the curtain over the place to make me think you were still there?"

Flora luminously considered; after which, with her little divine smile: "Because I don't like to frighten you!"

"But if I had, by your idea, gone out——?"

She absolutely declined to be puzzled; she turned her eyes to the flame of the candle as if the question were as irrelevant, or at any rate as impersonal, as Mrs. Marcet or nine-times-nine. "Oh, but you know," she quite adequately answered, "that you might come back, you dear, and that you *have!*" And after a little, when she had got into bed, I had, for a long time, by almost sitting on her to hold her hand, to prove that I recognized the pertinence of my return.

You may imagine the general complexion, from that moment, of my nights. I repeatedly sat up till I didn't know when; I selected moments when my roommate unmistakably slept, and, stealing out, took noiseless turns in the passage and even pushed as far as to where I had last met Quint. But I never met him there again; and I may as well say at once that I on no other occasion saw him in the house. I just missed, on the staircase, on the other hand, a different adventure. Looking down it from the top I once recognized the presence of a woman seated on one of the lower steps with her back presented to me, her body half-bowed and her head, in an attitude of woe, in her hands. I had been there but an instant, however, when she vanished without looking round at me. I knew, nonetheless, exactly what dreadful face she had to show; and I wondered whether, if instead of being above I had been below, I should have had, for going up, the same nerve I had lately shown Quint. Well, there continued to be plenty of chance for nerve. On the eleventh night after my latest encounter with that gentleman—they were all numbered now—I had an alarm that perilously skirted it and that indeed, from the particular quality of its unexpectedness, proved quite my sharpest shock. It was precisely the first night during this series that, weary with watching, I had felt that I might again without laxity lay myself down at my old hour. I slept immediately and, as I afterward knew till about one o'clock; but when I woke it was to sit straight up, as completely roused as if a hand had shook me. I had left a light burning, but it was now out, and I felt an instant certainty that Flora had extinguished it. This brought me to my feet and straight, in the darkness, to her bed, which I found she had left. A glance at the window enlightened me further, and the striking of a match completed the picture.

The child had again got up—this time blowing out the taper, and had again, for some purpose of observation or response, squeezed in behind the blind and was peering out into the night. That she now saw—as she had not, I had satisfied myself, the previous time—was proved to me by the fact that she was disturbed neither by my reillumination nor by the haste I made to get into slippers and into a wrap. Hidden, protected, absorbed, she evidently rested on the sill—the casement opened forward—and gave herself up. There was a great still moon to help her, and this fact had counted in my quick decision. She was face to face with the apparition we had met at the lake, and could now communicate with it as she had not then been able to do. What I, on my side, had to care for was, without disturbing her, to reach, from the corridor, some other window in the same quarter. I got to the door without her hearing me; I got out of it, closed it, and listened, from the other side, for some sound from her. While I stood in the passage I had my eyes on her brother's door, which was but ten steps off and which, indescribably, produced in me a renewal of the strange impulse that I lately spoke of as my temptation. What if I should go straight in and march to *his* window?—what if, by risking to his boyish bewilderment a revelation of my motive, I should throw across the rest of the mystery the long halter of my boldness?

This thought held me sufficiently to make me cross to his threshold and pause again. I preternaturally listened; I figured to myself what might portentously be; I wondered if his bed were also empty and he too were secretly at watch. It was a deep, soundless minute, at the end of which my impulse failed. He was quiet; he might be innocent; the risk was hideous; I turned away. There was a figure in the grounds—a figure prowling for a sight, the visitor with whom Flora was engaged; but it was not the visitor most concerned with my boy. I hesitated afresh, but on other grounds and only a few seconds; then I had made my choice. There were empty rooms at Bly, and it was only a question of choosing the right one. The right one suddenly presented itself to me as the lower one—though high above the garden—in the solid corner of the house that I have spoken of as the old tower. This was a large, square chamber, arranged with some state as a bedroom, the extravagant size of which made it so inconvenient that it had not for years, though kept by Mrs. Grose in exemplary order, been occupied. I had often admired it and I knew my way about in it; I had only, after just faltering at the first chill gloom of its disuse, to pass across it and unbolt as quietly as I could one of the shutters. Achieving this transit, I uncovered the glass without a sound and, applying my face to the pane, was able, the darkness without being much less than within, to see that I commanded the right direction. Then I saw something more. The moon made the night extraordinarily penetrable and showed me on the lawn a person, diminished by distance, who stood there motionless and as if fascinated, looking up to where I had appeared—looking, that is, not so much straight at me as at something that was apparently above me. There was clearly another person above me—there was a person on the tower; but the presence on the lawn was not in the least what I had conceived and had confidently hurried to meet. The presence on the lawn—I felt sick as I made it out—was poor little Miles himself.

XI

It was not till late next day that I spoke to Mrs. Grose; the rigor with which I kept my pupils in sight making it often difficult to meet her privately, and the more as we each felt the importance of not provoking —on the part of the servants quite as much as on that of the children—any suspicion of a secret flurry or of a discussion of mysteries. I drew a great security in this particular from her mere smooth aspect. There was nothing in her fresh face to pass on to others my horrible confidences. She believed me, I was sure, absolutely: if she hadn't I don't know what would have become of me, for I couldn't have borne the business alone. But she was a magnificent monument to the blessing of a want of imagination, and if she could see in our little charges nothing but their beauty and amiability, their happiness and cleverness, she had no direct communication with the sources of my trouble. If they had been at all visibly blighted or battered, she would doubtless have grown, on tracing it back, haggard enough to match them; as matters stood, however, I could feel her, when she surveyed them, with her large white arms folded and the habit of serenity in all her look, thank the Lord's mercy that if they were ruined the pieces would still serve. Flights of fancy gave place, in her mind, to a steady fireside glow, and I had already begun to perceive how, with the development of the conviction that—as time went on without a public accident—our young things could, after all, look out for themselves, she addressed her greatest solicitude to the sad case presented by their instructress. That, for myself, was a sound simplification: I could engage that, to the world, my face should tell no tales, but it would have been, in the conditions, an immense added strain to find myself anxious about hers.

At the hour I now speak of she had joined me, under pressure, on the terrace, where, with the lapse of the season, the afternoon sun was now agreeable; and we sat there together while, before us, at a distance, but within call if we wished, the children strolled to and fro in one of their most manageable moods. They moved slowly, in unison, below us, over the lawn, the boy, as they went, reading aloud from a storybook and passing his arm round his sister to keep her quite in touch. Mrs. Grose watched them with positive placidity; then I caught the suppressed intellectual creak with which she conscientiously turned to take from me a view of the back of the tapestry. I had made her a receptacle of lurid things, but there was an odd recognition of my superiority—my accomplishments and my function—in her patience under my pain. She offered her mind to my disclosures as, had I wished to mix a witch's broth and proposed it with assurance, she would have held out a large clean saucepan. This had become thoroughly her attitude by the time that, in my recital of the events of the night, I reached the point of what Miles had said to me when, after seeing him, at such a monstrous hour, almost on the very spot where he happened now to be, I had gone down to bring him in; choosing then, at the window, with a concentrated need of not alarming the house, rather that method than a signal more resonant. I had left her meanwhile in little doubt of my small hope of representing with success even to her actual sympathy my sense of the real splendor of the little inspiration with which, after I had got him into the house, the boy met my final articulate challenge. As soon as I appeared in the moonlight on the terrace, he had come to me as straight as possible; on which I had taken his hand without a word and led him, through the dark spaces, up the staircase where Quint had so hungrily hovered for him, along the lobby where I had listened and trembled, and so to his forsaken room.

Not a sound, on the way, had passed between us, and I had wondered—oh, how I had wondered!—if he were groping about in his little mind for something plausible and not too grotesque. It would tax his invention, certainly, and I felt, this time, over his real embarrassment, a curious thrill of triumph. It was a sharp trap for the inscrutable! He couldn't play any longer at innocence; so how the deuce would he get out of it? There beat in me indeed, with the passionate throb of this question, an equal dumb appeal as to how the deuce *I* should. I was confronted at last, as never yet, with all the risk attached even now to sounding my own horrid note. I remember in fact that as we pushed into his little chamber, where the bed had not been slept in at all and the window, uncovered to the moonlight, made the place so clear that there was no need of striking a match—I remember how I suddenly dropped, sank upon the edge of the bed from the force of the idea that he must know how he really, as they say, "had" me. He could do what he liked, with all his cleverness to help him, so long as I should continue to defer to the old tradition of the criminality of those caretakers of the young who minister to superstitions and fears. He "had" me indeed, and in a cleft stick; for who would ever absolve me, who would consent that I should go unhung, if, by the faintest tremor of an overture, I were the first to introduce into our perfect intercourse an element so dire? No, no: it was useless to attempt to convey to Mrs. Grose, just as it is scarcely less so to attempt to suggest here, how, in our short, stiff brush in the dark, he fairly shook me with admiration. I was of course thoroughly kind and merciful; never, never yet had I placed on his little shoulders hands of such tenderness as those with which, while I rested against the bed, I held him there well under fire. I had no alternative but, in form at least, to put it to him.

"You must tell me now—and all the truth. What did you go out for? What were you doing there?"

I can still see his wonderful smile, the whites of his beautiful eyes, and the uncovering of his little teeth shine to me in the dusk. "If I tell you why, will you understand?" My heart, at this, leaped into my mouth. *Would* he tell me why? I found no sound on my lips to press it, and I was aware of replying only with a vague, repeated, grimacing nod. He was gentleness itself, and while I wagged my head at him he stood there more than ever a little fairy prince. It was his brightness indeed that gave me a respite. Would it be so great if he were really going to tell me? "Well," he said at last, "just exactly in order that you should do this."

"Do what?"

"Think me—for a change—*bad!*" I shall never forget the sweetness and gaiety with which he brought out the word, nor how, on top of it, he bent forward and kissed me. It was practically the end of everything. I met his kiss and I had to make, while I folded him for a minute in my arms, the most stupendous effort not to cry. He had given exactly the account of himself that permitted least of my going behind it, and it was only with the effect of confirming my acceptance of it that, as I presently glanced about the room, I could say—

"Then you didn't undress at all?"

He fairly glittered in the gloom. "Not at all. I sat up and read."

"And when did you go down?"

"At midnight. When I'm bad I *am* bad!"

"I see, I see—it's charming. But how could you be sure I would know it?"

"Oh, I arranged that with Flora." His answers rang out with a readiness! "She was to get up and look out."

"Which is what she did do." It was I who fell into the trap!

"So she disturbed you, and to see what she was looking at, you also looked—you saw."

"While you," I concurred, "caught your death in the night air!"

He literally bloomed so from this exploit that he could afford radiantly to assent. "How otherwise should I have been bad enough?" he asked. Then, after another embrace, the incident and our interview closed on my recognition of all the reserves of goodness that, for his joke, he had been able to draw upon.

XII

The particular impression I had received proved in the morning light, I repeat, not quite successfully presentable to Mrs. Grose, though I reinforced it with the mention of still another remark that he had made before we separated. "It all lies in half a dozen words," I said to her, "words that really settle the matter. 'Think, you know, what I *might* do!' He threw that off to show me how good he is. He knows down to the ground what he 'might' do. That's what he gave them a taste of at school."

"Lord, you do change!" cried my friend.

"I don't change—I simply make it out. The four, depend upon it, perpetually meet. If on either of these last nights you had been with either child, you would clearly have understood. The more I've watched and waited the more I've felt that if there were nothing else to make it sure it would be made so by the systematic silence of each. Never, by a slip of the tongue, have they so much as alluded to either of their old friends, any more than Miles has alluded to his expulsion. Oh, yes, we may sit here and look at them, and they may show off to us there to their fill; but even while they pretend to be lost in their fairytale they're steeped in their vision of the dead restored. He's not reading to her," I declared; "they're talking of *them*—they're talking horrors! I go on, I know, as if I were crazy; and it's a wonder I'm not. What I've seen would have made you so; but it has only made me more lucid, made me get hold of still other things."

My lucidity must have seemed awful, but the charming creatures who were victims of it, passing and repassing in their interlocked sweetness, gave my colleague something to hold on by; and I felt how tight she held as, without stirring in the breath of my passion, she covered them still with her eyes. "Of what other things have you got hold?"

"Why, of the very things that have delighted, fascinated, and yet, at bottom, as I now so strangely see, mystified and troubled me. Their more than earthly beauty, their absolutely unnatural goodness. It's a game," I went on; "it's a policy and a fraud!"

"On the part of little darlings——?"

"As yet mere lovely babies? Yes, mad as that seems!" The very act of bringing it out really helped me to trace it—follow it all up and piece it all together. "They haven't been good—they've only been absent. It has been easy to live with them, because they're simply leading a life of their own. They're not mine—they're not ours. They're his and they're hers!"

"Quint's and that woman's?"

"Quint's and that woman's. They want to get to them."

Oh, how, at this, poor Mrs. Grose appeared to study them! "But for what?"

"For the love of all the evil that, in those dreadful days, the pair put into them. And to ply them with that evil still, to keep up the work of demons, is what brings the others back."

"Laws!" said my friend under her breath. The exclamation was homely, but it revealed a real acceptance of my further proof of what, in the bad time—for there had been a worse even than this!—must have occurred. There could have been no such justification for me as the plain assent of her experience to whatever depth of depravity I found credible in our brace of scoundrels. It was in obvious submission of memory that she brought out after a moment: "They were rascals! But what can they now do?" she pursued.

"Do?" I echoed so loud that Miles and Flora, as they passed at their distance, paused an instant in their walk and looked at us. "Don't they do enough?" I demanded in a lower tone, while the children, having smiled and nodded and kissed hands to us, resumed their exhibition. We were held by it a minute; then I answered: "They can destroy them!" At this my companion did turn, but the inquiry she launched was a silent one, the effect of which was to make me more explicit. "They don't know, as yet, quite how—but they're trying hard. They're seen only across, as it were, and beyond—in strange places and on high places, the top of towers, the roof of houses, the outside of windows, the further edge of pools; but there's a deep design, on either side, to shorten the distance and overcome the obstacle; and the success of the tempters is only a question of time. They've only to keep to their suggestions of danger."

"For the children to come?"

"And perish in the attempt!" Mrs. Grose slowly got up, and I scrupulously added: "Unless, of course, we can prevent!"

Standing there before me while I kept my seat, she visibly turned things over. "Their uncle must do the preventing. He must take them away."

"And who's to make him?"

She had been scanning the distance,

but she now dropped on me a foolish face. "You, miss."

"By writing to him that his house is poisoned and his little nephew and niece mad?"

"But if they are, miss?"

"And if I am myself, you mean? That's charming news to be sent him by a governess whose prime undertaking was to give him no worry."

Mrs. Grose considered, following the children again. "Yes, he do hate worry. That was the great reason——"

"Why those fiends took him in so long? No doubt, though his indifference must have been awful. As I'm not a fiend, at any rate, I shouldn't take him in."

My companion, after an instant and for all answer, sat down again and grasped my arm. "Make him at any rate come to you."

I stared, "To *me*?" I had a sudden fear of what she might do. " 'Him'?"

"He ought to *be* here—he ought to help."

I quickly rose, and I think I must have shown her a queerer face than ever yet. "You see me asking him for a visit?" No, with her eyes on my face she evidently couldn't. Instead of it even—as a woman reads another—she could see what I myself saw: his derision, his amusement, his contempt for the breakdown of my resignation at being left alone and for the fine machinery I had set in motion to attract his attention to my slighted charms. She didn't know —no one knew—how proud I had been to serve him and to stick to our terms; yet she nonetheless took the measure, I think, of the warning I now gave her. "If you should so lose your head as to appeal to him for me——"

She was really frightened. "Yes, miss?"

"I would leave, on the spot, both him and you."

XIII

It was all very well to join them, but speaking to them proved quite as much as ever an effort beyond my strength—offered, in close quarters, difficulties as insurmountable as before. This situation continued a month, and with new aggravations and particular notes, the note above all, sharper and sharper, of the small ironic consciousness on the part of my pupils. It was not, I am as sure today as I was sure then, my mere infernal imagination: it was absolutely traceable that they were aware of my predicament and that this strange relation made, in a manner, for a long time, the air in which we moved. I don't mean that they had their tongues in their cheeks or did anything vulgar, for that was not one of their dangers: I do mean, on the other hand, that the element of the unnamed and untouched became, between us, greater than any other, and that so much avoidance could not have been so successfully effected without a great deal of tacit arrangement. It was as if, at moments, we were perpetually coming into sight of subjects before which we must stop short, turning suddenly out of alleys that we perceived to be blind, closing with a little bang that made us look at each other —for, like all bangs, it was something louder than we had intended—the doors we had indiscreetly opened. All roads lead to Rome, and there were times when it might have struck us that almost every branch of study or subject of conversation skirted forbidden ground. Forbidden ground was the question of the return of the dead in general and of whatever, in especial, might survive, in memory, of the friends little children had lost. There were days when I could have sworn that one of them had, with a small invisible nudge, said to the other: "She thinks she'll do it this time—but she won't!" To "do it" would have been to indulge for instance—and for once in a way—in some direct reference to the lady who had prepared them for my discipline. They had a delightful endless appetite for passages in my own history, to which I had again and again treated them; they were in possession of everything that had ever happened to me, had had, with every circumstance the story of my smallest adventures and of those of my brothers and sisters and of the cat and the dog at home, as well as many particulars of the eccentric nature of my father, of the furniture and arrangement of our house, and of the conversation of the old women of our village. There were things enough, taking one with another, to chatter about, if one went very fast and knew by instinct when to go round. They pulled with an art of their own the strings of my invention and my memory; and nothing else perhaps, when I thought of such occasions afterward, gave me so the suspicion of being watched from under cover. It was in any case over my life, my past, and my friends alone that we could take anything like our ease—a state of affairs that led them sometimes without the least pertinence to break out into sociable reminders. I was invited—with no visible connection—to repeat afresh Goody Gosling's celebrated *mot* or to confirm the details already supplied as to the cleverness of the vicarage pony.

It was partly at such junctures as these and partly at quite different ones that, with the turn my matters had now taken, my predicament, as I have called it, grew most sensible. The fact that the days passed for me without another encounter ought, it would have appeared, to have done something toward soothing my nerves. Since the light brush, that second night on the upper landing, of the presence of a woman at the foot of the stair, I had seen nothing, whether in or out of the house, that one had better not have seen. There was many a corner round which I expected to have come upon Quint, and many a situation that, in a merely sinister way, would have favored the appearance of Miss Jessel. The summer had turned, the summer had gone; the autumn had dropped upon Bly and had blown out half our lights. The place, with its gray sky and withered garlands, its bared spaces and scattered dead leaves, was like a theater after the performance—all strewn with crumpled playbills. There were exactly states of the air, conditions of sound and of stillness, unspeakable impressions of the *kind* of ministering moment, that brought back to me, long enough to catch it, the feeling of the medium in which, that June evening out of doors, I had had my first sight of Quint, and in which, too, at those other instants, I had, after seeing him through the window, looked for him in vain in the circle of shrubbery. I recognized the signs, the portents— I recognized the moment, the spot. But they remained unaccompanied and empty, and I continued unmolested; if unmolested one could call a young woman whose sensibility had, in the most extraordinary fashion, not declined but deepened. I had said in my talk with Mrs. Grose on that horrid scene of Flora's by the lake—and had perplexed her by so saying—that it would from that moment distress me much more to lose my power than to keep it. I had then expressed what was vividly in my mind: the truth that, whether the children really saw or not—since, that is, it was not yet definitely proved—I greatly preferred, as a safeguard, the fullness of my own exposure. I was ready to know the very worst that was to be known. What I had then had an ugly glimpse of was that my eyes might be sealed just while theirs were most opened. Well, my eyes were sealed, it appeared, at present—a consummation for which it seemed blasphemous not to thank God. There was, alas, a difficulty about that: I would have thanked him with all my soul had I not had in a proportionate measure this conviction of the secret of my pupils.

How can I retrace today the strange steps of my obsession? There were times of our being together when I would have been ready to swear that, literally, in my presence, but with my direct sense of it closed, they had visitors who were known and were welcome. Then it was that, had I not been deterred by the very chance that such an injury might prove greater than the injury to be averted, my exultation would have broken out. "They're here, they're here, you little wretches," I would have cried, "and you can't deny it now!" The little wretches denied it with all the added volume of their sociability and their tenderness, in just the crystal depths of which—like the flash of a fish in a stream—the mockery of their advantage peeped up. The shock, in truth, had sunk into me still deeper than I knew on the night when, looking out to see either Quint or Miss Jessel under the stars, I had beheld the boy over whose rest I watched and who had immediately brought in with him—had straightway, there, turned it on me—the lovely upward look with which, from the battlements above me, the hideous apparition of Quint had played. If it was a question of a scare, my discovery on this occasion had scared me more than any other, and it was in the condition of nerves produced by it that I made my actual inductions. They harassed me so that sometimes, at odd moments, I shut myself up audibly to rehearse—it was at once a fantastic relief and a renewed despair—the manner in which I might come to the point. I approached it from one side and the other while, in my room, I flung myself about, but I always broke down in the monstrous utterance of names. As they died away on my lips, I said to myself that I should indeed help them to represent something infamous if, by pronouncing them, I should violate as rare a little case of instinctive delicacy as any schoolroom, probably, had ever known. When I said to myself: "They have the manners to be silent, and you, trusted as you are, the baseness to speak!" I felt myself crimson and I covered my face with my hands. After these secret scenes I chattered more than ever, going on volubly enough till one of our prodigious, palpable hushes occurred—I can call them nothing else—the strange, dizzy lift or swim (I try for terms!) into a stillness, a pause of all life, that had nothing to do with the more or less noise that at the moment we might be engaged in making and that I could hear through any deepened exhilaration or quickened recitation or louder strum of the piano. Then it was that the others, the outsiders, were there. Though they were not angels, they "passed," as the French say, causing me, while they stayed, to tremble with the fear of their addressing to their younger victims some yet more infernal message or more vivid image than they had thought good enough for myself.

What it was most impossible to get rid of was the cruel idea that, whatever I had seen, Miles and Flora saw more—things terrible and unguessable and that sprang from dreadful passages of intercourse in the past. Such things naturally left on the surface, for the time, a chill which we vociferously denied that we felt; and we had, all three, with repetition, got into such splendid training that we went, each time, almost automatically, to mark the close of the incident, through the very same movements. It was striking of the children, at all events, to kiss me inveterately with a kind of wild irrelevance and never to fail—one or the other—of the precious question that had helped us through many a peril. "When do you think he *will* come? Don't you think we *ought* to write?"—there was nothing like that inquiry, we found by experience, for carrying off an awkwardness. "He" of course was their uncle in Harley Street; and we lived in much profusion of theory that he might at any moment arrive to mingle in our circle. It was impossible to have given less encouragement than he had done to such a doctrine, but if we had not had the doctrine to fall back upon we should have deprived each other of some of our finest exhibitions. He never wrote to them—that may have been selfish, but it was a part of the flattery of his trust of me; for the way in which a man pays his highest tribute to a woman is apt to be but by the more festal celebration of one of the sacred laws of his comfort; and I held that I carried out the spirit of the pledge given not to appeal to him when I let my charges understand that their own letters were but charming literary exercises. They were too beautiful to be posted; I kept them myself; I have them all to this hour. This was a rule indeed which only added to the satiric effect of my being plied with the supposition that he might at any moment be among us. It was exactly as if my charges knew how almost more awkward than anything else that might be for me. There appears to me, moreover, as I look back, no note in all this more extraordinary than the mere fact that, in spite of my tension and of their triumph, I never lost patience with them. Adorable they must in truth have been, I now reflect, that I didn't in these days hate them! Would exasperation, however, if relief had longer been postponed, finally have betrayed me? It little matters, for relief arrived. I call it relief, though it was only the relief that a snap brings to a strain or the burst of a thunderstorm to a day of suffocation. It was at least change, and it came with a rush.

XIV

Walking to church a certain Sunday morning, I had little Miles at my side and his sister, in advance of us and at Mrs. Grose's, well in sight. It was a crisp, clear day, the first of its order for some time; the night had brought a touch of frost, and the autumn air, bright and sharp, made the church bells almost gay. It was an odd accident of thought that I should have happened at such a moment to be particularly and very gratefully struck with the obedience of my little charges. Why did they never resent my inexorable, my perpetual society? Something or other had brought nearer home to me that I had all but pinned the boy to my shawl and that, in the way our companions were marshaled before me, I might have appeared to provide against some danger of rebellion. I was like a gaoler with an eye to possible surprises and escapes. But all this belonged—I mean their magnificent little surrender—just to the special array of the facts that were most abysmal. Turned out for Sunday by his uncle's tailor, who had had a free hand and a notion of pretty waistcoats and of his grand little air, Miles's whole title to independence, the rights of his sex and situation, were so stamped upon him that if he had suddenly struck for freedom I should have had nothing to say. I was by the strangest of chances wondering how I should meet him when the revolution unmistakably occurred. I call it a revolution because I now see how, with the word he spoke, the curtain rose on the last act of my dreadful drama, and the catastrophe was precipitated. "Look here, my dear, you know," he charmingly said, "when in the world, please, am I going back to school?"

Transcribed here the speech sounds harmless enough, particularly as uttered in the sweet, high, casual pipe with which, at all interlocutors, but above all at his eternal governess, he threw off intonations as if he were tossing roses. There was something in them that always made one "catch," and I caught, at any rate, now so effectually that I stopped as short as if one of the trees of the park had fallen across the road. There was something new, on the spot, between us, and he was perfectly aware that I recognized it, though, to enable me to do so, he had no need to look a whit less candid and charming than usual. I could feel in him how he already, from my at first finding nothing to reply, perceived the advantage he had gained. I was so slow to find anything that he had plenty of time, after a minute, to continue with his suggestive but inconclusive smile: "You know, my dear, that for a fellow to be with a lady *always*——!" His "my dear" was constantly on his lips for me, and nothing could have expressed more the exact shade of the sentiment with which I desired to inspire my pupils than its fond familiarity. It was so respectfully easy.

But, oh, how I felt that at present I must pick my own phrases! I remember that, to gain time, I tried to laugh, and I seemed to see in the beautiful face with which he watched me how ugly and queer I looked. "And always with the same lady?" I returned.

He neither blanched nor winked. The whole thing was virtually out between us. "Ah, of course, she's a jolly, 'perfect' lady; but, after all, I'm a fellow, don't you see? that's—well, getting on."

I lingered there with him an instant ever so kindly. "Yes, you're getting on." Oh, but I felt helpless!

I have kept to this day the heartbreaking little idea of how he seemed to know that and to play with it. "And you can't say I've not been awfully good, can you?"

I laid my hand on his shoulder, for, though I felt how much better it would have been to walk on, I was not yet quite able. "No, I can't say that, Miles."

"Except just that one night, you know——!"

"That one night?" I couldn't look as straight as he.

"Why, when I went down—went out of the house."

"Oh, yes. But I forget what you did it for."

"You forget?"—he spoke with the sweet extravagance of childish reproach. "Why, it was to show you I could!"

"Oh, yes, you could."

"And I can again."

I felt that I might, perhaps, after all, succeed in keeping my wits about me. "Certainly. But you won't."

"No, not *that* again. It was nothing."

"It was nothing," I said. "But we must go on."

He resumed our walk with me, passing his hand into my arm. "Then when *am* I going back?"

I wore, in turning it over, my most responsible air. "Were you very happy at school?"

He just considered. "Oh, I'm happy enough anywhere!"

"Well, then," I quavered, "if you're just as happy here——!"

"Ah, but that isn't everything! Of course you know a lot——"

"But you hint that you know almost as much?" I risked as he paused.

"Not half I want to!" Miles honestly professed. "But it isn't so much that."

"What is it, then?"

"Well—I want to see more life."

"I see; I see." We had arrived within sight of the church and of various persons, including several of the household of Bly, on their way to it and clustered about the door to see us go in. I quickened our step; I wanted to get there before the question between us opened up much further; I reflected hungrily that, for more than an hour, he would have to be silent; and I thought with envy of the comparative dusk of the pew and of the almost spiritual help of the hassock on which I might bend my knees. I seemed literally to be running a race with some confusion to which he was about to reduce me, but I felt that he had got in first when, before we had even entered the churchyard, he threw out—

"I want my own sort!"

It literally made me bound forward. "There are not many of your own sort, Miles!" I laughed. "Unless perhaps dear little Flora!"

"You really compare me to a baby girl?"

This found me singularly weak. "Don't you, then, *love* our sweet Flora?"

"If I didn't—and you, too; if I didn't ——!" he repeated as if retreating for a jump, yet leaving his thought so unfinished that, after we had come into the gate, another stop, which he imposed on me by the pressure of his arm, had become inevitable. Mrs. Grose and Flora had passed into the church, the other worshippers had followed, and we were, for the minute, alone among the old, thick graves. We had paused, on the path from the gate, by a low, oblong, tablelike tomb.

"Yes, if you didn't——?"

He looked, while I waited, about at the graves. "Well, you know what!" But he didn't move, and he presently produced something that made me drop straight down on the stone slab, as if suddenly to rest. "Does my uncle think what *you* think?"

I markedly rested. "How do you know what I think?"

"Ah, well, of course I don't; for it strikes me you never tell me. But I mean does *he* know?"

"Know what, Miles?"

"Why, the way I'm going on."

I perceived quickly enough that I could make, to this inquiry, no answer that would not involve something of a sacrifice of my employer. Yet it appeared to me that we were all, at Bly, sufficiently sacrificed to make that venial. "I don't think your uncle much cares."

Miles, on this, stood looking at me. "Then don't you think he can be made to?"

"In what way?"

"Why, by his coming down."

"But who'll get him to come down?"

"*I* will!" the boy said with extraordinary brightness and emphasis. He gave me another look charged with that expression and then marched off alone into church.

XV

The business was practically settled from the moment I never followed him. It was a pitiful surrender to agitation, but my being aware of this had somehow no power to restore me. I only sat there on my tomb and read into what my little friend had said to me the fullness of its meaning; by the time I had grasped the whole of which I had also embraced, for absence, the pretext that I was ashamed to offer my pupils and the rest of the congregation such an example of delay. What I said to myself above all was that Miles had got something out of me and that the proof of it, for him, would be just this awkward collapse. He had got out of me that there was something I was much afraid of and that he should probably be able to make use of my fear to gain, for his own purpose, more freedom. My fear was of having to deal with the intolerable question of the grounds of his dismissal from school, for that was really but the question of the horrors gathered behind. That his uncle should arrive to treat with me of these things was a solution that, strictly speaking, I ought now to have desired to bring on; but I could so little face the ugliness and the pain of it that I simply procrastinated and lived from hand to mouth. The boy, to my deep discomposure, was immensely in the right, was in a position to say to me: "Either you clear up with my guardian the mystery of this interruption of my studies, or you cease to expect me to lead with you a life that's so unnatural for a boy." What was so unnatural for the particular boy I was concerned with was this sudden revelation of a consciousness and a plan.

That was what really overcame me, what prevented my gong in. I walked round the church, hesitating, hovering; I reflected that I had already, with him, hurt myself beyond repair. Therefore I could patch up nothing, and it was too extreme an effort to squeeze beside him into the pew: he would be so much more sure than ever to pass his arm into mine and make me sit there for an hour in close, silent contact with his commentary on our talk. For the first minute since his arrival I wanted to get away from him. As I paused beneath the high east window and listened to the sounds of worship, I was taken with an impulse that might master me, I felt, completely should I give it the least encouragement. I might easily put an end to my predicament by getting away altogether. Here was my chance; there was no one to stop me; I could give the whole thing up—turn my back and retreat. It was only a question of hurrying again, for a few preparations, to the house which the attendance at church of so many of the servants would practically have left unoccupied. No one, in short, could blame me if I should just drive desperately off. What was it to get away if I got away only till dinner? That would be in a couple of hours, at the end of which—I had the acute prevision—my little pupils would play at innocent wonder about my nonappearance in their train.

"What *did* you do, you naughty, bad thing? Why in the world, to worry us so—and take our thoughts off, too, don't you know?—did you desert us at the very door?" I couldn't meet such questions nor, as they asked them, their false little lovely eyes; yet it was all so exactly what I should have to meet that, as the prospect grew sharp to me, I at last let myself go.

I got, so far as the immediate moment was concerned, away; I came straight out of the churchyard and, thinking hard, retraced my steps through the park. It seemed to me that by the time I reached the house I had made up my mind I would fly. The Sunday stillness both of the approaches and of the interior, in which I met no one, fairly excited me with a sense of opportunity. Were I to get off quickly, this way, I should get off without a scene, without a word. My quickness would have to be remarkable, however, and the question of a conveyance was the great one to settle. Tormented, in the hall, with difficulties and obstacles, I remember sinking down at the foot of the staircase—suddenly collapsing there on the lowest step and then, with a revulsion, recalling that it was exactly where more than a month before, in the darkness of night and just so bowed with evil things, I had seen the specter of the most horrible of women. At this I was able to straighten myself; I went the rest of the way up; I made, in my bewilderment, for the schoolroom, where there were objects belonging to me that I should have to take. But I opened the door to find again, in a flash, my eyes unsealed. In the presence of what I saw I reeled straight back upon my resistance.

Seated at my own table in clear noonday light I saw a person whom, without my previous experience, I should have taken at the first blush for some housemaid who might have stayed at home to look after the place and who, availing herself of rare relief from observation and of the schoolroom table and my pens, ink, and paper, had applied herself to the considerable effort of a letter to her sweetheart. There was an effort in the way that, while her arms rested on the table, her hands with evident weariness supported her head; but at the moment I took this in I had already become aware that, in spite of my entrance, her attitude strangely persisted. Then it was—with the very act of its announcing itself—that her identity flared up in a change of posture. She rose, not as if she had heard me, but with an indescribable grand melancholy of indifference and detachment, and, within a dozen feet of me, stood there as my vile predecessor. Dishonored and tragic, she was all before me; but even as I fixed and, for memory, secured it, the awful image passed away. Dark as midnight in her black dress, her haggard beauty and her unutterable woe, she had looked at me long enough to appear to say that her right to sit at my table was as good as mine to sit at hers. While these instants lasted, indeed, I had the extraordinary chill of feeling that it was I who was the intruder. It was as a wild protest against it that, actually addressing her—"You terrible, miserable woman!"—I heard myself break into a sound that, by the open door, rang through the long passage and the empty house. She looked at me as if she heard me, but I had recovered myself and cleared the air. There was nothing in the room the next minute but the sunshine and a sense that I must stay.

XVI

I had so perfectly expected that the return of my pupils would be marked by a demonstration that I was freshly upset at having to take into account that they were dumb about my absence. Instead of gaily denouncing and caressing me, they made no allusion to my having failed them, and I was left, for the time, on perceiving that she too said nothing, to study Mrs. Grose's odd face. I did this to such purpose that I made sure they had in some way bribed her to silence; a silence that, however, I would engage to break down on the first private opportunity. This opportunity came before tea: I secured five minutes with her in the housekeeper's room, where, in the twilight, amid a smell of lately baked bread, but with the place all swept and garnished, I found her sitting in pained placidity before the fire. So I see her still, so I see her best: facing the flame from her straight chair in the dusky, shining room, a large clean image of the "put away"—of drawers closed and locked and rest without a remedy.

"Oh, yes, they asked me to say nothing; and to please them—so long as they were there—of course I promised. But what had happened to you?"

"I only went with you for a walk," I said. "I had then to come back to meet a friend."

She showed her surprise. "A friend—you?"

"Oh, yes, I have a couple!" I laughed. "But did the children give you a reason?"

"For not alluding to your leaving us? Yes; they said you would like it better. Do you like it better?"

My face had made her rueful. "No, I like it worse!" But after an instant I added: "Did they say why I should like it better?"

"No; Master Miles only said, 'We must do nothing but what she likes!'"

"I wish indeed he would! And what did Flora say?"

"Miss Flora was too sweet. She said, 'Oh, of course, of course!'—and I said the same."

I thought a moment. "You were too sweet, too—I can hear you all. But nonetheless, between Miles and me, it's now all out."

"All out?" My companion stared. "But what, miss?"

"Everything. It doesn't matter. I've made up my mind. I came home, my dear," I went on, "for a talk with Miss Jessel."

I had by this time formed the habit of having Mrs. Grose literally well in hand in advance of my sounding that note; so that even now, as she bravely blinked under the signal of my word, I could keep her comparatively firm. "A talk! Do you mean she spoke?"

"It came to that. I found her, on my return, in the schoolroom."

"And what did she say?" I can hear the good woman still, and the candor of her stupefaction.

"That she suffers the torments——!"

It was this, of a truth, that made her, as she filled out my picture, gape. "Do you mean," she faltered, "—of the lost?"

"Of the lost. Of the damned. And that's why, to share them——" I faltered myself with the horror of it.

But my companion, with less imagination, kept me up. "To share them——?"

"She wants Flora." Mrs. Grose might, as I gave it to her, fairly have fallen away from me had I not been prepared. I still held her there, to show I was. "As I've told you, however, it doesn't matter."

"Because you've made up your mind? But to what?"

"To everything."

"And what do you call 'everything'?"

"Why, sending for their uncle."

"Oh, miss, in pity do," my friend broke out.

"Ah, but I will, I *will!* I see it's the only way. What's 'out,' as I told you, with Miles is that if he thinks I'm afraid to—

and has ideas of what he gains by that—he shall see he's mistaken. Yes, yes; his uncle shall have it here from me on the spot (and before the boy himself, if necessary) that if I'm to be reproached with having done nothing again about more school——"

"Yes, miss——" my companion pressed me.

"Well, there's that awful reason."

There were now clearly so many of these for my poor colleague that she was excusable for being vague. "But—a—which?"

"Why, the letter from his old place."

"You'll show it to the master?"

"I ought to have done so on the instant."

"Oh, no!" said Mrs. Grose with decision.

"I'll put it before him," I went on inexorably, "that I can't undertake to work the question on behalf of a child who has been expelled——"

"For we've never in the least known what!" Mrs. Grose declared.

"For wickedness. For what else—when he's so clever and beautiful and perfect? Is he stupid? Is he untidy? Is he infirm? Is he ill-natured? He's exquisite—so it can be only *that*; and that would open up the whole thing. After all," I said, "it's their uncle's fault. If he left here such people——!"

"He didn't really in the least know them. The fault's mine." She had turned quite pale.

"Well, you shan't suffer," I answered.

"The children shan't" she emphatically returned.

I was silent awhile; we looked at each other. "Then what am I to tell him?"

"You needn't tell him anything. *I'll* tell him."

I measured this. "Do you mean you'll write——?" Remembering she couldn't, I caught myself up. "How do you communicate?"

"I tell the bailiff. *He* writes."

"And should you like him to write our story?"

My question had a sarcastic force that I had not fully intended, and it made her, after a moment, inconsequently break down. The tears were again in her eyes. "Ah, miss, you write!"

"Well—tonight," I at last answered; and on this we separated.

XVII

I went so far, in the evening, as to make a beginning. The weather had changed back, a great wind was abroad, and beneath the lamp, in my room, with Flora at peace beside me, I sat for a long time before a blank sheet of paper and listened to the lash of the rain and the batter of the gusts. Finally I went out, taking a candle; I crossed the passage and listened a minute at Miles's door. What, under my endless obsession, I had been impelled to listen for was some betrayal of his not being at rest, and I presently caught one, but not in the form I had expected. His voice tinkled out. "I say, you there—come in." It was a gaiety in the gloom!

I went in with my light and found him, in bed, very wide awake, but very much at his ease. "Well, what are you up to?" he asked with a grace of sociability in which it occurred to me that Mrs. Grose, had she been present, might have looked in vain for proof that anything was "out."

I stood over him with my candle. "How did you know I was there?"

"Why, of course I heard you. Did you fancy you made no noise? You're like a troop of cavalry!" he beautifully laughed.

"Then you weren't asleep?"

"Not much! I lie awake and think."

I had put my candle, designedly, a short way off, and then, as he held out his friendly old hand to me, had sat down on the edge of his bed. "What is it," I asked, "that you think of?"

"What in the world, my dear, but you?"

"Ah, the pride I take in your appreciation doesn't insist on that! I had so far rather you slept."

"Well, I think also, you know, of this queer business of ours."

I marked the coolness of his firm little hand. "Of what queer business, Miles?"

"Why, the way you bring me up. And all the rest!"

I fairly held my breath a minute, and even from my glimmering taper there was light enough to show how he smiled up at me from his pillow. "What do you mean by all the rest?"

"Oh, you know, you know!"

I could say nothing for a minute,

though I felt, as I held his hand and our eyes continued to meet, that my silence had all the air of admitting his charge and that nothing in the whole world of reality was perhaps at that moment so fabulous as our actual relation. "Certainly you shall go back to school," I said, "if it be that that troubles you. But not to the old place—we must find another, a better. How could I know it did trouble you, this question, when you never told me so, never spoke of it at all?" His clear, listening face, framed in its smooth whiteness, made him for the minute as appealing as some wistful patient in a children's hospital; and I would have given, as the resemblance came to me, all I possessed on earth really to be the nurse or the sister of charity who might have helped to cure him. Well, even as it was, I perhaps might help! "Do you know you've never said a word to me about your school—I mean the old one; never mentioned it in any way?"

He seemed to wonder; he smiled with the same loveliness. But he clearly gained time; he waited, he called for guidance. "Haven't I?" It wasn't for *me* to help him —it was for the thing I had met!

Something in his tone and the expression of his face, as I got this from him, set my heart aching with such a pang as it had never yet known; so unutterably touching was it to see his little brain puzzled and his little resources taxed to play, under the spell laid on him, a part of innocence and consistency. "No, never—from the hour you came back. You've never mentioned to me one of your masters, one of your comrades, nor the least little thing that ever happened to you at school. Never, little Miles—no, never—have you given me an inkling of anything that may have happened there. Therefore you can fancy how much I'm in the dark. Until you came out, that way, this morning, you had, since the first hour I saw you, scarce even made a reference to anything in your previous life. You seemed so perfectly to accept the present." It was extraordinary how my absolute conviction of his secret precocity (or whatever I might call the poison of an influence that I dared but half to phrase) made him, in spite of the faint breath of his inward trouble, appear as accessible as an older person—imposed him almost as an intellectual equal.

"I thought you wanted to go on as you are."

It struck me that at this he just faintly colored. He gave, at any rate, like a convalescent slightly fatigued, a languid shake of his head. "I don't—I don't. I want to get away."

"You're tired of Bly?"

"Oh, no, I like Bly."

"Well, then——?"

"Oh, you know what a boy wants!"

I felt that I didn't know so well as Miles, and I took temporary refuge. "You want to go to your uncle?"

Again, at this, with his sweet ironic face, he made a movement on the pillow. "Ah, you can't get off with that!"

I was silent a little, and it was I, now, I think, who changed color. "My dear, I don't want to get off!"

"You can't, even if you do. You can't, you can't!"—he lay beautifully staring. "My uncle must come down, and you must completely settle things."

"If we do," I returned with some spirit, "you may be sure it will be to take you quite away."

"Well, don't you understand that that's exactly what I'm working for? You'll have to tell him—about the way you've let it all drop: you'll have to tell him a tremendous lot!"

The exultation with which he uttered this helped me somehow, for the instant, to meet him rather more. "And how much will you, Miles, have to tell him? There are things he'll ask you!"

He turned it over. "Very likely. But what things?"

"The things you've never told me. To make up his mind what to do with you. He can't send you back——"

"Oh, I don't want to go back!" he broke in. "I want a new field."

He said it with admirable serenity, with positive unimpeachable gaiety; and doubtless it was that very note that most evoked for me the poignancy, the unnatural childish tragedy, of his probable reappearance at the end of three months with all this bravado and still more dishonor. It overwhelmed me now that I should never be able to bear that, and it made me let myself go. I threw myself upon him and in the tenderness of my pity I embraced him. "Dear little Miles, dear little Miles——!"

My face was close to his, and he let me kiss him, simply taking it with indulgent good humor. "Well, old lady?"

"Is there nothing—nothing at all that you want to tell me?"

He turned off a little, facing round toward the wall and holding up his hand to look at as one had seen sick children look. "I've told you—I told you this morning."

Oh, I was sorry for him! "That you just want me not to worry you?"

He looked round at me now, as if in recognition of my understanding him; then ever so gently, "To let me alone," he replied.

There was even a singular little dignity in it, something that made me release him, yet, when I had slowly risen, linger beside him. God knows I never wished to harass him, but I felt that merely, at this, to turn my back on him was to abandon or, to put it more truly, to lose him. "I've just begun a letter to your uncle," I said.

"Well, then, finish it!"

I waited a minute. "What happened before?"

He gazed up at me again. "Before what?"

"Before you came back. And before you went away."

For some time he was silent, but he continued to meet my eyes. "What happened?"

It made me, the sound of the words, in which it seemed to me that I caught for the very first time a small faint quaver of consenting consciousness—it made me drop on my knees beside the bed and seize once more the chance of possessing him. "Dear little Miles, dear little Miles, if you *knew* how I want to help you! It's only that, it's nothing but that, and I'd rather die than give you a pain or do you a wrong—I'd rather die than hurt a hair of you. Dear little Miles"—oh, I brought it out now even if I *should* go too far—"I just want you to help me to save you!" But I knew in a moment after this that I had gone too far. The answer to my appeal was instantaneous, but it came in the form of an extraordinary blast and chill, a gust of frozen air, and a shake of the room as great as if, in the wild wind, the casement had crashed in. The boy gave a loud, high shriek, which, lost in the rest of the shock of sound, might have seemed, indistinctly, though I was so close to him, a note either of jubilation or of terror. I jumped to my feet again and was conscious of darkness. So for a moment we remained, while I stared about me and saw that the drawn curtains were unstirred and the window tight. "Why, the candle's out!" I then cried.

"It was I who blew it, dear!" said Miles.

XVIII

The next day, after lessons, Mrs. Grose found a moment to say to me quietly: "Have you written, miss?"

"Yes—I've written." But I didn't add —for the hour—that my letter, sealed and directed, was still in my pocket. There would be time enough to send it before the messenger should go to the village. Meanwhile there had been, on the part of my pupils, no more brilliant, more exemplary morning. It was exactly as if they had both had at heart to gloss over any recent little friction. They performed the dizziest feats of arithmetic, soaring quite out of my feeble range, and perpetrated, in higher spirits than ever, geographical and historical jokes. It was conspicuous of course in Miles in particular that he appeared to wish to show how easily he could let me down. This child, to my memory, really lives in a setting of beauty and misery that no words can translate; there was a distinction all his own in every impulse he revealed; never was a small natural creature, to the uninitiated eye all frankness and freedom, a more ingenious, a more extraordinary little gentleman. I had perpetually to guard against the wonder of contemplation into which my initiated view betrayed me; to check the irrelevant gaze and discouraged sigh in which I constantly both attacked and renounced the enigma of what such a little gentleman could have done that deserved a penalty. Say that, by the dark prodigy I knew, the imagination of all evil *had* been opened up to him: all the justice within me ached for the proof that it could ever have flowered into an act.

He had never, at any rate, been such a little gentleman as when, after our early dinner on this dreadful day, he came round to me and asked if I shouldn't like him, for half an hour, to play to me. David playing to Saul could never have shown a finer sense of the occasion. It was literally a charming exhibition of tact, of magnanimity, and quite tantamount to his saying outright: "The true knights we love to read about never push an advantage too far. I know what you mean now: you mean that—to be let alone yourself and not followed up—you'll cease to worry and spy upon me, won't keep me so close to you, will let me go and come. Well, I 'come,' you see—but I don't go! There'll be plenty of time for that. I do really delight in your society, and I only want to show you that I contended for a principle." It may be imagined whether I resisted this appeal or failed to accompany him again, hand in hand, to the schoolroom. He sat down at the old piano and played as he had never played; and if there are those who think he had better have been kicking a football I can only say that I wholly agree with them. For at the end of a time that under his influence I had quite ceased to measure, I started up with a strange sense of having literally slept at my post. It was after luncheon, and by the schoolroom fire, and yet I hadn't really, in the least, slept: I had only done something much worse—I had forgotten. Where, all this time, was Flora? When I put the question to Miles, he played on a minute before answering and then could only say: "Why, my dear, how do I know?"—breaking moreover into a happy laugh which, immediately after, as if it were a vocal accompaniment, he prolonged into incoherent, extravagant song.

I went straight to my room, but his sister was not there; then, before going downstairs, I looked into several others. As she was nowhere about she would surely be with Mrs. Grose, whom, in the comfort of that theory, I accordingly proceeded in quest of. I found her where I had found her the evening before, but she met my quick challenge with blank, scared ignorance. She had only supposed that, after the repast, I had carried off both the children; as to which she was quite in her right, for it was the very first time I had allowed the little girl out of my sight without some special provision. Of course now indeed she might be with the maids, so that the immediate thing was to look for her without an air of alarm. This we promptly arranged between us; but when, ten minutes later and in pursuance of our arrangement, we met in the hall, it was only to report on either side that after guarded inquiries we had altogether failed to trace her. For a minute there, apart from observation, we exchanged mute alarms, and I could feel with what high interest my friend returned me all those I had from the first given her.

"She'll be above," she presently said—"in one of the rooms you haven't searched."

"No; she's at a distance." I had made up my mind. "She has gone out."

Mrs. Grose stared. "Without a hat?"

I naturally also looked volumes. "Isn't that woman always without one?"

"She's with *her*?"

"She's with *her*!" I declared. "We must find them."

My hand was on my friend's arm, but she failed for the moment, confronted with such an account of the matter, to respond to my pressure. She communed, on the contrary, on the spot, with her uneasiness. "And where's Master Miles?"

"Oh, *he*'s with Quint. They're in the schoolroom."

"Lord, miss!" My view, I was myself aware—and therefore I suppose my tone—had never yet reached so calm an assurance.

"The trick's played," I went on; "they've successfully worked their plan. He found the most divine little way to keep me quiet while she went off."

"'Divine'?" Mrs. Grose bewilderedly echoed.

"Infernal, then!" I almost cheerfully rejoined. "He has provided for himself as well. But come!"

She had helplessly gloomed at the upper regions. "You leave him——?"

"So long with Quint? Yes—I don't mind that now."

She always ended, at these moments, by getting possession of my hand, and in this manner she could at present still stay me. But after gasping an instant at my sudden resignation, "Because of your letter?" she eagerly brought out.

I quickly, by way of answer, felt for my letter, drew it forth, held it up, and then, freeing myself, went and laid it on the great hall table. "Luke will take it," I said as I came back. I reached the house door and opened it; I was already on the steps.

My companion still demurred: the storm of the night and the early morning had dropped, but the afternoon was damp and gray. I came down to the drive while she stood in the doorway. "You go with nothing on?"

"What do I care when the child has nothing? I can't wait to dress," I cried, "and if you must do so, I leave you. Try meanwhile, yourself, upstairs."

"With *them?*" Oh, on this, the poor woman promptly joined me!

XIX

We went straight to the lake, as it was called at Bly, and I daresay rightly called, though I reflect that it may in fact have been a sheet of water less remarkable than it appeared to my untraveled eyes. My acquaintance with sheets of water was small, and the pool of Bly, at all events on the few occasions of my consenting, under the protection of my pupils, to affront its surface in the old flat-bottomed boat moored there for our use, had impressed me both with its extent and its agitation. The usual place of embarkation was half a mile from the house, but I had an intimate conviction that, wherever Flora might be, she was not near home. She had not given me the slip for any small adventure, and, since the day of the very great one that I had shared with her by the pond, I had been aware, in our walks, of the quarter to which she most inclined. This was why I had now given to Mrs. Grose's steps so marked a direction—a direction that made her, when she perceived it, oppose a resistance that showed me she was freshly mystified. "You're going to the water, Miss?—you think she's *in*——?"

"She may be, though the depth is, I believe, nowhere very great. But what I judge most likely is that she's on the spot from which, the other day, we saw together what I told you."

"When she pretended not to see——?"

"With that astounding self-possession? I've always been sure she wanted to go back alone. And now her brother has managed it for her."

Mrs. Grose still stood where she had stopped. "You suppose they really *talk* of them?"

I could meet this with a confidence! "They say things that, if we heard them, would simply appal us."

"And if she *is* there——?"

"Yes?"

"Then Miss Jessel is?"

"Beyond a doubt. You shall see."

"Oh, thank you!" my friend cried, planted so firm that, taking it in, I went straight on without her. By the time I reached the pool, however, she was close behind me, and I knew that, whatever, to her apprehension, might befall me, the exposure of my society struck her as her least danger. She exhaled a moan of relief as we at last came in sight of the greater part of the water without a sight of the child. There was no trace of Flora on that nearer side of the bank where my observation of her had been most startling, and none on the opposite edge, where, save for a margin of some twenty yards, a thick copse came down to the water. The pond, oblong in shape, had a width so scant compared to its length that, with its ends out of view, it might have been taken for a scant river. We looked at the empty expanse, and then I felt the suggestion of my friend's eyes. I knew what she meant and I replied with a negative headshake.

"No, no; wait! She has taken the boat."

My companion stared at the vacant mooring place and then again across the lake. "Then where is it?"

"Our not seeing it is the strongest of proofs. She has used it to go over, and then has managed to hide it."

"All alone—that child?"

"She's not alone, and at such times she's not a child: she's an old, old woman." I scanned all the visible shore while Mrs. Grose took again, into the queer element I offered her, one of her plunges of submission; then I pointed out that the boat might perfectly be in a small refuge formed by one of the recesses of the pool, an indentation masked, for the hither side, by a projection of the bank and by a clump of trees growing close to the water.

"But if the boat's there, where on earth's *she?*" my colleague anxiously asked.

"That's exactly what we must learn." And I started to walk further.

"By going all the way round?"

"Certainly, far as it is. It will take us

but ten minutes, but it's far enough to have made the child prefer not to walk. She went straight over."

"Laws!" cried my friend again; the chain of my logic was ever too much for her. It dragged her at my heels even now, and when we had got halfway round—a devious, tiresome process, on ground much broken and by a path choked with overgrowth—I paused to give her breath. I sustained her with a grateful arm, assuring her that she might hugely help me; and this started us afresh, so that in the course of but few minutes more we reached a point from which we found the boat to be where I had supposed it. It had been intentionally left as much as possible out of sight and was tied to one of the stakes of a fence that came, just there, down to the brink and that had been an assistance to disembarking. I recognized, as I looked at the pair of short, thick oars, quite safely drawn up, the prodigious character of the feat for a little girl; but I had lived, by this time, too long among wonders and had panted to too many livelier measures. There was a gate in the fence, through which we passed, and that brought us, after a trifling interval, more into the open. Then, "There she is!" we both exclaimed at once.

Flora, a short way off, stood before us on the grass and smiled as if her performance was now complete. The next thing she did, however, was to stoop straight down and pluck—quite as if it were all she was there for—a big, ugly spray of withered fern. I instantly became sure she had just come out of the copse. She waited for us, not herself taking a step, and I was conscious of the rare solemnity with which we presently approached her. She smiled and smiled, and we met; but it was all done in a silence by this time flagrantly ominous. Mrs. Grose was the first to break the spell: she threw herself on her knees and, drawing the child to her breast, clasped in a long embrace the little tender, yielding body. While this dumb convulsion lasted I could only watch it—which I did the more intently when I saw Flora's face peep at me over our companion's shoulder. It was serious now—the flicker had left it; but it strengthened the pang with which I at that moment envied Mrs. Grose the simplicity of *her* relation. Still, all this while, nothing more passed between us save that Flora had let her foolish fern again drop to the ground. What she and I had virtually said to each other was that pretexts were useless now. When Mrs. Grose finally got up she kept the child's hand, so that the two were still before me; and the singular reticence of our communion was even more marked in the frank look she launched me. "I'll be hanged," it said, "if *I'll* speak!"

It was Flora who, gazing all over me in candid wonder, was the first. She was struck with our bareheaded aspect. "Why, where are your things?"

"Where yours are, my dear!" I promptly returned.

She had already got back her gaiety, and appeared to take this as an answer quite sufficient. "And where's Miles?" she went on.

There was something in the small valor of it that quite finished me: these three words from her were, in a flash like the glitter of a drawn blade, the jostle of the cup that my hand, for weeks and weeks, had held high and full to the brim and that now, even before speaking, I felt overflow in a deluge. "I'll tell you if you'll tell *me*——" I heard myself say, then heard the tremor in which it broke.

"Well, what?"

Mrs. Grose's suspense blazed at me, but it was too late now, and I brought the thing out handsomely. "Where, my pet, is Miss Jessel?"

XX

Just as in the churchyard with Miles, the whole thing was upon us. Much as I had made of the fact that this name had never once, between us, been sounded, the quick, smitten glare with which the child's face now received it fairly likened my breach of the silence to the smash of a pane of glass. It added to the interposing cry, as if to stay the blow, that Mrs. Grose, at the same instant, uttered over my violence—the shriek of a creature scared, or rather wounded, which, in turn, within a few seconds, was completed by a gasp of my own. I seized my colleague's arm. "She's there, she's there!"

Miss Jessel stood before us on the opposite bank exactly as she had stood the other time, and I remember, strangely, as the first feeling now produced in me, my thrill of joy at having brought on a proof. She was there, and I was justified; she was there, and I was neither cruel nor mad. She was there for poor scared Mrs. Grose, but she was there most for Flora; and no moment of my monstrous time was perhaps so extraordinary as that in which I consciously threw out to her—with the sense that, pale and ravenous demon as she was, she would catch and understand it—an inarticulate message of gratitude. She rose erect on the spot my friend and I had lately quitted, and there was not, in all the long reach of her desire, an inch of her evil that fell short. This first vividness of vision and emotion were things of a few seconds, during which Mrs. Grose's dazed blink across to where I pointed struck me as a sovereign sign that she too at last saw, just as it carried my own eyes precipitately to the child. The revelation then of the manner in which Flora was affected startled me, in truth, far more than it would have done to find her also merely agitated, for direct dismay was of course not what I had expected. Prepared and on her guard as our pursuit had actually made her, she would repress every betrayal; and I was therefore shaken, on the spot, by my first glimpse of the particular one for which I had not allowed. To see her, without a convulsion of her small pink face, not even feign to glance in the direction of the prodigy I announced, but only, instead of that, turn at me an expression of hard, still gravity, an expression absolutely new and unprecedented and that appeared to read and accuse and judge me—this was a stroke that somehow converted the little girl herself into the very presence that could make me quail. I quailed even though my certitude that she thoroughly saw was never greater than at that instant, and in the immediate need to defend myself I called it passionately to witness. "She's there, you little unhappy thing—there, there, *there*, and you see her as well as you see me!" I had said shortly before to Mrs. Grose that she was not at these times a child, but an old, old woman, and that description of her could not have been more strikingly confirmed than in the way in which, for all answer to this, she simply showed me, without a concession, an admission, of her eyes, a countenance of deeper and deeper, of indeed suddenly quite fixed, reprobation. I was by this time—if I can put the whole thing at all together—more appalled at what I may properly call her manner than at anything else, though it was simultaneously with this that I became aware of having Mrs. Grose also, and very formidably, to reckon with. My elder companion, the next moment, at any rate, blotted out everything but her own flushed face and her loud, shocked protest, a burst of high disapproval. "What a dreadful turn, to be sure, miss! Where on earth do you see anything?"

I could only grasp her more quickly yet, for even while she spoke the hideous plain presence stood undimmed and undaunted. It had already lasted a minute, and it lasted while I continued, seizing my colleague, quite thrusting her at it and presenting her to it, to insist with my pointing hand. "You don't see her exactly as we see? —you mean to say you don't now—*now*? She's as big as a blazing fire! Only look, dearest woman, *look*——!" She looked, even as I did, and gave me, with her deep groan of negation, repulsion, compassion—the mixture with her pity of her relief at her exemption—a sense, touching to me even then, that she would have backed me up if she could, I might well have needed that, for with this hard blow of the proof that her eyes were hopelessly sealed I felt my own situation horribly crumble, I felt—I saw—my livid predecessor press, from her position, on my defeat, and I was conscious, more than all, of what I should have from this instant to deal with in the astounding little attitude of Flora. Into this attitude Mrs. Grose immediately and violently entered, breaking, even while there pierced through my sense of ruin a prodigious private triumph, into breathless reassurance.

"She isn't there, little lady, and nobody's there—and you never see nothing, my sweet! How can poor Miss Jessel—when poor Miss Jessel's dead and buried? We know, don't we, love?"—and she appealed, blundering in, to the child. "It's all a mere mistake and a worry and a joke—and we'll go home as fast as we can!"

Our companion, on this, had responded with a strange, quick primness of propriety, and they were again, with Mrs.

Grose on her feet, united, as it were, in pained opposition to me. Flora continued to fix me with her small mask of reprobation, and even at that minute I prayed God to forgive me for seeming to see that, as she stood there holding tight to our friend's dress, her incomparable childish beauty had suddenly failed, had quite vanished. I've said it already—she was literally, she was hideously, hard; she had turned common and almost ugly. "I don't know what you mean. I see nobody. I see nothing. I never *have*. I think you're cruel. I don't like you!" Then, after this deliverance, which might have been that of a vulgarly pert little girl in the street, she hugged Mrs. Grose more closely and buried in her skirts the dreadful little face. In this position she produced an almost furious wail. "Take me away, take me away—oh, take me away from *her*!"

"From *me*?" I panted.

"From you—from you!" she cried.

Even Mrs. Grose looked across at me dismayed, while I had nothing to do but communicate again with the figure that, on the opposite bank, without a movement, as rigidly still as if catching, beyond the interval, our voices, was as vividly there for my disaster as it was not there for my service. The wretched child had spoken exactly as if she had got from some outside source each of her stabbing little words, and I could therefore, in the full despair of all I had to accept, but sadly shake my head at her. "If I had ever doubted, all my doubt would at present have gone. I've been living with the miserable truth, and now it has only too much closed round me. Of course I've lost you: I've interfered, and you've seen—under *her* dictation"—with which I faced, over the pool again, our infernal witness—"the easy and perfect way to meet it. I've done my best, but I've lost you. Good-bye." For Mrs. Grose I had an imperative, an almost frantic "Go, go!" before which, in infinite distress, but mutely possessed of the little girl and clearly convinced, in spite of her blindness, that something awful had occurred and some collapse engulfed us, she retreated, by the way we had come, as fast as she could move.

Of what first happened when I was left alone I had no subsequent memory. I only knew that at the end of, I suppose, a quarter of an hour, an odorous dampness and roughness, chilling and piercing my trouble, had made me understand that I must have thrown myself, on my face, on the ground and given way to a wildness of grief. I must have lain there long and cried and sobbed, for when I raised my head the day was almost done. I got up and looked a moment, through the twilight, at the gray pool and its blank, haunted edge, and then I took, back to the house, my dreary and difficult course. When I reached the gate in the fence the boat, to my surprise, was gone, so that I had a fresh reflection to make on Flora's extraordinary command of the situation. She passed that night, by the most tacit, and I should add, were not the word so grotesque a false note, the happiest of arrangements, with Mrs. Grose. I saw neither of them on my return, but, on the other hand, as by an ambiguous compensation, I saw a great deal of Miles. I saw—I can use no other phrase—so much of him that it was as if it were more than it had ever been. No evening I had passed at Bly had the portentous quality of this one; in spite of which—and in spite also of the deeper depths of consternation that had opened beneath my feet—there was literally, in the ebbing actual, an extraordinarily sweet sadness. On reaching the house I had never so much as looked for the boy; I had simply gone straight to my room to change what I was wearing and to take in, at a glance, much material testimony to Flora's rupture. Her little belongings had all been removed. When later, by the schoolroom fire, I was served with tea by the usual maid, I indulged, on the article of my other pupil, in no inquiry whatever. He had his freedom now—he might have it to the end! Well, he did have it; and it consisted—in part at least—of his coming in at about eight o'clock and sitting down with me in silence. On the removal of the tea things I had blown out the candles and drawn my chair closer: I was conscious of a mortal coldness and felt as if I should never again be warm. So, when he appeared, I was sitting in the glow with my thoughts. He paused a moment by the door as if to look at me; then—as if to share them—came to the other side of the hearth and sank into a chair. We sat there in absolute stillness; yet he wanted, I felt, to be with me.

XXI

Before a new day, in my room, had fully broken, my eyes opened to Mrs. Grose, who had come to my bedside with worse news. Flora was so markedly feverish that an illness was perhaps at hand; she had passed a night of extreme unrest, a night agitated above all by fears that had for their subject not in the least her former, but wholly her present, governess. It was not against the possible re-entrance of Miss Jessel on the scene that she protested—it was conspicuously and passionately against mine. I was promptly on my feet of course, and with an immense deal to ask; the more that my friend had discernibly now girded her loins to meet me once more. This I felt as soon as I had put to her the question of her sense of the child's sincerity as against my own. "She persists in denying to you that she saw, or has ever seen, anything?"

My visitor's trouble, truly, was great. "Ah, miss, it isn't a matter on which I can push her! Yet it isn't either, I must say, as if I much needed to. It has made her, every inch of her, quite old."

"Oh, I see her perfectly from here. She resents, for all the world like some high little personage, the imputation on her truthfulness and, as it were, her respectability. 'Miss Jessel indeed—*she!*' Ah, she's 'respectable' the chit! The impression she gave me there yesterday was, I assure you, the very strangest of all; it was quite beyond any of the others. I *did* put my foot in it! She'll never speak to me again."

Hideous and obscure as it all was, it held Mrs. Grose briefly silent; then she granted my point with a frankness which, I made sure, had more behind it. "I think indeed, miss, she never will. She do have a grand manner about it!"

"And that manner"—I summed it up —"is practically what's the matter with her now!"

Oh, that manner, I could see in my visitor's face, and not a little else besides! "She asks me every three minutes if I think you're coming in."

"I see—I see." I, too, on my side, had so much more than worked it out. "Has she said to you since yesterday—except to repudiate her familiarity with anything so dreadful—a single other word about Miss Jessel?"

"Not one, miss. And of course you know," my friend added, "I took it from her, by the lake, that, just then and there at least, there *was* nobody."

"Rather! And, naturally, you take it from her still."

"I don't contradict her. What else can I do?"

"Nothing in the world! You've the cleverest little person to deal with. They've made them—their two friends, I mean—still cleverer even than nature did; for it was wondrous material to play on! Flora has now her grievance, and she'll work it to the end."

"Yes, miss; but to *what* end?"

"Why, that of dealing with me to her uncle. She'll make me out to him the lowest creature——!"

I winced at the fair show of the scene in Mrs. Grose's face; she looked for a minute as if she sharply saw them together. "And him who thinks so well of you!"

"He has an odd way—it comes over me now," I laughed, "—of proving it! But that doesn't matter. What Flora wants, of course, is to get rid of me."

My companion bravely concurred. "Never again to so much as look at you."

"So that what you've come to me now for," I asked, "is to speed me on my way?" Before she had time to reply, however, I had her in check. "I've a better idea—the result of my reflections. My going *would* seem the right thing, and on Sunday I was terribly near it. Yet that won't do. It's *you* who must go. You must take Flora."

My visitor, at this, did speculate. "But where in the world——?"

"Away from here. Away from *them*. Away, even most of all, now, from me. Straight to her uncle."

"Only to tell on you——?"

"No, not 'only'! To leave me, in addition, with my remedy."

She was still vague. "And what *is* your remedy?"

"Your loyalty, to begin with. And then Miles's."

She looked at me hard. "Do you think he——?"

"Won't, if he has the chance, turn on me? Yes, I venture still to think it. At all events, I want to try. Get off with his sister as soon as possible and leave me with him alone." I was amazed, myself, at the spirit I had still in reserve, and therefore perhaps a trifle the more disconcerted at the way in which, in spite of this fine example of it, she hesitated. "There's one thing, of course," I went on: "they mustn't, before she goes, see each other for three seconds." Then it came over me that, in spite of Flora's presumable sequestration from the instant of her return from the pool, it might already be too late. "Do you mean," I anxiously asked, "that they *have* met?"

At this she quite flushed. "Ah, miss, I'm not such a fool as that! If I've been obliged to leave her three or four times, it has been each time with one of the maids, and at present, though she's alone, she's locked in safe. And yet—and yet!" There were too many things.

"And yet what?"

"Well, are you so sure of the little gentleman?"

"I'm not sure of anything but you. But I have, since last evening, a new hope. I think he wants to give me an opening. I do believe that—poor little exquisite wretch!— he wants to speak. Last evening, in the firelight and the silence, he sat with me for two hours as if it were just coming."

Mrs. Grose looked hard, through the window, at the gray, gathering day. "And did it come?"

"No, though I waited and waited, I confess it didn't, and it was without a breach of the silence or so much as a faint allusion to his sister's condition and absence that we at last kissed for good night. All the same," I continued, "I can't, if her uncle sees her, consent to his seeing her brother without my having given the boy—and most of all because things have got so bad —a little more time."

My friend appeared on this ground more reluctant than I could quite understand. "What do you mean by more time?"

"Well, a day or two—really to bring it out. He'll then be on *my* side—of which you see the importance. If nothing comes, I shall only fail, and you will, at the worst, have helped me by doing, on your arrival in town, whatever you may have found possible." So I put it before her, but she continued for a little so inscrutably embarrassed that I came again to her aid. "Unless, indeed," I wound up, "you really want *not* to go."

I could see it, in her face, at last clear itself; she put out her hand to me as a pledge. "I'll go—I'll go. I'll go this morning."

I wanted to be very just. "If you *should* wish still to wait, I would engage she shouldn't see me."

"No, no: it's the place itself. She must leave it." She held me a moment with heavy eyes, then brought out the rest. "Your idea's the right one. I myself, miss——"

"Well?"

"I can't stay."

The look she gave me with it made me jump at possibilities. "You mean that, since yesterday, you *have* seen——?"

She shook her head with dignity. "I've heard——!"

"Heard?"

"From that child—horrors! There!" she sighed with tragic relief. "On my honor, miss, she says things——!" But at this evocation she broke down; she dropped, with a sudden sob, upon my sofa and, as I had seen her do before, gave way to all the grief of it.

It was quite in another manner that I, for my part, let myself go. "Oh, thank God!"

She sprang up again at this, drying her eyes with a groan. " 'Thank God'?"

"It so justifies me!"

"It does that, miss!"

I couldn't have desired more emphasis, but I just hesitated. "She's so horrible?"

I saw my colleague scarce knew how to put it. "Really shocking."

"And about me?"

"About you, miss—since you must have it. It's beyond everything, for a young lady; and I can't think wherever she must have picked up——"

"The appalling language she applied to me? I can, then!" I broke in with a laugh that was doubtless significant enough.

It only, in truth, left my friend still more grave. "Well, perhaps I ought to also —since I've heard some of it before! Yet I can't bear it," the poor woman went on while, with the same movement, she glanced, on my dressing table, at the face of my watch. "But I must go back."

I kept her, however. "Ah, if you can't bear it——!"

"How can I stop with her, you mean? Why, just for that: to get her away. Far from this," she pursued, "far from them——"

"She may be different? She may be free?" I seized her almost with joy. "Then, in spite of yesterday, you believe—"

"In such doings?" Her simple description of them required, in the light of her expression, to be carried no further, and she gave me the whole thing as she had never done. "I believe."

Yes, it was a joy, and we were still shoulder to shoulder: if I might continue sure of that I should care but little what else happened. My support in the presence of disaster would be the same as it had been in my early need of confidence, and if my friend would answer for my honesty, I would answer for all the rest. On the point of taking leave of her, nonetheless, I was to some extent embarrassed. "There's one thing, of course—it occurs to me—to remember. My letter, giving the alarm, will have reached town before you."

I now perceived still more how she had been beating about the bush and how weary at last it had made her. "Your letter won't have got there. Your letter never went."

"What then became of it?"

"Goodness knows! Master Miles—"

"Do you mean he took it?" I gasped.

She hung fire, but she overcame her reluctance. "I mean that I saw yesterday, when I came back with Miss Flora, that it wasn't where you had put it. Later in the evening I had the chance to question Luke, and he declared that he had neither noticed nor touched it." We could only exchange, on this, one of our deeper mutual soundings, and it was Mrs. Grose who first brought up the plumb with an almost elated "You see!"

"Yes, I see that if Miles took it instead he probably will have read it and destroyed it."

"And don't you see anything else?"

I faced her a moment with a sad smile. "It strikes me that by this time your eyes are open even wider than mine."

They proved to be so indeed, but she could still blush, almost, to show it. "I make out now what he must have done at school." And she gave, in her simple sharpness, an almost droll disillusioned nod. "He stole!"

I turned it over—I tried to be more judicial. "Well—perhaps."

She looked as if she found me unexpectedly calm. "He stole *letters!*"

She couldn't know my reasons for a calmness after all pretty shallow; so I showed them off as I might. "I hope then it was to more purpose than in this case! The note, at any rate, that I put on the table yesterday," I pursued, "will have given him so scant an advantage—for it contained only the bare demand for an interview—that he is already much ashamed of having gone so far for so little, and that what he had on his mind last evening was precisely the need of confession." I seemed to myself, for the instant, to have mastered it, to see it all. "Leave us, leave us"—I was already, at the door, hurrying her off. "I'll get it out of him. He'll meet me—he'll confess. If he confesses, he's saved. And if he's saved——"

"Then *you* are?" The dear woman kissed me on this, and I took her farewell. "I'll save you without him!" she cried as she went.

XXII

Yet it was when she had got off—and I missed her on the spot—that the great pinch really came. If I had counted on what it would give me to find myself alone with Miles, I speedily perceived, at least, that it would give me a measure. No hour of my stay in fact was so assailed with apprehensions as that of my coming down to learn that the carriage containing Mrs. Grose and my younger pupil had already rolled out of the gates. Now I *was*, I said to myself, face to face with the elements, and for much of the rest of the day, while I fought my weakness, I could consider that I had been supremely rash. It was a tighter place still than I had yet turned round in; all the more that, for the first time, I could see in the aspect of others a confused reflection of the crisis. What had happened naturally caused them all to stare; there was too little of the explained, throw out whatever we might, in the suddenness of my colleague's act. The maids and the men looked blank; the effect of which on my nerves was an aggravation until I saw the necessity of making it a positive aid. It was precisely, in short, by just clutching the helm that I avoided total wreck; and I dare say that, to bear up at all, I became, that morning, very grand and very dry. I welcomed the consciousness that I was charged with much to do, and I caused it to be known as well that, left thus to myself, I was quite remarkably firm. I wandered with that manner, for the next hour or two, all over the place and looked, I have no doubt, as if I were ready for any onset. So, for the benefit of whom it might concern, I paraded with a sick heart.

The person it appeared least to concern proved to be, till dinner, little Miles himself. My perambulations had given me, meanwhile, no glimpse of him, but they had tended to make more public the change taking place in our relation as a consequence of his having at the piano, the day before, kept me, in Flora's interest, so beguiled and befooled. The stamp of publicity had of course been fully given by her confinement and departure, and the change itself was now ushered in by our nonobservance of the regular custom of the schoolroom. He had already disappeared when, on my way down, I pushed open his door, and I learned below that he had breakfasted—in the presence of a couple of the maids—with Mrs. Grose and his sister. He had then gone out, as he said, for a stroll; than which nothing, I reflected, could better have expressed his frank view of the abrupt transformation of my office. What he would now permit this office to consist of was yet to be settled: there was a queer relief, at all events—I mean for myself in especial—in the renouncement of one pretension. If so much had sprung to the surface, I scarce put it too strongly in saying that what had perhaps sprung highest was the absurdity of our prolonging the fiction that I had anything more to teach him. It sufficiently stuck out that, by tacit little tricks in which even more than myself he carried out the care for my dignity, I had had to appeal to him to let me off straining to meet him on the ground of his true capacity. He had at any rate his freedom now; I was never to touch it again; as I had amply shown, moreover, when, on his joining me in the schoolroom the previous night, I had uttered, on the subject of the interval just concluded, neither challenge nor hint. I had too much, from this moment, my other ideas. Yet when he at last arrived, the difficulty of applying them, the accumulations of my problem, were brought straight home to me by the beautiful little presence on which what had occurred had as yet, for the eye, dropped neither stain nor shadow.

To mark, for the house, the high state I cultivated I decreed that my meals with the boy should be served, as we called it, downstairs; so that I had been awaiting him in the ponderous pomp of the room outside of the window of which I had had from Mrs. Grose, that first scared Sunday, my flash of something it would scarce have done to call light. Here at present I felt afresh—for I had felt it again and again—how my equilibrium depended on the success of my rigid will, the will to shut my eyes as tight as possible to the truth that what I had to deal with was, revoltingly, against nature. I could only get on at all by taking "nature" into my confidence and my account, by treating my monstrous ordeal as a push in a direction unusual, of course, and unpleasant, but demanding, after all, for a fair front, only another turn of the screw of ordinary human virtue. No attempt, nonetheless, could well require more tact than just this attempt to supply, one's self, *all* the nature. How could I put even a little of that article into a suppression of reference to what had occurred? How, on the other hand, could I make reference without a new plunge into the hideous obscure? Well, a sort of answer, after a time, had come to me, and it was so far confirmed as that I was met, incontestably, by the quickened vision of what was rare in my little companion. It was indeed as if he had found even now—as he had so often found at lessons—still some other delicate way to ease me off. Wasn't there light in the fact which, as we shared our solitude, broke out with a specious glitter it had never yet quite worn?—the fact that (opportunity aiding, precious opportunity which had now come) it would be preposterous, with a child so endowed, to forego the help one might wrest from absolute intelligence? What had his intelligence been given him for but to save him? Mightn't one, to reach his mind, risk the stretch of an angular arm over his character? It was as if, when we were face to face in the dining room, he had literally shown me the way. The roast mutton was on the table, and I had dispensed with attendance. Miles, before he sat down, stood a moment with his hands in his pockets and looked at the joint, on which he seemed on the point of passing some humorous judgment. But what he presently produced was: "I say, my dear, is she really very awfully ill?"

"Little Flora? Not so bad but that she'll presently be better. London will set her up. Bly had ceased to agree with her. Come here and take your mutton."

He alertly obeyed me, carried the plate carefully to his seat, and, when he was established, went on. "Did Bly disagree with her so terribly suddenly?"

"Not so suddenly as you might think. One had seen it coming on."

"Then why didn't you get her off before?"

"Before what?"

"Before she became too ill to travel."

I found myself prompt. "She's *not* too ill to travel: she only might have become so if she had stayed. This was just the moment to seize. The journey will dissipate the influence"—oh, I was grand!—"and carry it off."

"I see, I see"—Miles, for that matter, was grand, too. He settled to his repast with the charming little "table manner" that, from the day of his arrival, had relieved me of all grossness of admonition. Whatever he had been driven from school for, it was not for ugly feeding. He was irreproachable, as always, today; but he was unmistakably more conscious. He was discernibly trying to take for granted more things than he found, without assistance, quite easy; and he dropped into peaceful silence while he felt his situation. Our meal was of the briefest—mine a vain pretense, and I had the things immediately removed. While this was done Miles stood again with his hands in his little pockets and his back to me—stood and looked out of the wide window through which, that other day, I had seen what pulled me up. We continued silent while the maid was with us—as silent, it whimsically occurred to me, as some young couple who, on their wedding journey, at the inn, feel shy in the presence of the waiter. He turned round only when the waiter had left us. "Well—so we're alone!"

XXIII

"Oh, more or less." I fancy my smile was pale. "Not absolutely. We shouldn't like that!" I went on.

"No—I suppose we shouldn't. Of course we have the others."

"We have the others—we have indeed the others," I concurred.

"Yet even though we have them," he returned, still with his hands in his pockets and planted there in front of me, "they don't much count, do they?"

I made the best of it, but I felt wan. "It depends on what you call 'much'!"

"Yes"—with all accommodation—"everything depends!". On this, however, he faced to the window again and presently reached it with his vague, restless, cogitating step. He remained there awhile, with his forehead against the glass, in contemplation of the stupid shrubs I knew and the dull things of November. I had always my hypocrisy of "work," behind which, now, I gained the sofa. Steadying myself with it there as I had repeatedly done at those moments of torment that I have described as the moments of my knowing the children to be given to something from which I was barred, I sufficiently obeyed my habit of being prepared for the worst. But an extraordinary impression dropped on me as I extracted a meaning from the boy's embarrassed back —none other than the impression that I was not barred now. This inference grew in a few minutes to sharp intensity and seemed bound up with the direct perception that it was positively *he* who was. The frames and squares of the great window were a kind of image, for him, of a kind of failure. I felt that I saw him, at any rate, shut in or shut out. He was admirable, but not comfortable: I took it in with a throb of hope. Wasn't he looking, through the haunted pane, for something he couldn't see?—and wasn't it the first time in the whole business that he had known such a lapse? The first, the very first: I found it a splendid portent. It made him anxious, though he watched himself; he had been anxious all day and, even while in his usual sweet little manner he sat at table, had needed all his small strange genius to give it a gloss. When he at last turned round to meet me, it was almost as if this genius had succumbed. "Well, I think I'm glad Bly agrees with me!"

"You would certainly seem to have seen, these twenty-four hours, a good deal more of it than for some time before. I hope," I went on bravely, "that you've been enjoying yourself."

"Oh, yes, I've been ever so far; all round about—miles and miles away. I've never been so free."

He had really a manner of his own, and I could only try to keep up with him. "Well, do you like it?"

He stood there smiling; then at last he put into two words—"Do you?"—more discrimination than I had ever heard two words contain. Before I had time to deal with that, however, he continued as if with the sense that this was an impertinence to be softened. "Nothing could be more charming than the way you take it, for of course if we're alone together now it's you that are alone most. But I hope," he threw in, "you don't particularly mind!"

"Having to do with you?" I asked. "My dear child, how can I help minding? Though I've renounced all claim to your company— you're so beyond me—I at least greatly enjoy it. What else should I stay on for?"

He looked at me more directly, and the expression of his face, graver now, struck me as the most beautiful I had ever found in it. "You stay on just for *that*?"

"Certainly. I stay on as your friend and from the tremendous interest I take in you till something can be done for you that may be more worth your while. That needn't surprise you." My voice trembled so that I felt it impossible to suppress the shake. "Don't you remember how I told you, when I came and sat on your bed the night of the storm, that there was nothing in the world I wouldn't do for you?"

"Yes, yes!" He, on his side, more and more visibly nervous, had a tone to master; but he was so much more successful than I that, laughing out through his gravity, he could pretend we were pleasantly jesting. "Only that, I think, was to get me to do something for you!"

"It was partly to get you to do something," I conceded. "But, you know, you didn't do it."

"Oh, yes," he said with the brightest superficial eagerness, "you wanted me to tell you something."

"That's it. Out, straight out. What you have on your mind, you know."

"Ah, then, is *that* what you've stayed over for?"

He spoke with a gaiety through which I could still catch the finest little quiver of resentful passion; but I can't begin to express the effect upon me of an implication of surrender even so faint. It was as if what I had yearned for had come at last only to astonish me. "Well, yes—I may as well make a clean breast of it. It was precisely for that."

He waited so long that I supposed it for the purpose of repudiating the assumption on which my action had been founded; but what he finally said was: "Do you mean now—here?"

"There couldn't be a better place or time." He looked round him uneasily, and I had the rare—oh, the queer!—impression of the very first symptom I had seen in him of the approach of immediate fear. It was as if he were suddenly afraid of me—which struck me indeed as perhaps the best thing to make him. Yet in the very pang of the effort I felt it vain to try sternness, and I heard myself the next instant so gentle as to be almost grotesque. "You want so to go out again?"

"Awfully!" He smiled at me heroically, and the touching little bravery of it was enhanced by his actually flushing with pain. He had picked up his hat, which he had brought in, and stood twirling it in a way that gave me, even as I was just nearly reaching port, a perverse horror of what I was doing. To do it in any way was an act of violence, for what did it consist of but the obtrusion of the idea of grossness and guilt on a small helpless creature who had been for me a revelation of the possibilities of beautiful intercourse? Wasn't it base to create for a being so exquisite a mere alien awkwardness? I suppose I now read into our situation a clearness it couldn't have had at the time, for I seem to see our poor eyes already lighted with some spark of a prevision of the anguish that was to come. So we circled about, with terrors and scruples, like fighters not daring to close. But it was for each other we feared! That kept us a little longer suspended and unbruised. "I'll tell you everything," Miles said—"I mean I'll tell you anything you like. You'll stay on with me, and we shall both be all right, and I *will* tell you—I *will*. But not now."

"Why not now?"

My insistence turned him from me and kept him once more at his window in a silence during which, between us, you might have heard a pin drop. Then he was before me again with the air of a person for whom, outside, someone who had frankly to be reckoned with was waiting. "I have to see Luke."

I had not yet reduced him to quite so vulgar a lie, and I felt proportionately ashamed. But, horrible as it was, his lies made up my truth. I achieved thoughtfully a few loops of my knitting. "Well, then, go to Luke, and I'll wait for what you promise. Only, in return for that, satisfy, before you leave me, one very much smaller request."

He looked as if he felt he had succeeded enough to be able still a little to bargain. "Very much smaller——?"

"Yes, a mere fraction of the whole. Tell me"—oh, my work preoccupied me, and I was offhand!—"if, yesterday afternoon, from the table in the hall, you took, you know, my letter."

XXIV

My sense of how he received this suffered for a minute from something that I can describe only as a fierce split of my attention—a stroke that at first, as I sprang straight up, reduced me to the mere blind movement of getting hold of him, drawing him close, and, while I just fell for support against the nearest piece of furniture, instinctively keeping him with his back to the window. The appearance was full upon us that I had already had to deal with here: Peter Quint had come into a view like a sentinel before a prison. The next thing I saw was that, from outside, he had reached the window, and then I knew that, close to the glass and glaring in through it, he offered once more to the room his white face of damnation. It represents but grossly what took place within me at the sight to say that on the second my decision was made; yet I believe that no woman so overwhelmed ever in so short a time recovered her grasp of the *act*. It came to me in the very horror of the immediate presence that the act would be, seeing and facing what I saw and faced, to keep the boy himself unaware. The inspiration—I can call it by no other name—was that I felt how voluntarily, how transcendently, I *might*. It was like fighting with a demon for a human soul, and when I had fairly so appraised it I saw how the human soul—held out, in the tremor of my hands, at arm's length—had a perfect dew of sweat on a lovely childish forehead. The face that was close to mine was as white as the face against the glass, and out of it presently came a sound, not low nor weak, but as if from much further away, that I drank like a waft of fragrance.

"Yes—I took it."

At this, with a moan of joy, I enfolded, I drew him close; and while I held him to my breast, where I could feel in the sudden fever of his little body the tremendous pulse of his little heart, I kept my eyes on the thing at the window and saw it move and shift its posture. I have likened it to a sentinel, but its slow wheel, for a moment, was rather the prowl of a baffled beast. My present quickened courage, however, was such that, not too much to let it through, I had to shade, as it were, my flame. Meanwhile the glare of the face was again at the window, the scoundrel fixed as if to watch and wait. It was the very confidence that I might now defy him, as well as the positive certitude, by this time, of the child's unconsciousness, that made me go on. "What did you take it for?"

"To see what you said about me."

"You opened the letter?"

"I opened it."

My eyes were now, as I held him off a little again, on Miles's own face, in which the collapse of mockery showed me how complete was the ravage of uneasiness. What was prodigious was that at last, by my success, his sense was sealed and his communication stopped: he knew that he was in presence, but knew not of what, and knew still less that I also was and that I did know. And what did this strain of trouble matter when my eyes went back to the window only to see that the air was clear again and—by my personal triumph—the influence quenched? There was nothing there. I felt that the cause was mine and that

I should surely get *all*. "And you found nothing!"—I let my elation out.

He gave the most mournful, thoughtful little headshake. "Nothing."

"Nothing, nothing!" I almost shouted in my joy.

"Nothing, nothing," he sadly repeated.

I kissed his forehead; it was drenched. "So what have you done with it?"

"I've burned it."

"Burned it?" It was now or never. "Is that what you did at school?"

Oh, what this brought up! "At school?"

"Did you take letters?—or other things?"

"Other things?" He appeared now to be thinking of something far off and that reached him only through the pressure of his anxiety. Yet it did reach him. "Did I *steal?*"

I felt myself redden to the roots of my hair as well as wonder if it were more strange to put to a gentleman such a question or to see him take it with allowances that gave the very distance of his fall in the world. "Was it for that you mightn't go back?"

The only thing he felt was a dreary little surprise. "Did you know I mightn't go back?"

"I know everything."

He gave me at this the longest and strangest look. "Everything?"

"Everything. Therefore *did* you——?" But I couldn't say it again.

Miles could, very simply. "No. I didn't steal."

My face must have shown him I believed him utterly; yet my hands—but it was for pure tenderness—shook him as if to ask him why, if it was all for nothing, he had condemned me to months of torment. "What then did you do?"

He looked in vague pain all round the top of the room and drew his breath, two or three times over, as if with difficulty. He might have been standing at the bottom of the sea and raising his eyes to some faint green twilight. "Well—I said things."

"Only that?"

"They thought it was enough!"

"To turn you out for?"

Never, truly, had a person "turned out" shown so little to explain it as this little person! He appeared to weigh my question, but in a manner quite detached and almost helpless. "Well, I suppose I oughtn't."

"But to whom did you say them?"

He evidently tried to remember, but it dropped—he had lost it. "I don't know!"

He almost smiled at me in the desolation of his surrender, which was indeed practically, by this time, so complete that I ought to have left it there. But I was infatuated—I was blind with victory, though even then the very effect that was to have brought him so much nearer was already that of added separation. "Was it to everyone?" I asked.

"No; it was only to——" But he gave a sick little headshake. "I don't remember their names."

"Were they then so many?"

"No—only a few. Those I liked."

Those he liked? I seemed to float not into clearness, but into a darker obscure, and within a minute there had come to me out of my very pity the appalling alarm of his being perhaps innocent. It was for the instant confounding and bottomless, for if he *were* innocent, what then on earth was *I?* Paralyzed, while it lasted, by the mere brush of the question, I let him go a little, so that, with a deep-drawn sigh, he turned away from me again; which, as he faced toward the clear window, I suffered, feeling that I had nothing now there to keep him from. "And did they repeat what you said?" I went on after a moment.

He was soon at some distance from me, still breathing hard and again with the air, though now without anger for it, of being confined against his will. Once more, as he had done before, he looked up at the dim day as if, of what had hitherto sustained him, nothing was left but an unspeakable anxiety. "Oh, yes," he nevertheless replied —"they must have repeated them. To those *they* liked," he added.

There was, somehow, less of it than I had expected; but I turned it over. "And these things came round——?"

"To the masters? Oh, yes!" he answered very simply. "But I didn't know they'd tell."

"The masters? They didn't—they've never told. That's why I ask you."

He turned to me again his little beautiful fevered face. "Yes, it was too bad."

"Too bad?"

"What I suppose I sometimes said. To write home."

I can't name the exquisite pathos of the contradiction given to such a speech by such a speaker; I only know that the next instant I heard myself throw off with homely force: "Stuff and nonsense!" But the next after that I must have sounded stern enough. "What were these things?"

My sternness was all for his judge, his executioner; yet it made him avert himself again, and that movement made me, with a single bound and an irrepressible cry, spring straight upon him. For there again, against the glass, as if to blight his confession and stay his answer, was the hideous author of our woe—the white face of damnation. I felt a sick swim at the drop of my victory and all the return of my battle, so that the wildness of my veritable leap only served as a great betrayal. I saw him, from the midst of my act, meet it with a divination, and on the perception that even now he only guessed, and that the window was still to his own eyes free, I let the impulse flame up to convert the climax of his dismay into the very proof of his liberation. "No more, no more, no more!" I shrieked, as I tried to press him against me, to my visitant.

"Is she here?" Miles panted as he caught with his sealed eyes the direction of my words. Then as his strange "she" staggered me and, with a gasp, I echoed it, "Miss Jessel, Miss Jessel!" he with a sudden fury gave me back.

I seized, stupefied, his supposition—some sequel to what we had done to Flora, but this made me only want to show him that it was better still than that. "It's not Miss Jessel! But it's at the window—straight before us. It's *there*—the coward horror, there for the last time!"

At this, after a second in which his head made the movement of a baffled dog's on a scent and then gave a frantic little shake for air and light, he was at me in a white rage, bewildered, glaring vainly over the place and missing wholly, though it now, to my sense, filled the room like the taste of poison, the wide, overwhelming presence. "It's *he*?"

I was so determined to have all my proof that I flashed into ice to challenge him. "Whom do you mean by 'he'?"

"Peter Quint—you devil!" His face gave again, round the room, its convulsed supplication. "*Where?*"

They are in my ears still, his supreme surrender of the name and his tribute to my devotion. "What does he matter now, my own?—what will he *ever* matter? *I* have you," I launched at the beast, "but he has lost you forever!" Then, for the demonstration of my work, "There, *there!*" I said to Miles.

But he had already jerked straight round, stared, glared again, and seen but the quiet day. With the stroke of the loss I was so proud of he uttered the cry of a creature hurled over an abyss, and the grasp with which I recovered him might have been that of catching him in his fall. I caught him, yes, I held him—it may be imagined with what a passion; but at the end of a minute I began to feel what it truly was that I held. We were alone with the quiet day, and his little heart, dispossessed, had stopped.

FOR DISCUSSION:

1. To what purpose does James use the introductory device of presenting the narrator, Douglas, as a member of a sociable group, telling ghost stories for mutual entertainment? Can it be said that he is an objective, impartial narrator?

2. Enumerate the various physical symptoms revealed by the governess's description of her own condition, starting from her first words (e.g., vertigo, insomnia).

3. Analyze the scene in which the governess and Mrs. Grose discuss the ghostly appearances of Quint. Who actually identifies the male spectre as Quint? What is the psychological significance of having him appear first on a tower, next peering through a window?

4. What is the psychological significance of having the female ghost appear first on a lake? How do the two ghost figures differ in their intents and purposes? According to the governess, is one ghost more dangerous than the other?

5. What is the significance of the letter from Miles's school? Does the reader ever learn the exact contents of this message?

6. If the behavior of Miles and Flora is

viewed objectively, quite apart from the governess's interpretation, is their conduct normal for young children? Are their statements typical of innocent children or can they be said to possess hidden meanings?

7. Is the governess educationally qualified for her position? What is her actual program of study for her young charges? What innovations does she make in their daily routine? Are these innovations educationally motivated?

8. In any of the episodes in which the governess encounters ghostly forms, are there other witnesses to the apparitions? If so, who are they?

9. Comment on the governess's attitude toward the children's guardian.

The Buried Life

MATTHEW ARNOLD

Light flows our war of mocking words, and yet,
Behold, with tears mine eyes are wet!
I feel a nameless sadness o'er me roll.
Yes, yes, we know that we can jest,
We know, we know that we can smile!
But there's a something in this breast,
To which thy light words bring no rest,
And thy gay smiles no anodyne.
Give me thy hand, and hush awhile,
And turn those limpid eyes on mine,   10
And let me read there, love! thy inmost soul.

Alas! is even love too weak
To unlock the heart, and let it speak?
Are even lovers powerless to reveal
To one another what indeed they feel?
I knew the mass of men conceal'd
Their thoughts, for fear that if reveal'd
They would by other men be met
With blank indifference, or with blame reproved;
I knew they lived and moved   20
Trick'd in disguises, alien to the rest
Of men, and alien to themselves—and yet
The same heart beats in every human breast!

But we, my love!—doth a like spell benumb
Our hearts, our voices?—must we too be dumb?

Ah! well for us, if even we,
Even for a moment, can get free
Our heart, and have our lips unchain'd;
For that which seals them hath been deep-ordain'd!
Fate, which foresaw   30
How frivolous a baby man would be—
By what distractions he would be possess'd,
How he would pour himself in every strife,
And well-nigh change his own identity—
That it might keep from his capricious play
His genuine self, and force him to obey
Even in his own despite his being's law,
Bade through the deep recesses of our breast
The unregarded river of our life
Pursue with indiscernible flow its way;   40
And that we should not see
The buried stream, and seem to be
Eddying at large in blind uncertainty,
Though driving on with it eternally.

But often, in the world's most crowded streets,

468

But often, in the din of strife,
There rises an unspeakable desire
After the knowledge of our buried life;
A thirst to spend our fire and restless force
In tracking out our true, original course;
A longing to inquire
Into the mystery of this heart which beats
So wild, so deep in us—to know
Whence our lives come and where they go.
And many a man in his own breast then delves,
But deep enough, alas! none ever mines.
And we have been on many thousand lines,
And we have shown, on each, spirit and power;
But hardly have we, for one little hour,
Been on our own line, have we been ourselves—
Hardly had skill to utter one of all
The nameless feelings that course through our breast,
But they course on for ever unexpress'd.
And long we try in vain to speak and act
Our hidden self, and what we say and do
Is eloquent, is well—but 'tis not true!
And then we will no more be rack'd
With inward striving, and demand
Of all the thousand nothings of the hour
Their stupefying power;
Ah yes, and they benumb us at our call!
Yet still, from time to time, vague and forlorn,
From the soul's subterranean depth upborne
As from an infinitely distant land,
Come airs, and floating echoes, and convey
A melancholy into all our day.

Only—but this is rare—
When a belovéd hand is laid in ours,
When, jaded with the rush and glare
Of the interminable hours,
Our eyes can in another's eyes read clear,
When our world-deafen'd ear
Is by the tones of a loved voice caress'd—
A bolt is shot back somewhere in our breast,
And a lost pulse of feeling stirs again.
The eye sinks inward, and the heart lies plain,
And what we mean, we say, and what we would, we know.
A man becomes aware of his life's flow,
And hears its winding murmur; and he sees
The meadows where it glides, the sun, the breeze.

And there arrives a lull in the hot race
Wherein he doth for ever chase
That flying and elusive shadow, rest.
An air of coolness plays upon his face,
And an unwonted calm pervades his breast.
And then he thinks he knows
The hills where his life rose,
And the sea where it goes.

FOR DISCUSSION:

1. In this poem is Arnold referring to conscious thoughts, unconscious drives, or both? How do you know?
2. Would Freud agree that "the same heart beats in every human breast"?
3. The buried life is symbolized as a river in line 39 and a mine in line 55. Are these appropriate images?
4. Is it significant that it is only during the expression of love that Arnold believes man "thinks he knows/The hills where his life rose"?

I Saw a Chapel All of Gold

WILLIAM BLAKE

I saw a chapel all of gold
That none did dare to enter in
And many weeping stood without
Weeping mourning worshipping

I saw a serpent rise between
The white pillars of the door
And he forcd & forcd & forcd
Down the golden hinges tore

And along the pavement sweet
Set with pearls & rubies bright   10
All his slimy length he drew
Till upon the altar white

Vomiting his poison out
On the bread & on the wine
So I turned into a sty
And laid me down among the swine

FOR DISCUSSION:

1. Is Blake's disgust at the end of the poem due to revulsion at the sex act or at the hypocrisy of the moral law which governs sexuality? Examine the poem and its phallic imagery in the light of these possibilities.

Kisses in the Train*

D. H. LAWRENCE

I saw the midlands
  Revolve through her hair;
The fields of autumn
  Stretching bare,
And sheep on the pasture
  Tossed back in a scare.

And still as ever
  The world went round,

My mouth on her pulsing
  Neck was found,   10
And my breast to her beating
  Breast was bound.

But my heart at the center
  Of all, in a swound
Was still as a pivot,
  As all the ground

---

* From THE COMPLETE POEMS OF D. H. LAWRENCE, Volume I, edited by Vivian de Sola Pinto & F. Warren Roberts. Copyright 1920 by B. W. Huebsch, Inc., renewed 1948 by Frieda Lawrence. Reprinted by permission of The Viking Press, Inc., William Heinemann Ltd., Laurence Pollinger Limited, and the Estate of the late Mrs. Frieda Lawrence.

On its prowling orbit
    Shifted round.

And still in my nostrils
    The scent of her flesh.
And still my wet mouth
    Sought her afresh;
And still one pulse
    Through the world did thresh.

And the world all whirling
    Around in joy
Like the dance of a dervish
    Did destroy
My sense—and my reason
    Spun like a toy.

But firm at the center
    My heart was found;
Her own to my perfect
    Heart-beat bound,
Like a magnet's keeper
    Closing the round.

FOR DISCUSSION:

1. Does Lawrence effectively integrate imagery and narrative in this poem? If so, how?

My Last Duchess

ROBERT BROWNING

FERRARA

That's my last Duchess painted on the wall,
Looking as if she were alive. I call
That piece a wonder, now: Frà Pandolf's hands
Worked busily a day, and there she stands.
Will 't please you sit and look at her? I said
"Frà Pandolf" by design, for never read
Strangers like you that pictured countenance,
The depth and passion of its earnest glance,
But to myself they turned (since none puts by
The curtain I have drawn for you, but I)
And seemed as they would ask me, if they durst,
How such a glance came there; so, not the first
Are you to turn and ask thus. Sir, 't was not
Her husband's presence only, called that spot
Of joy into the Duchess' cheek: perhaps
Frà Pandolf chanced to say "Her mantle laps
Over my lady's wrist too much," or "Paint
Must never hope to reproduce the faint
Half-flush that dies along her throat": such stuff
Was courtesy, she thought, and cause enough
For calling up that spot of joy. She had
A heart—how shall I say?—too soon made glad,
Too easily impressed; she liked whate'er
She looked on, and her looks went everywhere.
Sir, 't was all one! My favour at her breast,
The dropping of the daylight in the West,
The bough of cherries some officious fool
Broke in the orchard for her, the white mule
She rode with round the terrace—all and each

Would draw from her alike the approving speech, 30
Or blush, at least. She thanked men,—good! but thanked
Somehow—I know not how—as if she ranked
My gift of a nine-hundred-years-old name
With anybody's gift. Who'd stoop to blame
This sort of trifling? Even had you skill
In speech—(which I have not)—to make your will
Quite clear to such an one, and say, "Just this
Or that in you disgusts me; here you miss,
Or there exceed the mark"—and if she let
Herself be lessoned so, nor plainly set 40
Her wits to yours, forsooth, and made excuse,
—E'en then would be some stooping; and I choose
Never to stoop. Oh sir, she smiled, no doubt,
Whene'er I passed her; but who passed without
Much the same smile? This grew; I gave commands;
Then all smiles stopped together. There she stands
As if alive. Will't please you rise? We'll meet
The company below, then. I repeat,
The Count your master's known munificence
Is ample warrant that no just pretence 50
Of mine for dowry will be disallowed;
Though his fair daughter's self, as I avowed
At starting, is my object. Nay, we'll go
Together down, sir. Notice Neptune, though,
Taming a sea-horse, thought a rarity,
Which Claus of Innsbruck cast in bronze for me!

FOR DISCUSSION:

1. The poem is in the form of a dramatic monologue. To whom is the Duke speaking? What is the occasion?

2. The Duke claims he has no skill in speech. Is this true?

3. What are the motives of the Duke in speaking about his last Duchess?

4. As he speaks, does the Duke unconsciously betray his own personality? What are his main character traits? What are those of his last Duchess?

5. Browning critic Laurence Perrine observes, "The Duke while revealing himself as infinitely worse than he supposes himself to be is at the same time revealing his last Duchess as infinitely better than he supposes her to be." Comment on this observation.

Soliloquy of the Spanish Cloister

ROBERT BROWNING

I

Gr-r-r—there go, my heart's abhorrence!
　Water your damned flower-pots, do!
If hate killed men, Brother Lawrence,
　God's blood, would not mine kill you!
What? your myrtle-bush wants trimming?
　Oh, that rose has prior claims—
Needs its leaden vase filled brimming?
　Hell dry you up with its flames!

II

At the meal we sit together:
    Salve tibi! I must hear
Wise talk of the kind of weather,
    Sort of season, time of year:
Not a plenteous cork-crop: scarcely
    Dare we hope oak-galls, I doubt:
What 's the Latin name for "parsley"?
    What 's the Greek name for Swine's Snout?

III

Whew! We 'll have our platter burnished,
    Laid with care on our own shelf!
With a fire-new spoon we 're furnished,
    And a goblet for ourself,
Rinsed like something sacrificial
    Ere 't is fit to touch our chaps—
Marked with L. for our initial!
    (He-he! There his lily snaps!)

IV

Saint, forsooth! While brown Dolores
    Squats outside the Convent bank
With Sanchicha, telling stories,
    Steeping tresses in the tank,
Blue-black, lustrous, thick like horsehairs,
    —Can't I see his dead eye glow,
Bright as 't were a Barbary corsair's?
    (That is, if he 'd let it show!)

V

When he finishes refection,
    Knife and fork he never lays
Cross-wise, to my recollection,
    As do I, in Jesu's praise.
I the Trinity illustrate,
    Drinking watered orange-pulp—
In three sips the Arian frustrate;
    While he drains his at one gulp.

VI

Oh, those melons? If he 's able
    We 're to have a feast! so nice!
One goes to the Abbot's table,
    All of us get each a slice.

---

10. *Salve tibi!* Hail to thee, a salutation 39. Arian subscriber to the heretical doctrines of Arius, a fourth-century Syrian who denied the divinity of Christ and held Him to be inferior to God

How go on your flowers? None double?
 Not one fruit-sort can you spy?
Strange!—And I, too, at such trouble,
 Keep them close-nipped on the sly!

VII

There 's a great text in Galatians,
 Once you trip on it, entails
Twenty-nine distinct damnations,
 One sure, if another fails:
If I trip him just a-dying,
 Sure of heaven as sure can be,
Spin him round and send him flying
 Off to hell, a Manichee?

VIII

Or, my scrofulous French novel
 On grey paper with blunt type!
Simply glance at it, you grovel
 Hand and foot in Belial's gripe:
If I double down its pages
 At the woeful sixteenth print,
When he gathers his greengages,
 Ope a sieve and slip it in 't?

IX

Or, there's Satan!—one might venture
 Pledge one's soul to him, yet leave
Such a flaw in the indenture
 As he'd miss till, past retrieve,
Blasted lay that rose-acacia
 We 're so proud of! *Hy, Zy, Hine* ...
'St, there 's Vespers! *Plena gratiâ*
 Ave, Virgo! Gr-r-r—you swine!

FOR DISCUSSION:

1. What is the difference between a soliloquy and a monologue?
2. The speaker compares himself with Brother Lawrence. What does the comparison reveal about the speaker? About Brother Lawrence?
3. What is the effect of opening and closing the poem with "Gr-r-r"? Of closing the poem with a simultaneous prayer and curse?

56. Manichee follower of Manes, a third-century Persian who attempted to combine Orient religion with Christianity and maintained that two supreme principles govern the universe: light (goodness) and darkness (evil) 71. *Plena gratiâ* "Full of grace," from a prayer to the Virgin Mary

The Bishop Orders His Tomb at Saint Praxed's Church

ROBERT BROWNING

ROME, 15—

Vanity, saith the preacher, vanity!
Draw round my bed: is Anselm keeping back?
Nephews—sons mine . . . ah God, I know not!
    Well—
She, men would have to be your mother once,
Old Gandolf envied me, so fair she was!
What 's done is done, and she is dead beside,
Dead long ago, and I am Bishop since,
And as she died so must we die ourselves,
And thence ye may perceive the world 's a dream.
Life, how and what is it? As here I lie   10
In this state-chamber, dying by degrees,
Hours and long hours in the dead night, I ask
"Do I live, am I dead?" Peace, peace seems all.
Saint Praxed's ever was the church for peace;
And so, about this tomb of mine. I fought
With tooth and nail to save my niche, ye know:
—Old Gandolf cozened me, despite my care;
Shrewd was that snatch from out the corner South
He graced his carrion with, God curse the same!
Yet still my niche is not so cramped but thence   20
One sees the pulpit o' the epistle-side,
And somewhat of the choir, those silent seats,
And up into the aery dome where live
The angels, and a sunbeam 's sure to lurk:
And I shall fill my slab of basalt there,
And 'neath my tabernacle take my rest,
With those nine columns round me, two and two,
The odd one at my feet where Anselm stands:
Peach-blossom marble all, the rare, the ripe
As fresh-poured red wine of a mighty pulse.   30
—Old Gandolf with his paltry onion-stone,
Put me where I may look at him! True peach,
Rosy and flawless: how I earned the prize!
Draw close: that conflagration of my church
—What then? So much was saved if aught were missed!
My sons, ye would not be my death? Go dig
The white-grape vineyard where the oil-press stood,
Drop water gently till the surface sink,
And if ye find . . . Ah God, I know not, I! . . .
Bedded in store of rotten fig-leaves soft,   40
And corded up in a tight olive-frail,

---

1. Vanity, see Ecclesiastes I: 2

Some lump, ah God, of *lapis lazuli*,
Big as a Jew's head cut off at the nape,
Blue as a vein o'er the Madonna's breast . . .
Sons, all have I bequeathed you, villas, all,
That brave Frascati villa with its bath,
So, let the blue lump poise between my knees,
Like God the Father's globe on both his hands
Ye worship in the Jesu Church so gay,
For Gandolf shall not choose but see and burst! 50
Swift as a weaver's shuttle fleet our years:
Man goeth to the grave, and where is he?
Did I say basalt for my slab, sons? Black—
'T was ever antique-black I meant! How else
Shall ye contrast my frieze to come beneath?
The bas-relief in bronze ye promised me,
Those Pans and Nymphs ye wot of, and perchance
Some tripod, thyrsus, with a vase or so,
The Saviour at his sermon on the mount,
Saint Praxed in a glory, and one Pan 60
Ready to twitch the Nymph's last garment off,
And Moses with the tables . . . but I know
Ye mark me not! What do they whisper thee,
Child of my bowels, Anselm? Ah, ye hope
To revel down my villas while I gasp
Bricked o'er with beggar's mouldy travertine
Which Gandolf from his tomb-top chuckles at!
Nay, boys, ye love me—all of jasper, then!
'T is jasper ye stand pledged to, lest I grieve
My bath must needs be left behind, alas! 70
One block, pure green as a pistachio-nut,
There 's plenty jasper somewhere in the world—
And have I not Saint Praxed's ear to pray
Horses for ye, and brown Greek manuscripts,
And mistresses with great smooth marbly limbs?
—That 's if ye carve my epitaph aright,
Choice Latin, picked phrase, Tully's every word,
No gaudy ware like Gandolf's second line—
Tully, my masters? Ulpian serves his need!
And then how I shall lie through centuries, 80
And hear the blessed mutter of the mass,
And see God made and eaten all day long,
And feel the steady candle-flame, and taste
Good strong thick stupefying incense-smoke!
For as I lie here, hours of the dead night,
Dying in state and by such slow degrees,
I fold my arms as if they clasped a crook,
And stretch my feet forth straight as stone can point,
And let the bedclothes, for a mortcloth, drop
Into great laps and folds of sculptor's-work: 90
And as yon tapers dwindle, and strange thoughts

42. *lapus lazuli* a semi-precious blue stone 46. *Frascati* an exclusive suburb in the Alban hills near Rome 77. *Tully's Latin* Cicero's Latin, characterized by a high, elegant style 79. *Ulpian* a Latin writer whose style was inferior to that of Cicero

Grow, with a certain humming in my ears,
About the life before I lived this life,
And this life too, popes, cardinals and priests,
Saint Praxed at his sermon on the mount,
Your tall pale mother with her talking eyes,
And new-found agate urns as fresh as day,
And marble's language, Latin pure, discreet,
—Aha, ELUCESCEBAT quoth our friend?
No Tully, said I, Ulpian at the best! 100
Evil and brief hath been my pilgrimage.
All *lapis*, all, sons! Else I give the Pope
My villas! Will ye ever eat my heart?
Ever your eyes were as a lizard's quick,
They glitter like your mother's for my soul,
Or ye would heighten my impoverished frieze,
Piece out its starved design, and fill my vase
With grapes, and add a visor and a Term,
And to the tripod ye would tie a lynx
That in his struggle throws the thyrsus down, 110
To comfort me on my entablature
Whereon I am to lie till I must ask
"Do I live, am I dead?" There, leave me, there!
For ye have stabbed me with ingratitude
To death—ye wish it—God, ye wish it! Stone—
Gritstone, a-crumble! Clammy squares which sweat
As if the corpse they keep were oozing through—
And no more *lapis* to delight the world!
Well, go! I bless ye. Fewer tapers there,
But in a row: and, going, turn your backs 120
—Ay, like departing altar-ministrants,
And leave me in my church, the church for peace,
That I may watch at leisure if he leers—
Old Gandolf, at me, from his onion-stone,
As still he envied me, so fair she was!

FOR DISCUSSION:

1. Compare the technique of unconscious character revelation in this poem with that of the Duke of Ferrara and the Friar in the cloister in the two preceding poems.

2. In his delirium the Bishop shows that he is more concerned with the flesh than the spirit. Cite examples.

3. In what ways does paganism influence the dying Bishop's thinking as much as Christianity?

4. Is Browning's psychological portrayal of the Bishop an indictment of the Church as a whole or merely of one individual in it?

99. ELUCESCEBAT He was illustrious

Daddy

SYLVIA PLATH

You do not do, you do not do
Any more, black shoe
In which I have lived like a foot
For thirty years, poor and white,
Barely daring to breathe or Achoo.

Daddy, I have had to kill you.
You died before I had time——
Marble-heavy, a bag full of God,
Ghastly statue with one grey toe
Big as a Frisco seal   10

And a head in the freakish Atlantic
Where it pours bean green over blue
In the waters off beautiful Nauset.
I used to pray to recover you.
Ach, du.

In the German tongue, in the Polish town
Scraped flat by the roller
Of wars, wars, wars.
But the name of the town is common.
My Polack friend   20

Says there are a dozen or two.
So I never could tell where you
Put your foot, your root,
I never could talk to you.
The tongue stuck in my jaw.

It stuck in a barb wire snare.
Ich, ich, ich, ich,
I could hardly speak.
I thought every German was you.
And the language obscene   30

An engine, an engine
Chuffing me off like a Jew.
A Jew to Dachau, Auschwitz, Belsen.
I began to talk like a Jew.
I think I may well be a Jew.

---

* From *Ariel* by Sylvia Plath. Copyright © 1963 by Ted Hughes. Reprinted by permission of Harper & Row, Publishers, and by permission of Olwyn Hughes, for the Estate of Sylvia Plath.

33. Dachau, Auschwitz, Belsen most notorious of Nazi concentration camps in World War II

The snows of the Tyrol, the clear beer of Vienna
Are not very pure or true.
With my gypsy ancestress and my weird luck
And my Taroc pack and my Taroc pack
I may be a bit of a Jew.

I have always been scared of you,
With your Luftwaffe, your gobbledygoo.
And your neat moustache
And your Aryan eye, bright blue.
Panzer-man, panzer-man, O You——

Not God but a swastika
So black no sky could squeak through.
Every woman adores a Fascist,
The boot in the face, the brute
Brute heart of a brute like you.

You stand at the blackboard, daddy,
In the picture I have of you,
A cleft in your chin instead of your foot
But no less a devil for that, no not
Any less the black man who

Bit my pretty red heart in two.
I was ten when they buried you.
At twenty I tried to die
And get back, back, back to you.
I thought even the bones would do.

But they pulled me out of the sack,
And they stuck me together with glue.
And then I knew what to do.
I made a model of you,
A man in black with a Meinkampf look

And a love of the rack and the screw.
And I said I do, I do.
So daddy, I'm finally through.
The black telephone's off at the root,
The voices just can't worm through.

If I've killed one man, I've killed two——
The vampire who said he was you
And drank my blood for a year,
Seven years, if you want to know.
Daddy, you can lie back now.

There's a stake in your fat black heart
And the villagers never liked you.

---

39. *Taroc pack Taroc* is a popular card game in Central Europe; gypsies use the cards to tell fortunes
45. *Panzer-man Panzer* is a German word for *tank*
58. refers to an unsuccessful suicide attempt
65. *Mein Kampf My Struggle*, Adolph Hitler's autobiography

They are dancing and stamping on you.
They always knew it was you.
Daddy, daddy, you bastard, I'm through.   80

FOR DISCUSSION:

1. Trace the comparison of Daddy to the Nazis and the poetess to the condemned Jews.
2. Comment on the ambivalent love-hate attitude implicit in line 48, "Every woman adores a Fascist."

La Belle Dame Sans Merci

JOHN KEATS

Ah, what can ail thee, wretched wight,
   Alone and palely loitering;
The sedge is wither'd from the lake,
   And no birds sing.

Ah, what can ail thee, wretched wight,
   So haggard and so woe-begone?
The squirrel's granary is full,
   And the harvest's done.

I see a lily on thy brow,
   With anguish moist and fever dew;   10
And on thy cheek a fading rose
   Fast withereth too.

I met a Lady in the meads
   Full beautiful, a fairy's child;
Her hair was long, her foot was light,
   And her eyes were wild.

I set her on my pacing steed,
   And nothing else saw all day long;
For sideways would she lean, and sing
   A faery's song.   20

I made a garland for her head,
   And bracelets too, and fragrant zone;
She look'd at me as she did love,
   And made sweet moan.

She found me roots of relish sweet,
   And honey wild, and manna dew,
And sure in language strange she said,
   I love thee true.
She took me to her elfin grot,
   And there she gaz'd and sighed deep   30

And there I shut her wild sad eyes—
    So kiss'd to sleep.

And there we slumber'd on the moss,
    And there I dream'd, ah woe betide
The latest dream I ever dream'd
    On the cold hill side.

I saw pale kings, and princes too,
    Pale warriors, death-pale were they all;
Who cry'd—"La belle Dame sans merci
    Hath thee in thrall!"   40

I saw their starv'd lips in the gloom
    With horrid warning gaped wide,
And I awoke, and found me here
    On the cold hill side.

And this is why I sojourn here
    Alone and palely loitering,
Though the sedge is wither'd from the lake,
    And no birds sing.

FOR DISCUSSION:

1. Account for the speaker's profound melancholy at the end of the poem. Is he sad because his love affair with La Belle Dame has not been consummated, or because it has?

2. What is the significance of the speaker's dream?

3. Comment on the significance of the title. Why is the lady sans merci?

4. Is the theme of the poem that (a) man should be content with his mortal lot, (b) the quest for the ideal is doomed to frustration, (c) fulfillment and satiety breed disillusionment, (d) imagination makes its own reality?

Kubla Khan:

OR, A VISION IN A DREAM. A FRAGMENT

SAMUEL TAYLOR COLERIDGE

The following fragment is here published at the request of a poet of great and deserved celebrity,[1] and, as far as the Author's own opinions are concerned, rather as a psychological curiosity, than on the ground of any supposed *poetic* merits.

In the summer of the year 1797, the Author, then in ill health, had retired to a lonely farm-house between Porlock and Linton, on the Exmoor confines of Somerset and Devonshire. In consequence of a slight indisposition, an anodyne had been prescribed, from the effects of which he fell asleep in his chair at the moment that he was reading the following sentence, or words of the same substance, in 'Purchas's Pilgrimage': 'Here the Khan Kubla commanded a palace to be built, and a stately garden thereunto. And

---

[1] Lord Byron.

thus ten miles of fertile ground were inclosed with a wall.' The Author continued for about three hours in a profound sleep, at least of the external senses, during which time he has the most vivid confidence, that he could not have composed less than from two to three hundred lines; if that indeed can be called composition in which all the images rose up before him as *things*, with a parallel production of the correspondent expressions, without any sensation or consciousness of effort. On awaking he appeared to himself to have a distinct recollection of the whole, and taking his pen, ink, and paper, instantly and eagerly wrote down the lines that are here preserved. At this moment he was unfortunately called out by a person on business from Porlock, and detained by him above an hour, and on his return to his room, found, to his no small surprise and mortification, that though he still retained some vague and dim recollection of the general purport of the vision, yet, with the exception of some eight or ten scattered lines and images, all the rest had passed away like the images on the surface of a stream into which a stone has been cast, but, alas! without the after restoration of the latter!

>   Then all the charm
> Is broken—all that phantom-world so fair
> Vanishes, and a thousand circlets spread,
> And each mis-shape['s] the other. Stay awhile,
> Poor youth! who scarcely dar'st lift up thine eyes—
> The stream will soon renew its smoothness, soon
> The visions will return! And lo, he stays,
> And soon the fragments dim of lovely forms
> Come trembling back, unite, and now once more
> The pool becomes a mirror.[2]

Yet from the still surviving recollections in his mind, the Author has frequently purposed to finish for himself what had been originally, as it were, given to him. But the to-morrow is yet to come.

As a contrast to this vision, I have annexed a fragment of a very different character, describing with equal fidelity the dream of pain and disease.

>   In Xanadu did Kubla Khan
> A stately pleasure-dome decree:
> Where Alph, the sacred river, ran
> Through caverns measureless to man
>   Down to a sunless sea.
> So twice five miles of fertile ground
> With walls and towers were girdled round:
> And there were gardens bright with sinuous rills,
> Where blossomed many an incense-bearing tree;
> And here were forests ancient as the hills,   10
> Enfolding sunny spots of greenery.
>
> But oh! that deep romantic chasm which slanted
> Down the green hill athwart a cedarn cover!
> A savage place! as holy and enchanted
> As e'er beneath a waning moon was haunted
> By woman wailing for her demon-lover!
> And from this chasm, with ceaseless turmoil seething,
> As if this earth in fast thick pants were breathing,
> A mighty fountain momently was forced:
> Amid whose swift half-intermitted burst   20
> Huge fragments vaulted like rebounding hail,

---

[2] From *The Picture; or, the Lover's Resolution*, lines 91–100.

Or chaffy grain beneath the thresher's flail:
And 'mid these dancing rocks at once and ever
It flung up momently the sacred river.
Five miles meandering with a mazy motion
Through wood and dale the sacred river ran,
Then reached the caverns measureless to man,
And sank in tumult to a lifeless ocean:
And 'mid this tumult Kubla heard from far
Ancestral voices prophesying war!   30
  The shadow of the dome of pleasure
  Floated midway on the waves;
  Where was heard the mingled measure
  From the fountain and the caves.
It was a miracle of rare device,
A sunny pleasure-dome with caves of ice!

  A damsel with a dulcimer
  In a vision once I saw:
  It was an Abyssinian maid,
  And on her dulcimer she played,   40
  Singing of Mount Abora.
  Could I revive within me
  Her symphony and song,
  To such a deep delight 'twould win me,
That with music loud and long,
I would build that dome in air,
That sunny dome! those caves of ice!
And all who heard should see them there,
And all should cry, Beware! Beware!
His flashing eyes, his floating hair!   50
Weave a circle round him thrice,
And close your eyes with holy dread,
For he on honey-dew hath fed,
And drunk the milk of Paradise.

FOR DISCUSSION:

1. If, as Freud believed, dreams are an expression of the unconscious mind, what can be inferred about Coleridge's unconscious from this poem, which he states in his preface is a recollection of a dream?

2. In the preface Coleridge says the poem is fragmentary, but many modern critics have argued for the poem's psychological and aesthetic unity. What evidence is there to support their views despite a statement from the author to the contrary?

3. Is the dome mentioned in line 2 the same dome mentioned in lines 31, 36, and 46–47? How do you know? Does it make any difference?

4. Does Kubla Khan himself represent (a) the poet, (b) a poet, (c) a tyrannical force, (d) Mankind, (e) God?

5. Of what symbolic importance are the pleasure dome, the sacred river, the gardens, the chasm, the fountain, the icy caves, the damsel, and the honey-dew?

Goblin Market

CHRISTINA ROSSETTI

Morning and evening
Maids heard the goblins cry:

'Come buy our orchard fruits,
Come buy, come buy:
Apples and quinces,
Lemons and oranges,
Plump unpecked cherries,
Melons and raspberries,
Bloom-down-cheeked peaches,
Swart-headed mulberries,
Wild free-born cranberries,
Crab-apples, dewberries,
Pine-apples, blackberries,
Apricots, strawberries;—
All ripe together
In summer weather,—
Morns that pass by,
Fair eves that fly;
Come buy, come buy:
Our grapes fresh from the vine,
Pomegranates full and fine,
Dates and sharp bullaces,
Rare pears and greengages,
Damsons and bilberries,
Taste them and try:
Currants and gooseberries,
Bright-fire-like barberries,
Figs to fill your mouth,
Citrons from the South,
Sweet to tongue and sound to eye;
Come buy, come buy.'

   Evening by evening
Among the brookside rushes,
Laura bowed her head to hear,
Lizzie veiled her blushes:
Crouching close together
In the cooling weather,
With clasping arms and cautioning lips,
With tingling cheeks and finger tips.
'Lie close,' Laura said,
Pricking up her golden head:
'We must not look at goblin men,
We must not buy their fruits:
Who knows upon what soil they fed
Their hungry thirsty roots?'
'Come buy,' call the goblins
Hobbling down the glen.
'Oh,' cried Lizzie, 'Laura, Laura,
You should not peep at goblin men.'
Lizzie covered up her eyes,
Covered close lest they should look;
Laura reared her glossy head,
And whispered like the restless brook:
'Look, Lizzie, look, Lizzie,
Down the glen tramp little men.

One hauls a basket,
One bears a plate,
One lugs a golden dish
Of many pounds weight.
How fair the vine must grow
Whose grapes are so luscious;
How warm the wind must blow
Through those fruit bushes.'
'No,' said Lizzie: 'No, no, no;
Their offers should not charm us,
Their evil gifts would harm us.'
She thrust a dimpled finger
In each ear, shut eyes and ran:
Curious Laura chose to linger
Wondering at each merchant man.
One had a cat's face,
One whisked a tail,
One tramped at a rat's pace,
One crawled like a snail,
One like a wombat prowled obtuse and furry,
One like a ratel tumbled hurry skurry.
She heard a voice like voice of doves
Cooing all together:
They sounded kind and full of loves
In the pleasant weather.

    Laura stretched her gleaming neck
Like a rush-imbedded swan,
Like a lily from the beck,
Like a moonlit poplar branch,
Like a vessel at the launch
When its last restraint is gone.

    Backwards up the mossy glen
Turned and trooped the goblin men,
With their shrill repeated cry,
'Come buy, come buy.'
When they reached where Laura was
They stood stock still upon the moss,
Leering at each other,
Brother with queer brother;
Signalling each other,
Brother with sly brother.
One set his basket down,
One reared his plate;
One began to weave a crown
Of tendrils, leaves, and rough nuts brown
(Men sell not such in any town);
One heaved the golden weight
Of dish and fruit to offer her:
'Come buy, come buy,' was still their cry.
Laura stared but did not stir,
Longed but had no money:
The whisk-tailed merchant bade her taste

In tones as smooth as honey,
The cat-faced purr'd,
The rat-paced spoke a word
Of welcome, and the snail-paced even was heard;
One parrot-voiced and jolly
Cried 'Pretty Goblin' still for 'Pretty Polly;'—
One whistled like a bird.

But sweet-tooth Laura spoke in haste:
'Good folk, I have no coin;
To take were to purloin:
I have no copper in my purse,
I have no silver either,
And all my gold is on the furze
That shakes in windy weather
Above the rusty heather.'
'You have much gold upon your head,'
They answered all together:
'Buy from us with a golden curl.'
She clipped a precious golden lock,
She dropped a tear more rare than pearl,
Then sucked their fruit globes fair or red:
Sweeter than honey from the rock,
Stronger than man-rejoicing wine,
Clearer than water flowed that juice;
She never tasted such before,
How should it cloy with length of use?
She sucked and sucked and sucked the more
Fruits which that unknown orchard bore;
She sucked until her lips were sore;
Then flung the emptied rinds away
But gathered up one kernel stone,
And knew not was it night or day
As she turned home alone.

Lizzie met her at the gate
Full of wise upbraidings:
'Dear, you should not stay so late,
Twilight is not good for maidens;
Should not loiter in the glen
In the haunts of goblin men.
Do you not remember Jeanie,
How she met them in the moonlight,
Took their gifts both choice and many,
Ate their fruits and wore their flowers
Plucked from bowers
Where summer ripens at all hours?
But ever in the noonlight
She pined and pined away;
Sought them by night and day,
Found them no more but dwindled and grew grey;
Then fell with the first snow,
While to this day no grass will grow
Where she lies low:

I planted daisies there a year ago
That never blow.
You should not loiter so.'
'Nay, hush,' said Laura:
'Nay, hush, my sister:
I ate and ate my fill,
Yet my mouth waters still;
To-morrow night I will
Buy more:' and kissed her:
'Have done with sorrow;
I'll bring you plums to-morrow
Fresh on their mother twigs,
Cherries worth getting;
You cannot think what figs
My teeth have met in,
What melons icy-cold
Piled on a dish of gold
Too huge for me to hold,
What peaches with a velvet nap,
Pellucid grapes without one seed:
Odorous indeed must be the mead
Whereon they grow, and pure the wave they drink
With lilies at the brink,
And sugar-sweet their sap.'

Golden head by golden head,
Like two pigeons in one nest
Folded in each other's wings,
They lay down in their curtained bed:
Like two blossoms on one stem,
Like two flakes of new-fall'n snow,
Like two wands of ivory
Tipped with gold for awful kings.
Moon and stars gazed in at them,
Wind sang to them lullaby,
Lumbering owls forbore to fly,
Not a bat flapped to and fro
Round their nest:
Cheek to cheek and breast to breast
Locked together in one nest.

Early in the morning
When the first cock crowed his warning,
Neat like bees, as sweet and busy,
Laura rose with Lizzie:
Fetched in honey, milked the cows,
Aired and set to rights the house,
Kneaded cakes of whitest wheat,
Cakes for dainty mouths to eat,
Next churned butter, whipped up cream,
Fed their poultry, sat and sewed;
Talked as modest maidens should:
Lizzie with an open heart,
Laura in an absent dream;

One content, one sick in part;
One warbling for the mere bright day's delight,
One longing for the night.

   At length slow evening came:
They went with pitchers to the reedy brook;
Lizzie most placid in her look,
Laura most like a leaping flame.
They drew the gurgling water from its deep;
Lizzie plucked purple and rich golden flags,   220
Then turning homewards said: 'The sunset flushes
Those furthest loftiest crags;
Come, Laura, not another maiden lags,
No wilful squirrel wags,
The beasts and birds are fast asleep.'
But Laura loitered still among the rushes
And said the bank was steep.

   And said the hour was early still,
The dew not fall'n, the wind not chill:
Listening ever, but not catching   230
The customary cry,
'Come buy, come buy,'
With its iterated jingle
Of sugar-baited words:
Not for all her watching
Once discerning even one goblin
Racing, whisking, tumbling, hobbling;
Let alone the herds
That used to tramp along the glen,
In groups or single,   240
Of brisk fruit-merchant men.

   Till Lizzie urged, 'O Laura, come;
I hear the fruit-call but I dare not look:
You should not loiter longer at this brook:
Come with me home.
The stars rise, the moon bends her arc,
Each glowworm winks her spark,
Let us get home before the night grows dark:
For clouds may gather
Though this is summer weather,   250
Put out the lights and drench us through;
Then if we lost our way what should we do?'

   Laura turned cold as stone
To find her sister heard that cry alone,
That goblin cry,
'Come buy our fruits, come buy.'
Must she then buy no more such dainty fruit?
Must she no more such succous pasture find,
Gone deaf and blind?
Her tree of life drooped from the root: 260
She said not one word in her heart's sore ache;

But peering thro' the dimness, nought discerning,
Trudged home, her pitcher dripping all the way;
So crept to bed, and lay
Silent till Lizzie slept;
Then sat up in a passionate yearning,
And gnashed her teeth for baulked desire, and wept
As if her heart would break.

Day after day, night after night,
Laura kept watch in vain
In sullen silence of exceeding pain.
She never caught again the goblin cry:
'Come buy, come buy;'—
She never spied the goblin men
Hawking their fruits along the glen:
But when the noon waxed bright
Her hair grew thin and grey;
She dwindled, as the fair full moon doth turn
To swift decay and burn
Her fire away.

One day remembering her kernel-stone
She set it by a wall that faced the south;
Dewed it with tears, hoped for a root,
Watched for a waxing shoot,
But there came none;
It never saw the sun,
It never felt the trickling moisture run:
While with sunk eyes and faded mouth
She dreamed of melons, as a traveller sees
False waves in desert drouth
With shade of leaf-crowned trees,
And burns the thirstier in the sandful breeze.

She no more swept the house,
Tended the fowls or cows,
Fetched honey, kneaded cakes of wheat,
Brought water from the brook,
But sat down listless in the chimney-nook
And would not eat.

Tender Lizzie could not bear
To watch her sister's cankerous care
Yet not to share.
She night and morning
Caught the goblins' cry:
'Come buy our orchard fruits,
Come buy, come buy;'—
Beside the brook, along the glen,
She heard the tramp of goblin men,
The voice and stir
Poor Laura could not hear;
Longed to buy fruit to comfort her
But feared to pay too dear.

She thought of Jeanie in her grave,
Who should have been a bride;
But who for joys brides hope to have
Fell sick and died
In her gay prime,
In earliest Winter time,
With the first glazing rime,
With the first snow-fall of crisp Winter time.

   Till Laura dwindling 320
Seemed knocking at Death's door:
Then Lizzie weighed no more
Better and worse;
But put a silver penny in her purse,
Kissed Laura, crossed the heath with clumps of furze
At twilight, halted by the brook:
And for the first time in her life
Began to listen and look.

   Laughed every goblin
When they spied her peeping: 330
Came towards her hobbling,
Flying, running, leaping,
Puffing and blowing,
Chuckling, clapping, crowing,
Clucking and gobbling,
Mopping and mowing,
Full of airs and graces,
Pulling wry faces,
Demure grimaces,
Cat-like and rat-like,
Ratel- and wombat-like, 340
Snail-paced in a hurry,
Parrot-voiced and whistler,
Helter skelter, hurry skurry,
Chattering like magpies,
Fluttering like pigeons,
Gliding like fishes,—
Hugged her and kissed her:
Squeezed and caressed her:
Stretched up their dishes,
Panniers, and plates: 350
'Look at our apples
Russet and dun,
Bob at our cherries,
Bite at our peaches,
Citrons and dates,
Grapes for the asking,
Pears red with basking
Out in the sun,
Plums on their twigs;
Pluck them and suck them, 360
Pomegranates, figs.'—

'Good folk,' said Lizzie,
Mindful of Jeanie:
'Give me much and many:'—
Held out her apron,
Tossed them her penny.
'Nay, take a seat with us,
Honour and eat with us,'
They answered grinning:
'Our feast is but beginning.
Night yet is early,
Warm and dew-pearly,
Wakeful and starry:
Such fruits as these
No man can carry;
Half their bloom would fly,
Half their dew would dry,
Half their flavour would pass by.
Sit down and feast with us,
Be welcome guest with us,
Cheer you, and rest with us.'—
'Thank you,' said Lizzie: 'But one waits
At home alone for me:
So without further parleying,
If you will not sell me any
Of your fruits though much and many,
Give me back my silver penny
I tossed you for a fee.'—
They began to scratch their pates,
No longer wagging, purring,
But visibly demurring,
Grunting and snarling.
One called her proud,
Cross-grained, uncivil;
Their tones waxed loud,
Their looks were evil.
Lashing their tails
They trod and hustled her,
Elbowed and jostled her,
Clawed with their nails,
Barking, mewing, hissing, mocking,
Tore her gown and soiled her stocking,
Twitched her hair out by the roots,
Stamped upon her tender feet,
Held her hands and squeezed their fruits
Against her mouth to make her eat.

White and golden Lizzie stood,
Like a lily in a flood,—
Like a rock of blue-veined stone
Lashed by tides obstreperously,—
Like a beacon left alone
In a hoary roaring sea,
Sending up a golden fire,—
Like a fruit-crowned orange-tree

White with blossoms honey-sweet
Sore beset by wasp and bee,—
Like a royal virgin town
Topped with gilded dome and spire
Close beleaguered by a fleet
Mad to tug her standard down.

One may lead a horse to water,
Twenty cannot make him drink.
Though the goblins cuffed and caught her,
Coaxed and fought her,
Bullied and besought her,
Scratched her, pinched her black as ink,
Kicked and knocked her
Mauled and mocked her,
Lizzie uttered not a word;
Would not open lip from lip
Lest they should cram a mouthful in:
But laughed in heart to feel the drip
Of juice that syrupped all her face,
And lodged in dimples of her chin,
And streaked her neck which quaked like curd.
At last the evil people
Worn out by her resistance
Flung back her penny, kicked their fruit
Along whichever road they took,
Not leaving root or stone or shoot;
Some writhed into the ground,
Some dived into the brook
With ring and ripple,
Some scudded on the gale without a sound,
Some vanished in the distance.

In a smart, ache, tingle,
Lizzie went her way;
Knew not was it night or day;
Sprang up the bank, tore thro' the furze,
Threaded copse and dingle,
And heard her penny jingle
Bouncing in her purse,—
Its bounce was music to her ear.
She ran and ran
As if she feared some goblin man
Dogged her with gibe or curse
Or something worse:
But not one goblin skurried after,
Nor was she pricked by fear;
The kind heart made her windy-paced
That urged her home quite out of breath with haste
And inward laughter.

She cried 'Laura,' up the garden,
'Did you miss me?
Come and kiss me.

Never mind my bruises,
Hug me, kiss me, suck my juices
Squeezed from goblin fruits for you,
Goblin pulp and goblin dew.
Eat me, drink me, love me;
Laura, make much of me:
For your sake I have braved the glen
And had to do with goblin merchant men.'

Laura started from her chair,
Flung her arms up in the air,
Clutched her hair:
'Lizzie, Lizzie, have you tasted
For my sake the fruit forbidden?
Must your light like mine be hidden,
Your young life like mine be wasted,
Undone in mine undoing
And ruined in my ruin,
Thirsty, cankered, goblin-ridden?'—
She clung about her sister,
Kissed and kissed and kissed her:
Tears once again
Refreshed her shrunken eyes,
Dropping like rain
After long sultry drouth;
Shaking with aguish fear, and pain,
She kissed and kissed her with a hungry mouth.

Her lips began to scorch,
That juice was wormwood to her tongue,
She loathed the feast
Writhing as one possessed she leaped and sung,
Rent all her robe, and wrung
Her hands in lamentable haste,
And beat her breast.
Her locks streamed like the torch
Borne by a racer at full speed,
Or like the mane of horses in their flight,
Or like an eagle when she stems the light
Straight toward the sun,
Or like a caged thing freed,
Or like a flying flag when armies run.

Swift fire spread through her veins, knocked at her heart,
Met the fire smouldering there
And overbore its lesser flame;
She gorged on bitterness without a name:
Ah! fool, to choose such part
Of soul-consuming care!
Sense failed in the mortal strife:
Like the watch-tower of a town
Which an earthquake shatters down,
Like a lightning-stricken mast,
Like a wind-uprooted tree

Spun about,
Like a foam-topped waterspout
Cast down headlong in the sea,
She fell at last;
Pleasure past and anguish past,
Is it death or is it life?

 Life out of death.
That night long Lizzie watched by her,
Counted her pulse's flagging stir,
Felt for her breath,
Held water to her lips, and cooled her face
With tears and fanning leaves:
But when the first birds chirped about their eaves,
And early reapers plodded to the place
Of golden sheaves,
And dew-wet grass
Bowed in the morning winds so brisk to pass,
And new buds with new day
Opened of cup-like lilies on the stream,
Laura awoke as from a dream,
Laughed in the innocent old way,
Hugged Lizzie but not twice or thrice;
Her gleaming locks showed not one thread of grey,
Her breath was sweet as May
And light danced in her eyes.

 Days, weeks, months, years
Afterwards, when both were wives
With children of their own
Their mother-hearts beset with fears,
Their lives bound up in tender lives;
Laura would call the little ones
And tell them of her early prime,
Those pleasant days long gone
Of not-returning time:
Would talk about the haunted glen,
The wicked, quaint fruit-merchant men,
Their fruits like honey to the throat
But poisons in the blood;
(Men sell not such in any town:)
Would tell them how her sister stood
In deadly peril to do her good,
And win the fiery antidote:
Then joining hands to little hands
Would bid them cling together,
'For there is no friend like a sister
In calm or stormy weather;
To cheer one on the tedious way,
To fetch one if one goes astray,
To lift one if one totters down,
To strengthen whilst one stands.'

FOR DISCUSSION:

1. The goblin men and their wares obviously represent some sort of sensuous indulgence. Analyze carefully the imagery with which they and their fruits are described.

2. What is the significance of lines 183–198?

3. Characterize Lizzie and Laura. Can it be said that Lizzie is a superego figure and Laura an id figure? Develop this idea.

4. Discuss the use of imagery in lines 418–422.

5. Is it possible to interpret the poem as a psychoreligious experience? For example, can Lizzie's entreaty to Laura to "Eat me, drink me, love me" (line 471) be viewed as an invitation to partake of the Eucharist? Notice that sacrifice, atonement, redemption, and love are all implicit in this action. Examine this thesis in the light of other parts of the poem.

Original Sin: A Short Story*

ROBERT PENN WARREN

Nodding, its great head rattling a gourd,
And locks like seaweed strung on the stinking stone,
The nightmare stumbles past, and you have heard
It fumble your door before it whimpers and is gone:
It acts like the old hound that used to snuffle your door and moan.

You thought you had lost it when you left Omaha,
For it seemed connected then with your grandpa, who
Had a wen on his forehead and sat on the veranda
To finger the precious protuberance, as was his habit to do,
Which glinted in sun like rough garnet or the rich old brain bulging through.   10

But you met it in Harvard Yard as the historic steeple
Was confirming the midnight with its hideous racket,
And you wondered how it had come, for it stood so imbecile,
With empty hands, humble, and surely nothing in pocket:
Riding the rods, perhaps—or Grandpa's will paid the ticket.

You were almost kindly then, in your first homesickness,
As it tortured its stiff face to speak, but scarcely mewed.
Since then you have outlived all your homesickness,
But have met it in many another distempered latitude:
Oh, nothing is lost, ever lost! at last you understood.   20

It never came in the quantum glare of sun
To shame you before your friends, and had nothing to do
With your public experience or private reformation:
But it thought no bed too narrow—it stood with lips askew
And shook its great head sadly like the abstract Jew.

* From SELECTED POEMS: NEW AND OLD, 1923–1966, by Robert Penn Warren. © Copyright 1966 by Robert Penn Warren. Reprinted by permission of Random House, Inc.

Never met you in the lyric arsenical meadows
When children call and your heart goes stone in the bosom—
At the orchard anguish never, nor ovoid horror,
Which is furred like a peach or avid like the delicious plum.
It takes no part in your classic prudence or fondled axiom.   30

Not there when you exclaimed: "Hope is betrayed by
Disastrous glory of sea-capes, sun-torment of whitecaps
—There must be a new innocence for us to be stayed by."
But there it stood, after all the timetables, all the maps,
In the crepuscular clutter of *always, always,* or *perhaps.*

You have moved often and rarely left an address,
And hear of the deaths of friends with a sly pleasure,
A sense of cleansing and hope which blooms from distress;
But it has not died, it comes, its hand childish, unsure,
Clutching the bribe of chocolate or a toy you used to treasure.   40

It tries the lock. You hear, but simply drowse:
There is nothing remarkable in that sound at the door.
Later you may hear it wander the dark house
Like a mother who rises at night to seek a childhood picture;
Or it goes to the backyard and stands like an old horse cold in the pasture.

FOR DISCUSSION:

1. List the characteristics of "it" as described in the poem. To what does "it" refer? Some readers believe the subject of the poem is a psychological complex; others feel it is primordial guilt. Can both views be correct? Does the very vagueness of the subject contribute measurably to the poem's meaning?

2. In what way is the subtitle of the poem ironic?

3. Is the psychosexual imagery of stanza 6 (lines 26–30) effective, or unclear and ill-defined?

4. Comment on the images which depict psychological experiences in lines 40 and 44. How do the images relate to the subject of the poem?

IV Critical Perspective:
ARCHETYPAL

Introduction

In recent years a school of literary criticism has emerged that both accepts and rejects earlier critical methods. Led by Northrup Frye, Leslie Fiedler, Richard Chase, and Stanley Edgar Hyman, this school accepts the concept that a work of art is produced by a cultural climate, but one extending beyond the present or recent past. Although critics who start from this premise accept the technique of close, intensive, and analytical reading of the text, they deny that the work of art is self-sufficient. Sharing the psychological critic's interest in the unconscious mind, they explore collective rather than individual aspects of the human psyche. Since their approach frequently emphasizes myth in its analysis of literature, it is sometimes called mythic. More often, however, because it emphasizes repetitive patterns in man's life as revealed in his literature, only some of which are embodied in myths, this critical perspective is called archetypal, a word that refers to "a pattern from which copies are made."

The major difference between archetypal analysis and earlier critical perspectives is an awareness of what Frye has called "the total coherence of literature." By this he means that all literature is imbued with the same mythic world order, with the same cultural patterns that reveal and shape man's psychic and social life. Summarizing this view, he writes,

Total literary history moves from the primitive to the sophisticated, and here we glimpse the possibility of seeing literature as a complication of a relatively restricted and simple group of formulas that can be studied in primitive culture. If so, then the search for archetypes is a kind of literary anthropology concerned with the way that literature is informed by pre-literary categories such as ritual, myth, and folk-tale.

The basic contention of archetypal criticism is that literary expression is an unconscious product of the collective experience of the entire human species. As such, literature is therefore integrally related with man's cultural past. To support this assertion, archetypal criticism draws heavily on the nonliterary fields of man's historical and prehistorical past —religion, anthropology, folklore—in order to understand and interpret the creative mind. Of particular interest to these critics are man's civilizations—his rites, rituals, mores, folkways, and myths—that is, all the beliefs and practices that combine to form human cultural behavior.

At the base of the assertions of the archetypal critics are the theories of Carl Jung (1875–1961), a Swiss psychologist whose investigations into the nature of the human mind brought forth two ideas especially important and influential for literary criticism: the concept of the collective unconscious and the theory of the archetype. It will be helpful to discuss these ideas before applying them to the analysis of literature.

We have seen that Freud believed in a personal unconscious; each individual's psyche differs from all others. Jung accepted this basic idea but suggested, however, that one aspect of the individual's psyche is identical to the psyches of all other members of the same species. He believed that this part of the mind goes beyond personal experience and is the same in all minds because it draws upon a common source and foundation. For Jung, then, the experiences of the individual are conditioned by the experiences of the human race, of all who have gone before. The unconscious mental record of these experiences, Jung called the collective unconscious:

This psychic life is the mind of our ancient ancestors, the way in which they thought and felt, the way in which they conceived of life and the world, of gods and human beings. The existence of these historical layers is presumably the source of the belief in reincarnation and in memories of past lives. As the body is a sort of museum of its phylogenetic history, so is the mind. There is no reason for believing that the psyche, with its peculiar structure, is the only thing in the world that has no history beyond its individual manifestation. Even the conscious mind cannot be denied a history extending over at least five thousand years. It is only individual ego-consciousness that has forever a new beginning and an early end. But the unconscious psyche is not only immensely old, it is also able to grow increasingly into an equally remote future. It forms, and is part of, the human species just as much as the body, which is also individually ephemeral, yet collectively of immeasurable duration.

Jung believed further that the collective unconscious is not directly knowable but that it expresses itself in the form of an archetype, which he defined as

a figure, whether it be daemon, man or process, that repeats itself in the course of history wherever creative fantasy is fully manifested. Essentially, therefore, it is a mythological figure. If we subject these images to a closer investigation, we discover them to be the formulated resultants of countless experiences of our ancestors. They are, as it were, the psychic residua of numberless experiences of the same type.

The fundamental quality of the archetype, as Jung conceived it, is that it is primordial, a preconscious, instinctual expression of man's basic nature. Biologists have long recognized that such inborn behavior patterns exist in lower animals. The nesting of birds, the ritual dance of bees, the spinning instinct of spiders, and the migratory habits of certain birds are all examples of actions that are not acquired but that seem derived from the remotest beginnings of the species. Jung thought that in like manner, subtle psychophysical and atavistic forces concentrate man's behavior into perceptible patterns. He believed also that, although the archetypes may take on innumerable forms, their essential patterns grow out of man's nature as a social, psychological, and biological being.

Jung also asserted that the archetype is universal; it is generated by man's psyche regardless of time or place. The archetype's expression is as meaningful to a Bantu tribesman as to an advertising executive, as relevant to a Roman gladiator as to an astronaut. Since man's psychoneurological mechanism differs comparatively little from time to time and from place to place, and since man undergoes essentially the same kinds of basic experiences, the expression of his collective unconscious is bound to be the same.

The findings of many modern anthropologists lend credence to Jung's views. Research has shown amazing similarities between myths collected from widely different geographical and cultural areas. Stories explaining the creation of man and of the world, for example, seem to be universal. Ancient Mayans, Buddhists, Hindus, and Christians have all been confronted with the archetypal problem of understanding their own existence. Their explanations have been introduced into holy books, religious rituals, and sacramental practices that are strikingly similar.

Other universal or near-universal motifs reported by anthropologists are stories of the destruction of the world by flood, famine, plague, or earthquake; the slaying of monsters; incest myths; sibling rivalries; and Oedipus legends. To be sure, the details of these stories frequently vary greatly from culture to culture, but the basic patterns remain amazingly

INTRODUCTION

alike. Nor can the persistence of these stories be explained by an interaction among the peoples who originated them. So geographically remote are some of the areas concerned, and so unlikely the prospect of social intercourse, that many anthropologists have concluded with Jung that these and similar stories generate from the common problems of diverse peoples as they confront their universe, gods, parents, and children. That is, they believe the stories originate from experiences, attitudes, and problems that are universal rather than particular.

A final characteristic of the archetype is that it is recurrent. From prehistoric times until the end of the earth, it expresses man's reaction to essentially changeless situations. Each generation of readers unconsciously reacts to the archetype as it stimulates an image already in their collective unconscious. One of the major reasons we applaud the creation of such literary characters as Faust, Macbeth, and Huckleberry Finn is that they depict some eternal quality, some enduring feature of the human race. As the archetype reaches into the racial past and re-creates the spiritual progenitors of the present, each generation recognizes itself and responds emotionally. Jung believed that the creative process consists mainly of successive embodiments of the archetypes, of fashioning primordial images "into the language of the present which makes it possible for every man to find again the deepest springs of life which would otherwise be closed to him."

The number of possible archetypes is as unlimited as the variety of man's experiences. Their appearances, however, may be grouped in three major categories: (1) characters, (2) situations, and (3) symbols or associations.

CHARACTERS

A. The Hero—Lord Raglan in The Hero: A Study in Tradition, Myth, and Drama contends that this archetype is so well defined that the life of the protagonist can be clearly divided into a series of well-marked adventures, which strongly suggest a ritualistic pattern. Raglan finds that traditionally the hero's mother is a virgin, the circumstances of his conception are unusual, and at birth some attempt is made to kill him. He is, however, spirited away and reared by foster parents. We know almost nothing of his childhood, but upon reaching manhood he returns to his future kingdom. After a victory over the king or a wild beast, he marries a princess, becomes king, reigns uneventfully, but later loses favor with the gods. He is then driven from the city after which he meets a mysterious death, often at the top of a hill. His body is not buried, but nevertheless he has one or more holy sepulchers. Characters who exemplify this archetype to a greater or lesser extent are Oedipus, Theseus, Romulus, Perseus, Jason, Dionysos, Joseph, Moses, Elijah, Jesus Christ, Siegfried, Arthur, Robin Hood, Watu Gunung (Javanese), and Llew Llawgyffes (Celtic).

B. The Scapegoat—An animal or more usually a human whose death in a public ceremony expiates some taint or sin that has been visited upon a community (e.g., Shirley Jackson's "The Lottery").

C. The Outcast—A figure who is banished from a social group for some crime against his fellow man. The outcast is usually destined to become a wanderer from place to place (e.g., Cain, the Wandering Jew, the Ancient Mariner).

D. The Devil Figure—Evil incarnate, this character offers wordly goods, fame, or knowledge to the protagonist in exchange for possession of his soul (e.g., Lucifer, Mephistopheles, Satan, the Faust legend).

E. The Woman Figure

    1. The Earthmother—Symbolic of fruition, abundance, and fertility, this charac-

ter traditionally offers spiritual and emotional nourishment to those with whom she comes in contact (e.g., Mother Nature, Mother Country, alma mater).

  2. The Temptress—Characterized by sensuous beauty, this woman is one to whom the protagonist is physically attracted and who ultimately brings about his downfall (e.g., Delilah, the Sirens, Cleopatra).

  3. The Platonic Ideal—This woman is a source of inspiration and a spiritual ideal, for whom the protagonist or author has an intellectual rather than a physical attraction (e.g., Dante's Beatrice, Petrarch's Laura, most Shelleyan heroines).

  4. The Unfaithful Wife—A woman, married to a man she sees as dull and unimaginative, is physically attracted to a more virile and desirable man (e.g., Guinevere, Madame Bovary, Anna Karenina, Lady Chatterley).

F. The Star-Crossed Lovers—A young man and woman enter an ill-fated love affair which ends tragically in the death of either or both of the lovers (e.g., Romeo and Juliet, West Side Story, Tristan and Isolde, Hero and Leander).

SITUATIONS

A. The Quest—This motif describes the search for someone or some talisman which, when found and brought back, will restore fertility to a wasted land, the desolation of which is mirrored by a leader's illness and disability. Jessie L. Weston's From Ritual to Romance traces one facet of this archetype through the quests of Gawain, Perceval, and Galahad for the Holy Grail. This situation is also used in Tennyson's Idylls of the King as well as in shorter poems by Morris, Browning, and Arnold. Ahab's monomaniacal quest for the albino whale in Moby Dick is a variation on this archetype.

B. The Task—To save the kingdom, to win the fair lady, to identify himself so that he may reassume his rightful position, the Hero must perform some nearly superhuman deed (e.g., Odysseus must string the bow, Arthur must pull the sword from the stone, Beowulf must slay Grendel).

C. The Initiation—This usually takes the form of an initiation into life, that is, the depiction of an adolescent coming into maturity and adulthood with all the attendant problems and responsibilities that this process involves. An awakening, awareness, or an increased perception of the world and the people in it usually forms the climax of this archetypal situation (e.g., Holden Caulfield, Huckleberry Finn, Stephen Dedalus, Eugene Gant).

D. The Journey—Usually combined with any or all of the foregoing situational archetypes, the journey is used to send the Hero in search of information or some intellectual truth. A common employment of the journey archetype is the descent into hell (e.g., Odyssey, Aeneid, Inferno, Endymion, Joyce's Ulysses). A second use of this pattern is the depiction of a limited number of travellers on an airplane flight, sea voyage, bus ride, or walking trip for the purpose of isolating them and using them as a microcosm of society (e.g., The Canterbury Tales, Ship of Fools).

E. The Fall—This archetype describes a descent from a higher to a lower state of being. The experience involves spiritual defilement and/or a loss of innocence and bliss. The Fall is also usually accompanied by expulsion from a kind of paradise as penalty for disobedience and moral transgression (e.g., Paradise Lost, Billy Budd).

F. Death and Rebirth—The most common of all situational archetypes, this motif grows out of the parallel between the cycle of nature and the cycle of life. Thus, morning and springtime represent birth, youth, or rebirth; evening and winter suggest old age or death. Anthropologists believe that fertility rites and vegetative rituals usually took place in the spring because this is the time of physical regeneration of Nature, an appropriate time to enact ritualistic statements of spiritual rebirth and resurrection. In The Golden Bough Sir James Frazer cites many rites celebrating the rebirth of dying gods, especially among the peoples of Egypt and Western Asia. Tied closely to seasonal patterns is a variety of ritualistic observances to such annually resurrected gods as Osiris, Tammuz, Adonis, and Attis. Writers frequently make use of this archetype. For example, poems of death and despondency are usually set at night (e.g., Gray's "Elegy," Poe's "The Raven") or in the winter (e.g., Frost's "Stopping by Woods on a Snowy Evening"). A somewhat different use of the same archetype is shown in Tess of the D'Urbervilles. When Tess's life is spiritually fulfilled and emotionally satisfying, she works as a dairymaid on a farm where lush vegetation and agricultural abundance prevail. But when she loses all, when her life is empty and without purpose, she is employed on a farm that is all but barren and where vegetation is scant. Hardy thus mirrors her emotional condition in the physical conditions of the farms.

SYMBOLS AND ASSOCIATIONS

The collective unconscious makes certain associations between the outside world and psychic experiences. These associations become enduring and are passed from one generation to the next. Some of the more common archetypal associations are as follows:

A. Light-Darkness—Light usually suggests hope, renewal or intellectual illumination; darkness implies the unknown, ignorance, or despair (e.g., "Dover Beach").

B. Water-Desert—Because water is necessary to life and growth, it commonly appears as a birth or rebirth symbol. It is archetypally significant, anthropologists believe, that water is used in baptismal services, which solemnize spiritual birth. Similarly, the appearance of rain in a work of literature can suggest a character's regeneration or rebirth (e.g., The Ancient Mariner). Conversely, the aridity of the desert is often associated with spiritual sterility and desiccation (e.g., The Waste Land).

C. Heaven-Hell—Man has traditionally associated parts of the universe not accessible to him with the dwelling places of the primordial forces that govern his world. The skies and mountain tops house his gods; the bowels of the earth contain the diabolic forces that inhabit his universe (e.g., Mount Olympus, the Underworld, Paradise Lost, The Divine Comedy).

It should be noted that the primitive mind tends not to make fine discriminations but thinks rather in terms of polarities. Thus, when archetypes appear in a work of literature, they usually evoke their primordial opposites. Good is in conflict with evil; birth symbols are juxtaposed with death images; depictions of heaven are countered by descriptions of hell; and for every Penelope, there is usually a Circe to balance the archetypal scales.

The advantages of archetypal criticism are apparent. First, it relates literature to other areas of intellectual activity in a coherent, meaningful way. Secondly, by placing literature against an unfolding cultural panorama, it clarifies the author-work-audience relationship to a degree unmatched by other critical modes. As Stanley Hyman observes, archetypes "exist all along the chain of communication: as configurations in the [author's] unconscious, as recurring themes or image sequences in [literature], and as configurations in the reader's unconscious." Because of this threefold emphasis, archetypal criticism interprets a work of art simultaneously from psychological, aesthetic, and cultural points of view. No other approach can claim so much.

The Concept of the Collective Unconscious*

CARL JUNG

Probably none of my empirical concepts has met with so much misunderstanding as the idea of the collective unconscious. In what follows I shall try to give (1) a definition of the concept, (2) a description of what it means for psychology, (3) an explanation of the method of proof . . .

DEFINITION

The collective unconscious is a part of the psyche which can be negatively distinguished from a personal unconscious by the fact that it does not, like the latter, owe its existence to personal experience and consequently is not a personal acquisition. While the personal unconscious is made up essentially of contents which have at one time been conscious but which have disappeared from consciousness through having been forgotten or repressed, the contents of the collective unconscious have never been in consciousness, and therefore have never been individually acquired, but owe their existence exclusively to heredity. Whereas the personal unconscious consists for the most part of *complexes*, the content of the collective unconscious is made up essentially of *archetypes*.

The concept of the archetype, which is an indispensable correlate of the idea of the collective unconscious, indicates the existence of definite forms in the psyche which seem to be present always and everywhere. Mythological research calls them "motifs"; in the psychology of primitives they correspond to Lévy-Bruhl's concept of "représentations collectives," and in the field of comparative religion they have been defined by Hubert and Mauss as "categories of the imagination." Adolf Bastian long ago called them "elementary" or "primordial thoughts." From these references it should be clear enough that my idea of the archetype—literally a pre-existent form—does not stand alone but is something that is recognized and named in other fields of knowledge.

My thesis, then, is as follows: In addition to our immediate consciousness, which is of a thoroughly personal nature and which we believe to be the only empirical psyche (even if we tack on the personal unconscious as an appendix), there exists a second psychic system of a collective, universal, and impersonal nature which is identical in all individuals. This collective unconscious does not develop individually but is inherited. It consists of pre-existent forms, the archetypes, which can only become conscious secondarily and which give definite form to certain psychic contents.

---

* From THE COLLECTED WORKS OF C. G. JUNG, IX, Part I, translated by R. F. C. Hull. Copyright 1959 by the Bollingen Foundation and reprinted by its permission. Also from THE ARCHETYPES AND THE COLLECTIVE UNCONSCIOUS by C. G. Jung, translated by R. F. C. Hull, by permission of Routledge & Kegan Paul Ltd. [Footnotes omitted—Ed.]

THE PSYCHOLOGICAL MEANING OF THE COLLECTIVE UNCONSCIOUS

Medical psychology, growing as it did out of professional practice, insists on the *personal* nature of the psyche. By this I mean the views of Freud and Adler. It is a *psychology of the person*, and its aetiological or causal factors are regarded almost wholly as personal in nature. Nonetheless, even this psychology is based on certain general biological factors, for instance on the sexual instinct or on the urge for self-assertion, which are by no means merely personal peculiarities. It is forced to do this because it lays claim to being an explanatory science. Neither of these views would deny the existence of *a priori* instincts common to man and animals alike, or that they have a significant influence on personal psychology. Yet instincts are impersonal, universally distributed, hereditary factors of a dynamic or motivating character, which very often fail so completely to reach consciousness that modern psychotherapy is faced with the task of helping the patient to become conscious of them. Moreover, the instincts are not vague and indefinite by nature, but are specifically formed motive forces which, long before there is any consciousness, and in spite of any degree of consciousness later on, pursue their inherent goals. Consequently they form very close analogies to the archetypes, so close, in fact, that there is good reason for supposing that the archetypes are the unconscious images of the instincts themselves, in other words, that they are *patterns of instinctual behaviour*.

The hypothesis of the collective unconscious is, therefore, no more daring than to assume there are instincts. One admits readily that human activity is influenced to a high degree by instincts, quite apart from the rational motivations of the conscious mind. So if the assertion is made that our imagination, perception, and thinking are likewise influenced by inborn and universally present formal elements, it seems to me that a normally functioning intelligence can discover in this idea just as much or just as little mysticism as in the theory of instincts. Although this reproach of mysticism has frequently been levelled at my concept, I must emphasize yet again that the concept of the collective unconscious is neither a speculative nor a philosophical but an empirical matter. The question is simply this: are there or are there not unconscious, universal forms of this kind? If they exist, then there is a region of the psyche which one can call the collective unconscious. It is true that the diagnosis of the collective unconscious is not always an easy task. It is not sufficient to point out the often obviously archetypal nature of unconscious products, for these can just as well be derived from acquisitions through language and education. Cryptomnesia should also be ruled out, which it is almost impossible to do in certain cases. In spite of all these difficulties, there remain enough individual instances showing the autochthonous revival of mythological motifs to put the matter beyond any reasonable doubt. But if such an unconscious exists at all, psychological explanation must take account of it and submit certain alleged personal aetiologies to sharper criticism.

What I mean can perhaps best be made clear by a concrete example. You have probably read Freud's discussion of a certain picture by Leonardo da Vinci: St. Anne with the Virgin Mary and the Christ-child. Freud interprets this remarkable picture in terms of the fact that Leonardo himself had two mothers. This causality is personal. We shall not linger over the fact that this picture is far from unique, nor over the minor inaccuracy that St. Anne happens to be the grandmother of Christ and not, as required by Freud's interpretation, the mother, but shall simply point out that interwoven with the apparently personal psychology there is an impersonal motif well known to us from other fields. This is the motif of the *dual mother*, an archetype to be found in many variants in the field of mythology and comparative religion and forming the basis of numerous "représentations collectives." I might mention, for instance, the motif of the *dual descent*, that is, descent from human and divine parents, as in the case of Heracles, who received immortality through being unwittingly adopted by Hera. What was a myth in Greece was actually a ritual in Egypt: Pharoah was both human and divine by nature. In the birth chambers of the Egyptian temples Pharaoh's second, divine conception and birth is depicted on the walls; he is "twice-born." It is an idea that underlies all rebirth mysteries, Christianity included. Christ himself is "twice-born": through his baptism in the Jordan he was regenerated and reborn from water and spirit. Consequently, in the Roman liturgy the font is designated the "uterus ecclesiae," and, as you can read in the Roman missal, it is called this even today, in the "benediction of the font" on Holy Saturday before Easter. Further, according to an early Christian-Gnostic idea, the spirit which appeared in the form of a dove was interpreted as Sophia-Sapientia—Wisdom and the Mother of Christ. Thanks to this motif of the dual birth, children today, instead of having good and evil fairies who magically "adopt" them at birth with blessings or curses, are given sponsors—a "godfather" and a "godmother."

The idea of a second birth is found at all times and in all places. In the earliest beginnings of medicine it was a magical means of healing; in many religions it is the central mystical experience; it is the key idea in medieval, occult philosophy, and, last but not least, it is an infantile fantasy occurring in numberless children, large and small, who believe that their parents are not their real parents but merely foster-parents to whom they were handed over. Benvenuto Cellini also had this idea, as he himself relates in his autobiography.

Now it is absolutely out of the question that all the individuals who believe in a dual descent have in reality always had two mothers, or conversely that those few who shared Leonardo's fate have infected the rest of humanity with their complex. Rather, one cannot avoid the assumption that the universal occurrence of the dual-birth motif together with the fantasy of the two mothers answers an omnipresent human need which is reflected in these motifs. If Leonardo da Vinci did in fact portray his two mothers in St. Anne and Mary—which I doubt—he nonetheless was only expressing something which countless millions of people before and after him have believed. The vulture symbol (which Freud also discusses in the work mentioned) makes this view all the more plausible. With some justification he quotes as the source of the symbol the *Hieroglyphica* of Horapollo, a book much in use in Leonardo's time. There you read that vultures are female only and symbolize the mother. They conceive through the wind (*pneuma*). This word took on the meaning of "spirit" chiefly under the influence of Christianity. Even in the account of the miracle at Pentecost the pneuma still has the double meaning of wind and spirit. This fact, in my opinion, points without doubt to Mary, who, a virgin by nature, conceived through the pneuma, like a vulture. Furthermore, according to Horapollo, the vulture also symbolizes Athene, who sprang, unbegotten, directly from the head of Zeus, was a virgin, and knew only spiritual motherhood. All this is really an allusion to Mary and the rebirth motif. There is not a shadow of evidence that Leonardo meant anything else by his picture. Even if it is correct to assume that he identified himself with the Christ-child, he was in all probability representing the mythological dual-mother motif and by no means his own personal prehistory. And what about all the other artists who painted the same theme? Surely not all of them had two mothers?

Let us now transpose Leonardo's case to the field of the neuroses, and assume that a patient with a mother complex is suffering from the delusion that the cause of his neurosis lies in his having really had two mothers. The personal interpretation would have to admit that he is right—and yet it would be quite wrong. For in reality the cause of his neurosis would lie in the reactivation of the dual-mother archetype, quite regardless of whether he had one mother or two mothers, because, as we have seen, this archetype functions individually and historically without any reference to the relatively rare occurrence of dual motherhood.

In such a case, it is of course tempting to presuppose so simple and personal a cause, yet the hypothesis is not only inexact but totally false. It is admittedly difficult to understand how a dual-mother motif—unknown to a physician trained only in medicine—could have so great a determining power as to produce the effect of a traumatic condition. But if we consider the tremendous powers that lie hidden in the mythological and religious sphere in man, the aetiological significance of the archetype appears less fantastic. In numerous cases of neurosis the cause of the disturbance lies in the very fact that the psychic life of the patient lacks the co-operation of these motive forces. Nevertheless a purely personalistic psychology, by reducing everything to personal causes, tries its level best to deny the existence of archetypal motifs and even seeks to destroy them by personal analysis. I consider this a rather dangerous procedure which cannot be justified medically. Today you can judge better than you could twenty years ago the nature of the forces involved. Can we not see how a whole nation is reviving an archaic symbol, yes, even archaic religious forms, and how this mass emotion is influencing and revolutionizing the life of the individual in a catastrophic manner? The man of the past is alive in us today to a degree undreamt of before the war, and in the last analysis what is the fate of great nations but a summation of the psychic changes in individuals?

So far as a neurosis is really only a private affair, having its roots exclusively in personal causes, archetypes play no role at all. But if it is a question of a general incompatibility or an otherwise injurious condition productive of neuroses in relatively large numbers of individuals, then we must assume the presence of constellated archetypes. Since neuroses are in most cases not just private concerns, but *social* phenomena, we must assume that archetypes are constellated in these cases too. The archetype corresponding to the situation is activated, and as a result those explosive and dangerous forces hidden in the archetype come into action, frequently with unpredictable consequences. There is no lunacy people under the domination of an archetype will not fall a prey to. If thirty years ago anyone had dared to predict that our psychological development was tending towards a revival of the medieval persecutions of the Jews, that Europe would again tremble before the Roman fasces and the tramp of legions, that people would once more give the Roman salute, as two thousand years ago, and that instead of the Christian Cross an archaic swastika would lure onward millions of warriors ready for death—why, that man would have been hooted at as a mystical fool. And today? Surprising as it may seem, all this absurdity is a horrible reality. Private life, private aetiologies, and private neuroses have become almost a fiction in the world of today. The man of the past who lived in a world of archaic "représentations collectives" has risen again into very visible and painfully real life, and this not only in a few unbalanced individuals but in many millions of people.

There are as many archetypes as there are typical situations in life. Endless repetition has engraved these experiences into our psychic constitution, not in the form of images filled with content, but at first only as *forms without content*, representing merely the possibility of a certain type of perception and action. When a situation occurs which corresponds to a given archetype, that archetype becomes activated and a compulsiveness appears, which, like an instinctual drive, gains its way against all reason and will, or else produces a conflict of pathological dimensions, that is to say, a neurosis.

METHOD OF PROOF

We must now turn to the question of how the existence of archetypes can be proved. Since archetypes are supposed to produce certain psychic forms, we must discuss how and where one can get hold of the material demonstrating these forms. The main source, then, is *dreams*, which have the advantage of being involuntary, spontaneous products of the unconscious psyche and are therefore pure products of nature not falsified by any conscious purpose. By questioning the individual one can ascertain which of the motifs appearing in the dream are known to him. From those which are unknown to him we must naturally exclude all motifs which *might* be known to him, as for instance—to revert to the case of Leonardo—the vulture symbol. We are not sure whether Leonardo took this symbol from Horapollo or not, although it would have been perfectly possible for an educated person of that time, because in those days artists were distinguished for their wide knowledge of the humanities. Therefore, although the bird motif is an archetype par excellence, its existence in Leonardo's fantasy would still prove nothing. Consequently, we must look for motifs which could not possibly be known to the dreamer and yet behave functionally in his dream in such a manner as to coincide with the functioning of the archetype known from historical sources.

Another source for the material we need is to be found in "active imagination." By this I mean a sequence of fantasies produced by deliberate concentration. I have found that the existence of unrealized, unconscious fantasies increases the frequency and intensity of dreams, and that when these fantasies are made conscious the dreams change their character and become weaker and less frequent. From this I have drawn the conclusion that dreams often contain fantasies which "want" to become conscious. The sources of dreams are often repressed instincts which have a natural tendency to influence the conscious mind. In cases of this sort, the patient is simply given the task of contemplating any one fragment of fantasy that seems significant to him—a chance idea, perhaps, or something he has become conscious of in a dream—until its context becomes visible, that is to say, the relevant associative material in which it is embedded. It is not a question of the "free association" recommended by Freud for the purpose of dream-analysis, but of elaborating the fantasy by observing the further fantasy material that adds itself to the fragment in a natural manner.

This is not the place to enter upon a technical discussion of the method. Suffice it to say that the resultant sequence of fantasies relieves the unconscious and produces material rich in archetypal images and associations. Obviously, this is a method that can only be used in certain carefully selected cases. The method is not entirely without danger, because it may carry the patient too far away from reality. A warning against thoughtless application is therefore in place.

Finally, very interesting sources of archetypal material are to be found in the delusions of paranoiacs, the fantasies observed in trance-states, and the dreams of early childhood, from the third to the fifth year. Such material is available in profusion, but it is valueless unless one can adduce convincing mythological parallels. It does not, of course, suffice simply to connect a dream about a snake with the mythological occurrence of snakes, for who is to guarantee that the functional meaning of the snake in the dream is the same as in the mythological setting? In order to draw a valid parallel, it is necessary to know the functional meaning of the individual symbol, and then to find out whether the apparently parallel mythological symbol has a similar context and therefore the same functional meaning. Establishing such facts not only requires lengthy and wearisome researches, but is also an ungrateful subject for demonstration. As the symbols must not be torn out of their context, one has to launch forth into exhaustive descriptions, personal as well as symbological, and this is practically impossible in the framework of a lecture. I have repeatedly tried it at the risk of sending one half of my audience to sleep.

FOR DISCUSSION:

1. How does the collective unconscious differ from the personal unconscious?
2. What is an archetype?
3. What objections does Jung advance against Freud's interpretation of Da Vinci's painting?
4. What does Jung mean by saying that at first the archetypes are "forms without content"?
5. What role do dreams play in Jung's theory of the unconscious?

The Collective Unconscious, Myth, and the Archetype*

CARL JUNG

.... In the dream, as in the products of psychoses, there are numberless interconnections to which one can find parallels only in mythological associations of ideas (or perhaps in certain poetic creations which are often characterized by a borrowing, not always conscious, from myths). Had thorough investigation shown that in the majority of such cases it was simply a matter of forgotten knowledge, the physician would not have gone to the trouble of making extensive researches into individual and collective parallels. But, in point of fact, typical mythologems were observed among individuals to whom all knowledge of this kind was absolutely out of the question, and where indirect derivation from religious ideas that might have been known to them, or from popular figures of speech, was impossible. Such conclusions forced us to assume that we must be dealing with "autochthonous" revivals independent of all tradition, and, consequently, that "myth-forming" structural elements must be present in the unconscious psyche.

These products are never (or at least very seldom) myths with a definite form, but rather mythological components which, because of their typical nature, we can call "motifs," "primordial images," types or—as I have named them—*archetypes*. The child archetype is an excellent example. Today we can hazard the formula that the archetypes appear in myths and fairytales just as they do in dreams and in the products of psychotic fantasy. The medium in which they are embedded is, in the former case, an ordered and for the most part immediately understandable context, but in the latter case a generally unintelligible, irrational, not to say delirious sequence of images which nonetheless does not lack a certain hidden coherence. In the individual, the archetypes appear as involuntary manifestations of unconscious processes whose existence and meaning can only be inferred, whereas the myth deals with traditional forms of incalculable age. They hark back to a prehistoric world whose spiritual preconceptions and general conditions we can still observe today among existing primitives. Myths on this level are as a rule tribal history handed down from generation to generation by word of mouth. Primitive mentality differs from the civilized chiefly in that the conscious mind is far less developed in scope and intensity. Functions such as thinking, willing, etc. are not yet differentiated; they are pre-conscious, and in the case of thinking, for instance, this shows itself in the circumstance that the primitive does not think *consciously*, but that thoughts *appear*. The primitive cannot assert that he thinks; it is rather that "something thinks in him." The spontaneity of the act of thinking does not lie, causally, in his conscious mind, but in his unconscious. Moreover, he is incapable of any conscious effort of will; he must put himself beforehand into the "mood of willing," or let himself be put—hence his *rites d'entrée et de sortie*. His consciousness is

---

*From "The Child Archetype" in THE COLLECTED WORKS OF C. G. JUNG, IX, Part I, translated by R. F. C. Hull. Copyright 1959 by the Bollingen Foundation and reprinted by its permission. Also from THE ARCHETYPES AND THE COLLECTIVE UNCONSCIOUS by C. G. Jung, translated by R. F. C. Hull, by permission of Routledge & Kegan Paul Ltd. [Footnotes omitted—Ed.]

menaced by an almighty unconscious: hence his fear of magical influences which may cross his path at any moment; and for this reason, too, he is surrounded by unknown forces and must adjust himself to them as best he can. Owing to the chronic twilight state of his consciousness, it is often next to impossible to find out whether he merely dreamed something or whether he really experienced it. The spontaneous manifestation of the unconscious and its archetypes intrudes everywhere into his conscious mind, and the mythical world of his ancestors—for instance, the *alchera* or *bugari* of the Australian aborigines—is a reality equal if not superior to the material world. It is not the world as we know it that speaks out of his unconscious, but the unknown world of the psyche, of which we know that it mirrors our empirical world only in part, and that, for the other part, it moulds this empirical world in accordance with its own psychic assumptions. The archetype does not proceed from physical facts, but describes how the psyche experiences the physical fact, and in so doing the psyche often behaves so autocratically that it denies tangible reality or makes statements that fly in the face of it.

The primitive mentality does not *invent* myths, it *experiences* them. Myths are original revelations of the preconscious psyche, involuntary statements about unconscious psychic happenings, and anything but allegories of physical processes. Such allegories would be an idle amusement for an unscientific intellect. Myths, on the contrary, have a vital meaning. Not merely do they represent, they *are* the psychic life of the primitive tribe, which immediately falls to pieces and decays when it loses its mythological heritage, like a man who has lost his soul. A tribe's mythology is its living religion, whose loss is always and everywhere, even among the civilized, a moral catastrophe. But religion is a vital link with psychic processes independent of and beyond consciousness, in the dark hinterland of the psyche. Many of these unconscious processes may be indirectly occasioned by consciousness, but never by conscious choice. Others appear to arise spontaneously, that is to say, from no discernible or demonstrable conscious cause.

Modern psychology treats the products of unconscious fantasy-activity as self-portraits of what is going on in the unconscious, or as statements of the unconscious psyche about itself. They fall into two categories. First, fantasies (including dreams) of a personal character, which go back unquestionably to personal experiences, things forgotten or repressed, and can thus be completely explained by individual anamnesis. Second, fantasies (including dreams) of an impersonal character, which cannot be reduced to experiences in the individual's past, and thus cannot be explained as something individually acquired. These fantasy-images undoubtedly have their closest analogues in mythological types. We must therefore assume that they correspond to certain *collective* (and not personal) structural elements of the human psyche in general, and, like the morphological elements of the human body, are *inherited*. Although tradition and transmission by migration certainly play a part, there are, as we have said, very many cases that cannot be accounted for in this way and drive us to the hypothesis of "autochthonous revival." These cases are so numerous that we are obliged to assume the existence of a collective psychic substratum. I have called this the *collective unconscious*.

The products of this second category resemble the types of structures to be met with in myth and fairytale so much that we must regard them as related. It is therefore wholly within the realm of possibility that both, the mythological types as well as the individual types, arise under quite similar conditions. As already mentioned, the fantasy-products of the second category (as also those of the first) arise in a state of reduced intensity of consciousness (in dreams, delirium, reveries, visions, etc.). In all these states the check put upon unconscious contents by the concentration of the conscious mind ceases, so that the hitherto unconscious material streams, as though from opened side-sluices, into the field of consciousness. This mode of origination is the general rule.

Reduced intensity of consciousness and absence of concentration and attention, Janet's *abaissement du niveau mental*, correspond pretty exactly to the primitive state of consciousness in which, we must suppose, myths were originally formed. It is therefore exceedingly probable that the mythological archetypes, too, made their appearance in much the same manner as the manifestations of archetypal structures among individuals today.

The methodological principle in accordance with which psychology treats the products of the unconscious is this: Contents of an archetypal character are manifestations of processes in the collective unconscious. Hence they do not refer to anything that is or has been conscious, but to something essentially unconscious. In the last analysis, therefore, it is impossible to say what they refer to. Every interpretation necessarily remains an "as-if." The ultimate core of meaning may be circumscribed, but not described. Even so, the bare circumscription denotes an essential step forward in our knowledge of the pre-conscious structure of the psyche, which was already in existence when there was as yet no unity of personality (even today the primitive is not securely possessed of it) and no consciousness at all. We can also observe this pre-conscious state in early childhood, and as a matter of fact it is the dreams of this early period that not infrequently bring extremely remarkable archetypal contents to light.

If, then, we proceed in accordance with the above principle, there is no longer any question whether a myth refers to the sun or the moon, the father or the mother, sexuality or fire or water; all it does is to circumscribe and give an approximate description of an *unconscious core of meaning*. The ultimate meaning of this nucleus was never conscious and never will be. It was, and still is, only interpreted, and every interpretation that comes anywhere near the hidden sense (or, from the point of view of scientific intellect, nonsense, which comes to the same thing) has always, right from the beginning, laid claim not only to absolute truth and validity but to instant reverence and religious devotion. Archetypes were, and still are, living psychic forces that demand to be taken seriously, and they have a strange way of making sure of their effect. Always they were the bringers of protection and salvation, and their violation has as its consequence the "perils of the soul" known to us from the psychology of primitives. Moreover, they are the unfailing causes of neurotic and even psychotic disorders, behaving exactly like neglected or maltreated physical organs or organic functional systems.

An archetypal content expresses itself, first and foremost, in metaphors. If such a content should speak of the sun and identify with it the lion, the king, the hoard of gold guarded by the dragon, or the power that makes for the life and health of man, it is neither the one thing nor the other, but the unknown third thing that finds more or less adequate expression in all these similes, yet—to the perpetual vexation of the intellect—remains unknown and not to be fitted into a formula. For this reason the scientific intellect is always inclined to put on airs of enlightenment in the hope of banishing the spectre once and for all. Whether its endeavours were called euhemerism, or Christian apologetics, or Enlightenment in the narrow sense, or Positivism, there was always a myth hiding behind it, in new and disconcerting garb, which then, following the ancient and venerable pattern, gave itself out as ultimate truth. In reality we can never legitimately cut loose from our archetypal foundations unless we are prepared to pay the price of a neurosis, any more than we can rid ourselves of our body and its organs without committing suicide. If we cannot deny the archetypes or otherwise neutralize them, we are confronted, at every new stage in the differentiation of consciousness to which civilization attains, with the task of finding a new *interpretation* appropriate to this stage, in order to connect the life of the past that still exists in us with the life of the present, which threatens to slip away from it. If this link-up does not take place, a kind of rootless consciousness comes into being no longer oriented to the past, a consciousness which succumbs helplessly to all manner of suggestions and, in practice, is susceptible to psychic epidemics. With the loss of the past, now become "insignificant," devalued, and incapable of revaluation, the saviour is lost too, for the saviour is either the insignificant thing itself or else arises out of it. Over and over again in the "metamorphosis of the gods" he rises up as the prophet or first-born of a new generation and appears unexpectedly in the unlikeliest places (sprung from a stone, tree, furrow, water, etc.) and in ambiguous form (Tom Thumb, dwarf, child, animal, and so on).

This archetype of the "child god" is extremely widespread and intimately bound up with all the other mythological aspects of the child motif. It is hardly necessary to allude to the still living "Christ-child," who, in the legend of Saint Christopher, also has the typical feature of being "smaller than small and bigger than big." In folklore the child motif appears in the guise of the *dwarf* or the *elf* as personifications of the hidden forces of nature. To this sphere also belongs the little metal man of late antiquity, the ἀνθρωπάριον, who, till far into the Middle Ages, on the one hand inhabited the mine-shafts, and on the other represented the alchemical metals, above all Mercurius reborn in perfect form (as the hermaphrodite, *filius sapientiae*, or *infans noster*). Thanks to the religious interpretation of the "child," a fair amount of evidence has come down to us from the Middle Ages showing that the "child" was not merely a traditional figure, but a vision spontaneously experienced (as a so-called "irruption of the unconscious"). I would mention Meister Eckhart's vision of the "naked boy" and the dream of Brother Eustachius. Interesting accounts of these spontaneous experiences are also to be found in English ghost-stories, where we read of the vision of a "Radiant Boy" said to have been seen in a place where there are Roman remains. This apparition was supposed to be of evil omen. It almost looks as though we were dealing with the figure of a *puer aeternus* who had become inauspicious through "metamorphosis," or in other words had shared the fate of the classical and the Germanic gods, who have all become bugbears. The mystical character of the experience is also confirmed in Part II of Goethe's *Faust*, where Faust himself is transformed into a boy and admitted into the "choir of blessed youths," this being the "larval stage" of Doctor Marianus.

In the strange tale called *Das Reich ohne Raum*, by Bruno Goetz, a *puer aeternus* named Fo (= Buddha) appears with whole troops of "unholy" boys of evil significance. (Contemporary parallels are better let alone.) I mention this instance only to demonstrate the enduring vitality of the child archetype.

The child motif not infrequently occurs in the field of psychopathology. The "imaginary" child is common among women with mental disorders and is usually interpreted in a Christian sense. Homunculi also appear, as in the famous Schreber case, where they come in swarms and plague the sufferer. But the clearest and most significant manifestation of the child motif in the therapy of neuroses is in the maturation process of personality induced by the analysis of the unconscious, which I have termed the process of *individuation*. Here we are confronted with preconscious processes which, in the form of more or less well-formed fantasies, gradually pass over into the conscious mind, or become conscious as dreams, or, lastly, are made conscious through the method of active imagination. This material is rich in archetypal motifs, among them frequently that of the child. Often the child is formed after the Christian model; more often, though, it develops from earlier, altogether non-Christian levels—that is to say, out of chthonic animals such as crocodiles, dragons, serpents, or monkeys. Sometimes the child appears in the cup of a flower, or out of a golden egg, or as the centre of a mandala. In dreams it often appears as the dreamer's son or daughter or as a boy, youth, or young girl; occasionally it seems to be of exotic origin, Indian or Chinese, with a dusky skin, or, appearing more cosmically, surrounded by stars or with a starry coronet; or as the king's son or the witch's child with daemonic attributes. Seen as a special instance of "the treasure hard to attain" motif, the child motif is extremely variable and assumes all manner of shapes, such as the jewel, the pearl, the flower, the chalice, the golden egg, the quaternity, the golden ball, and so on. It can be interchanged with these and similar images almost without limit.

FOR DISCUSSION:

1. How does Jung account for myths? What is their relationship to archetypes?

2. What is meant by the statement, "The primitive mentality does not invent myths, it experiences them"?

3. In what ways does the archetype express itself?

4. Account for the widespread occurrence of the child archetype.

Archetype and Signature*
THE RELATIONSHIP OF POET AND POEM

LESLIE FIEDLER

I

A central dogma of much recent criticism asserts that biographical information is irrelevant to the understanding and evaluation of poems, and that conversely, poems cannot legitimately be used as material for biography. This double contention is part of a larger position which holds that history is history and art is art, and that to talk about one in terms of the other is to court disaster. Insofar as this position rests upon the immortal platitude that it is good to know what one is talking about, it is unexceptionable; insofar as it is a reaction based upon the procedures of pre-Freudian critics, it is hopelessly outdated; and insofar as it depends upon the extreme nominalist definition of a work of art, held by many "formalists" quite unawares, it is metaphysically reprehensible. It has the further inconvenience of being quite unusable in the practical sphere (all of its proponents, in proportion as they are sensitive critics, immediately betray it when speaking of specific works, and particularly of large bodies of work); and, as if that were not enough, it is in blatant contradiction with the assumptions of most serious practicing writers.

That the anti-biographical position was once "useful," whatever its truth, cannot be denied; it was even once, what is considerably rarer in the field of criticism, amusing; but for a long time now it has been threatening to turn into one of those annoying clichés of the intellectually middle-aged, proffered with all the air of a stimulating heresy. The position was born in dual protest against an excess of Romantic criticism and one of "scientific scholarship." Romantic aesthetics appeared bent on dissolving the formally realized "objective" elements in works of art into "expression of personality"; while the "scholars," in revolt against Romantic subjectivity, seemed set on casting out all the more shifty questions of value and *gestalt* as "subjective," and concentrating on the kind of "facts" amenable to scientific verification. Needless to say, it was not the newer psychological sciences that the "scholars" had in mind, but such purer disciplines as physics and biology. It was at this point that it became fashionable to talk about literary study as "research," and graphs and tables began to appear in analyses of works of art.

Both the "scholarly" and the Romantic approaches struck the anti-biographists as "reductive"—attempts to prove that the work of art was *nothing but* the personality of the Genius behind it, or the sum total of its genetic factors. In answer to both heresies of attack, the anti-biographist offered what he came to call the "intrinsic" approach, which turned out, alas, to be another *nothing but* under its show of righteous indignation—namely, the contention that a poem was *nothing but* "words," and its analysis therefore properly *nothing but* a study of syntax and semantics. An attempt to illuminate a poem by reference to its author's life came therefore to be regarded with horror, unless it confined itself to an examination of his "idiosyncratic use of words"! This is not parody, but direct quotation.

By this time a generation of critics has grown up, of whom I am one, to whom the contention that biographical material is irrelevant to the essential "experience" of a poem

---

* From *The Sewanee Review* (Spring 1952). Reprinted by permission of the editors and the author. Originally published and copyrighted by the University of the South.

was taught as the basic doctrine of all right-thinking readers. The word "experience" is important; it comes out of I. A. Richards at his most scientizing, and along with the "extrinsic-intrinsic" metaphor is a key to the anti-biographist point of view. It must be understood for what the word "experience" is being substituted: as an "experience," a poem is no longer regarded as an "imitation," in any of the received senses of the word; nor even as an "expression" in the Crocean sense; and above all not as a "communication." All three possible substitute terms imply a necessary interconnectedness between the art object and some *other* area of experience—or at least an essentially intended pointing outward or inward toward some independently existent *otherness*. This is distasteful to the anti-biographist, who shows the ordinary nominalist uneasiness at any suggestion that there are realities more comprehensive than particulars, to which words only refer.

An odd phenomenon is the support of a position to which nominalism is logically necessary, by many confirmed anti-scientizers and realists; they are betrayed into their ill-advised fellow-traveling, I think, by an excess of anti-Romanticism. It is no longer as fashionable as it once was to publicly anathematize Shelley and Swinburne, but the bias persists as a real force in current critical practice, and cuts off many, to whom the position would be temperamentally and metaphysically attractive, from Expressionism. What the modern sensibility finds particularly unsympathetic in some Romantic writing has been misleadingly called, I think, "the exploitation of personality"; it is rather a tendency toward the excessively "programmatic." Just as music and painting can be too "literary," so literature itself can be too "literary." In reaction against the programmatic, there are two possible paths: more deeply into and through the personalism of Romanticism to Expressionism; or outward and away toward the sort of "abstraction" achieved in cubist painting. As a matter of fact, there has been at work all along in our period an underground, and probably harmful, analogy between poetry and the plastic arts. A poem, the feeling has been, should be as "palpable and mute" not merely as an actual fruit, but as the fruit become pure color and texture of Picasso or Matisse. As pictures have become frankly paint, so should poems be frankly words. "A poem should not mean but be." There is the slogan of the movement!

It is a rather nice phrase in the limited context of MacLeish's little poem, but a dangerous full-blown aesthetic position. The notion that a work of art is, or should be, absolutely self-contained, a discrete set of mutually interrelated references, needs only to be stated clearly to seem the *reductio ad absurdum* which it is. Yet this belief in the poem as a closed system, "cut off" in ideal isolation, descends from the realm of theoretical criticism to practical criticism and classroom pedagogy (if not in practice, at least as an institutionalized hypocrisy) to become the leitmotif of the New Teacher: "Stay *inside* the poem!"

The narrative and dramatic poem, finally poetic drama itself, is assimilated to a formulation, even *apparently* applicable only to a lyric of the most absolute purity—and it becomes heretical to treat the work as anything but "words," to ask those questions which attest our conviction that the work of art is "real"; that in the poem, the whole is greater than the sum of its parts; that certain created actions and characters exist, in some sense, *outside* of their formalizations. How long was Hamlet in Wittenberg? How many children did Lady Macbeth have? In what sense does Prospero speak for Shakespeare? What developing sensibility can be inferred from the Shakespearian corpus and be called (what *else?*) Shakespeare? We cannot ask these questions in the dewy innocence with which they were first posed; we restate them on the second convolution, aware of all the arguments against them, and the more convinced that they are essential, and cannot be shelved any more than those questions about the ends and origins of existence which have also been recently declared "unreal."

Closely associated with the Richardsian experiential-semantic approach in the total, eclectic position of the anti-biographist, is the psychological notion of the poem as the "objective correlative" or a complex of "objective correlatives" of emotional responses to the given world. Mr. Eliot's term is as elusive as it is appealing; but I am concerned here (Mr. Eliseo Vivas has elsewhere criticized it as containing some "non-intrinsic" contradictions) only with the adjective "objective" in one of its possible implications. Whatever its origins, Mr. Eliot seems to be asserting, a poem succeeds, as a poem, insofar as it is detached from the subjectivity of its maker. The poem is achieved by a process of objectification, and can be legitimately examined and understood only as an "object." This formulation leaves a somewhat second-best use for the biographical approach, as a way of explaining the particular badness of certain kinds of bad poems, e.g., Romantic verse and Shakespeare's *Hamlet*.

From this presumed insight follows the deprivation of the poet's right to explain his own poem, or at least the challenging of his claim to speak with final authority about his own work. Once realized, the argument runs, the successful poem is detached; and the author no longer has any property rights in what now belongs to the tradition rather than to him. And if, benightedly, he protests against some critical analysis or interpretation which seems to him wrong on the basis of his special biographical knowledge, he reveals that either his poem is not truly "successful," or even worse, that he has never read "Tradition and the Individual Talent."

There are, in fact, two quite different contentions, one valid, one invalid, confused in most statements about the poet as commentator on his own work. First it is asserted (and with real truth) that a poem may contain more meanings than the maker is ever aware of; and second (this is false, of course) that nothing the poet can tell us about his own work is of any *decisive* importance, because the poet cannot help falling into the trap of talking about his "intentions." But the notion of "intention" implies the belief that there is a somehow existent something against which the achieved work of art can be measured; and although this has been for all recorded time the point of view of the practicing writer, every graduate student who has read Wimsatt and Beardsley's ponderous tract on the Intentional Fallacy knows that we are all now to believe that there is no poem except the poem of "words."

The fact that all recognized critics have consistently spoken of intention shows merely that in the unfortunate past the writer about literature has often (unfortunately!) spoken more like the poet than the scientific semanticist. This regrettable looseness of expression we can only hope will be amended in the future, now that we have been duly warned. It is difficult not to be tempted by analogy. Why, we want to ask, can we properly laugh at the visiting dignitary in the high hat when he slips on the steps to the platform, because of the disparity between the entrance he *intended* and the one he **achieved**; and still not speak of a bathetic disparity between what a poem obviously aims at and what it does? On what respectable grounds can it be maintained that a poem is all act and no potentiality?

It is difficult to understand the success of the anti-biographist tendency in more respectable critical circles and in the schools, in light of its own internal contradictions. The explanation lies, I suppose, in its comparative newness, and in the failure of its opponents to arrive at any *coherent* theory of the relationship between the life of the poet and his work; so long as biographers are content merely to place side by side undigested biographical data and uninspired paraphrases of poems—linking them together mechanically or pseudo-genetically: "Wordsworth lived in the country and therefore wrote Nature poetry," or even worse, so long as notes proving that Milton was born in one house rather than another continue to be printed in magazines devoted to the study of literature, people will be tempted into opposite though equal idiocies, which have at least not been for so long proved utterly bankrupt.

A recent phenomenon of some interest in this regard is the astonishing popularity of such texts as Thomas and Brown's classroom anthology called *Reading Poems*—the very title reveals the dogma behind the book; in a world of discrete, individual "experiences," of "close reading" (a cant phrase of the anti-biographist) as an ideal, one cannot even talk of so large an abstraction as poetry. It is only "poems" to which the student must be exposed, poems printed out of chronological order and without the names of the authors attached, lest the young reader be led astray by what (necessarily irrelevant) information he may have concerning the biography or social background of any of the poets. It is all something of a hoax, of course; the teacher realizes that the chances of any student knowing too much for his own good about such matters are slight indeed; and besides, there is an index in which the names are revealed, so that unless one is very virtuous, he can scarcely help looking up the anthologized pieces. In addition, the good teacher is himself aware to begin with of the contexts, social and biographical, of a large number of the pieces. Frankly, that is why they make sense to him; and even when he admonishes the young to "stay *inside*" the poems, he is bootlegging all kinds of rich relevancies which he possesses because he is capable of connecting.

I cannot help feeling that the chief problem of teaching anything in our atomized period lies precisely in the fact that the ordinary student cannot or will not connect the few facts he knows, the slim insights he has previously attained, the chance extensions of sensibility into which he has been once or twice tempted, into a large enough context to make sense of the world he inhabits, or the works of art he encounters. It is because the old-line biographist fails to connect his facts with the works they presumably illuminate, and not because he does connect them, that he is a poor critic. And the doctrinaire anti-biographist, like the doctrinaire biographist before him, secure in pride and ignorance of the newer psychologies, makes worse the endemic disease of our era—the failure to connect. There is no "work itself," no independent formal entity which is its own sole context; the poem is the sum total of many contexts, all of which must be known to know it and evaluate it. "Only connect!" should be the motto of all critics and teachers—and the connective link between the poem on the page and most of its rewarding contexts is precisely —biography.

The poet's life is the focusing glass through which pass the determinants of the shape of his work: the tradition available to him, his understanding of "kinds," the impact of special experiences (travel, love, etc.). But the poet's life is more than a burning glass; with his work, it makes up his total meaning. I do not intend to say, of course, that some meanings of works of art, satisfactory and as far as they go sufficient, are not available in the single work itself (only a really *bad* work depends for all substantial meaning on a knowledge of the life-style of its author); but a whole body of work will contain larger meanings, and, where it is available, a sense of the life of the writer will raise that meaning to a still higher power. The latter two kinds of meaning fade into each other; for as soon as two works by a single author are considered side by side, one has begun to deal with biography—that is, with an interconnectedness fully explicable only in terms of a personality, inferred or discovered.

One of the essential functions of the poet is the assertion and creation of a personality, in a profounder sense than any non-artist can attain. We ask of the poet a definition of man, at once particular and abstract, stated and acted out. It is impossible to draw a line between the work the poet writes and the work he lives, between the life he lives and the life he writes. And the agile critic, therefore, must be prepared to move constantly back and forth between life and poem, not in a pointless circle, but in a meaningful spiraling toward the absolute point.

To pursue this matter further, we will have to abandon at this point the nominalist notion of the poem as "words" or "only words." We have the best of excuses, that such terminology gets in the way of truth. We will not, however, return to the older notions of the poem as a "document" or the embodiment of an "idea," for these older conceptions are equally inimical to the essential concept of the "marvelous"; and they have the further difficulty of raising political and moral criteria of "truth" as relevant to works of art. To redeem the sense of what words are all the time pointing *to* and what cannot be adequately explained by syntactical analysis or semantics, I shall speak of the poem as Archetype and Signature, suggesting that the key to analysis is *symbolics*; and I shall not forget that the poet's life is also capable of being analyzed in those terms. We have been rather ridiculously overemphasizing *medium* as a differentiating factor; I take it that we can now safely assume no one will confuse a life with a poem, and dwell on the elements common to the two, remembering that a pattern of social behavior can be quite as much a symbol as a word, chanted or spoken or printed. In deed as in word, the poet composes himself as maker and mask, in accordance with some contemporaneous *mythos* of the artist. And as we all know, in our day, it is even possible to be a writer without having written anything. When we talk therefore of the importance of the biography of the poet, we do not mean the importance of every trivial detail, but of all that goes into making his particular life-style, whether he concentrate on recreating himself, like Shelley, in some obvious image of the Poet, or, like Wallace Stevens, in some witty anti-mask of the Poet. Who could contend that even the *faces* of Shelley and Stevens are not typical products of their quite different kinds of art!

The word "Archetype" is the more familiar of my terms; I use it instead of the word "myth," which I have employed in the past but which becomes increasingly ambiguous, to mean any of the immemorial patterns of response to the human situation in its most permanent aspects: death, love, the biological family, the relationship with the Unknown, etc., whether those patterns be considered to reside in the Jungian Collective Unconscious or the Platonic world of Ideas. The archetypal belongs to the infra- or meta-personal, to what Freudians call the id or the unconscious; that is, it belongs to the Community at its deepest, pre-conscious levels of acceptance.

I use "Signature" to mean the sum total of individuating factors in a work, the sign of the Persona or Personality through which an Archetype is rendered, and which itself tends to become a subject as well as a means of the poem. Literature, properly speaking, can be said to come into existence at the moment a Signature is imposed upon the Archetype. The purely archetypal, without signature elements, is the myth. Perhaps a pair of examples are in order (with thanks to Mr. C. S. Lewis). The story of Baldur the Beautiful and Shakespeare's *Tempest* deal with somewhat similar archetypal material of immersion and resurrection; but we recall *The Tempest* only in all its specificity: the diction, meter, patterns of imagery, the heard voice of Shakespeare (the Signature as Means); as well as the scarcely motivated speech on pre-marital chastity, the breaking of the fictional frame by the unconventional religious *plaudite* (the Signature as Subject). Without these elements, *The Tempest* is simply not *The Tempest*; but *Baldur* can be retold in any diction, any style, just so long as faith is kept with the bare plot—and it is itself, for it is pure myth. Other examples are provided by certain children's stories, retold and reillustrated without losing their essential identity, whether they be "folk" creations like *Cinderella* or art products "captured" by the folk imagination, like Southey's *Three Bears*.

In our own time, we have seen the arts (first music, then painting, last of all literature) attempting to become "pure," or "abstract"—that is to say, attempting to slough off all remnants of the archetypal in a drive toward becoming unadulterated Signature. It should be noticed that the *theory* of abstract art is completely misleading in this regard, speaking as it does about pure forms, and mathematics, and the disavowal of personality. The abstract painter, for instance, does not, as he sometimes claims, really "paint paint," but signs his name. So-called abstract art is the ultimate expression of personality; so that the spectator says of a contemporary painting, not what one would have said in the anonymous Middle Ages, "There's a *Tree of Jesse* or a *Crucifixion!*" or not even what is said of Renaissance art, "There's a Michelangelo *Last Judgment* or a Raphael *Madonna!*" but quite simply, "There's a Mondrian or a Jackson Pollock!" Analogously, in literature we recognize a poem immediately as "a Marianne Moore" or "an Ezra Pound" long before we understand, if ever, any of its essential meanings.

The theory of "realism" or "naturalism" denies both the Archetype and the Signature, advocating, in its extreme forms, that art merely "describes nature or reality" in a neutral style, based on the case report of the scientist. Art which really achieves such aims becomes, of course, something less than "poetry" as I have used the term here, becoming an "imitation" in the lowest Platonic sense, "thrice removed from the truth." Fortunately, the great "realists" consistently betray their principles, creating Archetypes and symbols willy-nilly, though setting them in a Signature distinguished by what James called "solidity of specification." The chief value of "realism" as a theory is that it helps create in the more sophisticated writer a kind of blessed stupidity in regard to what he is really doing, so that the archetypal material can well up into his work uninhibited by his intent; and in a complementary way, it makes acceptance of that archetypal material possible for an audience which thinks of itself as "science-minded" and inimical to the demonic and mythic. It constantly startles and pleases me to come across references to such creators of grotesque Archetypes as Dostoevsky and Dickens and Faulkner as "realists."

A pair of caveats are necessary before we proceed. The distinction between Archetype and Signature, it should be noted, does not correspond to the ancient dichotomy of Content and Form. Such "forms" as the structures of Greek Tragedy (*cf.* Gilbert Murray), New Comedy and Pastoral Elegy are themselves *versunkene* Archetypes, capable of being rerealized in the great work of art. (Elsewhere I have called these "structural myths.")

Nor does the present distinction cut quite the same way as that between "impersonal" (or even "nonpersonal") and "personal." For the Signature, which is rooted in the ego and superego, belongs, as the twofold Freudian division implies, to the social collectivity as well as to the individual writer. The Signature is the joint product of "rules" and "conventions," of the expectations of a community and the idiosyncratic responses of the individual poet, who adds a personal idiom or voice to a received style. The difference between the communal element in the Signature and that in the Archetype is that the former is *conscious*—that is, associated with the superego rather than the id. The relevant, archetypal metaphor would make the personal element the Son, the conscious-communal the Father and the unconscious-communal the Mother (or the Sister, an image which occurs often as a symbolic euphemism for the Mother)—in the biological Trinity.

It is not irrelevant that the Romantic movement, which combined a deliberate return to the archetypal with a contempt for the conscious communal elements in the Signature, made one of the leitmotifs of the lives of its poets, as well as of their poems, the flight of the Sister from the threat of rape by the Father (Shelley's *Cenci*, for instance) and the complementary desperate love of Brother and Sister (anywhere from Chateaubriand and Wordsworth to Byron and Melville).

Even the most orthodox anti-biographist is prepared to grant the importance of biographical information in the *understanding* of certain ego elements in the Signature—

this is what the intrinsicist calls the study of an author's "idiosyncratic use of words." But they deny vehemently the possibility of using biographical material for the purposes of evaluation. Let us consider some examples. For instance, the line in one of John Donne's poems, "A Hymne to God the Father," which runs, "When thou hast done, thou hast not done . . ." would be incomprehensible in such a collection without author's names as the Thomas and Brown *Reading Poems*. Without the minimum biographical datum of the name of the poet, the reader could not realize that a pun was involved, and he could not therefore even ask himself the evaluative question most important to the poem, namely, what is the value of the pun in a serious, even a religious, piece of verse? This is the simplest use of biography, referring us for only an instant outside of the poem, and letting us remain there once we have returned with the information. Other similar examples are plentiful in Shakespeare's sonnets: the references to his own first name, for instance, or the troublesome phrase "all *hewes* in his controlling."

A second example which looks much like the first to a superficial glance, but which opens up in quite a different way, would be the verse "they'are but *Mummy*, possest," from Donne's "Loves Alchymie." Let us consider whether we can sustain the contention that there is a pun on *Mummy*, whether deliberately planned or unconsciously fallen into. Can we read the line as having the two meanings: women, so fair in the desiring, turn out to be only dried-out corpses after the having; and women, once possessed, turn out to be substitutes for the Mother, who is the real end of our desiring? An analysis of the mere word does not take us very far; we discover that the *lallwort* "mummy" meaning "mother" is not recorded until 1830 in that precise spelling, but that there are attested uses of it in the form "mammy" (we remember, perhaps, that "mammy-apple" and "mummy-apple" are interchangeable forms meaning "papaya") well back into Donne's period, and that the related form "mome" goes back into Middle English. Inevitably, such evidence is inconclusive, establishing possibilities at best, and never really bearing on the question of probability, for which we must turn to his life itself, to Donne's actual relations with his mother; and beyond that to the science of such relationships.

When we have discovered that John Donne did, indeed, live in an especially intimate relationship with his mother throughout her long life (she actually outlived her son); and when we have set the possible pun in a context of other literary uses of a mythic situation in which the long-desired possessed turns at the moment of possession into a shriveled hag who is also a mother (Rider Haggard's *She*, Hilton's *Lost Horizon*, and, most explicitly, Flaubert's *L'Education Sentimentale*), we realize that our original contention is highly probable, for it is motivated by a traditional version of what the psychologists have taught us to call the Oedipus Archetype. It should be noticed in passing that the archetypal critic is delivered from the bondage of time, speaking of "confluences" rather than "influences," and finding the explication of a given work in things written later as well as earlier than the original piece. Following the lead opened up by "Mummy, possest," we can move still further toward an understanding of Donne, continuing to shuttle between life and work with our new clue, and examining, for instance, Donne's ambivalent relations to the greater Mother, the Roman Church, which his actual mother represented not only metaphorically but in her own allegiance and descent. This sort of analysis which at once unifies and opens up (one could do something equally provocative and rich, for instance, with the fact that in two of Melville's tales ships symbolic of innocence are called *The Jolly Bachelor* and *The Bachelor's Delight*) is condemned in some quarters as "failing to stay close to the actual meaning of the work itself"—as if the work were a tight little island instead of a focus opening on an inexhaustible totality.

The intrinsicist is completely unnerved by any reference to the role of the Archetype in literature, fearing such references as strategies to restore the criterion of the "marvelous" to respectable currency as a standard of literary excellence; for not only is the notion of the "marvelous" pre-scientific but it is annoyingly immune to "close analysis." Certainly, the contemplation of the Archetype pushes the critic beyond semantics, and beyond the kind of analysis that considers it has done all when it assures us (once again)! that the parts and whole of a poem cohere. The critic in pursuit of the Archetype finds himself involved in anthropology and depth psychology (not because these are New Gospels, but because they provide useful tools); and if he is not too embarrassed at finding himself in such company to look about him, he discovers that he has come upon a way of binding together our fractured world, of uniting literature and nonliterature *without the reduction of the poem.*

It is sometimes objected that though the archetypal critic can move convincingly between worlds ordinarily cut off from each other, he sacrifices for this privilege the ability to distinguish the essential qualities of literary works, and especially that of evaluating them. Far from being irrelevant to evaluation, the consideration of the archetypal content of works of art is essential to it! One of the earlier critics of Dante says someplace that poetry, as distinguished from rhetoric (which treats of the credible as credible), treats of the "marvelous" as credible. Much contemporary criticism has cut itself off from this insight—that is, from the realization of what poetry on its deepest levels *is.* It is just as ridiculous to attempt the evaluation of a work of art *purely* in formal terms (considering only the Signature as Means), as it would be to evaluate it *purely* in terms of the "marvelous," or the archetypal. The question, for instance, of whether *Mona Lisa* is just a bourgeoise or whether she "as Leda, was the mother of Helen of Troy, and, as St. Anne, was the mother of Mary" is just as vital to a final estimate of the picture's worth as any matter of control of the medium or handling of light and shadow.

The Romantics seem to have realized this, and to have reached, in their distinction between Fancy and Imagination, for rubrics to distinguish between the poetic method that touches the archetypal deeply and that which merely skirts it. Even the Arnoldian description of Pope as "a classic of our prose," right or wrong, was feeling toward a similar standard of discrimination. It is typical and ironic that Arnold in a moralizing age should have felt obliged to call the daemonic power of evoking the Archetype "High Seriousness." Certainly, the complete abandonment of any such criterion by the intrinsicist leaves him baffled before certain strong mythopoeic talents like Dickens or Stevenson; and it is the same lack in his system which prevents his understanding of the complementary relationship of the life and work of the poet.

II

The Archetype which makes literature itself possible in the first instance is the Archetype of the Poet. At the moment when myth is uncertainly becoming literature—that is, reaching tentatively toward a Signature—the poet is conceived of passively, as a mere vehicle. It is the Muse who is mythically bodied forth, the unconscious, collective source of the Archetypes, imagined as more than human, and, of course, female; it is she who mounts the Poet, as it were, in that position of feminine supremacy preferred in matriarchal societies. The Poet is still conceived more as Persona than Personality; the few characteristics with which he is endowed are borrowed from the prophet: he is a blind old man, impotent in his own right. That blindness (impotence as power, what Keats much later would call "negative capability") is the earliest version of the blessing-curse, without which the popular mind cannot conceive of the poet. His flaw is, in the early stages, at once the result and the pre-condition of his submitting himself to the dark powers of inspiration for the sake of the whole people.

But very soon the poet begins to assume a more individualized life-style, the lived Signature imposed on the Archetype, and we have no longer the featureless poet born in seven cities, his face a Mask through which a voice not his is heard, but Aeschylus, the Athenian citizen-poet; Sophocles, the spoiled darling of fate; or Euripides, the crowd-contemner in his Grotto. The mass mind, dimly resentful as the Vates becomes Poeta, the Seer a Maker, the Persona a Personality, composes a new Archetype, an image to punish the poet for detaching himself from the collective id—and the Poet, amused and baffled, accepts and elaborates the new image. The legend asserts that Euripides (the first completely self-conscious alienated artist?) dies torn to pieces by dogs or, even more to the point, by women. And behind the new, personalized application looms the more ancient mythos of the ritually dismembered Orpheus, ripped by the Maenads when he had withdrawn for lonely contemplation. The older myth suggests that a sacrifice is involved as well as a punishment—the casting-out and rending of the poet being reinterpreted as a death suffered for the group, by one who has dared make the first forays out of collectivity toward personality and has endured the consequent revenge of the group as devotees of the unconscious.

In light of this, it is no longer possible to think of the poète maudit as an unfortunate invention of the Romantics, or of the Alienated Artist as a by-product of mass communications. These are reinventions, as our archetypal history repeats itself before the breakdown of Christianity. Our newer names name only recent exacerbations of a situation as old as literature itself which in turn is coeval with the rise of personality. Only the conventional stigmata of the poet as Scape-Hero have changed with time: the Blind Man becomes the disreputable Player, the Atheist, the incestuous Lover, the Homosexual or (especially in America) the Drunkard; though, indeed, none of the older versions ever die, even the Homer-typus reasserting itself in Milton and James Joyce. Perhaps in recent times the poet has come to collaborate somewhat more enthusiastically in his own defamation and destruction, whether by drowning or tuberculosis or dissipation—or by a token suicide in the work (cf. Werther). And he helps ever more consciously to compose himself and his fellow poets—Byron, for instance, the poet par excellence of the mid-nineteenth century, being the joint product of Byron and Goethe—and, though most of us forget, Harriet Beecher Stowe! Some dramatic version of the poet seems necessary to every age, and the people do not care whether the poet creates himself in his life or work or both. One thinks right now of Fitzgerald, of course, our popular image of the artist.

The contemporary critic is likely to become very impatient with the lay indifference to the poetizing of life and the "biographizing" of poetry; for he proceeds on the false assumption that the poet's life is primarily "given" and only illegitimately "made," while his work is essentially "made" and scarcely "given" at all. This is the source of endless confusion.

In perhaps the greatest periods of world literature, the "given" element in poetry is made clear by the custom of supplying or, more precisely, of imposing on the poet certain traditional bodies of story. The poet in such periods can think of himself only as "working with" materials belonging to the whole community, emending by a dozen or sixteen lines the inherited plot. Greek myths, the fairy tales and novelle of the Elizabethans, the Christian body of legend available to Dante are examples of such material. (In our world a traditionally restricted body of story is found only in subart: the pulp Western, or the movie horse opera.) In such situations, Archetype and "story" are synonymous; one remembers that for Aristotle mythos was the word for "plot," and plot was, he insisted, the most important element in tragedy. That Aristotle makes his assertions on rationalistic grounds, with no apparent awareness of the importance of the Archetype as such, does not matter; it does not even matter whether the poet himself is aware of the implications of his material. As long as he works with such an inherited gift, he can provide the ritual satisfaction necessary to great art without self-consciousness.

A Shakespeare, a Dante or a Sophocles, coming at a moment when the Archetypes of a period are still understood as "given," and yet are not considered too "sacred" for rendering through the individual Signature, possesses immense initial advantages over the poet who comes earlier or later in the process. But the great poet is not simply the mechanical result of such an occasion; he must be able to rise to it, to be capable (like Shakespeare) at once of realizing utterly the archetypal implications of his material and of formally embodying it in a lucid and unmistakable Signature. But the balance is delicate and incapable of being long maintained. The brief history of Athenian tragedy provides the classic instance. After the successes of Sophocles come the attempts of Euripides; and in Euripides one begins to feel the encounter of Signature and Archetype as a *conflict*—the poet and the collectivity have begun to lose touch with each other and with their common pre-conscious sources of value and behavior. Euripides seems to feel his inherited material as a burden, tucking it away in prologue and epilogue, so that he can get on with his proper business—the imitation of particulars. The poem begins to come apart; the acute critic finds it, however "tragic," sloppy, technically inept; and the audience raises the familiar cry of "incomprehensible and blasphemous!" Even the poet himself begins to distrust his own impulses, and writes, as Euripides did in his *Bacchae*, a mythic criticism of his own sacrilege. The poetry of the struggle against the Archetype is especially moving and poignant, but to prefer it to the poetry of the moment of balance is to commit a gross lapse of taste.

After the Euripidean crisis, the Archetypes survive only in fallen form: as inherited and scarcely understood structures (the seeds of the genres which are structural Archetypes become structural platitudes); as type characters, less complex than the masks that indicate them; as "popular" stock plots. The "Happy Ending" arises as a kind of ersatz of the true reconciliation of society and individual in Sophoclean tragedy; and the audience which can no longer find essential reassurance in its poetry that the superego and the id can live at peace with each other content themselves with the demonstration that at least Jack has his Jill, despite the comic opposition of the Old Man. Still later, even the tension in Euripidean tragedy and New Comedy is lost, and the Signature comes to be disregarded completely; poetry becomes either completely "realistic," rendering the struggle between ego and superego in terms of the imitation of particulars; or it strives to be "pure" in the contemporary sense—that is, to make the Signature its sole subject as well as its means.

Can the Archetype be redeemed after such a fall? There are various possibilities (short of the emergence of a new, ordered myth system): the writer can, like Graham Greene or Robert Penn Warren, capture for serious purposes—that is, rerender through complex and subtle Signatures—debased "popular" Archetypes: the thriller, the detective story, the Western or science fiction; or the poet can ironically manipulate the shreds and patches of outlived mythologies, fragments shored against our ruins. Eliot, Joyce, Ezra Pound and Thomas Mann have all made attempts of the latter sort, writing finally not archetypal poetry but poetry *about* Archetypes, in which plot (anciently, *mythos* itself) founders under the burden of overt explication or disappears completely. Or the poet can, like Blake or Yeats or Hart Crane, invent a private myth system of his own. Neither of the last two expedients can reach the popular audience, which prefers its Archetypes rendered without self-consciousness of so intrusive a sort.

A final way back into the world of the Archetypes, available even in our atomized culture, is an extension of the way instinctively sought by the Romantics, down through the personality of the poet, past his particular foibles and eccentricities, to his unconscious core, where he becomes one with us all in the presence of our ancient Gods, the protagonists of fables we think we no longer believe. In fantasy and terror, we can return to our common source. It is a process to delight a Hegelian, the triple swing from a naïve communal to a personal to a sophisticated communal.

We must be aware of the differences between the thesis and the synthesis in our series. What cannot be re-created as Plot is reborn as Character—ultimately the character of the poet (what else is available to him?), whether directly or in projection. In the Mask of his life and the manifold masks of his work, the poet expresses for a whole society the ritual meaning of its inarticulate selves; the artist goes forth not to "re-create the conscience of his race," but to redeem its unconscious. We cannot get back into the primal Garden of the unfallen Archetypes, but we can yield ourselves to the dreams and images that mean paradise regained. For the critic, who cannot only yield but must also *understand*, there are available new methods of exploration. To understand the Archetypes of Athenian drama, he needs (above and beyond semantics) anthropology; to understand those of recent poetry, he needs (beyond "close analysis") depth analysis, as defined by Freud and, particularly, by Jung.

The biographical approach, tempered by such findings, is just now coming into its own. We are achieving new ways of connecting (or, more precisely, of understanding a connection which has always existed) the Poet and the poem, the lived and the made, the Signature and the Archetype. It is in the focus of the poetic personality that *Dichtung und Wahrheit* become one; and it is incumbent upon us, without surrendering our right to make useful distinctions, to seize the principle of that unity. "Only connect!"

FOR DISCUSSION:

1. What distinction does Fiedler make between literature and myth?

2. What does Fiedler mean when he says that it is erroneous to view a work of art as "a tight little island instead of a focus opening on an inexhaustible totality"?

3. Describe the interrelationship between Archetype and Signature. To what degree do they blend together? To what degree does each retain its idiosyncratic characteristics?

4. What is the difference between "archetypal poetry" and "poetry about archetypes"? Cite examples of each.

5. What possibilities are available for the redemption of the fallen archetypes?

6. Not all archetypal critics share Fiedler's biographical orientation. Does the concept of the literary archetype necessarily imply a study of the life of the author?

7. Why does Fiedler believe that "Only connect" is a better motto for literary critics than "A poem should not mean but be"?

SUGGESTIONS FOR ADDITIONAL READING:

Bodkin, Maud. *Archetypal Patterns in Poetry*. London, 1934.

Campbell, Joseph. *The Hero with a Thousand Faces*. New York, 1949.

Chase, Richard. *Quest for Myth*. Baton Rouge, 1949.

Frazer, Sir James. *The New Golden Bough*, ed. Theodor H. Gaster. New York, 1959.

Frye, Northrup. "The Archetypes of Literature," *Kenyon Review*, XIII (Winter 1951), 92–110.

Jacobi, Jolande. *Complex/ Archetype/ Symbol in the Psychology of C. G. Jung*. New York, 1959.

Kluckhohn, Clyde. "Recurrent Themes in Myths and Mythmaking," *Daedalus*, LXXXVIII (Spring 1959), 268–279.

Lane, Lauriat. "The Literary Archetype: Some Reconsiderations," *Journal of Aesthetics and Art Criticism*, XIII (December 1954), 226–232.

Murray, Henry, ed. *Myth and Myth Making*. New York, 1959.

Raglan, Lord. *The Hero: A Study in Tradition, Myth and Drama*. London, 1937.

Sebeok, Thomas A., ed. *Myth: A Symposium*. Bloomington, 1958.

Shumaker, Wayne. *Literature and the Irrational*. New York, 1960.

Slote, Bernice, ed. *Myth and Symbol*. Lincoln, 1963.

Vickery, John B., ed. *Myth and Literature*. Lincoln, 1966.

Weston, Jesse L. *From Ritual to Romance*. London, 1920.

Wheelwright, Philip. *The Burning Fountain*. Bloomington, 1954.

The Myth of Orpheus

CATHERINE B. AVERY

In Greek legend, Orpheus is a son of Oeagrus, king of Thrace and the muse Calliope and, some say, the brother of that Linus who was slain by Heracles. But according to some accounts, Orpheus was the son of Apollo. Whoever his father was, Orpheus was the most famous poet and musician in Greek legend. Apollo gave him the lyre and the Muses taught him to play it so beautifully that trees and stones danced to his music and wild beasts were tamed by it. He was taught the Mysteries of Rhea by the female Dactyls in Samothrace and on a visit to Egypt he saw the Mysteries of Osiris. In imitation of these latter he invented the Mysteries of Dionysus and instituted them in Thrace. He taught the Mysteries of Dionysus to Midas, the Phrygian king, among others.

Orpheus accompanied Jason and the Argonauts on the expedition to Colchis for the Golden Fleece. With his music he soothed quarrels that sprang up among the Argonauts, made the arduous labor of rowing seem lighter, and drowned out the songs of the Sirens, thus enabling the Argonauts to pass their island in safety on the return voyage. Only Butes succumbed to the charms of the Sirens and leaped overboard. According to some accounts, the Sirens were so chagrined at being out-charmed by Orpheus that they committed suicide, but in Homeric legend they were still on their island when Odysseus passed by a generation later. On the island of the Phaeacians Orpheus sang the marriage song at the wedding of Jason and Medea.

When he returned from the voyage of the *Argo* Orpheus married Eurydice and went to dwell among the Cicones of Thrace. One day as Eurydice was walking in the meadows, Aristaeus saw her and tried to ravish her. As she fled from him she stepped on a viper which bit her ankle, and she died of the poisoned sting. Orpheus was inconsolable and resolved to bring her back from the Underworld. He ascended to Tartarus, some say through an entrance in Thesprotia, and so charmed Charon that the ferryman freely carried him over the Styx. Cerberus, the watch-dog of Tartarus was also charmed by his music, and the judges of the Underworld interrupted their task to listen, and the tortures of the wicked were temporarily suspended. Even Hades' heart was softened, and he agreed to let Eurydice return to earth on condition that Orpheus was not to look back as she followed him until she reached the light of the sun. Orpheus gladly accepted this condition and led the way, playing upon his lyre. Eurydice followed, guided by the music. When he reached the light of the sun, he could wait no longer; he looked back eagerly to see Eurydice. But she had not yet stepped into the sunlight and so he lost her forever.

After this second loss he retired to Thrace and kept apart from all women. Many maidens sought to win his love but he scorned them and gave his attention to lads in the first bloom and beauty of youth.

When he played his lyre, the trees and rocks gathered to listen. One day as he was thus playing, he was set upon by the Ciconian women. Some say Dionysus inspired them with madness because Orpheus had neglected the worship of the god and now honored the sun above all. Orpheus protested against human sacrifice and objected to the orgies of the maenads. Others say the women set upon him in revenge for his scorn. While their husbands were worshiping in the temple the women rushed at Orpheus. One hurled a stone at him, but the stone, charmed by his music, dropped harmlessly at his feet. Then the clamor of the women was so great the music was drowned out. The women fell upon him and tore him limb from limb. They flung his head and lyre into the Hebrus River.

* From *The New Century Classical Handbook*, edited by Catherine B. Avery. Copyright © 1962 by Appleton-Century-Crofts, Inc. Reprinted by permission.

From there they floated, still singing, across the sea to the island of Lesbos. As the head lay on the shore of Lesbos a serpent approached to bite it, but Apollo appeared and turned the serpent to stone.

The head was placed in a cave at Antissa, where it prophesied continually until Apollo, fearful lest it become more famous than his oracle at Delphi, commanded it to cease prophesying. The lyre was first placed in the temple of Apollo at Lesbos and its image was placed in the heavens as a constellation. The Muses, grieving over the loss of the poet, gathered his limbs and buried them at the foot of Mount Olympus, and ever since, the nightingales of this region sing more sweetly than anywhere else in the world.

The Ciconian women sought to wash the blood of Orpheus from their hands in the Helicon River, but the river-god, not willing to be an accessory in any way in the murder of Orpheus, dived underground and did not reappear for several miles. The women were transformed where they stood into oak trees as a punishment for the murder of Orpheus, and there they stood throughout time. In Zone in Thrace was another ring of oak trees left standing in the midst of a dance they had been performing as Orpheus played for them.

A religious sect arose, perhaps in the 5th century B.C., called the Orphics. They claimed Orpheus as their founder and adopted some Oriental and Egyptian ideas of purification and expiation. According to the Orphics, Orpheus was a more ancient poet than Homer and they attributed many poems, hymns, and prayers to him, some of which survive.

Orpheus Descending*

TENNESSEE WILLIAMS

DOLLY HAMMA, } local residents, wives of
BEULAH BINNINGS, } small planters
PEE WEE BINNINGS, Beulah's husband
DOG HAMMA, Dolly's husband
CAROL CUTRERE, uninhibited member of one of the oldest and most distinguished families in the county.
EVA TEMPLE, } Jabe Torrance's cousins
SISTER TEMPLE, }
UNCLE PLEASANT, part Indian, part Negro "conjure man"
VAL XAVIER, restless, itinerant musician; in love with Lady
VEE TALBOTT, Sheriff Talbott's wife

LADY TORRANCE, proprietor of Torrance's Mercantile Store; in love with Val
JABE TORRANCE, Lady's husband; suffering from a fatal illness
SHERIFF TALBOTT, the local law enforcement officer
MR. DUBINSKY, the town druggist
WOMAN
DAVID CUTRERE, Carol's brother; at one time in love with Lady
NURSE PORTER, a nurse called in to care for Jabe
FIRST MAN
SECOND MAN

ACT I

Prologue

Scene. The set represents in nonrealistic fashion a general drygoods store and part of a connecting "confectionery" in a small Southern town. The ceiling is high and the upper walls are dark, as if streaked with moisture and cobwebbed. A great dusty window upstage offers a view of disturbing emptiness that fades into late dusk. The action of the play occurs during a rainy season, late winter and early spring, and sometimes the window turns opaque but glistening silver with sheets of rain. "TORRANCE MERCANTILE STORE" is lettered on the window in gilt of old-fashioned design.

Merchandise is represented very sparsely and it is not realistic. Bolts of pepperel and percale stand upright on large spools, the black skeleton of a dressmaker's dummy stands meaninglessly against a thin white column, and there is a motionless ceiling fan with strips of flypaper hanging from it.

There are stairs that lead to a landing and disappear above it, and on the landing there is a sinister-looking artificial palm tree in a greenish-brown jardiniere.

But the confectionery, which is seen partly through a wide arched door, is shadowy and poetic as some inner dimension of the play.

---

* *Orpheus Descending* by Tennessee Williams. Copyright © 1955, 1958 by Tennessee Williams. All rights reserved. CAUTION: Professionals and amateurs are hereby warned that *Orpheus Descending*, being fully protected under the copyright laws of the U.S.A., the British Empire, including Canada, and all other countries of the Copyright Union, is subject to a royalty. All rights, including professional, amateur, motion pictures, recitation, public reading, radio broadcasting, telecasting, and rights of translation into foreign languages are strictly reserved. For information contact New Directions Publishing Corporation, 333 Sixth Avenue, New York 14, N.Y. Reprinted by permission of the publisher, New Directions Publishing Corporation, and Audrey Wood.

Another, much smaller, playing area is a tiny bedroom alcove which is usually masked by an Oriental drapery which is worn dim but bears the formal design of a gold tree with scarlet fruit and fantastic birds.

At the rise of the curtain two youngish middle-aged women, DOLLY *and* BEULAH, *are laying out a buffet supper on a pair of pink-and-gray-veined marble-topped tables with gracefully curved black-iron legs, brought into the main area from the confectionery. They are wives of small planters and tastelessly overdressed in a somewhat bizarre fashion.*

A train whistles in the distance and dogs bark in response from various points and distances. The women pause in their occupations at the tables and rush to the archway, crying out harshly.

DOLLY. Pee Wee!
BEULAH. Dawg!
DOLLY. Cannonball is comin' into th' depot!
BEULAH. You all git down to th' depot an' meet that train!

[*Their husbands slouch through, heavy, red-faced men in clothes that are too tight for them or too loose, and mud-stained boots.*]

PEE WEE. I fed that one-armed bandit a hunnerd nickels an' it coughed up five.
DOG. Must have hed indigestion.
PEE WEE. I'm gonna speak to Jabe about them slots. [*They go out and a motor starts and pauses.*]
DOLLY. I guess Jabe Torrance has got more to worry about than the slot machines and pinball games in that confectionery.
BEULAH. You're not tellin' a lie. I wint to see Dr. Johnny about Dawg's condition. Dawg's got sugar in his urine again, an as I was leavin' I ast him what was the facks about Jabe Torrance's operation in Mimphis. Well—
DOLLY. What'd he tell you, Beulah?
BEULAH. He said the worse thing a doctor ever can say.
DOLLY. What's that, Beulah?
BEULAH. Nothin' a-tall, not a spoken word did he utter! He just looked at me with those big dark eyes of his and shook his haid like this!

DOLLY [*with doleful satisfaction*]. I guess he signed Jabe Torrance's death warrant with just that single silent motion of his haid.
BEULAH. That's exactly what passed through my mind. I understand that they cut him open—[*Pauses to taste something on the table.*]
DOLLY.—An' sewed him right back up!—that's what I heard . . .
BEULAH. I didn't know these olives had seeds in them!
DOLLY. You thought they was stuffed?
BEULAH. Uh-huh. Where's the Temple sisters?
DOLLY. Where d'you think?
BEULAH. Snoopin' aroun' upstairs. If Lady catches 'em at it she'll give those two old maids a touch of her tongue! She's not a Dago for nothin'!
DOLLY. Ha, ha, no! You spoke a true word, honey . . . [*Looks out door as car passes.*] Well, I was surprised when I wint up myself!
BEULAH. You wint up you'self?
DOLLY. I did and so did you because I seen you, Beulah.
BEULAH. I never said that I didn't. Curiosity is a human instinct.
DOLLY. They got two separate bedrooms which are not even connectin'. At opposite ends of the hall, and everything is so dingy an' dark up there. Y'know what it seemed like to me? A county jail! I swear to goodness it didn't seem to me like a place for white people to live in!—that's the truth . . .
BEULAH [*darkly*]. Well, I wasn't surprised. Jabe Torrance bought that woman.
DOLLY. Bought her?
BEULAH. Yais, he bought her, when she was a girl of eighteen! He bought her and bought her cheap because she'd been thrown over and her heart was broken by that—[*Jerks head toward a passing car, then continues.*]—that Cutrere boy. . . . Oh, what a—*Mmmm,* what a—*beautiful* thing he was. . . . And those two met like you struck two stones together and made a fire!—yes—fire . . .
DOLLY. What?
BEULAH. *Fire!*—Ha . . . [*Strikes another match and lights one of the candelabra. Mandolin begins to fade in. The following monologue should be treated frankly*

as exposition, spoken to audience, almost directly, with a force that commands attention. DOLLY *does not remain in the playing area, and after the first few sentences, there is no longer any pretense of a duologue.*]

—Well, that was a long time ago, before you and Dog moved into Two River County. Although you must have heard of it. Lady's father was a Wop from the old country and when he first come here with a mandolin and a monkey that wore a little green velvet suit, ha ha.

—He picked up dimes and quarters in the saloons—this was before Prohibition. . . .

—People just called him "The Wop," nobody knew his name, just called him "The Wop," ha ha ha. . . .

DOLLY [*Off, vaguely*]. Anh-hannnh. . . .

[BEULAH *switches in the chair and fixes the audience with her eyes, leaning slightly forward to compel their attention. Her voice is rich with nostalgia, and at a sign of restlessness, she rises and comes straight out to the proscenium, like a pitchman. This monologue should set the nonrealistic key for the whole production.*]

BEULAH. Oh, my law, well, that was Lady's daddy! Then come prohibition an' first thing ennyone knew, The Wop had took to bootleggin' like a duck to water! He picked up a piece of land cheap, it was on the no'th shore of Moon Lake which used to be the old channel of the river and people thought some day the river might swing back that way, and so he got it cheap. . . . [*Moves her chair up closer to proscenium.*] He planted an orchard on it; he covered the whole no'th shore of the lake with grapevines and fruit trees, and then he built little arbors, little white wooden arbors with tables and benches to drink in and carry on in, ha ha! And in the spring and the summer, young couples would come out there, like me and Pee Wee, we used to go out there, an' court up a storm, ha ha, just court up a—storm! Ha ha!—The county was dry in those days, I don't mean dry like now, why, now you just walk a couple of feet off the highway and whistle three times like a jaybird and a nigger pops out of a bush with a bottle of corn!

DOLLY. Ain't that the truth? Ha ha.

BEULAH. But in those days the county was dry for true, I mean bone dry except for The Wop's wine garden. So we'd go out to The Wop's an' drink that Dago red wine an' cut up an' carry on an' raise such cane in those arbors! Why, I remember one Sunday old Doctor Tooker, Methodist minister then, he bust a blood vessel denouncing The Wop in the pulpit!

DOLLY. Lawd have mercy!

BEULAH. Yes, ma'am!—Each of those white wooden arbors had a lamp in it, and one by one, here and there, the lamps would go out as the couples begun to make love . . .

DOLLY. Oh—oh . . .

BEULAH. What strange noises you could hear if you listened, calls, cries, whispers, moans—giggles. . . . [*Her voice is soft with recollection.*]—And then, one by one, the lamps would be lighted again, and The Wop and his daughter would sing and play Dago songs. . . . [*Bring up mandolin: voice under "Dicitencello Vuoi."*] But sometimes The Wop would look around for his daughter, and all of a sudden Lady wouldn't be there!

DOLLY. Where would she be?

BEULAH. She'd be with David Cutrere.

DOLLY. Awwwwww—ha ha . . .

BEULAH.—Carol Cutrere's big brother, Lady and him would disappear in the orchard and old Papa Romano, The Wop, would holler, "Lady, Lady!"—no answer whatsoever, no matter how long he called and no matter how loud. . . .

DOLLY. Well, I guess it's hard to shout back, "Here I am, Papa," when where you are is in the arms of your lover!

BEULAH. Well, that spring, no, it was late that summer . . . [DOLLY *retires again from the playing area.*]—Papa Romano made a bad mistake. He sold liquor to niggers. The Mystic Crew took action.—They rode out there, one night, with gallons of coal oil—it was a real dry summer—and set that place on fire!—They burned the whole thing up, vines, arbors, fruit trees. —Pee Wee and me, we stood on the dance pavilion across the lake and watched that fire spring up. Inside of tin minutes

the whole nawth shore of the lake was a mass of flames, a regular sea of flames, and all the way over the lake we could hear Lady's papa shouting, "Fire, fire, fire!"—as if it was necessary to let people know, and the whole sky lit up with it, as red as Guinea red wine!—Ha ha ha ha. . . . Not a fire engine, not a single engine pulled out of a station that night in Two River County! —The poor old fellow, The Wop, he took a blanket and run up into the orchard to fight the fire singlehanded—and burned alive. . . . Uh-huh! burned alive. . . .
[*Mandolin stops short.* DOLLY *has returned to the table to have her coffee.*]
You know what I sometimes wonder?

DOLLY. No. What do you wonder?

BEULAH. I wonder sometimes if Lady has any suspicion that her husband, Jabe Torrance, was the leader of the Mystic Crew the night they burned up her father in his wine garden on Moon Lake?

DOLLY. Beulah Binnings, you make my blood run cold with such a thought! How could she live in marriage twenty years with a man if she knew he'd burned her father up in his wine garden?

[*Dog bays in distance.*]

BEULAH. She could live with him in hate. People can live together in hate for a long time, Dolly. Notice their passion for money. I've always noticed when couples don't love each other they develop a passion for money. Haven't you seen that happen? Of course you have. Now there's not many couples that stay devoted forever. Why, some git so they just barely tolerate each other's existence. Isn't that true?

DOLLY. You couldn't of spoken a truer word if you read it out loud from the Bible!

BEULAH. Barely tolerate each other's existence, and some don't even do that. You know, Dolly Hamma, I don't think half as many married min have committed suicide in this county as the Coroner says has done so!

DOLLY [*with voluptuous appreciation of* BEULAH's *wit*]. You think it's their wives that give them the deep six, honey?

BEULAH. I don't think so, I know so. Why there's couples that loathe and despise the sight, smell and sound of each other before that round-trip honeymoon ticket is punched at both ends, Dolly.

DOLLY. I hate to admit it but I can't deny it.

BEULAH. But they hang on together.

DOLLY. Yes, they hang on together.

BEULAH. Year after year after year, accumulating property and money, building up wealth and respect and position in the towns they live in and the counties and cities and the churches they go to, belonging to the clubs and so on and so forth and not a soul but them knowin' they have to go wash their hands after touching something the other one just put down! ha ha ha ha ha!—

DOLLY. Beulah, that's an evil laugh of yours, that laugh of yours is evil!

BEULAH [*louder*]. Ha ha ha ha ha!—But you know it's the truth.

DOLLY. Yes, she's tellin' the truth! [*Nods to audience.*]

BEULAH. Then one of them—gits—cincer or has a—stroke or somethin'?—The other one—

DOLLY.—Hauls in the loot?

BEULAH. That's right, hauls in the loot! Oh, my, then you should see how him or her blossoms out. New house, new car, new clothes. Some of 'em even change to a different church!—If it's a widow, she goes with a younger man, and if it's a widower, he starts courtin' some chick, ha ha ha ha ha!
And so I said, I said to Lady this morning before she left for Memphis to bring Jabe home, I said, "Lady, I don't suppose you're going to reopen the confectionery till Jabe is completely recovered from his operation." She said, "It can't wait for anything that might take that much time." Those are her exact words. It can't wait for anything that might take that much time. Too much is invested in it. It's going to be done over, redecorated, and opened on schedule the Saturday before Easter this spring!—Why?—Because —she knows Jabe is dying and she wants to clean up quick!

DOLLY. An awful thought. But a true one. Most awful thoughts are.

[*They are startled by sudden light laughter from the dim upstage area. The light changes on the stage to mark a division.*]

Scene I

The women turn to see CAROL CUTRERE *in the archway between the store and the confectionery. She is past thirty and, lacking prettiness, she has an odd, fugitive beauty which is stressed, almost to the point of fantasy, by a style of makeup with which a dancer named Valli has lately made such an impression in the bohemian centers of France and Italy, the face and lips powdered white and the eyes outlined and exaggerated with black pencil and the lids tinted blue. Her family name is the oldest and most distinguished in the country.*

BEULAH. Somebody don't seem to know that the store is closed.
DOLLY. Beulah?
BEULAH. What?
DOLLY. Can you understand how anybody would deliberately make themselves look fantastic as that?
BEULAH. Some people have to show off, it's a passion with them, anything on earth to get attention.
DOLLY. I sure wouldn't care for that kind of attention. Not me. I wouldn't desire it. . . .

[*During these lines, just loud enough for her to hear them,* CAROL *has crossed to the payphone and deposited a coin.*]

CAROL. I want Tulane 0370 in New Orleans. What? Oh. Hold on a minute.

[EVA TEMPLE *is descending the stairs, slowly, as if awed by* CAROL's *appearance.* CAROL *rings open the cashbox and removes some coins; returns to deposit coins in phone.*]

BEULAH. She helped herself to money out of the cashbox.

[EVA *passes* CAROL *like a timid child skirting a lion cage.*]

CAROL. Hello, Sister.
EVA. I'm Eva.
CAROL. Hello, Eva.
EVA. Hello . . . [*Then in a loud whisper to* BEULAH *and* DOLLY.] She took money out of the cashbox.
DOLLY. Oh, she can do as she pleases, she's a Cutrere!
BEULAH. Shoot . . .
EVA. What is she doin' barefooted?
BEULAH. The last time she was arrested on the highway, they say that she was naked under her coat.
CAROL [*to operator*]. I'm waiting. [*Then to women.*]—I caught the heel of my slipper in that rotten boardwalk out there and it broke right off. [*Raises slippers in hand.*] They say if you break the heel of your slipper in the morning it means you'll meet the love of your life before dark. But it was already dark when I broke the heel of my slipper. Maybe that means I'll meet the love of my life before daybreak. [*The quality of her voice is curiously clear and childlike.* SISTER TEMPLE *appears on stair landing bearing an old waffle iron.*]
SISTER. Wasn't that them?
EVA. No, it was Carol Cutrere!
CAROL [*at phone*]. Just keep on ringing, please, he's probably drunk.
[SISTER *crosses by her as* EVA *did.*]
Sometimes it takes quite a while to get through the living-room furniture. . . .
SISTER. —She a sight?
EVA. Uh-huh!
CAROL. Bertie?—Carol!—Hi, doll! Did you trip over something? I heard a crash. Well, I'm leaving right now, I'm already on the highway and everything's fixed, I've got my allowance back on condition that I remain forever away from Two River County! I had to blackmail them a little. I came to dinner with my eyes made up and my little black sequin jacket and Betsy Boo, my brother's wife, said, "Carol, you going out to a fancy dress ball?" I said, "Oh, no, I'm just going jooking tonight up and down the Dixie Highway between here and Memphis like I used to when I lived here." Why, honey, she flew so fast you couldn't see her passing and came back in with the ink still wet on the check! And this will be done once a month as long as I stay away from Two

River County.... [*Laughs gaily.*]—How's Jackie? Bless his heart, give him a sweet kiss for me! Oh, honey, I'm driving straight through, not even stopping for pickups unless you need one! I'll meet you in the Starlite Lounge before it closes, or if I'm irresistibly delayed, I'll certainly join you for coffee at the Morning Call before the all-night places have closed for the day ... —I—Bertie? Bertie? [*Laughs uncertainly and hangs up.*]—let's see, now. ... [*Removes a revolver from her trench-coat pocket and crosses to fill it with cartridges back of counter.*]

EVA. What she looking for?

SISTER. Ask her.

EVA [*advancing*]. What're you looking for, Carol?

CAROL. Cartridges for my revolver.

DOLLY. She don't have a license to carry a pistol.

BEULAH. She don't have a license to drive a car.

CAROL. When I stop for someone I want to be sure it's someone I want to stop for.

DOLLY. Sheriff Talbott ought to know about this when he gits back from the depot.

CAROL. Tell him, ladies. I've already given him notice that if he ever attempts to stop me again on the highway, I'll shoot it out with him....

BEULAH. When anybody has trouble with the law—

[*Her sentence is interrupted by a panicky scream from* EVA, *immediately repeated by* SISTER. *The* TEMPLE SISTERS *scramble upstairs to the landing.* DOLLY *also cries out and turns, covering her face. A Negro* CONJURE MAN *has entered the store. His tattered garments are fantastically bedizened with many talismans and good-luck charms of shell and bone and feather. His blue-black skin is daubed with cryptic signs in white paint.*]

DOLLY. Git him out, git him out, he's going to mark my baby!

BEULAH. Oh, shoot, Dolly....

[DOLLY *has now fled after the* TEMPLE SISTERS, *to the landing of the stairs. The* CONJURE MAN *advances with a soft, rapid, toothless mumble of words that sound like wind in dry grass. He is holding out something in his shaking hand.*]

It's just that old crazy conjure man from Blue Mountain. He cain't mark your baby.

[*Phrase of primitive music or percussion as* NEGRO *moves into light.* BEULAH *follows* DOLLY *to landing.*]

CAROL [*very high and clear voice*]. Come here, Uncle, and let me see what you've got there. Oh, it's a bone of some kind. No, I don't want to touch it, it isn't clean yet, there's still some flesh clinging to it.

[*Women make sounds of revulsion.*]

Yes, I know it's the breastbone of a bird but it's still tainted with corruption. Leave it a long time on a bare rock in the rain and the sun till every sign of corruption is burned and washed away from it, and then it will be a good charm, a white charm, but now it's a black charm, Uncle. So take it away and do what I told you with it. ...

[*The* NEGRO *makes a ducking obeisance and shuffles slowly back to the door.*]

Hey, Uncle Pleasant, give us the Choctaw cry.

[NEGRO *stops in confectionery.*]

He's part Choctaw, he knows the Choctaw cry.

SISTER TEMPLE. Don't let him holler in *here!*

CAROL. Come on, Uncle Pleasant, you know it!

[*She takes off her coat and sits on the R. window sill. She starts the cry herself. The* NEGRO *throws back his head and completes it: a series of barking sounds that rise to a high sustained note of wild intensity. The women on the landing retreat further upstairs. Just then, as though the cry had brought him,* VAL *enters the store. He is a young man, about 30, who has a kind of wild beauty about him that the cry would suggest. He does not wear Levi's or a T-shirt, he has on a pair of dark serge pants, glazed from long wear and not excessively tight-fitting. His remarkable garment is a snakeskin jacket, mottled white, black and gray. He carries a guitar which is covered with inscriptions.*]

CAROL [*looking at the young man*]. Thanks, Uncle ...

BEULAH. *Hey, old man, you! Choctaw! Conjure man! Nigguh! Will you go out-a this sto'? So we can come back down stairs?*

[CAROL *hands* NEGRO *a dollar; he goes out right cackling.* VAL *holds the door open for* VEE TALBOTT, *a heavy, vague woman in her forties. She does primitive oil paintings and carries one into the store, saying:*]

VEE. I got m'skirt caught in th' door of the Chevrolet an' I'm afraid I tore it.
[*The women descend into store: laconic greetings, interest focused on* VAL.]
Is it dark in here or am I losin' my eyesight? I been painting all day, finished a picture in a ten-hour stretch, just stopped a few minutes fo' coffee and went back to it again while I had a clear vision. I think I got it this time. But I'm so exhausted I could drop in my tracks. There's nothing more exhausting than that kind of work on earth, it's not so much that it tires your body out, but it leaves you drained inside. Y'know what I mean? Inside? Like you was burned out by something? Well! Still!—You feel you've accomplished something when you're through with it, sometimes you feel—*elevated!* How are you, Dolly?
DOLLY. All right, Mrs. Talbott.
VEE. That's good. How are you, Beulah?
BEULAH. Oh, I'm all right, I reckon.
VEE. Still can't make out much. Who is that there? [*Indicates* CAROL's *figure by the window. A significant silence greets this question.* VEE, *suddenly.*]
Oh! I thought her folks had got her out of the county . . .
[CAROL *utters a very light, slightly rueful laugh, her eyes drifting back to* VAL *as she moves back into confectionery.*]
Jabe and Lady back yet?
DOLLY. Pee Wee an' Dawg have gone to the depot to meet 'em.
VEE. Aw. Well, I'm just in time. I brought my new picture with me, the paint isn't dry on it yet. I thought that Lady might want to hang it up in Jabe's room while he's convalescin' from the operation, cause after a close shave with death, people like to be reminded of spiritual things. Huh? Yes! This is the Holy Ghost ascending. . . .
DOLLY [*looking at canvas*]. You didn't put a head on it.
VEE. The head was a blaze of light, that's all I saw in my vision.
DOLLY. Who's the young man with yuh?
VEE. Aw, excuse me, I'm too worn out to have manners. This is Mr. Valentine Xavier, Mrs. Hamma and Mrs.—I'm sorry, Beulah. I never can get y' last name!
BEULAH. I fo'give you. My name is Beulah Binnings.
VAL. What shall I do with this here?
VEE. Oh, that bowl of sherbet. I thought that Jabe might need something light an' digestible so I brought a bowl of sherbet.
DOLLY. What flavor is it?
VEE. Pineapple.
DOLLY. Oh, goody, I love pineapple. Better put it in the icebox before it starts to melt.
BEULAH [*looking under napkin that covers bowl*]. I'm afraid you're lockin' th' stable after the horse is gone.
DOLLY. Aw, is it melted already?
BEULAH. Reduced to juice.
VEE. Aw, shoot. Well, put it on ice anyhow, it might thicken up.
[*Women are still watching* VAL.]
Where's the icebox?
BEULAH. In the confectionery.
VEE. I thought that Lady had closed the confectionery.
BEULAH. Yes, but the Frigidaire's still there.

[VAL *goes out R. through confectionery.*]

VEE. Mr. Xavier is a stranger in our midst. His car broke down in that storm last night and I let him sleep in the lockup. He's lookin' for work and I thought I'd introduce him to Lady an' Jabe because if Jabe can't work they're going to need somebody to help out in th' store.
BEULAH. That's a good idea.
DOLLY. Uh-huh.
BEULAH. Well, come on in, you all, it don't look like they're comin' straight home from the depot anyhow.
DOLLY. Maybe that wasn't the Cannonball Express.
BEULAH. Or maybe they stopped off fo' Pee Wee to buy some liquor.
DOLLY. Yeah . . . at Ruby Lightfoot's.

[*They move past* CAROL *and out of sight.* CAROL *has risen. Now she crosses into the main store area, watching* VAL *with the candid curiosity of one child observing another. He pays no attention but concentrates on his belt buckle which he is repairing with a pocketknife.*]

CAROL. What're you fixing?

VAL. Belt buckle.

CAROL. Boys like you are always fixing something. Could you fix my slipper?

VAL. What's wrong with your slipper?

CAROL. Why are you pretending not to remember me?

VAL. It's hard to remember someone you never met.

CAROL. Then why'd you look so startled when you saw me?

VAL. Did I?

CAROL. I thought for a moment you'd run back out the door.

VAL. The sight of a woman can make me walk in a hurry but I don't think it's ever made me run.—You're standing in my light.

CAROL [*moving aside slightly*]. Oh, excuse me. Better?

VAL. Thanks....

CAROL. Are you afraid I'll snitch?

VAL. Do what?

CAROL. Snitch? I wouldn't; I'm not a snitch. But I can prove that I know you if I have to. It was New Year's Eve in New Orleans.

VAL. I need a small pair of pliers....

CAROL. You had on that jacket and a snake ring with a ruby eye.

VAL. I never had a snake ring with a ruby eye.

CAROL. A snake ring with an emerald eye?

VAL. I never had a snake ring with any kind of an eye.... [*Begins to whistle softly, his face averted.*]

CAROL [*smiling gently*]. Then maybe it was a dragon ring with an emerald eye or a diamond or a ruby eye. You told us that it was a gift from a lady osteopath that you'd met somewhere in your travels and that any time you were broke you'd wire this lady osteopath collect, and no matter how far you were or how long it was since you'd seen her, she'd send you a money order for twenty-five dollars with the same sweet message each time. "I love you. When will you come back?" And to prove the story, not that it was difficult to believe it, you took the latest of these sweet messages from your wallet for us to see.... [*She throws back her head with soft laughter. He looks away still further and busies himself with the belt buckle.*]—We followed you through five places before we made contact with you and I was the one that made contact. I went up to the bar where you were standing and touched your jacket and said, "What stuff is this made of?" and when you said it was snakeskin, I said, "I wish you'd told me before I touched it." And you said something not nice. You said, "Maybe that will learn you to hold back your hands." I was drunk by that time which was after midnight. Do you remember what I said to you? I said, "What on earth can you do on this earth but catch at whatever comes near you, with both your hands, until your fingers are broken?" I'd never said that before, or even consciously thought it, but afterwards it seemed like the truest thing that my lips had ever spoken, what on earth can you do but catch at whatever comes near you with both your hands until your fingers are broken.... You gave me a quick, sober look. I think you nodded slightly, and then you picked up your guitar and began to sing. After singing you passed the kitty. Whenever paper money was dropped in the kitty you blew a whistle. My cousin Bertie and I dropped in five dollars, you blew the whistle five times and then sat down at our table for a drink, Schenley's with Seven Up. You showed us all those signatures on your guitar.... Any correction so far?

VAL. Why are you so anxious to prove I know you?

CAROL. Because I want to know you better and better! I'd like to go out jooking with you tonight.

VAL. What's jooking?

CAROL. Oh, don't you know what that is? That's where you get in a car and drink a little and drive a little and stop and dance a little to a juke box and then you drink a little more and drive a little more and stop and dance a little more to a juke box and then you stop dancing and you just drink and drive and then you stop driving and just drink, and then, finally, you stop drinking....

VAL.—What do you do, then?
CAROL. That depends on the weather and who you're jooking with. If it's a clear night you spread a blanket among the memorial stones on Cypress Hill, which is the local bone orchard, but if it's not a fair night, and this one certainly isn't, why, usually then you go to the Idlewild cabins between here and Sunset on the Dixie Highway. . . .
VAL.—That's about what I figured. But I don't go that route. Heavy drinking and smoking the weed and shacking with strangers is okay for kids in their twenties but this is my thirtieth birthday and I'm all through with that route. [*Looks up with dark eyes.*] I'm not young any more.
CAROL. You're young at thirty—I hope so! I'm twenty-nine!
VAL. Naw, you're not young at thirty if you've been on a Goddam party since you were fifteen!

[*Picks up his guitar and sings and plays "Heavenly Grass."* CAROL *has taken a pint of bourbon from her trench-coat pocket and she passes it to him.*]

CAROL. Thanks. That's lovely. Many happy returns of your birthday, Snakeskin.

[*She is very close to him.* VEE *enters and says sharply:*]

VEE. Mr. Xavier don't drink.
CAROL. Oh, ex-cuse me!
VEE. And if you behaved yourself better your father would not be paralyzed in bed!

[*Sound of car out front. Women come running with various cries.* LADY *enters, nodding to the women, and holding the door open for her husband and the men following him. She greets the women in almost toneless murmurs, as if too tired to speak. She could be any age between thirty-five and forty-five, in appearance, but her figure is youthful. Her face taut. She is a woman who met with emotional disaster in her girlhood; verges on hysteria under strain. Her voice is often shrill and her body tense. But when in repose, a girlish softness emerges again and she looks ten years younger.*]

LADY. Come in, Jabe. We've got a reception committee here to meet us. They've set up a buffet supper.

[JABE *enters. A gaunt, wolfish man, gray and yellow. The women chatter idiotically.*]

BEULAH. Well, look who's here!
DOLLY. Well, Jabe!
BEULAH. I don't think he's been sick. I think he's been to Miami. Look at that wonderful color in his face!
DOLLY. I never seen him look better in my life!
BEULAH. Who does he think he's foolin'? Ha ha ha!—not me!
JABE. Whew, Jesus—I'm mighty—tired. . . . [*An uncomfortable silence, everyone staring greedily at the dying man with his tense, wolfish smile and nervous cough.*]
PEE WEE. Well, Jabe, we been feedin' lots of nickels to those one-arm bandits in there.
DOG. An' that pinball machine is hotter'n a pistol.
PEE WEE. Ha ha.

[EVA TEMPLE *appears on stairs and screams for her sister.*]

EVA. Sistuh! Sistuh! Sistuh! Cousin Jabe's here!

[*A loud clatter upstairs and shrieks.*]

JABE. Jesus. . . .

[EVA *rushing at him—stops short and bursts into tears.*]

LADY. Oh, cut that out, Eva Temple!—What were you doin' upstairs?
EVA. I can't help it, it's so good to see him, it's so wonderful to see our cousin again, oh, Jabe, blessed!
SISTER. Where's Jabe, where's precious Jabe? Where's our precious cousin?
EVA. Right here, Sister!
SISTER. Well, bless your old sweet life, and lookit the color he's got in his face, will you?
BEULAH. I just told him he looks like he's been to Miami and got a Florida suntan, haha ha!

[*The preceding speeches are very rapid, all overlapping.*]

JABE. I ain't been out in no sun an' if you all will excuse me I'm gonna do my celebratin' upstairs in bed because I'm kind of—worn out. [*Goes creakily to foot of steps while* EVA *and* SISTER *sob into their handkerchiefs behind him.*]—I see they's been some changes made here. Uh-huh. Uh-huh. How come the shoe department's back here now? [*Instant hostility as if habitual between them.*]

LADY. We always had a problem with light in this store.

JABE. So you put the shoe department further away from the window? That's sensible. A very intelligent solution to the problem, Lady.

LADY. Jabe, you know I told you we got a fluorescent tube coming to put back here.

JABE. Uh-huh. Uh-huh. Well. Tomorrow I'll get me some niggers to help me move the shoe department back front.

LADY. You do whatever you want to, it's your store.

JABE. Uh-huh. Uh-huh. I'm glad you reminded me of it.

[LADY *turns sharply away. He starts up stairs.* PEE WEE *and* DOG *follow him up. The women huddle and whisper in the store.* LADY *sinks wearily into chair at table.*]

BEULAH. That man will never come down those stairs again!

DOLLY. Never in this world, honey.

BEULAH. He has th' death sweat on him! Did you notice that death sweat on him?

DOLLY. An' yellow as butter, just as yellow as—

[SISTER *sobs.*]

EVA. Sister, Sister!

BEULAH [*crossing to* LADY]. Lady, I don't suppose you feel much like talking about it right now but Dog and me are so worried.

DOLLY. Pee Wee and me are worried sick about it.

LADY.—About what?

BEULAH. Jabe's operation in Memphis. Was it successful?

DOLLY. Wasn't it successful?

[LADY *stares at them blindly. The women, except* CAROL, *close avidly about her, tense with morbid interest.*]

SISTER. Was it too late for surgical interference?

EVA. Wasn't it successful?

[*A loud, measured knock begins on the floor above.*]

BEULAH. Somebody told us it had gone past the knife.

DOLLY. We do hope it ain't hopeless.

EVA. We hope and pray it ain't hopeless.

[*All their faces wear faint, unconscious smiles.* LADY *looks from face to face; then utters a slight, startled laugh and springs up from the table and crosses to the stairs.*]

LADY [*as if in flight*]. Excuse me, I have to go up, Jabe's knocking for me. [LADY *goes upstairs. The women gaze after her.*]

CAROL [*suddenly and clearly, in the silence*]. Speaking of knocks, I have a knock in my engine. It goes knock, knock, and I say who's there. I don't know whether I'm in communication with some dead ancestor or the motor's about to drop out and leave me stranded in the dead of night on the Dixie Highway. Do you have any knowledge of mechanics? I'm sure you do. Would you be sweet and take a short drive with me? So you could hear that knock?

VAL. I don't have time.

CAROL. What have you got to do?

VAL. I'm waiting to see about a job in this store.

CAROL. I'm offering you a job.

VAL. I want a job that pays.

CAROL. I expect to pay you.

[*Women whisper loudly in the background.*]

VAL. Maybe sometime tomorrow.

CAROL. I can't stay here overnight; I'm not allowed to stay overnight in this county. [*Whispers rise. The word "corrupt" is distinguished.*]
[*Without turning, smiling very brightly.*] What are they saying about me? Can you hear what those women are saying about me?

VAL.—Play it cool. . . .

CAROL. I don't like playing it cool! What are they saying about me? That I'm corrupt?

VAL. If you don't want to be talked about,

why do you make up like that, why do you—

CAROL. *To show off!*

VAL. What?

CAROL. *I'm an exhibitionist!* I want to be noticed, seen, heard, felt! I want them to know I'm alive! Don't you want them to know you're alive?

VAL. I want to live and I don't care if they know I'm alive or not.

CAROL. Then why do you play a guitar?

VAL. Why do you make a Goddam show of yourself?

CAROL. That's right, for the same reason.

VAL. We don't go the same route. . . . [*He keeps moving away from her; she continually follows him. Her speech is compulsive.*]

CAROL. I used to be what they call a Christ-bitten reformer. You know what that is?—A kind of benign exhibitionist. . . . I delivered stump speeches, wrote letters of protest about the gradual massacre of the colored majority in the county. I thought it was wrong for pellagra and slow starvation to cut them down when the cotton crop failed from army worm or boll weevil or too much rain in summer. I wanted to, tried to, put up free clinics, I squandered the money my mother left me on it. And when that Willie McGee thing came along—he was sent to the chair for having improper relations with a white whore—[*Her voice is like a passionate incantation.*] I made a fuss about it. I put on a potato sack and set out for the capitol on foot. This was in winter. I walked barefoot in this burlap sack to deliver a personal protest to the Governor of the State. Oh, I suppose it was partly exhibitionism on my part, but it wasn't completely exhibitionism; there was something else in it, too. You know how far I got? Six miles out of town—hooted, jeered at, even spit on!—every step of the way—and then arrested! Guess what for? Lewd vagrancy! Uh-huh, that was the charge, "lewd vagrancy," because they said that potato sack I had on was not a respectable garment. . . . Well, all that was a pretty long time ago, and now I'm not a reformer any more. I'm just a "lewd vagrant." And I'm showing the "S.O.B.S." how lewd a "lewd vagrant" can be if she puts her whole heart in it like I do mine! All right. I've told you my story, the story of an exhibitionist. Now I want you to do something for me. Take me out to Cypress Hill in my car. And we'll hear the dead people talk. They do talk there. They chatter together like birds on Cypress Hill, but all they say is one word and that one word is "live," they say "Live, live, live, live, live!" It's all they've learned, it's the only advice they can give.—Just live. . . . [*She opens the door.*] Simple!—a very simple instruction. . . .

[*Goes out. Women's voices rise from the steady, indistinct murmur, like hissing geese.*]

WOMEN'S VOICES.—No, not liquor! Dope!
—Something not normal all right!
—Her father and brother were warned by the Vigilantes to keep her out of this county.
—She's absolutely degraded!
—Yes, corrupt!
—Corrupt! (Etc., etc.)

[*As if repelled by their hissing voices,* VAL *suddenly picks up his guitar and goes out of the store as—*VEE TALBOTT *appears on the landing and calls down to him.*]

VEE. Mr. Xavier! Where is Mr. Xavier?

BEULAH. Gone, honey.

DOLLY. You might as well face it, Vee. This is one candidate for salvation that you have lost to the opposition.

BEULAH. He's gone off to Cypress Hill with the Cutrere girl.

VEE [*descending*].—If some of you older women in Two River County would set a better example there'd be more decent young people!

BEULAH. What was that remark?

VEE. I mean that people who give drinkin' parties an' get so drunk they don't know which is their husband and which is somebody else's and people who serve on the altar guild and still play cards on Sundays—

BEULAH. Just stop right there! Now I've discovered the source of that dirty gossip!

VEE. I'm only repeating what I've been told by others. I never been to these parties!

BEULAH. No, and you never will! You're a public kill-joy, a professional hypocrite!

VEE. I try to build up characters! You and your drinkin' parties are only concerned with tearin' characters down! I'm goin' upstairs, I'm goin' back upstairs! [*Rushes upstairs.*]
BEULAH. Well, I'm glad I said what I said to that woman. I've got no earthly patience with that sort of hypocriticism. Dolly, let's put this perishable stuff in the Frigidaire and leave here. I've never been so thoroughly disgusted!
DOLLY. Oh, my Lawd. [*Pauses at stairs and shouts.*] PEE WEE! [*Goes off with the dishes.*]
SISTER. Both of those wimmen are as common as dirt.
EVA. Dolly's folks in Blue Mountain are nothin' at all but the poorest kind of white trash. Why, Lollie Tucker told me the old man sits on the porch with his shoes off drinkin' beer out of a bucket!— Let's take these flowers with us to put on the altar.
SISTER. Yes, we can give Jabe credit in the parish notes.
EVA. I'm going to take these olive-nut sandwiches, too. They'll come in handy for the Bishop Adjutant's tea.

[DOLLY *and* BEULAH *cross through.*]

DOLLY. We still have time to make the second show.
BEULAH [*shouting*]. Dog!
DOLLY. Pee Wee! [*They rush out of store.*]
EVA. Sits on the porch with his shoes off?
SISTER. Drinkin' beer out of a bucket! [*They go out with umbrellas, etc. Men descend stairs.*]
SHERIFF TALBOTT. Well, it looks to me like Jabe will more than likely go under before the cotton comes up.
PEE WEE. He never looked good.
DOG. Naw, but now he looks worse.

[*They cross to door.*]

SHERIFF. Vee!
VEE [*from landing*]. Hush that bawling. I had to speak to Lady about that boy and I couldn't speak to her in front of Jabe because he thinks he's gonna be able to go back to work himself.
SHERIFF. Well, move along, quit foolin'.
VEE. I think I ought to wait till that boy gits back.
SHERIFF. I'm sick of you making a goddam fool of yourself over every stray bastard that wanders into this county.

[*Car horn honks loudly.* VEE *follows her husband out. Sound of cars driving off. Dogs bay in distance as lights dim to indicate short passage of time.*]

Scene 2

A couple of hours later that night. Through the great window the landscape is faintly luminous under a scudding moonlit sky. Outside a girl's laughter, CAROL's, rings out high and clear and is followed by the sound of a motor, rapidly going off.

VAL *enters the store before the car sound quite fades out and while a dog is still barking at it somewhere along the highway. He says "Christ" under his breath, goes to the buffet table and scrubs lipstick stain off his mouth and face with a paper napkin, picks up his guitar which he had left on a counter.*

Footsteps descending: LADY *appears on the landing in a flannel robe, shivering in the cold air; she snaps her fingers impatiently for the old dog, Bella, who comes limping down beside her. She doesn't see* VAL, *seated on the shadowy counter, and she goes directly to the phone near the stairs. Her manner is desperate, her voice harsh and shrill.*

LADY. Ge' me the drugstore, will you? I know the drugstore's closed, this is Mrs. Torrance, my store's closed, too, but I got a sick man here, just back from the hospital, yeah, yeah, an emergency, wake up Mr. Dubinsky, keep ringing till he answers, it's an emergency! [*Pause: she mutters under her breath.*]—Porca la miseria! I wish I was dead, dead, dead. . . .
VAL [*quietly*]. No, you don't, Lady.

[*She gasps, turning and seeing him, without leaving the phone, she rings the cashbox open and snatches out something.*]

LADY. What're you doin' here? You know this store is closed!
VAL. I seen a light was still on and the door was open so I come back to—
LADY. You see what I got in my hand? [*Raises revolver above level of counter.*]
VAL. You going to shoot me?
LADY. You better believe it if you don't get out of here, mister!
VAL. That's all right, Lady, I just come back to pick up my guitar.
LADY. To pick up your guitar?
[*He lifts it gravely.*]
—Huh. . . .
VAL. Miss Talbott brought me here. I was here when you got back from Memphis, don't you remember?
LADY.—Aw. Aw, yeah. . . . You been here all this time?
VAL. No. I went out and come back.
LADY [*into the phone*]. I told you to keep ringing till he answers! Go on, keep ringing, keep ringing! [*Then to* VAL.] You went out and come back?
VAL. Yeah.
LADY. What for?
VAL. You know that girl that was here?
LADY. Carol Cutrere?
VAL. She said she had car trouble and could I fix it.
LADY.—Did you fix it?
VAL. She didn't have no car trouble, that wasn't her trouble, oh, she had trouble, all right, but *that* wasn't it. . . .
LADY. What was her trouble?
VAL. She made a mistake about me.
LADY. What mistake?
VAL. She thought I had a sign "Male at Stud" hung on me.
LADY. She thought you—? [*Into phone suddenly.*] Oh, Mr. Dubinsky, I'm sorry to wake you up but I just brought my husband back from the Memphis hospital and I left my box of luminal tablets in the—I got to have some! I ain't slep' for three nights, I'm going to pieces, you hear me, I'm going to pieces, I ain't slept in three nights, I got to have some tonight. Now you look here, if you want to keep my trade, you send me over some tablets. Then bring them yourself, God damn it, excuse my French! Because I'm going to pieces right this minute! [*Hangs up violently.*]—Mannage la miseria!—Christ. . . . I'm shivering!—It's cold as a Goddam ice-plant in this store, I don't know why, it never seems to hold heat, the ceiling's too high or something, it don't hold heat at all.—Now what do you want? I got to go upstairs.
VAL. Here. Put this on you.

[*He removes his jacket and hands it to her. She doesn't take it at once, stares at him questioningly and then slowly takes the jacket in her hands and examines it, running her fingers curiously over the snakeskin.*]

LADY. What is this stuff this thing's made of? It looks like it was snakeskin.
VAL. Yeah, well, that's what it is.
LADY. What're you doing with a snakeskin jacket?
VAL. It's a sort of a trademark; people call me Snakeskin.
LADY. Who calls you Snakeskin?
VAL. Oh, in the bars, the sort of places I work in—but I've quit that. I'm through with that stuff now. . . .
LADY. You're a—entertainer?
VAL. I sing and play the guitar.
LADY.—Aw? [*She puts the jacket on as if to explore it.*] It feels warm all right.
VAL. It's warm from my body, I guess. . . .
LADY. You must be a warm-blooded boy. . . .
VAL. That's right. . . .
LADY. Well, what in God's name are you lookin' for around here?
VAL.—Work.
LADY. Boys like you don't work.
VAL. What d'you mean by boys like me?
LADY. Ones that play th' guitar and go around talkin' about how warm they are. . . .
VAL. That happens t' be the truth. My temperature's always a couple degrees above normal the same as a dog's, it's normal for me the same as it is for a dog, that's the truth. . . .
LADY.—Huh!
VAL. You don't believe me?
LADY. I have no reason to doubt you, but what about it?
VAL.—Why—nothing. . . .

[LADY *laughs softly and suddenly;* VAL *smiles slowly and warmly.*]

LADY. You're a peculiar somebody all right, you sure are! How did you get around here?

VAL. I was driving through here last night and an axle broke on my car, that stopped me here, and I went to the county jail for a place to sleep out of the rain. Mizz Talbott took me in and give me a cot in the lockup and said if I hung around till you got back that you might give me a job in the store to help out since your husband was tooken sick.

LADY.—Uh-huh. Well—she was wrong about that.... If I took on help here it would have to be local help, I couldn't hire no stranger with a—snakeskin jacket and a guitar ... and that runs a temperature as high as a dog's! [*Throws back her head in another soft, sudden laugh and starts to take off the jacket.*]

VAL. Keep it on.

LADY. No, I got to go up now and you had better be going ...

VAL. I got nowhere to go.

LADY. Well, everyone's got a problem and that's yours.

VAL.—What nationality are you?

LADY. Why do you ask me that?

VAL. You seem to be like a foreigner.

LADY. I'm the daughter of a Wop bootlegger burned to death in his orchard!—Take your jacket....

VAL. What was that you said about your father?

LADY. Why?

VAL.—A "Wop bootlegger"?

LADY.—They burned him to death in his orchard! What about it? The story's well known around here.

[JABE *knocks on ceiling.*]

I got to go up, I'm being called for.

[*She turns out light over counter and at the same moment he begins to sing softly with his guitar:* "Heavenly Grass." *He suddenly stops short and says abruptly.*]

VAL. I do electric repairs.

[LADY *stares at him softly.*]

I can do all kinds of odd jobs. Lady, I'm thirty today and I'm through with the life that I've been leading. [*Pause: dog bays in distance.*] I lived in corruption but but I'm not corrupted. Here is why. [*Picks up his guitar.*] My life's companion! It washes me clean like water when anything unclean has touched me.... [*Plays softly, with a slow smile.*]

LADY. What's all that writing on it?

VAL. Autographs of musicians I run into here and there.

LADY. Can I see it?

VAL. Turn on that light above you.

[*She switches on green-shaded bulb over counter.* VAL *holds the instrument tenderly between them as if it were a child; his voice is soft, intimate, tender.*]

See this name? Leadbelly?

LADY. Leadbelly?

VAL. Greatest man ever lived on the twelve-string guitar! Played it so good he broke the stone heart of a Texas governor with it and won himself a pardon out of jail. ... And see this name Oliver? King Oliver? That name is immortal, Lady. Greatest man since Gabriel on a horn....

LADY. What's this name?

VAL. Oh. That name? That name is also immortal. The name Bessie Smith is written in the stars!—Jim Crow killed her, John Barleycorn and Jim Crow killed Bessie Smith but that's another story.... See this name here? That's another immortal!

LADY. Fats Waller? Is his name written in the stars, too?

VAL. Yes, his name is written in the stars, too....

[*Her voice is also intimate and soft: a spell of softness between them, their bodies almost touching, only divided by the guitar.*]

LADY. You had any sales experience?

VAL. All my life I been selling something to someone.

LADY. So's everybody. You got any character reference on you?

VAL. I have this—letter.

[*Removes a worn, folded letter from a wallet, dropping a lot of snapshots and cards of various kinds on the floor. He passes the letter to her gravely and crouches to collect the dropped articles while she peruses the character reference.*]

LADY [*reading slowly aloud*]. "This boy worked for me three months in my auto repair shop and is a real hard worker and is good and honest but is a peculiar talker

and that is the reason I got to let him go but would like to—[*Holds letter closer to light.*]—would like to—keep him. Yours truly."
[VAL *stares at her gravely, blinking a little.*] Huh!—Some reference!
VAL.—Is that what it says?
LADY. Didn't you know what it said?
VAL. No.—The man sealed the envelope on it.
LADY. Well, that's not the sort of character reference that will do you much good, boy.
VAL. Naw. I guess it ain't.
LADY.—However. . . .
VAL.—What?
LADY. What people say about you don't mean much. Can you read shoe sizes?
VAL. I guess so.
LADY. What does 75 David mean?
[VAL *stares at her, shakes head slowly.*]
75 means seven and one half long and David means "D" wide. You know how to make change?
VAL. Yeah, I could make change in a store.
LADY. Change for better or worse? Ha ha!—Well—[*Pause.*] Well—you see that other room there, through that arch there? That's the confectionery; it's closed now but it's going to be reopened in a short while and I'm going to compete for the night life in this county, the after-the-movies trade. I'm going to serve setups in there and I'm going to redecorate. I got it all planned. [*She is talking eagerly now, as if to herself.*] Artificial branches of fruit trees in flower on the walls and ceilings!—It's going to be like an orchard in the spring!—My father, he had an orchard on Moon Lake. He made a wine garden of it. We had fifteen little white arbors with tables in them and they were covered with—grapevines and—we sold Dago red wine an' bootleg whiskey and beer.—They burned it up! My father was burned up in it. . . .
[JABE *knocks above more loudly and a hoarse voice shouts* "Lady!" *Figure appears at the door and calls:* "Mrs. Torrance?"]
Oh, that's the sandman with my sleeping tablets. [*Crosses to door.*] Thanks, Mr. Dubinsky, sorry I had to disturb you, sorry I—
[*Man mutters something and goes. She closes the door.*]
Well, go to hell, then, old bastard. . . .
[*Returns with package.*]—You ever have trouble sleeping?
VAL. I can sleep or not sleep as long or short as I want to.
LADY. Is that right?
VAL. I can sleep on a concrete floor or go without sleeping, without even feeling sleepy, for forty-eight hours. And I can hold my breath three minutes without blacking out; I made ten dollars betting I could do it and I did it! And I can go a whole day without passing water.
LADY [*startled*]. Is *that* a fact?
VAL [*very simply as if he'd made an ordinary remark*]. That's a fact. I served time on a chain gang for vagrancy once and they tied me to a post all day and I stood there all day without passing water to show the sons of bitches that I could do it.
LADY.—I see what that auto repair man was talking about when he said this boy is a peculiar talker! Well—what else can you do? Tell me some more about your self-control!
VAL [*grinning*]. Well, they say that a woman can burn a man down. But I can burn down a woman.
LADY. Which woman?
VAL. Any two-footed woman.
LADY [*throws back her head in sudden friendly laughter as he grins at her with the simple candor of a child*].—Well, there's lots of two-footed women round here that might be willin' to test the truth of that statement.
VAL. I'm saying I could. I'm not saying I would.
LADY. Don't worry, boy. I'm one two-footed woman that you don't have to convince of your perfect controls.
VAL. No, I'm done with all that.
LADY. What's the matter? Have they tired you out?
VAL. I'm not tired. I'm disgusted.
LADY. Aw, you're disgusted, huh?
VAL. I'm telling you, Lady, there's people bought and sold in this world like carcasses of hogs in butcher shops!
LADY. You ain't tellin' me nothing I don't know.
VAL. You might think there's many and many kinds of people in this world but,

Lady, there's just two kinds of people, the ones that are bought and the buyers! No!—there's one other kind . . .
LADY. What kind's that?
VAL. The kind that's never been branded.
LADY. You will be, man.
VAL. They got to catch me first.
LADY. Well, then, you better not settle down in this county.
VAL. You know they's a kind of bird that don't have legs so it can't light on nothing but has to stay all its life on its wings in the sky? That's true. I seen one once, it had died and fallen to earth and it was light-blue colored and its body was tiny as your little finger, that's the truth, it had a body as tiny as your little finger and so light on the palm of your hand it didn't weigh more than a feather, but its wings spread out this wide but they was transparent, the color of the sky and you could see through them. That's what they call protection coloring. Camouflage, they call it. You can't tell those birds from the sky and that's why the hawks don't catch them, don't see them up there in the high blue sky near the sun!
LADY. How about in gray weather?
VAL. They fly so high in gray weather the Goddam hawks would get dizzy. But those little birds, they don't have no legs at all and they live their whole lives on the wing, and they sleep on the wind, that's how they sleep at night, they just spread their wings and go to sleep on the wind like other birds fold their wings and go to sleep on a tree. . . . [Music fades in.] —They sleep on the wind and . . . [His eyes grow soft and vague and he lifts his guitar and accompanies the very faint music.]—never light on this earth but one time when they die!
LADY.—I'd like to be one of those birds.
VAL. So'd I like to be one of those birds; they's lots of people would like to be one of those birds and never be—corrupted!
LADY. If one of those birds ever dies and falls on the ground and you happen to find it, I wish you would show it to me because I think maybe you just imagine there is a bird of that kind in existence. Because I don't think nothing living has ever been that free, not even nearly. Show me one of them birds and I'll say, Yes, God's made one perfect creature!—I sure would give this mercantile store and every bit of stock in it to be that tiny bird the color of the sky . . . for one night to sleep on the wind and—float!—around under th'—stars . . .

[JABE knocks on floor. LADY's eyes return to VAL.]

—Because I sleep with a son of a bitch who bought me at a fire sale, and not in fifteen years have I had a single good dream, not one—oh!—Shit . . . I don't know why I'm—telling a stranger—this. . . . [She rings the cashbox open.] Take this dollar and go eat at the Al-Nite on the highway and come back here in the morning and I'll put you to work. I'll break you in clerking here and when the new confectionery opens, well, maybe I can use you in there.—That door locks when you close it!—But let's get one thing straight.
VAL. What thing?
LADY. I'm not interested in your perfect functions, in fact you don't interest me no more than the air that you stand in. If that's understood we'll have a good working relation, but otherwise trouble! —Of course I know you're crazy, but they's lots of crazier people than you are still running loose and some of them in high positions, too. Just remember. No monkey business with me. Now go. Go eat, you're hungry.
VAL. Mind if I leave this here? My life's companion? [He means his guitar.]
LADY. Leave it here if you want to.
VAL. Thanks, Lady.
LADY. Don't mention it.

[He crosses toward the door as a dog barks with passionate clarity in the distance. He turns to smile back at her and says:]

VAL. I don't know nothing about you except you're nice but you are just about the nicest person that I have ever run into! And I'm going to be steady and honest and hard-working to please you and any time you have any more trouble sleeping, I know how to fix that for you. A lady osteopath taught me how to make little adjustments in the neck and spine that give you sound, natural sleep. Well, g'night, now.

[He goes out. Count five. Then she throws back her head and laughs as lightly and gaily as a young girl. Then she turns and wonderingly picks up and runs her hands tenderly over his guitar as the curtain falls.]

ACT II

Scene I

The store, afternoon, a few weeks later. The table and chair are back in the confectionery. LADY *is hanging up the phone.* VAL *is standing just outside the door. He turns and enters. Outside on the highway a mule team is laboring to pull a big truck back on the icy pavement. A Negro's voice shouts: "Hyyyyyyyy-up."*

VAL [*moving to R. window*]. One a them big Diamond T trucks an' trailors gone off the highway last night and a six mule team is tryin' t' pull it back on. . . . [*He looks out window.*]

LADY [*coming from behind to R. of counter*]. Mister, we just now gotten a big fat complaint about you from a woman that says if she wasn't a widow her husband would come in here and beat the tar out of you.

VAL [*taking a step toward her*]. Yeah?—Is this a small pink-headed woman?

LADY. *Pin*-headed woman did you say?

VAL. Naw, I said, "Pink!"—A little pink-haired woman, in a checkered coat with pearl buttons this big on it.

LADY. I talked to her on the phone. She didn't go into such details about her appearance but she did say you got familiar. I said, "How? by his talk or behavior?" And she said, "Both!"—Now I was afraid of this when I warned you last week, "No monkey business here, boy!"

VAL. This little pink-headed woman bought a valentine from me and all I said is my name is Valentine to her. Few minutes later a small colored boy come in and delivered the valentine to me with something wrote on it an' I believe I still got it. . . . [*Finds and shows it to* LADY *who goes to him.* LADY *reads it, and tears it fiercely to pieces. He lights a cigarette.*]

LADY. Signed it with a lipstick kiss? You didn't show up for this date?

VAL. No, ma'am. That's why she complained. [*Throws match on floor.*]

LADY. Pick that match up off the floor.

VAL. Are you bucking for sergeant, or something?

[*He throws match out the door with elaborate care. Her eyes follow his back.* VAL *returns lazily toward her.*]

LADY. Did you walk around in front of her that way?

VAL [*at counter*]. What way?

LADY. Slew-foot, slew-foot!
   [*He regards her closely with good-humored perplexity.*]
   Did you stand in front of her like that? That close? In that, that—*position?*

VAL. What position?

LADY. Ev'rything you do is suggestive!

VAL. Suggestive of what?

LADY. Of what you said you was through with—somethin'—Oh, shoot, you know what I mean.—Why'd 'ya think I give you a plain, dark business suit to work in?

VAL [*sadly*]. Un-hun. . . . [*Sighs and removes his blue jacket.*]

LADY. Now what're you takin' that off for?

VAL. I'm giving the suit back to you. I'll change my pants in the closet. [*Gives her the jacket and crosses into alcove.*]

LADY. Hey! I'm sorry! You hear me? I didn't sleep well last night. Hey! I said I'm sorry! You hear me? [*She enters alcove and returns immediately with* VAL's *guitar and crosses to D.R. He follows.*]

VAL. Le' me have my guitar, Lady. You find too many faults with me and I tried to do good.

LADY. I told you I'm sorry. You want me to get down and lick the dust off your shoes?

VAL. Just give me back my guitar.

LADY. I ain't dissatisfied with you. I'm pleased with you, sincerely!

VAL. You sure don't show it.

LADY. My nerves are all shot to pieces. [*Extends hand to him.*] Shake.

VAL. You mean I ain't fired, so I don't have to quit?

[*They shake hands like two men. She hands him guitar—then silence falls between them.*]

LADY. You see, we don't know each other, we're, we're—just gettin'—acquainted.

VAL. That's right, like a couple of animals sniffin' around each other....

[*The image embarrasses her. He crosses to counter, leans over and puts guitar behind it.*]

LADY. Well, not exactly like that, but—!

VAL. We don't know each other. How do people get to know each other? I used to think they did it by touch.

LADY. By what?

VAL. By touch, by touchin' each other.

LADY [*moving up and sitting on shoe-fitting chair which has been moved to R. window*]. Oh, you mean by close—contact!

VAL. But later it seemed like that made them more strangers than ever, uhh, huh, more strangers than ever....

LADY. Then how d'you think they get to know each other?

VAL [*sitting on counter*]. Well, in answer to your last question, I would say this: Nobody ever gets to know *no body*! We're all of us sentenced to solitary confinement inside our own skins, for life! You understand me, Lady?—I'm tellin' you it's the truth, we got to face it, we're under a lifelong sentence to solitary confinement inside our own lonely skins for as long as we live on this earth!

LADY [*rising and crossing to him*]. Oh, no, I'm not a big optimist but I cannot agree with something as sad as that statement!

[*They are sweetly grave as two children; the store is somewhat dusky. She sits in chair R. of counter.*]

VAL. Listen!—When I was a kid on Witches Bayou? After my folks all scattered away like loose chicken's feathers blown around by the wind?—I stayed there alone on the bayou, hunted and trapped out of season and hid from the law!—*Listen!*—All that time, all that lonely time, I felt I was—waiting for something!

LADY. What for?

VAL. What does anyone wait for? For something to happen, for anything to happen, to make things make more sense.... It's hard to remember what that feeling was like because I've lost it now, but I was waiting for something like if you ask a question you wait for someone to answer, but you ask the wrong question or you ask the wrong person and the answer don't come.

Does everything stop because you don't get the answer? No, it goes right on as if the answer was given, day comes after day and night comes after night, and you're still waiting for someone to answer the question and going right on as if the question was answered. And then—well —then....

LADY. Then what?

VAL. You get the make-believe answer.

LADY. What answer is that?

VAL. Don't pretend you don't know because you do!

LADY.—Love?

VAL [*placing hand on her shoulder*]. That's the make-believe answer. It's fooled many a fool besides you an' me, that's the God's truth, Lady, and you had better believe it.

[LADY *looks reflectively at* VAL *and he goes on speaking and sits on stool below counter.*]

—I met a girl on the bayou when I was fourteen. I'd had a feeling that day that if I just kept poling the boat down the bayou a little bit further I would come bang into whatever it was I'd been so long expecting!

LADY. Was she the answer, this girl that you met on the bayou?

VAL. She made me think that she was.

LADY. How did she do that?

VAL. By coming out on the dogtrot of a cabin as naked as I was in that flat-bottom boat! She stood there a while with the daylight burning around her as bright as heaven as far as I could see. You seen the inside of a shell, how white that is, pearly white? Her naked skin was like that.—Oh, God, I remember a bird flown out of the moss and its wings made a shadow on her, and then it sung a single, high clear note, and as if she was waiting for that as a kind of a signal to catch me, she turned and smiled, and walked on back in the cabin....

LADY. You followed?

VAL. Yes, I followed, I followed, like a bird's tail follows a bird, I followed!

I thought that she give me the answer to the question, I'd been waiting for, but afterwards I wasn't sure that was it, but from that time the question wasn't much plainer than the answer and—

LADY.—What?

VAL. At fifteen I left Witches Bayou. When the dog died I sold my boat and the gun. ... I went to New Orleans in this snakeskin jacket.... It didn't take long for me to learn the score.

LADY. What did you learn?

VAL. I learned that I had something to sell besides snakeskins and other wild things' skins I caught on the bayou. I was corrupted! That's the answer....

LADY. Naw, that ain't the answer!

VAL. Okay, you tell me the answer!

LADY. I don't know the answer, I just know corruption ain't the answer. I know that much. If I thought that was the answer I'd take Jabe's pistol or his morphine tablets and—

[A woman bursts into store.]

WOMAN. I got to use your pay-phone!

LADY. Go ahead. Help yourself.

[Woman crosses to phone, deposits coin. LADY crosses to confectionery. To VAL.] Get me a coke from the cooler.

[VAL crosses and goes out R. During the intense activity among the choral women, LADY and VAL seem bemused as if they were thinking back over their talk before. For the past minute or two a car horn has been heard blowing repeatedly in the near distance.]

WOMAN [at phone]. Cutrere place, get me the Cutrere place, will yuh? David Cutrere or his wife, whichever comes to the phone!

[BEULAH rushes in from the street to R.C.]

BEULAH. Lady, Lady, where's Lady! Carol Cutrere is—!

WOMAN. Quiet, please! I am callin' her brother about her!

[LADY sits at table in confectionery.]

[At phone.] Who's this I'm talking to? Good! I'm calling about your sister, Carol Cutrere. She is blowing her car horn at the Red Crown station, she is blowing and blowing her car horn at the Red Crown station because my husband give the station attendants instructions not to service her car, and she is blowing and blowing and blowing on her horn, drawing a big crowd there and, Mr. Cutrere, I thought that you and your father had agreed to keep that girl out of Two River County for good, that's what we all understood around here.

[Car horn.]

BEULAH [Listening with excited approval]. Good! Good! Tell him that if—

[DOLLY enters.]

DOLLY. She's gotten out of the car and—

BEULAH. Shhh!

WOMAN. Well, I just wanted to let you know she's back here in town makin' another disturbance and my husband's on the phone now at the Red Crown station—

[DOLLY goes outside and looks off.]

trying to get the Sheriff, so if she gits picked up again by th' law, you can't say I didn't warn you, Mr. Cutrere.

[Car horn.]

DOLLY [coming back in]. Oh, good! Good!

BEULAH. Where is she, where's she gone now?

WOMAN. You better be quick about it. Yes, I do. I sympathize with you and your father and with Mrs. Cutrere, but Carol cannot demand service at our station, we just refuse to wait on her, she's not— Hello? Hello? [She jiggles phone violently.]

BEULAH. What's he doin'? Comin' to pick her up?

DOLLY. Call the Sheriff's office!
[BEULAH *goes outside again.* VAL *comes back with a bottle of Coca-Cola—hands it to* LADY *and leans on juke box.*]
[*Going out to* BEULAH.] What's goin' on now?
BEULAH [*outside*]. Look, look, they're pushing her out of the station driveway.

[*They forget* LADY *in this new excitement. Ad libs continual. The short woman from the station charges back out of the store.*]

DOLLY. Where is Carol?
BEULAH. Going into the White Star Pharmacy!

[DOLLY *rushes back in to the phone.*]

BEULAH [*crossing to* LADY]. Lady, I want you to give me your word that if that Cutrere girl comes in here, you won't wait on her! You hear me?
LADY. No.
BEULAH.—What? Will you refuse to wait on her?
LADY. I can't refuse to wait on anyone in this store.
BEULAH. Well, I'd like to know why you can't.
DOLLY. Shhh! I'm on the phone!
BEULAH. Who you phonin' Dolly?
DOLLY. That White Star Pharmacy! I want to make sure that Mr. Dubinsky refuses to wait on that girl! [*Having found and deposited coin.*] I want the White Far Starmacy. I mean the—[*Stamps foot.*]—White Star Pharmacy!—I'm so upset my tongue's twisted!
[LADY *hands coke to* VAL. BEULAH *is at the window.*]
I'm getting a busy signal. Has she come out yet?
BEULAH. No, she's still in the White Star!
DOLLY. Maybe they're not waiting on her.
BEULAH. Dubinsky'd wait on a purple-bottom baboon if it put a dime on th' counter an' pointed at something!
DOLLY. I know she sat at a table in the Blue Bird Café half'n hour last time she was here and the waitresses never came near her!
BEULAH. That's different. They're not foreigners there!
[DOLLY *crosses to counter.*]
You can't ostracize a person out of this county unless everybody cooperates. Lady just told me that she was going to wait on her if she comes here.
DOLLY. Lady wouldn't do that.
BEULAH. Ask her! She told me she would!
LADY [*rising and turning at once to the women and shouting at them*]. Oh, for God's sake, no! I'm not going to refuse to wait on her because you all don't like her! Besides I'm delighted that wild girl is givin' her brother so much trouble! [*After this outburst she goes back of the counter.*]
DOLLY [*at phone*]. Hush! Mr. Dubinsky! This is Dolly Hamma, Mr. "Dog" Hamma's wife!
[CAROL *quietly enters the front door.*]
I want to ask you, is Carol Cutrere in your drugstore?
BEULAH. [*warningly*]. Dolly!
CAROL. No. She isn't.
DOLLY.—What?
CAROL. She's here.

[BEULAH *goes into confectionery.* CAROL *moves toward* VAL *to D.R.C.*]

DOLLY.—Aw!—Never mind, Mr. Dubinsky, I —[*Hangs up furiously and crosses to door.*]

[*A silence in which they all stare at the girl from various positions about the store. She has been on the road all night in an open car: her hair is blown wild, her face flushed and eyes bright with fever. Her manner in the scene is that of a wild animal at bay, desperate but fearless.*]

LADY [*finally and quietly*]. Hello, Carol.
CAROL. Hello, Lady.
LADY [*defiantly cordial*]. I thought that you were in New Orleans, Carol.
CAROL. Yes, I was. Last night.
LADY. Well, you got back fast.
CAROL. I drove all night.
LADY. In that storm?
CAROL. The wind took the top off my car but I didn't stop.

[*She watches* VAL *steadily; he steadily ignores her; turns away and puts bottles of Coca-Cola on a table.*]

LADY [*with growing impatience*]. Is something wrong at home, is someone sick?
CAROL [*absently*]. No. No, not that I know of, I wouldn't know if there was, they—may I sit down?
LADY. Why, sure.
CAROL [*crossing to chair at counter and sitting*].—They pay me to stay away so I wouldn't know. . . .
[*Silence.* VAL *walks deliberately past her and goes into alcove.*]
—I think I have a fever, I feel like I'm catching pneumonia, everything's so far away. . . .

[*Silence again except for the faint, hissing whispers of* BEULAH *and* DOLLY *at the back of the store.*]

LADY [*with a touch of exasperation*]. Is there something you want?
CAROL. Everything seems miles away. . . .
LADY. Carol, I said is there anything you want here?
CAROL. Excuse me!—yes. . . .
LADY. Yes, what?
CAROL. Don't bother now. I'll wait.

[VAL *comes out of alcove with the blue jacket on.*]

LADY. Wait for what, what are you waiting for! You don't have to wait for nothing, just say what you want and if I got it in stock I'll give it to you!

[*Phone rings once.*]

CAROL [*vaguely*].—Thank you—no. . . .
LADY [*to* VAL]. Get that phone, Val.

[DOLLY *crosses and hisses something inaudible to* BEULAH.]

BEULAH [*rising*]. I just want to wait here to see if she does or she don't.
DOLLY. She just said she would!
BEULAH. Just the same, I'm gonna wait!!
VAL [*at phone*]. Yes, sir, she is.—I'll tell her. [*Hangs up and speaks to* LADY.] Her brother's heard she's here and he's coming to pick her up.
LADY. David Cutrere is not coming in this store!
DOLLY. Aw-aw!

BEULAH. David Cutrere used to be her lover.
DOLLY. I remember you told me.
LADY [*wheels about suddenly toward the women*]. Beulah! Dolly! Why're you back there hissing together like geese? [*Coming from behind counter to R.C.*] Why don't you go to th'—Blue Bird and—have some hot coffee—talk there!
BEULAH. It looks like we're getting what they call the bum's rush.
DOLLY. I never stay where I'm not wanted and when I'm not wanted somewhere I never come back!

[*They cross out and slam door.*]

LADY [*after a pause*]. What did you come here for?
CAROL. To deliver a message.
LADY. To me?
CAROL. No.
LADY. Then who?
[CAROL *stares at* LADY *gravely a moment, then turns slowly to look at* VAL.]
—Him?—Him?
[CAROL *nods slowly and slightly.*]
OK, then, give him the message, deliver the message to him.
CAROL. It's a private message. Could I speak to him alone, please?

[LADY *gets a shawl from a hook.*]

LADY. Oh, for God's sake! Your brother's plantation is ten minutes from here in that sky-blue Cadillac his rich wife give him. Now look, he's on his way here but I won't let him come in, I don't even want his hand to touch the door-handle. I know your message, this boy knows your message, there's nothing private about it. But I tell you, that this boy's not for sale in my store!—Now—I'm going out to watch for the sky-blue Cadillac on the highway. When I see it, I'm going to throw this door open and holler and when I holler, I want you out of this door like a shot from a pistol!—that fast! Understand?

[*Note: Above scene is overextended. This can be remedied by a very lively performance. It might also help to indicate a division between the Lady-Val scene and the group scene that follows.*]

[LADY *slams door behind her. The loud noise of the door-slam increases the silence that follows.* VAL's *oblivious attitude is not exactly hostile, but deliberate. There's a kind of purity in it; also a kind of refusal to concern himself with a problem that isn't his own. He holds his guitar with a specially tender concentration, and strikes a soft chord on it. The girl stares at* VAL; *he whistles a note and tightens a guitar string to the pitch of the whistle, not looking at the girl. Since this scene is followed by the emotional scene between* LADY *and* DAVID, *it should be keyed somewhat lower than written; it's important that* VAL *should not seem brutal in his attitude toward* CAROL; *there should be an air between them of two lonely children.*]

VAL [*in a soft, preoccupied tone*]. You told the lady I work for that you had a message for me. Is that right, Miss? Have you got a message for me?

CAROL [*she rises, moves a few steps toward him hesitantly.* VAL *whistles, plucks guitar string, changes pitch*]. You've spilt some ashes on your new blue suit.

VAL. Is that the message?

CAROL [*moves away a step*]. No. No, that was just an excuse to touch you. The message is—

VAL. What?

[*Music fades in—guitar.*]

CAROL.—I'd love to hold something the way you hold your guitar, that's how I'd love to hold something, with such—*tender protection!* I'd love to hold you that way, with that same—*tender protection!* [*Her hand has fallen onto his knee, which he has drawn up to rest a foot on the counter stool.*]—Because you hang the moon for me!

VAL [*he speaks to her, not roughly but in a tone that holds a long history that began with a romantic acceptance of such declarations as she has just made to him, and that turned gradually to his present distrust. He puts guitar down and goes to her*]. Who're you tryin' t' fool beside you'self? You couldn't stand the weight of a man's body on you. [*He casually picks up her wrist and pushes the sleeve back from it.*] What's this here? A human wrist with a bone? It feels like a twig I could snap with two fingers.... [*Gently, negligently, pushes collar of her trench coat back from her bare throat and shoulders. Runs a finger along her neck tracing a vein.*] Little girl, you're transparent, I can see the veins in you. A man's weight on you would break you like a bundle of sticks....

[*Music fades out.*]

CAROL [*gazes at him, startled by his perception*]. Isn't it funny! You've hit on the truth about me. The act of love-making is almost unbearably painful, and yet, of course, I do bear it, because to be not alone, even for a few moments, is worth the pain and the danger. It's dangerous for me because I'm not built for child-bearing.

VAL. Well, then, fly away, little bird, fly away before you—get broke. [*He turns back to his guitar.*]

CAROL. Why do you dislike me?

VAL [*turning back*]. I never dislike nobody till they interfere with me.

CAROL. How have I interfered with you? Did I snitch when I saw my cousin's watch on you?

VAL [*Beginning to remove his watch*].— You won't take my word for a true thing I told you. I'm thirty years old and I'm done with the crowd you run with and the places you run to. The Club Rendezvous, the Starlite Lounge, the Music Bar, and all the night places. Here—[*Offers watch*]—take this Rolex Chronometer that tells the time of the day and the day of the week and the month and all the crazy moon's phases. I never stole nothing before. When I stole that I known it was time for me to get off the party, so take it back, now, to Bertie. ... [*He takes her hand and tries to force the watch into her fist. There is a little struggle, he can't open her fist. She is crying, but staring fiercely into his eyes. He draws a hissing breath and hurls watch violently across the floor.*]

—That's my message to you and the pack you run with!

CAROL [*flinging coat away*]. I RUN WITH NOBODY!—I hoped I could run with you.... [*Music stops short.*] You're in danger here, Snakeskin. You've taken off the jacket that said: "I'm wild, I'm alone!" and put on the nice blue uniform of a convict! . . . Last night I woke up thinking about you again. I drove all night to bring you this warning of danger. . . . [*Her trembling hand covers her lips.*]—The message I came here to give you was a warning of danger! I hoped you'd hear me and let me take you away before it's—too late.

[*Door bursts open.* LADY *rushes inside, crying out.*]

LADY. Your brother's coming, go out! He can't come in!
[CAROL *picks up coat and goes into confectionery, sobbing.* VAL *crosses toward door.*]
Lock that door! Don't let him come in my store!

[CAROL *sinks sobbing at table.* LADY *runs up to the landing of the stairs as* DAVID CUTRERE *enters the store. He is a tall man in hunter's clothes. He is hardly less handsome now than he was in his youth but something has gone: his power is that of a captive who rules over other captives. His face, his eyes, have something of the same desperate, unnatural hardness that* LADY *meets the world with.*]

DAVID. Carol?
VAL. She's in there. [*He nods toward the dim confectionery into which the girl has retreated.*]
DAVID [*crossing*]. Carol!
[*She rises and advances a few steps into the lighted area of the stage.*]
You broke the agreement.
[CAROL *nods slightly, staring at* VAL.]
[*Harshly:*] All right. I'll drive you back. Where's your coat?
[CAROL *murmurs something inaudible, staring at* VAL.]
Where is her coat, where is my sister's coat?

[VAL *crosses below and picks up the coat that* CAROL *has dropped on the floor and hands it to* DAVID. *He throws it roughly about* CAROL's *shoulders and propels her forcefully toward the store entrance.* VAL *moves away to D.R.*]

LADY [*suddenly and sharply*]. Wait, please!

[DAVID *looks up at the landing; stands frozen as* LADY *rushes down the stairs.*]

DAVID [*softly, hoarsely*]. How—are you, Lady?
LADY [*turning to* VAL]. Val, go out.
DAVID [*to* CAROL]. Carol, will you wait for me in my car?

[*He opens the door for his sister; she glances back at* VAL *with desolation in her eyes.* VAL *crosses quickly through the confectionery. Sound of door closing in there.* CAROL *nods slightly as if in sad response to some painful question and goes out of the store. Pause.*]

LADY. I told you once to never come in this store.
DAVID. I came for my sister. . . . [*He turns as if to go.*]
LADY. No, wait!
DAVID. I don't dare leave my sister alone on the road.
LADY. I have something to tell you I never told you before.
[*She crosses to him.* DAVID *turns back to her, then moves away to D.R.C.*]
—I—carried your child in my body the summer you quit me.

[*Silence.*]

DAVID.—I—didn't know. . .
LADY. No, no, I didn't write you no letter about it; I was proud then; I had pride. But I had your child in my body the summer they burned my father in his wine garden, and you, you washed your hands clean of any connection with a Dago bootlegger's daughter and—[*Her breathless voice momentarily falters and she makes a fierce gesture as she struggles to speak.*]—took that—society girl that—restored your homeplace and give you such—[*Catches breath.*]—wellborn children. . . .
DAVID.—I—didn't know. . .
LADY. Well, now you do know, you know now. I carried your child in my body the summer you quit me but I had it cut out of my body, and they cut my heart out with it!

DAVID.—I—didn't know.

LADY. I wanted death after that, but death don't come when you *want* it, it comes when you don't want it! I wanted death, then, but I took the next best thing. You sold *yourself.* I sold *my* self. You was bought. *I* was bought. You made whores of us both!

DAVID.—I—didn't know. . . .

[*Mandolin, barely audible, "Dicitincello Vuoi."*]

LADY. But that's all a long time ago. Some reason I drove by there a few nights ago; the shore of the lake where my father had his wine garden? You remember? You remember the wine garden of my father?

[DAVID *stares at her. She turns away.*]

No, you don't? You don't remember it even?

DAVID.—Lady, I don't—remember—anything else. . . .

LADY. The mandolin of my father, the songs that I sang with my father in my father's wine garden?

DAVID. Yes, I don't remember anything else. . . .

LADY. Core Ingrata! Come Le Rose! And we disappeared and he would call, "Lady? Lady?" [*Turns to him.*] How could I answer him with two tongues in my mouth! [*A sharp hissing intake of breath, eyes opened wide, hand clapped over her mouth as if what she said was unendurable to her. He turns instantly, sharply away.*]

[*Music stops short.* JABE *begins to knock for her on the floor above. She crosses to stairs, stops, turns.*]

I hold hard feelings!—Don't ever come here again. If your wild sister comes here, send somebody else for her, not you, not you. Because I hope never to feel this knife again in me.

[*Her hand is on her chest; she breathes with difficulty.*]

[*He turns away from her; starts toward the door. She takes a step toward him.*]

And don't pity me neither. I haven't gone down so terribly far in the world. I got a going concern in this mercantile store, in there's the confectionery which'll reopen this spring, it's being done over to make it the place that all the young people will come to, it's going to be like—

[*He touches the door, pauses with his back to her.*]

—the wine garden of my father, those wine-drinking nights when you had something better than anything you've had since!

DAVID. Lady—That's—

LADY.—What?

DAVID.—True! [*Opens door.*]

LADY. Go now. I just wanted to tell you my life ain't over.

[*He goes out as* JABE *continues knocking. She stands, stunned, motionless till* VAL *quietly re-enters the store. She becomes aware of his return rather slowly; then she murmurs.*]

I made a fool of myself. . . .

VAL. What?

[*She crosses to stairs.*]

LADY. I made a fool of myself!

[*She goes up the stairs with effort as the lights change slowly to mark a division of scenes.*]

Scene 2

Sunset of that day. VAL *is alone in the store, as if preparing to go. The sunset is fiery. A large woman opens the door and stands there looking dazed. It is* VEE TALBOTT.

VAL [*turning*]. Hello, Mrs. Talbott.

VEE. Something's gone wrong with my eyes. I can't see nothing.

VAL [*going to her*]. Here, let me help you. You probably drove up here with that setting sun in your face. [*Leading her to shoe-fitting chair at R. window.*] There now. Set down right here.

VEE. Thank you—so—much. . . .

VAL. I haven't seen you since that night you brought me here to ask for this job.

VEE. Has the minister called on you yet? Reverend Tooker? I made him promise he would. I told him you were new around here and weren't affiliated to any church yet. I want you to go to ours.

VAL.—That's—mighty kind of you.

VEE. The Church of the Resurrection, it's Episcopal.

VAL. Uh, huh.

VEE. Unwrap that picture, please.

VAL. Sure. [*He tears paper off canvas.*]

VEE. It's the Church of the Resurrection. I give it a sort of imaginative treatment. You know, Jabe and Lady have never darkened a church door. I thought it ought to be hung where Jabe could look at it, it might help to bring that poor dying man to Jesus. . . .

[VAL *places it against chair R. of counter and crouches before the canvas, studying it long and seriously.* VEE *coughs nervously, gets up, bends to look at the canvas, sits uncertainly back down.* VAL *smiles at her warmly, then back to the canvas.*]

VAL [*at last*]. What's this here in the picture?

VEE. The steeple.

VAL. Aw.—Is the church steeple red?

VEE. Why—no, but—

VAL. Why'd you paint it red, then?

VEE. Oh, well, you see, I—[*Laughs nervously, childlike in her growing excitement.*]—I just, just *felt* it that way! I paint a thing how I feel it instead of always the way it actually is. Appearances are misleading, nothing is what it looks like to the eyes. You got to have—vision—to see!

VAL.—Yes. Vision. Vision!—to see. . . . [*Rises, nodding gravely, emphatically.*]

VEE. I paint from vision. They call me a visionary.

VAL. Oh.

VEE [*with shy pride*]. That's what the New Orleans and Memphis newspaper people admire so much in my work. They call it a primitive style, the work of a visionary. One of my pictures is hung on the exhibition in Audubon Park museum and they have asked for others. I can't turn them out fast enough!—I have to wait for—visions, no, I—I can't paint without—visions . . . I couldn't *live* without visions!

VAL. Have you always had visions?

VEE. No, just since I was born, I—[*Stops short, startled by the absurdity of her answer. Both laugh suddenly, then she rushes on, her great bosom heaving with curious excitement, twisting in her chair, gesturing with clenched hands.*] I was born, I was born with a caul! A sort of thing like a veil, a thin, thin sort of a web was over my eyes. They call that a caul. It's a sign that you're going to have visions, and I did, I had them! [*Pauses for breath; light fades.*]—When I was little my baby sister died. Just one day old, she died. They had to baptize her at midnight to save her soul.

VAL. Uh-huh. [*He sits opposite her, smiling, attentive.*]

VEE. The minister came at midnight, and after the baptism service, he handed the bowl of holy water to me and told me, "Be sure to empty this out on the ground!"—I didn't. I was scared to go out at midnight, with, with—death! in the—house and—I sneaked into the kitchen; I emptied the holy water into the kitchen sink—thunder struck!—the kitchen sink turned black, the kitchen sink turned absolutely black!

[SHERIFF TALBOTT *enters the front door.*]

TALBOTT. Mama! What're you doin'?

VEE. Talkin'.

TALBOTT. I'm gonna see Jabe a minute, you go out and wait in th' car. [*He goes up. She rises slowly, picks up canvas and moves to counter.*]

VEE.—Oh, I—tell you!—since I got into this painting, my whole outlook is different. I can't explain how it is, the difference to me.

VAL. You don't have to explain. I know what you mean. Before you started to paint, it didn't make sense.

VEE.—What—what didn't?

VAL. Existence!

VEE [*slowly and softly*]. No—no, it didn't . . . existence didn't make sense. . . . [*She places canvas on guitar on counter and sits in chair.*]

VAL [*rising and crossing to her*]. You lived in Two River County, the wife of the county Sheriff. You saw awful things take place.

VEE. Awful! Things!

VAL. Beatings!
VEE. Yes!
VAL. Lynchings!
VEE. Yes!
VAL. Runaway convicts torn to pieces by hounds!

[*This is the first time she could express this horror.*]

VEE. Chain-gang dogs!
VAL. Yeah?
VEE. Tear fugitives!
VAL. Yeah?
VEE.—to pieces....

[*She had half risen: now sinks back faintly. VAL looks beyond her in the dim store, his light eyes have a dark gaze. It may be that his speech is too articulate: counteract this effect by groping, hesitations.*]

VAL [*moving away a step*]. But violence ain't quick always. Sometimes it's slow. Some tornadoes are slow. Corruption—rots men's hearts and—rot is slow....
VEE.—How do you—?
VAL. Know? I been a witness, I know!
VEE. I been a witness! I know!
VAL. We seen these things from seats down front at the show. [*He crouches before her and touches her hands in her lap. Her breath shudders.*] And so you begun to paint your visions. Without no plan, no training, you started to paint as if God touched your fingers. [*He lifts her hands slowly, gently from her soft lap.*] You made some beauty out of this dark country with these two, soft, woman hands....

[TALBOTT *appears on the stair landing, looks down, silent.*] Yeah, you made some beauty! [*Strangely, gently, he lifts her hands to his mouth. She gasps.* TALBOTT *calls out.*]

TALBOTT. Hey!
  [VEE *springs up, gasping.*]
  [*Descending.*] Cut this crap!
  [VAL *moves away to R.C.*]
  [*To* VEE.] Go out. Wait in the car. [*He stares at* VAL *till* VEE *lumbers out as if dazed. After a while.*]
Jabe Torrance told me to take a good look at you. [*Crosses to* VAL.] Well, now, I've taken that look. [*Nods shortly. Goes out of store. The store is now very dim. As door closes on* TALBOTT, VAL *picks up painting; he goes behind counter and places it on a shelf, then picks up his guitar and sits on counter. Lights go down to mark a division as he sings and plays* "Heavenly Grass."]

Scene 3

As VAL *finishes the song,* LADY *descends the stair. He rises and turns on a green-shaded light bulb.*

VAL [*to* LADY]. You been up there a long time.
LADY.—I gave him morphine. He must be out of his mind. He says such awful things to me. He says I want him to die.
VAL. You sure you don't?
LADY. I don't want no one to die. Death's terrible, Val.
  [*Pause. She wanders to the front window R. He takes his guitar and crosses to the door.*] You gotta go now?
VAL. I'm late.
LADY. Late for what? You got a date with somebody?
VAL.—No....
LADY. Then stay a while. Play something. I'm all unstrung....
  [*He crosses back and leans against counter; the guitar is barely audible, under the speeches.*]
  I made a terrible fool of myself down here today with—
VAL.—That girl's brother?
LADY. Yes, I—threw away—pride....
VAL. His sister said she'd come here to give me a warning. I wonder what of?
LADY [*sitting in shoe-fitting chair*].—I said things to him I should of been too proud to say....

[*Both are pursuing their own reflections; guitar continues softly.*]

VAL. Once or twice lately I've woke up with a fast heart, shouting something, and had to pick up my guitar to calm myself down. . . . Somehow or other I can't get used to this place, I don't feel safe in this place, but I—want to stay. . . .

[Stops short; sound of wild baying.]

LADY. The chain-gang dogs are chasing some runaway convict. . . .

VAL. Run boy! Run fast, brother! If they catch you, you never will run again! That's—[He has thrust his guitar under his arm on this line and crossed to the door.]—for sure. . . . [The baying of the dogs changes, becomes almost a single savage note.]—Uh-huh—the dogs've got him. . . . [Pause.] They're tearing him to pieces! [Pause. Baying continues. A shot is fired. The baying dies out. He stops with his hand on the door; glances back at her; nods; draws the door open. The wind sings loud in the dusk.]

LADY. Wait!
VAL.—Huh?
LADY.—Where do you stay?
VAL.—When?
LADY. Nights.
VAL. I stay at the Wildwood cabins on the highway.
LADY. You like it there?
VAL. Uh-huh.
LADY.—Why?
VAL. I got a comfortable bed, a two-burner stove, a shower and icebox there.
LADY. You want to save money?
VAL. I never could in my life.
LADY. You could if you stayed on the place.
VAL. What place?
LADY. This place.
VAL. Whereabouts on this place?
LADY [pointing to alcove]. Back of that curtain.
VAL.—Where they try on clothes?
LADY. There's a cot there. A nurse slept on it when Jabe had his first operation, and there's a washroom down here and I'll get a plumber to put in a hot an' cold shower! I'll—fix it up nice for you. . . . [She rises, crosses to foot of stairs. Pause. He lets the door shut, staring at her.]
VAL [moving D.C.].—I—don't like to be—obligated.
LADY. There wouldn't be no obligation, you'd do me a favor. I'd feel safer at night with somebody on the place. I would; it would cost you nothing! And you could save up that money you spend on the cabin. How much? Ten a week? Why, two or three months from now you'd—save enough money to—[Makes a wide gesture with a short laugh as if startled.] Go on! Take a look at it! See if it don't suit you!—All right. . . .

[But he doesn't move; he appears reflective.]

LADY [shivering, hugging herself]. Where does heat go in this building?
VAL [reflectively].—Heat rises. . . .
LADY. You with your dog's temperature, don't feel cold, do you? I do! I turn blue with it!
VAL.—Yeah. . . .

[The wait is unendurable to LADY.]

LADY. Well, aren't you going to look at it, the room back there, and see if it suits you or not?!
VAL.—I'll go and take a look at it. . . .

[He crosses to the alcove and disappears behind the curtain. A light goes on behind it, making its bizarre pattern translucent: a gold tree with scarlet fruit and white birds in it, formally designed. Truck roars; lights sweep the frosted window. LADY gasps aloud; takes out a pint bottle and a glass from under the counter, setting them down with a crash that makes her utter a startled exclamation: then a startled laugh. She pours a drink and sits in chair R. of counter. The lights turn off behind the alcove curtain and VAL comes back out. She sits stiffly without looking at him as he crosses back lazily, goes behind counter, puts guitar down. His manner is gently sad as if he had met with a familiar, expected disappointment. He sits down quietly on edge of counter and takes the pint bottle and pours himself a shot of the liquor with a reflective sigh. Boards creak loudly, contracting with the cold. LADY's voice is harsh and sudden, demanding.]

LADY. Well, is it okay or—what!
VAL. I never been in a position where I could turn down something I got for nothing in my life. I like that picture in

there. That's a famous picture, that "September Morn" picture you got on the wall in there. Ha ha! I might have trouble sleeping in a room with that picture. I might keep turning the light on to take another look at it! The way she's cold in that water and sort of crouched over in it, holding her body like that, that—might—ha ha!—sort of keep me awake....

LADY. Aw, you with your dog's temperature and your control of all functions, it would take more than a picture to keep you awake!

VAL. I was just kidding.

LADY. I was just kidding too.

VAL. But you know how a single man is. He don't come home every night with just his shadow.

[*Pause. She takes a drink.*]

LADY. You bring girls home nights to the Wildwood cabins, do you?

VAL. I ain't so far. But I would like to feel free to. That old life is what I'm used to. I always worked nights in cities and if you work nights in cities you live in a different city from those that work days.

LADY. Yes. I know, I—imagine....

VAL. The ones that work days in cities and the ones that work nights in cities, they live in different cities. The cities have the same name but they are different cities. As different as night and day. There's something wild in the country that only the night people know....

LADY. Yeah, I know!

VAL. I'm thirty years old!—but sudden changes don't work, it takes—

LADY.—Time—yes....

[*Slight pause which she finds disconcerting. He slides off counter and moves around below it.*]

VAL. You been good to me, Lady.—Why d'you want me to stay here?

LADY [*defensively*]. I told you why.

VAL. For company nights?

LADY. Yeah, to, to!—*guard the store*, nights!

VAL. To be a night watchman?

LADY. Yeah, to be a night *watchman*.

VAL. You feel nervous alone here?

LADY. Naturally now!—Jabe sleeps with a pistol next to him but if somebody broke in the store, he couldn't git up and all I could do is holler!—Who'd *hear* me? They got a telephone girl on the night shift with—sleepin' sickness, I think! Anyhow, why're you so suspicious? You look at me like you thought I was *plottin'*.—Kind people *exist:* Even me! [*She sits up rigid in chair, lips and eyes tight closed, drawing in a loud breath which comes from a tension both personal and vicarious.*]

VAL. I understand, Lady, but.... Why're you sitting up so stiff in that chair?

LADY. Ha! [*Sharp laugh; she leans back in chair.*]

VAL. You're still unrelaxed.

LADY. I know.

VAL. Relax. [*Moving around close to her.*] I'm going to show you some tricks I learned from a lady osteopath that took me in, too.

LADY. What tricks?

VAL. How to manipulate joints and bones in a way that makes you feel like a loose piece of string. [*Moves behind her chair. She watches him.*] Do you trust me or don't you?

LADY. Yeah, I trust you completely, but—

VAL. Well then, lean forward a little and raise your arms up and turn sideways in the chair.

[*She follows these instructions.*]

Drop your head. [*He manipulates her head and neck.*] Now the spine, Lady. [*He places his knee against the small of her backbone and she utters a sharp, startled laugh as he draws her backbone hard against his kneecap.*]

LADY. Ha, ha!—That makes a sound like, like, like!—boards contracting with cold in the building, ha, ha!

[*He relaxes.*]

VAL. Better?

LADY. Oh, yes!—much ... thanks....

VAL [*stroking her neck*]. Your skin is like silk. You're light skinned to be Italian.

LADY. Most people in this country think Italian people are dark. Some are but not all are! Some of them are fair ... very fair. ... My father's people were dark but my mother's people were fair. Ha ha!

[*The laughter is senseless. He smiles understandingly at her as she chatters to* cover confusion. He turns away, then goes above and sits on counter close to her.] My mother's mother's sister—come here from Monte Cassino, to die, with relations!—but I think people always die alone . . . with or without relations. I was a little girl then and I remember it took her such a long, long time to die we almost forgot her.—And she was so quiet . . . in a corner. . . . And I remember asking her one time, Zia Teresa, how does it feel to die?—Only a little girl would ask such a question, ha ha! Oh, and I remember her answer. She said—"It's a lonely feeling."

I think she wished she had stayed in Italy and died in a place that she knew. . . . [Looks at him directly for the first time since mentioning the alcove.] Well, there is a washroom, and I'll get the plumber to put in a hot and cold shower! Well—[Rises, retreats awkwardly from the chair. His interest seems to have wandered from her.] I'll go up and get some clean linen and make up that bed in there.

[She turns and walks rapidly, almost running, to stairs. He appears lost in some private reflection but as soon as she has disappeared above the landing, he says something under his breath and crosses directly to the cashbox. He coughs loudly to cover the sound of ringing it open; scoops out a fistful of bills and coughs again to cover the sound of slamming drawer shut. Picks up his guitar and goes out the front door of store. LADY returns downstairs, laden with linen. The outer darkness moans through the door left open. She crosses to the door and a little outside it, peering both ways down the dark road. Then she comes in furiously, with an Italian curse, shutting the door with her foot or shoulder, and throws the linen down on counter. She crosses abruptly to cashbox, rings it open and discovers theft. Slams drawer violently shut.] Thief! Thief!

[Turns to phone, lifts receiver. Holds it a moment, then slams it back into place. Wanders desolately back to the door, opens it and stands staring out into the starless night as the scene dims out. Music: blues—guitar.]

Scene 4

Late that night. VAL enters the store, a little unsteadily, with his guitar; goes to the cashbox and rings it open. He counts some bills off a big wad and returns them to the cashbox and the larger wad to the pocket of his snakeskin jacket. Sudden footsteps above; light spills onto stair landing. He quickly moves away from the cashbox as LADY appears on the landing in a white sateen robe; she carries a flashlight.

LADY. Who's that?

[Music fades out.]

VAL.—Me.

[She turns the flashlight on his figure.]

LADY. O, my God, how you scared me!
VAL. You didn't expect me?
LADY. How'd I know it was you I heard come in?

VAL. I thought you give me a room here.
LADY. You left without letting me know if you took it or not. [She is descending the stairs into store, flashlight still on him.]
VAL. Catch me turning down something I get for nothing.
LADY. Well, you might have said something so I'd expect you or not.
VAL. I thought you took it for granted.
LADY. I don't take nothing for granted.
[He starts back to the alcove.]
Wait!—I'm coming downstairs. . . . [She descends with the flashlight beam on his face.]
VAL. You're blinding me with that flashlight.

[He laughs. She keeps the flashlight on him. He starts back again toward the alcove.]

LADY. The bed's not made because I didn't expect you.
VAL. That's all right.

LADY. I brought the linen downstairs and you'd cut out.
VAL.—Yeah, well—
[*She picks up linen on counter.*]
Give me that stuff. I can make up my own rack. Tomorrow you'll have to get yourself a new clerk. [*Takes it from her and goes again toward alcove.*] I had a lucky night. [*Exhibits a wad of bills.*]
LADY. Hey!
[*He stops near the curtain. She goes and turns on green-shaded bulb over cashbox.*]
—Did you just open this cashbox?
VAL.—Why you ask that?
LADY. I thought I heard it ring open a minute ago, that's why I come down here.
VAL.—In your—white satin—kimona?
LADY. *Did you just open the cashbox?!*
VAL.—I wonder who did if I didn't. . . .
LADY. Nobody did if you didn't, but somebody did! [*Opens cashbox and hurriedly counts money. She is trembling violently.*]
VAL. How come you didn't lock the cash up in the safe this evening, Lady?
LADY. Sometimes I forget to.
VAL. That's careless.
LADY.—Why'd you open the cashbox when you come in?
VAL. I opened it twice this evening, once before I went out and again when I come back. I borrowed some money and put it back in the box an' got all this left over! [*Shows her the wad of bills.*] I beat a blackjack dealer five times straight. With this much loot I can retire for the season. . . . [*He returns money to pocket.*]
LADY. *Chicken-feed!*—I'm sorry for you.
VAL. You're sorry for me?
LADY. I'm sorry for you because nobody can help you. I was touched by your—strangeness, your strange talk.—That thing about birds with no feet so they have to sleep on the wind?—I said to myself, "This boy is a bird with no feet so he has to sleep on the wind," and that softened my fool Dago heart and I wanted to help you. . . . Fool, me!—I got what I should of expected. You robbed me while I was upstairs to get sheets to make up your bed!
[*He starts out toward the door.*]
I guess I'm a fool to even feel disappointed.
VAL [*stopping C. and dropping linen on counter*]. You're disappointed in me. I was disappointed in you.
LADY [*coming from behind counter*].—How did I disappoint you?
VAL. There wasn't no cot behind that curtain before. You put it back there for a purpose.
LADY. It was back there!—folded behind the mirror.
VAL. It wasn't back of no mirror when you told me three times to go and—
LADY [*cutting in*]. I left that money in the cashbox on purpose, to find out if I could trust you.
VAL. You got back th' . . .
LADY. No, no, no, I can't trust you, now I know I can't trust you, I got to trust anybody or I don't want him.
VAL. That's OK, I don't expect no character reference from you.
LADY. I'll give you a character reference. I'd say this boy's a peculiar talker! But I wouldn't say a real hard worker or honest. I'd say a peculiar slew-footer that sweet talks you while he's got his hand in the cashbox.
VAL. I took out less than you owed me.
LADY. Don't mix up the issue. I see through you, mister!
VAL. I see through you, Lady.
LADY. What d'you see through me?
VAL. You sure you want me to tell?
LADY. I'd love for you to.
VAL.—A not so young and not so satisfied woman, that hired a man off the highway to do double duty without paying overtime for it. . . . I mean a store clerk days and a stud nights, and—
LADY. God, no! You—! [*She raises her hand as if to strike at him.*] Oh, God no . . . you cheap little—[*Invectives fail her so she uses her fists, hammering at him with them. He seizes her wrists. She struggles a few moments more, then collapses, in chair, sobbing. He lets go of her gently.*]
VAL. It's natural. You felt—lonely. . . .

[*She sobs brokenly against the counter.*]

LADY. Why did you come back here?
VAL. To put back the money I took so you wouldn't remember me as not honest or grateful—[*He picks up his guitar and starts to the door nodding gravely. She catches her breath; rushes to intercept him,*

spreading her arms like a crossbar over the door.]

LADY. NO, NO, DON'T GO . . . I NEED YOU!!!

[He faces her for five beats. The true passion of her outcry touches him then, and he turns about and crosses to the alcove. . . . As he draws the curtain across it he looks back at her.]

TO LIVE. . . . TO GO ON LIVING!!!

[Music fades in—"Lady's Love Song"—guitar. He closes the curtain and turns on the light behind it, making it translucent. Through an opening in the alcove entrance, we see him sitting down with his guitar.

LADY picks up the linen and crosses to the alcove like a spellbound child. Just outside it she stops, frozen with uncertainty, a conflict of feelings, but then he begins to whisper the words of a song so tenderly that she is able to draw the curtain open and enter the alcove. He looks up gravely at her from his guitar. She closes the curtain behind her. Its bizarre design, a gold tree with white birds and scarlet fruit in it, is softly translucent with the bulb lighted behind it. The guitar continues softly for a few moments; stops; the stage darkens till only the curtain of the alcove is clearly visible.]

ACT III

Scene I

An early morning. The Saturday before Easter. The sleeping alcove is lighted. VAL is smoking, half dressed, on the edge of the cot. LADY comes running, panting downstairs, her hair loose, in dressing robe and slippers and calls out in a panicky, shrill whisper.

LADY. Val! Val, he's comin' downstairs!
VAL [hoarse with sleep]. Who's—what?
LADY. Jabe!
VAL. Jabe?
LADY. I swear he is, he's coming downstairs!
VAL. What of it?
LADY. Jesus, will you get up and put some clothes on? The damned nurse told him that he could come down in the store to check over the stock! You want him to catch you half dressed on that bed there?
VAL. Don't he know I sleep here?
LADY. Nobody knows you sleep here but you and me.

[Voices above.]

Oh, God!—they've started.
NURSE. Don't hurry now. Take one step at a time.

[Footsteps on stairs, slow, shuffling. The professional, nasal cheer of a nurse's voice.]

LADY [panicky]. Get your shirt on! Come out!
NURSE. That's right. One step at a time, one step at a time, lean on my shoulder and take one step at a time.

[VAL rises, still dazed from sleep. LADY gasps and sweeps the curtain across the alcove just a moment before the descending figures enter the sight-lines on the landing. LADY breathes like an exhausted runner as she backs away from the alcove and assumes a forced smile. JABE and the nurse, MISS PORTER, appear on the landing of the stairs and at the same moment scudding clouds expose the sun. A narrow window on the landing admits a brilliant shaft of light upon the pair. They have a bizarre and awful appearance, the tall man, his rusty black suit hanging on him like an empty sack, his eyes burning malignantly from his yellow face, leaning on a stumpy little woman with bright pink or orange hair, clad all in starched white, with a voice that purrs with the faintly contemptuous cheer and sweetness of those hired to care for the dying.]

NURSE. Aw, now, just look at that, that nice bright sun comin' out.
LADY. Miss Porter? It's—it's cold down here!

JABE. What's she say?
NURSE. She says it's cold down here.
LADY. The—the—the air's not warm enough yet, the air's not heated!
NURSE. He's determined to come right down, Mrs. Torrance.
LADY. I know but—
NURSE. Wild horses couldn't hold him a minute longer.
JABE [exhausted].—Let's—rest here a minute!
LADY [eagerly]. Yes! Rest there a minute!
NURSE. Okay. We'll rest here a minute. . . .

[They sit down side by side on a bench under the artificial palm tree in the shaft of light. JABE glares into the light like a fierce dying old beast. There are sounds from the alcove. To cover them up, LADY keeps making startled, laughing sounds in her throat, half laughing, half panting, chafing her hands together at the foot of the stairs, and coughing falsely.]

JABE. Lady, what's wrong? Why are you so excited?
LADY. It seems like a miracle to me.
JABE. What seems like a miracle to you?
LADY. You coming downstairs.
JABE. You never thought I would come downstairs again?
LADY. Not this quick! Not as quick as this, Jabe! Did you think he would pick up as quick as this, Miss Porter?

[JABE rises.]

NURSE. Ready?
JABE. Ready.
NURSE. He's doing fine, knock wood.
LADY. Yes, knock wood, knock wood!
[Drums counter loudly with her knuckles. VAL steps silently from behind the alcove curtain as the NURSE and JABE resume their slow, shuffling descent of the stairs.]
[Moving back to D.R.C.] You got to be careful not to overdo. You don't want another setback. Ain't that right, Miss Porter?
NURSE. Well, it's my policy to mobilize the patient.
LADY [to VAL in a shrill whisper]. Coffee's boiling, take the Goddamn coffee pot off the burner! [She gives VAL a panicky signal to go in the alcove.]
JABE. Who're you talking to, Lady?
LADY. To—to—to Val, the clerk! I told him to—get you a—chair!
JABE. Who's that?
LADY. Val, Val, the clerk, you know Val!
JABE. Not yet. I'm anxious to meet him. Where is he?
LADY. Right here, right here, here's Val!

[VAL returns from the alcove.]

JABE. He's bright and early.
LADY. The early bird catches the worm!
JABE. That's right. Where is the worm?
LADY [loudly]. Ha ha!
NURSE. Careful! One step at a time, Mr. Torrance.
LADY. Saturday before Easter's our biggest sales-day of the year, I mean second biggest, but sometimes it's even bigger than Christmas Eve! So I told Val here a half hour early.

[JABE misses his step and stumbles to foot of stairs. LADY screams. NURSE rushes down to him. VAL advances and raises the man to his feet.]

VAL. Here. Here.
LADY. Oh, my God.
NURSE. Oh, oh!
JABE. I'm all right.
NURSE. Are you sure?
LADY. Are you sure?
JABE. Let me go! [He staggers to lean against counter, panting, glaring, with a malignant smile.]
LADY. Oh, my God. Oh, my—God. . . .
JABE. This is the boy that works here?
LADY. Yes, this is the clerk I hired to help us out, Jabe.
JABE. How is he doing?
LADY. Fine, fine.
JABE. He's mighty good-looking. Do women give him much trouble?
LADY. When school lets out the high-school girls are thick as flies in this store!
JABE. How about older women? Don't he attract older women? The older ones are the buyers, they got the money. They sweat it out of their husbands and throw it away! What's your salary, boy, how much do I pay you?
LADY. Twenty-two fifty a week.
JABE. You're getting him cheap.
VAL. I get—commissions.

JABE. Commissions?
VAL. Yes. One percent of all sales.
JABE. Oh? Oh? I didn't know about that.
LADY. I knew he would bring in trade and he brings it in.
JABE. I bet.
LADY. Val, get Jabe a chair, he ought to sit down.
JABE. No, I don't want to sit down. I want to take a look at the new confectionery.
LADY. Oh, yes, yes! Take a look at it! Val, Val, turn on the lights in the confectionery! I want Jabe to see the way I done it over! I'm—real—proud!
[VAL crosses and switches on light in confectionery. The bulbs in the arches and the juke box light up.]
Go in and look at it, Jabe. I am real proud of it!

[He stares at LADY a moment; then shuffles slowly into the special radiance of the confectionery. LADY moves D.C. At the same time a calliope becomes faintly audible and slowly but steadily builds. MISS PORTER goes with the patient, holding his elbow.]

VAL [returning to LADY]. He looks like death.
LADY [moving away from him]. Hush!

[VAL goes up above counter and stands in the shadows.]

NURSE. Well, isn't this artistic.
JABE. Yeh. Artistic as hell.
NURSE. I never seen anything like it before.
JABE. Nobody else did either.
NURSE [coming back to U.R.C.]. Who done these decorations?
LADY [defiantly]. I did them, all by myself!
NURSE. What do you know. It sure is something artistic.

[Calliope is now up loud.]

JABE [coming back to D.R.]. Is there a circus or carnival in the county?
LADY. What?
JABE. That sounds like a circus calliope on the highway.
LADY. That's no circus calliope. It's advertising the gala opening of the Torrance Confectionery tonight!
JABE. Doing what did you say?
LADY. It's announcing the opening of our confectionery, it's going all over Glorious Hill this morning and all over Sunset and Lyon this afternoon. Hurry on here so you can see it go by the store. [She rushes excitedly to open the front door as the ragtime music of the calliope approaches.]
JABE. I married a live one, Miss Porter. How much does that damn thing cost me?
LADY. You'll be surprised how little. [She is talking with an hysterical vivacity now.] I hired it for a song!
JABE. How much of a song did you hire it for?
LADY [closing door]. Next to nothing, seven-fifty an hour! And it covers three towns in Two River County!

[Calliope fades out.]

JABE [with a muted ferocity]. Miss Porter, I married a live one! Didn't I marry a live one? [Switches off lights in confectionery.] Her daddy "The Wop" was just as much of a live one till he burned up.
[LADY gasps as if struck.]
[With a slow, ugly grin:] He had a wine garden on the north shore of Moon Lake. The new confectionery sort of reminds me of it. But he made a mistake, he made a bad mistake, one time, selling liquor to niggers. We burned him out. We burned him out, house and orchard and vines and "The Wop" was burned up trying to fight the fire. [He turns.] I think I better go up.
LADY.—Did you say "WE"?
JABE.—I have a kind of a cramp. . . .
NURSE [taking his arm]. Well, let's go up.
JABE.—Yes, I better go up. . . .

[They cross to stairs. Calliope fades in.]

LADY [almost shouting as she moves D.C.]. Jabe, did you say "WE" did it, did you say "WE" did it?
JABE [at foot of stairs, stops, turns]. Yes, I said "We" did it. You heard me, Lady.
NURSE. One step at a time, one step at a time, take it easy.

[They ascend gradually to the landing and above. The calliope passes directly before the store and a clown is seen, or heard, shouting through megaphone.]

CLOWN. Don't forget tonight, folks, the gala opening of the Torrance Confectionery, free drinks and free favors, don't forget it, the gala opening of the confectionery.

[*Fade.* JABE *and the* NURSE *disappear above the landing. Calliope gradually fades. A hoarse cry above. The* NURSE *runs back downstairs, exclaiming:*]

NURSE. He's bleeding, he's having a hemm'rhage! [*Runs to phone.*] Dr. Buchanan's office! [*Turns again to* LADY.] Your husband is having a hemm'rhage!

[*Calliope is loud still.* LADY *appears not to hear. She speaks to* VAL.]

LADY. Did you hear what he said? He said "We" did it, "WE" burned—house—vines—orchard—"The Wop" burned fighting the fire. . . .

[*The scene dims out; calliope fades out.*]

Scene 2

Sunset of the same day. At rise VAL *is alone. He is standing stock-still down center stage, almost beneath the proscenium, in the tense, frozen attitude of a wild animal listening to something that warns it of danger, his head turned as if he were looking off stage left, out over the house, frowning slightly, attentively. After a moment he mutters something sharply, and his body relaxes; he takes out a cigarette and crosses to the store entrance, opens the door and stands looking out. It has been raining steadily and will rain again in a while, but right now it is clearing: the sun breaks through, suddenly, with great brilliance; and almost at the same instant, at some distance, a woman cries out a great hoarse cry of terror and exaltation; the cry is repeated as she comes running nearer.*

VEE TALBOTT *appears through the window as if blind and demented, stiff, groping gestures, shielding her eyes with one arm as she feels along the store window for the entrance, gasping for breath.* VAL *steps aside, taking hold of her arm to guide her into the store. For a few moments she leans weakly, blindly panting for breath against the oval glass of the door, then calls out.*

VEE. I'm—struck blind!
VAL. You can't see?
VEE.—No; Nothing. . . .
VAL [*assisting her to stool below counter*]. Set down here, Mrs. Talbott.
VEE.—Where?
VAL [*pushing her gently*]. Here.
[VEE *sinks moaning onto stool.*] What hurt your eyes, Mrs. Talbott, what happened to your eyes?
VEE [*drawing a long, deep breath*]. The vision I waited and prayed for all my life long!
VAL. You had a vision?
VEE. I saw the eyes of my Saviour!—They struck me blind. [*Leans forward, clasping her eyes in anguish.*] Ohhhh, they burned out my eyes!
VAL. Lean back.
VEE. Eyeballs burn like fire. . . .
VAL [*going off R.*]. I'll get you something cold to put on your eyes.
VEE. I knew a vision was coming, oh, I had many signs!
VAL [*in confectionery*]. It must be a terrible shock to have a vision. . . . [*He speaks gravely, gently, scooping chipped ice from the soft-drink cooler and wrapping it in his handkerchief.*]
VEE [*with the naïveté of a child, as* VAL *comes back to her*]. I thought I would see my Saviour on the day of His passion, which was yesterday, Good Friday, that's when I expected to see Him. But I was mistaken, I was—disappointed. Yesterday passed and nothing, nothing much happened but—today—
[VAL *places handkerchief over her eyes.*]
—this afternoon, somehow I pulled myself together and walked outdoors and started to go to pray in the empty church and meditate on the Rising of Christ tomorrow. Along the road as I walked, thinking about the mysteries of Easter, veils!—

[*She makes a long, shuddering word out of "veils."*]—seemed to drop off my eyes! Light, oh, light! I never have seen such brilliance! It PRICKED my eyeballs like NEEDLES!

VAL.—Light?

VEE. Yes, yes, light. YOU know, you know we live in light and shadow, that's, that's what we live in, a world of—light and—shadow. . . .

VAL. Yes. In light and shadow. [*He nods with complete understanding and agreement. They are like two children who have found life's meaning, simply and quietly, along a country road.*]

VEE. A world of light and shadow is what we live in, and—it's—confusing. . . .

[*A man is peering in at store window.*]

VAL. Yeah, they—do get—mixed. . . .

VEE. Well, and then—[*Hesitates to recapture her vision.*]—I heard this clap of thunder! Sky!—Split open!—And there in the split-open sky, I saw, I tell you, I saw the TWO HUGE BLAZING EYES OF JESUS CHRIST RISEN!—Not crucified but Risen! I mean Crucified and then RISEN!—The blazing eyes of Christ Risen! And then a great—[*Raises both arms and makes a great sweeping motion to describe an apocalyptic disturbance of the atmosphere.*]—His hand!—Invisible!—I didn't see his hand!—But it touched me—here! [*She seizes* VAL's *hand and presses it to her great heaving bosom.*]

TALBOTT [*appearing R. in confectionery, furiously*]. VEE!

[*She starts up, throwing the compress from her eyes. Utters a sharp gasp and staggers backward with terror and blasted ecstasy and dismay and belief, all confused in her look.*]

VEE. You!

TALBOTT. VEE!

VEE. You!

TALBOTT [*advancing*]. VEE!

VEE [*making two syllables of the word "eyes"*].—The Ey—es! [*She collapses, forward, falls to her knees, her arms thrown about* VAL. *He seizes her to lift her. Two or three men are peering in at the store window.*]

TALBOTT [*pushing* VAL *away*]. Let go of her, don't put your hands on my wife! [*He seizes her roughly and hauls her to the door.* VAL *moves up to help* VEE.] Don't move. [*At door, to* VAL.] I'm coming back.

VAL. I'm not goin' nowhere.

TALBOTT [*to* DOG, *as he goes off L. with* VEE]. Dog, go in there with that boy.

VOICE [*outside*]. Sheriff caught him messin' with his wife.

[*Repeat:* ANOTHER VOICE *at a distance.* "DOG" HAMMA *enters and stands silently beside the door while there is a continued murmur of excited voices on the street. The following scene should be underplayed, played almost casually, like the performance of some familiar ritual.*]

VAL. What do you want?

[DOG *says nothing but removes from his pocket and opens a spring-blade knife and moves to D.R.* PEE WEE *enters. Through the open door—voices.*]

VOICES [*outside*].—Son of a low-down bitch foolin' with—
—That's right, ought to be—
—Cut the son of a—

VAL. What do you—?

[PEE WEE *closes the door and silently stands beside it, opening a spring-blade knife.* VAL *looks from one to the other.*]
—It's six o'clock. Store's closed.
[*Men chuckle like dry leaves rattling.* VAL *crosses toward the door; is confronted by* TALBOTT; *stops short.*]

TALBOTT. Boy, I said stay here.

VAL. I'm not—goin' nowhere. . . .

TALBOTT. Stand back under that light.

VAL. Which light?

TALBOTT. That light.
[*Points.* VAL *goes behind counter.*]
I want to look at you while I run through some photos of men wanted.

VAL. I'm not wanted.

TALBOTT. A good-looking boy like you is always wanted.
[*Men chuckle.* VAL *stands in hot light under green-shaded bulb.* TALBOTT *shuffles through photos he has removed from his pocket.*]
—How tall are you, boy?

VAL. Never measured.

TALBOTT. How much do you weigh?

VAL. Never weighed.
TALBOTT. Got any scars or marks of identification on your face or body?
VAL. No, sir.
TALBOTT. Open your shirt.
VAL. What for? [*He doesn't.*]
TALBOTT. Open his shirt for him, Dog.
[DOG *steps quickly forward and rips shirt open to waist.* VAL *starts forward; men point knives; he draws back.*]
That's right, stay there, boy. What did you do before?

[PEE WEE *sits on stairs.*]

VAL. Before—what?
TALBOTT. Before you come here?
VAL.—Traveled and—played. . . .
TALBOTT. Played?
DOG [*advancing to C.*]. What?
PEE WEE. With wimmen?

[DOG *laughs.*]

VAL. No. Played guitar—and sang. . . .

[VAL *touches guitar on counter.*]

TALBOTT. Let me see that guitar.
VAL. Look at it. But don't touch it. I don't let nobody but musicians touch it.

[*Men come close.*]

DOG. What're you smiling for, boy?
PEE WEE. He ain't smiling, his mouth's just twitching like a dead chicken's foot.

[*They laugh.*]

TALBOTT. What is all that writing on the guitar?
VAL.—Names. . . .
TALBOTT. What of?
VAL. Autographs of musicians dead and living.

[*Men read aloud the names printed on the guitar:* Bessie Smith, Leadbelly, Woody Guthrie, Jelly Roll Morton, *etc. They bend close to it, keeping the open knife blades pointed at* VAL's *body;* DOG *touches neck of the guitar, draws it toward him.* VAL *suddenly springs, with catlike agility, onto the counter. He runs along it, kicking at their hands as they catch at his legs. The* NURSE *runs down to the landing.*]

NURSE PORTER. What's going on?
TALBOTT [*at the same time*]. Stop that!

[JABE *calls hoarsely above.*]

NURSE PORTER [*excitedly, all in one breath, as* JABE *calls*]. Where's Mrs. Torrance? I got a very sick man up there and his wife's disappeared.
[JABE *calls out again.*]
I been on a whole lot of cases but never seen one where a wife showed no concern for a—

[JABE *cries out again. Her voice fades out as she returns above.*]

TALBOTT [*overlapping* NURSE's *speech*]. Dog! Pee Wee! You all stand back from that counter. Dog, why don't you an' Pee Wee go up an' see Jabe. Leave me straighten this boy out, go on, go on up.
PEE WEE. C'mon, Dawg. . . .

[*They go up.* VAL *remains panting on counter.*]

TALBOTT [*sits in shoe chair at R. window. In* TALBOTT's *manner there is a curious, half-abashed gentleness, when alone with the boy, as if he recognized the purity in him and was, truly, for the moment, ashamed of the sadism implicit in the occurrence*]. Awright, boy. Git on down off th' counter, I ain't gonna touch y'r guitar.
[VAL *jumps off counter.*]
But I'm gonna tell you something. They's a certain county I know of which has a big sign at the county line that says, "Nigger, don't let the sun go down on you in this county." That's all it says, it don't threaten nothing, it just says, "Nigger, don't let the sun go down on you in this county!"
[*Chuckles hoarsely. Rises and takes a step toward* VAL.]
Well, son! You ain't a nigger and this is not that county, but, son, I want you to just imagine that you seen a sign that said to you: "Boy, don't let the sun rise on you in this county." I said "rise," not "go down" because it's too close to sun-

set for you to git packed an' move on before that. But I think if you value that instrument in your hands as much as you seem to, you'll simplify my job by not allowing the sun tomorrow to rise on you in this county. 'S that understood, now, boy?

[VAL *stares at him, expressionless, panting.*]

[*Crossing to door*] I hope so. I don't like violence. [*He looks back and nods at* VAL *from the door. Then goes outside in the fiery afterglow of the sunset. Dogs bark in the distance. Music fades in: "Dog Howl Blues"—minor—guitar. Pause in which* VAL *remains motionless, cradling guitar in his arms. Then* VAL's *faraway, troubled look is resolved in a slight, abrupt nod of his head. He sweeps back the alcove curtain and enters the alcove and closes the curtain behind him. Lights dim down to indicate a division of scenes.*]

Scene 3

Half an hour later. The lighting is less realistic than in the previous scenes of the play. The interior of the store is so dim that only the vertical lines of the pillars and such selected items as the palm tree on the stair landing and the ghostly paper vineyard of the confectionery are plainly visible. The view through the great front window has virtually become the background of the action: A singing wind sweeps clouds before the moon so that the witchlike country brightens and dims and brightens again. The Marshall's hounds are restless: their baying is heard now and then. A lamp outside the door sometimes catches a figure that moves past with mysterious urgency, calling out softly and raising an arm to beckon, like a shade in the under kingdom.

At rise, or when the stage is lighted again, it is empty but footsteps are descending the stairs as DOLLY *and* BEULAH *rush into the store and call out, in soft shouts:*

DOLLY. Dawg?

BEULAH. Pee Wee?

EVA TEMPLE [*appearing on landing and calling down softly in the superior tone of a privileged attendant in a sick-chamber*]. Please don't shout!—Mr. Binnings and Mr. Hamma [*Names of the two husbands*] are upstairs sitting with Jabe. . . . [*She continues her descent. Then* EVA TEMPLE *appears, sobbing, on landing.*]

—Come down carefully, Sister.

SISTER. Help me, I'm all to pieces. . . .

[EVA *ignores this request and faces the two women.*]

BEULAH. Has the bleedin' quit yit?

EVA. The hemorrhage seems to have stopped. Sister, Sister, pull yourself together, we all have to face these things sometime in life.

DOLLY. Has he sunk into a coma?

EVA. No. Cousin Jabe is conscious. Nurse Porter says his pulse is remarkably strong for a man that lost so much blood. Of course he's had a transfusion.

SISTER. Two of 'em.

EVA [*crossing to* DOLLY]. Yais, an' they put him on glucose. His strength came back like magic.

BEULAH. She up there?

EVA. Who?

BEULAH. Lady!

EVA. No! When last reported she had just stepped into the Glorious Hill Beauty Parlor.

BEULAH. You don't mean it.

EVA. Ask Sister!

SISTER. She's planning to go ahead with—!

EVA.—The gala opening of the confectionery. Switch on the lights in there, Sister. [SISTER *crosses and switches on lights and moves off R. The decorated confectionery is lighted.* DOLLY *and* BEULAH *exclaim in awed voices.*]

—Of course it's not normal behavior; it's downright lunacy, but still that's no excuse for it! And when she called up at five, about one hour ago, it wasn't to ask about Jabe, oh, no, she didn't mention his name. She asked if Ruby Lightfoot had delivered a case of Seagram's. Yais, she just shouted that question and hung up the phone, before I could—[*She crosses and goes off R.*]

BEULAH [*going into confectionery*]. Oh, I understand, now! Now I see what she's up to! Electric moon, cut-out silver-paper stars and artificial vines? Why, it's her father's wine garden on Moon Lake she's turned this room into!

DOLLY [*suddenly as she sits in shoe chair*]. Here she comes, here she comes!

[*The* TEMPLE SISTERS *retreat from view in confectionery as* LADY *enters the store. She wears a hooded rain-cape and carries a large paper shopping bag and paper carton box.*]

LADY. Go on, ladies, don't stop, my ears are burning!

BEULAH [*coming in to U.R.C.*].—Lady, oh, Lady, Lady. . . .

LADY. Why d'you speak my name in that pitiful voice? Hanh? [*Throws back hood of cape, her eyes blazing, and places bag and box on counter.*] Val? Val! Where is that boy that works here?

[DOLLY *shakes her head.*]

I guess he's havin' a T-bone steak with French fries and coleslaw fo' ninety-five cents at the Blue Bird. . . .

[*Sounds in confectionery.*]

Who's in the confectionery, is that you, Val?

[TEMPLE SISTERS *emerge and stalk past her.*]

Going, girls?

[*They go out of store.*]

Yes, gone! [*She laughs and throws off rain-cape, onto counter, revealing a low-cut gown, triple strand of pearls and a purple satin-ribboned corsage.*]

BEULAH [*sadly*]. How long have I known you, Lady?

LADY [*going behind counter, unpacks paper hats and whistles*]. A long time, Beulah. I think you remember when my people come here on a banana boat from Palermo, Sicily, by way of Caracas, Venezuela, yes, with a grind-organ and a monkey, ha ha! You remember the monkey? The man that sold Papa the monkey said it was a very young monkey, but he was a liar, it was a very old monkey, it was on its last legs, ha ha ha! But it was a well-dressed monkey. [*Coming around to R. of counter.*] It had a green velvet suit and a little red cap that it tipped and a tambourine that it passed around for money, ha ha ha. . . . The grind-organ played and the monkey danced in the sun, ha ha!—"O Sole Mio, Da Da Da daaa . . . !" [*Sits in chair at counter.*]—One day, the monkey danced too much in the sun and it was a very old monkey and it dropped dead. . . . My Papa, he turned to the people, he made them a bow and he said, "The show is over, the monkey is dead." Ha ha!

[*Slight pause. Then* DOLLY *pipes up venomously.*]

DOLLY. Ain't it wonderful Lady can be so brave?

BEULAH. Yaiss, wonderful! Hanh. . . .

LADY. For me the show is not over, the monkey is not dead yet! [*Then suddenly.*] Val, is that you, Val?

[*Someone has entered the confectionery door, out of sight, and the draught of air has set the wind-chimes tinkling wildly.* LADY *rushes forward but stops short as* CAROL *appears. She wears a trench coat and a white sailor's cap with a turned-down brim, inscribed with the name of a vessel and a date, past or future, memory or anticipation.*]

DOLLY. Well, here's your first customer, Lady.

LADY [*going behind counter*].—Carol, that room ain't open.

CAROL. There's a big sign outside that says "Open Tonite!"

LADY. It ain't open to you.

CAROL. I have to stay here a while. They stopped my car, you see, I don't have a license; my license has been revoked and I have to find someone to drive me across the river.

LADY. You can call a taxi.

CAROL. I heard that the boy that works for you is leaving tonight and I—

LADY. Who said he's leaving?

CAROL [*crossing to counter*]. Sheriff Talbott. The County Marshall suggested I get him to drive me over the river since he'd be crossing it too.

LADY. You got some mighty wrong information!

CAROL. Where is he? I don't see him?
LADY. Why d'you keep coming back here bothering that boy? He's not interested in you! Why would he be leaving here tonight?
[Door opens off as she comes from behind counter.]
Val, is that you, Val?
[CONJURE MAN enters through confectionery, mumbling rapidly, holding out something. BEULAH and DOLLY take flight out the door with cries of revulsion.]
No conjure stuff, go away!
[He starts to withdraw.]
CAROL [crossing to U.R.C.]. Uncle! The Choctaw cry! I'll give you a dollar for it.

[LADY turns away with a gasp, with a gesture of refusal. The NEGRO nods, then throws back his turkey neck and utters a series of sharp barking sounds that rise to a sustained cry of great intensity and wildness. The cry produces a violent reaction in the building. BEULAH and DOLLY run out of the store. LADY does not move but she catches her breath. DOG and PEE WEE run down the stairs with ad libs and hustle the NEGRO out of the store, ignoring LADY, as their wives call: "PEE WEE!" and "DAWG!" outside on the walk. VAL sweeps back the alcove curtain and appears as if the cry were his cue. Above, in the sick room, hoarse, outraged shouts that subside with exhaustion. CAROL crosses downstage and speaks to the audience and to herself.]

CAROL. Something is still wild in the country! This country used to be wild, the men and women were wild and there was a wild sort of sweetness in their hearts, for each other, but now it's sick with neon, it's broken out sick, with neon, like most other places.... I'll wait outside in my car. It's the fastest thing on wheels in Two River County!

[She goes out of the store R. LADY stares at VAL with great asking eyes, a hand to her throat.]

LADY [with false boldness]. Well, ain't you going with her?
VAL. I'm going with no one I didn't come here with. And I come here with no one.
LADY. Then get into your white jacket. I need your services in that room there tonight.
[VAL regards her steadily for several beats.]
[Clapping her hands together twice] Move, move, stop goofing! The Delta Brilliant lets out in half'n hour and they'll be driving up here. You got to shave ice for the setups!
VAL [as if he thought she'd gone crazy]. "Shave ice for the setups"? [He moves up to counter.]
LADY. Yes, an' call Ruby Lightfoot, tell her I need me a dozen more half-pints of Seagram's. They all call for Seven-and-Sevens. You know how t' sell bottle goods under a counter? It's OK. We're gonna git paid for protection. [Gasps, touching her diaphragm]. But one thing you gotta watch out for is sellin' to minors. Don't serve liquor to minors. Ask for his driver's license if they's any doubt. Anybody born earlier than—let's see, twenty-one from—oh, I'll figure it later. Hey! Move! Move! Stop goofing!
VAL [placing guitar on counter].—You're the one that's goofing, not me, Lady.
LADY. Move, I said, move!
VAL. What kick are you on, are you on a benny kick, Lady? 'Ve you washed down a couple of bennies with a pot of black coffee t' make you come on strong for th' three o'clock show? [His mockery is gentle, almost tender, but he has already made a departure; he is back in the all-night bars with the B-girls and raffish entertainers. He stands at counter as she rushes about. As she crosses between the two rooms, he reaches out to catch hold of her bare arm and he pulls her to him and grips her arms.]
LADY. Hey!
VAL. Will you quit thrashin' around like a hooked catfish?
LADY. Go git in y'r white jacket an'—
VAL. Sit down. I want to talk to you.
LADY. I don't have time.
VAL. I got to reason with you.
LADY. It's not possible to.
VAL. You can't open a night-place here this night.
LADY. You bet your sweet life I'm going to!
VAL. Not me, not my sweet life!
LADY. I'm betting my life on it! Sweet or not sweet, I'm—

VAL. Yours is yours, mine is mine.... [*He releases her with a sad shrug.*]
LADY. You don't get the point, huh? There's a man up there that set fire to my father's wine garden and I lost my life in it, yeah, I lost my life in it, *three* lives was lost in it, two *born* lives and one—not.... I was made to commit a *murder* by him up there! [*Has frozen momentarily.*]—I want that man to see the wine garden come open again when he's dying! I want him to hear it coming open again when he's dying! I want him to hear it coming open again here tonight! While he's dying. It's necessary, no power on earth can stop it. Hell, I don't even want it, it's just necessary, it's just something's got to be done to square things away, to, to, to—be *not defeated*! You get me? Just to be *not defeated*! Ah, oh, I won't be defeated, not again, in my life! [*Embraces him.*] Thank you for staying here with me!—God bless you for it.... Now please go and get in your white jacket ...

[VAL *looks at her as if he were trying to decide between a natural sensibility of heart and what his life's taught him since he left Witches' Bayou. Then he sighs again, with the same slight, sad shrug, and crosses into alcove to put on a jacket and remove from under his cot a canvas-wrapped package of his belongings.* LADY *takes paper hats and carnival stuff from counter, crosses into confectionery and puts them on the tables, then starts back but stops short as she sees* VAL *come out of alcove with his snakeskin jacket and luggage.*]

LADY. That's not your white jacket, that's that snakeskin jacket you had on when you come here.
VAL. I come and I go in this jacket.
LADY. Go, did you say?
VAL. Yes, ma'am, I did, I said go. All that stays to be settled is a little matter of wages.

[*The dreaded thing's happened to her. This is what they call "the moment of truth" in the bull ring, when the matador goes in over the horns of the bull to plant the mortal sword-thrust.*]

LADY.—So you're—cutting out, are you?

VAL. My gear's all packed. I'm catchin' the southbound bus.
LADY. Uh-huh, in a pig's eye. You're not conning me, mister. She's waiting for you outside in her high-powered car and you're—

[*Sudden footsteps on stairs. They break apart,* VAL *puts suitcase down, drawing back into shadow, as* NURSE PORTER *appears on the stair landing.*]

NURSE PORTER. Miss Torrance, are you down there?
LADY [*crossing to foot of stairs*]. Yeah. I'm here. I'm back.
NURSE PORTER. Can I talk to you up here about Mr. Torrance?
LADY [*shouting to* NURSE]. I'll be up in a minute.
[*Door closes above.* LADY *turns to* VAL.] OK, now, mister. You're scared about something, ain't you?
VAL. I been threatened with violence if I stay here.
LADY. I got paid for protection in this county, plenty paid for it, and it covers you too.
VAL. No, ma'am. My time is up here.
LADY. Y' say that like you'd served a sentence in jail.
VAL. I got in deeper than I meant to, Lady.
LADY. Yeah, and how about me?
VAL [*going to her*]. I would of cut out before you got back to the store, but I wanted to tell you something I never told no one before. [*Places hand on her shoulder.*] I feel a true love for you, Lady! [*He kisses her.*] I'll wait for you out of this county, just name the time and the ...
LADY [*moving back*]. Oh, don't talk about love, not to me. It's easy to say "Love, Love!" with fast and free transportation waiting right out the door for you!
VAL. D'you remember some things I told you about me the night we met here?
LADY [*crossing to R.C.*]. Yeah, many things. Yeah, temperature of a dog. And some bird, oh, yeah, without legs so it had to sleep on the wind!
VAL [*through her speech*]. Naw, not that; not that.
LADY. And how you could burn down a woman? I said "Bull!" I take that back. You can! You can burn down a woman

and stamp on her ashes to make sure the fire is put out!

VAL. I mean what I said about gettin' away from . . .

LADY. How long've you held this first steady job in your life?

VAL. Too long, too long!

LADY. Four months and five days, mister. All right! How much pay have you took?

VAL. I told you to keep out all but—

LADY. Y'r living expenses. I can give you the figures to a dime. Eighty-five bucks, no, ninety! Chicken-feed, mister! Y'know how much you got coming? IF you get it? I don't need paper to figure, I got it all in my head. You got five hundred and eighty-six bucks coming to you, not, not chicken-feed, that. But, mister. [Gasps for breath]—If you try to walk out on me, now, tonight, without notice!—You're going to get just nothing! A great big zero. . . . [Somebody hollers at door off R.: "Hey! You open?" She rushes toward it shouting, "CLOSED! CLOSED! GO AWAY!"— VAL crosses to the cashbox. She turns back toward him, gasps.]

Now you watch your next move and I'll watch mine. You open that cashbox and I swear I'll throw open that door and holler, clerk's robbing the store!

VAL.—Lady?

LADY [fiercely]. Hanh?

VAL.—Nothing, you've—

LADY.—Hanh?

VAL. Blown your stack. I will go without pay.

LADY [coming to C.]. Then you ain't understood me! With or without pay, you're staying!

VAL. I've got my gear. [Picks up suitcase. She rushes to seize his guitar.]

LADY. Then I'll go up and git mine! And take this with me, just t'make sure you wait till I'm—[She moves back to R.C. He puts suitcase down.]

VAL [advancing toward her]. Lady, what're you—?

LADY [entreating with guitar raised]. Don't—

VAL.—Doing with—

LADY.—Don't!

VAL.—my guitar!

LADY. Holding it for security while I—

VAL. Lady, you been a lunatic since this morning!

LADY. Longer, longer than morning! I'm going to keep hold of your "life companion" while I pack! I am! I am goin' to pack an' go, if you go, where you go!

[He makes a move toward her. She crosses below and around to counter.]

You didn't think so, you actually didn't think so? What was I going to do, in your opinion? What, in your opinion, would I be doing? Stay on here in a store full of bottles and boxes while you go far, while you go fast and far, without me having your—forwarding address!—even?

VAL. I'll—give you a forwarding address. . . .

LADY. Thanks, oh, thanks! Would I take your forwarding address back of that curtain? "Oh, dear forwarding address, hold me, kiss me, be faithful!" [Utters grotesque, stifled cry; presses fist to mouth.] [He advances cautiously, hand stretched toward the guitar. She retreats above to U.R.C., biting lip, eyes flaring. JABE knocks above.]

Stay back! You want me to smash it!

VAL [D.C.]. He's—knocking for you. . . .

LADY. I know! Death's knocking for me! Don't you think I hear him, knock, knock, knock? It sounds like what it is! Bones knocking bones. . . . Ask me how it felt to be coupled with death up there, and I can tell you. My skin crawled when he touched me. But I endured it. I guess my heart knew that somebody must be coming to take me out of this hell! You did. You came. Now look at me! I'm alive once more! [Convulsive sobbing controlled: continues more calmly and harshly.]

—I won't wither in dark! Got that through your skull? Now. Listen! Everything in this rotten store is yours, not just your pay, but everything Death's scraped together down here!—but Death has got to die before you can go. . . . You got that memorized, now?—Then get into your white jacket!—Tonight is the gala opening— [Rushes through confectionery.]—of the confectionery—

[VAL runs and seizes her arm holding guitar. She breaks violently free.]

Smash me against a rock and I'll smash your guitar! I will, if you—

[Rapid footsteps on stairs.]

Oh, Miss Porter!

[She motions VAL back. He retreats into alcove. LADY puts guitar down beside juke-

box. MISS PORTER *is descending the stairs.*]
NURSE PORTER [*descending watchfully*]. You been out a long time.
LADY [*moving U.R.C.*]. Yeah, well, I had lots of—[*Her voice expires breathlessly. She stares fiercely, blindly, into the other's hard face.*]
NURSE PORTER.—Of what?
LADY. Things to—things to—take care of. . . . [*Draws a deep, shuddering breath, clenched fist to her bosom.*]
NURSE PORTER. Didn't I hear you shouting to someone just now?
LADY.—Uh-huh. Some drunk tourist made a fuss because I wouldn't sell him no— liquor. . . .
NURSE [*crossing to the door*]. Oh. Mr. Torrance is sleeping under medication.
LADY. That's good. [*She sits in shoe-fitting chair.*]
NURSE. I gave him a hypo at five.
LADY.—Don't all that morphine weaken the heart, Miss Porter?
NURSE. Gradually, yes.
LADY. How long does it usually take for them to let go?
NURSE. It varies according to the age of the patient and the condition his heart's in. Why?
LADY. Miss Porter, don't people sort of help them let go?
NURSE. How do you mean, Mrs. Torrance?
LADY. Shorten their suffering for them?
NURSE. Oh, I see what you mean. [*Snaps her purse shut.*]—I see what you mean, Mrs. Torrance. But killing is killing, regardless of circumstances.
LADY. Nobody said killing.
NURSE. You said "shorten their suffering."
LADY. Yes, like merciful people shorten an animal's suffering when he's. . . .
NURSE. A human being is not the same as an animal, Mrs. Torrance. And I don't hold with what they call—
LADY [*overlapping*]. Don't give me a sermon, Miss Porter I just wanted to know if—
NURSE [*overlapping*]. I'm not giving a sermon. I just answered your question. If you want to get somebody to shorten your husband's life—
LADY [*jumping up; overlapping*]. Why, how dare you say that I—
NURSE. I'll be back at ten-thirty.
LADY. Don't!
NURSE. What?

LADY [*crossing behind counter*]. Don't come back at ten-thirty, don't come back.
NURSE. I'm always discharged by the doctors on my cases.
LADY. This time you're being discharged by the patient's wife.
NURSE. That's something we'll have to discuss with Dr. Buchanan.
LADY. I'll call him myself about it. I don't like you. I don't think you belong in the nursing profession, you have cold eyes; I think you like to watch pain!
NURSE. I know why you don't like my eyes. [*Snaps purse shut.*] You don't like my eyes because you know they see clear.
LADY. Why are you staring at *me*?
NURSE. I'm not staring at you, I'm staring at the curtain. There's something burning in there, smoke's coming out! [*Starts toward alcove.*] Oh.
LADY. Oh, no, you don't. [*Seizes her arm.*]
NURSE [*pushes her roughly aside and crosses to the curtain.* VAL *rises from cot, opens the curtain and faces her coolly*]. Oh, excuse me! [*She turns to* LADY.]—The moment I looked at you when I was called on this case last Friday morning I knew that you were pregnant.
[LADY *gasps.*]
I also knew the moment I looked at your husband it wasn't by him. [*She stalks to the door.* LADY *suddenly cries out.*]
LADY. Thank you for telling me what I hoped for is true.
NURSE PORTER. You don't seem to have any shame.
LADY [*exalted*]. No. I don't have shame. I have—great—joy!
NURSE PORTER [*venomously*]. Then why don't you get the calliope and the clown to make the announcement?
LADY. You do it for me, save me the money! Make the announcement, all over!

[NURSE *goes out.* VAL *crosses swiftly to the door and locks it. Then he advances toward her, saying:*]

VAL. Is it true what she said?

[LADY *moves as if stunned to the counter; the stunned look gradually turns to a look of wonder. On the counter is a heap of silver and gold paper hats and trumpets for the gala opening of the confectionery.*]

VAL [*in a hoarse whisper*]. Is it true or not true, what that woman told you?
LADY. You sound like a scared little boy.
VAL. She's gone out to tell.

[*Pause.*]

LADY. You gotta go now—it's dangerous for you to stay here. . . . Take your pay out of the cashbox, you can go. Go, go, take the keys to my car, cross the river into some other county. You've done what you came here to do. . . .
VAL.—It's true then, it's—?
LADY [*sitting in chair of counter*]. True as God's word! I have life in my body, this dead tree, my body, has burst in flower! You've given me life, you can go!

[*He crouches down gravely opposite her, gently takes hold of her knotted fingers and draws them to his lips, breathing on them as if to warm them. She sits bolt upright, tense, blind as a clairvoyant.*]

VAL.—Why didn't you tell me before?
LADY.—When a woman's been childless as long as I've been childless, it's hard to believe that you're still able to bear!—We used to have a little fig tree between the house and the orchard. It never bore any fruit, they said it was barren. Time went by it, spring after useless spring, and it almost started to—die. . . . Then one day I discovered a small green fig on the tree they said wouldn't bear! [*She is clasping a gilt paper horn.*] I ran through the orchard, I ran through the wine garden shouting, "Oh, Father, it's going to bear, the fig tree is going to bear!"—It seemed such a wonderful thing, after those ten barren springs, for the little fig tree to bear, it called for a celebration—I ran to a closet, I opened a box that we kept Christmas ornaments in!—I took them out, glass bells, glass birds, tinsel, icicles, stars. . . . And I hung the little tree with them, I decorated the fig tree with glass bells and glass birds, and silver icicles and stars, because it won the battle and it would bear! [*Rises, ecstatic*] Unpack the box! Unpack the box with the Christmas ornaments in it, put them on me, glass bells and glass birds and stars and tinsel and snow! [*In a sort of delirium she thrusts the conical gilt paper hat on her head and runs to the foot of the stairs with the paper horn. She blows the horn over and over, grotesquely mounting the stairs, as* VAL *tries to stop her. She breaks away from him and runs up to the landing, blowing the paper horn and crying out:*] I've won, I've won, Mr. Death, I'm going to bear! [*Then suddenly she falters, catches her breath in a shocked gasp and awkwardly retreats to the stairs. Then turns screaming and runs back down them, her cries dying out as she arrives at the floor level. She retreats haltingly as a blind person, a hand stretched out to* VAL, *as slow, clumping footsteps and hoarse breathing are heard on the stairs. She moans.*]—Oh, God, oh—God. . . .

[JABE *appears on the landing, by the artificial palm tree in its dully lustrous green jardiniere, a stained purple robe hangs loosely about his wasted yellowed frame. He is death's self, and malignancy, as he peers, crouching, down into the store's dimness to discover his quarry.*]

JABE: Buzzards! Buzzards! [*Clutching the trunk of the false palm tree, he raises the other hand holding a revolver and fires down into the store.* LADY *screams and rushes to cover* VAL's *motionless figure with hers.* JABE *scrambles down a few steps and fires again and the bullet strikes her, expelling her breath in a great "Hah!" He fires again; the great "Hah!" is repeated. She turns to face him, still covering* VAL *with her body, her face with all the passions and secrets of life and death in it now, her fierce eyes blazing, knowing, defying and accepting. But the revolver is empty; it clicks impotently and* JABE *hurls it toward them; he descends and passes them, shouting out hoarsely.*] I'll have you burned! I burned her father and I'll have you burned! [*He opens the door and rushes out onto the road, shouting hoarsely.*] The clerk is robbing the store, he shot my wife, the clerk is robbing the store, he killed my wife!
VAL.—Did it—?
LADY.—Yes!—it did. . . .

[*A curious, almost formal, dignity appears in them both. She turns to him with the sort of smile that people offer in apology*

for an awkward speech, and he looks back at her gravely, raising one hand as if to stay her. But she shakes her head slightly and points to the ghostly radiance of her make-believe orchard and she begins to move a little unsteadily toward it. Music. LADY enters the confectionery and looks about it as people look for the last time at a loved place they are deserting.]
The show is over. The monkey is dead....

[Music rises to cover whatever sound Death makes in the confectionery. It halts abruptly. Figures appear through the great front window of the store, pocket-lamps stare through the glass and someone begins to force the front door open. VAL cries out.]

VAL. Which way!

[He turns and runs through the dim radiance of the confectionery, out of our sight. Something slams. Something cracks open. Men are in the store and the dark is full of hoarse, shouting voices.]

VOICES OF MEN [shouting].—Keep to the walls He's armed!
—Upstairs, Dog!
—Jack, the confectionery!
[Wild cry back of store.]
Got him. GOT HIM!
—They got him!
—Rope, git rope!
—Git rope from th' hardware section!
—I got something better than rope!
—What've you got?
—What's that, what's he got?
—A BLOWTORCH!
—Christ....
[A momentary hush.]
—Come on, what in hell are we waiting for?
—Hold on a minute, I wanta see if it works!
—Wait, Wait!
—LOOK here!
[A jet of blue flame stabs the dark. It flickers on CAROL's figure in the confectionery. The men cry out together in hoarse passion crouching toward the fierce blue jet of fire, their faces lit by it like the faces of demons.]
—Christ!
—It works!

[They rush out. Confused shouting behind. Motors start. Fade quickly. There is almost silence, a dog bays in the distance. Then—the CONJURE MAN appears with a bundle of garments which he examines, dropping them all except the snakeskin jacket, which he holds up with a toothless mumble of excitement.]

CAROL [quietly, gently]. What have you got there, Uncle? Come here and let me see.
[He crosses to her.]
Oh yes, his snakeskin jacket. I'll give you a gold ring for it.
[She slowly twists ring off her finger. Somewhere there is a cry of anguish. She listens attentively till it fades out, then nods with understanding.]
—Wild things leave skins behind them, they leave clean skins and teeth and white bones behind them, and these are tokens passed from one to another, so that the fugitive kind can always follow their kind....
[The cry is repeated more terribly than before. It expires again. She draws the jacket about her as if she were cold, nods to the old NEGRO, handing him the ring. Then she crosses toward the door, pausing halfway as SHERIFF TALBOTT enters with his pocket-lamp.]

SHERIFF. Don't no one move, don't move!
[She crosses directly past him as if she no longer saw him, and out the door. He shouts furiously.]
Stay here!
[Her laughter rings outside. He follows the girl, shouting.] Stop! Stop!
[Silence. The NEGRO looks up with a secret smile as the curtain falls slowly.]

FOR DISCUSSION:

1. What aspects of the Orpheus legend has Williams adapted to his play? Identify each character's mythic counterpart. What changes has Williams made in the myth? Try to account for these changes.

2. How does the physical set on stage meet the requirements of the Orpheus story?

3. What functions do Dolly and Beulah serve in the play? Are they individualized in any way?

4. What is the symbolic significance of (a) Val's snakeskin jacket, (b) his guitar, (c) his blue suit, (d) the bird without legs?

5. Discuss the aura of supernaturalism that permeates the play.

6. To what extent does Val meet the requirements of the archetypal poet?

7. Much of the play's imagery is concerned with light and darkness—Val worked nights in the city, the shoe section is in the darkest part of the building, Lady at one point wants Val to become a night watchman. Trace these and similar symbols throughout the play. Does Williams assign fixed values to light and darkness or does their meaning vary with the dramatic context?

8. Does the final act with its setting at Eastertime confuse the Orpheus legend with Christian symbolism? In this connection is the name Val Xavier appropriate for a character modeled on pagan myth?

9. Several archetypal themes run throughout Orpheus Descending—loss of innocence, spiritual resurrection, conflict between forces of light and darkness, essential loneliness of mankind. Trace these throughout the play.

10. Is Val's downfall caused by (a) too much sexuality, (b) too little sexuality, (c) too much rationality, (d) too little rationality, (e) forces over which he has no control?

Orpheus Descending*

SIGNI L. FALK

Tennessee Williams says of *Orpheus Descending*, a revision of *Battle of Angels*, which was rewritten after fifteen years of theatrical experience: "On the surface it was and still is the tale of a wild-spirited boy who wanders into a conventional community of the South and creates the commotion of a fox in a chicken coop.

"But beneath the now familiar surface it is a play about unanswered questions that haunt the hearts of people and the difference between continuing to ask them, a difference represented by the four major protagonists of the play, and the acceptance of prescribed answers that are not answers at all, but expedient adaptations or surrender to a state of quandary."

The theme of the poet in an unfriendly world is a recurrent one in Williams' plays. The last three stanzas of a poem, "Orpheus Descending," apostrophizes this special figure in rather flamboyant terms. Williams describes the unhappy life of the poet. He says to Orpheus that he must learn that some things, by their nature incomplete—an idea basic to the horror story, "Desire and the Black Masseur"—are to be sought for and abandoned; that it is in the nature of things that those who reach for the heights are destined to fall; that he, a fugitive and ashamed, must crawl within himself, for he is not the stars but the residue of victims torn by the avenging furies. The ambivalence of spirit and flesh within this character as described in the poem recall the symbolic figure of Alma Winemiller, the idealist turned prostitute, or the decadent aristocrat, Blanche Du Bois. Williams has given the classic myth his own interpretation and imposed it on the old play.

Orpheus is Val Xavier, the poet-itinerant-savior, who descends into the hell of a small southern town to rescue the dead Eurydice, or Lady (Myra of the old play), from Pluto, or Jabe Torrance, the cancer-doomed, flint-hearted husband who snatched her away from the romantic life she dreamed about. The particular corner of hell that Orpheus-Val Xavier enters is a grubby dry goods store with an adjacent confectionery which is done in shadowy poetic tones and which represents romantic memories of love and happiness. Preoccupied with the memory theme again, Williams makes this social parlor, refurbished during the play, represent the imitation of the Moon Lake Casino which Lady romantically associates with the rich boy who deserted her and with her father, called the Wop, who with his Casino was burned alive because he sold liquor to "niggers." And only in Williams' version of hell would there be the inevitable bedroom alcove, exotically curtained with an Oriental hanging in brilliant colors—a gold tree, scarlet fruit, tropical birds—obviously supposed to represent all that is not icy Puritanism.

The inhabitants of this hell are a motley assortment of commonplace townspeople, frowsy women, and silly and malicious gossips who savor recollections of "spooning" in the old Moon Lake Casino and reports of others' suffering. Their husbands—pot-bellied old boys who play with slot machines, guns, and bloodhounds—are remnants of the

---

* From *Tennessee Williams* by Signi L. Falk. Copyright 1961 by Twayne Publishers, Inc. and reprinted by their permission. [Footnotes omitted—Ed.]

Mystic Crew—a kind of Ku Klux Klan which keeps foreigners, like the Wop, and "niggers" in their places. A ghoulish primitive, the Conjure Man, with his bird bones and bloodcurdling Choctaw cry, seems to be Williams' own private symbol of pure freedom and death. But most important for Orpheus-Val Xavier are three women; for the play revolves around his relationship with them.

Val Xavier is a handsome southerner with an intimate, soft voice whose trademark of freedom, wild freedom, is still a snakeskin jacket instead of the job-holder's conventional blue business suit. He is now a man of thirty who is no longer sure that sex gives the answer to all questions. The guitar which he carries—that guitar for some critics is a phallic symbol—covered with names of famous singers, would also seem to be a symbol of his art and his purity. His art, he says, affords a purification after he has been contaminated by the world. Untainted in spite of his corrupt life "with the party"—is there a veiled reference here to homosexuality?—he belongs to neither of two classes, the buyers and the bought, but to those who are uncommitted and free. This man who admits that he has been penalized for vagrancy, seems to want, at thirty, to exchange some of his wild freedom for security.

An old companion of his vagabond-entertainer days is Carol Cutrere (Sandra Whiteside of the old play), who is still the poor little rich girl but an older and even more exotic one and more of an exhibitionist. She wears the exaggerated make-up of the theater. Asked why she makes such a display of herself, she tells of her earlier humanitarian ventures. She was at one time another kind of exhibitionist, a religious fanatic and reformer who made speeches, wrote protest letters about the brutal mistreatment of Negroes, spent her inheritance to build clinics, and made a particular exhibition of herself by dressing in burlap and walking barefoot to ask the governor to free a Negro taken with a white whore. Arrested for vagrancy herself, she has made that her career ever since. The early part of this biography hardly fits the character, or any resemblance of the character, who operates as Carol Cutrere, unless it is an extreme example of the idealist who fell deep into the mud. There is also a suggestion in this biography of a Williams attitude—a disinclination to take sides, to make judgments of good and evil, to become committed.

Frustrated in the humanitarian ventures she reports upon, she turns to sex—and with a terrible compulsion. She makes her usual proposition to Val who refuses, saying that heavy drinking and "shacking up" with strangers is for youngsters and not a thirty-year old. These two exchange confidences with an air "of two lonely children," but the topic is the same old line about sex, embroidered with tender words and blunt biological facts.

Val, as in the former version, courts disaster when he seeks to exchange his freedom for a job in the mercantile store and becomes involved with the love-starved wife. It is his poetic description of freedom and purity that seems to win her sympathy: "You know they's a kind of bird that don't have legs so it can't light on nothing but has to stay all its life on its wings in the sky? . . . You can't tell those birds from the sky and that's why the hawks don't catch them, don't see them up there in the high blue sky near the sun!" Robert Brustein calls this bird a symbol of innocence that stays free of the corrupting influences of the earth. If Val's purity is to be taken as a state of innocence before the corrupting experience of sex and if his commitment to the commercial world is another association with the dark forces, then Val Xavier is surely headed for trouble. For all the introduction of involved symbolism, the emphasis, however, is heavily placed on erotic scenes.

The relationship between Val and Lady affords Williams several opportunities to exemplify his familiar theories of human relationships. His touch theory is frequently illustrated: that love and understanding depend upon physical contact. Every character for whom Williams has any sympathy at all is lonesome. He has created a long, long procession of very lonely people. Val Xavier might be said to speak for them all: "Nobody ever gets to know *no body!* We're all of us sentenced to solitary confinement inside our own skins, for life! You understand me, Lady?—I'm tellin' you it's the truth, we got to face it, we're under a life-long sentence to solitary confinement inside our own lonely skins for as long as we live on this earth!" When Lady expresses the belief that the answer to loneliness is love, Val answers that it is a delusion that has fooled many people.

But he is soon taken in. When Lady suddenly sets up the sleeping arrangements in the little alcove and accuses him of robbing her cashbox, he makes a number of futile efforts to escape; and the mutual recriminations are ugly. Val's descriptions of Lady are nasty; he calls her an aging, unsatisfied woman who hired a stranger for a clerk by day but wanted him for a lover at night without paying extra. Invectives failing her, she strikes with her fists; but, when he turns to leave, she cries out in Tennessee Williams' double-sized, capital letters for him not to leave, that she needs him to go on living. Her uninhibited cries of passion are heightened by the appropriate mood music. Then Lady, a woman between thirty-five and forty-five, but described like a child in a trance, emotionally torn and hesitant, walks toward the alcove with the bedding in her arms. Encouraged by Val's whispered tenderness, she gathers strength to enter. He looks from his guitar to her—the old phallic guitar?—and the inevitable curtain suggests the bedroom scene.

Another aspect of the poetic spirit is represented by Vee Talbott, wife of an ignorant and brutal sheriff, who seeks release in her painting. A religious fanatic, she seems to work at her best in a frenzy, as when she painted the ascent of the Holy Ghost after a "vision." There is a curious, seemingly personal touch, in the playwright's account of the way in which she works: "I been painting all day, finished a picture in a ten-hour stretch, just stopped a few minutes fo' coffee and went back to it again while I had a clear vision. I think I got it this time. But I'm so exhausted I could drop in my tracks. There's nothing more exhausting than that kind of work on earth, it's not so much that it tires your body out, but it leaves you drained inside. Y'know what I mean? Inside? Like you was burned out by something? Well! Still!—You feel you've accomplished something when you're through with it, sometimes you feel—*elevated!*" She says of another painting, a Church of the Resurrection with a red steeple, "I just, just *felt* it that way! I paint a thing how I feel it instead of always the way it actually is. Appearances are misleading, nothing is what it looks like to the eyes. You got to have—*vision*—to see!"

These four main protagonists present interesting questions which should have been given fuller development. Unfortunately there are so many distractions and so much sensationalism that the stronger parts of the play are underdeveloped and obscured. Williams' inability to carry through a dramatic theme can be illustrated by the hysterical ending of the play—again, "something wild." Lady, as mercenary as her neighbors, corrupted obviously by her environment, for years a barren wife, ecstatically announces her pregnancy. The playwright gave this same final announcement to his heroines in *The Rose Tattoo* and in *Cat on a Hot Tin Roof*. Val Xavier, the life bringer, a symbol of wild and pure freedom, but trapped by love—the various sequences make this very hard to believe— wilts in reverence before this woman. But Jabe, the Pluto and the injured husband, in spite of severe hemorrhaging, described as a symbol of death as well as evil, is still able to hold a gun; he plugs Lady twice with a "hah!" and a curse; he threatens to burn her as he burned her father; his gleeful announcement tardily confirms Lady's suspicions.

Accompanied by a mob with blow torches, Sheriff Talbott—in drunken suspicion over the vagrant's attention to his wife, Vee, and also in response to Jabe's false charges of murder—drags Val away. There are terrible cries of anguish offstage. The Conjure Man returns shortly with the snakeskin jacket; Carol Cutrere drops from nowhere to deliver the final tribute to freedom: "Wild things leave skins behind them, they leave clean skins and teeth and white bones behind them, and these are tokens passed from one to another, so that the fugitive kind can always follow their kind. . . ." And then the cry of the tortured Val is repeated more terribly than before.

John Gassner, who called this play "one of the most chaotic contemporary works of genius," remarked that it is the violence rather than the meaning that remains uppermost. In a plot made up of a "multiplication of griefs, evils, and horrors," there are several levels of meaning; but "the snarled symbolism of the play" obscures both character and environment. "Myth is scrambled in the play when two legends about Orpheus become entangled in the symbolism of the work. The plot runs parallel to one legend of the bard's descent into the underworld; the other analogy is that of his being torn to pieces by the Bacchantes driven to frenzy by orgiastic religion." Translated in terms of this particular southern town and in those of a hero with so many different symbols blended together—"Val the poet, Val the idealized male pursued to his destruction by sex-hungry women, and Val the noble savage of Rousseauist romanticism" probably by way of D. H. Lawrence—the play attempts too much. The work is further complicated by Williams' presentation of two of his major themes conjointly: "the tragic isolation of the artist in the hell of modern society and the crucifixion of the pure male on the cross of sexuality." Though he considered the play a failure, Gassner recognized its value in relation to other contemporary attempts.

Donald Justice said of the play:

This is a key work to the understanding of Williams. A revision of his first important play, *Battle of Angels*, it sketches in the crude outlines of virtually undisguised fantasy a conflict basic to his imagination, one which received its best-known treatment in the conflict between the "poetic" Blanche and the "real" Stanley in *Streetcar*. There, too, the "poetic" was destroyed by the "real"; but a certain ambivalence was developing. No longer was the conflict simply between good and bad; Stanley, in spite of everything, remained not altogether unsympathetic. Sexual energy in *Orpheus* had been associated almost exclusively with the "poetic," but in *Streetcar*, as the "real" takes over some of this energy, Williams' sympathy goes along with it and, evidently, ours as well. The better balance of forces makes for a better play.

Henry Popkin gave some idea of the involved and confused pretensions and the garbled symbolism of the play when he described it in terms of the Christian references upon which it is built and the changes in those references from *Battle of Angels*. The last act has shifted from Good Friday to Holy Saturday; Myra, or Mary, has become Lady, or "Our Lady" a characteristic Williams' habit of imposing upon a universal religious figure his own fantasy—making the Mother of God a sex-starved, mercenary store keeper; Val becomes Orpheus and is associated with Christ, both of whom descend to hell, but Val-Orpheus is destroyed; Val's guitar, which is close enough to Orpheus' lyre, has a phallic significance, for the jealous, sexually unsuccessful townsmen approach Val with knives drawn as if to castrate him; Jabe, described as "like the very Prince of Darkness," destroys the lovers; a kind of symbolic resurrection seems to be implied by the shafts of light which play upon the scene; the final note of the play combines two familiar Williams themes—sexuality and religion—and a tribute to the snakeskin jacket is accompanied by a "religious chant."

Tennessee Williams renamed this play *The Fugitive Kind* for the movie version. In doing so he picked up a phrase used by decadent or aristocratic Sandra Whiteside of *Battle of Angels* as she describes herself and Val and tries to coax Val away from a commonplace life.

FOR DISCUSSION:

1. Does the blend of mythic patterns drawn from the Orpheus and Christ stories cited by Popkin in the essay weaken or strengthen the play. Why?

2. What are Williams's attitudes toward human relationships? How does Orpheus Descending reveal those views?

3. This essay describes the theme of Williams' play as a portrayal of "the poet in an unfriendly world." Is it really necessary for Williams's purpose that Val be a "poet"? Or is this merely a weak attempt to relate the play to the Orpheus myth? In what particular ways is the world unfriendly to Val? Is he unfriendly to the world?

4. What is meant by the statement that Orpheus Descending is a failure because it "attempts too much"?

King Solomon*

ISAAC ROSENFELD

WITH HIS WOMEN

Every year, a certain number of girls. They come to him, lie down beside him, place their hands on his breast and offer to become his slaves.

This goes on all the time. "I will be your slave," say the girls, and no more need be said. But Solomon's men, his counselors, can't bear it—what is this power of his? Some maintain it is no power at all, he is merely the King. Oh yes, admit the rest, his being the King has something to do with it —but there have been other kings, so it can't be that. Nor is it anything else. Consider how unprepossessing he is, what a poor impression he makes—why, most of the counselors are taller, handsomer, and leaner than he. To be sure, he has an excellent voice. But his voice comes through best on the telephone, and he has an unlisted number which no one would give out. Certainly not, say the men. Still the girls keep coming, and they lie down beside him with their hands on his breast.

It is not enough to say the counselors are jealous. After all, there is something strange here, the like of it has not been seen. But who shall explain the King?

Solomon himself makes no comment, he does not speak of his personal affairs. He may drop a hint or two, but these hints are contradictory and vague, and he drops them only for his own amusement; perhaps he, too, doesn't know. Every few years he publishes a collection of his sayings, most of which he has never said, but the sayings have little to do with the case, and their melancholy tone is held to be an affectation. The wisest counselors pay no attention to his words. If anything is to be learned, the wise men say, it had better be sought among his girls.

But the girls also say nothing. The rejected go away in tears—in which case one cannot expect them to speak coherently or with regard for truth; or they are determined yet to win his love—and again they will tell lies. As for the women he accepts, they are useless. Almost at once they become so much like Solomon, adopting his mannerisms of gesture and speech and sharing his views of things, that they say only what he would say—and Solomon does not speak his heart.

So it has become the custom in the court to study Solomon's women in their work; perhaps the manner in which they serve him will make it clear. The counselors watch over the harem, each chooses a woman to follow about the palace, over the grounds and through the town. One woman . . . there she goes! . . . sets out early in the morning with a basket, trailed by a counselor. She makes her way to the largest and most crowded kosher market, where she will stand in line for hours, haggling and hefting, crying highway robbery! And what delicacies does she buy? Surely pickles and spices, the rarest and the best. . . . Not necessarily, it may even be noodles. So who is the wiser? And as for the obvious conclusion—that Solomon sets store by economy—this has long since been drawn. He even lunches on left-overs.

Others clean his shoes, open and sort the mail, tend the garden and the vineyards, keep his instruments polished and in tune. A few go to the well for water— a curious assignment, as the palace has had hot and cold running water for years. Perhaps he sends them to the well on purpose, to confuse the counselors. But if this occupation serves only to deceive, why not all the rest? This may well be the case.

---

* Reprinted by permission of Mrs. Isaac Rosenfeld. Originally published in *Harper's Magazine*, July 1956.

King Solomon has a staff of regular servants, quite capable of looking after his needs.

Therefore nothing has been learned. The counselors are always confronted by the same questions at nightfall, when their need to know the King is greatest. Much of the time, he sits quietly with a girl or two, pasting stamps in an album, while they massage his scalp. On festive nights, the counselors note the revelry and participate, when invited, in the dancing and carousing. Not that this enchants them; many counselors complain that the King has no taste in entertainment, that he relies, for instance, too heavily on tambourines, which he has his dancing girls flutter in their hands till the jingling gives one a headache; that much the same or better amusements can be had in the cabarets about the town which—so much for Solomon's originality—have been the source of many a spectacle of the King's court—and they even have newspaper clippings to prove the point. Nevertheless, they succumb to the King's merrymaking, and even if it makes them puke with disdain, still they lose the essential detachment. And then at the hour when the King retires to his chamber with his chosen love, all is lost, the counselors are defeated and go disgruntled to their own quarters, to lie awake or dream enviously through the night.

All the same a pertinacious lot. What stratagems, disguising themselves as eunuchs or hiding in vases or behind the furniture to learn what goes on at night! Here, too, they have been disappointed. Though Solomon burns soft lights beside his couch, no one has witnessed anything—or at least has ever reported what he saw. At the last moment the hidden counselors have shut their eyes or turned away; no one has dared look at the King's nakedness, dared to witness his love. Still, sounds have been heard floating in deep summer air over the garden and the lily pond, mingling with the voices of frogs—but the intrusion has been its own punishment, maddening those who have overheard the King and driving them wild with lust or despair. Sooner or later, the counselors have been compelled to stopper their ears. Now when these sounds issue from the King's apartments, the counselors take up instruments and play, softly but in concert, to hide his sounds within their own.

None has seen the King's nakedness; yet all have seen him in shirt sleeves or suspenders, paunchy, loose-jowled, in need of a trim. Often in the heat of the day he appears bareheaded, and all have looked upon his baldness; sometimes he comes forth in his bare feet, and the men have observed bunions and corns. When he appears in this fashion with, say, a cigar in his mouth and circles under his eyes; his armpits showing yellowish and hairy over the arm holes of his undershirt; his wrinkles deep and his skin slack; a wallet protruding from one hip pocket and a kerchief from the other—at such moments, whether he be concerned with issues of government or merely the condition of the plumbing, he does show himself in human nakedness after all, he is much like any man, he even resembles a policeman on his day off or a small-time gambler. And sometimes, unexpectedly, he summons the cabinet to a game of pinochle—then all are aware he has again transcended them.

Of late, King Solomon has turned his attention to the young. He has organized bicycle races for children, entertained them with magicians, taken them on picnics and excursions to the zoo. He loves to sit on a shady bench with a youngster on either knee, a boy and a girl, about four or five in age. They pull at his beard, tug at his ears, and finger his spectacles till he can no longer see through the smudges. Sometimes, the children are his own, more often not. It makes no difference, the King has many sons and daughters. He tells stories, not nearly so amusing as they should be, old stories which the children grew tired of in the nursery, or poor inventions, rather pointless on the whole. And he seldom finishes a story but begins to nod in the telling, his words thicken and stumble; eventually he falls asleep. Solomon is a disappointment to the young, seldom will children come twice to his garden. Yet for them he is truly a king: robed and gowned, golden-sandaled, wearing a crown, his hair trimmed, his beard washed, lustrous, combed, and waved, and the hairs plucked out of his nostrils.

And in this splendor, in which he seldom appears, not even for the reception of ambassadors, he loves to bounce a rubber ball and play catch with the children. He is unskilled at these games, they call him butter-fingers. A man turning sixty, an aging king.

But how clear is the expression of his eyes as he plays with the children—if only one knew what it meant! Perhaps he longs to reveal himself but does not know how; or does not know that the people await this revelation; or is unable to see beyond the children, who are bored with him. Perhaps he has nothing to reveal, and all his wisdom lies scattered from his hand: he is merely this, that, and the other, a few buildings raised, roads leveled, a number of words spoken, unthinking, on an idle afternoon. Occasionally, when he recognizes the expectation of the people, he tries to remember an appropriate saying from one of the collections he has published. Most of the time, he is unaware of all this.

The children are fretful in the garden, they wait to be delivered. They have been brought by mothers, nurses, older sisters, who stand outside the gate, looking through the palings. The mothers and nurses whisper together, their feet and eyes and hands are restless, they look at his shining beard. Later in the afternoon, when the children have been led home, perhaps one of the older girls, one of the sisters, will enter the same garden, approach the spot where the King lies resting, lie down beside him, fold her hands upon his breast, and offer to become his slave.

THE QUEEN OF SHEBA

From all over they have come, and they keep coming, though the King is now an old man. It may be owing to his age that he has grown lenient, admitting women to concubinage whom, the counselors swear, he would have sent packing in the old days. He has reached the years when anything young looks good to him. This may not be true, there may be other reasons; but the counselors have a point in saying that the standards have fallen, and they tell the story of the Queen of Sheba.

A letter came, it was the first application to be received by mail. From a foreign country, the woman signed herself The Queen. She flattered Solomon's wisdom, word of which had reached her from afar; her own ears longed to hear his discourse, her own eyes, to behold his person. An unorthodox application, written in a powerful, forward-rushing though feminine hand on strangely scented paper: the King said it reminded him of jungles. He inspected the postmark, clipped off the stamp, and pasted it on a page by itself in his album. His expression was hidden in his beard.

The woman meant it. Boxes began to arrive, plastered with travel stickers. They came on sand-choked, sneezing camels, in long trains, attended by drivers, natives of the Land of Sheba. The next day, more boxes, and again on the third. Gifts of all description, of money and goods, spangles and bangles for the entire court. It made an excellent impression, but Solomon who distributed the gifts, did not seem pleased. . . . Here the counselors pretend to know the King's mind. First of all, they say, he was annoyed at having to put up so many camels, whole droves of them—his stables were crowded, and there was a shortage of feed for his own animals. Then the camel drivers, rough and barbarous men, were inflamed by the sight of Solomon's women, and the King had to double the guard and pay overtime; this killed him. But their greatest presumption lies in saying that Solomon thought, "*Adonai Elohenu!* Is she coming to stay?" No one knows what the King thought.

He may well have been glad that the Queen was coming. No queen had ever before asked to be his slave—and she was a queen for sure, and of a rich country, think of the gifts she had sent. Solomon put his economists to work and they submitted a report: the financial structure was sound, and the country led in the production of myrrh, pepper and oil. Now to be sure, the Queen's letter made no direct application; apart from the flattery, it merely said, *coming for a visit*, as an equal might say. But the interpretation was clear. An equal would not come uninvited, only one who meant to offer herself would do so—unless the Queen was rude; but the gifts she had sent took care of that. Yet as a queen, writing from her own palace, she could not have expressed the intention, it would have been treason to her own people. Nevertheless, she had every intention: otherwise, why would she have gone to the trouble? The fact is, there was rejoicing in the palace, Solomon himself led the dancing, and he declared a holiday when the Queen of Sheba arrived.

She came in a howdah, on a camel, preceded by troops of archers and trumpeters. Solomon helped her down, and washed and anointed her feet in the courtyard. This didn't come off so well. Sheba used coloring matter on her toenails and the soles of her feet, and the coloring ran; Solomon was out of practice, he tickled her feet a few times and made her laugh. The ceremony was supposed to be a solemn one, the people took it very seriously, and they were offended by her toenails—feet were supposed to be presented dusty: as for the giggling, it was unpardonable, and the priests took offense. A poor set of omens.

Besides, Sheba was not quite so young as the autographed picture, which she had sent in advance to Solomon, would have led one to expect. Her skin was nearly black, and her black hair, which she had apparently made some effort to straighten, had gone frizzled and kinky again in the heat of the desert crossing. She wore anklets of delicate chain, gold bracelets all over her arms, and jewels in both obvious and unexpected places, so that the eye was never done seeing them; their light was kept in constant agitation by the massive rhythm of her breathing, which involved her entire body. A sense of tremendous power and authenticity emanated from her breasts. Some thought she was beautiful, others, not.

No one knows what the King thought; but he may well have felt what everyone else did who came to witness her arrival—drawn, and at the same time, stunned.

But the King is glad in his heart as he leads Sheba to the table, where he has put on a great spread for her. He is attended by his court and surrounded by his women—and how lordly are his movements as he eats meat and rinses his mouth with wine! At the same time he is uneasy in the Queen's presence—after all, this is no maiden lurking in the garden to trip up to him and fold her hands upon his breast. The meal goes well enough: Sheba asks for seconds, and seems impressed with the napkins and silverware. But suddenly, right in the middle of dessert, she turns to him and demands, in front of everyone and that all may hear, that he show her his famous wisdom. This comes as something of a shock. The implication is two-fold: that so far he has spoken commonplaces; and secondly, that he is to suffer no illusions, it was really for the sake of his wisdom that she made the difficult trip. The people turn their eyes on the King, who handles the awkward moment with skill; he clears his throat on schedule, and raises his hand in the usual gesture, admonishing silence. But nothing comes.

In the official account of the visit, which Solomon had written to order, he was supposed to have

> ... told her all questions: There was not anything ... which he told her not. And when the Queen of Sheba had seen all Solomon's wisdom, and the house that he had built, and the meat of his table and the sitting of his servants ...

etc.,

> there was no more spirit in her. And she said to the King, It was a true report that I heard in mine own land, of thy acts and thy wisdom. Howbeit, I believed not the words, until I came and mine eyes had seen it; and behold, the half was not told me: Thy wisdom and prosperity exceedeth the fame which I heard. Happy are thy men ... which stand continually before thee and that hear thy wisdom.

After which there was supposed to have been a further exchange of compliments and gifts.

Now this is not only a bit thick, it gets round the question of Solomon's wisdom. What *did* the King say, when put to it by the Queen? That there were so many feet in a mile? That all circles were round? That the number of stars visible on a clear night from a point well out of town was neither more nor less than a certain number? Did he advise her what to take for colds, give her a recipe for salad dressing, or speak of building temples and ships? Just what does a man say under the circumstances?

Certainly, he hadn't the nerve, the gall,

to repeat the abominable invention to her face of the two women who disputed motherhood of a child. She would have seen through it right away. And surely he knew this was not the time to quote his sayings; besides, he always had trouble remembering them. Then what did he say?

His economists had worked up a report on the Land of Sheba. He may have sent for a copy; more likely, he knew the essential facts cold, and spoke what came to mind: industry, agrciulture, natural resources. Of the financial structure, the public debt, the condition of business. Of the production of pepper, myrrh, and oil, especially oil. Grant him his wisdom.

Certainly, the Queen was impressed, but one need not suppose that the spirit was knocked out of her or that she said, "It was a true report that I heard in mine own land . . ." etc. Chances are, she paid no attention to his words (except to note the drift) but watched him as he spoke, taking in the cut of his beard, the fit of his clothes, and wondering, betimes, what sort of man he was. She saw his initial uncertainty give way and his confidence grow as he reached the meaty part of his delivery. And all along, she observed how he drew on the admiring glances of his girls, soaked up their adoration, as they lay open-mouthed on couches and rugs at his feet, all criticism suspended, incapacitated by love. Love ringed him round, love sustained him, he was the splendid heart of their hearts. She must have forgotten the heat and sand images of the desert crossing, she, too, lapped from all sides and borne gently afloat. . . .

So much, one may imagine. But the Queen spent a number of days or weeks, perhaps even a month or two in the King's company, and of what happened during the time of her stay, let alone the subsequent events of the first night, the official chronicles say nothing. A merciful omission, according to the counselors, who report that it went badly from the start. When the King had finished his discourse, they say the Queen felt called upon to answer. But words failed her, or she felt no need of words: she was the Queen. What she did was to lean forward and, in utter disregard of the company, take his head into her hands, gaze at him for a long time with a smile on her thick lips, and at last bestow on him a kiss, which landed somewhere in his beard.

Then she jumped onto the table, commanded music, and danced among the cups and bowls, the dishes and the crumpled napkins. The counselors were shocked, the girls smirked painfully, the servants held their breath. Nor was Sheba so slender as the autographed picture may have led one to believe. When she set her feet down, the table shook, and the carafes of wine and sweetened water swayed and threatened to topple. Solomon himself hastily cleared a way for her, pushing the dishes to one side; his hands were trembling. But she proceeded with the dance, the chain anklets tinkled, her fingers snapped, the many jewels she wore flashed wealthily. Her toes left marks on the tablecloth, as though animals had run there. And run she did, back and forth over the length of the table, bending over the counselors to tweak this one's nose and that one's ear. But always she glanced back to see if she had the King's eye.

She had it, darker than usual. To her, this meant that he was admiring her, gravely, as befits King and Queen, and her feet quickened. How stern she was! Already she felt the King's love, harder than any courtier's and so much more severe. She increased the tempo, the musicians scrambling to keep up with her, and whirled. Round and round she sped, drawing nearer the end of the table where the King sat. It was a dance in the style of her country, unknown in these parts, and she did it with the abandon of a tribesgirl, though one must assume she was conscious, in her abandonment, that it was she, the Queen, none other than Sheba, who abandoned herself to King Solomon. That was the whole point of it, the mastery of the thing. Pride did not leave her face, it entered her ecstasy and raised it in degree. Already cries, guttural, impersonal, were barking in her throat; then with a final whoop she spun round and threw herself, arms outstretched and intertwined, like one bound captive, to fall before him on the table where his meal had been.

It was a terrible mistake. The women and the counselors knew the King so much better than she, and their hearts went out in pity. The Queen had offered herself in the only way she knew—majesty, power, and reign implied—throwing herself prone with a condescending crash for the King to rise and take her. What presumption! He did not move. He sat infinitely removed, almost sorrowing over this great embarrassment. The music had stopped, there was an unbearable silence in the banquet hall. The King rumbled something deep in his beard; perhaps he was merely clearing his throat, preparatory to saying a few words (if only his wisdom did not fail him!). Some of the servants took it to mean more wine, others, more meat, still others, fingerbowls. They ran in all directions. Sheba lowered herself into her seat at the King's side. Her dark face burned. . . . Somehow the time went by, and the evening was over. Solomon led Sheba off to his chamber, as courtesy demanded. Even as she went with him, it was apparent that she still went in hope; even at the last moment. The older women wept.

Day by day, the strain mounted. Sheba was sometimes with the King, they played chess or listened to the radio, they bent their heads over maps, discussed politics, and played croquet. But there were no festivities and she did not dance again. She bore herself with dignity, but she had grown pale, and her smile, when she forgot herself, was cringing and meek. Sometimes, when she was alone, she was seen to run her finger over the table tops and the woodwork, looking for dust. She could not bear the sight of her waiting women—lest the revival of her hope, as they did her toilet, become apparent to them—and would chase them out of the room; only to call them back, and help her prepare for an audience with the King. Finally, she quarreled with some of the girls of the harem. And when this happened, Sheba knew that the day had come and she began to pack.

A pinochle game was in progress when the Queen of Sheba, unannounced and without knocking, came into the room to say she wanted a word with the King. He dismissed his counselors, but one of them swears he managed to hide behind the draperies, where he witnessed the scene.

The King was in his undershirt, smoking a cigar. He apologized for his dishevelment and offered to repair it. The affairs of state, he explained, were so trying lately, he found he worked better in dishabille. Had he been working? asked the Queen with a smile. She thought this was some sort of game, and she fingered the cards with pictures of kings and queens. Solomon, knowing that women do not play pinochle, told her the cabinet had been in extraordinary session, trying fortunes with the picture cards. The times were good, but one must look to the future, and he offered to show her how it was done.

"No, I don't want to keep you," said the Queen of Sheba, "I beg only a few words."

"Speak," said Solomon.

"Solomon, Solomon," said the Queen, "I am going away. No, don't answer me. You will say something polite and regretful, but my decision can only be a relief to you." She paused, taking on courage. "You must not allow this to be a disappointment to you, you must let me take the whole expense of our emotion upon myself. I did a foolish thing. I am a proud woman, being a Queen, and my pride carried me too far. I thought I would take pride in transcending pride, in offering myself to the King. But still that was pride, you did wisely to refuse me. Yes, you are wise, Solomon, let no one question your wisdom. Yours is the wisdom of love, which is the highest. But your love is love only of yourself; yet you share it with others by letting them love you—and this is next to the highest. Either way you look at it, Solomon is wise enough. Understand me—" She took a step forward, a dance step, as though she were again on the table top, but her eyes spoke a different meaning.

"I am not pleading with you that you love me or allow me to love you. For you are the King, your taking is your giving. But allow me to say, your power rests on despair. Yours is the power of drawing love, the like of which has not been seen. But you despair of loving with your own heart. I have come to tell the King he must not despair. Surely, Solomon who has built temples and made the desert flourish is a powerful king, and he has the power to do what the simplest slave girl or washerwoman of his harem can do—to love with his own heart. And if he does not have this power, it will come to him, he need only accept the love which it is his nature to call forth in everyone, especially in us poor women. This is his glory. Rejoice in it, O King, for you are the King!"

The counselor who hid behind the drapes said he regretted his action, to see how his King stood burdened before the Queen. His own heart filled with loving shame. Solomon looked lost, deprived of his power, as though the years in the palace and the garden had never been. He made an effort to stand dignified in his undershirt, he bore his head as though he were wearing the crown, but it was pitiful to see him.

"The Queen is wise," said he. Then he broke down, and the counselor did not hear his next words. He did hear him say that the Queen was magnificent, that she had the courage of lions and tigers ... but by now his head was lowered. Suddenly, he clasped the Queen to his breast in an embrace of farewell, and the Queen smiled and stroked his curly beard. They did not immediately take leave of each other, but went on to speak of other matters. Before the Queen of Sheba left the country, King Solomon had leased her oil lands for ninety-nine years.

But on the day of her departure, he stood bareheaded in the crowded courtyard to watch her set out, with her trumpeters and archers mounted on supercilious camels. He extended his hand to help her up, and she, with her free hand, chucked him under the chin. Then she leaned out of the howdah to cry, "Long live the King!" King Solomon stood with bowed head to receive the ovation. Now more than ever they yearned for him.

When Sheba moved off, at the head of the procession, Solomon led the people onto the roof, to watch the camels file across the sand. He stood till evening fell, and the rump of the last plodding animal had twitched out of sight beyond the sand hills. Then he averted his face and wept silently lest the people see their King's tears.

WITH HIS FATHERS

So the counselors have a point when they say the standards have fallen. Once the Queen of Sheba herself was unable to make it; and now, look. But no wonder, her like will not come again, and besides, Solomon is old. He has been running the country forty years, and has begun to speak of retiring; but the people know he will never retire, and so they whisper, it is time for the King to die.

How does this strike him? To look at him—his beard is white, his spotted hands shake, he walks bent, his eyes are rheumy and dim—to look at him one would suppose he dwells on the thought of death. But he is no better known now than he was in his prime. The only certainty is that the King is old.

But what follows from this, how does it reveal him? Or this?—that he had an attack of pleurisy not long ago, and since then his side has been taped. And what does it mean to say that he now has more women than ever cluttering up the palace, one thousand in all, including seven hundred wives? (It is merely that the standards have fallen?) It was necessary to tear down the harem (while the women, to everyone's displeasure, were quartered in the town) and raise a new building, so large it has taken up ground formerly allotted to the garden. They are a great source of trouble to him, these women, and the counselors complain —that's where all the money is going, to support the harem. Harem? Why, it's a whole population, the country will be ruined! And the priests complain, every week they send fresh ultimatums, objecting to the fact that so many of Solomon's girls are heathen; they have even accused him of idolatry and threatened him with loss of the Kingdom and the wrath of God. And the people grumble, it's a shame, when they find his women loitering in beauty shops or quarrelling right out in the open, as they have begun to do, in the very streets. But Solomon ignores the discontent and goes on collecting women as he once collected stamps.

Why? Or what does this mean?—that he seldom takes the trouble to interview applicants, but establishes a policy for several months, during which time the rule is, no vacancies. Then he will change the rule and take on newcomers by the dozen, most of whom he does not even see, the work being done by the counselors. And how complicated the work has become, compared with the old days, when all that was necessary was for a girl to lie beside the King with her hands upon his breast. Now there are forms to fill out and letters of recommendation to obtain, several interviews and a medical examination to go through, and even then the girls must wait until their references have been checked. The filing cabinets have mounted to the ceiling. What sense does it make?

And above all in view of the following? The counselors vouch for it, they swear they have seen the proof. That King Solomon now takes to bed, not with a virgin, as his father, David, did in his old age, or even with a dancing girl, but with a hot water bottle. If this report is true, then doesn't something follow? For this is the extreme, between life and death, where all thoughts meet; an extreme, not a mean; and a wrong guess is impossible, everything is true, as at the topmost point, where all direction is down. It follows that he warms his hands on the water bottle, presses it to his cheek, passes it down along his belly.

Now when he thinks of his pride, he of all men must wonder: what was the glory of the King? Who bestowed the power, and what did it consist in? When he had it, he did not consider, and now it is gone. Passing the rubber bottle down to his feet and digging with his toes for warmth, he sees he did everything possible in his life, and left no possibility untouched, of manhood, statesmanship, love. What else can a man do? There is no answer. Except to say, he was in God's grace then? And now no longer? Or is he still in a state of grace, witness the water bottle at his feet? And perhaps he is only being tried, and may look forward to even greater rewards? Such are the advantages of being a believer. If he were one, he would know—at least believe that he knew. But a man who knows only that once love was with him, which now is no more—what does he know, what shall he believe, old, exhausted, shivering alone in bed at night with a hot water bottle, when all's quiet in the palace? And if all's not quiet, that's no longer his concern.

No, if there were any rewards, he'd settle for a good night's sleep. But sleep does not come. He hears strange noises in the apartment, scratching. . . . Mice? He must remember to speak to the caretakers. . . . At last he drowses off, to sleep a while. And if he does not sleep? Or later, when he wakes, and it is still the same night? . . . Does he think of the Queen of Sheba and wonder, whom is she visiting now? Does he remember how she danced upon the table? Or the song he wrote soon after her departure, with her words still fresh in his mind, when he resolved to pour out his love for her, but from the very first line poured out, instead, her love for him? *Let him kiss me with the kisses of his mouth, for thy love is better than wine.* It has been years since he heard from her. . . .

Meanwhile, the bottle has grown cold. Shall he ring for another? He shifts the bottle, kneads it between his knees. *And be thou like a young hart upon the mountains of spices.* Look forward, look back, to darkness, at the light, both ways blind. He raises the bottle to his breast; it does not warm him. He gropes for the cord, and while his hand reaches, he thinks, as he has thought many times, there is a time and a season for everything, a time to be born and a time to die. Is it time now? They will lay him out, washed, anointed, shrouded. They will fold his arms across his chest, with the palms turned in, completing the figure. Now his own hands will lie pressed to his breast, and he will sleep with his fathers.

FOR DISCUSSION:

1. Is Rosenfeld's portrayal of Solomon intended to be a depiction of the archetypal leader?

2. Is there any significance to the fact that the author has selected a religious leader rather than a political one as the protagonist of his story?

3. What is the effect of the anachronistic details, e.g., the radio, economic reports, oil rights, etc?

4. Solomon is shown as a very human leader with the inadequacies and shortcomings that humanity implies. Does Rosenfeld suggest why nations tend to ignore the weaknesses of their leaders and exaggerate their mental and physical powers?

5. What role does Sheba play in the story? The counselors?

Young Goodman Brown

NATHANIEL HAWTHORNE

Young Goodman Brown came forth at sunset into the street at Salem village; but put his head back, after crossing the threshold, to exchange a parting kiss with his young wife. And Faith, as the wife was aptly named, thrust her own pretty head into the street, letting the wind play with the pink ribbons of her cap while she called to Goodman Brown.

"Dearest heart," whispered she, softly and rather sadly, when her lips were close to his ear, "prithee put off your journey until sunrise and sleep in your own bed to-night. A lone woman is troubled with such dreams and such thoughts that she's afeard of herself sometimes. Pray tarry with me this night, dear husband, of all nights in the year."

"My love and my Faith," replied young Goodman Brown, "of all nights in the year, this one night must I tarry away from thee. My journey, as thou callest it, forth and back again, must needs be done 'twixt now and sunrise. What, my sweet, pretty wife, dost thou doubt me already, and we but three months married?"

"Then God bless you!" said Faith, with the pink ribbons; "and may you find all well when you come back."

"Amen!" cried Goodman Brown. "Say thy prayers, dear Faith, and go to bed at dusk, and no harm will come to thee."

So they parted; and the young man pursued his way until, being about to turn the corner by the meeting-house, he looked back and saw the head of Faith still peeping after him with a melancholy air, in spite of her pink ribbons.

"Poor little Faith!" thought he, for his heart smote him. "What a wretch am I to leave her on such an errand! She talks of dreams, too. Methought as she spoke there was trouble in her face, as if a dream had warned her what work is to be done to-night. But no, no; 't would kill her to think it. Well, she's a blessed angel on earth; and after this one night I'll cling to her skirts and follow her to heaven."

With this excellent resolve for the future, Goodman Brown felt himself justified in making more haste on his present evil purpose. He had taken a dreary road, darkened by all the gloomiest trees of the forest, which barely stood aside to let the narrow path creep through, and closed immediately behind. It was all as lonely as could be; and there is this peculiarity in such a solitude, that the traveller knows not who may be concealed by the innumerable trunks and the thick boughs overhead; so that with lonely footsteps he may yet be passing through an unseen multitude.

"There may be a devilish Indian behind every tree," said Goodman Brown to himself; and he glanced fearfully behind him as he added, "What if the devil himself should be at my very elbow!"

His head being turned back, he passed a crook of the road, and, looking forward again, beheld the figure of a man, in grave and decent attire, seated at the foot of an old tree. He arose at Goodman Brown's approach and walked onward side by side with him.

"You are late, Goodman Brown," said he. "The clock of the Old South was striking as I came through Boston, and that is full fifteen minutes agone."

"Faith kept me back a while," replied the young man, with a tremor in his voice, caused by the sudden appearance of his companion, though not wholly unexpected.

It was now deep dusk in the forest, and deepest in that part of it where these two were journeying. As nearly as could be discerned, the second traveller was about fifty years old, apparently in the same rank of life as Goodman Brown, and bearing a considerable resemblance to him, though perhaps more in expression than features.

Still they might have been taken for father and son. And yet, though the elder person was as simply clad as the younger, and as simple in manner too, he had an indescribable air of one who knew the world, and who would not have felt abashed at the governor's dinner table or in King William's court, were it possible that his affairs should call him thither. But the only thing about him that could be fixed upon as remarkable was his staff, which bore the likeness of a great black snake, so curiously wrought that it might almost be seen to twist and wriggle itself like a living serpent. This, of course, must have been an ocular deception, assisted by the uncertain light.

"Come, Goodman Brown," cried his fellow-traveller, "this is a dull pace for the beginning of a journey. Take my staff, if you are so soon weary."

"Friend," said the other, exchanging his slow pace for a full stop, "having kept covenant by meeting thee here, it is my purpose now to return whence I came. I have scruples touching the matter thou wot'st of."

"Sayest thou so?" replied he of the serpent, smiling apart. "Let us walk on, nevertheless, reasoning as we go; and if I convince thee not thou shalt turn back. We are but a little way in the forest yet."

"Too far! too far!" exclaimed the goodman, unconsciously resuming his walk. "My father never went into the woods on such an errand, nor his father before him. We have been a race of honest men and good Christians since the days of the martyrs; and shall I be the first of the name of Brown that ever took this path and kept"—

"Such company, thou wouldst say," observed the elder person, interpreting his pause. "Well said, Goodman Brown! I have been as well acquainted with your family as with ever a one among the Puritans; and that's no trifle to say. I helped your grandfather, the constable, when he lashed the Quaker woman so smartly through the streets of Salem; and it was I that brought your father a pitch-pine knot, kindled at my own hearth, to set fire to an Indian village, in King Philip's war. They were my good friends, both; and many a pleasant walk have we had along this path, and returned merrily after midnight. I would fain be friends with you for their sake."

"If it be as thou sayest," replied Goodman Brown, "I marvel they never spoke of these matters; or, verily, I marvel not, seeing that the least rumor of the sort would have driven them from New England. We are a people of prayer, and good works to boot, and abide no such wickedness."

"Wickedness or not," said the traveller with the twisted staff, "I have a very general acquaintance here in New England. The deacons of many a church have drunk the communion wine with me; the selectmen of divers towns make me their chairman; and a majority of the Great and General Court are firm supporters of my interest. The governor and I, too—But these are state secrets."

"Can this be so?" cried Goodman Brown, with a stare of amazement at his undisturbed companion. "Howbeit, I have nothing to do with the governor and council; they have their own ways, and are no rule for a simple husbandman like me. But, were I to go on with thee, how should I meet the eye of that good old man, our minister, at Salem village? Oh, his voice would make me tremble both Sabbath day and lecture day."

Thus far the elder traveller had listened with due gravity; but now burst into a fit of irrepressible mirth, shaking himself so violently that his snake-like staff actually seemed to wriggle in sympathy.

"Ha! ha! ha!" shouted he again and again; then composing himself, "Well, go on, Goodman Brown, go on; but, prithee, don't kill me with laughing."

"Well, then, to end the matter at once," said Goodman Brown, considerably nettled, "there is my wife, Faith. It would break her dear little heart; and I'd rather break my own."

"Nay, if that be the case," answered the other, "e'en go thy ways, Goodman Brown. I would not for twenty old women like the one hobbling before us that Faith should come to any harm."

As he spoke he pointed his staff at a female figure on the path, in whom Goodman Brown recognized a very pious and exemplary dame, who had taught him his catechism in youth, and was still his moral and spiritual adviser, jointly with the minister and Deacon Gookin.

"A marvel, truly, that Goody Cloyse should be so far in the wilderness at nightfall," said he. "But with your leave, friend,

I shall take a cut through the woods until we have left this Christian woman behind. Being a stranger to you, she might ask whom I was consorting with and whither I was going."

"Be it so," said his fellow-traveller. "Betake you to the woods, and let me keep the path."

Accordingly the young man turned aside, but took care to watch his companion, who advanced softly along the road until he had come within a staff's length of the old dame. She, meanwhile, was making the best of her way, with singular speed for so aged a woman, and mumbling some indistinct words—a prayer, doubtless—as she went. The traveller put forth his staff and touched her withered neck with what seemed the serpent's tail.

"The devil!" screamed the pious old lady.

"Then Goody Cloyse knows her old friend?" observed the traveller, confronting her and leaning on his writhing stick.

"Ah, forsooth, and is it your worship indeed?" cried the good dame. "Yea, truly is it, and in the very image of my old gossip, Goodman Brown, the grandfather of the silly fellow that now is. But—would your worship believe it?—my broomstick hath strangely disappeared, stolen, as I suspect, by that unhanged witch, Goody Cory, and that, too, when I was all anointed with the juice of smallage, and cinquefoil, and wolf's bane"—

"Mingled with fine wheat and the fat of a new-born babe," said the shape of old Goodman Brown.

"Ah, your worship knows the recipe," cried the old lady, cackling aloud. "So, as I was saying, being all ready for the meeting, and no horse to ride on, I made up my mind to foot it; for they tell me there is a nice young man to be taken into communion to-night. But now your good worship will lend me your arm, and we shall be there in a twinkling."

"That can hardly be," answered her friend. "I may not spare you my arm, Goody Cloyse; but here is my staff, if you will."

So saying, he threw it down at her feet, where, perhaps, it assumed life, being one of the rods which its owner had formerly lent to the Egyptian magi. Of this fact, however, Goodman Brown could not take cognizance. He had cast up his eyes in astonishment, and, looking down again, beheld neither Goody Cloyse nor the serpentine staff, but his fellow-traveller alone, who waited for him as calmly as if nothing had happened.

"That old woman taught me my catechism," said the young man; and there was a world of meaning in this simple comment.

They continued to walk onward, while the elder traveller exhorted his companion to make good speed and persevere in the path, discoursing so aptly that his arguments seemed rather to spring up in the bosom of his auditor than to be suggested by himself. As they went, he plucked a branch of maple to serve for a walking stick, and began to strip it of the twigs and little boughs, which were wet with evening dew. The moment his fingers touched them they became strangely withered and dried up as with a week's sunshine. Thus the pair proceeded, at a good free pace, until suddenly, in a gloomy hollow of the road, Goodman Brown sat himself down on the stump of a tree and refused to go any farther.

"Friend," said he, stubbornly, "my mind is made up. Not another step will I budge on this errand. What if a wretched old woman do choose to go to the devil when I thought she was going to heaven: is that any reason why I should quit my dear Faith and go after her?"

"You will think better of this by and by," said his acquaintance, composedly. "Sit here and rest yourself a while; and when you feel like moving again, there is my staff to help you along."

Without more words, he threw his companion the maple stick, and was as speedily out of sight as if he had vanished into the deepening gloom. The young man sat a few moments by the roadside, applauding himself greatly, and thinking with how clear a conscience he should meet the minister in his morning walk, nor shrink from the eye of good old Deacon Gookin. And what calm sleep would be his that very night, which was to have been spent so wickedly, but so purely and sweetly now, in the arms of Faith! Amidst these pleasant and praiseworthy meditations, Goodman Brown heard the tramp of horses along the road, and deemed it advisable to conceal himself within the verge of the forest, conscious of the guilty purpose that had brought him thither, though now so happily turned from it.

On came the hoof tramps and the voices of the riders, two grave old voices, conversing soberly as they drew near. These mingled sounds appeared to pass along the road, within a few yards of the young man's hiding-place; but, owing doubtless to the depth of the gloom at that particular spot, neither the travellers nor their steeds were visible. Though their figures brushed the small boughs by the wayside, it could not be seen that they intercepted, even for a moment, the faint gleam from the strip of bright sky athwart which they must have passed. Goodman Brown alternately crouched and stood on tiptoe, pulling aside the branches and thrusting forth his head as far as he durst without discerning so much as a shadow. It vexed him the more, because he could have sworn, were such a thing possible, that he recognized the voices of the minister and Deacon Gookin, jogging along quietly, as they were wont to do, when bound to some ordination or ecclesiastical council. While yet within hearing, one of the riders stopped to pluck a switch.

"Of the two, reverend sir," said the voice like the deacon's, "I had rather miss an ordination dinner than to-night's meeting. They tell me that some of our community are to be here from Falmouth and beyond, and others from Connecticut and Rhode Island, besides several of the Indian pow-wows, who, after their fashion, know almost as much deviltry as the best of us. Moreover, there is a goodly young woman to be taken into communion."

"Mighty well, Deacon Gookin!" replied the solemn old tones of the minister. "Spur up, or we shall be late. Nothing can be done, you know, until I get on the ground."

The hoofs clattered again; and the voices, talking so strangely in the empty air, passed on through the forest, where no church had ever been gathered or solitary Christian prayed. Whither, then, could these holy men be journeying so deep into the heathen wilderness? Young Goodman Brown caught hold of a tree for support, being ready to sink down on the ground, faint and overburdened with the heavy sickness of his heart. He looked up to the sky, doubting whether there really was a heaven above him. Yet there was the blue arch, and the stars brightening in it.

"With heaven above and Faith below, I will yet stand firm against the devil!" cried Goodman Brown.

While he still gazed upward into the deep arch of the firmament and had lifted his hands to pray, a cloud, though no wind was stirring, hurried across the zenith and hid the brightening stars. The blue sky was still visible, except directly overhead, where this black mass of cloud was sweeping swiftly northward. Aloft in the air, as if from the depths of the cloud, came a confused and doubtful sound of voices. Once the listener fancied that he could distinguish the accents of towns-people of his own, men and women, both pious and ungodly, many of whom he had met at the communion table, and had seen others rioting at the tavern. The next moment, so indistinct were the sounds, he doubted whether he had heard aught but the murmur of the old forest, whispering without a wind. Then came a stronger swell of those familiar tones, heard daily in the sunshine at Salem village, but never until now from a cloud of night. There was one voice, of a young woman, uttering lamentations, yet with an uncertain sorrow, and entreating for some favor, which, perhaps, it would grieve her to obtain; and all the unseen multitude, both saints and sinners, seemed to encourage her onward.

"Faith!" shouted Goodman Brown, in a voice of agony and desperation; and the echoes of the forest mocked him, crying, "Faith! Faith!" as if bewildered wretches were seeking her all through the wilderness.

The cry of grief, rage, and terror was yet piercing the night, when the unhappy husband held his breath for a response. There was a scream, drowned immediately in a louder murmur of voices, fading into far-off laughter, as the dark cloud swept away, leaving the clear and silent sky above Goodman Brown. But something fluttered lightly down through the air and caught on the branch of a tree. The young man seized it, and beheld a pink ribbon.

"My Faith is gone!" cried he, after one stupefied moment. "There is no good on earth; and sin is but a name. Come, devil; for to thee is this world given."

And, maddened with despair, so that he

laughed loud and long, did Goodman Brown grasp his staff and set forth again, at such a rate that he seemed to fly along the forest path rather than to walk or run. The road grew wilder and drearier and more faintly traced, and vanished at length, leaving him in the heart of the dark wilderness, still rushing onward with the instinct that guides mortal man to evil. The whole forest was peopled with frightful sounds—the creaking of the trees, the howling of wild beasts, and the yell of Indians; while sometimes the wind tolled like a distant church bell, and sometimes gave a broad roar around the traveller, as if all Nature were laughing him to scorn. But he was himself the chief horror of the scene, and shrank not from its other horrors.

"Ha! ha! ha!" roared Goodman Brown when the wind laughed at him. "Let us hear which will laugh loudest. Think not to frighten me with your deviltry. Come witch, come wizard, come Indian powwow, come devil himself, and here comes Goodman Brown. You may as well hear him as he fear you."

In truth, all through the haunted forest there could be nothing more frightful than the figure of Goodman Brown. On he flew among the black pines, brandishing his staff with frenzied gestures, now giving vent to an inspiration of horrid blasphemy, and now shouting forth such laughter as set all the echoes of the forest laughing like demons around him. The fiend in his own shape is less hideous than when he rages in the breast of man. Thus sped the demoniac on his course, until, quivering among the trees, he saw a red light before him, as when the felled trunks and branches of a clearing have been set on fire, and throw up their lurid blaze against the sky, at the hour of midnight. He paused, in a lull of the tempest that had driven him onward, and heard the swell of what seemed a hymn, rolling solemnly from a distance with the weight of many voices. He knew the tune; it was a familiar one in the choir of the village meeting-house. The verse died heavily away, and was lengthened by a chorus, not of human voices, but of all the sounds of the benighted wilderness pealing in awful harmony together. Goodman Brown cried out, and his cry was lost to his own ear by its unison with the cry of the desert.

In the interval of silence he stole forward until the light glared full upon his eyes. At one extremity of an open space, hemmed in by the dark wall of the forest, arose a rock, bearing some rude, natural resemblance either to an altar or a pulpit, and surrounded by four blazing pines, their tops aflame, their stems untouched, like candles at an evening meeting. The mass of foliage that had overgrown the summit of the rock was all on fire, blazing high into the night and fitfully illuminating the whole field. Each pendent twig and leafy festoon was in a blaze. As the red light arose and fell, a numerous congregation alternately shone forth, then disappeared in shadow, and again grew, as it were, out of the darkness, peopling the heart of the solitary woods at once.

"A grave and dark-clad company," quoth Goodman Brown.

In truth they were such. Among them, quivering to and fro between gloom and splendor, appeared faces that would be seen next day at the council board of the province, and others which, Sabbath after Sabbath, looked devoutly heavenward, and benignantly over the crowded pews, from the holiest pulpits in the land. Some affirm that the lady of the governor was there. At least there were high dames well known to her, and wives of honored husbands, and widows, a great multitude, and ancient maidens, all of excellent repute, and fair young girls, who trembled lest their mothers should espy them. Either the sudden gleams of light flashing over the obscure field bedazzled Goodman Brown, or he recognized a score of the church members of Salem village famous for their special sanctity. Good old Deacon Gookin had arrived, and waited at the skirts of that venerable saint, his revered pastor. But, irreverently consorting with these grave, reputable, and pious people, these elders of the church, these chaste dames and dewy virgins, there were men of dissolute lives and women of spotted fame, wretches given over to all mean and filthy vice, and suspected even of horrid crimes. It was strange to see that the good shrank not from the wicked, nor were the sinners abashed by the saints. Scattered also among their pale-faced enemies were the Indian priests, or powwows, who had often scared their native forest with more hideous incantations than any known to English witchcraft.

"But where is Faith?" thought Goodman Brown; and, as hope came into his heart, he trembled.

Another verse of the hymn arose, a slow and mournful strain, such as the pious love, but joined to words which expressed all that our nature can conceive of sin, and darkly hinted at far more. Unfathomable to mere mortals is the lore of fiends. Verse after verse was sung; and still the chorus of the desert swelled between like the deepest tone of a mighty organ; and with the final peal of that dreadful anthem there came a sound, as if the roaring wind, the rushing streams, the howling beasts, and every other voice of the unconcerted wilderness were mingling and according with the voice of guilty man in homage to the prince of all. The four blazing pines threw up a loftier flame, and obscurely discovered shapes and visages of horror on the smoke wreaths above the impious assembly. At the same moment the fire on the rock shot redly forth and formed a glowing arch above its base, where now appeared a figure. With reverence be it spoken, the figure bore no slight similitude, both in garb and manner, to some grave divine of the New England churches.

"Bring forth the converts!" cried a voice that echoed through the field and rolled into the forest.

At the word, Goodman Brown stepped forth from the shadow of the trees and approached the congregation, with whom he felt a loathful brotherhood by the sympathy of all that was wicked in his heart. He could have well-nigh sworn that the shape of his own dead father beckoned him to advance, looking downward from a smoke wreath, while a woman, with dim features of despair, threw out her hand to warn him back. Was it his mother? But he had no power to retreat one step, nor to resist, even in thought, when the minister and good old Deacon Gookin seized his arms and led him to the blazing rock. Thither came also the slender form of a veiled female, led between Goody Cloyse, that pious teacher of the catechism, and Martha Carrier, who had received the devil's promise to be queen of hell. A rampant hag was she. And there stood the proselytes beneath the canopy of fire.

"Welcome, my children," said the dark figure, "to the communion of your race. Ye have found thus young your nature and your destiny. My children, look behind you!"

They turned; and flashing forth, as it were, in a sheet of flame, the fiend worshippers were seen; the smile of welcome gleamed darkly on every visage.

"There," resumed the sable form, "are all whom ye have reverenced from youth. Ye deemed them holier than yourselves, and shrank from your own sin, contrasting it with their lives of righteousness and prayerful aspirations heavenward. Yet here are they all in my worshipping assembly. This night it shall be granted you to know their secret deeds: how hoary-bearded elders of the church have whispered wanton words to the young maids of their households; how many a woman, eager for widows' weeds, has given her husband a drink at bedtime and let him sleep his last sleep in her bosom; how beardless youths have made haste to inherit their fathers' wealth, and how fair damsels— blush not, sweet ones—have dug little graves in the garden, and bidden me, the sole guest, to an infant's funeral. By the sympathy of your human hearts for sin ye shall scent out all the places—whether in church, bed-chamber, street, field, or forest—where crime has been committed, and shall exult to behold the whole earth one stain of guilt, one mighty blood spot. Far more than this. It shall be yours to penetrate, in every bosom, the deep mystery of sin, the fountain of all wicked arts, and which inexhaustibly supplies more evil impulses than human power—than my power at its utmost —can make manifest in deeds. And now, my children, look upon each other."

They did so; and, by the blaze of the hell-kindled torches, the wretched man beheld his Faith, and the wife her husband, trembling before that unhallowed altar.

"Lo, there ye stand, my children," said the figure, in a deep and solemn tone, almost sad with its despairing awfulness, as if his once angelic nature could yet mourn for our miserable race. "Depending upon one another's hearts, ye had still hoped that virtue were not all a dream. Now are ye undeceived. Evil is the nature of mankind. Evil must be your only happiness. Welcome again, my children, to the communion of your race."

"Welcome," repeated the fiend worshippers, in one cry of despair and triumph.

And there they stood, the only pair, as it seemed, who were yet hesitating on the verge of wickedness in this dark world. A basin was hollowed, naturally, in the rock. Did it contain water, reddened by the lurid light, or was it blood? or, perchance, a liquid flame? Herein did the shape of evil dip his hand and prepare to lay the mark of baptism upon their foreheads, that they might be partakers of the mystery of sin, more conscious of the secret guilt of others, both in deed and thought, than they could now be of their own. The husband cast one look at his pale wife, and Faith at him. What polluted wretches would the next glance show them to each other, shuddering alike at what they disclosed and what they saw!

"Faith! Faith!" cried the husband, "look up to heaven, and resist the wicked one."

Whether Faith obeyed he knew not. Hardly had he spoken when he found himself amid calm night and solitude, listening to a roar of the wind which died heavily away through the forest. He staggered against the rock, and felt it chill and damp; while a hanging twig, that had been all on fire, besprinkled his cheek with the coldest dew.

The next morning young Goodman Brown came slowly into the street of Salem village, staring around him like a bewildered man. The good old minister was taking a walk along the graveyard to get an appetite for breakfast and meditate his sermon, and bestowed a blessing, as he passed, on Goodman Brown. He shrank from the venerable saint as if to avoid an anathema. Old Deacon Gookin was at domestic worship, and the holy words of his prayer were heard through the open window. "What God doth the wizard pray to?" quoth Goodman Brown. Goody Cloyse, that excellent old Christian, stood in the early sunshine at her own lattice, catechizing a little girl who had brought her a pint of morning's milk. Goodman Brown snatched away the child as from the grasp of the fiend himself. Turning the corner by the meeting-house, he spied the head of Faith, with the pink ribbons, gazing anxiously forth, and bursting into such joy at sight of him that she skipped along the street and almost kissed her husband before the whole village. But Goodman Brown looked sternly and sadly into her face, and passed on without a greeting.

Had Goodman Brown fallen asleep in the forest and only dreamed a wild dream of a witch-meeting?

Be it so if you will; but, alas! it was a dream of evil omen for young Goodman Brown. A stern, a sad, a darkly meditative, a distrustful, if not a desperate man did he become from the night of that fearful dream. On the Sabbath day, when the congregation were singing a holy psalm, he could not listen because an anthem of sin rushed loudly upon his ear and drowned all the blessed strain. When the minister spoke from the pulpit with power and fervid eloquence, and, with his hand on the open Bible, of the sacred truths of our religion, and of saintlike lives and triumphant deaths, and of future bliss or misery unutterable, then did Goodman Brown turn pale, dreading lest the roof should thunder down upon the gray blasphemer and his hearers. Often, awaking suddenly at midnight, he shrank from the bosom of Faith; and at morning or eventide, when the family knelt down at prayer, he scowled and muttered to himself, and gazed sternly at his wife, and turned away. And when he had lived long, and was borne to his grave a hoary corpse, followed by Faith, an aged woman, and children and grandchildren, a goodly procession, besides neighbors not a few, they carved no hopeful verse upon his tombstone, for his dying hour was gloom.

FOR DISCUSSION:

1. What is the symbolic nature of Goodman Brown's journey into the forest with the devil?

2. For what is Goodman Brown bartering his soul? Is this a variation of the Faust legend?

3. Comment on the symbolic purport of the characters' names, Faith's pink ribbons, and the initiation rites in the forest.

4. Specifically what does Brown discover that makes the remainder of his life one of gloom and despair?

5. At the end of the story the reader is not sure whether Brown's experience was a dream or reality. Does this uncertainty strengthen or weaken the tale? Why?

Blackberry Winter*

ROBERT PENN WARREN

It was getting into June and past eight o'clock in the morning, but there was a fire —even if it wasn't a big fire, just a fire of chunks—on the hearth of the big stone fireplace in the living room. I was standing on the hearth, almost into the chimney, hunched over the fire, working my bare toes slowly on the warm stone. I relished the heat which made the skin of my bare legs warp and creep and tingle, even as I called to my mother, who was somewhere back in the dining room or kitchen, and said: "But it's June, I don't have to put them on!"

"You put them on if you are going out," she called.

I tried to assess the degree of authority and conviction in the tone, but at that distance it was hard to decide. I tried to analyze the tone, and then I thought what a fool I had been to start out the back door and let her see that I was barefoot. If I had gone out the front door or the side door she would never have known, not till dinner time anyway, and by then the day would have been half gone and I would have been all over the farm to see what the storm had done and down to the creek to see the flood. But it had never crossed my mind that they would try to stop you from going barefoot in June, no matter if there had been a gully-washer and a cold spell.

Nobody had ever tried to stop me in June as long as I could remember, and when you are nine years old, what you remember seems forever; for you remember everything and everything is important and stands big and full and fills up Time and is so solid that you can walk around and around it like a tree and look at it. You are aware that time passes, that there is a movement in time, but that is not what Time is. Time is not a movement, a flowing, a wind then, but is, rather, a kind of climate in which things are, and when a thing happens it begins to live and keeps on living and stands solid in Time like the tree that you can walk around. And if there is a movement, the movement is not Time itself, no more than a breeze is climate, for all the breeze does is to shake a little the leaves on the tree which is alive and solid. When you are nine, you know that there are things that you don't know, but you know that when you know something you know it. You know how a thing has been and you know that you can go barefoot in June. You do not understand that voice from back in the kitchen which says that you cannot go barefoot outdoors and run to see what has happened and rub your feet over the wet shivery grass and make the perfect mark of your foot in the smooth, creamy, red mud and then muse upon it as though you had suddenly come upon that single mark on the glistening auroral beach of the world. You have never seen a beach, but you have read the book and how the footprint was there.

The voice had said what it had said, and I looked savagely at the black stockings and the strong, scuffed brown shoes which I had brought from my closet as far as the hearth rug. I called once more, "But it's June," and waited.

"It's June," the voice replied from far away, "but it's blackberry winter."

I had lifted my head to reply to that, to make one more test of what was in that tone, when I happened to see the man.

The fireplace in the living room was at the end; for the stone chimney was built, as in so many of the farmhouses in Tennessee, at the end of a gable, and there was a window on each side of the chimney. Out

---

* From THE CIRCUS IN THE ATTIC AND OTHER STORIES, copyright, 1947, by Robert Penn Warren. Reprinted by permission of Harcourt, Brace & World, Inc.

of the window on the north side of the fireplace I could see the man. When I saw the man I did not call out what I had intended, but, engrossed by the strangeness of the sight, watched him, still far off, come along the path by the edge of the woods.

What was strange was that there should be a man there at all. That path went along the yard fence, between the fence and the woods which came right down to the yard, and then on back past the chicken runs and on by the woods until it was lost to sight where the woods bulged out and cut off the back field. There the path disappeared into the woods. It led on back, I knew, through the woods and to the swamp, skirted the swamp where the big trees gave way to sycamores and water oaks and willows and tangled cane, and then led on to the river. Nobody ever went back there except people who wanted to gig frogs in the swamp or to fish in the river or to hunt in the woods, and those people, if they didn't have a standing permission from my father, always stopped to ask permission to cross the farm. But the man whom I now saw wasn't, I could tell even at that distance, a sportsman. And what would a sportsman have been doing down there after a storm? Besides, he was coming from the river, and nobody had gone down there that morning. I knew that for a fact, because if anybody had passed, certainly if a stranger had passed, the dogs would have made a racket and would have been out on him. But this man was coming up from the river and had come up through the woods. I suddenly had a vision of him moving up the grassy path in the woods, in the green twilight under the big trees, not making any sound on the path, while now and then, like drops off the eaves, a big drop of water would fall from a leaf or bough and strike a stiff oak leaf lower down with a small, hollow sound like a drop of water hitting tin. That sound, in the silence of the woods, would be very significant.

When you are a boy and stand in the stillness of woods, which can be so still that your heart stops beating and makes you want to stand there in the green twilight until you feel your very feet sinking into and clutching the earth like roots and your body breathing slow through its pores like the leaves—when you stand there and wait for the next drop to drop with its small, flat sound to a lower leaf, that sound seems to measure out something, to put an end to something, to begin something, and you cannot wait for it to happen and are afraid it will not happen, and then when it has happened, you are waiting again, almost afraid.

But the man whom I saw coming through the woods in my mind's eye did not pause and wait, growing into the ground and breathing with the enormous, soundless breathing of the leaves. Instead, I saw him moving in the green twilight inside my head as he was moving at that very moment along the path by the edge of the woods, coming toward the house. He was moving steadily, but not fast, with his shoulders hunched a little and his head thrust forward, like a man who has come a long way and has a long way to go. I shut my eyes for a couple of seconds, thinking that when I opened them he would not be there at all. There was no place for him to have come from, and there was no reason for him to come where he was coming, toward our house. But I opened my eyes, and there he was, and he was coming steadily along the side of the woods. He was not yet even with the back chicken yard.

"Mama," I called.

"You put them on," the voice said.

"There's a man coming," I called, "out back."

She did not reply to that, and I guessed that she had gone to the kitchen window to look. She would be looking at the man and wondering who he was and what he wanted, the way you always do in the country, and if I went back there now she would not notice right off whether or not I was barefoot. So I went back to the kitchen.

She was standing by the window. "I don't recognize him," she said, not looking around at me.

"Where could he be coming from?" I asked.

"I don't know," she said.

"What would he be doing down at the river? At night? In the storm?"

She studied the figure out the window, then said, "Oh, I reckon maybe he cut across from the Dunbar place."

That was, I realized, a perfectly rational explanation. He had not been down at the river in the storm, at night. He had come over this morning. You could cut across from the Dunbar place if you didn't mind breaking through a lot of elder and sassafras and blackberry bushes which had about taken over the old cross path, which nobody ever used any more. That satisfied me for a moment, but only for a moment. "Mama," I asked, "What would he be doing over at the Dunbar place last night?"

Then she looked at me, and I knew I had made a mistake, for she was looking at my bare feet. "You haven't got your shoes on," she said.

But I was saved by the dogs. That instant there was a bark which I recognized as Sam, the collie, and then a heavier, churning kind of bark which was Bully, and I saw a streak of white as Bully tore around the corner of the back porch and headed out for the man. Bully was a big, bone-white bull dog, the kind of dog that they used to call a farm bull dog but that you don't see any more, heavy chested and heavy headed, but with pretty long legs. He could take a fence as light as a hound. He had just cleared the white paling fence toward the woods when my mother ran out to the back porch and began calling, "Here you, Bully! Here you!"

Bully stopped in the path, waiting for the man, but he gave a few more of those deep, gargling, savage barks that reminded you of something down a stone-lined well. The red clay mud, I saw, was splashed up over his white chest and looked exciting, like blood.

The man, however, had not stopped walking even when Bully took the fence and started at him. He had kept right on coming. All he had done was to switch a little paper parcel which he carried from the right hand to the left, and then reach into his pants pocket to get something. Then I saw the glitter and knew that he had a knife in his hand, probably the kind of mean knife just made for devilment and nothing else, with a blade as long as the blade of a frog-sticker, which will snap out ready when you press a button in the handle. That knife must have had a button in the handle, or else how could he have had the blade out glittering so quick and with just one hand?

Pulling his knife against the dogs was a funny thing to do, for Bully was a big, powerful brute and fast, and Sam was all right. If those dogs had meant business, they might have knocked him down and ripped him before he got a stroke in. He ought to have picked up a heavy stick, something to take a swipe at them with and something which they could see and respect when they came at him. But he apparently did not know much about dogs. He just held the knife blade close against the right leg, low down, and kept on moving down the path.

Then my mother had called, and Bully had stopped. So the man let the blade of the knife snap back into the handle, and dropped it into his pocket, and kept on coming. Many women would have been afraid with the strange man who they knew had that knife in his pocket. That is, if they were alone in the house with nobody but a nine-year-old boy. And my mother was alone, for my father had gone off, and Dellie, the cook, was down at her cabin because she wasn't feeling well. But my mother wasn't afraid. She wasn't a big woman, but she was clear and brisk about everything she did and looked everybody and everything right in the eye from her own blue eyes in her tanned face. She had been the first woman in the county to ride a horse astride (that was back when she was a girl and long before I was born), and I have seen her snatch up a pump gun and go out and knock a chicken hawk out of the air like a busted skeet when he came over her chicken yard. She was a steady and self-reliant woman, and when I think of her now after all the years she has been dead, I think of her brown hands, not big, but somewhat square for a woman's hands, with square-cut nails. They looked, as a matter of fact, more like a young boy's hands than a grown woman's. But back then it never crossed my mind that she would ever be dead.

She stood on the back porch and watched the man enter the back gate, where the dogs (Bully had leaped back into the yard) were dancing and muttering and giving sidelong glances back to my mother to see if she meant what she had said. The man walked right by the dogs, almost brushing sidelong glances back to my mother to tion. I could see now that he wore old khaki pants, and a dark wool coat with stripes in it, and a gray felt hat. He had on a gray shirt with blue stripes in it, and no tie. But I could see a tie, blue and reddish, sticking in his side coat-pocket. Everything was wrong about what he wore. He ought to have been wearing blue jeans or overalls, and a straw hat or an old black felt hat, and the coat, granting that he might have been wearing a wool coat and not a jumper, ought not to have had those stripes. Those clothes, despite the fact that they were old enough and dirty enough for any tramp, didn't belong there in our back yard, coming down the path, in Middle Tennessee, miles away from any big town, and even a mile off the pike.

When he got almost to the steps, without having said anything, my mother, very matter-of-factly, said, "Good morning."

"Good morning," he said, and stopped and looked her over. He did not take off his hat, and under the brim you could see the perfectly unmemorable face, which wasn't old and wasn't young, or thick or thin. It was grayish and covered with about three days of stubble. The eyes were a kind of nondescript, muddy hazel, or something like that, rather bloodshot. His teeth, when he opened his mouth, showed yellow and uneven. A couple of them had been knocked out. You knew that they had been knocked out, because there was a scar, not very old, there on the lower lip just beneath the gap.

"Are you hunting work?" my mother asked him.

"Yes," he said—not "yes, mam"—and still did not take off his hat.

"I don't know about my husband, for he isn't here," she said, and didn't mind a bit telling the tramp, or whoever he was, with the mean knife in his pocket, that no man was around, "but I can give you a few things to do. The storm has drowned a lot of my chicks. Three coops of them. You can gather them up and bury them. Bury them deep so the dogs won't get at them. In the woods. And fix the coops the wind blew over. And down yonder beyond that pen by the edge of the woods are some drowned poults. They go out and I couldn't get them in. Even after it started to rain hard. Poults haven't got any sense."

"What are them things—poults?" he demanded, and spat on the brick walk. He rubbed his foot over the spot, and I saw that he wore a black, pointed-toe low shoe, all cracked and broken. It was a crazy kind of shoe to be wearing in the country.

"Oh, they're young turkeys," my mother was saying. "And they haven't got any sense. I oughtn't to try to raise them around here with so many chickens, anyway. They don't thrive near chickens, even in separate pens. And I won't give up my chickens." Then she stopped herself and resumed briskly on the note of business. "When you finish that, you can fix my flower beds. A lot of trash and mud and gravel has washed down. Maybe you can save some of my flowers if you are careful."

"Flowers," the man said, in a low, impersonal voice which seemed to have a wealth of meaning, but a meaning which I could not fathom. As I think back on it, it probably was not pure contempt. Rather, it was a kind of impersonal and distant marveling that he should be on the verge of grubbing in a flower bed. He said the word, and then looked off across the yard.

"Yes, flowers," my mother replied with some asperity, as though she would have nothing said or implied against flowers. "And they were very fine this year." Then she stopped and looked at the man. "Are you hungry?" she demanded.

"Yeah," he said.

"I'll fix you something," she said, "before you get started." She turned to me. "Show him where he can wash up," she commanded, and went into the house.

I took the man to the end of the porch where a pump was and where a couple of wash pans sat on a low shelf for people to use before they went into the house. I stood there while he laid down his little parcel wrapped in newspaper and took off his hat and looked around for a nail to hang it on. He poured the water and plunged his hands into it. They were big hands, and strong looking, but they did not have the creases and the earth-color of the hands of men who work outdoors. But they were dirty, with black dirt ground into the skin and under the nails. After he had washed his hands, he poured another basin of water and washed his face. He dried his face, and with the towel still dangling in his grasp, stepped over to the mirror on the house wall. He rubbed one hand over the stubble on his face. Then he carefully inspected his face, turning first one side and then the other, and stepped back and settled his striped coat down on his shoulders. He had the movements of a man who had just dressed up to go to church or a party— the way he settled his coat and smoothed it and scanned himself in the mirror.

Then he caught my glance on him. He glared at me for an instant out of the bloodshot eyes, then demanded in a low, harsh voice, "What you looking at?"

"Nothing," I managed to say, and stepped back a step from him.

He flung the towel down, crumpled, on the shelf, and went toward the kitchen door and entered without knocking.

My mother said something to him which I could not catch. I started to go in again, then thought about my bare feet, and decided to go back of the chicken yard, where the man would have to come to pick up the dead chicks. I hung around behind the chicken house until he came out.

He moved across the chicken yard with a fastidious, not quite finicking motion, looking down at the curdled mud flecked with bits of chicken-droppings. The mud curled up over the soles of his black shoes. I stood back from him some six feet and watched him pick up the first of the drowned chicks. He held it up by one foot and inspected it.

There is nothing deader looking than a drowned chick. The feet curl in that feeble, empty way which back when I was a boy, even if I was a country boy who did not mind hog-killing or frog-gigging, made me feel hollow in the stomach. Instead of looking plump and fluffy, the body is stringy and limp with the fluff plastered to it, and the neck is long and loose like a little string of rag. And the eyes have that bluish membrane over them which makes you think of a very old man who is sick about to die.

The man stood there and inspected the chick. Then he looked all around as though he didn't know what to do with it.

"There's a great big old basket in the shed," I said, and pointed to the shed attached to the chicken house.

He inspected me as though he had just discovered my presence, and moved toward the shed.

"There's a spade there, too," I added.

He got the basket and began to pick up the other chicks, picking each one up slowly by a foot and then flinging it into the basket with a nasty, snapping motion. Now and then he would look at me out of the bloodshot eyes. Every time he seemed on the verge of saying something, but he did not. Perhaps he was building up to say something to me, but I did not wait that long. His way of looking at me made me so uncomfortable that I left the chicken yard.

Besides, I had just remembered that the creek was in flood, over the bridge, and that people were down there watching it. So I cut across the farm toward the creek. When I got to the big tobacco field I saw that it had not suffered much. The land lay right and not many tobacco plants had washed out of the ground. But I knew that a lot of tobacco round the country had been washed right out. My father had said so at breakfast.

My father was down at the bridge. When I came out of the gap in the osage hedge into the road, I saw him sitting on his mare over the heads of the other men who were standing around, admiring the flood. The creek was big here, even in low water; for only a couple of miles away it ran into the river, and when a real flood came, the red water got over the pike where it dipped down to the bridge, which was an iron bridge, and high over the floor and even the side railings of the bridge. Only the upper iron work would show, with the water boiling and frothing red and white around it. That creek rose so fast and so heavy because a few miles back it came down out of the hills, where the gorges filled up with water in no time when a rain came. The creek ran in a deep bed with limestone bluffs along both sides until it got within three quarters of a mile of the bridge, and when it came out from between those bluffs in flood it was boiling and hissing and steaming like water from a fire hose.

Whenever there was a flood, people from half the county would come down to see the sight. After a gully-washer there would not be any work to do anyway. If it didn't ruin your crop, you couldn't plow and you felt like taking a holiday to celebrate. If it did ruin your crop, there wasn't anything to do except to try to take your mind off the mortgage, if you were rich enough to have a mortgage, and if you couldn't afford a mortgage you needed something to take your mind off how hungry you would be by Christmas. So people would come down to the bridge and look at the flood. It made something different from the run of days.

There would not be much talking after the first few minutes of trying to guess how high the water was this time. The men and kids just stood around, or sat their horses or mules, as the case might be, or stood up in the wagon beds. They looked at the strangeness of the flood for an hour or two, and then somebody would say that he had better be getting on home to dinner and would start walking down the gray, puddled limestone pike, or would touch heel to his mount and start off. Everybody always knew what it would be like when he got down to the bridge, but people always came. It was like church or a funeral. They always came, that is, if it was summer and the flood unexpected. Nobody ever came down in winter to see high water.

When I came out of the gap in the bowdock hedge, I saw the crowd, perhaps fifteen or twenty men and a lot of kids, and saw my father sitting his mare, Nellie Gray. He was a tall, limber man and carried himself well. I was always proud to see him sit a horse, he was so quiet and straight, and when I stepped through the gap of the hedge that morning, the first thing that happened was, I remember, the warm feeling I always had when I saw him up on a horse, just sitting. I did not go toward him, but skirted the crowd on the far side, to get a look at the creek. For one thing, I was not sure what he would say about the fact that I was barefoot. But the first thing I knew, I heard his voice calling, "Seth!"

I went toward him, moving apologetically past the men, who bent their large, red or thin, sallow faces above me. I knew some of the men, and knew their names, but because those I knew were there in a crowd, mixed with the strange faces, they seemed foreign to me, and not friendly. I did not look up at my father until I was almost within touching distance of his heel. Then I looked up and tried to read his face, to see if he was angry about my being barefoot. Before I could decide anything from that impassive, high-boned face, he had leaned over and reached a hand to me. "Grab on," he commanded.

I grabbed on and gave a little jump, and he said, "Up-see-daisy!" and whisked me, light as a feather, up to the pommel of his McClellan saddle.

"You can see better up here," he said, slid back on the cantle a little to make me more comfortable, and then, looking over my head at the swollen, tumbling water, seemed to forget all about me. But his right hand was laid on my side, just above my thigh, to steady me.

I was sitting there as quiet as I could, feeling the faint stir of my father's chest against my shoulders as it rose and fell with his breath, when I saw the cow. At first, looking up the creek, I thought it was just another big piece of driftwood steaming down the creek in the ruck of water, but all at once a pretty good-size boy who had climbed part way up a telephone pole by the pike so that he could see better yelled out, "Golly-damn, look at that-air cow!"

Everybody looked. It was a cow all right, but it might just as well have been driftwood; for it was dead as a chunk, rolling and rolling down the creek, appearing and disappearing, feet up or head up, it didn't matter which.

The cow started up the talk again. Somebody wondered whether it would hit one of the clear places under the top girder of the bridge and get through or whether it would get tangled in the drift and trash that had piled against the upright girders and braces. Somebody remembered how about ten years before so much driftwood had piled up on the bridge that it was knocked off its foundations. Then the cow hit. It hit the edge of the drift against one of the girders, and hung there. For a few seconds it seemed as though it might tear loose, but then we saw that it was really caught. It bobbed and heaved on its side there in a slow, grinding, uneasy fashion. It had a yoke around its neck, the kind made out of a forked limb to keep a jumper behind fence.

"She shore jumped one fence," one of the men said.

And another: "Well, she done jumped her last one, fer a fack."

Then they began to wonder about whose cow it might be. They decided it must belong to Milt Alley. They said that he had a cow that was a jumper, and kept her in a fenced-in piece of ground up the creek. I had never seen Milt Alley, but I knew who he was. He was a squatter and lived up the hills a way, on a shirt-tail patch of set-on-edge land, in a cabin. He was pore white trash. He had lots of children. I had seen the children at school, when they came. They were thin-faced, with straight, sticky-looking, dough-colored hair, and they smelled something like old sour buttermilk, not because they drank so much buttermilk but because that is the sort of smell which children out of those cabins tend to have. The big Alley boy drew dirty pictures and showed them to the little boys at school.

That was Milt Alley's cow. It looked like the kind of cow he would have, a scrawny, old, sway-backed cow, with a yoke around her neck. I wondered if Milt Alley had another cow.

"Poppa," I said, "do you think Milt Alley has got another cow?"

"You say 'Mr. Alley,'" my father said quietly.

"Do you think he has?"

"No telling," my father said.

Then a big gangly boy, about fifteen, who was sitting on a scraggly little old mule with a piece of croker sack thrown across the saw-tooth spine, and who had been staring at the cow, suddenly said to nobody in particular, "Reckin anybody ever et drownt cow?"

He was the kind of boy who might just as well as not have been the son of Milt Alley, with his faded and patched overalls ragged at the bottom of the pants and the mud-stiff brogans hanging off his skinny, bare ankles at the level of the mule's belly. He had said what he did, and then looked embarrassed and sullen when all the eyes swung at him. He hadn't meant to say it, I am pretty sure now. He would have been too proud to say it, just as Milt Alley would have been too proud. He had just been thinking out loud, and the words had popped out.

There was an old man standing there on the pike, an old man with a white beard. "Son," he said to the embarrassed and sullen boy on the mule, "you live long enough and you'll find a man will eat anything when the time comes."

"Time gonna come fer some folks this year," another man said.

"Son," the old man said, "in my time I et things a man don't like to think on. I was a sojer and I rode with Gin'l Forrest, and them things we et when the time come. I tell you. I et meat what got up and run when you taken out yore knife to cut a slice to put on the fire. You had to knock it down with a carbeen butt, it was so active. That-air meat would jump like a bullfrog, it was so full of skippers."

But nobody was listening to the old man. The boy on the mule turned his sullen sharp face from him, dug a heel into the side of the mule and went off up the pike with a motion which made you think that any second you would hear mule bones clashing inside that lank and scrofulous hide.

"Cy Dundee's boy," a man said, and nodded toward the figure going up the pike on the mule.

"Reckin Cy Dundee's young-uns seen times they'd settle fer drownt cow," another man said.

The old man with the beard peered at them both from his weak, slow eyes first at one and then at the other. "Live long enough," he said, "and a man will settle fer what he kin git."

Then there was silence again, with the people looking at the red, foam-flecked water.

My father lifted the bridle rein in his left hand, and the mare turned and walked around the group and up the pike. We rode on up to our big gate, where my father dismounted to open it and let me myself ride Nellie Gray through. When he got to the lane that led off from the drive about two hundred yards from our house, my father said, "Grab on." I grabbed on, and he let me down to the ground. "I'm going to ride down and look at my corn," he said. "You go on." He took the lane, and I stood there on the drive and watched him ride off. He was wearing cowhide boots and an old hunting coat, and I thought that that made him look very military, like a picture. That and the way he rode.

I did not go to the house. Instead, I went by the vegetable garden and crossed behind the stables, and headed down for Dellie's cabin. I wanted to go down and play with Jebb, who was Dellie's little boy about two years older than I was. Besides, I was cold.

I shivered as I walked, and I had goose-flesh. The mud which crawled up between my toes with every step I took was like ice. Dellie would have a fire, but she wouldn't make me put on shoes and stockings.

Dellie's cabin was of logs, with one side, because it was on a slope, set on limestone chunks, with a little porch attached to it, and had a little whitewashed fence around it and a gate with plow-points on a wire to clink when somebody came in, and had two big white oaks in the yard and some flowers and a nice privy in the back with some honeysuckle growing over it. Dellie and Old Jebb, who was Jebb's father and who lived with Dellie and had lived with her for twenty-five years even if they never had got married, were careful to keep everything nice around their cabin. They had the name all over the community for being clean and clever Negroes. Dellie and Jebb were what they used to call "white-folks' niggers." There was a big difference between their cabin and the other two cabins farther down where the other tenants lived. My father kept the other cabins weatherproof, but he couldn't undertake to go down and pick up after the litter they strewed. They didn't take the trouble to have a vegetable patch like Dellie and Jebb or to make preserves from wild plum, and jelly from crab apple the way Dellie did. They were shiftless, and my father was always threatening to get shed of them. But he never did. When they finally left, they just up and left on their own, for no reason, to go and be shiftless somewhere else. Then some more came. But meanwhile they lived down there, Matt Rawson and his family, and Sid Turner and his, and I played with their children all over the farm when they weren't working. But when I wasn't around they were mean sometimes to Little Jebb. That was because the other tenants down there were jealous of Dellie and Jebb.

I was so cold that I ran the last fifty yards to Dellie's gate. As soon as I had entered the yard, I saw that the storm had been hard on Dellie's flowers. The yard was, as I have said, on a slight slope, and the water running across had gutted the flower beds and washed out all the good black woods-earth which Dellie had brought in. What little grass there was in the yard was plastered sparsely down on the ground, the way the drainage water had left it. It reminded me of the way the fluff was plastered down on the skin of the drowned chicks that the strange man had been picking up, up in my mother's chicken yard.

I took a few steps up the path to the cabin, and then I saw that the drainage water had washed a lot of trash and filth out from under Dellie's house. Up toward the porch, the ground was not clean any more. Old pieces of rag, two or three rusted cans, pieces of rotten rope, some hunks of old dog dung, broken glass, old paper, and all sorts of things like that had washed out from under Dellie's house to foul her clean yard. It looked just as bad as the yards of the other cabins, or worse. It was worse, as a matter of fact, because it was a surprise. I had never thought of all that filth being under Dellie's house. It was not anything against Dellie that the stuff had been under the cabin. Trash will get under any house. But I did not think of that when I saw the foulness which had washed out on the ground which Dellie sometimes used to sweep with a twig broom to make nice and clean.

I picked my way past the filth, being careful not to get my bare feet on it, and mounted to Dellie's door. When I knocked, I heard her voice telling me to come in.

It was dark inside the cabin, after the daylight, but I could make out Dellie piled up in bed under a quilt, and Little Jebb crouched by the hearth, where a low fire simmered. "Howdy," I said to Dellie, "how you feeling?"

Her big eyes, the whites surprising and glaring in the black face, fixed on me as I stood there, but she did not reply. It did not look like Dellie, or act like Dellie, who would grumble and bustle around our kitchen, talking to herself, scolding me or Little Jebb, clanking pans, making all sorts of unnecessary noises and mutterings like an old-fashioned black steam thrasher engine when it has got up an extra head of steam and keeps popping the governor and rumbling and shaking on its wheels. But now Dellie just lay there on the bed, under the patchwork quilt, and turned the black face, which I scarcely recognized, and the glaring white eyes to me.

"How you feeling?" I repeated.

"I'se sick," the voice said croakingly

out of the strange black face which was not attached to Dellie's big, squat body, but stuck out from under a pile of tangled bedclothes. Then the voice added: "Mighty sick."

"I'm sorry," I managed to say.

The eyes remained fixed on me for a moment, then they left me and the head rolled back on the pillow. "Sorry," the voice said, in a flat way which wasn't question or statement of anything. It was just the empty word put into the air with no meaning or expression, to float off like a feather or a puff of smoke, while the big eyes, with the whites like the peeled white of hard-boiled eggs, stared at the ceiling.

"Dellie," I said after a minute, "there's a tramp up at the house. He's got a knife."

She was not listening. She closed her eyes.

I tiptoed over to the hearth where Jebb was and crouched beside him. We began to talk in low voices. I was asking him to get out his train and play train. Old Jebb had put spool wheels on three cigar boxes and put wire links between the boxes to make a train for Jebb. The box that was the locomotive had the top closed and a length of broom stick for a smoke stack. Jebb didn't want to get the train out, but I told him I would go home if he didn't. So he got out the train, and the colored rocks, and fossils of crinoid stems, and other junk he used for the load, and we began to push it around, talking the way we thought trainmen talked, making a chuck-chucking sound under the breath for the noise of the locomotive and now and then uttering low, cautious toots for the whistle. We got so interested in playing train that the toots got louder. Then, before he thought, Jebb gave a good, loud *toot-toot*, blowing for a crossing.

"Come here," the voice said from the bed.

Jebb got up slow from his hands and knees, giving me a sudden, naked, inimical look.

"Come here!" the voice said.

Jebb went to the bed. Dellie propped herself weakly up on one arm, muttering, "Come closer."

Jebb stood closer.

"Last thing I do, I'm gonna do it," Dellie said. "Done tole you to be quiet."

Then she slapped him. It was an awful slap, more awful for the kind of weakness which it came from and brought to focus. I had seen her slap Jebb before, but the slapping had always been the kind of easy slap you would expect from a good-natured, grumbling Negro woman like Dellie. But this was different. It was awful. It was so awful that Jebb didn't make a sound. The tears just popped out and ran down his face, and his breath came sharp, like gasps.

Dellie fell back. "Cain't even be sick," she said to the ceiling. "Git sick and they won't even let you lay. They tromp all over you. Cain't even be sick." Then she closed her eyes.

I went out of the room. I almost ran getting to the door, and I did run across the porch and down the steps and across the yard, not caring whether or not I stepped on the filth which had washed out from under the cabin. I ran almost all the way home. Then I thought about my mother catching me with the bare feet. So I went down to the stables.

I heard a noise in the crib, and opened the door. There was Big Jebb, sitting on an old nail keg, shelling corn into a bushel basket. I went in, pulling the door shut behind me, and crouched on the floor near him. I crouched there for a couple of minutes before either of us spoke, and watched him shelling the corn.

He had very big hands, knotted and grayish at the joints, with callused palms which seemed to be streaked with rust with the rust coming up between the fingers to show from the back. His hands were so strong and tough that he could take a big ear of corn and rip the grains right off the cob with the palm of his hand, all in one motion, like a machine. "Work long as me," he would say, "and the good Lawd'll give you a hand lak cass-ion won't nuthin' hurt." And his hands did look like cast iron, old cast iron streaked with rust.

He was an old man, up in his seventies, thirty years or more older than Dellie, but he was strong as a bull. He was a squat sort of man, heavy in the shoulders, with remarkably long arms, the kind of build they say the river natives have on the Congo from paddling so much in their boats. He had a round bullet-head, set on powerful shoulders. His skin was very black, and the thin hair on his head was now grizzled like tufts of old cotton batting. He had small eyes and a flat nose, not big, and the kindest and wisest old face in the world, the blunt, sad, wise face of an old animal peering tolerantly out on the goings-on of the merely human creatures before him. He was a good man, and I loved him next to my mother and father. I crouched there on the floor of the crib and watched him shell corn with the rusty cast-iron hands, while he looked down at me out of the little eyes set in the blunt face.

"Dellie says she's mighty sick," I said.

"Yeah," he said.

"What's she sick from?"

"Woman-mizry," he said.

"What's woman-mizry?"

"Hit comes on 'em," he said. "Hit just comes on 'em when the time comes."

"What is it?"

"Hit is the change," he said. "Hit is the change of life and time."

"What changes?"

"You too young to know."

"Tell me."

"Time come and you find out everything."

I knew that there was no use in asking him any more. When I asked him things and he said that, I always knew that he would not tell me. So I continued to crouch there and watch him. Now that I had sat there a little while, I was cold again.

"What you shiver fer?" he asked me.

"I'm cold. I'm cold because it's blackberry winter," I said.

"Maybe 'tis and maybe 'tain't," he said.

"My mother says it is."

"Ain't sayen Miss Sallie doan know and ain't sayen she do. But folks doan know everything."

"Why isn't it blackberry winter?"

"Too late fer blackberry winter. Blackberries done bloomed."

"She said it was."

"Blackberry winter just a leetle cold spell. Hit come and then hit go away, and hit is growed summer of a sudden lak a gunshot. Ain't no tellen hit will go way this time."

"It's June," I said.

"June," he replied with great contempt. "That what folks say. What June mean? Maybe hit is come cold to stay."

"Why"

"Cause this-here old yearth is tahrd. Hit is tahrd and ain't gonna perduce. Lawd let hit come rain one time forty days and forty nights, 'cause He wus tahrd of sinful folks. Maybe this-here old yearth say to the Lawd, Lawd, I done plum tahrd. Lawd, lemme rest. And Lawd say, Yearth, you done yore best, you give 'em cawn and you give 'em taters, and all they think on is they gut, and, Yearth, you kin take a rest."

"What will happen?"

"Folks will eat up everything. The yearth won't perduce no more. Folks cut down all the trees and burn 'em cause they cold, and the yearth won't grow no more. I been tellen 'em. I been tellen folks. Sayen, maybe this year, hit is the time. But they doan listen to me, how the yearth is tahrd. Maybe this year they find out."

"Will everything die?"

"Everything and everybody, hit will be so."

"This year?"

"Ain't no tellen. Maybe this year."

"My mother said it is blackberry winter," I said confidently, and got up.

"Ain't sayen nuthin' agin Miss Sallie," he said.

I went to the door of the crib. I was really cold. Running, I had got up a sweat and now I was worse.

I hung on the door, looking at Jebb, who was shelling corn again.

"There's a tramp came to the house," I said. I had almost forgotten the tramp.

"Yeah."

"He came by the back way. What was he doing down there in the storm?"

"They comes and they goes," he said, "and ain't no tellen."

"He had a mean knife."

"The good ones and the bad ones, they comes and they goes. Storm or sun, light or dark. They is folks and they comes and they goes lak folks."

I hung on the door, shivering.

He studied me a moment, then said, "You git on to the house. You ketch yore death. Then what yore mammy say?"

I hesitated.

"You git," he said.

When I came to the backyard, I saw that my father was standing by the back porch and the tramp was walking toward him. They began talking before I reached them, but I got there just as my father was saying, "I'm sorry, but I haven't got any work. I got all the hands on the place I need now. I won't need any extra until wheat thrashing."

The stranger made no reply, just looked at my father.

My father took out his leather coin purse, and got out a half-dollar. He held it toward the man. "This is for half a day," he said.

The man looked at the coin, and then at my father, making no motion to take the money. But that was the right amount. A dollar a day was what you paid them back in 1910. And the man hadn't even worked half a day.

Then the man reached out and took the coin. He dropped it into the right side pocket of his coat. Then he said, very slowly and without feeling: "I didn't want to work on your——farm."

He used the word which they would have frailed me to death for using.

I looked at my father's face and it was streaked white under the sunburn. Then he said, "Get off this place. Get off this place or I won't be responsible."

The man dropped his right hand into his pants pocket. It was the pocket where he kept the knife. I was just about to yell to my father about the knife when the hand came back out with nothing in it. The man gave a kind of twisted grin, showing where the teeth had been knocked out above the new scar. I thought that instant how maybe he had tried before to pull a knife on somebody else and had got his teeth knocked out.

So now he just gave that twisted, sickish grin out of the unmemorable, grayish face, and then spat on the brick path. The glob landed just about six inches from the toe of my father's right boot. My father looked down at it, and so did I. I thought that if that glob had hit my father's boot something would have happened. I looked down and saw the bright glob, and on one side of it my father's strong cowhide boots, with the brass eyelets and the leather thongs, heavy boots splashed with good red mud and set solid on the bricks, and on the other side the pointed-toe, broken, black shoes, on which the mud looked so sad and out of place. Then I saw one of the black shoes move a little, just a twitch first, then a real step backward.

The man moved in a quarter circle to the end of the porch, with my father's steady gaze upon him all the while. At the end of the porch, the man reached up to the shelf where the wash pans were to get his little newspaper-wrapped parcel. Then he disappeared around the corner of the house and my father mounted the porch and went into the kitchen without a word.

I followed around the house to see what the man would do. I wasn't afraid of him now, no matter if he did have the knife. When I got around in front, I saw him going out the yard gate and starting up the drive toward the pike. So I ran to catch up with him. He was sixty yards or so up the drive before I caught up.

I did not walk right up even with him at first, but trailed him, the way a kid will, about seven or eight feet behind, now and then running two or three steps in order to hold my place against his longer stride. When I first came up behind him, he turned to give me a look, just a meaningless look, and then fixed his eyes up the drive and kept on walking.

When we had got around the bend in the drive which cut the house from sight, and were going along by the edge of the woods, I decided to come up even with him. I ran a few steps, and was by his side, or almost, but some feet off to the right. I walked along in this position for a while, and he never noticed me. I walked along until we got within sight of the big gate that let on the pike.

Then I said: "Where did you come from?"

He looked at me then with a look which seemed almost surprised that I was there. Then he said, "It ain't none of yore business."

We went on another fifty feet.

Then I said, "Where are you going?"

He stopped, studied me dispassionately for a moment, then suddenly took a step toward me and leaned his face down at me. The lips jerked back, but not in any grin, to show where the teeth were knocked out and to make the scar on the lower lip come white with the tension.

He said: "Stop following me. You don't

stop following me and I cut yore throat, you little son-of-a-bitch."

Then he went on to the gate, and up the pike.

That was thirty-five years ago. Since that time my father and mother have died. I was still a boy, but a big boy, when my father got cut on the blade of a mowing machine and died of lockjaw. My mother sold the place and went to town to live with her sister. But she never took hold after my father's death, and she died within three years, right in middle life. My aunt always said, "Sallie just died of a broken heart, she was so devoted." Dellie is dead, too, but she died, I heard, quite a long time after we sold the farm.

As for Little Jebb, he grew up to be a mean and ficey Negro. He killed another Negro in a fight and got sent to the penitentiary, where he is yet, the last I heard tell. He probably grew up to be mean and ficey from just being picked on so much by the children of the other tenants, who were jealous of Jebb and Dellie for being thrifty and clever and being white-folks' niggers.

Old Jebb lived forever. I saw him ten years ago and he was about a hundred then, and not looking much different. He was living in town then, on relief—that was back in the Depression—when I went to see him. He said to me: "Too strong to die. When I was a young feller just comen on and seen how things wuz, I prayed the Lawd. I said, Oh, Lawd, gimme strength and make me strong fer to do and in-dure. The Lawd hearkened to my prayer. He give me strength. I was in-duren proud fer being strong and me much man. The Lawd give me my prayer and my strength. But now He done gone off and fergot me and left me alone with my strength. A man doan know what to pray fer, and him mortal."

Jebb is probably living yet, as far as I know.

That is what has happened since the morning when the tramp leaned his face down at me and showed his teeth and said: "Stop following me. You don't stop following me and I cut yore throat, you little son-of-a-bitch." That was what he said, for me not to follow him. But I did follow him, all the years.

FOR DISCUSSION:

1. Comment on the archetypal nature of the setting, characters, and situations in this story.

2. Why does Warren emphasize the fact that Seth wants to go outside barefoot?

3. What is the meaning of the final sentence?

4. In many ways Seth undergoes his own "Blackberry Winter." During the course of the story what specifically does the boy discover about nature, Negroes, the adult world, himself?

5. Is there any advantage to having the story told in retrospect, that is, from the vantage point of thirty-five years?

My Kinsman, Major Molineux

NATHANIEL HAWTHORNE

After the kings of Great Britain had assumed the right of appointing the colonial governors, the measures of the latter seldom met with the ready and general approbation which had been paid to those of their predecessors, under the original charters. The people looked with most jealous scrutiny to the exercise of power which did not emanate from themselves, and they usually rewarded their rules with slender gratitude for the compliances by which, in softening their instructions from beyond the sea, they had incurred the reprehension of those who gave them. The annuals of Massachusetts Bay will inform us, that of six governors in the space of about forty years from the surrender of the old charter, under James II., two were imprisoned by a popular insurrection; a third, as Hutchinson inclines to believe, was driven from the province by the whizzing of a musket-ball; a fourth, in the opinion of the same historian, was hastened to his grave by continual bickerings with the House of Representatives; and the remaining two, as well as their successors, till the Revolution, were favored with few and brief intervals of peaceful sway. The inferior members of the court party, in times of high political excitement, led scarcely a more desirable life. These remarks may serve as a preface to the following adventures, which chanced upon a summer night, not far from a hundred years ago. The reader, in order to avoid a long and dry detail of colonial affairs, is requested to dispense with an account of the train of circumstances that had caused much temporary inflammation of the popular mind.

It was near nine o'clock of a moonlight evening, when a boat crossed the ferry with a single passenger, who had obtained his conveyance at that unusual hour by the promise of an extra fare. While he stood on the landing-place, searching in either pocket for the means of fulfilling his agreement, the ferryman lifted a lantern, by the aid of which, and the newly risen moon, he took a very accurate survey of the stranger's figure. He was a youth of barely eighteen years, evidently country-bred, and now, as it should seem, upon his first visit to town. He was clad in a coarse gray coat, well worn, but in excellent repair; his under garments were durably constructed of leather, and fitted tight to a pair of serviceable and well-shaped limbs; his stockings of blue yarn were the incontrovertible work of a mother or a sister; and on his head was a three-cornered hat, which in its better days had perhaps sheltered the graver brow of the lad's father. Under his left arm was a heavy cudgel formed of an oak sapling, and retaining a part of the hardened root; and his equipment was completed by a wallet, not so abundantly stocked as to incommode the vigorous shoulders on which it hung. Brown, curly hair, well-shaped features, and bright, cheerful eyes were nature's gifts, and worth all that art could have done for his adornment.

The youth, one of whose names was Robin, finally drew from his pocket the half of a little province bill of five shillings, which, in the depreciation in that sort of currency, did but satisfy the ferryman's demand, with the surplus of a sexangular piece of parchment, valued at three pence. He then walked forward into the town, with as light a step as if his day's journey had not already exceeded thirty miles, and with as eager an eye as if he were entering London city, instead of the little metropolis of a New England colony. Before Robin had proceeded far, however, it occurred to him that he knew not whither to direct his steps; so he paused, and looked up and down the narrow street, scrutinizing the small and mean wooden buildings that were scattered on either side.

"This low hovel cannot be my kinsman's dwelling," thought he, "nor yonder old house, where the moonlight enters at the broken casement; and truly I see none hereabouts that might be worthy of him. It would have been wise to inquire my way of the ferryman, and doubtless he would have gone with me, and earned a shilling from the Major for his pains. But the next man I meet will do as well."

He resumed his walk, and was glad to perceive that the street now became wider, and the houses more respectable in their appearance. He soon discerned a figure moving on moderately in advance, and hastened his steps to overtake it. As Robin drew nigh, he saw that the passenger was a man in years, with a full periwig of gray hair, a wide-skirted coat of dark cloth, and silk stockings rolled above his knees. He carried a long and polished cane, which he struck down perpendicularly before him at every step; and at regular intervals he uttered two successive hems, of a peculiarly solemn and sepulchral intonation. Having made these observations, Robin laid hold of the skirt of the old man's coat, just when the light from the open door and windows of a barber's shop fell upon both their figures.

"Good evening to you, honored sir," said he, making a low bow, and still retaining his hold of the skirt. "I pray you tell me whereabouts is the dwelling of my kinsman, Major Molineux."

The youth's question was uttered very loudly; and one of the barbers, whose razor was descending on a well-soaped chin, and another who was dressing a Ramillies wig, left their occupations, and came to the door. The citizen, in the mean time, turned a long-favored countenance upon Robin, and answered him in a tone of excessive anger and annoyance. His two sepulchral hems, however, broke into the very centre of his rebuke, with most singular effect, like a thought of the cold grave obtruding among wrathful passions.

"Let go my garment, fellow! I tell you, I know not the man you speak of. What! I have authority, I have—hem, hem—authority; and if this be the respect you show for your betters, your feet shall be brought acquainted with the stocks by daylight, tomorrow morning!"

Robin released the old man's skirt, and hastened away, pursued by an ill-mannered roar of laughter from the barber's shop. He was at first considerably surprised by the result of his question, but, being a shrewd youth, soon thought himself able to account for the mystery.

"This is some country representative," was his conclusion, "who has never seen the inside of my kinsman's door, and lacks the breeding to answer a stranger civilly. The man is old, or verily—I might be tempted to turn back and smite him on the nose. Ah, Robin, Robin! even the barber's boys laugh at you for choosing such a guide! You will be wiser in time, friend Robin."

He now became entangled in a succession of crooked and narrow streets, which crossed each other, and meandered at no great distance from the water-side. The smell of tar was obvious to his nostrils, the masts of vessels pierced the moonlight above the tops of the buildings, and the numerous signs, which Robin paused to read, informed him that he was near the centre of business. But the streets were empty, the shops were closed, and lights were visible only in the second stories of a few dwelling-houses. At length, on the corner of a narrow lane, through which he was passing, he beheld the broad countenance of a British hero swinging before the door of an inn, whence proceeded the voices of many guests. The casement of one of the lower windows was thrown back, and a very thin curtain permitted Robin to distinguish a party at supper, round a well-furnished table. The fragrance of the good cheer steamed forth into the outer air, and the youth could not fail to recollect that the last remnant of his travelling stock of provision had yielded to his morning appetite, and that noon had found and left him dinnerless.

"Oh, that a parchment three-penny might give me a right to sit down at yonder table!" said Robin, with a sigh. "But the Major will make me welcome to the best of his victuals; so I will even step boldly in, and inquire my way to his dwelling."

He entered the tavern, and was guided by the murmur of voices and the fumes of tobacco to the public-room. It was a long and low apartment, with oaken walls, grown dark in the continual smoke, and a floor which was thickly sanded, but of no immaculate purity. A number of persons—the larger part of whom appeared to be mariners, or in some way connected with the sea—occupied the wooden benches, or leather-bottomed chairs, conversing on various matters, and occasionally lending their attention to some topic of general interest. Three or four little groups were draining as many bowls of punch, which the West India trade had long since made a familiar drink in the colony. Others, who had the appearance of men who lived by regular and laborious handicraft, preferred the insulated bliss of an unshared potation, and became more taciturn under its influence. Nearly all, in short, evinced a predilection for the Good Creature in some of its various shapes, for this is a vice to which, as Fast Day sermons of a hundred years ago will testify, we have a long hereditary claim. The only guests to whom Robin's sympathies inclined him were two or three sheepish countrymen, who were using the inn somewhat after the fashion of a Turkish caravansary; they had gotten themselves into the darkest corner of the room, and heedless of the Nicotian atmosphere, were supping on the bread of their own ovens, and the bacon cured in their own chimney-smoke. But though Robin felt a sort of brotherhood with these strangers, his eyes were attracted from them to a person who stood near the door, holding whispered conversation with a group of ill-dressed associates. His features were separately striking almost to grotesqueness, and the whole face left a deep impression on the memory. The forehead bulged out into a double prominence, with a vale between; the nose came boldly forth in an irregular curve, and its bridge was of more than a finger's breadth; the eyebrows were deep and shaggy, and the eyes glowed beneath them like fire in a cave.

While Robin deliberated of whom to inquire respecting his kinsman's dwelling, he was accosted by the innkeeper, a little man in a stained white apron, who had come to pay his professional welcome to the stranger. Being in the second generation from a French Protestant, he seemed to have inherited the courtesy of his parent nation; but no variety of circumstances was ever known to change his voice from the one shrill note in which he now addressed Robin.

"From the country, I presume, sir?" said he, with a profound bow. "Beg leave to congratulate you on your arrival, and trust you intend a long stay with us. Fine town here, sir, beautiful buildings, and much that may interest a stranger. May I hope for the honor of your commands in respect to supper?"

"The man sees a family likeness! the rogue has guessed that I am related to the Major!" thought Robin, who had hitherto experienced little superfluous civility.

All eyes were now turned on the country lad, standing at the door, in his worn three-cornered hat, gray coat, leather breeches, and blue yarn stockings, leaning on an oaken cudgel, and bearing a wallet on his back.

Robin replied to the courteous innkeeper, with such an assumption of confidence as befitted the Major's relative. "My honest friend," he said, "I shall make it a point to patronize your house on some occasion, when"—here he could not help lowering his voice—"when I may have more than a parchment three-pence in my pocket. My present business," continued he, speaking with lofty confidence, "is merely to inquire my way to the dwelling of my kinsman, Major Molineux."

There was a sudden and general movement in the room, which Robin interpreted as expressing the eagerness of each individual to become his guide. But the innkeeper turned his eyes to a written paper on the wall, which he read, or seemed to read, with occasional recurrences to the young man's figure.

"What have we here?" said he, breaking his speech into little dry fragments. " 'Left the house of the subscriber, bounden servant, Hezekiah Mudge,—had on, when he went away, gray coat, leather breeches, master's third-best hat. One pound currency reward to whosoever shall lodge him in any jail of the province.' Better trudge, boy; better trudge!"

Robin had begun to draw his hand towards the lighter end of the oak cudgel, but a strange hostility in every countenance induced him to relinquish his purpose of breaking the courteous innkeeper's head. As he turned to leave the room, he encountered a sneering glance from the bold-featured personage whom he had before noticed; and no sooner was he beyond the door, than he heard a general laugh, in which the innkeeper's voice might be distinguished, like the dropping of small stones into a kettle.

"Now, is it not strange," thought Robin, with his usual shrewdness,—"is it not strange that the confession of an empty pocket should outweigh the name of my kinsman, Major Molineux? Oh, if I had one of those grinning rascals in the woods, where I and my oak sapling grew up together, I would teach him that my arm is heavy though my purse be light!"

On turning the corner of the narrow lane, Robin found himself in a spacious street, with an unbroken line of lofty houses on each side, and a steepled building at the upper end, whence the ringing of a bell announced the hour of nine. The light of the moon, and the lamps from the numerous shop-windows, discovered people promenading on the pavement, and amongst them Robin hoped to recognize his hitherto inscrutable relative. The result of his former inquiries made him unwilling to hazard another, in a scene of such publicity, and he determined to walk slowly and silently up the street, thrusting his face close to that of every elderly gentleman, in search of the Major's lineaments. In his progress, Robin encountered many gay and gallant figures. Embroidered garments of showy colors, enormous periwigs, gold-laced hats, and silver-hilted swords glided past him and dazzled his optics. Travelled youths, imitators of the European fine gentlemen of the period, trod jauntily along, half dancing to the fashionable tunes which they hummed, and making poor Robin ashamed of his quiet and natural gait. At length, after many pauses to examine the gorgeous display of goods in the shop-windows, and after suffering some rebukes for the impertinence of his scrutiny into people's faces, the Major's kinsman found himself near the steepled building, still unsuccessful in his search. As yet, however, he had seen only one side of the thronged street; so Robin crossed, and continued the same sort of inquisition down the opposite pavement, with stronger hopes than the philosopher seeking an honest man, but with no better fortune. He had arrived about midway towards the lower end, from which his course began, when he overheard the approach of some one who struck down a cane on the flag-stones at every step, uttering, at regular intervals, two sepulchral hems.

"Mercy on us!" quoth Robin, recognizing the sound.

Turning a corner, which chanced to be close at his right hand, he hastened to pursue his researches in some other part of the town. His patience now was wearing low, and he seemed to feel more fatigue from his rambles since he crossed the ferry, than from his journey of several days on the other side. Hunger also pleaded loudly within him, and Robin began to balance the propriety of demanding, violently, and with lifted cudgel, the necessary guidance from the first solitary passenger whom he should meet. While a resolution to this effect was gaining strength, he entered a street of mean appearance, on either side of which a row of ill-built houses was straggling towards the harbor. The moonlight fell upon no passenger along the whole extent, but in the third domicile which Robin passed there was a half-opened door, and his keen glance detected a woman's garment within.

"My luck may be better here," said he to himself.

Accordingly, he approached the door, and beheld it shut closer as he did so; yet an open space remained, sufficing for the fair occupant to observe the stranger, without a corresponding display on her part. All that Robin could discern was a strip of scarlet petticoat, and the occasional sparkle of an eye, as if the moonbeams were trembling on some bright thing.

"Pretty mistress," for I may call her so with a good conscience, thought the shrewd youth, since I know nothing to the contrary,—"my sweet pretty mistress, will you be kind enough to tell me whereabouts I must seek the dwelling of my kinsman, Major Molineux?"

Robin's voice was plaintive and winning, and the female, seeing nothing to be shunned in the handsome country youth, thrust open the door, and came forth into the moonlight. She was a dainty little figure, with a white neck, round arms, and a slender waist, at the extremity of which her scarlet petticoat jutted out over a hoop, as if she were standing in a balloon. Moreover, her face was oval and pretty, her hair dark beneath the little cap, and her bright eyes possessed a sly freedom, which triumphed over those of Robin.

"Major Molineux dwells here," said this fair woman.

Now, her voice was the sweetest Robin had heard that night, the airy counterpart of a stream of melted silver; yet he could not help doubting whether that sweet voice spoke Gospel truth. He looked up and down the mean street, and then surveyed the house before which they stood. It was a small, dark edifice of two stories, the second of which projected over the lower floor, and the front apartment had the aspect of a shop for petty commodities.

"Now, truly, I am in luck," replied Robin, cunningly, "and so indeed is my kinsman, the Major, in having so pretty a housekeeper. But I prithee trouble him to step to the door; I will deliver him a message from his friends in the country, and then go back to my lodgings at the inn."

"Nay, the Major has been abed this hour or more," said the lady of the scarlet petticoat; "and it would be to little purpose to disturb him to-night, seeing his evening draught was of the strongest. But he is a kind-hearted man, and it would be as much as my life's worth to let a kinsman of his turn away from the door. You are the good old gentleman's very picture, and I could swear that was his rainy-weather hat. Also he has garments very much resembling those leather small-clothes. But come in, I pray, for I bid you hearty welcome in his name."

So saying, the fair and hospitable dame took our hero by the hand; and the touch was light, and the force was gentleness, and though Robin read in her eyes what he did not hear in her words, yet the slender-waisted woman in the scarlet petticoat proved stronger than the athletic country youth. She had drawn his half-willing footsteps nearly to the threshold, when the opening of a door in the neighborhood startled the Major's housekeeper, and, leaving the Major's kinsman, she vanished speedily into her own domicile. A heavy yawn preceded the appearance of a man, who, like the Moonshine of Pyramus and Thisbe, carried a lantern, needlessly aiding his sister luminary in the heavens. As he walked sleepily up the street, he turned his broad, dull face on Robin, and displayed a long staff, spiked at the end.

"Home, vagabond, home!" said the watchman, in accents that seemed to fall asleep as soon as they were uttered. "Home, or we'll set you in the stocks by peep of day!"

"This is the second hint of the kind," thought Robin. "I wish they would end my difficulties, by setting me there to-night."

Nevertheless, the youth felt an instinctive antipathy towards the guardian of midnight order, which at first prevented him from asking his usual question. But just when the man was about to vanish behind the corner, Robin resolved not to lose the opportunity, and shouted lustily after him,—

"I say, friend! will you guide me to the house of my kinsman, Major Molineux?"

The watchman made no reply, but turned the corner and was gone; yet Robin seemed to hear the sound of drowsy laughter stealing along the solitary street. At that moment, also, a pleasant titter saluted him from the open window above his head; he looked up, and caught the sparkle of a saucy eye; a round arm beckoned to him, and next he heard light footsteps descending the staircase within. But Robin, being of the household of a New England clergyman, was a good youth, as well as a shrewd one; so he resisted temptation, and fled away.

He now roamed desperately, and at random, through the town, almost ready to believe that a spell was on him, like that by which a wizard of his country had once kept three pursuers wandering, a whole winter night, within twenty paces of the cottage which they sought. The streets lay before him, strange and desolate, and the lights were extinguished in almost every house. Twice, however, little parties of men, among whom Robin distinguished individuals in outlandish attire, came hurrying along; but, though on both occasions they paused to address him, such intercourse did not at all enlighten his perplexity. They did but utter a few words in some language of which Robin knew nothing, and perceiving his inability to answer, bestowed a curse upon him in plain English and hastened away. Finally, the lad determined to knock at the door of every mansion that might appear worthy to be occupied by his kinsman, trusting that perseverance would overcome the fatality that had hitherto thwarted him. Firm in this resolve, he was passing beneath the walls of a church, which formed the corner of two streets, when, as he turned into the shade of its steeple, he encountered a bulky stranger, muffled in a cloak. The man was proceeding with the speed of earnest business, but Robin planted himself full before him, holding the oak cudgel with both hands across his body as a bar to further passage.

"Halt, honest man, and answer me a question," said he, very resolutely. "Tell me, this instant, whereabouts is the dwelling of my kinsman, Major Molineux!"

"Keep your tongue between your teeth, fool, and let me pass!" said a deep, gruff voice, which Robin partly remembered. "Let me pass, I say, or I'll strike you to the earth!"

"No, no, neighbor!" cried Robin, flourishing his cudgel, and then thrusting its larger end close to the man's muffled face. "No, no, I'm not the fool you take me for, nor do you pass till I have an answer to my question. Whereabouts is the dwelling of my kinsman, Major Molineux?"

The stranger, instead of attempting to force his passage, stepped back into the moonlight, unmuffled his face, and stared full into that of Robin.

"Watch here an hour, and Major Molineux will pass by," said he.

Robin gazed with dismay and astonishment on the unprecedented physiognomy of the speaker. The forehead with its double prominence, the broad hooked nose, the shaggy eyebrows, and fiery eyes were those which he had noticed at the inn, but the man's complexion had undergone a singular, or, more properly, a twofold change. One side of the face blazed an intense red, while the other was black as midnight, the division line being in the broad bridge of the nose; and a mouth which seemed to extend from ear to ear was black or red, in contrast to the color of the cheek. The effect was as if two individual devils, a fiend of fire and a fiend of darkness, had united themselves to form this infernal visage. The stranger grinned in Robin's face, muffled his particolored features, and was out of sight in a moment.

"Strange things we travellers see!" ejaculated Robin.

He seated himself, however, upon the steps of the church-door, resolving to wait the appointed time for his kinsman. A few moments were consumed in philosophical speculations upon the species of man who had just left him; but having settled this point shrewdly, rationally, and satisfactorily, he was compelled to look elsewhere for his amusement. And first he threw his eyes along the street. It was of more respectable appearance than most of those into which he had wandered; and the moon, creating, like the imaginative power, a beautiful strangeness in familiar objects, gave something of romance to a scene that might not have possessed it in the light of day. The irregular and often quaint architecture of the houses, some of whose roofs were broken into numerous little peaks, while others ascended, steep and narrow, into a single point, and others again were square; the pure snow-white of some of their complexions, the aged darkness of others, and the thousand sparklings, reflected from bright substances in the walls of many; these matters engaged Robin's attention for a while, and then began to grow wearisome. Next he endeavored to define the forms of distant objects, starting away, with almost ghostly indistinctness, just as his eye appeared to grasp them; and finally he took a minute survey of an edifice which stood on the opposite side of the street, directly in front of the church-door, where he was stationed. It was a large, square mansion, distinguished from its neighbors by a balcony, which rested on tall pillars, and by an elaborate Gothic window, communicating therewith.

"Perhaps this is the very house I have been seeking," thought Robin.

Then he strove to speed away the time, by listening to a murmur which swept continually along the street, yet was scarcely audible, except to an unaccustomed ear like his; it was a low, dull, dreamy sound, compounded of many noises, each of which was at too great a distance to be separately heard. Robin marvelled at this snore of a sleeping town, and marvelled more whenever its continuity was broken by now and then a distant shout, apparently loud where it originated. But altogether it was a sleep-inspiring sound, and, to shake off its drowsy influence, Robin arose, and climbed a window-frame, that he might view the interior of the church. There the moonbeams came trembling in, and fell down upon the deserted pews, and extended along the quiet aisles.

A fainter yet more awful radiance was hovering around the pulpit, and one solitary ray had dared to rest upon the open page of the great Bible. Had nature, in that deep hour, become a worshipper in the house which man had builded? Or was that heavenly light the visible sanctity of the place, —visible because no earthly and impure feet were within the walls? The scene made Robin's heart shiver with a sensation of loneliness stronger than he had ever felt in the remotest depths of his native woods; so he turned away and sat down again before the door. There were graves around the church, and now an uneasy thought obtruded into Robin's breast. What if the object of his search, which had been so often and so strangely thwarted, were all the time mouldering in his shroud? What if his kinsman should glide through yonder gate, and nod and smile to him in dimly passing by?

"Oh that any breathing thing were here with me!" said Robin.

Recalling his thoughts from this uncomfortable track, he sent them over forest, hill, and stream, and attempted to imagine how that evening of ambiguity and weariness had been spent by his father's household. He pictured them assembled at the door, beneath the tree, the great old tree, which had been spared for its huge twisted trunk and venerable shade, when a thousand leafy brethren fell. There, at the going down of the summer sun, it was his father's custom to perform domestic worship, that the neighbors might come and join with him like brothers of the family, and that the wayfaring man might pause to drink at that fountain, and keep his heart pure by freshening the memory of home. Robin distinguished the seat of every individual of the little audience; he saw the good man in the midst, holding the Scriptures in the golden light that fell from the western clouds; he beheld him close the book and all rise up to pray. He heard the old thanksgiving for daily mercies, the old supplications for their continuance, to which he had so often listened in weariness, but which were now among his dear remembrances. He perceived the slight inequality of his father's voice when he came to speak of the absent one; he noted how his mother turned her face to the broad and knotted trunk; how his elder brother scorned, because the beard was rough upon his upper lip, to permit his features to be moved; how the younger sister drew down a low hanging branch before her eyes; and how the little one of all, whose sports had hitherto broken the decorum of the scene, understood the prayer for her playmate, and burst into clamorous grief. Then he saw them go in at the door; and when Robin would have entered also, the latch tinkled into its place, and he was excluded from his home.

"Am I here, or there?" cried Robin, starting; for all at once, when his thoughts had become visible and audible in a dream, the long, wide, solitary street shone out before him.

He aroused himself, and endeavored to fix his attention steadily upon the large edifice which he had surveyed before. But still his mind kept vibrating between fancy and reality; by turns, the pillars of the balcony lengthened into the tall, bare stems of pines, dwindled down to human figures, settled again into their true shape and size, and then commenced a new succession of changes. For a single moment, when he deemed himself awake, he could have sworn that a visage—one which he seemed to remember, yet could not absolutely name as his kinsman's—was looking towards him from the Gothic window. A deeper sleep wrestled with and nearly overcame him, but fled at the sound of footsteps along the opposite pavement. Robin rubbed his eyes, discerned a man passing at the foot of the balcony, and addressed him in a loud, peevish, and lamentable cry.

"Hallo, friend! must I wait here all night for my kinsman, Major Molineux?"

The sleeping echoes awoke, and answered the voice; and the passenger, barely able to discern a figure sitting in the oblique shade of the steeple, traversed the street to obtain a nearer view. He was himself a gentleman in his prime, of open, intelligent, cheerful, and altogether prepossessing countenance. Perceiving a country youth, apparently homeless and without friends, he accosted him in a tone of real kindness, which had become strange to Robin's ears.

"Well, my good lad, who are you sitting here?" inquired he. "Can I be of service to you in any way?"

"I am afraid not, sir," replied Robin,

despondingly; "yet I shall take it kindly, if you'll answer me a single question. I've been searching, half the night, for one Major Molineux; now, sir, is there really such a person in these parts, or am I dreaming?"

"Major Molineux! The name is not altogether strange to me," said the gentleman, smiling. "Have you any objection to telling me the nature of your business with him?"

Then Robin briefly related that his father was a clegyman, settled on a small salary, at a long distance back in the country, and he and Major Molineux were brothers' children. The Major, having inherited riches, and acquired civil and military rank, had visited his cousin, in great pomp, a year or two before; had manifested much interest in Robin and an elder brother, and, being childless himself, had thrown out hints respecting the future establishment of one of them in life. The elder brother was destined to succeed to the farm which his father cultivated in the interval of sacred duties; it was therefore determined that Robin should profit by his kinsman's generous intentions, especially as he seemed to be rather the favorite, and was thought to possess other necessary endowments.

"For I have the name of being a shrewd youth," observed Robin, in this part of his story.

"I doubt not you deserve it," replied his new friend, good-naturedly; "but pray proceed."

"Well, sir, being nearly eighteen years old, and well grown, as you see," continued Robin, drawing himself up to his full height, "I thought it high time to begin the world. So my mother and sister put me in handsome trim, and my father gave me half the remnant of his last year's salary, and five days ago I started for this place, to pay the Major a visit. But, would you believe it, sir! I crossed the ferry a little after dark, and have yet found nobody that would show me the way to his dwelling; only, an hour or two since, I was told to wait here, and Major Molineux would pass by."

"Can you describe the man who told you this?" inquired the gentleman.

"Oh, he was a very ill-favored fellow, sir," replied Robin, "with two great bumps on his forehead, a hook nose, fiery eyes; and, what struck me as the strangest, his face was of two different colors. Do you happen to know such a man, sir?"

"Not intimately," answered the stranger, "but I chanced to meet him a little time previous to your stopping me. I believe you may trust his word, and that the Major will very shortly pass through this street. In the mean time, as I have a singular curiosity to witness your meeting, I will sit down here upon the steps and bear you company."

He seated himself accordingly, and soon engaged his companion in animated discourse. It was but of brief continuance, however, for a noise of shouting, which had long been remotely audible, drew so much nearer that Robin inquired its cause.

"What may be the meaning of this uproar?" asked he. "Truly, if your town be always as noisy, I shall find little sleep while I am an inhabitant."

"Why, indeed, friend Robin, there do appear to be three or four riotous fellows abroad to-night," replied the gentleman. "You must not expect all the stillness of your native woods here in our streets. But the watch will shortly be at the heels of these lads and"—

"Ay, and set them in the stocks by peep of day," interrupted Robin, recollecting his own encounter with the drowsy lantern-bearer. "But, dear sir, if I may trust my ears, an army of watchmen would never make head against such a multitude of rioters. There were at least a thousand voices went up to make that one shout."

"May not a man have several voices, Robin, as well as two complexions?" said his friend.

"Perhaps a man may; but Heaven forbid that a woman should!" responded the shrewd youth, thinking of the seductive tones of the Major's housekeeper.

The sounds of a trumpet in some neighboring street now became so evident and continual, that Robin's curiosity was strongly excited. In addition to the shouts, he heard frequent bursts from many instruments of discord, and a wild and confused laughter filled up the intervals. Robin rose from the steps, and looked wistfully towards a point whither people seemed to be hastening.

"Surely some prodigious merry-making is going on," exclaimed he. "I have laughed very little since I left home, sir, and should be sorry to lose an opportunity. Shall we step round the corner by that darkish house, and take our share of the fun?"

"Sit down again, sit down, good Robin," replied the gentleman, laying his hand on the skirt of the gray coat. "You forget that we must wait here for your kinsman; and there is reason to believe that he will pass by, in the course of a very few moments."

The near approach of the uproar had now disturbed the neighborhood; windows flew open on all sides; and many heads, in the attire of the pillow, and confused by sleep suddenly broken, were protruded to the gaze of whoever had leisure to observe them. Eager voices hailed each other from house to house, all demanding the explanation, which not a soul could give. Half-dressed men hurried towards the unknown commotion, stumbling as they went over the stone steps that thrust themselves into the narrow foot-walk. The shouts, the laughter, and the tuneless bray, the antipodes of music, came onwards with increasing din, till scattered individuals, and then denser bodies, began to appear round a corner at the distance of a hundred yards.

"Will you recognize your kinsman, if he passes in this crowd?" inquired the gentleman.

"Indeed, I can't warrant it, sir; but I'll take my stand here, and keep a bright lookout," answered Robin, descending to the outer edge of the pavement.

A mighty stream of people now emptied into the street, and came rolling slowly towards the church. A single horseman wheeled the corner in the midst of them, and close behind him came a band of fearful wind-instruments, sending forth a fresher discord now that no intervening buildings kept it from the ear. Then a redder light disturbed the moonbeams, and a dense multitude of torches shone along the street, concealing, by their glare, whatever object they illuminated. The single horseman, clad in a military dress, and bearing a drawn sword, rode onward as the leader, and, by his fierce and variegated countenance, appeared like war personified; the red of one cheek was an emblem of fire and sword; the blackness of the other betokened the mourning that attends them. In his train were wild figures in the Indian dress, and many fantastic shapes without a model, giving the whole march a visionary air, as if a dream had broken forth from some feverish brain, and were sweeping visibly through the midnight streets. A mass of people, inactive, except as applauding spectators, hemmed the procession in; and several women ran along the sidewalk, piercing the confusion of heavier sounds with their shrill voices of mirth or terror.

"The double-faced fellow has his eye upon me," muttered Robin, with an indefinite but an uncomfortable idea that he was himself to bear a part in the pageantry.

The leader turned himself in the saddle, and fixed his glance full upon the country youth, as the steed went slowly by. When Robin had freed his eyes from those fiery ones, the musicians were passing before him, and the torches were close at hand; but the unsteady brightness of the latter formed a veil which he could not penetrate. The rattling of wheels over the stones sometimes found its way to his ear, and confused traces of a human form appeared at intervals, and then melted into the vivid light. A moment more, and the leader thundered a command to halt: the trumpets vomited a horrid breath, and then held their peace; the shouts and laughter of the people died away, and there remained only a universal hum, allied to silence. Right before Robin's eyes was an uncovered cart. There the torches blazed the brightest, there the moon shone out like day, and there, in tar-and-feathery dignity, sat his kinsman, Major Molineux!

He was an elderly man, of large and majestic person, and strong, square features, betokening a steady soul; but steady as it was, his enemies had found means to shake it. His face was pale as death, and far more ghastly; the broad forehead was contracted in his agony, so that his eyebrows formed one grizzled line; his eyes were red and wild, and the foam hung white upon his quivering lip. His whole frame was agitated by a quick and continual tremor, which his pride strove to quell, even in those circumstances of overwhelming humiliation. But perhaps the bitterest pang of all was when his eyes met those of Robin; for he evidently knew him on the instant, as the youth stood witnessing the foul disgrace of a head grown gray in honor. They stared at each other in silence, and Robin's knees shook, and his hair bristled, with a mixture of pity and terror. Soon, however, a bewildering excitement began to seize upon his mind; the preceding adventures of the night, the unexpected appearance of the crowd, the torches, the confused din and the hush that followed, the spectre of his kinsman reviled by that great multitude,—all this, and, more than all, a perception of tremendous ridicule in the whole scene, affected him with a sort of mental inebriety. At that moment a voice of sluggish merriment saluted Robin's ears; he turned instinctively, and just behind the corner of the church stood the lantern-bearer, rubbing his eyes, and drowsily enjoying the lad's amazement. Then he heard a peal of laughter like the ringing of silvery bells; a woman twitched his arm, a saucy eye met his, and he saw the lady of the scarlet petticoat. A sharp, dry cachinnation appealed to his memory, and, standing on tiptoe in the crowd, with his white apron over his head, he beheld the courteous little innkeeper. And lastly, there sailed over the heads of the multitude a great, broad laugh, broken in the midst by two sepulchral hems; thus, "Haw, haw, haw,—hem, hem,—haw, haw, haw, haw!"

The sound proceeded from the balcony of the opposite edifice, and thither Robin turned his eyes. In front of the Gothic window stood the old citizen wrapped in a wide gown, his gray periwig exchanged for a nightcap, which was thrust back from his forehead, and his silk stockings hanging about his legs. He supported himself on his polished cane in a fit of convulsive merriment, which manifested itself on his solemn old features like a funny inscription on a tombstone. Then Robin seemed to hear the voices of the barbers, of the guests of the inn, and of all who had made sport of him that night. The contagion was spreading among the multitude, when all at once, it seized upon Robin, and he sent forth a shout of laughter that echoed through the street,—every man shook his sides, every man emptied his lungs, but Robin's shout was the loudest there. The cloud-spirits peeped from their silvery islands, as the congregated mirth went roaring up the sky! The Man in the Moon heard the far bellow. "Oho," quoth he, "the old earth is frolicsome to-night!"

When there was a momentary calm in that tempestuous sea of sound, the leader gave the sign, the procession resumed its march. On they went, like fiends that throng in mockery around some dead potentate, mighty no more, but majestic still in his agony. On they went, in counterfeited pomp, in senseless uproar, in frenzied merriment, trampling all on an old man's heart. On swept the tumult, and left a silent street behind.

"Well, Robin, are you dreaming?" inquired the gentleman, laying his hand on the youth's shoulder.

Robin started, and withdrew his arm from the stone post to which he had instinctively clung, as the living stream rolled by him. His cheek was somewhat pale, and his eye not quite as lively as in the earlier part of the evening.

"Will you be kind enough to show me the way to the ferry?" said he, after a moment's pause.

"You have, then, adopted a new subject of inquiry?" observed his companion, with a smile.

"Why, yes, sir," replied Robin, rather dryly. "Thanks to you, and to my other friends, I have at last met my kinsman, and he will scarce desire to see my face again. I begin to grow weary of a town life, sir. Will you show me the way to the ferry?"

"No, my good friend Robin,—not to-night, at least," said the gentleman. "Some few days hence, if you wish it, I will speed you on your journey. Or, if you prefer to remain with us, perhaps, as you are a shrewd youth, you may rise in the world without the help of your kinsman, Major Molineux."

FOR DISCUSSION:

1. *Can Robin's adventures be interpreted as part of an initiation rite psychologically preparing him for the final scene in which he confronts his kinsman? How?*

2. *How is color contrast, particularly the light-dark device, used by Hawthorne to illustrate the moral theme of the tale? Has he departed from the conventional meaning of innocence which is usually represented by white? Is Robin's innocence associated with*

brightness and illumination, or is it associated with the darkness of ignorance? Is innocence a positive quality here?

3. In his quest Robin mainly encounters men; since all the men are older than he, do they represent aspects of the father image: authority, power, security, order? What are Robin's reactions to these men? What do the women he meets represent?

4. Does the church scene bring relief and faith to Robin's mind, or does it increase his anxiety? Why is it followed immediately by a vision of home which concludes with the door being shut to Robin?

5. Is the final scene in which Robin encounters his kinsman similar to an initiation rite in which Robin is tested? If so, does he pass the rites satisfactorily? What is the meaning of his laughter?

Stopping by Woods on a Snowy Evening

ROBERT FROST

Whose woods these are I think I know.
His house is in the village though;
He will not see me stopping here
To watch his woods fill up with snow.

My little horse must think it queer
To stop without a farmhouse near
Between the woods and frozen lake
The darkest evening of the year.

He gives his harness bells a shake
To ask if there is some mistake.
The only other sound's the sweep
Of easy wind and downy flake.

The woods are lovely, dark and deep.
But I have promises to keep,
And miles to go before I sleep,
And miles to go before I sleep.

FOR DISCUSSION:

1. Why is it significant that the poem is set in the winter on the darkest evening of the year?

2. What do the woods and the horse represent?

3. How does the reader know that the speaker wants to enter the woods?

To Autumn

JOHN KEATS

I

Season of mists and mellow fruitfulness,
 Close bosom-Friend of the maturing sun;
Conspiring with him how to load and bless
 With fruit the vines that round the thatch-eaves run;
To bend with apples the moss'd cottage-trees,
 And fill all fruit with ripeness to the core;
  To swell the gourd, and plump the hazel shells
 With a sweet kernel; to set budding more,
And still more, later flowers for the bees,
Until they think warm days will never cease,
 For Summer has o'er-brimm'd their clammy cells.

II

Who hath not seen thee oft amid thy store?
 Sometimes whoever seeks abroad may find
Thee sitting careless on a granary floor,
 Thy hair soft-lifted by the winnowing wind;

---

* From COMPLETE POEMS OF ROBERT FROST. Copyright, 1923, 1930, 1939 by Holt, Rinehart and Winston, Inc. Copyright 1951, © 1958 by Robert Frost. Reprinted by permission of Holt, Rinehart and Winston, Inc. and Jonathan Cape Ltd.

    Or on a half-reap'd furrow sound asleep,
        Drows'd with the fume of poppies, while thy hook
          Spares the next swath and all its twined flowers:
    And sometimes like a gleaner thou dost keep
        Steady thy laden head across a brook;   20
        Or by a cyder-press, with patient look,
          Thou watchest the last oozings hours by hours.

III

    Where are the songs of Spring? Ay, where are they?
        Think not of them, thou hast thy music too,—
    While barred clouds bloom the soft-dying day,
        And touch the stubble-plains with rosy hue;
    Then in a wailful choir the small gnats mourn
        Among the river sallows, borne aloft
          Or sinking as the light wind lives or dies;
    And full-grown lambs loud bleat from hilly bourn;   30
        Hedge-crickets sing; and now with treble soft
    The red-breast whistles from a garden-croft;
        And gathering swallows twitter in the skies.

FOR DISCUSSION:

1. What exactly does autumn represent for Keats?

2. Why does Keats note in line 30 that the lambs are "full-grown"? Why are the swallows "gathering" in the skies in line 33?

3. In a criticism of "To Autumn," Walter Jackson Bate writes, "Each of the three stanzas concentrates on a dominant, even archetypal, aspect of autumn, but while doing so, admits and absorbs its opposite." Discuss.

Crossing the Bar

ALFRED, LORD TENNYSON

    Sunset and evening star,
        And one clear call for me!
    And may there be no moaning of the bar,
        When I put out to sea,

    But such a tide as moving seems asleep,
        Too full for sound and foam,
    When that which drew from out the boundless deep
        Turns again home.

    Twilight and evening bell,
        And after that the dark!   10
    And may there be no sadness of farewell,
        When I embark;

For tho' from out our bourne of Time and Place
  The flood may bear me far,
I hope to see my Pilot face to face
  When I have crost the bar.

FOR DISCUSSION:

1. Comment on the effectiveness of the journey image. In what way is God like a pilot?

2. Since a pilot's duties are usually limited to the harbor, is the image in lines 15–16 a poor one? Why? Why not?

3. Is Tennyson's attitude as he confronts death calm, fearful, or resigned? How does the poem's imagery reveal his feelings?

Ulysses

ALFRED, LORD TENNYSON

It little profits that an idle king,
By this still hearth, among these barren crags,
Match'd with an aged wife, I mete and dole
Unequal laws unto a savage race,
That hoard, and sleep, and feed, and know not me.
I cannot rest from travel: I will drink
Life to the lees: all times I have enjoy'd
Greatly, have suffer'd greatly, both with those
That loved me, and alone; on shore, and when
Thro' scudding drifts the rainy Hyades   10
Vext the dim sea: I am become a name;
For always roaming with a hungry heart
Much have I seen and known,—cities of men
And manners, climates, councils, governments,
Myself not least, but honour'd of them all,—
And drunk delight of battle with my peers,
Far on the ringing plains of windy Troy.
I am a part of all that I have met;
Yet all experience is an arch wherethro'
Gleams that untravell'd world whose margin fades 20
For ever and for ever when I move.
How dull it is to pause, to make an end,
To rust unburnish'd, not to shine in use!
As tho' to breathe were life. Life piled on life
Were all too little, and of one to me
Little remains: but every hour is saved
From that eternal silence, something more,
A bringer of new things; and vile it were
For some three suns to store and hoard myself,
And this gray spirit yearning in desire   30
To follow knowledge, like a sinking star,
Beyond the utmost bound of human thought.
  This is my son, mine own Telemachus,
To whom I leave the sceptre and the isle—

Well-loved of me, discerning to fulfill
This labour, by slow prudence to make mild
A rugged people, and thro' soft degrees
Subdue them to the useful and the good.
Most blameless is he, centred in the sphere
Of common duties, decent not to fail 40
In offices of tenderness, and pay
Meet adoration to my household gods,
When I am gone. He works his work, I mine.
   There lies the port: the vessel puffs her sail:
There gloom the dark broad seas. My mariners,
Souls that have toil'd, and wrought, and thought with me—
That ever with a frolic welcome took
The thunder and the sunshine, and opposed
Free hearts, free foreheads—you and I are old;
Old age hath yet his honour and his toil; 50
Death closes all: but something ere the end,
Some work of noble note, may yet be done,
Not unbecoming men that strove with Gods.
The lights begin to twinkle from the rocks:
The long day wanes: the slow moon climbs: the deep
Moans round with many voices. Come, my friends.
'T is not too late to seek a newer world.
Push off, and sitting well in order smite
The sounding furrows; for my purpose holds
To sail beyond the sunset, and the baths 60
Of all the western stars, until I die.
It may be that the gulfs will wash us down:
It may be we shall touch the Happy Isles,
And see the great Achilles, whom we knew.
Tho' much is taken, much abides; and tho'
We are not now that strength which in old days
Moved earth and heaven, that which we are, we are;
One equal temper of heroic hearts,
Made weak by time and fate, but strong in will
To strive, to seek, to find, and not to yield. 70

FOR DISCUSSION:

1. Tennyson's sources for this poem are the Odyssey, XI, 100–137 and Dante's Inferno, canto XXVI. What aspects of his sources does he emphasize?

2. Comment on Tennyson's Ulysses as a modified Faust figure.

The Lotos-Eaters

ALFRED, LORD TENNYSON

"Courage!" he said, and pointed toward the land,
"This mounting wave will roll us shoreward soon."
In the afternoon they came unto a land
In which it seemed always afternoon.

All round the coast the languid air did swoon,
Breathing like one that hath a weary dream.
Full-faced above the valley stood the moon;
And, like a downward smoke, the slender stream
Along the cliff to fall and pause and fall did seem.

A land of streams! some, like a downward smoke, 10
Slow-dropping veils of thinnest lawn, did go;
And some thro' wavering lights and shadows broke,
Rolling a slumbrous sheet of foam below.
They saw the gleaming rivers seaward flow
From the inner land: far off, three mountain-tops,
Three silent pinnacles of aged snow,
Stood sunset-flush'd; and, dew'd with showery drops,
Up-clomb the shadowy pine above the woven copse.

The charmed sunset linger'd low adown
In the red West; thro' mountain clefts the dale 20
Was seen far inland, and the yellow down
Border'd with palm, and many a winding vale
And meadow, set with slender galingale;
A land where all things always seem'd the same!
And round about the keel with faces pale,
Dark faces pale against that rosy flame,
The mild-eyed melancholy Lotos-eaters came.

Branches they bore of that enchanted stem,
Laden with flower and fruit, whereof they gave
To each, but whoso did receive of them 30
And taste, to him the gushing of the wave
Far far away did seem to mourn and rave
On alien shores; and if his fellow spake,
His voice was thin, as voices from the grave;
And deep-asleep he seem'd, yet all awake,
And music in his ears his beating heart did make.

They sat them down upon the yellow sand,
Between the sun and moon upon the shore;
And sweet it was to dream of Fatherland,
Of child, and wife, and slave; but evermore 40
Most weary seem'd the sea, weary the oar,
Weary the wandering fields of barren foam.
Then some one said, "We will return no more;"
And all at once they sang "Our island home
Is far beyond the wave; we will no longer roam."

CHORIC SONG

I

There is sweet music here that softer falls
Than petals from blown roses on the grass,
Or night-dews on still waters between walls
Of shadowy granite, in a gleaming pass;

Music that gentlier on the spirit lies,
Than tir'd eyelids upon tir'd eyes;
Music that brings sweet sleep down from the blissful skies.
Here are cold mosses deep,
And thro' the moss the ivies creep,
And in the stream the long-leaved flowers weep,
And from the craggy ledge the poppy hangs in sleep.

II

Why are we weigh'd upon with heaviness,
And utterly consumed with sharp distress,
While all things else have rest from weariness?
All things have rest: why should we toil alone,
We only toil, who are the first of things,
And make perpetual moan,
Still from one sorrow to another thrown:
Nor ever fold our wings,
And cease from wanderings,
Nor steep our brows in slumber's holy balm;
Nor harken what the inner spirit sings,
"There is no joy but calm!"
Why should we only toil, the roof and crown of things?

III

Lo! in the middle of the wood,
The folded leaf is woo'd from out the bud
With winds upon the branch, and there
Grows green and broad, and takes no care,
Sun-steep'd at noon, and in the moon
Nightly dew-fed; and turning yellow
Falls, and floats adown the air.
Lo! sweeten'd with the summer light,
The full-juiced apple, waxing over-mellow,
Drops in a silent autumn night.
All its allotted length of days
The flower ripens in its place,
Ripens and fades, and falls, and hath no toil,
Fast-rooted in the fruitful soil.

IV

Hateful is the dark-blue sky,
Vaulted o'er the dark-blue sea.
Death is the end of life; ah, why
Should life all labour be?
Let us alone. Time driveth onward fast,
And in a little while our lips are dumb.
Let us alone. What is it that will last?
All things are taken from us, and become
Portions and parcels of the dreadful Past.
Let us alone. What pleasure can we have
To war with evil? Is there any peace

In ever climbing up the climbing wave?
All things have rest, and ripen toward the grave
In silence; ripen, fall, and cease:
Give us long rest or death, dark death, or dreamful ease.

V

How sweet it were, hearing the downward stream,
With half-shut eyes ever to seem
Falling asleep in a half-dream!
To dream and dream, like yonder amber light,
Which will not leave the myrrh-bush on the height;
To hear each other's whisper'd speech:
Eating the Lotos days by day,
To watch the crisping ripples on the beach,
And tender curving lines of creamy spray;
To lend our hearts and spirits wholly
To the influence of mild-minded melancholy;
To muse and brood and live again in memory,
With those old faces of our infancy
Heap'd over with a mound of grass,
Two handfuls of white dust, shut in an urn of brass!

VI

Dear is the memory of our wedded lives,
And dear the last embraces of our wives
And their warm tears: but all hath suffer'd change;
For surely now our household hearths are cold:
Our sons inherit us: our looks are strange:
And we should come like ghosts to trouble joy.
Or else the island princes over-bold
Have eat our substance, and the minstrel sings
Before them of the ten years' war in Troy,
And our great deeds, as half-forgotten things.
Is there confusion in the little isle?
Let what is broken so remain.
The Gods are hard to reconcile:
'T is hard to settle order once again.
There *is* confusion worse than death,
Trouble on trouble, pain on pain,
Long labour unto aged breath,
Sore task to hearts worn out by many wars
And eyes grown dim with gazing on the pilot-stars.

VII

But, propt on beds of amaranth and moly,
How sweet—while warm airs lull us, blowing lowly—
With half-dropt eyelid still,
Beneath a heaven dark and holy,
To watch the long bright river drawing slowly
His waters from the purple hill—

To hear the dewy echoes calling
From cave to cave thro' the thick-twined vine—
To watch the emerald-colour'd water falling
Thro' many a wov'n acanthus-wreath divine!
Only to hear and see the far-off sparkling brine,
Only to hear were sweet, stretch'd out beneath the pine.

VIII

The Lotos blooms below the barren peak,
The Lotos blows by every winding creek;
All day the wind breathes low with mellower tone;
Thro' every hollow cave and alley lone
Round and round the spicy down the yellow Lotos-dust is blown.
We have had enough of action, and of motion we,
Roll'd to starboard, roll'd to larboard, when the surge was seething free,
Where the wallowing monster spouted his foam fountains in the sea.
Let us swear an oath, and keep it with an equal mind,
In the hollow Lotos-land to live and lie reclined
On the hills like Gods together, careless of mankind.
For they lie beside their nectar, and the bolts are hurl'd
Far below them in the valleys, and the clouds are lightly curl'd
Round their golden houses, girdled with the gleaming world:
Where they smile in secret, looking over wasted lands,
Blight and famine, plague and earthquake, roaring deeps and fiery sands,
Clanging fights, and flaming towns, and sinking ships, and praying hands.
But they smile, they find a music centred in a doleful song
Steaming up, a lamentation and an ancient tale of wrong,
Like a tale of little meaning tho' the words are strong;
Chanted from an ill-used race of men that cleave the soil,
Sow the seed, and reap the harvest with enduring toil,
Storing yearly little dues of wheat, and wine and oil;
Till they perish and they suffer—some, 't is whisper'd—down in hell
Suffer endless anguish, others in Elysian valleys dwell,
Resting weary limbs at last on beds of asphodel.
Surely, surely, slumber is more sweet than toil, the shore
Than labour in the deep mid-ocean, wind and wave and oar;
Oh, rest ye, brother mariners, we will not wander more.

FOR DISCUSSION:

1. Compare Tennyson's account with that described in the Odyssey, IX, 82 ff. What changes has Tennyson made? To what purpose?

2. This poem argues for a life of lassitude and self-indulgence. Show how the image, meter, and events are intended to create a mood of somnolence and rest.

3. The theme of "The Lotos-Eaters" is in direct contrast to Ulysses' belief that the way of the meaningful life is "to strive, to seek, to find and not to yield." Compare the two poems in theme.

Bacchus

RALPH WALDO EMERSON

Bring me wine, but wine which never grew
In the belly of the grape,
Or grew on vine whose tap-roots, reaching through
Under the Andes to the Cape,
Suffered no savor of the earth to scape.

Let its grapes the morn salute
From a nocturnal root,
Which feels the acrid juice
Of Styx and Erebus;
And turns the woe of Night, 10
By its own craft, to a more rich delight.

We buy ashes for bread;
We buy diluted wine;
Give me of the true,—
Whose ample leaves and tendrils curled
Among the silver hills of heaven,
Draw everlasting dew;
Wine of wine,
Blood of the world,
Form of forms, and mould of statures, 20
That I intoxicated,
And by the draught assimilated,
May float at pleasure through all natures;
The bird-language rightly spell,
And that which roses say so well.

Wine that is shed
Like the torrents of the sun
Up the horizon walls,
Or like the Atlantic streams, which run
When the South Sea calls. 30

Water and bread,
Food which needs no transmuting,
Rainbow-flowering, wisdom-fruiting
Wine which is already man,
Food which teach and reason can.

Wine which Music is,—
Music and wine are one,—
That I, drinking this,
Shall hear far Chaos talk with me;
Kings unborn shall walk with me; 40
And the poor grass shall plot and plan
What it will do when it is man.
Quickened so, will I unlock
Every crypt of every rock.

I thank the joyful juice
For all I know;—
Winds of remembering
Of the ancient being blow,
And seeming-solid walls of use
Open and flow.   50

Pour, Bacchus! the remembering wine;
Retrieve the loss of me and mine!
Vine for vine be antidote,
And the grape requite the lote!
Haste to cure the old despair,—
Reason in Nature's lotus drenched,
The memory of ages quenched;
Give them again to shine;
Let wine repair what this undid;
And where the infection slid,   60
A dazzling memory revive;
Refresh the faded tints,
Recut the aged prints,
And write my old adventures with the pen
Which on the first day drew,
Upon the tablets blue,
The dancing Pleiads and eternal men.

FOR DISCUSSION:

1. Wine is obviously being used symbolically in this poem. What does it represent?

2. Emerson conceives of himself in "Bacchus" as an archetypal poet. For what is he asking?

3. What is meant by line 52, "Retrieve the loss of me and mine"?

Oedipus*

EDWIN MUIR

I, Oedipus, the club-foot, made to stumble,
Who long in the light have walked the world in darkness,
And once in the darkness did that which the light
Found and disowned—too well I have loved the light,
Too dearly have rued the darkness. I am one
Who as in innocent play sought out his guilt,
And now through guilt seeks other innocence,
Beset by evil thoughts, led by the gods.

There was a room, a bed of darkness, once
Known to me, now to all. Yet in that darkness,   10
Before the light struck, she and I who lay

* From *Collected Poems* by Edwin Muir. Copyright © 1960 by Willa Muir. Reprinted by permission of Oxford University Press, Inc. and Faber & Faber Ltd.

There without thought of sin and knew each other
Too well, yet were to each other quite unknown
Though fastened mouth to mouth and breast to breast—
Strangers laid on one bed, as children blind,
Clear-eyed and blind as children—did we sin
Then on that bed before the light came on us,
Desiring good to each other, bringing, we thought,
Great good to each other? But neither guilt nor death.

Yet if that darkness had been darker yet,
Buried in endless dark past reach of light
Or eye of the gods, a kingdom of solid darkness
Impregnable and immortal, would we have sinned,
Or lived like the gods in deathless innocence?
For sin is born in the light; therefore we cower
Before the face of the light that none can meet
And all must seek. And when in memory now,
Woven of light and darkness, a stifling web,
I call her back, dear, dreaded, who lay with me,
I see guilt, only guilt, my nostrils choke
With the smell of guilt, and I can scarcely breathe
Here in the guiltless guilt-evoking sun.

And when young Oedipus—for it was Oedipus
And not another—on that long vanished night
Far in my night, at that predestined point
Where three paths like three fates crossed one another,
Tracing the evil figure—when I met
The stranger who menaced me, and flung the stone
That brought him death and me this that I carry,
It was not him but fear I sought to kill,
Fear that, the wise men say, is father of evil,
And was my father in flesh and blood, yet fear,
Fear only, father and fear in one dense body,
So that there was no division, no way past:
Did I sin then, by the gods admonished to sin,
By men enjoined to sin? For it is duty
Of god and man to kill the shapes of fear.

These thoughts recur, vain thoughts. The gods see all,
And will what must be willed, which guards us here.
Their will in them was anger, in me was terror
Long since, but now is peace. For I am led
By them in darkness; light is all about me;
My way lies in the light; they know it; I
Am theirs to guide and hold. And I have learned,
Though blind, to see with something of their sight,
Can look into that other world and watch
King Oedipus the just, crowned and discrowned,
As one may see oneself rise in a dream,
Distant and strange. Even so I see
The meeting at the place where three roads crossed,
And who was there and why, and what was done
That had to be done and paid for. Innocent
The deed that brought the guilt of father-murder. Pure

The embrace on the bed of darkness. Innocent
And guilty. I have wrought and thought in darkness,
And stand here now, an innocent mark of shame,
That so men's guilt might be made manifest
In such a walking riddle—their guilt and mine,
For I've but acted out this fable. I have judged
Myself, obedient to the gods' high judgment,　　　　　　　70
And seen myself with their pure eyes, have learnt
That all must bear a portion of the wrong
That is driven deep into our fathomless hearts
Past sight or thought; that bearing it we may ease
The immortal burden of the gods who keep
Our natural steps and the earth and skies from harm.

FOR DISCUSSION:

1. This poem uses the Oedipus myth to explore the nature of guilt. Does Muir believe Oedipus is guilty of incest and his father's murder? In what sense is Oedipus innocent of both?
2. How are images of light and darkness used both literally and metaphorically throughout the poem? What is their significance?
3. What conclusion does Muir reach about the necessity of guilt?
4. Is the conclusion ironic and bitter or resigned and reconciled?

Kilroy*

PETER VIERECK

I

Also Ulysses once—that other war.
   (Is it because we find his scrawl
   Today on every privy door
   That we forget his ancient rôle?)
Also was there—he did it for the wages—
When a Cathay-drunk Genoese set sail.
Whenever "longen folk to goon on pilgrimages,"
Kilroy is there;
        he tells The Miller's Tale.

II

At times he seems a paranoiac king　　　　　　　10
Who stamps his crest on walls and says, "My own!"
But in the end he fades like a lost tune,
Tossed here and there, whom all the breezes sing.
"Kilroy was here"; these words sound wanly gay,
   Haughty yet tired with long marching.

* "Kilroy" appeared in Peter Viereck's out of print *Terror and Decorum*, N.Y., 1948, which won the 1949 Pulitzer Prize, and in the Bobbs-Merrill edition of his *New and Selected Poems*, N.Y., 1966. Reprinted by permission of the author.

He is Orestes—guilty of what crime?—
   For whom the Furies still are searching;
   When they arrive, they find their prey
(Leaving his name to mock them) went away.
Sometimes he does not flee from them in time:
"Kilroy was——"
              (with his blood a dying man
   Wrote half the phrase out in Bataan.)

III

Kilroy, beware. "HOME" is the final trap
That lurks for you in many a wily shape:
In pipe-and-slippers plus a Loyal Hound
   Or fooling around, just fooling around.
Kind to the old (their warm Penelope)
But fierce to boys,
              thus "home" becomes that sea,
Horribly disguised, where you were always drowned,—
   (How could suburban Crete condone
The yarns you would have V-mailed from the sun?)—
And folksy fishes sip Icarian tea.

One stab of hopeless wings imprinted your
   Exultant Kilroy-signature
Upon sheer sky for all the world to stare:
   "I was there! I was there! I was there!"

IV

God is like Kilroy; He, too, sees it all;
That's how He knows of every sparrow's fall;
That's why we prayed each time the tightropes cracked
On which our loveliest clowns contrived their act.
The G. I. Faustus who was
              everywhere
Strolled home again. "What was it like outside?"
Asked Can't, with his good neighbors Ought and But
And pale Perhaps and grave-eyed Better Not;
For "Kilroy" means: the world is very wide.
       He was there, he was there, he was there!

And in the suburbs Can't sat down and cried.

FOR DISCUSSION:

1. "Kilroy was here" was a favorite phrase of U.S. servicemen during World War II, which they chalked on walls all over the world. Why does Viereck choose this modern mythic figure as the protagonist of his poem?

2. Explain the references to the Canterbury Tales (lines 7–8), Orestes and the Furies (lines 16–17), the Odyssey (lines 25–28), and Faust (line 41).

3. Explain the poem's final line.

Corinna's Going A-Maying

ROBERT HERRICK

Get up, get up for shame, the Blooming Morne
Upon her wings presents the god unshorne.
      See how Aurora throwes her faire
      Fresh-quilted colours through the aire:
      Get up, sweet-Slug-a-bed, and see
      The Dew-bespangling Herbe and Tree.
Each Flower has wept, and bow'd toward the East,
Above an houre since; yet you not drest,
      Nay! not so much as out of bed?
      When all the Birds have Mattens seyd,
      And sung their thankfull Hymnes: 'tis sin,
      Nay, profanation to keep in,
When as a thousand Virgins on this day,
Spring, sooner then the Lark, to fetch in May.

Rise; and put on your Foliage, and be seene
To come forth, like the Spring-time, fresh and greene;
      And sweet as *Flora*. Take no care
      For Jewels for your Gowne, or Haire:
      Feare not; the leaves will strew
      Gemms in abundance upon you:
Besides, the childhood of the Day has kept,
Against you come, some *Orient Pearls* unwept:
      Come, and receive them while the light
      Hangs on the Dew-locks of the night.
      And *Titan* on the Eastern hill
      Retires himselfe, or else stands still
Till you come forth. Wash, dresse, be briefe in praying:
Few Beads are best, when once we goe a Maying.

Come, my *Corinna*, come; and comming, marke
How each field turns a street; each street a Parke
      Made green, and trimm'd with trees: see how
      Devotion gives each House a Bough,
      Or Branch: Each Porch, each doore, ere this,
      An Arke a Tabernacle is
Made up of white-thorn neatly enterwove;
As if here were those cooler shades of love.
      Can such delights be in the street,
      And open fields, and we not see't?
      Come, we'll abroad; and let's obay
      The Proclamation made for May:
And sin no more, as we have done, by staying;
But my *Corinna*, come, let's goe a Maying.

There's not a budding Boy, or Girle, this day,
But is got up, and gone to bring in May.
      A deale of Youth, ere this, is come

Back, and with *White-thorn* laden home.
Some have dispatcht their Cakes and Creame,
Before that we have left to dreame:
And some have wept, and woo'd, and plighted Troth,
And chose their Priest, ere we can cast off sloth:
    Many a green-gown has been given;
    Many a kisse, both odde and even:
    Many a glance too has been sent
    From out the eye, Loves Firmament:
Many a jest told of the Keyes betraying
This night, and Locks pickt, yet w'are not a Maying.

Come, let us goe, while we are in our prime;
And take the harmlesse follie of the time.
    We shall grow old apace, and die
    Before we know our liberty.
    Our life is short; and our dayes run
    As fast away as do's the Sunne:
And as a vapour, or a drop of raine
Once lost, can ne'r be found againe:
    So when or you or I are made
    A fable, song, or fleeting shade;
    All love, all liking, all delight
    Lies drown'd with us in endlesse night.
Then while time serves, and we are but decaying;
Come, my *Corinna*, come, let's goe a Maying.

FOR DISCUSSION:

1. Is this poem in the Christian or pagan tradition?
2. What do the May rites represent for Herrick?
3. What is the philosophy of life advanced by this poem? Is it an irresponsible philosophy?
4. Corinna is another name for Persephone, the goddess of spring. One critic believes the poem to be addressed to this goddess, imploring her to awaken and inhabit the countryside now that May has arrived. Is this interpretation more plausible than the view that the speaker is asking an English girl to go a-Maying with him? Does the poem support both views?
5. Is this archetypal poetry or poetry about archetypes?

Sailing to Byzantium

WILLIAM BUTLER YEATS

That is no country for old men. The young
In one another's arms, birds in the trees,
—Those dying generations—at their song,
The salmon-falls, the mackerel-crowded seas,
Fish, flesh, or fowl, commend all summer long

* Reprinted by permission of the publisher from THE COLLECTED POEMS OF WILLIAM BUTLER YEATS. Copyright 1928 by The Macmillan Company, Copyright renewed 1956 by Georgie Yeats. Also reprinted by permission of M. B. Yeats and The Macmillan Company of Canada Ltd.

Whatever is begotten, born, and dies.
Caught in that sensual music all neglect
Monuments of unageing intellect.

An aged man is but a paltry thing,
A tattered coat upon a stick, unless
Soul clap its hands and sing, and louder sing
For every tatter in its mortal dress,
Nor is there singing school but studying
Monuments of its own magnificence;
And therefore I have sailed the seas and come
To the holy city of Byzantium.

O sages standing in God's holy fire
As in the gold mosaic of a wall,
Come from the holy fire, perne in a gyre,
And be the singing-masters of my soul.
Consume my heart away; sick with desire
And fastened to a dying animal
It knows not what it is; and gather me
Into the artifice of eternity.

Once out of nature I shall never take
My bodily form from any natural thing,
But such a form as Grecian goldsmiths make
Of hammered gold and gold enamelling
To keep a drowsy Emperor awake;
Or set upon a golden bough to sing
To lords and ladies of Byzantium
Of what is past, or passing, or to come.

FOR DISCUSSION:

1. Is this an optimistic or pessimistic poem?
2. What are Yeats's attitudes toward aging and death? Does he find any recompense for the deprivations of old age, any possibility of regeneration?
3. What does Byzantium represent to Yeats?
4. Is there a belief in a sort of reincarnation expressed in the poem's final stanza? If so, what kind?

19. perne whirl, spin

The Rime of the Ancient Mariner

IN SEVEN PARTS

SAMUEL TAYLOR COLERIDGE

Facile credo, plures esse Naturas invisibiles quam visibiles in rerum universitate. Sed horum omnium familiam quis nobis enarrabit? et gradus et cognationes et discrimina et singulorum munera? Quid agunt? quae loca habitant? Harum rerum notitiam semper ambivit ingenium humanum, nunquam attigit. Juvat, interea, non diffiteor, quandoque in animo, tanquam in tabulà, majoris et melioris mundi imaginem contemplari: ne mens assuefacta hodiernae vitae minutiis se contrahst nimis, et tota subsidat in pusillas cogitationes. Sed veritati interea invigilandum est, modusque servandus, ut certa ab incertis, diem a nocte, distinguamus.

T. BURNET, Archaeol. Phil. p. 68.

I readily believe that there are more invisible beings in the universe than visible. But who shall explain to us the nature, the rank and kinship, the distinguishing marks and graces of each? What do they do? Where do they dwell? The human mind has circled round this knowledge, but never attained to it. Yet there is a profit, I do not doubt, in sometimes contemplating in the mind, as in a picture, the image of a greater and better world, lest the intellect, habituated to the petty details of daily life, should be contracted within too narrow limits and settle down wholly on trifles. But meanwhile, a watchful eye must be kept on truth, and proportion observed, that we may distinguish the certain from the uncertain, day from night.

BURNET, transl. Ernest Bernbaum

ARGUMENT

How a Ship having passed the Line was driven by storms to the cold Country towards the South Pole; and how from thence she made her course to the tropical Latitude of the Great Pacific Ocean; and of the strange things that befell; and in what manner the Ancyent Marinere came back to his own Country.

PART I

It is an ancient Mariner,
And he stoppeth one of three.
"By thy long grey beard and glittering eye,
Now wherefore stopp'st thou me?

The Bridegroom's doors are opened wide,
And I am next of kin;
The guests are met, the feast is set:
May'st hear the merry din."

10 He holds him with his skinny hand,
"There was a ship," quoth he.
"Hold off! unhand me, grey-beard loon!"
Eftsoons his hand dropt he.

He holds him with his glittering eye—
The Wedding-Guest stood still,
And listens like a three years' child:
The Mariner hath his will.

The Wedding-Guest sat on a stone:
He cannot choose but hear;

An ancient Mariner meeteth three Gallants bidden to a wedding-feast, and detaineth one.

The Wedding-Guest is spellbound by the eye of the old seafaring man, and constrained to hear his tale.

And thus spake on that ancient man,
20   The bright-eyed Mariner.

"The ship was cheered, the harbour cleared,
Merrily did we drop
Below the kirk, below the hill,
Below the lighthouse top.

The Sun came up upon the left,
Out of the sea came he!
And he shone bright, and on the right
Went down into the sea.

Higher and higher every day,
30   Till over the mast at noon—"
The Wedding-Guest here beat his breast,
For he heard the loud bassoon.

The Mariner tells how the ship sailed southward with a good wind and fair weather, till it reached the Line.

The bride hath paced into the hall,
Red as a rose is she;
Nodding their heads before her goes
The merry minstrelsy.

The Wedding-Guest heareth the bridal music; but the Mariner continueth his tale.

The Wedding-Guest he beat his breast,
Yet he cannot choose but hear;
And thus spake on that ancient man,
40   The bright-eyed Mariner.

"And now the STORM-BLAST came, and he
Was tyrannous and strong:
He struck with his o'ertaking wings,
And chased us south along.

The ship driven by a storm toward the south pole.

With sloping masts and dipping prow,
As who pursued with yell and blow
Still treads the shadow of his foe,
And forward bends his head,
The ship drove fast, loud roared the blast,
50   And southward aye we fled.

And now there came both mist and snow,
And it grew wondrous cold:
And ice, mast-high, came floating by,
As green as emerald.

And through the drifts the snowy clifts
Did send a dismal sheen:
Nor shapes of men nor beasts we ken—
The ice was all between.

The land of ice, and of fearful sounds where no living thing was to be seen.

The ice was here, the ice was there,
60   The ice was all around:
It cracked and growled, and roared and howled,
Like noises in a swound!

At length did cross an Albatross,
Thorough the fog it came;
As if it had been a Christian soul,
We hailed it in God's name.

Till a great sea-bird, called the Albatross, came through the snow-fog and was received with great joy and hospitality.

It ate the food it ne'er had eat,
And round and round it flew.
The ice did split with a thunder-fit;
⁷⁰ The helmsman steered us through!

And a good south wind sprung up behind;
The Albatross did follow,
And every day, for food or play,
Came to the mariner's hollo!

And lo! the Albatross proveth a bird of good omen, and followeth the ship as it returned northward through fog and floating ice.

In mist or cloud, on mast or shroud,
It perched for vespers nine;
Whiles all the night, through fog-smoke white,
Glimmered the white Moon-shine."

"God save thee, ancient Mariner!
From the fiends, that plague thee thus!—
⁸⁰ Why look'st thou so?"—With my cross-bow
I shot the ALBATROSS.

The ancient Mariner inhospitably killeth the pious bird of good omen.

PART II

The Sun now rose upon the right:
Out of the sea came he,
Still hid in mist, and on the left
Went down into the sea.

And the good south wind still blew behind,
But no sweet bird did follow,
Nor any day for food or play
⁹⁰ Came to the mariner's hollo!

And I had done a hellish thing,
And it would work 'em woe:
For all averred, I had killed the bird
That made the breeze to blow.
Ah wretch! said they, the bird to slay,
That made the breeze to blow!

His shipmates cry out against the ancient Mariner, for killing the bird of good luck.

Nor dim nor red, like God's own head,
The glorious Sun uprist:
Then all averred, I had killed the bird
¹⁰⁰ That brought the fog and mist.
'Twas right, said they, such birds to slay,
That bring the fog and mist.

But when the fog cleared off, they justify the same, and thus make themselves accomplices in the crime.

The fair breeze blew, the white foam flew,
The furrow followed free;
We were the first that ever burst
Into that silent sea.

The fair breeze continues; the ship enters the Pacific Ocean, and sails northward, even till it reaches the Line.

Down dropt the breeze, the sails dropt down,   *The ship hath been suddenly*
'Twas sad as sad could be;   *becalmed.*
And we did speak only to break
110   The silence of the sea!

All in a hot and copper sky,
The bloody Sun, at noon,
Right up above the mast did stand,
No bigger than the Moon.

Day after day, day after day,
We stuck, nor breath nor motion;
As idle as a painted ship
Upon a painted ocean.

Water, water every where,   *And the Albatross begins to*
120   And all the boards did shrink;   *be avenged.*
Water, water every where,
Nor any drop to drink.

The very deep did rot: O Christ!
That ever this should be!
Yea, slimy things did crawl with legs
Upon the slimy sea.

About, about, in reel and rout
The death-fires danced at night;
The water, like a witch's oils,
130   Burnt green, and blue and white.

And some in dreams assuréd were   *A spirit had followed them;*
Of the Spirit that plagued us so;   *one of the invisible inhabi-*
Nine fathom deep he had followed us   *tants of this planet, neither*
From the land of mist and snow.   *departed souls nor angels;*
   concerning whom the learned
   Jew, Josephus, and the Pla-
And every tongue, through utter drought,   *tonic Constantinopolitan, Mi-*
Was withered at the root;   *chael Psellus, may be*
We could not speak, no more than if   *consulted. They are very*
We had been choked with soot.   *numerous, and there is no*
   climate or element without
   one or more.

Ah! well a-day! what evil looks   *The shipmates, in their sore*
140   Had I from old and young!   *distress, would fain throw the*
Instead of the cross, the Albatross   *whole guilt on the ancient*
About my neck was hung.   *Mariner: in sign whereof*
   they hang the dead sea-bird
   round his neck.

PART III

There passed a weary time. Each throat
Was parched, and glazed each eye.
A weary time! a weary time!
How glazed each weary eye,
When looking westward, I beheld   *The ancient Mariner be-*
A something in the sky.   *holdeth a sign in the element*
   afar off.

At first it seemed a little speck,
And then it seemed a mist;
It moved and moved, and took at last
A certain shape, I wist.

A speck, a mist, a shape, I wist!
And still it neared and neared:
As if it dodged a water-sprite,
It plunged and tacked and veered.

With throats unslaked, with black lips baked,   *At its nearer approach, it seemeth him to be a ship; and at a dear ransom he freeth his speech from the bonds of thirst.*
We could nor laugh nor wail;
Through utter drought all dumb we stood!
I bit my arm, I sucked the blood,
And cried, A sail! a sail!

With throats unslaked, with black lips baked,
Agape they heard me call:
Gramercy! they for joy did grin,   *A flash of joy;*
And all at once their breath drew in,
As they were drinking all.

See! see! (I cried) she tacks no more!   *And horror follows. For can it be a ship that comes onward without wind or tide?*
Hither to work us weal;
Without a breeze, without a tide,
She steadies with upright keel!

The western wave was all a-flame.
The day was well nigh done!
Almost upon the western wave
Rested the broad bright Sun;
When that strange shape drove suddenly
Betwixt us and the Sun.

And straight the Sun was flecked with bars,   *It seemeth him but the skeleton of a ship.*
(Heaven's Mother send us grace!)
As if through a dungeon-grate he peered
With broad and burning face.

Alas! (thought I, and my heart beat loud)
How fast she nears and nears!
Are those *her* sails that glance in the Sun,
Like restless gossameres?

Are those *her* ribs through which the Sun   *And its ribs are seen as bars on the face of the setting Sun.*
Did peer, as through a grate?
And is that Woman all her crew?
Is that a Death? and are there two?
Is Death that woman's mate?

Her lips were red, her looks were free,   *The Spectre-Woman and her Deathmate, and no other on board the skeleton ship.*
Her locks were yellow as gold:
Her skin was as white as leprosy,

The Night-mare Life-in-Death was she,
Who thicks man's blood with cold.

The naked hulk alongside came,   *Like vessel, like crew!*
And the twain were casting dice;
"The game is done! I've won! I've won!"   *Death and Life-in-Death have*
Quoth she, and whistles thrice.   *diced for the ship's crew, and she (the latter) winneth the ancient Mariner.*

200   The Sun's rim dips; the stars rush out: *No twilight within the courts*
At one stride comes the dark;   *of the Sun.*
With far-heard whisper, o'er the sea,
Off shot the spectre-bark.

We listened and looked sideways up!   *At the rising of the Moon,*
Fear at my heart, as at a cup,
My life-blood seemed to sip!
The stars were dim, and thick the night,
The steersman's face by his lamp gleamed white;
From the sails the dew did drip—
Till clomb above the eastern bar
210   The hornéd Moon, with one bright star
Within the nether tip.

One after one, by the star-dogged Moon,   *One after another,*
Too quick for groan or sigh,
Each turned his face with a ghastly pang,
And cursed me with his eye.

Four times fifty living men,   *His shipmates drop down*
(And I heard nor sigh nor groan)   *dead.*
With heavy thump, a lifeless lump,
They dropped down one by one.

220   The souls did from their bodies fly,—   *But Life-in-Death begins her*
They fled to bliss or woe!   *work on the ancient Mariner.*
And every soul, it passed me by,
Like the whizz of my cross-bow!

PART IV

"I fear thee, ancient Mariner!   *The Wedding-Guest feareth*
I fear thy skinny hand!   *that a Spirit is talking to*
And thou art long, and lank, and brown,   *him;*
As is the ribbed sea-sand.

I fear thee and thy glittering eye,
And thy skinny hand, so brown."—
230   Fear not, fear not, thou Wedding-Guest!   *But the ancient Mariner as-*
This body dropt not down.   *sureth him of his bodily life, and proceedeth to relate his horrible penance.*

Alone, alone, all, all alone,
Alone on a wide wide sea!

And never a saint took pity on
My soul in agony.

The many men, so beautiful!
And they all dead did lie:
And a thousand thousand slimy things
Lived on; and so did I.

240 I looked upon the rotting sea,
And drew my eyes away;
I looked upon the rotting deck,
And there the dead men lay.

I looked to heaven, and tried to pray;
But or ever a prayer had gusht,
A wicked whisper came, and made
My heart as dry as dust.

I closed my lids, and kept them close,
And the balls like pulses beat;
250 For the sky and the sea, and the sea and the sky
Lay like a load on my weary eye,
And the dead were at my feet.

The cold sweat melted from their limbs,
Nor rot nor reek did they:
The look with which they looked on me
Had never passed away.

An orphan's curse would drag to hell
A spirit from on high;
But oh! more horrible than that
260 Is the curse in a dead man's eye!
Seven days, seven nights, I saw that curse,
And yet I could not die.

The moving Moon went up the sky,
And no where did abide:
Softly she was going up,
And a star or two beside —

Her beams bemocked the sultry main,
Like April hoar-frost spread;
But where the ship's huge shadow lay,
270 The charmèd water burnt alway
A still and awful red.

Beyond the shadow of the ship,
I watched the water-snakes:
They moved in tracks of shining white,
And when they reared, the elfish light
Fell off in hoary flakes.

He despiseth the creatures of the calm,

And envieth that they should live, and so many lie dead.

But the curse liveth for him in the eye of the dead men.

In his loneliness and fixedness he yearneth towards the journeying Moon, and the stars that still sojourn, yet still move onward; and every where the blue sky belongs to them, and is their appointed rest, and their native country and their own natural homes, which they enter unannounced, as lords that are certainly expected and yet there is a silent joy at their arrival.

By the light of the Moon he beholdeth God's creatures of the great calm.

Within the shadow of the ship
I watched their rich attire:
Blue, glossy green, and velvet black,
They coiled and swam; and every track
Was a flash of golden fire.

O happy living things! no tongue *Their beauty and their happiness.*
Their beauty might declare:
A spring of love gushed from my heart,
And I blessed them unaware: *He blesseth them in his heart.*
Sure my kind saint took pity on me,
And I blessed them unaware.

The self-same moment I could pray; *The spell begins to break.*
And from my neck so free
The Albatross fell off, and sank
Like lead into the sea.

PART V

Oh sleep! it is a gentle thing,
Beloved from pole to pole!
To Mary Queen the praise be given!
She sent the gentle sleep from Heaven,
That slid into my soul.

The silly buckets on the deck, *By grace of the holy Mother, the ancient Mariner is refreshed with rain.*
That had so long remained,
I dreamt that they were filled with dew;
And when I awoke, it rained.

My lips were wet, my throat was cold,
My garments all were dank;
Sure I had drunken in my dreams,
And still my body drank.

I moved, and could not feel my limbs:
I was so light—almost
I thought that I had died in sleep,
And was a blessèd ghost.

And soon I heard a roaring wind: *He heareth sounds and seeth strange sights and commotions in the sky and the element.*
It did not come anear;
But with its sound it shook the sails,
That were so thin and sere.

The upper air burst into life!
And a hundred fire-flags sheen,
To and fro they were hurried about!
And to and fro, and in and out,
The wan stars danced between.

And the coming wind did roar more loud,
And the sails did sigh like sedge;

320 And the rain poured down from one black cloud;
The Moon was at its edge.

The thick black cloud was cleft, and still
The Moon was at its side:
Like waters shot from some high crag,
The lightning fell with never a jag,
A river steep and wide.

The loud wind never reached the ship,   *The bodies of the ship's*
Yet now the ship moved on!   *crew are inspired and the*
Beneath the lightning and the Moon   *ship moves on.*
330 The dead men gave a groan.

They groaned, they stirred, they all uprose,
Nor spake, nor moved their eyes;
It had been strange, even in a dream,
To have seen those dead men rise.

The helmsman steered, the ship moved on;
Yet never a breeze up-blew;
The mariners all 'gan work the ropes,
Where they were wont to do;
They raised their limbs like lifeless tools—
340 We were a ghastly crew.

The body of my brother's son
Stood by me, knee to knee:
The body and I pulled at one rope,
But he said nought to me.

"I fear thee, ancient Mariner!"   *But not by the souls of the*
Be calm, thou Wedding-Guest!   *men, nor by daemons of*
'Twas not those souls that fled in pain,   *earth or middle air, but by a*
Which to their corses came again,   *blessed troop of angelic*
But a troop of spirits blest: *spirits, sent down by the*
     invocation of the guardian
350 For when it dawned—they dropped their arms,   *saint.*
And clustered round the mast;
Sweet sounds rose slowly through their mouths,
And from their bodies passed.

Around, around, flew each sweet sound,
Then darted to the Sun;
Slowly the sounds came back again,
Now mixed, now one by one.

Sometimes a-dropping from the sky
I heard the sky-lark sing;
360 Sometimes all little birds that are,
How they seemed to fill the sea and air
With their sweet jargoning!

And now 'twas like all instruments,
Now like a lonely flute;

And now it is an angel's song,
That makes the heavens be mute.

It ceased; yet still the sails made on
A pleasant noise till noon,
A noise like of a hidden brook
370 In the leafy month of June,
That to the sleeping woods all night
Singeth a quiet tune.

Till noon we quietly sailed on,
Yet never a breeze did breathe:
Slowly and smoothly went the ship,
Moved onward from beneath.

Under the keel nine fathom deep,   *The lonesome Spirit from the*
From the land of mist and snow,   *south-pole carries on the ship*
The spirit slid: and it was he   *as far as the Line, in obedi-*
380 That made the ship to go.   *ence to the angelic troop,*
The sails at noon left off their tune,   *but still requireth vengeance.*
And the ship stood still also.

The Sun, right up above the mast,
Had fixed her to the ocean:
But in a minute she 'gan stir,
With a short uneasy motion—
Backwards and forwards half her length
With a short uneasy motion.

Then like a pawing horse let go,
390 She made a sudden bound:
It flung the blood into my head,
And I fell down in a swound.

How long in that same fit I lay,   *The Polar Spirit's fellow-dae-*
I have not to declare;   *mons, the invisible inhabi-*
But ere my living life returned,   *tants of the element, take*
I heard and in my soul discerned   *part in his wrong; and two*
Two voices in the air.   *of them relate, one to the*
    other, that penance long and
"Is it he?" quoth one, "Is this the man?   *heavy for the ancient Mariner*
By him who died on cross,   *hath been accorded to the*
400 With his cruel bow he laid full low   *Polar Spirit, who returneth*
The harmless Albatross.   *southward.*

The spirit who bideth by himself
In the land of mist and snow,
He loved the bird that loved the man
Who shot him with his bow."

The other was a softer voice,
As soft as honey-dew:
Quoth he, "The man hath penance done,
And penance more will do."

PART VI

FIRST VOICE

⁴¹⁰ "But tell me, tell me! speak again,
Thy soft response renewing—
What makes that ship drive on so fast?
What is the ocean doing?"

SECOND VOICE

"Still as a slave before his lord,
The ocean hath no blast;
His great bright eye most silently
Up to the Moon is cast—

If he may know which way to go;
For she guides him smooth or grim.
⁴²⁰ See, brother, see! how graciously
She looketh down on him."

FIRST VOICE

"But why drives on that ship so fast,
Without or wave or wind?"

SECOND VOICE

"The air is cut away before,
And closes from behind.

Fly, brother, fly! more high, more high!
Or we shall be belated:
For slow and slow that ship will go,
When the Mariner's trance is abated."

⁴³⁰ I woke, and we were sailing on
As in a gentle weather:
'Twas night, calm night, the moon was high;
The dead men stood together.

All stood together on the deck,
For a charnel-dungeon fitter:
All fixed on me their stony eyes,
That in the Moon did glitter.

The pang, the curse, with which they died,
Had never passed away:
⁴⁴⁰ I could not draw my eyes from theirs,
Nor turn them up to pray.

And now this spell was snapt: once more
I viewed the ocean green,
And looked far forth, yet little saw
Of what had else been seen—

Like one, that on a lonesome road
Doth walk in fear and dread,

The Mariner hath been cast into a trance; for the angelic power causeth the vessel to drive northward faster than human life could endure.

The super-natural motion is retarded; the Mariner awakes, and his penance begins anew.

The curse is finally expiated.

And having once turned round walks on,
And turns no more his head;
Because he knows, a frightful fiend
Doth close behind him tread.

But soon there breathed a wind on me,
Nor sound nor motion made:
Its path was not upon the sea,
In ripple or in shade.

It raised my hair, it fanned my cheek
Like a meadow-gale of spring—
It mingled strangely with my fears,
Yet it felt like a welcoming.

Swiftly, swiftly flew the ship,
Yet she sailed softly too:
Sweetly, sweetly blew the breeze—
On me alone it blew.

Oh! dream of joy! is this indeed
The light-house top I see?
Is this the hill? is this the kirk?
Is this mine own countree?

And the ancient Mariner beholdeth his native country.

We drifted o'er the harbour-bar,
And I with sobs did pray—
O let me be awake, my God!
Or let me sleep alway.

The harbour-bay was clear as glass,
So smoothly it was strewn!
And on the bay the moonlight lay,
And the shadow of the Moon.

The rock shone bright, the kirk no less,
That stands above the rock:
The moonlight steeped in silentness
The steady weathercock.

And the bay was white with silent light,
Till rising from the same,
Full many shapes, that shadows were,
In crimson colours came.

The angelic spirits leave the dead bodies,

A little distance from the prow
Those crimson shadows were:
I turned my eyes upon the deck—
Oh, Christ! what saw I there!

And appear in their own forms of light.

Each corse lay flat, lifeless and flat,
And, by the holy rood!
A man all light, a seraph-man,
On every corse there stood.

This seraph-band, each waved his hand:
It was a heavenly sight!
They stood as signals to the land,
Each one a lovely light;

This seraph-band, each waved his hand,
No voice did they impart—
No voice; but oh! the silence sank
Like music on my heart.

500 But soon I heard the dash of oars,
I heard the Pilot's cheer;
My head was turned perforce away
And I saw a boat appear.

The Pilot and the Pilot's boy,
I heard them coming fast:
Dear Lord in Heaven! it was a joy
The dead men could not blast.

I saw a third—I heard his voice:
It is the Hermit good!
510 He singeth loud his godly hymns
That he makes in the wood.
He'll shrieve my soul, he'll wash away
The Albatross's blood.

PART VII

This Hermit good lives in that wood   The Hermit of the Wood,
Which slopes down to the sea.
How loudly his sweet voice he rears!
He loves to talk with marineres
That come from a far countree.

He kneels at morn, and noon, and eve—
520 He hath a cushion plump:
It is the moss that wholly hides
The rotted old oak-stump.

The skiff-boat neared: I heard them talk,
"Why, this is strange, I trow!
Where are those lights so many and fair,
That signal made but now?"

"Strange, by my faith!" the Hermit said—   Approacheth the ship with
"And they answered not our cheer!   wonder.
The planks looked warped! and see those sails,
530 How thin they are and sere!
I never saw aught like to them,
Unless perchance it were

Brown skeletons of leaves that lag
My forest-brook along;

When the ivy-tod is heavy with snow,
And the owlet whoops to the wolf below,
That eats the she-wolf's young."

"Dear Lord! it hath a fiendish look—
(The Pilot made reply)
₅₄₀ I am a-feared"—"Push on, push on!"
Said the Hermit cheerily.

The boat came closer to the ship,
But I nor spake nor stirred;
The boat came close beneath the ship,
And straight a sound was heard.

Under the water it rumbled on,   *The ship suddenly sinketh.*
Still louder and more dread:
It reached the ship, it split the bay;
The ship went down like lead.

₅₅₀ Stunned by that loud and dreadful sound,   *The ancient Mariner is saved*
Which sky and ocean smote,   *in the Pilot's boat.*
Like one that hath been seven days drowned
My body lay afloat;
But swift as dreams, myself I found
Within the Pilot's boat.

Upon the whirl, where sank the ship,
The boat spun round and round;
And all was still, save that the hill
Was telling of the sound.

₅₆₀ I moved my lips—the Pilot shrieked
And fell down in a fit;
The holy Hermit raised his eyes,
And prayed where he did sit.

I took the oars: the Pilot's boy,
Who now doth crazy go,
Laughed loud and long, and all the while
His eyes went to and fro.
"Ha! ha!" quoth he, "full plain I see,
The Devil knows how to row."

₅₇₀ And now, all in my own countree,
I stood on the firm land!
The Hermit stepped forth from the boat,
And scarcely he could stand.

"O shrieve me, shrieve me, holy man!"   *The ancient Mariner earnest-*
The Hermit crossed his brow.   *ly entreateth the Hermit to*
"Say quick," quoth he, "I bid thee say—   *shrieve him; and the penance*
What manner of man art thou?"   *of life falls on him.*

535. ivy-tod ivy-plant

Forthwith this frame of mine was wrenched
With a woful agony,
580 Which forced me to begin my tale;
And then it left me free.

Since then, at an uncertain hour,   *And ever and anon through-*
That agony returns: *out his future life an agony*
And till my ghastly tale is told,   *constraineth him to travel*
This heart within me burns.   *from land to land;*

I pass, like night, from land to land;
I have strange power of speech;
That moment that his face I see,
I know the man that must hear me:
590 To him my tale I teach.

What loud uproar bursts from that door!
The wedding-guests are there:
But in the garden-bower the bride
And bride-maids singing are:
And hark the little vesper bell,
Which biddeth me to prayer!

O Wedding-Guest! this soul hath been
Alone on a wide wide sea:
So lonely 'twas, that God himself
600 Scarce seeméd there to be.

O sweeter than the marriage-feast,
'Tis sweeter far to me,
To walk together to the kirk
With a goodly company!—

To walk together to the kirk,
And all together pray,
While each to his great Father bends,
Old men, and babes, and loving friends
And youths and maidens gay!

610 Farewell, farewell! but this I tell   *And to teach, by his own*
To thee, thou Wedding-Guest!   *example, love and reverence*
He prayeth well, who loveth well   *to all things that God made*
Both man and bird and beast.   *and loveth.*

He prayeth best, who loveth best
All things both great and small;
For the dear God who loveth us,
He made and loveth all.

The Mariner, whose eye is bright,
Whose beard with age is hoar,
620 Is gone: and now the Wedding-Guest
Turned from the bridegroom's door.

He went like one that hath been stunned,
And is of sense forlorn:
A sadder and a wiser man,
He rose the morrow morn.

FOR DISCUSSION:

1. What precisely is the Mariner's crime? What act brings about his redemption? How does archetypal imagery highlight his spiritual redemption?

2. Some critics suggest that the killing of the albatross represents the Fall of man. Does the remainder of the poem support this view?

3. Is there a symbolic meaning in the Mariner's biting his arm to quench his thirst in line 160?

4. Why does the Wedding-Guest arise the next morning "a sadder and a wiser man"?

5. Cite examples where Coleridge uses physical imagery to convey spiritual states in this poem.

6. When a friend told Coleridge that she thought that The Ancient Mariner lacked a moral, he responded with "as to the want of a moral . . . in my own judgment, the poem had too much." What did he mean?

Lycidas*

JOHN MILTON

In this monody the author bewails a learned friend, unfortunately drowned in his passage from Chester on the Irish Seas, 1637. And by occasion foretells the ruin of our corrupted clergy then in their height.

> Yet once more, O ye laurels, and once more
> Ye myrtles brown, with ivy never sere,
> I come to pluck your berries harsh and crude,
> And with forced fingers rude,
> Shatter your leaves before the mellowing year.
> Bitter constraint, and sad occasion dear,
> Compels me to disturb your season due;
> For Lycidas is dead, dead ere his prime,
> Young Lycidas, and hath not left his peer.
> Who would not sing for Lycidas? he well knew   10
> Himself to sing, and build the lofty rhyme.
> He must not float upon his watery bier
> Unwept, and welter to the parching wind,
> Without the meed of some melodious tear.
>   Begin then, Sisters of the sacred well,
> That from beneath the seat of Jove doth spring,
> Begin, and somewhat loudly sweep the string.
> Hence with denial vain, and coy excuse;

---

* From THE POEMS OF JOHN MILTON, edited by James Holly Hanford. The Ronald Press Company, New York, 1936. Reprinted by permission of the publisher. [All notes are from this edition—Ed.]

The name *Lycidas* occurs frequently in pastoral poetry. It is used, for example, by Theocritus (*Idyll* 7), and by Virgil (*Eclogue* 9).

1. *Yet once more*, etc. Milton had written no English poetry since *Comus* in 1634; instead he had been engaged in studious preparation for a future career. Now feeling that his preparation is still inadequate, he takes up his pen only because of the urgent demands of the occasion.

1–2. *laurels . . . myrtles . . . ivy*, evergreens traditionally used for crowns of honor. Laurel, sacred to Apollo, is symbolic of learning and poetic skill. Myrtle and ivy, sacred respectively to Venus and Bacchus, suggest such qualities as youth, beauty, joy, and friendship. *never sere*, never dry or withered.

3. *harsh and crude*, unripe, lacking the mellowness of maturity. The allusion in this and the two following lines is to Milton's sense of unreadiness for writing great poetry.

6. *dear*, grievous. In Milton's day, the word was applied to anything arousing strong emotion, unpleasant as well as pleasant. Cf. Shakespeare, *Henry V*, II, ii, 181: "all your dear offences."

7. *compels*. The verb is singular because constraint and occasion are regarded as forming one idea.

9–10. Note the repetition used to heighten the pathetic effect. Cf. Spenser's "Astrophel," 7–8.
Young Astrophel, the pride of shepheard's praise,
Young Astrophel, the rusticke lasses love.

10. *Who would not sing*, etc. Cf. Virgil *Eclogue* 10.3. *Neget quis Carmina Gallo?* ("Who would refuse a song to Gallus?") *he well knew . . . to sing*. This is largely conventional, most pastoral elegies having been written for poets. King, however, was the author of at least a small amount of Latin verse.

14. *melodious tear*, i.e., a funeral elegy. The figure was more or less conventional; cf. Spenser's *Teares of the Muses*.

15. *Begin*, etc. This invocation follows a common pastoral formula. Cf. Theocritus, *Idyll* I, 64. "Begin, ye Muses dear, begin the pastoral song." *Sisters of the sacred well*, the nine muses. The sacred well probably refers to the Pierian spring at the foot of Mt. Olympus, although some editors connect it with the fountain of Agannippe, on Mt. Helicon. Olympus was the Homeric seat of Jove (line 16) and the birthplace of the muses. Their worship was later transferred to Helicon.

18. *coy*, offish, disdainful. This is a common seventeenth-century meaning.

So may some gentle muse
With lucky words favor my destined urn, 20
And as he passes turn,
And bid fair peace be to my sable shroud.
For we were nursed upon the self-same hill,
Fed the same flock, by fountain, shade, and rill.
    Together both, ere the high lawns appeared
Under the opening eyelids of the Morn,
We drove a-field, and both together heard
What time the gray-fly winds her sultry horn,
Battening our flocks with the fresh dews of night,
Oft till the star that rose, at evening, bright 30
Toward Heaven's descent had sloped his westering wheel.
Meanwhile the rural ditties were not mute,
Tempered to the oaten flute;
Rough Satyrs danced, and Fauns with cloven heel
From the glad sound would not be absent long,
And old Damœtas loved to hear our song.
    But O the heavy change, now thou art gone,
Now thou art gone, and never must return!
Thee Shepherd, thee the woods and desert caves,
With wild thyme and the gadding vine o'ergrown, 40
And all their echoes mourn.
The willows and the hazel copses green
Shall now no more be seen
Fanning their joyous leaves to thy soft lays.
As killing as the canker to the rose,
Or taint-worm to the weanling herds that graze,
Or frost to flowers that their gay wardrobe wear,
When first the white-thorn blows,
Such, Lycidas, thy loss to shepherd's ear.
    Where were ye Nymphs when the remorseless deep 50

19. *Muse,* i.e., poet. Note the *he* in line 21.
20. *lucky,* auspicious.
23 ff. *For we were nursed upon the self-same hill,* etc. In these pastoral terms, Milton is obviously recalling his life at the University in company with King. The allegory, however, is not to be interpreted too literally, as many details are introduced for their conventional propriety rather than for their correspondence to fact. For example, Cambridge is not located on a hill.
25. *high lawns,* spaces clear of trees, pastures.
28. *What time the gray-fly winds her sultry horn,* i.e., in the middle of the day. The allusion is obviously to the humming sound made by insects in the heat of noon, although the precise species of insect which Milton had in mind is an open question. *What time* was a common idiom; cf. Psalms 56:3, "What time I am afraid, I will trust in thee."
29. *Battening,* feeding.
30. *the star that rose at evening,* the evening star Hesperus, whose appearance was a signal for the shepherd to begin getting his flock into the fold, as in *Comus,* 93. *Rose* must be understood in the sense of "appeared," for the evening star is of course visible only in the west and for only a short time after sunset.

34. *Satyrs . . . Fauns,* sportive divinities of the fields and woods. The Satyrs belonged to Greek, the Fauns to Roman mythology; but by later writers they were commonly regarded as identical. Both were half-human, half-bestial in form. In introducing them here, Milton is following the example of Virgil, *Eclogue* 6.27.
36. *Damoetas,* a common pastoral name. Milton may have wished it to stand for some specific person, but the identification is uncertain.
45. *canker,* the canker-worm. Cf. Shakespeare, *Two Gentlemen of Verona,* I, i, 42–43.
    As in the sweetest bud
The eating canker dwells, etc.
46. *taint-worm,* some sort of animal parasite, possibly the *tainct* mentioned by Sir Thomas Browne in *Vulgar Errors,* III, xvii, 2.
48. *white-thorn,* the hawthorn of "L'Allegro," 68.
50 ff. *Where were ye, Nymphs,* etc. This is closely imitated from Theocritus, *Idyll* 1:66–69, which had been imitated by Virgil also in *Eclogue* 10.9–12, and by many later pastoralists. The places mentioned are near the scene of King's shipwreck.

Closed o'er the head of your loved Lycidas?
For neither were ye playing on the steep,
Where your old bards, the famous Druids, lie,
Nor on the shaggy top of Mona high,
Nor yet where Deva spreads her wizard stream.
Ay me, I fondly dream!
Had ye been there—for what could that have done?
What could the Muse herself that Orpheus bore,
The Muse herself, for her enchanting son
Whom universal Nature did lament,   60
When by the rout that made the hideous roar,
His gory visage down the stream was sent,
Down the swift Hebrus to the Lesbian shore.
   Alas! what boots it with uncessant care
To tend the homely slighted shepherd's trade,
And strictly meditate the thankless Muse?
Were it not better done as others use,
To sport with Amaryllis in the shade,
Or with the tangles of Neæra's hair?
Fame is the spur that the clear spirit doth raise   70
(That last infirmity of noble mind)
To scorn delights, and live laborious days;
But the fair guerdon when we hope to find,
And think to burst out into sudden blaze,
Comes the blind Fury with the abhorrèd shears,

---

52. *the steep*, etc. The exact spot is in doubt, although the promontory of Holyhead, close to the western shore of Anglesey, seems to fit the description best. It is a region associated with the Druids, and was famous as a burial place.

53. *your old bards, the famous Druids*. Cf. Milton's Latin epistle *Mansus*, 42–43: "The Druids, an ancient folk occupied with the rites of the gods, used to sing the praises of heroes and their deeds so worthy of emulation."

54. *Mona*, the island of Anglesey, off the northwest coast of Wales.

55. *Deva*, the river Dee, on which Chester, the port from which King sailed, is located. It is called a wizard stream because of its reputed powers of prophecy. Cf. Drayton, *Polyolbion*, X, 203–7.

A Brook, that was supposed much business to
  have seen,
Which had an ancient bound twixt Wales and
  England been,
And noted was by both to be an ominous
  Flood,
That changing of his fords, the future ill, or
  good,
Of either country told.

58. *Muse . . . that Orpheus bore*, Calliope. Even she, Milton says, was powerless to save her son from a fatal end. What, then, could the Nymphs have done for Lycidas?

59. *enchanting*, i.e., working enchantment by his music.

61 ff. Orpheus was torn in pieces by the frenzied Thracian women when he refused to join them in the orgies of Bacchus which they were celebrating. His head was thrown into the river Hebrus, and borne by the current to the island of Lesbos. Cf. Ovid *Metamorphoses* xi. 1 ff. Milton refers to the story again in *Paradise Lost*, VII, 32–38, identifying his own lot with that of Orpheus.

65. *shepherd's trade*, i.e., the profession of poetry.

66. *meditate*. Cf. *Comus*, 547, and note.

67. *Were it not better done*. These lines are modeled on Virgil *Eclogue* 2.14–15: "Were it not better to have endured the scorn of haughty Amaryllis?" etc. The names Amaryllis and Neaera, both of which occur frequently in pastoral verse, are mentioned together by Spenser in *Colin Clouts Come Home Againe*. *as others use*, as others are accustomed to do. Milton is momentarily questioning the value of his own high-minded poetic ideal in terms of the more earthy standards of his contemporaries. Cf. *Elegy VI*.

70. *clear*, pure, unsullied.

71. *That last infirmity of noble mind*. Cf. Tacitus *Historiae* iv. 6: "Even in the case of wise men the desire for glory is last cut off." But Milton's line is an exact quotation from the play *Barnevelt* (1622).

73. *guerdon*, recompense.

74. *blaze*, i.e., of fame. Cf. *Paradise Regained*, III, 47: "For what is glory but the blaze of fame?"

75. *the blind Fury*, Atropos, one of the three fates of classical mythology. Her function was to cut the thread of life spun by Clotho and measured by Lachesis. Milton here calls her a *Fury* (thus associating her with the Erinyes) because he wishes to emphasize her vindictiveness; he adds the epithet *blind* to account for her mad unreason.

And slits the thin-spun life. "But not the praise,"
Phœbus replied, and touched my trembling ears;
"Fame is no plant that grows on mortal soil,
Nor in the glistering foil
Set off to the world, nor in broad rumor lies,   80
But lives and spreads aloft by those pure eyes
And perfect witness of all-judging Jove;
As he pronounces lastly on each deed,
Of so much fame in Heaven expect thy meed."
  O fountain Arethuse, and thou honored flood,
Smooth-sliding Mincius, crowned with vocal reeds,
That strain I heard was of a higher mood.
But now my oat proceeds,
And listens to the Herald of the Sea
That came in Neptune's plea.   90
He asked the waves, and asked the felon winds,
What hard mishap hath doomed this gentle swain?
And questioned every gust of rugged wings
That blows from off each bekëd promontory;
They knew not of his story,
And sage Hippotades their answer brings,
That not a blast was from his dungeon strayed,
The air was calm, and on the level brine,
Sleek Panope with all her sisters played,
It was that fatal and perfidious bark,   100
Built in the eclipse, and rigged with curses dark,
That sunk so low that sacred head of thine.
  Next Camus, reverend sire, went footing slow,
His mantle hairy, and his bonnet sedge,
Inwrought with figures dim, and on the edge

---

76. Cf. Spenser, *The Shepheardes Calender*, X, 19-20.
"Cuddie, the prayse is better than the price
The glory eke much greater than the gayne."
77. *Phoebus*, Apollo, god of poetry—here the voice of divine wisdom. *touched . . . ears*. The allusion is probably to the story of Midas, who, declaring that Pan was a better musician than Phoebus, had his ears changed by the offended god to those of an ass, to indicate his stupidity. Milton likens his own doubtful utterance to the foolishness of Midas, and his ears tremble in anticipation of Phoebus's reproof. Cf. the phrase "Midas ears" in the "Sonnet to Henry Lawes."
79-80. *glistering foil*, gold or silver leaf placed under gems to increase their brilliance—hence anything bright and showy. Milton means that true fame does not consist in brilliant appearances exhibited to the world, nor in popular approval *(broad rumor)*.
81. *lives and spreads aloft*. The metaphor of the plant (line 78) is continued.
82. *all-judging Jove*. Milton of course means God, but he keeps the classical nomenclature for the sake of consistency.
85. *fountain Arethuse*, a spring located in the island of Ortygia, near the birthplace of Theocritus.
It is used here as symbolic of the Sicilian pastoralists.
86. *Mincius*, an Italian river near which Virgil was born. Here it typifies Virgil's pastorals. *vocal reeds*, i.e., reeds used for shepherd's pipes.
88. *my oat proceeds*, i.e., I resume my pastoral strain.
89. *Herald of the Sea*, Triton. Cf. note on *Comus*, 873.
90. *came in Neptune's plea*, came in Neptune's defense.
96. *Hippotades*, Aeolus, god of the winds.
98. *The air was calm*. The poem by Edward King's brother in the Cambridge collection has a contrary implication. Cf. the lines
    He, the fairest arm,
Is torn away by an unluckie storm.
99. *Panope*, a sea-nymph, one of the fifty daughters of Nereus.
103. *Camus*, the god of the river Cam, which flows by Cambridge. Here he stands for the University. *footing slow* appropriately describes the sluggish movement of the current as well as the grief of the University.
104. *bonnet sedge*, i.e., the coarse grass growing along the banks. Sedge is a conventional adornment of river deities. The terms mantle and bonnet are undoubtedly meant to suggest academic dress.

Like to that sanguine flower inscribed with woe.
"Ah, who hath reft" (quoth he) "my dearest pledge?"
Last came, and last did go,
The Pilot of the Galilean Lake;
Two massy keys he bore of metals twain   110
(The golden opes, the iron shuts amain).
He shook his mitred locks, and stern bespake,
"How well could I have spared for thee, young swain,
Enough of such as for their bellies' sake,
Creep and intrude and climb into the fold!
Of other care they little reckoning make,
Than how to scramble at the shearers' feast,
And shove away the worthy bidden guest;
Blind mouths! that scarce themselves know how to hold
A sheep-hook, or have learnt aught else the least   120
That to the faithful herdsman's art belongs!
What recks it them? What need they? They are sped;
And when they list, their lean and flashy songs
Grate on their scrannel pipes of wretched straw;
The hungry sheep look up, and are not fed,
But swoln with wind and the rank mist they draw,
Rot inwardly, and foul contagion spread;
Besides what the grim wolf with privy paw
Daily devours apace, and nothing said;

106. *that sanguine flower inscribed with woe,* the hyacinth. Hyacinthus, a mythical Spartan youth, was killed by Zephyrus through the unwitting agency of Apollo. Apollo thereupon caused a flower to spring from the slain youth's blood, and inscribed on its petals the words Αι, Αι (Alas!). Cf. Ovid *Metamorphoses* x. 210 ff.

107. *pledge,* child. This use of pledge is based on the parallel use in Latin of the word *pignus,* which often denotes a child (i.e., a pledge of love).

109. *the pilot of the Galilean Lake,* St. Peter.

110. *Two massy keys,* etc. Cf. Matt. 16:19: "And I will give unto thee the keys of the kingdom of heaven." The number of keys is traditional but the distinction of metals and function is apparently Milton's own idea.

111. *amain,* with force.

112. *mitred locks.* St. Peter appears in the garb of his office as first Bishop of the Church.

113 ff. This denunciation of the "corrupted clergy," one of the most notable passages in the poem, gives us a forecast of Milton's later antiprelatical writings, as well as indicating clearly his ecclesiastical views in 1637. While not attacking the established church as an institution, he condemns a large section of its ministers on three counts: (1) they are guided by unworthy motives (lines 114–18), (2) they are ignorant (lines 119–22), (3) they are negligent in performing their duties (lines 123–29). He concludes with a prophecy of speedy retribution (lines 130–31). The literary antecedents of the passage are numerous, the most important in English being the May Eclogue of Spenser's *Shepheardes Calender.* Ezek. 34:2–10 and John 10 furnish significant biblical parallels. The intensity of the passage and its combination of details suggest the inspiration of Dante, whose work Milton was studying about this time.

115. *Creep, and intrude, and climb into the fold.* Cf. John 10:1: "He that entereth not by the door into the sheepfold, but climbeth up some other way, the same is a thief and a robber."

118. *the worthy bidden guest.* Cf. Matt. 22:8: "they which were bidden were not worthy."

119. *Blind mouths,* i.e., blind and gluttonous men. The phrase is an example of extraordinary compression of thought. Ruskin's comment (*Sesame and Lilies,* 22) is illuminating: "A 'Bishop' means 'a person who sees.' A 'Pastor' means a person who feeds.' The most unbishoply character a man can have is therefore to be Blind. The most unpastoral is, instead of feeding, to want to be fed —to be a Mouth."

122. *recks it them,* matters it to them. Cf. *Comus,* 404 *sped,* provided for. Cf. Shakespeare, *The Merchant of Venice,* II, ix, 71: "So begone; you are sped."

123. *lean and flashy songs,* i.e., meager, watery sermons, devoid of spiritual substance.

124. *scrannel,* thin, harsh. The sound of the word effectively suggests its meaning.

126. *wind . . . rank mist,* i.e., empty and false doctrines.

128. *the grim wolf with privy paw.* Probably this refers to the Church of Rome which at the time was secretly acquiring many converts in England. But it may simply mean the Devil.

But that two-handed engine at the door 130
Stands ready to smite once, and smite no more."
    Return Alpheus, the dread voice is past
That shrunk thy streams; return Sicilian Muse,
And call the vales, and bid them hither cast
Their bells and flowrets of a thousand hues.
Ye valleys low where the mild whispers use
Of shades and wanton winds and gushing brooks,
On whose fresh lap the swart star sparely looks,
Throw hither all your quaint enamelled eyes,
That on the green turf suck the honied showers, 140
And purple all the ground with vernal flowers.
Bring the rathe primrose that forsaken dies,
The tufted crow-toe, and pale jessamine,
The white pink, and the pansy freaked with jet,
The glowing violet,
The musk-rose, and the well-attired woodbine,
With cowslips wan that hang the pensive head,
And every flower that sad embroidery wears.
Bid amaranthus all his beauty shed,
And daffadillies fill their cups with tears, 150
To strew the laureate hearse where Lycid' lies.
For so to interpose a little ease,
Let our frail thoughts dally with false surmise;
Ay me! whilst thee the shores and sounding seas
Wash far away, where'er thy bones are hurled,
Whether beyond the stormy Hebrides,
Where thou perhaps under the whelming tide
Visit'st the bottom of the monstrous world;
Or whether thou to our moist vows denied,

130. *that two-handed engine, etc.* This is the most famous crux in Milton. Interpretations range from the axe "laid unto the root of the trees" (Matt. 3:20; Luke 3:9) to the two houses of Parliament. Perhaps the most likely allusion is to the sword of God's vengeance, the sword which Michael wielded "with huge two-handed sway" (*Paradise Lost*, VI, 251) and which went before the Cherubim in Eden (XII, 632–33). The menacing vagueness of the figure adds to its effectiveness.

132. *Return Alpheus.* Here, as after the digression on Fame, Milton announces his return to the pastoral mood. Alpheus is the name of an Arcadian river, which, after flowing in an underground channel for some distance, rises in Ortygia and mingles its waters with the "fountain Arethuse." The "dread voice" is the invective just uttered by St. Peter.

136. *use,* are accustomed to dwell.

138. *swart star,* i.e., Sirius, the dog-star, which was believed to have a blackening effect on vegetation. In fact the name Sirius is derived from a Greek word meaning "scorching." *sparely,* seldom.

142–50. This flower passage, which the MS. shows to have been omitted in the original draft, may owe something to the April Eclogue of Spenser's *Shepheardes Calender.* Cf. lines 136 ff.
Bring better the pincke and purple cullambine,
    With gelliflowres;
Bring coronations, and sops in wine,
    Worne of paramoures, etc.

142. *rathe,* early. *that forsaken dies.* Milton first wrote "that unwedded dies." Cf. *The Winter's Tale,* IV, iv, 122–24.

144. *freaked,* variegated or spotted.

149. *amaranthus.* The name comes from the Greek, meaning "not fading."

151. *laureate hearse,* i.e., the bier which has been decorated with memorial verse. *Hearse* might signify almost anything connected with a funeral; here it evidently refers to the frame on which the coffin rested or to the coffin itself. It was a common custom to affix to this the manuscripts of poetic eulogies.

153. Milton has been letting his fancy play with the notion that King's body is actually present for burial—a false surmise. Now by acknowledging that the supposition is a frail one (for the body is ultimately of no consequence), he prepares the way for the loftier thought to be developed in the next paragraph.

158. *monstrous world,* i.e., the world of monsters. Cf. *Comus,* 533, "monstrous rout."

159. *moist vows,* tearful rites.

Sleep'st by the fable of Bellerus old, 160
Where the great Vision of the guarded mount
Looks toward Namancos and Bayona's hold;
Look homeward Angel now, and melt with ruth;
And, O ye dolphins, waft the hapless youth.
  Weep no more, woeful shepherds weep no more,
For Lycidas your sorrow is not dead,
Sunk though he be beneath the watery floor,
So sinks the day-star in the ocean bed,
And yet anon repairs his drooping head,
And tricks his beams, and with new-spangled ore, 170
Flames in the forehead of the morning sky:
So Lycidas, sunk low, but mounted high,
Through the dear might of Him that walked the waves,
Where other groves and other streams along,
With nectar pure his oozy locks he laves,
And hears the unexpressive nuptial song,
In the blest kingdoms meek of joy and love.
There entertain him all the saints above,
In solemn troops and sweet societies
That sing, and singing in their glory move, 180
And wipe the tears for ever from his eyes.
Now Lycidas, the shepherds weep no more;
Henceforth thou art the Genius of the shore,
In thy large recompense, and shalt be good
To all that wander in that perilous flood.
  Thus sang the uncouth swain to the oaks and rills,

160. *fable of Bellerus old*, i.e., the fabled abode of old Bellerus. The Roman name for Land's End, in the extreme southeast of Cornwall, was Bellerium; Milton connects the name with a mythical king or giant.

161. *the great Vision of the guarded mount*. The reference is to the archangel Michael, for whom St. Michael's Mount near Land's End, is named. According to tradition, the angel was occasionally visible on a craggy seat at the summit. Cf. *The Shepheardes Calender*, VII, 41–42.
  St. Michels mount who does not know,
  That wardes the Westerne coste?

162. *Namancos and Bayona's hold*, points on the coast of Spain, toward which Michael gazes in defiance. *Hold* of course means a stronghold or fortified castle.

163. *Angel*. St. Michael is bidden to turn his gaze from Spain to England and the cenotaph of Lycidas.

164. *ye dolphins*, etc. Milton undoubtedly has in mind the legend of Arion, a Greek poet and musician, who was borne ashore by dolphins after he had flung himself into the sea to escape being murdered by the sailors of a ship on which he was taking passage. Since the dolphins were supposed to be friendly to mankind and especially susceptible to the charms of music, they could properly be invoked to bring the body of Lycidas to shore.

165. *Weep no more*, etc. For a similar change in mood, cf. the November Eclogue of *The Shepheardes Calender*, 171 ff. But indeed the consolation had become traditional pastoral elegy.

168. *day-star*, the sun.

170. *tricks*, decks, adorns. *with new-spangled ore*, i.e., with renewed radiance. *Ore* may possibly have been associated in Milton's mind with *aurum* (gold).

173. *Him that walked the waves*. Cf. Matt. 14: 24–31.

175. *With nectar pure*, etc. Cf. *Comus*, 838. Although the imagery of the passage is primarily Christian, Milton retains a connection with pagan mythology.

176. *unexpressive*, inexpressible. *nuptial song*. Cf. Rev. 19:9: "Blessed are they which are called unto the marriage supper of the Lamb." Cf. also the closing lines of the *Epitaphium Damonis*.

181. *And wipe the tears*, etc. Cf. Rev. 7:17 and 21:4: "And God shall wipe away all tears from their eyes."

183. The idea may have been suggested by Virgil's fifth *Eclogue*, in which Daphnis, the subject of the elegy, is set forth as a deity and his favors invoked. Cf. lines 64–65: "A god is he, a god, Manalcas! O be thou good and gracious to thine own!"

  The concluding eight lines, which form a perfect stanza in ottava rima, are a narrative epilogue to the lament proper. The subdued ending is characteristic of the classic pastoral.

186–90. *the uncouth swain*, the unknown rustic poet.

While the still Morn went out with sandals gray;
He touched the tender stops of various quills,
With eager thought warbling his Doric lay.
And now the sun had stretched out all the hills, 190
And now was dropped into the western bay;
At last he rose, and twitched his mantle blue:
To-morrow to fresh woods, and pastures new.

FOR DISCUSSION:

1. The pastoral form is a traditional literary archetype for the English elegy. Is it merely artificial and stylized adornment, or does it serve a real purpose in "Lycidas"? What are some of the obvious conventions of the pastoral tradition as shown in the poem?

2. Milton extends conventional practice in the pastoral elegy by introducing several references to his own poetic career. Are these digressions, or does he relate them to Edward King's death? Is Milton's grief sincere? Is the real subject of the poem King or Milton?

3. One of the prevailing unifying motifs in "Lycidas" seems to be an archetypal pattern of death and rebirth. Show how not only the overall subject of the poem but also many of the specific images (e.g., the Alpheus and Arethusa legend; the rising and setting of the sun; the reference to the Orpheus myth) relate to this archetypal pattern.

4. Water imagery is significant in "Lycidas." Not only is Milton acutely aware that King died by drowning, but water images recur frequently throughout the poem (e.g., the tear, the river, the Galilean lake). Trace these images and attempt to show whether Milton's use of water is consistent, or whether its symbolic meaning changes with the poetic context.

5. Are the frequent references to pagan myth inconsistent with the Christian tenor of the poem? Why?

6. How is this poem an excellent example of what Leslie Fiedler means by a blend of "archetype and signature"?

---

188. *the tender stops of various quills.* The stops are the holes in a wind instrument—*tender* because responsive to the delicate touch of the fingers; *quills* are reed pipes. The adjective *various* is used in allusion to the shifting moods of the poem.

189. *Doric lay*, pastoral song. The Greek pastoralists (Theocritus, Bion, and Moschus) all used the Doric dialect.

190. *And now the sun had stretched out all the hills*, i.e., the shadows cast by the hills had lengthened. The image is probably drawn from the concluding line of Virgil's first *Eclogue*: "And longer shadows fall from the high mountains."

192. *twitched*, i.e., gathered about him.

193. *To-morrow to fresh woods and pastures new.* Cf. Fletcher, *The Purple Island*, VI, 77: "To-morrow shall ye feast in pastures new." Milton is thinking of new poetic ventures and perhaps also of the journey to Italy which he was to undertake six months after he wrote this poem.

The Waste Land*

T. S. ELIOT

'Nam Sibyllam quidem Cumis ego ipse oculis meis vidi in ampulla pendere, et cum illi pueri dicerent: Σίβυλλα τί θέλεις; respondebat illa: ἀποθανεῖν θέλω.'

["I saw the Sibyl at Cumae
(One said) with mine own eye.
She hung in a cage, and read her rune
To all the passers-by.
Said all the boys, 'What wouldst thou, Sibyl?'
She answered, 'I would die.' "]†

For Ezra Pound
il miglior fabbro. ‡

I. THE BURIAL OF THE DEAD

April is the cruellest month, breeding
Lilacs out of the dead land, mixing
Memory and desire, stirring
Dull roots with spring rain.
Winter kept us warm, covering
Earth in forgetful snow, feeding
A little life with dried tubers.
Summer surprised us, coming over the Starnbergersee
With a shower of rain; we stopped in the colonnade,
And went on in sunlight, into the Hofgarten,   10
And drank coffee, and talked for an hour.
Bin gar keine Russin, stamm' aus Litauen, echt deutsch.
And when we were children, staying at the arch-duke's,
My cousin's, he took me out on a sled,
And I was frightened. He said, Marie,
Marie, hold on tight. And down we went.
In the mountains, there you feel free.
I read, much of the night, and go south in the winter.

What are the roots that clutch, what branches grow
Out of this stony rubbish? Son of man,   20

---

* From COLLECTED POEMS 1909–1962 by T. S. Eliot, copyright, 1936, by Harcourt, Brace & World, Inc.; ©1963, 1964, by T. S. Eliot. Reprinted by permission of the publishers, Harcourt, Brace & World, Inc. and Faber & Faber Ltd. [Bracketed notes by the editor, all others by T. S. Eliot—Ed.]

† [Epigraph is from the *Satyricon* of Petronius. Poetic translation by D. G. Rossetti.]

‡ [For Ezra Pound—the better craftsman.] Not only the title, but the plan and a good deal of the incidental symbolism of the poem were suggested by Miss Jessie L. Weston's book on the Grail legend: *From Ritual to Romance* (Cambridge). Indeed, so deeply am I indebted, Miss Weston's book will elucidate the difficulties of the poem much better than my notes can do; and I recommend it (apart from the great interest of the book itself) to any who think such elucidation of the poem worth the trouble. To another work of anthropology I am indebted in general, one which has influenced our generation profoundly; I mean *The Golden Bough*; I have used especially the two volumes *Adonis, Attis, Osiris*. Anyone who is acquainted with these works will immediately recognize in the poem certain references to vegetation ceremonies.

[12. Bin gar . . . I am not Russian, I come from Lithuania, pure German.]

20. Cf. Ezekiel II, i.

You cannot say, or guess, for you know only
A heap of broken images, where the sun beats,
And the dead tree gives no shelter, the cricket no relief,
And the dry stone no sound of water. Only
There is shadow under this red rock,
(Come in under the shadow of this red rock),
And I will show you something different from either
Your shadow at morning striding behind you
Or your shadow at evening rising to meet you;
I will show you fear in a handful of dust. 30
    Frisch weht der Wind
    Der Heimat zu
    Mein Irisch Kind,
    Wo weilest du?
'You gave me hyacinths first a year ago;
'They called me the hyacinth girl.'
—Yet when we came back, late, from the hyacinth garden,
Your arms full, and your hair wet, I could not
Speak, and my eyes failed, I was neither
Living nor dead, and I knew nothing, 40
Looking into the heart of light, the silence.
Oed' und leer das Meer.
Madame Sosostris, famous clairvoyante,
Had a bad cold, nevertheless
Is known to be the wisest woman in Europe,
With a wicked pack of cards. Here, said she,
Is your card, the drowned Phoenician Sailor,
(Those are pearls that were his eyes. Look!)
Here is Belladonna, the Lady of the Rocks,
The lady of situations. 50
Here is the man with three staves, and here the Wheel,
And here is the one-eyed merchant, and this card,
Which is blank, is something he carries on his back,
Which I am forbidden to see. I do not find
The Hanged Man. Fear death by water.
I see crowds of people, walking round in a ring.
Thank you. If you see dear Mrs. Equitone,
Tell her I bring the horoscope myself:
One must be so careful these days.

  Unreal City, 60
Under the brown fog of a winter dawn,
A crowd flowed over London Bridge, so many,

---

23. Cf. Ecclesiastes XII, v.
31. V. *Tristan und Isolde*, I, verses 5–8.
[*Frisch weht . . . weilest du?*
 Fresh blows the wind
 From off the bow
 My Irish child
 Where do you linger?]
42. Id. III, verse 24. [Wide and empty the sea.]
46. I am not familiar with the exact constitution of the Tarot pack of cards, from which I have obviously departed to suit my own convenience. The Hanged Man, a member of the traditional pack, fits my purpose in two ways: because he is associated in my mind with the Hanged God of Frazer, and because I associate him with the hooded figure in the passage of the disciples to Emmaus in Part V. The Phoenician Sailor and the Merchant appear later; also the 'crowds of people', and Death by Water is executed in Part IV. The Man with Three Staves (an authentic member of the Tarot pack) I associate, quite arbitrarily, with the Fisher King himself.
60. Cf. Baudelaire:
'Fourmillante cité, cité pleine de rêves,
'Ou le spectre en plein jour raccroche le passant.'
[Teeming city, city full of dreams
Where ghosts by daylight cling to the passerby.]

I had not thought death had undone so many.
Sighs, short and infrequent, were exhaled,
And each man fixed his eyes before his feet.
Flowed up the hill and down King William Street,
To where Saint Mary Woolnoth kept the hours
With a dead sound on the final stroke of nine.
There I saw one I knew, and stopped him crying: 'Stetson!
'You who were with me in the ships at Mylae! 70
'That corpse you planted last year in your garden,
'Has it begun to sprout? Will it bloom this year?
'Or has the sudden frost disturbed its bed?
'O keep the Dog far hence, that's friend to men,
'Or with his nails he'll dig it up again!
'You! hypocrite lecteur!—mon semblable,—mon frère!'

II. A GAME OF CHESS

The Chair she sat in, like a burnished throne,
Glowed on the marble, where the glass
Held up by standards wrought with fruited vines
From which a golden Cupidon peeped out   80
(Another hid his eyes behind his wing)
Doubled the flames of sevenbranched candelabra
Reflecting light upon the table as
The glitter of her jewels rose to meet it,
From satin cases poured in rich profusion.
In vials of ivory and coloured glass
Unstoppered, lurked her strange synthetic perfumes,
Unguent, powdered, or liquid—troubled, confused
And drowned the sense in odours; stirred by the air
That freshened from the window, these ascended   90
In fattening the prolonged candle-flames,
Flung their smoke into the laquearia,
Stirring the pattern on the coffered ceiling.
Huge sea-wood fed with copper
Burned green and orange, framed by the coloured stone,
In which sad light a carvèd dolphin swam.
Above the antique mantel was displayed
As though a window gave upon the sylvan scene
The change of Philomel, by the barbarous king
So rudely forced; yet there the nightingale   100
Filled all the desert with inviolable voice

63. Cf. *Inferno*, III, 55–57:
  'si lunga tratta
di gente, ch'io non avrei mai creduto
che morte tanta n'avesse disfatta.'
  [so long a train
Of people that I ne'er would have believed
That ever Death so many had undone.
—Translations from the *Inferno* and *Purgatorio* of the *Divine Comedy* are by Henry Wadsworth Longfellow.]
64. Cf. *Inferno*, IV, 25–27:
'Quivi, secondo che per ascoltare,
'non avea pianto, ma' che di sospiri,
'che l'aura eterna facevan tremare.'
[There in so far as I had power to hear
Were lamentations none, but only sighs
That tremulous made the everlasting air.]

68. A phenomenon which I have often noticed.
74. Cf. the Dirge in Webster's *White Devil*.
76. V. Baudelaire, Preface to *Fleurs du Mal*.
[Hypocrite reader!—My twin!—My brother!]
77. Cf. *Antony and Cleopatra*, II, ii, l. 190.
92. Laquearia. V. *Aeneid*, I, 726:
  dependent lychni laquearibus aureis incensi, et noctem flammis funalia vincunt.
[lamps hang down from the golden ceilings and torches expel the darkness with flames.]
98. Sylvan scene. V. Milton, *Paradise Lost*, IV, 140.
99. V. Ovid, *Metamorphoses*, VI, Philomela.
100. Cf. Part III, l. 204.

And still she cried, and still the world pursues,
'Jug Jug' to dirty ears.
And other withered stumps of time
Were told upon the walls; staring forms
Leaned out, leaning, hushing the room enclosed.
Footsteps shuffled on the stair.
Under the firelight, under the brush, her hair
Spread out in fiery points
Glowed into words, then would be savagely still.   110

'My nerves are bad to-night. Yes, bad. Stay with me.
'Speak to me. Why do you never speak. Speak.
   'What are you thinking of? What thinking? What?'
'I never know what you are thinking. Think.'

I think we are in rats' alley
Where the dead men lost their bones.

'What is that noise?'
                    The wind under the door.
'What is that noise now? What is the wind doing?'
                    Nothing again nothing.   120
                                        'Do
'You know nothing? Do you see nothing? Do you remember
'Nothing?'

   I remember
Those are pearls that were his eyes.
'Are you alive, or not? Is there nothing in your head?'
                                                    But
O O O O that Shakespeherian Rag—
It's so elegant
So intelligent   130
'What shall I do now? What shall I do?'
'I shall rush out as I am, and walk the street
'With my hair down so. What shall we do to-morrow?
'What shall we ever do?'
                       The hot water at ten.
And if it rains, a closed car at four.
And we shall play a game of chess,
Pressing lidless eyes and waiting for a knock upon the door.

When Lil's husband got demobbed, I said—
I didn't mince my words, I said to her myself,   140
HURRY UP PLEASE ITS TIME
Now Albert's coming back, make yourself a bit smart.
He'll want to know what you done with that money he gave you
To get yourself some teeth. He did, I was there.
You have them all out, Lil, and get a nice set,
He said, I swear, I can't bear to look at you.
And no more can't I, I said, and think of poor Albert,
He's been in the army four years, he wants a good time,
And if you don't give it him, there's others will, I said.
Oh is there, she said. Something o' that, I said.   150

---

115. Cf. Part III, 1. 195.
118. Cf. Webster: 'Is the wind in that door still?'

126. Cf. Part I, 1. 37, 48.
138. Cf. the game of chess in Middleton's *Women beware Women*.

Then I'll know who to thank, she said, and give me a straight look.
HURRY UP PLEASE ITS TIME
If you don't like it you can get on with it, I said.
Others can pick and choose if you can't.
But if Albert makes off, it won't be for lack of telling.
You ought to be ashamed, I said, to look so antique.
(And her only thirty-one.)
I can't help it, she said, pulling a long face,
It's them pills I took, to bring it off, she said.
(She's had five already, and nearly died of young George.)   160
The chemist said it would be all right, but I've never been the same.
You are a proper fool, I said.
Well, if Albert won't leave you alone, there it is I said,
What you get married for if you don't want children?
HURRY UP PLEASE ITS TIME
Well, that Sunday Albert was home, they had a hot gammon,
And they asked me in to dinner, to get the beauty of it hot—
HURRY UP PLEASE ITS TIME
HURRY UP PLEASE ITS TIME
Goonight Bill. Goonight Lou. Goonight May. Goonight.   170
Ta ta. Goonight. Goonight.
Good night, ladies, good night, sweet ladies, good night, good night.

III. THE FIRE SERMON

The river's tent is broken: the last fingers of leaf
Clutch and sink into the wet bank. The wind
Crosses the brown land, unheard. The nymphs are departed.
Sweet Thames, run softly, till I end my song.
The river bears no empty bottles, sandwich papers,
Silk handkerchiefs, cardboard boxes, cigarette ends
Or other testimony of summer nights. The nymphs are departed.
And their friends, the loitering heirs of City directors;   180
Departed, have left no addresses.
By the waters of Leman I sat down and wept . . .
Sweet Thames run softly till I end my song,
Sweet Thames, run softly, for I speak not loud or long.
But at my back in a cold blast I hear
The rattle of the bones, and chuckle spread from ear to ear.

A rat crept softly through the vegetation
Dragging its slimy belly on the bank
While I was fishing in the dull canal
On a winter evening round behind the gashouse   190
Musing upon the king my brother's wreck
And on the king my father's death before him.
White bodies naked on the low damp ground
And bones cast in a little low dry garret,
Rattled by the rat's foot only, year to year.
But at my back from time to time I hear
The sound of horns and motors, which shall bring

---

176. V. Spenser, *Prothalamion*.
192. Cf. *The Tempest*, I, ii.
196. Cf. Marvell, *To His Coy Mistress*.
197. Cf. Day, *Parliament of Bees*:
    'When of the sudden, listening, you shall hear,

'A noise of horns and hunting, which shall bring
'Actaeon to Diana in the spring,
'Where all shall see her naked skin . . .'

Sweeney to Mrs. Porter in the spring.
O the moon shone bright on Mrs. Porter
And on her daughter
They wash their feet in soda water
Et O ces voix d'enfants, chantant dans la coupole!

Twit twit twit
Jug jug jug jug jug jug
So rudely forc'd.
Tereu

Unreal City
Under the brown fog of a winter noon
Mr. Eugenides, the Smyrna merchant
Unshaven, with a pocket full of currants
C.i.f. London: documents at sight,
Asked me in demotic French
To luncheon at the Cannon Street Hotel
Followed by a weekend at the Metropole.

At the violet hour, when the eyes and back
Turn upward from the desk, when the human engine waits
Like a taxi throbbing waiting,
I Tiresias, though blind, throbbing between two lives,

---

199. I do not know the origin of the ballad from which these lines are taken: it was reported to me from Sydney, Australia.

202. V. Verlaine, *Parsifal*. [And O! those voices of children singing in the choir-loft.]

210. The currants were quoted at a price 'cost insurance and freight to London'; and the Bill of Lading, etc., were to be handed to the buyer upon payment of the sight draft.

218. Tiresias, although a mere spectator and not indeed a 'character', is yet the most important personage in the poem, uniting all the rest. Just as the one-eyed merchant, seller of currants, melts into the Phoenician Sailor, and the latter is not wholly distinct from Ferdinand Prince of Naples, so all the women are one woman, and the two sexes meet in Tiresias. What Tiresias sees, in fact, is the substance of the poem. The whole passage from Ovid is of great anthropological interest:

'. . . Cum Iunone iocos et maior vestra profecto est
Quam, quae contingit maribus', dixisse, 'voluptas.'
Illa negat; placuit quae sit sententia docti
Quaerere Tiresiae: venus huic erat utraque nota.
Nam duo magnorum viridi coeuntia silva
Corpora serpentum baculi violaverat ictu
Deque viro factus, mirabile, femina septem
Egerat autumnos; octavo rursus eosdem
Vidit et 'est vestrae si tanta potentia plagae',
Dixit 'ut auctoris sortem in contraria mutet,
Nunc quoque vos feriam!' percussis anguibus isdem
Forma prior rediit genetivaque venit imago.
Arbiter hic igitur sumptus de lite iocosa
Dicta Iovis firmat; gravius Saturnia iusto
Nec pro materia fertur doluisse suique
Iudicis aeterna damnavit lumina nocte,
At pater omnipotens (neque enim licet inrita cuiquam
Facta dei fecisse deo) pro lumine adempto
Scire futura dedit poenamque levavit honore.

[Jested with Juno as she idled by.
Freely the god began: "Who doubts the truth?
The female's pleasure is a great delight
Much greater than the pleasure of a male."
Juno denied it; therefore 'twas agreed
To ask Tiresias to declare the truth,
Than whom none knew both male and female joys.
For wandering in a green wood he had seen
Two serpents coupling; and he took his staff
And sharply struck them, til they broke and fled.
'Tis marvelous, that instant he became
A woman from a man, and so remained
While seven autumns passed. When eight were told
Again he saw them in their former plight,
And thus he spoke; Since such a power was wrought,
By one stroke of a staff my sex was changed
Again I strike! And even as he struck
The same two snakes, his former sex returned;
His manhood was restored.
                    As both agreed
To choose him umpire of the sportive strife,
He gave decision in support of Jove;
From this the disappointment Juno felt
Surpassed all reason, and enraged, decreed
Eternal night should seal Tiresias' eyes.
Immortal deities may never turn
Decrees and Deeds of other gods to naught,
But Jove, to recompense his loss of sight,
Endowed him with the gift of prophecy.
—Translation from Brookes More's *Ovid's Metamorphoses*.]

Old man with wrinkled female breasts, can see
At the violet hour, the evening hour that strives   220
Homeward, and brings the sailor home from sea,
The typist home at teatime, clears her breakfast, lights
Her stove, and lays out food in tins.
Out of the window perilously spread
Her drying combinations touched by the sun's last rays,
On the divan are piled (at night her bed)
Stockings, slippers, camisoles, and stays.
I Tiresias, old man with wrinkled dugs
Perceived the scene, and foretold the rest—
I too awaited the expected guest.   230
He, the young man carbuncular, arrives,
A small house agent's clerk, with one bold stare,
One of the low on whom assurance sits
As a silk hat on a Bradford millionaire.
The time is now propitious, as he guesses,
The meal is ended, she is bored and tired,
Endeavours to engage her in caresses
Which still are unreproved, if undesired.
Flushed and decided, he assaults at once;
Exploring hands encounter no defence;   240
His vanity requires no response,
And makes a welcome of indifference.
(And I Tiresias have foresuffered all
Enacted on this same divan or bed;
I who have sat by Thebes below the wall
And walked among the lowest of the dead.)
Bestows one final patronising kiss,
And gropes his way, finding the stairs unlit . . .

She turns and looks a moment in the glass,
Hardly aware of her departed lover;   250
Her brain allows one half-formed thought to pass:
'Well now that's done: and I'm glad it's over.'
When lovely woman stoops to folly and
Paces about her room again, alone,
She smoothes her hair with automatic hand,
And puts a record on the gramophone.

'This music crept by me upon the waters'
And along the Strand, up Queen Victoria Street.
O City city, I can sometimes hear
Beside a public bar in Lower Thames Street,   260
The pleasant whining of a mandoline
And a clatter and a chatter from within
Where fishmen lounge at noon: where the walls
Of Magnus Martyr hold
Inexplicable splendour of Ionian white and gold.

---

221. This may not appear as exact as Sappho's lines, but I had in mind the 'longshore' or 'dory' fisherman, who returns at nightfall.

253. V. Goldsmith, the song in *The Vicar of Wakefield*.

257. V. *The Tempest*, as above.

264. The interior of St. Magnus Martyr is to my mind one of the finest among Wren's interiors. See *The Proposed Demolition of Nineteen City Churches*: (P. S. King & Son, Ltd.)

The river sweats
Oil and tar
The barges drift
With the turning tide
Red sails
Wide
To leeward, swing on the heavy spar.
The barges wash
Drifting logs
Down Greenwich reach
Past the Isle of Dogs.
    Weialala leia
    Wallala leialala

Elizabeth and Leicester
Beating oars
The stern was formed
A gilded shell
Red and gold
The brisk swell
Rippled both shores
Southwest wind
Carried down stream
The peal of bells
White towers
    Weialala leia
    Wallala leialala

'Trams and dusty trees.
Highbury bore me. Richmond and Kew
Undid me. By Richmond I raised my knees
Supine on the floor of a narrow canoe.'

'My feet are at Moorgate, and my heart
Under my feet. After the event
He wept. He promised "a new start."
I made no comment. What should I resent?'

'On Margate Sands.
I can connect
Nothing with nothing.
The broken fingernails of dirty hands.
My people humble people who expect
Nothing.'
    la la

---

266. The Song of the (three) Thames-daughters begins here. From line 292 to 306 inclusive they speak in turn. V. *Götterdämmerung*, III, i: the Rhine-daughters.

279. V. Froude, *Elizabeth*, Vol. I, ch. iv, letter of De Quadra to Philip of Spain: 'In the afternoon we were in a barge, watching the games on the river. (The queen) was alone with Lord Robert and myself on the poop, when they began to talk nonsense, and went so far that Lord Robert at last said, as I was on the spot there was no reason why they should not be married if the queen pleased.'

293. Cf. *Purgatorio*, V. 133:
'Ricorditi di me, che son la Pia;
'Siena mi fe', disfecemi Maremma.'
[Do thou remember me who am the Pia
Siena made me, unmade me Maremma.]

To Carthage then I came

Burning burning burning burning
O Lord Thou pluckest me out
O Lord Thou pluckest 310

burning

IV. DEATH BY WATER

Phlebas the Phoenician, a fortnight dead,
Forgot the cry of gulls, and the deep sea swell
And the profit and loss.
    A current under sea
Picked his bones in whispers. As he rose and fell
He passed the stages of his age and youth
Entering the whirlpool.
    Gentile or Jew
O you who turn the wheel and look to windward, 320
Consider Phlebas, who was once handsome and tall as you.

V. WHAT THE THUNDER SAID

After the torchlight red on sweaty faces
After the frosty silence in the gardens
After the agony in stony places
The shouting and the crying
Prison and palace and reverberation
Of thunder of spring over distant mountains
He who was living is now dead
We who were living are now dying
With a little patience 330

Here is no water but only rock
Rock and no water and the sandy road
The road winding above among the mountains
Which are mountains of rock without water
If there were water we should stop and drink
Amongst the rock one cannot stop or think
Sweat is dry and feet are in the sand
If there were only water amongst the rock
Dead mountain mouth of carious teeth that cannot spit
Here one can neither stand nor lie nor sit 340
There is not even silence in the mountains

---

307. V. St. Augustine's *Confessions*: 'to Carthage then I came, where a cauldron of unholy loves sang all about mine ears'.

308. The complete text of the Buddha's Fire Sermon (which corresponds in importance to the Sermon on the Mount) from which these words are taken, will be found translated in the late Henry Clarke Warren's *Buddhism in Translation* (Harvard Oriental Series). Mr. Warren was one of the great pioneers of Buddhist studies in the Occident.

309. From St. Augustine's *Confessions* again. The collocation of these two representatives of eastern and western asceticism, as the culmination of this part of the poem, is not an accident.

In the first part of Part V three themes are employed: the journey to Emmaus, the approach to the Chapel Perilous (see Miss Weston's book) and the present decay of eastern Europe.

But dry sterile thunder without rain
There is not even solitude in the mountains
But red sullen faces sneer and snarl
From doors of mudcracked houses
                      If there were water

   And no rock
   If there were rock
   And also water
   And water   350
   A spring
   A pool among the rock
   If there were the sound of water only
   Not the cicada
   And dry grass singing
   But sound of water over a rock
   Where the hermit-thrush sings in the pine trees
   Drip drop drip drop drop drop drop
   But there is no water

Who is the third who walks always beside you?   360
When I count, there are only you and I together
But when I look ahead up the white road
There is always another one walking beside you
Gliding wrapt in a brown mantle, hooded
I do not know whether a man or a woman
—But who is that on the other side of you?
What is that sound high in the air
Murmur of maternal lamentation
Who are those hooded hordes swarming
Over endless plains, stumbling in cracked earth   370
Ringed by the flat horizon only
What is the city over the mountains
Cracks and reforms and bursts in the violet air
Falling towers
Jerusalem Athens Alexandria
Vienna London
Unreal

A woman drew her long black hair out tight
And fiddled whisper music on those strings

---

357. This is *Turdus aonalaschkae pallasii*, the hermit-thrush which I have heard in Quebec Province. Chapman says (*Handbook of Birds of Eastern North America*) 'it is most at home in secluded woodland and thickety retreats.... Its notes are not remarkable for variety or volume, but in purity and sweetness of tone and exquisite modulation they are unequalled.' Its 'water-dripping song' is justly celebrated.

360. The following lines were stimulated by the account of one of the Antarctic expeditions (I forget which, but I think one of Shackleton's): it was related that the party of explorers, at the extremity of their strength, had the constant delusion that there was *one more member* than could actually be counted.

367–377. Cf. Hermann Hesse, *Blick ins Chaos*: 'Schon ist halb Europa, schon ist zumindest der halbe Osten Europas auf dem Wege zum Chaos, fährt betrunken im heiligen Wahn am Abgrund entlang und singt dazu, singt betrunken und hymnisch wie Dmitri Karamasoff sang. Ueber diese Lieder lacht der Bürger beleidigt, der Heilige und Seher hört sie mit Tränen.' [Already half of Europe, or at least half of Eastern Europe, is heading for chaos and, drunk with religious frenzy, is traveling on the brink of the abyss, drunkenly singing songs and hymns—like Dmitri Karamazov. Offended, the ordinary middle-class citizen laughs at these songs; the saint and seer hears them and weeps.]

And bats with baby faces in the violet light
Whistled, and beat their wings
And crawled head downward down a blackened wall
And upside down in air were towers
Tolling reminiscent bells, that kept the hours
And voices singing out of empty cisterns and exhausted wells

In this decayed hole among the mountains
In the faint moonlight, the grass is singing
Over the tumbled graves, about the chapel
There is the empty chapel, only the wind's home.
It has no windows, and the door swings,
Dry bones can harm no one.
Only a cock stood on the rooftree
Co co rico co co rico
In a flash of lightning. Then a damp gust
Bringing rain
Ganga was sunken, and the limp leaves
Waited for rain, while the black clouds
Gathered far distant, over Himavant.
The jungle crouched, humped in silence.
Then spoke the thunder
DA
Datta: what have we given?
My friend, blood shaking my heart
The awful daring of a moment's surrender
Which an age of prudence can never retract
By this, and this only, we have existed
Which is not to be found in our obituaries
Or in memories draped by the beneficent spider
Or under seals broken by the lean solicitor
In our empty rooms
DA
Dayadhvam: I have heard the key
Turn in the door once and turn once only
We think of the key, each in his prison
Thinking of the key, each confirms a prison
Only at nightfall, aethereal rumours
Revive for a moment a broken Coriolanus
DA
Damyata: The boat responded
Gaily, to the hand expert with sail and oar

---

402. 'Datta, dayadhvam, damyata' (Give, sympathize, control). The fable of the meaning of the Thunder is found in the Brihadaranyaka—Upanishad, 5, 1. A translation is found in Deussen's Sechzig Upanishads des Veda, p. 489.
408. Cf. Webster, The White Devil, V, vi:
'... they'll remarry
Ere the worm pierce your winding-sheet, ere the spider
Make a thin curtain for your epitaphs.'
412. Cf. Inferno, XXXIII, 46:
'ed io sentii chiavar l'uscio di sotto
all'orribile torre.'

[And I heard locking up the under door
Of the horrible tower.]
Also F. H. Bradley, Appearance and Reality, p. 346. 'My external sensations are no less private to myself than are my thoughts or my feelings. In either case my experience falls within my own circle, a circle closed on the outside; and, with all its elements alike, every sphere is opaque to the others which surround it.... In brief, regarded as an existence which appears in a soul, the whole world for each is peculiar and private to that soul.'

> The sea was calm, your heart would have responded
> Gaily, when invited, beating obedient
> To controlling hands
>   I sat upon the shore
> Fishing, with the arid plain behind me
> Shall I at least set my lands in order?
> London Bridge is falling down falling down falling down
> *Poi s'ascose nel foco che gli affina*
> *Quando fiam uti chelidon*—O swallow swallow
> *Le Prince d'Aquitaine à la tour abolie*
> These fragments I have shored against my ruins
> Why then Ile fit you. Hieronymo's mad againe.
> Datta. Dayadhvam. Damyata.
>   *Shantih   shantih   shantih*

430

FOR DISCUSSION:

1. What is the significance of the epigraph?

2. Explain what is meant by line 1, "April is the cruellest month"? Is this the traditional poetic concept of this month?

3. According to Eliot, one of the major sources of The Waste Land is the Grail legend. Show how the motifs of crop failures, drought, illness of the king, and the quest for restoration of the king's health and the land's fertility form the major part of the poem's imagery.

4. What is the symbolic value of water in the poem? Comment also on the use of desert and rock imagery.

5. The major theme of The Waste Land is death-in-life. Trace this concept throughout the poem's imagery showing particularly how Eliot shifts meaning from physical barrenness and waste to spiritual sterility. What role do vegetative rites, fertility myths, and Christian archetypes play in this shift of meaning? How are these related to the death-rebirth archetype?

6. Much of the poem is built upon a system of archetypal contrasts and opposites—male-female, hope-despair, drought-water, universal-personal. Show how these antitheses and others like them are woven into each of the five sections of the poem.

7. Describe the nature of human relationships as depicted in "A Game of Chess" and "The Fire Sermon."

8. Does it finally rain in "What the Thunder Said"? Does the poem offer any hope of redemption?

9. Can the poem be understood without knowing the specific importance of the Fisher King, Tiresias, the Phoenician Sailor, and the Sanskrit quotations? Does Eliot place an unfair burden on his readers by demanding acquaintance with obscure myths, rites, rituals, and literary allusions?

10. Ezra Pound called The Waste Land "the longest poem in the English language." What did he mean?

11. How helpful are Eliot's notes to his poem?

---

425. V. Weston: *From Ritual to Romance*; chapter on the Fisher King.

428. [*Poi . . . tour abolie*
Then he hid him in the fire which refines them
When shall I be as the swallow—O swallow swallow
The Prince of Aquitaine at the ruined tower.]
V. *Purgatorio*, XXVI, 148:
'"Ara vos prec per aquella valor
"que vos condus al som de l'escalina,
"sovegna vos a temps de ma dolor."
Poi s'ascose nel foco che gli affina.'

[Therefore do I implore you by that power
Which guides you to the summit of the stairs
Be mindful to assuage my suffering.
Then hid him in the fire that purifies them.]

429. V. *Pervigilium Veneris*. Cf. Philomela in Parts II and III.

430. V. Gerard de Nerval, Sonnet *El Desdichado*.

432. V. Kyd's *Spanish Tragedy*.

434. Shantih. Repeated as here, a formal ending to an Upanishad. 'The Peace which passeth understanding' is our equivalent to this word.

V Critical Perspectives on BILLY BUDD

Billy Budd*

(AN INSIDE NARRATIVE)

HERMAN MELVILLE

DEDICATED TO
JACK CHASE
ENGLISHMAN

Wherever that great heart may now be
Here on Earth or harbored in Paradise
Captain of the maintop in the year 1843
in the U.S. Frigate *United States*

PREFACE

The year 1797, the year of this narrative, belongs to a period which, as every thinker now feels, involved a crisis for Christendom was not exceeded in its undetermined momentousness at the time by any other era whereof there is record. The opening proposition made by the Spirit of that Age involved rectification of the Old World's hereditary wrongs. In France, to some extent, this was bloodily effected. But what then? Straightway the Revolution itself became a wrongdoer, one more oppressive than the kings. Under Napoleon it enthroned upstart kings, and initiated that prolonged agony of continual war whose final throe was Waterloo. During those years not the wisest could have foreseen that the outcome of all would be what to some thinkers apparently it has since turned out to be—a political advance along nearly the whole line for Europeans.

Now, as elsewhere hinted, it was something caught from the Revolutionary Spirit that at Spithead emboldened the man-of-war's men to rise against real abuses, long-standing ones, and afterwards at the Nore to make inordinate and aggressive demands—successful resistance to which was confirmed only when the ringleaders were hung for an admonitory spectacle to the anchored fleet. Yet, in a way analogous to the operation of the Revolution at large, the Great Mutiny, though by Englishmen naturally deemed monstrous at the time, doubtless gave the first latent prompting to most important reforms in the British navy.

I

In the time before steamships, or then more frequently than now, a stroller along the docks of any considerable seaport would occasionally have his attention arrested by a group of bronzed mariners, man-of-war's men or merchant-sailors in holiday attire ashore on liberty. In certain instances they would flank, or, like a bodyguard, quite surround, some superior figure of their own class, moving along with them like Aldebaran among the lesser lights of his constellation. That signal object was the "Handsome Sailor" of the less prosaic time alike of the military and merchant navies. With no perceptible trace of the vain-glorious about him, rather with the offhand unaffectedness of natural regality, he seemed to accept the spontaneous homage of his shipmates. A somewhat remarkable instance recurs to me.

---

* Reprinted by permission of the publishers from MELVILLE'S BILLY BUDD (Edited by Frederic Barron Freeman and corrected by Elizabeth Treeman) Cambridge, Mass.: Harvard University Press, Copyright, 1948, 1956, by the President and Fellows of Harvard College.

In Liverpool, now half a century ago, I saw under the shadow of the great dingy street-wall of Prince's Dock (an obstruction long since removed) a common sailor, so intensely black that he must needs have been a native African of the unadulterate blood of Ham. A symmetric figure much above the average height. The two ends of a gay silk handkerchief thrown loose about the neck danced upon the displayed ebony of his chest; in his ears were big hoops of gold, and a Scotch Highland bonnet with a tartan band set off his shapely head.

It was a hot noon in July, and his face, lustrous with perspiration, beamed with barbaric good humor. In jovial sallies right and left, his white teeth flashing into view, he rollicked along, the center of a company of his shipmates. These were made up of such an assortment of tribes and complexions as would have well fitted them to be marched up by Anacharsis Cloots before the bar of the first French Assembly as Representatives of the Human Race. At each spontaneous tribute rendered by the wayfarers to this black pagoda of a fellow—the tribute of a pause and stare, and less frequent an exclamation—the motley retinue showed that they took that sort of pride in the evoker of it which the Assyrian priests doubtless showed for their grand sculptured Bull when the faithful prostrated themselves.

To return.

If in some cases a bit of a nautical Murat in setting forth his person ashore, the handsome sailor of the period in question evinced nothing of the dandified Billy-be-Dam, an amusing character all but extinct now, but occasionally to be encountered, and in a form yet more amusing than the original, at the tiller of the boats on the tempestuous Erie Canal, or, more likely, vaporing in the groggeries along the towpath. Invariably a proficient in his perilous calling, he was also more or less of a mighty boxer or wrestler. It was strength and beauty. Tales of his prowess were recited. Ashore he was the champion, afloat the spokesman; on every suitable occasion always foremost. Close-reefing topsails in a gale, there he was, astride the weather yard-arm-end, foot in the Flemish horse as "stirrup," both hands tugging at the "earing" as at a bridle, in very much the attitude of young Alexander curbing the fiery Bucephalus. A superb figure, tossed up as by the horns of Taurus against the thunderous sky, cheerily hallooing to the strenuous file along the spar.

The moral nature was seldom out of keeping with the physical make. Indeed, except as toned by the former, the comeliness and power, always attractive in masculine conjunction, hardly could have drawn the sort of honest homage the Handsome Sailor in some examples received from his less gifted associates.

Such a cynosure, at least in aspect, and something such too in nature, though with important variations made apparent as the story proceeds, was welkin-eyed Billy Budd, or Baby Budd as more familiarly under circumstances hereafter to be given he at last came to be called, aged twenty-one, a foretopman of the British fleet toward the close of the last decade of the eighteenth century. It was not very long prior to the time of the narration that follows that he had entered the King's Service, having been impressed on the Narrow Seas from a homeward-bound English merchantman into a seventy-four outward-bound, H.M.S. *Indomitable*; which ship, as was not unusual in those hurried days having been obliged to put to sea short of her proper complement of men. Plump upon Billy at first sight in the gangway the boarding officer Lieutenant Ratcliffe pounced, even before the merchantman's crew was formally mustered on the quarter-deck for his deliberate inspection. And him only he elected. For whether it was because the other men when ranged before him showed to ill advantage after Billy, or whether he had some scruples in view of the merchantman being rather short-handed, however it might be, the officer contented himself with his first spontaneous choice. To the surprise of the ship's company, though much to the lieutenant's satisfaction, Billy made no demur. But, indeed, any demur would have been as idle as the protest of a goldfinch popped into a cage.

Noting this uncomplaining acquiescence, all but cheerful one might say, the shipmates turned a surprise glance of silent reproach at the sailor. The shipmaster was one of those worthy mortals found in every vocation, even the humbler ones—the sort of person whom everybody agrees in calling "a respectable man." And—nor so strange to report as it may appear to be—though a plowman of the troubled waters, lifelong contending with the intractable elements, there was nothing this honest soul at heart loved better than simple peace and quiet. For the rest, he was fifty or thereabouts, a little inclined to corpulence, a prepossessing face, unwhiskered, and of an agreeable color—a rather full face, humanely intelligent in expression. On a fair day with a fair wind and all going well, a certain musical chime in his voice seemed to be the veritable unobstructed outcome of the innermost man. He had much prudence, much conscientiousness, and there were occasions when these virtues were the cause of overmuch disquietude in him. On a passage, so long as his craft was in any proximity to land, no sleep for Captain Graveling. He took to heart those serious responsibilities not so heavily borne by some shipmasters.

Now while Billy Budd was down in the forecastle getting his kit together, the *Indomitable*'s lieutenant, burly and bluff, nowise disconcerted by Captain Graveling's omitting to proffer the customary hospitalities on an occasion so unwelcome to him, an omission simply caused by preoccupation of thought, unceremoniously invited himself into the cabin, and also to a flask from the spirit-locker, a receptacle which his experienced eye instantly discovered. In fact he was one of those sea dogs in whom all the hardship and peril of naval life in the great prolonged wars of his time never impaired the natural instinct for sensuous enjoyment. His duty he always faithfully did; but duty is sometimes a dry obligation, and he was for irrigating its aridity, whensoever possible, with a fertilizing decoction of strong waters. For the cabin's proprietor there was nothing left but to play the part of the enforced host with whatever grace and alacrity were practicable. As necessary adjuncts to the flask, he silently placed tumbler and water-jug before the irrepressible guest. But excusing himself from partaking just then, he dismally watched the unembarrassed officer deliberately diluting his grog a little, then tossing it off in three swallows, pushing the empty tumbler away, yet not so far as to be beyond easy reach, at the same time settling himself in his seat and smacking his lips with high satisfaction, looking straight at the host.

These proceedings over, the master broke the silence, and there lurked a rueful reproach in the tone of his voice: "Lieutenant, you are going to take my best man from me, the jewel of 'em."

"Yes, I know," rejoined the other, immediately drawing back the tumbler preliminary to a replenishing. "Yes, I know. Sorry."

"Beg pardon, but you don't understand, Lieutenant. See here now. Before I shipped that young fellow, my forecastle was a rat-pit of quarrels. It was black times, I tell you aboard the *Rights* here. I was worried to that degree my pipe had no comfort for me. But Billy came, and it was like a Catholic priest striking peace in an Irish shindy. Not that he preached to them or said or did anything in particular, but a virtue went out of him, sugaring the sour ones. They took to him like hornets to treacle; all but the buffer of the gang, the big shaggy chap with the fire-red whiskers. He indeed, out of envy, perhaps, of the newcomer, and thinking such a 'sweet and pleasant fellow,' as he mockingly designated him to the others, could hardly have the spirit of a gamecock, must needs bestir himself in trying to get up an ugly row with him. Billy forebore with him and reasoned with him in a pleasant way—he is something like myself, Lieutenant, to whom aught like a quarrel is hateful—but nothing served. So, in the second dog watch one day the Red Whiskers, in presence of the others, under pretense of showing Billy just whence a sirloin steak was cut—for the fellow had once been a butcher—insultingly gave him a dig under the ribs. Quick as lightning Billy let fly his arm. I dare say he never meant to do quite as much as he did, but anyhow he gave the burly fool a terrible drubbing. It took about half a minute, I should think. And, Lord bless you, the lubber was astonished at the celerity. And will you believe it, Lieutenant, the Red Whiskers now really loves Billy—loves him, or is the biggest hypocrite that ever I heard of. But they all love him. Some of 'em do his washing, darn his old trousers for him; the carpenter is at odd times making a pretty little chest of drawers for him. Anybody will do anything for Billy Budd; and it's the happy family here. But now, Lieutenant, if that young fellow goes—I know how it will be aboard the *Rights*. Not again very soon shall I, coming up from dinner, lean over the capstan smoking a quiet pipe—no, not very soon again, I think. Aye, Lieutenant, you are going to take away the jewel of 'em; you are going to take away my peacemaker!" And with that the good soul had really some ado in checking a rising sob.

"Well," said the officer, who had listened with amused interest to all this, and now waxing merry with his tipple, "well, blessed are the peacemakers, especially the fighting peacemakers! And such are the seventy-four beauties some of which you see poking their noses out of the portholes of yonder warship lying to for me," pointing through the cabin window at the *Indomitable*. "But courage! don't you look so downhearted, man. Why, I pledge you in advance the royal approbation. Rest assured that His Majesty will be delighted to know that in a time when his hardtack is not sought for by sailors with such avidity as should be, a time also when some shipmasters privily resent the borrowing from them a tar or two for the services, His Majesty, I say, will be delighted to learn that one shipmaster at least cheerfully surrenders to the King the flower of his flock, a sailor who with equal loyalty makes no dissent.—But where's my beauty? Ah," looking through the cabin's open door, "here he comes; and, by Jove—lugging along his chest—Apollo with his portmanteau!—My man," stepping out to him, "you can't take that big box aboard a warship. The boxes there are mostly shotboxes. Put your duds in a bag, lad. Boot and saddle for the cavalrymen, bag and hammock for the man-of-war's man."

The transfer from chest to bag was made. And, after seeing his man into the cutter and then following him down, the lieutenant pushed off from the *Rights-of-Man*. That was the merchant ship's name, though by her master and crew abbreviated in sailor fashion into *The Rights*. The hardheaded Dundee owner was a staunch admirer of Thomas Paine, whose book in rejoinder to Burke's arraignment of the French Revolution had then been published for some time and had gone everywhere. In christening his vessel after the title of Paine's volume the man of Dundee was something like his contemporary shipowner, Stephen Girard of Philadelphia, whose sympathies, alike with his native land and its liberal philosophers, he evinced by naming his ships after Voltaire, Diderot, and so forth.

But now, when the boat swept under the merchantman's stern, and officer and oarsmen were noting—some bitterly and others with a grin—the name emblazoned there, just then it was that the new recruit jumped up from the bow where the coxswain had directed him to sit, and waving his hat to his silent shipmates sorrowfully looking over at him from the taffrail, bade the lads a genial good-bye. Then, making a salutation as to the ship herself, "And good-bye to you too, old *Rights of Man*."

"Down, sir!" roared the lieutenant, instantly assuming all the rigor of his rank, though with difficulty repressing a smile.

To be sure, Billy's action was a terrible breach of naval decorum. But in that decorum he had never been instructed, in consideration of which the lieutenant would hardly have been so energetic in reproof but for the concluding farewell to the ship. This he rather took as meant to convey a covert sally on the new recruit's part, a sly slur at impressment in general, and that of himself in especial. And yet, more likely, if satire it was in effect, it was hardly so by intention, for Billy, though happily endowed with the gaiety of high health, youth, and a free heart, was yet by no means of a satirical turn. The will to it and the sinister dexterity were alike wanting. To deal in double meanings and insinuations of any sort was quite foreign to his nature.

As to his enforced enlistment, that he seemed to take pretty much as he was wont to take any vicissitude of weather. Like the animals, though no philosopher, he was, without knowing it, practically a fatalist. And it may be that he rather liked this adventurous turn in his affairs, which promised an opening into novel scenes and martial excitements.

Aboard the *Indomitable* our merchant-sailor was forthwith rated as an able seaman and assigned to the starboard watch of the foretop. He was soon at home in the service, not at all disliked for his unpretentious good looks and a sort of genial happy-go-lucky air. No merrier man in his mess, in marked contrast to certain other individuals included like himself among the impressed portion of the ship's company; for these when not actively employed were sometimes, and more particularly in the last dog watch when the drawing near of twilight induced reverie, apt to fall into a saddish mood which in some partook of sullenness. But they were not so young as our foretopman, and no few of them must have known a hearth of some sort; others may have had wives and children left, too probably, in uncertain circumstances, and hardly any but must have had acknowledged kith and kin, while for Billy, as will shortly be seen, his entire family was practically invested in himself.

II

Though our new-made foretopman was well received in the top and on the gun decks, hardly here was he that cynosure he had previously been among those minor ship's companies of the merchant marine, with which companies only had he hitherto consorted.

He was young, and, despite his all but fully developed frame, in aspect looked even younger than he really was, owing to a lingering adolescent expression in the as yet smooth face all but feminine in purity of natural complexion but where, thanks to his seagoing, the lily was quite suppressed and the rose had some ado visibly to flush through the tan.

To one essentially such a novice in the complexities of factitious life, the abrupt transition from his former and simpler sphere to the ampler and more knowing world of a great warship—this might well have abashed him had there been any conceit or vanity in his composition. Among her miscellaneous multitude, the *Indomitable* mustered several individuals who, however inferior in grade, were of no common natural stamp, sailors more signally susceptive of that air which continuous martial discipline and repeated presence in battle can in some degree impart even to the average man. As the *handsome sailor* Billy Budd's position aboard the seventy-four was something analogous to that of a rustic beauty transplanted from the provinces and brought into competition with the highborn dames of the court. But this change of circumstances he scarce noted. As little did he observe that something about him provoked an ambiguous smile in one or two harder faces among the bluejackets. Nor less unaware was he of the peculiar favorable effect his person and demeanor had upon the more intelligent gentlemen of the quarter deck. Nor could this well have been otherwise. Cast in a mould peculiar to the finest physical examples of those Englishmen in whom the Saxon strain would seem not at all to partake of any Norman or other admixture, he showed in face that humane look of reposeful good nature which the Greek sculptor in some instances gave to his heroic strong man, Hercules. But this again was subtly modified by another and pervasive quality. The ear, small and shapely, the arch of the foot, the curve in mouth and nostril, even the indurated hand dyed to the orange-tawny of the toucan's bill, a hand telling alike of the halyards and tar bucket; but, above all, something in the mobile expression, and every chance attitude and movement, something suggestive of a mother eminently favored by Love and the Graces; all this strangely indicated a lineage in direct contradiction to his lot. The mysteriousness here became less mysterious through a matter of fact elicited when Billy at the capstan was being formally mustered into the service. Asked by the officer, a small brisk little gentleman, as it chanced among other questions, his place of birth, he replied, "Please, sir, I don't know."

"Don't know where you were born?—Who was your father?"

"God knows, sir."

Struck by the straightforward simplicity of these replies, the officer next asked, "Do you know anything about your beginning?"

"No, sir. But I have heard that I was found in a pretty silk-lined basket hanging one morning from the knocker of a good man's door in Bristol."

"*Found* say you? Well," throwing back his head and looking up and down the new recruit; "well, it turns out to have been a pretty good find. Hope they'll find some more like you, my man; the fleet sadly needs them."

Yes, Billy Budd was a foundling, a presumable by-blow, and, evidently, no ignoble one. Noble descent was as evident in him as in a blood horse.

For the rest, with little or no sharpness of faculty or any trace of the wisdom of the serpent, nor yet quite a dove, he possessed that kind and degree of intelligence going along with the unconventional rectitude of a sound human creature, one to whom not yet has been proffered the questionable apple of knowledge. He was illiterate; he could not read, but he could sing, and like the illiterate nightingale was sometimes the composer of his own song.

Of self-consciousness he seemed to have little or none, or about as much as we may reasonably impute to a dog of Saint Bernard's breed.

Habitually living with the elements and knowing little more of the land than as a beach, or, rather, that portion of the terraqueous globe providentially set apart for dance-houses, doxies, and tapsters, in short what sailors call a "fiddlers' green," his simple nature remained unsophisticated by those moral obliquities which are not in every case incompatible with that manufacturable thing known as respectability. But are sailors, frequenters of fiddlers' greens, without vices? No; but less often than with landsmen do their vices, so called, partake of crookedness of heart, seeming less to proceed from viciousness than exuberance of vitality after long constraint; frank manifestations in accordance with natural law. By his original constitution aided by the cooperating influences of his lot, Billy in many respects was little more than a sort of upright barbarian, much such perhaps as Adam presumably might have been ere the urbane Serpent wriggled himself into his company.

And here be it submitted that, apparently going to corroborate the doctrine of man's fall, a doctrine now popularly ignored, it is observable that where certain virtues pristine and unadulterate peculiarly characterize anybody in the external uniform of civilization, they will upon scrutiny seem not to be derived from custom or convention, but rather to be out of keeping with these, as if indeed exceptionally transmitted from a period prior to Cain's city and citified man. The character marked by such qualities has to an unvitiated taste an untampered-with flavor like that of berries, while the man thoroughly civilized even in a fair specimen of the breed has to the same moral palate a questionable smack as of a compounded wine. To any stray inheritor of these primitive qualities found, like Kaspar Hauser, wandering dazed in any Christian capital of our time, the good-natured poet's famous invocation, near two thousand years ago, of the good rustic out of his latitude in the Rome of the Caesars, still appropriately holds:

Honest and poor, faithful in word and thought,
What has thee, Fabian, to the city brought?

Though our Handsome Sailor had as much of masculine beauty as one can expect anywhere to see, nevertheless, like the beautiful woman in one of Hawthorne's minor tales, there was just one thing amiss in him. No visible blemish indeed, as with the lady; no, but an occasional liability to a vocal defect. Though in the hour of elemental uproar or peril he was everything that a sailor should be, yet under sudden provocation of strong heart-feeling his voice, otherwise singularly musical, as if expressive of the harmony within, was apt to develop an organic hesitancy, in fact more or less of a stutter or even worse. In this particular Billy was a striking instance that the arch interferer, the envious marplot of Eden, still has more or less to do with every human consignment to this planet of earth. In every case, one way or another he is sure to slip in his little card, as much as to remind us —I too have a hand here.

The avowal of such an imperfection in the Handsome Sailor should be evidence not alone that he is not presented as a conventional hero, but also that the story in which he is the main figure is no romance.

III

At the time of Billy Budd's arbitrary enlistment into the *Indomitable* that ship was on her way to join the Mediterranean fleet. No long time elapsed before the junction was effected. As one of that fleet the seventy-four participated in its movements, though at times, on account of her superior sailing qualities, in the absence of frigates, despatched on separate duty as a scout and at times on less temporary service. But with all this the story has little concernment, restricted as it is to the inner life of one particular ship and the career of an individual sailor.

It was the summer of 1797. In the April of that year had occurred the commotion at Spithead, followed in May by a second and yet more serious outbreak in the fleet at the Nore. The latter is known, and without exaggeration in the epithet, as the Great Mutiny. It was indeed a demonstration more menacing to England than the contemporary manifestoes and conquering and proselyting armies of the French Directory.

To the British Empire the Nore mutiny was what a strike in the fire brigade would be to London threatened by general arson. In a crisis when the kingdom might well have anticipated the famous signal that some years later published along the naval line of battle what it was that upon occasion England expected of Englishmen, *that* was the time when at the mastheads of the three-deckers and seventy-fours moored in her own roadstead—a fleet, the right arm of a Power then all but the sole free conservative one of the Old World—the bluejackets, to be numbered by thousands, ran up with hurrahs the British colors with the union and cross wiped out; by that cancellation transmuting the flag of founded law and freedom defined into the enemy's red meteor of unbridled and unbounded revolt. Reasonable discontent growing out of practical grievances in the fleet had been ignited into irrational combustion as by live cinders blown across the Channel from France in flames.

The event converted into irony for a time those spirited strains of Dibdin—as a song-writer no mean auxiliary to the English Government at the European conjuncture—strains celebrating, among other things, the patriotic devotion of the British tar:

And as for my life, 'tis the King's!

Such an episode in the Island's grand naval story her naval historians naturally abridge, one of them (G. P. R. James) candidly acknowledging that fain would he pass it over did not "impartiality forbid fastidiousness." And yet his mention is less a narration than a reference, having to do hardly at all with details. Nor are these readily to be found in the libraries. Like some other events in every age befalling states everywhere including America, the Great Mutiny was of such character that national pride along with views of policy would fain shade it off into the historical background. Such events cannot be ignored, but there is a considerate way of historically treating them. If a well-constituted individual refrains from blazoning aught amiss or calamitous in his family, a nation in the like circumstance may without reproach be equally discreet.

Though after parleyings between Government and the ringleaders, and concessions by the former as to some glaring abuses, the first uprising—that at Spithead—with difficulty was put down, or matters for the time pacified; yet at the Nore the unforeseen renewal of insurrection on a yet larger scale, and emphasized in the conferences that ensued by demands deemed by the authorities not only inadmissible but aggressively insolent, indicated—if the Red Flag did not sufficiently do so—what was the spirit animating the men. Final suppression, however, there was, but only made possible perhaps by the unswerving loyalty of the marine corps and voluntary resumption of loyalty among influential sections of the crews.

To some extent the Nore Mutiny may be regarded as analogous to the distempering irruption of contagious fever in a frame constitutionally sound, and which anon throws it off.

At all events, of these thousands of mutineers were some of the tars who not so very long afterwards—whether wholly prompted thereto by patriotism, or pugnacious instinct, or by both—helped to win a coronet for Nelson at the Nile, and the naval crown of crowns for him at Trafalgar. To the mutineers those battles and especially Trafalgar were a plenary absolution and a grand one: For all that goes to make up scenic naval display, heroic magnificence in arms, those battles, especially Trafalgar, stand unmatched in human annals.

IV

Concerning "The greatest sailor since our world began."—TENNYSON

In this matter of writing, resolve as one may to keep to the main road, some bypaths have an enticement not readily to be withstood. I am going to err into such a bypath. If the reader will keep me company I shall be glad. At the least we can promise ourselves that pleasure which is wickedly said to be in sinning, for a literary sin the divergence will be.

Very likely it is no new remark that the inventions of our time have at last brought about a change in sea warfare in degree corresponding to the revolution in all warfare effected by the original introduction from China into Europe of gunpowder. The first European firearm, a clumsy contrivance, was, as is well known, scouted by no few of the knights as a base implement, good enough peradventure for weavers too craven to stand up crossing steel with steel in frank fight. But as ashore knightly valor, though shorn of its blazonry, did not cease with the knights, neither on the seas, though nowadays in encounters there a certain kind of displayed gallantry be fallen out of date as hardly applicable under changed circumstances, did the nobler qualities of such naval magnates as Don John of Austria, Doria, Van Tromp, Jean Bart, the long line of British Admirals and the American Decaturs of 1812, become obsolete with their wooden walls.

Nevertheless, to anybody who can hold the Present at its worth without being inappreciative of the Past, it may be forgiven, if to such an one the solitary old hulk at Portsmouth, Nelson's *Victory*, seems to float there, not alone as the decaying monument of a fame incorruptible, but also as a poetic reproach, softened by its picturesqueness, to the *Monitors* and yet mightier hulls of the European ironclads. And this not altogether because such craft are unsightly, unavoidably lacking the symmetry and grand lines of the old battleships, but equally for other reasons.

There are some, perhaps, who, while not altogether inaccessible to that poetic reproach just alluded to, may yet on behalf of the new order be disposed to parry it; and this to the extent of iconoclasm, if need be. For example, prompted by the sight of the star inserted in the *Victory's* quarterdeck designating the spot where the Great Sailor fell, these martial utilitarians may suggest considerations implying that Nelson's ornate publication of his person in battle was not only unnecessary, but not military, nay, savored of foolhardiness and vanity. They may add, too, that at Trafalgar it was in effect nothing less than a challenge to death, and death came; and that but for his bravado the victorious admiral might possibly have survived the battle, and so, instead of having his sagacious dying injunctions overruled by his immediate successor in command, he himself when the contest was decided might have brought his shattered fleet to anchor, a proceeding which might have averted the deplorable loss of life by shipwreck in the elemental tempest that followed the martial one.

Well, should we set aside the more disputable point whether for various reasons it was possible to anchor the fleet, then plausibly enough the Benthamites of war may urge the above.

But the *might-have-been* is but boggy ground to build on. And, certainly, in foresight as to the larger issue of an encounter, and anxious preparations for it—buoying the deadly way and mapping it out, as at Copenhagen—few commanders have been so painstakingly circumspect as this same reckless declarer of his person in fight.

Personal prudence, even when dictated by quite other than selfish considerations, surely is no special virtue in a military man; while an excessive love of glory, impassioning a less burning impulse, the honest sense of duty, is the first. If the name *Wellington* is not so much of a trumpet to the blood as the simpler name *Nelson*, the reason for this may perhaps be inferred from the above. Alfred in his funeral ode on the victor of Waterloo ventures not to call him the greatest soldier of all time, though in the same ode he invokes Nelson as "the greatest sailor since our world began."

At Trafalgar Nelson on the brink of opening the fight sat down and wrote his last brief will and testament. If under the presentiment of the most magnificent of all victories to be crowned by his own glorious death, a sort of priestly motive led him to dress his person in the jeweled vouchers of his own shining deeds; if thus to have adorned himself for the altar and the sacrifice were indeed vainglory, then affectation and fustian is each more heroic line in the great epics and dramas, since in such lines the poet but embodies in verse those exaltations of sentiment that a nature like Nelson, the opportunity being given, vitalizes into acts.

V

Yes, the outbreak at the Nore was put down. But not every grievance was redressed. If the contractors, for example, were no longer permitted to ply some practices peculiar to their tribe everywhere, such as providing shoddy cloth, rations not sound or false in the measure, not the less impressment, for one thing, went on. By custom sanctioned for centuries, and judicially maintained by a Lord Chancellor as late as Mansfield, that mode of manning the fleet, a mode now fallen into a sort of abeyance but never formally renounced, it was not practicable to give up in those years. Its abrogation would have crippled the indispensable fleet, one wholly under canvas, no steam power, its innumerable sails and thousands of cannon, everything in short, worked by muscle alone; a fleet the more insatiate in demand for men, because then multiplying its ships of all grades against contingencies present and to come of the convulsed Continent.

Discontent foreran the two mutinies, and more or less it lurkingly survived them. Hence it was not unreasonable to apprehend some return of trouble sporadic or general. One instance of such apprehensions: In the same year with this story, Nelson, then Vice Admiral Sir Horatio, being with the fleet off the Spanish coast, was directed by the admiral in command to shift his pennant from the *Captain* to the *Theseus*, and for this reason: that the latter ship, having newly arrived on the station from home, where it had taken part in the Great Mutiny, danger was apprehended from the temper of the men, and it was thought that an officer like Nelson was the one, not indeed to terrorize the crew into base subjection, but to win them, by force of his mere presence, back to an allegiance, if not as enthusiastic as his own, yet as true. So it was that for a time on more than one quarter-deck anxiety did exist. At sea, precautionary vigilance was strained against relapse. At short notice an engagement might come on. When it did, the lieutenants assigned to batteries felt it incumbent on them, in some instances, to stand with drawn swords behind the men working the guns.

VI

But on board the seventy-four in which Billy now swung his hammock, very little in the manner of the men and nothing obvious in the demeanor of the officers would have suggested to an ordinary observer that the Great Mutiny was a recent event. In their general bearing and conduct the commissioned officers of a warship naturally take their tone from the commander, that is if he have that ascendancy of character that ought to be his.

Captain the Honorable Edward Fairfax Vere, to give his full title, was a bachelor of forty or thereabouts, a sailor of distinction even in a time prolific of renowned seamen. Though allied to the higher nobility his advancement had not been altogether owing to influences connected with that circumstance. He had seen much service, been in various engagements, always aquitting himself as an officer mindful of the welfare of his men, but never tolerating an infraction of discipline; thoroughly versed in the science of his profession, and intrepid to the verge of temerity, though never injudiciously so. For his gallantry in the West Indian waters as flag-lieutenant under Rodney in that admiral's crowning victory over De Grasse, he was made a post-captain.

Ashore in the garb of a civilian scarce anyone would have taken him for a sailor, more especially that he never garnished unprofessional talk with nautical terms, and, grave in his bearing, evinced little appreciation of mere humor. It was not out of keeping with these traits that on a passage when nothing demanded his paramount action, he was the most undemonstrative of men. Any landsman observing this gentleman not conspicuous by his stature and wearing no pronounced insignia, emerging from his cabin to the open deck, and noting the silent deference of the officers retiring to leeward, might have taken him for the King's guest, a civilian aboard the King's ship, some highly honorable discreet envoy on his way to an important post. But in fact this unobtrusiveness of demeanor may have proceeded from a certain unaffected modesty of manhood sometimes accompanying a resolute nature, a modesty evinced at all times not calling for pronounced action, and which, shown in any rank of life, suggests a virtue aristocratic in kind.

As with some other engaged in various departments of the world's more heroic activities, Captain Vere, though practical enough upon occasion, would at times betray a certain dreaminess of mood. Standing alone on the weather side of the quarter-deck, one hand holding by the rigging, he would absently gaze off at the blank sea. At the presentation to him then of some minor matter interrupting the current of his thoughts he would show more or less irascibility, but instantly he would control it.

In the navy he was popularly known by the appellation "Starry Vere." How such a designation happened to fall upon one who, whatever his sterling qualities, was without any brilliant ones, was in this wise: A favorite kinsman, Lord Denton, a free-hearted fellow, had been the first to meet and congratulate him upon his return to England from his West Indian cruise; and but the day previous turning over a copy of Andrew Marvell's poems had lighted, not for the first time however, upon the lines entitled "Appleton House," the name of one of the seats of their common ancestor, a hero in the German wars of the seventeenth century, in which poem occur the lines,

> This 'tis to have been from the first
> In a domestic heaven nursed,
> Under the discipline severe
> Of Fairfax and the starry Vere.

And so, upon embracing his cousin fresh from Rodney's great victory wherein he had played so gallant a part, brimming over with just family pride in the sailor of their house, he exuberantly exclaimed, "Give ye joy, Ed; give ye joy, my starry Vere!" This got currency, and the novel prefix serving in familiar parlance readily to distinguish the *Indomitable*'s captain from another Vere his senior, a distant relative, an officer of like rank in the navy, it remained permanently attached to the surname.

VII

In view of the part that the commander of the *Indomitable* plays in scenes shortly to follow, it may be well to fill out that sketch of him outlined in the previous chapter.

Aside from his qualities as a sea officer Captain Vere was an exceptional character. Unlike no few of England's renowned sailors, long and arduous service, with signal devotion to it, had not resulted in absorbing and *salting* the entire man. He had a marked leaning toward everything intellectual. He loved books, never going to sea without a newly replenished library, compact but of the best. The isolated leisure, in some cases so wearisome, falling at intervals to commanders even during a war cruise, never was tedious to Captain Vere. With nothing of that literary taste which less heeds the thing conveyed than the vehicle, his bias was toward those books to which every serious mind of superior order occupying any active post of authority in the world naturally inclines: books treating of actual men and events no matter of what era—history, biography, and unconventional writers, who, free from cant and convention, like Montaigne, honestly and in the spirit of common sense philosophize upon realities.

In this love of reading he found confirmation of his own more reasoned thoughts—confirmation which he had vainly sought in social converse—so that, as touching most fundamental topics, there had got to be established in him some positive convictions, which he forefelt would abide in him essentially unmodified so long as his intelligent part remained unimpaired. In view of the troubled period in which his lot was cast this was well for him. His settled convictions were as a dike against those invading waters of novel opinion, social, political, and otherwise, which carried away as in a torrent no few minds in those days, minds by nature not inferior to his own. While other members of that aristocracy to which by birth he belonged were incensed at the innovators mainly because their theories were inimical to the privileged classes, not alone Captain Vere disinterestedly opposed them because they seemed to him incapable of embodiment in lasting institutions, but at war with the peace of the world and the true welfare of mankind.

With minds less stored than his and less earnest, some officers of his rank, with whom at times he would necessarily consort, found him lacking in the companionable quality, a dry and bookish gentleman as they deemed. Upon any chance withdrawal from their company one would be apt to say to another, something like this: "Vere is a noble fellow, Starry Vere. Spite the gazettes, Sir Horatio" meaning him with the Lord title "is at bottom scarce a better seaman or fighter. But between you and me now don't you think there is a queer streak of the pedantic running through him? Yes, like the King's yarn in a coil of navy-rope?"

Some apparent ground there was for this sort of confidential criticism, since not only did the captain's discourse never fall into the jocosely familiar, but in illustrating any point touching the stirring personages and events of the time he would be as apt to cite some historic character or incident of antiquity as that he would cite from the moderns. He seemed unmindful of the circumstance that to his bluff company such remote allusions, however pertinent they might really be, were altogether alien to men whose reading was mainly confined to the journals. But considerateness in such matters is not easy to natures constituted like Captain Vere's. Their honesty prescribes to them directness, sometimes far-reaching like that of a migratory fowl that in its flight never heeds when it crosses a frontier.

VIII

The lieutenants and other commissioned gentlemen forming Captain Vere's staff it is not necessary here to particularize, nor needs it to make any mention of any of the warrant officers. But among the petty officers was one who, having much to do with the story, may as well be forthwith introduced. His portrait I essay, but shall never hit it. This was John Claggart, the master-at-arms. But that sea title may to landsmen seem somewhat equivocal. Originally, doubtless, that petty officer's function was the instruction of the men in the use of arms, sword or cutlass. But very long ago, owing to the advance in gunnery making hand-to-hand encounters less frequent and giving to niter and sulphur the preeminence over steel, that function ceased; the master-at-arms of a great warship becoming a sort of chief of police charged among other matters with the duty of preserving order on the populous lower gun decks.

Claggart was a man about five-and-thirty, somewhat spare and tall, yet of no ill figure upon the whole. His hand was too small and shapely to have been accustomed to hard toil. The face was a notable one, the features all except the chin cleanly cut as those on a Greek medallion; yet the chin, beardless as Tecumseh's, had something of strange protuberant heaviness in its make that recalled the prints of the Rev. Dr. Titus Oates, the historic deponent with the clerical drawl in the time of Charles II and the fraud of the alleged Popish Plot. It served Claggart in his office that his eye could cast a tutoring glance. His brow was of the sort phrenologically associated with more than average intellect: silken jet curls partly clustering over it, making a foil to the pallor below, a pallor tinged with a faint shade of amber akin to the hue of time-tinted marbles of old. This complexion, singularly contrasting with the red or deeply bronzed visages of the sailors, and in part the result of his official seclusion from the sunlight, though it was not exactly displeasing, nevertheless seemed to hint of something defective or abnormal in the constitution and blood. But his general aspect and manner were so suggestive of an education and career incongruous with his naval function that when not actively engaged in it he looked like a man of high quality, social and moral, who for reasons of his own was keeping incog. Nothing was known of his former life. It might be that he was an Englishman, and yet there lurked a bit of accent in his speech suggesting that possibly he was not such by birth, but through naturalization in early childhood. Among certain grizzled sea gossips of the gun decks and forecastle went a rumor perdue that the master-at-arms was a *chevalier* who had volunteered into the king's navy by way of compounding for some mysterious swindle whereof he had been arraigned at the King's

Bench. The fact that nobody could substantiate this report was, of course, nothing against its secret currency. Such a rumor once started on the gun decks in reference to almost anyone below the rank of a commissioned officer would, during the period assigned to this narrative, have seemed not altogether wanting in credibility to the tarry old wiseacres of a man-of-war crew. And indeed a man of Claggart's accomplishments, without prior nautical experience entering the navy at mature life, as he did, and necessarily allotted at the start to the lowest grade in it; a man too who never made allusion to his previous life ashore, these were circumstances which in the dearth of exact knowledge as to his true antecedents opened to the invidious a vague field for unfavorable surmise.

But the sailors' dog-watch gossip concerning him derived a vague plausibility from the fact that now for some period the British navy could so little afford to be squeamish in the matter of keeping up the muster rolls, that not only were press gangs notoriously abroad both afloat and ashore, but there was little or no secret about another matter, namely that the London police were at liberty to capture any questionable fellow at large, and summarily ship him to the dockyard or fleet. Furthermore, even among voluntary enlistments there were instances where the motive thereto partook neither of patriotic impulse nor yet of a random desire to experience a bit of sea life and martial adventure. Insolvent debtors of minor grade, together with the promiscuous lame ducks of morality, found in the navy a convenient and secure refuge. Secure, because once enlisted aboard a King's ship, they were as much in sanctuary as the transgressor of the Middle Ages harboring himself under the shadow of the altar. Such sanctioned irregularities, which for obvious reasons the government would hardly think to parade at the time and which consequently, and as affecting the least influential class of mankind, have all but dropped into oblivion, lend color to something for the truth whereof I do not vouch, and hence have some scruple in stating; something I remember having seen in print, though the book I cannot recall; but the same thing was personally communicated to me now more than forty years ago by an old pensioner in a cocked hat with whom I had a most interesting talk on the terrace at Greenwich, a Baltimore Negro, a Trafalgar man. It was to this effect: In the case of a warship short of hands whose speedy sailing was imperative, the deficient quota, in lack of any other way of making it good, would be eked out by drafts culled direct from the jails. For reasons previously suggested it would not perhaps be easy at the present day directly to prove or disprove the allegation. But allowed as a verity, how significant would it be of England's straits at the time, confronted by those wars which like a flight of harpies rose shrieking from the din and dust of the fallen Bastille. That era appears measurably clear to us who look back at it, and but read of it. But to the grandfathers of us graybeards, the more thoughtful of them, the genius of it presented an aspect like that of Camöen's Spirit of the Cape, an eclipsing menace mysterious and prodigious. Not America was exempt from apprehension. At the height of Napoleon's unexampled conquests, there were Americans who had fought at Bunker Hill who looked forward to the possibility that the Atlantic might prove no barrier against the ultimate schemes of this French upstart from the revolutionary chaos who seemed in act of fulfilling judgment prefigured in the Apocalypse.

But the less credence was to be given to the gun-deck talk touching Claggart, seeing that no man holding his office in a man-of-war can ever hope to be popular with the crew. Besides, in derogatory comments upon anyone against whom they have a grudge, or for any reason or no reason mislike, sailors are much like landsmen—they are apt to exaggerate or romance it.

About as much was really known to the *Indomitable*'s tars of the master-at-arms' career before entering the service as an astronomer knows about a comet's travels prior to its first observable appearance in the sky. The verdict of the sea quidnuncs has been cited only by way of showing what sort of moral impression the man made upon rude uncultivated natures whose conceptions of human wickedness were necessarily of the narrowest, limited to ideas of vulgar rascality—a thief among the swinging hammocks during a night watch, or the man-brokers and land-sharks of the sea ports.

It was no gossip, however, but fact, that though, as before hinted, Claggart upon his entrance into the navy was, as a novice, assigned to the least honorable section of a man-of-war's crew, embracing the drudgery, he did not long remain there.

The superior capacity he immediately evinced, his constitutional sobriety, ingratiating deference to superiors, together with a peculiar ferreting genius manifested on a singular occasion, all this capped by a certain austere patriotism abruptly advanced him to the position of master-at-arms.

Of this maritime chief of police the ship's-corporals, so called, were the immediate subordinates, and compliant ones, and this, as is to be noted in some business departments ashore, almost to a degree inconsistent with entire moral volition. His place put various converging wires of underground influence under the chief's control, capable when astutely worked through his understrappers of operating to the mysterious discomfort, if nothing worse, of any of the sea commonalty.

IX

Life in the foretop well agreed with Billy Budd. There, when not actually engaged on the yards yet higher aloft, the topmen, who as such had been picked out for youth and activity, constituted an aerial club lounging at ease against the smaller stunsails rolled up into cushions, spinning yarns like the lazy gods, and frequently amused with what was going on in the busy world of the decks below. No wonder then that a young fellow of Billy's disposition was well content in such society. Giving no cause of offense to anybody, he was always alert at a call. So in the merchant service it had been with him. But now such a punctiliousness in duty was shown that his topmates would sometimes good-naturedly laugh at him for it. This heightened alacrity had its cause, namely, the impression made upon him by the first formal gangway punishment he had ever witnessed, which befell the day following his impressment. It had been incurred by a little fellow, young, a novice, an afterguardsman absent from his assigned post when the ship was being put about—a dereliction resulting in a rather serious hitch to that maneuver, one demanding instantaneous promptitude in letting go and making fast. When Billy saw the culprit's naked back under the scourge gridironed with red welts, and worse; when he marked the dire expression on the liberated man's face as with his woolen shirt flung over him by the executioner he rushed forward from the spot to bury himself in the crowd, Billy was horrified. He resolved that never through remissness would he make himself liable to such a visitation or do or omit aught that might merit even verbal reproof. What then was his surprise and concern when ultimately he found himself getting into petty trouble occasionally about such matters as the stowage of his bag or something amiss in his hammock, matters under the police oversight of the ship's-corporals of the lower decks, and which brought down on him a vague threat from one of them.

So heedful in all things as he was, how could this be? He could not understand it, and it more than vexed him. When he spoke to his young topmates about it they were either lightly incredulous or found something comical in his unconcealed anxiety. "Is it your bag, Billy?" said one; "well, sew yourself up in it, bully boy, and then you'll be sure to know if anybody meddles with it."

Now there was a veteran aboard who because his years began to disqualify him for more active work had been recently assigned duty as mainmastman in his watch, looking to the gear belayed at the rail roundabout that great spar near the deck. At off times the foretopman had picked up some acquaintance with him, and now in his trouble it occurred to him that he might be the sort of person to go to for wise counsel. He was an old Dansker long anglicized in the service, of few words, many wrinkles, and some honorable scars. His wizened face, time-tinted and weather-stained to the complexion of an antique parchment, was here and there peppered blue by the chance explosion of a gun cartridge in action. He was an *Agamemnon* man; some two years prior to the time of this story having served under Nelson when but Sir Horatio in that ship immortal in naval memory, and which, dismantled and in part broken up to her bare ribs, is seen a grand skeleton in Haydon's etching. As one of a boarding party from the

Agamemnon he had received a cut slantwise along one temple and cheek, leaving a long pale scar like a streak of dawn's light falling athwart the dark visage. It was on account of that scar and the affair in which it was known that he had received it, as well as from his blue-peppered complexion, that the Dansker went among the *Indomitable*'s crew by the name of "Board-her-in-the-smoke."

Now the first time that his small weazel eyes happened to light on Billy Budd, a certain grim internal merriment set all his ancient wrinkles into antic play. Was it that his eccentric unsentimental old sapience, primitive in its kind, saw or thought it saw something which in contrast with the warship's environment looked oddly incongruous in the Handsome Sailor? But after slyly studying him at intervals, the old Merlin's equivocal merriment was modified; for now when the twain would meet it would start in his face a quizzing sort of look, but it would be but momentary and sometimes replaced by an expression of speculative query as to what might eventually befall a nature like that, dropped into a world not without some man traps and against whose subtleties simple courage lacking experience and address and without any touch of defensive ugliness is of little avail; and where such innocence as man is capable of does yet in a moral emergency not always sharpen the faculties or enlighten the will.

However it was, the Dansker in his ascetic way rather took to Billy. Nor was this only because of a certain philosophic interest in such a character. There was another cause. While the old man's eccentricities, sometimes bordering on the ursine, repelled the juniors, Billy, undeterred thereby, revering him as a salt hero would make advances, never passing the old *Agamemnon*-man without a salutation marked by that respect which is seldom lost on the aged, however crabbed at times or whatever their station in life.

There was a vein of dry humor, or what not, in the mastman; and, whether in freak of patriarchal irony touching Billy's youth and athletic frame or for some other and more recondite reason, from the first in addressing him he always substituted "Baby" for "Billy," the Dansker in fact being the originator of the name by which the foretopman eventually became known aboard ship.

Well then, in his mysterious little difficulty going in quest of the wrinkled one, Billy found him off duty in a dog watch ruminating by himself seated on a shotbox of the upper gun deck now and then surveying with a somewhat cynical regard certain of the more swaggering promenaders there. Billy recounted his trouble, again wondering how it all happened. The salt seer attentively listened, accompanying the foretopman's recital with queer twitchings of his wrinkles and problematical little sparkles of his small ferret eyes. Making an end of his story, the foretopman asked, "And now, Dansker, do tell me what you think of it."

The old man, shoving up the front of his tarpaulin and deliberately rubbing the long slant scar at the point where it entered the thin hair, laconically said, "Baby Budd, *Jimmy Legs*" (meaning the master-at-arms) "is down on you."

"*Jimmy Legs!*" ejaculated Billy, his welkin eyes expanding; "what for? Why he calls me *the sweet and pleasant young fellow*, they tell me."

"Does he so?" grinned the grizzled one; then said "Ay, Baby Lad, a sweet voice has *Jimmy Legs*."

"No, not always. But to me he has. I seldom pass him but there comes a pleasant word."

"And that's because he's down upon you, Baby Budd."

Such reiteration along with the manner of it, incomprehensible to a novice, disturbed Billy almost as much as the mystery for which he had sought explanation. Something less unpleasingly oracular he tried to extract; but the old sea-Chiron, thinking perhaps that for the nonce he had sufficiently instructed his young Achilles, pursed his lips, gathered all his wrinkles together, and would commit himself to nothing further.

Years, and those experiences which befell certain shrewder men subordinated lifelong to the will of superiors, all this had developed in the Dansker the pithy guarded cynicism that was his leading characteristic.

X

The next day an incident served to confirm Billy Budd in his incredulity as to the

Dansker's strange summing up of the case submitted. The ship at noon going large before the wind was rolling on her course, and he below at dinner and engaged in some sportful talk with the members of his mess chanced in a sudden lurch to spill the entire contents of his soup pan upon the new scrubbed deck. Claggart, the master-at-arms, official rattan in hand, happened to be passing along the battery in a bay of which the mess was lodged, and the greasy liquid streamed just across his path. Stepping over it, he was proceeding on his way without comment, since the matter was nothing to take notice of under the circumstances, when he happened to observe who it was that had done the spilling. His countenance changed. Pausing, he was about to ejaculate something hasty at the sailor, but checked himself, and, pointing down to the streaming soup, playfully tapped him from behind with his rattan, saying in a low musical voice peculiar to him at times: "Handsomely done, my lad! And handsome is as handsome did it too!" And with that passed on. Not noted by Billy, as not coming within his view, was the involuntary smile, or rather grimace, that accompanied Claggart's equivocal words. Aridly it drew down the thin corners of his shapely mouth. But everybody taking his remark as meant for humorous, and at which therefore as coming from a superior they were bound to laugh, "with counterfeited glee" acted accordingly; and Billy, tickled, it may be, by the allusion to his being the Handsome Sailor, merrily joined in; then addressing his messmates exclaimed: "There now, who says that Jimmy Legs is down on me!" "And who said he was, Beauty?" demanded one Donald with some surprise. Whereat the foretopman looked a little foolish recalling that it was only one person, Board-her-in-the-smoke, who had suggested what to him was the smoky idea that this master-at-arms was in any peculiar way hostile to him. Meantime that functionary, resuming his path, must have momentarily worn some expression less guarded than that of the bitter smile, and usurping the face from the heart, some distorting expression perhaps, for a drummer-boy, heedlessly frolicking along from the opposite direction and chancing to come into light collision with his person, was strangely disconcerted by his aspect. Nor was the impression lessened when the official, impulsively giving him a sharp cut with the rattan, vehemently exclaimed: "Look where you go!"

XI

What was the matter with the master-at-arms? And, be the matter what it might, how could it have direct relation to Billy Budd, with whom, prior to the affair of the spilled soup, he had never come into any special contact official or otherwise? What indeed could the trouble have to do with one so little inclined to give offense as the merchant ship's *peacemaker*, even him who in Claggart's own phrase was "the sweet and pleasant young fellow"? Yes, why should *Jimmy Legs*, to borrow the Dansker's expression, be *down* on the Handsome Sailor? But, at heart and not for nothing, as the late chance encounter may indicate to the discerning, down on him, secretly down on him, he assuredly was.

Now to invent something touching the more private career of Claggart, something involving Billy Budd, of which something the latter should be wholly ignorant, some romantic incident implying that Claggart's knowledge of the young bluejacket began at some period anterior to catching sight of him on board the seventy-four—all this, not so difficult to do, might avail in a way more or less interesting to account for whatever of enigma may appear to lurk in the case. But in fact there was nothing of the sort. And yet the cause, necessarily to be assumed as the sole one assignable, is in its very realism as much charged with that prime element of Radcliffian romance, *the mysterious*, as any that the ingenuity of the author of the *Mysteries of Udolpho* could devise. For what can more partake of the mysterious than an antipathy spontaneous and profound, such as is evoked in certain exceptional mortals by the mere aspect of some other mortal however harmless he may be, if not called forth by this very harmlessness itself?

Now there can exist no irritating juxtaposition of dissimilar personalities comparable to that which is possible aboard a great warship fully manned and at sea. There, every day among all ranks, almost every man comes into more or less of contact with almost every other man. Wholly there to avoid even the sight of an aggravating object one must needs give it Jonah's toss or jump overboard himself. Imagine how all this might eventually operate on some peculiar human creature the direct reverse of a saint.

But for the adequate comprehending of Claggart by a normal nature these hints are insufficient. To pass from a normal nature to him one must cross "the deadly space between." And this is best done by indirection.

Long ago an honest scholar my senior said to me in reference to one who like himself is now no more, a man so unimpeachably respectable that against him nothing was ever openly said though among the few something was whispered, "Yes, X—— is a nut not to be cracked by the tap of a lady's fan. You are aware that I am the adherent of no organized religion, much less of any philosophy built into a system. Well, for all that, I think that to try and get into X——, enter his labyrinth and get out again, without a clue derived from some source other than what is known as *knowledge of the world*—that were hardly possible, at least for me."

"Why," said I, "X——, however singular a study to some, is yet human, and knowledge of the world assuredly implies the knowledge of human nature, and in most of its varieties."

"Yes, but a superficial knowledge of it, serving ordinary purposes. But for anything deeper, I am not certain whether to know the world and to know human nature be not two distinct branches of knowledge, which, while they may coexist in the same heart, yet either may exist with little or nothing of the other. Nay, in an average man of the world, his constant rubbing with it blunts that fine spiritual insight indispensable to the understanding of the essential in certain exceptional characters, whether evil ones or good. In a matter of some importance I have seen a girl wind an old lawyer about her little finger. Nor was it the dotage of senile love. Nothing of the sort. But he knew law better than he knew the girl's heart. Coke and Blackstone hardly shed so much light into obscure spiritual places as the Hebrew prophets. And who were they? Mostly recluses."

At the time my inexperience was such that I did not quite see the drift of all this. It may be that I see it now. And indeed, if that lexicon which is based on Holy Writ were any longer popular, one might with less difficulty define and denominate certain phenomenal men. As it is, one must turn to some authority not liable to the charge of being tinctured with the Biblical element.

In a list of definitions included in the authentic translation of Plato, a list attributed to him, occurs this: "Natural Depravity: a depravity according to nature." A definition which, though savoring of Calvinism, by no means involves Calvin's dogmas as to total mankind. Evidently its intent makes it applicable but to individuals. Not many are the examples of this depravity, which the gallows and jail supply. At any rate, for notable instances, since these have no vulgar alloy of the brute in them but invariably are dominated by intellectuality, one must go elsewhere. Civilization, especially if of the austerer sort, is auspicious to it. It folds itself in the mantle of respectability. It has its certain negative virtues serving as silent auxiliaries. It never allows wine to get within its guard. It is not going too far to say that it is without vices or small sins. There is a phenomenal pride in it that excludes them from anything mercenary or avaricious. In short the depravity here meant partakes nothing of the sordid or sensual. It is serious, but free from acerbity. Though no flatterer of mankind it never speaks ill of it.

But the thing which in eminent instances signalizes so exceptional a nature is this: though the man's even temper and discreet bearing would seem to intimate a mind peculiarly subject to the law of reason, not the less in his heart he would seem to riot in complete exemption from that law, having apparently little to do with reason further than to employ it as an *ambidexter* implement for effecting the irrational. That is to say: Toward the accomplishment of an aim which in wantonness of malignity would seem to partake of the insane, he will direct a cool judgment sagacious and sound.

These men are true madmen, and of the most dangerous sort, for their lunacy is not continuous but occasional, evoked by some special object; it is probably secretive, which is as much to say it is self-contained, so that when, moreover, most active, it is to the average mind not distinguishable from sanity, and for the reason above suggested, that, whatever its aims may be—and the aim is never declared—the method and the outward proceeding are always perfectly rational.

Now something such an one was Claggart, in whom was the mania of an evil nature, not engendered by vicious training or corrupting books or licentious living but born with him and innate, in short "a depravity according to nature."

XII

Lawyers, Experts, Clergy
An Episode

By the way, can it be the phenomenon, disowned or at least concealed, that in some criminal cases puzzles the courts? For this cause have our juries at times not only to endure the prolonged contentions of lawyers with their fees, but also the yet more perplexing strife of the medical experts with theirs?—But why leave it to them? Why not subpoena as well the clerical proficients? their vocation bringing them into peculiar contact with so many human beings, and sometimes in their least guarded hour, in interviews very much more confidential than those of physician and patient; this would seem to qualify them to know something about those intricacies involved in the question of moral responsibility; whether in a given case, say, the crime proceeded from mania in the brain or rabies of the heart. As to any differences among themselves these clerical proficients might develop on the stand, these could hardly be greater than the direct contradictions exchanged between the remunerated medical experts.

Dark sayings are these, some will say. But why? Is it because they somewhat savor of Holy Writ in its phrase "mysteries of iniquity"? If they do, such savor was enough far from being intended, for little will it commend these pages to many a reader of today.

The point of the present story turning on the hidden nature of the master-at-arms has necessitated this chapter. With an added hint or two in connection with the incident at the mess, the resumed narrative must be left to vindicate, as it may, its own credibility.

XIII

Pale ire, envy and despair

That Claggart's figure was not amiss, and his face, save the chin, well molded, has already been said. Of these favorable points he seemed not insensible, for he was not only neat but careful in his dress. But the form of Billy Budd was heroic; and if his face was without the intellectual look of the pallid Claggart's, not the less was it lit, like his, from within, though from a different source. The bonfire in his heart made luminous the rose-tan in his cheek.

In view of the marked contrast between the persons of the twain, it is more than probable that when the master-at-arms in the scene last given applied to the sailor the proverb *Handsome is as handsome does* he there let escape an ironic inkling, not caught by the young sailors who heard it, as to what it was that had first moved him against Billy, namely, his significant personal beauty.

Now envy and antipathy, passions irreconcilable in reason, nevertheless in fact may spring conjoined like Chang and Eng in one birth. Is Envy then such a monster? Well, though many an arraigned mortal has in hopes of mitigated penalty pleaded guilty to horrible actions, did ever anybody seriously confess to envy? Something there is in it universally felt to be more shameful than even felonious crime. And not only does everybody disown it but the better sort are inclined to incredulity when it is in earnest imputed to an intelligent man. But since its lodgment is in the heart, not the brain, no degree of intellect supplies a guarantee against it. But Claggart's was no vulgar form of the passion. Nor, as directed toward Billy Budd, did it partake of that streak of apprehensive jealousy that marred Saul's visage perturbedly brooding on the comely young David. Claggart's envy struck deeper. If askance he eyed the good looks, cheery health, and frank enjoyment of young life in Billy Budd, it was because these went along with a nature that, as Claggart magnetically felt, had in its simplicity never willed malice or experienced the reactionary bite of that serpent. To him, the spirit lodged within Billy and looking out from his welkin eyes as from windows, that ineffability it was which made the dimple in his dyed cheek, supplied his joints, and, dancing in his yellow curls, made him pre-eminently the Handsome Sailor. One person excepted, the master-at-arms was perhaps the only man in the ship intellectually capable of adequately appreciating the moral phenomenon presented in Billy Budd. And the insight but intensified his passion, which, assuming various secret forms within him, at times assumed that of cynic disdain—disdain of innocence——To be nothing more than innocent! Yet in an esthetic way he saw the charm of it, the courageous free-and-easy temper of it, and fain would have shared it, but he despaired of it.

With no power to annul the elemental evil in him, though readily enough he could hide it; apprehending the good, but powerless to be it; a nature like Claggart's surcharged with energy as such natures almost invariably are, what recourse is left to it but to recoil upon itself, and, like the scorpion for which the Creator alone is responsible, act out to the end the part allotted it.

XIV

Passion, and passion in its profoundest, is not a thing demanding a palatial stage whereon to play its part. Down among the groundlings, among the beggars and rakers of the garbage, profound passion is enacted. And the circumstances that provoke it, however trivial or mean, are no measure of its power. In the present instance the stage is a scrubbed gun deck, and one of the external provocations a man-of-war's-man's spilled soup.

Now when the master-at-arms noticed whence came that greasy fluid streaming before his feet, he must have taken it—to some extent willfully, perhaps—not for the mere accident it assuredly was, but for the sly escape of a spontaneous feeling on Billy's part more or less answering to the antipathy on his own. In effect a foolish demonstration he must have thought, and very harmless, like the futile kick of a heifer, which yet, were the heifer a shod stallion, would not be so harmless. Even so was it that into the gall of Claggart's envy he infused the vitriol of his contempt. But the incident confirmed to him certain telltale reports purveyed to his ear by "Squeak," one of his more cunning corporals, a grizzled little man, so nicknamed by the sailors on account of his squeaky voice and sharp visage ferreting about the dark corners of the lower decks after interlopers, satirically suggesting to them the idea of a rat in a cellar.

From his Chief's employing him as an implicit tool in laying little traps for the worriment of the foretopman—for it was from the master-at-arms that the petty persecutions heretofore adverted to had proceeded—the corporal, having naturally enough concluded that his master could have no love for the sailor, made it his business, faithful understrapper that he was, to foment the ill blood by perverting to his Chief certain innocent frolics of the good-natured foretopman, besides inventing for his mouth sundry contumelious epithets he claimed to have overheard him let fall. The master-at-arms never suspected the veracity of these reports, more especially as to the epithets, for he well knew how secretly unpopular may become a master-at-arms, at least a master-at-arms of those days zealous in his function, and how the bluejackets shoot at him in private their raillery and wit; the nickname by which he goes among them (*Jimmy Legs*) implying under the form of merriment their cherished disrespect and dislike.

But in view of the greediness of hate for patrolmen, it hardly needed a purveyor to feed Claggart's passion. An uncommon prudence is habitual with the subtler depravity, for it has everything to hide. And in case of an injury but suspected, its secretiveness voluntarily cuts it off from enlightenment or disillusion; and, not unreluctantly, action is taken upon surmise as upon certainty. And the retaliation is apt to be in monstrous disproportion to the supposed offense; for when in anybody was revenge in its exactions aught else but an inordinate usurer? But how with Claggart's conscience? For though consciences are unlike as foreheads, every intelligence, not excluding the Scriptural devils who "believe and tremble," has one. But Claggart's conscience, being but the lawyer to his will, made ogres of trifles, probably arguing that the motive imputed to Billy in spilling the soup just when he did, together with the epithets alleged, these, if nothing more, made a strong case against him; nay, justified animosity into a sort of retributive righteousness. The Pharisee is the Guy Fawkes prowling in the hid chambers underlying the Claggarts. And they can really form no conception of an unreciprocated malice. Probably, the master-at-arms' clandestine persecution of Billy was started to try the temper of the man; but it had not developed any quality in him that enmity could make official use of or even pervert into plausible self-justification; so that the occurrence at the mess, petty if it were, was a welcome one to the peculiar conscience assigned to be the private mentor of Claggart. And, for the rest, not improbably it put him upon new experiments.

XV

Not many days after the last incident narrated something befell Billy Budd that more graveled him than aught that had previously occurred.

It was a warm night for the latitude, and the foretopman, whose watch at the time was properly below, was dozing on the uppermost deck, whither he had ascended from his hot hammock, one of hundreds suspended so closely wedged together over a lower gun deck that there was little or no swing to them. He lay as in the shadow of a hillside, stretched under the lee of the booms, a piled ridge of spare spars amidships between foremast and mainmast and among which the ship's largest boat, the launch, was stowed. Alongside of three other slumberers from below, he lay near that end of the booms which approaches the foremast, his station aloft on duty as a foretopman being just over the deck station of the forecastlemen, entitling him according to usage to make himself more or less at home in that neighborhood.

Presently he was stirred into semiconsciousness by somebody, who must have previously sounded the sleep of the others, touching his shoulder, and then, as the foretopman raised his head, breathing into his ear in a quick whisper, "Slip into the lee forechains, Billy; there is something in the wind. Don't speak. Quick, I will meet you there," and disappeared.

Now Billy, like sundry other essentially good-natured ones, had some of the weaknesses inseparable from essential good nature, among these was a reluctance, almost an incapacity, of plumply saying *no* to an abrupt proposition not obviously absurd on the face of it, nor obviously unfriendly, nor iniquitous. And being of warm blood he had not the phlegm tacitly to negative any proposition by unresponsive inaction. Like his sense of fear, his apprehension as to aught outside of the honest and natural was seldom very quick. Besides, upon the present occasion, the drowse from his sleep still hung upon him.

However it was, he mechanically rose, and, sleepily wondering what could be in the wind, betook himself to the designated place, a narrow platform, one of six, outside of the high bulwarks and screened by the great deadeyes and multiple columned lanyards of the shrouds and backstays, and, in a great warship of that time, of dimensions commensurate to the hull's magnitude, a tarry balcony in short overhanging the sea, and so secluded that one mariner of the *Indomitable*, a nonconformist old tar of a serious turn, made it even in daytime his private oratory.

In this retired nook the stranger soon joined Billy Budd. There was no moon as yet; a haze obscured the starlight. He could not distinctly see the stranger's face. Yet from something in the outline and carriage, Billy took him to be, and correctly, one of the after-guard.

"Hist! Billy," said the man in the same quick cautionary whisper as before; "you were impressed, weren't you? Well, so was I," and he paused, as to mark the effect. But Billy, not knowing exactly what to make of this, said nothing. Then the other: "We are not the only impressed ones, Billy. There's a gang of us.—Couldn't you—help —at a pinch?"

"What do you mean?" demanded Billy, here thoroughly shaking off his drowse.

"Hist, hist!" the hurried whisper now growing husky, "see here"—and the man held up two small objects faintly twinkling in the nightlight—"see, they are yours, Billy, if you'll only——"

But Billy broke in, and in his resentful eagerness to deliver himself his vocal infirmity somewhat intruded: "D-D-Damme,

I don't know what you are d-driving at, or what you mean, but you had better g-g-go where you belong!" For the moment the fellow, as confounded, did not stir; and Billy, springing to his feet, said, "If you d-don't start I'll t-t-toss you back over the r-rail!" There was no mistaking this, and the mysterious emissary decamped, disappearing in the direction of the mainmast in the shadow of the booms.

"Hallo, what's the matter?" here came growling from a forecastleman awakened from his deck doze by Billy's raised voice. And as the foretopman reappeared and was recognized by him: "Ah, Beauty, is it you? Well, something must have been the matter for you st-st-stuttered."

"Oh," rejoined Billy, now mastering the impediment, "I found an after-guardsman in our part of the ship here and I bid him be off where he belongs."

"And is that all you did about it, foretopman?" gruffly demanded another, an irascible old fellow of brick-colored visage and hair, and who was known to his associate forecastlemen as "Red Pepper." "Such sneaks I should like to marry to the gunner's daughter!" by that expression meaning that he would like to subject them to disciplinary castigation over a gun.

However, Billy's rendering of the matter satisfactorily accounted to these inquirers for the brief commotion, since of all the sections of a ship's company the forecastlemen, veterans for the most part and bigoted in their sea prejudices, are the most jealous in resenting territorial encroachments, especially on the part of any of the after-guard, of whom they have but a sorry opinion, chiefly landsmen, never going aloft except to reef or furl the mainsail, and in no wise competent to handle a marlinspike or turn in a deadeye, say.

XVI

This incident sorely puzzled Billy Budd. It was an entirely new experience, the first time in his life that he had ever been personally approached in underhand intriguing fashion. Prior to this encounter he had known nothing of the after-guardsman, the two men being stationed wide apart, one forward and aloft during his watch, the other on deck and aft.

What could it mean? And could they really be guineas, those two glittering objects the interloper had held up to his eyes? Where could the fellow get guineas? Why even spare buttons are not so plentiful at sea. The more he turned the matter over, the more he was nonplussed, and made uneasy and discomfited. In his disgustful recoil from an overture which though he but ill comprehended he instinctively knew must involve evil of some sort, Billy Budd was like a young horse fresh from the pasture suddenly inhaling a vile whiff from some chemical factory and by repeated snortings tries to get it out of his nostrils and lungs. This frame of mind barred all desire of holding further parley with the fellow, even were it but for the purpose of gaining some enlightenment as to his design in approaching him. And yet he was not without natural curiosity to see how such a visitor in the dark would look in broad day.

He espied him the following afternoon in his first dog watch below, one of the smokers on that forward part of the upper gun deck allotted to the pipe. He recognized him by his general cut and build, more than by his round freckled face and glassy eyes of pale blue, veiled with lashes all but white. And yet Billy was a bit uncertain whether indeed it were he—yonder chap about his own age chatting and laughing in freehearted way, leaning against a gun, a genial young fellow enough to look at, and something of a rattlebrain, to all appearance. Rather chubby too for a sailor, even an afterguardsman. In short the last man in the world, one would think, to be overburthened with thoughts, especially those perilous thoughts that must needs belong to a conspirator in any serious project, or even to the underling of such a conspirator.

Although Billy was not aware of it, the fellow, with a sidelong watchful glance, had perceived Billy first, and then noting that Billy was looking at him thereupon nodded a familiar sort of friendly recognition as to an old acquaintance, without interrupting the talk he was engaged in with the group of smokers. A day or two afterwards, chancing in the evening promenade on a gun deck to pass Billy, he offered a flying word of good fellowship, as it were, which, by its unexpectedness and equivocalness under the circumstances, so embarrassed Billy that he knew not how to respond to it, and let it go unnoticed.

Billy was now left more at a loss than before. The ineffectual speculations into which he was led were so disturbingly alien to him that he did his best to smother them. It never entered his mind that here was a matter which, from its extreme questionableness, it was his duty as a loyal bluejacket to report in the proper quarter. And, probably, had such a step been suggested to him, he would have been deterred from taking it by the thought, one of novice magnanimity, that it would savor overmuch of the dirty work of a telltale. He kept the thing to himself. Yet upon one occasion he could not forbear a little disburthening himself to the old Dansker, tempted thereto perhaps by the influence of a balmy night when the ship lay becalmed; the twain, silent for the most part, sitting together on deck, their heads propped against the bulwarks. But it was only a partial and anonymous account that Billy gave, the unfounded scruples above referred to preventing full disclosure to anybody. Upon hearing Billy's version, the sage Dansker seemed to divine more than he was told, and, after a while meditation during which his wrinkles were pursed as into a point, quite effacing for the time that quizzing expression his face sometimes wore—"Didn't I say so, Baby Budd?"

"Say what?" demanded Billy.

"Why, *Jimmy Legs* is *down* on you."

"And what," rejoined Billy in amazement, "has *Jimmy Legs* to do with that cracked after-guardsman?"

"Ho, it was an after-guardsman then. A cat's-paw, a cat's-paw!" And with that exclamation, which, whether it had reference to a light puff of air just then coming over the calm sea, or subtler relation to the after-guardsman, there is no telling, the old Merlin gave a twisting wrench with his black teeth at his plug of tobacco, vouchsafing no reply to Billy's impetuous question, though now repeated, for it was his wont to relapse into grim silence when interrogated in skeptical sort as to any of his sententious oracles, not always very clear ones, rather partaking of that obscurity which invests most Delphic deliverances from any quarter.

Long experience had very likely brought this old man to that bitter prudence which never interferes in aught and never gives advice.

XVII

Yes, despite the Dansker's pithy insistence as to the master-at-arms being at the bottom of these strange experiences of Billy on board the *Indomitable*, the young sailor was ready to ascribe them to almost anybody but the man who, to use Billy's own expression, "always had a pleasant word for him." This is to be wondered at. Yet not so much to be wondered at. In certain matters, some sailors even in mature life remain unsophisticated enough. But a young seafarer of the disposition of our athletic foretopman is much of a child-man. And yet a child's utter innocence is but its blank ignorance, and the innocence more or less wanes as intelligence waxes. But in Billy Budd intelligence, such as it was, had advanced, while yet his simple-mindedness remained for the most part unaffected. Experience is a teacher indeed, yet did Billy's years make his experience small. Besides, he had none of that intuitive knowledge of the bad which in natures not good or incompletely so foreruns experience, and therefore may pertain, as in some instances it too clearly does pertain, even to youth.

And what could Billy know of man except of man as a mere sailor? And the old-fashioned sailor, the veritable man-before-the-mast, the sailor from boyhood up, he, though indeed of the same species as a landman, is in some respects singularly distinct from him. The sailor is frankness, the landsman is finesse. Life is not a game with the sailor, demanding the long head; no intricate game of chess where few moves are made in straightforwardness, and ends are attained by indirection; an oblique, tedious, barren game hardly worth that poor candle burnt out in playing it.

Yes, as a class, sailors are in character a juvenile race. Even their deviations are marked by juvenility. And this more especially holding true with the sailors of Billy's time. Then, too, certain things which apply to all sailors do more pointedly operate here and there upon the junior one. Every sailor, too, is accustomed to obey orders without debating them; his life afloat is externally ruled for him; he is not brought into that promiscuous commerce with mankind where unobstructed free agency on equal terms—equal superficially, at least—soon teaches one that unless upon occasion he exercise a distrust keen in proportion to the fairness of the appearance, some foul turn may be served him. A ruled undemonstrative distrustfulness is so habitual, not with businessmen so much, as with men who know their kind in less shallow relations than business, namely, certain men-of-the-world, that they come at last to employ it all but unconsciously, and some of them would very likely feel real surprise at being charged with it as one of their general characteristics.

XVIII

But after the little matter at the mess Billy Budd no more found himself in strange trouble at times about his hammock or his clothes bag or what not. While, as to that smile that occasionally sunned him, and the pleasant passing word, these were, if not more frequent, yet if anything more pronounced than before.

But, for all that, there were certain other demonstrations now. When Claggart's unobserved glance happened to light on belted Billy rolling along the upper gun deck in the leisure of the second dog watch, exchanging passing broadsides of fun with other young promenaders in the crowd, that glance would follow the cheerful sea-Hyperion with a settled meditative and melancholy expression, his eyes strangely suffused with incipient feverish tears. Then would Claggart look like the man of sorrows. Yes, and sometimes the melancholy expression would have in it a touch of soft yearning, as if Claggart could even have loved Billy but for fate and ban. But this was an evanescence, and quickly repented of, as it were, by an immitigable look, pinching and shriveling the visage into the momentary semblance of a wrinkled walnut. But sometimes catching sight in advance of the foretopman coming in his direction, he would, upon their nearing, step aside a little to let him pass, dwelling upon Billy for the moment with the glittering dental satire of a Guise. But upon any abrupt unforeseen encounter a red light would [flash] forth from his eye like a spark from an anvil in a dusk smithy. That quick fierce light was a strange one, darted from orbs which in repose were of a color nearest approaching a deeper violet, the softest of shades.

Though some of these caprices of the pit could not but be observed by their object, yet were they beyond the construing of such a nature. And the thews of Billy were hardly compatible with that sort of sensitive spiritual organization which in some cases instinctively conveys to ignorant innocence an admonition of the proximity of the malign. He thought the master-at-arms acted in a manner rather queer at times. That was all. But the occasional frank air and pleasant word went for what they purported to be, the young sailor never having heard as yet of the "too fair-spoken man."

Had the foretopman been conscious of having done or said anything to provoke the ill will of the official, it would have been different with him, and his sight might have been purged if not sharpened. As it was, innocence was his blinder.

So was it with him in yet another matter. Two minor officers—the armorer and captain of the hold, with whom he had never exchanged a word, his position in the ship not bringing him into contact with them—these men now for the first began to cast upon Billy when they chanced to encounter him that peculiar glance which evidences that the man from whom it comes has been some way tampered with and to the prejudice of him upon whom the glance lights. Never did it occur to Billy as a thing to be noted or a thing suspicious, though he well knew the fact, that the armorer and captain of the hold, with the ship's yeoman, apothecary, and others of that grade, were, by naval usage, messmates of the master-at-arms, men with ears convenient to his confidential tongue.

But the general popularity that our Handsome Sailor's manly forwardness upon occasion, and his irresistible good nature, indicating no mental superiority tending to excite an invidious feeling—this good will on the part of most of his shipmates made him the less to concern himself about such mute aspects toward him as those whereto allusion has just been made.

As to the after-guardsman, though Billy

for reasons already given necessarily saw little of him, yet when the two did happen to meet, invariably came the fellow's offhand cheerful recognition, sometimes accompanied by a passing pleasant word or two. Whatever that equivocal young person's original design may really have been, or the design of which he might have been the deputy, certain it was from his manner upon these occasions that he had wholly dropped it.

It was as if his precocity of crookedness (and every vulgar villain is precocious) had for once deceived him, and the man he had sought to entrap as a simpleton had, through his very simplicity, ignominiously baffled him.

But shrewd ones may opine that it was hardly possible for Billy to refrain from going up to the after-guardsman and bluntly demanding to know his purpose in the initial interview, so abruptly closed in the forechains. Shrewd ones may also think it but natural in Billy to set about sounding some of the other impressed men of the ship in order to discover what basis, if any, there was for the emissary's obscure suggestions as to plotting disaffection aboard. Yes, the shrewd may so think. But something more, or, rather, something else, than mere shrewdness is perhaps needful for the due understanding of such a character as Billy Budd's.

As to Claggart, the monomania in the man—if that indeed it were, as involuntarily disclosed by starts in the manifestations detailed, yet in general covered over by his self-contained and rational demeanor—this, like a subterranean fire was eating its way deeper and deeper in him. Something decisive must come of it.

XIX

After the mysterious interview in the forechains, the one so abruptly ended there by Billy, nothing especially germane to the story occurred until the events now about to be narrated.

Elsewhere it has been said that in the lack of frigates (of course better sailers than line-of-battle ships) in the English squadron up the Straits at the period, the *Indomitable* was occasionally employed not only as an available substitute for a scout, but at times on detached service of more important kind. This was not alone because of her sailing qualities, not common in a ship of her rate, but quite as much, probably, that the character of her commander, it was thought, specially adapted him for any duty where under unforeseen difficulties a prompt initiative might have to be taken in some matter demanding knowledge and ability in addition to those qualities implied in good seamanship. It was on an expedition of the latter sort, a somewhat distant one, and when the *Indomitable* was almost at her furthest remove from the fleet, that in the latter part of an afternoon watch she unexpectedly came in sight of a ship of the enemy. It proved to be a frigate. The latter perceiving through the glass that the weight of men and metal would be heavily against her, invoking her light heels crowded sail to get away. After a chase urged almost against hope and lasting until about the middle of the first dog watch, she signally succeeded in effecting her escape.

Not long after the pursuit had been given up, and ere the excitement incident thereto had altogether waned away, the master-at-arms ascending from his cavernous sphere made his appearance cap in hand by the mainmast respectfully waiting the notice of Captain Vere, then solitary walking the weather side of the quarter-deck, doubtless somewhat chafed at the failure of the pursuit. The spot where Claggart stood was the place allotted to men of lesser grades seeking some more particular interview either with the officer of the deck or the captain himself. But from the latter it was not often that a sailor or petty officer of those days would seek a hearing; only some exceptional cause would, according to established custom, have warranted that.

Presently, just as the commander absorbed in his reflections was on the point of turning aft in his promenade, he became sensible of Claggart's presence, and saw the doffed cap held in deferential expectancy. Here be it said that Captain Vere's personal knowledge of this petty officer had only begun at the time of the ship's last sailing from home. Claggart then for the first, in transfer from a ship detained for repairs, supplying on board the *Indomitable* the place of a previous master-at-arms disabled and ashore.

No sooner did the commander observe

who it was that now deferentially stood awaiting his notice, than a peculiar expression came over him. It was not unlike that which uncontrollably will flit across the countenance of one at unawares encountering a person who though known to him indeed has hardly been long enough known for thorough knowledge, but something in whose aspect nevertheless now for the first provokes a vaguely repellent distaste. But coming to a stand, and resuming much of his wonted official manner, save that a sort of impatience lurked in the intonation of the opening word, he said, "Well? what is it, Master-at-Arms?"

With the air of a subordinate grieved at the necessity of being a messenger of ill tidings, and while conscientiously determined to be frank, yet equally resolved upon shunning overstatement, Claggart, at this invitation or rather summons to disburthen, spoke up. What he said, conveyed in the language of no uneducated man, was to the effect following if not altogether in these words, namely, that during the chase and preparations for the possible encounter he had seen enough to convince him that at least one sailor aboard was a dangerous character in a ship mustering some who not only had taken a guilty part in the late serious troubles, but others also who, like the man in question, had entered His Majesty's service under another form than enlistment.

At this point Captain Vere with some impatience interrupted him: "Be direct, man; say impressed men."

Claggart made a gesture of subservience and proceeded.

Quite lately he (Claggart) had begun to suspect that on the gun decks some sort of movement prompted by the sailor in question was covertly going on, but he had not thought himself warranted in reporting the suspicion so long as it remained indistinct. But, from what he had that afternoon observed in the man referred to, the suspicion of something clandestine going on had advanced to a point less removed from certainty. He deeply felt, he added, the serious responsibility assumed in making a report involving such possible consequences to the individual mainly concerned, besides tending to augment those natural anxieties which every naval commander must feel in view of extraordinary outbreaks so recent as those which, he sorrowfully said it, it needed not to name.

Now at the first broaching of the matter Captain Vere, taken by surprise, could not wholly dissemble his disquietude. But as Claggart went on, the former's aspect changed into restiveness under something in the witness's manner in giving his testimony. However, he refrained from interrupting him. And Claggart, continuing, concluded with this:

"God forbid, your honor, that the *Indomitable's* should be the experience of the——"

"Never mind that!" here peremptorily broke in the superior, his face altering with anger, instinctively divining the ship that the other was about to name, one in which the Nore Mutiny had assumed a singularly tragical character that for a time jeopardized the life of its commander. Under the circumstances he was indignant at the purposed allusion. When the commissioned officers themselves were on all occasions very heedful how they referred to the recent events, for a petty officer unnecessarily to allude to them in the presence of his captain, this struck him as a most immodest presumption. Besides, to his quick sense of self-respect, it even looked under the circumstances something like an attempt to alarm him. Nor at first was he without some surprise that one who so far as he had hitherto come under his notice had shown considerable tact in his function should in this particular evince such lack of it.

But these thoughts and kindred dubious ones flitting across his mind were suddenly replaced by an intuitional surmise which though as yet obscure in form served practically to affect his reception of the ill tidings. Certain it is that, long versed in everything pertaining to the complicated gun-deck life, which like every other form of life has its secret mines and dubious side, the side popularly disclaimed, Captain Vere did not permit himself to be unduly disturbed by the general tenor of his subordinate's report. Furthermore, if in view of recent events prompt action should be taken at the first palpable sign of recurring insubordination, for all that, not judicious would it be, he thought, to keep the idea of lingering disaffection alive by undue forwardness in crediting an informer even if his own subordinate and charged among other things with police surveillance of the crew. This feeling would not perhaps have so prevailed with him were it not that upon a prior occasion the patriotic zeal officially evinced by Claggart had somewhat irritated him as appearing rather supersensible and strained. Furthermore, something even in the official's self-possessed and somewhat ostentatious manner in making his specifications strangely reminded him of a bandsman, a perjurious witness in a capital case before a court-martial ashore of which when a lieutenant he, Captain Vere, had been a member.

Now the peremptory check given to Claggart in the matter of the arrested allusion was quickly followed up by this: "You say that there is at least one dangerous man aboard. Name him."

"William Budd. A foretopman, your honor——"

"William Budd," repeated Captain Vere with unfeigned astonishment; "and mean you the man that Lieutenant Ratcliffe took from the merchantman not very long ago—the young fellow who seems to be so popular with the men—Billy, the Handsome Sailor, as they call him?"

"The same, your honor; but, for all his youth and good looks, a deep one. Not for nothing does he insinuate himself into the good will of his shipmates, since at the least all hands will at a pinch say a good word for him at all hazards. Did Lieutenant Ratcliffe happen to tell your honor of that adroit fling of Budd's, jumping up in the cutter's bow under the merchantman's stern when he was being taken off? It is even masked by that sort of good-humored air that at heart he resents his impressment. You have but noted his fair cheek. A man trap may be under his ruddy-tipped daisies."

Now the Handsome Sailor, as a signal figure among the crew, had naturally enough attracted the captain's attention from the first. Though in general not very demonstrative to his officers, he had congratulated Lieutenant Ratcliffe upon his good fortune in lighting on such a fine specimen of the *genus homo*, who in the nude might have posed for a statue of young Adam before the Fall. As to Billy's adieu to the ship *Rights-of-Man*, which the boarding lieutenant had indeed reported to him but in a deferential way more as a good story than aught else, Captain Vere, though mistakenly understanding it as a satiric sally, had but thought so much the better of the impressed man for it, as a military sailor, admiring the spirit that could take an arbitrary enlistment so merrily and sensibly. The foretopman's conduct, too, so far as it had fallen under the captain's notice, had confirmed the first happy augury, while the new recruit's qualities as a *sailorman* seemed to be such that he had thought of recommending him to the executive officer for promotion to a place that would more frequently bring him under his own observation, namely, the captaincy of the mizzentop, replacing there in the starboard watch a man not so young whom partly for that reason he deemed less fitted for the post. Be it parenthesized here that since the mizzentopmen, having not to handle such breadths of heavy canvas as the lower sails on the mainmast and foremast, a young man if of the right stuff not only seems best adapted to duty there, but in fact is generally selected for the captaincy of that top, and the company under him are light hands and often but striplings. In sum, Captain Vere had from the beginning deemed Billy Budd to be what in the naval parlance of the time was called a *"King's bargain,"* that is to say, for His Britannic Majesty's navy a capital investment at small outlay or none at all.

After a brief pause during which the reminiscences above mentioned passed vividly through his mind and he weighed the import of Claggart's last suggestion conveyed in the phrase "pitfall under the daisies," and the more he weighed it the less reliance he felt in the informer's good faith, suddenly he turned upon him and in a low voice: "Do you come to me, Master-at-Arms, with so foggy a tale? As to Budd, cite me an act or spoken word of his confirmatory of what you in general charge against him. Stay," drawing nearer to him, "heed what you speak. Just now, and in a case like this, there is a yardarm-end for the false witness."

"Ah, your honor!" sighed Claggart, mildly shaking his shapely head as in sad deprecation of such unmerited severity of tone. Then, bridling—erecting himself as in virtuous self-assertion, he circumstantially alleged certain words and acts, which collectively, if credited, led to presumptions mortally inculpating Budd. And for some of these averments, he added, substantiating proof was not far.

With gray eyes impatient and distrustful essaying to fathom to the bottom Claggart's calm violet ones, Captain Vere again heard him out, then for the moment stood ruminating. The mood he evinced, Claggart, himself for the time liberated from the other's scrutiny, steadily regarded with a look difficult to render—a look curious of the operation of his tactics, a look such as might have been that of the spokesman of the envious children of Jacob deceptively imposing upon the troubled patriarch the blood-dyed coat of young Joseph.

Though something exceptional in the moral quality of Captain Vere made him, in earnest encounter with a fellow man, a veritable touchstone of that man's essential nature, yet now as to Claggart and what was really going on in him his feeling partook less of intuitional conviction than of strong suspicion clogged by strange dubieties. The perplexity he evinced proceeded less from aught touching the man informed against —as Claggart doubtless opined—than from considerations how best to act in regard to the informer. At first indeed he was naturally for summoning that substantiation of his allegations which Claggart said was at hand. But such a proceeding would result in the matter at once getting abroad, which in the present stage of it, he thought, might undesirably affect the ship's company. If Claggart was a false witness—that closed the affair. And therefore before trying the accusation he would first practically test the accuser, and he thought this could be done in a quiet undemonstrative way.

The measure he determined upon involved a shifting of the scene, a transfer to a place less exposed to observation than the broad quarter-deck. For although the few gun-room officers there at the time had, in due observance of naval etiquette, withdrawn to leeward the moment Captain Vere had begun his promenade on the deck's weather side; and though during the colloquy with Claggart they of course ventured not to diminish the distance, and though throughout the interview Captain Vere's voice was far from high and Claggart's silvery and low, and the wind in the cordage and the wash of the sea helped the more to put them beyond earshot; nevertheless, the interview's continuance already had attracted observation from some topmen aloft and other sailors in the waist or further forward.

Having determined upon his measures, Captain Vere forthwith took action. Abruptly turning to Claggart he asked, "Master-at-Arms, is it now Budd's watch aloft?"

"No, your honor." Whereupon, "Mr. Wilkes!" summoning the nearest midshipman, "tell Albert to come to me." Albert was the captain's hammock-boy, a sort of sea-valet in whose discretion and fidelity his master had much confidence. The lad appeared. "You know Budd the foretopman?"

"I do, sir."

"Go find him. It is his watch off. Manage to tell him out of earshot that he is wanted aft. Contrive it that he speaks to nobody. Keep him in talk yourself. And not till you get well aft here, not till then let him know that the place where he is wanted is my cabin. You understand. Go.—Master-at-Arms, show yourself on the decks below, and when you think it time for Albert to be coming with his man, stand by quietly to follow the sailor in."

XX

Now when the foretopman found himself closeted there, as it were, in the cabin with the captain and Claggart, he was surprised enough. But it was a surprise unaccompanied by apprehension or distrust. To an immature nature essentially honest and humane, forewarning intimations of subtler danger from one's kind come tardily if at all. The only thing that took shape in the young sailor's mind was this: Yes, the captain, I have always thought, looks kindly upon me. Wonder if he's going to make me his coxswain. I should like that. And maybe now he is going to ask the master-at-arms about me.

"Shut the door there, sentry," said the commander; "stand without, and let nobody come in.—Now, Master-at-Arms, tell this man to his face what you told of him to me," and stood prepared to scrutinize the mutually confronting visages.

With the measured step and calm collected air of an asylum physician approaching in the public hall some patient beginning to show indications of a coming paroxysm, Claggart deliberately advanced within short range of Billy, and, mesmerically looking him in the eye, briefly recapitulated the accusation.

Not at first did Billy take it in. When he did, the rose-tan of his cheek looked struck as by white leprosy. He stood like one impaled and gagged. Meanwhile the accuser's eyes removing not as yet from the blue dilated ones, underwent a phenomenal change, their wonted rich violet color blurring into a muddy purple, those lights of human intelligence losing human expression, gelidly protruding like the alien eyes of certain uncatalogued creatures of the deep. The first mesmeric glance was one of serpent fascination; the last was as the hungry lurch of the torpedo-fish.

"Speak, man!" said Captain Vere to the transfixed one, struck by his aspect even more than by Claggart's. "Speak! defend yourself." Which appeal caused but a strange dumb gesturing and gurgling in Billy, amazement at such an accusation so suddenly sprung on inexperienced nonage; this, and, it may be, horror of the accuser, serving to bring out his lurking defect and in this instance for the time intensifying it into a convulsed tongue-tie; while the intent head and entire form straining forward in an agony of ineffectual eagerness to obey the injunction to speak and defend himself, gave an expression to the face like that of a condemned Vestal priestess in the moment of being buried alive, and in the first struggle against suffocation.

Though at the time Captain Vere was quite ignorant of Billy's liability to vocal impediment, he now immediately divined it, since vividly Billy's aspect recalled to him that of a bright young schoolmate of his whom he had once seen struck by much the same startling impotence in the act of eagerly rising in the class to be foremost in response to a testing question put to it by the master. Going close up to the young sailor, and laying a soothing hand on his shoulder, he said: "There is no hurry, my boy. Take your time, take your time." Contrary to the effect intended, these words so fatherly in tone doubtless touching Billy's heart to the quick, prompted yet more violent efforts at utterance—efforts soon ending for the time in confirming the paralysis, and bringing to his face an expression which was as a crucifixion to behold. The next instant, quick as the flame from a discharged cannon at night, his right arm shot out, and Claggart dropped to the deck. Whether intentionally or but owing to the young athlete's superior height, the blow had taken effect full upon the forehead, so shapely and intellectual-looking a feature in the master-at-arms, so that the body fell over lengthwise, like a heavy plank tilted from erectness. A gasp or two, and he lay motionless.

"Fated boy," breathed Captain Vere in tone so low as to be almost a whisper, "what have you done! But here, help me."

The twain raised the felled one from the loins up into a sitting position. The spare form flexibly acquiesced, but inertly. It was like handling a dead snake. They lowered it back. Regaining erectness Captain Vere with one hand covering his face stood to all appearance as impassive as the object at his feet. Was he absorbed in taking in all the bearings of the event and what was best, not only now at once to be done, but also in the sequel? Slowly he uncovered his face, and the effect was as if the moon emerging from eclipse should reappear with quite another aspect than that which had gone into hiding. The father in him, manifested toward Billy thus far in the scene, was replaced by the military disciplinarian. In his official tone he bade the foretopman retire to a stateroom aft (pointing it out) and there remain till thence summoned. This order Billy in silence mechanically obeyed. Then, going to the cabin door where it opened on the quarter-deck, Captain Vere said to the sentry without, "Tell somebody to send Albert here." When the lad appeared his master so contrived it that he should not catch sight of the prone one. "Albert," he said to him, "tell the surgeon I wish to see him. You need not come back till called." When the surgeon entered—a self-poised character of that grave sense and experience that hardly anything could take him aback—Captain Vere advanced to meet him, thus unconsciously intercepting his view of Claggart, and, interrupting the other's wonted ceremonious salutation, said, "Nay, tell me how it is with yonder man," directing his attention to the prostrate one.

The surgeon looked, and for all his self-command, somewhat started at the abrupt revelation. On Claggart's always pallid complexion, thick black blood was now oozing from nostril and ear. To the gazer's professional eye it was unmistakably no living man that he saw.

"Is it so then?" said Captain Vere, intently watching him. "I thought it. But verify it." Whereupon the customary tests confirmed the surgeon's first glance, who now, looking up in unfeigned concern, cast a look of intense inquisitiveness upon his superior. But Captain Vere, with one hand to his brow, was standing motionless. Suddenly, catching the surgeon's arm convulsively, he exclaimed, pointing down to the body—"It is the divine judgment on Ananias! Look!"

Disturbed by the excited manner he had never before observed in the *Indomitable*'s captain, and as yet wholly ignorant of the affair, the prudent surgeon nevertheless held his peace, only again looking an earnest interrogation as to what it was that had resulted in such a tragedy.

But Captain Vere was now again motionless, standing absorbed in thought. But again starting, he vehemently exclaimed—"Struck dead by an angel of God! Yet the angel must hang!"

At these passionate interjections, mere incoherences to the listener as yet unapprised of the antecedents, the surgeon was profoundly discomposed. But now, as recollecting himself, Captain Vere in less passionate tone briefly related the circumstances leading up to the event.

"But come, we must despatch," he added. "Help me to remove him (meaning the body) to yonder compartment," designating one opposite that where the foretopman remained immured. Anew disturbed by a request that, as implying a desire for secrecy, seemed unaccountably strange to him, there was nothing for the subordinate to do but comply.

"Go now," said Captain Vere with something of his wonted manner—"go now. I shall presently call a drumhead court. Tell the lieutenants what happened, and tell Mr. Mordant," meaning the captain of marines, "and charge them to keep the matter to themselves."

XXI

Full of disquietude and misgiving, the surgeon left the cabin. Was Captain Vere suddenly affected in his mind, or was it but a transient excitement, brought about by so strange and extraordinary a happening? As to the drumhead court, it struck the surgeon as impolitic, if nothing more. The thing to do, he thought, was to place Billy Budd in confinement and in a way dictated by usage, and postpone further action in so extraordinary a case to such time as they should rejoin the squadron, and then refer it to the admiral. He recalled the unwonted agitation of Captain Vere and his excited exclamations so at variance with his normal manner. Was he unhinged? But assuming that he is, it is not so susceptible of proof. What then can he do? No more trying situation is conceivable than that of an officer subordinate under a captain whom he suspects to be, not mad indeed, but yet not quite unaffected in his intellect. To argue his order to him would be insolence. To resist him would be mutiny.

In obedience to Captain Vere he communicated what had happened to the lieutenants and captain of marines, saying nothing as to the captain's state. They fully shared his own surprise and concern. Like him too they seemed to think that such a matter should be referred to the admiral.

XXII

Who in the rainbow can show the line where the violet tint ends and the orange tint begins? Distinctly we see the difference of the colors, but when exactly does the one first blendingly enter into the other? So with sanity and insanity. In pronounced cases, there is no question about them. But in some supposed cases, in various degrees supposedly less pronounced, to draw the exact line of demarcation few will undertake—though for a fee some professional experts will. There is nothing namable but that some men will undertake to do it for pay.

Whether Captain Vere, as the surgeon professionally and privately surmised, was really the sudden victim of any degree of aberration, one must determine for himself by such light as this narrative may afford.

That the unhappy event which has been narrated could not have happened at a worse juncture was but too true. For it was close on the heel of the suppressed insurrections, an aftertime very critical to naval authority, demanding from every English sea commander two qualities not readily interfusible —prudence and rigor. Moreover, there was something crucial in the case.

In the jugglery of circumstances preceding and attending the event on board the *Indomitable*, and in the light of that martial code whereby it was formally to be judged, innocence and guilt personified in Claggart and Budd in effect changed places. In a legal view the apparent victim of the tragedy was he who had sought to victimize a man blameless; and the indisputable deed of the latter, navally regarded, constituted the most heinous of military crimes. Yet more. The essential right and wrong involved in the matter, the clearer that might be, so much the worse for the responsibility of a loyal sea commander inasmuch as he was not authorized to determine the matter on that primitive basis.

Small wonder then that the *Indomitable*'s captain, though in general a man of rapid decision, felt that circumspectness not less than promptitude was necessary. Until he could decide upon his course, and in each detail, and not only so, but until the concluding measure was upon the point of being enacted, he deemed it advisable, in view of all the circumstances, to guard as much as possible against publicity. Here he may or may not have erred. Certain it is, however, that subsequently in the confidential talk of more than one or two gun rooms and cabins he was not a little criticized by some officers, a fact imputed by his friends and vehemently by his cousin Jack Denton to professional jealousy of "Starry Vere." Some imaginative ground for invidious comment there was. The maintenance of secrecy in the matter, the confining all knowledge of it for a time to the place where the homicide occurred, the quarter-deck cabin—in these particulars lurked some resemblance to the policy adopted in those tragedies of the palace which have occurred more than once in the capital founded by Peter the Barbarian.

The case indeed was such that fain would the *Indomitable*'s captain have deferred taking any action whatever respecting it further than to keep the foretopman a close prisoner till the ship rejoined the squadron and then submitting the matter to the judgment of his admiral.

But a true military officer is in one particular like a true monk. Not with more of self-abnegation will the latter keep his vows of monastic obedience than the former his vows of allegiance to martial duty.

Feeling that unless quick action was taken on it, the deed of the foretopman, so soon as it should be known on the gun decks, would tend to awaken any slumbering embers of the Nore among the crew, a sense of the urgency of the case overruled in Captain Vere every other consideration. But though a conscientious disciplinarian he was no lover of authority for mere authority's sake. Very far was he from embracing opportunities for monopolizing to himself the perils of moral responsibility, none at least that could properly be referred to an official superior or shared with him by his official equals or even subordinates. So thinking, he was glad it would not be at variance with usage to turn the matter over to a summary court of his own officers, reserving to himself as the one on whom the ultimate accountability would rest, the right of maintaining a supervision of it, or formally or informally interposing at need. Accordingly a drumhead court was summarily convened, he electing the individuals composing it, the first lieutenant, the captain of marines, and the sailing master.

In associating an officer of marines with the sea lieutenants in a case having to do with a sailor, the commander perhaps deviated from general custom. He was prompted thereto by the circumstance that he took that soldier to be a judicious person, thoughtful, and not altogether incapable of grappling with a difficult case unprecedented in his prior experience. Yet even as to him he was not without some latent misgiving, for withal he was an extremely good-natured man, an enjoyer of his dinner, a sound sleeper, and inclined to obesity. A man who though he would always maintain his manhood in battle might not prove altogether reliable in a moral dilemma involving aught of the tragic. As to the first lieutenant and the sailing master, Captain Vere could not but be aware that, though honest natures, of approved gallantry upon occasion, their intelligence was mostly confined to the matter of active seamanship and the fighting demands of their profession. The court was held in the same cabin where the unfortunate affair had taken place. This cabin, the commander's, embraced the entire area under the poop deck. Aft, and on either side, was a small stateroom, the one room temporarily a jail and the other a dead-house, and a yet smaller compartment leaving a space between, expanding forward into a goodly oblong of length coinciding with the ship's beam. A skylight of moderate dimension was overhead, and at each end of the oblong space were two sashed porthole windows easily convertible back into embrasures for short carronades.

All being quickly in readiness, Billy Budd was arraigned, Captain Vere necessarily appearing as the sole witness in the case, and as such temporarily sinking his rank, though singularly maintaining it in a matter apparently trivial, namely, that he testified from the ship's weather side, with that object having caused the court to sit on the lee side. Concisely he narrated all that had led up to the catastrophe, omitting nothing in Claggart's accusation and deposing as to the manner in which the prisoner had received it. At this testimony the three officers glanced with no little surprise at Billy Budd, the last man they would have suspected either of the mutinous design alleged by Claggart or the undeniable deed he himself had done.

The first lieutenant, taking judicial primacy and turning toward the prisoner, said, "Captain Vere has spoken. Is it or is it not as Captain Vere says?" In response came syllables not so much impeded in the utterance as might have been anticipated. They were these: "Captain Vere tells the truth. It is just as Captain Vere says, but it is not as the master-at-arms said. I have eaten the King's bread and I am true to the King."

"I believe you, my man," said the witness, his voice indicating a suppressed emotion not otherwise betrayed.

"God will bless you for that, Your Honor!" not without stammering said Billy, and all but broke down. But immediately was recalled to self-control by another question, to which with the same emotional difficulty of utterance he said, "No, there was no malice between us. I never bore malice against the master-at-arms. I am sorry that he is dead. I did not mean to kill him. Could I have used my tongue I would not have struck him. But he foully lied to my face and in presence of my captain, and I had to say something, and I could only say it with a blow, God help me!"

In the impulsive aboveboard manner of the frank one the court saw confirmed all that was implied in words that just previously had perplexed them, coming as they did from the testifier to the tragedy and promptly following Billy's impassioned disclaimer of mutinous intent—Captain Vere's words, "I believe you, my man."

Next it was asked of him whether he knew of or suspected aught savoring of incipient trouble (meaning mutiny, though the explicit term was avoided) going on in any section of the ship's company.

The reply lingered. This was naturally imputed by the court to the same vocal embarrassment which had retarded or obstructed previous answers. But in main it was otherwise here, the question immediately recalling to Billy's mind the interview with the after-guardsman in the forechains. But an innate repugnance to playing a part at all approaching that of an informer against one's own shipmates—the same erring sense of uninstructed honor which had stood in the way of his reporting the matter at the time though as a loyal man-of-war-man it was incumbent on him, and failure so to do if charged against him and proven, would have subjected him to the heaviest of penalties—this, with the blind feeling now his, that nothing really was being hatched, prevailed with him. When the answer came it was a negative.

"One question more," said the officer of marines, now first speaking and with a troubled earnestness. "You tell us that what the master-at-arms said against you was a lie. Now why should he have so lied, so maliciously lied, since you declare there was no malice between you?"

At that question unintentionally touching on a spiritual sphere wholly obscure to Billy's thoughts, he was nonplused, evincing a confusion indeed that some observers, such as can readily be imagined, would have construed into involuntary evidence of hidden guilt. Nevertheless he strove some way to answer, but all at once relinquished the vain endeavor, at the same time turning an appealing glance toward Captain Vere, as deeming him his best helper and friend. Captain Vere, who had been seated for a time, rose to his feet, addressing the interrogator. "The question you put to him comes naturally enough. But how can he rightly answer it? or anybody else? unless indeed it be he who lies within there," designating the compartment where lay the corpse. "But the prone one there will not rise to our summons. In effect, though, as it seems to me, the point you make is hardly material. Quite aside from any conceivable motive actuating the master-at-arms, and irrespective of the provocation to the blow, a martial court must needs in the present case confine its attention to the blow's consequence, which consequence justly is to be deemed not otherwise than as the striker's deed."

This utterance, the full significance of which it was not at all likely that Billy took in, nevertheless caused him to turn a wistful interrogative look toward the speaker, a look in its dumb expressiveness not unlike that which a dog of generous breed might turn upon his master, seeking in his face some elucidation of a previous gesture ambiguous to the canine intelligence. Nor was the same utterance without marked effect upon the three officers, more especially the soldier. Couched in it seemed to them a meaning unanticipated, involving a prejudgment on the speaker's part. It served to augment a mental disturbance previously evident enough.

The soldier once more spoke, in a tone of suggestive dubiety addressing at once his associates and Captain Vere: "Nobody is present—none of the ship's company, I mean —who might shed lateral light, if any is to be had, upon what remains mysterious in this matter."

"That is thoughtfully put," said Captain Vere; "I see your drift. Aye, there is a mystery; but, to use a Scriptural phrase, it is 'a mystery of iniquity,' a matter for psychologic theologians to discuss. But what has a military court to do with it? Not to add that for us any possible investigation of it is cut off by the lasting tongue-tie of— him—in yonder," again designating the mortuary stateroom. "The prisoner's deed—with that alone we have to do."

To this, and particularly the closing reiteration, the marine soldier, knowing not how aptly to reply, sadly abstained from saying aught. The first lieutenant, who at the outset had not unnaturally assumed primacy in the court, now overrulingly instructed by a glance from Captain Vere, a glance more effective than words, resumed that primacy. Turning to the prisoner, "Budd," he said, and scarce in equable tones, "Budd, if you have aught further to say for yourself, say it now."

Upon this the young sailor turned another quick glance toward Captain Vere; then, as taking a hint from that aspect, a hint confirming his own instinct that silence was now best, replied to the lieutenant "I have said all, sir."

The marine—the same who had been the sentinel without the cabin door at the time that the foretopman, followed by the master-at-arms, entered it—he, standing by the sailor throughout these judicial proceedings, was now directed to take him back to the after compartment originally assigned to the prisoner and his custodian. As the twain disappeared from view, the three officers, as partially liberated from some inward constraint associated with Billy's mere presence, simultaneously stirred in their seats. They exchanged looks of troubled indecision, yet feeling that decide they must and without long delay. As for Captain Vere, he for the time stood unconsciously with his back toward them, apparently in one of his absent fits, gazing out from a sashed porthole to windward upon the monotonous blank of the twilight sea. But the court's silence continuing, broken only at moments by brief consultations in low earnest tones, this seemed to arm him and energize him. Turning, he to-and-fro paced the cabin athwart, in the returning ascent to windward climbing the slant deck in the ship's lee roll, without knowing it symbolizing thus in his action a mind resolute to surmount difficulties even if against primitive instincts strong as the wind and the sea. Presently he came to a stand before the three. After scanning their faces he stood less as mustering his thoughts for expression than as one only deliberating how best to put them to well-meaning men not intellectually mature, men with whom it was necessary to demonstrate certain principles that were axioms to himself. Similar impatience as to talking is perhaps one reason that deters some minds from addressing any popular assemblies.

When speak he did, something both in the substance of what he said and his manner of saying it, showed the influence of unshared studies modifying and tempering the practical training of an active career. This, along with his phraseology now and then, was suggestive of the grounds whereon rested that imputation of a certain pedantry socially alleged against him by certain naval men of wholly practical cast, captains who nevertheless would frankly concede that His Majesty's navy mustered no more efficient officer of their grade than "Starry Vere."

What he said was to this effect: "Hitherto I have been but the witness, little more; and I should hardly think now to take another tone, that of your coadjutor, for the time, did I not perceive in you—at the crisis too—a troubled hesitancy, proceeding, I doubt not, from the clash of military duty with moral scruple—scruple vitalized by compassion. For the compassion, how can I otherwise than share it? But, mindful of paramount obligations, I strive against scruples that may tend to enervate decision. Not, gentlemen, that I hide from myself that the case is an exceptional one. Speculatively regarded, it well might be referred to a jury of casuists. But for us here acting not as casuists or moralists, it is a case practical, and under martial law practically to be dealt with.

"But your scruples: do they move as in a dusk? Challenge them. Make them advance and declare themselves. Come now: do they import something like this: If, mindless of palliating circumstances, we are bound to regard the death of the master-at-arms as the prisoner's deed, then does that deed constitute a capital crime whereof the penalty is a mortal one? But in natural justice is nothing but the prisoner's overt act to be considered? How can we adjudge to summary and shameful death a fellow creature innocent before God, and whom we feel to be so?—Does that state it aright? You sign sad assent. Well, I too feel that, the full force of that. It is Nature. But do these buttons that we wear attest that our allegiance is to Nature? No, to the King. Though the ocean, which is inviolate Nature primeval, though this be the element where we move and have our being as sailors, yet as the King's officers lies our duty in a sphere correspondingly natural? So little is that true that, in receiving our commissions, we in the most important regards ceased to be natural free agents. When war is declared are we, the commissioned fighters, previously consulted? We fight at command. If our judgments approve the war, that is but coincidence. So in other particulars. So now. For suppose condemnation to follow these present proceedings. Would it be so much we ourselves that would condemn as it would be martial law operating through us? For that law and the rigor of it, we are not responsible. Our vowed responsibility is in this: That however pitilessly that law may operate, we nevertheless adhere to it and administer it.

"But the exceptional in the matter moves the hearts within you. Even so too is mine moved. But let not warm hearts betray heads that should be cool. Ashore in a criminal case will an upright judge allow himself off the bench to be waylaid by some tender kinswoman of the accused seeking to touch him with her tearful plea? Well the heart here denotes the feminine in man, is as that piteous woman and, hard though it be, she must here be ruled out."

He paused, earnestly studying them for a moment, then resumed.

"But something in your aspect seems to urge that it is not solely the heart that moves in you, but also the conscience, the private conscience. But tell me whether or not, occupying the position we do, private conscience should not yield to that imperial one formulated in the code under which alone we officially proceed?"

Here the three men moved in their seats, less convinced than agitated by the course of an argument troubling but the more the spontaneous conflict within.

Perceiving which, the speaker paused for a moment, then, abruptly changing his tone, went on.

"To steady us a bit, let us recur to the facts.—In wartime at sea a man-of-war's-man strikes his superior in grade, and the blow kills. Apart from its effect, the blow itself is, according to the Articles of War, a capital crime. Furthermore——"

"Aye, sir," emotionally broke in the officer of marines, "in one sense it was. But surely Budd purposed neither mutiny nor homicide."

"Surely not, my good man. And before a court less arbitrary and more merciful than a martial one that plea would largely extenuate. At the Last Assizes it shall acquit. But how here? We proceed under the law of the Mutiny Act. In feature no child can resemble his father more than that Act resembles in spirit the thing from which it derives—War. In His Majesty's service—in this ship indeed—there are Englishmen forced to fight for the King against their will. Against their conscience, for aught we know. Though as their fellow creatures some of us may appreciate their position, yet as navy officers, what reck we of it? Still less recks the enemy. Our impressed men he would fain cut down in the same swath with our volunteers. As regards the enemy's naval conscripts, some of whom may even share our own abhorrence of the regicidal French Directory, it is the same on our side. War looks but to the frontage, the appearance. And the Mutiny Act, War's child, takes after the father. Budd's intent or nonintent is nothing to the purpose.

"But while, put to it by those anxieties in you which I cannot but respect, I only repeat myself—while thus strangely we prolong proceedings that should be summary—the enemy may be sighted and an engagement result. We must do; and one of two things must we do—condemn or let go."

"Can we not convict and yet mitigate the penalty?" asked the junior lieutenant here speaking, and falteringly, for the first.

"Lieutenant, were that clearly lawful for us under the circumstances, consider the consequences of such clemency. The people" (meaning the ship's company) "have native sense; most of them are familiar with our naval usage and tradition, and how would they take it? Even could you explain to them—which our official position forbids —they, long molded by arbitrary discipline, have not that kind of intelligent responsiveness that might qualify them to comprehend and discriminate. No, to the people the foretopman's deed, however it be worded in the announcement, will be plain homicide committed in a flagrant act of mutiny. What penalty for that should follow, they know. But it does not follow. Why? they will ruminate. You know what sailors are. Will they not revert to the recent outbreak at the Nore? Aye. They know the well-founded alarm—the panic it struck throughout England. Your clement sentence they would account pusillanimous. They would think that we flinch, that we are afraid of them—afraid of practicing a lawful rigor singularly demanded at this juncture lest it should provoke new troubles. What shame to us such a conjecture on their part, and how deadly to discipline. You see then, whither, prompted by duty and the law, I steadfastly drive. But I beseech you, my friends, do not take me amiss. I feel as you do for this unfortunate boy. But did he know our hearts, I take him to be of that generous nature that he would feel even for us on whom in this military necessity so heavy a compulsion is laid."

With that, crossing the deck he resumed his place by the sashed porthole, tacitly leaving the three to come to a decision. On the cabin's opposite side the troubled court sat silent. Loyal lieges, plain and practical, though at bottom they dissented from some points Captain Vere had put to them, they were without the faculty, hardly had the inclination, to gainsay one whom they felt to be an earnest man, one, too, not less their superior in mind than in naval rank. But it is not improbable that even such of his words as were not without influence over them, less came home to them than his closing appeal to their instinct as sea officers in the forethought he threw out as to the practical consequences to discipline, considering the unconfirmed tone of the fleet at the time, should a man-of-war's-man's violent killing at sea of a superior in grade be allowed to pass for aught else than a capital crime demanding prompt infliction of the penalty.

Not unlikely they were brought to something more or less akin to that harassed frame of mind which in the year 1842 actuated the commander of the U.S. brig-of-war *Somers* to resolve, under the so-called Articles of War, Articles modeled upon the English Mutiny Act, to resolve upon the execution at sea of a midshipman and two petty officers as mutineers designing the seizure of the brig. Which resolution was carried out though in a time of peace and within not many days sail of home—an act vindicated by a naval court of inquiry subsequently convened ashore. History, and here cited without comment. True, the circumstances on board the *Somers* were different from those on board the *Indomitable*. But the urgency felt, well-warranted or otherwise, was much the same.

Says a writer whom few know, "Forty years after a battle it is easy for a noncombatant to reason about how it ought to have been fought. It is another thing personally and under fire to direct the fighting while involved in the obscuring smoke of it. Much so with respect to other emergencies involving considerations both practical and moral, and when it is imperative promptly to act. The greater the fog the more it imperils the steamer, and speed is put on though at the hazard of running somebody down. Little ween the snug card-players in the cabin of the responsibilities of the sleepless man on the bridge."

In brief, Billy Budd was formally convicted and sentenced to be hung at the yardarm in the early morning watch, it being now night. Otherwise, as is customary in such cases, the sentence would forthwith have been carried out. In wartime, on the field or in the fleet, a mortal punishment decreed by a drumhead court—on the field sometimes decreed by but a nod from the general—follows without delay on the heel of conviction, without appeal.

XXIII

It was Captain Vere himself who of his own motion communicated the findings of the court to the prisoner, for that purpose going to the compartment where he was in custody and bidding the marine there to withdraw for the time.

Beyond the communication of the sentence, what took place at this interview was never known. But in view of the character of the twain briefly closeted in that stateroom, each radically sharing in the rarer qualities of our nature—so rare indeed as to be all but incredible to average minds however much cultivated—some conjectures may be ventured.

It would have been in consonance with the spirit of Captain Vere should he on this occasion have concealed nothing from the condemned one—should he indeed have frankly disclosed to him the part he himself had played in bringing about the decision, at the same time revealing his actuating motives. On Billy's side it is not improbable that such a confession would have been received in much the same spirit that prompted it. Not without a sort of joy indeed he might have appreciated the brave opinion of him implied in his captain making such a confidant of him. Nor as to the sentence itself could he have been insensible that it was imparted to him as to one not afraid to die. Even more may have been. Captain Vere in the end may have developed the passion sometimes latent under an exterior stoical or indifferent. He was old enough to have been Billy's father. The austere devotee of military duty letting himself melt back into what remains primeval in our formalized humanity may in the end have caught Billy to his heart even as Abraham may have caught young Isaac on the brink of resolutely offering him up in obedience to the exacting behest. But there is no telling the sacrament, seldom if in any case revealed to the gadding world, wherever under circumstances at all akin to those here attempted to be set forth two of great Nature's nobler order embrace. There is privacy at the time, inviolable to the survivor, and holy oblivion, the sequel to each diviner magnanimity, providentially covers all at last.

The first to encounter Captain Vere in act of leaving the compartment was the senior lieutenant. The face he beheld, for the moment one expressive of the agony of the strong, was to that officer, though a man of fifty, a startling revelation. That the condemned one suffered less than he who mainly had effected the condemnation was apparently indicated by the former's exclamation in the scene soon perforce to be touched upon.

XXIV

Of a series of incidents within a brief term rapidly following each other, the adequate narration may take up a term less brief, especially if explanation or comment here and there seem requisite to the better understanding of such incidents. Between the entrance into the cabin of him who never left it alive, and his who when he did leave it left it as one condemned to die, between this and the closeted interview just given, less than an hour and a half had elapsed. It was an interval long enough, however, to awaken speculations among no few of the ship's company as to what it was that could be detaining in the cabin the master-at-arms and the sailor; for a rumor that both of them had been seen to enter it and neither of them had been seen to emerge, this rumor had got abroad upon the gun decks and in the tops; the people of a great warship being in one respect like villagers taking microscopic note of every outward movement or nonmovement going on. When, therefore, in weather not at all tempestuous all hands were called in the second dog watch, a summons under such circumstances not usual in those hours, the crew were not wholly unprepared for some announcement extraordinary, one having connection too with the continued absence of the two men from their wonted haunts.

There was a moderate sea at the time, and the moon newly risen and near to being at its full, silvered the white spar-deck wherever not blotted by the clear-cut shadows horizontally thrown of fixtures and moving men. On either side the quarter-deck the marine guard under arms was drawn up; and Captain Vere, standing in his place surrounded by all the wardroom officers, addressed his men. In so doing his manner showed neither more nor less than that property pertaining to his supreme position aboard his own ship. In clear terms and concise he told them what had taken place in the cabin: that the master-at-arms was dead; that he who had killed him had been already tried by a summary court and condemned to death; and that the execution would take place in the early morning watch. The word *mutiny* was not named in what he said. He refrained too from making the occasion an opportunity for any preachment as to the maintenance of discipline, thinking perhaps that under existing circumstances in the navy the consequence of violating discipline should be made to speak for itself.

Their captain's announcement was listened to by the throng of standing sailors in a dumbness like that of a seated congregation of believers in hell listening to the clergyman's announcement of his Calvinistic text.

At the close, however, a confused murmur went up. It began to wax. All but instantly, then, at a sign, it was pierced and suppressed by shrill whistles of the boatswain and his mates piping down one watch.

To be prepared for burial Claggart's body was delivered to certain petty officers of his mess. And here, not to clog the sequel with lateral matters, it may be added that, at a suitable hour, the master-at-arms was committed to the sea with every funeral honor properly belonging to his naval grade.

In this proceeding, as in every public one growing out of the tragedy, strict adherence to usage was observed. Nor in any point could it have been at all deviated from, either with respect to Claggart or Billy Budd, without begetting undesirable speculations in the ship's company, sailors, and more particularly men-of-war's men, being of all men the greatest sticklers for usage.

For similar cause, all communication between Captain Vere and the condemned one ended with the closeted interview already given, the latter being now surrendered to the ordinary routine preliminary to the end. This transfer under guard from the captain's quarters was effected without unusual precautions—at least no visible ones.

If possible not to let the men so much as surmise that their officers anticipate aught amiss from them is the tacit rule in a military ship. And the more that some sort of trouble should really be apprehended, the more do the officers keep that apprehension to themselves, though not the less unostentatious vigilance may be augmented.

In the present instance the sentry placed over the prisoner had strict orders to let no one have communication with him but the chaplain. And certain unobtrusive measures were taken absolutely to insure this point.

XXV

In a seventy-four of the old order the deck known as the upper gun deck was the one covered over by the spar-deck, which last, though not without its armament, was for the most part exposed to the weather. In general it was at all hours free from hammocks; those of the crew swinging on the lower gun deck and berth deck, the latter being not only a dormitory but also the place for the stowing of the sailor's bags, and on both sides lined with the large chests or movable pantries of the many messes of the men.

On the starboard side of the *Indomitable*'s upper gun deck, behold Billy Budd under sentry lying prone in irons in one of the bays formed by the regular spacing of the guns comprising the batteries on either side. All these pieces were of the heavier caliber of that period. Mounted on lumbering wooden carriages, they were hampered with cumbersome harness of breeching and strong side tackles for running them out. Guns and carriages, together with the long rammers and shorter lintstocks lodged in loops overhead—all these, as customary, were painted black; and the heavy hempen breechings, tarred to the same tint, wore the like livery of the undertakers. In contrast with the funereal tone of these surroundings the prone sailor's exterior apparel, white jumper and white duck trousers, each more or less soiled, dimly glimmered in the obscure light of the bay like a patch of discolored snow in early April lingering at some upland cave's black mouth. In effect he is already in his shroud or the garments that shall serve him in lieu of one. Over him but scarce illuminating him, two battle lanterns swing from two massive beams of the deck above. Fed with the oil supplied by the war contractors (whose gains, honest or otherwise, are in every land an anticipated portion of the harvest of death) with flickering splashes of dirty yellow light, they pollute the pale moonshine, all but ineffectually struggling in obstructed flecks through the open ports from which the tompioned cannon protrude. Other lanterns at intervals serve but to bring out somewhat the obscurer bays, which, like small confessionals or side-chapels in a cathedral, branch from the long dim-vistaed broad aisle between the two batteries of that covered tier.

Such was the deck where now lay the Handsome Sailor. Through the rose-tan of his complexion no pallor could have shown. It would have taken days of sequestration from the winds and the sun to have brought about the effacement of that. But the skeleton in the cheekbone at the point of its angle was just beginning delicately to be defined under the warm-tinted skin. In fervid hearts self-contained some brief experiences devour our human tissue as secret fire in a ship's hold consumes cotton in the bale.

But now lying between the two guns, as nipped in the vice of fate, Billy's agony, mainly proceeding from a generous young heart's virgin experience of the diabolical incarnate and effective in some men—the tension of that agony was over now. It survived not the something healing in the closeted interview with Captain Vere. Without movement, he lay as in a trance. That adolescent expression previously noted as his, taking on something akin to the look of a slumbering child in the cradle when the warm hearth-glow of the still chamber at night plays on the dimples that at whiles mysteriously form in the cheek, silently coming and going there. For now and then in the gyved one's trance a serene happy light born of some wandering reminiscence or dream would diffuse itself over his face, and then wane away only anew to return.

The Chaplain coming to see him and finding him thus, and perceiving no sign that he was conscious of his presence, attentively regarded him for a space, then, slipping aside, withdrew for the time, peradventure feeling that even he, the minister of Christ, though receiving his stipend from Mars had no consolation to proffer which could result in a peace transcending that which he beheld. But in the small hours he came again. And the prisoner now awake to his surroundings noticed his approach and civilly, all but cheerfully, welcomed him. But it was to little purpose that in the interview following the good man sought to bring Billy Budd to some godly understanding that he must die, and at dawn. True, Billy himself freely referred to his death as a thing close at hand; but it was something in the way that children will refer to death in general, who yet among their other sports will play a funeral with hearse and mourners.

Not that like children Billy was incapable of conceiving what death really is. No; but he was wholly without irrational fear of it, a fear more prevalent in highly civilized communities than those so-called barbarous ones which in all respects stand nearer to unadulterate Nature. And, as elsewhere said, a barbarian Billy radically was; as much so, for all the costume, as his countrymen the British captives, living trophies, made to march in the Roman triumph of Germanicus. Quite as much so as those later barbarians, young men probably, and picked specimens among the earlier British converts to Christianity, at least nominally such and taken to Rome (as today converts from lesser isles of the sea may be taken to London) of whom the pope of that time, admiring the strangeness of their personal beauty so unlike the Italian stamp, their clear ruddy complexion and curled flaxen locks, exclaimed, "Angles" (meaning *English*, the modern derivative) "Angles do you call them? And is it because they look so like angels?" Had it been later in time one would think that the Pope had in mind Fra Angelico's seraphs, some of whom, plucking apples in gardens of the Hesperides, have the faint rose-bud complexion of the more beautiful English girls.

If in vain the good chaplain sought to impress the young barbarian with ideas of death akin to those conveyed in the skull, dial, and crossbones on old tombstones, equally futile to all appearance were his efforts to bring home to him the thought of salvation and a Saviour. Billy listened, but less out of awe or reverence perhaps than from a certain natural politeness, doubtless at bottom regarding all that in much the same way that most mariners of his class take any discourse abstract or out of the common tone of the workaday world. And this sailor-way of taking clerical discourse is not wholly unlike the way in which the pioneer of Christianity, full of transcendent miracles, was received long ago on tropic isles by any superior *savage* so called—a Tahitian, say, of Captain Cook's time or shortly after that time. Out of natural courtesy he received, but did not appropriate. It was like a gift placed in the palm of an outreached hand upon which the fingers do not close.

But the *Indomitable*'s chaplain was a discreet man, possessing the good sense of a good heart. So he insisted not in his vocation here. At the instance of Captain Vere, a lieutenant had apprised him of pretty much everything as to Billy; and since he felt that innocence was even a better thing than religion wherewith to go to Judgment, he reluctantly withdrew, but in his emotion not without first performing an act strange enough in an Englishman, and under the circumstances yet more so in any regular priest. Stooping over, he kissed on the fair cheek his fellow man, a felon in martial law, one, who, though on the confines of death, he felt he could never convert to a dogma; nor for all that did he fear for his future.

Marvel not that having been made acquainted with the young sailor's essential innocence (an irruption of heretic thought hard to suppress) the worthy man lifted not a finger to avert the doom of such a martyr to martial discipline. So to do would not only have been as idle as invoking the desert, but would also have been an audacious transgression of the bounds of his function, one as exactly prescribed to him by military law as that of the boatswain or any other naval officer. Bluntly put, a chaplain is the minister of the Prince of Peace serving in the host of the God of War—Mars. As such, he is as incongruous as that musket of Blücher, etc., at Christmas. Why then is he there? Because he indirectly subserves the purpose attested by the cannon; because too he lends the sanction of the religion of the meek to that which practically is the abrogation of everything but brute Force.

XXVI

The night so luminous on the spar-deck but otherwise on the cavernous ones below, levels so like the tiered galleries in a coal mine—the luminous night passed away. But, like the prophet in the chariot disappearing in heaven and dropping his mantle to Elisha, the withdrawing night transferred its pale robe to the breaking day. A meek shy light appeared in the East, where stretched a diaphanous fleece of white furrowed vapor. That light slowly waxed. Suddenly *eight bells* was struck aft, responded to by one louder metallic stroke from forward. It was four o'clock in the morning. Instantly the silver whistles were heard summoning all hands to witness punishment. Up through the great hatchways rimmed with racks of heavy shot, the watch below came pouring, overspreading with the watch already on deck the space between the mainmast and foremast, including that occupied by the capacious launch and the black booms tiered on either side of it, boat and booms making a summit of observation for the powder-boys and younger tars. A different group comprising one watch of topmen leaned over the rail of that sea-balcony, no small one in a seventy-four, looking down on the crowd below. Man or boy none spake but in whisper, and few spake at all. Captain Vere—as before, the central figure among the assembled commissioned officers—stood nigh the break of the poop deck facing forward. Just below him on the quarter-deck the marines in full equipment were drawn up much as at the scene of the promulgated sentence.

At sea in the old time, the execution by halter of a military sailor was generally from the foreyard. In the present instance, for special reasons the mainyard was assigned. Under an arm of that lee yard the prisoner was presently brought up, the chaplain attending him. It was noted at the time, and remarked upon afterwards, that in this final scene the good man evinced little or nothing of the perfunctory. Brief speech indeed he had with the condemned one, but the genuine Gospel was less on his tongue than in his aspect and manner toward him. The final preparations personal to the latter being speedily brought to an end by two boatswain's mates, the consummation impended. Billy stood facing aft. At the penultimate moment, his words, his only ones, words wholly unobstructed in the utterance, were these—"God bless Captain Vere!" Syllables so unanticipated coming from one with the ignominious hemp about his neck —a conventional felon's benediction directed aft toward the quarters of honor; syllables, too, delivered in the clear melody of a singing bird on the point of launching from the twig, had a phenomenal effect, not unenhanced by the rare personal beauty of the young sailor spiritualized now through late experiences so poignantly profound.

Without volition as it were, as if indeed the ship's populace were but the vehicles of some vocal current electric, with one voice from alow and aloft came a resonant sympathetic echo—"God bless Captain Vere!" And yet at that instant Billy alone must have been in their hearts, even as he was in their eyes.

At the pronounced words and the spontaneous echo that voluminously rebounded them, Captain Vere, either through stoic self-control or a sort of momentary paralysis induced by emotional shock, stood erectly rigid as a musket in the ship-armorer's rack.

The hull deliberately recovering from the periodic roll to leeward was just regaining an even keel, when the last signal, a preconcerted dumb one, was given. At the same moment it chanced that the vapory fleece hanging low in the East was shot through with a soft glory as of the fleece of the Lamb of God seen in mystical vision, and simultaneously therewith, watched by the wedged mass of upturned faces, Billy ascended, and, ascending, took the full rose of the dawn.

In the pinioned figure arrived at the yard-end, to the wonder of all no motion was apparent, none save that created by the ship's motion, in moderate weather so majestic in a great ship ponderously cannoned.

XXVII

A digression

When, some days afterward, in reference to the singularity just mentioned, the purser, a rather ruddy rotund person more accurate as an accountant than profound as a philosopher, said at mess to the surgeon, "What testimony to the force lodged in will power," the latter—saturnine, spare and tall, one in whom a discreet causticity went along with a manner less genial than polite, replied, "Your pardon, Mr. Purser. In a hanging scientifically conducted—and under special orders I myself directed how Budd's was to be effected—any movement following the completed suspension and originating in the body suspended, such movement indicates mechanical spasm in the muscular system. Hence the absence of that is no more attributable to will power as you call it than to horsepower—begging your pardon."

"But this muscular spasm you speak of, is not that in a degree more or less invariable in these cases?"

"Assuredly so, Mr. Purser."

"How then, my good sir, do you account for its absence in this instance?"

"Mr. Purser, it is clear that your sense of the singularity in this matter equals not mine. You account for it by what you call will power, a term not yet included in the lexicon of science. For me, I do not, with my present knowledge, pretend to account for it at all. Even should we assume the hypothesis that at the first touch of the halyards the action of Budd's heart, intensified by extraordinary emotion at its climax, abruptly stopped—much like a watch when in carelessly winding it up you strain at the finish, thus snapping the chain—even under that hypothesis how account for the phenomenon that followed?"

"You admit, then, that the absence of spasmodic movement was phenomenal."

"It was phenomenal, Mr. Purser, in the sense that it was an appearance the cause of which is not immediately to be assigned."

"But tell me, my dear sir," pertinaciously continued the other, "was the man's death effected by the halter, or was it a species of euthanasia?"

" 'Euthanasia,' Mr. Purser, is something like your 'will power': I doubt its authenticity as a scientific term—begging your pardon again. It is at once imaginative and metaphysical,—in short, Greek. But," abruptly changing his tone, "there is a case in the sick bay that I do not care to leave to my assistants. Beg your pardon, but excuse me." And rising from the mess he formally withdrew.

XXVIII

The silence at the moment of execution and for a moment or two continuing thereafter, a silence but emphasized by the regular wash of the sea against the hull or the flutter of a sail caused by the helmsman's eyes being tempted astray, this emphasized silence was gradually disturbed by a sound not easily to be verbally rendered. Whoever has heard the freshet-wave of a torrent suddenly swelled by pouring showers in tropical mountains, showers not shared by the plain; whoever has heard the first muffled murmur of its sloping advance through precipitous woods, may form some conception of the sound now heard. The seeming remoteness of its source was because of its murmurous indistinctness since it came from close-by, even from the men massed on the ship's open deck. Being inarticulate, it was dubious in significance further than it seemed to indicate some capricious revulsion of thought or feeling such as mobs ashore are liable to, in the present instance possibly implying a sullen revocation on the men's part of their involuntary echoing of Billy's benediction. But ere the murmur had time to wax into clamor it was met by a strategic command, the more telling that it came with abrupt unexpectedness.

"Pipe down the starboard watch, Boatswain, and see that they go."

Shrill as the shriek of the sea hawk the whistles of the boatswain and his mates pierced that ominous low sound, dissipating it; and yielding to the mechanism of discipline the throng was thinned by one half. For the remainder, most of them were set to temporary employments connected with trimming the yards and so forth, business readily to be got up to serve occasion by any officer-of-the-deck.

Now each proceeding that follows a mortal sentence pronounced at sea by a drumhead court is characterized by promptitude not perceptibly merging into hurry, though bordering that. The hammock, the one which had been Billy's bed when alive, having already been ballasted with shot and otherwise prepared to serve for his canvas coffin, the last offices of the sea-undertakers, the sailmaker's mates, were now speedily completed. When everything was in readiness a second call for all hands, made necessary by the strategic movement before mentioned, was sounded, and now to witness burial.

The details of this closing formality it needs not to give. But when the tilted plank let slide its freight into the sea, a second strange human murmur was heard, blended now with another inarticulate sound proceeding from certain larger seafowl, whose attention having been attracted by the peculiar commotion in the water resulting from the heavy sloped dive of the shotted hammock into the sea, flew screaming to the spot. So near the hull did they come that the stridor or bony creak of their gaunt double-jointed pinions was audible. As the ship under light airs passed on, leaving the burial spot astern, they still kept circling it low down with the moving shadow of their outstretched wings and the croaked requiem of their cries.

Upon sailors as superstitious as those of the age preceding ours, men-of-war's men, too, who had just beheld the prodigy of repose in the form suspended in air and now foundering in the deeps; to such mariners the action of the seafowl, though dictated by mere animal greed for prey, was big with no prosaic significance. An uncertain movement began among them, in which some encroachment was made. It was tolerated but for a moment. For suddenly the drum beat to quarters, which familiar sound, happening at least twice every day, had upon the present occasion a signal peremptoriness in it. True martial discipline long continued superinduces in average man a sort of impulse of docility whose operation at the official sound of command much resembles in its promptitude the effect of an instinct.

The drumbeat dissolved the multitude, distributing most of them along the batteries of the two covered gun decks. There, as wont, the guns' crews stood by their respective cannon erect and silent. In due course the first officer, sword under arm and standing in his place on the quarter-deck, formally received the successive reports of the sworded lieutenants commanding the sections of batteries below, the last of which reports being made, the summed report he delivered with the customary salute to the commander. All this occupied time, which in the present case was the object of beating to quarters at an hour prior to the customary one. That such variance from usage was authorized by an officer like Captain Vere, a martinet as some deemed him, was evidence of the necessity for unusual action implied in what he deemed to be temporarily the mood of his men. "With mankind," he would say, "forms, measured forms, are everything; and that is the import couched in the story of Orpheus with his lyre spellbinding the wild denizens of the wood." And this he once applied to the disruption of forms going on across the Channel and the consequences thereof.

At this unwonted muster at quarters, all proceeded as at the regular hour. The band on the quarter-deck played a sacred air, after which the chaplain went through the customary morning service. That done, the drum beat the retreat, and, toned by music and religious rites subserving the discipline and purpose of war, the men in their wonted orderly manner dispersed to the places allotted them when not at the guns.

And now it was full day. The fleece of low-hanging vapor had vanished, licked up by the sun that late had so glorified it. And the circumambient air in the clearness of its serenity was like smooth white marble in the polished block not yet removed from the marble dealer's yard.

XXIX

The symmetry of form attainable in pure fiction cannot so readily be achieved in a narration essentially having less to do with fable than with fact. Truth uncompromisingly told will always have its ragged edges; hence the conclusion of such a narration is apt to be less finished than an architectural finial.

How it fared with the Handsome Sailor during the year of the Great Mutiny has been faithfully given. But though properly the story ends with his life, something in way of sequel will not be amiss. Three brief chapters will suffice.

In the general rechristening under the Directory of the craft originally forming the navy of the French monarchy, the *St. Louis* line-of-battle ship was named the *Athéiste*. Such a name, like some other substituted ones in the Revolutionary fleet, while proclaiming the infidel audacity of the ruling power was yet, though not so intended to be, the aptest name, if one consider it, ever given to a war-ship, far more so indeed than the *Devastation*, the *Erebus* (the *Hell*) and similar names bestowed upon fighting ships.

On the return passage to the English fleet from the detached cruise during which occurred the events already recorded, the *Indomitable* fell in with the *Athéiste*. An engagement ensued, during which Captain Vere, in the act of putting his ship alongside the enemy with a view of throwing his boarders across her bulwarks, was hit by a musket ball from a porthole of the enemy's main cabin. More than disabled, he dropped to the deck and was carried below to the same cockpit where some of his men already lay. The senior lieutenant took command. Under him the enemy was finally captured and though much crippled was by rare good fortune successfully taken into Gibraltar, an English port not very distant from the scene of the fight. There Captain Vere with the rest of the wounded was put ashore. He lingered for some days, but the end came. Unhappily he was cut off too early for the Nile and Trafalgar. The spirit that spite its philosophic austerity may yet have indulged in the most secret of all passions, ambition, never attained to the fullness of fame.

Not long before death, while lying under the influence of that magical drug which, soothing the physical frame, mysteriously operates on the subtler element in man, he was heard to murmur words inexplicable to his attendant—"Billy Budd, Billy Budd." That these were not the accents of remorse would seem clear from what the attendant said to the *Indomitable's* senior officer of marines, who, as the most reluctant to condemn of the members of the drumhead court, too well knew, though here he kept the knowledge to himself, who Billy Budd was.

XXX

Some few weeks after the execution, among other matters under the head of *News from the Mediterranean*, there appeared in a naval chronicle of the time, an authorized weekly publication, an account of the affair. It was doubtless for the most part written in good faith, though the medium, partly rumor, through which the facts must have reached the writer, served to deflect and in part falsify them. The account was as follows:

"On the tenth of the last month a deplorable occurrence took place on board H.M.S. *Indomitable*. John Claggart, the ship's master-at-arms, discovering that some sort of plot was incipient among an inferior section of the ship's company, and that the ringleader was one William Budd, he, Claggart, in the act of arraigning the man before the captain was vindictively stabbed to the heart by the suddenly drawn sheath knife of Budd.

"The deed and the implement employed sufficiently suggest that, though mustered into the service under an English name, the assassin was no Englishman, but one of those aliens adopting English cognomens whom the present extraordinary necessities of the service have caused to be admitted into it in considerable numbers.

"The enormity of the crime and the extreme depravity of the criminal appear the greater in view of the character of the victim, a middle-aged man respectable and discreet, belonging to that minor official grade, the petty officers, upon whom, as none know better than the commissioned gentlemen, the efficiency of His Majesty's navy so largely depends. His function was a responsible one, at once onerous and thankless, and his fidelity in it the greater because of his strong patriotic impulse. In this instance, as in so many other instances in these days, the character of this unfortunate man signally refutes, if refutation were needed, that peevish saying attributed to the late Dr. Johnson, that patriotism is the last refuge of a scoundrel.

"The criminal paid the penalty of his crime. The promptitude of the punishment has proved salutary. Nothing amiss is now apprehended aboard H.M.S. *Indomitable*."

The above, appearing in a publication now long ago superannuated and forgotten, is all that hitherto has stood in human record to attest what manner of men respectively were John Claggart and Billy Budd.

XXXI

Everything is for a term remarkable in navies. Any tangible object associated with some striking incident of the service is converted into a monument. The spar from which the foretopman was suspended was for some few years kept trace of by the bluejackets. Their knowledge followed it from ship to dockyard and again from dockyard to ship, still pursuing it even when at last reduced to a mere dockyard boom. To them a chip of it was as a piece of the Cross. Ignorant though they were of the secret facts of the tragedy, and not thinking but that the penalty was somehow unavoidably inflicted from the naval point of view, for all that they instinctively felt that Billy was a sort of man as incapable of mutiny as of willful murder. They recalled the fresh young image of the Handsome Sailor, that face never deformed by a sneer or subtler vile freak of the heart within. Their impression of him was doubtless deepened by fact that he was gone, and in a measure mysteriously gone. At the time on the gun decks of the *Indomitable* the general estimate of his nature and its unconscious simplicity eventually found rude utterance from another foretopman, one of his own watch, gifted, as some sailors are, with an artless poetic temperament; the tarry hands made some lines which, after circulating among the shipboard crew for a while, finally got rudely printed at Portsmouth as a ballad. The title given to it was the sailor's.

Billy in the Darbies

Good of the Chaplain to enter Lone Bay
And down on his marrow-bones here and pray
For the likes just o' me, Billy Budd.—But look:
Through the port comes the moonshine astray!
It tips the guard's cutlass and silvers this nook;
But 'twill die in the dawning of Billy's last day.
A jewel-block they'll make of me tomorrow,
Pendant pearl from the yardarm-end
Like the eardrop I gave to Bristol Molly—
Oh, 'tis me, not the sentence they'll suspend.
Aye, Aye, all is up; and I must up too
Early in the morning, aloft from alow.
On an empty stomach, now, never it would do.
They'll give me a nibble—bit o' biscuit ere I go.
Sure, a messmate will reach me the last parting cup;
But, turning heads away from the hoist and the belay,
Heaven knows who will have the running of me up!
No pipe to those halyards.—But aren't it all sham?
A blur's in my eyes; it is dreaming that I am.
A hatchet to my hawser? all adrift to go?
The drum roll to grog, and Billy never know?
But Donald he has promised to stand by the plank;
So I'll shake a friendly hand ere I sink.
But—no! It is dead then I'll be, come to think.—
I remember Taff the Welshman when he sank.
And his cheek it was like the budding pink
But me they'll lash me in hammock, drop me deep.
Fathoms down, fathoms down, how I'll dream fast asleep.
I feel it stealing now. Sentry, are you there?
Just ease this darbies at the wrist, and roll me over fair,
I am sleepy, and the oozy weeds about me twist.

Herman Melville and the Forms—
Irony and Social Criticism in Billy Budd*

KARL E. ZINK

Billy Budd, Foretopman is a social allegory, the last of Herman Melville's criticisms of social injustice as he saw it in nineteenth century America. His critical observations began mildly and idealistically in Typee (1846) with his (for that time) daring denunciation of the Christian missionary in the South Pacific; and they were explicit and dramatic in White Jacket (1850) when Melville first symbolized the man-of-war society and damned, for example, the practice of flogging in the United States Navy. His censure of mid-century commercial American society in The Confidence Man (1857) was just as explicit, but a new element of irony gave this book a sophistication and power which transcended the raw rhetoric of White Jacket. The same basic strain of philosophical irony motivated Billy Budd thirty years later. In this last book he resorts to heavier symbolism and irony to dramatize his last charge against the artificial "forms" by which he saw men live blindly and passively. Billy Budd is a tragedy of society; not a tragedy of "hope and triumph in death," as Mr. Freeman asserts in summarizing his critique of the novel,[1] nor of "passive acceptance," or "necessity,"[131] as some thirty years of American criticism have uniformly reiterated.[2]

I

Despite its apparent historical authenticity, Billy Budd is not a realistic novel of events. It is rather heavy social allegory. The characters and situations operate clearly as symbols. Against the social frame of the ship—the man-of-war society—it develops anew the old struggle between the force for good and the force for evil, with a special ugly twist brought into being (Melville feels) by the inherent evil of the social machinery. Billy and John Claggart are the complex symbols for these forces. Claggart is aggressive evil; Billy is passive good, a comprehensive symbol of the sort of natural goodness that Adam lived before his fall, in large part only the ignorance of evil. He is possibly an agent of Divine justice. Evil in the world has the edge; it enjoys a strong survival factor, not because of greater power[3] but because it is nurtured and protected by the "forms" (potentially evil) by which the culture governs itself. A third symbolic character is Captain Vere, the enlightened

---

* From Accent: A Quarterly of New Literature, XII (Summer 1952), 131–139. Reprinted by permission of the author.

[1] F. Barron Freeman, Melville's Billy Budd. Cambridge: Harvard University Press, 1948.

[2] See Joseph Schiffman, "Melville's Final Stage, Irony: A Re-examination of Billy Budd Criticism." American Literature (May, 1950), for a long overdue re-appraisal of this century's criticism of Billy Budd, and a brief analysis of the essential irony of this novel.

[3] Billy always triumphs over evil until he runs afoul of the forms. Red Whiskers, the Afterguardsman, and Claggart are experiences with evil of increasing degrees of complexity. Claggart is his most complex experience of evil short of the social code that hangs him, against which he has not the necessary "touch of defensive ugliness."

mediator, symbol of Authority, who phrases and ponders the philosophical problem involved in Billy's fatal clash with Claggart, but who defends the harshness of the social code as ultimately best for the common good. It is Vere, as much as Billy, who dramatizes the awful power and blind impersonality of the forms. For although he, a good man, sensitive and intelligent, is fully aware (where Billy is not) of the injustice of the trial and the execution, he is too enmeshed in the forms himself not to enforce them. His dilemma is, of course, acute—he is many days away from the jurisdiction of the fleet admiral; the recency of the great mutinies is still an ever present threat to all naval authorities. The letter of the law simplifies; it softens the sting to the conscience of disturbing moral considerations. He too dies, soon after Billy, trammelled in his own fashion among the forms. And though Billy's name is on his lips when he dies he apparently does not regret his decision.

A fourth character, apparently overlooked for many years, is the crew of the *Indomitable*, the mass of mankind, dominated easily, often[132] brutally, by an authority they have learned to fear and respect. The symbolic behavior of the crew in response to the hanging has been long overlooked. Prior to Billy's hanging the crew do not act as a group; they enjoy no dynamic identity. But the execution of Billy galvanizes them into action and identity. They respond immediately as a mass, integrated by instinctive resistance to injustice. We shall see that in this instinctive, but pathetically abortive, reaction of the crew to the hanging Melville asserts his final judgment of nineteenth century America's dangerously immoral inclination.

II

Through the Christ imagery which surrounds Billy, Melville makes possible many ironic parallels between the story of Christ, fouled in the forms of pre-Christian Roman colonial administration, and the story of Billy Budd, nineteenth century man, helplessly fouled in the social machinery of his own century. In both cases, we remember, a force for good among men ran afoul of arbitrary rules for mass conduct and was destroyed inevitably in the meeting. Both men were accused of agitating, of questioning the status quo. Both were executed as an "admonitory spectacle" for the mob, each a warning against breaking the rules. Both were simple, "good" men, who suffered violent death passively. Both uttered before their death a benediction for the authority they had offended. In both cases an individual was sacrificed to inflexible forms by which men had chosen to live.

Melville deliberately points up this complex comparison with the illusion of Billy's glorification in "the full rose of the dawn"—his hanging is an apparent "ascension," an acceptance, a moral victory. But in the light of the crew's reaction to the hanging and the material presented in the following several chapters, Billy's "ascension" becomes a climactic irony. For the still figure at the yard end dramatizes more fittingly the evil of the forms, the awful impersonality that could thus shove goodness and innocence out of the world; that for the sake of immediate comfort, in order to frighten men into more complete docility, could perpetrate an injustice against man and God. Melville allows the Christ-like Billy to "accept" the necessity of his fate. But we are mistaken if we assume that Melville himself accepted it.

III

Every development which follows the hanging is an ironic comment on that event and underscores the final triumph of the forms:[133] (1) the unusual behavior of the crew—at the pronouncement of sentence, at the hanging, and at the burial; (2) the "something of a sequel" in the last three chapters, which records the death of Vere, the falsified official account of the story, the history of the spar Billy died on; and (3) the ballad.

(1) This crucial sequence of events begins, in fact, just before the hanging, when Vere summons all hands during the second dog-watch to pronounce sentence. The men betray an immediate, instinctive reaction against his announcement of Billy's fate. But their impulse is quickly overpowered by Authority:

> Their Captain's announcement was listened to by the throng of standing sailors in a dumbness like that of a seated congregation of believers in hell listening to the clergyman's announcement of his Calvinistic text.
> At the close, however, a confused murmur went up. It began to wax. All but instantly, then, at a sign, it was pierced and suppressed by shrill whistles of the Boatswain and his mates piping down one watch.[4]

We must note the beginning here of characteristic terms for the description, on the one hand, of Authority, and, on the other, of the unorganized mass: the *dumbness*, the *confused murmur of the men is pierced and suppressed by shrill whistles, piping.*

Later, only seconds after the awful moment of the execution, with Billy still warm and quiet against the yard, Melville is at pains to describe a second sullen murmur from the men; this too is firmly and efficiently silenced by Authority:

> The silence at the moment of execution and for a moment or two continuing thereafter, a silence but emphasized by the regular wash of the sea against the hull or the flutter of a sail caused by the helmsman's eyes being tempted astray, this emphasized silence was gradually disturbed by a sound not easily to be here verbally rendered. Whoever has heard the freshet-wave of a torrent suddenly swelled by pouring showers in the tropical mountains, showers not shared by the plain; whoever has heard the first muffled murmur of its sloping advance through precipitous woods, may form some conception of the sound now heard. The seeming remoteness of its source was because of its murmurous indistinctness since it came from close by, even from the men massed on the ship's open deck. Being inarticulate, it was dubious in significance further that it seemed to indicate some capricious revulsion of thought or feeling such as mobs ashore are liable to in the present instance possibly implying a sullen revocation on the men's part of their involuntary echoing of Billy's benediction. But ere the murmur had time to wax into clamor it was met by a strategic command, the more telling that it came with abrupt unexpectedness.
> "Pipe down the starboard watch, Boatswain, and see that they go."
> Shrill as the shriek of the sea-hawk the whistles of the Boatswain and his Mates pierced that ominous low sound, dissipating it; and yielding to the mechanism of discipline the throng was thinned by one half. For the remainer most of them were set to temporary employments connected with trimming the yards and so forth, business readily to be got up to serve occasion by any officer-of-the-deck.[5]

Again, the instinctive feelings of the group are quelled. Note they are described as *indistinct, inarticulate, murmurous; it is the mechanism of discipline* which thins the throng.

When Billy's shotted hammock is dropped over the side a few moments later (all hands called again, this time to witness burial), a third strange human murmur is heard, blended this time with another "inarticulate" sound—that of the great sea-fowl hovering hungrily over the spot, "circling it low down with the moving shadow of their outstretched wings and the cracked requiem of their cries." This motion was seen by the superstitious sailors as "big with no prosaic significance"—nature too rebelled—and immediately

> An uncertain movement began among them, in which some encroachment was made. It was tolerated but for a moment. For suddenly the drum beat to quarters, which familiar sound hap-

---

[4] Freeman, pp. 254–255.   [5] Freeman, pp. 269–270.

pening at least twice a day, had upon the present occasion some signal peremptoriness in it. True martial discipline long continued superinduces in an average man a sort of impulse of docility whose operation at the official sound of command much resembles in its promptitude the effect of an instinct.[6]

This time it is the drumbeat that dissipates the angry mood of the massed men. The movement is characteristically *uncertain,* but Authority as usual is brisk and sure. For the third time Melville has driven home his belief in the natural though inarticulate revulsion which the mass of men feel against the tyranny of the forms, and for the third time we have seen their vague "murmur" expertly quelled. He is most specific at this point that the average man has developed an[135] impulse of docility in the face of Authority that is practically instinctive.

Captain Vere immediately justifies the drumbeat to quarters (it is an hour earlier this Sunday morning) as necessary to counteract the temporary mood of his men:

"With mankind" he would say "forms, measured forms are everything; and that is the import couched in the story of Orpheus with his lyre spellbinding the wild denizens of the woods."[7]

This is the climactic, ironic cap to their *inarticulate* feelings of outrage—this easy, learned explanation, heightened by the classical allusion which betrays the great age of the entrenched power of the forms. For "Orpheus" read Vere; for "lyre" read *Boatswain's pipe, drum;* "spellbinding" and "wild denizens" have overtones which are immediately apparent. In the following paragraph the Chaplain conducts the customary morning service, the drum beats the retreat, and "toned by music and religious rites subserving the discipline and purpose of war, the men in their wonted orderly manner dispersed to the places allotted them when not at the guns."[8] Note the terms *wonted, orderly, allotted.* The forms have won out.

IV

(2) According to Mr. Freeman's editing of the *Billy Budd* manuscripts the short story, *Baby Budd, Sailor,* ends at this point, the burial, with the men dispersed and quieted. It is thus apparent that even in his initial conception of the tale, Melville included the crew's instinctive revulsions against the authority of the forms. To the novel Melville added three short chapters and the ballad, "Billy in the Darbies." These final chapters trace Billy's story forward in time and amplify Melville's final criticism of the forms. The first of these records the death of Captain Vere in the act of destroying the *Athéiste.*[9] The second records the further triumph of the impersonal forms in the ironic reversal of[136] character and fact which was preserved in the authorized weekly naval chronicle called *News from the Mediterranean*—"all that hitherto has stood in human record," Melville says with characteristic irony, "to attest what manner of men respectively were John Clag-

---

[6] Freeman, pp. 271–272.
[7] Freeman, p. 272.
[8] Freeman, pp. 272–273.
[9] The old *St. Louis* had been rechristened *Athéiste* under the Directory. Vere dies, interestingly enough, in the glorious act of destroying the *Athéiste,* a ship fighting in a cause which sought to eradicate a system of entrenched forms. It is thus, symbolically, the "natural" enemy of the *Indomitable* which has just rationalized a shocking injustice to a Christ-like sailor in the name of law and order and authority. We are reminded here of the terrible paradox that the brute *Indomitable* bore the "Minister of the Prince of Peace" aboard, the military chaplain, "serving in the host of the God of War—Mars." "Why is he there?" Melville asks bitterly. "Because he indirectly subserves the purpose attested by the cannon; because too he lends the sanction of the religion of the meek to that which practically is the abrogation of everything but brute force." (Freeman, p. 262)

gart and Billy Budd." For here, it will be remembered, John Claggart was "vindictively stabbed to the heart by the suddenly drawn sheath knife of Budd," whom he accused of "some sort of plot . . . among an inferior section of the ship's company." Because he used a knife, Billy is presumed no Englishman but an "assassin" of foreign origin serving in the English Navy. The "enormity" of his crime and the "extreme depravity of the criminal" are deplored. The exemplary character of Claggart is there said to refute Dr. Johnson's "peevish saying" that patriotism is the last refuge of a scoundrel. "The promptitude of the punishment has proved salutary. Nothing amiss is now apprehended aboard the *H.M.S. Indomitable*."[10] Authority speaks. Through the high impersonality and indifference of the forms to the individual lives they dominate Billy dies unjustly and his character in the annals of men is unjustly and carelessly defamed.

The last chapter briefly traces the history of the yard from which Billy hung, how chips of it came to be cherished as pieces of the Cross, and records the composition of the ballad and how it was in time printed at Portsmouth. But this perspective, too, only reiterates man's subservience to the forms, his docility. This is manifest in the uncritical, paradoxical feeling of the men regarding the rightness of the execution:

Ignorant though they were of the secret facts of the tragedy, and not thinking but that the penalty was somehow unavoidably inflicted from the naval point of view, for all that they instinctively felt that Billy was a sort of man as incapable of mutiny as of willful murder.[11]

Though they cherished splinters from his spar and in their hearts felt him incapable of murder and mutiny, somehow his execution must have been justified "from the naval point of view." The murmur grows weaker.

(3) There remains the folk record, the ballad, "Billy in the Darbies," which brings Melville's story of Billy Budd to a close. Composed by a watchmate of Billy's (a man who should have known him well), it is said to preserve "the general estimate of his nature and its unconscious simplicity."[12] But in no satisfactory sense does it do this. This folk record tells us as little about the Billy Budd the reader knows as did the organ of the forms, *News from the Mediterranean*.

It preserves the last reflections of the condemned man on the night before he was hanged (a longer speech than Billy made anywhere in the novel), not his narrative, as might be expected, or any suggestion of his symbolic or spiritual meaning. Rough as it is, there is about it a sophistication, a bizarre humor, grim puns, that no one who knew him well could have attributed to him. Preoccupation with the ugly details of death by halter and sea burial do not bespeak the undisturbed boy who slept like a baby before his hanging. It is even doubtful that Billy ever gave an eardrop to Bristol Molly. The ballad is too passive, for one thing, and too non-committal. If the facts of his story—and his spiritual significance, as well—are thus blurred in the folk mind as well as in the official record, then mankind's immersion in the forms is blind and dark indeed. Something is missing in a ballad which generations of sailors are supposed to have sung in memory of a hero. What is missing, I suggest, is the outraged murmur which sought articulation first when sentence was pronounced, again when Billy ascended to the yard, and again when he was dropped into the sea. No spark of that "instinctive," "inarticulate," "uncertain" but genuine outrage which the massed crew had intuitively felt and abortively expressed aboard ship appears even by implication in the folk record—where it belongs. We should expect their murmur at his death to survive. But it does not. Only blurred, sympathetic feelings

---

[10] Freeman, p. 277.
[11] Freeman, p. 278.
[12] Freeman, pp. 278–279.

survive. Inasmuch as the ballad is no more valuable a record of the real Billy and no more sensitive to the spiritual Billy than it is, Melville's implication, his irony, seems clear. The men were incapable of understanding—incapable of realizing just how rare, and how innocent, and how important Billy was to the ship and to themselves. We know that Authority withheld the central facts. The several mass reactions we see the crew make are all non-rational, intuitive. (The crew's echo of Billy's benediction of Vere is irrational, coming as it does between clear manifestations of revolt.) Because their response to the injustice of the hanging was intuitive and inarticulate, it could be controlled. Melville stresses this. Apparently the men were no more capable of a vital, resistant articulation in words, than they were in action. And thus Authority perpetuates itself. This is the last of the chain of ironies following the hanging which illuminate the brute, insidious power of the forms—the great danger to the individual resident in the machinery by which the group manages itself.[138]

V

We have seen resistance to the forms grow weaker with each remove from the deck of the *Indomitable*. Vere dies convinced that his decision was justified—his last words, "Billy Budd," were not the "accents of remorse." The only official documentary record of Billy's story was hopelessly distorted. His mates, cherishing splinters from his spar, knowing in their hearts he was incapable of murder and mutiny, docilely accepted the penalty as "unavoidably inflicted from the naval point of view." And, finally, the ballad, the folk record, is also a distortion, which betrays subtly the undiscriminating docility of the pliable crew. This is Melville's final irony. The murmur has been lost. The triumph of the forms is complete. And Melville's tragic allegory of nineteenth century American society is finished.

That Billy Budd had to die is to the eternal shame of the inflexible machinery that could shove him off. For it was "the forms" that nurtured and protected the evil Claggart, and an apologist for the forms (Vere) who, fully awake to Billy's moral innocence, condemned the man to die who had rid the world (symbolically) of natural evil. Mr. Schiffman reminds us of the terrible dramatic irony of Billy's benediction of Captain Vere. And there is deep irony in the repetition of Billy's words—"God bless Captain Vere"—by the "wedged mass of upturned faces," the docile crew, inured to passive acceptance of the rules, to worship, almost of their administrators. "God bless Captain Vere" is the last thing they would knowingly have uttered. But with Billy alone in their hearts and in their eyes, their emotional identification with him is so complete that momentarily they too reflect his own special innocence of their true dilemma. The lesson is not that Billy learns to accept the necessary harshness of the forms, but that in their high impersonality there is a dangerous lack of discrimination—dangerous to the individual and to the social structure itself. For in justifying Billy's death, the structure deprived itself symbolically of the force for good. And part of the lesson is that men tolerate this inherent evil of the structure passively, uncritically. Moral integrity is often, unhappily, endangered by or sacrificed to the impersonal dicta of the forms. Civilization has come to compromise men's cherished natural integrity and constitutes a threat to itself. Something like this, it seems to me, is the tenor of Melville's thought in *Billy Budd*. It is ironic social criticism, not acceptance.[139]

The Ceremony of Innocence*

WILLIAM YORK TINDALL

Billy Budd seems to make something almost too tidy out of what remains uncertain in *Moby Dick*. Melville's story of the captain, the villain, and the tar, apparently less a story than a commentary on one, may strike the hasty reader as a product of reason rather than imagination, as something reduced to discourse for ready apprehension by basic Englishmen. What had to be said has been said by Captain Vere or Melville himself. As critics, therefore, we may feel frustrated, as Romantics we may prefer a little teasing mystery around, and as esthetes, confronted with discourse, we are sure that talking about a thing is less admirable than embodying it in image or action. Of Kierkegaard's three categories, the esthetic, the moral, and the divine, Melville seems to have chosen the second—to the applause of some and the departure of others, for *Don Giovanni* maybe.

That the matter of *Billy Budd* gratifies what Melville calls "the moral palate" is plain from the plainest rehearsal. The scene is a British frigate during the Napoleonic wars. Two mutinies have justified fears of more. Against this ominous background, Billy, an innocent aboard, is accused for no good reason by Claggart, a petty officer, of plotting mutiny. The captain, a reasonable man, doubts Claggart's story and brings Billy in to confront his lying accuser. Overcome by a stutterer's indignation, the innocent foretopman, unable to speak a word, strikes Claggart dead with a fist like a ham. Captain Vere is faced with a dilemma. Though he believes in Billy's innocence, naval law and prudence alike demand punishment for the impetuous seaman while pity and reason counsel mercy. Internal debate inclines the captain toward conviction, and Billy, condemned despite the "troubled conscience" of his judges, is hanged.

The subject is a quandary or what Melville calls "the intricacies involved in the question of moral responsibility." As the captain ponders "the moral phenomenon presented in Billy Budd" and the "elemental evil" of Claggart, he fathoms the "mystery of iniquity." The case of Billy seems, as the captain says, a matter for "psychologic theologians."

Although, as T. S. Eliot observes in *After Strange Gods*, "It is . . . during moments of moral and spiritual struggle . . . that men [in fiction] . . . come nearest being real," Billy and Claggart, who represent almost pure good and pure evil, are too simple and too extreme to satisfy the demands of realism; for character demands admixture. Their all but allegorical blackness and whiteness, however, are functional in the service of Vere's problem, and Vere, goodness knows, is real enough. Claggart is black because, as Philipp G. Frank once observed, a sinner is necessary for the realization of a moral code; and an innocent is almost equally instructive. These abstractions, a sacrifice of verisimilitude to tactical necessity, reveal the "moral quality" of the captain's mind, which becomes a theater for contending opposites and eventual choice. Such dramatic crises are not only the favorite stuff of novelists but of philosophers and poets as well: Kierkegaard wrote *Either/Or* and Yeats "The Choice."

---

* "The Ceremony of Innocence" by William York Tindall from GREAT MORAL DILEMMAS edited by R. M. MacIver. Copyright 1956 by The Institute for Religious and Social Studies. Reprinted by permission of Harper & Row, Publishers, and the author.

Not only rational, Vere's choice involves his whole sensitive, adult being. Agony shows on his face as he emerges from his interview with Billy, and a final exclamation shows how deeply he is stirred. Involving more than black and white, the captain's choice is between two moral codes, military and natural. The first is evident; the second is either that of the noble savage, in whom Melville was interested, or what Western culture takes for granted. In other words, the captain's conflict is between the balanced claims of justice and equity, order and confusion, law and grace, reason and feeling, or, as Melville puts it, "military duty" and "moral scruple." Vere's eloquent and moving speech to the drumhead court, the climax of such drama as there is, leaves little to add about these issues and his dilemma.[74]

The conflict of military with natural may occupy the stage, but Melville recognizes other codes, that of custom or respectability, for example. Claggart's "natural depravity" appears in respectable guise. Melville also recognizes the cultural, psychological, and absolute bases of morality, and hints in a very modern way at their operation.

"Moral," Melville's favorite word—in this book at least—is one which, though commonly taken for granted, is slippery. I have read a thing in which "moral" means something else on every page. What Yvor Winters means by it escapes me. Vague and general like F. R. Leavis's "awareness of life" or narrow and definite like the *quid agas* of Scholastic philosophers, the word needs fixing before use. As I shall use it and as I think Melville did, morality implies not only action but motive, attitude, and being. It involves a sense of obligation to self, community, and the absolute, which provide a frame by conscience, law, tradition, or revelation. If we demand a single equivalent, Melville's "responsibility" will do.

Vere's action, however sudden and whether we approve of it or not, is plainly responsible. Billy and Claggart act, to be sure: one bears false witness and the other delivers a blow, but neither actor follows reason and each is more important for what he is than what he does. If being as well as action can be moral, however, they are moral figures, too, existing like cherubs or fiends in a moral atmosphere. Good or bad, they occupy the region of good and evil.

It is agreed by most that moral substance is necessary for the novel. Not the pure form of Flaubert's desire, and falling far short of the condition of music, the novel is an arrangement of references to vital issues, without which it is empty. A value of Joyce's *Ulysses*, for example, is the feeling and idea of charity. That moral substance fails to insure greatness, however, is proved by the works of Horatio Alger; and that it fails to guarantee moral effect is proved by those of Mickey Spillane. The errors of censors and formalists show the folly of judging by morality alone or arrangement alone. Not moral idea but its embodiment in what Eliot called objective correlatives, suitably arranged, determines value. Far from inciting action as moralizing does, embodied morality invites contemplation, and to become an object of contemplation, substance must be distanced by form. The[75] question is not how much morality is there but how much is under control, how fully insight and moral intelligence have submitted to esthetic discipline. Our problem, then, is not morality itself but moral art or morally significant form.

Captain Vere's speech to the court adequately embodies the idea of "moral responsibility" in dramatic form; but we must find if Billy's history has found fitting embodiment. At first reading, that history seems a curious and eccentric structure of essays on ethics, digressions or "bypaths," character sketches, and chronicles of the navy, an arrangement that after uncertain progress tails inconclusively off. Such image and action as we find, failing to halt the lamentable decline, seem occasions for analysis or digression, like biblical texts in a pulpit. Since the crucial interview between Vere and Billy is disappointingly offstage, Melville seems to have avoided the dramatic possibilities of his theme. That the book calls for the dramatization he failed to give it, is proved by attempts at play and opera, which, while affirming excellence of theme, imply that action or image are better ways of presenting it. But something that continues to fascinate us in its present form and calls forth responses beyond the capacity of discourse, suggests art of another kind. Maybe Melville avoided drama in the interests of a less obvious medium.

Moby Dick assures us that Melville was an artist, not a lecturer on ethics. He not only worked three years on *Billy Budd*, but he seems to have regarded the result with far from senile favor. The first version, recently detected in manuscript by F. Barron Freeman, reveals more action and less discourse; yet this version, which corresponds more happily to what we think fiction should be, is not so effective as the one before us with all its weight of digression and analysis.

That Melville was aware of form is clear from passages in *Billy Budd*. When Captain Vere says, "With mankind forms, measured forms, are everything," he probably means usage and custom; but Melville himself, applying Vere's remark to esthetics, says that the symmetry of form desirable in pure fiction cannot be achieved in factual narrative like this. The story is not factual in fact. But Melville, wanting it to seem so, excuses apparent formlessness as a form for[76] giving the illusion of a bare report; for truth, he continues, will always have its ragged edges and matters of fact must lack the finish of an "architectural finial." Aware of loose structure and inconclusive ending, he justifies them for what seem wrong reasons. Not reasons, however, but what he made must detain us while we scout further possibilities. The curious form he made may be functional and, for all our hasty impression and his explanation, effective. Is the book as shapeless as he implies? Or, if shapeless, is shapelessness a kind of shape? Is the book as pedestrian, discursive, and factual as he claims and as we had supposed on first looking into it?

What seems at first to be factual is presented, we find, in part by images and allusions that are incompatible with a pretense of factuality. Though unapparent, those images are livelier than we thought. Consider the coloring of the scene between decks before the execution as Billy lies in white amid profound blackness. Catching up the abstract whiteness and blackness of Billy and Claggart, this image of black and white embodies them. At the execution the rosy dawn that seems "the fleece of the Lamb of God seen in mystical vision" promises a kind of renewal while implying much else. Circling birds after the burial at sea offer by the aid of tradition some spiritual import. And that spilt soup, perhaps more action than image, carries suggestions beyond the demands of plot, suggestions so indefinite, what is more, that they confound its rational progress. Even the names of ships, though serving a more comprehensible purpose, are as significant as those in *Moby Dick*. Billy is removed from the *Rights of Man*, for instance, and Vere is mortally wounded by a shot from the *Athéiste*.

The words of *Billy Budd* carry more than denotation. "Sinister dexterity," at once witty and desolating, sounds like something from *Finnegans Wake*, where, indeed, it reappears. Vere's last words, "Billy Budd," are equivocal. Do they imply feeling, regret, self-realization, understanding? Are they a form for something incompletely realized? However "factual" the words of this pseudoreport, they function like the words of poetry.

Not only last words and indeterminate images but a number of hints about Billy's "all but feminine" nature plague our assumptions.[77] Roses and lilies dye his cheeks. He comports himself like a "rustic beauty" at times and like a vestal virgin at others. These qualities and appearances, astonishing in an able seaman, calling forth an "ambiguous smile" from one or another of his shipmates, suggest psychological depths and motives below the level of the plain report. By virtue of such intimations Billy seems at once more and less bottomless than we had supposed, and so do the motives of Claggart, if not those of the captain himself. Among such suggestions, avoidance of the obviously dramatic becomes implicit embodiment that escapes the limits of drama.

What pleases me most, however, is the accompaniment of biblical allusions which, however unobtrusive and irregular, recurs like Wagnerian *leitmotiv*. Time and again Billy is compared to Adam and Jesus. Billy's innocence is as much that of Adam before the Fall as that of the more secular noble savage. As a "peacemaker," a term implying beatitude, Billy seems destined for "crucifixion"; and his hanging, condensing events, becomes an ascension. Vere is compared to Abraham about to sacrifice Isaac, obeying God's will with fear and trembling. Becoming a shadow of God, Vere weighs the claims of Adam and Satan. Claggart, whose denunciation is reported in Mosaic terms as "false witness," is compared not only to the Serpent of Eden but to Ananias and to one struck dead by an angel of God, "yet," as the captain says, "the angel must hang!" Man's fall and redemption and all troubles between seem suggested by this large though not fully elaborated analogy, which, bringing to mind the mythical parallels in *Ulysses* and *The Waste Land*, removes Billy a little farther from the abstraction to which, for all his stutter and those rosy cheeks, he seems committed. However incapable of supporting this mythical burden, he becomes by its aid almost as portentous as choosing Vere. The sailors, whose testimony cannot be ignored, are more impressed by Billy than by Vere, reason and all. Not only being and secular victim, Billy becomes saint and martyr and his hanging an omen. Pieces of the spar to which he quietly ascends are venerated like pieces of the true cross, suitable for reliquaries or the holiest of duffle bags. By the aid of myth and military ritual the[78] story of Billy, transformed from an essay on good, evil, and choice, approaches what Yeats called "the ceremony of innocence."

We must conclude that Melville avoided the attractions of the obvious in the interests of indefinite suggestiveness and myth. His work, whatever its air of the factual and the discursive, is symbolist and richer for scarcity of drama and image. Such drama and images as are there function more intensely in their abstract context than profusion could. That the structure as a whole also serves esthetic purpose is likely. As we have seen, the book is a queer arrangement of discourse, action, image, and allusion, with discourse predominating. We have seen how image and action work in this mixture; but we must examine the function of discourse. In such context, discourse, increasing tension, makes allusion and image dramatic or enlarges them, and, working with allusion, image, and action may produce a third something by juxtaposition as in Eliot's *Four Quartets*, or Wallace Stevens' *Notes Toward a Supreme Fiction*. Seeming now a structure of conflicts, not only of men and codes but of methods, which become a technical echo of the theme, the book emerges as a structural drama or a drama of structure. An ending that seemed weak afterthought (and was not there in the first version) now unifies all. Vere's exclamation, the saint's legend, and inconclusiveness, working together, comprise a form, which may tail off but tails suggestively off, leaving endless reverberations in our minds. There is more mystery around than we had thought, and we may agree with dying Gertrude Stein that answers are less important than questions. What at a superficial reading had the appearance of exhaustive discourse becomes inexhaustible. The shapeless thing becomes suggestive shape. Neither as loose nor as tight as it once seemed, the strange sequence of precise discourse and indefinite suggestiveness corresponds to our experience of life itself. That the form Melville made fascinates while it eludes and teases is shown no less by popular favor than by the abundance of critical comment.

However different it looks, *Billy Budd* is not altogether different in kind from *Moby Dick*, another structure of digression, discourse, action, and image. The proportions and impact may be different, the[79] images of *Moby Dick* may be more compelling, but both serve symbolic suggestion and both are forms for offering a vision of reality. Not the tidy discourse of our first impression, the work is almost as inexplicable as *Moby Dick*.

What exactly does this form present? It is impossible to answer this question for any symbolist work; for works of this kind escape discursive accounting. We may say that *Billy*

Budd is a vision of man in society, a vision of man's moral quandary or his responsibility; but its meaning is more general than these, and that is why it haunts us. So haunted, I find the work not an essay on a moral issue but a form for embodying the feeling and idea of thinking about a moral issue, the experience of facing, of choosing, of being uneasy about one's choice, of trying to know. Not a conclusion like a sermon, *Billy Budd* is a vision of confronting what confronts us, of man thinking things out with all the attendant confusions and uncertainties. Disorder is a form for this and the apparently formless book a formal triumph. To do what it does it has to be a fusion of tight-loose, shapeless-shaped, irrelevant-precise, suggestive-discursive—a mixture of myth, fact, and allusion that has values beyond reference. The discursive parts represent our attempts at thinking, while the action, images, and allusions represent what we cannot think but must approximate. Arrangement of these discordant elements forms a picture of a process.

From my guess at meaning it follows that the center of this form is neither Vere nor Billy but rather the teller of the story or Melville himself. Though ghostlier, he is not unlike the Marlow of Conrad's *Lord Jim* and *Heart of Darkness* or the Quentin of Faulkner's *Absalom, Absalom!* Using Vere and Billy as materials, Melville's thought-process, like those of Marlow and Quentin, is the heart of this darkness and its shape the objective correlative, a form for something at once imperfectly understood and demanding understanding. Morality, the substance of this form, becomes an element that limits and directs the feelings and ideas created by the whole. Moral substance, what is more, may be what engages our minds while the form does its work. Value, not from morality alone, issues from the form that includes it and in which it serves. If the form[80] concerned less, I repeat, it would be trivial, but without its formal presentation the morality would remain in Sunday school.

United now, the beautiful and the good create a vision larger than either, a vision transcending the case of Billy Budd or the quandary of Captain Vere. The teller, now any man, presents man's feeling in the face of any great dilemma. Thought and feeling, outdistancing themselves, become objects of contemplation, remote yet immediate. The effect of this form is moral in the sense of enlarging our awareness of human conditions or relationships and of improving our sensitivity. In such a form Kierkegaard's esthetic, moral, and divine become a single thing.[81]

Billy Budd: The Plot Against the Story*

LEE T. LEMON

Billy Budd rubs against the grain, and it rubs intensely and persistently enough to be irritating. Our sympathies are all with the innocent Billy, and we are accustomed to having authors exploit our sympathies directly. Most typically, a pattern of meaning emerges from a narrative because our responses to the pattern of values embodied in the hero and his story are reinforced by the thematic implications of the setting, characterization, tone, symbolism, authorial intrusions, and so on. If there is an ironic discrepancy between hero and theme, we expect an author to let us know what it is.

In a relatively simple novel like *For Whom the Bell Tolls*, Robert Jordan seems to embody Hemingway's ethic, and Jordan's world is conveniently built to make that ethic appear acceptable. If I may simplify somewhat, we know that Jordan is good because he is for Good Things and against Bad Things; and where the morality of the things is doubtful, we judge it by Jordan's response. Generally, we sympathize with Jordan because he is on the side of humanity; and because we sympathize, we judge the world as he judges it. This, at least, is the way Hemingway's novel seems designed to work. Similarly, when we have a rogue hero, as in Fielding's *Jonathan Wild*, we know which way our sympathies are supposed to run because the hero's actions and fate are in accord with the context the author has created.

Even in much more complicated works like *Light in August* or *Crime and Punishment*, the context in which the hero acts out his drama still generally supports the value system implicit in that drama. Our responses to Raskolnikov may be more complex than our responses to Robert Jordan, but the patterns of value Dostoevsky provides for him and his world in the novel are compatible. If a generous spirituality is good in Sonia, it is also good in Raskolnikov; if progressivism is evil for Lebeziatnikov, it is equally evil for Raskolnikov.[32]

The Russian Formalist critic Victor Shklovskij[1] originated a distinction that may help explain my meaning. The distinction is between *story* and *plot*: the story is the sequence of events in their causal-temporal relationship; whatever falls outside that relationship or distorts it belongs to the plot. All literary narratives have both, and they can be roughly separated by reducing the narrative to its essential story pattern—that "A happened, which caused B, which in turn caused C . . ." and so on. A novel may have two or more related stories, as in *Light in August* or *Vanity Fair*. Thus if one were telling Becky Sharp's "story," much of the detail about Amelia would be totally irrelevant in tracing Becky's fate. Likewise, much of the description of clothes, social customs, Thackeray's intrusions, and the like, would be irrelevant. All such irrelevancies would, however, be part of the plot.

---

* From *Studies in Short Fiction*, II (Fall 1964), 32–43. Reprinted by permission of the editor and the author.

[1] *Razvertyvanie sjuzheta* and *Tristam Shandy Stern'a i teorija i romana* (*Plot Development and Sterne's Tristam Shandy and the Theory of the Novel*), published separately in Petrograd, 1921. These and other Russian Formalist essays have been translated into English by L. T. Lemon and M. J. Reis; their first printing in English will be by the University of Nebraska Press in 1965.

My point is that in most narratives story and plot involve the same, or at least compatible, patterns of sympathy and revulsion. In *Vanity Fair* it seems clear that Thackeray wants us to be repelled by Becky's grasping ambition. The plot—including the material centering around Amelia—directly reinforces this theme. We know how bad Becky is partly by her effect on Amelia, partly by the contrast between the two women, partly by the dictums of Thackeray's that "All is vanity," and partly by the emptiness of her temporary success. Quite simply, the plot reinforces the thematic implications of the story.

I shall argue that in *Billy Budd* the thematic implications of the plot and those of the story are often in direct opposition and that this causes much of the confusion about the book. But I want to argue further that the opposition is itself functional and leads to a more subtle and more mature theme than could either aspect alone.

Put in its most general terms, *Billy Budd* is the familiar story of a young man forced into strange circumstances who, having unintentionally incurred the enmity of a person more powerful than himself, is hounded until he strikes out in self-defense and is murdered by society. From the outline of the story, nothing could be clearer than that our sympathies are to be with Billy and against society. When society kills innocence, right thinking men bristle naturally, and authors make such natural responses the basis of their themes. Moreover, Melville goes to great lengths to impress[33] his readers with Budd's innocence and society's guilt; parts of the plot, in other words, work conventionally to reinforce the sympathies and revulsions aroused by the story. Others work ambiguously, and still others work unconventionally—that is, against the story. I shall begin with what seem the most conventionally used elements of the plot and work through to the more unconventional.

For a number of reasons, Melville develops Claggart, the antagonist, least ambiguously. In the story he is unalloyed evil. He hates Billy for no reason, plots against him, and tries to destroy him; nothing in the cause and effect sequence of the story alleviates Claggart's evil—he even lacks all normal human motivation. In the plot, Melville goes out of his way to inform the reader that Claggart is born with "a depravity according to nature"; he is one of those "madmen, . . . of the most dangerous sort"[2] whose very rationality is a threat. On the level of plot he assumes a specific symbolic identity that comes as much from what we do not know about him as from what we do know. He appears to be a man "who for reasons of his own was keeping incog" [p. 681]. None of the crew's speculations on Claggart's origins reflects credit on him. He is possibly a swindler and certainly not a native Englishman; the only hint as to his nationality is the word *chevalier*, which suggests that he is French and therefore, in the context of *Billy Budd*, an enemy of the established social order. We know as little of Claggart's background "as an astronomer knows about a comet's travels prior to its first observable appearance in the sky" [p. 682].

I am belaboring that we do not know about Claggart, because we lack the same information about Billy. Like Claggart, he has no antecedents, although he appears to be unalloyed English, with "a mother eminently favored by Love and the Graces" and a noble father. But a curious exchange occurs when Billy is questioned about his parents:

". . . . Who was your father?"
"God knows, Sir." [p. 675]

On the strength of this I shall not attempt to make Billy into a Christ figure; at this point I merely want to emphasize that Melville is at great pains to hint that neither he nor Clag-

---

[2] [Textual references to *Billy Budd* in this article were originally to the Hayford-Sealts edition (Chicago, 1962). Page references have been changed to refer to the edition appearing in this text on pp. 671-712—Ed.]

gart is of this world, as if Melville were preparing us for a confrontation of a good and an evil whose purity is unalloyed by anything earthly.[3][34]

The purity of Claggart's evil is so beyond the range of human experience that Melville cannot trust himself to present it dramatically; instead, he stops the story at Chapter 11 to speculate on natural depravity and to suggest a radical discontinuity between the moral and the social worlds. To understand Claggart, "to pass from a normal nature to him one must cross 'the deadly space between'" [p. 686]. Possibly "to know the world and to know human nature [are] . . . two distinct branches of knowledge," so that one may know either and yet know "little or nothing of the other" [p. 686]. In fact, natural depravity or complete moral evil has so little to do with the everyday business of the world that society fosters the former and condemns the latter.

Symbolically (hence still on the level of plot) Claggart is linked with the serpent of the Garden of Eden. Claggart's henchman gains the attention of pre-lapsarian Billy by saying "Hist," and again, "Hist, hist!" [p. 689]—the sound of a serpent. When Claggart himself confronts Billy, "the first mesmeristic glance was one of serpent fascination" [p. 697]; when the sailors carry away the dead Claggart, "it was like handling a dead snake" [p 697]. Both the narrative thread of the story and the supplementary details of the plot combine to condemn Claggart, as in any conventional narrative. The plot serves merely to specify symbolically the nature of Claggart's evil.

The same conventional plot-story relationship holds true for Billy, but only in part. The story requires that we sympathize with this example of hounded innocence, and the plot defines that sympathy by defining its object. I have already pointed out that Billy, like Claggart, is not of this world. "God knows" who his father is, and he is constantly referred to as a kind of noble savage. The "natural regality" [p. 671] of this type specifically contrasts with Claggart's "natural depravity." His virtues are strength and beauty rather than the more civilized understanding and cunning. It should not be necessary to press the point that whenever Billy is compared to something, it is always something either before or beyond civilization. Claggart, who the narrator tells us is "intellectually capable of adequately appreciating the moral phenomenon presented in Billy Budd" understands that Billy is "nothing more than innocent" [p. 688]. If we try to make a Christ or an Adam of Billy, we are attributing both too much and too little to him; symbols, even literary and mythic symbols, are seldom mutually convertible. At[35] most we can say that Billy is Christ-like and Adam-like in his innocence and Christ-like in his role as victim.

Melville further specifies the innocence as both moral and social. His moral innocence makes the conflict with Claggart inevitable; his social innocence dooms him. He is, no matter how regrettably, "Baby Budd" in a social world that requires manhood. It is fitting that the world in which Baby Budd is most at home is the world of the *Rights-of-Man* which, Melville tells us, is named after Paine's book; the world of the rights of man is a "natural" world just as Budd is a "natural" man. On board the *Rights-of-Man*, discipline, which would seem to be social if anything is, is clearly and certainly presented as natural. It is not enforced by authority (the honest but rather ineffectual Captain Graveling) but rather by Billy: "'Not that he preached to them or said or did anything in particular; but a virtue went out of him, sugaring the sour ones'" [p. 673]. Even when Billy quiets the last trouble maker, Red Whiskers, he does it naturally by instinctively striking out, not by civilized or social means. The natural world—or, if the oxymoron is permissible, natural society—is better for Billy's presence. Yet Billy himself leaves that world with no regrets, as if Melville were telling us that Billy himself knows that he is twenty-one and must become a man. Thus he has no complaints when he is separated from his rights and im-

---

[3] Captain Vere, on the other hand, is earthly. As the novel's representative of social order it is appropriate that Melville tells us much about his background.

pressed on board the *Bellipotent*,* a warship in hostile waters and so a fitting symbol for society at its most organized and most authoritarian. As he changes ships, he shouts, " 'And good-bye to you too, old *Rights-of-Man*' " [p. 674]. He is, in fact, leaving the world of natural rights. The lieutenant, the representative of authority at this point, "roars," " 'Down, Sir!' "

All of this plot material functions quite conventionally, enlisting our sympathies with the hero and defining them. But a question about Billy should be taking form: can the natural man assume the responsibilities of the social man? The plot tells us that he cannot. Perhaps the most telling incident is his response to the temptation by Claggart's henchman.[4] Billy is utterly confused, for this is "the first time in his life that he had ever been personally approached in underhand intriguing fashion" [p. 690]. More important than his confusion, however, is his refusal to report the incident; because of his "novice magnanimity" he feels that informing "would savour overmuch of the dirty work of a telltale" [p. 691]. His attitude here[36] is essentially adolescent; he neither understands the importance of the event nor conceives of a duty higher than that to his private moral code. Equally important, he lies to Red Pepper, telling him that the tempter was only an afterguardsman on the prowl, and lies again at the court-martial. Both times, and this is significant, Billy lies deliberately, so deliberately that he even overcomes his speech impediment. On the second occasion,

> The reply lingered . . . the question immediately recalling to Billy's mind the interview with the afterguardsman in the forechains. But an innate repugnance to playing a part at all approaching that of an informer against one's shipmates—the same erring sense of uninstructed honor which had stood in the way of his reporting the matter at the time, though as a loyal man-of-war's man it was incumbent on him, and failure so to do, if charged against him and proven, would have subjected him to the heaviest of penalties; this, with the blind feeling now his that nothing really was being hatched, prevailed with him. When the answer came it was a negative. [p. 700]

I have quoted this passage at length because in it the narrator (whom we have no reason to distrust; I find the arguments that the narrator is ironic singularly unconvincing) specifically accuses Billy of a crime punishable by death. The crime can be thought of narrowly in terms of severe military justice; but it can also be thought of broadly as Billy's failure to protect the society he has joined. Billy is not only irresponsible, he is not responsible—in the sense in which children and feeble-minded persons are not responsible.

I am being very hard on Billy because critics generally have been too easy on him. And with good reason, for as I have shown, the story and much of the plot material built around him are designed to make him appealing. To state the case somewhat more fairly, Baby Budd has morally and intellectually never left the world of the *Rights-of-Man*, although we are told that at twenty-one he bade the rights good-bye and cheerfully entered the world of social responsibility, of duties as contrasted with rights.

To put this in a way hinted at earlier, Melville is opposing two ethical systems, the natural and the social, and he makes the former as attractive as possible by his description of the relaxed informality aboard Captain Graveling's ship and by the "natural regality" of Billy, the representative of the natural. Unfortunately, Billy has outgrown the natural, although in his simplicity he does not understand that he has to make a choice—or better,

---

* [The Hayford-Sealts edition substitutes *Bellipotent* for *Indomitable* as the name of Vere's ship —Ed.]

[4] I would include the temptation scene as part of the plot rather than the story because it is inconsequential; Claggart does not refer to it when he accuses Billy and, on the level of the story, it results in no further action.

that by the mere fact[37] that he is twenty-one a choice has been made and that he has been placed in a social world where responsibilities must be accepted.

It might be instructive to compare the responses of students to both *Billy Budd* and *Walden*. I have found that students usually dislike *Walden* because (once we decide that Thoreau probably did not expect all mankind to settle by a pond) their good sense tells them that a society of individualists would be intolerable; if each man marches to his own drummer, each stumbles over the other. Yet they accept *Billy Budd*, failing to see that Billy instinctively follows Thoreau's advice—he settles issues that affect others on a purely personal basis. In a sense, we may read *Billy Budd* as Melville's final answer to Thoreau, Emerson, Paine, and in general to that whole strain of ultra-individualistic feeling that pervaded nineteenth-century American thought.

At the end Billy seems finally to accept his social responsibility, not passively (as is usually argued) but actively. Actually, for all his innocence, Billy is not a passive creature. When taunted loutishly on board the *Rights*, he strikes out at his tormentor; when accused falsely by Claggart, he again strikes out. He may not be subtle enough to detect covert harassment (as the incident of the bags and the episode at the mess show), but he is certainly a man who defends himself when he is unjustly imposed upon. Yet he does not lash out when Captain Vere tells him that he must hang. On the contrary, Melville does everything within his power to show that Billy accepts Vere's judgment, even to the point of guessing at what might have happened when Vere told Billy of his sentence after the court-martial: "Not without a sort of joy, indeed, he might have appreciated the brave opinion of him implied in his captain's making such a confidant of him" [p. 704]. Does Billy's joy come from his natural and personal response to the meeting of two individuals? Or does it come from his sensing that acceptance of Vere's jurisdiction has placed him within the social system? I do not know, and the sections of the text dealing with Billy help very little. Billy's final exclamation, "God bless Captain Vere" [p. 708], could support either alternative, although the fact that the crew echo it, and thereby affirm their allegiance to the Captain and through him to society, supports the second.

If I have been reading aright—in outline, if not in all details—what we have seen is a growing opposition of the values implicit in the story by those in the plot. The villain of the story is the naturally depraved Claggart, the hero the naturally good Billy; the[38] action of the story is designed to arouse our *natural* responses towards villains and heroes. But as the plot thickens we find just enough emotional correspondence between it and the story to help the latter along and to keep the reader reminded of his natural emotional reactions; additional elements of the plot seem calculated to evoke an unnatural, a *social*, response. Nowhere is this better illustrated than in the development of Captain Vere.

The story of Billy's hanging requires that Vere have certain characteristics, for not everyone has conviction enough to demand the death of an appealing and innocent young man. The story requires that Vere have a certain hardness, a certain stubbornness, and a quickness of judgment coupled with prudence. The plot gives Vere these qualities, but qualifies them in important ways. Vere is "always . . . mindful of the welfare of his men, but never tolerating an infraction of discipline" [p. 679]. His convictions are "settled," yet settled against a floodtide of opinion "which carried away as in a torrent . . . minds by nature not inferior to his own" [p. 680]. He is also "resolute" [p. 680] and "bluff" [p. 681]. If one reads the section on Vere quickly enough and wants to make a villain of him, one can conclude that Vere is a prejudiced, cowardly, and inhuman martinet—precisely the kind of man who would kill Billy. Yet each of the unfavorable traits is qualified. His prejudice is "disinterested" [p. 680] and comes from reading writers "free from cant and convention" [p. 680]; an officer who keeps discipline, yet is "mindful of the welfare of his men" is, I believe, an exceptionally fine officer; I shall say more about the cowardice later.

The implied adverse criticism of Vere is—and I believe this point is crucial—just sufficient to substantiate the value system implicit in the story. It is there simply because without it Vere would not be the man to demand Billy's death; without it, the story would be unconvincing. What is far more interesting is the material that is irrelevant to the story, the material that qualifies and perhaps even reverses our attitude towards Vere's severity. Perhaps I can summarize briefly by noting that the story requires a *Captain* Vere and all the military sternness of that rank; the story does not require a *Starry* Vere and all the intellectuality, dreaminess, and idealism suggested by *Starry*.

Actually, Melville works the plot very hard to make Starry Vere appealing; he must, because in terms of the story he is a villain. Since there is a great deal of controversy about the goodness or evil of Vere, I shall present the strongest evidence of Vere's essential[39] goodness before taking up the more dubious. Most obvious is Vere's conversation with Billy after the court-martial—the scene that Melville, in a sense, did not write. The usual argument at this point, that Billy is Christ and Vere Pilate, fails because Vere's decision to confront the condemned is most un-Pilate-like and because the specific biblical allusion is to Isaac and Abraham, the sacrificial son and the father mournfully going about what he believes is God's will. The Pilate analogy probably carries over from the trial scene, in which Vere convinces the jury that Billy must hang by appealing to expediency, much as Pilate acted expediently when he turned Jesus over to the mob. Yet here the analogy breaks down quickly. Vere does not refuse to judge; he insists upon judging, and even forces a judgment against the will of the court. And furthermore, Melville explicitly shows that Vere's own decision is not based on expediency. Vere ignores naval custom, Melville tells us, by appointing an officer of the Marines to the court because he thinks the officer "a judicious person, thoughtful, and not altogether incapable of grappling with a difficult case unprecedented in his prior experience," although Vere does have misgivings [p. 699]. Vere does understand that the case is beyond the experience of the usual officer, tries to choose the best court he can, but must settle for what he can get. When he argues his case, he is forced to present two distinct arguments. At first he tries to argue the moral issue, which, bluntly, is the difference between natural justice and social justice and the necessity of accepting the latter within the framework of society. Vere argues from expediency only after noticing that "the three men moved in their seats, less convinced than agitated. . . . Perceiving which, the speaker paused for a moment; then abruptly changing his tone, went on" [p. 702]. Vere clearly argues from expediency only as a last resort, only because his listeners understand no other argument. If the officers could have understood Vere's moral argument, Billy's hanging would have been unnecessary—the moral universe would be the social universe.

A number of other elements, major and minor, seem clearly designed to make Vere appealing. He quickly recognizes Claggart's evil and is as repelled by it as the reader is; he is equally quick in recognizing Billy's moral innocence. Generally, he is described as exceptional, as superior in all ways to his fellow officers.

With one exception, and with that exception we turn to the less obviously pro-Vere elements. The exception is the passage on Nelson, and the issue is whether Vere is compared or contrasted with[40] the great admiral. The problem is an important one, because the whole section on Nelson is totally irrelevant to the story except, if the purpose is to contrast, to prepare for Vere as villain by showing that he is not the man Nelson was. The telling passage is this: "it was thought that an officer like Nelson was the one, not indeed to terrorize the crew into base subjection, but to win them, by force of his mere presence and heroic personality, back to an allegiance if not as enthusiastic as his own yet as true" [p. 679]. It would seem, on the surface, that Vere does "terrorize the crew into base subjection," unless it be remembered that, with Billy in their hearts, they bless Vere after the hanging.[5] Furthermore, the quality that Melville seems to admire most in Nelson is his lack of "personal prudence" [p. 678], which Nelson proves by being shot down on the deck of his ship, just as Vere is. The obvious point, I believe, is that Vere compares favorably with "the greatest sailor since our world began" [p. 678].

At first sight, the fears of the surgeon concerning Vere's sanity would seem at least as damaging as the comparison with Nelson, but again the difficulties not only vanish when placed in their proper light, but the incident puts Vere in even a better position. The surgeon, who we are told is "as yet unapprised of the antecedents," was profoundly discomposed and wondered if Vere were "unhinged" [p. 698]. This seems damning, especially since a surgeon would be the most likely person to assess Vere's sanity; but Melville is at great pains to inform us that the surgeon is incapable of understanding. He, not Vere, is like Pilate, for despite his conviction of Vere's guilt he does not act. Immediately thereafter we learn that few dare to pronounce on a man's sanity except professional experts "for a fee" [p. 698]. The surgeon, clearly, is not a man to be trusted. Later the surgeon and the purser discuss Billy's stillness at the moment of the hanging; the surgeon doubts anything that is not scientific, which is another way of saying that he has no moral understanding, which is another way of saying that he is the person least qualified to express judgment on any moral issue. Actually, the whole tone of the conversation between the surgeon and the purser shows the latter's complete obtuseness and perhaps thereby insists on Vere's sanity, especially since Melville has told us that Vere and Billy share "in the rarer qualities of our nature—so rare indeed as to be all but incredible to average minds however much cultivated" [p. 704].[41]

Even though the bulk of the plot material relating to Vere either clearly or indirectly presents him as an ideal, the final meaning of *Billy Budd* is not the simple acceptance of Vere and the social morality he represents. To show the complexity both of Melville's acceptance and of his technique, I shall retell the story once more, and then repeat it, the second time emphasizing the elements of the plot. The story is that a young sailor, impressed aboard a British man-o'-war, incurs the unmotivated enmity of one of the crew, is falsely accused by him, kills him in a flash of instinctive anger, and is tried and hanged. The story, along with those elements of the plot which support it, especially the many allusions to Billy's natural innocence and Claggart's natural depravity, recognizes that evil exists in the world and that it is powerful enough to destroy the good; the story is bleakly pessimistic.

The plot, though, is a different matter. Baby Budd, who has just reached the age of manhood, is forced to go from the *Rights-of-Man* to His Majesty's Ship the *Bellipotent*, commanded by Edward (guardian of the realm) Fairfax (fair facts) Vere (truth, manliness). Baby Budd is tempted by the serpent; although he does not yield to the temptation, he does yield to his naive (primitive, natural) nature by refusing to act responsibly. He is accused of a crime of which he is not guilty (a formal, "social" mutiny; he is guilty of a private mutiny), and kills the accuser-tempter-serpent. The Captain forces a court-martial and accuses Baby Budd of the right crime—failure to accept his social responsibility—but is forced to punish him for the technical crime because of the limited understanding of his officers. Billy is eventually executed, and Vere is mortally wounded in a successful engagement with the *Athée* (the Atheist). Is it too much to suggest that the battle with the *Athée* is an externalization of Vere's personal engagement with Billy? Billy, after all,

---

[5] The difficulty here might result from the unfinished state of the manuscript of *Billy Budd*.

is a creature of the *Rights-of-Man*, a ship named after a book written in defense of the French Revolution. If so, then Billy, like the French Revolution, is an instance of the impossibility of translating an ideal morality into a less than ideal social world.

The opposition between the story and the major elements of the plot, then, embodies the conflict in Melville's own mind between the claims of natural moral law and social law; and further, the growing attention he gave to Vere as the manuscript grew and the sheer bulk and importance of those plot elements that run counter[42] to the thematic implications of the story show that Melville was forced—reluctantly, regretfully, and even painfully—to the realization that man, because he must live in the social world, must abide by its laws.[43]

The "Ineludible Gripe" of Billy Budd*

ROBERT ROGERS

> Melville could not conceal
> Guilt he could not utter;
> So Billy Budd must stutter.
>
> R. W. STALLMAN

No visible blemish mars the masculine beauty of Melville's Handsome Sailor. Billy Budd's only noticeable flaw is an occasional "vocal defect," a stutter which develops "under sudden provocation of strong heart—feeling."[1] Melville regards this defect as "a striking instance that the arch interferer, the envious marplot of Eden, still has more or less to do with every human consignment to this planet." In mentioning Billy's defect Melville contrasts it to the visible blemish which appears in the shape of a tiny hand on Georgiana's cheek in Hawthorne's story, "The Birthmark." A passage in that story, one which Melville had underlined in his own copy of *Mosses from an Old Manse*, describes the birthmark as "the fatal flaw of humanity" which Nature stamps on all her productions, a crimson hand expressing "the ineludible gripe in which mortality clutches the highest and purest of earthly mould."

That Billy ranks as one of the highest and purest of earthly mould need not be labored. That the vocal defect confers humanity on an otherwise almost too-perfect character, much as Prince Myshkin's epilepsy functions in Dostoevsky's *Idiot*, need not be labored either. And that Billy's fatal flaw serves admirably in making the Christ-like sailor's murderous blow to the Master-at-Arms' head seems plausible is obvious enough. Yet why should the flaw take the curious form of a stutter, an incongruous sort of fault in a noble hero? Imagine Hamlet mumbling, "T-t-to be, or n-n-not to be—that is the q-question." Perhaps some deeper significance of the stutter outweighs the problem of incongruity. Perhaps, too, the stutter symbolizes more than Georgiana's blemish, which carries no hint of moral imperfection such as is conveyed by Melville's intimation that Satan has placed his mark on Billy.[2] That the vocal defect does in fact betray a moral flaw in the seemingly so innocent sailor is a major premise of this paper. This "ineludible gripe" represents a passion which inexorably grips all men who struggle for selfhood and autonomy, and[9] its significance provides the key to a fuller appreciation of this complex and ambiguous novel.

Ambiguous? Is it not about good and evil, about The Fall, about the temporal impotence (though ultimate triumph) of the truly innocent in the hands of the iniquitous?

---

* From *Literature and Psychology*, XIV (Winter 1964), 9–22. Reprinted by permission of the editor and the author.

[1] Though originally based on the F. Barron Freeman text of *Billy Budd* (*Melville's Billy Budd*, Cambridge: Harvard University Press, 1948), this paper has been checked with care at all relevant points against the painstaking new edition by Harrison Hayford and Merton M. Sealts, Jr. (University of Chicago Press, 1962), which supersedes all previous ones.

[2] Simon O. Lesser, in his admirable analysis of Hawthorne's tale in *Fiction and the Unconscious* (New York: Vintage Books, 1962), pp. 87–98, notes that the crimson hand symbolizes sexuality.

That may be. But if the reader, after satisfying himself on this score, later examines the many conflicting lucubrations lavished on *Billy Budd* by that hardy breed, The Melville Scholar, he may then feel as helpless to unravel the tangled critical strands as is the naive Captain Amasa Delano in "Benito Cereno" to untie the symbolic knot tossed him by the old Spanish sailor, a Gordian knot that looks to Delano like "a combination of double-bowline-knot, treble-crow-knot, back-handed-well-knot, knot-in-and-out-knot, and jamming-knot." Captain Delano does not even know there's a problem; at least the reader of commentary on *Billy Budd* will be aware that certain nagging questions have been asked. Is Billy innocent? If so, is the novel a tragedy? Or a tragedy manquée? Or a satire? Is the novel a great work or merely an "impressive last word . . . unevenly written . . . more a postscript than a testament," as Harry Levin claims?[3] Is Captain Vere a wise, just man, regretfully doing his duty—or a mad martinet? Is Claggart a latent homosexual, and if so, does it matter? Does the novel represent Melville's "testament of acceptance" or the final, slashing, ironic rejoinder in his perpetual quarrel with God?

Lawrence Thompson espouses the last view. Having discovered irony, and that Melville sometimes uses it, Professor Thompson decides that the "stupid" narrator fails to comprehend his own story; that Billy is "stupid"; that Vere is "inexcusably stupid" and ultimately as evil as Claggart; that Billy's responses to the evils of human experience are viewable as "amusing, ridiculous, pathetic, but never tragic"; and that the book stands as "a bitter comedy, in the satiric tradition of Lucian and Voltaire and Tom Paine"—a long, subtle, insidious allegorical *tour de force* calculated to mock gullible Christians.[4]

Of the more ambitious interpretations, the only other one to be considered in any detail here is the sensitive, insightful,[10] always interesting analysis of the late Richard Chase, who claims that "the real theme of *Billy Budd* is castration and cannibalism, the ritual murder and eating of the Host." Chase regards the novel as a brilliant piece of writing which unfortunately falls far short of the pure tragedy that Melville presumably meant it to be. Billy is a hero manqué. An "hermaphrodite Christ" and "beatified child," he seeks his own castration, "desiring to yield up his vitality to an authoritative but kindly father, whom he finds in Captain Vere." Because of Billy's fatal passivity, Chase thinks, we must look on Captain Vere as the true tragic hero of the work—insofar as it attains to tragedy at all.[5]

Chase's mythic—psychoanalytic approach provides a useful point of departure for the attempt in this paper to demonstrate that Billy does in fact fulfill the classic Aristotelian requirements for the tragic hero: in brief, that he be a morally imperfect though basically good man of noble or heroic stature, possessed of *hubris*, who precipitates his downfall by his own actions. The present discussion assumes, by the way, that *Billy Budd* is no more a "hideous intolerable allegory" than is *Moby Dick*, even though Melville's prodigally allusive pen compares his Handsome Sailor to such heroes as Apollo, Hercules, Achilles, Hyperion, Adam, and Christ. It further assumes the presence of multiple levels of meaning and the legitimacy of various critical approaches, though the psychoanalytic receives the most emphasis.

To view Billy as a conventional hero is to assume that he takes a tragic stance—that he maintains a typical posture with respect to the gods or the idea of moral order in the universe. Therefore it is crucial that all conflict in *Billy Budd* relates to the concepts of law, order, and authority. If the archetypal repository of authority is the father, then we must heed the pervasive search-for-the-father motif in Melville's writing, the presence of which

---

[3] *The Power of Blackness* (New York: Vintage Books, 1960), p. 194.

[4] *Melville's Quarrel with God* (Princeton University Press, 1952), pp. 356-357 and 384.

[5] *Herman Melville* (New York: Macmillan, 1949), pp. 258-277.

may be accounted for partly because Allan Melville died when his son was only thirteen years old. Newton Arvin considers this occurrence the most dire and decisive event in Herman Melville's early life and says that the author "was to spend much of his life divided between the attempt to retaliate upon his father for this abandonment and the attempt, a still more passionate one, to recover the closeness and confidence of[11] happy sonhood." *Pierre* furnishes one biographical parallel: the hero's father dies when Pierre is twelve. The protagonist of the more autobiographical *Redburn*, having heard that sea captains are "fathers to their crew . . . severe and chastising fathers, fathers whose sense of duty overcomes the sense of love [like Captain Vere]," responds to Captain Riga's initial friendliness with "tenderness and love," only to find himself rejected by Riga after the ship puts to sea. Redburn's obsession to retrace his father's footsteps in Liverpool by the aid of an old guidebook provides the most transparent example of this theme in Melville. F. O. Matthiessen offers a compelling statement of the theme as it appears in *Billy Budd* when he compares the relationship of Vere and Billy with the story of Abraham's willingness to sacrifice Isaac: "Here the search for a father, if latent in all Melville's Ishmaels, and in all the questings of his homeless spirit for authority, is enacted in an elemental pattern. . . . If Billy is young Adam before the Fall, and Claggart is almost the Devil Incarnate, Vere is the wise Father, terribly severe but righteous."[6]

Vere is not the only father surrogate in the novel, however. With a Protean-like dexterity Melville sketches a veritable pageant of them, the father appearing in no less than eight different guises. Captain Graveling, the aging "ploughman of the troubled waters" who skippers the *Rights-of-Man* from which Billy is impressed, functions as a gentle father who, during Billy's presence aboard, governs a "happy family" on the *Rights*. On *H. M. S. Indomitable* [the *Bellipotent* in the Hayford and Sealts edition], the ancient, wizened, gruff old Dansker manifests a streak of "patriarchal irony touching Billy's youth and athletic frame"; he persistently refers to Billy as "Baby Budd"; and he serves as an advisor by warning him that "Jemmy Legs" Claggart is "down" on him. The Chaplain, both as man and priest, plays a paternal role. He comes to Billy as he lies manacled on the gun deck, looking like "a slumbering child in the cradle," and after endeavoring to minister to the "young barbarian's" spiritual needs—an act ironically gratuitous for the Christ-like Billy—the Chaplain stoops over to kiss the sailor's cheek with paternal gentleness. Though Billy does not come in contact with him, Admiral Nelson, who is transferred to the *Theseus* after her participation in the Great Mutiny on the theory that his charisma[12] will win over the disgruntled sailors, represents an idealized nautical patriarch. The ample attention that critics have accorded to Captain Vere's paternal relation to Billy makes further comment unnecessary, though it might be noted in passing that Vere is "old enough to have been Billy's father," speaks to him in a "fatherly tone," and as Captain of the ship represents a higher father, His Majesty the King. One need not belabor, on the religious and psychological levels, how God fulfills the role of Father. Finally, John Claggart figures to some extent as a father by virtue of the authority vested in him as Master-at-Arms, a minor officer in the service of the King.

That this extraordinary multiplication of father imagoes is fraught with significance will be clear only in the light of Billy's relationship to them. He obviously views such men as the old Dansker with filial respect and devotion. But how does he relate to the father as an embodiment of authority? Is he rebellious or loyal? The consensus of critical opinion represents him as completely loyal. Newton Arvin, for example, says that "Billy is no rebel against divine justice, and he is not guilty, even symbolically, of disobeying some transcendent will. He is an unwitting, impulsive offender against the Mutiny Act."[7] For Milton

[6] *American Renaissance* (New York: Oxford University Press, 1941), p. 509.

[7] *Herman Melville* (New York: The Viking Press, 1957), p. 297.

R. Stern, Billy is "the childlike barbarian, the pure creature whose only experience is just the experience of his own inner purity and idealism."[8] E. L. Grant Watson insists that in his last novel Melville is no longer a rebel, arguing that Billy has not, "even under the severest provocation, any element of rebellion in him."[9] The defenders of Billy's innocence, after discussing his ingenuous, naive, and virgin heart, invariably quote the statement he makes during the court-martial: "I have eaten the King's bread and I am true to the King." The advocates of Billy's innocence at the critical bar never tire of pleading that he is Christ-like, that he is Adam before the Fall, and that—as Melville states—he has "not yet been proffered the questionable apple of knowledge"—ignoring the fact that the last quotation refers in context to Billy's illiteracy and that in the same paragraph Melville declares that while Billy shows no trace "of the wisdom of the serpent" he nevertheless is not "yet quite a dove." On the other hand, the attorneys for the prosecution[13] adduce little evidence in support of their brief that Billy should be considered a rebel. They assume it. They do not substantiate it.[10]

If Billy is entirely innocent, then the rebel who bulks so large in Melville's other works is conspicuous by his absence in this one. Where are the Tommos, Tajis, Pierres, Steelkilts, Ahabs, Jack Chases, and White Jackets, all of whom—like Melville himself in real life—are deserters or mutineers or both, in fact or in wish? (White Jacket, for instance, is ready to murder Captain Claret rather than submit to being flogged, and Ishmael's "splintered heart and maddened hand" are turned against "the wolfish world.") Certainly Claggart, as an allegorical Satan, cannot fill the role of rebel in *Billy Budd* as some commentators seem to believe. Structural and other considerations, among them that Claggart is not the protagonist, forbid it. No. Only Billy can be the rebel. Only he is accused. Only he is punished. Only he can be guilty. And we know he is guilty. His stutter, amounting to a *lapsus linguae*, betrays him, for the stutterer's tongue involuntarily conspires with his psychic censor to block the expression of hostility.[11]

Most of the critics politely ignore Billy's stutter. The only one to point out its hostile implications is Richard Chase, and he, recognizing the fact that the stutterer represses his impulses out of castration fear, ends by stressing *the act of repression* rather than *what is repressed*, with the result that Billy is seen as "fatally passive," the hermaphroditic Christ[14] submissive to his fate. If it can be demonstrated that Billy's "ineludible gripe" does reflect hostility, however, the reader will then perceive that Billy conforms to the role of the rebellious tragic hero.

That he does repress unconscious hostility can easily be seen when the only three occurrences of stuttering in the novel are correlated, a task no one has undertaken. In each episode someone challenges Billy's submissiveness to authority. In every case his stutter

---

[8] *The Fine Hammered Steel of Herman Melville* (Urbana: University of Illinois Press, 1957), p. 26.

[9] "Melville's Testament of Acceptance," in *Melville's Billy Budd and the Critics*, ed. William T. Stafford (San Francisco: Wadsworth, 1961), p. 76.

[10] Hayford and Sealts do show that the earliest draft of the ballad about Billy (out of which the novel grew) indicates that he was originally conceived to be guilty of rebellion (pp. 3–4). Later elaborations of the story translate this guilt from the realm of action to that of thought or wish.

[11] There are, to be sure, many other theories of the etiology of stuttering in the literature of aphasia, and no doubt the phenomenon can result from more than one cause; the psychoanalytic theory is adopted here as a working hypothesis. According to Otto Fenichel (see *The Psychoanalytic Theory of Neurosis* [New York: W. W. Norton & Co., Inc., 1945], pp. 311–317), stuttering is a conversion symptom "exacerbated in the presence of prominent or authoritative persons, that is, paternal figures against whom the unconscious hostility is most intense." When a patient is particularly eager to prove a point, he has concealed behind his apparent zeal "a hostile or sadistic tendency to destroy his opponent by means of words, and the stuttering is both the blocking of and the punishment for this tendency." Fenichel also remarks that when occasional (as distinct from habitual) stuttering "occurs regularly as a response to a specific stimulus, knowledge of the stimulus can be used as a starting point for an analysis of the disturbing factor." Billy, be it noted, stutters only occasionally and then only under specific circumstances, as will be shown.

betrays repressed hostility, specifically toward the King and by extension toward God and other parental figures. The first instance takes place when the afterguardsman, a "catspaw" for Claggart, tries to implicate Billy in mutiny by offering him money. Even though he fails to comprehend the situation, Billy recoils in disgust from the overture and threatens to throw the sailor overboard, in which connection it should be borne in mind that what matters psychologically is not the nature of an idea or action so much as the amount of psychic energy with which it is invested. In this case Billy feels the mere imputation of disloyalty to be an overwhelming threat. The second instance of stuttering occurs when an authoritarian figure, the Master-at-Arms, challenges Billy's loyalty in the presence of a higher authority and father figure, Captain Vere, who in turn represents still higher authority, the King, with the tragic result that Billy's inability to articulate his denial verbally causes him to express it physically with the fatal blow to Claggart's skull. The third and last time Billy stutters is in court just after he affirms that he is true to the King. When Captain Vere says with suppressed emotion, "I believe you, my man," Billy replies, "God will bless you for that, your honor," stammering as he speaks. Again, the authoritarian context is manifest.

Melville tells us that Billy stutters "under sudden provocation of strong heart-feeling." That the impediment crops up under very special circumstances, depending on the kind of stress involved, is corroborated by Melville's assertion that "in the hour of elemental uproar or peril Billy is everything a sailor should be." In the execution scene, a specific instance of what must be called strong heart-feeling but where the question of loyalty to authority no longer obtains (having in effect been answered by the sentence of the court martial), Billy issues at the penultimate moment his dying benediction: "God bless Captain Vere!" Melville emphasizes the fact that Billy's words are "*wholly unobstructed in the utterance*" (stress added). In fact,[15] Billy's articulation at this fateful moment is so perfect that the syllables are described as "delivered in the clear melody of a singing-bird on the point of launching from the twig." Thus Billy stutters *only* when his castration anxiety is mobilized by the insinuation that he hates authority. His antagonism is unconscious. Like Oedipus, he denies with vehemence his deepest longings.

A full understanding of the complex role of authority in the novel requires insight into Claggart's "Pale ire, envy, and despair," the phrase from *Paradise Lost* which Melville so artfully applies to Claggart's malady, his "depravity according to nature." To comprehend this depravity we must perceive Claggart's emotional relationship to both Billy and Captain Vere, and to do this requires some knowledge of the nature of homosexuality.[12]

Few critics mention Claggart's homosexuality. Those who do tend to slight it or else deny it, alleging that the words "the depravity here meant partakes nothing of the sordid or sensual" prove the absence of any sexual pathology. Not necessarily. The quotation indicates only the absence of any *overt* pathology and possibly shows Melville's unawareness of the underlying sexual problem. More important, it points to Claggart's own lack of awareness. The essence of his sickness lies in his elaborate paranoid defenses against his sexual impulses, not in the impulses themselves; in other words, his remedy is worse than his disease. Because of these paranoid defenses he cannot possibly understand his own depravity. In fact, there is no reason to doubt that Claggart really believes Billy to be a mutineer and that he tempts Billy through the offices of the afterguardsman not to "frame" him but in order to verify his own smoldering (paranoid) suspicions.

Melville provides ample textual evidence of Claggart's homosexual orientation (one

---

[12] The involved problem of Melville's psychosexual orientation lies outside the scope of this paper. Suffice it to say for the moment that if Melville tends to praise masculine beauty more often than feminine, he unquestionably rejects effeminacy, as scrutiny of the magnificent lyrical interlude in *Moby Dick* entitled "The Tail" confirms beyond doubt.

which, by the way, he seems to share with a number of other notable literary villains, such as Shakespeare's Iago, Dostoevsky's Smerdyakov, Mann's Cipolla, and Faulkner's Jason Compson). Despite the profound ambiguity of style Melville uses when discussing the Master-at-Arms, Claggart emerges as physically effeminate, as the sobriquet "Jemmy Legs" (O. E. D.: "dandified, foppish, effeminate") corroborates. Melville[16] hints at "something defective or abnormal in the constitution and blood." Submissive to authority, Claggart shows "a certain austere patriotism" and behaves with great obsequiousness to Captain Vere. He avoids wine, which might endanger his defenses. He looks at the handsome Billy with a melancholy expression,

. . . his eyes strangely suffused with incipient feverish tears. . . . Yes, and sometimes the melancholy expression would have in it a touch of soft yearning, as if Claggart could even have loved Billy but for fate and ban.

His paranoia damns him more than anything else: he makes "ogres of trifles," as when he thinks Billy spilled the soup on purpose; and in contrast to Billy's feeble intellect and large heart Claggart reveals the paranoid's desperate reliance on reason, though Melville, not without humor, leaves it an open question whether he suffers from "mania in the brain or rabies of the heart."[13] Thus Melville shows deep insight in remarking that Claggart employs reason "as an ambidexter implement for effecting the irrational." A look at two of Claggart's prototypes further substantiates the presence of a homosexual syndrome. Bland, the "neat and gentlemanly villain" in *White Jacket*, breaks his biscuit with a dainty hand, possesses a "wickedly delicate" mouth and a "snaky black eye," and shuns all indelicacy, such as swearing.[14] Jackson, the villain in *Redburn*, is a "clever, cunning man" with a "cold, and snaky, and deadly" eye who appears to be fond of boys. Though he tries to tyrannize over others, he befriends the handsome orphaned young Lancashire lad; but when the boy instinctively shrinks from him, Jackson's love changes to hatred. Exactly the same thing "happens" on the *Indomitable*: Claggart envies and therefore desires Billy's beauty; he recognizes the healthiness and robustness of Billy's masculinity and therefore despairs of possessing it; and he responds to what amounts to a rejection of his advances with "pale ire."

Theories on the etiology of homosexuality abound. Inversion may, of course, result from different causes or a combination of them. In any case, a substantial body of professional opinion holds that the problem of identification is basic.[15] The[17] absence of a suitable father figure with whom to identify (as in broken homes; or when the father dies early; or when the father is himself too passive and feminine; or when the mother is too dominating) may precipitate a feminine orientation in the male child. A similarly faulty identification may result if the father be so tyrannical that the child in effect castrates himself by adopting a passive, propitiating, and sexually feminine role. Seen in this connection, the multiplication of father figures and the manner in which Billy relates to them become highly significant.

Thus far Billy and Claggart have been discussed as though they were separate and autonomous psychological entities, that is, two separate people. In fact, they are *alter egos*, and at one level they may be regarded as two sides of a composite character. Billy and Claggart as fictional representatives of these two sides of a "decomposed" single character

---

[13] Freeman edition, chapter XII, deleted in the Hayford and Sealts edition.

[14] Hayford and Sealts (pp. 31–32) suggest that Melville based Bland on a corrupt Master-at-Arms (described by William McNally in *Evils and Abuses in the Naval and Merchant Service* [Boston: 1839]) named Sterritt, who was castrated by his shipmates.

[15] See, for one instance, Charles Berg and Clifford Allen, *The Problem of Homosexuality* (New York: Citadel Press, 1958), esp. pp. 46 ff.

engage in a sort of sexual dialectic or *agon*, a veiled but dramatic struggle between the normal and abnormal. In terms of their psychological kinship, both are sons to Captain Vere. One infers the existence of this relationship on several grounds: first, psychological (complementary sexual orientations to the father); second, allegorical (Claggart-Satan, the Bad Angel of God; Billy-Christ-Adam, the Good Angel of God); third, relation to authority (Captain Vere as father to all of his crew); fourth, the mystery common to both their backgrounds (the "family romance"); fifth, the complementary nature of most of their attributes (e.g., Claggart as head, Billy as heart). Finally, both are as sons to Jacob. As he speaks before the mainmast, Claggart regards Captain Vere with "a look such as might have been that of the spokesman of the envious children of Jacob deceptively imposing upon the troubled patriarch the blood-dyed coat of young Joseph," that is, Vere is Jacob, Billy is Joseph, and Claggart one of his brothers. While Richard Chase—and only Chase—perceives that Claggart and Billy are sons to Vere, he reverses their psychological relationship to him, stating that Claggart assumes the aggressive and hostile role of the father and Billy the passive one of the mother. Quite the opposite is true, as the following discussion will bear out.

The crucial accusation scene in Captain Vere's cabin dramatizes the psycho-sexual dialectic between Claggart and Billy. Claggart's indictment, if false on the story level, is ironically[18] true on the symbolic level. Rightly surmising the rebellion lurking behind Billy's placid exterior, Claggart charges him with it. He accuses Billy not of any old crime but of the only one Billy can possibly be guilty of. In effect he says to Vere, "I am your good, loyal, passive, obedient, submissive son, but Billy is your rebellious sexual rival, a potential parricide and mutineer." To be sure, Claggart appears aggressive enough in this scene, for his thwarted lust has turned to hostility; but it is directed at his *alter ego*, not at his father, toward whom he is passive. Accused of rebellion, Billy predictably manifests acute castration anxiety—precisely the appropriate, normal response. He stands like one "impaled and gagged." His face, "a crucifixion to behold," reminds Vere of a schoolmate whom he had seen "struck by much the same startling impotence." Billy's expression resembles "that of a condemned vestal priestess in the moment of being buried alive, and in the first struggle against suffocation." Yet it must be insisted that while gagging, suffocation, and fear of being buried alive may represent fear of castration as Chase points out, it does not necessarily follow that a person who endures castration anxiety—a universal phenomenon—desires castration or considers himself impotent. In this scene, furthermore, Billy reveals his virile power through action, while Claggart succumbs without resistance, static and symbolically limp in death. Billy's arm, "quick as the flame from a discharged cannon at night," proves potent enough. The assertion that lifting Claggart's "spare," "flexible," "inert" body is "like handling a dead snake" demonstrates beyond doubt that it is Claggart who figures as the flaccid, impotent, castrated son, not Billy.

But since Billy's blow unveils his repressed antipathy for authority, he is guilty and must be punished. Therefore "the father in him" which Vere has thus far "manifested toward Billy" is "replaced by the military disciplinarian." This disposition predominates until the court condemns Billy, after which time Vere reverts to his role as the tender, compassionate father. The affection between Vere and Billy during this period symbolizes the peaceful father-son love which follows the resolution of Oedipal conflict.[16][19]

Doubts as to Billy's masculinity which have confounded critics relate not only to his apparent passivity but to the feminine imagery, especially the flower metaphors, which

---

[16] Allowing for the indifference of primary process "thinking" toward considerations of time, space, and logical consistency, there seems to be no reason why Billy should be regarded at all times during the "story" as a simple, unchanging psychological entity; therefore he can be conceived as depicted variously at the pre-Oedipal, Oedipal, and post-Oedipal stages of psychic development.

Melville often uses to describe him. Besides according him a symbolic surname, Melville refers to Billy as a "bud." His "as yet" smooth face has a complexion "feminine in purity," though "the lily" is suppressed and "the rose" struggles to show through the tan. His position aboard the *Indomitable* is "analogous to that of a rustic beauty" from the provinces now in competition with "the high-born dames of court." Such attributes should not beget confusion. Melville, who remarks in *Moby Dick* that "real strength never impairs beauty or harmony, but it often bestows it," frequently uses sexual imagery without respect to gender to show these qualities. In taking note of Melville's sexual imagery, we must always remember to distinguish between the *effeminate*, which Billy is not, and the *feminine*, which in some ways he is, and we must regard such imagery in the light of the total context of the work. If Melville does not want us to make such distinctions, why else does he go out of his way to establish that Billy is not sexually innocent, that in fact he frolics on "fiddler's green" along with the rest of his sex-starved shipmates? And why does he insist on Billy's prowess at boxing and wrestling? Why call him "an upright barbarian"? Why have him trounce "Red Whiskers" aboard the *Rights-of-Man?* Why repeatedly compare him to such as Hercules?

To recapitulate the main points so far, the *hubris* of the tragic hero in Billy, who is not so innocent as he seems, is revealed by his stutter, which manifests itself only on occasions when his loyalty is impugned. Billy's role as the normal son in the Oedipal phase of development, the son who rebels instead of submitting, is confirmed by the presence of a contrasting counterpart in Claggart, the feminine, submissive son whose death is a symbolic sexual victory for Billy.

Besides being the rebellious, masculine-oriented son on the psychological level, Billy conforms to the role of the tragic hero in other ways. For one thing, he shares with the hero his mysterious birth, the myth of unknown royal or noble parents—known psychoanalytically as the "family romance." Instead of the archetype's customary dual set of parents, one high-born and one humble, Billy possesses a number of fathers, both high and low; no mothers appear. The original prose fragment which evolved into *Billy Budd* bears out the relative importance of this feature, for it describes Billy as possessing "a frame and natural[20] carriage indicating a lineage contradicting his lot." Billy's response, "God knows, Sir," to the question, "Who was your father?" if taken literally tends to establish him as the son of God at both the religious and mythic levels, reinforcing the allegorical role of Billy as Christ. In any event, Melville informs us that noble descent is "as evident in him as in a blood horse," and that as a foretopman he belongs to the aristocratic elite of the sailors aboard ship.

The Handsome Sailor accepts the homage of his shipmates "with no perceptible trace of the vainglorious" but rather with "the off-hand unaffectedness of natural regality." Although Billy seems here to lack the arrogance of the tragic hero, some evidence of *hubris* in him, besides that inherent in the symbolic crime of striking a superior, is revealed by his reaction to corporal punishment. He feels "horrified" while watching a flogging, so much so that he resolves he will never make himself liable for such punishment. While Billy's resolve seems natural, the intensity of his concern suggests a physical and spiritual pride so great that he could never submit to such a punishment, that he would rebel—like White Jacket—before submitting to the lash.

The historical elements of the novel lend further support to the idea that Billy is a rebel. Melville presents the political background of the story in such a way as to indicate that mutiny may be justifiable under certain circumstances, that rebellion may be good as well as evil. In fact he concludes the first paragraph of the supposed preface to the tale (a section deleted by Hayford and Sealts) by saying with implied approval that "some thinkers regard the outcome of the French Revolution to be a political advance along nearly the whole line for Europeans." Appropriately then, Vere is politically conservative; Billy is symbolically impressed from the *Rights-of-Man*; and Vere remarks that the "last Assizes" will acquit Billy for his violation of the Mutiny Act.

Finally, Melville solemnly advises us that his protagonist's vocal defect "should be evidence not alone that he is not presented as a conventional hero, but also that the story in which he is the main figure is no romance." While this assertion may only mean that Billy is not the faultless hero of the old romances, it may also imply that Melville intended to write a tragedy and that he associated Billy's stutter with the conventional flaw of the tragic hero.[21]

Many levels of meaning in this novel may now be seen to coalesce. On the psychological plane the story embodies the rebellion of the basically good but morally imperfect autonomous self, the natural conflict of father and son, and the antinomies of homosexual and heterosexual orientation; on the theological, man against the God who created him imperfect, to dwell in an imperfect world; on the political, man against the social order when order proves tyrannous; on the metaphysical, man against the chill clutch of circumstance. So long as no rigid, one-to-one correspondence at all points between all levels of meaning be demanded, harmony can be found between the layers of tension in *Billy Budd*. And some of the problems of the work vanish. Billy is both innocent and guilty. Vere is good, yet the righteous and authoritarian administrator of a necessarily arbitrary and limited code of order. As for genre, the work can only be a tragedy.

A huge manila hawser when under sufficient tension parts at the stroke of a sharp knife as easily as a feeble thread. Billy, though essentially genial and restrained under normal conditions, breaks out of control when provoked beyond endurance and thereby succumbs to the ineludible gripe of his imperfect nature. His apparent Apollonian calm should not beguile us into ignoring his hidden Dionysian rage. His story represents the ritual, not of the Eucharist, but of the familiar dying god—the scapegoat hero who acts out our universal guilt in his rebellion, like Prometheus or Oedipus or Hamlet, and through whose punishment we are all purged of that guilt. In presenting Billy's story Melville not only succeeds in writing the nearest thing to classic Aristotelian tragedy in all of American literature, he fashions his tale in so extraordinary a manner that if, as Keats suggests, the excellence of every art is its intensity, then the "last Assizes" of criticism must judge *Billy Budd* a work of genius on the grounds of its richly ambiguous texture; its psychological profundity; its allegorical bravura; and its mythic range and universality, that is, the general sense of being in touch with the ultimate rhythms of life which reading conveys.[22]

Innocence and Infamy

RICHARD CHASE

Melville's last book, a short novel written between 1888 and 1891 and called *Billy Budd, Foretopman*, has generally been praised for qualities it does not possess. It is natural, of course, to wish to see in *Billy Budd* the last ripe word of the aged Melville. And there has been a great temptation, especially on the liberal-religious left, to see in *Billy Budd*, as one writer says, Melville's final "testament of acceptance"—his final acceptance of a "tragic" view of life involving an apotheosis of the common man as Christ and an assertion that what is needed in American life is a leavening of individualism and law by the sympathetic passions of the heart. And *Billy Budd* is said to be Melville's definitive moral statement. But this estimate of *Billy Budd* will do our author no service if, as I think, the moral situation in the book is deeply equivocal.

In Melville's writings there are two basic kinds of hero, both akin, in their several variations, to the central figure of Prometheus. The first kind of hero is the false Prometheus, who in one way or another violates the deep-running, natural, and psychic rhythms of life which are necessary for all creative enterprise. The second kind of hero is the Handsome Sailor: the true hero in whom Prometheus tends to put on the full tragic manhood of Oedipus. This second kind of hero is briefly sketched or symbolized as Marnoo, Jack Chase, Bulkington, and Ethan Allen. In each case, he is a full-statured man, great in body, heart, and intellect, a man with great pain of experience behind him, a young man, but still so fully created a man that, in the case of Jack Chase, Ishmael is moved to call him "sire." At the beginning of *Billy Budd*, the Handsome Sailor is again symbolized, in the following manner:

> In the time before steamships, or then more frequently than now, a stroller along the docks of any considerable seaport would occasionally[258] have his attention arrested by a group of bronzed mariners, man-of-war's men or merchant sailors in holiday attire ashore on liberty. In certain instances, they would flank, or, like a bodyguard, quite surround some superior figure of their own class, moving along with them like Aldebaran among the lesser lights of his constellation. That signal object was the "Handsome Sailor" of the less prosaic time, alike of the military and merchant navies. With no perceptible trace of the vain-glorious about him, rather with the off-hand unaffectedness of natural regality, he seemed to accept the spontaneous homage of his shipmates. A somewhat remarkable instance recurs to me. In Liverpool, now half a century ago I saw under the shadow of the great dingy street-wall of Prince's Dock (an obstruction long since removed) a common sailor, so intensely black that he must needs have been a native African of the unadulterate blood of Ham. A symmetric figure, much above the average height. The two ends of a gay silk handkerchief thrown loose about the neck danced upon the displayed ebony of his chest; in his ears were big hoops of gold, and a Scotch Highland bonnet with a tartan band set off his shapely head.

The emblem of Lucy Tartan enlightens the forehead of the Handsome Sailor as he emerges from the depths of Night into the consciousness of Day. He moves as ponderously,

---

* Reprinted by permission of The Macmillan Company from HERMAN MELVILLE: A CRITICAL STUDY by Richard Chase. Copyright 1949 by Richard Chase.

but with as much strength and beauty, as Bulkington in *Moby-Dick*, or as revolutionary America itself, setting forth on the path of civilization.

Still, this magnificent and momentous figure does not appear at full scale in any of Melville's books. But Melville made two attempts to portray him fully: one in *Pierre* and one in *Billy Budd*. Not the least part of the wisdom which Melville had achieved at the end of *Pierre* was his realization that he could not portray this heroic figure, except as a perpetual adolescent whose suicide was entirely justified by the fact that he was no match for the realities of the world. At the end of *Pierre*, civilization was shown to be in the hands of conventional society, military power, and Laodicean liberalism. In *Billy Budd* civilization is shown to be in approximately the same hands. And the hero who opposes these forces is no more capable of doing so than Pierre.

Yet *Billy Budd* is a brilliant piece of writing, nicely constructed and balanced between swift, stark action and moral-philosophical comment. Though it falls sadly short of the pure tragedy Melville[259] apparently wanted to write, it is still a moving drama, if a drama only of pathos. And though the portrait of Billy Budd is unacceptable, the other main characters bear the stamp of the author's great intellectual powers as few of his characters do.

As in *Israel Potter*, the scene is the revolutionary days of the late eighteenth century, a period whose still "undetermined momentousness" Melville thought unsurpassed in the whole range of history. This period, as we have noted, seemed to Melville to be America's primeval time, when its first great acts were performed and its best hopes discovered. But the spirit of heroism and liberation could be felt in other nations too, and Billy Budd, though he might as easily have been an American, is in fact an Englishman. He is a youth of twenty-one. His physical strength and beauty no less than his frank simplicity and good will make him a favorite aboard the merchant ship *Rights-of-Man*, where we first discover him. Homeward bound near England, the *Rights-of-Man* is stopped by the outward bound frigate H.M.S. *Indomitable*. The frigate is shorthanded and Billy Budd is impressed aboard and given a post in the foretop. He easily gains the affection and respect of the men and officers—with one exception. The exception is Claggart, the wonderfully conceived and depicted master-at-arms. For no easily determined reason Claggart is "down on" Billy Budd, as an oracular old sailor suggests when Billy comes to him for counsel. With an inhuman cunning Claggart sets his trap for Billy Budd, contriving in various ways to cast suspicion on him. The story takes place shortly after the British Navy has been badly shaken by unprecedented waves of mutiny in the ranks. And so Claggart's best strategy is to involve Billy Budd in a charge of insurrection. He goes to the quarterdeck and tells Captain Vere that Budd is plotting mutiny. The captain, though more suspicious of Claggart than of the accused man, calls them both to his cabin. There Claggart, looking deeply and unflinchingly into Billy Budd's eyes with a kind of savage sharklike hunger and hatred, repeats his charge. Billy Budd has always been handicapped by a stammer which overcomes his power of speech in moments of excitement. He is unable to answer the charge, even though the captain benevolently puts his hand on Billy's shoulder and tells him to take his time. The blocked utterance bursts forth not in the form of speech, but as a tremendous[260] blow on Claggart's forehead from Billy Budd's fist—and the master-at-arms is killed on the spot. A drumhead court is quickly summoned, and though the court and the captain himself are tormented with a deep compunction, they soon sentence Billy Budd to be hanged at dawn—a sentence which is summarily carried out. Billy Budd dies murmuring, "God bless Captain Vere."

It is often said that *Billy Budd* shows Melville's final admission of the tragic necessity of law in human society. The fact of the matter is that Melville had admitted this forty years earlier in *White-Jacket* and had reaffirmed it in *Moby-Dick* by showing that the tragic dilemma of Ahab was in part due to his necessary commitment to the external forms of command. He makes no discovery of law in Billy Budd; he simply deals with the subject more carefully than he had before. Captain Vere's examination and defense of law in a man-of-war world and his decision that a human life must be sacrificed to this law is impeccable, irrefutable, and fully conscious of the pathetic irony of the situation. The flaw in the book is that Melville does not fully conceive of that which, in a genuine tragedy, has to be opposed to law.

Captain Vere and Claggart are perfectly portrayed. The captain's name—Edward Fairfax Vere—perhaps indicates what he is. He is Man (vir), but civilized Man. Though personally superior to the laws of "Cain's City," he nevertheless in all practical matters lives according to these laws. He is a superior type of "citified man." Captain Vere is a bachelor of forty-odd years. He is brave without being foolhardy, a disciplinarian but considerate of the interests of his men. He is inclined to be grave and practical; some of his acquaintances call him humorless and observe a streak of pedantry in his character. Yet he is sometimes given to moments of absentmindedness, and when he is seen at the ship's rail gazing meditatively into the blankness of space his nickname, Starry Vere, seems especially to fit him. He has no brilliant qualities but is intellectually superior to his associates. He is a reader of books, preferring authors who deal with actual men and events or who philosophize, like Montaigne, in the spirit of common sense. And though his training has made his mind a "dyke" against the spate of revolutionary ideas coming out of France, his arguments against them are reasoned.[261]

Captain Vere is profoundly moved by the plight of Billy Budd, and Melville tells us that the ordeal of the sentence and the hanging was worse for Vere than it was for Billy. Deciding to communicate the decision of the court to Billy in person, he assumes the relationship we have met so often in Melville's books. He becomes a father to a son. The possibility that Vere may in fact be Billy Budd's father is not contradicted by the author; for Billy was a foundling and, as the author suggests, a by-blow of some English nobleman. In Billy Budd the father whom the young hero seeks is shown to be purely mundane; he is "citified man" rather than Zeus or Jehovah. Captain Vere's short interview with Billy Budd, the sacred actualities of which Melville only hints at, is a kind of consummation of a quest he has been making all his life. The whole affair has so shaken him that the ship's surgeon suspects a touch of madness, a question which Melville carefully leaves open. Perhaps the captain's touch of madness is only his own terrible consciousness of having finally fulfilled the destiny of "citified man"—to recognize oneself as Caesar and one's son as Christ.

Melville describes Claggart as being about thirty-five. He is spare and tall, with the clean-cut features, except for a disproportionate heaviness of the chin, of a head on a Greek medallion. His hand is rather too small and there is a sort of intellectual pallor on his forehead. He has a trace of a foreign accent and though nothing is known of his origins, he has affinities, perhaps, with some Mediterranean culture. To say that Claggart is a version of the confidence man—the mysterious impostor from the East—may be surprising, but it is true.[1] Or rather he is the confidence man plus an actively evil nature. The figure in Melville's satire was not the evil man so[262] much as "the moderate man, the inveterate

---

[1] The more we look into Melville's works, the more wonderfully complex grows the character of the confidence man. In the chapter on Israel Potter we had occasion to note the kinship of the confidence man with Benjamin Franklin and even with such a character as Babbalanja of Mardi. The Reverend Mr. Falsgrave and Plinlimmon of Pierre and Derwent of Clarel are first cousins of the confidence man. So also is the figure of the "master-at-arms," whom we meet as Bland in White-Jacket and Claggart in Billy Budd. With the confidence man in mind, compare the following phrases used to describe (the appropriately named) Bland:

"There was a fine polish about his whole person, and a pliant, insinuating style in his conversation, that was, socially, quite irresistible. . . ."

"Ashore such a man might have been an irreproachable mercantile swindler, circulating in polite society. . . ."

"I pitied the continual gnawing which, under all his deftly donned disguises, I saw lying at the bottom of his soul."

understrapper to the evil man." Claggart is the confidence man invested with a "natural depravity" willed by paranoiac guile and controlled by superior intellect. In his campaign against Billy Budd, he employs all the devices of "confidence." Subtly obsequious, outwardly frank and friendly, he is a "fair-spoken man," speaking in silvery accents with a "confidential" tongue. Conducting himself, as is his wont, with an "uncommon prudence" and speaking with a Pharisaical sense of "retributive righteousness," he sells his case to Captain Vere:

What he said, conveyed in the language of no uneducated man, was to the effect following if not altogether in these words, namely, that . . . he had seen enough to convince him that at least one sailor aboard was a dangerous character in a ship mustering some who not only had taken a guilty part in the late serious trouble, but others also who, like the man in question, had entered His Majesty's service under another form than enlistment.

Contemptuous of this rhetoric, the captain interrupts with: "Be direct, man; say impressed men." But the sweet voice continues, using the confidence trick of misrepresenting the nature of a man. Billy Budd, says Claggart, is a "deep one"; under the fair exterior there is a "man-trap." This is an argument the captain cannot ignore; Claggart has merely to enunciate the charge and his case is won. The full character of Claggart emerges *in spite of* Melville's statement that he is "depraved according to nature." Melville states this, perhaps, because he wishes to oppose two "natural" men—Billy Budd, good by nature, and Claggart, depraved by nature—to "citified man," Captain Vere, who is presumably both good and depraved by nature. But to say that one character is good by nature and another depraved can have only a symbolic value. Claggart becomes evil as a civilized man. He becomes evil in the only way which allows us to understand what evil is: by living in Cain's city and making choices of action. It is, indeed, only his being a certain kind of "citified man" which allows his "natural depravity" or his kinship with the torpedo fish a meaningful symbolic value.

So highly "citified" is Claggart's depraved mind that, like the mind of mankind, it generates a compensatory vision of innocence. And this vision is at the root of his ambivalent feeling toward Billy[263] Budd, finding its expression to some extent in a homosexual attraction. Billy Budd's "harmlessness" fills Claggart with both longing and revulsion at the same time that Budd's physical beauty attracts him. Like Milton's Satan, thinking of the Garden, Claggart is capable of looking at Billy Budd and weeping "feverish tears." He weeps at being unable to put off the burden of civilization and be "harmless." But in less regressive moments he can feel the active bitterness of the ambiguous attraction-repulsion which Billy rouses in him. "To be nothing more than innocent!" Such a being is in the deepest sense a mutineer, an apostate from Cain's city. It is very difficult not to agree with Claggart.

The weakness of *Billy Budd* is the central character himself. The trouble is that he is not in any meaningful sense what Claggart says he is: "deep" and a "man-trap." He *ought* to be "deep" and in some inescapable human way a "man-trap." Otherwise he cannot function meaningfully in a tragedy which tries to demonstrate the opposition between human nature and the heart on the one hand and law on the other. Otherwise he cannot possibly be the Handsome Sailor. It is surely significant of uncertainty that Melville, though outwardly identifying Billy Budd as the Handsome Sailor, actually hedges. Melville's dedication of his book to Jack Chase inferentially compares Billy Budd with the Handsome Sailor of *White-Jacket*. After describing the Handsome Sailor and symbolizing him as the giant negro, Melville writes: "Such a cynosure, at least in aspect, and something such too in nature, though with important variations made apparent as the story proceeds, was welkineyed Billy Budd, or Baby Budd." Melville is determined apparently to have his cake and eat it too when it comes to the question of what manner of man his hero actually is. After thus presenting Billy Budd as a Handsome Sailor "with important variations," Melville goes on to ignore all possible "variations," referring to his hero throughout the rest of the book as the Handsome Sailor. Obviously Jack Chase and Billy Budd have many things in common, but the abyss between them is prodigious. And Melville could not admit this to himself.

Billy Budd is simple, direct, and kindly. He is a sort of Adam, the Adam as yet untainted by the "urbane serpent." He has the "humane look of reposeful good nature" sometimes shown in [264] statues of Hercules. Lacking powers of reflection, he is a fatalist as animals are fatalists. He is primeval, unspoiled man wandering, as if dazed, in Cain's city. In describing Billy, Melville grows hazily rhetorical: "he possessed that kind and degree of intelligence which goes along with the unconventional rectitude of a sound human creature—one to whom not as yet had been proffered the questionable apple of knowledge. He is a "childman." "He had none of the intuitive knowledge of the bad which in natures not good or incompletely so, foreruns experience, and therefore may pertain, as in some instances it too clearly does pertain, even to youth." One cannot understand the character of Billy Budd except as the final, and almost the first—first *crucial*—self-indulgence of a great intelligence. Looking backward almost fifty years, trying to convince himself that such a man might actually have existed, Melville tries to re-create life on a man-of-war in the image of Eden, insisting that sailors have a particular kind of "innocence" not found in the generality of mankind. And while this may be true in a certain sense—there is no doubt a kind of innocence or at least sexual and mental juvenility in a sailor's life—we must take *White-Jacket* to be Melville's clear account of life on a man-of-war; and in that book he had concluded that man-of-war's men were on the whole less innocent than the rest of mankind. The character of Billy Budd is meaningful only as a moving and revealing comment on Melville's last years.

The author makes an attempt to show that in the course of the story Billy Budd finds the consummation of his destiny. Having been sentenced to die by the man who may possibly be his father, Billy Budd can at last drop the role of Ishmael and become Isaac, the lawful heir of Abraham. When he first begins to be troubled by the evidence of a plot against him, Billy Budd seeks advice from an old sailor described as the mainmastman of the ship. We remember from *White-Jacket* that the patriarchal mainmastman was referred to as an Abraham, and though he is not called that in *Billy Budd*, the parallel is suggestive. It is this old sailor who has given Billy the name of Baby Budd; he refuses or is unable to play the part of Billy's father, as Abraham refuses Ishmael. Later Melville suggests that Billy finds his atonement with Captain Vere: "The austere devotee of military duty, letting himself melt back into what [265] remains primeval in our formalized humanity, may in the end have caught Billy to heart, even as Abraham may have caught young Isaac on the brink of resolutely offering him up in obedience to the exacting behest." This atonement is the logical conclusion to Melville's Ishmael theme, more fully and exactly stated here, in the strict terms of the Ishmael myth, than in *White-Jacket*. In *White-Jacket* the recognition and final meeting of father and son was presented as an act of maturity on the part of the son, a recognition of human depravity, an admission of law, form, and patriarchal majesty, and a consequent liberation of the son's creative energy. In *Billy Budd*, Melville insists on trying to have it both ways: there are suggestions that Billy has experienced a metamorphosis of character through an "agony mainly proceeding from a generous young heart's virgin experience of the diabolical incarnate and effective," and that he is "spiritualized now through late experiences so poignantly profound." The reader accepts this gratefully and with belief. And he reflects that, after all, Melville is going to say that Billy Budd is now the Ishmael who has become Isaac, the harmless Adam who has become the fallen Adam, the foundling of noble antecedents who has become Oedipus the tragic hero. All this would indicate that Billy Budd's agony has made of him a fully tragic, fully suffering, fully knowing man.

But not so. Billy Budd is hanged after sleeping the night out with the serene happy light of babyhood playing over his features. When a man is hanged, certain mechanical-physical spasms take place in his body; his bowels are emptied, his penis erects, and there is an ejaculation of semen. When Billy Budd is hanged, there is a total "absence of spasmodic movement." The tragedy of Melville's heroes had always been that they were "unmanned" by circumstances or the effect of their own moral decisions. Billy Budd was unmanned by Melville himself. There is a hint that the hanging of Billy Budd was a miraculous euthanasia. We recall that in *The Confidence Man* an "invalid Titan" had violently quarreled with the peddler of the Samaritan Pain Dissuader for claiming that his balm was "a certain cure for any pain in the world." In portraying Billy Budd, not as Isaac or the fallen Adam or Oedipus, but as the hermaphrodite Christ who ascends serenely to the yardarm of the *Indomitable*, Melville apparently forgot his "invalid Titan."[266]

II

Billy Budd is a syncretic work of art, and though we must not overemphasize its importance, it is a measure of Melville's final position. It demands to be considered as a "natural" tragedy as the tragedies of Sophocles and Shakespeare are "natural." But it is also a beatific vision, a vision of the hermaphrodite Christ who is mentioned in *Moby-Dick* and who always dimly haunted Melville—that shadowy Christ who, as we have noted, slept restively in Melville's mind after the writing of *Pierre*. If the Rolfe of *Clarel* had appeared in *Billy Budd*, we might have had a fully tragic hero. As it is, we have the Handsome Sailor minus Rolfe, the tragic human core. The residue is something less and more than human, a child or a flower or a radiance. The fall of Simon Magus symbolizes not only the decline of the pagan magic which created *Moby-Dick*; it also symbolizes a reaffirmation of Christianity—more particularly a fresh commitment to the infantile Christ who seeks entrance in *Pierre*, *Bartleby the Scrivener*, *Israel Potter*, *The Confidence Man*, and *Clarel*, and who is finally admitted in *Billy Budd*. It is surely not true, as some writers, including Charles Olson, have alleged, that Melville's weakness for the hermaphrodite Christ is the reason for the disintegration of his art after *Moby-Dick*. For one thing, as I hope I have been able to show, Melville's art did not disintegrate after his best book; it merely changed in various ways, even though these ways were journeys less bracing than the ascent of the magician. Furthermore, in the light of *Billy Budd*, the remarkable thing is that the hermaphrodite Christ appears so little in Melville's other writings; and this is especially remarkable of *Clarel*, the work in which Melville tried most explicitly to deal with moral problems and intellectual positions.

Billy Budd, the "Rose" of Melville's last work, is himself a syncretic conception, the product of nineteenth century nature worship and the image of the divine child-man. Though of all nineteenth century writers Melville is the least open to the charge of entertaining a superficial view of nature (indeed his superiority over Wordsworth and Emerson is his *tragic* view of nature), he nevertheless paid something of the romantic homage to the violet by the mossy stone. The frightening insistence with which, after[267] *Pierre*, nature presented itself to him as a stony waste land or a Medean muck, together with his feeling that "Niebuhr & Strauss" had robbed the world of its "bloom," led him to seek for whatever Rose nature in some mysterious or paradoxical way might produce. In the short stories of the 1850's, the Rose, as in *Jimmy Rose*, is a symbol of life reviving triumphantly and with quiet beauty in a hostile environment, a beautiful extrusion from the dark muck and suffering of earth and human life. In "After the Pleasure Party," the Rose is a symbol of sexual fertility and artistic creation. In *Clarel*, as we have seen, the Rose is identified with Ruth, who like Billy Budd himself is both a beautiful product of nature and an angel. In "Weeds and Wildings, with a Rose or Two"—a group of poems written late in life and tenderly dedicated to his wife—Melville uses the Rose as a principle of life which sustains itself though it feeds on nothing but snow or virginity; again the Rose is like the Promethean hearth fire; or it sheds light in a sepulcher, blooming in the very atmosphere of death. The idea that nature, dark and hostile as it may be, paradoxically creates the good and the beautiful is restated in *Billy Budd*, where the young hero is said to embody natural goodness and beauty, a flower of nature, which paradoxically also produces a Claggart. As a social symbol Billy Budd has close affinities with the "natural man" or "noble savage," an idea celebrated by the period in which the story takes place.

But if Billy Budd is natural goodness, he is also divine goodness. He is that peculiarly American god, the beatified boy. His career is like that of Christ; he is persecuted by a satanic Claggart and rebuffed and sacrificed by "citified man." With a loose similarity, Wellingborough Redburn had been persecuted by Jackson and rebuffed by Captain Riga. But Redburn is a creature acting in what Rolfe called "Circumstance" and "Time." At the overt levels of human tragedy, Bully Budd is not a definably human being. The moral content of his character is self-contradictory and obscure. Innocence, Mortmain had said in *Clarel*, is the act of the true heart reflecting upon evil. This is, perhaps, the only kind of innocence we want to take seriously or believe in.

Surely we are not more likely to be moved by *Billy Budd* as beatific vision than by *Billy Budd* as natural tragedy. Yet the story is strangely moving. Let us look below the clutter of its overt levels.[268]

III

At the deep levels of *Billy Budd* there is a massive and terrible image, which, it seems to me, moved the aged Melville so overpoweringly that he was unable to give it direct expression. As Melville says at one point in *Billy Budd*, "every . . . form of life has its secret mines and dubious sides; the side popularly disclaimed." On the night before Billy Budd's execution, the ship, with its decks, is like the story itself. "The night was luminous on the spar-deck, but otherwise in the cavernous ones below—levels so very like the tiered galleries in a coal-mine."

The *real theme* of *Billy Budd* is castration and cannibalism, the ritual murder and eating of the Host. During his trial Billy proclaims his faithfulness to the King and to Captain Vere by saying, "I have eaten the King's bread, and I am true to the King." When, "without remorse," the dying Captain Vere murmurs, "Billy Budd, Billy Budd," he expresses faithfulness, dependence, and longing. He had eaten of the Host, and he was true to the Host. After forty years Melville had returned to the theme of *Typee*. In that book the young hero had extricated himself from the valley by a sudden exchange of passivity for action. Billy Budd is fatally passive, his acts of violence being unconsciously calculated to ensure his final submission. All of Billy's conscious acts are toward passivity, the first one being his quick acquiescence in his impressment, an act which causes the hero-worshiping sailors to regard him with "surprise" and "silent reproach." In symbolic language, Billy Budd is seeking his own castration—seeking to yield up his vitality to an authoritative but kindly father, whom he finds in Captain Vere. When anyone else stirs the depths of Billy's longing, threatening to bring his unconscious thoughts to consciousness, he flies into a sudden rage. When Red-Whiskers, a sailor who had once been a butcher, maliciously digs Billy in the ribs to show him "just whence a sirloin steak was cut," Billy gives him a "terrible drubbing." And when the minion of Claggart approaches Billy on the moonlit deck and, holding out two shining guineas, says, "See, they are yours, Bill," Billy Budd stammeringly threatens to toss him over the rail. The persistent feminine imagery Melville associates with Billy and his statement that "above all" there was "something in the mobile[269] expression, and every chance attitude and movement suggestive of a mother eminently favored by Love and the Graces," indicate that Billy has identified himself with the mother at a pre-Oedipean level and has adopted the attitude of harmlessness and placation toward the father in order to avoid the hard struggle of the Oedipus conflict. The Oedipus conflict entails, of course, the idea of one's incestuous guilt and one's desire to kill one's father. The psychoanalyst might say that Billy Budd has avoided the Oedipus struggle by forming an attachment to the *mother* at the prephallic level of "oral eroticism" and has allayed his fears of castration by symbolically castrating himself (by being consciously submissive) and by repressing his rage and hostility against the father in order to placate him. That all Billy's rage and hostility against the father are unconscious is symbolized by the fact that whenever it is aroused it cannot find expression in spoken language. Billy can only stutter and use his fists. This is a mechanism for keeping himself from admitting his own guilt and his own destructiveness. For indeed Billy destroys not only Claggart but himself—and even Captain Vere. For a cloud seems to pass over Vere in his last days, and he dies without achieving the rewards his character had seemed to predestine him to achieve; he dies longing for a "child-man" he had once known.

The food symbolism need not be labored. It recurs frequently, and it is the symbolism which takes us down most swiftly into the coherent lower strata of the story, where there is "a subterranean fire . . . eating its way deeper and deeper." Melville even symbolizes moral qualities by their taste, the innocent character having an "untampered-with flavor like that of berries" as against the guilty character, which has the "questionable smack of a compounded wine." Frequently Billy Budd is compared with animals—a heifer, a horse, a dog, a nightingale, a goldfinch. When he is hanged, he ascends to the yardarm like a "singing-bird," watched from below by a "wedged mass of upturned faces"—as if the sailors were birds expecting to be fed. It is said of Billy Budd (the Lamb of God) that the serpent has never bitten him, but after the accusation Claggart is described as a snake.

The idea of Billy as Host is established early in the story. When the lieutenant of the *Indomitable* goes aboard the *Rights-of-Man* in[270] search of new hands and immediately selects Billy Budd, he drinks some of the captain's grog almost as if conscious of performing a ritual. "Lieutenant," says the captain, "you are going to take my best man from me, the jewel of 'em." " 'Yes, I know,' rejoined the other, immediately drawing back the tumbler preliminary to a replenishing; 'yes, I know. Sorry.' " The captain, referring to the pacifying effect Billy has had on his troublesome sailors, then says, "A virtue went out of him, sugaring the sour ones. They took to him like hornets to treacle." Metaphors such as these evoke the primitive rite of slaughtering the young hero in order to eat his flesh and thus obtain his "virtue," his strength, or his heroic quality.

Later in the story Billy Budd spills his soup at mess, and Claggart, happening to pass by at the moment, is inwardly enraged, though outwardly he is only suavely and ambiguously satrical. Melville seems to feel that the enormous eruption of hostile emotion in Claggart may strike the reader as excessive and hence unbelievable. He therefore prefaces one of his comments on the spilled soup with a paragraph which says in effect that the most ordinary event may be a symbolic act which can arouse momentous passions:

Passion, and passion in its profoundest, is not a thing demanding a palatial stage whereupon to play its part. Down among the groundlings, among the beggars and rakers of the garbage, profound passion is enacted. And the circumstances that provoke it, however trivial or mean, are no measure of its power.

The palatial stage is surely the conscious mind or the realm of conscious art, and the abode of beggars and rakers of the garbage is the unconscious mind. There are "beggars" in the unconscious mind, calling the ego back among the rakers of garbage, as Billy Budd calls his own ego back. And is not this whole passage intended as a statement that *Billy Budd* does not present the reader with a "palatial stage" where profoundest passions are being enacted "down among the groundlings"? This comes close to telling us not only what is wrong with the story—simply that its profound passions do not find adequate objective representation—but also what is wrong with Billy Budd as tragic hero—that there is no "palatial stage" in his[271] personality, no conscious structure, no mind whose disintegration we should watch with pity and terror rather than merely with bewilderment and an obscure sense of loss.

When Claggart spies the spilled soup, it seemed to him "the sly escape of a spontaneous feeling on Billy's part more or less answering to the antipathy on his own." He feels that Billy has insulted him. But what is the nature of the insult? Presumably that, in spilling the soup, Billy has symbolically exposed himself to Claggart as the Host, the vessel from which issues "virtue." (Handsomely done, my lad!" cries Claggart. "And handsome is as handsome did it, too!") The spilled soup has also exposed Claggart's guilt as an eater of the Host and, furthermore, Claggart's fear of his own unconscious desire to be like Billy; for the psychological content of Claggart's desire to share Billy's innocence is his desire to be the passive Host.

Melville tells us that Claggart's jaw is heavy out of proportion with his otherwise delicately shaped face—Claggart's unconscious motives center upon orality. This occurs to us when, for example, he smiles at Billy Budd with an ambiguously "glittering dental satire." One of Claggart's "cunning corporals" is called Squeak, "so nicknamed by the sailors on account of his squeaky voice and sharp visage ferreting about the dark corners of the lower decks after interlopers, satirically suggesting to them the idea of a rat in a cellar." Squeak spies on Billy Budd and in this capacity is described as the "purveyor" who "feeds Claggart's passions."

I am sure that much of the sacramental symbolism in *Billy Budd* is conscious and intended. But some of it may be less conscious. One cannot be sure how much Melville means by pointing out that two other partisans of Claggart in compromising Billy Budd (two of Claggart's "messmates," they are called) are the Armourer and the Captain of the Hold; but it is a haunting idea that the Armourer represents Teeth and the Captain of the Hold represents Belly. Nor can one say what Thyestean implications there may be in the use of parts of the body in referring to Claggart, whose nickname is Jimmy Legs and whose official title is Master-at-Arms.

As the story concludes, the grim symbolism occurs more frequently and with more intensity. In the captain's cabin Claggart's "mesmeric glance," which Melville compares with "the hungry[272] lurch of the torpedo fish," quickly determines Billy's fate. It is the overt threat of castration which always sets off the explosion of Billy's unconscious fears and resentments. There is a terrible up-welling of his passive emotions, as if in a last attempt to control their aggressive counterparts. Briefly Billy has the expression of "a condemned vestal priestess at the moment of her being buried alive, and in the first struggle against suffocation"—images which convey both the desire for, and the fear of, castration.[2] But such emotions as these Billy cannot express consciously. He stutters, and strikes Claggart.

Describing the scene in which Vere informs Billy Budd of the sentence, Melville says, "there is no telling the sacrament." There is no telling; but the sacrament can be symbolized. Lying manacled on the deck during the night, Billy is like "a patch of discolored snow . . . lingering at some upland cave's black mouth." His terrible experiences are of the order that "devour our human tissues." The skeleton begins to show under Billy's cheek for the first time; he lies between two cannon as if "nipped in the vise of fate." After the hanging of this Lamb of God, after the chaplain has knelt down "on his marrow bones" to pray (as the ballad of "Billy in the Darbies" says), after the night has passed and it is full day, "the fleece of low-hanging vapor had vanished, licked up by the sun that late had so glorified it." The very patriarch of the universe feeds on Billy Budd.

The passage Melville calls a "Digression" is difficult and obscure; but I venture the following account. The purser and the surgeon discuss the absence of spasm in Billy's body. (They are at mess during this discussion: we are continually reminded in *Billy Budd* of the verbal kinship of "mess" with the ritual word "mass.") The purser is "a rather ruddy, rotund person, more accurate as an accountant than profound as a philosopher." The surgeon is "spare[273] and tall" (the same words used to describe Claggart): he is caustic, austere, and something of an intellectual. The two men are opposite types. The purser is the unthinking human animal who kills, vicariously, in order to eat. He is the simple cannibal, as is indicated by his placid rotundity (his being like a purse) and by his crude belief that Billy controlled his spasm by "will power." The surgeon is, like Claggart, a lean, emotionally complex and ambivalent sadist: he is more interested in murder than in food, as may be symbolized by his hastily leaving the mess table to get back to a patient in the sick bay. Thus, this very horrifying passage is not really a digression: it is a brief scene which universalizes the theme of the story by presenting two opposite mythical types of man lingering, as it were, over the body.

As the body of Billy Budd, wrapped in canvas and weighted with cannon balls, slides over the rail, the sailors "who had just beheld the prodigy of repose in the form suspended in air" think of the same form "foundering in the deeps"—an image of the act of eating. Over the spot where Billy has sunk, gaunt sea birds wheel and scream; and though the birds are predictably moved by "mere animal greed for prey," the sight has a surprising effect on the sailors. "An uncertain movement began among them, in which some encroachment was made." It is a brief moment of potentially mutinous commotion, which we can understand by noticing that the captain and his officers are symbolically connected with the birds, a connection the sailors unconsciously make. Immediately after the hanging, there had been a similar murmurous impulse to mutiny among the sailors. But the ship's officers had acted quickly. Their authoritative voice was heard in the whistle of the boatswain and his mates, which was "shrill as the shriek of the sea-hawk," which "pierced the low ominous sound" and "dissipated" it, so that in a moment or two "the throng was thinned by one half."

In a man-of-war world, Melville is saying, law feeds on man, being only a translation into social forms of that "horrible vulturism of earth" of which he had spoken in *Moby-Dick*. And with a complex human vulturism Captain Vere feeds on Billy Budd. Notice

---

[2] The psychoanalysts tell us that suffocation is sometimes identified in the unconscious with castration. In connection with the cabin scene, the following passage is significant: "Quite often a patient begins to stutter when he is particularly eager to prove a point. Behind his apparent zeal he has concealed a hostile or sadistic tendency to destroy his opponent by means of words, and the stuttering is both a blocking of and a punishment for this tendency. Still more often stuttering is exacerbated by the presence of prominent or authoritative persons, that is, of paternal figures against whom the unconscious hostility is most intense." O. Fenichel, *The Psychoanalytic Theory of Neuroses*, pp. 312–313.

the sexual-sacramental character of Vere's reaction to Billy's spontaneous "God bless Captain Vere." At these words, "Captain Vere, either through stoic self-control or a sort of momentary[274] paralysis induced by emotional shock, stood erectly rigid as a musket in the ship-armor's rack." The sexual spasm does not occur in Billy Budd because Billy's vitality or "virtue" has been symbolically transferred to Vere. And yet the transference is ambiguous; paralysis and rigidity suggest death just as surely as erection and the potentiality of the musket suggest life. New vitality has been given to Vere as captain and exponent of martial law (Vere as "musket"), but as man and father he has been stricken.

The intimation of Melville's passages about Lord Nelson is that had Nelson been aboard the *Indomitable* instead of Vere (the two are inferentially compared on several occasions), all this might not have happened, or—and perhaps this is the central point—if it had happened, no subsequent cloud would have passed over Nelson, as it does over Vere. Nelson is the invulnerable and fully mature father, a mythical hero standing behind Captain Vere, a less majestic figure. Nelson already has the qualities of Billy Budd, so that the ritual transference of vitality need not ruin him with its cruel ambiguities. Nelson has the heroic vitality of Billy Budd and the brilliance and audacity of the "jewel" among sailors; it is Nelson's fatherhood which allows him to make "ornate publication" of the very qualities, in sublimated form, which Billy Budd, in the form of infantile rage and hostility, represses. As Melville presents him, Nelson, the "Great Sailor," is the ultimate heroic possibility of the man-of-war world. But he is not of that order of hero represented by Jack Chase; Jack Chase symbolizes a culture beyond the boundaries of Nelson's world. Nelson would never leave his ship to take part in a republican revolution, as Jack Chase did. He is the mythical father whose very presence on board ship, as Melville says, is enough to forestall an incipient mutiny—the uprising, that is, of the sons against the father.

The imposing structure of personality Melville attributes to Nelson is beyond the reach of Captain Vere because Vere's moral stability is not proof against the uprising of the sons. In Claggart he sees his own hostility toward Billy Budd. (The relation of Vere to Claggart and Billy is the relation of a father to his sons, one of whom assumes the aggressive and hostile role of the father and the other of whom assumes the passive role of the mother.) In Billy Budd, Captain Vere sees his own imperfectly redeemed childhood.[275] Vere, imposing and even heroic as he is, must repeatedly return to his own childhood to feed on it and to murder it. For him there is no other way of supporting, of nourishing, the structure of consciousness, order, authority, and legality which constitutes the man-of-war world. The man-of-war world destroys itself by feeding on its own vitality, as the vulture feeds upon Prometheus.

This is in itself a moving idea; and so is the implied identification of Billy Budd with Christ. But is there not still another source of the massive emotion which rests uneasily beneath the imperfect surface of *Billy Budd?* Consider the connections Melville makes between the captains and literature. Nelson's ship is "poetic"; it has "symmetry" and "grand lines." Of Nelson at Trafalgar, Melville writes:

> If under the presentiment of the most magnificent of all victories, to be crowned by his own glorious death, a sort of priestly motive led him to dress his person in the jewelled vouchers of his own shining deeds; if thus to have adorned himself for the altar and the sacrifice were indeed vainglory, then affectation and fustian is each truly heroic line in the great epics and dramas, since in such lines the poet embodies in verse those exaltations of sentiment that a nature like Nelson, the opportunity being given, vitalizes into acts.

Homer is a kind of Nelson. They are the same mythical hero—great captains of the mind, the sea, and the man-of-war world. The author of *Moby-Dick* was such a captain.

Captain Vere "loved books." His name, "Vere," signifies (besides "man") "truth"; he is a speaker of the truth. Both his mien and his interests connect him with different kinds of literature than that associated with Nelson. He likes books "treating of actual men and events, no matter of what era." Such a man of truth is Herman Melville, who writes concerning *Billy Budd:* "The symmetry of form attainable in pure fiction cannot so readily be achieved in a narration essentially having less to do with fable than with fact. Truth uncompromisingly told will always have its ragged edges."

In *Typee*, Melville had already pictured himself as Billy Budd, the youth with the nameless malady who shrank with such inexplicable fear from the tattooing instrument, tipped with a shark's tooth, and who discovered that his elders—the fathers and the warriors of the tribe—were cannibals.[276]

Lord Nelson is not on "the main road"; he is on "a bypath." The central autobiographical figure in *Billy Budd* is Captain Vere. The dark and moving image of the book is Melville as the devourer of his own childhood. An old man with sons of his own,[3] Melville is overwhelmingly moved with pity for the passive, hermaphrodite youth, an image of himself, who must continuously be killed in the rite of the sacrament if books are to be written or the man-of-war world sustained—or indeed if life is to go on at all.

IV

Surely, then—to recall the restrictions on *Billy Budd* which I tried to make in the first sections of this chapter—I contradict myself. Billy Budd *is* a deep one and a man-trap (but if he is, he cannot be "innocent"!). His personality has extensive moral significance and psychological reality. He is highly effective, since he kills Claggart and even Captain Vere. And Captain Vere, not Billy Budd, is the tragic hero of the story.

It seems to me, however, that how one judges *Billy Budd* depends on what level of the story one is talking about. Potentially the story is one of the great tragedies of Western literature. But the upper level, the conscious structure, the "palatial stage" is far too uncreated, self-contradictory, and noncommittal to articulate the underlying images. At the explicit symbolic and dramatic levels of the story Melville draws back in awe from Billy Budd and can speak of him only by painful acts of will which in the very process of becoming articulate cut themselves off from the deepest sources of emotion and thus remain inexpressive. Billy Budd's stammering is Melville's own. When Billy Budd speaks articulately, he misrepresents his own deepest emotions. So does Melville.[277]

---

[3] Melville's first son Malcolm shot himself accidentally or on purpose in 1869, when he was twenty and Melville was fifty. The Melville family cherished a phrase spoken by the baby Malcolm in reference to his father: "Where dat old man?"

Billy Budd: Adam or Christ?*

H. E. HUDSON, IV

Melville's immortal *Moby Dick* ends with the destruction of the whaler *Pequod* and the loss of all hands save one, Ishmael. His lesser-known novel, *Billy Budd*, concludes its main action with the sacrifice of only one and the survival of all others. This significant difference has suggested a new, more hopeful aspect of Herman Melville. *Billy Budd* has therefore been enjoying a re-discovery, or properly speaking a process of discovery since it was not published in America until 1928. The Ustinov film production, released in the Fall of 1962, is most successful and impressive.

The unmistakable religious symbolism in *Billy Budd* suggests the need for a study of its theological themes and the meanings that they hold for religious liberals. It is the contention of this paper that Melville's character, Billy Budd, represents both the mythological Adam and the figure of "the Christ." Before taking up these themes it will be helpful to recount briefly the history of the story and to summarize its contents.

I

Almost all of Melville's prose fiction was written between 1845 and 1857, a period of only twelve years. From 1857 to 1888 Melville devoted himself almost exclusively to poetry. Then, on November 16, 1888 he began *Billy Budd*. Although much shorter than his early novels *Billy Budd* took three years in the writing. It was finished on April 19, 1891. Five months later Melville died.

Thus, *Billy Budd* occupies a singular position in Melville's writings. It is the last and apparently most carefully written of his works. As Ronald Mason says in his book, *The Spirit Above the Dust*, Melville "seems to have taken far more pains with the detailed construction of this one story than ever did with any of[62] his previous writings. . . ."[1] It was almost as if he had something very important to say.

In 1949 *Billy Budd* became the basis of the play *Uniform of Flesh*, written by Louis O. Coxe and Robert Chapman. This play ran for seven performances at the Lenox Hill Playhouse. The play was then re-written and opened at the Biltmore Theatre under the title *Billy Budd*. Here it narrowly missed the Drama Critics Award for the best play in the 1950–51 season.

II

Such is the history of *Billy Budd*. Before proceeding with an interpretation of its themes, it might be best to summarize the contents of the novel.

The action takes place in 1798 on the high seas when England and France are still at war. This is the year of the naval mutinies at Spithead and Nore when English sailors,

---

* From *Crane Review*, VII (1965), 62–67. Reprinted by permission of the editor and the author, Herbert E. Hudson, IV.

[1] Ronald Mason, *The Spirit Above the Dust* (London: John Lehmann Press, 1951), p. 246.

infected by the spirit of revolution, protest such abuses as impressment, flogging and capital punishment.

Billy Budd, a slim, handsome boy of nineteen is impressed from the merchantman, *The Rights of Man*, to serve on the man-of-war, *H.M.S. Indomitable*, commanded by Captain Vere. Of a cheerful, cooperative nature, Budd quickly adapts to navy life. His frank, trusting disposition makes him well-liked by his shipmates. His very presence seems to create a sense of good-will and confidence—with all except one, the ship's master-at-arms, John Claggart. The spiritual antithesis of Budd, Claggart's nature is sinister and evil. As Melville wrote:

> ... [in Claggart was] an evil nature, not engendered by vicious training or corrupting books or licentious living, but born with him and innate, in short "a depravity according to nature."[2]

Claggart becomes obsessed by the need to hurt Billy Budd. He plots with his assistant, Squeak, to discredit Budd by sabotaging his gear. He insults him and tries to provoke him, but to no avail. Soon it becomes clear that Claggart will not rest until he has destroyed Budd. One night he has Squeak try to tempt Budd into mutinous behavior by offering the young seaman two gold guineas. When this fails, Claggart executes his masterstroke. He goes to Captain Vere and accuses Budd of mutiny. Captain Vere knows Budd is not guilty and has long suspected Claggart of improprieties, so he sees this as an opportunity to catch Claggart on a perjury charge (a capital offense).[63]

Summoning Billy to his cabin Vere has Claggart repeat the charges. Standing falsely accused, Billy is shocked, tongue-tied, enraged. Although he had been known to stammer when under stress, this is the first time he completely loses control of himself. Billy is choked with anger, his face twisted, his body almost convulsed. Not able to answer in any other way, his arm strikes out and catches Claggart squarely on the temple. There is a groan and Claggart topples over dead.

Suddenly the plot turns, violently the roles are reversed. Now Budd is guilty of deed if not of intent. A court martial ensues and we cannot believe that Budd will be convicted. But there is no choice for the tormented Captain Vere: Budd has killed a ship's officer; it is in time of war; he must hang!

Before we can fully grasp what has happened, the crew is summoned together to witness punishment, Budd is marched forward and executed. The crew stands by, fixed in horror. Just before Billy is lifted from the deck he shouts—for he has trusted Captain Vere implicitly and bears him no malice—"God bless Captain Vere!"

The story then follows the history of the *H.M.S. Indomitable* and Captain Vere, who is soon killed in a naval engagement, but concludes shortly thereafter.

III

Throughout the story certain themes and religious symbolism emerge which we are now in a position to interpret. Two minor images suggested are David felling Goliath and Abraham being called upon to sacrifice his son. The relationship of trust and affection between Vere and Budd is much like that of father and son. As Vere says in the play, "If I had a son, I'd hope for one like Budd."[3] Since Budd is illegitimate yet of noble bearing, the possibility is never dismissed that Vere could in fact be his father.

---

[2] Herman Melville, "Billy Budd," In *Selected Writings of Herman Melville* (New York: The Modern Library, 1952), p. 843.

[3] John Gassner (ed.)., "Billy Budd" by Louis O. Coxe and Robert Chapman, *Best American Plays, Third Series 1945–1951* (New York: Crown Publishers, 1952), p. 381.

By far, however, the dominant images which Budd embodies are those of the mythological Adam before the Fall, and "the Christ" figure.

Billy Budd clearly embodies the qualities of Adam. Budd, as he arrives from *The Rights of Man*, is simple, completely natural. His innocence, carried almost to the point of naiveté, make this association with Adam inescapable. In this handsome young sailor there is only one flaw, an impediment of speech which proves his undoing, as did the fatal flaw of Adam, curiosity. Melville himself[64] calls attention to this similarity at several points in the text of the novel. Melville describes Billy as "a sort of upright barbarian, much such perhaps as Adam presumably might have been ere the urbane Serpent wriggled himself into his company."[4]

Yet the serpent does find his way into Budd's company: in the form of Claggart and his false accusations Budd is tempted to the limit of his endurance and commits an act of anger and violence. In striking Claggart, Budd has finally recognized the evil in the master-at-arms and found the potentiality for it in himself, and in this knowledge he falls from the state of innocence that he previously held.

So, the Adam theme is completed. This would be story enough. For the first time the character of Budd is believable, but Melville is not content to effect the Fall if Budd simply struck Claggart out of hatred and anger; through a quirk of fate Melville has Budd *kill* him. Nor is Melville going to let him off at the court martial to live as Fallen Man. Captain Vere asserts the need to fulfill the law, and Budd, because of his human failing, is condemned and sacrificed.

Thus, Melville set into motion yet another theme, that of the Christ. Budd's character is still one somewhat of innocence, but it is described by one critic as a "dynamic pervasive innocence credited to Jesus."[5] Throughout the entire story, as with the Adam theme, there are frequent parallels between Budd and Jesus. Budd is confronted with the temptation of the two gold guineas, as Jesus is said to have been tempted by Satan. Both Budd and Jesus were falsely accused of the same crime—treason. Both were equally innocent. One was convicted under the Mosaic law and the other under the Mutiny Act. Neither, when accused, uttered a word in his own defense. The friends of both stood by helplessly while they were killed. When the chaplain saw Billy before the execution, he stooped and kissed him on the cheek, reminiscent of the act of Judas. Budd's cry as he was being executed, "God Bless Captain Vere!" echoes that other cry of compassion, "Forgive them for they know not what they do!" Melville's own description of Budd's execution and the appearance of the early morning sky cannot be ignored:

> ... it chanced that the vapory fleece hanging low in the East, was shot through with a soft glory as of the fleece of the Lamb of God seen in mystical vision and simultaneously therewith, watched by the wedged mass of upturned faces, Billy ascended; and, ascending, took the full rose of the dawn.[6][65]

It has been suggested that it is no coincidence that Billy is described as "ascending." Following his death Melville reports that sailors followed the spar from which Budd was hanged "from ship to dock-yard and again from dock-yard to ship, still pursuing it even when at last reduced to a mere dockyard boom. To them a chip of it was as a piece of the Cross."[7]

In Billy Budd, then, we have a figure who was admired by his fellows for his strength and goodness and who was revered after his tragic death. Throughout his time aboard the *Indomitable* his spirit was one that transformed the circumstances of hardship and suf-

---

[4] Melville, op. cit., p. 817.
[5] Mason, op. cit., p. 250.
[6] Melville, op. cit., p. 894.
[7] Melville, op. cit., p. 902.

fering to joy and hope. There is even reason to believe that death was for him something that could be accepted with trust, something that did not vanquish his sense of good-will and serenity. Thus his final words were unmarked by a trace of stammer.

Our interpretation, then, is that Billy Budd represents both Adam and Christ. He is not completely either, yet a curious combination of both. By character he is very much Adam; by circumstances he is forced to play out the role of the Christ. As Milton Stern said in his excellent work, *The Fine Hammered Steel of Herman Melville:*

> . . . in *Billy Budd* Melville tells his history of humanity in a reworking of the Adam-Christ story, placing prelapsarian Adam and the Christ on a man-of-war, and demonstrating the inevitability of the Fall and the necessity of the Crucifixion.[8]

IV

This being our interpretation, what does it mean—to Melville, to us? If the Adam-Christ interpretation of *Billy Budd* is as Melville intended, it is clear that this final work is categorically different from his earlier novels. In the earlier works man is locked in deadly combat with the inscrutable forces of evil. In Ahab's defiance and Pierre's despair there is no reconciliation to life, only struggle and crushing defeat. In *Billy Budd*, however, Melville suggests a degree of resolution and transcendence over the forces of evil not hitherto expressed. Billy Budd rises above the annihilating circumstances of life and death, and asserts his spirit of goodness and acceptance.

If this is the meaning Melville intended, the consequences are far-reaching. It means that Melville underwent a transition not only in literary out-look but in his own convictions about life. "Towards the end," said Auden in his poem on Melville, "he sailed into an extraordinary mildness."[9] Ronald Mason remarked:

> . . . [*Billy Budd*] is a calm and authoritative revelation; the doubts which had tormented [Melville's] . . . most vigorous and productive moments have by years and years of unrecorded wrestling, both of intellect and imagination, been resolved.[10]

If this is so, it means that *Billy Budd* is one of Melville's most important novels, that it cannot be ignored as a natural sequel to the greatest of the earlier works such as *Moby Dick*.

Some scholars are skeptical, however, whether Melville intended *Billy Budd* to be taken seriously, or whether instead the work is a misleading effort at ironic, satiric comedy. They suggest that since Melville was negative about religion and Christianity throughout his life it is too much to expect that he could make such a transition; they feel that a deathbed recantation is somehow too pat. Lawrance Thompson, a chief spokesman of this point of view, states in his book, *Melville's Quarrel With God:*

> My suggestion is that *Billy Budd* should be viewed as Melville's most subtle triumph in triple-talk; that it was designed to conceal and reveal much the same notions as expressed years earlier in *Moby Dick* and *Pierre* and *The Confidence-Man*; that Melville came to the end of his life still harping on the notion that the world was put together wrong and that God was to blame . . .[11]

---

[8] Milton R. Stern, *The Fine Hammered Steel of Herman Melville* (Urbana, Ill.: University of Illinois Press, 1957), p. 211.

[9] Mason, op. cit., p. 246.

[10] Mason, op. cit., p. 245.

[11] Lawrance Thompson, *Melville's Quarrel With God* (Princeton, N. J.: Princeton University Press, 1952), p. 332.

We could understand such skepticism if *Billy Budd* were something Melville dashed off in a few months. We could imagine him spending no more time on a satiric comedy. But the present writer finds it improbable that Melville would take longer than he ever had taken on works many times the size, that he would summon the last of his strength and occupy his final moments simply restating what had earlier received classic form.

What Melville intended is perhaps something we shall never know. What the story means to us, however, is another matter. We are free to accept it at face value, as this writer is inclined to, as a positive treatment of the Adam and Christ themes and for the meaning these symbols hold. As such the story becomes a commentary on man's epic struggle for goodness. The struggle takes place in a world of imperfections and human failings—but it is not without hope. Man has resources of compassion, joy, and courage upon which he may draw. In *Billy Budd* we have the promise that even in the stark world of Herman Melville the goodness in man's heart cannot be vanquished.[67]

Billy Budd—Acceptance or Irony*

RICHARD HARTER FOGLE

There appear to be three principal conceptions of the meaning of Melville's *Billy Budd*: the first, and most heavily supported, that it is Melville's "Testament of acceptance," his valedictory and his final benediction. "There are not many final works," remarks Newton Arvin, "that have so much the air as *Billy Budd, Foretopman* has of being a Nunc Dimittis. Everyone has felt this benedictory quality about it." The second view, a reaction against the first, holds that *Billy Budd* is ironic, and that its real import is precisely the opposite of its ostensible meaning. Lawrance Thompson feels that Melville is still quarreling with God. Still a third interpretation denies that intepretation is possible; a work of art has no meaning at all that can be abstracted from it, nor is a man's work in any way an index of his character or his opinions. Thus Stanley Edgar Hyman in a lively and malicious survey of Melville scholarship denies the possibility of any certain conclusions about what manner of man Melville actually was: "If all these basic questions about Melville, from his view of the absolute to his sexual leanings, are unanswerable, and if Melville is like Shakespeare ultimately unknowable, it is due to our inability to penetrate this mask, which is simply the mask or persona of art. Behind it the artist sits in darkness and anonymity, perhaps, as Joyce suggests, paring his nails. 'Strike through the mask,' Ahab exhorts us. How can we? Why in fact should we? In the last analysis it is the mask itself we want, and the face we see mirrored in it can only be our own."

All three of these views of *Billy Budd* are in their own sense true. As a highly complex work of art *Billy Budd* provides ample evidence for all. Melville certainly accepts his own imagined characters, action, and situation in good faith. Billy, Vere, and Claggart[107] are treated with seriousness and dignity, as is the tragic complication which destroys them. On the other hand, it is also true that *Billy Budd* is pervasively ironic. Yet its irony is neither the irony of concealment nor the irony of deceit; it does not change the boldly delineated face of the story, nor its explicit and fundamental affirmations. With whatever allowances one wishes to make, Billy and Vere are still good men, Claggart is still evil, and the action is still tragic. *Billy Budd* is both ironic and ambiguous, but its ironies and ambiguities are Melville's acceptance of the limits of interpretation: they are intended neither to confuse nor to mock. His world is as always organically one and yet incomprehensible, containing the conception of an absolute truth which is yet too complex and too far away for the vision of man to encompass. There is also in *Billy Budd* the effect of an ambiguity which is not the ambiguity of art, and which needs to be taken into account. Carefully written as it no doubt was, it is not quite a finished product ready for publication. It is sometimes tentative simply for lack of a final decision which would have had to be made.

One sees how the "ironic" interpretation has arisen. It would be easy, for example, to read a devastating irony into the sequence of events immediately following Billy's execution. Step by step the crew, the natural men of the story, are diverted, misled, diffused into impotence by their officers, themselves the automatons of the mutiny act by which their world is governed. Step by step tradition and law are subtly perverted to meet the circumstances, as the starboard watch is dismissed to thin the crowd, all hands are again

---

* From *Tulane Studies in English*, VIII (1958), 107–113. Reprinted by permission of the author.

called together swiftly for the funeral, to be dispersed again by the drum beating to quarters. Everything is orderly but a little out of order; and the sequence of displacement follows the same pattern as Captain Vere's illegal bolstering of the law at Billy's trial. We remember that strict observation of the forms would have demanded delay until the *Indomitable* had rejoined the fleet, and Billy could be brought before the admiral. From the general point of view for the moment proposed here a single sentence could be used to epitomize the whole: "Shrill as the shriek of the sea-hawk the whistles of the Boatswain and his Mates pierced that ominous low sound, dissipating it; and yielding to the mechanism of discipline the throng was thinned by one half." The boatswains' whistles could well be the exultant scream of the bird of heaven, the sky-god's emissary, over the defeat and death of poor humanity. One recalls Tashtego and the sea-hawk at the sinking of the *Pequod*.[108] The hawk at once exults and commands. Vere's use of form and ceremony constitutes a definite pattern.

This is not, however, the true emphasis of *Billy Budd*. To suppose it was would be to conceive an impossible perversion of values, would render Melville a crafty masochist and madman. Such an interpretation, furthermore, would have to be imported from without, and would present a distorted picture which laid inordinate stress upon Melville's rebelliousness and his reliance upon eighteenth century rationalism. The action of Captain Vere in skilfully checking incipient revolt is based upon the settled and disinterested beliefs of a lifetime, in terms of the preparation which Melville has laid down; Vere acts for the general welfare. " 'With mankind' he would say 'forms, measured forms are everything; and that is the import couched in the story of Orpheus with his lyre spellbinding the wild denizens of the woods.' And this he once applied to the disruption of forms going on across the Channel and the consequences thereof." There is perhaps a lurking irony in this Orpheus passage, but it signifies not a total reversal of its ostensible meaning but a consciousness of its incompleteness. As with all general maxims, it leaves something more to be said.

Billy Budd is, it seems to me, entirely comprehensible as Melville's version of tragedy. But to affirm this it is necessary to provide some definition both of tragedy and of irony as the terms are used here, though no more is attempted than an informal description sufficient for the immediate purpose. Tragedy, then, is a heightened and dignified action, intentionally so complicated as to involve its personae in the greatest conceivable difficulties, in order to elicit from them in their struggle the fullest potentialities of which they are capable. As to irony, we know that there are many notions of it, and perhaps no certain center can be found. We shall need to distinguish between different usages in order to specify the respects in which *Billy Budd* is or is not ironic. It is not ironic in the sense of irony ordinarily used by those who claim that it is; that is, a more or less complete reversal of the ostensible meaning, with, to add the words of A. R. Thompson in *The Dry Mock*, an effect of painful mockery. It is not painful, it is not sharp-edged, except by distortion of a part to misrepresent the total effect. It is ironic in that it frequently means more—not other—than it seems to say. Correspondingly *Billy Budd* is ironic in the modern sense of irony somewhat overworked by T. S. Eliot[109]—who called it wit—, I. A. Richards, and the New Critics: that is, a consciousness of the difficulties which any belief or attitude must face, an awareness of complexity. Indeed, one might concede to *Billy Budd* any ironies, of character, word, situation, or general attitude, which do not impeach its essential good faith and render verbalization itself a worthless currency. But precisely this destructive irony is what the ironist critics have fixed upon.

Billy Budd can like *Moby Dick* be justly described as Melville's nineteenth century version of classical tragedy, with old forms revivified by new issues. According to Aristotelean prescription it portrays men as better than they are. The principals are exceptional: Billy, Captain Vere, and Claggart stand high in the hierarchy of natural man, above the limited comprehension of the mere worldly-wise. The last meeting of Vere and Budd is too sacred for the common view. "But there is no telling the sacrament, seldom if in any case revealed to the gadding world wherever under circumstances at all akin to those here attempted to be set forth two of great Nature's nobler order embrace." As to Claggart, his evil is an object of moral and aesthetic appreciation, a quality to be savored by connoisseurs.

To heighten and dignify the tragic action Melville, as in *Moby Dick* with Ahab, magnifies his characters by investing them in heroic myth, legend, and history. The background is "a crisis for Christendom not exceeded in its undetermined momentousness at the time by any other era of which there is record." The Handsome Sailor has mythical proportions. He is Alderbaran, a pagod, a grand Assyrian bull; at the yard-arm he is "young Alexander curbing the fiery Bucephalus. A superb figure, tossed up as by the horns of Taurus against the thunderous sky." He is Hercules refined by the influence of Venus, in him "something suggestive of a mother eminently favored by Love and the Graces." Melville thus states the problem of this modern tragedy: "Passion, and passion in its profoundest, is not a thing demanding a palatial stage whereon to play its part. Down among the groundlings, among the beggars and rakers of the garbage, profound passion is enacted. And the circumstances that provoke it, however trivial or mean, are no measure of its power. In the present instance the stage is a scrubbed gun-deck, and one of the external provocations a man-of-war's man's spilled soup." But his stage is so framed and so lighted as to display the tragic patterns to the best dramatic advantage. Antique myth,[110] Christian allusion at its most spacious, and finally the aesthetic distance of a more poetic age of sail are all utilized to magnify and embellish. (One may remark here in passing that it is a waste of ingenuity to prove that Billy is not the Handsome Sailor. Insofar as the Sailor is mythic hero he cannot be, for this is not a man but an archetype. Billy is as close to being the Handsome Sailor as any human, closely scanned, is likely to get. How much use was Melville able to get out of Bulkington in *Moby Dick*?) One final comment upon magnification: there is a commemorative quality about *Billy Budd* which very interestingly fuses the tragedy of hero and common man, which blends the diverse tones of *Moby Dick* and *John Marr and Other Sailors*. It is a tale at once of Lord Nelson and of Greenwich pensioners, of mutiny, age-old oppression and pain, and of military splendor. "To the mutineers those battles and especially Trafalgar were a plenary absolution; and a grand one; for all that goes to make up scenic naval display and heroic magnificence in arms. Those battles especially Trafalgar stand unmatched in human annals."

Like classical tragedy, *Billy Budd* makes a clear distinction between the sphere of the actual and the sphere of the ideal. True judgment of Billy lies with natural law, here also divine, the realm of absolute justice—chronometrical, as Plotinus Plinlimmon would have it in *Pierre*. "'At the last Assizes it shall acquit,'" says Vere. But Vere is equally clear on the distinction between a natural and a man-of-war world. The killing of Claggart is divine justice, but on the *Indomitable* it is the murder of a superior officer under wartime conditions. "'Struck dead by an angel of God. Yet the angel must hang!'" "'We proceed under the law of the Mutiny Act.'" In *Billy Budd* this tragic discrepancy is born of the dogma of the Fall of Man, which inevitably brings it into being. The low of the mutiny act is the law of a fallen world, in which an unfallen man like Billy cannot long exist. The immediate tragedy originates in a second Fall, the mutiny at the Nore, which has made any union of these worlds impossible. Age-old abuses of government, first rationally and properly protested at Spithead, have finally roused the "red meteor" of the Nore. "Reasonable discontent growing out of practical grievances in the fleet had been ignited into irrational combustion as by live cinders blown across the Channel from France in flames." The Revolution, one sees, is also a Fall. Many parallels with Melville's early writing have been suggested by critics of[1111] *Billy Budd*. At this point one might add to the list *The Encantadas*, and most particularly Sketch Seventh, "Charles's Isle and the Dog-King." The Encantadas are a fallen world in which no rational government can flourish, in which oppression on the one hand is countered on the other by unbridled license.

In still another respect *Billy Budd* follows the classic formula of tragedy. The mainspring of the plot is a reversal, the *peripateia* defined by Aristotle as a hallmark of the complex tragic action, in which carefully laid plans produce results directly opposite to expectation, with, if well-managed, an artistic effect of combined surprise and inevitability. Thus Vere's well-planned arrangements lead to the killing of Claggart and the execution of Billy. He is not, we recall, deceived by Claggart's accusation. He brings the two men privately to his cabin, in order to confront the liar with truth in a manner as little harmful as possible to the general welfare. He fully understands Billy's inability to speak, but by his very kindness he brings on the fatal blow. "Contrary to the effect intended, these words so fatherly in tone, doubtless touching Billy's heart to the quick, prompted yet more violent efforts at utterance—efforts soon ending for the time in confirming the paralysis, and bringing to the face an expression which was as a crucifixion to behold. The next instant, quick as the flame from a discharged cannon at night, his right arm shot out, and Claggart dropped to the deck." Inevitability accompanies surprise, as Aristotle has laid down, for Melville has carefully paved the way by his references to Billy's stutter—his one connection with a fallen world— and his sudden violence once before aboard the merchantman *Rights of Man*. " 'Quick as lightning Billy let fly his arm. I dare say he never meant to do quite as much as he did, but anyhow he gave the burly fool a terrible drubbing.' "

With so many of the traits and qualities of tragedy, *Billy Budd* can claim also the final attribute of tragic reconciliation. In his defeat and passion the tragic hero yet brings about a partial redemption, he keeps alive some hope for the future, some confidence that goodness survives. So the story of Billy does not die, but is preserved and transmitted among seamen, and bits of the boom from which he was hanged are kept like pieces of the true Cross. This effect and survival of his memory might be contrasted with the effect of the announcement by Vere of Billy's impending execution, which "was listened to by the throng of standing sailors in a dumbness[1112] like that of a seated congregation of believers in hell listening to the clergyman's announcement of his Calvinistic text."

This reconciliation is not precisely Greek, nor yet the Hebraic catharsis of *Samson Agonistes*—"nothing is here to wail, nothing for tears." There is no firm base of belief on which to ground it. The system with which we are to be reconciled is too vast and ambiguous. In one dimension of meaning Captain Vere is certainly God the Father, as Billy is God the Son; but as Nathalia Wright has well remarked Vere is not omnipotent. He acts in accordance with a law that is not of his own framing. There is something beyond him. It would be interesting to compare other nineteenth century experiments in meaning through myth, especially Byron's *Manfred*, in which level after level of the personified supernatural is tried and discarded, even Ahrimanes, the lord of all that is; or perhaps Shelley's *Prometheus Unbound*, in which Jupiter is eclipsed by the mighty shadow of Demogorgon, a formless, shapeless gloom.

As tragedy *Billy Budd* undoubtedly possesses tragic irony, the irony of fate. Its ironies would seem bitter to those who are inclined to view them bitterly. One might well think that Melville is presenting in *Billy Budd* a second crucifixion, which in this man-of-war world will inevitably be reenacted whenever Christ should reassume the estate of man. His irony, however, is the natural attitude of a capacious, energetic, and subtle mind in pursuit of as much meaning as it can grasp, and its honest admission of the presence in reality of a something finally ungraspable. It magnifies and intensifies, it deepens and enriches, rather than diminishing by a mere irony of wailing mockery. Viewed in the full context of the tragedy of *Billy Budd*, this irony is neither a scream nor a sneer.[1113]

The Problem of Billy Budd*

EDWARD H. ROSENBERRY

When a monumental new edition of *Billy Budd* appeared in 1962, it was the hope of the editors that their exhaustive scholarship might contribute to a definitive interpretation of the novel. Such a wish might seem unnecessarily restrictive, but the extreme critical divergence on *Billy Budd* has created a genuine threat to its artistic integrity as a result of its apparent failure to support a demonstrable reading. This essay is an attempt to end the war, or to make the end more predictable.

Let it be clear at the outset that I am not proposing to limit the range of parallel and compatible interpretations. *Billy Budd* is sufficiently complex to present the many-layered phenomenon which criticism rightly expects in a fine work of art. The kind of imaginative but disciplined discussion which has been generated by, say, "Rappaccini's Daughter" is constructive and I have no quarrel with it. The kind which will not do and which this study is expressly committed to combat is the kind that has plagued *The Turn of the Screw*: a factious dialog between two mutually exclusive points of view, one of which is more ingenious than the other but less soundly supported by the available evidence in and out of the text.[1]

Fundamentally, the problem of *Billy Budd* is not unlike that of Ivan Karamazov's youthful article on ecclesiastical government, which was taken to favor both churchmen and atheists and finally suspected of "impudent satirical burlesque." *Billy Budd* has been read as a parable of God the Father sacrificing His Son for a fallen world, and alternatively of Pontius Pilate selling out Jesus for present and personal convenience; and finally its sober voice has been taken for a dry mock protesting God and the whole created scheme of things. As in the case of Ivan's article, the problem hinges largely on the question of tone, though there are crucial points of substance and reasoning to be considered as well. The issues are intricately interconnected, since after all what we have to deal with is meaning in an organic work of art; but in as orderly a manner as possible I shall try to analyze the causes of critical error, as they appear to me, and then to show, by examining first the tone of the novel and then its ethical logic, that the plainest reading of this disputed book is the only valid reading possible.

---

* Reprinted by permission of the Modern Language Association from *PMLA*, LXXX (December 1965), 489–498. Also by permission of the author.

[1] Alexander Jones's admirable survey of this familiar quarrel in "Point of View in *The Turn of the Screw*," *PMLA*, LXXIV (March 1959), 112–122, is a model of corrective criticism. See also Wayne Booth, *The Rhetoric of Fiction* (Chicago, 1961), pp. 311–315.

By now any scholarly reassessment of works like these carries a Bunyanesque burden of prior study which it is impractical to spread out for detailed inspection, even in footnotes. The latest annotated text of *Billy Budd*, edited by Harrison Hayford and Merton Sealts (Chicago, 1962), to which this study refers throughout, lists 161 items in its bibliography, and a selection of this material edited by William Stafford under the title *Melville's Billy Budd and the Critics* (San Francisco, 1961) lists nearly a hundred in addition to the twenty-odd it wholly or partly reprints. Between them these sources (most concisely the former, pp. 24–27) tell all that the average reader of the novel or of this essay will want to know about the *Billy Budd* controversy. In the interest of progress and brevity I shall omit a good deal of the argument and formal documentation accessible in these compendia.

DELUSIONS

A good starting point for this conservative case was provided several years ago by Richard Harter Fogle, who identified two "heresies" of *Billy Budd* criticism and dismissed them with entire justification, in my opinion, but without the formal refutation evidently needed to lay such stubborn ghosts.[2] He complained of the widespread attribution to Melville of an ironic tone resulting in a sardonic reversal of the story's ostensible meaning; and he complained particularly of Lawrance Thompson's invention (in *Melville's Quarrel with God*) of a quasi-authorial narrator in whose "bland" and "stupid" vision the apparent straightforwardness of the narration may be conveniently discounted. Thompson's idea is spectacular enough to deserve special mention, but it is basically the ironist heresy tricked out with a supporting device which no other ironist has been clever enough to bring to his case. In effect, it only postpones the collapse of the case by one step, because there is no evidence that such a mediator between author and reader exists. Despite Wayne Booth's proper insistence on every author's "undramatized narrator" or "implicit second self,"[3] never altogether identical with the man behind the mask of art, a considerable burden of proof falls on the claim that these psychic twins are militantly opposed, and the obligation is not discharged by showing that the alter ego *must* be present if the meaning of the novel is to be reversed. Thompson's argument is simply circular and would perhaps have raised more general objection than it has if he had not invented also an "alert reader" who always adopts his views and [489] with whom one is instinctively reluctant to dissociate himself. The real issue lies behind this little smoke screen: are we to take Melville at his word and read *Billy Budd* as a parable of the plight of innocence in a "man-of-war world," or are we to find beneath its tragic benediction a satiric attack on the complacency of earthly and heavenly authority?

Since the latter reading would render the novel, in Fogle's words, "cheap, puerile, and perverse" (witness *Pierre*), no one entertained that possibility until, in 1950, one adventurous essay[4] loosed a spate of ironist interpretations from the scholarly presses. The reasons for this, I am convinced, must be sought in the critics and their milieu rather than in the book. Wayne Booth makes the valuable point that a book tends to mean what we expect it to mean, "and the last several decades have produced—for whatever reasons—an audience that has been thrown off balance by a barrage of ironic works."[5] Irony-hunting has joined symbol-hunting as a fashionable indoor sport, which has so conditioned us to the expectation of obliquity and ambiguity that, as Booth says, "We can't accept a straight and simple statement when we read one." The popular mystique of close reading inclines us to see weasels in clouds and exposes contemporary criticism to what Plinlimmon would have called "strange, *unique* follies and sins." The most conspicuous of these in reading Melville is mistaking an occasional romantic petulance of temper for a considered philosophic posture.

In fact, our expectations of Melville constitute as real a source of error as did the very different expectations of his contemporaries. For them he was "the man who lived among the cannibals," and the leap from Typee to Saddle Meadows, or even to the try-works, was too much for them. For us he is the voice of Ahab and the Confidence-Man,

---

[2] R. H. Fogle, "*Billy Budd*: The Order of the Fall," *Nineteenth Century Fiction*, xv (December 1960), 189–205.
[3] *The Rhetoric of Fiction*, pp. 151–152.
[4] Joseph Schiffman, "Melville's Final Stage, Irony: A Re-examination of *Billy Budd* Criticism," *American Literature*, xxii (May 1950), 128–136.

[5] *The Rhetoric of Fiction*, p. 366. The entire section labeled (after Saul Bellow) "Deep Readers of the World, Beware!" is worth reading on this topic.

the sayer of "No! in thunder." We easily forget that the nay-saying he praised was Hawthorne's and not Beckett's or Sartre's, and that the remark was not made in *Billy Budd* or within thirty years of it. The ironist critics are at least partly disabled by the same prejudice that afflicts the anti-Stratfordians: the man in their minds could not possibly have written this work.

Reinforcing the *idée fixe* about the author is an equally powerful preconception of the characters in *Billy Budd*. The norms of the novel and the rhetoric that expresses them are clear enough in themselves, but they encounter resistance in the natural interests and sympathies of the reader. Booth has commented on the force in literature of "our irresistible sympathy for the innocent victim,"[6] a sympathy so strongly generated by "Baby Budd" as to tempt the most wary of us (in Merlin Bowen's words) "to risk the luxury of at least following our own conscience."[7] Abetting this reaction is the equal and opposite inclination against Captain Vere. Melville, as I shall try to show, made Vere as attractive as he could in the face of his official austerity; but Billy, just as he stands, is an American Adam, loved from the start, and fit to be forgiven anything after he has struck his sacrificial blow at oppressive authority. We must resent his judge, irrespective of the merits of the case, on precisely the ground Melville once supposed to underlie the popular opinion of God: "The reason the mass of men fear God, and *at bottom dislike* Him, is because they rather distrust his heart, and fancy him all brain like a watch."[8] It is belief rather than disbelief which it is difficult to suspend in such a story as *Billy Budd*. Yet to be ruled by indignation, however righteous, is to subvert tragedy to melodrama. It happens to every freshman who lets himself be carried away by the "injured innocence" of Oedipus into the mistake of casting the oracle as villain. It is instructive to reflect on the critical abuse *Billy Budd* would deservedly draw if it really said what the ironists claim it says. *Weltschmerz* has never had much survival value as art.

Several allied faults of interpretation, more logical than emotional, though perhaps emotionally conditioned, may be briefly added to the indictment. Most basic is the rejection of *donnée*, the refusal to honor the author's proffered coin of meaning. The critic with a thesis to prove or with simply a sophisticated aversion to the obvious—pandemic in our time—can follow the bent of his ingenuity to any predetermined conclusion, undeterred by patent narrative facts often reinforced by pointed authorial comment. Reviewing the notorious *Turn of the Screw* case, Wayne Booth hangs between amusement and dismay, "wishing for more signs of respect for standards of proof" (p. 315). One characteristic misuse of evidence in *Billy Budd* criticism is reasoning categorically from prior works. *White-Jacket*, because of obvious resemblances in character and setting, has been a fertile field for such deductions. Since the *Somers* affair of 1842 is one of the sources of *Billy Budd* (though by no means the primary one, as once supposed), a condemnation of it in *White-Jacket* as "murder" has been taken as symptomatic of Melville's attitude toward it in *Billy Budd*. In the later book, however, the purpose and context of the citation (Ch. xxi) are totally different: what was once a loaded exhibit in a reform polemic is now "history, and here cited without comment," to illustrate the exigencies of naval command. In the same way, Billy's response to punitive flogging is read in the light of the sensational attack on naval discipline in *White-Jacket*, while more moderate and pertinent references in both the early fiction and the late verse are ignored.[9] The correctives are many and

---

[6] Ibid., p. 132. Booth is referring here specifically to Joyce's *Portrait of the Artist*, but the problem of sympathy is explored at large in Chs. v, ix, and x.

[7] Merlin Bowen, *The Long Encounter* (Chicago, 1960) p. 233. The full case against the argument from conscience will be made from another point of view further on.

[8] Letter to Hawthorne, June 1851.

[9] Good discussions of both issues may be found in the notes to the Chicago text, pp. 157, 181–183.

evident, not the least of them the differences among these works as art. *White-Jacket*, like all the early books (until well into *Moby-Dick*), has a fully dramatized narrator with his own created opinions, attitudes, and purposes; *Billy Budd* is narrated by an unmediated author who, unlike Chaucer, gives no hint that his "wit is short" or his artistic distance great. More defensible is reasoning from the poems, which both time and rhetoric link closely with *Billy Budd*; and both of the studies I have seen making such comparisons conclude as I do that Melville's tone in this last novel was affirmative and his point of view conservative.[10]

Most pervasive of the fallacies I have noticed in the *Billy Budd* literature is the confusion of dramatic facts with the personal views of author or reader. The whole "testament" controversy is shot through with this flaw or the threat of it—the danger, that is, of allowing no artistic distance at all in the narrative or of imposing on the fiction one's own norms in place of those provided, implicitly or explicitly, by the author. Much print has been devoted to the problem of whether Billy's benediction to Captain Vere expresses Melville's feeling or its opposite. Since Billy is an imaginary figure in an imaginary situation contrived by a professional novelist who plainly labels the cry "conventional," there is no reason to suppose that the question is even relevant. In the case of Vere, as much time has been wasted agitating the question of whether the reader would have acted as he did, or whether Captain Mackenzie of the *Somers* did so, or whether naval law (British of 1797? American of 1842? or 1888?) required a commander to act in such a way—all matters having nothing to do with the self-consistency of the fictional character in question.

TONE

The assumption that a fictional character can be taken as a reliable spokesman for his author is boggy ground to build on. Yet somewhere within every successful fiction there must be adequate clues to that much-disputed but still indispensable value, the author's intention. What I mean by intention, let it be clear, is not belief but tone—that is, the belief-making mechanism of the story as we have it. Does the author's apparent attitude invite acceptance or rejection of the value system on which the story is based?

Some of the critical confusion which has beclouded *Billy Budd* has arisen out of an initial failure to define the "irony" which is supposed to throw its belief-making mechanism into reverse. So far as I know, R. H. Fogle is the only commentator to have illuminated this crucial point by observing that while *Billy Budd* is ironic enough in the Aristotelian sense (reversal of fortune, the "irony of fate"), it is not ironic in the rhetorical sense (reversal of meaning, the irony of satire).[11] Unhappily, the presence or absence of this latter irony is difficult to prove, and proof has so far been largely limited to assertion and counter-assertion. The critic peers into the text and sees, like Thurber at the microscope, his own eye. It helps, but it does not solve all problems, to say that irony is grounded in absurdity. In much contemporary literature absurdity is the norm, and even in fiction based on traditional norms the author's notion of what is out of joint, or his way of expressing it, may differ sharply from the reader's. One can only inspect what clues the text provides with an impartial eye and in the perspective of a scale of values as nearly exempt from the dangers of subjective manipulation as possible.

Much of the textual scrutiny has already been done piecemeal and only needs to be

---

[10] Fogle, op. cit. (note 2, above); Lawrence Barrett, "The Differences in Melville's Poetry," *PMLA*, LXX (September 1955), 606–623.

[11] R. H. Fogle, "Billy Budd—Acceptance or Irony," *Tulane Studies in English*, VIII (1958), 109–110, 112.

reviewed here.[12] There is first the fact of the novel's dedication to Jack Chase—simple, direct, reverent, memorializing the "great heart" of the most admirable man Melville had ever met. It may be, as Warner Berthoff has proposed, that this theme of [491] magnanimity is the central strain of the narrative; at the very least it provides a keynote unmistakable in its sincerity and quite lacking in the ironic potential of the dedication of *Pierre* to Mount Greylock or of *Israel Potter* to the Bunker Hill monument.

This keynote is consistently echoed in Melville's portrayal of his principals. Capping his introductory sketch of Captain Vere in Chapter vii, Melville emphasizes that natures like Vere's are rare in that "honesty prescribes to them directness." Characterizing the common seaman in Chapter xvi he writes with simple nostalgia of the "old-fashioned sailor" whose "frankness" stands in contrast to the landsman's "finesse," "long head," "indirection," and "distrustfulness." In describing the life ashore Melville anticipates our popular concept of gamesmanship: "an oblique, tedious, barren game hardly worth that poor candle burnt out in playing it." In the following chapter he appeals for acceptance of his simple protagonist by disarming the anticipated skepticism of the sophisticated reader and demanding in its place "something else than mere shrewdness." His only devious and ironical character is the villain Claggart, and to him he has Captain Vere say, "Be direct, man." Here, in short, is an internal scale of values as poorly contrived to nourish an ironic tone as can well be imagined.[13]

As the story develops, it becomes steadily plainer that the irony is all in the case and not in the author's attitude toward it. Into his climactic episode in Chapter xxi Melville built a classic Aristotelian irony by which "innocence and guilt . . . changed places" and it became a fact as unalterable as the parricide of Oedipus that Billy had killed an officer in performance (however badly) of his duty. Then, in the next breath, Melville extended his *donnée* to include the inevitable judgment of the captain, who "was not authorized to determine the matter on [the] primitive basis [of] essential right and wrong." At the end of the chapter, as a further inducement to our acceptance of that decision, he appended a warning to the "snug card players in the cabin" not to pass judgment on the actions "under fire" of "the sleepless man on the bridge." In the face of such rhetoric one might rather expect to find an author reproached for excessive explicitness than debated as an enigma.

On the other hand, if it seems impossible for the ironists to be right, it is not wholly their fault that they are wrong. The seal of reconciliation which the condemned Billy is made to place upon his captain's intransigent sentence is mystical and as hard to accept as the forgiveness of Christ on the cross. On such a scene as their final interview in Chapter xxii, the author felt obliged to draw the curtain and to content himself with hinting at the passionate consonance supposed to have welled up in the spirits of these two "phenomenal" natures. His allusion to them as Abraham and Isaac is a clue to both his sincerity and his difficulty. The originals are accepted (when they are accepted) by a suspension of disbelief in which poetic faith is immeasurably assisted by religious faith. Melville can only invoke his biblical counterparts by allusions and hope for the best. That he fears the worst, however, is apparent from the nervous manner in which he reminds us of the "rarer qualities" in the natures of his "Abraham" and "Isaac"—"so rare indeed as to be all but incredible to average minds however much cultivated." This is diffidence, and well founded, but not irony. Melville is not mocking belief but pleading for it. The ironists are simply those readers with whom his appeal has failed.

[12] Among the many pertinent studies listed in the bibliography of Hayford and Sealts, I have found especially useful those of Berthoff (1960), Braswell (1957), Fogle (1958, 1960), and Miller (1958). A very important contribution of W. G. Kilbourne, Jr., will be discussed in another connection.

[13] Some of this very evidence is used by Wayne Booth, p. 178, in citing *Billy Budd* as an example of "reliable" narration.

Finally we must consider the sources of what dubious testimony he allowed to stand in his manuscript. It is notable that all the reservations about Vere are held by minor characters with patently inferior vision: his fellow officers, whose imputations of pedantry must be written off to professional jealousy; the surgeon, whose suspicions of his captain's sanity are an almost comical reflection of his own lack of information, involvement, and insight;[14] the chaplain, who is presumed to disapprove the sentence on grounds of higher morality but who lacks perception or authority to influence the course of events. Melville's attitude toward this chaplain is instructive. We are not to hold the clergyman accountable, we are told, for his failure to protest Billy's sentence, since such a protest would have been both "idle as invoking the desert" and "an audacious transgression of the bounds of his function." On the other hand, the idea of a chaplain on a warship is treated as an absurdity—"incongruous as a musket would be on the altar at Christmas." The contrast in tone is palpable: Melville is struck by the irony of the chaplain's institutional or symbolic presence, but not by his personal sufferance of the double standard he is anomalously bound to. This is not the Melville who once pilloried clerical hypocrisy in the Rev. Mr. Falsgrave but it is a possibly [492] more mature writer for whom the eternal dilemma of man's dual allegiance is not resolved by romantic gestures.

Outside the text itself, the search for tone is reduced to conjecture. The ironists have tried to deduce from Melville's earlier writings what his attitude might have been in this one. It seems to me at least as legitimate to apply the touchstone method instead, holding up to *Billy Budd* parallel passages from works by other authors in which the intention is not in doubt, and in this way confining the problem to purely rhetorical grounds.

From the outer limit of the ironic scale we may take a piece of gross satire like *Some Adventures of Captain Simon Suggs* by Johnson Jones Hooper (1845, reprinted 1846, 1848, 1881). The tone of this book is signaled by the moral code of its frontier anti-hero: "It is good to be shifty in a new country." Suggs cheats his way through a series of escapades, two of which were borrowed by Mark Twain for *Huckleberry Finn*,[15] and another of which (Ch. viii) bears enough resemblance to the crucial episode of *Billy Budd* to provide a measure of extreme contrast in tone. As self-appointed captain of the "Tallapoosa Volunteers," Suggs impounds a motley group of frightened civilians, declares martial law, and threatens to shoot anyone who fails to "walk the chalk." When a harmless widow sneaks out for a pinch of tobacco, Suggs convenes a drum-head court, seconded by his next-in-command ("Lewtenants ought allers to think jist as their captings do"), and terrorizes the old lady with a death sentence, ultimately commuted to a $25 fine. His addresses to court and culprit neatly parody Vere's: "It's a painful duty, Lewtenant! a very painful duty, Lewtenant Snipes; and very distressin'. But the rules of war is very strict, you know! . . . And officers must do their duty, come what may. [And to the widow] It ain't me that's a-gwine to kill you; it's the Rules of War . . . You've 'fessed the crime, . . . and ef me and the Lewtenant wanted to let you off ever so bad, the rules of war would lay us liable ef we was to." Any comparison of such outlandish farce with *Billy Budd* may seem impertinent, but, apart from dialect, nothing really separates them except the absurdity built into Hooper's story by a conscious and exploited incongruity between word and fact.

Vere is sometimes treated as if he were a Simon Suggs: either hypocritical, in not really believing what he says, or cowardly, in not daring to break the rules. This is not so much, I think, because Vere himself is misunderstood as because Melville's world is

---

[14] Cf. Shaw's *Candida*, in which everyone thinks everyone else "mad" for precisely these reasons.

[15] Walter Blair, *Mark Twain and Huck Finn* (Berkeley, Calif., 1960), pp. 280, 329.

mistaken for Hooper's, in which there is no real moral dilemma at all—in which what poses as moral dilemma is plainly the crowning absurdity of the whole affair. But there is nothing inherently absurd either in the dilemma Vere faces or in the choice he makes, as a very different sort of touchstone may illustrate.

In Chapter xxv of Ignazio Silone's *Bread and Wine* the central character, an erstwhile Communist named Pietro Spina, hears a confession of political duplicity from a young revolutionary torn between conflicting loyalties. Though he is no longer an active leader in the movement, it is significant that Spina makes no judgment on the boy's conduct without first defining the ethical posture from which he must speak:

"If I were head of a party, or of a political group, . . . I would have to judge you according to the party's rules. Every party has its morality, codified in rules. These rules are often very close to those which moral sentiment inspires in every man; but they are sometimes the precise opposite. . . . But here and now I am just an ordinary man, and if I must judge another man I can be guided only by my conscience."

Compare the statement of Melville's Vere from the alternative position:

"Do these buttons that we wear attest that our allegiance is to Nature? No, to the King. . . . We fight at command. If our judgments approve the war, that is but a coincidence. . . . For [martial] law and the vigor of it, we are not responsible. . . . Tell me whether or not, occupying the position we do, private conscience should not yield to that imperial one formulated in the code under which alone we officially proceed?"

The rhetoric, in context, is decisive. If an author's intention is to ridicule the Organization Man for his lack of independence, he will sound something like this: "The Roman sword would never have conquered the world if the grand fabric of Roman Law had not been elaborated to save the man behind the sword from having to think for himself. In the same way the British Empire is the outcome of College and School discipline and of the Church Catechism."[16] Nothing resembling this tone is to be found in either Silone or Melville. On the contrary, both were at pains to create strikingly non-conformist characters, so independent as to be dramatically isolated from the mass of men.[493]

But the character of Billy has troubled the dissenting critics as much as that of Vere. After all, they reason, Melville did make his Handsome Sailor a kind of Christ figure, innocent of blood lust if not of blood, and could hardly have contemplated such a fate as Billy's without giving it, however subtly, the colors of legal murder. Again, my denial of this view may be defended by a comparison of Melville's story with a parallel tale which is clearly activated by irony. The rhetorical contrast must speak for itself. In *The Brothers Karamazov* the story of Richard ("a charming pamphlet, translated from the French") is recounted by Ivan to his brother Alyosha as part of the psychological preparation for the shattering ironic legend of the Grand Inquisitor. Richard, a foundling, brutalized by circumstance, drifts into murder as a young man and is promptly condemned to die for it. ("There are no sentimentalists there," Dostoevsky's narrator remarks.) Once in jail, Richard is suddenly showered with all the benevolent attentions formerly withheld by the Christian society that ruined and doomed him; and in the end, converted, repentant, and limp with fear, he faces death parroting, "This is my happiest day. I am going to the Lord!" Then, says Ivan, "covered with his brothers' kisses, Richard is dragged to the scaffold. . . . And they chopped off his head in a brotherly fashion, because he had found grace."

[16] F. M. Cornford, *Microcosmographia Academica*, 5th ed. (Cambridge, Eng., 1953), p. 11.

There is moral absurdity, and there is the rhetoric of irony by which it is effectively exposed. I contend that Melville chose not to use such rhetoric because the story he had to tell was not morally absurd.

ETHICS

Although no one piece of evidence on the norms of the novel is conclusive, the most compelling to my mind is a passage in Chapter vii citing Montaigne as one of Vere's favorite authors. In this fact we have not only Montaigne's philosophical posture to guide us, but Vere's reasons for approving it as well, reinforced by Melville's own recorded opinions on the subject. The case has not been made in detail, and it is one that deserves a full hearing. The heart of the matter, as a recent pioneer study has indicated, is that Montaigne had an overriding respect for law, however fallible, as against personal judgment, which he held to be still more fallible: "Private reason has only a private jurisdiction."[17] To this central point the argument constantly returns and refers.

The effort to see Vere's thought through Montaigne's, however, runs into paradox directly when we read that what Vere got from the philosopher was "settled convictions, . . . a dike against [the] invading waters of novel opinion." This may be thought to smack of rigidity quite alien to the open-mindedness of the skeptic whose motto was "Que sais-je?" Rigidity is in fact the chief stick Vere's critics like to beat him with.[18] But what Vere responds to in Montaigne, Melville makes clear, is not opinions but an attitude—honest, realistic, "free from cant and convention"; a mind not lacking in principles, but proof against convictions resulting from habit thinking and interested motives. Montaigne argued, on the one hand, the kind of moral relativism which Melville saw in Hamlet's remark that "nothing is either good or bad but thinking makes it so,"[19] and on the other hand the supreme wisdom of ordering human conduct by fixed principles—"always to will the same things, and always to oppose the same things."[20] He was of course aware that the will cannot always be just, and for precisely that reason he insisted that men must live by definite laws superior to the will. These laws, it is important to understand, are civil statutes, "still supremely the judges of their judges," as distinct from the so-called "laws of conscience, which we say are born of nature" but which in fact "are born of custom."[21]

This distinction, pervasive in Montaigne, may be further instanced in the "Apology for Raymond Sebond" (II. xii), from which Melville had earlier taken one of his whaling extracts for *Moby-Dick*. Here he stresses the common basis of all law in "possession and usage," that is, custom. And custom, like a river, takes its force from growth, beginning in insignificance but ending in sometimes irresistible power (p. 440). This, for Montaigne, was the current of civilization, the organized movement of society, which ought to define the general course of a man's moral life through the laws which describe it. The alternative

---

[17] "Of Custom, and Not Easily Changing an Accepted Law," *Complete Works of Montaigne*, trans. Donald Frame (Stanford, Calif., 1957) I.xxiii. The conservative implications of this and certain other passages have been explored by W. G. Kilbourne, Jr., "Montaigne and Captain Vere," *American Literature*, xxxiii (January 1962), 514–517.

[18] Lawrance Thompson takes the observation that Vere found in Montaigne's "confirmation" of his inmost thoughts as evidence that he was reading his own opinions into the text. I think that the "shock of recognition" was probably what Melville had in mind—Keats's "almost a remembrance," or Emerson's own experience with Montaigne, as recorded in *Representative Men*: "It seemed to me as if I had myself written the book, in some former life, so sincerely it spoke to my thought and experience."

[19] Melville labeled this sentiment "Montaignism" in the margin of his Shakespeare: Jay Leyda, *The Melville Log* (New York, 1951), p. 291.

[20] "Of the Inconsistency of Our Actions," II.i.

[21] "Of Custom," I. xxiii.

was ethical anarchy: "If it is from ourselves that we derive the ruling of our conduct, into what confusion do we cast ourselves!" (p. 436).

Earlier in the same essay (p. 419) he quotes Epicurus and Plato on the necessity of laws, that even the worst of them are needed to keep men from eating one another; and the remark is reminiscent of Hobbes, another philosopher whom Melville quoted on whales and who may have influenced his thinking. In the *Leviathan* laws are pictured as the "reason and will" of the social body; without their indispensable controls the life of man becomes, in the famous phrase, "solitary, poor, nasty, brutish, and short." In his biting critique of ideal morality Hobbes uses Melville's very image of the unordered society, the "man-of-war world": men unchecked by civil power "are in that condition which is called war." Society can survive only when its members "reduce their wills unto one will" in a surrender of moral sovereignty which presupposes the unreliability of private conscience and the necessity of some personal sacrifice for the general welfare. For Hobbes the exercise of private judgment in social decisions is tantamount to the state of "war" which exists when there are no public norms at all. Quite possibly Melville arrived at this conclusion independently, but the *Leviathan,* if only coincidentally, illuminates the tragic predicament of Captain Vere, caught between two warring worlds, one armed by legal tyranny and the other by legal anarchy. Melville criticism has given much sentimental attention to the former, and with reasons obviously shared by Vere; but it is the latter which the philosopher in him fears more profoundly and is doomed to fear alone.

The reader who dismisses Vere as a shallow formalist is taking part of Melville's *donnée* for the whole. When Vere proclaims his unalterable allegiance to the King's "buttons," it is possible to think of him simply as a man in a sailor suit, "accustomed," as Melville describes the species in Chapter xvi, "to obey orders without debating them." What must be kept in mind is the hard prior debate inside "Starry" Vere which could alone persuade a thoughtful man to don the King's buttons in the first place. What was threatened in the Nore Mutiny, Melville reminds us in Chapter iii, was not just naval authority but "the flag of founded law and freedom defined." It is this symbol to which Vere has sworn his difficult allegiance, an allegiance reaffirmed in his disputed reflections at the close of Chapter xxvii on the human need for "measured forms." Like Hobbes, Vere sees unbridled man as a beast, and law (in Melville's provocative image) as "Orpheus with his lyre spellbinding the wild denizens of the wood."[22]

Legality as music is a figure seemingly out of keeping with the harsh spirit of that "child of War," the Mutiny Act. Yet in a world in which mutiny is a serviceable metaphor for the moral and theological condition of man, an imposed order is the only kind that is possible, and the articles under which Captain Vere takes his authority are not radically different from those under which Moses took his.[23] With respect to the taking of life, neither the military nor the biblical statute goes beyond a general prohibition. The extenuations of circumstance, as Melville well knew, are as infinitely adjustable as the "Protean easy-chair" of the Confidence-Man, built to "ease human suffering [by] endlessly changeable accommodations" in which "the most tormented conscience must, somehow and somewhere, find rest." *Billy Budd,* I contend, was conceived as the kind of story in which such accommodations are not available. It invites comparison in its ethical structure, not to "The Birthmark," the one tale of Hawthorne to which Melville acknowledged a specific debt, but to *The Scarlet Letter.* Both stories deal with the collision of private morality

---

[22] See the discussion of this controversial passage, with a review of the principal scholarship on it, in the notes of Hayford and Sealts, pp. 195–196.

[23] The point is interestingly made in *Paradise Lost* XII. 300–306, as quoted and discussed by Norman H. Pearson, "Billy Budd: 'The King's Yarn'," *American Quarterly,* III (Summer 1951), 99–114. Another valuable essay on Melville's conservative and anti-romantic conception of law is Frederick I. Carpenter, "Melville and the Men-of-War," *American Literature and the Dream* (New York, 1955), pp. 73–82. Carpenter quotes an instructive passage from *Mardi* (Ch. clxi): "Though an army be all volunteers, martial law must prevail."

and the law in a tight little community which admits no extenuations. They have a number of features in common—a devil figure, self-destroyed; a child of nature, innocent but flawed—but most importantly a central sensibility impaled on a dilemma precisely defined by the opposition of statutory and romantic law. Billy's exoneration, like Dimmesdale's marriage, is made in heaven but can only be recognized there. One irreducible fact gets all but lost in the personal sympathy generated by both characters: no law can sanction the execution of bad officers by their men or the [495] extra-marital intercourse of clergymen with their parishioners.

Vere has been abused for his instant observation that "the angel must hang," as though he were prejudging Billy and making a mockery of his trial. But it is hard to see how such a sentiment can prevail in any reasoned estimate of the story. If one sees a man commit murder, one knows that he ought to suffer the penalty; and one also knows that in a civilized society the guilt, however obvious, must be determined and the penalty exacted by due process. Vere's remark may sound unsportsmanlike, but it cannot be regarded as unjust. If he blunders at all at this point, it is not in anticipating judgment but in assessing character. Here and here only he displays prejudice: he likes Billy and dislikes Claggart. The reader allows him these feelings because he shares them and has privileged information which justifies them. But Vere does not have this information and decides on intuition alone that he has seen an "Ananias . . . struck dead by an angel of God." If Claggart were a sympathetic character, our indignation would be justly turned against the superior who treated him with peremptory contempt, was prepared to take a subordinate's word against his, and laid him open to a judgment which not only preceded but precluded trial. The death of Claggart is exactly like that of a soldier Montaigne tells of in "Of Conscience" (II.v), whose stomach was cut open to determine whether he had stolen food as charged. It appeared that he had, but, as Montaigne ironically remarked, what "an instructive condemnation!"

Unwittingly Vere misleads us in the direction of allegory. His word "angel" too effectively polarizes the principals of the drama in his cabin. It is a touch of romance which we can surely forgive in a character sometimes thought to lack heart; but it increases difficulty for both himself and the reader. Forgetting the patent symbolism of Billy's stammer and the reality of the crime it makes him commit, and ignoring Melville's explicit disclaimer of romantic intentions (end of Chapter ii), we are apt to mistake a human tragedy for the Death of Innocence in a morality play. And the tendency is aggravated by an equal and opposite gravitation, dramatized by the officers of the court, toward compromise rather than categorical decision in the matter of punishment. What shouldn't happen to a dog is happening to an "angel," and we quarrel with that uncongenial part of the author's *donnée* expressed in Vere's indubitable mandate to "condemn or let go."[24]

All of the problems of *Billy Budd* somehow converge on the fundamental issue of absolute versus relative values. Most of Melville's critics have recognized in his work the uneasy co-existence of anti-Platonism and romantic idealism, and some of them have tried to resolve this discordance by appeal to the Plinlimmon pamphlet in *Pierre*, the one document in which Melville dealt with it explicitly, if not in his own voice.[25] Broadly, the case rests on a presumed correspondence between the alternatives confronting Captain

---

[24] The groundwork which Melville laid for acceptance of Vere's alternatives is most clearly seen in the second paragraph of Chapter xviii, where, as prelude to Claggart's accusation, he describes the dangerous situation of the *Bellipotent* and the unique qualification of her commander to exercise "prompt initiative" in "unforeseen difficulties."

[25] Melville's general opposition to absolutism and idealism is admirably analyzed by Milton Stern in the opening chapter of *The Fine Hammered Steel of Herman Melville* (Urbana, Ill., 1957). The Plinlimmon case is most fully argued by Wendell Glick, "Expediency and Absolute Morality in *Billy Budd*," PMLA, LXVIII (March 1953), 103–110; and James E. Miller, Jr., "*Billy Budd*: The Catastrophe of Innocence," MLN, LXXIII (March 1958), 168–176.

Vere in the judgment of Billy and the two systems of morality predicated by Plotinus Plinlimmon. Plinlimmon's "chronometrical" or heavenly morality is supposed to be the same as Vere's "natural law" or the "last assizes" at which Billy will be acquitted; and the contrasting "horological" or earthly morality is equated with the martial or statutory law by which Billy is condemned. The inference is that the chronometrical standard is an ideal of universal perfection to which Vere has not the courage to aspire, and the horological a temporizing expedient on which he seizes to stay out of trouble.

No doubt the best corrective for this astonishing conclusion is to keep the Plinlimmon pamphlet out of *Billy Budd*, particularly in view of the uncertainty of its tone; but if it is to continue to raise its head it will have to do an about-face. It is not the law which is partial, local, "horological," but ideal morality. Since the "chronometrical" is a Platonic idea, it can only be imitated, and law is man's imitation of it. Imperfect as it is in operation, law is in principle a universal and absolute good, and it is the only one we have. The higher morality, on the other hand, by which Vere would presumably free Billy or mitigate his punishment, is only a benign expedient by which this killer under these conditions is to be exempted from the normal (and normally correct) judgment. It is, in fact, precisely horological—of this time, of that place. The advocates of absolute morality are pleading Portia's case: "The quality of mercy is not strained." But this means it is not[496] codified, it is gratuitous, a product of individual will and not susceptible to the disciplines of social architecture. The fact that Portia's problem was solved by the letter of the law demonstrates what we have to build on.

At bottom the Plinlimmon argument is radically misleading because the analogy is false. As Henry Murray long ago pointed out, there is no rigid dichotomy between real and ideal morality,[26] and what discrepancy there is cannot be described by a mathematical differential. An apter image, and one closer to the Melville of *Billy Budd*, is the one Dostoevsky uses in Ivan Karamazov's analysis of the same problem. Drawing his figure from geometry rather than chronometry, Ivan describes man's mind as "Euclidian" and refers to the realms of the ideal and the real as those in which parallel lines do or do not meet (v, iii). Melville evidently had the same idea, and in nearly the same terms, when he warned in *Moby-Dick* (Ch. xxxv) against the navigator "who offers to ship with the Phaedon instead of Bowditch in his head." Later, in *The Encantadas* (Sketch Second), a similar thought took form as he watched a Galapagos tortoise butting patiently against a mast and saw in its hopeless inflexibility "the curse [of] straightforwardness in a belittered world." These are figures which keep clear, as the Plinlimmon figure does not, the crucial distinction between expediency and practicality. Seen in this light, Vere's problem is one of moral navigation, and its solution is dictated by a respect for his charts which is both characteristic and heroic.

A MODERN INSTANCE

My plea for straightforwardness in literary criticism may be thought to labor under the curse of the tortoise. In this case, however, it is the "straight" reading which respects the author's sensitively wrought image of a tragically belittered world. It is the ironists who would oversimplify the work of art by stripping it of its mute, suspended ambiguities, its terribly insoluble perplexities, and leave us with an underdone sophomoric bleat. Notwithstanding the temperamental clarity I have claimed for it, *Billy Budd* bears an unex-

---

[26] Notes to his edition of *Pierre* (New York, 1949), p. 477. Recall also the quotation from *Bread and Wine*, above, p. 493: "These rules are often very close to those which moral sentiment inspires in every man."

pected philosophic and aesthetic—sometimes even verbal—resemblance to the provocative "parable of the law" with which Kafka concluded Chapter ix of *The Trial*.[27]

In this dream-like tale an official doorkeeper of the temple of Law refuses a suppliant admission to the inner sanctum of ideal justice. The suppliant, in consequence, pines away his life on the threshold, though he perceives the "radiance that streams immortally from the door." Like Vere, the doorkeeper is compassionate yet intransigent, at once father and enemy. He is somewhat "pedantic" in appearance, and "where his duty is concerned he is to be moved neither by pity nor rage." Disturbingly, he performs a mechanical function without being himself mechanical; it is the paradox of his nature that (in the words of one commentator) "he represents without being responsible for what he represents."[28] This is the crux of the *Billy Budd* problem as of the problem in Kafka's parable. Among the points of view explained to Joseph K. is one which, despite important differences in legal circumstance, expresses well enough the case for Captain Vere: "that the story confers no right on anyone to pass judgment on the doorkeeper. Whatever he may seem to us, he is yet a servant of the Law; that is, he belongs to the Law and as such is set above human judgment."

Enveloping the parable of the doorkeeper Kafka has created a still more relevant parable in the controversy over its meaning. In the crazy gamut of sophistical interpretations which the narrator reviews there is parodied every earnest critical battle that has been waged over problematical fictions like *Billy Budd* and *The Turn of the Screw*. Out of the whole patchwork of plausibility the only statement that emerges with the sure ring of authorial sincerity is the one that undercuts all the others: "You must not pay too much attention to them. The scriptures are unalterable and the comments often enough merely express the commentator's bewilderment."

It is not sneering at the great body of *Billy Budd* criticism to suggest, in conclusion, that it has expressed bewilderment. It is only saying that some very good thinking has chosen some very bad grounds. Unlike "The Lady or the Tiger?" *Billy Budd* was never conceived as a puzzle for our solution or a choice for our decision, but rather as a course of events for our contemplation. Unfortunately, the polemical virus runs strong in the scholar-critic, and the natural effect of being drawn into the story is to take sides on its warring values. A firm will is needed to remember, with Tindall, that *Billy Budd* is "not a conclusion, like a sermon, [but] a vision of confronting what confronts us, of man thinking things out with all the attendant confusions and uncertainties."[29] This is a Sophoclean Melville in *Billy Budd*, speaking with a detachment and a respect for fact that criticism must emulate if it is to get at his meaning.

---

[27] There are congruities between Kafka and the Melville of "Bartleby" and *The Confidence-Man* which deserve their own study, but they are beyond the scope of this one.

[28] Heinz Politzer, *Franz Kafka: Parable and Paradox* (Ithaca, N.Y., 1962), p. 183. Cf. Vere's remark to the court in Chapter xxi: "For that law and the rigor of it, we are not responsible."

[29] William York Tindall, "The Ceremony of Innocence," *Great Moral Dilemmas in Literature*, ed. R. M. MacIver (New York, 1956), p. 80.

APPENDIX:
What to Say About Literature

What to Say About a Play

DOUGALD B. MacEACHEN

One of the major problems of the student who has to read a poem, a play, or a novel is what he should do with it. Until he has been given specific directions he doesn't know what he should look for; he doesn't know how to divide and conquer. If he is told to go to the reserve shelf and consult some lengthy book on the art of poetry or drama or fiction, he soon finds himself lost in an overabundance of instruction. He now has a double problem: what to do with the literary work and what to do with the manual on the particular art form. A battery of mimeographed questions can provide the student with most of the direction he needs. The question form of analysis gives him the pleasant feeling that he is being granted complete independence and not being made the prisoner of a closed system. The following set of questions on the drama may at the very least inspire a better one.

CHARACTERS

1. Who is the protagonist or main character? What are his or her main character traits? His or her chief weaknesses and virtues?

2. What are the special functions of the other characters? Do any of them serve to bring out certain aspects of the character of the protagonist? How do they do this? Is there a character in the play who seems to be the special vehicle for the author's own comment on the play?

3. Who is the antagonist, if there is one? Is he a complex character, a mixture of good or bad?

4. If the play is a tragedy, what is the main character's "tragic flaw" or weakness? A moral defect, an error of judgment? What part does chance or accident play in his downfall? Is he of sufficient nobility of character, no matter what his social position is, to win our admiration and sympathy in spite of his shortcomings?

5. What means does the playwright use to characterize? Stage directions? Self-revelation by monologue or conversation? Actions? Comments of other characters? Characteristic habits, such as the repetition of some cliché or a little eccentricity? Does the playwright try to create his characters in depth or does he merely give one or two facets of them? Are there type or stock characters in the play?

PLOT

1. What are the main elements of the plot? Into how many "chapters of action" is it divided, regardless of the act divisions? Can you summarize each chapter of action after you have finished reading it? Is the progress of the action clear or confused?

2. Is the plot of sufficient scope and importance to engage our deepest interest?

3. What brings on the dramatic conflict? At what point does the play begin?

4. Are the incidents well and plausibly connected? Is there sufficient causation supplied?

5. Is the resolution sufficiently inevitable, or is the denouement brought about by arbitrary coincidence?

6. Is there dramatic irony present? To what degree? What does it achieve in each case?

SETTING

1. What is the setting? Does it change? If it does, does the change weaken the play in any way? Is the change of setting a necessary and natural one?

2. How does the setting contribute to

* From *College English*, XXV (April 1964), 549–550. Reprinted with the permission of the National Council of Teachers of English and Dougald B. MacEachen. Originally published under the title "Analyzing a Play."

the theme and characterization? Is the particular setting important to the play?

THEME

1. What is the moral or human significance of the play? Does it have universal significance through its theme, plot, and characters? Does it stimulate thought about any important problems of life? Does it supply answers by implication or direct statement?

2. Does the play clearly reveal any overall view of the universe on the part of the dramatist? Is his view sentimental, romantic, Christian humanist, cynical, etc.? Does he content himself with showing evil and leave the conclusions up to the reader, or does he use devices to help form the reader's conclusions?

LANGUAGE

1. If verse, what kind? Is the dramatist hampered by his verse forms?

2. Is the language elevated, or close to that of real life? Is it swollen, bombastic, stilted, artificial?

3. Does it contribute significantly to enjoyment of the play?

4. Is the language used by each character specially adapted to him, used to help characterize him?

GENERAL

1. Does the author observe the unities of time, place, and action? Does his play gain or lose by the unities he observes?

2. Would you like to give the play a second or even third reading? Why or why not?

What to Say About Fiction*

ROBERT W. LEWIS, JR.

This outline is merely a tool of analysis, and being put in the form of questions, it should constantly remind its user that only he can provide answers. Hopefully, we can talk to one another about literature, and exchange informed and reasoned opinions about it, but if a given work of fiction is to mean anything to us, if we are to feel and know it completely, we must at one stage wrestle with the work bare-handed, without others as guides or informants. If one were to answer in detail each of the following questions, he would most certainly understand and, hopefully, feel the work thoroughly. Not every question is relevant to every work; and in many cases complete answers will overlap with other ones. Also the good reader may well devise new questions to help him examine special kinds of fiction such as science fiction or black humor. The short story, while like the novel in many respects, is a distinct form for which all these questions will not be generally relevant. In general, however, these questions should alert the reader beforehand and afterward help him verbalize or conceptualize his thoughts and feelings, whether of the short story or the novel.

Only in section one, the questions about historical background, would the reader need any source other than the work itself to arrive at answers. And this section should clearly and emphatically be considered as what it is: mere *background* to the work itself. For some critical purposes, these questions can be ignored altogether, and in other cases such questions might only be answered *after* a thorough analysis based on the other sections. Quite often, an introduction or preface will provide answers to these

---

* Adapted by the author from "Analyzing a Novel," *College English*, XIX (April 1958), 306–309. Reprinted with the permission of the National Council of Teachers of English and Robert W. Lewis, Jr.

questions, but literary reference works, histories, and biographies, as well as the author's own comments in his journals, letters, essays, or autobiography, may sometimes provide useful information that may then be tested against the integrity of the work itself as you understand it.

To paraphrase Socrates, "The unexamined story is not worth reading." These questions should help one to answer the larger and older questions that, for all their commonplaceness, are still fundamental: What is the author trying to do? How has he done it? and Was it worth doing? Ultimately we should not shun judgment of the story, but we should be certain through our analytical but sympathetic inquiry that we have opened our minds to a unique creation and tried to understand it.

ANALYZING FICTION

I. HISTORICAL BACKGROUND

A. When was the work written? What relation or significance does this date have to preceding, contemporary, and succeeding events—biographical events, literary publications, and important political, economic, or social occurrences? Is the author qualified to treat the subject? Is he biased or inaccurate?

B. Does the story significantly relate to the work of other writers or to source materials?

C. What place does the story hold in the author's total work?

D. Are any circumstances of special interest associated with the composition of the work? Do these circumstances in any way aid in the better understanding of the story itself?

E. Does the author make any useful comments concerning this story or his work in general in his letters, essays, journals, autobiography?

II. PLOT

A. Can you give a brief synopsis of the story?

B. Does the plot grow out of the characters or out of chance or coincidence? Within its own terms, is it logical and believable?

C. Is there a well unified beginning, middle, and end? At the beginning do we learn what happened, to whom did it happen, when did it happen, where did it happen?

D. Is there a strong center of interest and how is it determined—by the author's statements (but beware the "intentional fallacy") or by space, emphasis, and recurrence? Is there a central crucial episode or is the plot more episodic with no one outstanding event?

E. If there is more than one action in the story, which is the main and which the subordinate plots (sub-plots)?

F. Is anything seemingly irrelevant to the main plot? If so, does it serve any purpose?

G. What is the nature of the conflict (or conflicts)? Are there complications to the main problem? Identify the protagonist and the antagonist. Where is the climax or turning point?

H. Is our curiosity aroused? How?

I. What of dilemmas, irony, foreshadowing, flashbacks?

J. Is the conclusion satisfactory? Does the story end with a bang or a whimper?

K. Is the title a good one? Is it helpful in any way?

III. SETTING

A. What is the historic time, place, and social background of the story?

B. Has the setting any influence on plot or characters?

C. Are any scenes especially appropriate for the action that takes place there?

D. Is there any use of symbolism in the setting? (Cf. H.)

E. How much time does the action cover? How does the author treat time gaps?

F. Which are the most interesting, striking, or important scenes? How does the author handle them?

G. How is the setting presented? With photographic detail? Impressionistically through a few suggestive details? Indirectly through thoughts and actions?

H. Is the setting detailed or generalized? Realistic or stylized? Is it thematically functional or casual, arbitrary, or atmospheric? (Would it make any difference if the story were set someplace else?) Is the setting allegorical or symbolical or merely literal?

IV. CHARACTERS

A. Can you sum up the appearance and

important characteristics of each major character?

B. Are there any marked similarities or contrasts among the characters? (Cf. F.)

C. Are they "masters of their fate" or "victims of circumstance"?

D. Which characters change as the story proceeds? Do they change for the better or the worse? (Cf. H.)

E. Which characters are distinct individuals (round) and what are types (flat)?

F. Does every character have a function in the story? What are the functions of the minor characters? (Any foils?) Are these minor characters interesting in themselves?

G. How are the principal characters presented? By the author's description and comment? By representation of the thoughts and actions of the characters themselves? By observations and comments of the other characters?

H. Are the characters at once realistically consistent and also sufficiently motivated for whatever change occurs in them?

I. Toward which characters does the author show sympathy? Toward which antipathy?

J. Are the characters' names suitable or in any way significant? (Characternyms?)

V. STYLE

A. What are the outstanding qualities or features of the style?

B. How would you describe the author's style? Simple and clearcut, complex and involved? Smooth and graceful, abrupt and harsh? Richly suggestive and implying much, lean and direct? Poetic, sentimental, restrained? Literal or figurative? Concrete or abstract? Specific or general? Formal or informal or colloquial? Consistent or variable?

C. Does the author's style have individuality? Could another story of his be recognized by the style alone?

D. Is there any humor in the story? Is it quiet or broad?

E. Is the dialog appropriate to the speakers?

F. How frequent are dramatic situations? How are they reached, by anticipation or surprise? How treated, by suggestion or in detail? How rendered, by dialog or by description?

G. Are there any different rates of movement in the story? Where and why?

H. Do you note abuse of digression?

I. From what point of view is the story written? Is the point of view consistent? Could it have been changed for the better?

    1. Omniscient

        a. Editorial omniscient: author present as narrator and commentator who summarizes, analyzes, interprets.

        b. Neutral omniscient: author narrates but does not comment directly; but he may use a spokesman character.

    2. Limited

        a. Third person narration, but point of view of a single character; roving narrator, a variation.

        b. First-person narrator is the protagonist.

        c. First-person narrator is a minor character or merely an onlooker; Lubbock's "central intelligence."

    3. Wholly dramatic narration (effaced narrator—extremely rare).

What are the discernible reasons for the choice of the particular point of view? The effects of the choice?

J. Are any of the sentences or paragraphs particularly striking, meaningful, or remarkable for their freshness of statement?

K. From the many possibilities, what materials has the author *selected*, and what does his selectivity indicate?

L. What kind of action or scene does the author choose to expand? What kind to dramatize and what kind to narrate? Significance of his selection?

M. What effects does his style produce: atmosphere or mood (effect on reader); tone (author's attitude toward his material); irony; understatement; hyperbole; sentimentality.

VI. CLASSIFICATION

A. On what levels can the story profitably be read? (Plot, character, emotional effect, theme.) Is this a story of character with the primary interest being in personalities? Of action, primary interest in events? Of setting, primary interest in environment? Of idea, primary interest in thesis or ethical significance?

B. What is the theme or total meaning of the story? Do all the elements support that meaning? Are there other comments of significance—i.e., minor themes? Does the author raise questions or try to solve them? Is what he says worth saying?

(Beware, however, of reduction, distortion, or inflation of the story by a specific statement of theme.)

C. What is the ideological climate of the story? What ideas seem to be unconscious assumptions of the author and thus operate tacitly? What ideas become subject matter by being themes? And how are they presented, discursively or dramatically?

D. In what general literary tradition was the story written? Realistic—attempting to see life as it is with emphasis on the difficulties, absurdities, animalities, and ironies? Romantic—attempting to see larger truths beyond the literal and factual with emphasis on the imagination and sentiment? Naturalistic, fantastic, symbolistic, allegorical, picaresque, etc.

E. Does the author make any use of allegory, parable, symbolism, or myth?

F. Can you now make a judgment of the story?

What to Say About a Poem*

WILLIAM K. WIMSATT

What to say about a poem. How to say something special about a poem, different from what is said by the ordinary reader, different quite likely from what would be said by the poet himself. Our professional preoccupation as teachers, scholars, critics, sometimes conceals from us the fact that our kind of interest in poems is after all a very special thing—a vocational or shop interest, somewhat strained perhaps at moments, even somewhat uncouth. Poems, a cultivated person might suppose, are made to be read and enjoyed. If I read a poem and enjoy it, why should I then proceed to dwell on it as an object about which something deliberate and elaborate has to be *said*—unless in a surreptitious effort to borrow or emulate some of the self-expression enjoyed by the poet? What a critic or a teacher does with a poem is not, certainly, the main thing the poem is intended for or fit for. The poem is not the special property of these professionals. What they do with it in any deeper sense, what their purpose and methods are, we had better not try to say too quickly. It is the problem of this essay.

II

Many centuries of literary theory have equipped us with a large array of now more or less standard topics, handles or labels, for the analysis of poems. We are disciplined to speak of the *theme* (the most abstractive and assertive kind of meaning which the poem has), and we wish to distinguish this from its realization or more concrete definition in various expressive features conceived as denser, more real, than theme, and yet translucent with meaning. We speak of *diction, imagery, metaphor, symbol* (above all symbol); we sometimes resurrect such older terms as *personification, allegory, fable*. And in our most ambitious, or in our vaguer and more portentous, moments, we sum up such terms and magnify them into the name of *myth*. At the same time, we speak of the movement of the poem in time, its *rhythm*, and more precisely its *meter*, its *lines, stanzas, rhymes, alliteration* and *assonance*, its echoes, turns, agnominations, and puns, and also the more directly imitative qualities

---

*From HATEFUL CONTRARIES by William K. Wimsatt, Copyright 1965 by the University of Kentucky Press. Reprinted by permission of the publishers, the University of Kentucky Press, and the author. [Footnotes omitted—Ed.]

of its sound, the *onomatopoeia*, representative meter, and sound symbolism, the orchestration, and all that. Sound tangles with meaning. A whole poem has a *pattern*, both of meaning and of sound, interacting. It is an act of speech and hence a *dramatization* of a meaning; it is set in a landscape or a decor, an *atmosphere*, a world, a place full of flora and fauna, constellations, furniture, accoutrements, all "symbolic" of course. It is spoken by some person, fictitious, or fictive, if we rightly conceive him, a *persona*, a mask, a mouthpiece, and hence it has a point of view and a variety of emotive endowments, an attitude toward its materials, and toward the speaker himself, a self-consciousness, and a *tone* of voice towards you and me the readers or *audience*. And often we too, if we rightly conceive ourselves, are a part of the fiction of the poem. Or at least we read only over the shoulder of some person or group that is the immediate and fictive audience. The poem is furthermore (especially if we are historical critics) a poem of a certain type or *genre* (tragic, comic, epic, elegiac, satiric, or the like), and this conception implies certain *rules*, a tradition, a decorum, convention, or expectancy. The genre and its aspects are in truth a part of the language of the sophisticated poet, a backdrop for his gestures, a sounding board against which he plays off his effects. Often enough, or perhaps always, the exquisite poem presents a sort of finely blended or dramatically structured opposition of attitudes and of the meanings which lie behind them—their *objective correlatives*. Hence the poem has *tension* (stress and distress), it lives in conflict; its materials are warped, its diction strained, dislocated. Catachresis is only normal. That is to say, the poem is *metaphoric*. The metaphoric quality of the meaning turns out to be the inevitable counterpart of the mixed feelings. Sometimes this situation is so far developed as to merit the name of *paradoxical, ambiguous, ironic*. The poem is subtle, elusive, tough, *witty*. Always it is an indirect stratagem of its finest or deepest meaning.

I have been running over some of the main terms of our inherited grammar of criticism and attempting just a hint at some of their relationships—the pattern, if not of the poem, at least of criticism itself. I hope it is evident that I am in no sense unfriendly to this grammar of criticism or to any one of the terms of which it is composed. I am all in favor of a grammar of criticism and of our making it as sober, tight, accurate, and technically useful as may be possible. The grammar, for instance, must be especially firm in the areas of syntax and prosody, where the poet himself has, at various times in various languages and poetic traditions, been compelled to be, or has allowed himself to be, most tight and technical. It is important, for instance, to know that *Paradise Lost* is written in iambic pentameter, and if we let ourselves be pushed around at the whim of random musical or linguistic theory into finding three, four or seven or eight metrical beats in a Miltonic line of blank verse, we are making sad nonsense of literary history and of what this particular poet did and said. An analogous difficulty would be the enterprise of talking about the poet John Donne without the use of any such terms at all as paradox, metaphysical wit, irony.

On the other hand, grammar is grammar. And I will confess to a decided opinion that the kind of technical and quasi-technical matters which I have been naming ought to be discussed mainly at the level of generalization—they ought to be taken mainly as the preliminaries, the tuning-up exercises, the calisthenics of criticism. An essay on the theme of metaphor, of symbol, of lyrical dramatics, of irony, of meter, of rhyme or pun, is one sort of thing—it is likely to be extremely interesting and useful. But an interpretation or appreciation of a specific poem by the means mainly of an appeal to categories expressed by such terms is another sort of thing—this is likely in my opinion to be somewhat less interesting.

The purpose of any poem cannot be simply to be a work of art, to be artificial, or to embody devices of art. A critic or appreciator of a poem ought scarcely to be conceived as a person who has a commitment to go into the poem and bring out trophies under any of the grammatical heads, or to locate and award credits for such technicalities—for symbols, for ironies, for meter. These and similar terms will likely enough be useful in the course of the critic's going into and coming out of a given poem. But that is a different thing. To draw a crude analogy: It would be an awkward procedure to introduce one human being to another (one of our friends to another) with allusions to commonplaces of his anatomy, or labels of his race, creed, or type of neurosis. The analogy, as I have said, is crude. Poems are not persons. Still there may be a resemblance here sufficient to give us ground for reflection.

I am supposing that the specific thing we are discussing is what to say about a given poem—rather than how to make a survey of poetry in general in order to write a grammar of poetry. Not the most precisely definable and graded features of poems in general, the accepted grammar, but something in a sense even more generic, the basic activity of our own minds by which we examine a given individual poem—this is what I now wish to talk for a while about. This activity of our own in examining a poem, let me add immediately and firmly, does suppose that an object, with definable features, is there, independent of us, for us to examine.

III

Let us, for one thing, remember, and observe in passing, that as teachers, for instance, we are likely to put ourselves in a Socratic relation to our pupils—setting them exercises, asking them questions. So that our own first question, what to *say* about a poem, is likely enough to assume the shape: what to *ask* about a poem. This I think is a very special, intrinsic and difficult aspect of our professional problem. If we assume that we do know, roughly, the correct things to say about a poem, how can these be transposed into good questions? Sometimes the very attempt will reveal the emptiness of what we thought we had to say. This question about questions is obviously a matter of art and tact, our own personality and that of our pupils, and I believe that nobody ought to presume to write any manuals about it. But let me stay long enough to suggest that a good question about a poem should have at least two qualities—it should stand in a middle ground between two kinds of fault. That is, in the first place, it should have in mind an answer that is better than arbitrary or prescriptive. It should not mean in effect merely: "Guess what I am thinking about. Or, tell me what I ought to be thinking about." "How does the imagery, or the meter, in this poem accomplish its purpose?" We may look on such a question, if we like, as setting an exercise, a way of eliciting or demanding an overnight paper. It is scarcely a part of a Socratic discussion. But then in the second place, the question ought not to be so good that it betrays or implies its own answer or the terms of its answer. "Is the imagery of the dead trees in this poem well suited to express the idea of mortality?" The answer that is being angled for ought to be more than simply yes or no—unless perhaps as a mere preliminary to some further and more real question. Sometimes, oddly enough, the two faults of question-making turn out to be the same thing—or at least some of our more careless questions will invite being taken in either of two ways, both empty. Rather accurate parodies of the world of discourse we teachers are capable of creating appear sometimes in the jokes, gags, or riddles (learned I suppose mostly over breakfast radio) which become the favorites of our youngest pupils. "What is large and red and eats rocks?" A certain father tried to be the ingenious pupil and answered, "A large poem by William Blake." But that of course was wrong. The answer was: "A large red rock-eater." A good question should have a definite answer—different from the question and yet entailed by it. Some questions the teacher will ask mainly for the sake of giving himself the occasion for reciting the answer. (I do not say that is always bad.) A good question about a poem will be less like the example I have already given than like this other from the same source—though not exactly like this either. "What is the difference between a lead pipe and an infatuated Dutchman?" The father, though a teacher of poetry, gave up. The answer of course is that one is a hollow cylinder, the other is a silly Hollander.

IV

At the outset what can we be sure of? Mainly that a person says or means something, or ought to mean something (or ought to if we as teachers have any business with it—perhaps that is the safe minimum).

The meaning of the poem may be quite obscure and difficult (rough, opaque and resistant to first glance), or it may be smooth and easy, perhaps deceptively smooth and easy, a nice surface and seemingly transparent. For either kind of poem, the simplest, but not the least important, kind of observation we can make, the simplest question we can ask, is the kind which relates to the dictionary. What does a certain word or phrase mean? We are lucky enough, I am assuming, to have a poem which contains some archaic, technical, or esoteric expression, which the class, without previous research, will not understand. If we are even luckier, the word has another, a modern, an easy and plausible meaning, which conceals the more difficult meaning. (Ambiguity, double or simultaneous meaning, our grammar instructs us, is a normal situation in poems.) In any case, we can put our question in two stages: "Are there any difficulties or questions with this stanza?" "Well, in that case, Miss Proudfit, what does the word braw mean?" "What does kirkward mean?" "When six braw gentlemen kirkward shall carry ye." We are lucky, I say, not simply that we have a chance to teach the class something—to earn our salary in a clear and measurable way. But of course because we hereby succeed in turning the attention of the class to the poem, to the surface, and then through the surface. They may begin to suspect the whole of this surface. They may ask a few questions of their own. This is success. A person who has been a teacher for a number of years masters the problem of knowing his lesson only to experience the more difficult problem of trying to remember what it is like not to know it.

V

The answers to the kind of questions we have just noticed lie in a clean, dictionary region of meaning. This kind of meaning is definitely, definably, and provably there—some of our pupils just did not happen to be aware of it. Let us call this *explicit* meaning. I believe it is important to give this kind of meaning a name and to keep it fixed. The act of expounding this meaning also needs a name. Let us call it *explanation*—explanation of the explicit.

Obviously, our talking about the poem will not go far at this level—not much farther than our translation of Caesar or Virgil in a Latin reading class.

And so we proceed, or most often we do, to another level of commentary on the poem—not necessarily second *in order* for every teacher or for every poem, but at least early and fundamental, or in part so. This level of commentary may usefully be called *description* of a poem—not explanation, just description. There is no way of describing the weather report, except to repeat what it says—describing the weather. A poem, on the other hand, not only says something, but *is* something. "A poem," we know, "should not mean but be." And so the poem itself especially invites description.

The meter of a poem, for instance, is of certain kind, with certain kinds of variations and certain relations to the syntax; one kind of word rhymes with another kind (*Aristotle* with *bottle*, in Byron; *Adam* with *madam*, in Yeats); some conspicuous repetition or refrain in a poem shows partial variations ("On the Ecchoing Green. . . . On the darkening Green." "Could frame thy fearful symmetry. . . . Dare frame thy fearful symmetry"). Some unusual word is repeated several times in a short poem, or a word appears in some curious position. Some image (or "symbol") or cluster of images recurs in a tragedy or is played against some other image or cluster. Shakespeare's *Hamlet*, for instance, may be described as a dramatic poem which concerns the murder of a father and a son's burden of exacting revenge. At the same time it is a work which exhibits a remarkable number and variety of images relating to the expressive arts and to the criticism of the arts—music, poetry, the theater. "That's an ill phrase, a vile phrase; 'beautified' is a vile phrase." "Speak the speech, I pray you . . . trippingly on the tongue." "Govern these ventages with your finger and thumb . . . it will discourse most eloquent music."

Description in the most direct sense moves inside the poem, accenting the parts and showing their relations. It may also, however, look outside the poem. *Internal* and *external* are complementary. The external includes all the kinds of history in which the poem has its setting. A specially important kind of history, for example, is the literary tradition itself. The small neat squared-off quatrains of Andrew Marvell's *Horatian Ode* upon Oliver Cromwell go in a very exact way with the title and with the main statement of the poem. Both in ostensible theme and in prosody the poem is a kind of echo of Horatian alcaics in honor of Caesar Augustus. The blank verse of Milton's *Paradise Lost* and the couplets of Dryden's translation of the *Aeneid* are both attempts to find an equivalent for, or a vehicle of reference to, the hexameters of Greek and Latin epic poetry. A poem in William Blake's *Songs of Innocence* is written in simple quatrains, four rising feet or three to a line, with perhaps alternate rhymes. These are something like the stanzas of a folk ballad, but they are more like something else. A more immediate antecedent both of Blake's metric and of his vocabulary of childlike piety, virtues and vices, hopes and fears, is the popular religious poetry of the eighteenth century, the hymns sung at the evangelical chapels, written for children by authors like Isaac Watts or Christopher Smart.

VI

We can insist, then, on *description* of poems, both *internal* and *external*, as a moment of critical discourse which has its own identity and may be usefully recognized and defined. Let us hasten to add, however, that in making the effort to define this moment we are mainly concerned with setting up a platform for the accurate construction of something further.

The truth is that description of a poetic structure is never simply a report on appearances (as it might be, for instance, if the object were a painted wooden box). Description of a poetic structure is inevitably also an engagement with *meanings* which inhere in that structure. It is a necessary first part of the engagement with certain kinds of meaning. (Certain kinds—in the long run we shall want to lay some emphasis on that qualification. But for the moment the point is that there is meaning.) In the critic's discourse "pure description" will always have a hard time taking the "place of sense."

Perhaps we shall feel guilty of stretching the meaning of the word *meaning* slightly, but unless we are willing to leave many kinds of intimation out of our account of poetry, we shall have to say, for example, that Byron meant that criticism had fallen on evil days—and that it didn't matter very much. "Longinus o'er a bottle, Or, Every Poet his own Aristotle." We shall have to say, surely we shall wish to say, that Milton in the opening of his *Paradise Lost* means, "This is the language and style of epic, the greatest kind of poetry; and this is the one theme that surpasses those of the greatest epics of antiquity." ("This"—in a sense—"is an epic to end all epics." As it did.) Alexander Pope in his *Epistle to Augustus* means, "This is a poem to the King of England which sounds curiously like the Epistle of Horace to the Emperor Augustus. Let anybody who cares or dares notice how curious it sounds." Shakespeare means that the action of *Hamlet* takes place on a stage, in a world, where relations between appearance and reality are manifold and some of them oddly warped.

Through description of poems, then, we move back to meaning—though scarcely to the same kind of meaning as that with which we were engaged in our initial and simple explanation of words. Through description, we arrive at a kind of meaning which ought to have its own special name. We can safely and usefully, I think, give it the simple name of the *implicit*. What we are doing with it had better too be given a special name. Perhaps *explication* is the best, though the harsher word *explicitation* may seem invited. The realms of the explicit and the implicit do not, of course, constitute sealed-off separate compartments. Still there will be some meanings which we can say are clearly explicit, and some which are clearly but implicit.

I believe that we ought to work to keep ourselves keenly aware of two things concerning the nature of implicit meaning. One of these is the strongly directive and selective power of such meaning—the power of the *pattern*, of the main formally controlling purpose in the well-written poem (in terms of Gestalt psychology, the principle of "closure"). It is this which is the altogether sufficient and compelling reason in many of our decisions about details of meaning which we proceed, during our discussion of the poem, to make quite explicit—though the dictionary cannot instruct us. In the third stanza of Marvell's *Garden:* "No white or red was ever seen / So am'rous as this lovely green." How do we know that the words *white* and *red* refer to the complexions of the British ladies?—and not, for instance, to white and red roses? The word *am'rous* gives a clue. The whole implicit pattern of meaning in the poem proves it. In these lines of this poem the words can mean nothing else. In Marvell's *Ode* on Cromwell: ". . . now the *Irish* are asham'd to see themselves in one Year tam'd. . . . They can affirm his Praises best, And have, though overcome, confest How good he is, how just, And fit for highest Trust." How do we show that these words do not express simply a complacent English report, for the year 1650, on the ruthless efficiency of Cromwell in Ireland? Only by appealing to the delicately managed intimations of the whole poem. The cruder reading, which might be unavoidable in some other context, will here reveal (in the interest of a supposedly stolid historical accuracy) a strange critical indifference to the extraordinary finesse of Marvell's poetic achievement. "Proud Maisie is in the wood, Walking so early. . . . 'Tell me, thou bonny bird, When shall I marry me?'—'When six braw gentlemen Kirkward shall carry ye.'" How do we know, how do we prove to our freshman class, that the word *proud* does not mean in the first place—does not necessarily mean at all—conceited, unlikable, nasty, unlovable, that Maisie does not suffer a fate more or less well deserved (withered and grown old as a spinster—an example of poetic justice)? Only, I think, by appealing to the whole contour and intent of this tiny but exquisitely complete poem.

"Who makes the bridal bed,
　Birdie, say truly?"—
"The gray-headed sexton
　That delves the grave duly.

"The glow-worm o'er grave and stone
　Shall light thee steady.
The owl from the steeple sing,
　'Welcome, proud lady.'"

The second thing concerning implicit meaning which I think we ought to stress is exactly its character as implicit—and this in reaction against certain confused modes of talk which sometimes prevail. It was a hard fight for criticism, at one time not so long past, to gain recognition of the formal and implicit at all as a kind of meaning. But that fight being in part won, perhaps a careless habit developed of talking about all sorts and levels of meaning as if they all were meaning in the same direct and simple way. And this has brought anguished bursts of protest from more sober and literal scholars. The critic seems all too gracefully and readily to move beyond mere explanation (being a sophisticated man, he feels perhaps the need to do relatively little of this). He soars or plunges into descriptions of the colors and structures of the poem, with immense involvements of meaning, manifold explicitations—yet all perhaps in one level tone of confident and precise insistence, which scarcely advertises or even admits what is actually going on. The trouble with this kind of criticism is that it knows too much. Students, who of course know too little, will sometimes render back and magnify this kind of weakness in weird parodies, innocent sabotage. "I am overtired / Of the great harvest I myself desired," proclaims the man who lives on the farm with the orchard, the cellar bin, the drinking trough, and the woodchuck, in Robert Frost's *After Apple-Picking.* "This man," says the student in his homework paper, "is tired of life. He wants to go to sleep and die." This we mark with a red pencil. Then we set to work, somehow, in class, to retrieve the "symbolism." This monodrama of a tired applepicker, with the feel of the ladder rungs in his instep, bears nearly the same relation to the end of a country fair, the end of a victorious football season, of a long vacation, or of a full lifetime, as a doughnut bears to a Christmas wreath, a ferris wheel, or the rings of Saturn. *Nearly* the same relation, let us say. A poem is a kind of shape, a cunning and precise shape of words and human experience, which has something of the indeterminacy of a simpler physical shape, round or square, but which at the same time invites and justifies a very wide replication or reflection of itself in the field of our awareness.

Till the little ones, weary
No more can be merry;
The sun does descend,
And our sports have an end.
Round the laps of their mothers
Many sisters and brothers,
Like birds in their nest,

Are ready for rest,
And sport no more seen
On the darkening Green.

What experience has any member of the class ever had, or what experiences can he think of or imagine, that are parallel to or concentric to that of the apple-picker? of the Ecchoing Green?—yet the words of the poem do not *mean* these other experiences in the same way that they mean the apples, the ladder, the man, the sport and the green. The kind of student interpretation which I have mentioned may be described as the fallacy of the literal feedback. Proud Maisie translated into conceited Maisie may be viewed as a miniature instance of the same. And this will illustrate the close relation between the two errors of implicit reading which I have just been trying to describe. The uncontrolled reading is very often the over-explicit reading.

VII

Explanation, then—of the explicit and clearly ascertainable but perhaps obscure or disguised meanings of words; description—of the poem's structure and parts, its shape and colors, and its historical relations; explication—the turning of such description as far as possible into meaning. These I believe are the teacher-critic's staple commitments—which we may sum up, if we wish, in some such generic term as *elucidation* or *interpretation*.

It is difficult to illustrate these matters evenly from any single short poem. Let me, nevertheless, make the effort. Not to show the originality of my own critical judgment, but to keep within the area of what is readily available and plausible, I choose the four quatrains of William Blake's *London* in his *Songs of Experience*.

I wander thro' each charter'd street
Near where the charter'd Thames does flow,
And mark in every face I meet
Marks of weakness, marks of woe.

In every cry of every Man,
In every infant's cry of fear,
In every voice, in every ban,
The mind-forg'd manacles I hear.

How the Chimney-sweeper's cry
Every black'ning Church Appalls;
And the hapless Soldier's sigh
Runs in blood down Palace walls.

But most thro' midnight streets I hear
How the youthful Harlot's curse
Blasts the new born Infant's tear,
And blights with plagues the Marriage hearse.

Let me remark briefly that Blake engraved and printed and illuminated this poem as part of a pictorially designed page. But I believe that this poem (if perhaps not all of Blake's similarly illustrated poems) can be fully understood without any picture.

A further special remark is required by the fact that an early draft of this poem, which is available in Blake's notebook, the celebrated Rossetti manuscript, gives us several variant readings, even variants of key words in the poem. Such avenues of access to the poet's process of composition, a favorite kind of resort for the biographical detective, may also I believe be legitimately enough invoked by a teacher as an aid to exposition. Surely the variant reading, the fumbled and rejected inspiration, makes a convenient enough focus on the actual reading. We suppose that the poet did improve his composition, and usually he did. So if word A is worse, why is word B better, or best? Comparison opens inquiry, promotes realization. Sometimes the discovery of such an unravelled thread, in our learned edition of the poet, will save a classroom discussion which was otherwise moving toward vacuity. Nevertheless I choose here not to invoke the interesting variants to Blake's poem, because I believe the existence and the exhibition of such genetic vestiges is not intrinsic to the confrontation of our minds with the poem. Not that to invoke the variants would be unfair—it is simply unnecessary. If we really need inferior variants, we can make up some of our own. And perhaps we ought to.

Perhaps there is no single word in this poem which calls for the simple dictionary work which I have defined as the level of mere explanation. But the word *charter'd*, used twice in the first two lines, is nearly such a word. At any rate, its emphatic and reiterated assertion, its somewhat curious ring in its context, as well as its position at the start of the poem, make it a likely word to begin with. How is a street chartered? How is the Thames chartered? A charter is a written document, delivered by a governmental authority and granting privileges, recognizing rights, or creating corporate entities, boroughs, universities, trading companies, utilities. It is privilege, immunity, publicly conceded right. The Great Charter (*Magna Charta*) is a glorious instance of the concept in the history of men who speak English. I have been following, where it led me, the article under the word *Charter* in the *Oxford English Dictionary on Historical Principles*. But surely the great Dictionary is mistaken when under meaning 3.2 figurative. "Privileged, licensed," it quotes Shakespeare's *Henry the Fifth*, "When he speakes, The Ayre, a Charter'd Libertine, is still," and shortly after that, Blake, *Songs of Experience*, "Near where the charter'd Thames does flow." Surely the eminent Victorian person who compiled that entry was little given to the modern critical sin of looking for ironies in poetry. The force of that reiterated word in the first two lines of Blake's poem must have something to do with a tendency of the word, in the right context (and Blake's poem is that context), to mean nearly the opposite of those meanings of advantage listed in the Dictionary. For chartered privilege is a legalistic thing, which sounds less good when we call it vested interest, and which entails an inevitable obverse, that is, restriction or restraint. How indeed could the street or the river be chartered in any of the liberating senses listed in the Dictionary? It is the traffic on them or the right to build houses along them that is chartered in the sense of being conceded—to somebody. And this inevitably means that for somebody else—probably for you and me—the privilege is the restriction. Thus the strange twisted aptness, the happy catachresis, of the wanderer's calling so mobile and natural a force as the river chartered at all. The fact is that this meaning of the word *chartered* is not listed in the *Oxford Dictionary*.

We began with the Dictionary, but we have had to go beyond it, to correct it in a specific point, and even to reverse its general drift. Examples of dictionary explanation of words in poems almost always turn out to be not quite pure.

To turn away from the attempt at such explanation, then—what opportunities do we find for simply *describing* this poem—and first, with regard to its immediate historical contexts? Perhaps some note on the chimney sweeper will be needed for our twentieth-century American pupils. We can look a little to one side and see Blake's angry poem *The Chimney Sweeper* in the *Songs of Experience*: "A little black thing among the snow, Crying 'weep!' 'weep!' in notes of woe!" We can look back and see the companion *Chimney Sweeper*, tenderly comical, poignant, in the *Songs of Innocence*. ". . . I said 'Hush, Tom! never mind it, for when your head's bare You know that the soot cannot spoil your white hair.'" An Act of Parliament of 1788 had attempted to prohibit the employment of chimney sweeps until they were eight years old. In winter they began work at 7 a.m., in summer at 5. Their heads were shaved to reduce the risk of their hair catching fire from pockets of smouldering soot. An essay on the eighteenth-century London practice of chimney-sweeping would of course be an explication, *in extenso*, of the third stanza of this poem. We could add notes too for this stanza on the wars and armies of the period, on the condition of the London churches (the blackening of Portland limestone outside—suppositions about the failure of the ministry inside, priestly symbols of oppression in other lyrics by Blake), or for the fourth stanza we could investigate harlots in eighteenth-century London. But I believe it is part of the power of this particular poem that it scarcely requires any very elaborate descriptive explications of this sort. "We can do pretty well with the poem," says one commentator, "in contexts of our own manufacture or out of our own experience."

Another external point of reference, a part of Blake's immediate literary and religious tradition, has already been named—that is, when we alluded to the simple metrics and the innocent language of the eighteenth-century evangelical hymns. Blake's *Songs of Innocence and of Experience*, says one critic, are "almost a parody" of such popular earlier collections as the *Divine Songs Attempted in Easy Language for the Use of Children* by the nonconformist minister and logician Isaac Watts. Blake knew that collection well. And thus, a certain *Song* entitled *Praise for Mercies Spiritual and Temporal*.

> Whene'er I take my walks abroad,
>   How many poor I see;

> What shall I render to my God
>   For all his gifts to me.
>
> . . . .
>
> How many children in the street,
>   Half naked I behold!
> While I am cloth'd from head to feet,
>   And cover'd from the cold.

The echoes of such socially innocent hymnology in the minds and ears of Blake and his generation make, as I have suggested, a part of the meaning of his vocabulary and rhythm, part of a historic London sounding board, against which we too can enjoy a more resonant reading of the bitterness and irony of the wanderer in the chartered streets.

But to turn back to the words of our poem and to inquire whether any *internal* features of it deserve descriptive notice: For one thing, I should want a class to notice how the simple hymn-like stanzas of this poem are fortified or specialized in a remarkable way by a kind of phonemic tune, or prominent and stark, almost harsh, succession of similar emphatic syllables. This tune is announced in the opening verb *wander*, then immediately picked up and reiterated, doubly and triply:—*chartered* street, *chartered* Thames, "And *mark* in every face . . . *Marks* of Weakness, *marks* of woe." The word *mark* indeed, the inner mental act, the outer graven sign, is the very motif of this marking repetition. It was more than a semantic or dictionary triumph when Blake revising his poem hit on the word *chartered*—rejecting the other quite different-sounding word which we need not mention, which appears in the Rossetti manuscript.

The student of the poem will easily pick out the modulations of the theme through the rest of the poem: the rhyme words *man* and *ban*, the emphatic syllable of *man*acles, the *black*'ning Church, the *hap*less sigh, the *Pal*ace *Walls* . . . *Har*lot, *Blasts*, and *Mar*riage. But what is the meaning of this phonetic pattern? A certain meaning, not in the sense necessarily of what Blake fully intended or would have confessed or defined if we had asked him, but in the sense of something which is actually conveyed if we will let it be conveyed, has been pretty much implied in the very description of the pattern. According to our temperaments and our experiences, and as our imagination is more auditory, eidetic, or kinesthetic, we will realize the force of this phonetic marking in images of insistently wandering, tramping feet, in a savage motion of the arms and head, in a bitter chanting, a dark repetition of indictments. Any one of these images, as I attempt to verbalize it, is perhaps excessive; no one is specifically necessary. But all of these and others are relevant.

We have said that the word *chartered* when applied to the street and even more when applied to the river is an anomaly. A close inspection of this poem will reveal a good many curiosities in its diction. Notice, for example, the word *cry*, which occurs three times in the course of stanzas two and three. Why do men cry in the streets of London? In addition to various random cries of confusion, hurry, and violence (which we are surely entitled to include in the meaning of the word), there is the more special and more continuous London street cry, the "proclamation," as the Dictionary has it, of wares or of services. If we had plenty of time for history we could read Addison's *Spectator* on "Street Cries." A more immediately critical interest is served when we notice that the steadily clamorous background of the London scene of charter and barter merges by a kind of metaphoric glide, in the next two lines, into a medley of other vocal sounds, "cries," in another sense, of fear, "voices," "bans"—that is to say, legal or official yells, proclamations, summonses, prohibitions, curses. Are the kinds of cries really separate, or are all much the same? In the next line the infant cry of fear merges literally with the cry of service—"sweep, sweep," or "weep, weep," as we learn the pronunciation from Blake's two Chimney Sweeper songs. The whole poem proceeds not only by pregnant repetitions but by a series of extraordinary conjunctions and compressions, by a pervasive emergence of metaphoric intimation from the literal details of the Hogarthian scene. Consider, for instance, how to *appall* is to dismay or terrify, and etymologically perhaps to make *pale*. Doubtless the syntax says here in the first place that the unconsciously accusing cry of the infant sweep strikes dismay, even a kind of pallor, into these irrelevant, mouldering, and darkening fabrics. At the same time the syntax does not forbid a hint of the complementary sense that the walls throw back the infant cry in ineffectual and appalled echoes. The strange assault of pitiful sounds upon the very color of the walls, which is managed in these first two lines by verbal intimation, erupts in the next two beyond verbalism into the bold, surrealistically asserted vision of the *sigh* which attaches itself as blood to palace walls.

But most thro' midnight streets I hear
How the youthful Harlot's curse
Blasts the new born Infant's tear,
And blights with plagues the Marriage hearse.

The devotee of Blake may, by consulting the Rossetti manuscript, discover that the poet took extraordinary pains with this last stanza of the poem (which was an afterthought): he wrote it and rewrote it deleting words and squeezing alternatives onto his already used-up page. Clearly he intended that a lot of meaning should inhere in this densely contrived stanza—the climax, the *most* appalling instance, of the assault of the city sounds upon the citadels, the institutions, the persons of the chartered privilege. The new role of the infant in this stanza, lying between the harlot and the major target of her curse, and the impatient energy, the crowding of sense, from the harlot and her curse, through the blight, the plague, to the ghastly paradox of that final union of words—the marriage hearse—perhaps we had better leave this to a paper by our students, rather than attempt to exhaust the meaning in class.

I have perhaps already said too much about this one short poem. Yet I have certainly not said all that might be said. Relentless criticism of a poem, the technique of the lemon-squeezer, is not to my mind an ideal pedagogic procedure. It is not even a possibility. A descriptive explication of a poem is both more and less than a multiple and exhaustive précis. Our aim I think should be to say certain selected, intelligible things about a poem, enough to establish the main lines of its technical achievement, of its symbolic shape. When we have done that much, we understand the poem—even if there are grace notes and overtones which have escaped our conscious notice.

VIII

Let me back off then from the poem by William Blake and return once more, briefly, to my main argument. *Explanation, description,* and *explication:* we can recognize three phases of our interpretation of the poem, though they prove to be more closely entangled and merged with one another than we might have realized at the beginning. But are they all? Is there not another activity which has been going on in our minds, almost inevitably, all this while? The activity of *appreciation.* All this time, while reading the poem so carefully, have we not also been liking it or disliking it? Admiring it or despising it? Presumably we have. And presumably we ought now to ask ourselves this further question: Is there any connection between the things we have managed so far to say about the poem and the kind of response we experience toward it? Our liking it or our disliking it? Are we inclined to try to explain why we like the poem? Do we know how to do this? More precisely: Would a statement of our liking the poem, an act of praise or appreciation, be something different from (even though perhaps dependent upon) the things we have already been saying? Or has the appreciation already been sufficiently implied or entailed by what we have been saying?

At the first level, that of simple dictionary explanation, very little, we will probably say, has been implied. And very little, we will most likely say, in many of our motions at the second level, the simply descriptive. It is not a merit in a poem, or surely not much of a merit, that it should contain any given vocabulary, say of striking or unusual words, or even that it should have metaphors, or that it should have meter or any certain kind of meter, or rhymes, as any of these entities may be purely conceived.

But that—as we have been seeing—is to put these matters of simple explanation and simple description more simply and more abstractly than they are really susceptible of being put. We pass imperceptibly and quickly beyond these matters. We are inevitably and soon caught up in the demands of explication—the realization of the vastly more rich and interesting implicit kinds of meaning. We are engaged with features of a poem which—given always other features too of the whole context—do tend to assert themselves as reasons for our pleasure in the poem and our admiration for it. We begin to talk about patterns of meaning; we encounter structures or forms which are radiant or resonant with meaning. Patterns and structures involve coherence (unity, coherence, and emphasis), and coherence is an aspect of truth and significance. I do not think that our evaluative intimations will often, if ever, advance to the firmness and completeness of a demonstration. Perhaps it is hardly conceivable that they should. But our discourse upon the poem will almost inevitably be charged with implications of its value. It will be more difficult to keep out these intimations than to let them in. Critics who have announced the most resolute programs of neutrality have found this out. Take care of the weight, the color, the shape of the poem, be fair to the explanation and description, the indisputable parts of the formal explication—the appreciation will be there, and it will be difficult to avoid having expressed it.

Explicatory criticism (or explicatory evaluation) is an account of a poem which exhibits the relation between its form and its meaning. Only poems which are worth something are susceptible of this kind of account. It is something like a definition of poetry to say that whereas rhetoric—in the sense of mere persuasion or sophistic—is a kind of discourse the power of which diminishes in proportion as the artifice of it is understood or seen through—poetry, on the other hand, is a kind of discourse the power of which—or the satisfaction which we derive from it—is actually increased by an increase in our understanding of the artifice. In poetry the artifice is art. This comes close I think to the center of the aesthetic fact.

IX

One of the attempts at a standard of poetic value most often reiterated in past ages has been the doctrinal—the explicitly didactic. The aim of poetry, says the ancient Roman poet, is double, both to give pleasure and to teach some useful doctrine. You might get by with only one or the other, but it is much sounder to do both. Or, the aim of poetry is to teach some doctrine—and to do this convincingly and persuasively, by means of vividness and pleasure—as in effect the Elizabethan courtier and the eighteenth-century essayist would say. But in what does the pleasure consist? Why is the discourse pleasurable? Well, the aim of poetry is really to please us by means of or through the act of teaching us. The pleasure is a dramatized moral pleasure. Thus in effect some theories of drama in France during the seventeenth century. Or, the pleasure of poetry is a pleasure simply of tender and morally good feelings. Thus in effect the philosophers of the age of reason in England and France. And at length the date 1790 and Immanuel Kant's *Critique of Judgment*: which asserts that the end or effect of art is not teaching certainly, and not pleasure in anything like a simple sensuous way—rather it is something apart, a feeling, but precisely its own kind of feeling, the aesthetic. Art is autonomous—though related symbolically to the realm of moral values. Speaking from this nondidactic point of view, a critic ought to say, I should think, that the aesthetic merit of Blake's *London* does not come about because of the fact that London in that age witnessed evils which cried to Heaven for remedy, or because Blake was a Prophet Against Empire, or a Visionary Politician, or because at some time, perhaps a few years after he had written the poem, he may have come to view it as one article or moment in the development of an esoteric philosophy of imagination, a Fearful Symmetry of Vision, expanded gradually in allegorical glimpses during several phases of his life into a quasi-religious revelation or privilege which in some sense, at moments, he believed in. Blake's *London* is an achievement in words, a contained expression, a victory which resulted from some hours, or days, of artistic struggle, recorded by his pen on a page of the Rossetti manuscript.

Between the time of Immanuel Kant, however, and our own, some complications in the purity of the aesthetic view have developed. Through the romantic period and after, the poetic mind advanced pretty steadily in its own autonomous way, toward a claim to be in itself the creator of higher values—to be perhaps the only creator. Today there is nothing that the literary theorist —at least in the British- and American-speaking world—will be more eager to repudiate than any hint of moral or religious didacticism, any least intimation that the poem is to measure its meaning or get its sanction from any kind of authority more abstract or more overtly legislative than itself. But on the other hand there has probably never been a generation of teachers of literature less willing to admit any lack of high seriousness, of implicit and embodied ethical content, even of normative vision in the object of their study. Despite our reiterated denials of didacticism, we live in an age, we help to make an age, of momentous claims for poetry—claims the most momentous conceivable, as they advance more and more under the sanction of an absolutely creative and autonomous visionary imagination. The Visionary imagination perforce repudiates all but the tautological commitment to itself. And thus, especially when it assumes (as now it begins to do) the form of what is called the "Tragic Vision" (not "The Vision of Tragedy"), it is the newest version of the *Everlasting No*. Vision *per se* is the vision of itself. "Tragic Vision" is the nearly identical vision of "Absurdity." (War-weariness and war-horror, the developing mind and studies of a generation that came out of the second War and has been living in expectation of the third may go far to explain the phenomenon, but will not justify it.) Antidoctrine is of course no less a didactic energy than doctrine itself. It is the reverse of doctrine. No more than doctrine itself, can it be located or even approached by a discussion of the relation between poetic form and poetic meaning. Antidoctrine is actually asserted by the poems of several English romantic poets, and notably, it would appear, though it is difficult to be sure, by the "prophecies" of William Blake. The idea of it may be hence a part of these poems, though never their achieved result or expression. Any more than an acceptable statement of Christian doctrine is Milton's achieved expression in *Paradise Lost*, or a statement of Aristotelian ethics is the real business of Spenser's *Faerie Queene*. Today I believe no prizes are being given for even the best doctrinal interpretation of poems. (The homiletic or parabolic interpretation of Shakespeare, for example, has hard going with the reviewer.) On the other hand, if you are willing to take a hand in the exploitation of the neuroses, the misgivings, the anxieties, the infidelities of the age—if you have talents for the attitudes of Titanism, the graces needed by an impresario of the nuptials of Heaven and Hell, you are likely to find yourself in some sense rewarded. It is obvious I hope that I myself do not believe the reward will consist in the achievement of a valid account of the relation between poetic form and poetic meaning.

INDEX

(Authors in capitals, titles of selections in oblique, first lines in roman)

A poem should be palpable and mute 255
Act of Faith, 78–86
After Apple-Picking, 267–268
Again the Native Hour Lets Down the Locks, 150
Again the native hour lets down the locks 150
"Ah, Are You Digging on My Grave?" 254
"Ah, are you digging on my grave 254
Ah, what can ail thee, wretched wight, 480
AIKEN, CONRAD, 403–412
ALGREN, NELSON, 92–99
Also Ulysses once—that other war. 628
April is the cruellest month, breeding 657
Araby, 238–241
Archetype and Signature, 515–525
ARNOLD, MATTHEW, 144; 486–469
Ars Poetica, 255–256
As Rochefoucault his Maxims drew 125
As virtuous men passe mildly away, 277
AUDEN, W. H., 145
Autobiography, 138–143
AVERY, CATHERINE B., 527–528

Bacchus, 625–626
Bartleby the Scrivener, 101–119
Billy Budd, 671–712
Billy Budd—Acceptance or Irony, 758–761
Billy Budd: Adam or Christ? 753–757
Billy Budd: The Plot Against the Story, 724–731
Bishop Orders His Tomb at Saint Praxed's Church, The, 475–477
Blackberry Winter, 594–605
BLAKE, WILLIAM, 470
Bottle of Milk for Mother, A, 92–99
Bring me wine, but wine which never grew 625
BROOKS, CLEANTH, 167–171
BROWNING, ROBERT, 471–472; 472–474; 475–477
Buried Life, The, 468–469
BURNS, ROBERT, 122–123

Ceremony of Innocence, The, 719–723
Charge of the Light Brigade, The, 122
CHASE, RICHARD, 741–752
CLOUGH, ARTHUR HUGH, 137
COLERIDGE, SAMUEL TAYLOR, 481–483; 633–648
Collar, The, 261–262
Collective Unconscious, Myth, and the Archetype, The, 510–514

Concept of the Collective Unconscious, The, 504–508
Corinna's Going A-Maying, 630–631
"Courage!" he said, and pointed toward the land, 620
CRANE, STEPHEN, 225–237
Criticism and Sociology, 7–18
CROMPTON, LOUIS, 67–77
Crossing the Bar, 618–619
CUMMINGS, E. E., 124–125

Daddy, 478–480
DAICHES, DAVID, 7–18
Death of the Ball Turret Gunner, The, 257
DICKEY, JAMES, 151–154
DICKINSON, EMILY, 255
Dissection of the Psychical Personality, The, 288–301
DONNE, JOHN, 258–259; 277–278
Dover Beach, 144

Easter-Wings, 260
Elegy Written in a Country Churchyard, 147–150
Elementary School Classroom in a Slum, An, 146
ELIOT, T. S., 657–668
EMERSON, RALPH WALDO, 625–626

FALK, SIGNI L., 574–577
Far far from gusty waves, these children's faces 146
FERLINGHETTI, LAWRENCE, 138–143
Fern Hill, 276–277
FIEDLER, LESLIE, 515–525
Flight, 215–224
FOGLE, RICHARD HARTER, 758–761
Force that Through the Green Fuse Drives the Flower, The, 275
Formalist Critics, The, 167–171
FREUD, SIGMUND, 288–301
Freud and Literature, 302–313
From my mother's sleep I fell into the State, 257
FROST, ROBERT, 267–268; 617

Get up, get up for shame, the Blooming Morne 630
Goblin Market, 483–494
Goe, and catche a falling starre, 258
Good news. It seemed he loved them after all. 155
GRAY, THOMAS, 147–150

793

INDEX

G-r-r-r—there go, my heart's abhorrence! 472

Half a league, half a league, 122
Hamlet, 315–378
HARDY, THOMAS, 254
HAWTHORNE, NATHANIEL, 587–593; 606–615
HEMINGWAY, ERNEST, 242–253
HERBERT, GEORGE, 260; 261–262
Herman Melville and the Forms—Irony and Social Criticism in Billy Budd, 713–718
HERRICK, ROBERT, 630–631
HOPKINS, GERARD MANLEY, 274
HUDSON, H. E., IV, 753–757

I am leading a quiet life 138
I caught this morning morning's minion, king- 274
I Never Lost as Much but Twice, 255
I never lost as much but twice 255
I, Oedipus, the club-foot, made to stumble, 626
I Saw a Chapel All of Gold, 470
I saw a chapel all of gold 470
I saw the midlands 470
I struck the board, and cry'd, No more. 261
I Will Arise and Go Now, 121
If my dear love were but the child of state, 260
In far Tibet 121
In the great place the great house is gone from in the sun 151
In Xanadu did Kubla Khan 482
"Ineludible Gripe" of Billy Budd, The, 732–740
Innocence and Infamy, 741–752
It is an ancient Mariner, 633
It little profits that an idle king, 619

JACKSON, SHIRLEY, 87–91
JAMES, HENRY, 413–466
JARRELL, RANDALL, 257
JONES, ERNEST, 379–387
JOYCE, JAMES, 238–241
JUNG, CARL, 504–508; 510–514

KEATS, JOHN, 258; 278–280; 480–481; 617–618
Kilroy, 628–629
King Solomon, 579–586
Kisses in the Train, 470–471
Kubla Khan, 481–483

La Belle Dame Sans Merci, 480–481
Latest Decalogue, The, 137
LATTIMORE, RICHMOND, 204–214
LAWRENCE, D. H., 470–471
LEMON, LEE T., 724–731
LEWIS, ROBERT W., JR., 778–781
Light flows our war of mocking words, and yet, 467
Lord, who createdst man in wealth and store, 260
Lotos-Eaters, The, 620–624
Lottery, The, 87–91
Lycidas, 649–656

MACEACHEN, DOUGALD B., 777–778
MACLEISH, ARCHIBALD, 255–256
Major Barbara, 19–66
Major Barbara: Shaw's Challenge to Liberalism, 67
MELVILLE, HERMAN, 101–119; 671–712
MILTON, JOHN, 649–656
Mr. Arcularis, 403–412
Morning and evening 483
Much have I travelled in the realms of gold, 258
MUIR, EDWIN, 626–628
My Kinsman, Major Molineux, 606–615
My Last Duchess, 471–472
My long two-pointed ladder's sticking through a tree 267–268
Myth of Orpheus, The, 527–528

NASH, OGDEN, 121
next to of course god america i, 124–125
"next to of course god america i 124
Nodding, its great head rattling a gourd, 495
Now as I was young and easy under the apple boughs 276

O wild West Wind, thou breath of Autumn's being, 262
Ode on a Grecian Urn, 278–280
Ode to the West Wind, 262–264
Oedipus, 626–628
Oedipus Rex, 173–202
Oedipus Tyrannus, 204–214
On First Looking into Chapman's Homer, 258
Open Boat, The, 225–237
Original Sin: A Short Story, 495–496
Orpheus, The Myth of, 527–528
Orpheus Descending (essay), 574–577
Orpheus Descending (play), 529–572

POE, EDGAR ALLAN, 392–402
PLATH, SYLVIA, 478–480
Problem of Billy Budd, The, 762–773
Psycho-Analytic Solution to Hamlet's Character, The, 379–387

Rime of the Ancient Mariner, The, 633–648
ROGERS, ROBERT, 732–740
ROSENBERRY, EDWARD H., 762–773
ROSENFELD, ISAAC, 579–586
ROSSETTI, CHRISTINA, 483–494

Sailing to Byzantium, 631–632
Season of mists and mellow fruitfulness, 617
Secret Life of Walter Mitty, The, 388–390
SHAKESPEARE, WILLIAM, 259; 260–261; 315–378
SHAW, BERNARD, 19–66
SHAW, IRWIN, 78–86
SHELLEY, PERCY BYSSHE, 262–264; 264–267
Slave Quarters, 151–154
Snows of Kilimanjaro, The, 242–253
Soliloquy of the Spanish Cloister, 472–474
Song About Major Eatherly, A, 155–158

Song: Goe and Catche a Falling Starre, 258–259
Sonnet 124, 260–261
Sonnet 73, 259
SOPHOCLES, 173–202
SPENDER, STEPHEN, 146
STEINBECK, JOHN, 215–224
Stopping by Woods on a Snowy Evening, 617
Sunset and evening star, 618
SWIFT, JONATHAN, 125–137

TATE, ALLEN, 150
Tears, Idle Tears, 256–257
Tears, idle tears, I know not what they mean, 256
Tennyson, Alfred, Lord, 122; 256–257; 618–619; 619–620; 620–624
That is no country for old men. The young 631
That time of year thou mayst in me behold 259
That's my last Duchess painted on the wall, 471
The curfew tolls the knell of parting day, 147
The force that through the green fuse drives the flower 275
The sea is calm to-night, 144
The world is too much with us; late and soon, 124
THOMAS, DYLAN, 275; 276–277
Thou shalt have one God only; who 137
Thou still unravish'd bride of quietness, 278
THURBER, JAMES, 388–390
TINDALL, WILLIAM YORK, 719–723
To a Mouse, 122–123
To a Skylark, 264–267
To Autumn, 617–618
Tragedy of Hamlet, Prince of Denmark, The, 315–378
TRILLING, LIONEL, 302–313

Ulysses, 619–620
Unknown Citizen, The, 145

Valediction: Forbidding Mourning, A, 277–278
Vanity, saith the preacher, vanity! 475
Verses on the Death of Dr. Swift, D.S.P.D., 125–137
VIERICK, PETER, 628–629

WAIN, JOHN, 155–158
WARREN, ROBERT PENN, 495–496; 594–605
Waste Land, The, 657–668
Wee, sleekit, cowrin, tim'rous beastie, 122
What to Say About a Play, 777–778
What to Say About a Poem, 781–792
What to Say About Fiction, 778–781
When Lilacs Last in the Dooryard Bloom'd, 268–273
When lilacs last in the dooryard bloom'd, 268
WHITMAN, WALT, 268–273
Whose woods these are I think I know. 617
William Wilson, 392–402
WILLIAMS, TENNESSEE, 529–572
WIMSATT, WILLIAM K., 781–792
Windhover, The, 274
WORDSWORTH, WILLIAM, 124
World is Too Much with Us; Late and Soon, The, 124

YEATS, WILLIAM BUTLER, 631–632
Yet once more, O ye laurels, and once more 649
You do not do, you do not do 478
Young Goodman Brown, 587–593

ZINK, KARL E., 713–718